# The Airman's C

I am an American Airman.
I am a Warrior.
I have answered my Nation's call.

I am an American Airman.
My mission is to Fly, Fight, and Win.
I am faithful to a Proud Heritage,
A Tradition of Honor,
And a Legacy of Valor.

I am an American Airman.
Guardian of Freedom and Justice,
My Nation's Sword and Shield,
Its Sentry and Avenger.
I defend my Country with my Life.

I am an American Airman.
Wingman, Leader, Warrior.
I will never leave an Airman behind,
I will never falter,
And I will not fail.

ACCESSIBILITY: Publications and forms are available for downloading or ordering on the e-Publishing Web site at http://www.e-publishing.af.mil/.

RELEASABILITY: There are no releasability restrictions on this publication

| OPR: AETC/A3/AADD | Certified by: HQ USAF/A1 (GINA M. GROSSO, Lt Gen, USAF) |
|---|---|
| Supersedes: AFH1, 1 October 2015 | Pages: 574 |

This handbook implements AFPD 36-22, *Air Force Military Training*. Information in this handbook is primarily from Air Force publications and contains a compilation of policies, procedures, and standards that guide Airmen's actions within the Profession of Arms. This handbook applies to the Regular Air Force, Air Force Reserve and Air National Guard. This handbook contains the basic information Airmen need to understand the professionalism required within the Profession of Arms. Attachment 1 contains references and supporting information used in this publication.

This handbook is the sole source reference for the development of study guides to support the enlisted promotion system. Enlisted Airmen will use these study guide to prepare for their Promotion Fitness Examination (PFE) or United States Air Force Supervisory Examination (USAFSE). These study guides are available at www.studyguides.af.mil. Send recommendations for changes, additions, or deletions to this handbook to HQ AETC/A3 Airman Advancement Division (AAD), Professional Development Branch (AAD/AADD), 1550 5th Street East, Randolph AFB TX 78150-4449; DSN 487-4075; AAD/AADD Workflow email: pdg@us.af.mil. This publication may not be supplemented or further implemented or extended.

Ensure that all records created as a result of processes prescribed in this publication are maintained IAW Air Force Manual (AFMAN) 33-363, *Management of Records,* and disposed of IAW Air Force Records Information Management System (AFRIMS) Records Disposition Schedule (RDS). The use of the name or mark of any specific manufacturer, commercial product, commodity, or service in this publication does not imply endorsement by the Air Force.

*SUMMARY OF CHANGES*

There are several minor updates within this edition of the Air Force Handbook 1, AIRMAN. The first major changes are the complete revision of chapters 5, 11, and 25. The second major change is the revision of the section Doctrine within chapter 4. The final major change involves the major revision of the section enlisted force structure within chapter 9. This publication was substantially revised by 125 Air Force level subject matter experts (SME) and must be completely reviewed.

**Chapter 11—OFFICER AND ENLISTED EVALUATION SYSTEMS AND CIVILIAN PERFORMANCE PROGRAM**

**Forward**

| | | |
|---|---|---|
| **Assistant Secretaries of War for Air Secretaries of the Air Force** | F. Trubee Davison | 1926-1932 |
| | Robert A. Lovett | 1941-1946 |
| | W. Stuart Symington | 1946-1947 |
| **Secretaries of the Air Force** | W. Stuart Symington | 1947-1950 |
| | Thomas K. Finletter | 1950-1953 |
| | Harold E. Talbott | 1953-1955 |
| | Donald A. Quarles | 1955-1957 |
| | James H. Douglas, Jr. | 1957-1959 |
| | Dudley C. Sharp | 1959-1961 |
| | Eugene M. Zuckert | 1961-1965 |
| | Harold Brown | 1965-1969 |
| | Robert C. Seamans, Jr. | 1969-1973 |
| | John L. McLucas | 1973-1975 |
| | James Plummer (acting) | 1975-1976 |
| | Thomas C. Reed | 1976-1977 |
| | John C. Stetson | 1977-1979 |
| | Hans M. Mark | 1979-1981 |
| | Verne Orr | 1981-1985 |
| | Russell A. Rourke | 1985-1986 |
| | Edward C. Aldridge, Jr. | 1986-1988 |
| | James McGovern (acting) | 1988-1989 |
| | John J. Welch, Jr. (acting) | 1989-1989 |
| | Donald B. Rice | 1989-1993 |
| | Michael Donley (acting) | 1993-1993 |
| | Sheila E. Widnall | 1993-1997 |
| | F. Whitten Peters (acting) | 1997-1999 |
| | F. Whitten Peters | 1999-2001 |
| | Dr. Lawrence Delaney (acting) | 2001-2001 |
| | Dr. James G. Roche | 2001-2005 |
| | Michael W. Wynne | 2005-2008 |
| | Michael B. Donley | 2008-2013 |
| | Eric K. Fanning (acting) | 2013-2013 |
| | Deborah L. James | 2013-2016 |
| | Lisa S. Disbrow (acting) | 2017-2017 |
| | Heather A. Wilson | 2017-Present |
| **Military Air Chiefs** | Capt Charles D. Chandler | 1907-1910 |
| | Capt Arthur S. Cowan | 1910-1911 |
| | Capt Charles D. Chandler | 1911-1912 |
| | Lt Henry H. Arnold | 1912-1913 |
| | Col Samuel Reber | 1913-1916 |
| | Brig Gen George Squier | 1916-1917 |
| | Lt Col John B. Bennet | 1917 |
| | Brig Gen Benjamin Foulois | 1917 |
| | Brig Gen Alexander Dade | 1917-1918 |
| | Maj Gen William Kenly | 1918-1919 |
| | Maj Gen Mason M. Patrick | 1921-1927 |
| | Maj Gen James E. Fechet | 1927-1931 |
| | Maj Gen Benjamin Foulois | 1931-1935 |
| | Maj Gen Oscar Westover | 1935-1938 |
| | Gen Henry H. Arnold | 1938-1946 |
| | Gen Carl A. Spaatz | 1946-1947 |

| U.S. Air Force Chiefs of Staff | | |
|---|---|---|
| | Gen Carl A. Spaatz | 1947-1948 |
| | Gen Hoyt S. Vandenberg | 1948-1953 |
| | Gen Nathan F. Twining | 1953-1957 |
| | Gen Thomas D. White | 1957-1961 |
| | Gen Curtis E. LeMay | 1961-1965 |
| | Gen John P. McConnell | 1965-1969 |
| | Gen John D. Ryan | 1969-1973 |
| | Gen George S. Brown | 1973-1974 |
| | Gen David C. Jones | 1974-1978 |
| | Gen Lew Allen, Jr. | 1978-1982 |
| | Gen Charles A. Gabriel | 1982-1986 |
| | Gen Larry D. Welch | 1986-1990 |
| | Gen Michael J. Dugan | 1990-1990 |
| | Gen John M Loh (acting) | 1990-1990 |
| | Gen Merrill A. McPeak | 1990-1994 |
| | Gen Ronald R. Fogleman | 1994-1997 |
| | Gen Ralph Eberhart (acting) | 1997-1997 |
| | Gen Michael E. Ryan | 1997-2001 |
| | Gen John P. Jumper | 2001-2005 |
| | Gen T. Michael Moseley | 2005-2008 |
| | Gen Norton A. Schwartz | 2008-2012 |
| | Gen Mark A. Welsh III | 2012-2016 |
| | Gen David L. Goldfein | 2016-Present |

**Chief Master Sergeants of the Air Force**

Refer to Chapter 9, The Noncommissioned Officer
Paragraph 9.5.3.4 for a list of CMSAF

## We Are America's Airmen

We are America's Airmen—a Total Force of active, guard, reserve, and civilian patriots that make us the greatest air force in the world. Every single day Airmen around the world provide the air, space, and cyberspace power necessary to protect America and our way of life. We *fly, fight,* and *win* whenever and wherever our nation needs us.

Our Air Force reflects the vision of the founders of airpower. We foster innovation in the development of the world's most professional Airmen, and are the heart and soul of our unique fighting force. The emerging global environment in which we operate demands that our Air Force continues to develop innovative Airmen who find better and smarter ways to *fly, fight,* and *win* by embracing strategic agility and inclusiveness to succeed in our mission and overcome unforeseen challenges that lay ahead.

You have joined a team of Airmen who have a rich history, and play an unparalleled role in the defense of America. Our Air Force is the greatest air force in the world because of the generations of professional Airmen who devoted their lives to serving their country. Airmen today recognize and honor their historic achievements and unique contributions to fighting and winning America's wars.

# Chapter 1

## AIR FORCE HERITAGE

### Section 1A—Overview

**1.1. Introduction.**

As preparation for your entry into the Air Force, this section will introduce the Air Force mission and their evolution, the machines and technology associated with air and space flight and most importantly, the legacy of the men and women of the United States Air Force. By surveying the history of aviation, you will discover our heritage, appreciate Air Force traditions, and understand your role in our nation's defense. This United States Air Force Historical Perspective is by Dr. John T. Farquhar from the United States Air Force Academy Department of History and contributing editor George W. Bradley III, the Air Force Space Command Historian. The enlisted portions of this document were provided by the Air Force Enlisted Heritage Research Institute's historian, Mr. William I. Chivalette. Dr. John Q. Smith, Senior Air Force Historian, assisted with additional editing.

### Section 1B—Dawn of Flight, Early Days of Aviation, First Air War and the 1920s and 1930s Airpower

**1.2. The Dawn of Flight:**

**Inflating the Civil War balloon *Intrepid*, 1862**

1.2.1. The dream of flight recurs in myth and legend from ancient times, but not until two French brothers, Joseph Michel and Jacques Etienne Montgolfier, launched a hot air balloon on 15 October 1783, with passenger Jean François Pilatre de Rozier, did man first "fly." The military potential of aviation was noted in 1794, when the French "Aerostatic Corps" balloons accompanied the armies of the French Revolution until 1798.

1.2.2. In September 1861, a "Balloon Corps" provided aerial observation for the Union Army during the American Civil War. However, the early balloons proved fragile, vulnerable to weather, and of limited value.

1.2.3. Aviation languished in the United States, but in Europe, balloons, gliders, and aerodynamics advanced rapidly. By 1853, Britain's Sir George Cayley created a glider with fixed wings, cambered airfoil, and horizontal and vertical stabilizers. Continuing Cayley's work, German engineer Otto Lilienthal produced flying machines similar to today's hang gliders. From 1891 until his death five years later, Lilienthal greatly advanced aerodynamic theory. The publicity generated by Lilienthal spurred on imaginative people on both sides of the Atlantic, including Orville and Wilbur Wright.

1.2.4. The Wrights furthered Lilienthal's experiments with the assistance of American Octave Chanute, whose book, *Progress in Flying Machines*, provided their foundation in aeronautics. From 1900 to 1902, the Wrights conducted more than 1,000 glides from Kill Devil Hills near Kitty Hawk, North Carolina. After perfecting wing warping, elevators and rudders, and a water-cooled engine, they attempted the first powered flight on 14 December 1903. On that try, the aircraft stalled upon takeoff and crashed three seconds later. Success came at 10:35, on 17 December 1903, when Orville Wright flew 120 feet in 12 seconds. Alternating pilot duties, the brothers made three more flights with Wilbur flying 852 feet and staying aloft 59 seconds on the fourth attempt.

1.2.5. American military authorities rejected the Wrights' flyer, reacting in part to the highly publicized failure of Samuel P. Langley's steam-powered Aerodrome in October 1903. Although a highly respected scientist and Secretary of the Smithsonian Institution, Langley and the Army were subjected to public ridicule and Congressional criticism for the "waste" of a $50,000 government grant. Only when President Theodore Roosevelt intervened was an aeronautical division established in the United States Army's Signal Corps on 1 August 1907.

1.2.6. With the establishment of an aeronautical division the army was in possession of several balloons. The Army required trained enlisted men to conduct balloon inflations and effect necessary repairs. Effective 2 July 1907, Eddy Ward and Jason Barrett reported to the Leo Stevens' balloon factory in New York City. They would become the first enlisted men assigned to the Signal Corps' small Aeronautical Division, which in time evolved into the United States Air Force enlisted corps.

1.2.7. When Ward and Barrett reported, the division did not officially exist. The Army had disbanded the minuscule Civil War balloon service in 1863, and the corps' attempts to revive military aviation met with little success. At the balloon factory, the two men were

The enlisted men of the 1908 Aeronautical Division Left to right (back row), Pfc. Vernon L. Burge, Pfc. Charles De Kim, Pvt. Eldred O. Eldred; (middle row) Pvt. Stewart K. Rosenberger, Corporal Edward Ward, Pvt. Cecil R. Colle, Pvt. William E. McConnell. Seated are Pvt. John Crotty (left) and Pvt. Benjamin Schmidt.

schooled in the rudiments of fabric handling, folding, and stitching; in the manufacturing of buoyant gases; and in the inflation and control of the Army's "aircraft."

1.2.8. On 13 August 1907, Ward and Barrett were ordered to report to Camp John Smith outside Norfolk, Virginia, to participate in the Jamestown Exposition celebrating the 300th anniversary of the first settlement of Virginia. Over the next few years, the detachment participated in numerous air shows and moved from location to location. Barrett left the Army to complete a career in the Navy, but the enlisted detachment was soon expanded to include eight others. These nine men were the nucleus from which America's enlisted air arm grew. They were the first of a small band of enlisted Airmen who, during the decade before World War I, shared in the experimental and halting first steps to establish military aviation as a permanent part of the Nation's defense. Never numbering more than a few hundred individuals, the enlisted crews of the Signal Corps' Aeronautical Division provided day-to-day support for a handful of officer pilots, learned the entirely new skills of airplane "mechanician"—and later, mechanic, rigger, and fitter—met daunting transportation and logistical challenges, and contributed mightily to the era's seat-of-the-pants technological advances.

1.2.9. A few enlisted men, against official and semi-official military prejudice, learned to fly. The majority of enlisted men were absorbed in the tasks of getting the fragile balloons and even flimsier planes of the day into the air and keeping them there. Of necessity flexible and innovative, early crews often had to rebuild aircraft from the ground up after every crash—and, in those early days of flight; crashes were the rule rather than the exception. Enlisted crews not only repaired the planes, they labored to make some of the more ill-designed craft airworthy in the first place.

### 1.3.  The Early Days of the United States Army Aviation (1907-1917):

**Wright brothers at Kitty Hawk**

1.3.1. By December 1907, the new Aeronautical Division of the Signal Corps established specifications for an American military aircraft. The flying machine had to carry two people (with a combined weight of 350 pounds or less), and fly for 125 miles at an average speed of 40 miles per hour (mph). The Army received 41 bids, but only one, submitted by the Wright brothers, produced a flyable aircraft. By September 1908, the Wright Type "A" Military Flyer flew for more than an hour at a maximum altitude of 310 feet, carrying the first military observer, Lieutenant Frank P. Lahm. A subsequent test on 17 September 1908 resulted in the first military aviation fatality: Lieutenant Thomas E. Selfridge. On 30 July 1909, pilot Orville Wright and Lieutenant Benjamin D. Foulois flew from Fort Myer to Alexandria, Virginia, at an average speed of 42.6 mph. The Army accepted the plane 2 August 1909 and awarded the Wrights $25,000 and a $5,000 bonus.

1.3.2. The United States Army's early air operations were not promising. In October 1909, Wilbur Wright trained Lieutenants Frank P. Lahm and Frederic E. Humphreys to fly; on 26 October, they were the first Army pilots to fly solo. By 5 November, they crashed the Army's plane and within weeks were transferred out of aviation. In March 1910, Lieutenant Foulois received orders to become the Signal Corps' pilot. Chief of the Signal Corps, Gen James Allen, told him, "Don't worry. You'll learn the techniques as you go along...just take plenty of spare parts and teach yourself to fly."

1.3.3. United States military aviation was falling behind Europe. By the end of 1911, the French had produced 353 aviators versus 26 American pilots, of whom only eight were military. By 1913, France and Germany each had spent $22 million on military aviation; Russia spent $12 million; and even Belgium spent $2 million, compared to just $430,000 for the United States.

1.3.4. Increased appropriations over the ensuing two years allowed the Army to purchase more aircraft. By October 1912, the Aeronautical Division had 11 aircraft, 14 flying officers, and 39 enlisted mechanics. On 28 September 1912, one of these mechanics, Corporal Frank Scott, became the first enlisted person to die in an accident in a military aircraft. A crew chief, Scott was flying as a passenger when the aircraft's pilot lost control and the aircraft dived to earth. Scott Field, now Scott Air Force Base, in Illinois, was named in his honor. On 5 March 1913, the 1st Aero Squadron (Provisional) was activated becoming the oldest Air Force squadron.

1.3.5. After years of testing, improvising, and operating on little more than dedication and a shoestring, Army aviation finally received official status by the passage of United States House Resolution 5304 on 18 July 1914. This bill authorized the Signal Corps to establish an aviation section consisting of 60 officers and 260 enlisted men. The bill created the military rating of aviation mechanician, which called for a 50 percent pay increase for enlisted men "instructed in the art of flying" while they were on flying status. The number of such personnel was limited to 40, and the law specified that no more than a dozen enlisted men could be trained as aviators.

1.3.6. America's first aviation combat experience demonstrated that the air arm was not prepared. After Francisco "Pancho" Villa's Mexican forces raided Columbus, New Mexico, in March 1916, President Woodrow Wilson ordered the 1st Aero Squadron to accompany a force he was organizing to protect the border and to apprehend Pancho Villa. The squadron, commanded by Captain Foulois, sought to provide aerial scouting for the ground forces. Mustering 11 pilot officers, 82 enlisted men, and one civilian mechanic, the squadron departed from San Antonio with eight Curtiss JN-3 "Jennies," ten trucks, and six motorcycles. On the train, Foulois picked up two enlisted hospital corpsmen. An officer and 14 enlisted men of the engineering section joined them. In spite of the 1st Aero Squadron's reconnaissance flights and several deliveries of mail and dispatches, readily apparent was the squadron's JN type aeroplane was not powerful enough to operate at the 5,000-foot elevations of the Casa Grande, and mountain weather, dust, and extreme temperatures wreaked havoc with Foulois' underpowered, dilapidated Curtis JN-3 Jennies. By 19 April, only two of the eight planes were in working condition. The rest had fallen victim to landing accidents and forced landings, and all had suffered from the heat and sand.

1.3.7. After 11 months of fruitless campaigning, the so-called Punitive Expedition was recalled in February 1917, and Villa continued to lead rebels in northern Mexico until 1920. Yet, poorly equipped as it was the 1st Aero Squadron had acquitted itself admirably. In his final report on the mission, Major Foulois praised his pilots, who because of poor climbing characteristics of the aircraft, could not carry sufficient food or even adequate clothing. Foulois also commended the willingness of his pilots to fly clearly dangerous aircraft. He did not neglect the enlisted personnel; he praised them for their dedication and willingness to work day and night to keep the aircraft flying. If the performance was admirable, the fact remains that the results of this first demonstration of American air power were deeply disappointing. Yet Foulois and the others learned valuable lessons about the realities of aviation under field conditions. Adequate maintenance was essential, as were plenty of backup aircraft, which could be rotated into service while other airplanes were removed from the line and repaired. Enlisted and civilian mechanics faced a myriad of problems; in particular, the laminated wood propellers pulled apart. In response, the mechanics developed a humidor facility to maximize the life of the props.

1.3.8. Army brass persisted in discouraging the training of enlisted men, and if not for officers such as Billy Mitchell and Hap Arnold, who developed a deep and abiding respect for enlisted personnel in military aviation, there probably would have been even fewer enlisted aviators than the law allowed. The Signal Corps authority to train more enlisted men was largely through the efforts of Mitchell and the National Defense Act of 3 June 1916. When the United States entered World War I, however, there were no more than a dozen non-officers qualified as pilots.

## 1.4. The First Air War:

1.4.1. Aircraft and aerial warfare evolved during the first World War, 1914-1918. Observation, artillery spotting, and reconnaissance emerged as the airplane's most important war missions. By 1915, pursuit aircraft were developed to deny the enemy use of the air. After early attempts to down enemies with handguns, French pilot Roland Garros attached steel plates to the propeller of his Morane-Saulnier Type L monoplane, enabling him to fire a machine gun through the propeller arc. He earned wide acclaim as the war's first "ace." When engine trouble forced Garros to land behind enemy lines on 19 April 1915, the Germans studied his innovation. Dutch-born Anthony Fokker then created the first true fighter plane, the Fokker Eindecker, using an interrupter gear to enable a machine gun to fire through the propeller. By the end of World War I, Airmen had pioneered most of today's aerial missions, including photographic reconnaissance, close air support for ground troops, battlefield interdiction, and day and nighttime strategic bombardment. The German air service inaugurated long-range strategic bombardment as early as 1915 with their massive Zeppelin dirigibles.

1.4.2. Despite the importance of reconnaissance and artillery spotting, fighter pilots captured the public's imagination. Newspapers portrayed the daring, skill, and chivalry of the "knights of the air." Following Roland Garros, the French produced such aces as Rene Fonck, with 75 kills, and Georges Guynemer, with 54 aerial victories.

1.4.3. Like the allies, Germany publicized "aces" to foster public support for the war effort. Germany's first ace, Max Immelmann, developed a revolutionary technique to reverse direction of an aircraft in flight. The technique still bears his name. Manfred von Richtofen, perhaps the most famous ace of all, flew a scarlet Fokker triplane, earning him the name, "the Red Baron." Shortly after his 80th victory, Richtofen was shot down and killed on 21 April 1918.

1.4.4. Not to be outdone by the French and Germans, Britain exulted in the exploits of fighter pilots. Britain's leading ace, with 73 kills, was Edward "Mick" Mannock, who was killed by ground fire while aiding a novice wingman.

1.4.5. As early as 1915, Americans flew in the European war, both with the French and the British—though it was the American-manned Lafayette Escadrille of France that earned the greatest and most enduring fame. The French air service established the *Escadrille Americaine* for American volunteers on 21 March 1916. Later renamed the *Lafayette Escadrille*, this squadron flew French Nieuport 17 fighters and provided valuable experience when the United States entered the war. French-born American Raoul Lufbery shot down 17 German planes before transferring to the American Air Service, where he commanded the famous "Hat in the Ring" 94th Aero Squadron, before his death on 19 May 1918.

1.4.6. A little-acknowledged fact about the Lafayette Escadrille is the roster of aviators included an enlisted man who was also an African-American—one of the very few enlisted Americans to fly in the war Corporal Eugene Bullard was

the son of a Georgia former slave. As a member of the French Foreign Legion, he was awarded the Croix de Guerre (one of 15 decorations from the French government) and was wounded four times before the legion gave him a disability discharge. During his convalescence in Paris, he bet an American $2,000 that he could learn to fly and become a combat aviator. Corporal Bullard won the bet by completing training and joining the Lafayette Escadrille. Styling himself the "Black Swallow of Death," he claimed two victories. Despite his record of daring and dedication, he was grounded at the request of American officers attached to the escadrille. When the escadrille pilots were reorganized and incorporated into the American Expeditionary Force, Bullard was denied the officer's commission accorded to other American escadrille aviators and to most of the handful of white enlisted men who had earned their wings in regular United States Army outfits.

**Corporal Eugene Bullard**

1.4.7. Of the 767 United States pilots and 481 observers in action in 1918, Capt Edward V. "Eddie" Rickenbacker and Lieutenant Frank Luke, Jr., achieved the most fame. Rickenbacker was a renowned race car driver before the war. Older than most pilots, the 28-year-old became America's "Ace of Aces" with 26 confirmed kills. Frank Luke was the only pilot awarded the Medal of Honor during the war (Rickenbacker would be awarded one in 1931). Known as the "Arizona Balloon Buster," Luke downed 14 German balloons and four aircraft in 17 days. His spectacular career ended on 29 September 1918 during a solo attack, when he shot down three enemy balloons and two aircraft before enemy ground fire forced him down. Seriously wounded, he died with a pistol in his hand.

1.4.8. Enlisted men flew before, during, and after World War I—but their status remained vague. On 22 January 1919, the commanding officer of the Air Mechanics School at Kelly Field sought to clarify the situation by asking the Office of Military Aeronautics for a

**2nd. Lt. Frank Luke, Jr.**

definition of "enlisted aviator" and "aerial flier." The Kelly commanding officer wanted to know who exactly was entitled to wear the enlisted aviator insignia on the upper-right shoulder of his tunic. The reply came on 31 January, " you are advised that although uniform regulations and specifications provide for an insignia to be worn by enlisted aviators, the grade itself has never been created and consequently there is no one in the service entitled to wear the

insignia provided for such grade." In other words, enlisted aviators, who had served as instructors, ferry pilots, test pilots, and mechanical flight-check pilots, did not exist—at least not officially.

1.4.9. Vernon Burge and the handful of World War I enlisted aviators who immediately followed him were the first of some 3,000 enlisted personnel who would fly between the wars and into the early months of World War II. The military withheld official flying status from these men until Congress enacted Public Law 99 in 1941, which provided for training enlisted "aviation students," who were "awarded the rating of pilot and warranted as a staff sergeant." Late in 1942, however, Congress

**Sergeant William C. Ocker**

passed the Flight Officer Act (Public Law 658), which automatically promoted sergeant pilots produced by the Staff Sergeant Pilot Program to flight officers. Thus, the cockpit was effectively reserved "for the commissioned." One enlisted pilot, Sergeant William C. Ocker, inspired to fly by watching Vernon Burge, received his commission in January 1917 and commanded a flight school in Pennsylvania. However, before this his flying skills made Ocker a valuable commodity in the Aviation Section. Known as the "Father of Blind Flight," Ocker flight-tested modified aircraft, served as a flight instructor, and was hand-picked to scout various parcels for future airfields near the Potomac River. One of the tracts he selected became Bolling Field, Washington District of Columbia.

1.4.10. Master Sergeant George H. Holmes was the last of about 2,500 men who graduated from enlisted pilot training. He became a pilot in 1921 and was eventually promoted to lieutenant colonel during World War II. When the war ended, he chose to revert to his enlisted rank of master sergeant. He was the last enlisted pilot to serve and retired in 1957.

**George H. Holmes (as a corporal)**

1.4.11. In addition to the specialized roles directly associated with flying, Air Service enlisted personnel performed a wide variety of general support functions in administration, mess, transport, and the medical corps. Construction personnel, who built the airfields, hangars, barracks, and other buildings, were often the first enlisted men stationed at various overseas locations.

1.4.12. World War I Airmen were not combat soldiers as such, but enlisted men who stood guard and operated base defense. Given the static nature of the war, there was relatively little danger of a base being overrun by ground troops.

Air attacks, however, happened frequently. Aerial bombardment and strafing techniques improved later in the war, and enlisted men received training in the operation of antiaircraft machine guns.

1.4.13. Enlisted personnel also served as observers for both the aircraft and balloon corps. In this capacity Sergeant Fred C. Graveline of the 20th Aero Squadron was able to receive the Distinguished Flying Cross. Graveline served as an observer and aerial gunner from 30 September to 5 November 1918 on 15 missions in the back seat of a DH-4. In one 35-minute battle in which Graveline remarked he "aged 10 years," he helped drive off nearly two dozen German planes, shooting down two.

1.4.14. While he was not an ace, William "Billy" Mitchell emerged as one of the outstanding American air combat commanders of the war, in essence the first Combined Forces Air Component Commander, as he directed British, French, and American airpower. Supremely confident about the efficacy of airpower, Mitchell sometimes clashed with his superiors, including aviation pioneer General Foulois. Nevertheless, Foulois recognized Mitchell's leadership and recommended him for the top combat position, Chief of Air Service, 1st Army.

**Sergeant Fred C. Graveline (shown as a corporal)**

In September 1918, Mitchell massed 1,481 aircraft of American, French, British, and Italian units to support General Pershing's St. Mihiel offensive. Mitchell emphasized concentrated, mass attacks to overwhelm enemy airpower and punish German ground forces. In four days, Allied Airmen flew 3,300 combat sorties and dropped 75 tons of explosives. Lauded as a success by General Pershing, Mitchell refined his tactics during the Meuse-Argonne offensive of 26 September 1918, where 700 American aircraft faced 500 German planes. By 1918, based upon his outstanding performance directing Air Service combat units over the Château-Thierry area, the St. Mihiel salient, and the Meuse-Argonne, Mitchell earned the Distinguished Service Cross for valor and temporary promotion to brigadier general.

**Brig. Gen. William "Billy" Mitchell**

1.4.15. By the Armistice of 11 November 1918, airpower had played an important role in the Allied victory. Although observation, reconnaissance, and artillery spotting remained the most significant missions, close air support, interdiction, and strategic bombardment showed promise. Eclipsing all other roles, the image of the glamorous fighter ace with his brightly painted aircraft, leather jacket, and flying scarf captured public attention. The Army Air Service destroyed 781 enemy aircraft and 73 balloons at a cost of 289 American aircraft, 48 balloons, and 569 battle casualties.

1.4.16. At the end of the war, more than 190,000 men were serving in the Air Service, 74,000 of them overseas with the American expeditionary force. On the same day, the Air Service halted all inductions of enlisted recruits and began the process of dissolving its forces. Combat groups and wings in Europe were disbanded immediately, but squadrons remained intact to serve initially as the basic demobilization unit structures. Since the Air Service had no clear idea of the authorized final strength for the postwar peacetime, it cut loose men in wholesale batches. The Army, in general, and the air service, in particular, took considerable pains to help discharged enlisted men find jobs after leaving the service. The Army worked closely with Federal officials to aid veterans and even allowed some men to remain in the service temporarily beyond their discharge if they had no prospects for work. Air service commanding officers provided special letters of recommendation to former mechanics and technically trained enlisted men in an effort to help them find employment.

1.4.17. On 20 May 1918, President Woodrow Wilson issued an Executive Order that transferred Army aviation from under the Signal Corps control to the Secretary of War. Later that same month, the Army officially recognized the Bureau of Aircraft Production and the Division of Military Aeronautics as the Air Service. World War I showed the difficulty of coordinating air activities under the existing organization, thus the Army Reorganization Act of 1920 made the Air Service an official combat arm of the Army.

## 1.5. Controversy and Records, 1920s Airpower:

1.5.1. Budget cutbacks reduced the 1918 Air Service from 190,000 men to fewer than 20,000. Likewise, the $460 million allocated for military aviation in 1919 fell to $25 million in 1920. Even worse from a technology viewpoint, Congress demanded that new military aircraft use the surplus Liberty engines produced during the World War I buildup. Consequently, First World War vintage Curtiss Jennies and Liberty DH-4 bombers remained in service until the 1930s, despite technological advances in airframe and engine design.

1.5.2. As far back as 1919, while Congress debated the size of the postwar establishment, the Air Service mounted shows for all occasions. Scarcely a county fair or patriotic gathering within flying distance of a military airfield operated without an aerial demonstration. Enlisted mechanics might lecture on how to repair the Liberty engine, while pilots flew acrobatics overhead. The traveling air shows, known as circuses, coincided with Victory Loan rallies and in later years provided entertainment at Armistice Day or Washington's Birthday celebrations. Enlisted pilots also took part in air shows, including a trio of intrepid flying sergeants who in 1923 put together an act that involved flying a tight "V" formation while their planes were tied together with cords. Other enlisted pilots offered more routine skills, such as dropping demonstration smoke bombs.

**Lt. James H. Doolittle, 1922**

1.5.3. A concerted effort to achieve records in speed, altitude, endurance, and other areas helped spur aviation advances in the 1920s. In September 1922, Lieutenant James "Jimmy" Doolittle became the first man to fly across the United States in less than a day. Seven months later, Lieutenants Oakley Kelley and John Macready flew a Fokker T-2 on the first nonstop transcontinental flight. On 6 April 1924, a team of Army pilots departed Seattle in four Douglas World Cruisers, christened the *Chicago, Boston, Seattle,* and *New Orleans,* in an effort to fly around the world. Although the *Seattle* and *Boston* were lost to a mountain crash and engine failure, respectively, the remaining aircraft completed the circuit 175 days later. In 1925, Jimmy Doolittle achieved further fame by winning the Schneider Trophy, an over–water seaplane race, and established a world seaplane record at 245.71 miles per hour. Although less publicized, Doolittle also played a major role in designing and testing instruments for all–weather flying, including an altimeter, gyro, artificial horizon, and radio navigation aids. On 24 September 1929, Doolittle was the first pilot to take off, fly a set course, and land using instruments alone.

1.5.4. Air activities through the mid-1920s were relatively limited and generally focused on establishing records, testing equipment, and garnering headlines. Master electrician Jack Harding and Sergeant First Class Jerry Dobias served aboard a Martin bomber that flew "around the rim" of the country, starting at Bolling Field on 24 July 1919. Totaling 100 flights and 9,823 miles, Dobias kept the effort from ending almost before it began. Almost immediately after taking off from Bolling, he crawled out on the aircraft's left wing, without a parachute, to repair a leaky engine. In 1920, the Air Corps flew a round-trip flight of four DH-4Bs from Mitchell Field on Long Island to Nome, Alaska. The flight took three months and covered 9,000 miles and the safety record was largely attributable to Master Sergeant Albert Vierra.

1.5.5. Toward the end of the decade, Airmen were ready to demonstrate even more impressive records. New Year's Day 1929, a team of Airmen destined for fame took off in a Fokker C-2 featuring a large question mark on the fuselage. The question was simple: how long could they stay in the air? Using a crude air refueling technique pioneered in 1923, Major Carl "Tooey" Spaatz, Capt Ira Eaker, Lieutenant Harry Halverson, Lieutenant Elwood "Pete" Quesada, and Staff Sergeant Roy Hooe flew the *Question Mark* 150 hours and 40 minutes, taking on 5,600 gallons of hand-pumped fuel during 37 air-to air refuelings, to travel 11,000 miles. This endurance test proved the unlimited range available with air refueling. The quest for world records in the 1920s honed the skills of Airmen, advanced aviation technology, and kept military aviation in the limelight.

**Refueling the *Question Mark***

**Aerial view of the *Ostfriesland***

1.5.6. An important group of demonstrations during the 1920s was more closely related to the airplane as an advanced weapon of war. As early as the beginning of the decade, Brigadier General Mitchell was convinced of airpower's potential as the primary component of national defense and a war-winning weapon and aggressively promoted his cause to create an independent Air Force. Hoping to make this the nation's first line of defense, he challenged the United States Navy, arguing that bombers rendered battleships obsolete. Reluctantly, the Navy agreed to allow Mitchell to test his Martin MB-2 bombers against some captured German ships. Mitchell's Airmen sank the 27,000-ton battleship, *Ostfriesland* on 21 July 1921. Despite the four-layer armored hull and watertight compartments, the battleship eventually disappeared into the water. Although Mitchell failed to convince the War or Navy departments, the bombing tests spurred carrier-based aviation development.

1.5.7. Despite previous air service successes, the Navy remained unconvinced about their vulnerability from the air. Officials eventually turned over two World War I battleships, the USS *New Jersey* (BB-16) and the USS *Virginia,* for further testing. A young bombardier, Sergeant Ulysses "Sam" Nero, earned a slot among the 12 aircrews selected by General Mitchell to try to sink the battleships.

1.5.8. On 5 September 1923, 11 aircraft reached the targets just off the North Carolina coast—the 12th returned to base because of engine trouble. Ten of the aircraft dropped their ordnance far from the *New Jersey.* Nero, using different tactics than General Mitchell instructed, scored two hits. General Mitchell disqualified Nero and his pilot from further competition but reconsidered when the remainder of the crews failed to hit the *Virginia* until they dropped down to 1,500 feet.

1.5.9. Nero and the Martin-Curtiss NBS-1 pilot approached the *New Jersey* at 85 miles per hour at an altitude of 6,900 feet, from about 15 degrees off the port beam. Using an open wire site, Nero dropped his first 600-pound bomb right down the ship's smokestack. A delayed explosion lent suspense to the result, but a billowing black cloud signaled the *New Jersey's* demise, which went down in just over three minutes. Having one bomb left and no *New Jersey* to drop it on, Nero's aircraft proceeded to the floundering *Virginia,* where Nero proceeded to administer the *coup de grace* on the stricken craft—his bomb landed directly on the *Virginia's* deck. General Mitchell promoted Nero during the next cycle.

**Sergeant Ulysses Nero**

1.5.10. Frustrated by what he perceived as a lack of progress, Mitchell's public statements were increasingly incendiary. When the Navy airship *Shenandoah* crashed on 5 September 1925, Mitchell issued a press release charging the Department of the Navy and the War Department with "incompetency, criminal negligence, and almost treasonable administration of our national defense." During the ensuing court martial, Mitchell attempted to transform the trial into a public hearing on airpower. Found guilty of "conduct of a nature to bring discredit upon the military service," the court sentenced Mitchell to a five-year suspension from the service without pay. On 1 February 1926, Mitchell resigned from the Air Service to continue the fight for an independent air force. Until his death in 1936, Mitchell fought tenaciously for his vision. He placed his indelible stamp on United States air combat practice and doctrine with his emphasis on massed forces and offensive operations.

1.5.11. Mitchell's efforts produced some success for the fledgling Air Corps. The Air Corps Act of 1926 greatly improved the status of aviation within the Army. This transformed the Air Service into the Air Corps, provided representation on the General Staff, added an Assistant Secretary of War for Air, and promised expansion to a force of 1,650 officers, 15,000 enlisted men, and 1,800 serviceable aircraft within five years. However, funding never matched the goal established.

## 1.6. Air Corps Tactical School and the Rise of the Bomber (1930s Air Corps):

1.6.1. Although technological advances continued into the 1930s, the Great Depression dominated the decade. The technological promise of all-metal construction, monoplane design, and advanced power plants met the harsh realities of a shoe-string budget caused by reduced tax revenues and economic malaise. Toward the latter half of the decade, powerful totalitarian states, including Fascist Italy, Nazi Germany, Nationalist Japan, and the Communist Union of Soviet Socialist Republics, threatened western democracies, but powerful isolationist sentiment limited the United States military response.

1.6.2. Within the Air Corps, leading Airmen emphasized doctrinal development through the Air Corps Tactical School. Doctrine, the concepts that are the basis of how to fight, provided ideas for technological requirements, aircraft procurement, strategy, and tactics. The Air Corps Tactical School served as the military aviation doctrine center from their founding in 1920 as the Air Service Field Officer School, Langley Field, Virginia. In 1922, the school was renamed the Air Service Tactical School before becoming the Air Corps Tactical School in 1926. Even before the Air Corps Tactical School moved to Maxwell Field, Alabama, in 1931, the school attracted the best and brightest Airmen to their faculty, including Harold L. George, Kenneth Walker, Donald Wilson, George C. Kenney, Haywood S. Hansell, and Muir S. Fairchild. Influenced by Billy Mitchell, Italy's Giulio Douhet, and Britain's Hugh Trenchard, the Air Corps Tactical School faculty emphasized long-range strategic bombardment.

1.6.3. According to Air Corps Tactical School lectures, massed bombers would penetrate enemy defenses, bypass field armies and navies, and strike enemy "vital centers" whose destruction would collapse the enemy's economy. Proper target selection would destroy an enemy's capability and will to fight. In an era before radar, airpower theorists believed effective air defense would be impossible. They looked to high altitude, speed, and internal armament for defense. These ideas ultimately led United States Airmen to emphasize the high altitude precision daylight bombardment that characterized much of the air operations during the Second World War.

1.6.4. During the interwar period, aircraft mechanics received formal technical training at Chanute Field, Illinois, at what became the Air Corps Technical School in 1926. Perhaps the key to the success of the technical school was the air service system of trade testing. While other branches of the Army returned to the apprentice system of assignment and training, the Army Air Corps continued to use and develop a combination of the Army Alpha Test, aptitude tests, and counseling. Enlisted men who wanted to apply for technical training had to qualify as high school graduates or the equivalent and pass a mathematics proficiency test in addition to the alpha test. Finally, a trade test specialist familiar with the actual work personally interviewed each enlisted man.

1.6.5. Classes at the technical school started in the fall and usually continued until the following spring. Students had to pay their own transportation to Illinois and, during some periods, lived in relatively crude conditions. Still, the training grew in popularity, and by 1938; the technical school had outgrown Chanute, with new branches opening at Lowry Field near Denver, Colorado, and at Scott Field in downstate Illinois.

**Sergeant Ralph W. Bottriell**

1.6.6. Enlisted men participated in a range of experimental work, including altitude flights, blind flying, aerial photography, and cosmic ray research and the development of the parachute. Whether they were selected as guinea pigs or because they were just interested, enlisted men served as the first to try out new parachute designs, and they eventually took over most of the testing and training. The most prominent enlisted parachutist was Sergeant Ralph Bottriell who tested the first backpack-style, freefall parachute on 19 May 1919. Bottriell eventually became chief parachute instructor at Kelly Field, Texas, and earned the Distinguished Flying Cross in 1933 for service as an experimental parachute tester.

1.6.7. Coinciding with Air Corps Tactical School doctrine, the American aviation industry introduced a series of advanced bombers that encouraged airpower advocates. In 1931, the Boeing Airplane Company introduced the B-9, an all-metal, stressed-skin bomber with retractable landing gear capable of 188 mph. A few months later, the Martin B-10 overshadowed the open-cockpit B-9. The B-10 also featured an all metal, monoplane design with retractable landing gear, enclosed cockpit, a glazed gun turret, variable pitch propellers, wing flaps, and an internal bomb bay with power-driven doors. On 19 July 1934, Colonel Henry H. "Hap" Arnold led a squadron of B-10s from Washington, District of Columbia, to Anchorage, Alaska, covering 4,000 miles in 25 flying hours. Bomber theorists saw this exploit as a validation of their ideas

1.6.8. In February 1934, a crisis arose that tested both the leadership and the flying skills of the Air Corps when President Franklin D. Roosevelt cancelled airmail contracts with civilian airlines. Without a thorough analysis of Air Corps capabilities, General Foulois asserted that the Air Corps would pick up the slack until contracts were renewed. However, the Air Corps underestimated the challenge posed. Army Airmen attempted to fly mail routes in open-cockpit planes with primitive instruments in one of the worst winters recorded. In three months, the Air Corps lost 66 aircraft and suffered 18 fatalities. The airmail fiasco forced Foulois to resign and led to a Congressional investigation known as the Baker Board.

1.6.9. The Baker Board scrutinized Air Corps operations and recommended the creation of a single command for all combat aircraft, known as General Headquarters Air Force. Brig Gen Frank Andrews assumed command 1 March 1935. Airmen applauded the action as a means to consolidate command, centralize doctrine, and integrate training. The initial cadre included 17 combat units: three wings, ten groups, and four squadrons. Today's Air Combat Command traces their heritage to General Headquarters Air Force. Among other measures, the General Headquarters Air Force called for a bomber capable of carrying a 2,000-pound payload for 1,020 miles, at a speed of 200 mph. The Martin and Douglas companies advanced designs, but the Boeing's Model 299 was what excited the General Headquarters Air Force staff. In August 1935, the four-engine aircraft flew 2,100 miles nonstop from Seattle, Washington, to Dayton, Ohio, averaging 232 mph. The B-17 "Flying Fortress," paired with the Norden bombsight, revolutionized bombardment and promised to validate Air Corps Tactical School theories.

*Section 1C—General Headquarters, Air Corps Prepares for War, and Airpower in World War II*

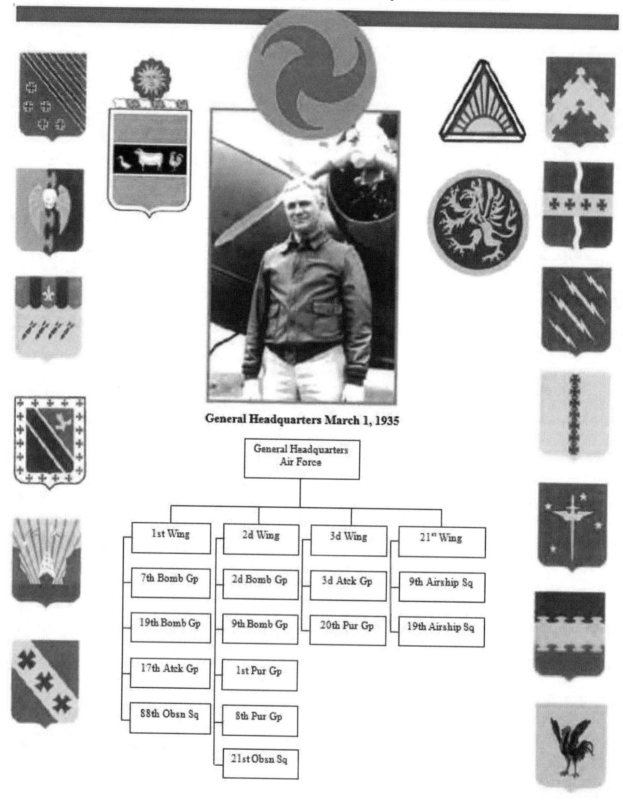

**General Headquarters March 1, 1935**

General Headquarters
Air Force

| 1st Wing | 2d Wing | 3d Wing | 21" Wing |
|---|---|---|---|
| 7th Bomb Gp | 2d Bomb Gp | 3d Atck Gp | 9th Airship Sq |
| 19th Bomb Gp | 9th Bomb Gp | 20th Pur Gp | 19th Airship Sq |
| 17th Atck Gp | 1st Pur Gp | | |
| 88th Obsn Sq | 8th Pur Gp | | |
| | 21st Obsn Sq | | |

## 1.7. General Headquarters Air Force (1935-1939):

1.7.1. The resulting reorganization established a General Headquarters Air Force (a measure that set up a tactical air force under the direct control of the Army General Headquarters but left the day-to-day organization of the Air Corps mostly intact—a confusing half-step toward an independent air force) and recognized that technological advances in aircraft would eventually make air power a significant military force apart from its early role of solely supporting ground troops. The appearance of the B-17 bomber and the threat of global war ushered in an era of greater expenditure, manpower expansion, and more specialized and more sophisticated training.

1.7.2. The General Headquarters Air Force resumed the practice of sending demonstration teams to fairs and expositions and expanded the scope and scale of publicity flights to include large gestures such as goodwill missions to South America. These expeditions also provided opportunities to test the new long-range big bombers. In February 1938, the air force flew six B-17s with full crews, including enlisted men, to Buenos Aires to mark the inauguration of the new Argentine president.

1.7.3 Even before the actual outbreak of hostilities in Europe in the fall of 1939, the General Headquarters Air Force had begun the massive expansion program that would blossom during the following years into the largest air organization in the Nation's history. In 1939, President Franklin Delano Roosevelt asked for an appropriation of $300 million for military aviation. The Air Corps planned for 24 operational combat-ready groups by 1941, which called for greatly enhanced manpower, training, and equipment.

## 1.8. The Air Corps Prepares for War.

In 1938, when the United States first took seriously the signs of war in Europe, the army's air arm was still split into two cumbersome command organizations, the Army Air Corps and General Headquarters Air Force. The total force included less than 20,000 enlisted Airmen. In 1940, Congress passed the first peacetime conscription law in United States history. By March 1944 when the air force manpower reached their high point, 2,104,405 enlisted men and women were serving in a virtually independent branch of the armed services. Moreover, they operated a sophisticated machine of air war that covered nearly the entire globe.

## 1.9. Airpower in World War II: The European Theater:

1.9.1. If the First World War signaled airpower's promise, the Second World War fulfilled the vision. In every aspect of aerial combat, airpower served as a force multiplier and a vital component of the joint, combined arms campaign. Air superiority proved a prerequisite for successful land, sea, or air operations.

1.9.2. On 1 September 1939, Adolf Hitler launched a massive assault on Poland that opened the greatest war in history and spawned the term Blitzkrieg, or "lightning war." The German Air Force (*Luftwaffe*) employed Messerschmitt Me-109 fighters to gain air superiority; Heinkel He-111 and Dornier Do-17 twin-engined bombers to pound Poland's capital, Warsaw; and Junkers Ju-87 *Stuka* dive bombers to attack Polish ground forces and terrorize refugees. Commanded by Hermann Göring, the *Luftwaffe* emphasized speed and concentration of forces to crush the enemy.

1.9.3. In April 1940, German forces surprised neutral Denmark and Norway, where *Luftwaffe* aircraft inflicted significant damage to Britain's Royal Navy, protected inferior German naval forces, and airlifted German troops to Norwegian airfields. In May, Hitler's forces invaded the Netherlands and Belgium. The speed of the German advance and the ruthlessness of the bombing of Rotterdam shocked the West. German paratroopers and glider forces surprised Belgium's famed Eban Emael fortress, considered the strongest in Europe. When German forces attacked France, the *Luftwaffe* gained air superiority, masked the movement of German panzers through the Ardennes forest, and hindered Allied attempts to rally.

1.9.4. Following the defeat of France in June 1940, the victorious *Luftwaffe* faced Britain's Royal Air Force in the Battle of Britain, the first all-air campaign in history. On paper, the *Luftwaffe* appeared to have a decisive edge, with 1,232 medium bombers, 406 dive bombers, 813 single-engine fighters, 282 twin-engine fighters, and 50 long-range reconnaissance aircraft manned by experienced crews. Opposing them, Air Marshal Sir Hugh Dowding's Fighter Command assembled 704 operational aircraft, including roughly 400 Hawker Hurricanes, suited for attacking bombers, and 200 Supermarine Spitfires, a fighter equal to German Messerschmitts.

1.9.5. Despite the apparent mismatch, the German Air Force suffered from serious weaknesses. Substantial losses had eroded *Luftwaffe* strength; in particular, the forces in France badly needed rest and refitting. Equally significant, German training, equipment, and experience proved ill-suited for a long-range strategic air campaign. Although the Me-109 was a superb fighter, the short range limited the Me-109 combat time and tactical flexibility over England. The long-range Me-110 proved hopelessly outclassed by Royal Air Force Spitfires and Hurricanes. On the other hand, Dowding's Fighter Command had been preparing for a German onslaught since 1937. Using Sir Robert Watson-Watt's innovation, radar, the British created an effective, integrated air defense system. Dowding also exploited a breakthrough in code breaking with the use of the Enigma machine. Any information gained from Enigma was top secret and known as ULTRA. This gave British intelligence forewarning of major attacks and invaluable insight on the status of German maintenance and logistics.

1.9.6. Plagued by poor intelligence, Göring and other *Luftwaffe* leaders miscalculated, leading to a battle of attrition won by the Royal Air Force. Failing to appreciate the value of British radar stations, the Germans first attacked Royal Air Force airfields and then after the Royal Air Force bombed Berlin 24 August, switched to a terror bombing campaign against London. Against German losses of 1,733 aircraft, the Royal Air Force lost 915 planes. By 15 September 1940, Hitler abandoned his planned invasion of Britain. In tribute to the Royal Air Force Fighter Command, Prime Minister Winston Churchill stated, "Never in the field of human conflict was so much owed by so many to so few."

1.9.7. The fall of France in June 1940 galvanized President Franklin Roosevelt's resolve to fight Nazi tyranny. Knowing the isolationist sentiment of many Americans, Roosevelt turned to airpower as a major weapon. The President called for American industry to build 50,000 military aircraft. Considering that in 1939, the United States Army Air Corps numbered roughly 1,800 aircraft and 18,000 men, this figure stunned air leaders and industrialists alike. American industry proved equal to the task, but aeronautical designs, blueprints, tools, dies, air frames, and engines, not to mention factories, skilled workers, and the countless other components of an aviation industry required time to develop. Air logisticians such as Major General Oliver P. Echols began the most massive aircraft procurement program in history. Until December 1940, the United States built aircraft at a rate of only 800 per month. By 1942, American factories produced 47,800 aircraft, and by 1944, an astronomical 96,300 planes. American industrial production emerged as a key to Allied victory.

**Women working in an aircraft factory**

1.9.8. To manage growing American airpower, a major reorganization created the United States Army Air Forces. General Henry "Hap" Arnold was appointed Commanding General of the United States Army Air Forces and Deputy Chief of Staff, Air Force to General George C. Marshall. In August 1941, a group of ex-Air Corps Tactical School instructors created a doctrinal blueprint, Air War Planning Document 1, for the conduct of a strategic air campaign against the Axis. Led by Lieutenant Colonel Harold "Hal" George, Major Lawrence Kuter, Major Kenneth Walker, and Captain Haywood "Possum" Hansell, the team created the conceptual framework for the American air effort in World War II. Reflecting 1930s Air Corps Tactical School doctrine of using massive force to destroy the enemy's will and capability to fight through long-range strategic bombardment, Air War Planning Document 1 called for 239 combat groups; 26,416 combat aircraft, including 7,500 heavy bombers; 37,051 training planes; 150,000 trained aircrews; and 2.2 million personnel.

1.9.9. On 7 December 1941, "a date which will live in infamy," Imperial Japan dealt a devastating blow to the United States Pacific Fleet at Pearl Harbor. Two waves of 350 Japanese aircraft sank or heavily damaged all eight United States battleships. Concerned over the prospect of sabotage, the United States Army ground commander ordered United States Army Air Forces aircraft parked in tight rows that made prime targets for Japanese aviators. To make matters worse, a few hours later, Japanese forces caught United States aircraft on the ground refueling in the Philippines and destroyed B-17s and assorted fighters. On 8 December, the United States declared war on Japan; three days later, Germany and Italy were at war with the United States as allies of Japan. Despite the fact the attack on Pearl Harbor was what formally brought the United States into the war, the war in Europe and the defeat of Germany would take precedence.

1.9.10. As America entered the war, the Royal Air Force tried to persuade the United States Army Air Forces to switch to night operations, like those of Royal Air Force Bomber Command. Under Air Marshal Sir Arthur Harris, Royal Air Force bombing doctrine embraced night area bombing of German cities to displace German workers. To United States Army Air Forces leaders, night bombing was ineffective, inefficient, and indiscriminate with regard to civilian casualties. After tough negotiations, the Casablanca Directive of January 1943 inaugurated the Combined Bomber Offensive, codenamed Operation POINTBLANK, combining American precision daylight bombing and British night area bombing.

1.9.11. In February 1942, Brig Gen Ira C. Eaker established the VIII Bomber Command, flying from bases in England in preparation for the United States Army Air Forces buildup. General Spaatz assumed command of the "Mighty Eighth" in June 1942. On 17 August 1942, a dozen B-17Es from the 97th Bomb Group conducted the first American operational bombing mission. The strike against a railroad marshalling yard in Rouen, France, barely penetrated the German defenses, but the mission and a series of others known as the "Freshman Raids" showed promise for American daylight bombardment.

**B–24 Liberators over Ploesti**

1.9.12. Three disastrous missions in the late summer and fall of 1943 illustrated United States Army Air Forces theory flaws. Eager to strike Hitler's oil supply, 177 B-24 Liberators based in North Africa attacked oil refineries at Ploesti, Romania, on 1 August 1943. Ploesti was one of the most heavily defended targets in Europe, so success depended on a 2,700-mile flight (much at low-level to avoid radar detection), accurate open-water navigation, good weather, and surprise. But a combination of bad weather, human error, and bad luck scattered the bomber formations and resulted in a nightmare for surviving crews. As the careful plan imploded, bombers improvised striking targets of opportunity in the face of determined fighter opposition and hundreds of anti-aircraft guns. The attacking force lost 54 B-24s; 41 in combat. Of the 177 aircraft, only 30 emerged unscathed. Although the strike reduced oil-refining capacity by 40 percent, within a few days a new facility opened, negating the damage.

1.9.13. After finally assembling enough trained crews to strike deep into Germany, Eighth Air Force planners targeted German ball bearing factories in an effort to destroy a "vital center" in the enemy's industrial web. They devised an ambitious double raid upon the Messerschmitt aircraft factory at Regensburg and the top-priority Schweinfurt ball bearing plants. The plan called for a wave of the 3d Air Division to fight through German fighters, hit Regensburg, and proceed to North Africa to land, followed 30 minutes later by a second bomber wave that would strike Schweinfurt as German fighters on the ground rearmed and refueled.

1.9.14. On 17 August 1943, General LeMay's 3d Air Division launched the first wave. Thick fog delayed the second wave and prevented fighter escorts from taking off. When the fog lifted, almost the entire German fighter force pounced upon the ill-fated 1st Air Division. The Eighth Air Force staggered under the loss of 60 out of 361 B-17s and 600 trained aircrew members, more casualties in a day than during the previous six months. To make matters worse, the Schweinfurt ball bearing plants required reattack.

1.9.15. Known as "Black Thursday," the 14 October 1943 mission against Schweinfurt effectively ended the United States Army Air Forces unescorted bombing campaign. Determined to destroy the top priority target, General Eaker ordered 291 B-17s to run the gauntlet of German fighters. This time, bombing accuracy improved significantly and the mission severely damaged the factories, but another 60 bombers were shot down; seven were destroyed upon landing in England, and 138 B-17s suffered battle damage.

1.9.16. While warplanners devoted the bulk of American airpower to daylight strategic bombing, in October 1943, heavily modified, mission-unique bombers from the Special Flight Section, 5th Bombardment Wing, Twelfth Air Force, along with England-based 801st Bombardment Group "Carpetbaggers," provided clandestine support for allied partisans and guerilla units in occupied territories, rescuing hundreds of downed aircrews trapped behind enemy lines.

1.9.17. Some technological and production breakthroughs reversed the course of the air war over the winter of 1943-1944. During the initial campaigns, effective long-range escort fighters appeared to be technically impossible. In order to carry the fuel necessary for long-range flight, fighters required at least twin engines, but the increased size sacrificed speed and maneuverability. The long-range Lockheed P-38 Lightning offered a partial solution, but the P-38's performance lagged at high altitudes. In mid-1943, the United States Army Air Forces introduced 75-gallon, and later 108-gallon, drop tanks that extended the combat radius of the Republic P-47 Thunderbolt fighter from 175 miles to 280 miles and 325 miles, respectively. The P-47's extended range proved an important step, but only a partial answer to the escort problem.

1.9.18. The North American Aviation P-51 Mustang revolutionized the air war over Europe. Designed in only 100 days during the spring of 1940, the Mustang was to supplement the Royal Air Force's Spitfire. The initial Allison engine for the P-51 proved inadequate; but when the Spitfire's Rolls-Royce Merlin engine replaced the original power plant, the results stunned aviators. At 440 mph, the P-51B was faster and could out turn and out dive the latest models of Me-109 and the new Focke-Wulf FW-190. With a basic range of 500 miles, augmentable to 850 miles, the Mustang flew farther than a B-17 with normal payload. Introduced in December 1943, the P-51 had to wait until late February 1944 before weather permitted full flight operations and was a technological marvel: a plane with a bomber's range and a fighter's performance.

1.9.19. The P-47 and P-51 team seized the air superiority from the *Luftwaffe* in the spring of 1944. Complementing the technological improvements, Allied factories poured out large numbers of new aircraft and stateside training bases produced well-trained air crews. At the helm of the VIII Fighter Command, Brigadier General William E. Kepner maximized his advantage by introducing new tactics. Fighters would no longer be required to "stick to the bombers." Numerical superiority permitted fighter sweeps and aggressive scouting; superior range allowed fighters to strafe German airfields and attack targets of opportunity.

**B-17s flying over Europe**

1.9.20. Armed with new aircraft, tactics, and superior numbers, Spaatz, Doolittle, and Kepner launched Operation ARGUMENT with the objective of winning air superiority and crippling Germany's aircraft industry. Between 20 and 25 February 1944, the 8th Air Force flew 3,300 heavy bomber sorties; the Fifteenth Air Force added 500 missions from Italy; and Royal Air Force Bomber Command flew 2,750 night attacks aimed at German aircraft manufacturing plants. Protecting them involved nearly 4,000 fighter sorties. At a cost of 226 American bombers, 114 British heavies, and 41 United States Army Air Forces fighters, Operation ARGUMENT destroyed 355 *Luftwaffe* fighters, damaged 155 fighters, and killed 400 fighter pilots. Although the *Luftwaffe* replaced its aircraft, it could not replace the 2,262 experienced pilots killed in the five months preceding D-Day, the invasion of Normandy.

1.9.21. By 6 June 1944, Allied air forces dominated the skies of Europe. On the first day of the invasion, the Allies directed 8,722 United States Army Air Forces and 5,676 Royal Air Force sorties against German defenses in France. In response, the once vaunted *Luftwaffe* could launch fewer than 100 sorties and only two German aircraft inflicted damage on the invasion beaches. Allied bombers and fighters trumped the German integrated air defense network.

1.9.22. After the Normandy invasion, the Combined Bomber Offensive devastated Germany. Approximately 75 percent of the 1.5 million tons of bombs dropped were after June 1944. In contrast to the horrific losses experienced at Schweinfurt, Regensburg, and Ploesti in 1943, American losses fell to "acceptable" rates. By 1945, some raids reported negligible losses: one bomber lost out of 1,094 sent to Kassel, five out of 1,310 at Chemnitz-Magdeburg, and zero losses out of 1,219 at Nuremburg. At its peak, the United States Army Air Forces and Royal Air Force massed 7,904 heavy bombers in the theater and 28,000 combat planes total. By 16 April 1945, General Spaatz declared the strategic air war against Germany ended since all significant targets were considered destroyed.

**Crew of the *Memphis Belle***

1.9.23. From 1942 to 1945, the Combined Bomber Offensive was the longest, bloodiest, air campaign in history. According to the United States Strategic Bombing Survey, the Allies flew 1.69 million combat sorties and dropped 1.5 million tons of bombs, killing and wounding more than a million Germans, and destroying 3.6 million buildings: 20 percent of the nation's total. Airpower emerged as a dominant weapon in Western Europe during World War II.

**Tech. Sgt. Paul Airey, May 1945**

1.9.24. Enlisted personnel served with honor throughout World War II. For example, a raid against the last operational Nazi oil refinery on 15 March 1945 was successful, but cost the life of one of the enlisted force's most decorated Airmen. Sergeant Sandy Sanchez flew 44 missions as a gunner with the 95th Bomb Group, 19 more than required to complete his tour. After returning home for a brief period, rather than accept an assignment as a gunnery instructor, he returned to Europe. Flying with the 353d Bombardment Squadron in Italy, Sanchez's aircraft was hit by ground fire. Nine of the 10-member crew bailed out successfully, but Sanchez never made it from the stricken aircraft. Sanchez was the only enlisted airman to have a B-17 named for him.

1.9.25. At the age of 20, on a mission to bomb the oil refineries outside Vienna, Technical Sergeant Paul Airey and his fellow crewmen were shot down on their 28th mission. He was held as a prisoner of war for 10 months, surviving a 90-day march from the Baltic Sea to Berlin before being liberated by the British Army in 1945. Promoted to Chief Master Sergeant in 1962, Airey became the first Chief Master Sergeant of the Air Force in 1967. In 1988, he received the first Air Force prisoner of war medal.

*Section 1D—Tuskegee Airmen, Air War in the Pacific, Air Force Independence, Cold War, and Cuban Missile Crisis*

**1.10. The Tuskegee Airmen:**

1.10.1. In 1941, President Franklin D. Roosevelt directed the Army Air Corps to accept black Americans into aviation cadet training. The Air Corps, like all other components of the United States Armed Forces, decided to segregate black aviators into all-black squadrons. By the end of World War II, nearly a thousand black Americans had earned their wings as Army flyers. Fired by a determination to prove their patriotism, valor, and skill in combat, these black aviators, forever called the Tuskegee Airmen, struck a significant blow against racism in America.

**The Tuskegee Airmen**
*Colonel Alan L. Grossman, USAF (Ret)*

1.10.2. The first Tuskegee Airmen to fight were members of the 99th Fighter Squadron, a unit commanded by black West Point graduate and future Air Force general officer, Colonel Benjamin O. Davis, Jr. On 27 January 1944, over Anzio, pilots from the 99th Fighter Squadron, flying obsolete P-40s, downed nine superior Focke-Wulf 190s. As the 99th Fighter Squadron continued scoring kills, the 332d Fighter Group, another unit manned by Tuskegee Airmen, arrived in Italy with obsolete P-39 ground-attack fighters. In the spring of 1944, these segregated units transitioned to P-47 Thunderbolts and to P-51 Mustangs a month later, when they began flying bomber escort missions.

1.10.3. The 332d Fighter Group flew escort missions from 9 June 1944 until the German surrender in the spring of 1945. By a large margin, the Tuskegee Airmen destroyed more aircraft than they lost. They shot down 111 enemy aircraft in air-to-air combat, losing 66 of their own aircraft to all causes, including seven shot down. A tribute to their skill, courage, and determination, the Tuskegee Airmen amassed a distinguished combat record on 200 escort missions into Germany.

1.10.4. While the 332d Fighter Group fought in Europe, the segregated 477th Bomb Group, manned by Tuskegee Airmen, was activated in 1944, at Selfridge Field, Michigan. Their ability to prepare for war was hampered by frequent relocations and segregation-imposed training barriers. Nevertheless, the Tuskegee Airmen struck a significant blow to the poison of racism in America, fighting bigotry by their actions in the skies over North Africa, the Mediterranean, Sicily, Italy, Austria, Yugoslavia, France, Romania, and Germany. With their record, they dispelled myths, opened eyes, rewrote history, and prepared the United States Air Force to be the first armed service to integrate racially.

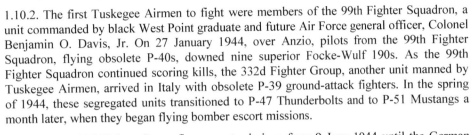

**Pilots from Tuskegee Airmen
Class 43A**

**1.11. Air War in the Pacific:**

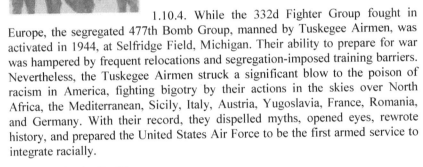

**Flying Tiger P-40**

1.11.1. America's first combat experience in the Pacific Theater of World War II occurred before the declaration of war. In early 1941, former Air Corps Tactical School instructor Claire Lee Chennault organized the American volunteer group, known as the "Flying Tigers," to aid Nationalist China against Japanese invaders. Famous for shark mouths painted on their Curtis P-40 Warhawks, the Flying Tigers amassed an impressive 286 confirmed victories, losing only 12 pilots, before being disbanded in July 1942.

1.11.2. The Japanese forces appeared invincible during the first six months of conflict, and America needed a strong offensive strike against the Japanese to boost sagging morale. On 18 April 1942, Lieutenant Colonel James "Jimmy" Doolittle led 16 North American B-25 Mitchell medium bombers, launching from the carrier USS *Hornet*, in a bombing raid on various targets in Tokyo, Kobe, and Nagoya. The Doolittle Raid inflicted little damage, but the gesture shocked Japanese military leaders and cheered the American public. Upon his return to the United States in May 1942, Doolittle received the Medal of Honor and promotion to brigadier general.

**B-25 launching from the USS *Hornet***

1.11.3. Not many fliers have had a popular song written about them, but an exception was a soft-spoken United States Army Air Force enlisted man, John D. Foley. Although he never received aerial gunnery training, he volunteered as a gunner and was assigned to a B-26 crew. On his first mission, Foley shot down at least one Japanese enemy aircraft.

Other 19th Bomb Squadron members confirmed his victory and he was nicknamed "Johnny Zero" by a war correspondent. Corporal Foley became a hero and the subject of a popular song, "Johnny Got a Zero." Commercial firms capitalized on his fame and produced such items as "Johnny Zero" watches and boots. During his 31 other Pacific combat missions, Foley shared in the destruction of at least six more enemy aircraft and survived three crashes. Malaria forced his return to the United States in 1943 where he toured factories promoting war production. He volunteered to fly again and completed 31 missions over Europe. He returned to the United States again and was preparing for a third overseas tour when World War II ended. But before the war ended, Foley became an Army Air Force legend by being decorated a total of eight times for heroism including personal recognition by Generals MacArthur, Eisenhower, and Doolittle.

1.11.4. Naval aviation played a vital role in the Pacific War. Under the leadership of Admirals Chester Nimitz, Frank "Jack" Fletcher, Raymond Spruance, and William "Bull" Halsey, United States carrier-based aviation proved the value of airpower at sea. The Battle of Coral Sea, fought 4-8 May 1942, marked the first naval battle fought entirely by air. At the Battle of Midway, 4 June 1942, United States Navy pilots sank four Japanese carriers and turned the tide of the war in the Pacific.

1.11.5. The primary United States Army Air Forces contribution to the Pacific counterattack was made by the Fifth Air Force, attached to the Southwest Pacific Theater under General Douglas MacArthur's command. While Admiral Nimitz' carrier task forces struck from the Central Pacific, MacArthur's command thrust across New Guinea toward the Philippines. Because of the "Europe First" strategy, Fifth Air Force flew second string aircraft out of primitive bases, struggling to overcome its low resource priority level and a 10,000 mile supply chain.

1.11.6. In July 1942, Major General George C. Kenney assumed command of the Fifth Air Force. Kenney maximized the resource-poor command's combat power. In a theater where range dominated employment decisions, Kenney used the Lockheed P-38 Lightning with locally developed 150-gallon drop tanks. Kenney encouraged an ingenious subordinate, Maj Paul "Pappy" Gunn, to mount quad .50-caliber machine guns in the nose of A-20 and B-25 aircraft, creating deadly attack planes. Other Fifth Air Force innovations included parachutes attached to fragmentation bombs and low-level "skip" bombing techniques.

1.11.7. An even lower a priority than Fifth Air Force, Allied forces in the China-Burma-India Theater faced logistical challenges at the end of the war's longest supply chain. Called to transport vital supplies across the Himalayas, Air Transport Command crews, flying C-46s and C-47s, braved perilous weather conditions to deliver 650,000 tons of supplies to Chinese and American forces. Flying the "Hump" was one of the most hazardous military air operations of World War II. Enterprise architect William H. Tunner developed many maintenance and cargo-handling techniques that later proved invaluable during the Berlin Airlift.

1.11.8. In addition to Air Transport Command efforts in the China-Burma-India Theater, the 1st Air Commando Group, led by Lieutenant Colonel Phillip G. Cochran and John R. Allison, provided assistance to British "Chindit" forces conducting long-range penetration missions against the Japanese during Operation Thursday, using unconventional air warfare to support British ground forces. America's first Air Commandos demonstrated that air power could support unconventional warfare any place, any time. The 1st Air Commando Group also demonstrated its ingenuity, conducting the first helicopter combat rescue.

**B-29 Superfortress**

1.11.9. Allied soldiers, sailors, and marines pushed back the borders of the Japanese empire and airmen sought to destroy Japan through strategic bombardment. General Arnold hoped to clinch victory through airpower alone in order to avoid a costly land invasion. In November 1939, Air Corps leaders selected the primary campaign instrument: the Boeing XB-29. With a pressurized crew compartment, remotely controlled guns, and new radial engines, the B-29 was an aircraft of unprecedented size and capability. The United States Army Air Forces ordered 1,664 before the prototype had even flown. The rush to produce the plane led to substantial technical problems. Nevertheless, by April 1944, B-29s appeared in the China-Burma-India to conduct Operation MATTERHORN, the designation for B-29 operations out of bases in India and China to carry out strategic bombing of Japanese force.

1.11.10. At first, XX Bomber Command crews attempted to reproduce high-altitude daylight precision bombing, with disappointing results. Flying from bases in China with logistical staging from India, XX Bomber Command engine problems were amplified by distance and weather. By October 1944, B-29 operations shifted to Saipan, significantly reducing supply lines. Former Air Corps Tactical School instructor Haywood S. Hansell renewed efforts for a daylight precision bombing campaign. Impatient with the results, General Arnold replaced Hansell in January 1945 with Major General Curtis E. LeMay, a proven combat commander from the European theater.

**34**

1.11.11. LeMay drastically altered B-29 tactics. To avoid the jet stream and high-altitude engine problems, LeMay ordered low-altitude night attacks with bombers stripped of defensive machine guns, reduced fuel loads, and increased bomb loads. Much like the Royal Air Force, LeMay's B-29s relied on darkness for protection and pummeled enemy cities with incendiary bombs. From March-August 1945, American firebomb raids destroyed 66 Japanese cities and burned 178 square miles of urban landscape. Civilian casualties were severe; in one raid against Tokyo an estimated 80,000 people perished.

1.11.12. Following a successful atomic test on 18 July 1945, the Allied powers issued an ultimatum on 26 July calling for the Japanese government to surrender or suffer "prompt and utter destruction." Specially modified B-29s from the 393d Bombardment Squadron, a component of the 509th Composite Group, delivered the first operational atomic bombs. On 6 August 1945, Colonel Paul Tibbets piloted the Enola Gay which dropped a uranium bomb, known as "Little Boy," over Hiroshima destroying nearly five square miles of the city and killing 80,000 people. Japan did not surrender. On 9 August 1945, the B-29 Bockscar, commanded by Major Charles W. Sweeney, released a plutonium bomb called "Fat Man" on Nagasaki. Because Nagasaki was partially protected by hilly terrain, the bomb devastated 1.5 square miles, killed 35,000, and injured 60,000. Faced with a defeated army, destroyed navy and air force, burned cities, a declaration of war by the Soviet Union, and atomic weapons, the Japanese government surrendered 14 August 1945. In the Pacific Theater, airpower proved even more decisive than in Europe. The industrial might of the United States overwhelmed Japanese forces. The geographic circumstances and immense distances involved made airpower the preeminent weapon.

Loading the atomic bomb onto the Enola Gay.

## 1.12. Air Force Independence and the Cold War:

1.12.1. With victory in World War II, the American public returned to normal life. Airpower and military affairs, in general, decreased in importance. From a wartime strength of more than 79,000 aircraft and 2.4 million people, forces dwindled to 24,000 aircraft and 304,000 people by May 1947. Nevertheless, airpower's impact on warfare led to the realization of Billy Mitchell's dream. On 26 July 1947, President Harry S. Truman signed into law the National Security Act of 1947, which provided for a separate Department of the Air Force. On 18 September 1947, Stuart Symington became the first Secretary of the Air Force and officially established the United States Air Force as an independent, coequal service. Under the leadership of General Spaatz as the first Chief of Staff, Air Force and that of his successor, General Hoyt S. Vandenberg, the Air Force clarified roles and missions and organized to meet the challenges of the growing Cold War.

1.12.2. In many areas, the establishment of the Air Force had little impact on the lives of most Airmen until months or even years had passed. What were designated as "organic" service units were taken over as newly designated Air Force units. Units that provided a common service to both the Army and the Air Force were left intact. Until 1950, for example, if an Airman became seriously ill, he was likely treated by Army doctors in an Army hospital. There was also, at first, no change in appearance. The distinctive blue uniforms of the United States Air Force were introduced only after large stocks of Army clothing were used up. Familiar terms slowly gave way to new labels. By 1959, enlisted Airmen ate in "dining halls" rather than "mess halls," were eyed warily by "air police" instead of "military police," and bought necessities at the "base exchange" instead of the "post exchange."

1.12.3. Initially, the enlisted rank system remained as it had been in the United States Army Air Force. Corporal was removed from NCO status in 1950. Then, in 1952, the Air Force officially changed the names of the lower four ranks from private to Airman basic; private first class to Airman, third class; corporal to Airman, second class; and sergeant to Airman, first class. These changes were in response to a development that surfaced during World War II, and the rank structure would continue to evolve over time. Promotion and specialization went hand-in-hand with training in the new Air Force. When the new organization established Air Force specialty codes as standard designations for functional and technical specialties, qualification for an advanced Air Force specialty code became part of the criteria for promotion. During the late 1940s, the Air Force also began an Airman Career Program that attempted to encourage long-term careers for enlisted specialists.

**Berlin airlift**

1.12.4. The Berlin Crisis awakened Americans to the impact of the Cold War between the United States and the Union of Soviet Socialist Republics. On 24 June 1948, the Soviets blockaded railroad and road corridors serving the 2.5 million residents of West Berlin, deep within Communist East Germany. United States Air Forces in Europe Commander General LeMay organized a makeshift airlift of food, medicine, and coal. United States Air Forces in Europe C-47 and C-54 cargo aircraft established a precise schedule of flights every three minutes, 24-hours-a-day. After the first month, Major General William H. Tunner assumed command of an expanded effort that would include 300 American and 100 British aircraft flown by aircrews who would apply lessons learned while flying the "Hump" during World War II. On 15 April 1949, 1,398 aircraft delivered a one-day record 12,941 tons of supplies. By 1949, the Soviets acknowledged the airlift's success and lifted the blockade. Operation VITTLES tallied 277,804 flights delivering 2.3 million tons of supplies. This nonviolent use of airpower defused a potentially disastrous confrontation.

1.12.5. Throughout the airlift, enlisted personnel served as cargo managers and loaders (with a major assist from German civilians), air traffic controllers, communications specialists, and weather and navigation specialists. Of all the enlisted functions, perhaps the most critical to the success of the airlift was maintenance. The Soviets' eventual capitulation and dismantling of the surface blockade represented one of the great Western victories of the cold war—without a bomb having been dropped—and laid the foundation for the North Atlantic Treaty Organization (NATO).

1.12.6. The 1948 Berlin Crisis and 1949 Soviet detonation of an atomic device motivated the Air Force to improve war readiness. As the new Strategic Air Command commander, General LeMay emphasized rigorous training, exacting performance standards, and immediate readiness. In the late 1940s, SAC incorporated the B-50 (a more powerful version of the B-29) and the massive Convair B-36 Peacemaker (the first bomber with intercontinental range) into the inventory. Behind the scenes, the Air Force conducted a highly secret, extensive electronic reconnaissance program that included covert flights over the Union of Soviet Socialist Republic to assess Communist air defenses.

1.12.7. Jet aircraft technological breakthroughs changed the face of aviation. Although the Bell XP-59 Airacomet first flew 1 October 1942, the Lockheed P-80 (later redesignated F-80) entered service in December 1945 as the Air Force's first operational jet fighter. On 14 October 1947, Charles "Chuck" Yeager seized headlines as the first man to break the sound barrier. His Bell X-1 "Glamorous Glennis" reached Mach 1.06 at 43,000 feet after a launch from a B-29 mother ship. In the early 1950s, Strategic Air Command upgraded to an all-jet bomber force, activating the Boeing B-47 Stratojet and the Boeing B-52 Stratofortress.

**X-1 and the B-29**

1.12.8. On 25 June 1950, Communist North Korea launched a massive invasion of United States-backed South Korea. Three days later, American B-26 bombers attacked advancing North Korean troops in the first major flare-up of the Cold War. For six weeks, Far East Air Forces, commanded by Lieutenant General George E. Stratemeyer, gained air superiority to help United Nations forces shut down the North Korean assault. The initial phase of the Korean War illustrated the dangers of being unprepared, as American Airmen struggled to relearn close air support and interdiction skills. In addition, the F-80's limited range

**Chuck Yeager and the X-1**

inhibited the time over target required for tactical operations. About 100 Far East Air Forces Bomber Command B-29s conducted strategic operations to destroy the enemy's will and capacity to fight. Although United Nations forces controlled the skies and destroyed North Korea's industrial base, multiple limitations frustrated hopes of decisive victory.

1.12.9. General MacArthur's amphibious assault at Inchon and successive operations shattered the North Korean Army, but the United Nations advance into North Korea led to Communist Chinese intervention. The entry of half a million Chinese troops in November 1950 drastically changed the war. Within weeks, advanced Soviet-made MiG-15 fighters appeared. Flown by North Korean, Chinese, and Soviet pilots, the MiG-15 outperformed American F-51, F-80, and F-84 aircraft. Lieutenant Russell Brown, flying an F-80C, shot down a MiG-15 in the world's first all-jet air battle on 8 November 1950. In response to the enemy's superior speed and altitude, Air Force leaders rushed the North American F-86 Sabre into action. The F-86 matched the MiG's speed and proved a more stable gun platform.

1.12.10. On 9 November 1950, Corporal Harry LaVene of the 91st Strategic Reconnaissance Squadron, serving as gunner, scored the first B-29 victory over a jet by downing a MiG-15. LaVene's victory was the first of 27 MiGs shot down by B-29 gunners during the course of the war. Sergeant Billie Beach, a tail gunner on an Okinawa-based B-29, shot down two MiGs on 12 April 1951, a feat unmatched by any other gunner. His own plane was so shot up, however, that it and the crew barely survived an emergency landing with collapsed gear at an advanced fighter strip.

**Pilots heading to their F-86 Sabres**

1.12.11. As the war on the ground settled into stalemate, F-86s battled over "MiG Alley," where superior training and experience prevailed. F-86 pilots destroyed 792 MiGs and 18 other enemy aircraft at a cost of 76 Sabres lost to MiGs, and 142 to other causes.

1.12.12. During the Korean War, the Air Rescue Service medically evacuated more than 9,600 wounded soldiers, and rescued nearly 1,000 personnel shot down over enemy territory. In addition, Air Resupply and Communication Service wings executed unconventional warfare and counterinsurgency operations against enemy forces.

**Joseph McConnell and James Jabara**

1.12.13. During the Korean War, a new group of Air Force pilots entered the pantheon of fighter aces. The F-86 pilots established a remarkable 10-to-1 kill ratio. Captain Joseph McConnell, a B-24 navigator in World War II, led the pack with a score of 16, closely followed by Captain James Jabara who tallied 15 kills. Jabara gained recognition as the world's first jet ace. Unlike the mass squadron formations often flown in World War II, Korean War pilots devised new tactics based on flights of only four F-86s.

1.12.14. Despite success in the air war, the Korean War frustrated American airpower. Accustomed to the commitment of World War II, Korean War era leaders struggled under political, technological, and resource limitations inherent in the Cold War. Worried that the conflict in Korea foreshadowed a Soviet invasion of Europe, American policy makers limited operations in Asia in order to build up North Atlantic Treaty Organization forces. Nevertheless, United Nations forces repelled two communist invasions of South Korea, and American airpower secured the skies against enemy air attack.

1.12.15. After the Korean conflict, Air Force missile and space capabilities developed rapidly. In late 1953, Assistant Secretary of the Air Force for Research and Development, Trevor Gardner, convened a group of experts known as the Teapot Committee to examine the field of long-range missiles. The committee's 10 February 1954 report recommended accelerating intercontinental ballistic missile development. Based on the recommendation, the Air Research and Development Command, on 1 July 1954, established the Western Development Division in Inglewood, California, to develop and field intercontinental ballistic missiles. On 2 August 1954, Brigadier General Bernard Schriever assumed command of the new organization.

1.12.16. Concurrent with efforts to develop long-range missiles, the United States also pursued space-based technology that could provide accurate information on Soviet military intentions. On 27 November 1954, Air Force senior leaders followed the recommendation of the RAND Corporation's Project Feed Back report, issuing Weapon System Requirement No. 5, directing development of an electro-optical reconnaissance satellite. Weapon System Requirement

No. 5 later became weapon system 117L. The scope of weapon system 117L eventually broadened to include other space-based missions, such as meteorology, missile warning, and multispectral imaging.

1.12.17. On 4 October 1957, the course of missile and satellite development changed when the Soviet Union successfully launched the Sputnik I satellite into earth orbit. The Soviet success marked the beginning of the space age and sparked the space race between the United States and Soviet Union. Over the next two decades the Air Force played a major role in the developing national space programs, assuming the mantle of America's air and space force. In response to the Sputnik I launch, President Eisenhower accelerated United States civil and military space efforts; a decision that would prove crucial throughout the Cold War.

1.12.18. In 1958, the Air Force developed plans for a manned military presence in space, but President Eisenhower reserved manned missions for the National Aeronautics and Space Agency. However, the Air Force's plan formed the basis of the Mercury, Gemini, and Apollo Programs. The Atlas rocket, which began as a United States Army Air Corps ballistic missile in October 1945, was used to launch the MERCURY missions. The Titan-II booster, also originally a ballistic missile, launched the Gemini astronauts. In fact, the Air Force and its contractors planned, built, and launched all of the Titan-II rockets in Project Gemini.

1.12.19. In 1960, the National Reconnaissance Office was formed to take charge of highly classified reconnaissance satellites. President Eisenhower undertook several initiatives to help prevent a surprise nuclear attack against the United States, including establishing the classified Corona satellite photo reconnaissance program. This system, known publicly as the Discoverer research program, achieved its first successful launch

**Atlas rocket launching**

of the Discoverer XIII, 10 August 1960. Corona employed a payload capsule that jettisoned from the orbiter, returned to earth by parachute, and was captured by an aircraft. Discoverer XIV, launched a week after recovering Discoverer XIII, shot over 3,000 feet of reconnaissance film from space, heralding the beginning of America's space-based photo reconnaissance capability.

1.12.20. The Air Force concentrated on unmanned missions to fulfill national security needs. Space reconnaissance satellites, for instance, supported strategic deterrence throughout the Cold War, providing invaluable knowledge of the Soviet Union's nuclear inventory, and verifying arms control treaty compliance. Space systems also provided early warning of any missile attack on North America, and worldwide communications platforms for strategic command and control.

## 1.13. Cuban Missile Crisis (1962):

1.13.1. In 1959, Fidel Castro overthrew the dictator of Cuba, initially promising free elections, but instead he instituted a socialist dictatorship. Hundreds of thousands of Cubans fled their island, many coming to the United States. In late 1960, President Eisenhower authorized the Central Intelligence Agency to plan an invasion of Cuba using Cuban exiles as troops. President Eisenhower hoped that, in conjunction with the invasion, the Cuban people would overthrow Castro and install a pro-United States government. The President's second term ended before the plan could be implemented. President John F. Kennedy ordered the invasion to proceed. In mid-April 1961, the Cuban exiles landed at the Bay of Pigs and suffered a crushing defeat.

**U-2 "Dragon Lady" in flight**

1.13.2. Following the failure of the United States-supported Bay of Pigs invasion of Cuba by Cuban exiles in April 1961, the Soviet Union increased economic and military aid to Cuba. In August 1962, the Soviets and Cubans started constructing intermediate- and medium-range ballistic missile complexes on the island. Suspicious, the United States intelligence community called for photographic investigation and verification of the activity. In October, Strategic Air Command U-2 aircraft deployed to McCoy Air Force Base, Florida, and began flying high-altitude reconnaissance flights over Cuba. On 15 October, photographs obtained on flights the previous day confirmed the construction of launch pads that, when completed, could be used to employ nuclear-armed missiles with a range up to 5,000 miles. Eleven days later, RF-101s and RB-66s began conducting low-level reconnaissance flights, verifying data gathered by the U-2s and gathering prestrike intelligence.

1.13.3. In the event an invasion of Cuba became necessary, Tactical Air Command deployed F-84, F-100, F-105, RB-66, and KB-50 aircraft to numerous bases in Florida. Meanwhile, Strategic Air Command prepared for general war by dispersing nuclear-capable B-47 aircraft to approximately 40 airfields in the United States and keeping numerous B-52 heavy bombers in the air ready to strike.

1.13.4. Meanwhile, President Kennedy and his advisors on the national security team debated the most effective course of action. Many on the Joint Chiefs of Staff favored invasion, but President Kennedy took the somewhat less drastic step of imposing a naval blockade of the island, which was designed to prevent any more materiel from reaching Cuba. Still technically an act of war, the blockade nevertheless had the advantage of not turning the cold war into a hot one.

1.13.5. Confronted with the photographic evidence of missiles, the Soviet Union initially responded belligerently. Soviet Premier Nikita Khrushchev accused the United States of degenerate imperialism and declared that the Union of Soviet Socialist Republic would not observe the illegal blockade. In the ensuing days, Khrushchev softened, and then hardened, his position and demands. Tensions increased on 27 October when Cuban air defenses shot down a U-2 piloted by Major Rudolf Anderson.

1.13.6. The Joint Chiefs of Staff recommended an immediate air strike against Cuba, but President Kennedy decided to wait. The increasing tempo in the military, however, continued unabated. While United States military preparations continued, the United States agreed not to invade Cuba in exchange for removal of Soviet missiles from the island. Secretly, the United States also agreed to remove American missiles from Turkey. The Soviets turned their Cuban-bound ships around, packed up the missiles in Cuba, and dismantled the launch pads. As the work progressed, the Air Force started to deploy aircraft back to home bases and lower the alert status.

1.13.7. The Cuban Missile Crisis brought the United States and the Soviet Union dangerously close to nuclear war; the world breathed a sigh of relief when it ended. The strategic and tactical power of the United States Air Force, coupled with the will and ability to use it, provided the synergy to deter nuclear war with the Union of Soviet Socialist Republic and convince the Soviet leaders to remove the nuclear weapons from Cuba.

## Section 1E—Vietnam, Desert Storm and Operations (1992-2014)

### 1.14. Vietnam, 1961-1973:

1.14.1. After eight years, during which the Air Force worked to build America's strategic nuclear forces, President Kennedy's administration faced national wars of liberation backed by the Soviet Union. Responding to Communist efforts in Laos and South Vietnam, President Kennedy in April 1961 ordered Operation FARMGATE; the covert deployment of the 4400th Combat Crew Training Squadron (Jungle Jim) to train the South Vietnamese Air Force. Flying North American T-28 Trojans, Douglas A-26 Invaders, and Douglas A-1E Skyraiders, American pilots launched attack missions under the umbrella of combat training. Following the August 1964 Gulf of Tonkin incident, when North Vietnamese torpedo boats attacked the USS *Maddox*, President Lyndon B. Johnson lifted the shroud of secrecy and ordered an orchestrated

air attack as a show of force. By December 1964, North American F-100 Super Sabres, McDonnell RF-101 Voodoos, and Republic F-105 Thunderchiefs, with Boeing KC-135 Stratotanker support, conducted Operation BARRELL ROLL, attacking Communist forces in Laos.

**B-52s attacking enemy forces**

1.14.2. Faced with a deteriorating political and military situation in South Vietnam, President Johnson ordered Operation ROLLING THUNDER; a sign of American support to South Vietnam and a signal of United States resolve. Beginning on 2 March 1965, Rolling Thunder was "a program of measured and limited air action against selected military targets in North Vietnam remaining south of the 19th Parallel." Closely managed by the White House, Rolling Thunder sought to apply incrementally announced military power to undermine the North Vietnamese will to wage war. However, the United States underestimated the enemy's resiliency and determination. Air Force leaders chafed at rules of engagement that negated the speed, surprise, and flexibility of massed airpower. They believed periodic bombing pauses intended to signal American intentions allowed the enemy to recover. In 1965, North Vietnamese air defenses multiplied, including Soviet-made SA-2 surface-to-air missiles. Hanoi established an advanced radar-controlled air defense system that combined surface-to-air missiles, antiaircraft artillery, and Soviet-produced MiG-17 and MiG-21 interceptors. Consequently, United States losses mounted without any visible effect from the air campaign. By the fall of 1968, Air Force tactical aircraft had flown 166,000 sorties over North Vietnam, and Navy attack aircraft added 144,500. In the process, the enemy downed 526 Air Force aircraft: surface-to-air missiles accounted for 54, MiGs destroyed 42, and antiaircraft artillery claimed the remainder. Personnel losses were equally heavy. Of the 745 Air Force crew members shot down over North Vietnam, 145 were rescued, 255 were confirmed killed, 222 were captured, and 123 were classified missing in action. Air Force leaders found these results intolerable for an air campaign with virtually complete air superiority.

1.14.3. Complementing operations over North Vietnam, the air war over South Vietnam demonstrated the full spectrum of airpower. Air Force aircraft and helicopters provided close air support, interdiction, reconnaissance, airlift, tanker support, and search-and-rescue capabilities. Air Force resources ranged from one-man Cessna O-1 Bird Dogs, used by forward air controllers to mark enemy targets for strikers, to mammoth B-52Ds modified to drop as many as 27 750-pound bombs, and 84 500-pound bombs for Operation ARC LIGHT interdiction missions. Vintage World War II aircraft, like AC-47 Puff the Magic Dragon gunships, joined state-of-the-art platforms like the General Dynamics swing-wing, advanced terrain-following radar F-111 Aardvark.

1.14.4. The January 1968 siege of Khe Sanh displayed the potential of Air Force close air support. When more than 20,000 North Vietnamese troops, protected by hilly, covered terrain, surrounded 6,000 United States Marines, General William Momyer applied massive firepower during Operation NIAGARA. A flight of three B-52s hit the enemy every 90 minutes for most of the 77-day siege. To prevent the enemy from overrunning the base, American aircraft dropped 100,000 tons of bombs, two-thirds of those from B-52s.

1.14.5. Following the 1968 bombing halt, President Richard M. Nixon initiated a phased withdrawal from the frustrating conflict. From 536,000 United States troops in 1968, American personnel numbered fewer than 100,000 by 1972. When the North Vietnamese launched the Easter Offensive in Spring 1972, Nixon resolved to achieve peace with honor. Reinforcing ground troops was politically impossible, so Nixon employed Operation LINEBACKER to blunt the Communist attack.

1.14.6. Unlike Rolling Thunder, military leaders were allowed to use appropriate strategy and tactics, in part because the administration significantly reduced restrictions. With the acquisition of precision-guided munitions, new television and laser-guided smart bombs dramatically increased strike accuracy.

1.14.7. On 13 May 1972, 16 McDonnell-Douglas F-4 Phantoms hit the Than Hoa bridge with 24 smart bombs, destroying a target that had eluded American Airmen for years. From April to October 1972, Air Force and Navy aircraft dropped 155,548 tons of bombs on North Vietnamese troops. The era's first war aces earned their marks during Linebacker, as well. On 28 August 1972, Captain Steve Ritchie shot down his fifth MiG- 21. Within weeks, two F-4 weapons systems officers joined the fraternity of aces: Captain Charles De Bellevue with six kills and Captain Jeffrey Feinstein with five. When North Vietnamese negotiators accepted specific peace conditions, President Nixon terminated the air campaign.

1.14.8. In December 1972, North Vietnamese intransigence over the final peace agreement prompted President Nixon to initiate Linebacker II, an intense 11-day air campaign to pressure enemy compliance. From 18-29 December, American aircraft pounded military and industrial targets in North Vietnam. For the first time, the White House authorized B-52 strikes near Hanoi. In less than two weeks, 729 B-52 sorties dropped 15,000 tons of bombs and fighter-bombers added another 5,000 tons. Despite the loss of 26 aircraft, including 15 B-52s, airpower broke the impasse. Peace talks resumed 8 January 1973, and a comprehensive ceasefire was signed 23 January.

1.14.9. During Vietnam, airpower demonstrated its versatility and wide ranging impact, as well as its limitations. Despite an impressive military showing, the United States did not win decisively in Vietnam. Although the Air Force flew more than five million sorties and dropped six million tons of bombs, North Vietnamese forces eventually conquered South Vietnam in April 1975. Airpower did not prevent the collapse of the South Vietnamese government or the change in American political climate.

1.14.10. The Vietnam War saw a number of notable and heroic achievements by Air Force enlisted members, including two winners of the Medal of Honor, who will be discussed in detail in a later section of this chapter. While not a Medal of Honor recipient, Duane Hackney became one of the most honored heroes of the Vietnam War, the recipient of 28 decorations for valor in combat (more than 70 awards and decorations in all), and winner of the Cheney Award for 1967, an honor presented for valor or self-sacrifice in a humanitarian effort. Hackney enlisted in the Air Force a few days after graduation, volunteering for pararescue training. An honor graduate in every phase of the tough, year-long course, he had his choice of assignments. Airman Second Class Hackney turned down assignments in Bermuda and England for Detachment 7, 38th Aerospace Rescue and Recovery Squadron, at Da Nang. Hackney flew more than 200 combat missions in three and a half years of Vietnam duty, all as a volunteer. He earned four Distinguished Flying Crosses for specific acts of heroism and 18 Air Medals, many for single acts of valor. He also received the Air Force Cross, the Silver Star, the Airman's Medal, the Purple Heart, and several foreign decorations. Hackney's most celebrated mission was on 6 February 1967. That morning he

**Duane Hackney**

descended from a HH-3E Jolly Green Giant to look for a downed pilot near Mu Gia pass. The pilot had stopped his radio transmissions, a clue that enemy troops were nearby. For two hours, Hackney searched for the man, dodging enemy patrols, until the mission was called off because of weather. Late that afternoon, the downed pilot came back on the air, and Hackney's crew headed for the rescue area to get him out before dark. This time Hackney found his man, badly injured but alive, got him onto the forest penetrator, and started up to the chopper, drawing small-arms fire all the way. As the men were hauled aboard, the helicopter took a direct hit from a 37-mm antiaircraft gun and burst into flame. Wounded by shell fragments and suffering third-degree burns, Hackney, knowing that the HH-3 was not going to make it, put his own parachute on the rescued pilot and got him out of the doomed chopper. Groping through dense smoke, he found an oil-soaked chute and slipped it on. Before he could buckle the chute, a second 37-mm shell hit the HH-3, blowing him out the door. He did not remember pulling the ripcord of the unbuckled chute before hitting trees 250 feet below, then plunging 80 feet to a rock ledge in a crevasse. When he regained consciousness, enemy troops were leaping across the crevasse a few feet above him Once they were gone, Hackney popped his smoke and was picked up by the backup chopper. There were no other survivors from the rescue helicopter. For that mission, Hackney received the Air Force Cross. In 1973, Hackney left the Air Force, one of the most decorated pararescuemen of the Vietnam War. Four years later, missing the camaraderie of Air Force life, he enlisted again, returning to duty as a pararescue instructor. In 1981, he suffered a severe heart attack, the result of a rescue operation, and was permanently grounded. Altogether, he served in the United States Air Force from 1965 to 1991, retiring as a Chief Master Sergeant.

1.14.11. In December 1972, B-52 tail gunner Staff Sergeant Samuel Turner shot down an enemy MiG, the first of only two confirmed shootdowns by enlisted Airmen during the war—both victories from gunners belonging to the 307th Strategic Wing at U-Tapao, Thailand. Credit for the fifth overall MiG-21 kill during Linebacker II also went to an enlisted Airman, Airman First Class Albert E. Moore.

1.14.12. Chief Master Sergeant Wayne Fisk was directly involved in the famed Son Tay prisoner of war camp raid and the rescue of the crew of the USS *Mayaquez*. When the USS *Mayaquez* was highjacked by Cambodian Communist forces in May 1975, Fisk was a member of the assault force that successfully recovered the ship, the crew, and the entrapped United States Marines. For his actions, Fisk was presented with his second Silver Star. Concluding the *Mayaquez* mission, he was recognized as the last American serviceman to engage Communist forces in ground combat in Southeast Asia. In 1979, he was the first Air Force enlisted recipient of the United States Jaycees Ten Outstanding Young Men of America. In 1986, Fisk became the first director of the Air Force Enlisted Heritage Hall on Maxwell Air Force Base-Gunter Annex.

**Wayne Fisk**
**(as a staff sergeant)**

### 1.15. The Post-Vietnam Era and the end of the Cold War:

1.15.1. Rebuilding the conventional Air Force after Vietnam began with personnel changes. The Vietnam-era Air Force included many members who had entered its ranks in World War II. President Nixon ended the draft in 1973 in favor of an all-volunteer American military. The Air Force attracted recruits as best it could but encountered problems with the racial friction and alcohol and drug abuse that reflected America's social problems. Enough Vietnam career veterans remained, however, to direct the new service and implement changes. One of the most notable of those changes was more realistic- more dangerous- combat training. In combat simulations, Air Force pilots flew as aggressors employing enemy tactics. By 1975, training had evolved into Red Flag at the United States Air Force Weapons and Tactics Center, Nellis Air Force Base, Nevada. Red Flag aircrews flew both individual sorties and formations in realistic situations to gain application experience before actual combat. Colonel Richard "Moody" Suter is the founder of Red Flag. As a major, working in the Pentagon in 1975, he saw his vision through to fruition. Red Flag revolutionized Air Force training. According to senior leaders at the time, Colonel Suter's efforts resulted in a program that made the United States Air Force the premier air arm of the world.

1.15.2. An innovative genius, Suter flew more than 200 combat missions in Vietnam and was the first F-15 Eagle squadron commander. In addition to Red Flag, he is credited with founding the Air Force aggressor squadron, and the Einsiedlerhof Air Station, Germany Warrior Preparation Center, used to train senior battle commanders in the art of war. Suter was the driving force behind Checkmate, the Air Force think tank for wartime scenarios. After his death in January 1996, the Warrior Preparation Center Command Section Building and Red Flag Building, Nellis Air Force Base, Nevada, were named in his honor.

1.15.3. Post-Vietnam rebuilding included applying technology improvements. The battle for control of the skies over North Vietnam emphasized the need for a highly maneuverable dogfighting aircraft armed with missiles and cannon. The F-15 Eagle and F-16 Fighting Falcon filled this need. The danger posed by radar-guided antiaircraft artillery and surface-to-air missiles in Vietnam drove the Air Force to develop stealth technology: special paints, materials, and designs to reduce or eliminate aircraft radar, thermal, and electronic signatures. Operational by October 1980, the F-117 Nighthawk stealth fighter featured detection avoidance.

**A-10 Thunderbolt II**

1.15.4. Other Vietnam War technologies included precision-guided munitions and smart bombs. From April 1972 to January 1973, the United States used more than 4,000 early smart weapons to destroy bridges and enemy tanks. Laser-guided bombs, electro-optically-guided missiles, and other precision technologies changed Air Force doctrine from its focus on strategic bombing to pinpoint bombing focused on destroying enemy's industrial web chokepoints with economy of force and no collateral damage. To overcome numerically superior Warsaw Pact forces, the Air Force worked with the Army to update the air-land battle tactical doctrine published in Field Manual 100-5. The Air Force would make deep air attacks on an enemy army to isolate it on the battlefield, conduct battlefield air interdiction to prevent enemy reinforcements from reaching the front, disrupt the movement of secondary forces to the front, and provide close air support to Army ground forces. The Air Force procured the A-10 Thunderbolt II in the 1970s to support such missions.

1.15.5. Operation RICE BOWL, the April 1980 attempt to rescue American hostages from the United States embassy in Iran, ended in disaster at the Desert One refueling site. Inquiries led to the reorganization and revitalization of United States Special Operations Forces. Crisis support missions during the 1980s allowed the Air Force to test new ideas and technologies. During Operation URGENT FURY, October 1983, American forces rescued American students and restored order to Grenada. The Air Force primarily transported troops and cargo, but discovered problems with command, control, planning, and intraservice & interservice coordination during the operation. In April 1986, President Reagan mobilized England-based F-111s to strike Libya during Operation ELDORADO CANYON. The counterterrorism operation exposed on-going target identification and intelligence difficulties, punctuated by inaccurate bombing. Finally, Operation JUST CAUSE in 1989 tested air operations; this time in Panama. The Air Force primarily airlifted troops and supplies, but also debuted the F-117 Nighthawk stealth fighter, with an AC-130 Spectre gunship, intimidating Panamanian troops loyal to dictator Manuel Noriega.

1.15.6. President Kennedy's flexible-response nuclear war doctrine of the early 1960s lacked the technology to match its vision of adapting to meet various Cold War crises. Advances in geodesy, cartography, missile and satellite guidance system integrated circuits significantly improved missile accuracy. Technology improvements resulted in better targeting systems and smaller, more effective warheads. Because they were smaller and lighter, more warheads could be mounted to intercontinental ballistic missiles and submarine launched ballistic missiles. In the early 1970s, the Department of Defense developed multiple independently targetable reentry vehicles, allowing three or more warheads to be mounted on each intercontinental ballistic missile and submarine launched ballistic missiles. The Air Force arsenal peaked at 1,054 Titan and Minuteman intercontinental ballistic missiles, but many carried three multiple independently targetable reentry vehicles, as opposed to earlier models that carried a single warhead. In spite of technological advances, planned targets continued to support the doctrine of mutually assured destruction or the capacity to eradicate an enemy's society, even after an attack on United States forces.

1.15.7. Mutually assured destruction doctrine was based on the theory that superpower strategic nuclear forces could be sized and protected to survive a nuclear attack in order to retaliate with sufficient force to destroy the other side. Such retaliatory destruction was deterrent insurance because no rational leader would consider starting a nuclear war knowing that the result would be nuclear destruction.

1.15.8. For two decades the Air Force developed more capable satellite systems, such as the Missile Defense Alarm System, which was the first attempt at a space-based long-range missile attack detection and warning system. Missile Defense Alarm System 7, launched 9 May 1963, validated the concept of infrared sensing from a nearly circular 2,000-mile orbit. The need for accurate information on Soviet nuclear testing led to the development of a space-based system that could specifically detect nuclear explosions. In September 1959, Department of Defense directed the Advanced Research Projects Agency to develop the Vela Hotel nuclear detection program; a low-cost, automated nuclear detection satellite constellation. The first pair of Vela satellites was launched from Cape Canaveral, 16 October 1963, and detected a nuclear blast the next day. Extensive United States and Soviet spending for weapons and related systems escalated into what appeared to be an unlimited strategic arms race.

1.15.9. However, on 26 May 1972, the United States and the Union of Soviet Socialist Republics signed the Anti-Ballistic Missile Treaty, limiting each country to two Anti-Ballistic Missile sites: one to protect the national capital and an intercontinental ballistic missile complex. The treaty served to reinforce the notion of the mutually assured destruction doctrine as a deterrent. The Strategic Arms Limitation Treaty, which was signed at the same time, limited the number of nuclear weapons, with the objective of obtaining a verified freeze on the numerical growth and destabilizing characteristics of each side's strategic nuclear forces.

1.15.10. Satellite advances significantly enhanced weather and communications support. The Air Force vision of weather satellites was realized with the development of a dedicated military weather satellite system known initially as the Defense Satellite Applications Program. Early Defense Satellite Applications Program military weather satellites were relatively unsophisticated, weighing about 430 pounds. The Initial Defense Satellite Communications Program, launched 16 June 1966, was one of the earliest Air Force satellite communication systems. Another benefit of early satellites was improved navigation. Although the Navy produced the first working satellite navigation system (Transit), an early Air Force navigation satellite program was designed to provide precise time and navigation information in three dimensions. Later, a joint Air Force and Navy program would result in what became known as the NAVSTAR Global Positioning System.

1.15.11. Increased defense spending during the early 1980s resulted in more mature space and missile programs (most of which are still in service) to replace the systems developed in the 1960s and 1970s. These included the Defense Support Program, the Defense Meteorological Satellite Program, the Defense Satellite Communications System, and the Global Positioning System. Concurrently, the Air Force developed the ground-based infrastructure to support, augment, and complement the space-based portions of the systems. Ground-based systems included the Ballistic Missile Early Warning System; orbiting space object surveillance using Baker-Nunn cameras; and the Air Force Satellite Control Network. In addition, the Air Force developed launch support bases necessary to get satellites into space – one at Cape Canaveral, Florida, and the other at Vandenberg Air Force Base, California. The launch bases provided support not only for Department of Defense sponsored systems but also for National Aeronautics and Space Agency, other United States government agencies, and commercial requirements.

1.15.12. In the late 1970s and early 1980s, the time had come to substantially reorganize the way the service managed its space systems. Chief of Staff, Air Force General Lew Allen appeared with Under Secretary of the Air Force Pete Aldridge, 21 June 1982 to announce the formation of Space Command, with activation slated for 1 September 1982. Air Force Space Command's responsibilities grew quickly over the ensuing decade as it absorbed programs from Aerospace Defense Command, Air Force Systems Command, and Strategic Air Command. Eventually command missions included missile warning, space surveillance, satellite control, space defense, space support to operational forces, and launch operations. The organizational changes that led to the establishment of Space Command reflected a growth in the use of space systems in support of worldwide joint operations.

**Berlin Wall—symbol of the Cold War**

1.15.13. In a 23 March 1983 address, President Ronald Reagan proposed replacing the doctrine of mutually assured destruction with one of assured survival, through implementation of the Strategic Defense Initiative. Strategic Defense Initiative would include a combination of defensive systems such as space-based lasers, particle beams, railguns, and fast ground-launched missiles, among others, to intercept intercontinental ballistic missiles in the earth's outer atmosphere and ballistic path in space. The end of the Cold War and collapse of the Soviet Union eliminated the justification for the level of research and development associated with the project, although research continued at a much-lower level under the Ballistic Missile Defense Organization.

1.15.14. Beginning in March 1985, Soviet Communist Party General-Secretary Mikhail Gorbachev initiated major changes in Soviet-American relations. The Intermediate Range Nuclear Forces Treaty, in December 1987, eliminated medium-range nuclear missiles, including United States Air Force ground-launched cruise missiles. Gorbachev's announcement in May 1988 that the Soviet Union, after nine years of inconclusive combat, would withdraw from the war in Afghanistan resulted in reduced Cold War tension, but it was only a hint of the rapid changes ahead. Relatively free and open Russian national elections in March 1989, followed by a coal miner strike in July, shook the foundations of Communist rule. East Germany opened the Berlin Wall in November which led to German reunification in October 1990. The August 1991 coup against Gorbachev, led by Boris Yeltsin, resulted in the dissolution of the Soviet Union, replaced 25 December 1991 by the Commonwealth of Independent States.

1.15.15. American nuclear strategy changed significantly in response to these changes. Under the Strategic Arms Reduction Treaty I, signed by the United States and the Soviet Union in July 1991, the Air Force would reduce arms to 6,000 total warheads on deployed intercontinental ballistic missiles, submarine launched ballistic missiles, and heavy bombers. Strategic Arms Reduction Treaty II, signed in January 1993, would reduce total deployed warheads up to a range of 3,500 nautical miles. The resulting force structure (determined during the Nuclear Posture Review process overseen by then Secretary of Defense Les Aspin), would ultimately lead to the deployment of 500 single-warhead Minuteman III intercontinental ballistic missiles, 66 B-52H, and 20 B-2 heavy bombers. Ninety-four B-1 heavy bombers would be reoriented to a conventional role by 2003, and all Peacekeeper intercontinental ballistic missiles would be removed from active inventory and associated silo launchers eliminated. The Air Force, by presidential direction in September 1991, notified Strategic Air Command to remove heavy bombers from alert status. Strategic Air Command was subsequently inactivated in June 1992. United States Strategic Command, a unified combatant command, replaced Strategic Air Command and assumed control of all remaining Air Force and Navy strategic nuclear forces.

### 1.16. Desert Storm (The Air Campaign against Iraq, 1990-1991):

1.16.1. On 2 August 1990, Iraqi dictator Saddam Hussein ordered 100,000 troops to invade oil-rich Kuwait, claiming Kuwait as Iraq's 19th province. International condemnation followed, and on 6 August the United Nations authorized an economic embargo. The same day, President George H. W. Bush announced Operation DESERT SHIELD, the deployment of United States air and ground units to defend Saudi Arabia and Persian Gulf states. Within 18 hours of the order, Air Force Military Airlift Command C-141 and C-5 transports delivered the Army 82d Airborne Division and elements of the Air Force 1st Tactical Fighter Wing (whose 48 F-15Cs flew direct).

1.16.2. Operation DESERT SHIELD eclipsed the Berlin Airlift as the greatest air deployment in history. Military Airlift Command cargo planes delivered defensive forces 7 August - 8 November 1990, brought counteroffensive material 9 November - January 1991. The air bridge spanned more than 7,000 miles and included 20,500 strategic airlift missions. Desert Shield validated the C-5A Galaxy and C-141 Starlifter large capacity heavy lifters, which carried 534,000 passengers and 542,000 tons of cargo during the Gulf War.

**Coalition aircraft, Desert Shield/Storm**

1.16.3. The Gulf War represents the first, extensive, broad-based employment of space support capabilities. Coalition forces employed more than 60 military satellites, as well as commercial and civil sector systems during the conflict. Defense Meteorological Satellite Program provided dedicated meteorological support in theater, which helped provide safe, highly effective combat power planning and application in a harsh environment characterized by sandstorms and oil fires. Satellite-based systems delivered more than 90 percent of all communications to and from the theater due to the sheer volume and the lack of ground-based infrastructure. At the height of the conflict, 700,000 phone calls and 152,000 messages per day flowed over satellite links.

1.16.4. At 0100, 17 January 1991, three Air Force Special Operations MH-53J Pave Low helicopters led nine Army Apaches on the first strike mission of Operation DESERT STORM.

**Destroyed Iraqi column, Highway 8**

1.16.5. Within hours, the world watched live television coverage of Iraqi skies filled with antiaircraft artillery fire. F-117A Nighthawks struck heavily defended targets with unprecedented precision. Under the command of Lieutenant General Charles A. Horner, United States Central Command Air Forces, 2,700 aircraft from 14 countries and services implemented the master attack plan. The coalition effort overwhelmed the Iraqi air defense system with speed, surprise, precision, and mass. A flight of seven B-52Gs flew nonstop from Barksdale Air Force Base Louisiana to strike Iraqi power stations and communications facilities with Air Launched Cruise Missiles. At 35 hours round-trip, the 14,000-mile raid was the longest combat mission up to that time and proof of America's global reach.

1.16.6. The first week of Desert Storm focused on achieving air supremacy and destroying the enemy's command and control system. Captain Jon K. "JB" Kelk, flying an F-15C, scored the first air-to-air kill, downing an Iraqi MiG-29. All total, coalition aircraft shot down 41 Iraqi aircraft, with Captain Thomas N. "Vegas" Dietz and First Lieutenant Robert W. "Gigs" Hehemann each credited with three kills. Additionally, Allied air forces destroyed 375 enemy aircraft and 594 hardened bunkers. Faced with coalition air dominance, 148 Iraqi aircraft fled to neighboring Iran.

1.16.7. The air campaign then prepared the battlefield by isolating Iraqi ground units, interdicting supplies, and reducing enemy combat power. A-10 Thunderbolt II "Warthogs" and F-15Es introduced a new term -tank plinking - as they destroyed the enemy's armored forces. F-111F "Aardvarks" dropped 4,600 of the 8,000 precision-guided munitions. EF-111A electronic warfare aircraft provided tactical jamming, while combined RC- 135 Rivet Joint, E-8 Joint Surveillance Target Attack Radar System (Joint STARS), and E-3 Airborne Warning and Control System aircraft provided intelligence and command and control. Perhaps the most spectacular element: B-52s shattered Iraqi Army morale with massive bomb drops. When one Iraqi commander asserted that he surrendered because of B-52 strikes, his interrogator pointed out that his position had never been attacked by the B-52. "That is true, but I saw one that had been attacked," said the Iraqi.

1.16.8. Not all aspects of the air campaign were successful. Early in the campaign, Iraq launched modified Soviet Scud missiles against Israel, Saudi Arabia, and the Persian Gulf states. On 18 January 1991, United States Air Force A-10s,

F-16s, and F-15Es with Low-Altitude Navigation and Targeting Infrared for Night pods commenced the Great Scud Hunt. Despite 2,767 sorties (22 percent of the strategic air phase), air patrols did not destroy a significant number of the missiles. Iraqi camouflage, decoys, and employment tactics frustrated the effort. The enemy launched 88 Scuds, including one that struck a United States Army Reserve unit at Dhahran, killing 28 soldiers and wounding 98. The anti-Scud effort did limit Scud launches after the first 2 weeks of fighting and reduced the political impact of the weapon.

1.16.9. The Desert Storm air campaign demonstrated airpower's impact on a conventional battlefield. Air Force space assets provided precision positioning and navigation to joint and coalition forces with the combat debut of the Global Positioning System. Space forces also provided the coalition and allies with advanced Iraqi Scud launch warnings. Defense Support Program gave timely warning of the launch of Iraqi Scud missiles to United States forces in theater and allowed Patriot batteries in Israel, Saudi Arabia, and Kuwait sufficient time to engage the incoming Iraqi intermediate range ballistic missiles. Space force capabilities influenced Israel to remain neutral, thereby preserving the integrity of the allied coalition. Over the course of the 44-day air campaign, the coalition flew 118,661 sorties, of which the Air Force flew 60 percent. The 1991 Persian Gulf War brought military space operations to the joint community. The Gulf War was the first conflict to highlight the force enhancement capabilities of space-based communications, intelligence, navigation, missile warning, and weather satellites. Desert Storm also demonstrated the impact of precision-guided munitions on modern war. Although precision-guided munitions accounted for only eight percent of the 88,500 tons of bombs dropped, they were responsible for 80 percent of the destroyed targets. While coalition ground forces delivered General Schwarzkopf's famous Hail Mary outflanking maneuver that applied the final blow to the Iraqi military forces, airpower set the stage for victory. As the Gulf War Air Power Survey stated: It was not the number of Iraqi tanks or artillery pieces destroyed, or the number of Iraqi soldiers killed that mattered. It was the effectiveness of the air campaign in breaking apart the organizational structure and cohesion of enemy military forces and in reaching the mind of the Iraqi soldier that counted.

## 1.17. Operations PROVIDE RELIEF, IMPRESSIVE LIFT, and RESTORE HOPE—Somalia (1992-1994):

1.17.1. Civil unrest in the wake of a two-year civil war contributed to a famine in Somalia that killed up to 350,000 people in 1992. As many as 800,000 refugees fled the stricken country. The United Nations-led relief effort began in July 1992. To relieve the suffering of refugees near the Kenya-Somalia border and then Somalia itself, the United States initiated Operation PROVIDE RELIEF in August 1992. By December, the United States airlifted 38 million pounds of food into the region, sometimes under the hail of small arms fire. Continued civil war and clan fighting within Somalia, however, prevented much of the relief supplies from getting into the hands of those who most desperately needed them.

1.17.2. First, the United Nations, then the United States, attempted to alleviate the problem. In September, the United States initiated Operation IMPRESSIVE LIFT to airlift hundreds of Pakistani soldiers under the United Nations banner to Somalia. Despite the increased security from the United Nations forces, the problems continued. On 4 December, President George Bush authorized Operation RESTORE HOPE to establish order in the country so that food could reach those in need. Marines landed and assumed control of the airport, allowing flights in and out of Mogadishu, Somalia, to resume. C-5 Galaxies, C-141 Starlifters, C-130 Hercules, and even KC-10 tankers rushed supplies into the country. Further, the Operation RESTORE HOPE airlift brought 32,000 United States troops into Somalia. In March 1993, the United Nations once again assumed control of the mission, and Operation RESTORE HOPE officially ended 4 May 1993. Fewer than 5,000 of the 25,000 United States troops originally deployed remained in Somalia. Unfortunately, factional fighting within the country caused the relief effort to unravel yet again. On 3 October 1993, United States special forces troops, in an effort to capture members of one clan, lost 18 personnel and suffered 84 wounded.

**MSgt. Timothy A. Wilkinson**

1.17.3. In the late afternoon of 3 October 1993, Technical Sergeant Timothy A. Wilkinson, a pararescueman with the 24th Special Tactics Squadron, responded with his crew to the downing of a United States UH-60 helicopter in the streets of Mogadishu, Somalia. Wilkinson repeatedly exposed himself to intense enemy small arms fire while extracting the wounded and dead crewmembers from the crashed helicopter. Despite his own wounds, he provided life-saving medical treatment to the wounded crewmembers. With the helicopter crew taken care of, he turned to aid the casualties of a ranger security element engaged in an intense firefight across an open four-way intersection from his position where he began immediate medical treatment. His decisive actions, personal courage, and bravery under heavy enemy fire were integral to the success of all casualty treatment and evacuation efforts conducted in the intense 18-hour combat engagement. Wilkinson was awarded the Air Force Cross for his actions.

1.17.4. The losses sustained on 3 and 4 October prompted Operation RESTORE HOPE II, the airlifting of 1,700 United States troops and 3,100 tons of cargo into Mogadishu between 5 and 13 October 1993. The troops and equipment were tasked with only stabilizing the situation: President Clinton refused to commit the United States to "nation building" and promised to remove United States forces by March 1994. Operation RESTORE HOPE II officially ended 25 March 1994 when the last C-5 carrying United States troops departed Mogadishu. While Operation RESTORE HOPE II allowed United States forces to get out of the country without further casualties, anarchy ruled in Somalia, and the threat of famine remained.

### 1.18. Operation ALLIED FORCE:

1.18.1. The post-Cold War breakup of Yugoslavia proved to be NATO's greatest challenge in the 1990s. Militant Serbian nationalism and a policy of ethnic cleansing, promoted by Yugoslavian President Slobodan Milosevic, created a crisis in Kosovo in 1999. Meanwhile, Albanian separatists in the Kosovo Liberation Army fanned the flames of violence. When diplomacy failed, NATO worried about the possibility of a genocidal civil war and destabilization throughout the Balkans. As NATO debated intervention, President Milosevic unleashed a ruthless offensive designed to crush the Kosovo Liberation Army and drive ethnic Albanians out of Kosovo. Faced with a massive humanitarian crisis, NATO turned to airpower.

1.18.2. After Desert Storm in early 1992, Chief of Staff, Air Force General Merrill McPeak, introduced a revamped Air Force mission: Defend the United States through control and exploitation of air and space. Resultant organizational changes permitted the Air Force to attain an unprecedented level of integration between air and space capabilities by the time the Air War over Serbia commenced in 1999. During Air War over Serbia, Air Force Space Command deployed nearly 150 space professionals to nine locations in theater. During the conflict, multisource Tactical System/Combat Track I modifications to five B-52s and two B-1s allowed near real-time information to flow to the cockpits. The space-enabled information included threats, target updates, imagery, and secure communications with the wing operations center. Global Positioning System satellites provided terminal guidance data for Joint Direct Attack Munitions, Conventional Air Launched Cruise Missiles, and Tomahawk Land Attack Missile deliveries. This conflict was the first operational employment of Joint Direct Attack Munitions, demonstrating precision adverse weather delivery of multiple weapons against multiple aim points on a single pass.

1.18.3. Optimistic policymakers looked to NATO's successful two-week Operation DELIBERATE FORCE in 1995 that brought relative peace to Bosnia. On 24 March 1999, President Bill Clinton commenced Operation ALLIED FORCE, announcing three objectives: demonstrate NATO's opposition to aggression; deter Milosevic from escalating attacks on civilians; and damage Serbia's capability to wage war against Kosovo. Milosevic and Serbian forces presented United States and NATO forces with an opponent with a capacity for skilled propaganda and utter ruthlessness. The ensuing 78-day battle was directed against both the Serbian military and Milosevic's propaganda efforts.

1.18.4. From 24 March to 9 June 1999, NATO air forces walked a political tightrope. In over 38,000 sorties, 13 of NATO's 19 nations attempted to pressure Milosevic, destroy Serbian fielded forces engaged in Kosovo, and maintain popular support for intervention. Initially, 214 strike aircraft followed a limited air campaign against approximately 50 targets.

**B-2 Spirit in flight**

1.18.5. The B-2 Spirit stealth bomber flew its first combat missions from Whiteman Air Force Base, Missouri, delivering 650 Joint Direct Attack Munitions in 49 30-hour sorties. On 27 March 1999, Serb air defenses shot down an Air Force F-117, but Combat Search and Rescue personnel recovered the pilot. After weeks of caution and frustration, NATO expanded the scale of the air campaign: 563 United States Air Force aircraft and 13,850 American Airmen deployed to 24 locations.

1.18.6. By June 1999, NATO airpower accomplished its objectives, although complex political constraints, abysmal flying weather, and a Serbian-manufactured refugee crisis hampered progress. Despite a concerted effort to avoid civilian casualties, at least 20 major incidents occurred, including the 7 May 1999 accidental bombing of the Chinese embassy.

1.18.7. The 1999 air campaign against Serbia reinforced historical lessons on employing air and space power. Despite limitations, air and space forces proved precise, effective, and rapid. In many ways, a limited air campaign represented the only means available to coerce an implacable foe. Assessments of Operation ALLIED FORCE concluded that air and ground commanders must agree on the enemy's centers of gravity, and micromanaging the targeting process limits military effectiveness.

### 1.19. Operations NOBLE EAGLE, ENDURING FREEDOM, and IRAQI FREEDOM (Global War on Terrorism):

1.19.1. On 11 September 2001, 19 Islamic extremist Al Qaeda terrorists highjacked four airliners and flew them into the World Trade Center, the Pentagon, and a remote field in Pennsylvania, killing about 3,000 people. In response, President

George W. Bush declared a global war on terrorism. Operation NOBLE EAGLE immediately focused on protecting the United States homeland from both internal and external air attacks of the nature used on September 11. United States Air Force fighter, tanker, and surveillance air assets provided 24-hour intercept response coverage for virtually the entire United States in the form of ground alert and airborne combat air patrols over designated locations.

1.19.2. Operation ENDURING FREEDOM focused on forming and acting with an international coalition, which included forces from the United Kingdom, Australia, Canada, the Czech Republic, Denmark, France, Germany, Italy, Japan, Jordan, the Netherlands, New Zealand, Norway, Pakistan, Poland, Russia, Spain, Turkey, and other nations to remove Afghanistan's Taliban government. The Taliban sponsored Al Qaeda terrorism and provided a safe haven for Osama bin Laden, its leader.

**USAF combat controller on horseback**

1.19.3. On 7 October 2001, 15 Air Force bombers, 25 Navy carrier-strike aircraft, and 50 United States and British sea-launched Tomahawk cruise missiles launched the first wave of Operation ENDURING FREEDOM military operations. In the opening days of the campaign, joint airpower destroyed Taliban air defenses, command centers, and other fixed targets, and protected humanitarian relief missions to the Afghan people. In contrast to Desert Storm and Allied Force, Taliban and Al Qaeda forces presented few fixed targets suitable for air attack. Instead, Air Force B-52 bombers carrying Global Positioning System-guided Joint Direct Attack Munitions flew to engagement zones where ground-based forces directed attacks. Global Positioning System-guided munitions were employed with great accuracy, enabling air planners to reduce the number of air sorties required to destroy a particular objective. Combat operations in Afghanistan began with small groups of elite American military forces deployed to support anti-Taliban Afghani fighters. A number of the deployed troops carried 2.75-pound Precision Lightweight Global Positioning System Receivers and satellite-based communications devices. Air Force combat controllers were among the 300 or so Army, Navy, and Air Force special operations personnel augmenting the Afghan Northern Alliance. On 13 November 2001, the Afghanistan capital, Kabul, fell to coalition forces.

1.19.4. One relatively small but quite significant operation took place on 4 March 2002. The Pentagon called it Operation ANACONDA and the press referred to it as the battle at Shah-I-Kot Mountain, but the men who fought there called it the battle of Robert's Ridge. In the early morning hours, on a mountaintop called Takur Ghar in southeastern Afghanistan, al Qaeda soldiers fired on an MH-47E helicopter, causing a Navy SEAL to fall to the ground, and a chain of events ensued culminating in one of the most intense small-unit firefights of the war against terrorism, the death of all the al Qaeda terrorists defending the mountaintop, and the death of seven United States servicemen. Despite these losses, the United States forces involved in this fight distinguished themselves by conspicuous bravery. Their countless acts of heroism demonstrated the best of America's Special Operations Forces as Air Force, Army, and Navy special operators fought side by side to save one of their own and each other, and in the process secured the mountaintop and inflicted serious loss on al Qaeda.

**Tech. Sgt. John A. Chapman**

1.19.5. On 10 January 2003, Secretary of the Air Force posthumously awarded the Air Force Cross to Technical Sergeant John A. Chapman. It was only the third time since the end of the Vietnam conflict that an enlisted Airman received the Air Force Cross and the second time that it went to one of the enlisted Airman who died in what became a 17-hour ordeal on top of Takur Ghar mountain in Afghanistan. Chapman's helicopter came under enemy fire, causing a Navy SEAL to fall out of a MH-47 helicopter during an insertion under fire. The helicopter landed 4.5 miles away from where the SEAL was killed. Once on the ground, Chapman provided directions to another helicopter to pick them up. After being rescued, Chapman and the team volunteered to rescue their mission team member from the enemy stronghold. After landing, Chapman killed two enemy soldiers and, without regard for his own life, kept advancing toward a dug-in machinegun nest. The team came under fire from three directions. Chapman exchanged fire from minimum personal cover and succumbed to multiple wounds. His engagement and destruction of the first enemy position and advancement to the second enabled his team to move to cover and break enemy contact. He is credited with saving the lives of the entire rescue team.

1.19.6. Afghanistan's rugged terrain, complex political relationships, and distance from operating bases challenged coalition forces. (Navy aircraft flew 700 miles one way from carriers, and Air Force bombers ventured 2,500 miles one way from Diego Garcia.) Air Force KC-135 tankers, C-17 and C-130 airlifters, Red Horse civil engineer teams, space-based Global Positioning System and intelligence-gathering satellites, and other support functions proved to be unsung heroes of the campaign. Their effectiveness reduced combat troop casualties. In the first 18 months, the Air Force flew more than 85,000 sorties (75 percent of the total effort), dropped 30,750 munitions, delivered 487,000 tons of cargo, and provided 3,025 intelligence, surveillance, and reconnaissance missions. Even after the defeat of the Taliban, operations in Afghanistan remained hazardous, as United States and coalition forces there faced extended counterinsurgency operations.

1.19.7 On 19 March 2003 a coalition of American and allied forces entered Iraq to end the regime of Saddam Hussein and to free the Iraqi people, kicking off Operation IRAQI FREEDOM. Much like the Gulf War, Operation IRAQI FREEDOM came as no surprise to anyone besides Saddam Hussein. On 17 March 2003, President George W. Bush announced a 48-hour ultimatum for Saddam and his sons to leave Iraq or face conflict. Saddam rejected President Bush's ultimatum to flee, and on 20 March a salvo of missiles and laser-guided bombs hit targets where coalition forces believed Saddam and his sons and other leaders gathered. Thus the war began.

1.19.8. More than 300,000 troops were deployed to the Gulf region to form a multinational coalition. Combat operations took longer than the 24-hour war of Operation DESERT STORM. Operation IRAQI FREEDOM officially began on 20 March 2003, and the primary combat phase ended on 1 May 2003. The Pentagon unleashed air strikes so devastating they would leave Saddam's soldiers unable or unwilling to fight. Between 300 and 400 cruise missiles were fired at targets, more than the number launched during the entire first Gulf War. On the second day, the plan called for launching another 300 to 400 missiles. The battle plan was based on a concept developed at the National Defense University. Called "Shock and Awe," it focused on the psychological destruction of the enemy's will to fight rather than the physical destruction of the opposing military force. The concept relies on a large number of precision-guided weapons hitting the enemy simultaneously, much like a nuclear weapon strike that takes minutes instead of days or weeks to work.

1.19.9. Heavy sand storms slowed the coalition advance, but soldiers reached within 50 miles of Baghdad by 24 March. Missile attacks hit military facilities in Baghdad on 30 March, and by 2 April, the Baghdad and Medina divisions of Iraq's Republican Guard were defeated. United States soldiers seized bridges over the Tigris and Euphrates rivers and then advanced within 25 miles of Baghdad. The next day, United States Army units along with Air Force special tactics combat controllers, pararescuemen, and combat weathermen attacked Saddam International Airport, 10 miles southwest of the capital. Two days later American-armored vehicles drove through Baghdad after smashing through Republican Guard units. On 7 April, United States tanks rumbled through downtown Baghdad and a B–1B bomber attack hit buildings thought to hold Saddam and other leaders.

SSgt. Scott D. Sather

1.19.10. On 8 April 2003, Staff Sergeant Scott Sather, a combat controller, became the first Airman killed in Operation IRAQI FREEDOM. The 29-year-old Michigan native earned seven medals, including the bronze star, during his Air Force career. The citation accompanying Sather's Bronze Star Medal with Valor reads, "He led this reconnaissance task force on combat operations into Iraq on the first day of the ground war, breeching enemy fortifications during the Iraqi border crossing. During the next several days Sergeant Sather covered countless miles conducting specialized reconnaissance in the Southwestern Iraqi desert supporting classified missions. With only minimal sleep he assumed a leadership role in the reconnaissance of an enemy airfield opening up the first of five airheads used by a joint task force to conduct critical resupply of fielded troops, and provide attack helicopter rearming facilities enabling deep battlefield offensive operations. Sergeant Sather was then employed to an area of heavy enemy concentration tasked to provide critical reconnaissance and intelligence on enemy movement supporting direct action missions against enemy forces. Exposed to direct enemy fire on numerous occasions he continued to provide vital information to higher headquarters in direct support of ongoing combat operations. His magnificent skills in the control of close air support aircraft and keen leadership under great pressure were instrumental in the overwhelming success of these dangerous missions. Sergeant Sather's phenomenal leadership and bravery on the battlefield throughout his deployment were instrumental in the resounding successes of numerous combat missions performing a significant role in the success of the war and complete overthrow of the Iraqi regime."

1.19.11. The withdrawal of American military forces from Iraq had been a contentious issue within the United States since the beginning of the Iraq War. As the war progressed from its initial 2003 invasion phase to a multi-year occupation, United States public opinion turned in favor of troop withdrawal. In late April 2007, the United States Congress passed a supplementary spending bill for Iraq that set a deadline, but President Bush vetoed this bill soon afterwards. All United States Forces were mandated to withdraw from Iraqi territory by 31 December 2011 under the terms of a bilateral agreement signed in 2008 by President Bush.

1.19.12. As the deadline for withdrawal drew nearer, the mission of United States forces in Iraq continued to move away from combat, and 1 September 2010 marked the transition from Operation IRAQI FREEDOM to Operation NEW DAWN, signifying a formal end to United States military combat operations. The transition to a supporting role and stability operations was made possible by increased capability of Iraqi Security Forces and their improved ability to combat terrorists and provide security for the Iraqi people. As part of Operation NEW DAWN, United States Forces had three primary missions: advising, assisting, and training the Iraqi security forces; conducting partnered counterterrorism operations; and providing support to provincial reconstruction teams and civilian partners as they help build Iraq's civil capacity. The United States troop withdrawal from Iraq was completed on 18 December 2011, early Sunday morning.

1.19.13. On 20 March 2011 a collection of aircraft launched in support of Operation ODYSSEY DAWN to enforce United Nations Security Council Resolution 1973, centered on protecting Libyan citizens from further harm from Libyan leader Moammar Gadhafi's regime. Following the initial launch of Tomahawk missiles, three United States aircraft led strikes on a variety of strategic targets over Libya. United States fighter aircraft created airspace where no enemy forces could advance on Libyan opposition troops.

1.19.14. As already stated, the war in Afghanistan had begun in 2001, with the stated goal of dismantling the al-Qaeda terrorist organization and ending its use of Afghanistan as a base. The United States also said that it would remove the Taliban regime from power and create a viable democratic state. More than a decade into the war, NATO forces continued to battle a widespread Taliban insurgency, and the war expanded into the tribal area of neighboring Pakistan. On 21 May 2012 the leaders of the NATO-member countries signed off on President Barack Obama's exit strategy from Afghanistan that called for an end to combat operations in 2013 and the withdrawal of the United States-led international military force by the end of 2014.

1.19.15. On 9 June 2012 French President Francois Hollande announced his plan to withdraw combat forces by year's end. In December of that year, France pulled its last troops engaged directly in combat out of Afghanistan. The remaining French troops, about 1,500, remained for approximately six months removing equipment and helping to train Afghan forces. Also on 2 September 2012 United States Special Operations Forces temporarily suspended training of some 1,000 Afghan local police recruits while they double-checked the background of the current police force, following a rise in insider attacks against NATO troops by Afghan forces. On September 20, 2012 the surge of United States forces in Afghanistan ended and the last several hundred surge troops left the country. On 18 June 2013 Afghan National Security Forces formally took over combat operations. Canada's military mission in Afghanistan ended on 12 March 2014, and on 27 May, President Obama announced that the United States combat mission in Afghanistan would end in December.

1.19.16. For most United States' and NATO forces, the war in Afghanistan was over by the end of 2014. At NATO's International Security Assistance Force headquarters in Kabul, a ceremony marked the end of International Security Assistance Force's mission and the transition to the NATO-led Resolute Support. The new NATO presence would be more than 12,500 troops to focus on Afghan security forces stability, and United States personnel would number almost 11,000, including approximately 2,500 Airmen, in January 2015. The United States Operation ENDURING FREEDOM would be replaced by Operation FREEDOM'S SENTINEL, the name of the United States portion of NATO's Resolute Support. Airmen would continue to work at standing up the Afghan Air Force, and their mission could continue until the Afghan Air Force becomes fully independent.

1.19.17. In the latter part of 2014, a new and ominous threat emerged that resulted in United States Airmen again involved in operations in the skies over Iraq. The enemy, calling themselves the Islamic State of Iraq and Levant, was an extremist Sunni jihadist organization. Aided by a number of worldwide recruits and sympathizers, Islamic State of Iraq and Levant gained control of territory in Syria and northern Iraq (including the cities of Mosul and Fallujah) exceeding the size of Great Britain, leaving savage atrocities in their wake, including mass murders and ruthless executions of innocent civilians. Their brutality resulted in nearly universal condemnation—even Al Qaeda repudiated them—and President Obama authorized United States forces, in cooperation with partner nations, to conduct carefully targeted air strikes over Syria and Iraq, beginning in August, with the aim of degrading and defeating Islamic State of Iraq and Levant. This operation, under the name of INHERENT RESOLVE, was still ongoing at the end of 2014.

## 1.20. Historical Perspective Conclusion:

1.20.1. From Kitty Hawk to Afghanistan, the record of air and space power emphasizes powerful themes. The interplay of doctrine, technology, tactics, and strategy must be sustained by training, logistics, supply, and support infrastructure. Although history may not provide hard and fast lessons, it offers inspiration, insight, and examples to spur your thinking. Today's Airmen draw from a proud heritage of sacrifice, valor, and success. Just as our predecessors triumphed over the challenges at St. Mihiel, Schweinfurt, and MiG Alley, you will face new challenges with courage, skill, innovation, and perseverance.

1.20.2. From the skies over the Rio Grande to those over Iraq and Afghanistan nearly 100 years later, air power has evolved from an ineffective oddity to the dominant form of military might in the world. Its applications and effectiveness have increased with each succeeding conflict; in World War I air power played a minor role, in Kosovo it played the only role. In addition to their air combat role, airmen have bravely and successfully carried out a large number of humanitarian missions, demonstrating the ability to save lives and alleviate suffering in the face of both natural and man-made disasters. This chapter has looked at the development of air power through the nation's many conflicts and contingencies, spotlighting just a few of the many contributions of enlisted personnel.

*Section 1F—Airman Exemplars*

**1.21. Airman Exemplars.** The following Airmen are representative of the diverse individuals whose exceptional contributions shaped and influenced our Air Force and continue to inspire today's Airmen.

1.21.1. **Orville and Wilbur Wright.** The Wright brothers, bicycle manufacturers from Dayton, Ohio, achieved the first powered, sustained, controlled airplane flight in 1903, heralding the age of heavier-than-air aviation. Wilbur was born 16 April 1867, near Millville, Indiana, and Orville was born 19 August 1871, in Dayton, Ohio. They became interested in mechanical flight after reading about Otto Lilienthal's successful glider experiments in Germany during the 1890s. In contrast to other experimenters, the Wrights concentrated their efforts on a three-dimensional system of control, using an elevator and twisting the wings (called warping) in combination with a vertical rudder. A series of biplane gliders in 1902 led to a development of a perfectly controllable glider capable of generating sufficient lift. Subsequently, the brothers designed and built a relatively lightweight gasoline engine and revolutionary, highly efficient propellers for the 1903 flyer. Using that aircraft, they successfully flew four manned missions 17 December 1903 at Kitty Hawk, North Carolina. In 1904 and 1905, the Wright brothers conducted experiments at Huffman Prairie, near Dayton, and introduced a new improved aircraft each year. The 1905 Wright flyer is generally recognized as the first practical airplane. It could turn, bank, fly figure eights, and remain aloft for over 30 minutes. It was not until 1907 that the Signal Corps established an Aviation Section and  issued a bid for a military airplane. Tests of the Wright military machine began at Fort Myer, Virginia, in 1908. A crash 17 September 1908, however, seriously injured Orville, killed passenger Lieutenant Thomas E. Selfridge, and temporarily interrupted testing. A new machine accepted in the fall of 1909 was the United States Army's first airplane: Signal Corps No. 1. Subsequently the Wright brothers trained several United States Army pilots, including Henry H. "Hap" Arnold, future commander of the United States Army Air Forces during World War II. The Wright Aircraft Company sold the Army several airplanes. The Wrights, however, remained wedded to the wing warping system of control and their airplanes became increasingly inferior and uncompetitive, while those of rivals like Glenn Curtiss improved rapidly in performance. Wilbur died of typhoid fever 30 May 1912, and Orville later sold the Wright Company and assumed a less active role in aviation. He remained, however, the "father" of flying and a highly honored individual until his death 30 January 1948.

1.21.2. **Colonel William "Billy" Mitchell.** Colonel Mitchell was an airpower visionary who saw the airplane dominating warfare and called for an air force independent of the United States Army.

1.21.2.1. Born to wealthy American parents in Nice, France, on 29 December 1879, he grew up in Wisconsin. He attended Racine College and Columbian College (now George Washington University in Washington, District of Columbia) but abandoned college at the beginning of the Spanish-American War and enlisted in the military. His father, a United States Senator, applied influence and he received a commission. Intelligent, able, and aggressive, Mitchell was the youngest captain ever selected to join the General Staff (1912).

1.21.2.2. In 1915, Mitchell joined the Aviation Section of the Signal Corps and the following year he took private flying lessons. During much of 1918, he commanded most of the United States air combat units at the front. He added the use of aircraft in mass to overwhelm the enemy to the British doctrine of taking the offensive. In September 1918, he massed more than 1,500 United States and Allied aircraft in support of the St. Mihiel offensive. In April 1921, Mitchell became Assistant to the Chief of the Air Service. His outspoken advocacy of a separate air force, critical remarks about the poor quality of the Air Service, and criticism of superiors caused considerable controversy. Worse was his methodology, which relied on appeals to

Congress and the public outside the chain of command, often in violation of direct orders. His claims that the airplane could sink battleships ultimately led to bombing trials in June 1921. During these trials, the 1st Provisional Air Brigade under Mitchell's leadership sank the former German battleship *Ostfriesland*, which was probably the high point of Mitchell's military career.

1.21.2.3. Major General Mason Patrick, Air Service commander after the bombing trials, was able to keep Mitchell out of trouble for a time, but in 1925 further activities led the War Department to refuse to reappoint him as Assistant Chief. Mitchell reverted to his permanent rank of colonel and was assigned to Fort Sam Houston, Texas.

1.21.2.4. Even from Texas, Mitchell used the press to continue to advocate an independent air force. After the Navy dirigible *Shenandoah* was destroyed in a storm, he charged senior military leadership with incompetence. President Coolidge personally ordered Mitchell's court-martial, and he was found guilty of insubordination. Mitchell resigned his commission 1 February 1926 and died 19 February 1936.

1.21.3. **Major General Benjamin D. "Benny" Foulois.** Foulois was a pioneer aviator and the first commander of an American air unit in the field. He was born in Connecticut, 9 December 1879. He enlisted in the Army at the time of the Spanish-American War and was commissioned during his service in the Philippines in 1901. In 1907, Foulois entered the Aviation Section of the Signal Corps. In 1908 and 1909, Foulois participated in the acceptance tests of the Army's first semirigid dirigible and its first airplane, a Wright flyer designated Signal Corps No. 1. In 1910, Foulois took Signal Corps No. 1 to Fort Sam Houston, Texas, where he conducted tests to demonstrate its military usefulness. He remained in aviation until his retirement in 1935. In subsequent years, Foulois participated in all aspects of early United States Army aviation and in 1915, completed the organization of the Army's first operational unit, the 1st Aero Squadron. Foulois commanded the squadron during the Mexican Punitive Expedition in 1916-1917; the first deployment of a United States Army air unit to the field. Following the Punitive Expedition, Foulois went to Washington, District of Columbia,  where he played a major role in planning and implementing the $640 million aviation program begun after the United States entered World War I. Foulois was promoted to brigadier general and named Chief of the Air Service for the American Expeditionary Force in November 1917.

1.21.3.1. He was unsuccessful, however, and was replaced by General Patrick in May 1918. Foulois' subsequent work, especially as Patrick's assistant, however, played a major role in Air Service success during the war.

1.21.3.2. In 1927, he moved to Washington, District of Columbia, to become Assistant Chief of the Air Service, and in 1931 was promoted to major general and named Chief of the Air Corps. Foulois proved a less-than-effective Air Corps leader. A hands-on individual, he tried to spend more time in the cockpit and less in the office. A firm advocate of strategic bombardment and an independent air force, his testimony before Congress was usually blunt and straightforward.

1.21.3.3. In 1934, Foulois agreed on short notice that the Air Corps could fly the United States mail. The service proved ill-equipped for the effort, which damaged Foulois' reputation. However, during his tenure, the Air Corps acquired its first B-17 heavy bombers and he helped organize General Headquarters Air Force in 1935; a significant step toward Air Force independence. General Foulois retired 31 December 1935 and died 25 April 1967.

1.21.4. **General of the Air Force Henry H. "Hap" Arnold.** General Arnold was an aviation pioneer and is generally  recognized as the father of the modern United States Air Force, commanding the United States Army Air Forces during World War II. Arnold was born in Gladwyne, Pennsylvania, 25 June 1886, and graduated from West Point in 1907. Originally an infantryman, he became a flyer in 1911. His career paralleled the early development of United States military aviation. In April 1911, the Signal Corps sent Arnold to Dayton, Ohio, where Wilbur and Orville Wright taught him to fly. In 1912, he won the first Mackay Trophy for making the most meritorious military flight of the year. *Promoted* to temporary colonel, Arnold spent most of World War I as the highest-ranking flying officer in Washington, District of Columbia. He would apply the lessons he learned during the Great War to the development of the United States Army Air Forces. Arnold began his rise to command of the Army Air Corps during the interwar years, serving in Air Service headquarters in Washington, District of Columbia, and in several of the most important operational flying commands in the field. Promotion to lieutenant colonel came in 1931 and with it command of March Field, California. In 1934, he took command of the western zone of the United States.

1.21.4.1. In 1934, Arnold again won the Mackay Trophy, leading a flight of 10 B-10 bombers from Washington, District of Columbia, to Fairbanks, Alaska. On 29 September 1938, he was named Chief of the Air Corps. On 30 June 1941, he became Commanding General of the United States Army Air Forces.

1.21.4.2. General Arnold commanded America's aerial war effort in World War II. Under his direction, the United States Army Air Forces expanded from 22,000 members and 3,900 aircraft to nearly 2.5 million members and 75,000 aircraft. Throughout the war he remained committed to strategic bombardment, laying the foundation for a post-war independent air force. He directly commanded the 20th Air Force B-29s during their 1944 and 1945 assault on Japan. Supervising the air war on a global scale proved a strenuous task. Arnold had a severe heart attack that led to his 30 June 1946 retirement.

1.21.4.3. On 7 May 1949, Congress appointed Arnold the first and only five-star General of the Air Force. (He was a five-star General of the Army in 1944.) General Arnold died at his home in Sonoma, California, 15 January 1950.

1.21.5. **General Carl A. "Tooey" Spaatz**. General Spaatz, first Chief of Staff of the United States Air Force, was born 28 June 1891, in Boyertown, Pennsylvania. He graduated from West Point in 1914, entered the Aviation Section of the Signal Corps in October 1915, and earned his wings in 1916. During World War I, Spaatz served in France. He flew in combat for only three weeks but still shot down three German planes. General Spaatz was one of the pioneering aviators of the interwar years. For nearly a week, 1-7 January 1929, Spaatz and several other officers kept the Question Mark, a Fokker trimotor, aloft over California. During the 151-hour flight, the Question Mark refueled in the air 37 times, nine of those after dark. In June 1933, he was assigned to Washington, District of Columbia, as Chief of the Air Corps Training and Operations Division. While attending the Command and General Staff School at Fort Leavenworth, Kansas, in September 1935, he was promoted to lieutenant colonel. In 1936, Spaatz was assigned as the executive officer, 2d Bomb Wing, Langley Field, Virginia. He returned to Washington in 1939 to serve as Assistant Executive Officer to the Chief  of the Air Corps. In November 1939, he was promoted to colonel and transferred to England to serve as a military observer. In October 1940, Spaatz returned to Washington to accept a promotion to brigadier general and an assignment as Assistant to the Chief of the Air Corps.

1.21.5.1. After the war began, Spaatz advanced rapidly through a succession of jobs. He commanded Eighth Air Force before accepting command of the Northwest African Air Forces. On 6 January 1944, he assumed command of United States Strategic Air Forces in Europe, tasked with softening up Hitler's Fortress Europe, before the Allied invasion. General Spaatz pinned on his fourth star in March 1945, prior to assuming command of United States Strategic Air Forces in the Pacific Theater. He oversaw the final strategic bombing campaign against Japan, including the 1945 use of atomic weapons against Hiroshima and Nagasaki.

1.21.5.2. In February 1946, Spaatz was promoted to Commanding General of the Army Air Forces and in September 1947, President Harry S. Truman appointed him Chief of Staff of the United States Air Force. He retired 30 June 1948, after which he served as the Civil Air Patrol Chairman and Air Force Association Chairman of the Board from 1940 to 1951. A leading advocate of an Air Force Academy, General Spaatz died in Washington, District of Columbia, 14 July 1974.

1.21.6. **Lieutenant General Frank M. Andrews**. General Andrews was one of the founding fathers of the modern Air Force and commander of the first combat Air Force. Killed in an aircraft accident near Iceland, 3 May 1943, General Andrews was one of the most promising Army Air Forces generals. Born in Nashville, Tennessee, 3 February 1884, he graduated from West Point in 1906 and entered the cavalry. He served at several posts, from the Philippines to Vermont, before joining the Aviation Division in August 1917, serving in the Office of the Chief Signal Officer. In 1918, he was assigned to the Army General Staff Plans Division. He was assigned to Germany in August 1920, where he served for three years in public relations and civil affairs. Andrews returned to Kelly Field, Texas, in 1923, to serve as executive officer and, eventually, Commandant of Flying. After attending the Air Corps Tactical School, he was assigned to 2d Wing Headquarters, Langley Field, Virginia, as a staff officer. Andrews completed the Army War College in May 1933, and subsequently, became Commander, 1st Pursuit Group at Selfridge Field, Michigan. In October 1934, he returned to Washington for a second tour on the General Staff.

1.21.6.1. In March 1935, General Andrews assumed command of the newly created General Headquarters Air Force. In August 1939, he was named the Army Assistant Chief of Staff for Operations and Training. In 1940, Andrews pinned on his second star and in September 1941 was named Commanding General, Caribbean Defense Command.

1.21.6.2. Andrews was promoted to lieutenant general after America entered World War II, when he assumed command of United States Forces in the Middle East. In February 1943, he accepted command of United States Forces in the European Theater. His premature death ended a career that showed great promise. In June 1949, Andrews Air Force Base in Maryland was named in his honor.

1.21.7. **General Ira C. Eaker**. General Eaker, aviation pioneer and articulate advocate of aerospace power, was born in Field Creek, Texas, 13 April 1896. In 1917, he graduated from Southeastern State Teachers College. After accepting a commission in the Army Reserve, he attended flight school. His first assignment was to the Philippines, where he did graduate work at the University of the Philippines before returning to Mitchel Field, New York, in 1922. While serving in New York, he studied law at Columbia University.

1.21.7.1. General Eaker was a daring and innovative aviator. He participated in the Pan-American goodwill tour of 1926 and 1927, and flew in the first extended aerial refueling experiment in 1929, during which the crew kept a plane aloft for 151 hours.

1.21.7.2. In the 1930s, as war loomed over Europe, Eaker returned to Washington, District of Columbia, to serve in the office of the Chief of the Air Corps. In 1940, as a lieutenant colonel, he accepted command of the 20th Pursuit Group at Hamilton Field, California. In January 1942, shortly after the United States entered World War II, Eaker took command of the VIII Bomber Command and was promoted to brigadier general. A strong advocate of daylight strategic bombardment, he convinced Prime Minister Winston Churchill that it had merit. Eaker directed the daylight campaigns that pounded the German military and industrial base of Nazi-occupied Europe and Germany.

1.21.7.3. In September 1943, after promotion to lieutenant general, he served as commander of the Mediterranean Allied Air Forces. After the war and until his August 1947 retirement, General Eaker was Deputy Commander, United States Army Air Forces and Chief of the Air Staff.

1.21.7.4. In 1947, General Eaker accepted a position as vice president of Hughes Tool Company. He served as a vice president of Douglas Aircraft from 1957-1961. In retirement, General Eaker was an active writer, with regularly published articles and columns in numerous newspapers and military journals. President Reagan promoted him to four-star general, 10 April 1985. He died 6 August 1987.

1.21.8. **Major General Oliver P. Echols**. General Echols, a pioneer logistician who coordinated the rapid expansion of America's air arsenal during World War II, was born in Charlottesville, Virginia, on 4 March 1892. Logistics play a vital role in warfare, and his contribution was notable.

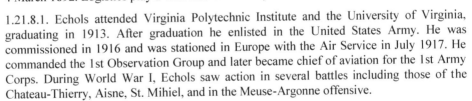

1.21.8.1. Echols attended Virginia Polytechnic Institute and the University of Virginia, graduating in 1913. After graduation he enlisted in the United States Army. He was commissioned in 1916 and was stationed in Europe with the Air Service in July 1917. He commanded the 1st Observation Group and later became chief of aviation for the 1st Army Corps. During World War I, Echols saw action in several battles including those of the Chateau-Thierry, Aisne, St. Mihiel, and in the Meuse-Argonne offensive.

1.21.8.2. After the war, following several flying assignments, Echols served in the Air Corps Experimental Engineering Section from 1927 to 1930. The following year he became chief of the Air Corps Procurement Section. After graduating from the Air Corps Tactical School in 1932, Echols returned to the procurement field as Chief Engineer, Air Corps Materiel Division. In 1938, he was promoted to assistant chief, and earned his first star and the promotion to division chief in October 1940. During World War II, General Echols coordinated the most massive aircraft procurement program in history, as Chief, Army Air Forces Materiel Division. In 1947, he retired, accepting an offer to run the Aircraft Industries Association. He died 15 May 1954.

1.21.9. **Captain Lillian K. Keil**. A pioneer in passenger care, Captain Keil successfully combined two careers (airline flight attendant and Air Force flight nurse) to become the most decorated woman in United States military history. Keil was one of the first stewardesses hired by United Airlines when the United States entered World War II. She was later accepted into the Army Air Forces and by the summer of 1943, she was in England pulling wounded and frostbitten crewmen out of B-17s returning from bombing raids over Europe. D-Day, 6 June 1944, found her aboard a C-47, heading for Normandy to collect the wounded. During the war, Keil made 250 evacuation flights, 23 of which were transatlantic.

1.21.9.1. After World War II, Keil returned to United Airlines as an assistant chief stewardess. In 1950, she returned to duty as an Air Force flight nurse and flew to Korea. During the next 16 months, she flew 175 air evacuations, logging 1,400 hours of flight time while assigned to the 801st Medical Air Evacuation Transportation Squadron.

1.21.9.2. The Army Air Forces captain attended to more than 10,000 wounded soldiers, sailors, and marines in the air. She was awarded 19 medals, including a European Theater medal with 4 battle stars, a Korean service medal with 7 battle stars, 4 air medals, and a Presidential Citation from the Republic of Korea.

1.21.9.3. Honored several times by her hometown of Covina Hills, California, she was active in the Covina Hills Veterans of Foreign Wars chapter until her death 30 June 2005.

1.21.10. **General George C. Kenny**. The United States Army Air Forces produced many great operational air commanders in World War II. Leaders like Spaatz, Eaker, LeMay, and Doolittle richly deserve acclaim, but some historians rank General Kenney first among equals for his ability to overcome severe organizational, logistical, personnel, technical, and strategic difficulties.

1.21.10.1. Kenney distinguished himself in World War I, flying 75 missions, downing two German planes, and receiving the Distinguished Service Cross and Silver Star.

1.21.10.2. His Army Air Corps experiences enabled him to command air forces with such success during World War II. He was the quintessential Air Corps officer in the sense that his experience encompassed a broad range of functions, from maintenance, supply, and production to strategy, tactics, and operations. He gained a reputation as a technical and tactical innovator.

1.21.10.3. During World War II, as commander of the Southwest Pacific Area Allied Air Forces and the Fifth Air Force, Kenney was General MacArthur's Airman. He created clear lines of authority, instituted new supply and maintenance programs, commanded with authority, and earned the respect and admiration of his men. Perhaps the most daring and innovative commander of the war, Kenney gained MacArthur's confidence because he knew how to run combat air forces and produced results quickly.

1.21.10.4. Toward the end of the war in the Pacific, General Arnold cabled Kenney: "It may truthfully be said that no air commander ever did so much with so little." MacArthur wrote: "Of all the commanders of our major Air Forces engaged in World War II, none surpassed General Kenney in those three great essentials of successful combat leadership - aggressive vision, mastery over air strategy and tactics, and the ability to exact the maximum in fighting quality from both men and equipment." General Kenney died 9 August 1977.

1.21.11. **General James "Jimmy" Doolittle**. In a career defined by variety, General Doolittle was a renaissance man: an air leader, aeronautical engineer, airplane racer, businessman, commanding general, oil company executive, special assistant to the Chief of Staff of the United States Air Force, and holder of the Medal of Honor. Doolittle was born 14 December 1896, in Alameda, California. After a year at the California School of Mines, he joined the Signal Corps Reserve in 1917 and earned his wings in 1918. Over the next 4 years he accepted a variety of assignments in the Signal Corps aviation section, demonstrating exceptional ability as a pilot and as a daredevil. He also continued his education, earning a bachelor's degree from the University of California in 1922, a master's degree from the Massachusetts Institute of Technology in 1924, and a Ph.D. from Massachusetts Institute of Technology in 1925.

1.21.11.1. His aviation accomplishments are legendary. In September 1922, he flew a DH-4 coast-to-coast in 22 hours, 35 minutes, with only one refueling stop. In 1925, he won the Schneider Trophy Races, setting a seaplane speed record of 245.713 mph. He helped develop fog-flying equipment in 1928, which led to widespread use of the artificial horizontal and directional gyroscopes. He made the first "blind" flight, completely dependent on instruments, for which he won the Harmon Trophy.

1.21.11.2. He served as Army advisor on the building of Floyd Bennett Field, New York City's first municipal airport.

1.21.11.3. Doolittle resigned his regular commission in 1930 to manage Shell Oil's aviation department. As part of his duties with Shell, he helped develop high-octane gasoline and sold the Air Corps on the development of high-compression engines using that fuel.

1.21.11.4. General Arnold brought Doolittle back to active duty in 1940 to troubleshoot engine and aircraft development, but Doolittle is best remembered for leading the 18 April 1942 B-25 raid on Tokyo, launched from the deck of the aircraft carrier Hornet. Though all 16 aircraft were lost, the raid restored American morale and damaged Japanese confidence. It also earned Doolittle the Medal of Honor and promotion to brigadier general.

1.21.11.5. Promoted to major general in November 1942, he commanded Twelfth Air Force in North Africa and in January 1944 took command of Eighth Air Force in England. He was promoted to lieutenant general 13 March 1944.

1.21.11.6. After World War II, Doolittle returned to civilian life as vice president of Shell Oil. He was promoted to four-star General on the Air Force retired list in June 1985 and died 27 September 1993.

1.21.12. **Major General Claire L. Chennault**. Nicknamed "Old Leatherface," General Chennault, famed leader of the Flying Tigers, was born 6 September 1890 in Commerce, Texas. He grew up in Louisiana and attended Louisiana State University before joining the United States Army.

1.21.12.1. Chennault was commissioned a first lieutenant in November 1917 and earned his wings at Kelly Field, Texas, in 1919. During the 1920s, Chennault earned a reputation as a talented "stick and rudder man" and an absolute master of pursuit (fighter) tactics. As a captain, Chennault graduated from the Air Corps Tactical School in 1931, then remained at the school as an instructor, eventually becoming head of the Pursuit Section. During the 1930s, such Air Corps Tactical School instructors as Harold George, Robert Olds, and Kenneth Walker developed doctrine advocating high altitude, daylight, precision bombing of key enemy industrial and military targets using heavy bombers. In contrast, Chennault stressed the importance of pursuit aviation, and advocated a system of air defense based upon early warning of an enemy attack. Technology in the 1930s was not in Chennault's favor. Bombers like the B-10 and B-17 became larger and faster, and pursuers fell increasingly behind.

1.21.12.2. Forced to retired in 1937 for health reasons, Chennault went to China shortly after to train pilots for the Chinese Air Force.

1.21.12.3. In 1941, Chennault recruited American military pilots and organized the American Volunteer Group under a carefully hidden Roosevelt Administration program to provide an air force for Chinese leader Chiang Kai-shek. Chennault trained three squadrons of "Flying Tigers" in tactics he had developed that took advantage of the strengths of his Curtiss P-40s and exploited enemy weaknesses.

1.21.12.4. Though the American Volunteer Group did not enter combat until after Pearl Harbor, the unit gained fame for its victorious exploits during the first six months of World War II. In April 1942, the United States Army Air Forces recalled Chennault to active duty, in the grade of major general, to command Fourteenth Air Force in China. In that capacity, he fought two wars: one against the Japanese and another against supply and equipment problems in isolated China.

1.21.12.5. In October 1945, General Chennault retired again and in 1946 became president of the China-based Civil Air Transport Company, assisting Chiang Kai-shek's losing fight against Chinese Communist forces. On 18 July 1958, the Air Force promoted Chennault to the honorary rank of lieutenant general. He died nine days later, 27 July 1958.

1.21.13. **General Curtis E. LeMay**. General LeMay, who made Strategic Air Command the world's premier force, was born 15 November 1906. He attended the Ohio State University and was commissioned through the Reserve Officer Training Corp program in 1928. His military career began in September 1928 with flight training at March Field, California.

1.21.13.1. General LeMay flew pursuit planes until 1937, when he transferred to the 2d Bomb Group, Langley Field, Virginia. There, he earned a reputation as an outstanding pilot and exceptional navigator. Accordingly, in late 1937 and early 1938, he served as lead navigator for two mass flights of B-17s to South America.

1.21.13.2. LeMay was promoted to captain in January 1940, major in March 1941, and lieutenant colonel in January 1942. He pinned on eagles three months later, when he took command of the 305th Bombardment Group at Muroc, California. Later that year, his group joined the Eighth Air Force in England. LeMay's no-nonsense approach to combat earned him his first and second stars in September 1943 and March 1944. In August 1944, he assumed command of the XX Bomber Command in the Pacific. His B-29s were charged with destroying Japan's war-making potential. After the war, LeMay served at the Pentagon before his promotion and assignment as Commander, United States Forces in Europe, in October 1947. His success at directing the Berlin Airlift in 1948 made him the obvious choice for Strategic Air Command commander-in-chief, in October 1948.

1.21.13.3. LeMay made Strategic Air Command the world's most powerful nuclear force. In the days before the deployment of guided missiles, LeMay developed Strategic Air Command's policy of constant alert, keeping some bombers aloft at all times, ready to respond to a Soviet attack.

1.21.13.4. In 1957, General LeMay became Air Force Vice Chief of Staff, and in June 1961 rose to Chief of Staff of the United States Air Force. He held that post until his retirement in February 1965. In 1968 he became the vice presidential candidate on the American Independent Party ticket, headed by Alabama Governor George C. Wallace. Defeated in November, LeMay returned to private life as chairman of the board of an electronics firm. He died 1 October 1990.

1.21.14. **Lieutenant General William H. Tunner**. Known as the Air Force's outstanding practitioner of air logistics and

air mobility, General Tunner was born in Elizabeth, New Jersey, in 1906. After graduating from the United States Military Academy in 1928, he entered the Air Corps and during the 1930s earned a reputation as an excellent pilot and hardworking intelligence officer. During World War II, Tunner helped create the United States Army Air Forces Ferrying Command. By the time it became Air Transport Command, it was delivering 10,000 aircraft monthly from stateside factories to worldwide theaters of operation.

1.21.14.1. In 1944, Tunner assumed command of the "Hump" airlift operation, supplying China from India over some of the world's highest mountain ranges. The often appalling terrain and weather, equipment, facilities, and aircraft shortages made the "Hump" a difficult operation. Tunner refined and standardized every element of the operation, implementing assembly-line maintenance, systemizing cargo-handling procedures, emphasizing flight safety, and imbuing the operation with a driving commitment to increase tonnage. In July 1945 alone, Air Transport Command delivered 71,042 tons of cargo. In June 1948, Air Transport Command and the Naval Air Transport Service merged, becoming the Military Air Transport Service, and Tunner assumed command of its Atlantic Division

1.21.14.2. On 24 June 1948, the Soviet Union blockaded the surface routes between Berlin and the Western occupation zones in Germany. Allied leaders ordered an airlift to supply Berlin, 26 June. On 28 July, Tunner assumed command of the airlift, Operation VITTLES. Tunner developed an intricate bridge of aircraft that flowed in a steady stream through narrow corridors in and out of Berlin. Before the Soviet Union lifted the blockade 12 May 1949, Operation VITTLES delivered 2.3 million tons of cargo to Berlin. Under Tunner, the Berlin Airlift emerged as an epic enterprise, demonstrating the peaceful use of airpower as a political instrument.

1.21.14.3. When the Korean War broke out in June 1950, General Tunner took command of Combat Cargo Command (Provisional). Tunner illustrated how a fleet of cargo aircraft was sufficiently flexible to handle airborne assault while airdropping supplies, and moving cargo and personnel through a combat theater. In the mid-1950s, Tunner commanded United States Air Forces in Europe.

1.21.14.4. His 1958 assumption of command of Military Air Transport Service provided the platform from which he advocated large, jet-powered transports to support the global mission. General Tunner retired in May 1960 and died 6 April 1983.

1.21.15. **General Charles P. Cabell**. General Cabell was a pioneer in the field of air intelligence. He was born in Dallas, Texas, in 1903, graduated from the United States Military Academy, 12 June 1925, and accepted a commission in the Field Artillery. Five years later he transferred to the Air Corps Primary Flying School at Brooks Field, Texas, graduating in February 1931. He then completed the observation course at Kelly Field, Texas, where he remained as a flying instructor.

1.21.15.1. A lieutenant at the time, Cabell joined the 7th Observation Squadron at France Field, Panama Canal Zone, as adjutant in October 1931. He subsequently served as commanding officer of the 44th Observation Squadron, the 24th Pursuit Squadron, and the 74th Pursuit Squadron, successively, at Albrook Field, Panama.

1.21.15.2. In September 1938, he entered the Air Corps Tactical School at Maxwell Field, Alabama, graduating in June 1939. The following June, Cabell, a major, was assigned to the Photographic Laboratory at Wright Field, Ohio. After a period as an observer with the Royal Air Force, he transferred to Washington, District of Columbia, in April 1941, to command the Office of the Chief of the Air Corps Photo Unit.

1.21.15.3. In February 1942, Cabell, a lieutenant colonel, was named assistant executive for technical planning and coordination. The following month, he became chief of the advisory council to the commanding general of the Army Air Forces.

1.21.15.4. From June to October 1943, Cabell attended the first Army and Navy Staff College course. He was assigned to the Eighth Air Force in the European Theater in October and in December, assumed command of the 45th Combat Bombardment Wing. In April 1944, he became director of plans for the United States Strategic Air Force in Europe and three months later was named director of operations and intelligence for the Mediterranean Allied Air Forces, headquartered at Caserta, Italy.

1.21.15.5. General Cabell later served as chief of the Strategy and Policy Division, Office of the Assistant Chief of Air Staff for Plans. In December 1945, he was assigned to the Military Staff Committee of the United Nations, followed by a promotion to Chief, Air Intelligence Requirements Division, Office of the Director of Intelligence in November 1947. On 15 May 1948, he was appointed Director of Intelligence. On 1 November 1951 he was named director of the Joint Staff. He and was appointed deputy director of the Central Intelligence Agency on 23 April 1953. Gen Cabell retired 31 January 1962; he died 25 May 1971.

1.21.16. **General Bernard A. Schriever**. Born in Germany, 14 September 1910, General Schriever is recognized as the architect of Air Force ballistic missile and military space programs. He came to America in 1917 and was naturalized in 1923. Raised in San Antonio, Texas, he graduated from Texas A&M in 1931 with a bachelor of science degree in engineering. He was commissioned in the Field Artillery but in July 1932 began flight training at Randolph Field, earning his Air Corps wings and commission at Kelly Field in June 1933. He was a bomber pilot at March and Hamilton Fields, California.

1.21.16.1. He participated in the ill-fated Army airmail program during the winter of 1934. He served at Albrook Field, but in September 1937, he resigned from the Air Corps to become a commercial pilot. Schriever returned to active duty in October 1938, serving with the 7th Bomb Group at Hamilton, and a year later became a test pilot at Wright Field. While there, he also attended the Air Corps Engineering School, graduating in July 1941. He then earned his master of science degree in aeronautical engineering at Stanford University.

1.21.16.2. Schriever distinguished himself during World War II, flying combat missions in the Pacific theater. He took part in the Bismarck Archipelago, Leyte, Luzon, Papua, North Solomon, South Philippine, and Ryukyu campaigns. After the war, Schriever, a colonel, transferred to Headquarters Army Air Forces to serve as chief scientific liaison in the Materiel directorate. In June 1950, he graduated from the National War College and returned to the Pentagon. In June 1953 he was promoted to brigadier general. Schriever began his long association with Air Research and Development Command, later Systems Command, in June 1954 as assistant to the commander. He was later appointed to head the Western Development Division to organize and form what would become the ballistic missile and space divisions that produced the Atlas, Titan, Thor, and Minuteman. He also produced the launchers and space systems that supported the National Aeronautics and Space Administration and other government agencies.

1.21.16.3. In April 1959, Schriever was named to head Air Research and Development Command. Two years later, he was promoted to four-star general, and named to head the new Air Force Systems Command.

1.21.16.4. He brought his systems approach to Air Force Systems Command and applied it to major aeronautics and space programs. Schriever established 437L, an antisatellite system, as part of his efforts to extend the Air Force mission to include space and personally headed the Manned Orbiting Laboratory Project. He retired in August 1966 and died 20 June 2005.

**1.21.17. Colonel Jacqueline "Jackie" Cochran.** Colonel Cochran was born in 1910 in Pensacola, Florida. She was the first female pilot to break the sound barrier, doing so 18 May 1953.

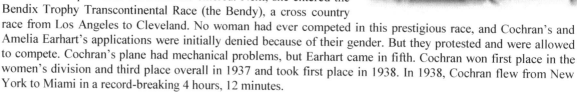

1.21.17.1. After flying lessons at Roosevelt Field, Long Island, in 1932, she obtained her license in 2 ½ weeks, bought a plane, and began taking additional flying lessons from Ted Marshall, a Navy pilot.

1.21.17.2. In 1934, after obtaining a commercial pilot's license, she entered the MacRobertson Trophy Air Race from London to Melbourne, Australia. Although she didn't win the 12,000-mile race, she won the first leg.

1.21.17.3. In 1935, she founded a cosmetic company and used the business to help finance the races she entered. Next, she entered the Bendix Trophy Transcontinental Race (the Bendy), a cross country race from Los Angeles to Cleveland. No woman had ever competed in this prestigious race, and Cochran's and Amelia Earhart's applications were initially denied because of their gender. But they protested and were allowed to compete. Cochran's plane had mechanical problems, but Earhart came in fifth. Cochran won first place in the women's division and third place overall in 1937 and took first place in 1938. In 1938, Cochran flew from New York to Miami in a record-breaking 4 hours, 12 minutes.

1.21.17.4. In 1939, she set a new altitude and international speed record and became the first woman to make a blind landing. In 1940, she broke the 2,000-kilometer international speed record. She received the Clifford Burke Harmon Trophy as the outstanding woman flier in the world in 1938, 1939, and 1940.

1.21.17.5. During World War II, she organized 25 women to fly for Great Britain and became the first woman to fly a bomber across the Atlantic. She received the Distinguished Service Medal for her services during the War.

1.21.17.6. In 1943, she was appointed to the staff of the United States Army Air Forces and director of the Women's Air Force Service Pilots. She also set nine international speed, distance, and altitude jet records.

1.21.17.7. In 1971, she was inducted into the National Aviation Hall of Fame, "for outstanding contributions to aviation by her devotion to the advancement of the role of women in all of its aspects, and by establishing new performance records that advanced aeronautics." In 1975, she was the first woman to be honored with a permanent display of her memorabilia at the United States Air Force Academy. Colonel Cochran died 7 August 1980.

**1.21.18. General Benjamin O. Davis, Jr.** General Davis was the commander of the famed World War II Tuskegee Airmen. At the time of his retirement in 1970, General Davis was the senior African American officer in the armed forces. He was born in Washington, District of Columbia, 18 December 1912, the son of Benjamin O. Davis, Sr., the first black general in the United States Army.

1.21.18.1. After attending Case Western Reserve University and the University of Chicago, General Davis graduated from West Point in 1936. Commissioned an infantry officer, Davis was a Reserve Officer Training Corp instructor at Tuskegee Institute from 1938 to 1941, when he became one of the first African Americans admitted to pilot training.

1.21.18.2. Davis advanced rapidly in rank, making first lieutenant in June 1939, captain in September 1940, and major and lieutenant colonel in the same month, May 1942. In early 1942, soon after the United States entered the war, Davis organized the 19th Fighter Squadron, an all-black unit that saw action over North Africa, Sicily, and Italy. The following year, he organized the 332d Fighter Group, which flew in Italy, Germany, and the Balkans. In May 1944, Davis was promoted to colonel.

1.21.18.3. After World War II, he commanded Dogman Field, Kentucky, from 1945 to 1946, and the 332d Fighter Wing at Lockbourne Field, Ohio. After graduating from the Air War College in 1950, he was named Chief, Fighter Development Branch, Headquarters United States Air Force.

1.21.18.4. Davis transferred to the Far East in 1953 to command the 51st Fighter Interceptor Wing in Korea. He pinned on his first star in October 1954, after which he was named Director of Operations, Headquarters, Far East Air Forces, Tokyo.

1.21.18.5. The general transferred to Ramstein, Germany, in 1957 serving as Chief of Staff, Twelfth Air Force. In June 1959, he became the first African American officer in any service to hold the rank of Major General. From 1959 to 1961, he was Deputy Chief for Operations, United States Air Forces Europe. In 1961, Davis became Director of Manpower and Organization at Headquarters United States Air Force, where he served until 1965. Following promotion to lieutenant general, he was named Chief of Staff for United States Forces and the United Nations Command in Korea. From 1968 until his retirement in 1970, General Davis was Deputy Commander, United States Strike Command, at MacDill Air Force Base, Florida.

1.21.18.6. General Davis remained active after retirement. In 1970, he organized a special force of sky marshals to help combat aircraft hijacking. In July 1971, he was appointed Assistant Secretary of Transportation, a position he held until he retired in 1975. In an 8 December 1998 White House ceremony, President Clinton promoted him to the rank of four-star general. General Davis died 4 July 2002.

1.21.19. **General Daniel "Chappie" James, Jr**. General James distinguished himself as a leader in three wars: World War II, Korea, and Vietnam. General James was born in Pensacola, Florida, in 1920. After graduating from high school in 1937, James continued his studies at Tuskegee Institute, Alabama. With war looming, James enrolled in the Civilian Pilot Training Program, which opened for the first time to African Americans.

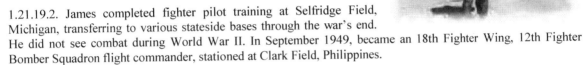

1.21.19.1. From the beginning of World War II until 1943, James served as a civilian flight instructor at Tuskegee Army Airfield. In July 1943, following completion of flight training, he accepted a commission as a second lieutenant, and joined the ranks of the famed Tuskegee Airmen.

1.21.19.2. James completed fighter pilot training at Selfridge Field, Michigan, transferring to various stateside bases through the war's end. He did not see combat during World War II. In September 1949, became an 18th Fighter Wing, 12th Fighter Bomber Squadron flight commander, stationed at Clark Field, Philippines.

1.21.19.3. In the skies over Korea, James faced his first combat experience while piloting F-51 and F-80 aircraft. He flew more than 100 combat missions during the war. In mid-1951, James was reassigned stateside as the flight operations officer, 58th Fighter Interceptor Squadron, Otis Air Force Base, Massachusetts, flying fighter jets.

1.21.19.4. In April 1953, he assumed command of the 60th Fighter- Interceptor Squadron in Massachusetts.

1.21.19.5. James' career continued to rise when he was assigned to Air Force headquarters as a staff officer, Air Defense Division, Office of the Deputy Chief of Staff for Operations. In July 1960, James transferred to Great Britain, where he held numerous leadership positions in the 81st Tactical Fighter Wing, including commander of the 92d Tactical Fighter Squadron, Royal Air Force, Bentwaters, England. He later became the deputy commander for operations of the 81st Tactical Fighter Wing.

1.21.19.6. James saw combat during the Vietnam War, as well. In June 1967, he became the vice commander, 8th Tactical Fighter Wing, flying 80 combat missions over North Vietnam. In the summer of 1969, James accepted command of the 7272d Fighter Training Wing, Wheelus Air Base, Libya.

1.21.19.7. In September 1974, he served as the vice commander, Military Airlift Command, and in 1975, was promoted to four-star general, assuming command of the North American Air Defense Command and United States Air Defense Command in September. James served as special assistant to the Chief of Staff of the United States Air Force in December 1977.

1.21.19.8. After a long and distinguished career, he retired 1 February 1978 and died 25 February 1978.

1.21.20. **Airman First Class John Lee Levitow.**

1.21.20.1. Airman Levitow, an AC-47 gunship loadmaster, is the lowest ranking Airman ever to receive the Medal of Honor for exceptional heroism during wartime. Born in Hartford, Connecticut, Levitow attended Glastonbury High School. He was trained in the civil engineering career field and later retrained into the loadmaster field. After flying on C-130s out of McGuire Air Force Base, New Jersey, he was deployed to Vietnam.

1.21.20.2. On 24 February 1969, Airman Levitow was handling Mark 24 magnesium flares aboard "Spooky 71" when his pilot threw the AC-47 and its eight-man crew into a turn to engage Viet Cong whose muzzle flashes were visible outside the United States Army Depot at Long Binh. The aircraft, an armed version of the C-47 Skytrain transport, had been flying a night mission in the Tan Son Nhut air base area when Long Binh came under attack.

1.21.20.3. Suddenly, Spooky 71 was jarred by a tremendous explosion and bathed in a blinding flash of light. A North Vietnamese Army 82-millimeter mortar shell had landed on top of the right wing and exploded inside the wing frame. The blast raked the fuselage with flying shrapnel. Everyone in the back of Spooky 71 was wounded. Despite his wounds, Levitow rescued a fellow crewmember who was perilously close to the open cargo door. As he dragged his buddy toward the center of the cabin, Levitow saw a loose, burning 27-pound magnesium flare rolling amid ammunition cans that contained 19,000 live rounds.

1.21.20.4. Through a haze of pain and shock, Levitow, with 40 shrapnel wounds in his legs, side, and back, fighting a 30–degree bank, crawled to the flare, but was unable to grasp it to pick it up. He threw himself on the burning flare, hugging it to his body, and dragged himself to the rear of the aircraft, leaving a trail of blood behind. He hurled it through the open cargo door, and at that instant, the flare separated and ignited in the air, fortunately clear of the aircraft. When the aircraft returned to the base, the extent of the danger was apparent: The AC-47 had more than 3,500 holes in the wings and fuselage, one measuring more than three feet long. Levitow spent 2 1/2 months in a hospital and upon his recovery, returned to Vietnam for another tour. He returned to the United States to receive the Medal of Honor from President Nixon during a 14 May 1970 Armed Forces Day ceremony at the White House.

1.21.20.5. Levitow was promoted to sergeant before his honorable discharge four years later. On 22 January 1998, Air Mobility Command struck a resounding chord with the Air Force enlisted corps when it named a C-17 Globemaster II "The Spirit of John Levitow."

1.21.20.6. Levitow designed veterans' programs for the state of Connecticut until his 8 November 2000 death after a lengthy battle with cancer. He was buried with military honors 17 November 2000 at Arlington National Cemetery.

1.21.20.7. In his memory, the Levitow Honor Graduate Award is presented to the top Air Force Airman Leadership School graduate from each class. The Headquarters Building, 737th Training Group, Lackland Air Force Base, Texas, was also dedicated in his honor.

1.21.21. **Staff Sergeant William H. Pitsenbarger**. On 11 April 1966, a 21-year-old known as "Pits" to his friends was killed while defending wounded comrades. For his bravery and sacrifice, Pararescueman Pitsenbarger was posthumously awarded the nation's highest military decorations: the Medal of Honor and the Air Force Cross. He was the first enlisted Airman to receive both medals posthumously.

1.21.21.1. Pitsenbarger was born in 1945 and grew up in Piqua, Ohio, a small town near Dayton. He joined the Air Force on New Year's Eve 1962 and after pararescue training in 1965, reported to Detachment 6, 38th Air Rescue and Recovery Squadron, Bien Hoa Air Base, near Saigon, Republic of South Vietnam. His unit, composed of five aircrews, flew three HH-43F Kaman "Huskie" helicopters. His commander, Major Maurice Kessler, referred to Pitsenbarger as "one of a special breed; alert and always ready to go on any mission." Pitsenbarger flew almost 300 rescue missions in Vietnam, routinely risking his life to rescue downed soldiers and Airmen.

1.21.21.2. On 11 April 1966, Airman Pitsenbarger was aboard a rescue helicopter responding to a call to evacuate casualties from an ongoing firefight approximately 35 miles east of Saigon. When he arrived at the site, he descended from the helicopter to organize and coordinate rescue efforts, care for the wounded, prepare casualties for evacuation, and insure the recovery operation was smooth and orderly. Several times he refused to evacuate.

1.21.21.3. Rescue helicopters transported wounded to an aid station, returning to evacuate more injured. One helicopter was hit by enemy fire as it lowered a litter basket to Pitsenbarger. When its engine began to lose power, the pilot realized he had to get it away from the area. Pitsenbarger chose to remain with the Army troops on the ground, waving off the helicopter. Because of the heavy mortar and small-arms fire, the helicopters couldn't return to the site.

1.21.21.4. As the battle raged, Pitsenbarger repeatedly exposed himself to enemy fire in order to pull wounded to safety and care for them, returning fire when possible. During the fight, he was wounded three times. When others ran low on ammunition, he gathered ammo clips from the dead and distributed them to the living. Having administered aid, he picked up a rifle, joining the soldiers to help hold off the Viet Cong. Pitsenbarger was killed by Viet Cong snipers later that night. When his body was recovered the next day, one hand still held a rifle and the other clutched a medical kit.

1.21.21.5. Although Pitsenbarger didn't escape alive, nine men did, thanks to his courage and devotion to duty. On 8 December 2000, Pitsenbarger's parents, William and Alice, accepted the Medal of Honor from Secretary of the Air Force Whit Peters. The audience included battle survivors, hundreds of pararescue airmen, a Congressional representative, and the Air Force Chief of Staff. Pitsenbarger was posthumously promoted to staff sergeant, and the Navy named an Air Force munitions preposition ship the "MV A1C William H. Pitsenbarger" in his honor.

1.21.22. **Colonel Eileen M. Collins**. Colonel Collins was the first woman to command a space shuttle mission. An Air

Force officer and National Aeronautics and Space Administration astronaut, Colonel Collins was born 19 November 1956, in Elmira, New York. She earned a bachelor of arts degree in mathematics and economics at Syracuse University in 1978; a master of science degree in operations research from Stanford University in 1986; and a master of arts degree in space systems management from Webster University in 1989. Collins graduated from Air Force Undergraduate Pilot Training at Vance Air Force Base, Oklahoma, in 1979, served as a T-38 instructor pilot at Vance, and in 1983 became a C-141 aircraft commander and instructor pilot at Travis Air Force Base, California. From 1986 to 1989, she was an assistant professor of mathematics and a T-41 instructor pilot at the United States Air Force Academy. By the time she retired from the Air Force in 2005, Colonel Collins logged more than 6,750 hours in 30 different types of aircraft.

1.21.22.1. In January 1990, National Aeronautics and Space Administration selected Colonel Collins for the astronaut program while she was attending the Air Force Test Pilot School at Edwards Air Force Base, California. She became an astronaut in July 1991, initially assigned to orbiter engineering support. She served on the astronaut support team responsible for orbiter prelaunch checkout, final launch configuration, crew ingress/egress, and landing/recovery, and also worked as a mission control spacecraft communicator. She also served as the astronaut office spacecraft systems branch chief, chief information officer, shuttle branch chief, and astronaut safety branch chief.

1.21.22.2. A veteran of four space flights, Collins logged over 872 hours in space. STS-63 was the first flight of the new joint Russian-American Space Program. Mission highlights included the rendezvous with the Russian Space Station Mir, an astronomy shuttle deployment and retrieval, and a space-walk. On this mission, Colonel Collins became the first female pilot of a space shuttle.

1.21.22.3. She flew on STS-84 aboard the Atlantis 15-24 May 1997. It was National Aeronautics and Space Administration's sixth Shuttle mission to rendezvous and dock with the Russian Space Station Mir. During the flight, the crew transferred nearly four tons of supplies and experimental equipment.

1.21.22.4. During STS-93, flown by the Columbia, 22-27 July 1999, she became the first woman to command a shuttle mission. This mission featured deployment of the Chandra X-Ray Observatory.

1.21.22.5. STS-114 Discovery, 26 July-9 August 2005, was the return to flight mission during which the shuttle docked with the International Space Station and the crew tested and evaluated new procedures for flight safety and shuttle inspection and repair techniques. After a two-week, 5.8 million-mile-journey in space, the orbiter and its seven-astronaut crew returned, landing at Edwards Air Force Base, California.

1.21.22.6. Colonel Collins retired from National Aeronautics and Space Administration in May 2006.

1.21.23. **Senior Airman Jason D. Cunningham**. Born 27 March 1975, Senior Airman Cunningham earned the Air Force Cross for extraordinary heroism in military operations, presented posthumously by the President of the United States, against an opposing armed force while serving as a pararescueman near the village of Marzak, Paktia Province, Afghanistan, 4 March 2002.

1.21.23.1. That day, Senior Airman Cunningham was the primary Air Force combat search and rescue medic assigned to a quick reaction force that had been tasked to rescue two American servicemen from austere terrain occupied by Al Qaeda and Taliban forces.

1.21.23.2. Shortly before landing, his MH-47E helicopter took rocket-propelled grenade and small arms fire, severely disabling the aircraft. The assault force formed a hasty defense and immediately suffered three fatalities and five critical casualties.

1.21.23.3. Facing enemy fire, risking his own life, Senior Airman Cunningham remained in the burning fuselage in order to treat the wounded. He moved his patients to a more secure location under mortar attack, disregarding the extreme danger, exposing himself to enemy fire on seven separate occasions.

1.21.23.4. When the second casualty collection point was also compromised, Senior Airman Cunningham braved intense small arms and rocket-propelled grenade attack to reposition the wounded to a third collection point. Mortally wounded and quickly fading, he continued to direct patient movement, transferring care to another medic. His selfless efforts resulted to the delivery of ten gravely wounded Americans to life-saving medical treatment.

1.21.24. **Chief Master Sergeant Richard L. Etchberger**. Born in 1933, Richard Loy "Dick" Etchberger grew up in Pennsylvania, joining the Air Force in 1951. After completing basic training, he attended a technical school at Keesler

Air Force Base, Mississippi, studying electronics, which would launch his career in radar bomb scoring. One of the Air Force's most highly trained radar technicians, he volunteered for a highly classified mission at Lima Site 85 in Laos. He was the crew chief of a radar team there when North Vietnamese forces overran his radar site 11 March 1968. Under heavy fire, he continued to defend his comrades, called in air strikes, and directed an air evacuation. When a rescue helicopter arrived, the chief put himself in the line of fire to load three other Airmen in rescue slings. He was fatally wounded by enemy ground fire as he was being rescued. His fierce defense prevented the enemy from closing on his position, which saved his comrades lives, although he lost his own. For extraordinary heroism and superb leadership, Chief Etchberger was posthumously awarded the Air Force Cross, but the award remained a secret for two decades. He was awarded the Medal of Honor on 21 September 2010, the first E-9 to receive this award.

*Section 1G—Medal of Honor*

**1.22. The Medal of Honor.**

The Medal of Honor is the highest award for heroism in military action that the Nation can bestow on a member of its Armed Forces.

1.22.1. The Air Force-designed Medal of Honor was created in April 14, 1965. This medal was first presented by President Lyndon B. Johnson on January 19, 1967, to Major Bernard F. Fisher for action in South Vietnam.

1.22.2. The Medal of Honor is award for conspicuous gallantry and intrepidity at the risk of life above and beyond the call of duty

1.22.3. Pictured below are members of the Air Force and its predecessor organizations who have earned four Medals of Honor in World War I, 38 in World War II, four in the Korean Conflict and 14 in the Vietnam War.

# MEDAL OF HONOR RECIPIENTS

2d Lt Erwin R. Bleckley
Wichita, KS
6 Oct 1918

1st Lt Harold E. Goetler
Chicago, IL
6 Oct 1918

2d Lt Frank Luke Jr..
Phoenix, AZ
29 Sep 1918

1st Lt Edward V.
Rickenbacker
Columbus, OH
25 Sep 1918

Lt Col Addison Earl Baker
Chicago, IL
1 Aug 1943

Maj Richard Ira Bong
Poplar, WI
10 Oct – 15 Nov 1944

Maj Horace S. Carswell
Jr.
Fort Worth, TX
26 Oct 1944

BG Frederick W.
Castle
Manila, Philippines
24 Dec 1944

Maj Ralph Cheli
San Francisco, CA
18 Aug 1943

Col Demas T. Craw
Traverse City, MI
8 Nov 1942

BG James H. Doolittle
Alameda, CA
18 Apr 1942

SSgt Henry E. Erwin
Adamsville, AL
12 Apr 1945

# MEDAL OF HONOR RECIPIENTS

2d Lt Robert E. Femoyer
Huntington, WV
2 Nov 1944

1st Lt Donald Joseph Gott
Arnett, OK
9 Nov 1944

Lt Col Pierpoint Hamilton
Tuxedo Park, NY
8 Nov 1942

Lt Col James H.
Howard
Canton, China
11 Jan 1944

2d Lt Lloyd Herbert
Hughes
Alexandria, LA
1 Aug 1943

Maj John Louis Jerstad
Racine, WI
1 Aug 1943

Col Leon William
Johnson
Columbia, MO
1 Aug 1943

Col John Riley Kane
McGregor, TX
1 Aug 1943

Col Neel E. Kearby
Wichita Falls, TX
11 Oct 1943

2d Lt David R. Kingsley
Portland, OP
23 Jun 1944

1st Lt Raymond L. Knight
Houston, TX
25 Apr 1945

1st Lt William R.
Lawley Jr.
Leeds, AL
20 Feb 1944

# MEDAL OF HONOR RECIPIENTS

Capt Darrell Robins
Lindsey
Jefferson, IA
9 Aug 1944

Sgt Archibald Mathies
Scotland
20 Feb 1944

1st Lt Jack W. Mathis
San Angelo, TX
18 Mar 1943

Maj Thomas B.
McGuire Jr.
Ridgewood, NJ
25-26 Dec 1944

Lt William E. Metzger Jr.
Lima, OH
9 Nov 1944

1st Lt Edward S. Michael
Chicago, IL
11 Apr 1944

2d Lt John Cary Morgan
Vernon, TX
28 Jul 1943

Capt Harl Pease Jr.
Plymouth, NH
7 Aug 1942

1st Lt Donald Dale Pucket
Longmont, CO
9 Jul 1944

2d Lt Joseph R. Sarnoski.
Simpson, PA
16 Jun 1943

Maj William A. Shomo
Jeannette, PA
11 Jan 1945

Sgt Maynard H. Smith
Caro, MI
1 May 1943

# MEDAL OF HONOR RECIPIENTS

2d Lt Walter E. Truemper
Aurora, IL
20 Feb 1944

Lt Col Leon R. Vance Jr.
Enid, OK
5 Jun 1944

TSgt Forrest L. Vosler
Lyndonville, NY
20 Dec 1943

BG Kenneth N. Walker
Cerritos, NM
5 Jan 1943

Maj Raymond H. Wilkins
Portsmouth, VA
2 Nov 1943

Maj Jay Zeamer
Carlisle, PA
16 Jun 1943

Maj George A. Davis Jr.
Dublin, TX
10 Feb 1952

Maj Charles J. Loring
Jr.
Portland, ME
22 Nov 1952

Maj Louis Joseph Sebille
Harbor Beach, MI
5 Aug 1950

Capt John S. Walmsley Jr.
Baltimore, MD
14 Sep 1951

Capt Steven L. Bennett
Palestine, TX
29 Jun 1972

Maj George E "BUD"
Day
Sioux City, IA
26 Aug 1967

# MEDAL OF HONOR RECIPIENTS

Maj Merlyn H. Dethlefsen
Greenville, IA
10 Mar 1967

CMSgt Richard Etchberger
Hamburg, PA
11 Mar 1968

Maj Bernard F. Fisher
San Bernardino, CA
10 Mar 1966

1st Lt James P. Fleming
Sedalia, MO
26 Nov 1968

Lt Col Joe M. Jackson
Newman, GA
12 May 1968

Col William A. Jones III
Warsaw, VA
1 Sep 1968

A1C John Levitow
South Windsor, CT
24 Feb 1969

A1C William
Pitsenbarger
Piqua, OH
11 Apr 1966

Capt Lance Peter Sijan
Milwaukee, WI
9 Nov 1967

Col Leo Thorsness
Walnut Grove, MN
19 Apr 1967

Capt Hilliard a. Wilbanks
Cornelia, GA
24 Feb 1967

Capt Gerald O. Young
Chicago, IL
9 Nov 1967

**1.23. Conclusion.**

This chapter documents the lives and activities of Airmen so you, the reader, will gain an understanding of what it means to be an Airman. From Kitty Hawk to Afghanistan 108 years later, the United States Air Force has grown into the finest Air Force in the world. You can take pride in the efforts and accomplishments of enlisted pioneers of the United States Air Force and its predecessor organizations who, through their own sacrifices, made the Air Force enlisted corps what it is today. Without their many contributions, none of that would have been possible.

## Chapter 2

## ENLISTED HISTORY

*Section 2A—Overview*

### 2.1. Introduction.

The history of the Air Force enlisted corps is long and varied. The United States Air Force traces their origin to the establishment of the Aeronautical Division, created on 1 August 1907. The Army, however, first used "aerial devices" for military purposes during the American Civil War, when President Lincoln created an unofficial balloon section. From Benjamin Franklin to the second Seminole War in 1840 to the war with Mexico in 1846, the Army has been interested in using balloons for military purposes but never did. Consequently, enlisted support for United States military aviation began with Civil War balloon operations. This chapter examines how enlisted participation in the many wars and conflicts throughout our history helped develop the United States Air Force into the greatest Air Force in the World. Enlisted Airmen historically comprised some 80 percent of America's air forces. From humble beginnings to today's great United States Air Force, the enlisted corps deserves much of the credit for their development and great accomplishments. Finally, the purpose for including this chapter within AFH 1, *Airman* is to provide enlisted Airmen reference material to support their promotion tests.

*Section 2B—Milestones of World War I and World War II*

### 2.2. Milestones of World War I (1917-1918):

2.2.1. When the first shots of the Great War were fired in Europe in August 1914, the 1st Aero Squadron mustered a dozen officers, 54 enlisted men, and 6 aircraft. By the end of 1915, the squadron counted 44 officers, 224 enlisted men, and 23 airplanes. This constituted the entire air arm of the United States Armed Forces.

2.2.2. By 1916, a second aero squadron was added, assigned to duty in the Philippine Islands, and new training facilities were added. In October 1916, plans were laid for 24 squadrons: 7 to serve with the regular Army, 12 with the National Guard, and 5 for coastal defense, supplementing balloon units for the field and coast artillery. Each squadron was to muster a dozen aircraft. The regular Army squadrons were either organized or in the process of being organized by the end of 1916, and all 24 squadrons were formed by early 1917, but only the 1st Aero Squadron was fully equipped, manned, and organized when the United States declared war on Germany 6 April 1917.

2.2.3. By April 1917, the United States Army Aviation Section consisted of 131 officers (virtually all pilots or pilots-in-training), 1,087 enlisted men, and had fewer than 250 airplanes. Even as the war in Europe dragged on, the United States Congress refused to appropriate significant funds for Army aeronautics. The Army's poor state of preparedness could not be laid entirely at Congress' feet. The Army had no plan to enable them to build an air force and did not send trained observers to Europe. General staff officers were so out of touch with modern aerial warfare requirements that their chief complaint about air personnel was the disrespectful manner in which flying officers flouted regulations by refusing to wear their cavalry spurs while flying airplanes.

2.2.4. Tradition dictated that pilots be drawn from the ranks of commissioned officers, but the Aviation Section soon realized the pressing need for trained enlisted personnel to perform duties in supply and construction and to serve specialized functions in the emerging aviation-related fields of photo reconnaissance and radio. Most of all, the Aviation Section needed mechanics. The war demanded engine mechanics, armament specialists, welders, riggers, and sail makers. The Army first pressed factories into service as training sites, but by the end of 1917, the Aviation Section began training mechanics and others at a number of special schools and technical institutions. The two largest were in St Paul Minnesota and at Kelly Field Texas. Later, mechanics and other enlisted specialists were also trained at fields and factories in Great Britain and France.

2.2.5. In addition to the specialized roles directly associated with flying, Air Service enlisted personnel performed a wide variety of administration, mess, transport, and medical corps support functions. Construction personnel, who built the airfields, hangars, barracks, and other buildings, were often the first enlisted men stationed at various overseas locations.

### 2.3. Milestones of World War II (1939-1945).

Even before the outbreak of hostilities in Europe, the General Headquarters Air Force had begun a massive expansion program that would balloon during the following years into the largest air organization in the nation's history. In 1939, President Franklin D. Roosevelt asked for $300 million for military aviation. The Air Corps planned to have 24 operational combat-ready groups by 1941 which would require greatly enhanced manpower, training, and equipment.

#### 2.3.1. The Air Corps Prepares for War:

2.3.1.1. In 1938, when the United States first took seriously the signs of war in Europe, the Army's air arm was still under two cumbersome command organizations: the Army Air Corps and General Headquarters Air Force. The total force included less than 20,000 enlisted members. In 1940, Congress passed the first peacetime conscription law in United States history. By March 1944 when Air Force manpower reached their high point, 2,104,405 enlisted men and women were serving in a virtually independent branch of the armed services. Moreover, they operated a sophisticated machine of air war that covered nearly the entire globe.

2.3.1.2. From 1939 until 1941, the concept of training did not change drastically, but the scale did. Training centers expanded and multiplied. Ever larger numbers of new Airmen passed through advanced training as the overall goals for assembling combat-ready groups increased. The air corps simply could not build housing fast enough or find qualified instructors in sufficient numbers to keep up with the pace. Army officials turned to private schools to help meet the demand, and many mechanics, for example, received training in one of the 15 civilian schools.

### 2.3.2. **World War II - The Great Central, Cataclysmic 20th Century Event:**

2.3.2.1. More than 2 million enlisted Airmen served in the United States Army Air Forces during the largest war ever. Most of them—aside from a small number of prewar soldiers—were not professional warriors. Some carried out routine duties in safe if unfamiliar surroundings, while others endured extreme conditions in faraway places for years. Tens of thousands died in combat, and scarcely any remained unchanged by the war.

2.3.2.2. Before the United States could engage the enemy, they needed more personnel, training, and equipment. Thus, 1942 was a year of buildup and training; processes that continued throughout the war. According to one former 8th Air Force gunner, "It took an average of about 30 men to support a bomber—I'm talking about a four-engine bomber, whether a B-24 or a B-17, they are about the same thing—yet you had to have somebody riding a gasoline truck, oil trucks; you had to have a carburetor specialist and armaments and so forth, sheet metal work; if you got shot up, they had to patch the holes. These people were very important and they worked 18 to 20 hours a day when you came back."

2.3.2.3. If anything, the gunner underestimated the number of guys on the ground required to keep planes in the air. No accurate figure exists across the board for World War II, but taking into account all the support personnel in the Army Air Corps, the ratio was probably closer to 70 men to 1 airplane. During the war, the great majority of the more than 2 million enlisted Airmen served in roles that never took them into the air, but without their efforts, even the most mundane or menial, no bombs would have dropped and no war would have been waged.

**Figure 2.1. Women's Army Auxiliary Corps.**

Courtesy of the Airmen Memorial Museum

2.3.2.4. Women served with distinction in the United States Army Air Forces, replacing men who could then be reassigned to combat and other vital duties. The Women's Army Auxiliary Corps was created in May 1942 (Figure 2.1). Top priority for assignment of Women's Army Auxiliary Corps was to serve at aircraft warning service stations. In the spring of 1943, the Women's Army Auxiliary Corps became the Women's Army Corps. Almost half of their peak strength served with the United States Army Air Forces with many assigned to clerical and administrative duties, while others worked as topographers, medical specialists, chemists, and even aircraft mechanics. Some commanders were reluctant to accept women into their units, but by mid-1943, the demand for them far exceeded the numbers available.

2.3.2.5. When the Air Force became a distinct service in 1947, segregation policies were transferred, but the new organization confronted special difficulties in maintaining the separation, especially in the case of enlisted Airmen. Official restrictions that forced black Airmen to serve either in all-black units or in segregated service squads robbed the Air Force of a major talent pool. On 11 May 1949, Air Force Letter 35.3 was published, mandating that black Airmen be screened for reassignment to formerly all-white units according to qualifications. Astoundingly, within a year, virtually the entire Air Force was integrated, with few incidents.

2.3.2.6. In the spring of 1945, after 3 ½ years of carnage, the end of the war seemed inevitable. The 1944 invasion of Europe and Allied ground forces' grinding advance toward Berlin finally destroyed Germany. The Third Reich surrendered in May 1945. With Europe calmed, American forces turned their attention to Japan. The American high command expected the final struggle in the Pacific would require relentless attacks against a fanatical foe. Despite widespread destruction of Japanese cities by low-level B-29 fire bombings throughout the spring and summer of 1945, Japan continued to resist. United States commanders realized that only an American invasion of the Japanese islands and subjugation of the Japanese would force the empire to surrender unconditionally, as the Allies demanded.

2.3.2.7. United States Army Air Forces enlisted crews flew thousands of combat missions during World War II, but there were two missions over Japan in August 1945 that changed the world. They were the flight of the *Enola Gay* (Figure 2.2), 6 August 1945, to drop the world's first nuclear bomb on Hiroshima; and the flight of *Bock's Car* (Figure 2.3), 3 days later to drop the second bomb on the city of Nagasaki.

**Figure 2.2. Enlisted Men of the Enola Gay Flight**

*From the Air Force Link - Photo History*

**Figure 2.3. Aircrew of the Bock's Car Flight**

*Courtesy of the Airmen Memorial Museum*

*Section 2C—Cold War, Berlin Airlift, Korean War, and War in Southeast Asia*

**2.4. The Cold War (1948-1991).**

Although the United States and their Western allies had counted on the Soviet Union as a heroic nation struggling with them against Hitler. Apparent even before World War II ended was that the alliance would not survive the ideological gulf that separated capitalist democracies from the Communist giant. In 1945, the Big Three—British Prime Minister Winston Churchill, Soviet Premier Josef Stalin, and American President Franklin D. Roosevelt—met to discuss the postwar division of Europe. The meeting did not go well, but did lay the foundation for what would become the United Nations. In 1946, the fledgling United Nations took up the issue of controlling nuclear weapons. By June 1946, a United Nations-appointed commission completed a plan for the elimination of nuclear weaponry based on inspectors who would travel the globe to ensure no country was making atomic bombs, and to supervise the dismantling of existing weapons. Unfortunately, the plan was vetoed by the Soviet Union, resulting in almost five decades of cold war.

**2.5. The Berlin Airlift (1948-1949):**

2.5.1. In June 1948, the Soviet Union exploited the arrangements under which the United States, Great Britain, and France had occupied Germany by closing off all surface access to the city of Berlin. If left unchallenged, the provocative actions of the communists may not only have won them an important psychological victory, but may also have given them permanent control over all of Berlin. Worried that an attempt to force the blockade on the ground could precipitate World War III, the allies instead built a Luftbrücke—an air bridge—into Berlin.

2.5.2. For their part, the Soviets did not believe resupply of the city by air was feasible, let alone practical. The Air Force turned to Major General William Tunner, who led the Hump airlift over the Himalayan Mountains to supply China during World War II. As the nation's leading military air cargo expert, he thoroughly analyzed United States airlift capabilities and requirements and set in motion an airlift operation that would save a city.

2.5.3. For 15 months, the 2.2 million inhabitants of the Western sectors of Berlin were sustained by airpower alone as the operation flew in 2.33 million tons of supplies on 277,569 flights (Figure 2.4). Although airlift came of age during World War II, full potential was achieved during the Berlin airlift, which was arguably airpower's single-most decisive contribution to the Cold War, unquestionably achieving a profound strategic effect.

**2.6. The Korean War (1950-1953):**

2.6.1. The 25 June 1950 surprise invasion of South Korea by North Korean armed forces caught the United States Air Force ill-prepared to deal with a conventional war in a remote corner of the world. The resulting confusion and makeshift responses fell short of requirements during the active course of the war; conditions made even more difficult by the drastic swings of military fortune during 1950 and 1951 on the Korean peninsula. The conflict imposed acute difficulties on enlisted Airmen, and throughout the Korean War, Airmen were called on to serve under the most dangerous and frustrating conditions.

**Figure 2.4. C-47s in Berlin.**

*Courtesy of the Airmen Memorial Museum*

2.6.2. By 1950, most United States ground and air strength in the Pacific was in Japan. Although the Far East Air Forces, led by General George Stratemeyer, claimed more than 400 aircraft in Japan, Guam, Korea, and the Philippines, the numbers were misleading. The force consisted largely of F-80 jets, which did not have the range necessary to reach Korea from Japan. The first aerial combat between the United States and North Korea took place over Kimpo, South Korea 27 June 1950. On 29 June, B-26 gunner Staff Sergeant Nyle S. Mickley shot down a North Korean YaK-3, the first such victory recorded during the war. Enlisted personnel served as gunners aboard the B-26 for the first several months of the conflict, and on B-29 aircraft throughout the war.

2.6.3. On 15 September 1950, United States forces spearheaded by the First Marine Division successfully landed at Inchon, near Seoul, South Korea, effectively cutting North Korean Army supply lines deep in the south, threatening the rear (Figure

**Figure 2.5. Combat Command Personnel and Supplies**

*Courtesy of the Airmen Memorial Museum*

2.5). The United States Eighth Army launched their own offensive from Pusan a day later, and what once was a stalled North Korean offensive became a disorganized retreat. So complete was the rout that less than a third of the 100,000-strong North Korean Army escaped to the north. On 27 September 1950, President Truman authorized United States forces to pursue the beaten Army north of the 38th parallel.

2.6.4. Airpower played a significant role in the Allied offensive. Airlift actions ranged from the spectacular, to include the drop of the 187th Airborne Regimental Combat Team to cut off retreating North Korean troops, to the more mundane but critical airlift of personnel and supplies. Foreshadowing the versatility that was exhibited by the B-52 in later decades, Far East Air Forces B-29s performed a number of missions not even considered before the war, to include interdiction, battlefield support, and air superiority (counter airfield).

**2.7. The War in Southeast Asia (1950-1975).**

The Truman Administration did not pursue total victory in Korea, in part to maintain United States defensive emphasis on Western Europe. The next major conflict for the United States Armed Forces, however, once again took place in Asia.

2.7.1. **The Early Years (1950-1964):**2.7.1.1. In the 1950s, the United States' involvement in Vietnam began as a cold war operation. Vietnam was essentially a French battle. However, the post-World War II policy of containment of communism prompted President Truman to intervene. He increased aid and ordered eight C-47 transports directly to Saigon, the first American Air Force presence in Vietnam. On 3 August 1950, the first contingent of the United States Military Assistance Advisory Group arrived in Saigon.

**Figure 2.6. Enlisted Technicians.**

2.7.1.2. By 1952, the United States supplied one-third of the cost of the French military effort in Vietnam, yet what was becoming apparent was that the French were losing heart. On 4 January 1953, the United States deployed the first sizable contingent of Air Force personnel (other than those attached to the Military Assistance Advisory Group). This group included a complement of enlisted technicians (Figure 2.6) to handle supply and aircraft maintenance.

2.7.1.3. In April 1953, the Viet Minh (under Ho Chi Minh's direction) staged a major offensive, advancing into Laos and menacing Thailand. President Eisenhower authorized C-119 transports (aircraft only, not crews) to the area, and in 1954 loaned

*Courtesy of the Airmen Memorial Museum*

additional cargo planes to the French. Because French air units were seriously undermanned, United States officials made the fateful decision on 31 January 1954 to dispatch 300 Airmen to service aircraft at Tourane and Do Son Airfield near Haiphong, North Vietnam.

2.7.1.4. As Air Force presence increased in the early 1960s, so did the need for support personnel. Priorities included construction of airfields and barracks, and intelligence-gathering.

*Section 2D—The Air War Expands, Vietnamization, Humanitarian Airlift, and Post-Vietnam Conflicts*

## 2.8. The Air War Expands (1965-1968):

2.8.1. On 7 February 1965, the Viet Cong attacked Camp Holloway near Pleiku, killing eight Americans. The President responded with Operation FLAMING DART, a series of strikes against military barracks near Dong Hoi in North Vietnam, as well as other targets. Increased airstrikes against targets in the northern half of the country, code name Rolling Thunder, began less than a month later on 2 March. Rolling Thunder was the first sustained bombing campaign of the war against North Vietnam, lasting through 1968.

2.8.2. As offensive air operations increased, United States Air Force presence in Southeast Asia also increased. About 10,000 Air Force personnel served in Vietnam in May 1965, doubling by the end of the year. As 1968 drew to a close, 58,000 Airmen served in the country. Airmen performed various duties, including support, combat and rescue (Figure 2.7). Prime BEEF personnel, for example, built revetments, barracks, and other facilities. Rapid engineering and heavy operational repair squadron, engineering (REDHORSE) teams provided more long-range civil engineer services.

**Figure 2.7. Medical Evacuation System**

*Courtesy of the Airmen Memorial Museum*

In the realm of combat operations, Air Force gunners flew aboard gunships as well as B-57s and B-52s. In December 1972, B-52 tail gunner Staff Sergeant Samuel Turner shot down an enemy MiG, the first of only two confirmed shoot-downs by enlisted Airmen during the war. Both victories were from gunners belonging to the 307th Strategic Wing at U-Tapao, Thailand. Credit for the fifth overall MiG-21 kill during Linebacker II also went to an enlisted member, Airman First Class Albert E. Moore.

2.8.3. Enlisted personnel also served on gunships during the war as both aerial gunners and as loadmasters. With the Gatling-style guns actually aimed by the pilot through speed, bank, and altitude, the responsibility of the aerial gunners was to keep the quick-firing guns reloaded. Crewmembers occupying this position were particularly vulnerable to ground fire. Meanwhile, loadmasters released flare canisters over target areas during night missions, another hazardous undertaking.

2.8.4. Air Force enlisted members faced combat on the ground as well. With the continuing threat of guerrilla attack, air base defense became a monumental undertaking performed almost exclusively by Air Force security police squadrons. Staff Sergeant William Piazza, 3d Security Police Squadron earned the Silver Star for helping defend Bien Hoa during the North Vietnamese Tet Offensive of 1968.

## 2.9. Vietnamization and Withdrawal (1969-1973):

2.9.1. Since the Eisenhower years, American presidents wanted the Vietnam conflict to be fought and resolved by the Vietnamese. Through 1963 and much of 1964, American forces operated under restrictive rules of engagement in an effort to maintain the United States role as advisory only. On 22 November 1963, embroiled in a deteriorating situation in Vietnam, President Kennedy was assassinated and Vice President Lyndon B. Johnson took office. After the Gulf of Tonkin incident and the Senate resolution of 1964, the advisory role rapidly evolved into one of combat operations. Yet the Air Force never stopped working with the Vietnamese Air Force to develop an ability to prosecute the war itself. In January 1969, shortly after taking office, President Nixon announced an end to United States combat in Southeast Asia as a primary goal of his administration. He charged the Secretary of Defense with making Vietnamization of the war a top priority.

2.9.2. Enlisted Airmen played key roles, especially in training Vietnamese operational and training crews. As the Vietnamese took over air operations, the nation's air force grew to become the fourth largest in the world. In May 1969, the withdrawal of United States Army ground units from Vietnam began in earnest, while air support units lingered. In 1972, taking advantage of reduced American ground presence, Communist forces of the National Liberation Front crossed the demilitarized zone, President Nixon ordered harbors mined, and Peace talks broke down completely.

2.9.3. President Nixon ordered 11 days of intensive bombing of Vietnamese cities, with B-52s from Andersen Air Force Base, Guam carrying out the mission called "Linebacker II." Linebacker II succeeded in breaking the deadlock, and the North Vietnamese resumed negotiations. A cease-fire agreement was hammered out by 28 January 1973.

2.9.4. While Linebacker II was a success, Vietnam was no ordinary war. The cease-fire did not bring an end to the fighting, and the punishment aircrews delivered did not bring victory. Nevertheless, the United States was committed to withdrawal. On 27 January 1973, the military draft ended; on 29 March, the last United States troop left the country; and even though another cease-fire agreement was drawn up to end previous cease-fire violations, fighting continued until April 22 when the president of South Vietnam resigned. North and South Vietnam were officially unified under a Communist regime on 2 July 1976.

**2.10. Humanitarian Airlift:**

2.10.1. The history of humanitarian airlift by United States Armed Forces is almost as old as the history of flight itself. Army aircraft flying out of Kelly Field Texas, for example, dropped food to victims of a Rio Grande flood in 1919, one of the first known uses of an aircraft to render assistance. Many early domestic humanitarian flights were flown in response to winter emergencies. In March 1923, Aberdeen Proving Ground Maryland sent airplanes to bomb an ice jam on the Delaware River and an aircraft from Chanute Field Illinois dropped food to stranded people on South Fox Island in Lake Michigan. From blizzards and floods to volcanic eruptions and earthquakes, Army Air Corps personnel and aircraft provided relief.

2.10.2. Army aircraft also flew humanitarian missions to foreign nations before the United States Air Force was established. In February 1939, the 2d Bombardment Wing delivered medical supplies to earthquake victims in Chile Four years later, in the midst of World War II, a B-24 from a base in Guatemala dropped a life raft with the diphtheria vaccine to a destroyer escorting a British aircraft carrier. The destroyer delivered the vaccine to the carrier, preventing a shipboard epidemic. In September 1944, United States Army Air Forces planes dropped food to starving French citizens; in May 1945, B-17s delivered food to hungry people in the Netherlands during Operation CHOWHOUND.

2.10.3. Humanitarian efforts continued after the Air Force became a separate service and through the ensuing decades During Operation SAFE HAVEN I and II, in 1956 and 1957, the Military Air Transport Service 1608th Air Transport Wing, Charleston Air Force Base South Carolina, and 1611th Air Transport Wing, McGuire Air Force Base New Jersey, airlifted over 10,000 Hungarian refugees to the United States. President Eisenhower approved asylum for the refugees who fled Hungary after Soviet forces crushed an anticommunist uprising there. In May 1960, earthquakes followed by volcanic eruptions, avalanches, and tidal waves ripped through southern Chile, leaving nearly 10,000 people dead and a quarter of a million homeless. The United States Department of Defense and State Department agreed to provide assistance. During the month-long "Amigos Airlift," the 63d Troop Carrier Wing from Donaldson Air Force Base South Carolina and the 1607th, 1608th, and 1611th Air Transport Wings airlifted over 1,000 tons of material to the stricken area.

2.10.4. America's commitment to South Vietnam led to many relief flights to that country during the 1960s and 1970s. In November 1964, three typhoons dumped 40-plus inches of rain on the country's central highlands, killing 7,000 people and destroying 50,000 homes. HH-43F helicopters from Detachment 5, Pacific Air Rescue Center, plucked 80 Vietnamese from rooftops and high ground in the immediate aftermath of the storms. Over the next 2 months, various Air Force units moved more than 2,000 tons of food, fuel, boats, and medicine to the ravaged area. Less than a year later, in August 1965, fighting in Da Nang displaced 400 orphaned children. To move them out of harm's way, 315th Air Division C-130s airlifted the orphans to Saigon. In 1975, following the fall of Cambodia and South Vietnam to Communist forces, transports from 11 Air Force wings and other units airlifted more than 50,000 refugees to the United States. This airlift, which included Operations BABYLIFT, NEW LIFE, FREQUENT WIND, and NEW ARRIVALS, was the largest aerial evacuation in history. In addition to refugees, Air Force units also moved 5,000 relief workers and more than 8,500 tons of supplies.

2.10.5. Aside from the Vietnamese evacuation of the 1970s and the Berlin airlift in the late 1940s, the most significant humanitarian airlift operations took place in the 1990s. In 1991, following the Persian Gulf War, Iraqi leader Saddam Hussein attacked the Kurdish population in northern Iraq. In response to the unfolding human tragedy, Air Force transports in support of Operation PROVIDE COMFORT provided more than 7,000 tons of blankets, tents, food, and more to the displaced Kurds, and airlifted thousands of refugees and medical personnel. Operation SEA ANGEL, in which the Air Force airlifted 3,000 tons of supplies to Bangladesh, followed a 1991 typhoon. Operation PROVIDE HOPE in 1992 and 1993 provided 6,000 tons of food, medicine, and other cargo to republics of the former Soviet Union. In 1994, the Air Force carried 3,600 tons of relief supplies to Rwandan refugees in war-torn central Africa.

**2.11. Post-Vietnam Conflicts:**

2.11.1. **Operation URGENT FURY, Grenada (1983):**

2.11.1.1. In October 1983, a military coup on the tiny Caribbean island nation of Grenada aroused United States attention. Coup leaders arrested and then assassinated Prime Minister Maurice Bishop, imposed a 24-hour shoot-on-sight curfew, and closed the airport at Pearls on the east coast, about 12 miles from the capital of St. George's, located on the opposite side of the island. President Ronald W. Reagan, who did not want a repetition of the Iranian hostage crisis a few years earlier, considered military intervention to rescue hundreds of United States citizens attending medical school on the island.

2.11.1.2. Twenty-six Air Force wings, groups, and squadrons supported the invasion by 1,900 United States Marines and Army Rangers. Airlift and special operations units from the Military Airlift Command comprised the bulk of the Air Force fighting force. AC-130 gunships in particular proved their worth repeatedly, showing more versatility and accuracy than naval bombardment and land artillery. Several Air Force enlisted personnel were among 10 Air Force Grenada veterans cited for special achievement who received special praise for their efforts. Among them, Sergeant Charles Tisby, a loadmaster, saved the life of an unidentified paratrooper in his aircraft. When his C-130 banked sharply to avoid antiaircraft fire, one paratrooper's static line fouled and left the trooper still attached to the aircraft. Tisby, with the help of paratroopers still on board, managed—at significant personal risk—to haul the man back in.

2.11.2. **El Dorado Canyon, Libya (1986):**

2.11.2.1. In 1969, a group of junior military officers led by Muammar Qadhafi overthrew the pro-Western Libyan Arab monarchy. By the mid-1980s, Libya was one of the leading sponsors of worldwide terrorism. In addition to subversion or direct military intervention against other African nations and global assassinations of anti-Qadhafi Libyan exiles and other "state enemies," Qadhafi sponsored terrorist training camps within Libya and supplied funds, weapons, logistical support, and safe havens for numerous terrorist groups.

2.11.2.2. Between January 1981 and April 1986, terrorists worldwide killed over 300 Americans and injured hundreds more. With National Security Decision Directive 138 signed on 3 April 1984, President Reagan established in principle a United States policy of preemptive and retaliatory strikes against terrorists. On 27 December 1985, terrorists attacked passengers in the Rome and Vienna airports. Despite the strong evidence that connected Libya to the incident, the United States administration determined they did not have sufficient proof to order retaliatory strikes against Libya. President Reagan imposed sanctions against Libya, publicly denounced Qadhafi for sponsoring the operation, and sent the 6th Fleet to exercise off the coast of Libya.

2.11.2.3. In Berlin, 5 April 1986, a large bomb gutted a discotheque popular with United States service members. This time President Reagan had the evidence he sought. On 9 April, he authorized an air strike against Libya and attempted to obtain support from European allies. Great Britain gave permission for the United States Air Force to use British bases; however, the governments of France and Spain denied permission to fly over their countries, thereby increasing the Air Force's round trip to almost 6,000 miles. By 14 April 1986, all Air Force forces were gathered and ready.

2.11.2.4. Politically, the raid against the terrorist state was extremely popular in the United States and almost universally condemned or "regretted" by the United States' European allies who feared that the raid would spawn more violence. The operation spurred Western European governments to increase their defenses against terrorism and their intelligence agencies began to share information. The Air Force was saddened by the loss of an F-111F crew, but the loss of one out of over a 100 aircraft used in the raid statistically was not a high toll. Despite the high abort rate, collateral damage, and loss of innocent lives—after a flight of more than 6 hours and in the face of strong enemy opposition—the Air Force successfully hit three targets previously seen only in photographs.

2.11.3. **Operation JUST CAUSE, Panama (1989):**

2.11.3.1. Since Panama's declaration of independence from Colombia in 1903, the United States has maintained a special interest in this small Central American country. The United States controlled and occupied the Panama Canal Zone, through which they built a 40-mile long canal to connect the Atlantic and Pacific Oceans. President Woodrow Wilson formally opened the canal on 12 July 1915. Political and domestic conditions in Panama remained stable until 1968, when a military ruler deposed the country's president. A new treaty took effect 1 October 1979, granting Panama complete control of the canal and dictating withdrawal of United States military forces by 1 January 2000.

2.11.3.2. A 1981 leadership struggle culminated in 1983; General Manuel Noriega prevailed. Noriega maintained ties with the United States intelligence community, furnishing information on Latin American drug trafficking and money laundering, while at the same time engaging in such activities. By 1987, brutal repression of his people was enough for the United States Senate to issue a resolution calling for the Panamanians to oust him. Noriega in turn ordered an attack on the United States Embassy, causing an end to United States military and economic aid. In 1988, a Miami federal grand jury indicted Noriega on drug-trafficking and money-laundering charges. Noriega intensified his harassment against his own people and all Americans. By 1989, President George H. W. Bush decided to invade Panama.

2.11.3.3. All four branches of the United States Armed Forces played a role in Operation JUST CAUSE. Air Force participation included elements of 18 wings, 9 groups, and 17 types of aircraft. On the first night of the operation, 84 aircraft flying 500 feet above the ground dropped nearly 5,000 troops, the largest nighttime airborne operation since World War II. The airdrop also featured the first Air Force personnel use of night vision goggles during a contingency.

2.11.3.4. Operation JUST CAUSE was the largest and most complex air operation since Vietnam and involved more than 250 aircraft. American forces eliminated organized resistance in just 6 days. Manuel Noriega surrendered 3 January 1990 and was flown to Miami Florida to face trial. Less than a year later, many of the same Airmen that made Operation JUST CAUSE a resounding success would build and travel another, larger air bridge during Operation DESERT SHIELD.

## Section 2E—Gulf War, Military Operations (1991-2003), and Iraq and Afghanistan

### 2.12. Gulf War I (1990):

2.12.1. **Persian Gulf War and Subsequent Operations:**

2.12.1.1. The Gulf War was no surprise to anyone except perhaps Saddam Hussein. After prevailing in an 8-year war with Iran that was so costly this war nearly led to a military coup, Saddam Hussein invaded and attempted to annex the small, oil-rich nation of Kuwait on 2 August 1990. During his occupation of the country, he plundered it and brutalized the population. The invasion put Iraq, with the fourth largest Army in the world and an extensive program to develop nuclear weapons, on the doorstep of Saudi Arabia with vast petroleum reserves. If the Saudis also fell to Iraq, the dictator would control 50 percent of the world's oil.

2.12.1.2. The United States sought and received a United Nations sanction to act against Iraq and joined 27 other nations to launch Operation DESERT SHIELD, a massive military buildup in Saudi Arabia near the border of Iraq, aimed first at deterring Saddam Hussein from aggression against the Saudis and then to prepare the way for a counter invasion, if necessary. United States President George Bush demanded the immediate withdrawal of Iraqi forces from Kuwait. Saddam believed that, since Vietnam, the American public lacked the stomach for war. For more than 6 months he alternated between defiance and vague promises of compliance.

2.12.2. **Operation DESERT SHIELD and Operation DESERT STORM, Kuwait and Iraq (1990-1991):**

2.12.2.1. By the time President Bush launched Operation DESERT SHIELD, the United States Air Force and the sister services had moved a considerable distance toward a unified conventional warfighting capability. The defensive deployment in itself was an impressive accomplishment. On 8 August 1990, 24 F-15Cs landed in Saudi Arabia after taking off 15 hours earlier from Langley Air Force Base Virginia, some 8,000 miles away. Within 5 days, C-5 and C-141 airlifters had escorted in five fighter squadrons, an airborne warning and control system contingent, and an airborne brigade: 301 planes altogether. On 21 August, Secretary of Defense Richard Cheney announced that sufficient force was in place to defend Saudi Arabia. A month into the crisis, 1,220 Allied aircraft were in theater and combat ready. When Saddam Hussein missed the final deadline to withdraw his troops from Kuwait, Operation DESERT STORM began 15 January 1991.

2.12.2.2. Within the first 24 hours of Desert Storm, the air war was essentially won. The Iraqi air force hardly showed their face. Having established air dominance, coalition air forces turned their attention to entrenched ground forces, pounding them into a frightened mass ready to surrender to the first allied troops they saw. In the final stages of the air war, the Air Force began "tank plinking," or destroying Iraqi tanks on the ground one at a time (Figure 2.8).

2.12.2.3. Maintenance was a key to the air campaign success. Air Force historian Dr. Richard Hallion said, "From the suppliers to the line crews sweating under the desert sun, the coalition's maintainers worked miracles, enabling ever-higher sortie rates as the war progressed—essentially, a constant

**Figure 2.8. Loading an A-10.**

*Courtesy of AF Link*

surge." Not all enlisted Airmen worked on maintenance crews. In addition to traditional enlisted functions, there were new duties, some of which were quite high tech. Two less known jobs were electronic emissions collection and analysis, undertaken with electronic warfare officers and airborne intelligence technicians. Electronic intelligence was characterized by long hours of work on station and meticulous, patient review of enemy transmissions, shot through with brief but urgently explosive moments when life or death information was quickly transmitted to the right people.

2.12.2.4. On 28 February 1991, scarcely 48 hours after the air war ended and the land invasion took center stage, Iraq surrendered to the coalition. In the 43-day war, the Air Force was, for the first time in modern combat, the equal partner of land and sea power. The Air Force went into the Gulf talking in cold war terms about air superiority and sustainable casualties and came out trumpeting air supremacy with minimum casualties. Within 6 months, 27 September 1991, strategic bomber crews were ordered to stand down from their decades-long round-the-clock readiness for nuclear war. The Cold War was officially over, a new world had arrived, and the role of enlisted Airmen changed.

## 2.13. Operations PROVIDE COMFORT and NORTHERN WATCH, Iraq (1991-2003):

2.13.1. When the American-led international coalition bombed Iraq and drove the forces of Iraq from Kuwait in 1991, Saddam Hussein's power was weakened. Rebellious Kurds in northern Iraq, whom Hussein brutally suppressed with chemical weapons 3 years earlier, launched an uprising in early March 1991. When Iraqi government troops defeated the rebellion a month later, threatening to repeat the massacres of the past, more than a million Kurds fled to Iran and Turkey. Hundreds of thousands more gathered on cold mountain slopes on the Iraqi-Turkish border. Lacking food, clean water, clothing, blankets, medical supplies, and shelter, the refugees suffered enormous mortality rates.

2.13.2. On 3 April 1991, the United Nations Security Council authorized a humanitarian relief effort for the Iraqi Kurds. During the first week in April, the United States organized a combined task force for Operation PROVIDE COMFORT. About 600 pallets of relief supplies were delivered per day, but airdrops alone proved inadequate. Moreover, the operation failed to address the root of the problem. The refugees could not stay where they were, and Turkey, faced with a restless Kurdish population of their own, refused to admit them in large numbers. Operation PROVIDE COMFORT, therefore, evolved into a larger-phased operation for American ground troops.

2.13.3. After 1993, Saddam Hussein rarely challenged coalition aircraft patrolling the no-fly zones, but United States units remained wary. On 14 April 1994, two American F-15s patrolling the northern no-fly zone accidentally shot down two UH-60 Black Hawk helicopters, killing 26 people, including 15 Americans. Misidentifying the helicopters as hostile, the F-15 pilots failed to receive contrary information from either the helicopters or an orbiting E-3 aircraft. The friendly fire incident aroused negative public opinion and a demand for changes to prevent such accidents in the future.

2.13.4. Phase II of Operation PROVIDE COMFORT ended in December 1996, thanks largely to infighting among Kurdish factions vying for power. When one Kurdish group accepted Iraqi backing to drive another from the northern Iraqi city of Irbil, United States transports participating in Operations QUICK TRANSIT I, II, and III airlifted many displaced Kurds to safe areas in Turkey. During Operation PACIFIC HAVEN, 7,000 refugees proceeded to Guam for settlement in the United States.

2.13.5. Operation NORTHERN WATCH, which began 1 January 1997 with an initial mandate of 6 months, succeeded Operation PROVIDE COMFORT. Operation NORTHERN WATCH officially ended 17 March 2003, 2 days before Operation IRAQI FREEDOM began.

## 2.14. Operation SOUTHERN WATCH, Iraq (1992-2003):

2.14.1. On 26 August 1992, to discourage renewed Iraqi military activity near Kuwait, President George H. W. Bush announced a no-fly zone in southern Iraq in support of United Nations Security Council Resolution 688, Operation SOUTHERN WATCH.

2.14.2. The resolution protected Shiite Muslims under aerial attack from the Iraqi regime of Saddam Hussein in the aftermath of Operation DESERT STORM and enforced other United Nations sanctions against Iraq. The Iraqi regime complied with the restrictions of the no-fly zone until 27 December 1992. F-16s shot down one Iraqi MiG-25 and chased a second aircraft back across the border.

2.14.3. Less than a month later, Air Force aircraft attacked surface-to-air missile sites threatening coalition aircraft. In June, the United States launched cruise missile strikes against the Iraq Intelligence Service Headquarters in Baghdad as retaliation for the planned assassination of former United States President George Bush during an April 1993 visit to Kuwait.

2.14.4. In October 1994, Iraqi troops, including elite Republican Guard units, massed at the Kuwaiti border. The United States responded with Operation VIGILANT WARRIOR, the introduction of thousands of additional United States Armed

Forces personnel into the theater. Operation SOUTHERN WATCH became the United States Air Force test for the Air and Space Expeditionary Force concept in October 1995, when a composite unit designed to replace temporarily a United States Navy carrier air wing leaving the gulf area arrived to support flying operations. The Air and Space Expeditionary Force arrived fully armed and began flying within 12 hours of landing. The Air and Space Expeditionary Force concept proved sound. Additional Air and Space Expeditionary Forces have since deployed to support Operation SOUTHERN WATCH.

2.14.5. In 1997, in response to Iraqi aggression against Kurdish rebels in northern Iraq, President William Clinton expanded the Operation SOUTHERN WATCH no-fly zone to the 33d parallel, just south of Baghdad. The expansion meant that most of Iraqi airspace fell into no-fly zones.

2.14.6. One of the most important improvements in both flying operations and the quality of life for members resulted directly from the 1996 bombing at Khobar Towers, Dhahran Air Base. In the aftermath, the Air Force reviewed their entire security police, law enforcement, and force protection programs. In 1998, the Air Force reorganized existing security police units into new security forces groups and squadrons that trained and specialized in all aspects of force protection, including terrorist activity and deployed force security. Operation SOUTHERN WATCH officially ended 26 August 2003.

## 2.15. Operations PROVIDE RELIEF, IMPRESSIVE LIFT, and RESTORE HOPE—Somalia (1992-1994).

In 1992, America's armed forces took part in several major humanitarian operations across the globe. One of those places was Somalia. Refer to Chapter 1 Enlisted Heritage paragraph 1.17 for information on enlisted Airman's involvement with these operations.

## 2.16. Operation UPHOLD DEMOCRACY, Haiti (1994):

2.16.1. The United States decided to intervene in Haiti on 8 September 1994. The United States Atlantic Command developed two different Operation UPHOLD DEMOCRACY plans: one for forcible entry and the other for passive entry. United States Air Force planners worked through evolving variations, not knowing which plan would be implemented. At nearly the last minute, a diplomatic proposal that former President James (Jimmy) E. Carter offered persuaded the military leader in Haiti to relinquish control. The unexpected decision caused a mission change from invasion to insertion of a multinational peacekeeping force. On 19 September 1994, the Joint Chief of Staff directed execution of the passive-entry plan. For the Air Force, this meant activating an aerial force of more than 200 aircraft: transports, special operations, and surveillance planes.

2.16.2. United States Air Force participation effectively ended 12 October 1994 when resupply of United States forces became routinely scheduled airlift missions and deployed aircraft and crews returned home. On 15 October 1994, the Haitian president returned to his country, the beneficiary of a strong United States response to an oppressive dictator. As in Panama, the Air Force brought to bear an overwhelming force of fighters, command and control aircraft, gunships and other special operations aircraft, reconnaissance airplanes, aerial refueling tankers, and thousands of troops aboard the airlift fleet of strategic and tactical aircraft. The successful adaptation to the last-minute change in mission, from military invasion force to airlifting peacekeeping troops, was a major indicator of the flexibility airpower offers United States military and political leaders in fulfilling foreign policy objectives.

## 2.17. Operation PROVIDE PROMISE, Sarajevo and Bosnia-Herzegovina (1992-1996):

2.17.1. By 1991, the collapse of communism in Eastern Europe and the Soviet Union, coupled with the disintegration of the Soviet Union itself, dissolved the political cement that bound ethnically diverse Yugoslavia into a single nation. Freed from the threat of external domination, Roman Catholic Slovenia and Croatia declared their independence from the Yugoslav federation dominated by Eastern Orthodox Serbia. In early 1992, predominantly Muslim Bosnia-Herzegovina (Bosnia) also severed ties to the Federation. Fearing their minority status, armed Serbs within Bosnia began forming their ethnic state by seizing territory and, in the spring, besieging the Bosnian capital of Sarajevo.

2.17.2. In April 1992, the United States recognized Bosnia's independence and began airlifting relief supplies to Sarajevo. On 3 July 1992, the United States designated operations in support of the United Nations airlift Operation PROVIDE PROMISE and United States Air Forces in Europe C-130s began delivering food and medical supplies.

2.17.3. Most United States Air Force missions flew out of Rhein-Main Air Base in Frankfurt, Germany. C-130s from the 435th and 317th Airlift Wings flew the initial Operation PROVIDE PROMISE missions, but over the course of the operation, Air Force Reserve, Air National Guard, and Regular Air Force units rotated from the United States on 3-week deployments. Although the United States was only one of at least 15 countries airlifting relief supplies to Sarajevo, by the end of 1992, United States airplanes had delivered more than 5,400 tons of food and medical supplies.

2.17.4. Inaugurated during the Bush administration, Operation PROVIDE PROMISE expanded significantly after President Clinton took office. He acted in response to continued attacks by Bosnian Serbs on Sarajevo and on the relief aircraft themselves. A secondary mission, Operation PROVIDE SANTA, took place in December 1993 when C-130s dropped 50 tons of toys and children's clothes and shoes over Sarajevo. A month later, an Operation PROVIDE PROMISE C-130 was the first United States Air Force aircraft to suffer damage from the operation when strucked by an artillery shell at the Sarajevo airport. Despite the fact there were no injuries and the damage was minor, the United Nations suspended flights for a week.

2.17.5. On 14 December 1995, warring factions signed peace accords at Wright-Patterson Air Force Base Ohio. The last humanitarian air-land delivery into Sarajevo took place on 4 January 1996. During the 3½ year operation, aircraft supporting the United Nations-relief operation withstood 279 incidents of ground fire.

## 2.18. Operation DENY FLIGHT, Bosnia (1993-1995):

2.18.1. North Atlantic Treaty Organization (NATO) Operation DENY FLIGHT was an effort to limit the war in Bosnia through imposition of a no-fly zone over the country. There was only one non-American in the NATO Operation DENY FLIGHT command chain, although many other nations participated, including the United Kingdom, France, the Netherlands, Spain, Germany, and Turkey.

2.18.2. Over the first 18 months of Operation DENY FLIGHT, the operation's mission expanded and aircraft engaged United Nations resolution violators. On 28 February 1994, NATO aircraft scored the first aerial combat victories in their 45-year history. Two United States Air Force F-16s from the 526th Fighter Squadron intercepted six Bosnian Serb jets and shot down four.

2.18.3. Despite NATO actions, Operation DENY FLIGHT did not stop the Bosnian Serb attacks or effectively limit the war. Bosnian Serbs often took members of lightly armed United Nations forces hostage to compel NATO to discontinue airstrikes. In May 1995, Operation DENY FLIGHT aircraft struck a munitions depot, after which Bosnian Serbs took 370 United Nations soldiers hostage. The United Nations vetoed further strikes. In June, Bosnian Serbs shot down a United States Air Force F-16 patrolling over Bosnia.

2.18.4. Operation DELIBERATE FORCE served notice to Bosnian Serb forces that they would be held accountable for their actions. Airstrikes came not only against targets around Sarajevo, but also against Bosnian Serb targets throughout the country. The results were dramatic. Operation DELIBERATE FORCE marked the first campaign in aerial warfare where precision munitions outweighed conventional bombs. The incessant air campaign, with only a few days respite in early September, as well as ground advances by Croatian and other forces against the Serbs, garnered the desired results. On 14 September, the Serbs agreed to NATO terms and the bombing stopped.

2.18.5. Operation DELIBERATE FORCE officially ended 21 September 1995 with the December signing in Paris of peace accords among the warring parties. Operation JOINT ENDEAVOR, whose mission was to implement the agreements, were replaced in 1996.

## 2.19. Operation ALLIED FORCE, Kosovo (1999):

2.19.1. The conclusion of Operations DELIBERATE FORCE and DENY FLIGHT did not mean the end to strife in the region. After revoking the province of Kosovo's autonomy in 1989, the Serbian government slowly began to oppress the ethnic Albanian population. That oppression eventually turned to violence and mass killings, and the international community began to negotiate with Serbian leaders in the spring of 1998 for a solution acceptable to all parties. The Serbs, led by President Slobodan Milosevic, considered the matter an internal one. A final effort to negotiate a settlement began in January 1999 at Rambouillet, France, but talks broke down following a large offensive against Albanian civilians in March.

2.19.2. To prevent a repeat of the "ethnic cleansing" that took place in Bosnia, on 24 March 1999 NATO forces began flying operations to force Serbia to accept NATO terms to end the conflict in Kosovo. Named Operation ALLIED FORCE, NATO leaders hoped a few days of airstrikes to demonstrate NATO's resolve would force Milosevic to capitulate. That was not the case and took 78 days with more than 38,000 sorties for NATO to secure their objective.

2.19.3. The primary factor in the conclusion of Operation ALLIED FORCE was NATO's unity and resolve. NATO was tough and became progressively tougher throughout the campaign. This lesson was clear to Milosevic, who had hoped he could outwait NATO. In addition, the precision and the persistence of the air campaign were fundamental factors in convincing Milosevic to end the fight. The air campaign started slowly but gathered momentum as the air campaign went on and became increasingly damaging to Milosevic's entire military infrastructure, not just the forces in the field in Kosovo, but throughout the entire country.

## 2.20. Operations NOBLE EAGLE and ENDURING FREEDOM:

2.20.1. Four unprecedented acts of violence in three locations spreading from New York City to western Pennsylvania to Washington, District of Columbia on 11 September 2001 left thousands dead, thousands more grieving, and a nation wondering what would happen next. This fanatical hatred carried out by a hidden handful manifested and exploded, causing two of the world's tallest buildings to crumble, scarring the nation's military nerve center, and forcing the President of the United States aboard Air Force One to seek safe haven. Following the attacks on the World Trade Center, the Air Force community realized the depth and scope of the hatred. In the days that followed, stories circulated of service members and civilians pulling comrades from burning buildings, fighting fires, providing medical attention, and volunteering to do whatever they could.

**Figure 2.9. C-17 in Afghanistan.**

*US Air Force Photo by SSgt Steven Pearsall*

2.20.2. The Air Force responded quickly to the attack. The day of the attack, American fighter aircraft began combat air patrols in the skies of America in support of Operation NOBLE EAGLE. Six months later, North American Aerospace Defense Command, with more than 100 Air National Guard, Air Force Reserve, and Regular Air Force fighters from 26 locations, continued to monitor American airspace. More than 80 percent of the pilots flying Operation NOBLE EAGLE missions belonged to the Air National Guard. Nearly as many Air Force Reserve, Air National Guard, and active duty members (more than 11,000) deployed to support Operation NOBLE EAGLE (Figure 2.9) as for the other thrust of the United States response to the attack, Operation ENDURING FREEDOM.

2.20.3. Operation ENDURING FREEDOM would take the fight to the Nation's enemies overseas, most notably Afghanistan, an impoverished country where the United States focus was twofold: provide humanitarian airlift to the oppressed people of Afghanistan and conduct military action to root out terrorists and their supporters. When the Taliban, Afghanistan's ruling government, refused President George W. Bush's demand that suspected terrorists be turned over and all terrorist training camps closed, the President ordered United States forces to the region. Approximately 350 United States aircraft, including B-1 and B-52 bombers, F-15 and F-16 fighters, special operations aircraft, RQ-1B and RQ-4A unmanned aerial vehicles, and Navy fighters, deployed to bases near Afghanistan, including some in the former Soviet Union. On 7 October 2001, following continued Taliban refusal to hand over suspected terrorists, United States, British, and French aircraft began a sustained campaign against terrorist targets in Afghanistan.

2.20.4. Working closely with United States special operations troops and Afghan opposition forces, airpower employed precision weapons to break the Taliban's will and capacity to resist. Organized resistance began to collapse in mid-November, and the Taliban abandoned the last major town under their control, Kandahar, in December 2001. In addition to strike operations, the Air Force flew humanitarian relief, dropping nearly 2.5 million humanitarian rations.

**2.21. Operation ANACONDA.**

One of the most crucial joint combat operations in Afghanistan was Operation ANACONDA, designed and executed to remove the last remaining organized Taliban resistance. Operation ANACONDA, conducted in the Shahikot Valley of Afghanistan during early March 2002, was a complex battle fought in rugged mountainous terrain under difficult conditions. The battle ended as an American victory at the cost of eight United States military personnel killed and more than 50 wounded. But the difficult early stages of the battle provide insights for thinking about how to organize, train, and equip United States forces for future joint expeditionary operations and how to pursue transformation. Refer back to Chapter 1, Air Force Heritage paragraphs 1.19.4 to 1.19.6 for the enlisted perspective for this operation.

**2.22. Operation IRAQI FREEDOM:**

2.22.1. The primary political goal of Operation IRAQI FREEDOM was to create "a stable Iraq, with their territorial integrity intact and a broad based government that renounces Weapons of Mass Destruction development and use, and no longer supports terrorism or threaten their neighbors." Based on that primary objective, the combined force commander's top three objectives were to "defeat or compel capitulation of Iraqi forces, neutralize regime leadership, and neutralize Iraqi theater ballistic missile/ Weapons of Mass Destruction delivery systems." For some additional information on the enlisted perspective for this operation refer back to Chapter 1, Air Force Heritage paragraphs 1.19.7 to 1.19.9.

2.22.2. Meanwhile, British forces took Basra, control of which was essential to delivering humanitarian aid. American commanders declared Saddam's regime was no longer in control of Baghdad on 9 April. Before the city fell, jubilant crowds toppled a 40-foot statue of Saddam. Iraq's science advisor surrendered to United States forces, the first on the 55 most-wanted leaders list issued by the coalition.

2.22.3. In a speech delivered on 2 May 2003 aboard the aircraft carrier USS *Abraham Lincoln*, President Bush announced victory in Iraq. The President's announcement was based on an assessment given to him 3 days earlier by General Tommy Franks, the top United States military commander in the Gulf. Meanwhile, in a speech delivered by Secretary of the Air

Force James G. Roche on 25 April 2003 to attendees of the Command Chief Master Sergeant Conference in Gunter Annex, Maxwell Air Force Base Alabama, Secretary Roche assessed how United States combat air forces performed during Operation IRAQI FREEDOM. Secretary Roche mentioned that in the past month in Iraq, coalition forces liberated an oppressed people and began the process of rebuilding a very different tribal and political climate.

## 2.23. Iraq and Afghanistan:

2.23.1. Operation ENDURING FREEDOM in Afghanistan began after the attacks of September 11, 2001. Small, highly-mobile Army, Navy and United States Air Force special operation forces were inserted deep into the hostile mountains of Afghanistan to find, capture, and destroy elusive Taliban and Al Qaeda forces. United States Air Force enlisted personnel played key roles in the attempt to drive the Taliban out and they were quickly removed from power. But that wasn't the end of the conflict. Air Force Airmen continued searching for terrorists hiding in the mountains.

2.23.2. United States Air Force Airmen remained an essential part of United States military operations worldwide as Operation ENDURING FREEDOM continued. They established forward assault landing strips, directed close air support strikes, and recovered downed and wounded personnel. In Iraq, United States Air Force Airmen, in joint operations with other United States unconventional forces, and conducted missions that paralyzed 11 Iraqi divisions making the land drive to Baghdad less difficult.

2.23.3. On July 19, 2003, Technical Sergeant Kevin Whalen, a Tactical Air Control Party Terminal Attack Controller (Figure 2.10), was supporting an Afghan Military Forces and United States Special Forces combat patrol in the Gayan Valley, Afghanistan. The patrol was hit in a well-coordinated ambush by a numerically superior enemy force. Whalen returned effective fire with an automatic grenade launcher and remained exposed to enemy fire from three directions while the rest of the team took cover. The grenade launcher was hit six times, but Whalen remained at his post. While he was trying to fix the launcher, Whalen was hit three times: one bullet hit his body armor, another his Gerber tool and the third struck him in the left arm. Whalen dropped out of the turret and began first aid to stop the bleeding. At the same time, he recovered his radio and calmly called in close air support. When the engagement was over, Whalen insisted that all other wounded be evacuated first so he could keep control of the close air support. After two days in the hospital, he refused to stay and went back to the team to continue combat missions. For his actions, Technical Sergeant Whalen was awarded the Silver Star.

**Figure 2.10. Technical Sergeant Whalen on a Humvee in Afghanistan**

Courtesy of NMUSAF

2.23.4. The bombing of the Khobar Towers on 25 June, 1996 drove major changes in how we conduct Basic Military Training. Since that time, the United States Air Force has placed a strong emphasis on the preparation of our young airmen for combat. While the intense training has become longer it also has shifted to include a deployment phase. In 2005 this deployment phase, was called the BEAST and places the trainees in an environment similar to those they may experience once they deploy. In addition to tackling the BEAST, and the massive obstacle courses, other training includes defending and protecting their base of operations, directing search and recovery, basic self-aid and buddy care, they begin leadership training. As deployments continue our airmen are much more prepared in 2012 as a result of lessons learned at Khobar Towers.

**Figure 2.11. Senior Master Sergeant Colon-Lopez**

Courtesy of NMUSAF

2.23.5. Senior Master Sergeant Ramon Colon-Lopez, a pararescueman deployed to Afghanistan March 11, 2004 (Figure 2.11). He was part of an advanced force operations team and along with elements of the Afghan national strike unit to capture a high-value target—a drug king-pin who was funding terrorism—and to prevent the proliferation of chemical weapons. Colon-Lopez was on an operation in Afghanistan. Colon-Lopez was on the first of four helicopters, which took sustained small-arms fire and was seriously damaged as they landed. With rounds impacting all around him and unsure of the size of the enemy force, he pressed forward, overrunning enemy positions. His action suppressed enemy fire against the other three helicopters. Colon-Lopez and the team drove the enemy away. The raid resulted in two enemy kills, 10 enemy apprehensions and the destruction of rocket-propelled grenades and small caliber weapons. As a result of this action, he became one of the first six recipients of the Combat Action medal. Additionally he received the Bronze Star with Valor for his actions during the engagement.

2.23.6. Because of budget constraints the United States Air Force reduced size of the active-duty force in 2007, to roughly 64% of that of the United States Air Force at the end of the Gulf War in 1991. In 2008 the United States Air Force went from 360,000 active duty personnel to 330,000 personnel. Consequently crews flying training hours were also reduced.

2.23.7. In late January 2007, two United States Army Special Forces teams that included United States Air Force Combat Controllers Technical Sergeant Bryan Patton and Staff Sergeant David Orvosh responded to help Iraqi police in Najaf who tried to arrest what they thought were only 30 members of the fanatical "Soldiers of Heaven" sect. Instead they were ambushed by about 800 heavily-entrenched insurgents. A large battle ensued and Patton and Orvosh successfully brought in close air support that strafed and bombed the enemy. More help arrived and was quickly pinned down, which included Combat Controller Staff Sergeant Ryan Wallace (Figure 2.12). Thanks to Wallace and several others their actions would turn the tide of the battle. At a key time in the battle, Wallace called in a 500-lb laser-guided bomb against the enemy position 100 meters away ("danger close") and killed or stunned the 40 insurgents in the position. Then, at great risk to their lives Wallace and two others charged the position and killed the remaining enemy. About 370 insurgents were killed, mostly by air attack, and more than 400 were captured (including 14 high-value targets). The destruction of this strongpoint proved to be the turning point in the battle. The three Combat Controllers' actions were essential to victory in this battle.

**Figure 2.12. Staff Sergeant Ryan Wallace**

Courtesy of NMUSAF

2.23.8. The withdrawal of American military forces from Iraq has been a contentious issue within the United States since the beginning of the Iraq War. As the war has progressed from the initial 2003 invasion phase to a multi-year occupation, United States public opinion has turned in favor of troop withdrawal. In late April 2007, the United States Congress passed a supplementary spending bill for Iraq that set a deadline for troop withdrawal, but President Bush vetoed this bill soon afterwards. All United States Forces were mandated to withdraw from Iraqi territory by 31 December 2011 under the terms of a bilateral agreement signed in 2008 by President Bush. The United States troop withdrawal from Iraq was completed on 18 December 2011 early Sunday morning.

**Figure 2.13. Master Sergeant Delorean Sheridan**

Courtesy of USAF

2.23.9. In March 2013, Technical Sergeant Delorean Sheridan (Figure 2.13.) was completing a routine pre-brief for a combat control mission at his deployed location in Wardak Province, Afghanistan. While his team loaded gear into their vehicles, an Afghan National Police Officer suddenly turned and opened fire with a truck-mounted machine gun 25 feet away. Simultaneously, 15 to 20 insurgents just outside the village engaged the base with heavy machine gunfire. With rounds striking and killing his teammates surrounding him, Technical Sergeant Sheridan closed in on the gunman with a pistol and M-4 Rifle, neutralizing the immediate threat with deadly accuracy. Still under heavy attack from outside insurgents, Technical Sergeant Sheridan exposed himself to heavy machine gunfire three more times to drag his wounded teammates out of the line of fire to a protected casualty collection point. Once his wounded teammates were pulled to safety, Technical Sergeant Sheridan directed close air support and surveillance aircraft to pinpoint, engage and eliminate the additional insurgents. During these efforts, Technical Sergeant Sheridan also aided in assessing and moving his wounded teammates, while directing the entrance and exit of six medical evacuation helicopters. Sergeant Sheridan's calmness and leadership in the face of danger helped saved 23 lives and allowed for the evacuation of his critically wounded teammates. For these actions, Technical Sergeant Sheridan was awarded the Silver Star. He also received one of the Air Force's most prestigious awards, the 2013 Lance P. Sijan United States Air Force Leadership Award. Lastly he was selected as one of the 12 Outstanding Airmen of the Year for 2014.

2.23.10. For most United States and NATO forces, the war in Afghanistan will be over by the end of 2014. The mission of roughly 300 American airmen could continue for years after the 12-year-old war is technically over. Those Airmen are helping stand up the Afghan air force, and their mission is expected to continue until the Afghan air force becomes fully independent in 2017. President Obama announced on 19 August 2014 that he planned to withdraw the last American troops from Afghanistan by the end of 2016. Under a new timetable the 32,000 American troops now in Afghanistan would be reduced to 9,800 after this year (2014). That number would be cut in half by the end of 2015, and by the end of 2016, there would be only a vestigial force to protect the embassy in Kabul and to help the Afghans with military purchases and other security matters. At the height of American involvement, in 2011, the United States had 101,000 troops in the country. Besides carrying out operations against the remnants of Al Qaeda, the troops that stay behind will train Afghan security forces. But from 2015 onward, they will be quartered at Bagram Airfield and in Kabul, the capital. While they will be supplemented by NATO troops, alliance members should follow America's lead in pulling out by the end of 2016. The shift in focus is from Al Qaeda in Afghanistan and Pakistan to Al Qaeda threats that have sprung up from Syria to Nigeria. We will go from the United States-led Operation ENDURING FREEDOM to NATO's Operation RESOLUTE SUPPORT.

2.23.11. The Air Force Cross is awarded to United States and Foreign military personnel and civilians who have displayed extraordinary heroism in one of the following situations: while engaged in action against a U.S. enemy, while engaged in military operations involving conflict with a foreign force, or while serving with a Friendly nation engaged in armed conflict against a force in which the United States is not a belligerent party. The Air Force Cross is awarded when the heroic actions fall just short of warranting the Congressional Medal of Honor. A complete listing of recipients with a brief, chronological       account       of       their       heroic       events       leading       to       their       decoration       is       located       at http://afehri.maxwell.af.mil/pages/afcross/afcross.htm

## 2.24. Conclusion.

From the skies over the Rio Grande to those over Iraq and Afghanistan nearly 100 years later, air power has evolved from an ineffective oddity to the dominant form of military might in the world. The applications and effectiveness have increased with each succeeding conflict; in World War I air power played a minor role, and in Kosovo the only role. This chapter looked at the development of air power through the nation's many conflicts and just a few of the many contributions of enlisted personnel.

**Chapter 3**

**ORGANIZATION**

*Section 3A—Overview*

### 3.1. Introduction.

The Armed Forces of the United States are not separate and independent parts of the government; rather, they compose one of the instruments of national policy. Since the birth of the Nation, policies and directives have been made by civilians assigned to the military and to the executive and legislative branches of the government. Military leaders do not make national military policy decisions. Civilian leadership is a key concept in the military organization, beginning with the President's role as Commander in Chief. This chapter begins with a discussion of the President's role. The chapter highlights the structure of the Department of Defense and defines the roles of the military departments, Joint Chiefs of Staff, unified combatant commands, and combined commands. Finally, this chapter emphasizes the key elements of the Department of the Air Force, focuses on force structure and major commands, and includes a discussion about the structure and functions of the various lower levels of command and Air Reserve Components.

*Section 3B—Command Authority and Department of Defense*

### 3.2. Commander in Chief.

The United States Constitution establishes the basic principle of civilian control of the Armed Forces. As Commander in Chief, the President has final command authority. However, as head of the executive branch, he is subject to the checks and balances system of the legislative and judicial branches.

### 3.3. Department of Defense.

Established by the National Security Act of 1947, the Department of Defense's function is to maintain and employ Armed Forces. The Department of Defense includes the Office of the Secretary of Defense; the Joint Chiefs of Staff; the Joint Staff; and the Departments of the Army, Navy (including the United States Marine Corps), and Air Force. Furthermore, the Department of Defense includes the unified combatant commands and forces dedicated to combined commands, defense agencies, and Department of Defense field activities. As the civilian head of the Department of Defense, the Secretary of Defense reports directly to the President.

### 3.4. Secretary of Defense.

The President appoints the Secretary of Defense with the advice and consent of the Senate. The Secretary of Defense serves as principal defense policy advisor to the President and is responsible for the formulation of general defense policy, policy related to all matters of direct and primary concern to the Department of Defense, and for the execution of approved policy. The operational chain of command runs from the President to the Secretary of Defense to the combatant commanders. A specific responsibility of the Secretary of Defense is providing written policy guidance for Department of Defense component chief's use to prepare and review program recommendations and budget proposals. The Secretary's guidance includes national security objectives and policies, military mission priorities, and the projected levels for available resources. The Secretary of Defense also provides the Chairman, Joint Chiefs of Staff with written policy guidance to prepare and review contingency plans. The Secretaries of the military departments and the commanders of the combatant commands are provided written guidelines to direct the effective detection and monitoring of all potential aerial and maritime threats to the national security of the United States.

#### 3.4.1. The Armed Forces Policy Council.

The Armed Forces Policy Council assists in matters requiring a long-range view and in formulating broad defense policy. The council advises the Secretary of Defense on matters of broad policy and reports on other matters as requested. The council consists of the Secretary of Defense (Chairman); the Deputy Secretary of Defense; Secretaries of the Army, Navy, and Air Force; the Chairman, Joint Chiefs of Staff; Under Secretaries of Defense for Policy and for Acquisition, Technology, and Logistics; the Deputy under Secretary of Defense for Acquisition and Technology; and the four service chiefs. Sometimes other departments and agencies in the executive branch are invited to attend specific meetings.

#### 3.4.2. Under Secretaries of Defense.

There are five Under Secretaries of Defense (Policy; Comptroller; Personnel and Readiness; Acquisition, Technology and Logistics; and Intelligence) who assist the Secretary of Defense. The Secretary of Defense receives staff assistance through a number of special agencies, such as the Defense Threat Reduction Agency, Security Service, and Defense Logistics Agency, which provide special skills, expertise, and advice.

## 3.5. Chairman, Joint Chiefs of Staff.

Appointed by the President, by and with the advice and consent of the Senate, the Chairman, Joint Chiefs of Staff is selected from the officers of the regular components of the Armed Forces. The Chairman, while so serving, holds the grade of general or, in the case of the Navy, holds the grade of admiral, and outranks all other officers of the Armed Forces. However, the Chairman may not exercise military command over the Joint Chiefs of Staff or any of the Armed Forces. The operational chain of command runs from the President to the Secretary of Defense to the combatant commanders. However, a provision of the Goldwater-Nichols Department of Defense Reorganization Act of 1986 permits the President to authorize communications through the Chairman, Joint Chiefs of Staff. Consequently, DoDD 5100.01, *Functions of the Department of Defense and Its Major Components,* places the Chairman, Joint Chiefs of Staff in the communications chain of command. The Chairman, Joint Chiefs of Staff is the principal military advisor to the President, the National Security Council, and the Secretary of Defense. Further, the Secretary of Defense may assign responsibility for overseeing the activities of the combatant commands to the Chairman, Joint Chiefs of Staff.

### 3.5.1. Vice Chairman, Joint Chiefs of Staff.

The Vice Chairman, appointed by the President, by and with the advice and consent of the Senate, is a member of the Joint Chiefs of Staff, and performs such duties as prescribed by the Chairman, with the approval of the Secretary of Defense. The Vice Chairman cannot be from the same Uniformed Service as the Chairman, and serves a tour of 2 years and may be reappointed for two additional terms. The Vice Chairman serves as the Acting Chairman in the absence, vacancy or disability of the Chairman.

### 3.5.2. Senior Enlisted Advisor to the Chairman.

Senior Enlisted Advisor to the Chairman (SEAC) is a military position within the United States Department of Defense and is designated the senior noncommissioned officer in the United States Armed Forces. The SEAC is appointed by the Chairman of the Joint Chiefs of Staff (CJCS) to serve as an advisor to the Chairman and the Secretary of Defense on all matters involving joint and combined total force integration, utilization, health of the force, and joint development for enlisted personnel. The SEAC also serves as a spokesperson to leaders and organizations on applicable issues affecting the total enlisted force

## 3.6. Joint Chiefs of Staff:

3.6.1. Subject to the authority, direction, and control of the President and the Secretary of Defense, members of the Joint Chiefs of Staff serve as advisors to the President, Secretary of Defense, and the National Security Council. They provide the strategic direction of the Armed Forces. They review major materiel and personnel requirements of the Armed Forces according to strategic and logistic requirements and establish joint doctrine. Members of the Joint Chiefs of Staff are also responsible for the assignment of logistic responsibilities to the military services, formulation of policies for joint training, and coordination of military education.

3.6.2. Members of the Joint Chiefs of Staff are the Chairman, Joint Chiefs of Staff; Vice Chairman, Joint Chiefs of Staff; Chief of Staff, United States Army; Chief of Naval Operations; Chief of Staff, United States Air Force; Commandant of the Marine Corps; and Chief of the National Guard Bureau. The Chairman, Joint Chiefs of Staff presides over the Joint Chiefs of Staff and furnishes the recommendations and views of the Joint Chiefs of Staff to the President, National Security Council, or the Secretary of Defense. Other members of the Joint Chiefs of Staff may also provide advice to these bodies, when requested. If a member disagrees with an opinion of the Chairman, Joint Chiefs of Staff, the Chairman, Joint Chiefs of Staff must present this advice in addition to his or her own. For the service chiefs (United States Army, Chief of Naval Operations, Chief of Staff, United States Air Force, Commandant of the Marine Corps), their Joint Chiefs of Staff duties take precedence over all other duties. Consequently, as the military heads of their respective services, Joint Chiefs of Staff members delegate many duties to their vice chiefs of staff while retaining overall responsibility.

## 3.7. Joint Staff.

The Joint Staff assists members of the Joint Chiefs of Staff in carrying out their assigned responsibilities of strategic direction, unified operation of combatant commands, and the integration of all land, naval, and air forces into an efficient force. By law, the direction of the Joint Staff rests exclusively with the Chairman, Joint Chiefs of Staff. The Chairman normally manages the Joint Staff through the Director of the Joint Staff. The Director of the Joint Staff is selected by the Chairman, after consultation with other members of the Joint Chiefs of Staff and with the approval of the Secretary of Defense. The staff's more than 1,500 military and civilian personnel are composed of approximately equal numbers of officers from the Army, Navy, and Air Force. Marines make up about 20 percent of the number allocated to the Navy. The Joint Staff is prohibited from functioning as a General Staff, and has no executive authority.

## 3.8. Unified Combatant Commands and Combined Commands:

### 3.8.1. Unified Combatant Commands.

The President, assisted by the Chairman, Joint Chiefs of Staff through the Secretary of Defense, establishes unified combatant commands for the performance of military missions. The Secretary of Defense assigns military missions through the Unified Command Plan. A unified combatant command has a broad, continuing mission and is composed of forces from two or more military departments. The combatant commander deploys, directs, controls, and coordinates the action of the command's forces; conducts joint training exercises; and controls certain support functions. Combatant commanders are responsible to both the Secretary of Defense and the President. Unified combatant commands are organized geographically or functionally. Geographic unified combatant commands include the United States European Command, United States Pacific Command, United States Northern Command, United States Southern Command, and the United States Central Command. Functional Unified Combatant Commands include the United States Special Operations Command, United States Transportation Command, and United States Strategic Command. Once assigned to a unified combatant commands by the Secretary of Defense, a force cannot be transferred except by authority of the Secretary of Defense or under special procedures of the Secretary of Defense office with the approval of the President. All units assigned to a unified combatant command remain under the combatant command authority of the unified combatant command commander and the administrative control authority of the respective Service Component Commander.

### 3.8.2. Combined Commands.

Combined commands consist of forces from more than one allied nation. Since combined commands are binational or multinational, their missions and responsibilities (including command responsibilities) must establish, assign, and conform to binational and multinational agreements. Normally a combined command operates under the terms of a treaty, alliance, or bilateral agreement between or among the nations concerned. The North American Aerospace Defense Command, Combined Forces Command Korea, and Allied Command Operations are examples of multinational commands.

## 3.9. Military Departments.

The military departments consist of the Army, Navy (including the Marine Corps and, in wartime, the Coast Guard), and the Air Force. The Service Secretaries are responsible for providing efficiently organized, trained, and equipped forces to the combatant commanders. Although operational command of the forces rests with the combatant commanders under the direction of the Secretary of Defense, the Service Secretaries assist the Secretary of Defense in managing the administrative, training, and logistic functions of the military departments. Except in operational matters, the Secretary of Defense can issue orders to a Service through their Secretary. Each Service develops and trains their forces to perform functions that support the efforts of other Services to accomplish the overall military objectives. The military departments share general and specific functions as outlined below, and the Air Force has primary functions designed to support the general and specific functions of the military departments.

### 3.9.1. General Functions.

The traditional roles and mission of each branch of Service are commonly referred to as functions. Besides specific combat roles, they furnish operational forces to unified commands. The Secretary of Defense and the Joint Chiefs of Staff established the functions of each branch of the Armed Forces in the Key West Agreement of 1948. The Key West Agreement was revised in 1953 and again in 1958. The general functions of the Armed Forces are to:

3.9.1.1. Support and defend the United States Constitution against all enemies, foreign and domestic.

3.9.1.2. Ensure, by timely and effective military action, the security of the United States, its possessions, and areas vital to its interests.

3.9.1.3. Uphold and advance the national policies and interests of the United States.

### 3.9.2. Specific Functions.

Along with general functions, military departments also have some specific functions they share. These include, but are not limited to:

3.9.2.1. Preparing forces and establishing reserves of personnel, equipment, and supplies for effective prosecution of war and military operations short of war, and planning for the expansion of peacetime components to meet the needs of war.

3.9.2.2. Maintaining, in readiness, mobile reserve forces properly organized, trained, and equipped for deployment in an emergency.

3.9.2.3. Preparing and submitting to the Secretary of Defense budgets for their respective departments, and justifying (before Congress) budget requests as approved by the Secretary of Defense.

3.9.2.4. Administering the funds made available for maintaining, equipping, and training the forces of their respective departments, including those assigned to unified commands.

3.9.2.5. Assisting each other in accomplishing their respective functions, including the provision of personnel, intelligence, training, facilities, equipment, supplies, and services.

*Section 3C—Department of the Air Force*

### 3.10. Overview.

Headquarters Air Force and the field units (identified in paragraph 3.17) comprise the Department of the Air Force. They are responsible for preparing the air, space and cyber forces necessary for the effective prosecution of war and military operations short of war for the expansion of the peacetime components of the Air Force to meet the needs of war.

### 3.11. Primary Functions of the Air Force.

The primary functions of the Air Force include, but are not limited to the following:

3.11.1. Organize, train, equip, and provide forces for the conduct of prompt and sustained combat operations in the air and space—specifically, forces to defend the United States against air and space attack, gain and maintain air and space supremacy, defeat enemy air and space forces, and conduct space operations.

3.11.2. Organize, train, equip, and provide forces for strategic air and missile warfare.

3.11.3. Organize, equip, and provide forces for joint amphibious, space, and airborne operations, in coordination with the other military Services, and provide for their training according to joint doctrines.

3.11.4. Organize, train, equip, and provide forces for close air support and air logistic support to the Army and other forces, as directed, including airlift, air support, resupply of airborne operations, aerial photography, tactical air reconnaissance, and air interdiction of enemy land forces and communications.

3.11.5. Organize, train, equip, and provide forces, as directed, to operate air and space lines of communications.

3.11.6. Organize, train, equip, and provide forces for the support and conduct of psychological operations.

3.11.7. Provide equipment, forces, procedures, and doctrine necessary for effective electronic warfare operations.

### 3.12. Secretary of the Air Force.

The Secretary of the Air Force is a civilian appointed by the President, by and with the advice and consent of the Senate. The Secretary of the Air Force is the head of the Department of the Air Force and is subject to the authority, control, and direction of the Secretary of Defense. The Secretary of the Air Force is responsible for recruiting, organizing, supplying, equipping (including research and development), training, servicing, mobilizing, demobilizing, and administering personnel (morale and welfare programs); maintaining, constructing, outfitting, and repairing military equipment; constructing, maintaining, and repairing buildings, structures, and utilities; and acquiring real property and interests in real property necessary to carry out the responsibilities specified in Title 10, United States Code, Section 8013.

### 3.13. Chief of Staff, United States Air Force.

The Chief of Staff, United States Air Force is an Air Force general officer appointed for 4 years by the President, by and with the advice and consent of the Senate. The Chief of Staff, United States Air Force is subject to the authority, direction, and control of the Secretary of the Air Force, and presides over the Air Staff. The Chief of Staff, United States Air Force acts as an agent in carrying out Air Staff approved recommendations or plans by the Secretary of the Air Force; exercises supervision consistent with the authority assigned to commanders of unified or specified combatant commands and organizations of the Air Force as the Secretary determines. The Chief of Staff, United States Air Force is a member of the Joint Chiefs of Staff and informs the Secretary of the Air Force regarding military advice rendered by the Joint Chiefs of Staff on matters affecting the Department of the Air Force to the extent that such action does not impair the independence of the Chief of Staff in the performance of his duties as a member of the Joint Chiefs of Staff.

### 3.14. Headquarters United States Air Force.

The headquarters of the Air Force consists of two major entities: the Secretariat (including the Secretary of the Air Force and the Secretary's principal staff) and the Air Staff headed by the Chief of Staff.

### 3.15. Air Staff.

The function of the Air Staff is to assist the Secretary of the Air Force in carrying out his or her responsibilities. The Air Staff is composed of the following: (1) Chief of Staff, (2) Vice Chief of Staff, (3) Deputy Chiefs of Staff, (4) Assistant Chiefs of Staff, (5) Surgeon General of the Air Force, (6) The Judge Advocate General of the Air Force, (7) Chief of the Air Force Reserve, (8) other members of the Air Force assigned or detailed to the Air Staff, and (9) civilian employees in the Department of the Air Force assigned or detailed to the Air Staff.

### 3.16. Air National Guard.

The National Guard Bureau is a joint activity of the Department of Defense, located in the Pentagon. The Air National Guard is one of the seven Reserve components of the United States Armed Forces that augment the active components in the performance of their missions. **Note:** The Air National Guard is not a major command, but is a component of the Total Force in offensive, defensive, and relief operations.

#### 3.16.1. Mission.

The Air National Guard has both a federal and state mission. The dual mission, a provision of the United States Constitution, results in each guardsman holding membership in the National Guard of his or her state and in the National Guard of the United States.

#### 3.16.2. Federal Mission.

The Air National Guard's federal mission is to maintain well-trained, well-equipped units available for prompt mobilization during war and provide assistance during national emergencies (such as natural disasters or civil disturbances). During peacetime, the combat-ready units and support units are assigned to most Air Force major commands to carry out missions compatible with training, mobilization readiness, humanitarian and contingency operations such as Operation Enduring Freedom in Afghanistan.

#### 3.16.3. State Mission.

When Air National Guard units are not mobilized or under federal control, they report to the governor of their respective state, territory (Puerto Rico, Guam, Virgin Islands) or the commanding general of the District of Columbia National Guard. Each of the 54 National Guard organizations is supervised by the adjutant general of the state or territory. Under state law, the Air National Guard provides protection of life, property and preserves peace, order and public safety. These missions are accomplished through emergency relief support during natural disasters such as floods, earthquakes and forest fires; search and rescue operations; support to civil defense authorities; maintenance of vital public services and counterdrug operations.

#### 3.16.4. Force Structure.

The primary sources of full-time support for Air National Guard units are the dual-status military technician and Active Guard and Reserve personnel. These people perform day-to-day organization, administration, recruitment, instruction, training and maintenance support to the unit. By law, dual-status military technicians are civil service employees of the federal government who must be military members of the unit that employs them. Technicians train with the unit and are mobilized with the unit when federalized. Active Guard and Reserve serve under the command authority of their respective state or territorial governors until mobilized for federal duty. The Air National Guard has more than 105,000 officers and enlisted people who serve in 90 flying units and 579 mission support units.

### 3.17. Field Units.

The Department of the Air Force field units includes major commands, field operating agencies, and direct reporting units.

#### 3.17.1. Major Commands.

The Air Force is organized functionally in the United States and geographically overseas. A major command represents a major Air Force subdivision having a specific portion of the Air Force mission. Each major command is directly subordinate to headquarters United States Air Force. Major commands are interrelated and complementary, providing offensive, defensive, and support elements. An operational command consists (in whole or in part) of strategic, tactical, space, or defense forces, or of flying forces that directly support such forces. A support command may provide supplies, weapon systems, support systems, operational support equipment, combat material, maintenance, surface transportation, education and training, or special services and other supported organizations. The major commands in the United States Air Force include:

**3.17.1.1. Air Combat Command (ACC).** Air Combat Command, with headquarters at Langley Air Force Base Virginia, was created 1 June 1992, which combined its predecessors, Strategic Air Command and Tactical Air Command.

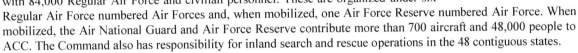

**3.17.1.1.1. Mission.** To support global implementation of national security strategy, ACC operates fighter, reconnaissance, battle-management and electronic-combat aircraft. ACC also provides command, control, communications and intelligence systems, and conducts global information operations.

**3.17.1.1.2. Personnel and Resources.** The command operates more than 1,300 aircraft, 34 wings, 25 bases, and has more than 230 worldwide operating locations with 84,000 Regular Air Force and civilian personnel. These are organized under six Regular Air Force numbered Air Forces and, when mobilized, one Air Force Reserve numbered Air Force. When mobilized, the Air National Guard and Air Force Reserve contribute more than 700 aircraft and 48,000 people to ACC. The Command also has responsibility for inland search and rescue operations in the 48 contiguous states.

**3.17.1.1.3. Organization.** As a force provider and Combat Air Forces lead agent, ACC organizes, trains, equips and maintains combat-ready forces for rapid deployment and employment while ensuring strategic air defense forces are ready to meet the challenges of peacetime air sovereignty and wartime air defense. Additionally, ACC develops strategy, doctrine, concepts, tactics, and procedures for air and space-power employment. The command provides conventional and information warfare forces to all unified commands to ensure air, space and information superiority for warfighters and national decision-makers. The command can also be called upon to assist national agencies with intelligence, surveillance and reconnaissance capabilities. ACC numbered Air Forces provide the air component to United States Central, Southern and Northern Commands. ACC also augments forces to United States European, Pacific, Africa-based and Strategic Commands.

**3.17.1.2. Air Mobility Command (AMC). Air Mobility Command,** with headquarters at Scott Air Force Base Illinois, was created 1 June 1992. AMC, the Air Force component to United States Transportation Command, provides America's global reach. This rapid, flexible, and responsive air mobility promotes stability in regions by keeping America's capability and character highly visible.

**3.17.1.2.1. Mission:** Air Mobility Command's is to provide global air mobility ... right effects, right place, right time. The command also plays a crucial role in providing humanitarian support at home and around the world. AMC Airmen— Regular Air Force, Air National Guard, Air Force Reserve and civilians—provide airlift and aerial refueling for all of America's armed forces. Many special duty and operational support aircraft and stateside aeromedical evacuation missions are also assigned to AMC. United States forces must be able to provide a rapid, tailored response with a capability to intervene against a well-equipped foe, hit hard and terminate quickly. Rapid global mobility lies at the heart of United States strategy in this environment, without the capability to project forces, there is no conventional deterrent. As United States forces stationed overseas continue to decline, global interests remain, making the unique capabilities only AMC can provide even more in demand.

**3.17.1.2.2. Personnel and Resources.** AMC has nearly 136,000 Regular Air Force and Air Reserve Component military and civilian personnel. AMC's mobility aircraft include the C-5 Galaxy, KC-10 Extender, C-17 Globemaster III, C-130 Hercules and KC-135 Stratotanker. Operational support aircraft are the VC-25 (Air Force One), C-9, C-20, C-21, C-32, C-37, C-40 and UH-1.

**3.17.1.2.3. Organization.** AMC has one numbered Air Force, the 18th Air Force, with headquarters at Scott Air Force Base, is charged with tasking and executing all air mobility missions. Units reporting to 18th Air Force include all AMC wings and groups based in the continental United States, as well as two expeditionary mobility task forces, the 15th Expeditionary Mobility Task Force at Travis Air Force Base, California and the 21st Expeditionary Mobility Task Force at McGuire AFB, New Jersey. The 15th and 21st Expeditionary Mobility Task Forces serve as lead agencies for conducting mobility operations worldwide. They are key to the execution phase of war fighting by providing worldwide expeditionary mobility support.

3.17.1.2.3.1. The 618th Tanker Airlift Control Center, located at Scott Air Force Base, also reports to 18th Air Force and serves as the organization's air operations hub, planning and directing tanker and transport aircraft operations around the world.

3.17.1.2.3.2. AMC's Regular Air Force bases are: Joint Base Charleston, South Carolina.; Dover Air Force Base, Delaware.; Fairchild Air Force Base, Washington.; Grand Forks Air Force Base, North Dakota.; Little Rock Air

Force Base, Arkansas.; MacDill Air Force Base, Florida.; McChord Air Force Base, Washington; McConnell Air Force Base, Kansas; McGuire Air Force Base, New Jersey; Pope Field, North Carolina.; Scott Air Force Base, Illinois; and Travis Air Force Base, California. In addition, the 89th Airlift Wing at Joint Base Andrews, Maryland; the 19th Air Refueling Group at Robins Air Force Base, Georgia; and the 317th Airlift Group at Dyess Air Force Base, Texas, are assigned to AMC.

3.17.1.2.3.3. The U.S. Air Force Expeditionary Center is the Air Force's Center of Excellence for advanced mobility and combat support training and education. Located at Joint Base McGuire-Dix-Lakehurst, N.J., the center also has direct oversight for en route and installation support, contingency response and partner capacity-building mission sets within the global mobility enterprise. The center provides administrative control for six wings and two groups within Air Mobility Command, to include the 87th Air Base Wing and the 621 Contingency Response Wing at Joint Base McGuire-Dix-Lakehurst; the 515 Air Mobility Operations Wing at Joint Base Pearl Harbor-Hickam, Hawaii; the 521 Air Mobility Operations Wing at Ramstein AFB, Germany; the 628th Air Base Wing at Joint Base Charleston, S.C.; the 43rd Air Mobility Operations Group at Pope Field, N.C.; and 627th Air Base Group at Joint Base Lewis-McChord, Washinton.

3.17.1.3. **Air Force Space Command (AFSPC).** Air Force Space Command, activated 1 September 1982, is headquartered at Peterson Air Force Base Colorado. AFSPC provides military-focused space and cyberspace capabilities with a global perspective to the joint warfighting team. AFSPC organizes, equips, trains and maintains mission-ready space and cyberspace forces and capabilities for North American Aerospace Defense Command, United States Strategic Command and other combatant commands around the world.

3.17.1.3.1. **Mission.** Provide resilient and affordable space and cyberspace capabilities for the Joint Force and the Nation.

3.17.1.3.2. **Personnel and Resources.** The command comprises approximately 38,000 space and cyberspace professionals assigned to 134 locations worldwide. AFSPC acquires, operates and supports the Global Positioning System, Defense Satellite Communications System, Defense Meteorological Satellite Program, Defense Support Program, Wideband Global SATCOM system, Milstar satellite communications system, Advanced Extremely High Frequency system, Global Broadcast Service, the Space-Based Infrared System, Geosynchronous Space Situational Awareness Program and the Space Based Space Surveillance satellite. AFSPC's launch operations include the Eastern and Western ranges and range support for all launches. The command maintains and operates a worldwide network of satellite tracking stations, called the Air Force Satellite Control Network, to provide communications links to satellites.

3.17.1.3.2.1. Ground-based radars used primarily for ballistic missile warning include the Ballistic Missile Early Warning System, Upgraded Early Warning Radar System, PAVE Phased Array Warning System and Perimeter Acquisition Radar Attack Characterization System. The Maui Optical Tracking Identification Facility, Ground-based Electro-Optical Deep Space Surveillance System, phased-array and mechanical radars provide primary space surveillance coverage. New transformational space programs are continuously being researched and developed to enable AFSPC to stay on the leading-edge of technology.

3.17.1.3.3. **Organization.** Fourteenth Air Force is located at Vandenberg Air Force Base, California, and provides space capabilities for the joint fight through the operational missions of spacelift; position, navigation and timing; satellite communications; missile warning and space control.

3.17.1.3.3.1. Twenty-fourth Air Force is located at Joint Base San Antonio - Lackland, Texas, and its mission is to provide combatant commanders with trained and ready cyber forces which plan and conduct cyberspace operations. The command extends, operates, maintains and defends its assigned portions of the Department of Defense network to provide capabilities in, through and from cyberspace.

3.17.1.3.3.2. The Space and Missile Systems Center at Los Angeles Air Force Base, California, designs and acquires all Air Force and most Department of Defense space systems. It oversees launches, completes on-orbit checkouts and then turns systems over to user agencies. It supports the Program Executive Office for Space on the Global Positioning, Defense Satellite Communications and MILSTAR systems. Space and Missile Systems Center also supports the Evolved Expendable Launch Vehicle, Defense Meteorological Satellite and Defense Support programs and the Space-Based Infrared System.

3.17.1.3.3.3. The Air Force Network Integration Center at Scott Air Force Base, Illinois, is the Air Force's premier organization for Air Force network integration, cyber simulation, and network standards, architecture and engineering services. Through these specialized technical services, Air Force Network Integration Center supports the nation's warfighters with decisive cyber capabilities for mission success.

3.17.1.3.3.4. The Air Force Spectrum Management Office, located in Fort Meade, Maryland, is responsible for planning, providing and preserving access to the electromagnetic spectrum for the Air Force and selected Department of Defense activities in support of national policy objectives, systems development and global operations. Air Force Spectrum Management Office defends and articulates Air Force spectrum access to regulatory agencies at the joint, national and international levels, and is responsible for all Air Force spectrum management-related matters, policy and procedures. Additionally, the agency oversees the Air Force spectrum management career field and manages the payment of the approximately $4 million Air Force spectrum fee each year.

3.17.1.3.3.5. AFSPC major installations include: Schriever, Peterson and Buckley Air Force Bases in Colorado; Los Angeles and Vandenberg Air Force Bases in California; and Patrick Air Force Base in Florida. Major AFSPC units also reside on bases managed by other commands in New Mexico, Texas, Illinois, Virginia and Georgia. AFSPC manages many smaller installations and geographically separated units in Massachusetts, North Dakota, Alaska, Hawaii and across the globe.

3.17.1.4. **Pacific Air Forces (PACAF).** Pacific Air Forces is headquartered at Joint Base Pearl Harbor-Hickam, Hawaii. When the North Koreans crossed the 38th parallel on 25 June 1950, Far East Air Forces consisted of 5th Air Force, 13th Air Force, 20th Air Force, and the Far East Materiel Command. Four years after the Korean War armistice, Far East Air Forces was redesignated as PACAF and the headquarters transferred to Hickam Air Force Base.

3.17.1.4.1. **Mission.** PACAF's primary mission is to provide United States Pacific Command integrated expeditionary Air Force capabilities to defend the Homeland, promote stability, dissuade/deter aggression, and swiftly defeat enemies. PACAF delivers rapid and precise air, space, and cyberspace capabilities to protect and defend the United States, its territories and our allies and partners; provides integrated air and missile warning and defense; promotes interoperability throughout the area of responsibility; maintains strategic access and freedom of movement across all domains; and is postured to respond across the full spectrum of military contingencies in order to restore regional security.

3.17.1.4.2. **Personnel and Resources.** The command has approximately 45,000 military and civilian personnel serving in nine strategic locations and numerous smaller facilities, primarily in Hawaii, Alaska, Japan, Guam and the Republic of Korea. Approximately 340 fighter and attack aircraft are assigned to the command with approximately 100 additional deployed aircraft rotating on Guam. PACAF is home to three of the seven F-22 fighter squadrons currently programmed, and is already home to the only two C-17 units based outside the continental United States. PACAF's Airmen are postured to deploy at any given time in support of the Overseas Contingency Operations, many participating in non-traditional missions such as convoy and detainee operations.

3.17.1.4.3. **Organization.** PACAF's major units are 5th Air Force, Yokota Air Base, Japan; 7th Air Force, Osan Air Base, Republic of Korea; 11th Air Force, and Elmendorf Air Force Base, Alaska. Major units also include 374th Airlift Wing, Yokota Air Base, Japan; 35th Fighter Wing, Misawa Air Base, Japan; 18th Wing, Kadena Air Base, Japan (Okinawa); 51st Fighter Wing, Osan Air Base, Republic of Korea; 8th Fighter Wing, Kunsan Air Base, Republic of Korea; 3d Wing, Joint Base Elmendorf-Richardson, Alaska; 354th Fighter Wing, Eielson Air Force Base, Alaska; 673d Air Base Wing, Joint Base Elmendorf-Richardson, Alaska; 15th Airlift Wing, Hickam Air Force Base, Hawaii; and the 36th Wing, Andersen Air Force Base, Guam.

3.17.1.5. **United States Air Forces in Europe (USAFE).** United States Air Forces in Europe is headquartered at Ramstein Air Base Germany. USAFE originated as the 8th Air Force in 1942 and flew heavy bombardment missions over the European continent during World War II. In August 1945, the command was given its current name, United States Air Forces in Europe.

3.17.1.5.1. **Mission.** As the air component for both United States European Command and United States Africa Command, USAFE-Air Forces Africa executes the Air Force, United States European Command and United States Africa Command missions with forward-based airpower and infrastructure to conduct and enable theater and global operations. USAFE-Air Force Africa directs air operations in a theater spanning three continents, covering more than 15 million square miles, containing 104 independent states, and possessing more than one-fifth of the world's population and more than a quarter of the world's gross domestic product.

3.17.1.5.2. **Personnel and Resources.** More than 35,000 Regular Air Force, Reserve, Air National Guard and civilian employees are assigned to USAFE-Air Forces Africa. Equipment assets include about 217 fighter, attack, rotary wing, tanker, and transport aircraft, and a full complement of conventional weapons.

3.17.1.5.3. **Organization.** USAFE-Air Forces Africa consists of one numbered Air Force, seven main operating bases and 114 geographically separated locations. Third Air Force supports United States European Command and United States Africa Command as the component numbered Air Force responsible for maintaining continuous theater-wide situational awareness and providing the commander of Air Force forces here the capability to command and control assigned and attached Airmen. The USAFE-Air Force Africa main operating bases are: Royal Air Force Lakenheath and Royal Air Force Mildenhall in the United Kingdom; Ramstein and Spangdahlem Air Bases in Germany; Aviano Air Base, Italy; Lajes Field in the Azores; and Incirlik Air Base, Turkey. These bases report to Third Air Force for day-to-day and contingency operations.

3.17.1.6. **Air Education and Training Command (AETC).** Air Education and Training Command, with headquarters at Joint Base San Antonio-Randolph Texas, was established 1 July 1993, with the realignment of Air Training Command and Air University. AETC's role makes it the first command to touch the life of almost every Air Force member. The 2005 Base Realignment and Closure plan renamed Randolph Air Force Base, Joint Base San Antonio-Randolph.

3.17.1.6.1. **Mission.** Recruit, train and educate Airmen to deliver airpower for America. We take America's sons and daughters – young men and women who have volunteered to serve their country in a time of war – and develop them into Airmen. Develop denotes more than educating or training them – it implies bringing them to embrace our culture, teaching them (by our example) our core values of integrity, service before self and excellence in all we do.

3.17.1.6.2. **Personnel and Resources.** More than 28,000 Regular Air Force members 6,500 Air National Guard and Air Force Reserve personnel, and 14,000 civilian personnel make up AETC. The command also has more than 10,000 contractors assigned. AETC flies approximately 1,390 aircraft.

3.17.1.6.3. **Organization.** AETC includes Air Force Recruiting Service, two numbered Air Forces and the Air University. The command operates 12 major installations and supports tenant units on numerous bases across the globe. There are also 16 Regular Air Force and seven Reserve wings.

3.17.1.7. **Air Force Materiel Command (AFMC).** Air Force Materiel Command, headquartered at Wright-Patterson Air Force Base, Ohio, is a major command created July 1, 1992. The command conducts research, development, test and evaluation, and provides acquisition management services and logistics support necessary to keep Air Force weapon systems ready for war.

3.17.1.7.1. **Mission.** AFMC equips the Air Force for world-dominant airpower. AFMC delivers war-winning expeditionary capabilities to the warfighter through development and transition of technology, professional acquisition management, exacting test and evaluation, and world-class sustainment of all Air Force weapon systems. From cradle-to-grave, AFMC provides the work force and infrastructure necessary to ensure the United States remains the world's most respected Air and Space Force.

3.17.1.7.2. **Personnel and Resources.** AFMC employs a highly professional and skilled command work force of some 80,000 military and civilian employees.

3.17.1.7.3. **Organization.** AFMC fulfills its mission of equipping the Air Force with the best weapon systems through the Air Force Research Laboratory and several unique centers which are responsible for the "cradle-to-grave" oversight for aircraft, electronic systems, missiles and munitions.

3.17.1.8. **Air Force Special Operations Command (AFSOC).** Air Force Special Operations Command, headquartered at Hurlburt Field Florida, was established 22 May 1990. AFSOC is the Air Force component of United States Special Operations Command.

**3.17.1.8.1. Mission.** AFSOC provides Air Force special operations forces for worldwide deployment and assignment to regional unified commands. The command's special operation forces are composed of highly trained, rapidly deployable Airmen, conducting global special operations missions ranging from precision application of firepower, to infiltration, exfiltration, resupply and refueling of special operation forces operational elements. The command's core missions include battlefield air operations, agile combat support, aviation foreign internal defense, information operations/military information support operations, precision strike, specialized air mobility; command and control; and intelligence, surveillance and reconnaissance.

**3.17.1.8.2. Personnel and Resources.** AFSOC has more than 19,500 Regular Air Force, Air Force Reserve, Air National Guard and civilian personnel. The command's special tactics squadrons combine combat controllers, special operations weathermen, pararescuemen, and tactical air control party specialists with other service special operation forces to form versatile joint special operations teams. AFSOC's Regular Air Force and reserve component flying units operate fixed and rotary-wing aircraft, including the CV-22B, AC-130, EC-130, MC-130, MQ-9, U-28A, C-145A, C-146A and MC-12.

**3.17.1.8.3. Organization.** The command's forces are organized under the following units: 1st Special Operations Wing at Hurlburt Field, Florida; the 24th Special Operations Wing at Hurlburt Field, Florida; the 27th Special Operations Wing at Cannon Air Force Base, New Mexico; the 352nd Special Operations Wing at Royal Air Force Mildenhall, England; the 353rd Special Operations Group at Kadena Air Base, Japan; the 919th Special Operations Wing at Duke Field, Florida, Air Force Reserve; the 137th Special Operations Wing at Will Rodgers Air National Guard Base, Oklahoma, and the 193rd Special Operations Wing at Harrisburg, Pennsylvania, are both Air National Guard units. The Air Force Special Operations Air Warfare Center, headquartered at Hurlburt Field, Florida, organizes, trains, educates and equips forces to conduct special operations missions; leads major command Irregular Warfare activities; executes special operations test and evaluation and lessons learned programs; and develops doctrine, tactics, techniques and procedures for Air Force Special Operations Forces.

**3.17.1.9. Air Force Global Strike Command (AFGSC).** Air Force Global Strike Command, activated 7 August 2009, is headquartered at Barksdale Air Force Base, Louisiana. AFGSC is responsible for the nation's three intercontinental ballistic missile wings, the Air Force's entire bomber force, to include B-52, B-1 and B-2 wings, the Long Range Strike Bomber program, and operational and maintenance support to organizations within the nuclear enterprise.

**3.17.1.9.1. Mission.** The Command's mission is to provide strategic deterrence, global strike and combat support.

**3.17.1.9.2. Personnel and Resources.** Approximately 31,000 professionals are assigned to two numbered Air Forces, nine wings, two geographically-separated squadrons and one detachment in the continental United States and deployed to locations around the globe.

**3.17.1.9.3. Organization.** Responsible for the nation's three intercontinental ballistic missile wings, the Air Force's entire bomber force, to include B-52, B-1 and B-2 wings, the Long Range Strike Bomber program, and operational and maintenance support to organizations within the nuclear enterprise.

**3.17.1.10. Air Force Reserve Command (AFRC).** Air Force Reserve Command, headquartered at Robins Air Force Base Georgia, became an Air Force major command on 17 February 1997. Previously, the AFRC was a Field Operating Agency.

**3.17.1.10.1. Mission.** The mission of AFRC is to provide combat-ready forces to fly, fight and win in defense of the United States and its interests.

**3.17.1.10.2. Personnel and Resources.** AFRC has nearly 70,000 officer and enlisted personnel, over 4,000 civilian personnel, and 323 aircraft assigned to accomplish its diverse missions. AFRC is organized into three numbered Air Forces: 4th, 10th, and 22d. Together these numbered Air Forces lead the activities of 35 flying wings; 10 independent groups. In addition, there are various mission support units located at 9 Reserve bases, 57 Regular Air Force, Joint Reserve and Air National Guard bases, as well as miscellaneous locations and ranges.

**3.17.1.10.3. Organization.** AFRC has several mission support groups that provide a wide range of services, including medical and aeromedical evacuation, aerial port, civil engineer, security forces, intelligence, communications, mobility support, logistics and transportation operations.

**3.17.2. Field Operating Agencies.**

Field operating agencies are subdivisions of the Air Force directly subordinate to a Headquarters Air Force functional manager. A field operating agency performs field activities beyond the scope of the major commands.

The activities are specialized or associated with an Air Force-wide mission and do not include functions performed in management headquarters (such as Headquarters AMC), unless specifically directed by a Department of Defense authority. Two examples are the Air Force Personnel Center under the Deputy Chief of Staff for Manpower, Personnel, and Services, and the Air Force Office of Special Investigations under the Inspector General. Similar organizations at major command level are called major command field operating agencies.

### 3.17.3. **Direct Reporting Units.**

Direct reporting units are Air Force subdivisions directly subordinate to the Chief of Staff, Air Force. A direct reporting unit performs a mission that does not fit into any of the major commands. A direct reporting unit has many of the same administrative and organizational responsibilities as a major command. Two examples are the Air Force District of Washington and the United States Air Force Academy.

## 3.18. **Lower Levels of Command.**

Below major commands are several levels of command. The Air Force component numbered Air Forces and numbered Air Forces administratively report directly to the major command. Wings, groups, squadrons, and flights report to either a component numbered Air Force or a numbered Air Force, whichever is appropriate.

### 3.18.1. **Air Force Component Numbered Air Forces.**

The Air Force currently has ten Air Force component numbered Air Forces dedicated, to supporting the unified/sub-unified combatant command and joint task force commanders. These component numbered Air Forces (nicknamed warfighting headquarters), when established, are the primary operational-level warfighting component commands. The component numbered Air Forces headquarters normally consists of an Air Force forces staff and an assigned air and space operations center or operations center. They are dedicated to supporting the unified combatant commander and subordinate joint force commanders across the full range of military operations. The component numbered Air Force commander supporting a geographic combatant command will normally be prepared to assume responsibilities as the joint force air component commander for joint military operations in his or her respective area of operations, and command a joint task force as required. Component numbered Air Forces include 1$^{st}$ Air Force (Air Force North), 3$^{d}$ Air Force (Air Force Europe), 7$^{th}$ Air Force (Air Force Korea), 8$^{th}$ Air Force (Air Force Strategic Command's Task Force 204), United States Air Forces Central Command, 11$^{th}$ Air Force, 12$^{th}$ Air Force (Air Forces Southern), 14$^{th}$ Air Force (Air Forces Strategic), 18$^{th}$ Air Force (Air Forces Transportation) and 24$^{th}$ Air Force (Air Forces Cyber). Note: The parenthetical in the name of a component numbered Air Force indicates the combatant command to which they are assigned.

### 3.18.2. **Numbered Air Force.**

The numbered Air Force is an administrative level of command directly under a major command. Numbered Air Forces provide intermediate level operational leadership and supervision. They do not have complete functional staffs. In non-component numbered Air Forces, the number of personnel assigned varies but should not exceed 99 manpower authorizations without an approved waiver from Headquarters Air Force/A1M. A numbered Air Force is assigned subordinate units, such as wings, groups, and squadrons.

### 3.18.3. **Wing.**

The wing is a level of command below the numbered Air Force and has a distinct mission with significant scope. A wing is responsible for maintaining the installation and may have several squadrons in more than one dependent group. The different types of wings are operational, air base, or specialized mission. Wings will have a minimum adjusted population of at least 1,000 (750 for Air National Guard and Air Force Reserve Command wings). This will include manpower authorizations, students, and a percentage of contractor workforces. See Figure 3.1 for a common wing structure.

3.18.3.1. **Operational Wing.** An operational wing is one that has an operations group and related operational mission activity assigned. When an operational wing performs the primary mission of the base, it usually maintains and operates the base. In addition, an operational wing is capable of self-support in functional areas such as maintenance and munitions, as needed. When an operational wing is a tenant organization, the host command provides it with varying degrees of base and logistics support.

3.18.3.2. **Air Base Wing.** An air base wing performs a support function rather than an operational mission. This type of wing maintains and operates a base. An air base wing often provides functional support to a major commands headquarters.

3.18.3.3. **Specialized Mission Wing.** A specialized mission wing performs a specialized mission and usually does not have aircraft or missiles assigned. Examples include intelligence wings, training wings, and so on. This wing is either a host or a tenant wing, depending on whether it maintains and operates the base.

**3.18.4. Group.**

A group is a level of command below the wing. Like the numbered Air Force, a group is a tactical echelon with minimal staff support. A group usually has two or more subordinate units. A dependent group is a mission, logistics, support, medical, or large functional unit, such as a civil engineer group. Such groups may possess small supporting staff elements that are organized as sections, such as standardization and evaluation or quality control. An independent group has the same functions and responsibilities as a like-type wing, but its scope and size do not warrant wing-level designation. Groups will have a minimum adjusted population of at least 400 (200 for Air National Guard and Air Force Reserve Command groups). This includes manpower authorizations, students, and a percentage of contractor workforces.

**Figure 3.1. Wing Organization.**

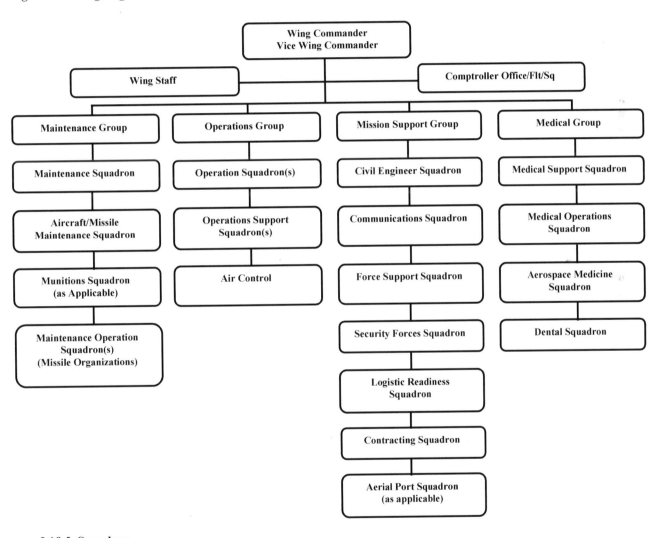

**3.18.5. Squadron.**

The squadron is the basic unit in the Air Force. The different types of squadrons are either a mission unit, such as an operational flying squadron, or a functional unit, such as a civil engineer, security forces, or logistics readiness squadron. Squadrons vary in size according to responsibility. Squadrons will have a minimum adjusted population of at least 35. This includes manpower authorizations, students, and a percentage of contractor workforces.

**3.18.6. Flight.**

If internal subdivision is required, a flight may consist of sections, then elements. The different types of flights are numbered/named, alpha, or functional.

3.18.6.1. **Numbered/Named Flight.** This is the lowest level unit in the Air Force. A numbered or named flight primarily incorporates smaller elements into an organized unit. The administrative characteristics for this type of flight include, strength reporting, like those of a squadron.

3.18.6.2. **Alpha Flight.** Alpha flights are part of a squadron (usually a mission squadron) and composed of several elements that perform identical missions. Because an alpha flight is not a unit, this type of a flight is not subject to unit reporting.

3.18.6.3. **Functional Flight.** Functional flights are usually part of a squadron and composed of elements that perform specific missions. Because a functional flight is not a unit, this type of a flight is not subject to unit reporting.

## 3.19. Air Reserve Component:

### 3.19.1. Components.

The Air National Guard and Air Force Reserve form a significant part of our aerospace capability. Together they are called the Air Reserve Component. Forces are drawn from the Air Reserve Component when circumstances require the active force to rapidly expand. AFPD 10-3, *Air Reserve Component Forces,* establishes policy to fully integrate the Air National Guard, Air Force Reserve, and active Air Force into a single Total Force.

### 3.19.2. Staffing and Equipping.

Air Reserve Component forces are staffed and trained to meet the same training standards and readiness levels as active component forces and are supplied with the same equipment on an equal priority. The active force can only withdraw, divert, or reassign equipment for other commitments with the Secretary of Defense's written approval. To ensure responsiveness and combat readiness, Air Reserve Component forces are continuously evaluated and modernized.

### 3.19.3. Use.

AFPD 10-3 states, under the Total Force policy established by Department of Defense in 1973, that both regular and reserve assets are considered parts of a single United States military resource. All aspects of regular and reserve forces are considered when determining an appropriate force mix. Significant factors include contribution of forces to national security; availability of forces in view of time, statutory or regulatory constraints; and the cost to equip and maintain forces. Considerations unique to Air National Guard units include their dual state and federal missions.

### 3.19.4. Organization.

Air National Guard and Air Force Reserve unit organization parallels similar Regular Air Force units with one exception: Air Reserve Component units are sometimes separated to take advantage of state or regional demographics and are not centralized at major, multisquadron bases, as is the case with Regular Air Force resources. This exception is beneficial because it implements a strong relationship with the civilian community and builds public support for the Air Force as a whole.

### 3.19.5. Jurisdiction.

Command jurisdiction for nonmobilized Air National Guard units is vested in the governor of the state, commonwealth, or possession, or in the President, who in essence is the governor of the District of Columbia. The President delegates authority to the Secretary of the Army to carry out the powers of the President as "governor" of the District of Columbia. Command of nonmobilized Air Force Reserve units is exercised through the Commander, Air Force Reserve Command, who, in turn, is responsible to the Chief of Staff, Air Force. Command of nonmobilized Air Force Reserve individual mobilization augmentees is exercised concurrently through Air Force Reserve Command and the unit of attachment. Whenever the President authorizes mobilization, the Secretary of Defense delegates authority to the Services who order Air National Guard and Air Force Reserve forces to active duty. When activated, operational command of Air Reserve Component forces transfers to the major command commander who is also responsible for establishing training resources for all assigned or attached Air Reserve Component forces.

## 3.20. Civil Air Patrol (CAP) / United States Air Force Auxiliary (AFAUX).

The Civil Air Patrol is a congressionally chartered, non-profit corporation for the public good that may be utilized as a civilian volunteer auxiliary of the Air Force. The Secretary of the Air Force can employ the services of CAP in lieu of or to supplement Air Force resources to fulfill the non-combat programs and missions of the Air Force. As a partner in the Total Force, when approved and assigned by the Air Force, CAP conducts missions as Airmen of the AFAUX.

3.20.1. **Mission.** CAP conducts three primary programs: Emergency Services and Civil Support, Aerospace Education, and Cadet Programs. CAP maintains the capability to meet Air Force requirements to assist federal, state, local agencies, and non-governmental organizations during routine and emergency situations. Such services may include, but are not limited to, Air Force-assigned missions in support of homeland security operations, consequence management, search and rescue, and other civil support. CAP aerospace education programs provide educational materials for both senior and cadet members and the general public. The Cadet Programs' focus is to motivate American youth to become responsible citizens through aviation-centered activities.

3.20.2. **Personnel and Resources.** CAP has over 55,000 senior member and cadet volunteers throughout the United States, Puerto Rico and the Virgin Islands. CAP maintains a fleet of over 500 aircraft, comprised mostly of Cessna 172, 182, and 206; and GA-8 high-wing, single-engine light aircraft. These aircraft are well suited for flying associated with aerial assessment, low-level route surveys, fighter intercept training, courier operations, and search and rescue. CAP maintains a fleet of over 900 vehicles of passenger vans, sedans, and pick-up trucks suited for light transportation of personnel and equipment, mobile communications units, and ground damage assessment. Most vehicles are equipped with radios able to communicate with CAP aircraft and other ground-based CAP stations. CAP maintains a nationwide communications capability including high frequency, very high frequency-AM, and very high frequency-FM fixed, mobile, and repeater systems. Finally, CAP maintains a state-of-the-art cell phone forensics cell at its National Operations Center that assists with search and rescue operations.

3.20.3. **Organization.** CAP is a non-profit corporation under Title 36 of United States Code, and the official Air Force Auxiliary under Title 10 of United States Code. CAP is governed by an 11-member Board of Governors. As a non-profit corporation, CAP is organized under a Chief Executive Officer and national staff. As the Air Force Auxiliary, the Chief Executive Officer serves as the National Commander. CAP is organized into eight geographic regions, each led by a regional commander, and 52 state-level wings (in each state, the District of Columbia, and Puerto Rico / U.S. Virgin Islands). Approximately 1,500 total individual units comprise the lower-level echelons of CAP within the state-level wings. The Air Force Auxiliary is aligned under Air Combat Command for fiscal and operational oversight and utilization.

**3.21. Air Force Junior Reserve Officer Training Corps (AFJROTC).**

AFJROTC is not an USAF accessions program and cadets are never under any obligation to join the military. AFJROTC is a Title 10 US Code mandated citizenship training program that is designed to educate and train high school cadets in citizenship, promote community service, instill personal responsibility, character, and self-discipline. The program achieves this through classroom education in air and space fundamentals and hands on learning opportunities in a number of fun and challenging extra-curricular activities.

3.21.1. **Mission.** Develop citizens of character dedicated to serving their nation and community.

3.21.2. **Personnel and Resources.** The Air Force Junior Reserve Officer Training Corps staff includes 31 headquarters' personnel and more than 1,910 retired Air Force officer and enlisted military instructors. There are 870 Air Force Junior ROTC units with nearly 120,000 cadets in high schools across the United States and selected Department of Defense Dependent Schools in Europe and the Pacific and public schools in Puerto Rico and Guam. The Air Force plans to continue expansion efforts to 955 units by 2020 when funds are available. With the addition of new units, AFJROTC is expected to reach more than 135,000 cadets worldwide.

3.21.3. **Organization.** Air Force JROTC provides leadership training and an aerospace science program for high school students. Secondary school students who enroll in the AFJROTC program are offered a wide variety of curricular and extra-curricular activities. The program explores the historic and scientific aspects of aerospace technology and teaches high school students self-reliance, self-discipline and other characteristics found in good leaders. The AFJROTC program is open to 9th-12th grade students who are citizens of the United States. The program is not a recruiting tool for the military services and those students who participate in AFJROTC do not incur any obligation to the Air Force.

3.21.3.1. The objectives of Air Force Junior ROTC are to educate and train high school cadets in citizenship and life skills; promote community service; instill a sense responsibility; develop character and self-discipline through education and instruction in air and space fundamentals and the Air Force's core values of "integrity first, service before self, and excellence in all we do."

*Section 3D—Functions of Other Services*

**3.22. Common Missions of the Armed Forces of the United States are:**

3.22.1. To support and defend the Constitution of the United States against all enemies, foreign or domestic.

3.22.2. To maintain, by timely and effective military action, the security of the United States, its possessions and areas vital to its interest.

3.22.3. To uphold and advance the national policies and interests of the United States.

3.22.4. To safeguard the internal security of the United States as directed by higher authority.

3.22.5. To conduct integrated operations on the land, on the sea, and in the air necessary for these purposes.

3.22.6. In order to facilitate the accomplishment of the foregoing missions the armed forces shall formulate integrated plans and make coordinated preparations. Each service shall observe the general principles and fulfill the specific functions outlined in paragraphs 3.21 to 3.24, and shall make use of the personnel, equipment and facilities of the other services in all cases where economy and effectiveness will thereby be increased.

### 3.23. Functions of the United States Army.

The United States Army includes land combat and service forces and such aviation and water transport as may be organic therein. It is organized, trained and equipped primarily for prompt and sustained combat incident to operations on land. The Army is responsible for the preparation of land forces necessary for the effective prosecution of war, and, in accordance with integrated joint mobilization plans, for the expansion of peacetime components of the Army to meet the needs of war.

3.23.1. The specific functions of the United States Army are to organize, train and equip land forces for; (1) Operations on land, including joint operations, (2) the seizure or defense of land areas, including airborne and joint amphibious operations, and (3) the occupation of land areas.

3.23.2. To develop weapons, tactics, technique, organization and equipment of Army combat and service elements, coordinating with the Navy and the Air Force in all aspects of joint concern, including those which pertain to amphibious and airborne operations.

3.23.3. To provide, as directed by proper authority, such missions and detachments for service in foreign countries as may be required to support the national policies and interests of the United States.

3.23.4. To assist the Navy and Air Forces in the accomplishment of their missions, including the provision of common services and supplies as determined by proper authority.

### 3.24. Functions of the United States Navy and Marine Corps.

The United States Navy includes naval combat and service forces, naval aviation, and the United States Marine Corps. It is organized, trained and equipped primarily for prompt and sustained combat at sea. The Navy is responsible for the preparation of naval forces necessary for the effective prosecution of war, and in accordance with integrated joint mobilization plans, for the expansion of the peacetime components of the Navy to meet the needs of war.

3.24.1. The specific functions of the United States Navy are to organize, train and equip naval forces for; (1) operations at sea, including joint operations, (2) the control of vital sea areas, the protection of vital sea lanes, and the suppression of enemy sea commerce, (3) the support of occupation forces as required, (4) the seizure of minor enemy shore 'positions capable of reduction by such landing forces as may be comprised within the fleet organization, (5) naval reconnaissance, antisubmarine warfare, and protection of shipping. The air aspects of those functions shall be coordinated with the Air Force, including the development and procurement of aircraft, and air installations located on shore, and use shall be made of Air Force personnel, equipment and facilities in all cases where economy and effectiveness will thereby be increased. Subject to the above provision, the Navy will not be restricted as to types of aircraft maintained and operated for these purposes, and (6) the air transport necessary for essential internal administration and for air transport over routes of sole interest to naval forces where the requirements cannot be met by normal air transport facilities.

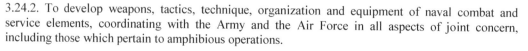

3.24.2. To develop weapons, tactics, technique, organization and equipment of naval combat and service elements, coordinating with the Army and the Air Force in all aspects of joint concern, including those which pertain to amphibious operations.

3.24.3. To provide, as directed by proper authority, such missions and detachments for service in foreign countries as may be required to support the national policies and interests of the United States.

3.24.4. To maintain the United States Marine Corps whose specific functions are; (1) to provide Marine Forces together with supporting air components, for service with the Fleet in the seizure or defense of advanced naval bases and for the conduct of limited land operations in connection therewith, (2) to develop, in coordination with the Army and the Air Force those phases of amphibious operations which pertain to the tactics, technique and equipment employed by landing forces; (3) to provide detachments and organizations for service on armed vessels of the Navy, (4) to provide security detachments for protection of naval property at naval stations and bases, and (5) to provide, as directed by proper authority, such missions and detachments for service in foreign countries as may be required to support the national policies and interests of the United States.

3.24.5. To assist the Army and the Air Force in the accomplishment of their missions, including the provision of common services and supplies as determined by proper authority.

## 3.25. Functions of the United States Air Force.

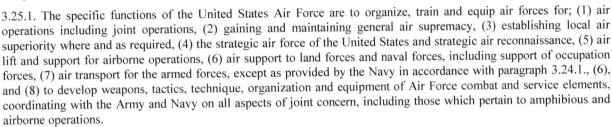

The United States Air Force includes all military aviation forces, both combat and service, not otherwise specifically assigned, and is organized, trained, and equipped primarily for prompt and sustained air offensive and defensive operations. The Air Force is responsible for the preparation of the air forces necessary for the effective prosecution of war except as otherwise assigned and, in accordance with integrated joint mobilization plans, for the expansion of the peacetime components of the Air Force to meet the needs of war.

3.25.1. The specific functions of the United States Air Force are to organize, train and equip air forces for; (1) air operations including joint operations, (2) gaining and maintaining general air supremacy, (3) establishing local air superiority where and as required, (4) the strategic air force of the United States and strategic air reconnaissance, (5) air lift and support for airborne operations, (6) air support to land forces and naval forces, including support of occupation forces, (7) air transport for the armed forces, except as provided by the Navy in accordance with paragraph 3.24.1., (6), and (8) to develop weapons, tactics, technique, organization and equipment of Air Force combat and service elements, coordinating with the Army and Navy on all aspects of joint concern, including those which pertain to amphibious and airborne operations.

3.25.2. To provide, as directed by proper authority, such missions and detachments for service in foreign countries as may be required to support the national policies and interests of the United States.

3.25.3. To provide the means for coordination of air defense among all services.

3.25.4. To assist the Army and Navy in accomplishment of their missions, including the provision of common services and supplies as determined by proper authority.

## 3.26. Functions of the United States Coast Guard.

The Coast Guard is a military service and a branch of the Armed Forces of the United States at all times. It is a service in the Department of Homeland Security except when operating as part of the Navy on declaration of war or when the President directs.

3.26.1. Some of the major functions of the Coast Guard are to: (1) enforce or assist in the enforcement of all applicable Federal laws on, under, and over the high seas and waters subject to the jurisdiction of the United States, (2) engage in maritime air surveillance or interdiction to enforce or assist in the enforcement of the laws of the United States, (3) administer laws and promulgate and enforce regulations for the promotion of safety of life and property on and under the high seas and waters subject to the jurisdiction of the United States, covering all matters not specifically delegated by law to some other executive department, (4) develop, establish, maintain, and operate, with due regard to the requirements of national defense, aids to maritime navigation, icebreaking facilities, and rescue facilities for the promotion of safety on, under, and over the high seas and waters subject to the jurisdiction of the United States, (5) pursuant to international agreements, develop, establish, maintain, and operate icebreaking facilities on, under, and over waters other than the high seas and waters subject to the jurisdiction of the United States, (6) engage in oceanographic research of the high seas and in waters subject to the jurisdiction of the United States, and (7) maintain a state of readiness to function as a specialized service in the Navy in time of war, including the fulfillment of Maritime Defense Zone command responsibilities.

## 3.27. Conclusion.

Organized with civilian leadership throughout, the Armed Forces of the United States are not separate and independent parts of the government but serve as instruments of national policy. This chapter began with a discussion of the President's role as Commander in Chief and continued with the Department of Defense, Joint Chief of Staff, unified combatant commands, and combined commands. In addition, this chapter contained information on the Department of the Air Force and focused on force structure and major commands. Finally, the chapter included a discussion of the structure and functions of the various lower levels of command and Air Reserve components.

## Chapter 4

## AIR FORCE DOCTRINE, AIR EXPEDITIONARY FORCE (AEF), AND JOINT FORCE

*Section 4A—Overview*

### 4.1. Introduction:

4.1.1. America's Air Force faces significant challenges. We have been engaged in combat while transforming into a smaller, leaner, and more capable force. Fiscal constraints combined with operational challenges and a dynamic international security environment translate into risks we continue to manage and mitigate in order to provide capabilities America needs. The Air Force continues to fight the war on terrorism and prepares to face new threats and conflicts of the future. In order to remain dominant, we must maintain our airpower advantages over potential adversaries. Modern warfare is changing. This is not new for America's Airmen, whose heritage spans and embraces change and whose culture embodies courage and innovation.

4.1.2. Meeting the challenges in this rapidly changing world requires we understand and apply Air Force doctrine. Airmen may not have understood or consistently applied doctrine. The complexity of integrating fighting elements according to joint, Air Force and multinational doctrine and the uncertainty inherent in rapidly developing contingency operations demand that planning and employment be understood and repeatable. We must learn and practice our own doctrine. We know how to do it right; we have taken the time to research, write it down, and publish it. We must understand what it means to be an Airman, and we must be able to articulate what air power can bring to the joint fight. Volume 1, *Air Force Basic Doctrine,* is the Air Force's premier statement of our beliefs, and the cornerstone upon which our service identity is based. Air Force Doctrine is developed by the LeMay Center for Doctrine Development and Education at Maxwell Air Force Base, Alabama. Air Force doctrine is web-based, and is available at https://doctrine.af.mil/.

4.1.3. Air Force forces are presented to a joint force commander as an air expeditionary task force, or may be composed of the air component to the joint task force or combatant commander (CCDR) as the C-Numbered Air Force or C-Major Command. The AEF is the Air Force methodology to provide Air Force forces and support on a rotational, predictable basis. Three principles are the foundation upon which the AEF is structured and executed: transparency, predictability, and equitability. Transparency is the sense that there is no mystery to the process; when, why, and how should be visible and understandable by every Airman. Every Air Force member is responsible for knowing and understanding the AEF original structure, how we deploy today's AEF, and our goals for the future. By aligning forces in AEF bands and utilizing the teaming concept our Air Force is able to determine who goes first, defines our battle rhythm, and provides a logically organized structure during surge periods to support CCDRs. The AEF is merely a vehicle for managing and scheduling Air Force forces for expeditionary purposes; it is not a warfighting organization. The Air Expeditionary Task Force (AETF) is normally the warfighting organization attached to the JFC.

4.1.4. Joint warfare is team warfare. Over time, the American experience in war increasingly demanded cooperation, coordination, and integration of all U.S. military Services. Today, joint operations are routine and, thus, routinely practiced. Effectively integrated joint forces are able to rapidly and efficiently identify and engage adversary weak points and vulnerabilities, without exposing their own weak points or seams, to ensure mission accomplishment. Whether there are years to prepare and plan (as in the World War II Normandy invasion), months (as in Operation DESERT STORM), or only a few weeks (as in Operation ENDURING FREEDOM), American armed forces must always be ready to operate in smoothly functioning, joint teams.

*Section 4B—Air Force Doctrine*

### 4.2. Uses of Doctrine.

One way to explore good doctrine is to use a "compare and contrast" model to walk through some key issues. This technique also amplifies the point that doctrine should be written broadly, allowing decision makers latitude in interpretation and flexibility in application, yet be specific enough to provide informed guidance. This technique also illustrates the use of doctrine in explaining contentious issues and how doctrine can be used to think more effectively about the best means to integrate various aspects of military power and organization. In the following discussion, there may be overlap among some of the principles expressed; this is desirable in that often there are different aspects or nuances to a particular issue. In doctrine, language is important. Finally, the following discussion presents an Air Force perspective; not all Services may entirely agree with these points. (Reference: Volume 1 – Basic Doctrine)

4.2.1. Doctrine is about *warfighting*, not *physics*. This principle specifically addresses the perceived differences between operations in air, space, and cyberspace. Air, space, and cyberspace are separate domains requiring exploitation of different sets of physical laws to operate in, but are linked by the effects they can produce together. To achieve a common purpose, air, space, and cyberspace capabilities need to be integrated. Therefore, Air Force doctrine focuses on the best means to obtain warfighting effects regardless of the medium in which a platform operates. As an example, Airmen should be concerned with the best means of employing intelligence, surveillance, and reconnaissance capabilities, not whether a particular intelligence, surveillance, and reconnaissance platform is airborne or in orbit. This is requisite to achieving true integration across any given collection of forces.

4.2.2. Doctrine is about *effects*, not *platforms*. This focuses on the desired outcome of a particular action, not on the system or weapon itself that provides the effect. For example, doctrine states that Airmen should seek to achieve air superiority, but doctrine does not focus on which platforms should be used to achieve that effect. A parallel example of this is seen in the recognition that bombers are not "strategic," nor are fighters "tactical." Similarly, it does not matter if an F-16 or a B-52 accomplishes a given task, or whether a particular platform is manned or unmanned, or whether a C-17 or a C-130 delivers a certain load; the outcome of the mission, the effect achieved, is what's important. Thus, Air Force doctrine does not explicitly tie specific weapon systems to specific tasks or effects.

4.2.3. Doctrine is about *using mediums*, not *owning mediums*. This illustrates the importance of properly using a medium to obtain the best warfighting effects, not of carving up the battlespace based on Service or functional parochialism. Focusing on using a medium is a vital first step to integration of efforts. "Ownership" arguments eventually lead to suboptimal (and usually at best tactical) application of efforts at the expense of the larger, total effort.

4.2.4. Doctrine is about *organization*, not *organizations*. Modern warfare demands that disparate parts of different Services, different nations, and even differing functions within a single Service be brought together intelligently to achieve unity of command and unity of effort. However, merely placing different organizations together in an area of operations is insufficient to meet these demands. A single, cohesive organization is required with clearly defined lines of command and commanders with requisite authorities at appropriate levels. Doctrine explains why certain organizational structures are preferred over others and describes effective command relationships and command authorities; this facilitates the rapid standup of joint and Service organizations during rapidly evolving situations. Ultimately, doctrine is not about whether one particular element of a joint force is more decisive than another, nor about positing that element as the centerpiece of joint operations; it's the total, tailored joint force that's decisive. Getting to that effective joint force requires smart organization and a thorough understanding of Service and joint doctrine.

4.2.5. Doctrine is about *synergy*, not *segregation*. True integration of effort cannot be achieved by merely carving up the operational environment. While segregation may have some benefit and may appear the simplest way, from a command and control viewpoint, to manage elements of a diverse joint force, it may actually suboptimize the overall effort. It guarantees that the whole will never be greater than the sum of its parts. For example, Airmen should have access to the entire theater of operations to maximize their ability to achieve joint force commander objectives; they should not be restricted from any area due to unnecessarily restrictive fire control measures. Also, segregating the battlespace into smaller areas of operation may create competition for scarce, high-demand, low-density capabilities and reduce combat effectiveness.

4.2.6. Doctrine is about *integration*, not just *synchronization*. Synchronization is defined as "the arrangement of military actions in time, space, and purpose to produce maximum relative combat power at a decisive place and time" (Joint Publication 1-02). Integration, by comparison, is defined as "the arrangement of military forces and their actions to create a force that operates by engaging as a whole" (Joint Publication 1-02). Synchronization is, in essence, deconfliction in time and space between different units. A useful means is to plan and execute operations and to prevent fratricide. However, it doesn't scale up to the operational level and hence is not the best means for achieving the maximum potential of a joint force. Synchronization emphasizes timing, while integration considers priority and effect to be both efficient and effective with scarce resources. Synchronization is bottom-up; integration, on the other hand, starts at the top with a single cohesive plan and works downward. Synchronization is an additive "sum of the parts" model, while integration may produce geometric results.

4.2.7. Doctrine is about *the right force*, not just *equal shares of the force*. This addresses the proper mix of Service components within a joint force. Some believe that a joint force requires equal parts of all the Services. This is an incorrect view. As one senior Air Force officer said, "joint warfighting is not like Little League baseball, where everybody gets a chance to play." Any given joint force should be tailored appropriately for the task at hand. Some operations will be land-centric, others air-centric, others maritime-, cyberspace-, or information-centric. The composition of the joint force and the tasks assigned its various elements should reflect the needs of the situation.

## 4.3. Levels of Airpower Doctrine.

As implemented in the Air Force, doctrine affects operations at three levels: basic, operational, and tactical. These levels speak to the intellectual content of the doctrinal concepts, not to the architectural structure of doctrine publications. (Reference: Volume 1 – Basic Doctrine)

4.3.1. **Basic doctrine** states the most fundamental and enduring beliefs that describe and guide the proper use, presentation, and organization of forces in military action. Basic doctrine describes the "elemental properties" of airpower and provides the Airman's perspective. Because of its fundamental and enduring character, basic doctrine provides broad and continuing guidance on how Air Force forces are organized, employed, equipped, and sustained. Because it expresses broad, enduring fundamentals, basic doctrine changes relatively slowly compared to the other levels of doctrine. As the foundation of all doctrine, basic doctrine also sets the tone and vision for doctrine development for the future. Air Force Doctrine Volume 1 is the Air Force's basic doctrine publication.

4.3.2. **Operational doctrine** contained in doctrine annexes describe more detailed organization of forces and applies the principles of basic doctrine to military actions. Operational doctrine guides the proper organization and employment of air, space, and cyberspace forces in the context of distinct objectives, force capabilities, broad functional areas, and operational environments. Operational doctrine provides the focus for developing the missions and tasks to be executed through tactical doctrine. Doctrine at this level changes a bit more rapidly than basic doctrine, but usually only after deliberate internal Service debate.

4.3.3. **Tactical doctrine** describes the proper employment of specific Air Force assets, individually or in concert with other assets, to accomplish detailed objectives. Tactical doctrine considers particular objectives (stopping the advance of an armored column) and conditions (threats, weather, and terrain) and describes how Air Force assets are employed to accomplish the tactical objective (B-1 bombers dropping anti-armor cluster munitions). Air Force tactical doctrine is codified as tactics, techniques, and procedures in Air Force (Air Force tactics, techniques, and procedures) -3 series manuals. Because tactical doctrine is closely associated with the employment of technology and emerging tactics, change will likely occur more rapidly than other levels of doctrine. Also, due to their sensitive nature, many tactics, techniques, and procedures are classified.

## 4.4. Airpower:

4.4.1. **Airpower is defined as "the ability to project military power or influence through the control and exploitation of air, space, and cyberspace to achieve strategic, operational, or tactical objectives."** The proper application of airpower requires a comprehensive doctrine of employment and an Airman's perspective. As the nation's most comprehensive provider of military airpower, the Air Force conducts continuous and concurrent air, space, and cyberspace operations. The air, space, and cyberspace capabilities of the other Services serve primarily to support their organic maneuver paradigms; the Air Force employs air, space, and cyberspace capabilities with a broader focus on theater-wide and national-level objectives. Through airpower, the Air Force provides the versatile, wide-ranging means towards achieving national objectives with the ability to deter and respond immediately to crises anywhere in the world. (Reference: Volume 1 – Basic Doctrine)

4.4.2. **Airpower exploits the third dimension of the operational environment; the electromagnetic spectrum; and time to leverage speed, range, flexibility, precision, tempo, and lethality to create effects from and within the air, space, and cyberspace domains.** From this multi-dimensional perspective, Airmen can apply military power against an enemy's entire array of diplomatic, informational, military, and economic instruments of power, at long ranges and on short notice. Airpower can be applied across the strategic, operational, and tactical levels of war simultaneously, significantly increasing the options available to national leadership. Due to its range, speed, and flexibility, airpower can compress time, controlling the tempo of operations in our favor. Airpower should be employed with appropriate consideration of land and maritime power, not just during operations against enemy forces, but when used as part of a team that protects and aids friendly forces as well.

4.4.2.1. Much of what airpower can accomplish from within these three domains is done to critically affect events in the land and maritime domains—this is the heart of joint domain integration, a fundamental aspect of airpower's contribution to United States (U.S.) national interests. Airmen integrate capabilities across air, space, and cyberspace domains to achieve effects across all domains in support of joint force commander objectives. For example, a remotely piloted aircraft operating from a ground station in the continental U.S. relies on space and cyberspace capabilities to support operations overseas. While all Services rely more and more on such integration, cross-domain integration is fundamental to how Airmen employ airpower to complement the joint force.

4.4.2.2. Airmen exploit the third dimension, which consists of the entire expanse above the earth's surface. The third dimensions lower limit is the earth's surface (land or water), and the upper limit reaches toward infinity. This third dimension consists of the air and space domains. From an operational perspective, the air domain can be described as that region above the earth's surface in which aerodynamics generally govern the planning and conduct of military operations, while the space domain can be described as that region above the earth's surface in which astrodynamics generally govern the planning and conduct of military operations. Airmen also exploit operational capabilities in cyberspace. Cyberspace is "a global domain within the information environment consisting of the interdependent network of information technology infrastructures, including the Internet, telecommunications networks, computer systems, and embedded processors and controllers." In contrast to our surface-oriented sister Services, the Air Force uses air, space, and cyberspace capabilities to create effects, including many on land and in the maritime domains, that are ends unto themselves, not just in support of predominantly land or maritime force activities.

4.4.2.3. The evolution of contemporary airpower stems from the Airman's original vision of combat from a distance, bypassing the force-on-force clash of surface combat. Originally manifest in long-range aircraft delivering kinetic weapons, airpower has evolved over time to include many long-range supporting capabilities, notably the conduct of networked information-related operations. This evolution has accelerated as Airmen conduct a greater percentage of operations not just over-the-horizon but globally, expanding operations first through space and now also in cyberspace. Just as airpower grew from its initial use as an adjunct to surface operations, space and cyberspace have likewise grown from their original manifestations as supporting capabilities into warfighting arenas in their own right.

4.4.3. **Air Force doctrine presents airpower as a unitary construct.** The Air Force acknowledges the importance of the space and cyberspace domains. However, Air Force doctrine should address what unifies Airmen. Thus, in the Air Force's senior doctrine product, the use of concepts and language that bind Airmen together instead of presenting the Air Force as a collection of tribes broken out in technological stovepipes according to the domains of air, space, and cyberspace is appropriate. Other subordinate doctrine products delve into the differences and interdependencies of the core functions and missions conducted within and across the air, space, and cyberspace domains, and within the context of more specific types of operations. Where appropriate, this product will also mention air, space, and cyberspace forces or capabilities.

**4.5. The Airman's Perspective.**

The practical application of "airmindedness" results in the Airman's unique perspective, which can be summarized as follows. (Reference: Volume 1 – Basic Doctrine)

4.5.1. **Control of the vertical dimension is generally a necessary precondition for control of the surface.** The first mission of an air force is to defeat or neutralize the enemy air forces so friendly operations on land, sea, in the air, and in space can proceed unhindered, while at the same time one's own military forces and critical vulnerabilities remain safe from air attack.

4.5.2. **Airpower is an inherently strategic force.** War and peace are decided, organized, planned, supplied, and commanded at the strategic level of war. Air Force forces can hold an enemy's strategic centers of gravity and critical vulnerabilities directly at risk immediately and continuously. Airpower also has great strategic capability for non-lethal strategic influence, as in humanitarian relief and building partnership activities.

4.5.3. **Airpower can exploit the principles of mass and maneuver simultaneously to a far greater extent than surface forces.** There are no natural lateral boundaries to prevent air, space, and cyberspace capabilities from quickly concentrating their power (physically or in terms of delivered effects) at any point, even when starting from widely dispersed locations. Airpower dominates the fourth dimension—time—and compresses the tempo of events to produce physical and psychological shock.

4.5.4. **Airpower can apply force against many facets of enemy power.** Air Force provided capabilities can be brought to bear against any lawful target within an enemy's diplomatic, informational, military, economic, and social structures simultaneously or separately. They can be employed in support of national, combined/joint, or other component objectives. They can be integrated with surface power or employed independently.

4.5.5. **Air Force forces are less culturally intrusive in many scenarios.** Surface forces are composed of many people and vehicles which, when arrayed for operations, cover a significant area. Thus, their presence may be very visible to local populations and may create resentment during certain types of stability operations and in counterinsurgency operations. Air Force forces, operating from bases over the horizon or from just a few bases in-country, have a smaller footprint for the effects they provide. Space and cyberspace forces have a negligible in-theater footprint relative to the capabilities they provide.

4.5.6. **Airpower's inherent speed, range, and flexibility combine to make it one of the most versatile components of military power.** This versatility component allows it to be rapidly employed against strategic, operational, and tactical objectives simultaneously. The versatility of airpower derives not only from the inherent characteristics of air forces themselves, but also from the manner in which they are organized and controlled.

4.5.7. **Airpower results from the effective integration of capabilities, people, weapons, bases, logistics, and all supporting infrastructure.** No one aspect of air, space, and cyberspace capabilities should be treated in isolation since each element is essential and interdependent. Ultimately, the Air Force depends on the performance of the people who operate, command, and sustain air, space, and cyberspace forces.

**4.5.8. The choice of appropriate capabilities is a key aspect in the realization of airpower.** Weapons should be selected based on their ability to create desired effects on an adversary's capability and will. Achieving the full potential of airpower requires timely, actionable intelligence and sufficient command and control capabilities to permit commanders to exploit precision, speed, range, flexibility, and versatility.

**4.5.9. Supporting bases with their people, systems, and facilities are essential to launch, recovery, and sustainment of Air Force forces.** One of the most important aspects of the Air Force has proved to be its ability to move anywhere in the world quickly and then rapidly begin operations. However, the need for mobility should be balanced against the need to operate at the deployment site. The availability and operability of suitable bases can be the dominant factor in employment planning and execution.

**4.5.10. Airpower's unique characteristics necessitate that it be centrally controlled by Airmen.** Airpower can quickly intervene anywhere, regardless if used for strategic or tactical purposes. Thus, Airmen tend to take a broader view of war, because the capabilities they command have effects at broader levels of war. Airmen apply airpower through the tenet of centralized control and decentralized execution.

**4.6. Principles of Joint Operations:**

4.6.1. Throughout the history of conflict, military leaders have noted certain principles that tended to produce military victory. Known as the principles of war, they are those aspects of warfare that are universally true and relevant. As members of the joint team, Airmen should appreciate how these principles apply to all forces, but should most fully understand them as they pertain to Air Force forces. Airpower, no matter which Service operates the systems and no matter which type of platform is used, provides unique capabilities.

4.6.2. Valid principles, despite how deeply they are held, are no substitute for sound, professional judgment; however, ignoring them completely assumes unnecessary risk. The complexity of war in general, and the unique character of each war in particular, preclude commanders from using these principles as a checklist to guarantee victory. Rather, they serve as valuable guides to evaluate potential courses of action. The principles are independent, but tightly fused in application. No one principle should be considered without due consideration of the others. These principles are not all inclusive; the art of developing airpower strategies depends upon the Airman's ability to view these principles from a three-dimensional perspective and integrate their application accordingly. The principles of war, combined with the additional tenets of airpower discussed elsewhere, provide the basis for a sound and enduring doctrine for the air, space, and cyberspace forces of America's joint force. (Reference: Volume 1 – Basic Doctrine)

4.6.3. The principles of war are:

4.6.3.1. **Unity of command ensures concentration of effort for every objective under one responsible commander.** This principle emphasizes that all efforts should be directed and coordinated toward a common objective. Airpower's operational-level perspective calls for unity of command to gain the most effective and efficient application. Coordination may be achieved by cooperation; however, coordination is best achieved by vesting a single commander with the authority and the capability to direct all force employment in pursuit of a common objective. In many operations, the wide-ranging interagency and nongovernmental organizations involved may dilute unity of command. Effective information-sharing arrangements may preserve unity of effort to ensure common focus and mutually supporting actions.

4.6.3.1.1. Unity of command is vital in employing airpower. Airpower is the product of multiple capabilities, and centralized control is essential to effectively fuse these capabilities and provide unity of command.

4.6.3.2. **The principle of objective is to direct military operations toward a defined and attainable objective that contributes to strategic, operational, and tactical aims.** In application, this principle refers to unity of effort in purpose, space, and time. In a broad sense, this principle holds that political and military goals should be complementary and clearly articulated. A clear National Military Strategy provides focus for defining campaign or theater objectives. At the operational level, campaign or theater objectives determine military priorities.

4.6.3.2.1. The objective is important due to the flexibility and versatility of airpower. From the outset, airpower can pursue tactical, operational, or strategic objectives, in any combination, or all three simultaneously. By integrating the potential offered by air, space, and cyberspace capabilities, Airmen can overcome the challenges imposed by distance and time. From an Airman's perspective, then, the principle of objective shapes priorities to allow airpower to concentrate on theater or campaign priorities and seeks to avoid the siphoning of force elements to fragmented objectives.

4.6.3.3. **The purpose of an offensive action is to seize, retain, and exploit the initiative.** The offensive aim is to act rather than react and to dictate the time, place, purpose, scope, intensity, and pace of operations. The initiative should be seized as soon as possible. The principle of the offensive holds that offensive action, or initiative, provides the means for joint forces to dictate operations. Once seized, the initiative should be retained and fully exploited.

4.6.3.3.1. This principle is particularly significant to airpower and is best used as an offensive weapon. While defense may be dictated by the combat situation, success in war is generally attained only while on the offensive. Even highly successful defensive air campaigns such as the World War II Battle of Britain were based upon selective offensive engagements.

4.6.3.3.2. The speed and range of attacking airpower gives it a significant offensive advantage over other forces. In an air attack, for example, the defender often requires more forces to defend a given geospatial area than the attacker requires to strike a set of specific targets. The integration of air, space, and cyberspace capabilities enhances the advantages of speed, range and persistence found in airpower.

4.6.3.3.3. Although all military forces have offensive capabilities, airpower's ability to mass and maneuver, and its ability to operate independently or simultaneously at the tactical, operational, and/or strategic levels of war, provides joint force commanders a resource with global reach to directly and rapidly seize the initiative. Whether deploying forces and supplies into a region, conducting combat operations, or maintaining information assurance, airpower provides the joint force commander the means to take the offensive. Through prompt and sustained offensive actions designed to attain operational and strategic objectives, airpower causes the enemy to react rather than act, denies them the offensive, and shapes the remainder of the conflict.

4.6.3.4. **The purpose of mass is to concentrate the effects of combat power at the most advantageous place and time to achieve decisive results.** Concentration of military power is a fundamental consideration in all military operations. At the operational level of war, this principle suggests that superior, concentrated combat power is used to achieve decisive results.

4.6.3.4.1. Airpower is singularly able to launch an attack from widely dispersed locations and mass combat power at the objective, whether that objective is a single physical location or a widely dispersed enemy system or systems. From an Airman's perspective, mass is not based solely on the quantity of forces and materiel committed. Airpower achieves mass through effectiveness of attack, not just overwhelming numbers. Contemporary airpower has altered the concept of massed forces. The speed, range, and flexibility of airpower—complemented by the accuracy and lethality of precision weapons and advances in information technologies—allow it to achieve mass faster than other forces.

4.6.3.4.2. Air Force cyberspace capabilities, often enabled by space systems, allow dispersed forces to collaborate to rapidly find, fix, track, and target fleeting targets and mass a response in new ways. Previously, operators and planners worked in relative proximity within the same theater of operations; today, those same planners and operators leverage distributed capabilities to apply precise effects around the globe.

4.6.3.4.3. Airlift and air refueling provide a significant and critical capability to mass lethal and nonlethal forces on a global scale. The capability of airpower to act quickly and mass effects, along with its capability to mass other lethal and nonlethal military power, combine the principle of mass with the principle of maneuver.

4.6.3.5. **Maneuver places the enemy in a position of disadvantage through the flexible application of combat power in a multidimensional combat space.** Airpower's ability to conduct maneuver is not only a product of its speed and range, but also flows from its flexibility and versatility during the planning and execution of operations. Maneuver, like the principle of offensive, forces the enemy to react, allowing the exploitation of successful friendly operations and reducing friendly vulnerabilities. Airpower maneuver allows engagement anywhere, from any direction, at any time, forcing the adversary to be on guard everywhere.

4.6.3.5.1. The principle of maneuver is not limited to simple weapons delivery. Maneuver may involve the strategic positioning of capabilities that bring potential airpower to bear within striking distance of potential or actual adversaries. Forward deployment of airpower assets is one example of maneuver that, by its very presence, can reassure allies and deter aggressors. Also, in airlift operations such as SUPPORT HOPE in Rwanda, PROVIDE HOPE in the former Soviet Union, or PROVIDE PROMISE in Bosnia; focused civil-military operations and exercises that support theater security cooperation goals, such as PACIFIC ANGEL; or combat operations such as ALLIED FORCE in Serbia, ENDURING FREEDOM in Afghanistan, or IRAQI FREEDOM in Iraq, airpower has played a critical role in American national security by providing unmatched maneuverability. Whether it involves airlift or attack aircraft, in small or large numbers, the versatility and responsiveness of airpower allow the simultaneous application of mass and maneuver.

**4.6.3.6. Economy of force is the judicious employment and distribution of forces.** Its purpose is to allocate minimum essential resources to secondary efforts. This principle calls for the rational use of force by selecting the best mix of air, space, and cyberspace capabilities. To ensure overwhelming combat power is available, maximum effort should be devoted to primary objectives. At the operational level of war, commanders ensure that any effort made towards secondary objectives does not degrade achievement of the larger operational or strategic objectives. This principle requires Airmen to maintain a broader operational view even as they seek to obtain clearly articulated objectives and priorities.

4.6.3.6.1. Economy of force may require a commander to establish a balance in the application of airpower between attacking, defending, delaying, or conducting other operations such as information operations, depending on the importance of the area or the priority of the objective or objectives. Also, priorities may shift rapidly; friendly troops in contact might drive a change in priority from one type of mission (e.g., interdiction) to another (e.g., close air support). Although this principle suggests the use of overwhelming force in one sense, it also recommends guarding against the "overkill" inherent in the use of more force than reasonably necessary. This is particularly relevant when excessive force can diminish the legitimacy and support for an operation.

**4.6.3.7. The purpose of security is to never permit the enemy to acquire unexpected advantage.** Friendly forces and their operations should be protected from enemy action that could provide the enemy with unexpected advantage. The lethal consequences of enemy attack make the security of friendly forces a paramount concern.

4.6.3.7.1. Critical to security is the understanding that it embraces physical security, operations security, and security of the information environment. Information has always been part of air, land, and sea warfare; now, with the proliferation of advanced communications and computer technologies, it becomes even more central to the outcome of a conflict.

4.6.3.7.2. **Aircraft are most vulnerable on the ground.** Thus, force protection is an integral part of airpower employment. Fixed bases are especially vulnerable as they not only should withstand aerial, ground, and cyberspace attacks, but should also sustain concentrated and prolonged air, space, and cyberspace activities against the enemy.

4.6.3.7.3. From an Airman's perspective, **security also may be obtained by staying beyond the enemy's reach, physically and virtually.** Airpower is uniquely suited to capitalize on this through its ability to operate over the horizon. Not only can airpower reach and strike at extended range, but it also can distribute data and analysis as well as command and control across a worldwide span.

4.6.3.7.4. Security from physical and electronic enemy intrusion conceals our capabilities and intentions, while allowing friendly forces the freedom to gather information on the adversary—the type of information that creates the opportunity to strike the enemy where least expected. By exploiting the vertical mediums of air and space, Airmen provide security for our nation and friendly forces by detecting enemy actions and determining intentions even in denied areas.

4.6.3.7.5. Commanders have an obligation to protect their forces, but the threat and the means for countering it are quite different in contingency operations. The threat varies depending on local circumstances, but the commander must be aware that it always exists. Although U.S. forces have a right to self-defense, Airmen must bear in mind the concepts of necessity and proportionality when exercising that right (as discussed in the standing rules of engagement). **Necessity** exists when a hostile act occurs or when a force demonstrates hostile intent; use of force is then authorized while the force continues to commit hostile acts or exhibit hostile intent. **Proportionality** means the use of force should be sufficient to respond decisively, and may exceed the means and intensity of the hostile act/intent, but the nature, duration and scope of force should not exceed what is required.

4.6.3.7.6. The concepts of necessity and proportionality as applicable to self-defense should not be confused with those of military necessity and proportionality as applicable in the law of armed conflict, which together seek to minimize collateral damage during offensive or defensive operations during armed conflict. Indeed, the defense of friendly forces against enemy attack during armed conflict would not (subject to prevailing rules of engagement) involve the concept of self-defense at all.

**4.6.3.8. Surprise leverages the principle of security by attacking the enemy at a time, place, or in a manner for which they are not prepared.** The speed and range of air, space, and cyberspace capabilities, coupled with their flexibility and versatility, allow air forces to achieve surprise more readily than other forces. The final choice of timing and tactics rests with the air component commander because terrain and distance are not inhibiting factors.

4.6.3.8.1. Surprise is one of airpower's strongest advantages. Operation EL DORADO CANYON (the U.S. raid on Libya) and the opening day of the air campaign during Operation DESERT STORM highlight examples where airpower achieved surprise.

4.6.3.8.2. Airpower can enhance and empower other forces to achieve surprise as well. The rapid global reach of airpower can enable surface forces to reach foreign destinations quickly, thus seizing the initiative through surprise.

4.6.3.9. **Simplicity calls for avoiding unnecessary complexity in organizing, preparing, planning, and conducting military operations.** Simplicity ensures that guidance, plans, and orders are as simple and direct as the objective allows. Simple guidance allows subordinate commanders the freedom to operate creatively within their portion of the operational environment, supporting the concept of decentralized execution. Common equipment, a common understanding of Service and joint doctrine, and familiarity with procedures through joint exercises and training, can help overcome complexity. Straightforward plans, unambiguous organization, and clearly-defined command relationships are central to reducing complexity as well.

4.6.4. **Additional Principles of Operations.**

In addition to the traditionally-held principles of war, an additional set of principles has been developed as a result of experience in contingency operations. These were first cast as "principles of military operations other than war" and later as "the political dimension of smaller-scale contingencies." A distinguishing characteristic of such operations has been the degree to which political objectives influence operations and tactics. (Note that joint doctrine does not contain unity of effort as an additional principle.) These additional principles are:

4.6.4.1. **Often the military is not the sole, or even the lead, agency in contingency operations.** Some operations are, by their nature, predominantly military. In most situations, however, the military will likely be one agency of many. As is especially common in stability operations, military forces often find themselves supporting the other instruments of national power. While unity of command is critical within the military forces, most of these operations demand unity of effort among a wide range of agencies to ensure that they coordinate their resources and focus on the same goal.

4.6.4.1.1. **Unity of effort becomes critical during interagency operations and can best be achieved through consensus building.** Whereas the main effort in military planning is on developing courses of action, the main effort in interagency planning should be to develop a shared, detailed understanding of the situation. This allows the various agencies to better understand how they can best apply their respective capabilities and measure success.

4.6.4.2. **Restraint is the disciplined application of military force appropriate to the situation.** Commanders should recognize that in some types of operations, use of more force than the minimum that is reasonably necessary (even though under or at the maximum permissible) may lead to escalation to a higher intensity conflict; could adversely affect efforts to gain or maintain legitimacy; and may impede the attainment of both short- and long-term goals.

4.6.4.2.1. Air component commanders should begin developing a force structure by outlining the necessary capabilities needed for an operation and then follow up by deploying the appropriate "tailored" air, space, and cyberspace force mix. In order to maintain effective security while also exercising restraint, commanders should develop very clear rules on the use of force and rules of engagement. The rules of engagement for contingency operations are often more restrictive, detailed, and sensitive to political concerns than in sustained combat operations. Moreover, these rules may change frequently during operations. For all operations, Airmen should understand that restraint in the use of force is appropriate and more easily justified. However, restraint does not preclude the ability to use armed force, both lethal and nonlethal, when necessary in self-defense.

4.6.4.3. **The principle of perseverance encompasses the patient, resolute, and persistent pursuit of national goals and objectives, for as long as necessary to achieve them.** Some contingency operations involve a one-time occurrence or a short-term operation to maintain stability until local authorities can take over. Many missions, however, especially peace operations and building partner capacity, require a long-term commitment. The U.S. should be prepared to stay involved in a region for a protracted time in order to achieve its strategic goals. Complex problems often cannot be solved quickly; if a situation has been building for a long time, it may take the same amount of time or longer to resolve it. With this in mind, objectives should be established for the conditions under which forces may leave, rather than simply by a timetable for departure.

4.6.4.4. **In order to reduce the threat to U.S. forces and to enable them to work toward their objective, the U.S. should be viewed as a legitimate actor in the mission, working towards multi-lateral interests including our own.** While legitimacy is principally generated by U.S. political leadership, legitimacy in the eyes of the host nation or target population could be affected more by the actions of the military. One key means of promoting legitimacy for certain types of contingency operations is through robust and effective military public affairs operations. Commanders should work closely with the host-nation government (if, in fact, there is one) at all levels to help preserve and foster the sense of legitimacy of mission.

**4.7. Tenets of Airpower.**

The application of airpower is refined by several fundamental guiding truths. These truths are known as tenets. They reflect not only the unique historical and doctrinal evolution of airpower, but also the current appreciation for the nature of airpower. The tenets of airpower complement the principles of joint operations. While the principles of war provide general guidance on the application of military forces, the tenets provide more specific considerations for the employment of airpower. The tenets of airpower are identified below. (Reference: Volume 1 – Basic Doctrine)

4.7.1. **The tenet of centralized control and decentralized execution is critical to effective employment of airpower.** Indeed, they are the fundamental organizing principles for airpower, having been proven over decades of experience as the most effective and efficient means of employing it. This tenet enables the principle of mass while maintaining economy of force. Because of airpower's unique potential to directly affect the strategic and operational levels of war, it should be controlled by a single Airman who maintains the broad, strategic perspective necessary to balance and prioritize the use of a powerful, highly desired yet limited force. A single air component commander, focused on the broader aspects of an operation, can best balance or mediate urgent demands for tactical support against longer-term strategic and operational requirements. The ability to concentrate the air effort to fulfill the highest priorities for effects and to quickly shift the effort can only be accomplished through centralized control. On the other hand, the flexibility to take advantage of tactical opportunities and to effectively respond to shifting local circumstances can only be achieved through decentralized execution.

4.7.1.1. This tenet is best appreciated as a general philosophy for the command and control of airpower. The construct of centralized control is an encapsulation of a hard-learned truth: that control of a valuable yet scarce resource (airpower) should be commanded by a single Airman, not parceled out and hardwired to subordinate surface echelons as it was prior to 1943. Tied to this fundamental truth is the recognition that no single Airman is capable of making all decisions, and should thus empower subordinates to respond in accordance with senior leader intent.

4.7.1.2. Centralized control should be accomplished by an Airman at the functional component commander level who maintains a broad focus on the joint force commander's objectives to direct, integrate, prioritize, plan, coordinate, and assess the use of air, space, and cyberspace assets across the range of military operations. Centralized control may be manifest at different levels within a combatant command depending on how the air component(s) is (are) organized and the nature of the supporting command and control architecture (functional or geographic). Also, due to the dynamics of the operational environment, control over some capabilities may, over time, shift up or down the command chain according to changes in priorities.

4.7.1.3. Centralized control empowers the air component commander to respond to changes in the operational environment and take advantage of fleeting opportunities, and embodies the tenet of flexibility and versatility. Some would rather this be just "centralized planning and direction." From an Airman's perspective, "planning and directing" do not convey all aspects of control implied in "centralized control," which maximizes the flexibility and effectiveness of airpower. Centralized control is thus pivotal to the determination of continuing advantage. However, it should not become a recipe for micromanagement, stifling the initiative subordinates need to deal with combat's inevitable uncertainties.

4.7.1.4. Decentralized execution is defined as the "delegation of authority to designated lower-level commanders" and other tactical-level decision makers to achieve effective span of control and to foster disciplined initiative and tactical flexibility. It allows subordinates, all the way down to the tactical level, to exploit situational responsiveness and fleeting opportunities in rapidly changing, fluid situations. The benefits inherent in decentralized execution, however, are maximized only when a commander clearly communicates intent and subordinate commanders frame their actions accordingly.

4.7.1.5. Centralized control and decentralized execution of airpower provide broad global or theater-wide focus while allowing operational flexibility to meet military objectives. They assure concentration of effort while maintaining economy of force. They exploit airpower's versatility and flexibility to ensure that it remains responsive, survivable, and sustainable.

4.7.1.6. Execution should be decentralized within a C2 architecture that exploits the ability of front-line decision makers (such as strike package leaders, air battle managers, forward air controllers) to make on-scene decisions during complex, rapidly unfolding operations. Modern communications technology may tempt commanders to take direct control of distant events and override the decisions of forward leaders, even when such control is not operationally warranted. This should be resisted at all costs in all functional components—not just air. Despite impressive gains in data exploitation and automated decision aids, a single person cannot, with confidence, achieve and maintain detailed situational awareness over individual missions when fighting a conflict involving many simultaneous engagements taking place throughout a large area, or over individual missions conducted in locally fluid and complex environments.

4.7.1.7. There may be some situations where there may be valid reasons for control of specific operations at higher levels, most notably when the JFC (or perhaps even higher authorities) may wish to control strategic effects, even at the sacrifice of tactical efficiency. However, such instances should be rare, as in the short notice prosecution of high-value, time-sensitive targets, or when the operational climate demands tighter control over selected missions due to political sensitivities, such as the potential for collateral damage or mistargeting, or in the case of nuclear employment. In all cases, senior commanders balance overall campaign execution against the pressing need for tactical effectiveness. As long as a subordinate's decision supports the superior commander's intent and meets campaign objectives, subordinates should be allowed to take the initiative during execution.

4.7.2. Although often used interchangeably, flexibility and versatility are different.

4.7.2.1. **Flexibility allows airpower to exploit mass and maneuver simultaneously.** Flexibility allows airpower to shift from one campaign objective to another, quickly and decisively; to "go downtown" on one sortie, then hit fielded enemy forces the next; to re-role assets quickly from a preplanned mission to support an unanticipated need for close air support of friendly troops in contact with enemy forces.

4.7.2.2. **Versatility is the ability to employ airpower effectively at the strategic, operational, and tactical levels of war and provide a wide variety of tasks in concert with other joint force elements.** Airpower has the potential to achieve this unmatched synergy through asymmetric and parallel operations. Space and cyberspace capabilities are especially able to simultaneously support multiple taskings around the globe and support tasks at all levels of warfare.

4.7.3. **Synergistic Effects. The proper application of a coordinated force across multiple domains can produce effects that exceed the contributions of forces employed individually.** The destruction of a large number of targets through attrition warfare is rarely the key objective in modern war. Instead, the objective is the precise, coordinated application of the various elements of airpower and surface power to bring disproportionate pressure on enemy leaders to comply with our national will (affecting their intent) or to cause functional defeat of the enemy forces (affecting their capability). Airpower's ability to observe adversaries allows joint force commanders to counter enemy movements with unprecedented speed and agility. Airpower is unique in its ability to dictate the tempo and direction of an entire warfighting effort regardless of the scale of the operation.

4.7.4. **Persistence. Air, space, and cyberspace operations may be conducted continuously against a broad spectrum of targets.** Airpower's exceptional speed and range allow its forces to visit and revisit wide ranges of targets nearly at will. Airpower does not have to occupy terrain or remain constantly in proximity to areas of operation to bring force upon targets. Space forces in particular hold the ultimate high ground, and as space systems continue to advance and proliferate, they offer the potential for persistent overhead access; unmanned aircraft systems offer similar possibilities from the atmosphere.

4.7.4.1. Examples of persistent operations might be maintaining a continuous flow of materiel to peacetime distressed areas; Air Force intelligence, surveillance, and reconnaissance capabilities monitoring adversaries to ensure they cannot conduct actions counter to those agreed upon; assuring that targets are kept continually out of commission; or ensuring that resources and facilities are denied an enemy or provided to an ally during a specified time. The end result would be to deny the opponent an opportunity to seize the initiative and to directly accomplish assigned tasks.

4.7.4.2. Factors such as enemy resilience, effective defenses, or environmental concerns may prevent commanders from quickly attaining their objectives. However, for many situations, airpower provides the most efficient and effective means to attain national objectives. Commanders must persist in the conduct of operations and resist pressures to divert resources to other efforts unless such diversions are vital to attaining theater goals or to survival of an element of the joint force. Given sufficient time, even the most devastating strategic effects can be circumvented by resourceful enemies; the goal is to keep pressure on and not allow the enemy that time.

4.7.5. **Concentration. One of the most constant and important trends throughout military history has been the effort to concentrate overwhelming power at the decisive time and place.** The principles of mass and economy of force deal directly with concentrating overwhelming power at the right time and the right place (or places). The versatility of airpower with its lethality, speed, and persistence makes it an attractive option for many tasks. With capabilities as flexible and versatile as airpower, the demand for them often exceeds the available forces and may result in the fragmentation of the integrated airpower effort in attempts to fulfill the many demands of the operation. Depending on the operational situation, such a course of action may court the triple risk of failing to achieve operational-level objectives, delaying or diminishing the attainment of decisive effects, and increasing the attrition rate of air forces—and consequently risking defeat. Airmen should guard against the inadvertent dilution of airpower effects resulting from high demand.

4.7.6. **Priority. Commanders should establish clear priorities for the use of airpower.** Due to its inherent flexibility and versatility, the demands for airpower may likely exceed available resources. If commanders fail to establish priorities, they can become ineffective. Commanders of all components need to effectively prioritize their requirements for coordinated airpower effects to the joint force commander, and only then can effective priorities for the use of airpower flow from an informed dialogue between the joint force commander and the air component commander. The air component commander should assess the possible uses of component forces and their strengths and capabilities to support the overall joint campaign. Limited resources require that airpower be applied where it can make the greatest contribution to the most critical current joint force commander requirements. The application of airpower should be balanced among its ability to conduct operations at all levels of war, often simultaneously. The principles of mass, offensive, and economy of force, the tenet of concentration, and the Airman's strategic perspective all apply to prioritizing airpower.

4.7.7. **Balance is an essential guideline for air commanders. Much of the skill of an air component commander is reflected in the dynamic and correct balancing of the principles of joint operations and the tenets of airpower to bring Air Force capabilities together to produce synergistic effects.** An air component commander should balance combat opportunity, necessity, effectiveness, efficiency, and the impact on accomplishing assigned objectives against the associated risk to friendly forces.

> 4.7.7.1. An Airman is uniquely—and best—suited to determine the proper theater-wide balance between offensive and defensive air operations, and among strategic, operational, and tactical applications. Air, space, and cyberspace assets are normally available only in finite numbers; thus, balance is a crucial determinant for an air component commander.

*Section 4C—Air Expeditionary Force*

**4.8. Air Expeditionary Force:**

> 4.8.1. **AEF Concept.**
>
> > The AEF concept provides forces and support on a rotational and relatively more predictable basis. The AEF 'force generation' construct establishes a predictable, standardized battle rhythm to ensure operational forces are organized, trained, equipped, and ready to respond to CCDRs' requests for forces. Using a rotational capacity construct, deployed units undergo a period of dwell (i.e., time spent at home station) before entering another deployment/mobilization vulnerability period.
>
> 4.8.2. **Expeditionary Capabilities.**
>
> > The Air Force relies on the AEF as a force management tool to sustain capabilities while rapidly responding to emerging crises. The Air Force supports global combatant commander requirements through a combination of assigned, attached (rotational), and mobility forces that may be forward deployed, transient, or operating from home station. There are four major elements of the AEF structure: readily available force, enabler force, in-place support, and institutional force. The first three elements are components that primarily constitute the Air Force's warfighting capability and are therefore postured in unit type codes.
> >
> > 4.8.2.1. **Readily Available Force.** The readily available force is the primary pool from which the Air Force fulfills Global Force Management Allocation Plan requirements. To meet these requirements, the Air Force aligns its warfighting capabilities (i.e. forces from combat, combat support, and combat service support organizations) based on requirements relative to assigned rotational capabilities for each vulnerability period.
> >
> > 4.8.2.2. **In-place Support. In-place Support.** There are two types of in-place support; forces that almost exclusively employ in direct support of a combatant commander mission, and those that represent the minimum number of requirements to support critical home station operations. In-place support forces are also included in the AEF Concepts.

4.8.2.3. **Demand Force Team.** Demand Force Teams include user assets with a unique set of mission capabilities, such as global mobility forces, Special Operation Forces, personnel recovery forces, space forces, and other uniquely categorized forces that provide support to authorized organizations within and outside the Department of Defense. Most high demand/low supply assets, like these are postured as Demand Force Teams and will rotate as operational requirements dictate. Due to their unique nature, they cannot be easily aligned in AEF battle rhythm; however, every effort must be made to develop a sustainable plan by the Headquarters Air Force/major command functional area managers as a part of the enabler nomination request package.

4.8.2.4. **Institutional Force.** The institutional force consists of those forces assigned to organizations responsible for Secretary of the Air Force directed Title 10 functions at the Air Force level (such as organize, train, equip, recruit, supply, etc.). Examples of these forces include: Military Training Instructors, technical school instructors, and personnel assigned to major commands and Headquarters staff. These organizations will not posture unit type codes in the unit type code availability, unless a waiver is granted by Headquarters Air Force. Although these organizations do not represent a war-fighting capability, the individuals assigned to these organizations are deployable.

4.8.2.5. **AEF Battle Rhythm.** The AEF operates on a 24-month life cycle. This cycle includes periods of normal training, preparation, and deployment vulnerability.

4.8.2.5.1. For most forces, the majority of the AEF battle rhythm is spent in normal training during which forces concentrate on unit missions and basic proficiency events in accordance with applicable Air Force directives and Air Force Specialty Code requirements. This may include Joint, Air Force, or major command exercise participation such as Red Flag and Silver Flag. Most contingency and deployment training should take place during this period. This training and exercise period is also used to fill the unit's assigned/committed mission requirements, filling contingency requirements for 30 days or less and crisis response needs including humanitarian response operations and operational plans.

4.8.2.5.2. Post-deployment reconstitution is included in this period. During the month immediately after deployment, the unit is focused on recovery. Permanent change of station or permanent change of assignment moves into and out of the unit will be de-conflicted to the maximum extent possible to occur during the 3-month period immediately after the vulnerability period.

4.8.2.5.3. For forces aligned in the Enabler force, unit commanders should develop a deployment schedule that provides a measure of predictability to associated Airmen. However, operational requirements may force deviations from the applicable battle rhythm. Major command vice commanders will ensure appropriate mechanisms are in place to ensure Airmen postured as Enablers are provided a measure of predictability/stability

4.8.3. **Global Force Management.**

Global force management is the process the Secretary of Defense and the Chairman of the Joint Chiefs of Staff use to assign forces to combatant commander for mission accomplishment and allocate additional forces to combatant commanders in the event of contingency operations and apportion forces for combatant commander planning in the event contingency operations escalate. Global force management also provides senior decision makers a process to quickly and accurately assess the impact and risk of proposed changes in force assignment, apportionment, and allocation.

4.8.4. **AEF Schedule.**

The AEF schedule operates on two 12-month life cycles that align with the global force management cycle and coincide with fiscal years. Prior to the beginning of every AEF cycle, Air Force specialty functional area managers will revalidate the deployment to dwell period alignment of their respective capability areas and realign forces if necessary. The Air Force goal is that functional areas align to the least strenuous deployment to dwell baseline to minimize risk to the force. Every 12 months a new 24-month AEF schedule will be established

4.8.5. **AEF Teaming Construct.**

The Air Force has transitioned to the AEF Teaming concept. This construct provides a better teaming concept through larger groupings of unit type codes from fewer units/bases in order to allow Airmen to deploy with their supervisors and members of their unit/base. This allows for shared common experiences throughout the deployment process. However, it should be noted, there will be no change to how the Air Force presents forces (air expeditionary task force (rotational), Component-major command-Numbered Air Force (in-place)).

**4.9. Air Expeditionary Force Schedule and Posturing:**

4.9.1. **Posturing.**

The basic building block used in force planning and the deployment of forces is the unit type code. A unit type code is a Joint Chiefs of Staff developed and assigned code, five-character alphanumeric designator uniquely identifying each type unit in the Armed Forces, and its force capability with personnel and/or equipment requirements. The assignment of a unit type code categorizes each type organization into a class or kind of unit having common distinguishing characteristics. All Air Force personnel contribute to the AEF and are inherently deployable or employable in-place. Those organizations identified as a Combat, Combat Support, or Combat Service Support or "war-fighting" organizations will posture unit type codes. Institutional organizations identified as "other" will not posture unit type codes. Posturing unit type codes is based on an organization's funded military authorizations as shown in unit manpower document.

4.9.1.1. AEF forces can be postured as forces *ready to deploy* to support combatant commander worldwide requirements, home station requirements, or reach back support to combatant commanders. This provides balanced war-fighting capabilities across the AEF Construct to support combatant commander requirements. With unit chain-of-command involvement and major command leadership and/or AEF cell oversight, major command functional area managers must determine which unit type codes to posture based on operational need, organizational specifics, and posturing codes within their functional area. Not all unit type codes will be postured, units may be tasked to support a unit type codes they have not postured as long as the unit can meet the unit type code's mission capability statement.

4.9.1.2. The various posturing codes (P-codes) indicate the number of unit type codes that are required for assigned/committed missions, critical home station requirements, and the number of unit type codes available to be simultaneously tasked for deployment.

4.9.1.2.1. **DP.** The minimum number of unit type codes required to accomplish the unit's assigned/committed missions either deployed or in-place. Assigned/committed missions include CCDR missions as well as those of external organizations/agencies that the unit must accomplish.

4.9.1.2.2. **DX.** Represents the minimum number of unit type code requirements to support critical home station operations. These missions are not associated with the assigned/committed mission; failure to accomplish these missions would not impact the assigned/committed mission requirements of the unit.

4.9.1.2.3. **DW.** Represents the maximum number of unit type code requirements available to support CCDR's rotational mission.

4.9.2. **AEF Indicators:**

4.9.2.1. All Airmen will be given an AEF indicator within 15-days of Date Arrive Station. For individuals assigned to readily available forces, their AEF indicator will correspond to the same AEF period as the unit's unit type codes. For individuals assigned to the Institutional Force, the AEF indicator will correspond to an AEF vulnerability period determined by the Airman's commander or equivalent. Except in cases of reaching forward, individuals will deploy during their associated AEF vulnerability period. Changing an individual's AEF indicator will be done only under extenuating circumstances, along with permanent change of station or permanent change of assignment.

4.9.2.2. AEF indicator Association Review. Prior to the start of each AEF Schedule, unit commanders will review AEF indicator codes of assigned Airmen to ensure they match unit type code alignment. In the case of the institutional force, organization commanders (or equivalent) will review AEF indicator codes to ensure equal distribution across the five vulnerability periods to the maximum extent possible while meeting the needs of the organization.

**4.10. Deployment Planning Systems and Tools:**

4.10.1. **Adaptive Planning and Execution System (APEX).** Joint operation planning occurs within a system of joint policies, procedures, and reporting structures known as APEX. APEX is supported by communications and information technology that is used by the joint planning and execution community to monitor, design, plan, execute, and assess mobilization, deployment, employment, sustainment, redeployment, and demobilization activities associated with joint operations. APEX formally integrates the planning activities of the joint planning and execution community and facilitates the seamless transition from planning to execution during times of crisis. APEX is the physical, virtual, and policy structure through which national strategic guidance is translated all the way down to levels used by the Air Force to plan and execute deployment activities. National strategic guidance proceeds through the following levels down to Air Force-specific guidance on deployment and support for the AEF.

4.10.1.1. **National-Level Strategies**. The National Security Strategy is prepared by the president for Congress, outlining our nation's major security concerns and how the administration plans to address them using all instruments of national power (diplomatic, informational, and economic as well as military). The National Defense Strategy describes how the Department of Defense will support the objectives lined out in the National Security Strategy, as well as providing a framework for other Department of Defense guidance, specifically on deliberate planning, force development, and intelligence. The National Military Strategy provides the Chairman Joint Chief of Staff advice regarding the security environment; it also defines national-level military objectives (i.e., ends), how to accomplish these objectives (ways), and addresses the military capabilities required to execute the strategy (means). The Quadrennial Defense Review helps articulate the latest National Security Strategy and National Defense Strategy by defining force structure, modernization plans, and budget plans.

4.10.1.2. **Unified Command Plan.** The Unified Command Plan establishes combatant command missions and responsibilities, addresses assignment of forces, delineates geographic areas of responsibility for geographic combatant commanders, and specifies responsibilities for functional combatant commanders.

4.10.1.3. **Guidance for Employment of the Force.** The Guidance for Employment of the Force provides two-year direction to combatant commands for operational planning, force management, security cooperation, and posture planning. The Guidance for Employment of the Force is the method through which the Secretary of Defense translates strategic priorities in the National Security Strategy, National Defense Strategy, and Quadrennial Defense Review into implementable direction for operational activities.

4.10.1.4. **Joint Strategic Capabilities Plan.** The Joint Strategic Capabilities Plan is the primary vehicle through which the Joint Chiefs of Staff exercise responsibility for directing the preparation of joint plans. The Joint Strategic Capabilities Plan provides military strategic- and operational-level guidance to combatant commanders, Service Chiefs, combat support agencies, and applicable Department of Defense agencies for preparation of combatant commanders' ongoing, steady-state campaign plans, as well as plans for specific contingencies or operations, *based on current military capabilities*. The Joint Strategic Capabilities Plan is the link between strategic guidance provided in the Guidance for Employment of the Force and joint operation planning activities and products that accomplish that guidance.

4.10.2. **U.S. Air Force War and Mobilization Plan (WMP).** The WMP is the Air Force's five-volume supporting document to the Joint Strategic Capabilities Plan. The WMP volumes provide the Air Staff, planners, and commanders with current policies, planning factors, and Chairman Joint Chief of Staff-apportioned forces for conducting and supporting operations. The five volumes consist of:

4.10.2.1. **Volume 1, Basic Plan and Supporting Supplements (WMP-1)**, provides a consolidated reference source for general policies and guidance for mobilization planning and the support of combat forces in war and other operations.

4.10.2.2. **Volume 2, Plans Listing and Summary (WMP-2)**, is the single-source listing of all active plans with time-phased force and deployment data, or at least the Air Force portions of the time-phased force and deployment data). Part 1 lists all combatant commander plans required by the Joint Strategic Capabilities Plan. Part 2 consists of the supporting plans written by component headquarters in support of Part 1, including the Air Force Service component.

4.10.2.3. **Volume 3, Combat and Support Forces (WMP-3)**, contains four parts: Part 1 lists combat forces. *When building the Air Force time-phased force and deployment data to accompany plans, component headquarters use only forces identified in Vol. 3, Part 1.* Part 2 lists the Air Force unit type code availability, containing all postured unit type code capability in the Air Force. Part 3 contains the Air Force Readiness Spares Package authorization document. Part 4 contains the capability annexes to the AEF Force Presence Policy, which describes how the Air Force makes its forces available through assignment, apportionment, and allocation to combatant commanders.

4.10.2.4. **Volume 4, Wartime Aircraft Activity (WMP-4)**, documents aircraft movement and operation by geographic location in plans, listed by current year (Part 1) and one year out (Part 2). It also provides guidance for and lists war reserve materiel, mission oriented items, and non-aircraft unit related ration requirements, again by location.

4.10.2.5. **Volume 5, Basic Planning Factors and Data (WMP-5)**, provides approved U.S. Air Force planning factors by aircraft type and theater, serving as a basis for establishing worldwide support for programmed force levels, based on aircraft apportioned in the WMP-3 in support of the Joint Strategic Capabilities Plan.

4.10.3. The information contained in the WMP's volumes provides the basis for Air Force component-level planning in support of combatant commanders' theater and functional campaign plans. These specify strategies for the combatant commands' steady-state, ongoing operations in support of national guidance. The WMP also supports deliberate planning for specific contingency operations, which are generally specific branches or sequels of combatant commanders' campaign plans, and which may be developed into detailed "on-the-shelf" concept plans (with or without an Air Force time-phased force and deployment data) or operation plans. These concept plans and operation plans then often form the basis of crisis action planning for related contingencies. Such plans will contain tasking for the Air Force Service component as well as the joint or combined functional air component. Crisis action planning will further develop requirements into specific operation orders (such as warning, planning, alert, and execute orders) applicable to particular units. It is important to realize, however, that commanders and planners can "reach down" from any of the levels explained above and require base- or unit-level deployment planning (and sometimes execution)—from theater campaign plans all the ways down to crisis execution orders.

4.10.4. **Base Level Deployment Planning and Execution:**

4.10.4.1. **Force Presence.** All Air Force personnel contribute to the AEF. Air Force Personnel Center (or other designated force manager) supports AEF operations by identifying the most ready and available forces as part of unit type codes or as individuals to meet the stated requirement.

4.10.4.2. **Designed Operational Capabilities Statement.** Document prepared by a parent major command that consolidates reporting criteria and information based on Authoritative Data Sources requirements and Functional Manager inputs. The designed operational capabilities statement compiles Core Mission Essential Task List, War and Mobilization Plan, unit type code Availability and specific resources units are required to report. The designed operational capabilities statement ensures standards of reporting and to assist the units and commanders with gathering and reporting readiness data.

4.10.4.3. **Mission Capability Statement.** A short paragraph describing the mission capabilities that higher headquarters planners expect of a specific unit type code. The statement usually contains pertinent information such as the type of base where commanders will deploy the unit, the unit's functional activities, and other augmentation requirements necessary to conduct specific missions.

4.10.4.4. **Operation Plan.** An operation plan is any plan for the conduct of military operations prepared in response to actual or potential contingencies. They are based upon stated assumptions and are in the form of directive employed by higher authority to permit subordinate commanders to prepare supporting plans and orders. Combatant commanders create operation plans in response to strategic-level guidance and commanders of subordinate commands may also create them in response to requirements tasked by the establishing unified commander. Operation plans are prepared in either complete format, containing a full description of the concept of operations, all annexes applicable to the plan, and a time-phased force and deployment data, or as a concept plan, with or without a time-phased force and deployment data.

4.10.4.5. **Time Phased Force and Deployment Data.** When developing or executing plans, a time phased force and deployment data is the data base used to coordinate the movement of forces into their operational locations, almost like a baseball team's batting order. The time-phased force and deployment data includes forces from all Services and their movement requirements. A time-phased force and deployment data contains critical information to include the time phasing of forces by C-Dates to specific destinations (called routing data). Additionally, through the use of unit type codes, this information includes personnel and equipment details. A time-phased force and deployment data is a deployment planning and execution tool containing live data that changes frequently. Time-phased force and deployment data provide a prioritized list of what unit type codes deploy in support of a particular plan, catalog combatant commander requirements, route forces, and establish transportation requirements. time-phased force and deployment data must be prioritized due to all Services competing for the movement assets.

4.10.4.6. **Installation Deployment Readiness Cell.** Centralized function aligned under the Logistic Readiness Squadron commander and located within the Logistic Readiness Squadron responsible for identifying, validating, and distributing deployment taskings and information. The installation deployment readiness cell is the day-to-day focal point for all deployment and execution operations. The permanent staff consists of the installation deployment officer, Logistic Readiness Squadron/Logistics Plans and Integration, and Force Support Squadron/Personnel Readiness Flight personnel.

4.10.4.7. **Installation Deployment Officer.** The designated military or federal civilian fully qualified logistics readiness officer that acts on behalf of the host installation/wing commander in directing, controlling, coordinating, and executing the deployment of in-place (home station) and aggregated contingency forces and installation deployment exercises (to include tenant units). Figure 4.1., provides the steps involved within a tasking process.

**Figure 4.1. Tasking Process.**

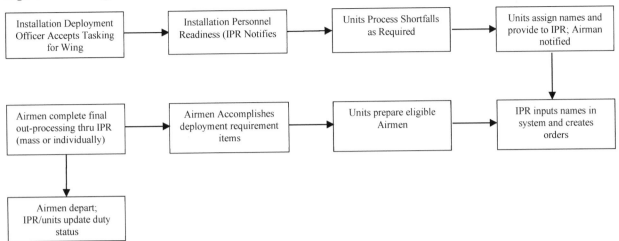

4.10.4.8. **Installation Personnel Readiness.** The Installation Personnel Readiness is an office in the Force Support Squadron responsible for providing installation wide personnel deployment planning and execution and personnel support in matters pertaining to; deployment availability information, personnel accountability, and duty status reporting for contingency, exercise, and deployments. Installation Personnel Readiness responsibilities are covered in the following five categories: planning, global command and control system, accountability, deployment processing, and general.

4.10.4.9. **Unit Deployment Manager.** The Unit Deployment Manager is appointed by the unit commander to manage all deployment readiness and training aspects for deployable personnel and equipment within their unit to ensure they are deployment ready. In addition, unit deployment managers support redeployed personnel in the redeployment support process, and serve as the primary liaison to the unit training manager, flight/squadron leadership, wing training functions regarding deployment related issues, and installation deployment readiness cell.

4.10.4.10. **AEF Online.**

4.10.4.10.1. **Commander's Toolkit.** Commander's Toolkit is a nonsecure internet protocol router-net based system that provides information on deployment readiness, including individual medical readiness data at the unit level for commanders via the "Commander's Toolkit" tab on every page of AEF Online (nonsecure internet protocol router). This tool was specifically built for base-level commanders, unit deployment managers, and other key staff, to monitor and manage the deployment status of their units and e-mail unit members with outstanding requirements directly from the tool.

4.10.4.10.2. **Personal Deployment Preparedness Tool.** The Personal Deployment Preparedness Tool provides personalized information at the individual level for all uniformed Airmen. The information provided includes; member's duty status, security clearance, AEF Indicator, medical requirements (immunizations, medical equipment, deployment availability codes, dental status, preventive health assessment and laboratory requirements), and total force awareness training and Basic Airman Readiness, expeditionary skills proficiency pre-deployment training requirements extracted from the advanced distributed learning system.

4.10.4.10.3. **AEF Unit Type Code Reporting Tool.** AEF reporting tool measures AEF readiness at the unit type code level. Force providers are involved in AEF reporting tool reporting as AEF reporting tool monitors or as suppliers/receivers of AEF reporting tool reporting information. AFI 10-244, *Reporting Status of Aerospace Expeditionary Forces*, provides guideline for assessing and reporting unit type code capabilities, reporting guidelines, and details daily maintenance requirements. Through their unit AEF reporting tool monitors, commanders report the ability of a unit type code to perform its mission capability statement anywhere in the world at the time of the assessment. AEF reporting tool highlights missing resources and quantifies missing requirements for additional justification when submitting budgets.

4.10.4.10.3.1. AEF reporting tool is the only assessment system that reports at the unit type code level and is the primary system used to source unit type codes for taskings and contingencies. Commanders ensure AEF reporting tool is accurate and up-to-date. Inaccurate AEF reporting tool reporting leads to taskings that exceed capability, shortfalls/reclamas, delays in filling combatant commander requirements, and Airmen receiving short-notice taskings.

4.10.4.10.3.2. Commanders conduct two types of unit type code assessments in AEF reporting tool: Readiness Assessments and Tasking Assessments. Readiness stoplight assessments (Green, Yellow, or Red) indicate whether a unit type code can perform its mission capability statement anywhere in the world at the time of the assessment. To report accurately, commanders and unit AEF reporting tool Monitors, who may also be the unit deployment manager, must know their unit type codes requirements and the status of their personnel and equipment and actions required to bring all unit type codes to "Green".

## Section 4D—The Joint Force

### 4.11. Introduction.

This section assists Airmen to successfully operate as members of a joint team. Specifically, this section discusses the foundations of joint doctrine, characterizes doctrine governing unified direction of armed forces, outlines the functions of the Department of Defense and its major components, describes the fundamental principles for joint command and control, details doctrine for joint commands, describes joint planning, provides guidance for multinational operations.

### 4.12. Foundations of Joint Doctrine.

Joint doctrine promotes a common perspective from which to plan, train, and conduct military operations. The foundations of joint doctrine represents what is taught, believed, and advocated as what is right (that is, what works best). U.S. military service is based on values that U.S. military experience has proven to be vital for operational success.

### 4.13. Fundamental Principles for Joint Command and Control:

4.13.1. Unity of command means all forces operate under a single commander with the requisite authority to direct all forces employed in pursuit of a common purpose. Unity of effort, however, requires coordination and cooperation among all forces toward a commonly recognized objective, although they are not necessarily part of the same command structure.

4.13.2. The President and the Secretary of Defense exercise authority, direction and control of the Armed Forces through two distinct branches of the chain of command and control. The operational branch, used for executing missions, runs from the President, through the Secretary of Defense to the combatant commander. The operational branch includes the following types of command authorities:

4.13.2.1. Combatant command authority is the authority of a combatant commander to perform those functions of command over assigned forces involving organizing and employing commands and forces, assigning tasks, designating objectives, and giving authoritative direction over all aspects of military operations, joint training (or in the case of U.S. special operations command, training of assigned forces), and logistics necessary to accomplish the missions assigned to the command. It cannot be delegated or transferred.

4.13.2.2. Operational control is the command authority that may be exercised by commanders at any echelon at or below the level of combatant command and may be delegated within the command. Operational control is inherent in combatant command and is the authority to perform those functions of command over subordinate forces involving organizing and employing commands and forces, assigning tasks, designating objectives, and giving authoritative direction necessary to accomplish the mission. Operational control includes authoritative direction over all aspects of military operations and joint training necessary to accomplish missions assigned to the command; it does not include authoritative direction for logistics or matters of administration, discipline, internal organization, or unit training.

4.13.2.3. Tactical control is the command authority over assigned or attached forces or commands, or military capability or forces made available for tasking that is limited to the detailed direction and control of movements or maneuvers within the operational area necessary to accomplish assigned missions or tasks. Tactical control is inherent in operational control and may be delegated to and exercised by commanders at any echelon at or below the level of combatant command.

4.13.2.4. A support relationship is established by a superior commander between subordinate commanders when one organization should aid, protect, complement, or sustain another force. Support may be exercised by commanders at any echelon at or below the combatant command level. This includes the Secretary of Defense designating a support relationship between combatant commanders as well as within a combatant command. The designation of supporting relationships is important as it conveys priorities to commanders and staffs that are planning or executing joint operations. The support command relationship is, by design, a somewhat vague but very flexible arrangement. The establishing authority (the common superior commander) is responsible for ensuring that both the supported commander and supporting commanders understand the degree of authority that the supported commander is granted.

4.13.3. The administrative branch of the chain of command, from the President through the Secretary of Defense to the Secretaries of the military departments to the service chiefs, provides the authority for the Secretary of the military department to accomplish those functions and responsibilities of administration and support described in 10 United States Code.

4.13.3.1. Administrative control is direction or exercise of authority over subordinate or other organizations in respect to administration and support, including organization of service forces, control of resources and equipment, personnel management, unit logistics, individual and unit training, readiness, mobilization, demobilization, discipline, and other matters not included in the operational missions of the subordinate or other organizations.

4.13.3.2. Administrative control is a service command authority, and flows through service, not joint, channels. This authority is not an operational command authority but provides the requisite authority for Services to execute their individual "organize, train, and equip" functions.

4.13.4. All National Guard and Reserve forces (except those specifically exempted) are assigned by the Secretary of Defense to the combatant commands. However, those forces are available for operational missions only when mobilized for specific periods, by law, or when ordered to Regular Air Force after being validated for employment by their parent service.

**4.14. Joint Force Organization:**

4.14.1. Joint forces are established at three levels: unified commands, subordinate unified commands, and joint task forces, and can be established on either a geographic area or functional basis (Figure 4.2). These organizations are commanded by a joint force commander. A joint force commander is a general term applied to a combatant commander, subunified commander, or joint force commander authorized to exercise combatant command (command authority) or operational control over a joint force.

4.14.1.1. A unified command is a command with broad continuing missions under a single commander, composed of forces from two or more military departments, and established by the President, through the Secretary of Defense, with the advice and assistance of the Chairman, Joint Chief of Staff.

4.14.1.2. A specified command is a command that has broad continuing missions and is established by the President, through the Secretary of Defense, with the advice and assistance of the Chairman, Joint Chief of Staff. Currently, there are no specified commands designated.

**Figure 4.2. Types of Joint Force Organizations**

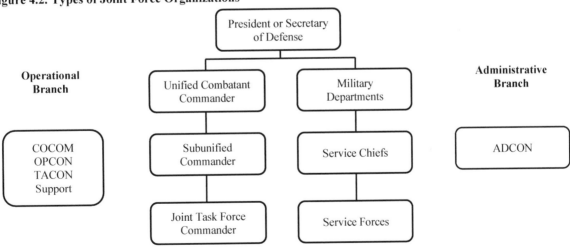

4.14.1.3. When authorized by the Secretary of Defense through the Chairman, Joint Chief of Staff, commanders of unified commands may establish subordinate unified commands to conduct operations on a continuing basis using the criteria set forth for unified commands.

4.14.1.4. A joint task force is a joint force that is constituted and so designated by the Secretary of Defense, a combatant commander, a subordinate unified commander, or an existing joint task force commander. A joint task force may be established on a geographical area or functional basis when the mission has a specific limited objective and does not require overall centralized control of logistics.

4.14.2. The key to successful employment of Air Force forces as part of a joint force effort is providing a single Air Force commander with the responsibility and authority to properly organize, train, equip and employ Air Force forces to accomplish assigned functions and tasks. The title of this commander is Commander, Air Force Forces. Operationally, the Commander, Air Force Forces should be prepared to employ Air Force forces as directed by the joint force commander, and if directed be prepared to employ joint air forces as the joint force air component commander. In either event, the Commander, Air Force Forces should also ensure that Air Force forces are prepared to execute the missions assigned by the joint force commander. The requirements and responsibilities of the COMAFFOR and joint force air component commander are inextricably linked; both are critical to operational success.

4.14.2.1. Although all Air Force units, regardless of level, have an Air Force commander, the title of Commander, Air Force Forces is reserved exclusively to the single Air Force commander of an Air Force Service component assigned or attached to a joint force commander at the unified combatant command, subordinate unified command, or joint task force level. The Secretary of Defense/combatant commander may elect to permanently establish a subordinate unified command or temporarily establish a subordinate joint task force as part of his/her organizational structure. The commanders of these subordinate joint forces are, by joint and Air Force doctrine, joint force commanders at a lower level than the combatant commander. If Air Force forces are assigned or attached to subordinate joint force commanders, that action creates an Air Force Service component with a separate Commander, Air Force Forces directly responsible to the appropriate joint force commander.

4.14.2.2. The Commander, Air Force Forces should normally be designated at a command level above the operating forces and should not be dual-hatted as commander of one of the subordinate operating units. This allows the Commander, Air Force Forces to focus at the operational level of war, while subordinate commanders lead their units at the tactical level.

4.14.2.3. The Commander, Air Force Forces commands the Air Force Service component to the joint force commander. At the combatant command or subordinate unified command level this is normally a standing permanently assigned organization. At the joint task force level the Air Force Service component will normally be an air expeditionary task force. At whatever level, the Air Force Service component presents a joint force commander with a task-organized, integrated package with the appropriate balance of force, sustainment, control, and force protection. Every Air Force Service component presents a scalable, tailorable organization with three elements: a single commander, embodied in the Commander, Air Force Forces; appropriate command and control mechanisms; and tailored and fully supported forces.

4.14.2.4. The air expeditionary task force will be tailored to the mission; this includes not only forces, but also the ability to command and control those forces for the missions assigned. When forming an air expeditionary task force, the Commander, Air Force Forces should draw first from in-theater resources, if available. If augmentation is needed, or if in-theater forces are not available, the Air Force will draw as needed from the AEF currently on rotation. These forces, whether in-theater or deployed from out of theater, should be fully supported with the requisite maintenance, logistical support, health services, and administrative elements. These forces will form up within the air expeditionary task force as expeditionary wings, groups, squadrons, flights, detachments, or elements, as necessary to provide reasonable spans of control and command elements at appropriate levels and to provide unit identity.

4.14.2.5. Air expeditionary task force command and control mechanisms are in place and are usually known as an air operations center. An air operations center may be regional or functional, aligning with the purpose of the unified command they support. The Commander, Air Force Forces requires command activities as tools to assist in exercising operational control, tactical control, and administrative control. The Commander, Air Force Forces uses an air operations center to exercise control of air and space operations, and a service component staff (commonly called the Air Force forces staff) to exercise support operations and administrative control. The character of the operations center may vary, depending on the nature of the forces. For air mobility operations, the operations center may be the 618th Air Operations Center (formerly the Tanker Airlift Control Center) at Scott Air Force Base, while space operations would leverage the 614th Air Operations Center at Vandenberg Air Force Base.

4.14.2.6. An air expeditionary task force also needs a command entity responsible for the deployment and sustainment of Air Force forces. The Air Force forces staff is the mechanism through which the Commander, Air Force Forces exercises service responsibilities. These sustainment activities are sometimes referred to as "beds, beans, and bullets." The Air Force forces staff is also responsible for the long-range planning and theater engagement operations that fall outside the air operation center's current operational focus.

4.14.2.7. The core capabilities of the air operations center and Air Force forces staff should be well-established, but tailored in size and function according to the theater and the operation. Not all operations require a full-up air operations center with over 1,000 people or a large Air Force forces staff. Smaller operations, such as some humanitarian operations, can make do with a small control center that does little more than scheduling and reporting.

4.14.3. Combatant commanders and commanders of subordinate unified commands and joint task force commanders have the authority to establish functional component commands to control military operations (Figure 4.3). Joint force commanders may decide to establish a functional component command to integrate planning; reduce their span of control; and/or significantly improve combat efficiency, information flow, unity of effort, weapon systems management, component interaction, and control over the scheme of maneuver.

**Figure 4.3. Joint Force Organization with Functional and Service Component**

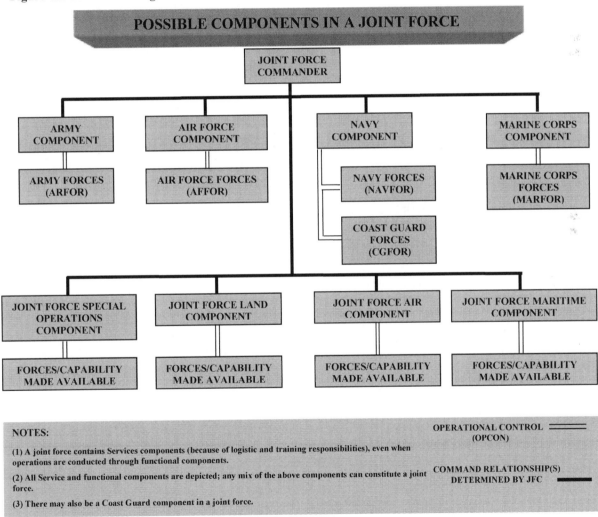

4.14.3.1. If air assets from more than one service are present within a joint force, the joint force commander normally will designate a joint force air component commander to exploit the full capabilities of joint air operations. The a joint force air component commander should be the service component commander with the preponderance of air capabilities and the ability to plan, task, and control joint air operations. If working with allies in a coalition or alliance operation, the joint force air component commander may be designated as the combined force air component commander. Both joint and U.S. Air Force doctrine state that one individual will normally be dual-hatted as commander, Air Force forces and a joint force air component commander/combined force air component commander. The U.S. Air Force prefers—and in fact, plans and trains—to employ through a commander, Air Force forces who is then prepared to assume responsibilities as aa joint force air component commander if so designated. The joint force air component commander recommends the proper employment of air forces from multiple components. The a joint force air component commander also plans, coordinates, allocates tasks, executes, and assesses air and space operations to accomplish assigned operational missions. Because of the wide scope of air operations, the joint force air component commander will typically maintain the same joint operating area/theater-wide perspective as the joint force commander. The joint force air component commander, as with any component commander, should not also be dual-hatted as the joint force commander.

4.14.3.2. Functional component commanders normally exercise tactical control of forces made available to them by the joint force commander. Thus, a Commander, Air Force Forces exercises operational control of Air Force forces and, acting as a joint force air component commander, normally exercises tactical control of any Navy, Army, Marine, and coalition air assets made available for tasking (i.e., those forces not retained for their own service's organic operations).

*"In preparing for battle I have always found that plans are useless, but planning is indispensable."*

General Dwight D. Eisenhower
34th president of the United States, 1953–1961
(1890–1969)

**4.15. Joint Operation Planning.**

Joint operation planning consists of planning activities associated with joint military operations by combatant commanders and their subordinate joint force commanders in response to contingencies and crises. Joint operation planning transforms national strategic objectives into activities by development of operational products that include planning for the mobilization, deployment, employment, sustainment, redeployment, and demobilization of joint forces. Furthermore, joint operation planning ties the military instrument of national power to the achievement of national security goals and objectives and is essential to securing strategic end states across the range of military operations. Planning begins with the end state in mind, providing a unifying purpose around which actions and resources are focused.

4.15.1. Joint operation planning provides a common basis for discussion, understanding, and change for the joint force, its subordinate and higher headquarters, the joint planning and execution community, and the national leadership. The APEX system facilitates iterative dialogue and collaborative planning between the multiple echelons of command to ensure that the military instrument of national power is employed in accordance with national priorities, and that the plan is continuously reviewed and updated as required and adapted according to changes in strategic guidance, resources, or the operational environment. Joint operation planning also identifies capabilities outside Department of Defense required for achieving the strategic objectives to reach the end state by providing a forum that facilitates the inter-organizational coordination that enables unified action.

4.15.2. The APEX system operates in a networked, collaborative environment, which facilitates dialogue among senior leaders, concurrent and parallel plan development, and collaboration across multiple planning levels. The joint planning and execution community uses the APEX system to monitor, plan, and execute mobilization, deployment, employment, sustainment, redeployment, and demobilization activities associated with joint operations. Clear strategic guidance and frequent interaction between senior leaders and planners promote early understanding of, and agreement on, planning assumptions, considerations, risks, and other key factors.

4.15.3. In peacetime, combatant commanders develop campaign plans to delineate their strategies for ongoing, steady-state operations intended to deliver continuing strategic advantage to the U.S. and its allies. Planners develop branch and sequel plans to these campaign plans to cover particular potential contingencies within their areas of responsibility. These contingency plans can be elaborated into one of four levels of detail, each with characteristic planning products:

4.15.3.1. **Commander's Estimate**. Produces multiple potential courses of action to address the contingency and complete the mission. It contains the supported commander's evaluation of the potential courses of action along with a recommended courses of action.

4.15.3.2. **Base Plan**. This describes a concept of operations that addresses the contingency, based on a selected course of action. It identifies major forces involved, the concept of support, and anticipated timelines for completing the mission (often expressed in "lines of effort"). It normally does not contain annexes or time-phased force deployment data.

4.15.3.3. **Concept of Plan**. This is an operation plan in abbreviated format. It normally includes a plan summary, a base plan, and several crucial annexes (such as those delineating command relations and interagency coordination requirements.). It may or may not include a time-phased force deployment data.

4.15.3.4. **Operation Plan**. A complete and detailed joint plan containing a comprehensive description of the concept of operations, including identification of specific forces, functional support, and resources required; all annexes applicable to the plan; and a time-phased force deployment data. It can be quickly developed in to an operation order.

4.15.4. In a crisis, the joint planning and execution community employs combat air patrol to accomplish planning in a time-sensitive manner, producing orders that describe the mission, situation, and objectives; establish command relationships; identify planning assumptions; and identify and/or task forces and strategic mobility resources, or request them. The types of joint operation orders are:

4.15.4.1. **Warning Order**. Initiates development and evaluation of course of actions by supported commander. Requests commander's estimate.

4.15.4.2. **Planning Order**. Begins execution planning for a particular course of action. Directs preparation of an operation order or contingency plan. Conveys anticipated course of action selection by the President or Secretary of Defense.

4.15.4.3. **Alert Order**. Begins execution planning for a selected course of action, directing preparation of and operation order or contingency plan. Conveys course of action selection by the President or Secretary of Defense.

4.15.4.4. **Prepare to Deploy Order**. Increases or decreases deployability posture of units.

4.15.4.5. **Deployment (or Redeployment) Order**. Deploys or redeploys forces, increases deployability posture, establishes a joint task force, and/or establishes a C-day/L-hour (day or hour on which the deployment operation commences).

4.15.4.6. **Execute Order**. Implements the President's or Secretary of Defense's decision to execute a course of action or operation order.

4.15.4.7. **Operation Order**. Directs the coordinated execution of an operation. Issued by a commander to subordinate commanders.

4.15.4.8. **Fragmentary Order**. Issued as needed to change or modify an operation order execution.

4.15.5. Planning is conducted at every echelon of command and across the range of military operations. Joint operation planning employs an integrated process for orderly analytical, and coordinated problem solving and decision-making known as the joint operation planning process. In its peacetime application, the process is highly structured to support the thorough and fully coordinated development of deliberate plans. In crisis, the process can be shortened as needed to support the dynamic requirements of changing events. In wartime, the process adapts to accommodate greater decentralization of joint operation planning activities. Joint operation planning process consists of a set of logical steps to examine a mission; develop, analyze, and compare alternative course of actions, select the best course of action, develop a concept of operations, and produce a plan or order. **Joint operation planning process is thus the process used to derive all the types of plans—and many of the orders—described above. Joint operation planning process is also the process used to derive subordinate plans for employment and support of forces, including those created for use by Air Force forces.** Joint operation planning process consists of seven steps:

4.15.5.1. **Planning Initiation**. An appropriate authority (such as the President, Secretary of Defense, or combatant commander) recognizes potential for employing military capability in a particular contingency or crisis and decides to develop military options.

4.15.5.2. **Mission Analysis**. A crucial output of this step is the mission statement: The joint force's mission is the task, or set of tasks, together with the purpose, that indicates the action to be taken and the reason for doing so. Key mission analysis activities include such things as review of initial planning guidance and intelligence; developing the mission statement; determining known facts and developing planning assumptions; conducting an initial force allocation review; and developing mission success criteria (measures of effectiveness for the mission). Mission analysis concludes with a mission analysis brief to the commander and involves approval of the mission statement.

4.15.5.3. **Course of Action Development**. A course of action is a potential way (solution, method) to accomplish the assigned mission. Staffs develop course of actions to provide unique choices to the commander, all oriented on accomplishing the military end state. course of actions describe *who* will take action, *what type* of military action will take place, *when* the action will occur, *where* the action will occur, *why* the action is required (the purpose), and *how* the action will take place (the method of employment of forces). Each course of action should explain the objectives, end state, key tasks, and task organization.

4.15.5.4. **Course of Action Analysis**. This step closely examines potential course of actions to reveal details that will allow the commander and staff to evaluate them in order to identify advantages and disadvantages. The primary means of conducting this analysis is wargaming. Wargaming is a conscious effort to visualize the flow of an operation, given friendly and adversary dispositions, capabilities, strengths, and possible course of actions. A critical element of wargaming is the "red team/cell," which role-plays and models the adversary, aggressively pursuing the adversary's point of view and objectives. Wargaming can be as simple as a turn-by-turn table-top affair, or as complex as a Department of Defense-adjudicated game hosted on mainframe computers. Wargaming allows the planning staff and commander to asses each course of action for feasibility— to answer questions like, "can it be supported?" "Is more combat capability need?" "Can the adversary effectively counter or prevent friendly action?" The outputs of this step feed the next:

4.15.5.5. **Course of Action Comparison**. Comparison is a subjective process whereby the course of action are independently evaluated against a set of criteria established by the commander and staff. This step should identify and recommend the course of action that has the greatest probability of success against the adversary course of action that is of most concern to the commander. Often, the staff develops an evaluation matrix that compares all the friendly course of action against the established set of criteria; this may help identify the best course of action. Ultimately, the staff develops a brief recommending their selection for "best" course of action.

4.15.5.6. **Course of Action Approval**. In this step, the staff briefs the commander on the course of action comparison and wargaming results and recommends a course of action for approval. The commander may approve the course of action or modify it, or direct the staff to reiterate portions of the joint operation planning process. From the final course of action selection, the commander and staff prepare a commander's estimate (previously described) and direct further plan or order development.

4.15.5.7. **Plan or Order Development**. The commander's staff and subordinate functional or Service component staffs develop more detailed plans, supporting plans, or orders, as required by the mission (and as described above).

4.15.6. For further information concerning the joint force and planning, see Joint Publication 5-0, *Joint Operation Planning*.

4.15.7. Subordinate and supporting commands and staffs use the JOPP process to create their own plans and orders. **When the Air Force Service component or the joint force air component accomplish this process, it is known as the joint operation planning process for air**. When the joint force air component accomplishes the joint operation planning process for air, it produces a plan known as the joint air operations plan, or joint air operations plan. During execution, the joint air operations plan is divided into time-defined (usually daily) "slices" known as air operation directives. Air operation directives, then, are the basis for the daily air tasking orders, which govern accomplishment of the air tasking and targeting cycles—the mechanisms of joint air employment of forces. Following execution, these cycles guide the staffs and commander through assessment of operations: "Are we doing the right things and are we doing things right in order to accomplish the mission?" "What is our progress toward accomplishment?" The Air Force Service component produces an Air Force Service component plan to support the joint force air component and the joint force overall. Most all of the planning described in this paragraph takes place in the air operations center, or air operation center, although some Service component planning may take place elsewhere. For more information on Air Force and air component planning, see Air Force Doctrine Annex 3-0, *Operations and Planning*.

## Section 4E— *Joint and Coalition Capabilities*

*"…. we will lead, and we will enable others to lead. Moreover, we will do this-always-by coordinating military power with the diplomacy and development efforts of our government and those of our allies and partners."*

> Martin E. Dempsey
> General U.S. Army
> 18th Chairman of the Joint Chiefs of Staff

## 4.16. Joint and Coalition Capabilities:

4.16.1. As our Nation and armed forces are confronted with a multitude of priorities, from a shrinking force and limited resources, to fiscal constraints, we must be mindful to advance only the necessary resources to ensure that the right capabilities are integrated and interoperable across all domains of air, space, and cyberspace. Competing priorities today must now be carefully measured against all military capabilities, ensuring that quality—not necessarily quantity—smartly contributes to a faster, more flexible, agile and response force. That said, we must rely on the strengths of others, or be interdependent, and meanwhile ensure all capabilities can effectively intertwine, or be interoperable with each other to achieve an overarching objective. One of the founding initiatives, which addressed joint interdependence and joint interoperability, was the Goldwater-Nichols Department of Defense Reorganization Act of 1986.

4.16.2. One of the first successful operational actions of combining joint and coalition integration was experienced during Operations DESERT SHIELD and DESERT STORM. These operations demonstrated an unmistakable fashion the value and effectiveness of joint and combined military operations. The unique capabilities of each of the U.S. military Services, and those of each of our allies, were exploited during various phases of both operations. The combined force provided a synergistic combat capability which brought the greatest possible military power of the coalition force to bear against the opponent. Likewise, our experience also reaffirmed the importance of joint and combined training, the value of forward presence and the validity of joint force sequencing for power-projection. A good example of this was through the use of the Air Force's domain of space. After the Gulf War there was a near unanimous agreement that space-based systems greatly increased the overall effectiveness of coalition forces.

4.16.3. Clearly, history proved that collectively, the strengths, resources, and training of one Service or nation in today's increasingly complex environment, increases and/or balances the successful outcome of a military objective. This was seen in Iraq, Libya, and Afghanistan…throughout all aspects of the global war on terrorism and through other worldwide security challenges.

4.16.4. The U.S. Air Force's unity of effort, through the application of air, space, and cyberspace, provides unique capabilities that bridge a comprehensive joint and coalition approach. This unity of effort involves the coordination and cooperation toward common objectives, even if the participants are not necessarily part of the same command or organization, but the product of successful unified action (Joint Publication 1-02).

4.16.5. Our doctrine continues to evolve; we now rarely see any one Service or any one country unilaterally plan, organize, or execute an operation, but we see inclusiveness with joint, coalition, and sometimes interagency partners, whereby we depend on each other to succeed in today's complex environment. Through this interdependence we are able to select the right resources and capabilities from each other. These capabilities simply do not get used when a contingency arises, but are synergized and tested through such venues as exercises and operations to ensure all joint, and when necessary, coalition partners can meet the desired objectives at the right time and right place.

4.16.6. Each Service and coalition brings a unique balance to every operation and, depending upon the circumstances, the balance may shift from one Service or nation due to the different operating environments and applications necessary to support the best options. Our Air Force tenet of centralized control, decentralized execution is a great example of this. When employing strategic air attack as a line of operations, which defines the interior or exterior orientation of the force in relation to the enemy or that connects actions on nodes and/or decisive points related in time and space to an objective, we will require a high degree of centralization under an air commander, known as the joint force air component commander. The joint force air component commander must have authority over all forces, foreign or domestic, to direct operations, including attack sequencing and make adjustments as operations unfold. On the contrary, if tactical air operations are necessary to support ground troops using close air support, these air resources are best when decentralized to support ground commanders. The tenet of Airpower is never prosecuted alone, but space and cyberspace, which belongs to no one state, remains a vital imperative for joint force operations.

4.16.7. A good example of this was played out during Operation ODYSSEY DAWN over Libya in 2011. During this operation, the joint and combined operations provided one of the greatest uses of joint and coalition capabilities in our recent history. In an effort to support multi-national efforts necessary to protect civilians in Libya from attacks by the regime of Libyan leader Muammar al-Qadhafi, the U.S. Africa Command task force was assigned to provide operational and tactical command and control of U.S. military forces supporting the international response to the unrest in Libya and enforcement of United Nations Security Council Resolution 1973. At the start of operations, U.S. Africa Command, commanded by General Carter Ham, exercised strategic command. Tactical command in the theater of operations was executed from USS *Mount Whitney* in the Mediterranean Sea under supported command of Admiral Sam Locklear, Commander, U.S. Naval Forces Africa. U.S. Secretary of Defense Robert Gates indicated that control of the operation would be transferred to French and British authorities, or North Atlantic Treaty Organization, within days. The Joint Task Force was called Joint Task Force ODYSSEY DAWN.

4.16.8. As a joint team, the supporting commands (commanders) were the Joint Force Maritime Component Commander Vice Admiral Harry B. Harris who controlled maritime assets aboard the USS *Mount Whitney,* and Joint Force Air Component Commander Major General Margaret Woodward.

4.16.9. As the Libyans began joining other Arab populations across North Africa in conducting antigovernment protests and demonstrations, time passed and the Qadhafi regime increasingly began to use military force against its citizens in efforts to repress the uprising. The Arab League meeting in Cairo asked the United Nations Security Council to impose a no-fly zone over Libya to protect civilians from air attack and declaring that the Qadhafi government had lost its sovereignty. The United Nations Security Council passed Resolution 1973 authorizing all necessary measures to protect civilians in Libya. The resolution authorized the use of force and the enforcement of a no-fly zone over Libya. The U.S. Secretary of Defense approved and ordered the use of U.S. military forces in strikes against the government of Libya. The International Coalition took measures to begin enforcement of United Nations Security Council Resolution 1973, to include the imposition of a no-fly zone, launched strikes against Libyan military sites and air defense systems.

4.16.10. To illustrate effective interdependence and interoperability, the following joint and coalition capabilities over Libya was a good example. The following representation was captured within the first few days of Operation ODYSSEY DAWN:

4.16.10.1. As Major General Woodward commanded the air campaign, French aircraft destroyed four Libyan tanks in air strikes to the southwest of the city of Benghazi. The French military claimed that its aircraft had also flown reconnaissance missions over all Libyan territory. On the same day, British Prime Minister David Cameron confirmed that Royal Air Force jets were also in action and reports suggested that the U.S. Navy had fired the first cruise missile. CBS News correspondent David Martin reported that three B-2 stealth bombers from Whiteman Air Force base Missouri flew nonstop from the U.S. to drop 40 bombs on a major Libyan airfield. Martin further reported that U.S. fighter jets were searching for Libyan ground forces to attack. The Pentagon and the British Ministry of Defense confirmed that, jointly, British ship HMS *Triumph* and U.S. Navy ships (including USS *Barry*) and submarines fired more than 110 Tomahawk cruise missiles, supported with air attacks on military installations, both inland and on the coast. Days later, several Storm Shadow missiles were launched by British jets. Nineteen U.S. planes conducted strike operations in Libya. The planes included Marine Corps AV-8B Harriers, U.S. Navy EA-18G Growlers, which were diverted from operations over Iraq and jammed Libyan radar and communications, and Air Force F-15 and F-16 fighter jets. A military convoy was destroyed south of Benghazi by air strikes. Seventy military vehicles were destroyed and multiple loyalist ground troop casualties were also reported. Four Danish F-16 fighters left Italy's Sigonella Air Base for a successful 5-hour long high-risk mission, and four Italian Tornados (electronic combat/reconnaissance), accompanied by four Italian aircraft. Operations continued and on 31 March 2011 at 0600 Greenwich Mean Time, North Atlantic Treaty Organization took command of all operations in Libya with subsequent operations being conducted as part of North Atlantic Treaty Organization-driven operation unified protector.

4.16.10.2. Operation ODYSSEY DAWN was a complete success and supported the necessity of, not only joint and coalition capabilities, but how air, space, and cyberspace domains intertwined all facets of the operation to guarantee success. General Dempsey said it best when he stated [Joint and Coalition] *"means building and presenting forces that can be molded to context—not just by adding and subtracting, but by leaders combining capabilities in innovative ways. It means interdependence services that rely on each other to achieve objectives and create capabilities that do not exist except when combined. It means a regionally postured, but globally networked and flexible force that can be scaled and scoped to demand."*

4.16.11. Today, not one military contingency or operation, whether in peacetime or wartime, can optimize its objective without space or cyberspace. Airpower offers speed, agility, flexibility, range, and responsiveness to virtually every need, and airpower has demonstrated its success to meet our homeland and international security challenges by leveraging our respective capabilities and maximizing resulting synergy. Cyber operations guarantee our capability to operate in any contested cyber domain to support vital land, sea, air, and space missions by developing capabilities to protect essential military cyber systems and to speed their recovery if an attack does occur. In these interdependent domains the Air Force possesses unique capabilities for ensuring global mobility, long-range strike, and intelligence, surveillance, and reconnaissance. The benefits of airpower extend beyond the air domain, and operations among the air, land, maritime, space, and cyber domains are increasingly interdependent upon each other for the success of any and all national military objectives. Together, the domains of air, space, and cyberspace, effectively combined with joint and coalition capabilities, has proven to be the most valuable means of supporting the National Security Strategy of the U.S. and our allies.

### Section 4F— *Adaptive Planning and Execution*

### 4.17. Adaptive Planning and Execution (APEX):

4.17.1. APEX is used by the joint planning and execution community to monitor, plan, assess, and execute joint operations. APEX formally integrates the strategic-theater and operational planning activities of the Joint Planning and Execution Community and facilitates the joint force commander's seamless transition from planning to execution during times of crises. APEX activities span many organizational levels, including the interaction between Secretary of Defense and Combatant Commanders, which ultimately helps the President and Secretary of Defense decide when, where, and how to commit U.S. military forces. APEX is used to facilitate the joint operation planning process.

4.17.2. The focus of the joint operation planning process is at the combatant commander level, which use it to determine the best method of accomplishing assigned tasks and direct the actions necessary to accomplish the mission. Joint operation planning is designed to facilitate timely building and maintenance of plans and rapid development of effective options through adaptation of approved operation plans during crisis. Joint operation planning allows for the effective management of operations in execution across the spectrum of mobilization, deployment, employment, sustainment, redeployment and demobilization. Joint operation planning is supported by a networked suite of automated data processing applications, tools, and databases, which reside on the Global Command and Control System. Joint operation planning and execution system is an automated data processing systems include the mechanisms to create and maintain time-phased force deployment data and to submit combatant commander movement requirements to the U.S. Transportation Command.

4.17.3. Governance for Joint Operation Planning are the Chairman, Joint Chief of Staff manuals and Joint Publication 5-0, *Joint Operation Planning*. For Air Force planning the primary governance is AFI 10-401.

> 4.17.3.1. Chairman, Joint Chief of Staff manual 3122.01A, *Joint Operation Planning and Execution System (JOPES) Volume I (Planning Policies and Procedures)*. This publication sets forth planning policies, processes, and procedure to govern the joint operation planning and execution activities and performance of the Armed Forces of the U.S. **Note:** Upon the next release this manual will be renamed CJCSM 3130.02.

> 4.17.3.2. Chairman, Joint Chief of Staff manual 3130.03, *Adaptive Planning and Execution Planning Formats and Guidance*. This publication prescribes standard formats and minimum content requirements for operation plans and concept plans.

> 4.17.3.3. Chairman, Joint Chief of Staff manual 3122.02D, *Joint Operation Planning and Execution System (JOPES) Volume III (Time-Phased Force Deployment Data Development and Deployment Execution)*. This publication establishes procedures for the development of Time-Phased Force Deployment Data and establishes policy, processes, and procedures to plan and execute joint deployment and redeployment operations. **Note:** Upon the next release this manual will be renamed CJCSM 3130.04.

**Note:** Chairman, Joint Chief of Staff manuals are reviewed periodically by the Joint Staff and service headquarters. Recommended changes may be submitted at any time to the war and mobilization plans division (AF/A3OD). Air Force component headquarters are required to send an information copy of these recommendations to their parent unified command.

## 4.18. Deliberate and Crisis Action Planning and Execution Segments.

Deliberate and Crisis Action Planning and Execution Segments is the Air Force's war planning system and provides an Air Force feed to Joint Operation Planning and Execution System automated data processing. The objective of Deliberate and Crisis Action Planning and Execution Segments is to enable improved and streamlined operations planning and execution processes which include associated policy and procedures, along with organizational and technology improvements. Deliberate and Crisis Action Planning and Execution Segments provides standard data files, formats, application programs, and management procedures that are Air Force unique, joint guidance compliant, and used primarily for force planning, sourcing equipment, personnel requirements, transportation feasibility estimation, civil engineering support, and medical planning. Deliberate and Crisis Action Planning and Execution Segments is detailed in AFI 10-401. Deliberate and Crisis Action Planning and Execution Segments supports all phases of operations planning and execution at the headquarters Air Force, major command, component, and wing/squadron level. It provides data manipulation capability to Air Force planners to perform rapid operation plan development, conduct feasibility capability analyses, support mobilization, deployment, sustainment, redeployment, demobilization, reconstitution, and personnel accounting of forces.

## 4.19. Conclusion.

The nature of the challenges to the U.S. and its interests demand that the Armed Forces operate as a fully integrated joint team across the range of military operations. This chapter provided essential information that all members of the joint force should understand. It covered levels of air and space doctrine, key doctrine concepts, AEF concepts, AEF force management, and joint force components and planning operations. Finally, it provided the JOPES used within the joint community for interagency coordination and for U.S. military involvement in multiagency and multinational operations.

## Chapter 5

## EMERGENCY MANAGEMENT

*Section 5A—Overview*

### 5.1. Introduction.

The ability of the United States Air Force to carry out its mission of Global Vigilance, Global Reach, and Global Power directly depends on continuance of the mission in the face of adversity. Challenges to mission accomplishment take many forms ranging from natural disasters, man-made incidents, terrorist use of weapons of mass destruction, and hostile attacks that threaten United States interests. The Air Force Emergency Management Program was developed to ensure the readiness of our Total Force to prepare for, respond to, and recover from the effects of incidents that endanger the lives of personnel and jeopardize mission accomplishment. Airmen may be called upon to serve the program in a variety of ways; from attending localized emergency preparedness briefings to being a member of a specialized team. In today's threat-laden environment, every Airman must play their part to ensure their installation has a successful Emergency Management program.

*Section 5B—Emergency Management Program and Air Force Incident Management System*

### 5.2. Air Force Emergency Management Program.

Protection of personnel and operational resources is essential to successful Air Force operations. The Air Force Emergency Management program develops and implements measures for, and manages activities related to, emergency preparedness, incident management, response and recovery operations, chemical, biological, radiological, and nuclear defense, and consequence management.

5.2.1. The primary mission of the Air Force Emergency Management Program is to save lives; minimize the loss or degradation of resources; and continue, sustain, and restore operational capability in an all-hazards physical threat environment at Air Force installations worldwide. The ancillary missions are to support homeland defense and civil support operations and to provide support to civil and host nation authorities according to Department of Defense publications and through the appropriate combatant command. These missions are accomplished using the Air Force Incident Management System, which employs the installation disaster response force, as the structure for all responses.

5.2.2. The Air Force Emergency Management Program contributes to mission assurance, which is defined as the process to protect or ensure the continued function and resilience of capabilities and assets—including personnel, equipment, facilities, networks, information, and information systems, infrastructure, and supply chains in any operating environment or condition, and the continuation of mission essential functions necessary to perform the operations of the installation in support of the national military strategy.

### 5.3. The Five Emergency Management Mission Areas.

The Air Force Emergency Management program mission areas (Figure 5.1.) include prevention, protection, response, recovery, and mitigation. They are met through preparedness, which includes actions to plan, organize, equip, train, and exercise prior to disasters and incidents.

**Figure 5.1. Mission Areas.**

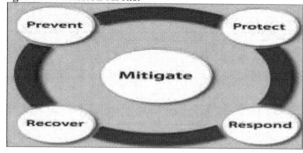

#### 5.3.1. Prevention.

Prevention includes the capabilities necessary to avoid, prevent, or stop a threatened or actual act of terrorism.

#### 5.3.2. Protection.

Protection provides the capabilities necessary to protect the installation against all threats and hazards, and manmade or natural disasters.

#### 5.3.3. Response.

Response includes actions taken to save lives, protect property, and mitigate the effects of an incident.

#### 5.3.4. Recovery.

Recovery includes operations such as implementing casualty treatment, unexploded explosive ordnance safing, personnel and resource decontamination, airfield damage repair, and facility restoration. Response contains three essential elements; notification, response, and protective actions.

#### 5.3.5. Mitigation.

Mitigation comprises the capabilities necessary to reduce the loss of life and property by lessening the impact of future disasters. These capabilities are designed to reduce or eliminate risks to persons or property or to lessen the actual or potential effects or consequences of a disaster or incident.

### 5.4. Air Force Incident Management System.

The Emergency Management program accomplishes its mission through the Air Force Incident Management System which utilizes the disaster response force. Air Force Incident Management System aligns Emergency Management planning and response with Homeland Security Directive 5, *Management of Domestic Incidents;* the National Incident Management System; the National Response Framework, and Office of the Secretary of Defense guidance while preserving unique military requirements. The system provides the Air Force with a single, comprehensive approach to incident management while allowing scalable and flexible response options to organize field-level operations for a broad spectrum of emergencies.

### 5.5. Air Force Emergency Management Structure.

The Air Force Emergency Management program has two structural elements; a strategic planning and management staff to maintain the Emergency Management program and a disaster response force to manage or conduct incident response operations (Figure 5.2.). The planning and management staff provide an overall cross-functional installation risk management program for developing threat and hazard plans and budget, and is comprised of four functions; the office of emergency management, unit emergency management representatives, the emergency management working group, and the wing inspection team. See AFI 10-2501, *Air Force Emergency Management Program*, for definitions of planning and management functions. The disaster response force are the organizational functions that respond to disasters or accidents to establish command and control and support disaster operations. The disaster response force includes the Crisis Action Team, Emergency Operations Center, unit control centers, Command Post, incident commander, first and emergency responders, and specialized and support recovery teams.

#### 5.5.1. Crisis Action Team.

The Crisis Action Team directs strategic actions supporting the installation's mission. This team is activated to provide a command, control, and communication link to higher headquarters and comparable civilian agencies and to coordinate the incident response.

#### 5.5.2. Emergency Operations Center.

The Emergency Operations Center is the command and control support element that coordinates information and resources to the installation actions before, during, and after an incident.

#### 5.5.3. Unit Control Center.

Unit control centers provide response and recovery support to the Incident Commander as directed by the Emergency Operations Center and mission support to the installation commander as directed by Crisis Action Team. Unit control centers provide a focal point within an organization to maintain unit command and control, relay information to and from unit personnel, provide expertise to the emergency operations center or the incident commander, and leverage unit resources to respond to and mitigate the incident.

**Figure 5.2. Installation Emergency Management Program Structure – Disaster Response Force.**

#### 5.5.4. Command Post.

As a command and control node, the command post assists in directing installation emergency management and response actions. The command post maintains notification rosters, provides and collects information from the unit control centers, and coordinates with the crisis action team and the Emergency Operations Center.

#### 5.5.5. Incident Commander.

The incident commander is a trained and experienced responder that provides on-scene tactical control using subject matter experts and support from other functions. Fire Emergency Services is the incident commander for all incidents involving two or more response agencies.

5.5.6. **First Responders.**

First responders deploy immediately to the scene to provide initial command and control, to save lives, and to suppress and control hazards. First responders include fire and emergency services, security forces, and medical personnel.

5.5.7. **Emergency Responders.**

Emergency responders deploy after the first responders to expand command and control and provide additional support. Emergency responders include emergency management, explosive ordnance disposal, bioenvironmental engineering personnel and may include other subject matter experts.

5.5.8. **Specialized and Support Recovery Teams.**

Specialized teams are formed from the existing installation and unit personnel resources to support emergency response operations. Specialized teams include the emergency management support team, shelter management team, contamination control team, post-attack reconnaissance team, and other specialized teams.

*Section 5C—Protective Measures and Response Procedures*

**5.6. Protective Measures.**

Threats and hazards that may affect your installation could be natural, man-made, or technological. Disasters or incidents resulting from a threat or hazard can occur at any time with little or no advance warning. These incidents can be local or widespread, predictable or unpredictable. There are ways to prepare for and cope with these events, regardless of the type of incident. Take time to think; then act according to the situation. Installations, as well as individuals, need to identify local threats and hazards, prepare early, and develop emergency plans. For preparation guidance, contact the installation readiness and emergency management flight and visit the Air Force "Be Ready" website (http://www.beready.af.mil/).

**5.7. Air Force Emergency Notification Signals.**

Every Air Force installation must have a rapid and effective system to quickly disseminate emergency information such as watches, warnings, evacuation routes, and protective actions. When a disaster or incident affecting the base is imminent or in-progress, personnel must respond to directions communicated over mass notification and warning systems (Figure 5.3). These messages may be visual or audible. Make sure you know how notifications and warnings are executed at your installation to ensure you are promptly informed and ready to properly respond to local emergencies.

**Figure 5.3. U.S. Air Force Emergency Notification Signals.**

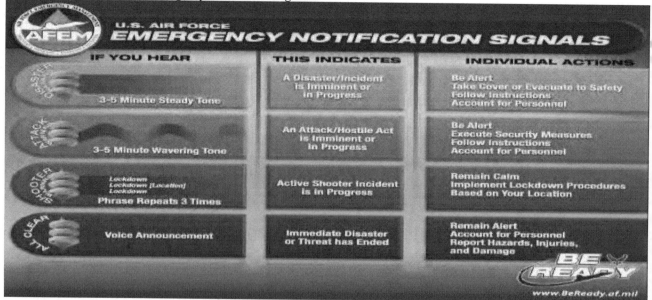

**5.8. Personnel Sheltering.**

All installations are required to conduct threat-based shelter planning. Shelter selection is based on structural and personnel housing capabilities in relation to the types of disasters. Personnel must know where their shelter is located and understand shelter-processing procedures. Shelter-in-place is used to provide temporary protection in a structure for short or no-notice emergencies, such as hazardous material incident or a tornado, when the type or extent of the hazard is unknown and/or evacuation at the time would be dangerous. Active shooter lock-down procedures are not the same as those used for shelter-in-place. Refer to AFMAN 10-2502, *Air Force Incident Management Standards and Procedures*, for shelter planning information. Wartime sheltering addressed in paragraph 5.17.4 and AFMAN 10-2503, *Operations in a Chemical, Biological, Radiological, Nuclear, and High-Yield Explosives (CBRNE) Environment*.

## 5.9. Response Procedures.

Commanders must be able to maintain the primary installation mission, save lives, mitigate damage, and restore mission-essential resources following disasters or incidents. Response levels will depend on the magnitude of the incident and degree of damage. Each installation must develop disaster response plans and policies to address local threats and hazards. The installation emergency management plan 10-2 is the vehicle for installation planning and response. The plan provides comprehensive guidance for emergency response to natural (geological, meteorological, and biological hazards), human-caused (accidental and intentional) or technological incidents. These categories are detailed in the following sections.

## *Section 5D – Natural Disaster, Man-Made Physical and Technological Hazards*

## 5.10. Natural Disasters.

Natural disasters and severe weather can create emergency conditions that vary widely in scope, urgency, and degree of damage and destruction. The installations must develop plans for the hazards likely to affect their location. Specific actions taken in response, mitigation, and recovery will vary. A national-level response may be required to help an Air Force installation recover from large-area natural disasters.

5.10.1. Natural disasters are categorized as geological, meteorological, or biological hazards. Natural geological hazards include earthquake, tsunami, volcano, landslide, and mudslide, subsidence (i.e. sinkholes, glacier, and iceberg). Natural meteorological hazards include: flood, flash flood, tidal surge, drought, fire, snow, ice, hail, sleet, avalanche, windstorm, tropical cyclone, hurricane, tornado, water spout, dust or sand storm, extreme temperature (heat, cold), lightning strikes, and geomagnetic storm. Natural biological hazards include diseases that impact humans or animals such as plague, anthrax, botulism, smallpox, tularemia, viral hemorrhagic fevers, West Nile Virus, foot and mouth diseases, severe acute respiratory syndrome, and pandemic disease.

## 5.11. Human Caused Hazards.

Installations are threatened with the possibility of catastrophic man-made hazards, whether accidental or intentional. All installations must prepare for, and quickly respond to major accidents to prevent the loss of life, preserve valuable resources, and protect the environment.

5.11.1. The Department of Defense is responsible for responding to incidents involving its resources or resulting from Department of Defense activities. The military installation, regardless of size, nearest the scene of the accident or incident will respond to the event unless otherwise directed by higher headquarters. Upon witnessing an accident or incident, personnel should alert others in the immediate area and report the incident to security forces, fire and emergency services, or installation command and control. After reporting the accident, personnel should:

5.11.1.1. Stay uphill and upwind. Avoid inhaling fumes, smoke, or vapors.

5.11.1.2. Attempt to rescue and care for casualties.

5.11.1.3. Avoid handling any material or component involved in the accident/incident.

5.11.1.4. Evacuate the area if rescue or containment is impractical, or if directed to evacuate.

5.11.2. **Man-Made Accidental.**

Man-made accidental incidents include hazardous materials (for example, explosive, flammable liquid, flammable gas, flammable solid, oxidizer, poison, radiological, corrosive) spill or release. An explosion or fire; transportation accident; building or structure collapse; energy, power, or utility failure; fuel or resource shortage; air or water pollution or contamination; dam, levee, or other water control structure failure; financial issues including economic depression, inflation, financial system collapse; and communication system interruption.

5.11.3. **Man-Made Intentional.**

Man-made intentional incidents include terrorism, sabotage, civil disturbance, public unrest, riot, strike or labor dispute, disinformation, criminal activity (vandalism, arson, theft, fraud, embezzlement, and data theft), electromagnetic pulse, physical or information security breach, active shooter, and product defect or contamination. An overview of man-made intentional incidents involving enemy or terrorist use chemical, biological, radiological, and nuclear is provided in Section 5E.

5.11.3.1. An active shooter is an individual actively engaged in killing or attempting to kill people, most often in populated areas. In most cases, active shooters use firearms and there is no pattern or method to their selection of victims. In some cases, active shooters use improvised explosive devices to create additional victims and impede first responders.

5.11.3.1.1. Lockdown is declared to protect personnel from an Active Shooter incident and is a base-wide protective action used to restrict the movement of personnel and to aid law enforcement first responders in neutralizing the shooting suspect as quickly as possible. During lockdown, no person may exit or enter another area until the all clear is broadcasted; unless movement is required to escape from a dangerous place or situation.

5.11.3.1.2. If you find yourself involved in an active shooter situation, remain calm, quickly determine the most reasonable way to protect your own life. If an escape route is accessible, evacuate the immediate area. If evacuation is not possible, find a place to create a barricade between you and the active shooter. As a last resort, and only when your life is in imminent danger, attempt to disrupt and/or incapacitate the shooter.

5.11.4. **Technological.**

Technologically caused incidents include central computer, mainframe, software, or application (internal and external) ancillary support equipment; telecommunications; and energy, power, utility, or nuclear power plant failure.

*Section 5E— Enemy Attack and Terrorist Use of Chemical, Biological, Radiological, and Nuclear Weapons*

**5.12. Chemical, Biological, Radiological, and Nuclear Hazards.**

Chemical, biological, radiological, and nuclear, as well as toxic industrial material, hazards cause adverse effects through deliberate release and dissemination. Installation chemical, biological, radiological, and nuclear defense requires an installation wide team that includes all personnel to plan, prepare, respond and recover from a chemical, biological, radiological, and nuclear incident. Chemical, biological, radiological, and nuclear preparedness and defense measures are intended to balance mission continuation with force survivability to maximize mission effectiveness within a chemical, biological, radiological, and nuclear environment. An awareness of the hazards and protective actions will help you protect yourself in the event of a chemical, biological, radiological, and nuclear attack.

**5.13. Chemical, Biological, Radiological, and Nuclear Threat Agents.**

Each chemical, biological, radiological, and nuclear threat agent presents a unique hazard. Airmen should know the importance of understanding what the characteristics, symptoms, and protective factors are for all chemical, biological, radiological, and nuclear threat agents relative to the deployed location.

5.13.1. **Chemical.** Chemical agents are chemical substances that are intended for use in military operations to kill, seriously injure, or incapacitate mainly through their physiological effects. Chemical agents are categorized according to their physiological effects: lung damaging agents (choking), blister agents, blood agents, incapacitating agents, and nerve agents. Also included in the chemical hazards classification are toxic industrial chemicals. Chemical agents can be delivered through a variety of means such as tactical ballistic missiles, bombs, artillery, grenades, mines, and spray attacks. Due to their persistent nature, nerve and blister pose the primary threat to air bases.

5.13.2. **Biological.** A biological agent is a microorganism (or a toxin derived from it) that causes disease in personnel, plants, or animals or causes the deterioration of materiel. Biological agents include viruses, bacteria, fungi, and toxins cultured from living organisms. Biological agents may be found as liquid droplets, aerosols, or dry powders and can be adapted for use as an adversarial weapon. Biological agents can be delivered through a variety of means such as spray attacks, aerosol releases, or covert attacks. Personnel may not experience symptoms immediately after being exposed to biological agents. Each agent has a different exposure (or incubation) period before infection.

5.13.3. **Radiological and Nuclear.** Radiation is a broad term that applies to a wide range of phenomena. Light (infrared to ultraviolet), radiofrequency emissions and microwaves are all forms of radiation known as nonionizing radiation. In general, nonionizing radiation produces heat when it interacts with the body. In contrast, ionizing radiation has sufficient energy to produce ions when it interacts with matter (including the human body). Radiation causes harmful effects to personnel because the ionization and excitation alters or destroys cell processes and structures essential for the normal functioning of the cell.

5.13.3.1. **Radiological Delivery Means.** Adversaries may disseminate radioactive materials by utilizing a radiological dispersal device. This device disseminates radioactive material across an area without a nuclear detonation. A radiological dispersal device could function as a terror weapon or terrain-denial mechanism. For example, a radiological dispersal device could function by using conventional explosives to blow-up and scatter radioactive source debris across a relatively small area; this device is also known as a dirty bomb.

5.13.3.2. **Nuclear Delivery Means.** Nuclear weapons can be detonated at various altitudes to include subsurface, surface, airburst, or high altitude. The primary concerns of a nuclear detonation include blast/shock, thermal radiation (heat), ionizing radiation, and ballistic debris for surface and shallow subsurface bursts. Nuclear blasts may also pose an electromagnetic pulse hazard that can cause widespread communications and/or electrical problems. Each type of burst has a different level of hazard ratio in regards to ionizing radiation, thermal radiation, and blast/shock. For example, a subsurface burst may produce a high level of blast and shock, but very little (if any) ionizing radiation penetrating outside the surface of the earth.

5.13.4. **Toxic Industrial Material.** Toxic industrial material hazards consist of toxic industrial chemicals, toxic industrial biologicals, and toxic industrial radiological material. Toxic industrial materials may be manufactured, stored, distributed, or transported in close proximity to airbases. These widely available toxic industrial materials are potential tools for asymmetric attacks against airbases. Most present a vapor (inhalation) hazard. Toxic industrial materials may also reduce the oxygen concentration below that required to support life. If there is a toxic industrial material incident, the most important action is immediate evacuation outside the hazard's path (if feasible). Airmen must note that the protective mask, ensemble, and military standard collective protection filters are not designed to provide protection from toxic industrial materials. If evacuation is impractical, implement shelter-in-place procedures.

## 5.14. Enemy Chemical, Biological, Radiological, and Nuclear Attack.

The Armed Forces of the United States must be prepared to conduct prompt, sustained, and decisive combat operations in chemical, biological, radiological, and nuclear environments. An adversary's chemical, biological, radiological, and nuclear capabilities can have a profound impact on United States and multinational objectives, campaign plans, and supporting actions, and therefore must be taken into account in planning. Adversaries use chemical, biological, radiological, and nuclear to disrupt efficient airbase mission operations, incapacitate and kill personnel, and contaminate equipment, rendering it unusable or dangerous to use. Deterring an adversary's use of chemical, biological, radiological, and nuclear weapons depends to a significant degree on effective preparations by the defender to deny the adversary any meaningful advantage from the employment of such weapons.

## 5.15. Chemical, Biological, Radiological, and Nuclear Defense Actions.

Operations in a chemical, biological, radiological, and nuclear environment are intended to balance mission continuation with force survivability to maximize mission effectiveness during and after a chemical, biological, radiological, and nuclear event. In-place and deployed forces must be prepared to conduct combat operations as required by Air Force, major command, or theater directives. When a crisis or conflict arises, mobility operations and force deployment begin.

## 5.16. Installation Command and Control.

Effective chemical, biological, radiological, and nuclear command and control is essential to mission accomplishment and base survivability. Effective wartime operations require coordinated and integrated actions at all levels. Installation command and control, in conjunction with the emergency operations center and unit control centers, implements operational plans and priorities, controls and monitors mission-generation capabilities, and ensures installation survivability.

## 5.17. Individual Protection:

5.17.1. Individual protection is comprised of singular use or a combination of individual protective equipment, vaccinations and prophylaxis, protective shelters, evacuation, relocation, exposure control, contamination control, and warning and notification systems. Measures are taken in stages equal to the urgency and nature of the threat. Command and theater-specific instructions will direct the proper individual protective postures.

5.17.2. Regardless of the type of agent, concentration, or method of attack, the best immediate protective equipment against chemical agents is the ground crew ensemble, a whole-body system which protects the wearer against chemical-biological warfare agents, toxins, and radiological particulates. Individual protection includes a protective mask with filters, overgarment, protective gloves, and footwear covers or overboots, and includes M8 and M9 detector paper, reactive skin decontamination lotion and M295 decontamination kits.

5.17.3. **Nerve Agent Antidote.** Medical representatives issue nerve agent antidotes and pretreatment during increased readiness. Additionally, medical representatives will issue pyridostigmine bromide tablets (P-tabs) if they anticipate use of a specific type of nerve agent. Members will take these tablets only if/when directed by the commander. The tablets, when combined with the antidote, will limit the effect of certain types of nerve agent poisoning.

5.17.4. **Chemical, Biological, Radiological, and Nuclear Wartime Sheltering.** The installation commander is responsible for establishing a shelter plan and should designate unit responsibility for preparing and operating each shelter during a chemical, biological, radiological, and nuclear event. Shelters are structures that protect personnel from chemical, biological, radiological, and nuclear effects over extended periods. Walls, doors, and windows offer limited physical barriers to chemical, biological, radiological, and nuclear hazards penetration. Heating, ventilation, and cooling systems should be shut off to prevent chemical, biological, radiological, and nuclear hazard spread. Personnel may be required to shelter-in-place in the event the type or extent of the hazard is unknown and/or evacuation at the time would be dangerous.

5.17.5. **Collective Protection Systems**. These systems provide protection from chemical, biological, radiological, and nuclear agents using an overpressure system to keep threat agents outside the facility, ultimately allowing the occupants to work or rest inside the facility without wearing protective gear. Many of these facilities will have integrated contamination control areas meaning contaminated personnel are able to enter the facility once decontaminated. Installations with collective protection systems should develop local procedures and provide base populace training, as required.

## 5.18. Chemical, Biological, Radiological, and Nuclear Incident Management Phases.

Air Force units must take actions to prepare for, respond to, and recover from or mitigate the effects of a chemical, biological, radiological, and nuclear attack or event. These actions will ensure we can conduct prompt, sustained, and decisive combat operations in chemical, biological, radiological, and nuclear environments.

5.18.1. In each phase, consistent approaches or actions are designed to save lives and to restore and sustain mission operations. Airbase attack preparation begins before a potential attack. Attack response actions focus primarily on individual and weapon systems survival, and recovery actions focusing on saving lives, detecting and mitigating hazards, mission restoration, and sustainment.

## 5.19. Preparedness.

Countering chemical, biological, radiological, and nuclear threats requires extraordinary preparedness. Conducting preparedness actions effectively and efficiently will increase the protection of mission critical resources and force survivability. These actions should be considered mission critical and given a high priority when the threat of enemy attack using chemical, biological, radiological, and nuclear agents is high. Your installation will establish several actions to counter chemical, biological, radiological, and nuclear attacks during the preparedness phase. These actions will be dependent on your installation's threat probabilities and Airmen should understand the importance of knowing these actions well before a chemical, biological, radiological, and nuclear attack. They include actions associated with alarm conditions, mission-oriented protective postures, split mission oriented protective posture, and contamination control. Actions begin upon receipt of the warning order or when the in-place forces are directed to transition to wartime operations. Installations will refer to their risk management plan and implement actions according to major command and theater guidance.

### 5.19.1. Alarm Conditions and Mission-Oriented Protective Posture Levels.

Attack warning signals are established and used to notify base populace of emergency conditions. The warnings may be communicated as audible alarms, through base public address and/or giant voice systems, display of alarm condition flags, or through other communication channels. The Air Force uses a standardized alarm system (see Figure 5.4) and mission-oriented protective posture levels to communicate the appropriate defense posture for in-place forces to take to transition to wartime chemical, biological, radiological, and nuclear operations. Attack warning signals are used to posture air base for attacks, warn of attacks in progress, initiate post attack recovery actions, and return the airbase to a normal wartime state of readiness. Attack warning signal variations may be used in some geographical regions. If used, Airmen will be notified of the variations before departure from home station or upon arrival into the region. For example, Alarm Blue is used instead of Alarm Red in South Korea. Mission-oriented protective postures are used in conjunction with alarm conditions quickly increase or decrease protection against chemical, biological, radiological, and nuclear threats.

### 5.19.2. Mission-Oriented Protective Postures.

Mission Oriented Protective Postures levels (Figure 5.5) are established to quickly communicate required individual protective equipment and protection levels. The levels are designed to allow a rapid increase or decrease personal protective equipment in response to chemical, biological, radiological, and nuclear attack alarm conditions. The installation commander determines the initial level, based on mission-oriented protective posture analysis, and adjusts levels as chemical, biological, radiological, and nuclear risks and mission priorities change.

### 5.19.3. Split Mission-Oriented Protective Posture.

Chemical, biological, radiological, and nuclear attacks can affect an entire airbase, but it is also possible that the attack may only affect specific areas. Split mission-orientated protective posture is a tactic used to split or divide an installation or operating location into two or more chemical, biological, radiological, and nuclear zones. Prior to hostilities, planners identify installation chemical, biological, radiological, and nuclear zones based on installation geography and mission. These zones enable the commander to tailor mission-oriented protective posture levels and alarm conditions within each zone to better reflect the current hazard and mission priorities. By using split mission-oriented protective postures the commander can divide the installation into contaminated or non-contaminated zones, instead of declaring the entire installation contaminated. This allows the installation to stay operational and effective. Unit control centers control movement between one zone to another. Personnel must be aware what alarm condition and mission-oriented protective posture level applies before entering a zone.

**Figure 5.4. U.S. Air Force Attack Warning Signals for Chemical, Biological, Radiological, and Nuclear Medium and High Threat Areas.**

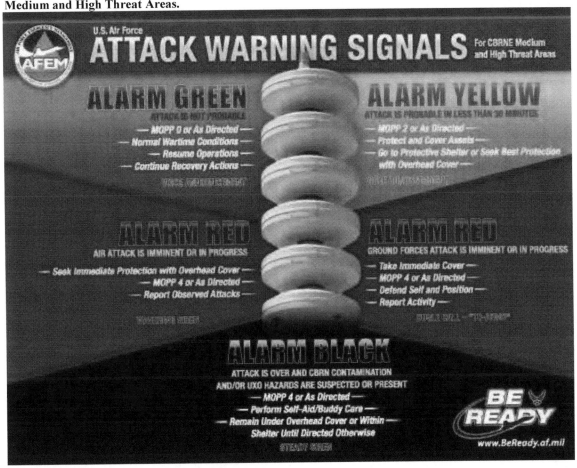

**Figure 5.5. Mission Oriented Protective Postures.**

### 5.19.3. Split Mission-Oriented Protective Posture.

Chemical, biological, radiological, and nuclear attacks can affect an entire airbase, but it is also possible that the attack may only affect specific areas. Split mission-orientated protective posture is a tactic used to split or divide an installation or operating location into two or more chemical, biological, radiological, and nuclear zones. Prior to hostilities, planners identify installation chemical, biological, radiological, and nuclear zones based on installation geography and mission. These zones enable the commander to tailor mission-oriented protective posture levels and alarm conditions within each zone to better reflect the current hazard and mission priorities. By using split mission-oriented protective postures the commander can divide the installation into contaminated or non-contaminated zones, instead of declaring the entire installation contaminated. This allows the installation to stay operational and effective. Unit control centers control movement between one zone to another. Personnel must be aware what alarm condition and mission-oriented protective posture level applies before entering a zone.

### 5.19.4. Contamination Avoidance Measures.

In chemical, biological, radiological, and nuclear threat areas, contamination avoidance is the key to preventing assets and personnel from becoming contaminated. Implementing quality avoidance procedures will ensure mission critical assets are available for use when needed and allow for the survival of the base populace to employ those resources.

### 5.19.5. Protect Critical Resources.

Prior to a chemical, biological, radiological, and nuclear attack, every unit must determine which equipment and assets can be stored, protected, or covered to protect against chemical, biological, radiological, and nuclear contamination. Protecting these vital resources will minimize or completely remove the requirement to decontaminate and make the resource available for mission use quickly after an attack. To the maximum extent possible, aircraft, vehicles, aerospace ground equipment, and munitions should be covered or moved inside. Bulk supplies should be placed in shelters or under overhead cover. If equipment cannot be placed under overhead cover, it must be covered or wrapped with at least one layer of barrier material to prevent contamination. However, the use at least two layers of barrier material to cover the top, so any contamination can be easily removed, safely discarded, and replaced is best. Resource protection provides you with survival and sustainment measures for operations after chemical, biological, radiological, and nuclear warfare events.

### 5.19.6. Facility Protection.

To ensure the inside of facilities do not become contaminated, occupants will close all windows, doors, and turn off ventilation systems at the time of the suspected chemical, biological, radiological, and nuclear attack.

## 5.20. Response.

Response actions during and after a chemical, biological, radiological, and nuclear attack are critical to not only ensure the Air Force mission is continued but more importantly for your survival. During attacks, the primary focus of the base populace should be directed toward force survivability to ensure attack warning signals and mission-oriented protective posture levels are disseminated to the lowest level rapidly. However, Airmen who recognize an attack in progress should take immediate action regardless if mass notification has been disseminated.

### 5.20.1. Notification.

Typically, the command post will disseminate the attack warning signals via giant voice and other mass notification means. Alarm signals and mission-oriented protective posture level changes come to the command post from the Crisis Action Team based on recommendations from the Emergency Operations Center.

### 5.20.2. Seek Cover.

Airmen need to use their best judgment regarding how far they can run during an attack to gain overhead cover or protection versus taking cover in an open area. Each situation is different, therefore it is important for Airmen to gain situational awareness and familiarize themselves with the surrounding environment before an attack takes place. When Alarm Red is declared, or attack begins without notification, drop to the ground, don protective mask (if not donned already), crawl to closest available protection, don remaining individual protective equipment, and immediately check every member of your unit to make sure they are protected and have donned the proper equipment. After taking cover remain there until directed otherwise. If your location becomes too dangerous to maintain, move to a safer area. Assist injured personnel if possible.

5.20.3. **Render Self-Aid and Buddy Care.**

Self-aid and buddy care can be performed immediately, without transition into Alarm Black. Airmen who provide self-aid and buddy care under fire should do so with caution to ensure they do not become injured. Each situation is different and handled using good judgment and risk analysis.

5.20.4. **Report.**

If you observe attacks or enemy personnel movement, report it up your chain of command immediately. Use the SALUTE reporting method (Table 5.1) as a quick and effective way to communicate attack information. SALUTE reports are submitted by the observer upon encountering enemy activity, to your unit control center or work center through the most secure means.

**Table 5.1. SALUTE Reporting.**

| LINE | A<br>Report Area | B<br>Information to Report |
|---|---|---|
| 1 | (S)ize | The number of persons and vehicles seen or the size of an object |
| 2 | (A)ctivity | Description of enemy activity (assaulting, fleeing, observing) |
| 3 | (L)ocation | Where the enemy was sighted (grid coordinate or reference point) |
| 4 | (U)nit | Distinctive signs, symbols, or identification on people, vehicles, aircraft, or weapons (numbers, patches, or clothing type) |
| 5 | (T)ime | Time activity was observed |
| 6 | (E)quipment | Equipment and vehicles associated with the activity |

**5.21. Recovery.**

Reestablishing the mission is a top priority. Minimizing the amount of personnel exposed to post attack hazards is critical for mission continuation and force survivability. Successful base recovery efforts require a coordinated and integrated approach. The recovery concept involves a combined effort from personnel trained to operate as a team, using specialized equipment to spearhead recovery efforts. Immediate actions are necessary to treat casualties, assess damage, and control contamination.

5.21.1. **Reconnaissance.** This base-wide effort is initiated by the installation commander. The installation commander will direct when base specialized and unit reconnaissance teams begin post-attack chemical, biological, radiological, and nuclear surveys. Unit control centers will be directed to release post attack reconnaissance teams to collect information about the effects of the attack. Post attack reconnaissance teams or resource owners are responsible for marking and reporting contamination, including contaminated equipment, to ensure approaching personnel are aware of the hazard associated with that resource. This will allow those approaching to don the appropriate protective gear to ensure they are protected before coming too close to the hazard. Additionally, the post attack reconnaissance team or resource owner must report information to their unit control center. The unit control center will forward unit survey information to the Emergency Operations Center.

5.21.1.1. If you are not on a reconnaissance team, your immediate recovery actions include performing immediate decontamination (if contaminated) and remain under cover unless otherwise directed.

5.21.2. **Post Attack Reporting.** Effective communication between post attack reconnaissance teams and leadership is invaluable. The Emergency Operations Center is the primary command and control function for collecting and consolidating post attack information. The Emergency Operations Center director up channels information and makes recommendations regarding alarm signals and mission-oriented protective posture levels to the Crisis Action Team based on the information collected by specialized and unit reconnaissance teams.

5.21.3. **Split Mission-Oriented Protective Posture Operations.** Commanders may implement split mission-oriented protective posture for each pre-established airbase chemical, biological, radiological, and nuclear zone based on the current hazard and mission priorities within that area. Normal operations continue within areas unaffected by the incident or at lower risk from the threat. Certain conditions and procedures must be followed when moving equipment or members between clean and contaminated areas.

5.21.4. **Zone Transition Points.** If movement or travel between zones is necessary, use zone transition points. Zone transition points are clear access routes into and out of zones. Zone transition points help to contain contamination while allowing the movement of people, equipment, and needed supplies. Unit control centers control movement of their personnel and equipment between zones.

5.21.5. **Decontamination.** Units will assess and determine what methods of decontamination, if any, can be reasonably put into action. If a chemical agent gets on the skin or protective equipment, it must be removed immediately. The reactive skin decontamination lotion and M295 individual decontamination kits are the most effective methods of removing chemical agents. In the absence of an individual decontamination kit, a 5-percent chlorine solution will remove the chemical agent from equipment and a 0.5 percent chlorine solution will remove agents from the skin. The eyes are very vulnerable when exposed to nerve and blister agents. If one of these agents gets in the eyes, the eyes should be irrigated with water.

5.21.6. **Contamination Control Area.** Should personnel become contaminated with chemical, biological, or radiological agents, they decontaminate by processing through the contamination control area within 24 hours of contact. If the individual has positive indication of contamination on their M9 paper, they should report contamination to their unit control center. Contaminated personnel and equipment should not enter any facility. Unit control centers will direct personnel to go to the contamination control area at the appropriate time.

5.21.7. **Chemically Contaminated Object Rule.** The chemically contaminated object rule for mission oriented protective posture reduction is often applied by commanders for operations in and near areas with contaminated objects. The chemically contaminated object rule is a risk management philosophy designed to warn people of chemically contaminated objects. It does not direct long duration maintenance in, or on chemically contaminated resources. Although there is an increased degree of risk when working in these areas, the rule provides guidance for protecting personnel by specifying the type of individual protective equipment required.

## 5.22. Terrorist Use of Chemical, Biological, Radiological, and Nuclear Material.

Air Force installations must prepare for the full range of terrorist threats, including use of chemical, biological, radiological and nuclear weapons.

5.22.1. Terrorist threat or use of chemical, biological, radiological, and nuclear material is among the emerging transnational threats. The overwhelming capability of the United States Armed Forces greatly limit adversary options. Increasingly, nations and terrorist groups are compelled to make use of asymmetric measures to accomplish their goals.

5.22.2. Traditionally, the perceived threat of terrorism was directed toward installations in foreign countries. Today, the terrorist use of chemical, biological, radiological, and nuclear material is clearly an emerging worldwide threat. Air Force personnel, equipment, and facilities at home and abroad are highly visible targets for terrorist attacks. Therefore, chemical, biological, radiological, and nuclear threat planning and response are high-priority. The installation commander is responsible for protecting installation personnel, facilities, and resources.

5.22.3. Protective measures include evacuation, relocation, exposure control, contamination control, warning and notification, and sheltering-in-place. Protective measures are taken in stages equal to the urgency and nature of the threat; a warning for an increased terrorist attack or threat forces will increase defense readiness, according to declared force protection conditions measures. Commanders at overseas locations will ensure units receive specific instruction and guidance on personnel and resource protection. Personnel deploying to overseas areas will ensure they are briefed, before and on arrival, on the enemy attack threat, protective actions, and use of protective equipment.

## 5.23. Conclusion.

The United States Air Force is the most ready and capable air and space force in the world today. The Air Force's ability to achieve its mission hinges on readiness. Each installation is different, but across the Air Force, one element is constant; as an Airman you have an inherent responsibility to maintain readiness within your unit and ensure your role in the installation's Emergency Management program is executed and ultimately successful. Air Force members should use emergency management fundamentals in concert with security and standards of conduct to ensure readiness.

## Chapter 6

## STANDARDS OF CONDUCT

### *Section 6A—Overview*

### 6.1. Introduction.

In 1757, Lieutenant Colonel George Washington said "discipline is the soul of an Army" and those words still hold true in today's Air Force. Air Force standards must be uniformly known, consistently applied and non-selectively enforced. Accountability is critically important to good order and discipline of the force. To navigate the necessary course of action and ensure mission accomplishment, a leader must be willing to use more than one approach. Failure to ensure accountability will destroy the trust of the American public, the very people living under the Constitution we swore to support and defend, and who look to us, the members of their Nation's Air Force, to embrace and live by the standards that are higher than those in the society we serve. This chapter discusses the Law of Armed Conflict, Code of Conduct, and general standards of conduct. Airmen must learn these standards well enough not only to be able to follow them, but be able to articulate them clearly to subordinates and enforce proper observation by other members. Used in concert with information presented in Chapter 5 and Chapter 19, this chapter covers issues vital to mission effectiveness, especially in light of the Air Force global mission.

### *Section 6B—Law of Armed Conflict*

### 6.2. Law of Armed Conflict Defined.

The Law of War, as defined by the Department of Defense (DoD), is that part of international law that regulates the resort to armed force; the conduct of hostilities and the protection of war victims in both international and non-international armed conflict; belligerent occupation; and the relationships between belligerent, neutral, and non-belligerent States. The law of war is often called the Law of Armed Conflict. While DoD uses the term Law of War, most Air Force doctrine and publications continue to use the term "Law of Armed Conflict". The Law of Armed Conflict arises from civilized nations' humanitarian desire to lessen the effects of conflicts. Law of Armed Conflict protects combatants, noncombatants and civilians from unnecessary suffering, and provides certain fundamental protections for persons who fall into the hands of the enemy, particularly prisoners of war, civilians, and military wounded, sick, and shipwrecked. The law also tries to keep conflicts from degenerating into savagery and brutality, thereby helping to restore peace.

### 6.3. Law of Armed Conflict Policy.

DoDD 2311.01E, *Department of Defense Law of War Program*, requires each military department to design a program that ensures Law of Armed Conflict observance, prevents violations, ensures prompt reporting of alleged violations, appropriately trains all forces, and completes a legal review of new weapons. Law of Armed Conflict training is an obligation of the U.S. under provisions of the 1949 Geneva Conventions other law of war treaties and customary international law. AFI 51-401, *Training and Reporting to Ensure Compliance with the Law of Armed Conflict*, requires that all Air Force personnel receive instruction on the principles and rules of the Law of Armed Conflict commensurate with each member's duties and responsibilities. The training is of a general nature; however, certain groups such as aircrews, medical personnel, and security forces receive additional, specialized training to address the unique situations they may encounter.

### 6.4. International and Domestic Law.

The Law of Armed Conflict is embodied in both customary international law and treaties. Customary international law, reflected in practices nations have come to accept as legally binding, establishes many of the oldest rules that govern the conduct of military operations in armed conflict. Article VI of the U.S. Constitution states that treaty obligations of the U.S. are the "supreme law of the land," and the U.S. Supreme Court has held that U.S. international legal obligations, to include custom, is part of U.S. law. This means that treaties and international agreements with the U.S. enjoy equal status to laws passed by Congress and signed by the President. Therefore, all persons subject to U.S. law must observe the U.S. Law of Armed Conflict obligations. Military personnel, civilians, and contractors authorized to accompany the armed forces in combat must consider the Law of Armed Conflict to plan and execute operations and must obey Law of Armed Conflict in combat. Those who commit violations may be criminally liable and court-martialed under the Uniform Code of Military Justice.

### 6.5. Principles.

Five important Law of Armed Conflict principles govern armed conflict: military necessity, distinction, proportionality, humanity, and honor.

### 6.5.1. Military Necessity:

6.5.1.1. Military necessity is the principle that justifies the use of all measures needed to defeat the enemy as quickly and efficiently as possible that are not prohibited by the law of war.

6.5.1.2. Attacks must be limited to military objectives. Certain classes of persons are military objectives and may be made the object of attack. These classes of persons include: combatants, or unprivileged belligerents; and civilians taking a direct part in hostilities. Military objectives, insofar as objects are concerned, include any objects which by its nature, location, purpose, or use make an effective contribution to military action and whose total or partial destruction, capture, or neutralization, in the circumstances ruling at the time, offer a definite military advantage. Examples include tanks, military aircraft, bases, supplies, lines of communications, and headquarters.

6.5.1.3. Military necessity does not authorize all military action and destruction. Under no circumstances may military necessity authorize actions specifically prohibited by the law of war, such as the murder of prisoners of war, ill treatment of prisoners of war or internees, the taking of hostages, or execution or reprisal against a person or object specifically protected from reprisal.

### 6.5.2. Humanity:

Although military necessity justifies certain actions necessary to defeat the enemy as quickly and efficiently as possible, military necessity cannot justify actions not necessary to achieve this purpose, such as cruelty or wanton violence. Moreover, once a military purpose has been achieved, inflicting more suffering is unnecessary and should be avoided. For example, if an enemy combatant has been placed hors de combat (e.g., incapacitated by being severely wounded or captured), no military purpose is served by continuing to attack him or her. Thus, the principle of humanity forbids making enemy combatants who have been placed hors de combat the object of attack. Humanity animates certain law of war rules, including prohibitions on weapons that are calculated to cause superfluous injury; and prohibitions on weapons that are inherently indiscriminate. For example, the 1907 Hague Convention prohibits the use of poison or poisoned weapons in combat. Also, indiscriminate chemical, biological, and bacterial weapons are banned by treaties because they cause unnecessary suffering. However, using rifles to shoot prisoners of war, strafing civilians, firing on shipwrecked mariners or downed aircrews are lawful weapons that may be used unlawfully.

### 6.5.3. Distinction:

6.5.3.1. This principle imposes a requirement to distinguish (also termed "discriminate") between the civilian population (or individual civilians not taking a direct part in the hostilities) and combatant forces when engaged in military operations. Military force may be directed only against military objects or objectives, and not against civilian objects.

6.5.3.1.1. Civilian objects are protected from attack and include such objects as places of worship, schools, hospitals, and dwellings.

6.5.3.1.2. Civilian objects can lose their protected status if they are used to make an effective contribution to military action.

6.5.3.2. A defender has an obligation to separate civilians and civilian objects (either in the defender's country or in an occupied area) from military targets. Employment of voluntary or involuntary human shields to protect military objectives or individual military units or personnel is a fundamental violation of the law of war principle of distinction.

### 6.5.4. Proportionality:

6.5.4.1. Proportionality may be defined as the principle that even where one is justified in acting, one must not act in way that is unreasonable or excessive. Proportionality generally weighs the justification for acting against the expected harms to determine whether the latter are disproportionate in comparison to the former. In war, incidental damage to the civilian population and civilian objects is unfortunate and tragic, but inevitable. Thus, applying the proportionality rule in conducting attacks does not require that no incidental damage result from attacks. Rather, this rule obliges persons to refrain from attacking where the expected harm incidental to such attacks would be excessive in relation to the military advantage anticipated to be gained.

6.5.4.2. Proportionality most often refers to the standard applicable to persons conducting attacks. Proportionality considerations, however, may also be understood to apply to the party subject to attack, which must take feasible precautions to reduce the risk of incidental harm. Proportionality also plays a role in assessing whether weapons are prohibited because they are calculated to cause unnecessary suffering.

6.5.4.3. Damages and casualties must be consistent with mission accomplishment and allowable risk to the attacking force (for example, the attacker need not expose its forces to extraordinary risks simply to avoid or minimize civilian losses).

### 6.5.5. Honor:

6.5.5.1. Honor requires a certain amount of fairness in offense and defense. In requiring a certain amount of fairness in offense and defense, honor reflects the principle that parties to a conflict must accept that certain limits exist on their ability to conduct hostilities. Honor also forbids resort to means, expedients, or conduct that would constitute a breach of trust with the enemy.

6.5.5.2. For example, enemies must deal with one another in good faith in their non-hostile relations. And even in the conduct of hostilities, good faith prohibits: (1) killing or wounding enemy persons by resort to perfidy; (2) misusing certain signs; (3) fighting in the enemy's uniform; (4) feigning non-hostile relations in order to seek a military advantage; and (5) compelling nationals of a hostile party to take part in the operations of war directed against their own country. Honor, however, does not forbid parties from using ruses and other lawful deceptions against which the enemy ought to take measures to protect itself.

## 6.6. The Protection of War Victims and Classes of Persons.

Some of the most important Law of Armed Conflict rules come from the Geneva Conventions of 1949. The Geneva Conventions consist of four separate international treaties that aim to protect all persons taking no active part in hostilities, including members of armed forces who have laid down their arms and those placed hors de combat by sickness, wounds, detention, or any other cause. These treaties also seek to protect civilians and private property.

### 6.6.1. Categories of Personnel:

6.6.1.1. **Geneva Convention Distinctions.** The Geneva Conventions distinguish between combatants, noncombatants, and civilians.

6.6.1.1.1. **Combatants.** Three classes of persons qualify as "lawful" or "privileged" combatants: (1) members of the armed forces of a State that is a party to a conflict, aside from certain categories of medical and religious personnel; (2) under certain conditions, members of militia or volunteer corps that are not part of the armed forces of a State, but belong to a State; and (3) inhabitants of an area who participate in a kind of popular uprising to defend against foreign invaders, known as a *levée en masse*. A combatant is commanded by a person responsible for subordinates; wears fixed distinctive emblems recognizable at a distance, such as uniforms; carries arms openly; and conducts his or her combat operations according to Law of Armed Conflict. Lawful or privileged combatants are entitled to Prisoner of war Status if captured and cannot be prosecuted for their lawful conduct in an armed conflict.

6.6.1.1.2. **Noncombatants.** Noncombatants include certain military personnel who are members of the Armed Forces not authorized to engage in combatant activities, such as permanent medical personnel and chaplains. Noncombatants must be respected and protected and may not be made the object of attack.

6.6.1.1.3. **Civilians.** Civilians are also protected persons and may not be made the object of direct attack. They may, however, suffer injury or death incident to a direct attack on a military objective without such an attack violating Law of Armed Conflict, if such attack is on a lawful target by lawful means. With limited exceptions, the Law of Armed Conflict does not authorize civilians to take an active or direct part in hostilities. Civilians who take a direct part in hostilities without authority to do so are unprivileged belligerent and can be made the object of attacked when participating in hostiles.

6.6.1.2. **Unprivileged Belligerents: A Distinction Not Made by the Geneva Conventions.** The term unprivileged belligerent is not used in the Geneva Conventions. The term "unprivileged belligerent", as defined in the DoD Manual on the Law of War, includes "lawful combatants who have forfeited the privileges of combatant status by engaging in spying or sabotage, and private persons who have forfeited one or more of the protections of civilian status by engaging in hostilities." An unprivileged belligerent is an individual who is not authorized by a state that is party to a conflict to take part in hostilities but does so anyway. For example, civilians who plant improvised explosive devices are unprivileged belligerents.

### 6.6.2. Undetermined Status.

Should doubt exist as to whether a captured individual is a lawful combatant, noncombatant, or an unprivileged belligerent, the individual will receive the protections of the Geneva Prisoner of War Convention until status is determined.

## 6.7. Military Objectives.

The Law of Armed Conflict governs the conduct of aerial warfare. The principle of military necessity authorizes aerial attacks on combatants and other lawful military objectives. Military objectives are limited to those objects or installations that by their own nature, location, purpose, or use make an effective contribution to military action and whose total or partial destruction, capture, or neutralization in the circumstances existing at the time offer a definite military advantage.

### 6.7.1. Protection of Civilians and Civilian Objects.

Law of Armed Conflict protects civilian populations. Military attacks against cities, towns, or villages not justified by military necessity are forbidden. Attacking civilians for the sole purpose of terrorizing them is also prohibited. Although civilians may not be made the object of a direct attack, Law of Armed Conflict recognizes that a military objective need not be spared because its destruction may cause collateral damage that results in the unintended death or injury to civilians or damage to their property. Commanders and their planners must take into consideration the extent of damage to civilian objects and casualties anticipated as a result of an attack on a military objective and seek to avoid or minimize civilian casualties and destruction. Anticipated damage to civilian objects and civilian casualties must not be disproportionate to the military advantage sought. Judge advocate, intelligence, and operations personnel play a critical role in determining the propriety of a target and the choice of weapon to be used under the particular circumstances known to the commander when planning an attack.

### 6.7.2. Protected Objects.

The Law of Armed Conflict provides specific protection to certain objects, including medical units or establishments; transports of wounded and sick personnel; military and civilian hospital ships; safety zones established under the Geneva Conventions; religious, cultural, and charitable buildings; monuments; and prisoner of war camps. However, if these protected objects are used for military purposes, they lose their protected status. Protected objects near lawful military objectives that suffer collateral damage when the nearby military objectives are lawfully engaged does not violate Law of Armed Conflict.

## 6.8. Aircraft and Combat:

### 6.8.1. Enemy Military Aircraft and Aircrew.

Enemy military aircraft may be attacked and destroyed wherever found, unless in neutral airspace or territory. Airmen who parachute from a disabled aircraft and offer no resistance may not be attacked. Airmen who resist in descent or are downed behind their own lines and who continue to fight may be subject to attack. The rules of engagement for a particular operation often include additional guidance for attacking enemy aircraft consistent with Law of Armed Conflict obligations.

### 6.8.2. Enemy Civilian Aircraft.

An enemy's public and private nonmilitary aircraft are generally not subject to attack unless used for a military purpose. Since World War II, nations have increasingly recognized the necessity to avoid attacking civil aircraft. Under exceptional conditions, however, civil aircraft in flight may be lawfully attacked. If a civil aircraft initiates an attack, it may be considered an immediate military threat and may be lawfully attacked. An immediate military threat justifying an attack may also exist when reasonable suspicion exists of a hostile intent, such as when a civil aircraft approaches a military base at high speed, or enters enemy territory without permission and disregards signals or warnings to land or proceed to a designated place.

### 6.8.3. Military Medical Aircraft.

Military medical aircraft are used exclusively for the removal of the wounded and sick and for the transport of medical personnel and equipment. Military medical aircraft are entitled to protection from attack by enemy combatants while flying at heights, times, and on routes specifically agreed upon between the parties to the conflict. Under Law of Armed Conflict, a military medical aircraft could be lawfully attacked and destroyed if Military Medical Aircraft:

6.8.3.1. Initiates an attack.

6.8.3.2. Does not bear a clearly marked Red Cross, Red Crescent, or other recognized symbol and is not otherwise known to be engaged in medical operations at the time.

6.8.3.3. Does not fly at heights, at times, and on routes specifically agreed to by the parties to the conflict and is not otherwise known to be engaged in medical operations at the time.

6.8.3.4. Flies over enemy territory or enemy-occupied territory (unless otherwise agreed upon by the parties) and is not otherwise known to be engaged in medical operations at the time.

6.8.3.5. Approaches enemy's territory or a combat zone and disregards a summons to land and is not otherwise known to be engaged in medical operations at the time.

## 6.9. Enforcing Law of Armed Conflict Rules:

### 6.9.1. Prosecution.

Military members who violate Law of Armed Conflict are subject to criminal prosecution and punishment. Criminal prosecutions may take place in a national or international forum. U.S. Armed Forces could be prosecuted by courts-martial under the Uniform Code of Military Justice or through an international military tribunal, such as those used in Nuremberg and Tokyo after World War II. "I was only following orders," generally is not accepted by national or international tribunals as a war crime defense. Individual Airmen are responsible for their actions and must comply with Law of Armed Conflict. Commanders can also be held criminally responsible for the actions of their subordinates through the doctrine of command responsibility. Commanders can be held criminally liable for the conduct of their subordinates when they issued illegal orders or when they either knew or should have known that their subordinates were committing war crimes.

### 6.9.2. Reprisal.

Reprisals are the commission of otherwise illegal acts that, under the circumstances, may be justified as a last resort to put an end to illegal acts committed first by the adversary. For example, if any enemy employs illegal weapons against a state, the victim may resort to the use of weapons that would otherwise be unlawful in order to compel the enemy to cease using the weapon. Reprisals can be legally justified if they meet certain requirements. Authority to approve reprisals is held at the highest decision-making level. Only the President of the U.S., as Commander in Chief, may authorize U.S. forces to take such an action.

## 6.10. Reporting Violations.

AFPD 51-4 includes guidance for personnel who suspect or have information which might reasonably be viewed as a violation of the Law of Armed Conflict committed by or against U.S. personnel, enemy personnel or any other individual shall promptly report the violation to their immediate commander. An Air Force member who knows or receives a report of an apparent Law of Armed Conflict violation must inform his or her commander. This includes violations by the enemy, allies, U.S. Armed Forces, or others. If the allegation involves or may involve a U.S. commander, the report should be made to the next higher U.S. command authority. Particular circumstances may require that the report be made to the nearest judge advocate, inspector general, a special agent in the Office of Special Investigations, or a security forces member.

## 6.11. Rules of Engagement.

Rules of engagement exist to ensure use of force in an operation occurs according to national policy goals, mission requirements, and the rule of law. In general, rules of engagement set parameters for when, where, how, why, and against whom commanders and their Airmen may use force. Mission-specific rules of engagement present a more detailed application of Law of Armed Conflict principles tailored to the political and military nature of a mission which are contained in execution orders, operations plans, and operations orders. All Airmen have a duty and a legal obligation to understand, remember, and apply mission rules of engagement. Failure to comply with rules of engagement may be punishable under the Uniform Code of Military Justice. The U.S. standing rules of engagement, approved by the President and Secretary of Defense and issued by the Chairman, Joint Chiefs of Staff, provide implementation guidance on the inherent right of self-defense and the application of force for mission accomplishment. Commanders at every echelon have an obligation to ensure that mission rules of engagement comply with the standing rules of engagement.

### 6.11.1. Self Defense.

The fundamental U.S. policy on self-defense is repeatedly stated throughout the standing rules of engagement: "These rules do not limit a commander's inherent authority and obligation to use all necessary means available to take all appropriate actions in self-defense of the commander's unit and other U.S. forces in the vicinity." Self-defense methods include national, collective, unit, and individual. Several elements must be considered before undertaking the use of force in self-defense.

6.11.1.1. **De-escalation.** When time and circumstances permit, the forces committing hostile acts or hostile intent should be warned and given the opportunity to withdraw or cease threatening actions.

6.11.1.2. **Necessity.** Rules of engagement necessity exists if a hostile act is committed or hostile intent is demonstrated against U.S. forces or other designated persons or property. A hostile act is defined as force used against the U.S., U.S. forces, designated persons and property, or intended to impede the mission of U.S. forces. Hostile intent is the threat of imminent use of force against the U.S., U.S. forces, designated persons and property, or intended to impede the mission of U.S. forces. Rules of engagement necessity relates to the threat perceived by an individual and is different from the Law of Armed Conflict concept of military necessity.

6.11.1.3. **Proportionality.** In self-defense, U.S. forces may only use the amount of force necessary to decisively counter a hostile act or a demonstration of hostile intent and ensure the continued safety of U.S. forces or other designated persons and property. Force used must be reasonable in intensity, duration, and magnitude compared to the threat based on facts known to the commander at the time. Rules of engagement proportionality refers to the reasonableness of the response to a threat and is different to the law of armed conflict concept of proportionality.

6.11.1.4. **Pursuit.** U.S. forces can pursue and engage a hostile force that has committed a hostile act or demonstrated a hostile intent, if those forces continue to commit hostile acts or demonstrate hostile intent. (Applicable rules of engagement may restrict or place limitations on U.S. forces ability to pursue or engage a hostile force across an international border.)

*Section 6C—Code of Conduct*

## 6.12. Policy.

The Code of Conduct outlines basic responsibilities and obligations of members of the U.S. Armed Forces. All members are expected to measure up to the standards described in the Code of Conduct. Although developed for prisoners of war, the spirit and intent are applicable to service members subject to other hostile detention. Such service members should consistently conduct themselves in a manner that brings credit to them and their country. The six articles of the Code of Conduct address situations and decision areas that any member could encounter to some degree. The Code of Conduct includes basic information useful to prisoners of war to help them survive honorably while resisting captors' efforts to exploit them. Such survival and resistance require knowledge and understanding of the articles.

## 6.13. Training.

DoD personnel who plan, schedule, commit, or control members of the Armed Forces must fully understand the Code of Conduct and ensure personnel have the training and education necessary to abide by it. How much knowledge members need depends on how likely they are to be captured, their exposure to sensitive information, and how useful or valuable a captor considers them. Training is conducted at three levels:

6.13.1. **Level A—Entry Level Training.**

Level A represents the minimum level of understanding needed for all members of the Armed Forces. This level is imparted to all personnel during entry training.

6.13.2. **Level B—Training After Assumption of Duty Eligibility.**

Level B is the minimum level of understanding needed for service members whose military jobs, specialties, or assignments entail moderate risk of capture, such as members of ground combat units. Training is conducted for such service members as soon as their assumption of duty makes them eligible.

6.13.3. **Level C—Training Upon Assumption of Duties or Responsibilities.**

Level C is the minimum level of understanding needed for military service members whose military jobs, specialties, or assignments entail significant or high risk of capture and whose position, rank, or seniority makes them vulnerable to greater-than-average exploitation efforts by a captor. Examples include aircrews and special mission forces such as Air Force pararescue teams. Training for these members is conducted upon their assumption of the duties or responsibilities that make them eligible.

## 6.14. The Articles of the Code of Conduct.

President Dwight D. Eisenhower first published the Code of Conduct for members of the Armed Forces of the U.S. on 17 August 1955. In March 1988, President Ronald W. Reagan amended the code with gender-neutral language.

6.14.1. **ARTICLE I.**

*I am an American, fighting in the forces which guard my country and our way of life. I am prepared to give my life in their defense.*

6.14.1.1. **Explanation.** Article I applies to all members at all times. A member of the Armed Forces has a duty to support U.S. interests and oppose U.S. enemies regardless of the circumstances, whether in active combat or captivity.

6.14.1.2. **Training.** Familiarity with the wording and basic meaning is necessary to understand that:

6.14.1.2.1. Past experience of captured Americans reveals that honorable survival in captivity requires a high degree of dedication and motivation.

6.14.1.2.2. Maintaining these qualities requires knowledge of and a strong belief in the advantages of American democratic institutions and concepts.

6.14.1.2.3. Maintaining these qualities also requires a love of and faith in the U.S. and a conviction that the U.S. cause is just.

6.14.1.2.4. Honorable survival in captivity depends on faith in and loyalty to fellow prisoners of war.

**Note:** Possessing the dedication and motivation fostered by such beliefs and trust may help prisoners of war survive long, stressful periods of captivity, and has helped many return to their country and families with their honor and self-esteem intact.

6.14.2. **ARTICLE II.**

*I will never surrender of my own free will. If in command, I will never surrender the members of my command while they still have the means to resist.*

6.14.2.1. **Explanation.** Members of the Armed Forces may never surrender voluntarily. Even when isolated and no longer able to inflict casualties on the enemy or otherwise defend themselves, their duty is to evade capture and rejoin the nearest friendly force. Only when evasion is impossible and further fighting would lead to their death with no significant loss to the enemy may the means to resist or evade be considered exhausted.

6.14.2.2. **Training.** Service members who are cut off, shot down, or otherwise isolated in enemy-controlled territory must make every effort to avoid capture. Actions available include concealment until recovered by friendly rescue forces, evasive travel to a friendly or neutral territory, and evasive travel to other prebriefed areas. Members must understand that capture is not dishonorable if all reasonable means of avoiding it have been exhausted, and the only alternative is death. Service members must understand and have confidence in search and recovery forces rescue procedures and techniques, and proper evasion destination procedures.

6.14.3. **ARTICLE III.**

*If I am captured, I will continue to resist by all means available. I will make every effort to escape and aid others to escape. I will accept neither parole nor special favors from the enemy.*

6.14.3.1. **Explanation:**

6.14.3.1.1. An Armed Forces member's duty to continue to resist enemy exploitation by all means available is not lessened by the misfortune of capture. Contrary to the 1949 Geneva Conventions, enemies U.S. forces have engaged since 1949 have treated the prisoner of war compound as an extension of the battlefield. The prisoner of war must be prepared for this.

6.14.3.1.2. Enemies have used a variety of tactics to exploit prisoners of war for propaganda purposes or to obtain military information, in spite of Geneva Conventions prohibition. Physical and mental harassment, general mistreatment, torture, medical neglect, and political indoctrination have all been used, and the enemy has tried to tempt prisoners of war to accept special favors or privileges in return for statements or information, or for a pledge by the prisoner of war not to attempt escape.

6.14.3.1.3. A prisoner of war must not seek special privileges or accept special favors at the expense of fellow prisoners of war. Under the guidance and supervision of the senior military person, the prisoner of war must be prepared to take advantage of escape opportunities. In communal detention, the welfare of the prisoners of war who remain behind must be considered. Additionally, prisoners of war should not sign or enter into a parole agreement. Parole agreements are promises the prisoners of war make to the captor to fulfill stated conditions, such as not to bear arms, in exchange for special privileges, such as release or lessened restraint.

6.14.3.2. **Training.** Members should understand that captivity involves continuous control by a captor who may attempt to use the prisoner of war as a source of information for political purposes or as a potential subject for political indoctrination. Members must familiarize themselves with prisoner of war and captor rights and obligations under the Geneva Conventions, understanding that some captors have accused prisoners of war of being war criminals simply because they waged war against them. Continued efforts to escape are critical because a successful escape causes the enemy to divert forces that may otherwise be fighting, provides the U.S. valuable information about the enemy and other prisoners of war, and serves as a positive example to all members of the Armed Forces.

6.14.4. **ARTICLE IV.**

*If I become a prisoner of war, I will keep faith with my fellow prisoners. I will give no information or take part in any action which might be harmful to my comrades. If I am senior, I will take command. If not, I will obey the lawful orders of those appointed over me and will back them up in every way.*

6.14.4.1. **Explanation.** Officers and NCOs continue to carry out their responsibilities and exercise authority in captivity. Informing, or any other action detrimental to a fellow prisoner of war, is despicable and expressly forbidden. Prisoners of war must avoid helping the enemy identify fellow prisoners of war who may have valuable knowledge to the enemy. Strong leadership is essential to discipline. Without discipline, camp organization, resistance, and even survival may be impossible. Personal hygiene, camp sanitation, and care of the sick and wounded are imperative. Wherever located, prisoners of war must organize in a military manner under the senior military prisoner of war, regardless of military service. If the senior prisoner of war is incapacitated or otherwise unable to act, the next senior prisoner of war assumes command.

6.14.4.2. **Training.** Members must be trained to understand and accept leadership from those in command and abide by the decisions of the senior prisoner of war, regardless of military service. Failing to do so may result in legal proceedings under the Uniform Code of Military Justice. Additionally, a prisoner of war who voluntarily informs or collaborates with the captor is a traitor to the U.S. and fellow prisoners of war and, after repatriation, is subject to punishment under the Uniform Code of Military Justice. Service members must be familiar with the principles of hygiene, sanitation, health maintenance, first aid, physical conditioning, and food utilization.

## 6.14.5. **ARTICLE V.**

*When questioned, should I become a prisoner of war, I am required to give name, rank, service number, and date of birth. I will evade answering further questions to the utmost of my ability. I will make no oral or written statements disloyal to my country and its allies or harmful to their cause.*

6.14.5.1. **Explanation:**

6.14.5.1.1. When questioned, a prisoner of war is required by the Geneva Conventions, and permitted by the Uniform Code of Military Justice, to give name, rank, service number, and date of birth. Under the Geneva Conventions, the enemy has no right to try to force a prisoner of war to provide any additional information. However, it is unrealistic to expect a prisoner of war to remain confined for years reciting only name, rank, service number, and date of birth. Many prisoner of war camp situations exist in which certain types of conversation with the enemy are permitted. For example, a prisoner of war is allowed, but not required by the Code of Conduct, the Uniform Code of Military Justice, or the Geneva Conventions, to fill out a Geneva Conventions capture card, to write letters home, and to communicate with captors on matters of health and welfare. The senior prisoner of war is required to represent prisoners of war in matters of camp administration, health, welfare, and grievances.

6.14.5.1.2. A prisoner of war must resist, avoid, or evade, even when physically and mentally coerced, all enemy efforts to secure statements or actions that may further the enemy's cause. Examples of statements or actions prisoners of war should resist include giving oral or written confessions, answering questionnaires, providing personal history statements, and making propaganda recordings and broadcast appeals to other prisoners of war to comply with improper captor demands. Additionally, prisoners of war should resist appealing for U.S. surrender or parole, engaging in self-criticism, or providing oral or written statements or communication that are harmful to the U.S., its allies, the Armed Forces, or other prisoners of war. Experience has shown that, although enemy interrogation sessions may be harsh and cruel, a prisoner of war can usually resist if there is a will to resist. The best way for a prisoner of war to keep faith with the U.S., fellow prisoners of war, and him or herself is to provide the enemy with as little information as possible.

6.14.5.2. **Training.** Service members familiarize themselves with the various aspects of interrogation, including phases, procedures, and methods and techniques, as well as the interrogator's goals, strengths, and weaknesses. Members should avoid disclosing information by such techniques as claiming inability to furnish information because of previous orders, poor memory, ignorance, or lack of comprehension. They should understand that, short of death, a prisoner of war may prevent a skilled enemy interrogator, using all available psychological and physical methods of coercion, from obtaining some degree of compliance by the prisoner of war is unlikely. However, the prisoner of war must recover as quickly as possible and resist successive efforts to the utmost.

## 6.14.6. **ARTICLE VI.**

*I will never forget that I am an American, fighting for freedom, responsible for my actions, and dedicated to the principles which made my country free. I will trust in my God and in the United States of America.*

6.14.6.1. **Explanation.** A member of the Armed Forces remains responsible for personal actions at all times. When repatriated, prisoners of war can expect their actions to be subject to review, both circumstances of capture and conduct during detention. The purpose of such a review is to recognize meritorious performance and, if necessary, investigate any allegations of misconduct. Such reviews are conducted with due regard for the rights of the individual and consideration for the conditions of captivity.

6.14.6.2. **Training.** Members must understand the relationship between the Uniform code of Military Justice and the Code of Conduct and realize that failure to follow the guidance may result in violations punishable under the Uniform Code of Military Justice, and they may be held legally accountable for their actions. They should also understand that the U.S. Government will use every available means to establish contact with prisoners of war, to support them, and to obtain their release. Furthermore, U.S. laws provide for the support and care of dependents of the Armed Forces, including prisoners of war family members. Military members must ensure their personal affairs and family matters are up to date at all times.

## 6.15. Detention of U.S. Military Personnel in Operations Other than War:

### 6.15.1. Policy.

U.S. military personnel isolated from U.S. control are still required to do everything in their power to follow DoD and Air Force policy and survive with honor. DoDI 1300.21, *Code of Conduct (CoC) Training and Education,* Enclosure 3, provides guidance to military members who find themselves isolated during operations other than war or in a situation not addressed specifically in the Code of Conduct. All military departments establish procedures to ensure U.S. military personnel are familiar with the guidance in this publication.

### 6.15.2. Rationale.

Because of their wide range of activities, U.S. military personnel are subject to detention by unfriendly governments or captivity by terrorist groups. When a hostile government or terrorist group detains or captures U.S. military personnel, the captor is often attempting to exploit both the individual and the U.S. Government for its own purposes. As history has shown, exploitation can take many forms, such as hostage confessions to crimes never committed, international news media exploitation, and substantial ransom demands, all of which can lead to increased credibility and support for the detainer.

### 6.15.3. Responsibility:

6.15.3.1. U.S. military personnel detained by unfriendly governments or held hostage by a terrorist group must do everything in their power to survive with honor. Furthermore, whether U.S. military personnel are detained or held hostage, they can be sure the U.S. Government will make every effort to obtain their release. To best survive the situation, military personnel must maintain faith in their country, in fellow detainees or captives and, most importantly, in themselves. In any group captivity situation, military captives must organize, to the fullest extent possible, under the senior military member present. If civilians are part of the group, they should be encouraged to participate.

6.15.3.2. U.S. military personnel must make every reasonable effort to prevent captors from exploiting them and the U.S. Government. If exploitation cannot be prevented, military members must attempt to limit it. If detainees convince their captors of their low propaganda value, the captors may seek a quick end to the situation. When a detention or hostage situation ends, military members who can honestly say they did their utmost to resist exploitation will have upheld DoD policy, the founding principles of the U.S., and the highest traditions of military service.

### 6.15.4. Military Bearing and Courtesy.

U.S. military personnel shall maintain their military bearing, regardless of the type of detention or captivity, or harshness of treatment. They should make every effort to remain calm, courteous, and project personal dignity. That is particularly important during the process of capture and the early stages of internment when the captors may be uncertain of their control over the captives. Discourteous, nonmilitary behavior seldom serves the long-term interest of a detainee or hostage and often results in unnecessary punishment that serves no useful purpose. Such behavior often results in punishment that serves no useful purpose. In some situations, such behavior may jeopardize survival and severely complicate efforts to gain release of the detainee or hostage.

### 6.15.5. Guidance for Detention by Governments:

6.15.5.1. Detainees in the custody of a hostile government, regardless of the circumstances that resulted in the detention, are subject to the laws of that government. Detainees must maintain military bearing and avoid aggressive, combative, or illegal behavior that may complicate their situation, legal status, or efforts to negotiate a rapid release. As American citizens, detainees should ask immediately and continually to see U.S. embassy personnel or a representative of an allied or neutral government. U.S. military personnel who become lost or isolated in a hostile foreign country during operations other than war will not act as combatants during evasion attempts. During operations other than war, there is no protection afforded under the Geneva Convention. The civil laws of that country apply.

6.15.5.2. A detainer's goal may be maximum political exploitation. Therefore, detained U.S. military personnel must be cautious in all they say and do. In addition to asking for a U.S. representative, detainees should provide name, rank, service number, date of birth, and the innocent circumstances leading to their detention. They should limit further discussions to health and welfare matters, conditions of their fellow detainees, and going home.

6.15.5.3. Detainees should avoid signing any document or making any statement, oral or otherwise. If forced, they must provide as little information as possible and then continue to resist. Detainees are not likely to earn their release by cooperation. Rather, release may be gained by resisting, thereby reducing the value of the detainee. U.S. military detainees should not refuse release, unless doing so requires them to compromise their honor or cause damage to the U.S. Government or its allies. Escape attempts must be made only after carefully considering the risk of violence, chance of success, and detrimental effects on detainees remaining behind. Jailbreak in most countries is a crime. Escape attempts can provide the detainer further justification to hold the individual.

### 6.15.6. Terrorist Hostage:

6.15.6.1. Capture by terrorists is generally the least predictable and structured form of operations, other than war captivity. Capture can range from a spontaneous kidnapping to a carefully planned hijacking. In either situation, hostages play an important role in determining their own fate because terrorists rarely expect to receive rewards for providing good treatment or releasing victims unharmed. U.S. military members should assume their captors are genuine terrorists when unclear if they are surrogates of a government.

6.15.6.2. A terrorist hostage situation is more volatile than a government detention, so members must take steps to lessen the chance of a terrorist indiscriminately killing hostages. In such a situation, DoD policy accepts and promotes efforts to establish rapport between U.S. hostages and the terrorists in order to establish themselves as people in the terrorist's mind, rather than a stereotypical symbol of a country the terrorist may hate. DoD policy recommends U.S. personnel talk to terrorists about nonsubstantive subjects such as family, sports, and hobbies. They should stay away from topics that could inflame terrorist sensibilities, such as their cause, politics, or religion. Listening can be vitally important when survival is at stake. Members should take an active role in the conversation, but should not argue, patronize, or debate issues with the captors. They should try to reduce tension and make it as hard as possible for terrorists to identify U.S. personnel as troublemakers, which may mark them for murder.

### Section 6D—Everyday Conduct

### 6.16. Overview.

The importance of the Air Force mission and responsibility to the nation requires members adhere to higher standards than nonmilitary members. Every person is accountable for his or her own actions on duty and off. Supervisors must hold subordinates accountable and take corrective action if they do not fulfill their responsibilities. Members must remember and reflect the Air Force Core Values—Integrity First, Service Before Self, and Excellence in All We Do—in everything they do.

### 6.17. Policy.

DoDD 5500.07, *Standards of Conduct,* DoD 5500.07-R, *The Joint Ethics Regulation (JER), and* AFI 1-1, *Air Force Standards* provide guidance to Air Force personnel on standards of conduct. Military members who violate the punitive provisions may be prosecuted under the Uniform Code of Military Justice. Civilian violations may result in disciplinary action without regard to the issue of criminal liability. Military members and civilian employees who violate these standards, even if such violations do not constitute criminal misconduct, are subject to administrative actions, such as reprimands. Contact the base legal office for assistance.

### 6.18. Ethical Values.

Ethics are standards of conduct based on values. Values are core beliefs, such as duty, honor, and integrity that motivate attitudes and actions. Not all values are ethical values (integrity is; happiness is not). Ethical values relate to what is right and wrong and thus take precedence over nonethical values when making ethical decisions. DoD employees who make decisions as part of their official duties should carefully consider ethical values. Primary ethical values include:

### 6.18.1. Honesty.

Being truthful, straightforward, and candid are aspects of honesty:

6.18.1.1. Truthfulness is required. Deceptions are usually easily uncovered. Lies erode credibility and undermine public confidence. Untruths told for seemingly altruistic reasons (to prevent hurt feelings, to promote good will, etc.) are nonetheless resented by the recipients.

6.18.1.2. Straightforwardness adds frankness to truthfulness and is usually necessary to promote public confidence and to ensure effective, efficient conduct of operations. Truths presented in such a way as to lead recipients to confusion, misinterpretation, or inaccurate conclusions are not productive. Such indirect deceptions can promote ill will and erode openness, especially when there is an expectation of frankness.

6.18.1.3. Candor is the forthright offering of unrequested information. This ethical value is necessary according to the gravity of the situation and the nature of the relationships. Candor is required when a reasonable person would feel betrayed if the information was withheld. In some circumstances, silence is dishonest; yet in other circumstances, disclosing information would be wrong and perhaps unlawful.

### 6.18.2. **Integrity.**

Being faithful to one's convictions is part of integrity. Following principles, acting with honor, maintaining independent judgment, and performing duties with impartiality help to maintain integrity and avoid conflicts of interest and hypocrisy.

### 6.18.3. **Loyalty.**

Fidelity, faithfulness, allegiance, and devotion are all synonyms for loyalty. Loyalty is the bond that holds the Nation and the U.S. Government together and the balm against dissension and conflict. This ethical value is not blind obedience or unquestioning acceptance of the status quo. Loyalty requires careful balance among various interests, values, and institutions in the interest of harmony and cohesion.

### 6.18.4. **Accountability.**

DoD employees are required to accept responsibility for their decisions and the resulting consequences. This includes avoiding even the appearance of impropriety. Accountability promotes careful, well-thought-out decisions, and limits thoughtless action.

### 6.18.5. **Fairness.**

Open mindedness and impartiality are important aspects of fairness. DoD employees must be committed to justice in the performance of their official duties. Decisions must not be arbitrary, capricious, or biased. Individuals must be treated equally and with tolerance.

### 6.18.6. **Caring.**

Compassion is an essential element of good government. Courtesy and kindness, both to those we serve and to those with whom we work, help to ensure individuals are not treated solely as a means to an end. Caring for others is the counterbalance against the temptation to pursue the mission at any cost.

### 6.18.7. **Respect.**

To treat people with dignity, to honor privacy, and to allow self-determination are critical in a government of diverse people. Lack of respect leads to a breakdown of loyalty and honesty within a government and brings chaos to the international community.

### 6.18.8. **Promise-Keeping.**

No government can function for long if its commitments are not kept. DoD employees are obligated to keep their promises in order to promote trust and cooperation. Because of the importance of promise-keeping, DoD employees must only make commitments within their authority.

### 6.18.9. **Responsible Citizenship.**

Responsible citizenship is the duty of every citizen, especially DoD employees, to exercise discretion. Public servants are expected to engage (employ) personal judgment in the performance of official duties within the limits of their authority so that the will of the people is respected according to democratic principles. Justice must be pursued and injustice must be challenged through accepted means.

### 6.18.10. **Pursuit of Excellence.**

In public service, competence is only the starting point. DoD employees are expected to set an example of superior diligence and commitment. They are expected to strive beyond mediocrity.

## 6.19. Professional and Unprofessional Relationships.

Professional relationships are essential to the effective operation of all organizations, military and civilian, but the nature of the military mission requires absolute confidence in command and an unhesitating adherence to orders that may result in inconvenience, hardships, injury, or death. While personal relationships between Air Force members are normally matters of individual choice and judgment, they become matters of official concern when they adversely affect or have the reasonable potential to adversely affect the Air Force by eroding morale, good order, discipline, respect for authority, unit cohesion, or mission accomplishment. AFI 36-2909, *Professional and Unprofessional Relationships,* establishes responsibilities for maintaining professional relationships.

### 6.19.1. Professional Relationships.

Professional relationships contribute to the effective operation of the Air Force. The Air Force encourages personnel to communicate freely with their superiors regarding their careers and performance, duties, and missions. This type of communication enhances morale and discipline and improves the operational environment while at the same time preserving proper respect for authority and focus on the mission. Participation by members of all grades in organizational activities, such as base intramural, interservice, and intraservice athletic competitions, unit-sponsored events, religious activities, community welfare projects, and youth programs, enhances morale and contributes to unit cohesion.

### 6.19.2. Unprofessional Relationships.

Unprofessional relationships, whether pursued on or off-duty, are those relationships that detract from the authority of superiors or result in, or reasonably create the appearance of, favoritism, misuse of office or position, or the abandonment of organizational goals for personal interests. Unprofessional relationships can exist between officers, between enlisted members, between officers and enlisted members, and between military personnel and civilian employees or contractor personnel. Familiar relationships in which one member exercises supervisory or command authority and relationships that involve shared living accommodations, vacations, transportation, or off-duty interests on a frequent or recurring basis in the absence of any official purpose or organizational benefit present a high risk of becoming unprofessional.

### 6.19.3. Fraternization.

Fraternization is an aggravated form of unprofessional relationship. As defined by the manual for courts-martial, fraternization is a personal relationship between an officer and an enlisted member that violates the customary bounds of acceptable behavior in the Air Force and prejudices good order and discipline, discredits the Armed Services, or operates to the personal disgrace or dishonor of the officer involved. The custom recognizes that officers will not form personal relationships with enlisted members on terms of military equality, whether on or off duty. Although the custom originated in an all-male military, fraternization is gender neutral. Fraternization can occur between males, between females, and between males and females. Because of the potential damage fraternization can do to morale, good order, discipline, and unit cohesion, fraternization is specifically prohibited in the manual for courts-martial and punishable under Article 134 of the Uniform Code of Military Justice.

## 6.20. General Guidelines on Avoiding Unprofessional Relationships Including Fraternization.

Military experience has shown that certain kinds of personal relationships present a high risk for being (or developing into) unprofessional relationships. Unprofessional relationships negatively impact morale and discipline. While some personal relationships are not initially unprofessional, they may become unprofessional when circumstances change. For example, factors that can change an otherwise permissible relationship into an unprofessional relationship include the members' relative positions in the organization and the members' relative positions in the supervisory and command chains. Air Force members, both officer and enlisted, must be sensitive to forming these relationships and consider the probable impact of their actions on the Air Force in making their decisions. The rules regarding these relationships must be somewhat elastic to accommodate differing conditions. However, the underlying standard is that Air Force members are expected to avoid relationships that negatively affect morale and discipline. When economic constraints or operational requirements place officers and enlisted members of different grades in close proximity with one another (such as combined or joint clubs, joint recreational facilities, or mixed officer and enlisted housing areas), military members are expected to maintain professional relationships. Although maintaining professional relationships is more difficult under certain circumstances, it does not excuse a member's responsibility to maintain standards.

### 6.20.1. Relationships within an Organization.

Unduly familiar relationships between members in which one member exercises supervisory or command authority over the other can easily be or become unprofessional. Similarly, as differences in grades increase, even in the absence of a command or supervisory relationship, there may be more risk that the relationship will become, or is perceived to be, unprofessional because senior members in military organizations normally exercise authority or have some direct or indirect organizational influence over more junior members. The danger for abuse of authority is always present. A senior member's ability to directly or indirectly influence assignments, promotion recommendations, duties, awards, or other privileges and benefits places both the senior and junior members in a vulnerable position. Once established, such relationships do not go unnoticed by other members of the unit. Service members must also avoid unprofessional relationships (including fraternization) between members of different services, particularly in joint service operations, because such relationships may have the same impact on morale and discipline as they would for members assigned to the same service.

### 6.20.2. Relationships with Civilian Employees.

Civilian employees and contractor personnel are an integral part of the Air Force. They contribute directly to readiness and mission accomplishment. Consequently, military members of all grades must maintain professional relationships with civilian employees, particularly those whom they supervise or direct. They must avoid relationships that adversely affect or reasonably might adversely affect morale, discipline, and respect for authority, or that violate law or regulation.

### 6.20.3. Dating and Close Friendships.

Dating, intimate relationships, and close friendships between men and women are subject to the same policy considerations as are other relationships. Like any personal relationship, they become a matter of official concern when they adversely affect morale, discipline, unit cohesion, respect for authority, or mission accomplishment. Members must recognize that these relationships can adversely affect morale and discipline, even when the members are not in the same chain of command or unit. The formation of such relationships between superiors and subordinates within the same chain of command or supervision is prohibited because such relationships invariably raise the perception of favoritism or misuse of position and erode morale, discipline and unit cohesion.

### 6.20.4. Shared Activities.

Sharing living accommodations, vacations, transportation, and off-duty interests on a frequent or recurring basis can be perceived as unprofessional. Often the frequency of these activities or the absence of an official purpose or organizational benefit is what causes them to become, or to be perceived as, unprofessional. While an occasional round of golf, game of racquetball, or similar activity between a supervisor and subordinate could remain professional, daily or weekly occurrences could result in at least the perception of an unprofessional relationship. Similarly, while it may be appropriate for a first sergeant to play golf with a different group of officers from his or her organization each weekend in order to get to know them better, playing with the same officers every weekend may be, or be perceived as, unprofessional.

### 6.20.5. Training, Schools, and Professional Military Education.

Personal relationships between recruiters and potential recruits during the recruiting process or between students and faculty or staff in training schools or professional military education settings are generally prohibited. These interpersonal relationships are especially susceptible to abuse of position, partiality or favoritism, or can easily create the appearance of such. This is particularly true during the recruiting process and in basic military training, because the potential recruit or junior military member is often unfamiliar with Air Force standards and dependent on the senior member, and the senior member is in a position to directly affect, positively or negatively, the career of the junior member.

### 6.20.6. Other Relationships.

Other relationships not specifically addressed, depending on the circumstances, can lead to actual or perceived favoritism or preferential treatment, and must be avoided. Examples of activities that may adversely impact morale, discipline, and respect for authority include gambling, partying with subordinates, soliciting or making solicited sales to subordinates, joint business ventures, or soliciting (or making solicited sales) to members junior in rank, grade, or position.

## 6.21. Consequences of Unprofessional Conduct.

Military members are subject to lawful orders. When a military member has been lawfully ordered to cease an unprofessional relationship or refrain from certain conduct, the military member is subject to prosecution under the Uniform Code of Military Justice for violating the order. Similarly, all military members are subject to prosecution for criminal offenses committed incidental to an unprofessional relationship (such as gambling, adultery, or assault).

## 6.22. Responsibilities for Professional Relationships:

### 6.22.1. Individuals.

All military members share the responsibility for maintaining professional relationships. However, the senior member (officer or enlisted) in a personal relationship bears primary responsibility for maintaining professional relationships. Leadership requires personnel to exercise maturity and judgment and avoid relationships that undermine respect for authority or have a negative impact on morale, discipline, or the mission of the Air Force.

This is especially true of officers and noncommissioned officers who are expected to exhibit the highest standards of professional conduct and to lead by example. The senior member in a relationship is in the best position to appreciate the effect the relationship could have on an organization and is in the best position to terminate or limit the extent of the relationship. However, all members should expect to be, and must be, held accountable for how their conduct impacts the Air Force.

6.22.2. **Commanders and Supervisors.**

Commanders and supervisors at all levels have the authority and responsibility to maintain good order, discipline, and morale within their units. They may be held accountable for failing to act in appropriate cases.

## 6.23. Actions in Response to Unprofessional Relationships.

If a relationship is prohibited by AFI 36-2909 or is causing (or if good professional judgment and common sense indicate that a relationship may reasonably result in) a degradation of morale, good order, discipline or unit cohesion, a commander or supervisor should take corrective action. Actions should normally be the least severe necessary to terminate the unprofessional aspects of a relationship, but a full spectrum of administrative actions is available and should be considered. Administrative actions include, but are not limited to; counseling, reprimand, creation of an unfavorable information file, removal from position, reassignment, demotion, delay of or removal from a promotion list, adverse or referral comments in performance reports, and administrative separation. One or more complementary actions can be taken. Experience has shown that counseling is often an effective first step in curtailing unprofessional relationships. More serious cases may warrant administrative action or nonjudicial punishment. An order to terminate a relationship, or the offensive portion of a relationship, can and should be given whenever it is apparent that lesser administrative action may not be effective. Officers or enlisted members who violate such orders are subject to action under the Uniform Code of Military Justice for violation of the order. Instances of actual favoritism, partiality, or misuse of grade or position may constitute independent violations of the Uniform Code of Military Justice or the punitive provisions of the Joint Ethics Regulation.

## 6.24. Financial Responsibility.

AFI 36-2906, *Personal Financial Responsibility*, establishes administrative and management guidelines for alleged delinquent financial obligations and for processing financial claims against Air Force members. The AFI also outlines basic rules for garnishment.

6.24.1. **Responsibilities.**

Military members will:

6.24.1.1. Pay their just financial obligations in a proper and timely manner.

6.24.1.2. Provide adequate financial support of a spouse, child or any other relative for which the member receives additional support allowances. Members will also comply with the financial support provisions of a court order or written support agreement.

6.24.1.3. Respond to applications for involuntary allotments of pay within the suspense dates established by the Defense Finance and Accounting Service or the commander.

6.24.2. **Handling Complaints.**

Complainants are often unfamiliar with Air Force organizational addresses or do not know the member's actual unit of assignment, and so frequently address correspondence to the installation commander, staff judge advocate, or force support squadron. The complaint is forwarded for action to the individual's commander, who attempts to respond within 15 days. If the member has had a permanent change of station, the complaint is forwarded to the new commander, and the complainant is notified of the referral. If the member has separated with no further military service or has retired, the complainant is notified and informed that the member is no longer under Air Force jurisdiction and the Air Force is unable to assist. (**Exception:** Retired members' retirement pay can be garnished for child support or alimony obligations.) Commanders must actively monitor complaints until they are resolved. Failure to pay debts or support dependents can lead to administrative or disciplinary action. If the commander decides the complaint reflects adversely on the member, this action should be included in the unfavorable information file.

6.24.3. **Personal Financial Management Program.**

The personal financial management program is an Airman and Family Readiness Center program that offers information, education, and personal financial counseling to help individuals and families maintain financial stability and reach their financial goals. Personal financial management program provides education to all personnel upon arrival at their first duty station. Personal financial management program education includes, at minimum, facts about personal financial management program, checkbook maintenance, budgeting, credit buying, state or country liability laws, and local fraudulent business practices. The personal financial management program also provides refresher education for all senior airmen and below upon arrival at a new installation. Personal financial management program services are free.

## Section 6E—Ethics and Conflict of Interest Prohibitions

### 6.25. Overview.

DoD policy requires a single, uniform source of standards on ethical conduct and ethics guidance be maintained within DoD. Each DoD agency will implement and administer a comprehensive ethics program to ensure compliance.

### 6.26. Bribery and Graft.

DoD employees and military members are directly or indirectly prohibited from giving, offering, promising, demanding, seeking, receiving, accepting, or agreeing to receive anything of value to influence any official act. They are prohibited from influencing the commission of fraud on the U.S., inducing commitment or omission of any act in violation of a lawful duty, or from influencing testimony given. They are prohibited from accepting anything of value for, or because of, any official act performed or to be performed. These prohibitions do not apply to the payment of witness fees authorized by law or certain travel and subsistence expenses.

### 6.27. Compensation from Other Sources.

DoD employees and military members are prohibited from receiving pay or allowance or supplements of pay or benefits from any source other than the U.S. for the performance of official service or duties unless specifically authorized by law. A task or job performed outside normal work hours does not necessarily allow employees to accept payment for performing it. If the undertaking is part of one's official duties, pay for its performance may not be accepted from any source other than the U.S. regardless of when it was performed.

### 6.28. Additional Pay or Allowance.

DoD employees and military members may not receive additional pay or allowance for disbursement of public money or for the performance of any other service or duty unless specifically authorized by law. Subject to certain limitations, civilian DoD employees may hold two distinctly different federal government positions and receive salaries for both if the duties of each are performed. Absent specific authority, however, military members may not do so because any arrangement by a military member for rendering services to the federal government in another position is incompatible with the military member's actual or potential military duties. The fact that a military member may have leisure hours during which no official duty is performed does not alter the result.

### 6.29. Commercial Dealings Involving DoD Personnel.

On or off duty, a DoD employee or military member shall not knowingly solicit or make solicited sales to DoD personnel who are junior in rank, grade, or position, or to the family members of such personnel. In the absence of coercion or intimidation, this does not prohibit the sale or lease of a DoD employee's or military member's noncommercial personal or real property or commercial sales solicited and made in a retail establishment during off-duty employment. This prohibition includes the solicited sale of insurance, stocks, mutual funds, real estate, cosmetics, household supplies, vitamins, and other goods or services. Solicited sales by the spouse or other household member of a senior-ranking person to a junior person are not specifically prohibited but may give the appearance that the DoD employee or military member is using public office for personal gain. If in doubt, consult an ethics counselor. Several related prohibitions in this area include:

6.29.1. Engaging in off-duty employment or outside activities that detract from readiness or pose a security risk, as determined by the employee's or member's commander or supervisor.

6.29.2. Engaging in outside employment or activities that conflict with official duties.

6.29.3. Receiving honoraria for performing official duties or for speaking, teaching, or writing that relates to one's official duties.

6.29.4. Misusing an official position, such as improper endorsements or improper use of nonpublic information.

6.29.5. Certain post-government service employment. See DoD 5500.07-R, Chapter 9, for specific guidance.

### 6.30. Gifts from Foreign Governments.

AFI 51-901, *Gifts from Foreign Governments,* requires all Air Force military and civilian personnel, and their dependents, to report gifts from foreign governments if the gift, or combination of gifts, at one presentation exceeds a U.S. retail value of $375. Gifts in excess of this minimal value may be accepted on behalf of the Air Force and a request for disposition instructions should be forwarded to SAF/AA within 60 days of receiving the gift. This requirement includes gifts that recipients want to keep for official use or display. The U.S. Attorney General may bring a civil action in any court of the U.S. against any person who knowingly solicits or accepts a gift from a foreign government that is not approved by Congress, or who fails to deposit or report such a gift, as required by AFI 51-901. Failure to report gifts valued in excess of $375 could result in a penalty not to exceed the retail value of the gift plus $5,000. **Note:** The limit on gifts from foreign governments is set by Congress and changes periodically. Be sure to confirm the most current limit with your ethics counselor when considering foreign gift issues.

## 6.31. Contributions or Presents to Superiors:

6.31.1. On an occasional basis, including any occasion when gifts are traditionally given or exchanged, the following may be given to an official supervisor by a subordinate or other employees receiving less pay:

6.31.1.1. Items, other than cash, with an aggregate market value of $10 or less.

6.31.1.2. Items such as food and refreshments to be shared in the office among several employees.

6.31.1.3. Personal hospitality provided at a residence and items given in connection with personal hospitality, which is of a type and value customarily provided by the employee to personal friends.

6.31.2. A gift appropriate to the occasion may be given to recognize special, infrequent occasions of personal significance, such as marriage, illness, or the birth or adoption of a child. Contributions or presents are also permissible upon occasions that terminate a subordinate-official supervisor relationship, such as retirement, separation, or reassignment. Regardless of the number of employees contributing, the market value of the gift cannot exceed $300. Even though contributions are voluntary, the maximum contribution one DoD employee may solicit from another cannot exceed $10.

## 6.32. Federal Government Resources.

Federal government resources, including personnel, equipment, and property, will be used by DoD employees and military members for official purposes only. Agencies may, however, permit employees or military members to make limited personal use of resources other than personnel, such as a computer, calculators, libraries, etc., if the use:

6.32.1. Does not adversely affect the performance of official duties by the employee, military member, or other DoD personnel.

6.32.2. Is of reasonable duration and frequency and is made during the employee's or military member's personal time, such as after duty hours or during lunch periods.

6.32.3. Serves a legitimate public interest, such as supporting local charities or volunteer services to the community.

6.32.4. Does not reflect adversely on the DoD.

6.32.5. Creates no significant additional cost to the DoD or government agency.

## 6.33. Communication Systems.

Federal Government communication systems and equipment including telephones, fax machines, electronic mail, and Internet systems will be used for official use and authorized purposes only. Official use includes emergency communications and, when approved by commanders in the interest of morale and welfare, may include communications by DoD personnel deployed for extended periods on official DoD business. Authorized purposes include brief communication while traveling on government business to notify family members of official transportation or schedule changes. Also authorized are personal communications from the DoD employee's or military member's usual workplace that are most reasonably made while at the workplace, such as checking in with spouse or minor children; scheduling doctor, auto, or home repair appointments; brief Internet searches; and emailing directions to visiting relatives, when the agency designee permits. However, many restrictions do apply. Consult DoD 5500.07-R for additional guidance; then consult the organizational point of contact.

## 6.34. Gambling, Betting, and Lotteries.

While on federally owned or leased property or while on duty, a DoD employee or military member will not participate in any gambling activity except:

6.34.1. Activities by organizations composed primarily of DoD personnel or their dependents for the benefit of welfare funds for their own members or for the benefit of other DoD personnel or their dependents, subject to local law and DoD 5500.07-R.

6.34.2. Private wagers among DoD personnel if based on a personal relationship and transacted entirely within assigned government living quarters and subject to local laws.

6.34.3. Lotteries authorized by any state from licensed vendors.

*Section 6F—Political Activities*

**6.35. Overview.**

It is Air Force policy to encourage Regular Air Force members to carry out their rights and responsibilities of U.S. citizenship. While on Regular Air Force members are prohibited from engaging in certain political activities in order to maintain good order and discipline and to avoid conflicts of interest and the appearance of improper endorsement in political matters. For more guidance, see DoDD 1344.10, *Political Activities by Members of the Armed Forces*, and AFI 51-902, *Political Activities by Members of the U.S. Air Force*.

**6.36. Rights.**

In general, a member on Regular Air Force may register to vote, vote, and express his or her personal opinion on political candidates and issues, but not as a representative of the Armed Forces. Members may make monetary contributions to a political party, organization or committee that favors a political candidate or slate of candidates. They may attend partisan and nonpartisan political meetings or rallies as spectators when not in uniform.

**6.37. Prohibitions.**

A member on Regular Air Force will not use his or her official authority or influence to interfere with an election, affect the course or outcome of an election, solicit votes for a particular candidate or issue, or require or solicit political contributions from others. A member cannot participate in partisan political management, campaigns, or conventions. Members who engage in any of the prohibited activities listed in paragraph 4.1 of AFI 51-902, are subject to prosecution under Article 92, UCMJ, in addition to any other applicable provision of the UCMJ or Federal law. A member may not be a candidate for, or hold, civil office except as outlined in paragraph 6.37.1.

   6.37.1. **Candidacy for Elected Office.**

   A member may not campaign as a nominee or as a candidate for nomination. However, enlisted members may seek and hold nonpartisan civil office, such as a notary public or school board member, neighborhood planning commission, or similar local agency, as long as such office is held in a private capacity and does not interfere with the performance of military duties. There are also specific exceptions to the prohibition on holding elected office that permit reservists in certain elected or appointed civil offices in federal, state, and local government to remain in office when called to Regular Air Force for no more than 270 days.

   6.37.2. **Additional Specific Prohibitions.**

   A member may not:

   6.37.2.1. Allow, or cause to be published, partisan political articles signed or authorized by the member for soliciting votes for or against a partisan political party or candidate.

   6.37.2.2. Serve in any official capacity or be listed as a sponsor of a partisan political club.

   6.37.2.3. Speak before a partisan political gathering of any kind for promoting a partisan political party or candidate.

   6.37.2.4. Conduct a political opinion survey under the auspices of a partisan political group or distribute partisan political literature.

   6.37.2.5. Perform clerical or other duties for a partisan political committee during a campaign or on Election Day.

   6.37.2.6. March or ride in a partisan political parade.

   6.37.2.7. Use contemptuous words against the officeholders described in Title 10, U.S. Code, Section 888, *Contempt Toward Officials* (officers only).

   6.37.2.8. Display a large political sign, banner, or poster (as distinguished from a bumper sticker) on a private vehicle.

   6.37.2.9. Display a political sign, banner or poster on the outside of a residence in government (including privatized) housing.

   6.37.2.10. For additional prohibitions refer to AFI 51-902, paragraph 4.1.

**6.38. Voting.**

The DoD Federal Voting Assistance Program is responsible for administering the Uniformed and Overseas Citizens Absentee Voting Act. Specifically, the DoD Federal Voting Assistance Program mission is to inform and educate U.S. citizens worldwide of their right to vote; foster voting participation; and protect the integrity of and enhance the electoral process at the Federal, state, and local levels. The Uniformed and Overseas Citizens Absentee Voting Act requires that states and territories allow certain groups of citizens, including military members on Regular Air Force and their families, to register and vote absentee in elections for federal offices. In many states, laws exist that allow military members and their families to vote absentee in state and local elections. The Uniformed and Overseas Citizens Absentee Voting Act requires each federal department and agency with personnel covered by the act to have a voting assistance program. Critical to the success of this program are the voting assistance officers. These individuals, military and civilian, are responsible for providing accurate nonpartisan voting information and assistance to all of the citizens they are appointed to help. They aid in ensuring citizens understand their voting rights, to include providing procedures on how to vote absentee.

6.38.1. The DoD Federal Voting Assistance Program is responsible for administering the Uniformed and Overseas Citizens Absentee Voting Act and the Military and Overseas Voter Empowerment Act. Enacted in 1986, Uniformed and Overseas Citizens Absentee Voting Act protects the right of service members to vote in federal elections regardless of where they are stationed. This law requires that states and territories allow members of the U.S. Uniformed Services and merchant marine, their family members and U.S. citizens residing outside the United States to register and vote absentee in elections for federal offices. In many states, laws exist that allow military members and their families to vote absentee in state and local elections. Uniformed and Overseas Citizens Absentee Voting Act was expanded significantly in 2009, when Congress passed the Military and Overseas Voter Empowerment Act to provide greater protections for service members, their families and other overseas citizens. Among other provisions, the Military and Overseas Voter Empowerment Act requires states to transmit validly-requested absentee ballots to Uniformed and Overseas Citizens Absentee Voting Act voters no later than 45 days before a federal election, when the request has been received by that date, except where the state has been granted an undue hardship waiver approved by the Department of Defense for that election.

6.38.2. The DoD Federal Voting Assistance Program mission is to inform and educate U.S. citizens worldwide of their right to vote; foster voting participation; and protect the integrity of and enhance the electoral process at the Federal, state, and local levels. Uniformed and Overseas Citizens Absentee Voting Act requires each federal department and agency with personnel covered by the act to have a voting assistance program. Critical to the success of this program are the voting assistance officers. These individuals, military and civilian, are responsible for providing accurate nonpartisan voting information and assistance to all of the citizens they are appointed to help. They aid in ensuring citizens understand their voting rights, to include providing procedures on how to vote absentee. More information about the Air Force program can be found in AFI 36-3107, *Voting Assistance Program.*

## 6.39. Dissident and Protest Activities.

Air Force commanders have the inherent authority and responsibility to take action to ensure the mission is performed and to maintain good order and discipline. This authority and responsibility includes placing lawful restriction on dissident and protest activities. Air Force commanders must preserve the service member's right of expression to the maximum extent possible, consistent with good order, discipline, and national security. To properly balance these interests, commanders must exercise calm and prudent judgment and should consult with the staff judge advocate. For more detail, review AFI 51-903, *Dissident and Protest Activities.*

### 6.39.1. Possessing or Distributing Printed Materials.

Air Force members may not distribute or post any printed or written material other than publications of an official government agency or base-related activity within any Air Force installation without permission of the installation commander or that commander's designee. Members who violate this prohibition are subject to disciplinary action under Article 92 of the Uniform Code of Military Justice.

### 6.39.2. Writing for Publications.

Air Force members may not write for unofficial publications, including blogs and other electronic social media journalistic forums during duty hours. While unofficial publication, such as an "underground newspaper," are not prohibited, they may not be produced using government or non-appropriated fund property or supplies on or off-duty. Any publication that contains language, the utterance of which is punishable by the Uniform Code of Military Justice or other federal laws, may subject a person involved in its printing, publishing, or distribution to prosecution or other disciplinary action.

### 6.39.3. Off-Limits Action.

Action may be initiated under AFJI 31-213, *Armed Forces Disciplinary Control Boards and Off-Installation Liaison and Operations,* to make certain establishments off limits. An establishment runs the risk of being off limits if its activities include counseling service members to refuse to perform their duties or to desert, or when involved in acts with a significant adverse effect on health, welfare, or morale of military members.

### 6.39.4. Prohibited Activities.

Military personnel must reject participation in organizations that espouse supremacist causes; attempt to create illegal discrimination based on race, color, gender, religion, national origin, or ethnic group; advocate the use of force or violence; otherwise engage in the effort to deprive individuals of their civil rights; or knowingly wear gang colors, clothes, tattoos, or body markings. Active participation, such as publicly demonstrating or rallying, fundraising, recruiting and training members, organizing or leading such organizations, or otherwise engaging in activities the commander finds to be detrimental to good order, discipline, or mission accomplishment, is incompatible with military service and prohibited. Members who violate this prohibition are subject to disciplinary action under Article 92 of the Uniform Code of Military Justice.

### 6.39.5. Demonstrations and Similar Activities.

Demonstrations or other activities within an Air Force installation that could result in interfering with or preventing the orderly accomplishment of a mission of the installation or which present a clear danger to loyalty, discipline, or morale of members of the Armed Forces are prohibited and are punishable under Article 92 of the Uniform Code of Military Justice. Air Force members are prohibited from participating in demonstrations when they are on duty, in a foreign country, in uniform, involved in activities that constitute a breach of law and order, or when violence is likely to result.

## 6.40. Public Statements.

When making public statements, AFI 35-101, *Public Affairs Responsibilities and Management,* governs members. Each Air Force member has a personal responsibility for the success of the Air Force Public Affairs Program. As representatives of the service in both official and unofficial contact with the public, members have many opportunities to contribute to positive public opinions toward the Air Force. Therefore, each person must strive to make contacts show the highest standards of conduct and reflect the Air Force core values.

### 6.40.1. Do.

Specifically, each Air Force member is responsible for obtaining the necessary review and clearance, starting with public affairs, before releasing any proposed statement, text, or imagery to the public. This includes digital products being loaded on an unrestricted Web site. Members must ensure the information revealed, whether official or unofficial, is appropriate for release according to classification requirements in DoDI 5200.01, *Department of Defense Information Security Program and Protection of Sensitive Compartmented Information*, and AFPD 31-4, *Information Security*.

### 6.40.2. Don't.

Air Force members must not use their Air Force association, official title, or position to promote, endorse, or benefit any profit-making agency. This does not prohibit members from assuming character or modeling roles in commercial advertisement during their nonduty hours; however, they cannot wear their uniform or allow their Air Force title or position to be affixed to the advertisement in any manner or imply Air Force endorsement of the product or service being promoted. Additionally, they must not make any commitment to provide official Air Force information to any non-DoD member or agency, including news media, before obtaining approval through command or public affairs channels.

## 6.41. Conclusion.

This chapter explained Air Force standards of conduct. Airmen must learn these standards well enough to be able to clearly explain them to subordinates, observe these standards, and always enforce their observation by other members. Used in concert with information presented in Chapters 5 and 19, this information covered essential issues vital to good order and discipline and mission effectiveness.

## Chapter 7

## ENFORCING STANDARDS AND LEGAL ISSUES

### Section 7A—Overview

**7.1. Introduction.**

Air Force commanders at all levels are required to continuously evaluate force readiness and organizational economy, efficiency and effectiveness. The inspection system provides the commander with a credible, independent assessment process to measure the capabilities of assigned forces. Supervisors at all levels play an integral part in this process through continual assessment of personnel, programs and the areas of responsibilities they supervise. Furthermore, when systematic, programmatic or procedural weaknesses are suspected, or to further ensure resources are used effectively and efficiently, Airmen at all levels may visit the Inspector General to report these areas as well as potential fraud, waste or abuse cases. This chapter provides information on the Air Force Inspection System, the Inspector General Complaints Program, and individual standards and punitive actions. All four areas are necessary to enable the Air Force to fulfill our national security obligations efficiently and effectively.

### Section 7B—Air Force Inspection System

**7.2. Purpose.**

The Inspectors General mission is defined in headquarters Air Force mission directive 1-20, *The Inspector General*, and AFPD 90-2, *Inspector General – The Inspection System*. The overall purpose of the Air Force inspection system is to enable and strengthen commanders' effectiveness and efficiency, motivate and promote military discipline, improve unit performance and management excellence up and down the chain of command, in units and staffs, as well as identify issues interfering with effectiveness, efficiency, compliance, discipline, readiness, performance, surety and management excellence. The Inspectors General reports on readiness, economy, efficiency, and state of discipline of Air Force organizations to the Secretary of the Air Force and the Chief of Staff of the Air Force.

**7.3. Philosophy.**

Inspection is an inherent function of command exercised at every level to evaluate readiness, economy, efficiency and state of discipline. Inspection preparation, if not directly aligned with mission readiness, is inherently wasteful. Units will be inspection ready when commander's focus on mission readiness and on building a culture of disciplined compliance in which every Airmen does their job right the first time even when no one's looking. The intent of the Inspector General is to continuously improve the Air Force inspection system so there is an ever-shrinking difference – both real and perceived – between mission readiness and inspection readiness. Each major command commander and Wing commander will appoint an Inspector General who will establish an inspection program consistent with major command mission requirements to inspect unit effectiveness, surety and other inspection program elements. Major Command Inspectors General establish inspection programs consistent with command mission requirements and in accordance with this instruction to assess unit readiness, economy, efficiency, and state of discipline.

**7.4. Inspection Types:**

7.4.1. **Commander's Inspection Program.** A validated and trusted commander's inspection program is the cornerstone of the Air Force inspection system. The Wing Inspector General is responsible to validate and verify self-assessment programs and independently assess the performance of organizations below the Wing level. The commander's inspection program should give the Wing Commander, subordinate commanders and wing Airmen the right information at the right time to assess risk, identify areas of improvement, determine root cause and precisely focus limited resources; all aligned with the commander's priorities and on the commander's timeline. The commander's inspection program also facilitates requests for targeted assistance from the major command commander and staff when and where needed. The commander's inspection program produces two key components: (1) the self-assessment program; and (2) the Wing's Inspection Program executed under the authority of the Wing Inspector General to validate and verify commander self-assessments are accurate and timely, and independently assess effectiveness of subordinate units and programs. These components provide critical data to leadership about the adequacy of policy, training, manpower, funds, equipment, and facilities.

7.4.2. **Unit Effectiveness Inspection.** The unit effectiveness inspection integrates elements of compliance and readiness using specific Inspector General Inspection elements to assess the effectiveness of a unit. Conducted by Major Command Inspectors General and the Air Force Inspection Agency on Wings and Wing-equivalents, the unit effectiveness inspection is a continual evaluation of performance throughout the inspection period. This is a photo album versus a snapshot. The unit effectiveness inspection inspects the following four Major Graded Areas: Managing Resources, Leading People, Improving the Unit, and Executing the Mission. The unit effectiveness inspection validates and verifies a wing commander's inspection program for accuracy and adequacy, and provides an independent assessment of the Wing's resource management, leadership, process improvement efforts and ability to execute the mission. A unit effectiveness inspection is a multi-year, continual inspection of the unit's effectiveness, and is intended to help the wing commander understand the areas of greatest risk from undetected non-compliance. The next inspection period begins immediately following the Unit Effectiveness Inspection Capstone event.

7.4.3. **Nuclear Surety Inspection.** Nuclear Surety Inspections are an integral part of the Air Force Inspection System and are considered a snapshot within a wing's Unit Effectiveness Inspection cycle. Major Command Inspector General's use performance and compliance-based inspections to evaluate a unit's ability to manage nuclear resources while complying with all nuclear surety standards. Additionally, during a Nuclear Surety Inspection a unit's capability to safely and reliably receive, store, secure, assemble, transport, maintain, load, mate, lock/unlock, test, render safe and employ nuclear weapons is evaluated.

## 7.5. Inspection Elements:

7.5.1. **Self-Assessment Program.** Led by unit commanders in accordance with Title 10, United States Code, Section 8583, the self-assessment program provides commanders with a means for internal assessment of a Wing's overall health and complements external assessments. The primary purpose of the self-assessment program for the commander is to accurately identify and report issues to the command chain. Self-Assessment programs may include a wide variety of internal assessments or evaluations. At a minimum, Commanders must utilize Management Internal Control Toolset and applicable self-assessment communicators. Commanders are encouraged to include additional measures as directed by superior Commanders, functional directives, or proven lessons and experience.

7.5.2. **Management Internal Control Toolset.** Management Internal Control Toolset is an Air Force program of record used to facilitate self-assessments and communicate compliance, risk and program health. Management Internal Control Toolset provides the supervisor and command chain, from Squadron Commander to Secretary of the Air Force, tiered visibility into user-selected compliance reports and program status. Management Internal Control Toolset also allows functional area managers the ability to virtually monitor unit performance and status. Additionally, Management Internal Control Toolset can assist Inspectors General by informing the risk-based sampling strategy and formulating specific inspection methodology and Inspector General Team composition for the commander's inspection program and on-site unit effectiveness inspection events.

7.5.3. **Self-Assessment Communicator.** A Self-Assessment Communicator is a two-way communication tool designed to improve compliance with published guidance and communicate risk and program health up and down the chain of command in near real-time. Compliance with a self-assessment communicator does not relieve individual Airmen from complying with all statutory and regulatory requirements in Air Force instructions and directives at the local, state or federal level. As a self-assessment tool, Self-Assessment Communicators ask Airmen at the shop-level to self-report compliance or non-compliance. While the responses are assumed to be truthful and timely, self-assessment communicators are frequently verified for accuracy and currency by wing Inspectors General and major command Inspectors General.

7.5.4. **Inspector General's Evaluation Management System.** The Inspectors General Evaluation Management System is the official program of record for the Air Force Inspection System. Inspectors General will use Inspectors General Evaluation Management System to record the unit's overall rating, identify deficiencies, track corrective action plans, and post the final inspection report.

## 7.6. Gatekeeper Program.

The Gatekeeper program is used to build schedules, synchronize and align Air Force and non-Air Force inspection requirements.

## Section 7C—Inspector General Complaints Program

## 7.7. Program Policy and Mission Focus.

The Air Force Inspector General Complaints program is a leadership tool that indicates where command involvement is needed to correct systematic, programmatic, or procedural weaknesses. The program also ensures effective and efficient use of resources; resolves problems affecting the Air Force mission promptly and objectively; creates an atmosphere of trust in which issues can be objectively and fully resolved without retaliation or fear of reprisal; and assists commanders in instilling confidence in Air Force leadership. The primary charge of the Inspector General is to sustain a credible Air Force Inspector General system by ensuring the existence of responsive complaint investigations, and fraud, waste, and abuse programs characterized by objectivity, integrity, and impartiality. Only the Inspector General may investigate allegations of reprisal and restriction under the Military Whistleblower's Protection Act. The Inspector General ensures the concerns of Regular Air Force, Reserve, and Guard members; civilian employees; family members; retirees; and the best interests of the Air Force are addressed through objective fact-finding.

### 7.8. Installation Inspector General Program.

The concept of separate, full-time installation Inspectors General was implemented to remove any perceived conflict of interest, lack of independence, or apprehension by Air Force personnel. This came as a result of the previous practice of assigning a chain of command and Inspector General roles to the same official. The installation Inspector General is organized as a staff function reporting directly to the installation commander.

#### 7.8.1. Inspector General Role.

Inspectors General are the "eyes and ears" of the commander. They execute the commander's inspection program, validating and verifying unit self-assessments and providing the commander an independent assessment of unit effectiveness: (1) they inform the commander of potential areas of concern as reflected by trends; (2) function as the fact finder and honest broker in the resolution of complaints; (3) educate and train commanders and members of the base population on their rights and responsibilities in regard to the Air Force Inspector General system; and (4) help commanders prevent, detect, and correct fraud, waste and abuse; and mismanagement. Personal complaints and fraud, waste, and abuse disclosures help commanders discover and correct problems that affect the productivity and morale of assigned personnel. Resolving the underlying cause of a complaint may prevent more severe symptoms or costly consequences, such as reduced performance, accidents, poor quality work, poor morale, or loss of resources. Even though allegations may not be substantiated, the evidence or investigation findings may reveal systemic morale or other problems that impede efficiency and mission effectiveness.

#### 7.8.2. Investigations Not Covered and Complaints Not Appropriate.

The following are not covered under the Inspector General Complaint Resolution program:

7.8.2.1. Administrative inquiries or investigations governed by other policy directives and instructions. These inquiries and investigations include:

7.8.2.1.1. Commander-directed inquiries and investigations.

7.8.2.1.2. Air Force Office of Special Investigations or security forces investigations.

7.8.2.1.3. Investigations of civilian employees who have specific appeal rights under law or labor union agreements.

7.8.2.2. Investigations under the authority of the Uniform Code of Military Justice (UCMJ) or the *Manual for Courts-Martial*, line of duty or report of survey investigations, quality assurance in the Air Force medical service boards, Air Force mishap or safety investigations, military equal opportunity treatment or civilian equal employment opportunity programs, and medical incident investigations.

7.8.2.3. Matters normally addressed through other established grievance or appeal channels unless there is evidence these channels mishandled the matter or process. If a policy directive or instruction provides a specific means of redress or appeal to a grievance, complainants must exhaust these means before filing an Inspector General complaint. Complainants must provide some relevant evidence that the process was mishandled or handled prejudicially before an Inspector General channel will process a complaint of mishandling. Dissatisfaction or disagreement with the outcome or findings of an alternative grievance or appeal process is not a sufficient basis to warrant an Inspector General investigation. **Note:** AFI 90-301, *Inspector General Complaints Resolution*, Table 3.6, assists Inspectors General in determining if a complaint belongs in other channels.

#### 7.8.3. Filing an Inspector General Complaint.

Air Force military members and civilian employees have a duty to promptly report fraud, waste and abuse or gross mismanagement; a violation of law, policy, procedures, or regulations; an injustice; abuse of authority, inappropriate conduct, or misconduct; and a deficiency or like condition to an appropriate supervisor or commander, to an Inspector General or other appropriate inspector, or through an established grievance channel. Complainants should attempt to resolve the issues at the lowest possible level using command channels before addressing them to a higher level or the Inspector General. The immediate supervisory command chain can often resolve complaints more quickly and effectively than a higher level not familiar with the situation. Use the Inspector General system when referral to the chain of command is futile, and there is fear of reprisal.

#### 7.8.4. Procedures for Filing a Complaint.

Table 7.1 outlines the procedures for filing an Inspector General complaint. Complainants complete an Air Force Form 102, *Inspector General Personal and Fraud, Waste and Abuse Complaint Registration*, briefly outlining the facts and relevant background information related to the issue or complaint. AFI 90-301 outlines the procedures. Complainants may also file anonymously through an Air Force fraud, waste, and abuse hotline, the Defense hotline, or directly with an Inspector General.

**Table 7.1. How to File an Inspector General Complaint.**

| Step | Action |
|---|---|
| 1 | If unable to resolve the complaint in supervisory channels, review AFI 90-301, Table 3.6, to determine if the complaint should be filed with the Inspector General. Complainants should file a complaint if they reasonably believe inappropriate conduct has occurred or a violation of law, policy, procedure, instruction, or regulation has been committed. |
| 2 | Complete the personal data information on Air Force Form 102 (typed or printed legibly), the preferred format for submitting complaints, so it may easily be reproduced. |
| 3 | Briefly outline the facts and relevant background information related to the issue or complaint on Air Force Form 102 in chronological order. The complainant should include witnesses who can corroborate the allegations or provide additional evidence relevant to the issues. The complainant is responsible for describing what each recommended witness can provide regarding the issues and/or allegations. |
| 4 | List the allegations of wrongdoing briefly, in general terms, and provide supporting narrative detail including chronology and documents later when interviewed. Allegations should be written as bullets and should answer:<br>1. When did the issue occur?<br>2. Where did the issue occur?<br>3. Who took the action in question 1 (e.g., Major John A. Smith, XXSQ/CC)?<br>4. What did the person (or people) in question 3 do (e.g., gave a letter of reprimand, wasted resources)?<br>5. To whom did the action in question 4 happen (e.g., complainant, Staff Sergeant Smith, etc)?<br>6. What law, regulation or policy was violated (e.g., AFI 36-2803, Title 10, United States Code., etc)?<br>7. What remedy is being sought? |
| 5 | If more than one year has elapsed since learning of the alleged wrong, the complainant should also include:<br>1. The date the complainant first became aware of the conduct.<br>2. How the complainant become aware of the conduct.<br>3. Why the complainant delay filing the complaint. |
| 6 | Submit the completed Air Force Form 102 to any Air Force Inspector General and set up a follow-on meeting to discuss the complaint. |
| 7 | If the Inspector General is named in the complaint, contact the next higher-level Inspector General. |

**7.8.5. Complainants' Rights.**

Complainants have the right to:

7.8.5.1. File an Inspector General complaint at any level without notifying or following the chain of command.

7.8.5.2. File a complaint with an Inspector General without fear of reprisal.

7.8.5.3. Request withdrawal of their complaint in writing; however, Inspectors General may still look into the allegations at their discretion.

7.8.5.4. Request the next higher level Inspector General review their case within 90 days of receiving a final Inspector General response. Must give specific reasons as to why the complainant believes the original investigation was not valid or adequate; simply disagreeing with the findings is not sufficient for an additional Inspector General review.

7.8.5.5. Submit complaints anonymously.

7.8.5.6. Submit a complaint on behalf of another individual or even when not the wronged party.

7.8.5.7. Request whistleblower protection after making or planning to make a protected communication.

7.8.5.7.1. Reprisal occurs when a responsible management official takes (or threatens to take) an unfavorable personnel action; or withholds (or threatens to withhold) a favorable personnel action, to retaliate against a member of the armed forces who made, or prepared to make, a protected communication. Any lawful communication, regardless of the subject, to an Inspector General or Congress, is considered protected. Additionally, this type of communication is protected when a member who reasonably believes he/she has evidence of a violation of law or regulation (regardless of whether he/she is the victim), discloses this to an authorized recipient in the form of a lawful communication.

7.8.5.7.2. Title 10, United States Code, Section 1034, *Protected Communications; Prohibition of Retaliatory Personnel Actions*, also states that a military member may not be restricted or prohibited from making a lawful communication to the Inspector General or a member of Congress (for example, making a protected communication). Restriction can result from either private or public statements that may reasonably discourage Air Force members from contacting the Inspector General or a member of Congress. For example, a first sergeant who directs a member to stay within his chain of command because the member told his supervisor he was going to complain to his Congressman about an upcoming deployment has probably restricted.

7.8.5.7.3. The Department of Defense Inspector General provides a quarterly report to Congress detailing the Services' Inspector General allegations of reprisal, and restricted (if substantiated, amounts to a violation of Federal law). In the Air Force, most allegations in these areas are against First Sergeants and senior enlisted personnel.

### 7.8.6. Complainants' Responsibilities.

Complainants must file within one year of learning of the alleged wrong. Inspector General complaints not reported within one year may seriously impede the gathering of evidence and testimony. The Inspector General may dismiss a complaint if, given the nature of the alleged wrong and the passage of time, there is reasonable probability that insufficient information can be gathered to make a determination, or no special Air Force interests exist to justify investigating the matter. Complainants must cooperate with investigators by providing factual and relevant information regarding the issues. Complainants must understand that they are submitting official statements; therefore, they remain subject to punitive action for knowingly making false statements and submitting other unlawful communications.

### 7.8.7. Confidentiality Policy.

The Inspector General makes every effort to protect the identity of complainants from anyone outside Inspector General channels. Inspectors General may release the name of a complainant only on an official need-to-know basis. Investigating officers do not divulge a complainant's name to a subject or witness or permit them to read the complaint without the Inspectors General or appointing authority's written permission.

## Section 7D—Individual Standards

## 7.9. Enforcing Individual Standards.

Commanders, supervisors, and other persons in authority can issue administrative counseling, admonitions, and reprimands. These actions are intended to improve, correct, and instruct subordinates who depart from standards of performance, conduct, bearing, and integrity, on or off duty, and whose actions degrade the individual and unit's mission. Written administrative counseling, admonitions, and reprimands are subject to the rules of access, protection, and disclosure outlined in the Privacy Act of 1974. The same rules apply to copies kept by supervisors and commanders and those filed in an individual's unfavorable information file or the unit's personnel information file. Raters must consider making comments on performance reports when the ratee receives any of these adverse actions. The following paragraphs discuss actions a commander may take to correct an individual's behavior without resorting to punishment under the UCMJ.

## 7.10. Administrative Counseling, Admonitions, and Reprimands.

Administrative counseling, admonitions, and reprimands are quality force management tools available to supervisors, superiors, and commanders. These tools are corrective in nature, not punitive. When properly used, they help maintain established Air Force standards and enhance mission accomplishment. When a member departs from standards, there are many factors to consider in determining what action, if any, is appropriate.

### 7.10.1. AFI 36-2907, Unfavorable Information File (UIF) Program.

7.10.1.1. Chapter 4 contains guidance on administrative counseling, admonitions, and reprimands. The decision to issue a letter of counseling, admonition, or reprimand should be based primarily on two factors.

7.10.1.1.1. First is the nature of the incident. Administrative counseling, admonitions, and reprimands may be administered for any departure from Air Force standards. Unlike nonjudicial punishment under Article 15 of the UCMJ, they are NOT limited to offenses punishable by the UCMJ. (These disciplinary measures may also be issued to Reserve members who commit an offense while in civilian (non-Title 10) status.) The seriousness of the departure should be considered before deciding what type of action is appropriate to take.

7.10.1.1.2. Second is the previous disciplinary record of the member. Counseling, admonitions, and reprimands should be used as part of a graduated pattern of discipline in response to repeated departures from standards. In other words, each time a service member departs from standards, the response should usually be more severe.

7.10.1.2. **Standard of Proof**. While no specific standard of proof applies to administrative action proceedings, commanders should utilize the "preponderance of the evidence" standard when evaluating the evidence and every element of the offenses committed. A preponderance of the evidence means simply the greater weight of credible evidence. Whether such proof is available should be considered before initiating the administrative action. If such proof is lacking, administrative action is susceptible to being found to be legally unsupportable and, as a result, could be set aside. There is no requirement to prove any allegation beyond a reasonable doubt."

**7.10.2. Letter of Counseling and Air Force IMT 174, Record of Individual Counseling.**

A letter of counseling is the lowest level of administrative action. Counseling helps people develop good judgment, assume responsibility, and face and solve their problems. Counselors help subordinates develop skills, attitudes, and behaviors consistent with maintaining the Air Force readiness. First-line supervisors, first sergeants, and commanders routinely counsel individuals verbally or in writing, giving advice and reassuring subordinates about specific situations. A verbal counseling may be recorded on a record of individual counseling.

**7.10.3. Letter of Admonishment.**

An admonishment is more severe than a letter of counseling or a record of individual counseling. Use an admonishment to document an infraction serious enough to warrant a letter of admonishment. Do not use it when a reprimand is more appropriate.

**7.10.4. Letter of Reprimand.**

A reprimand is more severe than a letter of counseling or letter of admonishment and indicates a stronger degree of official censure. Commanders may elect to file a letter of reprimand in a UIF for enlisted personnel.

**7.10.5. Issuing the Letter of Counseling, Record of Individual Counseling, Letter of Admonishments, or Letter of Reprimands.**

Counseling, admonitions, and reprimands may be either verbal or written. The counseling, admonition, or reprimand should be in writing because the corrective action is more meaningful to the member and the infraction is documented. Letter of counseling, letter of admonishments and letter of reprimands should be typed on letterhead and must comply with the requirements listed below. Failure to follow the requirements for drafting and maintaining these documents could limit the use of the documents in a subsequent proceeding. Failing to include the second endorsement noting the consideration of a response, for example, will likely render a letter of reprimand inadmissible in a later court-martial or discharge proceeding.

7.10.6. Written letter of counseling, letter of admonishments and letter of reprimands must state the following:

7.10.6.1. What the member did or failed to do, citing specific incidents and their dates.

7.10.6.2. What improvement is expected.

7.10.6.3. That further deviation may result in more severe action.

7.10.6.4. That the individual has 3 duty days to respond and provide rebuttal matters (45 days for non-extended Regular Air Force reservists).

7.10.6.5. That all supporting documents become part of the record.

7.10.6.6. That the person who initiates the letter of counseling, letter of admonishments and letter of reprimands has three duty days to advise the individual of their decision regarding any comments submitted by the individual.

**7.11. UIF.**

The UIF provides commanders with an official and single means of filing derogatory data concerning an Air Force member's personal conduct and duty performance. With some exceptions, the commander has wide discretion as to what should be placed in a UIF and what should be removed.

7.11.1. **Mandatory Documents.** (See AFI 36-2907, Table 2.2 for additional guidance relating to mandatory UIFs)

The commander must place the following documents in a UIF:

7.11.1.1. Suspended or unsuspended Article 15 punishment of more than 1 month (31 days or more).

7.11.1.2. Court-martial conviction.

7.11.1.3. A civilian conviction where the penalty or actions equivalent to a finding of guilty of an offense which resulted in confinement of 1 year or more or could have resulted in a penalty of confinement for more than one year or death.

7.11.1.4. Control roster actions (see paragraph 7.12).

7.11.2. **Optional Documents.**

The commander may place the following documents, among others, into a UIF for up to one year:

7.11.2.1. Article 15 when punishment is not suspended or does not exceed one month.

7.11.2.2. A record of conviction by a civilian court or an action equivalent to a finding of guilty for an offense where the maximum confinement penalty authorized for the offense is one year or less.

7.11.2.3. Written letters of reprimand, admonition, or counseling.

7.11.2.4. Confirmed incidents involving discrimination or sexual harassment of personnel.

7.11.3. **Initiating and Controlling UIFs.**

Commanders at all levels; vice commanders, staff directors, and directors at major commands, field operating agencies, and direct reporting units; and the senior Air Force officer assigned to a joint command have the authority to establish, remove, or destroy UIFs. Commanders refer optional documents (letters of admonishment, letters of counseling, and letters of reprimand) to the offending member along with an Air Force IMT 1058, *Unfavorable Information File Action*, before establishing a UIF. **Note:** Mandatory items, such as Articles 15 with punishment exceeding 1 month and court-martial or civilian court convictions, are not referred via Air Force IMT 1058. The individual has 3 duty days to acknowledge the intended actions and provide pertinent information before the commander makes the final decision on placing optional documents in the UIF. The commander advises the individual of his or her final decision; and, if the commander decides to file the information in a UIF, the individual's response is also filed.

7.11.4. **Accessing and Reviewing UIFs:**

7.11.4.1. In the course of their Air Force duties, the following individuals are authorized access to a member's UIF: the member, commander, first sergeant, enlisted performance report reporting and rating officials, force support squadron personnel, Inspector General, inspection team, legal office personnel, military equal opportunity personnel, law enforcement personnel and substance abuse counselors authorized by the commander to review the document in the course of their official Air Force duties.

7.11.4.2. All UIFs require periodic review to ensure continued maintenance of documents in the UIF is proper. The unit commander must review all UIFs within 90 days of assuming or being appointed to command. UIFs are also reviewed when individuals are considered for promotion, reenlistment, permanent change of station, permanent change of assignment, and voluntary or mandatory reclassification or retraining. UIFs are also reviewed annually, with the assistance of the staff judge advocate.

7.11.5. **Removing UIFs or Documents within UIFs.**

Commanders keep the UIF and documents for the disposition period unless early removal is clearly warranted. AFI 36-2907, *Unfavorable Information File (UIF) Program,* contains additional guidance on disposition dates. Commanders initiate removal action via Air Force IMT 1058, and the individual acknowledges the action.

**7.12. Control Roster.**

The control roster is a rehabilitative tool commanders may use to establish a 6-month observation period for individuals whose duty performance is substandard or who fail to meet or maintain Air Force standards of conduct, bearing, and integrity, on or off duty. A single incident of substandard performance or an isolated breach of standards, not likely to be repeated, should not ordinarily be a basis for a control roster action. Commanders should consider prior incidents, acts, failures, counseling, and rehabilitative efforts.

7.12.1. **Use.**

A commander may direct an enlisted performance report before entering or removing an individual from the roster, or both. The commander cannot place an individual on the roster as a substitute for more appropriate administrative, judicial, or nonjudicial action. Being on the roster does not shield an individual from other actions. An individual cannot remain on the roster for more than 6 consecutive months. If a member is not rehabilitated in this time, the commander initiates more severe action.

7.12.2. **Initiating and Maintaining the Control Roster.**

Commanders place an individual on the control roster by using Air Force IMT 1058, which puts the member on notice that his/her performance and behavior must improve or he/she will face more severe administrative action or punishment. The individual acknowledge receipt of the action and has 3 duty days to respond and submit a statement on his or her behalf before the Air Force IMT 1058 is finalized. Placement on the control roster is a mandatory UIF entry. The 6-month time period begins the day the Air Force IMT 1058 is finalized and ends at 2400 hours 6 months later. For example, if placed on the roster 1 January, this action expires at 2400 on 30 June. An individual's time does not stop and start for periods of temporary duty, ordinary leave, or a change in immediate supervisor. The commander can remove an enlisted member early from the control roster using Air Force IMT 1058.

**7.13. Administrative Demotion of Airmen.**

The group or equivalent-level commander may demote Master Sergeants and below. Major command, field operating agency, and direct reporting unit commanders may demote Senior Master Sergeants and Chief Master Sergeants.

7.13.1. **Reasons for Demotion.**

Common reasons for the administrative demotion of Airmen include failure to:

7.13.1.1. Complete officer transitional training for reasons of academic deficiency, self-elimination, or misconduct. Trainees will be demoted to the grade they formerly held.

7.13.1.2. Maintain or attain the appropriate grade and skill level.

7.13.1.3. Fulfill the responsibilities of a noncommissioned officer (NCO) as prescribed in AFI 36-2618, *The Officer and Enlisted Force Structures*.

7.13.1.4. Attain or maintain fitness program standards as prescribed in AFI 36-2905, *Fitness Program*.

7.13.1.5. Termination of student status of members attending temporary duty Air Force schools.

7.13.2. **Demotion Procedure:**

7.13.2.1. The immediate commander notifies the member in writing of the intention to recommend demotion, citing the paragraph, the demotion authority if other than the initiating commander, and the recommended grade. The notification must also include the specific reasons for the demotion and a complete summary of the supporting facts.

7.13.2.2. The commander informs the member of their right to counsel and the right to respond within 3 duty days. The commander must also inform eligible members of their right to apply for retirement in lieu of demotion. Following the member's response, if the commander elects to continue the proceedings, the case file is forwarded with a summary of the member's written and verbal statements to the force support squadron for processing prior to forwarding to the demotion authority. The member must be notified in writing of the decision to forward the action to the demotion authority. The demotion authority obtains a written legal review before making a decision.

7.13.3. **Appeal Policy.**

Airmen may appeal a demotion decision. The appellate authority for Airmen in the grades of Airman through Master Sergeant is the next level commander above the group commander. The appellate authority for Airmen in the grades of Senior Master Sergeant and Chief Master Sergeant is the Air Force Vice Chief of Staff, unless the major command, field operating agency, or direct reporting unit commander delegated demotion authority to a subordinate level. If delegated, the major command, field operating agency, or direct reporting unit commander then becomes the appellate authority for demotion appeals of Senior Master Sergeants and Chief Master Sergeants.

**7.14. Administrative Separations.**

The suitability of persons to serve in the Air Force is judged on the basis of their conduct and their ability to meet required standards of duty performance and discipline. Separating members failing to meet standards of performance, conduct, or discipline, promotes Air Force readiness and strengthens our standards of military service. Commanders and supervisors must identify enlisted members who show likelihood for early separation and make reasonable efforts to help these members meet Air Force standards. Members who do not show potential for further service should be discharged. Commanders must consult the servicing staff judge advocate and military personnel flight before initiating the involuntary separation of a member.

7.14.1. **Service Characterization.**

Airmen who do not qualify for reenlistment receive a discharge without regard to their remaining Military Service Obligation. The character of the member's service is honorable. The service of members separating at their expiration of term of service, or voluntarily or involuntarily separating for the convenience of the Government, is characterized as honorable. The service of members administratively discharged under AFI 36-3208, *Administrative Separation of Airmen*, may be characterized as honorable, general (under honorable conditions), or under other than honorable conditions. The service characterization depends upon the reason for the discharge and the member's military record in the current enlistment or period of service.

7.14.1.1. Honorable: Appropriate when the quality of the member's service generally has met Air Force standards of acceptable conduct and performance of duty, or a member's service is otherwise so meritorious that any other characterization would be inappropriate.

7.14.1.2. General (under honorable conditions): Appropriate if a member's service has been honest and faithful, but significant negative aspects of the member's conduct or performance outweigh positive aspects of military record.

7.14.1.3. Under Other Than Honorable Conditions: Appropriate if based on a pattern of behavior or one or more acts or omissions constituting a significant departure from the conduct expected of Airmen. This characterization can be given only if the member is offered an administrative discharge board or if a discharge is unconditionally requested in lieu of trial by court-martial.

7.14.1.4. A commander must initiate discharge processing or seek a waiver of the discharge if the reason for discharge is for fraudulent or erroneous enlistment; civil court conviction for an offense for which a punitive discharge and confinement for one year or more would be authorized under the UCMJ; drug abuse; or sexual assault. A commander must make a discharge or retention recommendation when a member remains in a poor fitness category for a continuous 12-month period or receives 4 poor fitness assessments in a 24-month period.

7.14.2. **Reasons for Separation.**

Airmen are entitled to separate at expiration of term of service unless there is a specific authority for retention or they consent to retention. Nevertheless, a separation is not automatic; members remain in the service until separation action is initiated. Many different reasons for separation exist. The following discussion cannot cover all of them; its purpose is to briefly identify major reasons for separation and a concise discussion of each:

7.14.2.1. **Required Separation:**

7.14.2.1.1. Airmen who will continue to serve in another military status must separate; for example, an Airman may separate to serve with the Air Force Reserve or Air National Guard. An Airman may also separate to accept an appointment as a commissioned officer of the Air Force or to accept an appointment as a warrant or commissioned officer of another branch of service.

7.14.2.1.2. Airmen with insufficient retainability for permanent change of station must separate.

7.14.2.2. **Voluntary Separation.** Airmen may ask for early separation for the convenience of the Government if they meet the criteria. Entering an officer training program, pregnancy, conscientious objection, hardship, and early release to attend school are some of the reasons for which members may be allowed to separate.

7.14.2.3. **Involuntary Separation.** Physical conditions that interfere with duty performance or assignment availability, inability to cope with parental responsibilities or military duty, or insufficient retainability for required retraining are reasons for involuntary discharge for the convenience of the Government. Defective enlistment (fraudulent or erroneous) is also a basis for discharge. Airmen are subject to discharge for cause based on such factors as unsatisfactory performance, substance abuse, misconduct, or in the interest of national security.

7.14.2.4. **Discharge Instead of Trial by Court-Martial.** If charges have been preferred against an Airman and if the UCMJ authorizes punitive discharge as punishment for the offense, the Airman may request an administrative discharge instead of trial by court-martial. There is no guarantee, however, that the Airman's request will be granted.

*Section 7E—Punitive Actions*

### 7.15. Military Law, a Separate Judicial System.

Effective leadership is the most desirable means of maintaining standards. Military law provides commanders the tools, including court-martial and nonjudicial punishment, to deal with criminal conduct. The purpose of military law is to promote justice, to assist in maintaining good order and discipline in the Armed Forces, to promote efficiency and effectiveness in the military establishment, and to thereby strengthen the national security of the U.S.

**Figure 7.1. The Military Justice System Pillars.**

7.15.1. **The U.S. Constitution.**

The U.S. Constitution is the primary source of our military law. The framers of the U.S. Constitution gave Congress the authority to make rules for the military, and Congress and the President have used their combined authority to create the military justice system currently in place (Figure 7.1). The U.S. Constitution designates the President as Commander in Chief of the Armed Forces and vests the power to carry out the responsibilities of this position. Congress has the power to raise an Army and Navy, control the military budget, and make rules for the government of the Army and Navy. This separation of power is an important element of our military justice system.

**7.15.2. UCMJ and the Manual for Courts-Martial:**

7.15.2.1. **UCMJ.** In 1950, Congress enacted the UCMJ, and President Harry S. Truman signed it into law. The UCMJ became effective 31 May 1951.

7.15.2.2. **The Manual for Courts-Martial.** In 1951, President Truman created the Manual for Courts-Martial by executive order. The Manual for Courts-Martial sets out rules for evidence, procedure, maximum punishments, and provides standardized forms. The Manual for Courts-Martial is intended to provide military law guidance to commanders and judge advocates and is revised annually. Furthermore, the manual contains a wide range of materials, including the U.S. Constitution, the UCMJ (including text and discussion of the punitive articles, as well as sample specifications), rules for courts-martial, and military rules of evidence.

**7.15.3. Legal Rights.**

Members of the Armed Forces retain virtually all the legal rights they held as civilians before entering the military, including protection against involuntary self-incrimination and the right to counsel.

7.15.3.1. **Self-incrimination:**

7.15.3.1.1. **Involuntary Self-incrimination.** The Fifth Amendment to the Constitution states that no person shall be compelled to be a witness against him or herself. Article 31, UCMJ, and military rules of evidence 304 reflect this right and prohibit involuntary statements from being used against an accused. A statement is "involuntary" when obtained in violation of the Fifth Amendment, Article 31, or through the use of coercion, unlawful influence, or unlawful inducement. The UCMJ requires that prior to interrogation or any requests for a statement from a person suspected of an offense, the person must be first told of the nature of the accusation, advised that he or she does not have to make any statement regarding the offense, and that any statement he or she makes may be used as evidence against him or her in a trial by court-martial. Prior to interrogation, the suspect is entitled to consult with counsel and to have such counsel present at the interrogation. If counsel is requested, questioning must cease until counsel is present.

7.15.3.1.2. **Statements.** Once properly advised of his or her rights, a person may waive these rights and choose to make a statement. Assuming this waiver is made freely, knowingly, and intelligently, any subsequent statement can be used as evidence in a court-martial or other judicial or administrative proceedings.

7.15.3.2. **Right to Counsel:**

7.15.3.2.1. The UCMJ provides an accused the right to be represented by a military attorney before summary, special, and general courts-martial; Article 32 preliminary hearings; and in the Article 15 process free of charge. The area defense counsel program provides Air Force members independent legal representation. Airmen suspected of an offense or facing adverse administrative actions receive confidential legal advice from an experienced judge advocate general outside the local chain of command, avoiding conflicts of interest or command influence.

7.15.3.2.2. The area defense counsel program, established in 1974, made the Air Force the first service to create a totally independent defense function. Area defense counsel are assigned to the Air Force Judiciary, which falls under the Air Force Legal Operations Agency at Joint Base Andrews-Naval Air Facility Washington. Although located at most major bases, the area defense counsel works for a separate chain of command and reports only to senior defense attorneys. The area defense counsel does not report to anyone at base level, including the wing commander and the base staff judge advocate. This separate chain of command ensures undivided loyalty to the client.

7.15.3.2.3. Area defense counsel work to protect a client's individual interests and ensure the independent and zealous representation of a client facing military justice action or other adverse actions, thereby promoting discipline and strengthening confidence in justice. Most area defense counsel are selected from the local base legal office, but to ensure further independence, they are not rotated back to the base legal office when their area defense counsel assignments are completed.

7.15.3.2.4. Before selection as an area defense counsel, a judge advocate will be carefully screened for the proper level of judgment, advocacy skills, and courtroom experience. Additionally, other experienced trial advocates (senior defense counsel) travel to assist in the defense of particularly complex courts-martial. Area defense counsel are supported by defense paralegals, who are enlisted personnel.

**7.16. Military Jurisdiction in Action:**

**7.16.1. Apprehension and Pretrial Restraint:**

7.16.1.1. **Apprehension.** Apprehension is the act of taking a person into custody and the equivalent of a civilian "arrest." Military law enforcement officers, military criminal investigators and persons on guard or performing police duties are authorized to apprehend persons subject to UCMJ jurisdiction, and arrest and temporarily detain persons subject to the military extraterritorial jurisdiction act, when there is probable cause that an offense has been committed and that the person committed it. Although all commissioned, warrant, petty, and noncommissioned officers on Regular Air Force may apprehend persons subject to UCMJ jurisdiction, absent exigent circumstances, the apprehension of civilians should be done by law enforcement personnel.

7.16.1.1.1. An apprehension is made by clearly notifying the person orally or in writing that he or she is in custody. The simple statement, "You are under apprehension," is usually sufficient to provide notice. During apprehension, such force and means as are reasonably necessary under the circumstances to effect the apprehension are authorized.

7.16.1.1.2. NCOs not otherwise performing law enforcement duties may apprehend commissioned or warrant officers only on specific orders from a commissioned officer or when such apprehension prevents disgrace to the service or to prevent the commission of a serious offense or escape of someone who has committed a serious offense. The immediate commander of an apprehended person should be promptly notified.

7.16.1.2. **Pretrial Restraint.** Pretrial restraint is moral or physical restraint on a person's liberty that is imposed before and during the disposition of offenses. Pretrial restraint may include conditions on liberty, restrictions, arrest, or confinement. Only an officer's commander can order pretrial restraint of an officer; this authority cannot be delegated. Any commissioned officer may order pretrial restraint of any enlisted person. An enlisted person's commander may also delegate such restraint authority to an NCO.

7.16.1.2.1. **Conditions on Liberty.** Conditions on liberty are imposed directing a person to do or refrain from doing specified acts; examples include orders to report periodically to a specified official, orders to stay away from a certain place (such as the scene of the alleged offense), and orders not to associate with specified persons (such as the alleged victim or potential witnesses). However, conditions on liberty must not hinder pretrial preparation.

7.16.1.2.2. **Restrictions in Lieu of Arrest.** Restriction imposes restraint on a person to remain within specified limits, but is less severe than arrest. The geographic limits are usually broader (for example, restriction to the limits of the installation), and the offender will perform full military duties unless otherwise directed.

7.16.1.2.3. **Arrest.** In the Armed Forces, the term "arrest" means the limiting of a person's liberty. Arrest is not imposed as punishment for an offense. The notification of arrest directs a person to remain within specified limits. Arrest is a moral restraint; no physical restraint is exercised to prevent a person from breaking arrest. A person in arrest is not expected to perform full military duties.

7.16.1.2.4. **Confinement.** Confinement is physical restraint, such as imprisonment in a confinement facility. Individuals are put in pretrial confinement only when lesser forms of pretrial restraint are inadequate. When a person is ordered into confinement they have the right to retain civilian counsel (at their own expense) or to request military counsel be assigned (at no expense to the accused). They also have the right to a prompt review of their status.

7.16.1.3. **Use of Pretrial Restraint.** Pretrial restraint may only be ordered if there is a reasonable belief that the person committed an offense triable by court-martial and the circumstances require restraint. Factors to consider in ordering pretrial restraint include whether one can foresee that the person will not appear at trial or will engage in serious criminal misconduct while awaiting court-martial. Pretrial restraint should not be more rigorous than the circumstances require.

7.16.2. **Search and Seizure:**

7.16.2.1. The fourth amendment to the U.S. Constitution protects against unreasonable searches and seizures. The authorization to search must be based on probable cause and particularly describe the place to be searched and the persons or things to be seized.

7.16.2.2. Probable cause to search exists when there is a reasonable belief that the person, property, or evidence sought is located in the place or on the person to be searched.

7.16.2.3. "Authorization to search" is the military equivalent of a civilian search warrant. A search authorization is an express permission, written or oral, issued by a competent military authority to search a person or an area for specified property or evidence or to search for a specific person and to seize such property, evidence, or person.

7.16.2.4. Commanders, as well as military judges, installation commanders, and magistrates, are authorized to direct inspections of persons and property under your command and to authorize probable cause searches and seizures over anyone subject to military law or at any place on the installation. However, a commander who authorizes a search or seizure must be neutral and detached from the case and facts. Therefore, the command functions of gathering facts and maintaining overall military discipline must remain separate from the legal decision to grant search authorization.

7.16.2.5. The installation commander has discretion to appoint, in writing, up to two military magistrates who may also authorize search and seizure (including apprehension) requests. Each magistrate must receive training provided by the staff judge advocate on search and seizure issues.

### 7.16.3. Inspections.

An inspection is of a person, property or premises for the primary purpose of determining and ensuring the security, military fitness, or good order and discipline of a unit, organization or installation. Commanders may conduct inspections of their units. Inspections are not searches. The distinction between a search and an inspection is that an inspection is not conducted for the primary purpose of obtaining evidence for use in a trial or other disciplinary proceedings and does not focus on a particular suspect or individual. Contraband seized during an inspection (for example, vehicle entry checks, and random drug testing) is admissible in court.

## 7.17. Nonjudicial Punishment—Article 15.

Nonjudicial punishment is authorized under Article 15, UCMJ. Often referred to as an "Article 15," nonjudicial punishment provides commanders with an essential and prompt means of maintaining good order and discipline without the stigma of a court-martial conviction. An Article 15 may be imposed for minor offenses. Any Air Force member can be punished by Article 15. Commanders are encouraged to take nonpunitive disciplinary actions, such as counseling and administrative reprimand, before resorting to Article 15. However, such measures are not required before an Article 15 can be offered. An Article 15 should not be offered unless the commander is prepared to proceed with court-martial charges because an Article 15 cannot be imposed upon a member who demands trial by court-martial.

### 7.17.1. Minor Offense.

Whether an offense is minor depends on several factors and is a matter left to the imposing commander's discretion. Besides the nature of the offense, the commander should also consider the offender's age, grade, duty assignments, record, experience, and the maximum sentence imposable for the offense if tried by a general court-martial. Ordinarily, a minor offense is an offense in which the maximum sentence imposable would not include a dishonorable discharge or confinement for more than 1 year if tried by a general court-martial.

### 7.17.2. Punishments Under Article 15.

The type and permissible extent of punishment are limited by both the imposing commander's grade and the offender's grade as reflected in Table 7.2. Punishments may include reduction in grade, forfeiture of pay, restrictions, extra duties, and/or correctional custody.

### 7.17.3. Procedures:

7.17.3.1. While no specific standard of proof is applicable to nonjudicial punishment proceedings, commanders should recognize that a member is entitled to demand trial by court-martial, where proof beyond a reasonable doubt by competent evidence is required for conviction. Commanders should consider whether such proof is available before initiating action under Article 15. If not, nonjudicial punishment is usually not warranted. Commanders must confer with the staff judge advocate, or a designee, before initiating nonjudicial punishment proceedings and before imposing punishment. The staff judge advocate advises and helps the commander evaluate the facts and determine what offense was committed. However, the commander makes the decision to impose punishment and the degree of punishment imposed. The military justice section of the base legal office prepares the Air Force IMT 3070, *Record of Nonjudicial Punishment Proceedings*.

7.17.3.2. After the commander determines that nonjudicial punishment is appropriate, the staff judge advocate prepares an Air Force Form 3070A, *Record of Nonjudicial Punishment Proceedings (AB thru SSgt)*; Air Force Form 3070B, *Record of Nonjudicial Punishment Proceedings (TSgt thru CMSgt)*; or Air Force Form 3070C, *Record of Nonjudicial Punishment Proceedings (Officer)*. The commander notifies the member that he or she is considering punishment under Article 15 by signing the Air Force Form 3070A/B/C and providing it to the member. The Air Force Form 3070A/B/C includes a statement of the alleged offenses, the member's rights, and the maximum punishment allowable. After receiving the Air Force Form 3070A/B/C, the member has a right to examine all statements and evidence available to the commander. In practice, the member or the area defense counsel is provided copies of the evidence used to support the alleged offenses.

7.17.3.3. Once offered nonjudicial punishment, a member must first decide whether to accept. The member has 3 duty days (72 hours) to make the decision. Before making the decision, the member may consult with area defense counsel. A member's decision to accept the Article 15 is not an admission of guilt but is a choice of forum. The member may present matters orally, in writing, or both and may present witnesses. The member is not required to present any matters or make any statement and has the right to remain silent under Article 31(b), UCMJ.

**Table 7.2. Permissible Nonjudicial Punishments on Enlisted Members.** (Notes 1, 2, 3, and 4)

| RULE | A Punishment | | B Imposed by Lieutenant or Captain | C Imposed by Major | D Imposed by Lieutenant Colonel or Above |
|---|---|---|---|---|---|
| 1 | Additional restrictions | | May not impose nonjudicial punishment on Chief or Senior Master Sergeant | May not impose nonjudicial punishment on Chief or Senior Master Sergeant | See note 2 for reduction of Chief or Senior Master Sergeant |
| 2 | Correctional custody | | Up to 7 days | 30 days | 30 days |
| 3 | Reduction in Grade (note 2) | Chief Master Sergeant | No | No | Note 2 |
| 4 | | Senior Master Sergeant | No | No | Note 2 |
| 5 | | Master Sergeant | No | No | One grade |
| 6 | | Technical Sergeant | No | One grade | One grade |
| 7 | | Staff Sergeant | One grade | One grade | One grade |
| 8 | | Senior Airman | One grade | To Airman Basic | To Airman Basic |
| 9 | | Airman First Class | One grade | To Airman Basic | To Airman Basic |
| 10 | | Airman | One grade | To Airman Basic | To Airman Basic |
| 12 | Reprimand | | Yes | Yes | Yes |
| 13 | Restriction | | 14 days | 60 days | 60 days |
| 14 | Extra duties | | 14 days | 45 days | 45 days |
| 15 | Forfeiture | | 7 days pay | ½ of 1 month's pay per month for 2 months | ½ of 1 month's pay per month for 2 months |

**Notes:**

1. See Manual for Courts-Martial, part V, paragraph 5d, for further limitations on combinations of punishments.

2. Chief or Senior Master Sergeant may be reduced one grade only by major command commanders, commanders of unified or specified commands, or commanders to whom promotion authority to theses grades has been delegated. See AFI 36-2502, *Airman Promotion Program*. AFI 51-202, *Nonjudicial Punishment,* Table 3.1, note 2.

3. Bread and water and diminished rations punishments are not authorized.

4. Frocked commanders may exercise only that authority associated with their actual pay grade. No authority is conferred by the frocked grade.

7.17.3.4. After carefully considering all matters submitted by the member and consulting with the staff judge advocate, the commander will indicate one of the following decisions and annotate the Air Force Form 3070A/B/C accordingly:

7.17.3.4.1. The member did not commit the offenses alleged, or nonjudicial punishment is not appropriate, and the proceedings are terminated. In light of matters in extenuation and mitigation, nonjudicial punishment is not appropriate, and the proceedings are terminated.

7.17.3.4.2. The member committed one or more of the offenses alleged. (The commander must line out and initial any offenses he or she determines were not committed.)

7.17.3.4.3. The member committed one or more lesser-included offenses rather than the offenses listed.

7.17.3.5. If the commander finds the member committed an offense, he or she will determine the appropriate punishment and serve it on the member, notifying the member of the right to appeal.

7.17.3.6. Members are entitled to appeal nonjudicial punishment to the next superior authority in the commander's chain of command. The member may appeal when he or she considers the punishment to be unjust or disproportionate to the offense. A member may assert the punishment was unjust because the offense was not committed. Thus, the guilty finding, the punishment, or both may be appealed. The member has 5 calendar days to submit a written appeal—an oral statement is not acceptable. Punishments are not stayed during the appeal process. However, if the commander and/ or appellate authority fail to take action on an appeal within five days after submission, and if the member so requests, any unexecuted punishment involving restraint or extra duties will be delayed until after appeal. The appellate authority may deny all relief, grant partial relief, or grant all relief requested by the member. The appellate authority's decision is final.

**7.17.4. Suspension, Remission, Mitigation, and Set-Aside Actions.**

A commander has the power to suspend, remit, or mitigate punishment of an Article 15.

**7.17.4.1. Suspension.** To suspend punishment is to postpone application of all or part for a specific probationary period with the understanding that the punishment will be automatically remitted (cancelled) at the end of this period if the member does not engage in further misconduct. The probationary period may not exceed 6 months. Suspension may occur when the commander imposes the punishment or within 4 months of executing the punishment. The Manual for Courts-Martial and Air Force policy encourage the use of suspended sentences as a corrective tool for first-time offenders to provide both an observation period and an incentive for good behavior.

**7.17.4.2. Remission.** Remission is an action whereby any portion of the unexecuted punishment is cancelled, normally used as a reward for good behavior or when determined the punishment imposed was too severe for the particular offense.

**7.17.4.3. Mitigation.** Mitigation is a reduction in either the quantity or quality of a punishment. Commanders may, at any time, mitigate any part or amount of the unexecuted portion of the punishment by changing to a less severe form or reduce the quantity. For example, a reduction in grade can be mitigated to a forfeiture of pay.

**7.17.4.4. Set Aside.** Setting aside is an action whereby the punishment, whether executed or unexecuted, is set aside and any property, privilege, or rights affected by the portion of the punishment set aside are restored. Commanders use this action only when they believe that under all the circumstances of the case the punishment has resulted in clear injustice.

**7.18. Types of Courts-Martial:**

**7.18.1. Summary Court-Martial.**

A Summary Court-Martial tries minor offenses. Instead of a military judge, an Regular Air Force commissioned officer is appointed as the Summary Court-Martial officer. The accused may have assistance from the area defense counsel. The Summary Court-Martial considers the evidence, including witness testimony, and then makes a finding. If the finding is guilty, the Summary Court-Martial considers any additional evidence before deciding an appropriate sentence. Only enlisted service members may be tried by Summary Court-Martial and only if they consent to being tried in that forum. Sentences are limited as set out in Table 7.3, Line 1, Column F.

**7.18.2. Special Court-Martial.**

Any service member may be tried by a Special Court-Martial. A Special Court-Martial is the intermediate-level court in the military system. The Special Court-Martial usually consists of a military judge and a panel (similar to a civilian jury) of three or more members. Enlisted accused may request at least one-third of the panel consist of enlisted members. The accused may request trial by military judge alone. The proceedings include a trial counsel (prosecutor), defense counsel, the accused, and a court reporter to record the proceedings. A sentence in a Special Court-Martial may include any punishment authorized by the Uniform Code of Military Justice except death, dishonorable discharge, dismissal (in the case of an officer), or confinement in excess of 1 year.

**7.18.3. General Court-Martial.**

A General Court-Martial tries the most serious offenses. Cases cannot be referred for trial by General Court-Martial without a preliminary hearing under Article 32, Uniform of Military Justice. The General Court-Martial is composed of a military judge and at least a five-member panel, and may include at least one-third enlisted members, if so requested by an enlisted accused. The accused may request trial by a military judge alone, except in a capital case (when a sentence to death may be adjudged). The maximum authorized punishment this court-martial may impose is the maximum allowable under the UCMJ for the offenses charged. For some offenses, the maximum allowable sentence may include death.

**7.19. Court-Martial Procedures:**

**7.19.1. Trial.**

When a case is referred to trial, the convening authority, generally the wing or numbered Air Force commander selects the court-martial panel. Panel members must be senior in grade to the accused and be the best qualified. Throughout the court-martial process, commanders and convening authorities are expressly forbidden to exercise any improper influence on the action of the court.

**7.19.2. Findings and Sentence.**

The verdict of a court-martial is called the "findings." An accused cannot be found guilty unless guilt is proved beyond a reasonable doubt. A finding of guilty does not require a unanimous agreement, but requires at least two-thirds of the members to vote for a finding of guilty. Voting is by secret written ballot. In the event of a not-guilty verdict (acquittal), the trial ends. If there is a finding of guilty, a pre-sentencing procedure follows immediately to help the court determine an appropriate sentence. A sentence of death requires a unanimous vote by a panel of twelve members, while a sentence of confinement in excess of 10 years requires the concurrence of three-fourths of panel members.

**Table 7.3. Composition, Appointment, and Jurisdiction of Courts-Martial.**

| LINE | A Court | B Required Membership | C Convening Authority | D Persons Triable | E Offenses Triable | F Maximum Punishment |
|------|---------|------------------------|------------------------|--------------------|---------------------|-----------------------|
| 1 | Summary | One commissioned officer (Rule for Court-Martial 1301(a), Art. 16, UCMJ) | The officer exercising General Court-Martial or Special Court-Martial convening authority over the accused, or the commander of a detached squadron or other detachment (Rule for Court-Martial 1302, Article 24, UCMJ) | Enlisted members. If an accused objects to trial by Summary Court-Martial, the convening authority may order trial by Special Court-Martial or General Court-Martial (Rules for Court-Martial 1301(c) and 1303, Article 20, UCMJ) | Any noncapital offense punishable under UCMJ. Summary Court-Martial normally used to try minor offenses for which the accused was first offered nonjudicial punishment (Rule for Court-Martial 1301(c), Art. 20, UCMJ) | 1 month's confinement, hard labor without confinement for 45 days, restriction for 2 months, forfeiture of 2/3 of 1 month's pay, reduction to AB, reprimand, and a fine (Rule for Court-Martial 1301 (d)(1), Article 20, UCMJ). If the accused is Staff Sergeant or above, a Summary Court-Martial may not impose a sentence of confinement, hard labor without confinement, or reduction except to the next pay grade (Rule for Court-Martial 1301 (d)(2), UCMJ) |
| 2 | Special | Three or more members and a military judge or, if requested, a military judge only (Rule for Court-Martial 501 (a)(2), Article 16, UCMJ) | The officer exercising General Court-Martial convening authority over the accused; the commander of a base, wing, group, or separate squadron when expressly authorized by the major command commander or designated Secretary of the Air Force; or any commander designated by the Secretary of the Air Force (Rule for Court-Martial 504 (b)(2), Article 23a, UCMJ) | Any person subject to the UCMJ (Rule for Court-Martial 201 (b)(4), Article 19, UCMJ) | Any noncapital offense punishable under the UCMJ (Rule for Court-Martial 201(b)(5), Article 19, UCMJ) | **Upon enlisted members:** The maximum punishment authorized by the UCMJ, which may include a bad conduct discharge (enlisted members only), confinement for 1 year (enlisted members only), hard labor without confinement for 3 months (enlisted members only), restriction for 2 months, forfeiture of 2/3 pay per month for 1 year, reduction to AB (enlisted members only), reprimand, and a fine (Rules for Court-Martial 201 (f)(2)(B)(i), Article 19, UCMJ) |
| 3 | General | A military judge and at least five members, or a military judge only in noncapital cases (Rule for Court-Martial 501(a)(1), Article 16, UCMJ) | The President, Secretary of the Air Force, the commander of an air command, an air force, an air division or a separate wing of the Air Force, or any commander when designated by the President or Secretary of the Air Force (Rule for Court-Martial 504 (b)(1), Article 22, UCMJ) | Any person subject to the UCMJ (Rule for Court-Martial 201 (b)(4), Article 18, UCMJ) | Any offense punishable under the UCMJ (Rule for Court-Martial 201(b)(5), Article 18, UCMJ) | The maximum punishment authorized by the UCMJ, which may include death, a punitive separation (dismissal, dishonorable discharge, or bad conduct discharge), confinement for life or a specified period, hard labor without confinement for 3 months (enlisted members only), restriction for 2 months, forfeiture of all pay and allowances, reduction to AB (enlisted members only), reprimand, and a fine (Rule for Court-Martial 201 (f)(1)(A)(ii), Article 18, UCMJ) |

**7.19.3. Post-Trial.**

When the court reporter completes the record of trial, the military judge ensures the record accurately reflects the proceedings. Before the convening authority approves, disapproves, or reduces all or part of the findings and sentence, the complete record must be submitted to the staff judge advocate for review. When applicable, the staff judge advocate will provide the convening authority a clear and concise written recommendation. The accused and any victim named in a charge of which the accused was convicted may provide matters for the convening authority's consideration in making his or her clemency decision.

## 7.20. Initial Review of Trial Records.

The convening authority must act on every case. Pursuant to Article 60, UCMJ, the convening authority has limited authority to disapprove the findings or sentence.

## 7.21. Appellate Review:

### 7.21.1. The Judge Advocate General.

Following the court-martial, the record of the trial is reviewed for legal sufficiency. The records of trail in each general court-martial is not otherwise reviewed under Article 66 of the UCMJ shall be examined in the Office of The Judge Advocate General if there is a finding of guilty and the accused does not waive or withdraw his or her right to appellate review under Article 61.

### 7.21.2. The U.S. Air Force Court of Criminal Appeals.

The Air Force court of criminal appeals is the first level of formal appellate review. The court may approve, disapprove, or modify the convening authority's findings and sentence. The court reviews records of trial that include a death sentence; dismissal of a commissioned officer; a punitive discharge; or confinement of 1 year or more.

### 7.21.3. The U.S. Court of Appeals for the Armed Forces.

The United States court of appeals for the Armed Forces is composed of five civilian judges appointed by the President and is the highest appellate court in the military justice system. The court reviews all cases in which the death sentence was imposed and cases previously reviewed by the Air Force court of criminal appeals forwarded on the judge advocate general's order. The accused may also petition to have his or her case reviewed.

### 7.21.4. The U.S. Supreme Court.

Decisions of the U.S. court of appeals for the Armed Forces may be reviewed by the U.S. Supreme Court.

## 7.22. NCO Military Justice Responsibilities.

The military justice system is one tool used to correct breaches of discipline. NCOs have a general responsibility to be familiar with the UCMJ and correct marginal or substandard behavior or duty performance of their subordinates. NCOs must:

7.22.1. Support their commander in the application of the military justice system for maintaining order and discipline.

7.22.2. Become involved when breaches of discipline occur in their presence and report all such violations to the proper authorities.

7.22.3. Be prepared to investigate incidents when ordered to do so. This means that NCOs should be familiar with both the right against self-incrimination and resources available to assist in conducting the investigation and should not hesitate to seek advice before acting.

7.22.4. Be familiar with the rules in the UCMJ for apprehending, arresting, and confining violators of the UCMJ.

7.22.5. Be prepared to generally counsel Airmen on their legal rights under the UCMJ and refer them to proper legal authorities for guidance.

7.22.6. Provide leadership and counseling to obtain the maximum positive behavior change in the member receiving Article 15 punishment.

## Section 7F—Legal Issues

## 7.23. Evolution of the Military Justice System:

7.23.1. The strength of the military depends on disciplined service members ready to fight and win our Nation's wars. Military justice strengthens national security by providing commanders with an efficient and effective means of maintaining good order and discipline. Furthermore, the military justice system is a separate criminal justice system that does not look to the civilian courts to dispose of disciplinary problems. As a separate system, it allows the military to handle unique military crimes that civilian courts would be unable to handle.

7.23.2. In addition, a separate system enables the military to address crimes committed by service members at worldwide locations in times of war or peace. The military needs a justice system that goes wherever the troops go to provide uniform treatment regardless of locale or circumstances. No other judicial system in the U.S. provides such expansive coverage. As our separate military justice system has evolved, this system has balanced two basic interests: discipline (essential to warfighting capability) and justice (a fair and impartial system essential to the morale of those serving their country).

7.23.3. While military justice can be traced to the time of the Roman armies, the historical foundation for the U.S. military law and criminal justice system is the British Articles of War. In fact, the first codes predated the U.S. Constitution and Declaration of Independence. These codes were the Articles of War, applicable to the Army, and the Articles for the Government of the Navy. Through World War I, these codes went through some amendments and revisions but were substantially unchanged for more than 100 years. Throughout most of this time, the U.S. had a very small standing military. Those who entered the military understood they were going to fall under a different system of justice with unique procedures and punishments. While some people had bad experiences with the military justice system during this time, there was no overwhelming demand for change.

7.23.4. This changed with World War II when the U.S. had over 16 million men and women serving in the U.S. Armed Forces. Incredibly, there were about 2 million courts-martial during hostilities. There were approximately 80,000 general courts-martial during World War II. An average of more than 60 general courts-martial convictions occurred per day for the duration of the war.

7.23.5. The soldiers and sailors of World War II were regular citizens who volunteered or were drafted. Many of these citizens had some very unpleasant experiences with the military justice system, which looked quite different than today. The military justice system did not offer members the protections afforded by the civilian court system, and many American citizens disapproved of the way criminal laws were being applied in the military. Following the war, many organizations studied and made proposals to improve the military criminal legal system, and Congress conducted hearings on the military justice system.

7.23.6. After unification of the Armed Services under the Department of Defense in 1947, Secretary James V. Forrestal, the first Secretary of Defense, decided there should not be separate criminal law rules for the different branches of Service. He desired a uniform code that would apply to all services and address the abuses from World War II. His efforts set the stage for a new uniform system of discipline. In 1950, Congress enacted the UCMJ; this legislation is contained in Title 10, United States Code, Sections 801 through 946. The UCMJ is the military's criminal code applicable to all branches of service.

7.23.7. The UCMJ became effective in 1951 and provided substantial procedural guarantees of an open and fair process that continues today. The UCMJ required attorneys to represent the accused and the Government in all general courts-martial, prohibited improper command influence, and created the appellate court system. Furthermore, the UCMJ established Air Force, Army, Navy, and Coast Guard Boards of Review as the first level of appeal in the military justice system and the U.S. Court of Military Appeals as the second level of appeal. The Court of Military Appeals, composed of five civilian judges, was perhaps the most revolutionary change that brought the checks and balances of civilian control of the U.S. Armed Forces into the military justice system. In October 1994, the Court of Military Appeals was renamed the U.S. Court of Appeals for the Armed Forces to bring the name more in line with our civilian counterparts.

7.23.8. In addition to changing courts-martial processes and procedures, the UCMJ provided a complete set of criminal laws. Moreover, the UCMJ included many crimes punished under civilian law (for example, murder, rape, drug use, larceny, drunk driving, etc.), and also punished other conduct that affects good order and discipline. These unique military crimes include such offenses as desertion, absence without leave, disrespect toward superiors, failure to obey orders, dereliction of duty, wrongful disposition of military property, drunk on duty, malingering, and conduct unbecoming an officer. The UCMJ also included provisions punishing misbehavior before the enemy, improper use of countersign, misbehavior of a sentinel, misconduct as a prisoner, aiding the enemy, spying, and espionage.

7.23.9. The UCMJ has been amended on a number of occasions. For example, the Military Justice Act of 1968 created the position of military judge, authorized trial by military judge alone, required an attorney to act as defense counsel in all Special Court-Martials when the authorized punishment included a bad conduct discharge, prohibited trial by Summary Court-Martial if the accused objected, and changed service boards of review to courts of review.

7.23.10. The next significant change was the Military Justice Act of 1983, which streamlined pretrial and post-trial procedures. The act also provided for direct appeals to the U.S. Supreme Court from the Court of Military Appeals in appropriate cases, without the need to first pursue an appeal through the civilian appellate courts. The act also established a separate punitive article (112a) for drug offenses. Today's UCMJ reflects centuries of experience in criminal law and military justice and guarantees service members rights and privileges similar to and, in many cases, greater than those enjoyed by civilians.

## 7.24. Constitutional Underpinnings:

Two provisions in the U.S. Constitution grant powers to the legislative and executive branches providing the legal foundation for our military justice system.

### 7.24.1. Powers Granted to Congress.

The U.S. Constitution, Article I, Section 8, provides that Congress is empowered to declare war; raise and support armies; provide and maintain a navy; make rules for the government and regulation of the land and naval forces; provide for calling forth the militia; and organize, arm, and discipline the militias, and govern such part of them as may be employed in the service of the U.S.. Congress is also responsible for all laws deemed necessary and proper for carrying into execution the foregoing powers and all other powers vested by the U.S. Constitution in the U.S. Government. Congress has exercised their responsibilities over military justice by enacting the UCMJ.

### 7.24.2. Authority Granted to the President.

The U.S. Constitution, Article II, Section 2, provides that the President serves as commander in chief of the U.S. Armed Forces and of the militia of the states (National Guard) when called to federal service. By virtue of authority as commander in chief, the President has the power to issue executive orders to govern the U.S. Armed Forces as long as these orders do not conflict with any basic constitutional or statutory provisions. Article 36, UCMJ, specifically authorizes the President to prescribe the procedures, including rules of evidence, to be followed in courts-martial. In accordance with Article 36, UCMJ, President Harry S. Truman established the Manual for Courts-Martial in 1951 to implement the UCMJ. The Manual for Courts-Martial, like the UCMJ, has undergone a number of revisions.

## 7.25. Jurisdiction of Military Courts.

Courts-martial jurisdiction is concerned with the question of personal jurisdiction (Is the accused a person subject to the UCMJ?) and subject-matter jurisdiction (Is the conduct prohibited by the UCMJ?). If the answer is "yes" in both instances, then (and only then) does a court-martial have jurisdiction to decide the case.

### 7.25.1. Personal Jurisdiction:

7.25.1.1. Personal jurisdiction involves status, that is, the accused must possess the legal status of a service member or a person otherwise subject to the UCMJ before personal jurisdiction can attach.

7.25.1.2. Article 2, UCMJ, includes the following as persons subject to court-martial jurisdiction: (1) members of a regular component of the Armed Forces; including those awaiting discharge after expiration of their terms of enlistment; (2) cadets, aviation cadets, and midshipmen; (3) members of a Reserve component while on inactive duty training (but, in the case of members of the Army National Guard and Air National Guard, only when in Federal service); (4) retired members of a Regular component of the Armed Forces who are entitled to pay; (5) persons in custody of the Armed Forces serving a sentence imposed by court-martial; (6) prisoners of war in custody of the Armed Forces; and (7) in time of declared war or a contingency operation, persons serving with or accompanying an armed force in the field.

7.25.1.3. While the UCMJ previously provided for jurisdiction over civilians serving with or accompanying an armed force in the field in time of war, the U.S. court of appeals for the Armed Forces held that the phrase "in time of war" meant a war formally declared by Congress. The U.S. court of appeals for the Armed Forces decided this issue in reviewing a case (*U.S. v. Averette*, 1970) in which a civilian had been tried during the Vietnam Conflict for crimes committed within the combat zone. In the National Defense Authorization Act for Fiscal Year 2007, Congress amended Article 2(a)(10) to provide for UCMJ jurisdiction over civilians serving with or accompanying an armed force in the field in time of declared war or a contingency operation.

### 7.25.2. Subject-Matter Jurisdiction:

7.25.2.1. Courts-martial have the power to try any offense under the code except when prohibited from doing so by the U.S. Constitution. Courts-martial have exclusive jurisdiction when a purely military offense such as desertion, failure to obey orders, or disrespect toward superiors is involved. However, if the offense violates both the UCMJ and a civilian code, concurrent jurisdiction may exist. For example, if an Regular Air Force military member is caught shoplifting at an off-base merchant, the member can be tried by court-martial for larceny in violation of Article 121, UCMJ, and tried by a civilian court for a larceny offense recognized in the local jurisdiction.

7.25.2.2. The determination as to whether a military or a civilian authority will try the member is normally made through consultation or prior agreement between appropriate military authorities (ordinarily the staff judge advocate) and appropriate civilian authorities. A member to be tried by both a court-martial and a state court for the same act is constitutionally permissible and a member who has been tried by a state court normally will not be tried by court-martial for the same act. Only the Secretary of the Air Force may approve such prosecutions, and only in the most unusual cases, when the ends of justice and discipline can be met in no other way.

**7.26. Commander Involvement:**

7.26.1. Military commanders are responsible for maintaining law and order in the communities over which they have authority and for maintaining the discipline of the fighting force. Reports of crimes may come from law enforcement or criminal investigative agencies, as well as reports from supervisors or individual service members. One of the commander's greatest powers in the administration of military justice is the exercise of discretion—to decide how misconduct committed by a member of his or her command will be resolved. Each commander in the chain of command has independent, yet overlapping, discretion to dispose of offenses within the limits of that officer's authority. A commander may dispose of the case by taking no action, initiating administrative action against the member, offering the member nonjudicial punishment under Article 15, UCMJ, or preferring court-martial charges. Ordinarily, the immediate commander determines how to dispose of an offense; however, a superior commander may withhold that authority. The staff judge advocate is available to provide advice, but the commander ultimately decides how to dispose of alleged misconduct.

7.26.2. If a commander believes preferred charges should be disposed by court-martial, the charges are forwarded to the convening authority. Convening authorities are superior commanders or officials who possess the authority to convene specific levels of courts-martial (wing and numbered Air Force commanders in most cases). A convening authority convenes a court-martial by issuing an order that charges previously preferred against an accused will be tried by a specified court-martial. The convening authority must personally make the decision to refer a case to trial; delegation of this authority is not allowed. Charges may be referred to one of three types of court-martial: summary, special, or general.

**7.27. Roles of the Parties in the Adversarial System.**

In courts-martial, both Government and the accused have legal counsel. In addition, detailed defense counsel must include judge advocates, graduates of an accredited law school, and members of the bar of a federal court or the highest court of a state. Moreover, counsel must have certification to perform duties by a service's judge advocate general. The trial counsel prosecutes in the name of the U.S. and presents evidence against the accused. The defense counsel represents the accused and zealously seeks to protect the accused's rights.

7.27.1. **Trial Counsel:**

7.27.1.1. Trial counsel are similar to prosecutors in civilian criminal trials. They represent the Government, and their objective is justice, not merely securing a conviction. They zealously present evidence they believe is admissible and seek to persuade the court that the accused committed the alleged offenses. Trial counsel argues the inferences most strongly supporting the charges. Highly experienced trial advocates (senior trial counsel) are available to assist in the prosecution of particularly complex courts-martial.

7.27.1.2. Trial counsel also presents evidence and arguments to address defenses raised on behalf of the accused. Trial counsel may not ethically permit the continuance of the cause of action against the accused knowing the charges are not supported by probable cause. Additionally, trial counsel have an affirmative duty to disclose to the defense any evidence that negates the accused's guilt, mitigates the degree of guilt, or reasonably tends to reduce the punishment of the accused.

7.27.1.3. No person who has acted as accuser (one who prefers charges), preliminary hearing officer, military judge, or court member in any case may act later as trial counsel or assistant trial counsel in the same case. No person who has acted for the prosecution may act later in the same case for the defense, nor may any person who has acted for the defense act later in the same case for the prosecution.

7.27.2. **Defense Counsel Representation.**

In a trial by court-martial, the accused is entitled to an area defense counsel free of charge. The accused may also hire a civilian lawyer at his or her own expense. An accused may request representation by a particular military lawyer, and this officer will serve if he or she is reasonably available. Defense counsel will zealously, within the bounds of the law, guard the interests of the accused.

7.27.3. **Military Judge.**

A military trial judge presides over each open session of the court-martial. Military trial judges are selected from highly qualified, experienced judge advocates. Like defense counsel, military judges are assigned to the Air Force Legal Operations Agency and do not report to anyone at base level. No person is eligible to act as military judge in a case if he or she was the accuser, is a witness for the prosecution, or has acted as preliminary hearing officer or a counsel in the same case. The military judge of a court-martial may not consult with the members of the court except in the presence of the accused, trial counsel, and defense counsel, nor does he or she vote with the members of the court. In noncapital cases, an accused may elect to be tried by military judge alone. If such an election is made, the military judge will make a finding of guilty or not guilty and, if guilty, determine the sentence.

**7.27.4. Court Members:**

7.27.4.1. Members detailed to a court-martial are those persons who, in the opinion of the convening authority, are best qualified for the duty by reason of their age, education, training, experience, length of service, and judicial temperament.

7.27.4.2. Court panels are normally only composed of officers senior to the accused. If the accused is enlisted and makes a timely request that enlisted members be included on the court, the panel must consist of at least one-third enlisted personnel.

7.27.4.3. Court members determine whether the accused has been proved guilty beyond a reasonable doubt and, if guilty, adjudge (decide) a proper sentence based on the evidence and according to the instructions of the military judge. No member may use grade or position to influence another member. Voting is done by secret, written ballot.

**7.27.5. Ethical Standards.**

Both trial and defense counsels are bound by the ethical standards detailed in AFI 51-110, *Professional Responsibility Program*. These standards cover a variety of matters. For example, counsel may not:

7.27.5.1. Present testimony known to be perjured or other evidence known to be false.

7.27.5.2. Intentionally misrepresent any piece of evidence or matter of law.

7.27.5.3. Unnecessarily delay or prolong the proceedings.

7.27.5.4. Obstruct communications between prospective witnesses and counsel for the other side.

7.27.5.5. Use illegal means or condone the use of illegal means to obtain evidence.

7.27.5.6. Inject his or her own personal opinions or beliefs into arguments to the court.

7.27.5.7. Appeal to passion or prejudice.

7.27.5.8. Attempt to influence court members by currying favor or communicating privately with them.

**7.28. Post-trial Matters and Appellate Review:**

**7.28.1. Post-trial Matters.**

The convening authority must act on every case. When taking action on a case, the convening authority must consider the results of trial, written recommendation of the staff judge advocate when required, and written matters submitted by the accused and any victim named in a charge of which the accused was convicted. Convening authorities may also consider the record of trial, personnel records of the accused, and other matters they deem appropriate. Pursuant to Article 60, UCMJ, the convening authority has limited authority to disapprove the findings or sentence

7.28.1.1. The convening authority may, but is not required to, grant clemency on the findings. If the convening authority so chooses, some clemency on findings may be given, subject to regulatory and statutory limitations. The convening authority must provide a written explanation for such action.

7.28.1.2. Regardless of the offenses charged, the convening authority may not disapprove, commute, or suspend in whole or in part an adjudged sentence of confinement for more than 6 months or a punitive discharge, unless exceptions apply.

**7.28.2. Appellate Review.**

Following the convening authority's action is appellate review. The type of appellate review depends upon the adjudged and approved sentence.

7.28.2.1. The judge advocate general is the review authority in general court-martial cases where the sentence does not include death, dismissal, punitive discharge, or confinement for 1 year or more. The judge advocate general may also elect to certify (refer) any case reviewed by The Judge Advocate General's office to the Air Force Court of Criminal Appeals. The Air Force Court of Criminal Appeals is an independent appellate judicial body authorized by Congress and established by the judge advocate general pursuant to direction of Title 10, United States Code, Section 866(a) (1994). The court hears and decides appeals of Air Force court-martial convictions and appeals during litigation. The Air Force court of criminal appeals appellate judges are judge advocates appointed by the judge advocate general.

7.28.2.2. Unless appellate review is waived by an appellant, the Air Force court of criminal appeals automatically reviews all cases involving a sentence that includes death, dismissal, a punitive discharge, or confinement of 1 year or more. However, appellate review cannot be waived in death penalty cases. In this forum, the appellant is provided a military counsel (free of charge) who is an experienced trial advocate and a full-time appellate counsel. Civilian appellate counsel may be retained at the appellant's own expense. The Government is represented by appellate Government counsel.

7.28.2.3. The Air Force court of criminal appeals must consist of a panel of at least three military judges, reviews the case for legal error, and determines if the record of trial supports both the findings and sentence as approved by the convening authority. The Air Force court of criminal appeals has the power to dismiss the case, change a finding of guilty to one of not guilty or guilty to a lesser-included offense, reduce the sentence, or order a rehearing. However, the appeal may not change a finding of not guilty to one of guilty. The judge advocate general instructs convening authorities to take action according to the court's decisions.

7.28.2.4. If the Air Force court of criminal appeals rules against the appellant, he or she may request review by the U.S. court of appeals for the Armed Forces. The U.S. court of appeals for the Armed Forces must review all death penalty cases and any other case directed by The Judge Advocate General of each service. Review in other cases is discretionary upon petition of the appellant and upon good cause shown. Air Force appellate defense counsel are appointed to represent the appellant before the U.S. court of appeals for the Armed Forces. If an appellant's case is reviewed and relief is not granted by the U.S. court of appeals for the Armed Forces, the appellant may petition the Supreme Court of the U.S. for further review.

7.28.2.5. The Secretary of the Air Force automatically reviews cases involving dismissal of an Air Force officer or cadet. Dismissal is a punishment that punitively separates officers from the service. The dismissal cannot be executed until the Secretary, or appointed designee, approves the sentence.

7.28.2.6. If the sentence extends to death, the individual cannot be put to death until the President approves this part of the sentence. The President has clemency powers over all courts-martial cases and may commute, remit, or suspend any portion of the sentence. However, the President may not suspend the part of the sentence that provides for death.

## 7.29. Punitive Articles.

This paragraph focuses on unique military offenses that do not have a counterpart in civilian law.

### 7.29.1. Absence Offenses.

For an armed force to be effective, they must have sufficient members present to carry out the mission. One way this can be accomplished is by deterring members from being absent without authority, whether the absences are permanent or temporary. The circumstances under which the absence occurs, as well as the intent of the accused, determines the severity of the offense. Absence offenses include desertion and being absent without official leave.

#### 7.29.1.1. Desertion:

7.29.1.1.1. Article 85, UCMJ, may occur under the following categories: (1) unauthorized absence with the intent to remain away permanently; (2) quitting the unit or place of duty to avoid hazardous duty or shirk important service; or (3) desertion by an officer before notice of acceptance of resignation. More severe punishment is authorized if the desertion is terminated by apprehension instead of a voluntary surrender or if the desertion occurs in wartime. Desertion may be charged as a capital offense (which authorizes the death penalty) during wartime.

7.29.1.1.2. Absence with the specific intent to remain away permanently is the most commonly charged type of desertion. The unauthorized absence may be from the accused's place of duty, unit, or organization. The specific intent to remain away permanently may exist at the beginning of the absence or may be formed at any time during the absence. Thus, when a member leaves without permission, intending to return after a period of time, but later decides never to return, the member has committed the offense of desertion. However, proving intent is often difficult and may be shown by a number of factors, including the length of the absence, use of an alias, disposal of military identification and clothing items, concealment of military status, distance from duty station, and the assumption of a permanent-type civilian status or employment. The accused's voluntary return to military control is not a defense to desertion. The essential issue is whether the accused, at any time, formed the intent to remain away permanently.

#### 7.29.1.2. Absent Without Official Leave:

7.29.1.2.1. Article 86, UCMJ, addresses other cases where the member is not at the place where he or she is required to be at a prescribed time. This includes failure to go to the appointed place of duty; going from the appointed place of duty; absence from unit, organization, or other place of duty; abandoning watch or guard; and absence with intent to avoid maneuvers or field exercises.

7.29.1.2.2. Proving a failure to go to an appointed place of duty requires showing the accused actually knew he or she was required to be at the appointed place of duty at the prescribed time. The offense of going from the appointed place of duty requires proof the accused left his or her place of duty without proper authority, rather than failing to report in the first place. The accused must have reported for and begun the duty before leaving without proper authority.

7.29.1.2.3. Absence from the unit, organization, or other place of duty is a common absent without official leave charge. The authorized maximum punishment for this offense varies with the duration of the absence.

7.29.1.2.4. "Inability to return from leave" is a defense if the accused encountered unforeseeable circumstances beyond his or her control. For example, if Technical Sergeant Jane Doe's authorized 10-day period of leave expired on 1 December and she failed to report to her unit until 3 December, she would not be guilty of absent without official leave if she could establish she was at a distant city and had purchased an airline ticket on a flight that was cancelled due to a blizzard. Even though she has a defense, she is not excused from calling her unit and requesting an extension of leave. Inability would not be a defense where a military member took space-available transportation to Europe while on leave and then claimed he or she was unable to return on the date planned because he or she was unable to get space-available transportation back when he or she had hoped.

7.29.1.2.5. Other absences include abandoning watch or guard and absence from the unit, organization, or place of duty with intent to avoid maneuvers or field exercises. In addition, Article 87, UCMJ, provides that missing a movement is an offense that applies when the member, through neglect or design, misses the movement of a ship, aircraft, or unit.

### 7.29.2. False Official Statements.

Article 107, UCMJ, covers both the making and signing of false official statements and official documents. An "official" statement or document is any statement or document made in the line of duty. "In the line of duty" pertains to a matter within the jurisdiction of any U.S. department or agency. Furthermore, you must be able prove that the accused knew the statement or document was false and had a specific intent to deceive. Examples include falsely identifying oneself to a base gate guard or falsely listing a person as one's dependent to gain base privileges. However, material gain is not an element of the offense.

### 7.29.3. General Article.

The General Article (Article 134) is designed to address unspecified offenses punishable because of their effect on the U.S. Armed Forces. Article 134 generally provides for those offenses not specifically mentioned elsewhere in the punitive articles of the UCMJ. A military member can be punished under Article 134 for any and all disorders and neglects that are prejudicial to good order and discipline in the Armed Forces, for conduct of a nature to bring discredit upon the Armed Forces, and for crimes and offenses not capital.

7.29.3.1. **Disorders and Neglects Prejudicial to Good Order and Discipline.** Article 134, UCMJ, seeks to protect the internal operation of the U.S. Armed Forces. The issue is the effect of the accused's act on good order and discipline within the Armed Forces. The effect must be reasonably direct and tangible. Disorders and neglects prejudicial to good order and discipline include breach of customs of the service, fraternization, impersonating an officer, disorderly conduct, gambling with a subordinate, and incapacitating oneself for duty through prior indulgence in intoxicating liquors.

7.29.3.2. **Conduct of a Nature To Bring Discredit upon the Armed Forces.** The concern here is the potential effect of the accused's act on the reputation of the U.S. Armed Forces (how the military is perceived by the civilian sector). The conduct must tend to bring the Service into disrepute or lower it in public esteem. Thus, violations of local civil law or foreign law may be punished if they bring discredit upon the Armed Forces, such as dishonorable failure to pay debts, indecent exposure, fleeing the scene of an accident, bigamy, adultery, or pandering.

7.29.3.3. **Crimes and Offenses Not Capital.** Acts or omissions not chargeable under other articles of the UCMJ, but are crimes or offenses under federal statutes, are charged under Article 134; for example, counterfeiting. This crime is not specifically listed in the UCMJ but is still a violation of federal law. Also, if a military member commits an act in an area over which the military exercises exclusive or concurrent jurisdiction with the state and no UCMJ article or federal law prohibits the act—only the law of the state prohibits the act—then the Federal Assimilative Crimes Act allows the member to be tried by a court-martial under Article 134.

### 7.29.4. Offenses Related to War.

The UCMJ includes a number of offenses related to war. These offenses include misbehaving before the enemy, aiding the enemy, compelling surrender, improperly using countersigns, mishandling captured or abandoned property, committing misconduct as a prisoner of war, and making disloyal statements. Two especially egregious offenses related to war are misbehavior before the enemy and misconduct as a prisoner of war.

7.29.4.1. **Misbehavior Before the Enemy.** Article 99, UCMJ, provides that running away before the enemy and cowardly conduct are capital offenses punishable by death.

7.29.4.1.1. The term "enemy" (as used in "running away before the enemy") includes both civilian and military organized forces of the enemy in time of war and any opposing hostile bodies including rebellious mobs or bands of renegades. The term is not restricted to the enemy Government or their Armed Forces. If the misbehavior were caused by fear, the offense is charged as "cowardly conduct," rather than "running away." Whether a person is "before the enemy" is not a question of definite distance, but one of tactical relation.

7.29.4.1.2. The critical element in the offense of cowardly conduct is fear that results in the abandonment or refusal to perform one's duty. Fear is a natural apprehension going into battle, and the mere display of apprehension does not constitute this offense. Cowardice is misbehavior motivated by fear. Genuine or extreme illness or other disability at the time of the alleged misbehavior may be a defense.

7.29.4.2. **Misconduct as a Prisoner of War.** Article 105, UCMJ, recognizes two types of offenses arising in prisoner of war situations. One offense involves unauthorized conduct by an accused who secures favorable treatment to the detriment of other prisoners. The other offense prohibits maltreatment of a prisoner of war by a person in a position of authority. The purpose of this article is to protect all persons held as prisoners, whether military or civilian and regardless of their nationality.

7.29.5. **Insubordination:**

7.29.5.1. Insubordinate conduct may be expressed in many different ways and toward many different persons in the military community. Insubordination is judged both by the means used and the relative relationship in the military hierarchy of the parties involved.

7.29.5.2. Article 89, UCMJ, prohibits disrespectful acts or language used toward a superior commissioned officer in his or her capacity as an officer or as a private individual. Therefore, the superior commissioned officer does not need to be in the execution of his or her office at the time of the disrespectful behavior. However, it must be established that the accused knew the person against whom the acts or words were directed was the accused's superior commissioned officer. Disrespect may include neglecting the customary salute or showing a marked disdain, indifference, insolence, impertinence, undue familiarity, or other rudeness toward the superior officer. Truth is no defense. A superior commissioned officer is one who is superior in rank or command.

7.29.5.3. Article 91, UCMJ, similarly prohibits insubordinate conduct toward a warrant officer, NCO, or petty officer. However, unlike Article 89 violations, the insubordinate conduct must occur while the individual being disrespected is in the execution of his or her duties. In addition, Article 91 does not require a superior-subordinate relationship as an element of the prescribed offense and can only be committed by enlisted members.

7.29.5.4. Another form of insubordination involves striking or assaulting a superior officer. Article 90(1), UCMJ, prohibits assaults and batteries against superior commissioned officers in the execution of their duties. Article 91 prohibits similar conduct toward warrant officers, NCOs, and petty officers. "In the execution of his office" includes any act or service the officer is required or authorized to do by statute, regulation, orders, or customs. An essential element is the accused's knowledge that the person is a superior officer or superior warrant officer, NCO, or petty officer. In time of war, striking a superior commissioned officer can be a capital offense.

7.29.6. **Disobedience Offenses:**

7.29.6.1. **Disobeying a Superior Officer.** Article 90(2), UCMJ, prohibits the intentional or willful disobedience of the lawful orders of a superior officer.

7.29.6.2. **Failure to Obey Orders or Regulations.** Article 92, UCMJ, provides that members are subject to court-martial if they: (1) violate or fail to obey any lawful general order or regulation; (2) having knowledge of a lawful order issued by a member of the Armed Forces, which is their duty to obey, fail to obey the order; or (3) are derelict in the performance of their duties.

7.29.6.2.1. **Lawful General Order or Regulation.** This term relates to general orders or regulations that are properly published by the President, the Secretary of Defense, the Secretary of a military department, an officer having General Court-Martial jurisdiction, a general officer in command, or a commander superior to one of the former. (A squadron commander does not have the authority to issue general orders.) Once issued, a general order or regulation remains in effect even if a subsequent commander assumes command. Knowledge of the order is not an element of the offense, and a lack of knowledge is not a defense. Only those general orders or regulations that are "punitive" are enforceable under Article 92(1). A punitive order or regulation specifically states a member may be punished under the UCMJ if violated. Regulations that only supply general guidelines or advice for conducting military functions are not "punitive" and cannot be enforced under Article 92(1).

**7.29.6.2.2. Other Lawful Orders or Regulations.** This offense includes violations of written regulations that are not general regulations. The key requirements are that the accused had a duty to obey the order and had actual knowledge of the order. Such knowledge is usually proven through circumstantial evidence. The accused cannot be convicted of this offense merely because he or she should have known about the order. Failure to obey a wing-level directive that prohibits overnight guests in the dormitory is an example.

**7.29.6.2.3. Dereliction of Duty.** Dereliction of duty is comprised of three elements: (1) the accused had certain duties; (2) the accused knew or reasonably should have known of the duties; and (3) the accused was derelict in performing the duties, either by willfully failing to carry them out or by carrying them out in a negligent or culpably inefficient manner. "Willfully" means performing an act knowingly and purposely while specifically intending the natural and probable consequences of the act. "Negligently" means an act or omission of a person who is under a duty to use due care that exhibits a lack of this degree of care that a reasonably prudent person would have exercised under the same or similar circumstances. "Culpable inefficiency" means an inefficiency for which there is no reasonable or just excuse. Merely being inept in the performance of duty will not support a charge of dereliction of duty, that is, officers or enlisted members cannot be punished for inadequate performance if they make a good faith effort but fall short because of a lack of aptitude or ability. Such performance may be grounds for administrative demotion or administrative discharge, but is not a crime.

**7.29.7. Lawfulness of Orders:**

7.29.7.1. A lawful order must be: (1) reasonably in furtherance of or connected to military needs; (2) specific as to time and place and definite and certain in describing the thing or act to be done or omitted; and (3) not otherwise contrary to established law or regulation.

7.29.7.2. An order is in furtherance of, or connected to, military needs when it involves activities reasonably necessary to accomplish a military mission or to safeguard or promote the morale, discipline, and usefulness of command. Such an order may interfere with private rights or personal affairs, provided a valid military purpose exists. Furthermore, the dictates of a person's conscience, religion, or personal philosophy cannot justify or excuse disobedience of an otherwise lawful order. An order requiring the performance of a military duty or act may be inferred to be lawful and is disobeyed at the peril of the subordinate. This inference does not apply to a patently illegal order, such as one that directs the commission of a crime. An accused cannot be punished for disobeying or failing to obey an unlawful order.

**7.30. Conclusion:**

7.30.1. Air Force commanders must continuously evaluate force readiness and organizational efficiency and effectiveness. The inspection system provides the commander with a credible, independent assessment process to measure the capability of assigned forces. Inspectors benchmark best practices and exchange lessons learned and innovative methods.

7.30.2. Criminal activity and intelligence operations against the Air Force threaten national security. When Air Force personnel commit criminal offenses, illegal activity occurs on an Air Force installation, or Air Force security is breached or compromised, the Air Force must thoroughly investigate criminal allegations and intelligence threats and refer them to appropriate authorities for action.

7.30.3. The mission of the U.S. Air Force is to defend the U.S. and protect its interests through air, space and cyberspace. Many aspects of carrying out this job involve legal issues. This chapter provided information on the Air Force Inspection System, the Inspector General Complaints Program, individual standards, and punitive actions. All four areas are necessary to enable the Air Force to fulfill our national security obligations efficiently and effectively.

## Chapter 8

## MILITARY CUSTOMS, COURTESIES, AND PROTOCOL FOR SPECIAL EVENTS

*Section 8A—Overview*

### 8.1. Introduction.

Military customs and courtesies are proven traditions that explain what should and should not be done in many situations. They are acts of respect and courtesy when dealing with other people, and have evolved as a result of the need for order, as well as the mutual respect and sense of fraternity that exists among military personnel. Military customs and courtesies go beyond basic politeness; they play an extremely important role in building morale, esprit de corps, discipline, and mission effectiveness. Customs and courtesies ensure proper respect for the military members and build the foundation for self-discipline. Customs and courtesies are outlined in four sections: Symbols, Professional Behavior, Drill and Ceremony, and Honor Guard. Not all-inclusive, this chapter highlights many of the customs and courtesies that make the Air Force and its people special.

*Section 8B—Symbols*

### 8.2. The United States (U.S.) Flag.

*The flag of the U.S. has not been created by rhetorical sentences in declarations of independence and in bills of rights. It has been created by the experience of a great people, and nothing is written upon it that has not been written by their life. It is the embodiment, not of a sentiment, but of a history.*

President Woodrow Wilson

#### 8.2.1. Laws of the U.S. Flag.

The laws relating to the flag of the U.S. of America are outlined in detail in the United States Code. Title 4, United States Code, *Flag and Seal, Seat of Government, and the States*, Chapter 1, pertains to the U.S. flag; Chapter 2 pertains to the seal; Chapter 3 pertains to the seat of the Government; and Chapter 4 pertains to the States; and Title 36, United States Code, *Patriotic and National Observances, Ceremonies, and Organizations*, Chapter 1, pertains to patriotic customs and observances. Executive orders and Presidential proclamations supplement these laws. See AFI 34-1201, *Protocol*, and AFPAM 34-1202, *Guide to Protocol*, for Air Force-specific guidance on protocol, decorum, customs and courtesies for Air Force ceremonies, conferences, and social events.

#### 8.2.2. Sizes, Types, and Occasions for Display.

Sizes, types, and occasions for display of the flag of the U.S. are as follows:

8.2.2.1. **Installation Flag.** This flag is lightweight nylon bunting material, 8 feet 11 3/8 inches by 17 feet and is only displayed in fair weather from an installation flagstaff. This is the typical flag used at Air Force installations.

8.2.2.2. **All-Purpose Flags.** The following are types of authorized all-purpose flags:

8.2.2.2.1. **All-Weather (Storm) Flag.** This flag is a lightweight nylon bunting material, 5 feet by 9 feet 6 inches. Use this size as an alternate for the installation flag in inclement weather.

8.2.2.2.2. **"All-Purpose" Flag.** This flag is made of rayon bunting material, 3 feet by 4 feet. This size can be used for outdoor display with flags of friendly foreign nations, in arrival ceremonies for international dignitaries or to indicate joint occupancy of a building by two or more countries. Also, commonly used as the flag presented at retirements.

8.2.2.3. **Ceremonial Flag.** This flag is rayon or synthetic substitute material, 4 feet 4 inches by 5 feet 6 inches, trimmed on three edges with yellow rayon fringe 2 inches wide.

8.2.2.4. **Organizational Flag.** This flag is rayon or synthetic substitute material and is 3 feet by 4 feet. This flag is trimmed on three edges with rayon fringe 2 inches wide.

8.2.2.5. **Interment Flag.** This flag is 5 feet by 9 feet 6 inches of any approved material. The interment flag is authorized for deceased military personnel and for deceased veterans. This is the size flag used to drape over a closed casket. To receive a flag, fill out Veterans Affair Form 27-2008, *Application for U.S. Flag for Burial Purposes* (available at http://www.cem.va.gov/burial_benefits/burial_flags.asp), and take it to any Veterans Administration regional office or U.S. Post Office.

**8.2.2.6. Retirement Flag.** This flag may be either 3 feet by 4 feet or 3 feet by 5 feet. Members retiring from the Air Force are entitled to presentation of a U.S. flag. Base Organization and Maintenance funds are authorized for this purchase. For details, refer to AFI 65-601, Volume 1, *Budget Guidance and Procedures*.

**8.2.2.7. Automobile Flags.** There are two sizes of this U.S. flag, each with specific uses.

8.2.2.7.1. The 12- by 18-inch flag is trimmed on three sides with yellow fringe, 1 inch wide. This flag is displayed with the individual automobile flag of the President and Vice President of the U.S.

8.2.2.7.2. The 18- by 26-inch flag is trimmed on three sides with yellow fringe, 1 inch wide. This flag is displayed on government automobiles of individuals who are authorized positional colors.

**8.2.3. Time and Occasions for Display.**

The universal custom is to display the flag only from sunrise to sunset on buildings and on stationary flagstaffs in the open. However, when a patriotic effect is desired, the flag may be displayed 24 hours a day if properly illuminated during the hours of darkness. All flags should be illuminated when displayed with the flag of the U.S.

8.2.3.1. Air Force installations are authorized to fly one installation flag from reveille to retreat, normally on a flagstaff placed in front of the installation headquarters. Additional flagstaffs and flags are authorized adjacent to each dependent school on the installation. Written requests for exceptions to policy are sent to the appropriate major command vice commander for approval. The installation protocol office will maintain the approval memorandum.

8.2.3.2. The flag should be hoisted briskly and lowered ceremoniously.

8.2.3.3. The flag should not be displayed on days when the weather is inclement, except when an all-weather flag is used.

8.2.3.4. The flag should be displayed on all days, especially on New Year's Day, January 1; Inauguration Day, January 20; Martin Luther King Jr.'s birthday, third Monday in January; Lincoln's Birthday, February 12; Washington's Birthday, third Monday in February; Easter Sunday (variable); Mother's Day, second Sunday in May; Armed Forces Day, third Saturday in May; Memorial Day (half-staff until noon), the last Monday in May; Flag Day, June 14; Father's Day, third Sunday in June; Independence Day, July 4; National Korean War Veterans Armistice Day, July 27; Labor Day, first Monday in September; Constitution Day, September 17; Columbus Day, second Monday in October; Navy Day, October 27; Veterans Day, November 11; Thanksgiving Day, fourth Thursday in November; Christmas Day, December 25; and such other days as may be proclaimed by the President of the U.S.; the birthdays of States (date of admission); and on State holidays.

8.2.3.5. The flag should be displayed daily on or near the main administration building of every public institution.

8.2.3.6. The flag should be displayed during school days in or near every schoolhouse.

**8.2.4. Position and Manner of Display.**

The following rules will be observed:

8.2.4.1. When carried in a procession with another flag or flags, the flag of the U.S. should be either on the marching right; that is, to the flag's own right (to the far right of all others) (Figure 8.1), or, if there is a line of other flags, in front of the center line. This also applies when flags are displayed in a stationary position. Flags carried by Airmen are never at half-staff.

8.2.4.2. The U.S. flag, when displayed with another flag against a wall from crossed staffs, should be on the right, the flag's own right (observer's left), and the staff should be in front of the staff of the other flag (Figure 8.2).

8.2.4.3. When the U.S. flag is displayed from a flagstaff with other flags, the following applies:

8.2.4.3.1. When a number of flags are grouped and displayed from staffs radiating from a central point, and no foreign flags are in the display, the U.S. flag will be in the center and at the highest point of the group as shown in Figure 8.3.

8.2.4.3.2. When a number of flags are displayed from staffs set in a line, all staffs will be of the same height and same finial. The U.S. flag will be at the right, which is to the left of an observer facing the display (Figure 8.4). However, if no foreign national flags are involved in the display, the U.S. flag may be placed at the center of the line when displayed at a higher level than the other flags in the display (Figure 8.5).

**Figure 8.1. U.S. Flag Carried in Procession with Another Flag.**

**Figure 8.2. U.S. Flag and Another Flag Displayed with Crossed Staffs.**

**Figure 8.3. U.S. Flag Displayed with Other Flags Radiating from a Central Point.**

**Figure 8.4. U.S. Flag Displayed in a Line with Other Flags at Equal Height.**

8.2.4.3.3. When flags of two or more nations are displayed, they are flown from separate staffs of the same height. The flags should be of equal size. International usage prescribes the display of the flag of one nation equal to that of another nation in time of peace. The flags are displayed in a line, alphabetically, using the English alphabet, with the U.S. flag at its own right (the observer's left). When in North Atlantic Treaty Organization countries, North Atlantic Treaty Organization member country flags are displayed in French alphabetical order.

8.2.4.3.4. When the U.S. flag is displayed from a staff projecting horizontally or at an angle from the windowsill, balcony, or front of a building, the union (or blue field) of the flag should be placed at the peak of the staff (Figure 8.6).

8.2.4.3.5. When displayed either horizontally or vertically against a wall, the union should be uppermost and to the flag's own right; that is, to the observer's left (Figure 8.7). When displayed in a window, the flag should be displayed in the same way, with the union to the left of observer in the street (Figure 8.8).

**Figure 8.5. U.S. Flag Displayed in a Line with Other Flags at Lower Level.**

**Figure 8.6. U.S. Flag Projected from a Building**

**Figure 8.7. U.S. Flag Positioned Vertically on Wall or Window**

**Figure 8.8. U.S. Flag Positioned Horizontally on Wall or Window.**

8.2.4.3.6. When the flag is displayed over the middle of the street, the flag should be suspended vertically with the union to the north on an east and west street or to the east on a north and south street.

8.2.4.3.7. When used on a speaker's platform, the flag, if displayed flat, should be displayed above and behind the speaker (Figure 8.9). When displayed from a staff in a church or public auditorium, the U.S. flag should hold the position of superior prominence and in the position of honor at the clergyman's or speaker's right as he or she faces the audience. Any other flag so displayed should be placed on the left of the clergyman or speaker or to the right of the audience (Figure 8.10).

**Figure 8.9. United States Flag Displayed Flat at Speaker's Platform**

**Figure 8.10. United States Flag Displayed from a Staff on Stage with Speaker.**

8.2.4.3.8. When the flag is suspended across a corridor or lobby in a building with only one main entrance, the flag should be suspended vertically with the union of the flag to the observer's left upon entering. If the building has more than one main entrance, the flag should be suspended vertically near the center of the corridor or lobby with the union to the north when entrances are to the east and west or to the east when entrances are to the north and south. If there are entrances in more than two directions, the union should be to the east. This includes aircraft hangars.

8.2.4.3.9. When three flag staffs are positioned outside a building, there may be two display options. If the flag staffs are in a straight line, then the flags should be of the same height with the U.S. flag to its own right. Use the building looking out to the flags as the point of reference for flag placement when flags are in line. If the flag is positioned on the center staff, then the center staff must be higher than the other two staffs.

8.2.4.3.10. On a closed casket, place the flag lengthwise with the union at the head and over the left shoulder of the deceased (Figure 8.11). When a full-couch casket is opened, remove the flag, fold to the triangular shape of a cocked hat, and place in the lid at the head end of the casket and just above the decedent's left shoulder. When a half-couch casket is opened, fold the flag on the lower half of the casket in the same relative position as when displayed full length on a closed casket. Do not lower the flag into the grave, and do not allow the flag to touch the ground. The interment flag may be given to the next of kin at the conclusion of the interment.

8.2.4.3.11. Drape the flag left to right when posted and also when used in official photographs. The blue field is on top with stripes running left to right.

8.2.4.3.12. When painted or displayed on an aircraft or vehicle, the union is toward the front and the stripes trail.

8.2.5. **Respect for the U.S. Flag.**

No disrespect should be shown to the U.S. flag; the flag will not be dipped to any person or thing. Regimental colors, state flags, and

**Figure 8.11. U.S. Flag Draped Over a Closed Casket.**

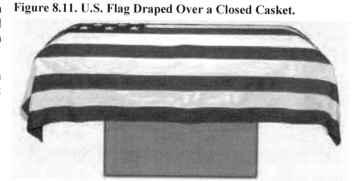

organizational or institutional flags are always dipped as a mark of respect to the U.S. flag. However, the Air Force flag and organizational flags will be dipped as appropriate. Military members will render the military salute as appropriate. At no time will a foreign national flag be dipped.

8.2.5.1. The flag should never be displayed with union down, except as a signal of dire distress in instances of extreme danger to life or property.

8.2.5.2. The flag should never touch anything beneath it, such as the ground, the floor, water, or merchandise. The flag should never be used as the covering for a statue or monument, although the flag could form a distinctive feature in a ceremony of the unveiling of a statue or monument.

8.2.5.3. The flag should never be carried flat or horizontally, but always aloft and free.

8.2.5.4. The flag should never be used as wearing apparel, bedding, or drapery. The flag should never be festooned, drawn back, up, or in folds, but always allowed to fall free (for example, the flag should not be used to cover a speaker's podium, drape the front of a platform, or for other decoration. A proper substitute is bunting of blue, white, and red, always arranged with the blue above, the white in the middle, and the red below).

8.2.5.5. The flag should never be fastened, displayed, used, or stored in such a manner as to permit the flag to be easily torn, soiled, or damaged.

8.2.5.6. The flag should never be used as a covering for a ceiling.

8.2.5.7. The flag should never have placed upon it, nor on any part of it, nor attached to it any mark, insignia, letter, word, figure, design, picture, or drawing of any nature.

8.2.5.8. The flag should never be used as a receptacle for receiving, holding, carrying, or delivering anything.

8.2.5.9. The flag should never be used for advertising purposes or be embroidered on such articles as cushions or handkerchiefs. Moreover, the flag should not be printed or otherwise impressed on paper napkins or boxes or anything that is designed for temporary use and discard. Advertising signs should not be fastened to a staff or halyard from which the flag is flown.

8.2.5.10. No part of the flag should be used as a costume or athletic uniform. However, a flag patch may be affixed to the uniform of military personnel, firemen, policemen, and members of patriotic organizations. A lapel flag pin, being a replica of the flag, should be worn on the left lapel near the heart. Patches worn on uniforms depicting the U.S. flag should be worn on the left shoulder, with the union to the viewer's left.

8.2.5.11. The flag should not be displayed on a float in a parade except from a staff.

8.2.5.12. The flag should not be draped over the hood, top, sides, or back of a vehicle, railroad train, or boat. When the flag is displayed on an automobile, the staff should be fixed firmly to the chassis or clamped to the right fender.

8.2.5.13. No other flag or pennant should be placed above or, if on the same level, to the right (observer's left) of the U.S. flag, except during church services conducted by naval chaplains at sea when the church pennant may be flown above the flag during church services for the personnel of the Navy.

8.2.6. **Display of the U.S. Flag at Half-staff.**

The U.S. flag is flown at half-staff throughout the U.S., territories and possessions on all Department of Defense buildings, grounds, and naval vessels on several days throughout the year according to DoDI 1005.06, *Display of the National Flag at Half-Staff* (Figures 8.12 and 8.13).

**Figure 8.12. U.S. Flag at Full Staff.**          **Figure 8.13. U.S. Flag at Half-staff.**

8.2.6.1. The following days apply:

8.2.6.1.1. On Memorial Day, fly the flag at half-staff until noon, then raise to the top of the staff.

8.2.6.1.2. On Peace Officers Memorial Day, 15 May, unless that day is also Armed Forces Day.

8.2.6.1.3. On Patriot Day, 11 September.

8.2.6.1.4. On National Pearl Harbor Remembrance Day, 7 December.

8.2.6.1.5. Each year in honor of the National Fallen Firefighters Memorial Service according to Public Law 107-51. This date is usually the first Sunday in October and is announced annually by Presidential Proclamation.

8.2.6.1.6. On the death of individuals in accordance with AFI 34-1201.

8.2.6.1.7. When so directed by the President of the U.S. or the Secretary of Defense.

8.2.6.2. The responsible military commander ensures the procedures for flying the flag at half-staff are executed as follows:

8.2.6.2.1. The term "half-staff" means the position of the flag when the flag is one-half the distance between the top and bottom of the staff.

8.2.6.2.2. When flown at half-staff, first hoist the flag to the peak for an instant and then lower to the half-staff position. Raise the flag again to the peak position before lowering the flag for the end of the day.

8.2.6.3. The flag is flown at half-staff outside the U.S. on Department of Defense buildings, grounds, and naval vessels even if another nation's flag is flown full staff next to the U.S. flag.

8.2.6.4. All flags displayed with the U.S. flag are flown at half-staff when the U.S. flag is flown at half-staff, with the exception of foreign national flags, unless the foreign country has granted permission for their flag to also be at half-staff.

8.2.6.5. The Heads of Department of Defense components may direct that the flag be flown at half-staff on buildings, grounds, or naval vessels under their jurisdiction on occasions when they consider the flag be flown at half-staff proper and appropriate. Within the Air Force, this authority is delegated to the installation commander. Any time an installation commander decides to fly the flag at half-staff based on this local authority for a local death, state the reason on the base marquees to avoid confusion.

8.2.7. **Care and Disposition of U.S. Flags.**

Exercise extreme care to ensure proper handling and cleaning of soiled flags. Professionally mend a torn flag, but destroy a badly torn or tattered flag. Title 4, U.S. Code, Chapter 1, states: "The flag, when it is in such condition that it is no longer a fitting emblem for display, should be destroyed in a dignified way, preferably by burning." There may be instances when a flag is retired from service and preserved because of its historical significance. In this case, the unit must request disposition instructions from the proper authority, such as the installation honor guard or protocol office.

8.2.8. **How to Obtain a Flag Flown Over the Capitol.**

Constituents may arrange to purchase flags flown over the Capitol by getting in touch with their Senator or Representative. A certificate signed by the Architect of the Capitol accompanies each flag. Ordering procedures are outlined at the following web site: www.aoc.gov/flags.

**8.3. Department of the Air Force Seal:**

8.3.1. **Description.**

**Figure 8.14. Air Force Seal**

The official Air Force colors of ultramarine blue and Air Force yellow are reflected in the Air Force Seal; the circular background is ultramarine blue, and the trim is Air Force yellow (Figure 8.14). The 13 white stars represent the original 13 colonies. The Air Force yellow numerals under the shield stand for 1947, the year the Department of the Air Force was established. The band encircling the whole design is white edged in Air Force yellow with black lettering reading "Department of the Air Force" on the top and "U.S. of America" on the bottom. Centered on the circular background is the Air Force Coat of Arms, consisting of the crest and shield.

8.3.1.1. The crest consists of the eagle, wreath, and cloud form. The American bald eagle symbolizes the U.S. air power, and appears in natural colors. The wreath under the eagle is made up of six alternate folds of metal (white, representing silver) and light blue. This repeats the metal and color used in the shield. The white clouds behind the eagle denote the start of a new sky.

8.3.1.2. The shield, directly below the eagle and wreath, is divided horizontally into two parts by a nebular line representing clouds. The top part bears an Air Force yellow thunderbolt with flames in natural color that shows striking power through the use of aerospace. The thunderbolt consists of an Air Force yellow vertical twist with three natural color flames on each end crossing a pair of horizontal wings with eight lightning bolts. The background of the top part is light blue representing the sky. The lower part is white representing metal silver.

### 8.3.2. **Authorized and Unauthorized Uses of the Seal and Coat of Arms.**

Title 18, United States Code, Section 506, *Seals of Departments or Agencies*, protects the Air Force seal from unauthorized use. Falsely making, forging, counterfeiting, mutilating, or altering the seal or knowingly using or possessing with fraudulent intent any such altered seal is punishable by law. AFMAN 33-326, *Preparing Official Communications,* Attachment 2, outlines the authorized users and uses of the seal or any part thereof. The Coat of Arms is authorized for unofficial use when approved by the Secretary of the Air Force of Public Affairs (SAF/PA). This approving authority was delegated to the Air Force Public Affairs Agency (AFPAA), a Field Operating Agency of SAF/PA.

### 8.4. **Official Air Force Symbol:**

8.4.1. The Air Force Symbol (Figure 8.15) was designated the official symbol of the U.S. Air Force on 5 May 2004. The Symbol honors the heritage of our past and represents the promise of our future. Furthermore, the symbol retains the core elements of our Air Corps heritage—the "Arnold" wings and star with circle—and modernizes them to reflect our air and space force of today and tomorrow.

**Figure 8.15. Air Force Symbol**

8.4.2. The Symbol has two main parts. In the upper half, the stylized wings represent the stripes of our strength—our enlisted men and women. The wings are drawn with great angularity to emphasize our swiftness and power and are divided into six sections which represent our distinctive capabilities—air and space superiority, global attack, rapid global mobility, precision engagement, information superiority, and agile combat support.

8.4.3. In the lower half are a sphere, a star, and three diamonds. The sphere within the star represents the globe. Moreover, the symbol reminds us of our obligation to secure our Nation's freedom with global vigilance, reach, and power. The globe also reminds us of our challenge as an expeditionary force to respond rapidly to crises and to provide decisive air and space power worldwide.

8.4.4. The area surrounding the sphere takes the shape of a star. The star has many meanings. The five points represent the components of our one force and family—our Regular Air Force, civilians, Guard, Reserve, and retirees. The star symbolizes space as the high ground of our nation's air and space force. The rallying symbol in all our wars, the star also represents our officer corps, central to our combat leadership.

8.4.5. The star is framed with three diamonds that represent our core values—integrity first, service before self, and excellence in all we do. The elements come together to form one symbol that presents two powerful images—at once an eagle, the emblem of our Nation; and a medal, representing valor in service to our Nation.

8.4.6. The Air Force Symbol is a registered trademark (registration number 2,767,190) and must be protected against unauthorized use or alterations to approved versions. Approved versions of the Symbol are available for download on the Air Force Portal, under the "Library & Resources" tab. Instructions for the proper use and display of the Symbol can be found in AFI 35-114, *Air Force Branding and Trademark Licensing Program*, in Department of Defense's *Important Information and Guidelines About the Use of Department of Defense Seals, Logos, Insignia, and Service Medals*, and at **www.trademark.af.mil**. Department of Defense employees and their immediate families may use the Symbol on personal items such as printed materials, clothing, literature, briefings, coins, web sites, and food; however, use must adhere to the resources above. Furthermore, these personal items must not be used in advertising, intended for personal gain, made available for sale, or create perceived/potential endorsements. Any individual, group, organization, or company wishing to use the Symbol beyond the scope of "personal items" should be directed to the Air Force Branding and Trademark Licensing Office.

*Section 8C—Professional Behavior*

### 8.5. Respect for the Flag.

The procedures to use when showing respect to the flag and the national anthem include:

8.5.1. When outdoors, all personnel in uniform, except those in formation must face the flag and salute during the raising and lowering of the flag. Upon the first note of the national anthem or "To the Colors," all personnel in uniform who are not in formation will stand at attention, face the flag (or the sound of the music, if the flag is not visible), and salute. Hold the salute until the last note of the national anthem or "To the Colors" is played.

8.5.2. All vehicles in motion will pull to the side of the road and stop. All occupants sit quietly until the last note of the national anthem or "To the Colors" has played.

8.5.3. When in civilian clothes, face the flag (or the sound of the music if the flag is not visible) and stand at attention with the right hand placed over the heart or render a salute.

8.5.4. If indoors during retreat or reveille, there is no need to stand or salute. However, everyone must stand during the playing of the national anthem before a showing of a movie while in the base theater. When listening to a radio or watching television, no specific action is necessary. Additionally, a folded flag is considered cased; therefore, a salute is not necessary.

### 8.6. Saluting.

The salute is a courteous exchange of greetings, with the junior member always saluting the senior member first. A salute is also rendered to the flag as a sign of respect. Any Airman, NCO, or officer recognizing a need to salute or a need to return a salute may do so anywhere at any time. When returning or rendering an individual salute, the head and eyes are turned toward the flag or person saluted. Guidance when exchanging salutes includes:

8.6.1. **Outdoors.**

Salutes are exchanged upon recognition between officers or warrant officers and enlisted members of the Armed Forces when they are in uniform. Saluting outdoors means salutes are exchanged when the persons involved are outside of a building. For example, if a person is on a porch, a covered sidewalk, a bus stop, a covered or open entryway, or a reviewing stand, the salute will be exchanged with a person on the sidewalk outside of the structure or with a person approaching or in the same structure. This applies both on and off military installations. The junior member should initiate the salute in time to allow the senior officer to return it. To prescribe an exact distance for all circumstances is not practical; however, good judgment should dictate when salutes are exchanged. Superiors carrying articles in both hands need not return the salute, but should nod in return or verbally acknowledge the salute. If the junior member is carrying articles in both hands, verbal greetings should be exchanged. Also, use the same procedures when greeting an officer of a foreign nation. Use these procedures in:

8.6.1.1. **Formation.** Members do not salute or return a salute unless given the command to do so. The person in charge salutes and acknowledges salutes for the whole formation.

8.6.1.2. **Groups, But Not in Formation.** When a senior officer approaches, the first individual noticing the officer calls the group to attention. All members face the officer and salute. If the officer addresses an individual or the group, all remain at attention (unless otherwise ordered) until the end of the conversation, at which time they salute the officer.

8.6.1.3. **Public Gatherings.** Salutes between individuals are not required in public gatherings, such as sporting events, meetings, or when a salute would be inappropriate or impractical.

8.6.1.4. **Moving Military Vehicles.** Exchange of salutes between military pedestrians (including gate sentries) and officers in moving military vehicles is not mandatory. However, when officer passengers are readily identifiable (for example, officers in appropriately marked staff vehicles), the salute must be rendered.

8.6.1.5. **The Presence of Civilians.** Persons in uniform may salute civilians. The President of the U.S., as Commander in Chief of the Armed Forces, is always accorded the honor of a salute. AFI 34-1201 provides additional guidance. In addition, if the exchange of salutes is otherwise appropriate, customs encourage military members in civilian clothes to exchange salutes upon recognition.

8.6.1.6. **A Work Detail.** In a work detail, individual workers do not salute. The person in charge salutes for the entire detail.

8.6.1.7. **Military Funeral.** When at a military funeral in uniform, salute the caisson or hearse as it passes and the casket as it is carried by your position. You also salute during the firing of volleys and the playing of "Taps."

**8.6.2. Indoors.**

Except for formal reporting, salutes are not rendered.

**8.7. Military Etiquette.**

Etiquette is defined as common, everyday courtesy. The military world, like the civilian world, functions more smoothly and pleasantly when members practice good manners.

8.7.1. Simple things like saying "please" and "thank you" help the organization run smoother because people respond more enthusiastically when asked in a courteous manner to do something. They also appreciate knowing their efforts are recognized when told "thank you."

8.7.2. One of the most valuable habits anyone can develop is to be on time for appointments. Granted, sometimes a person cannot avoid being late. When this happens, the best course of action is to call ahead or to reschedule the appointment. Do not keep others waiting.

8.7.3. Address civil service employees properly. As a rule, address them appropriately as "Mr.," "Mrs.," "Miss," or "Ms." and their last name, unless requested to do otherwise. Always address a superior formally. This is especially important in most foreign countries where using first names on the job is much more limited than in the U.S.

8.7.4. Don't gossip. A discussion of personal habits, problems, and activities (real or rumored) of others often results in quarrels and disputes among people who work together. The morale of any unit may suffer because of feuds that arise from gossip. The best policy is not to gossip and to discourage others from gossiping.

8.7.5. Use proper telephone etiquette. Always be polite and identify yourself and your organization. When an individual is not available to take a call, ask: "May I take a message?" or "Is there something I may help you with?" If taking a message to return a call, write down the individual's name, organization, telephone number, the message, and then pass this information along to the intended recipient.

8.7.6. Do not lean or sit on desks. Also, do not lean back in a chair or put feet on desks. This type of conduct doesn't present a professional military image.

8.7.7. In general, use common sense, be considerate of other people, and insist your subordinates do the same.

**8.8. Courtesies to Other Services:**

8.8.1. The collective efforts of the Air Force, Army, Navy, Marines, and Coast Guard provide for the defense of the country against aggression. All Services are part of the military team; therefore, extend the same military courtesies to members of the other Services. While there is a friendly natural rivalry between the Services, military courtesies among Services remain the same. Thus, the members of the other Services are as much comrades-in-arms as are any Airmen.

8.8.2. This is equally true of the friendly armed forces of the United Nations. Salute all commissioned officers and pay the same respect to the national anthems and flags of other nations as rendered the U.S. national anthem and flag. While not necessary to learn the identifying insignia of the military grades of all nations, you should learn the insignia of the most frequently contacted nations, particularly during an overseas assignment or deployment.

**8.9. Respect and Recognition:**

**8.9.1. Common Acts of Courtesy.**

Common acts of courtesy among all Air Force personnel aid in maintaining discipline and promoting the smooth conduct of affairs in the military establishment. When courtesy falters within a unit, discipline ceases to function, and accomplishing the mission is endangered. Many of the Air Force courtesies involve the salute. There are, however, many other courtesies commonly extended to superiors, subordinates, and working associates. Some acts of courtesies include:

8.9.1.1. Giving the senior person, enlisted or commissioned, the position of honor when walking, riding, or sitting with him or her at all times. The junior person takes the position to the senior's left.

8.9.1.2. When reporting to an officer indoors, knock once and enter when told to do so. Upon entering, march to approximately two paces from the officer or desk, halt, salute, and report in this manner: "Sir (Ma'am), Airman Smith reports as ordered," or "Sir (Ma'am), Airman Smith reports." When the conversation is completed, execute a sharp salute and hold until the officer acknowledges the salute, then perform the appropriate facing movements and depart.

8.9.1.3. Unless told otherwise, rise and stand at attention when a senior official enters or departs a room. If more than one person is present, the person who first sees the officer calls the group to attention. However, if an officer is already in the room who is equal to or has a higher rank than the officer entering the room, do not call the room to attention.

8.9.1.4. Military personnel enter automobiles and small boats in reverse order of rank. Juniors will enter a vehicle first and take their appropriate seat on the senior's left. The senior officer will be the last to enter the vehicle and the first to leave.

8.9.2. **Terms of Address.** For the proper terms of address, refer to Figure 8.16.

**Figure 8.16. Terms of Address.**

| Rank | Abbreviations | Terms of Address |
|---|---|---|
| **SNCO Tier** | | |
| Chief Master Sergeant of the Air Force | CMSAF | Chief Master Sergeant of the Air Force or Chief |
| Chief Master Sergeant | CMSgt | Chief Master Sergeant or Chief |
| Senior Master Sergeant | SMSgt | Senior Master Sergeant or Sergeant |
| Master Sergeant | MSgt | Master Sergeant or Sergeant |
| **NCO Tier** | | |
| Technical Sergeant | TSgt | Technical Sergeant or Sergeant |
| Staff Sergeant | SSgt | Staff Sergeant or Sergeant |
| **Airman Tier** | | |
| Senior Airman | SrA | Senior Airman or Airman |
| Airman First Class | A1C | Airman First Class or Airman |
| Airman | Amn | Airman |
| Airman Basic | AB | Airman Basic or Airman |

*Section 8D—Drill and Ceremony*

**8.10. Flag Ceremonies:**

8.10.1. **Reveille.**

The signal for the start of the official duty day is the reveille. Because the time for the start of the duty day varies between bases, the commander designates the specified time for reveille. If the commander desires, a reveille ceremony may accompany the raising of the flag. This ceremony takes place after sunrise near the base flagstaff. In the unit area, reveille is normally held using the formation of squadron in line. This formation is used when a reveille ceremony is not held at the base flagstaff. Procedures for reveille include:

8.10.1.1. Shortly before the specified time, Airmen march to a pre-designated position near the base flagstaff, halt, face toward the flagstaff, and dress. The flag security detail arrives at the flagstaff at this time and remains at attention.

8.10.1.2. The unit commander (or senior participant) commands "Parade, REST."

8.10.1.3. At the specified time for reveille, the unit commander commands "SOUND REVEILLE." The flag detail assumes the position of attention, moves to the flagstaff, and attaches the flag to the halyards.

8.10.1.4. After reveille is played, the unit commander commands "Squadron, ATTENTION" and "Present, ARMS" and then faces the flagstaff and executes present arms. On this signal, the national anthem or "To the Colors" is sounded.

8.10.1.5. On the first note of the national anthem or "To the Colors," the flag security detail begins to raise the flag briskly. The senior member of the detail holds the flag to keep the flag from touching the ground.

8.10.1.6. The unit commander holds the salute until the last note of the national anthem or "To the Colors" is played. Then he or she executes order arms, faces about, and commands "Order, ARMS." The Airmen are then marched back to the dismissal area.

8.10.2. **Raising the Flag:**

8.10.2.1. When practical, a detail consisting of one NCO and two Airmen hoists the flag. This detail should carry sidearms if the special equipment of the guard includes sidearms.

8.10.2.2. The detail forms in line with the NCO carrying the flag in the center. The detail then marches to the flagstaff and halts, and the flag is attached to the halyards. The flag is always raised and lowered from the leeward side of the flagstaff. The two Airmen attend the halyards, taking a position facing the staff to hoist the flag without entangling the halyards.

8.10.2.3. The NCO continues to hold the flag until hoisted clear of his or her grasp, taking particular care that no portion of the flag touches the ground. When the flag is clear of the grasp, the NCO comes to attention and executes present arms.

8.10.2.4. On the last note of the national anthem, "To the Colors," or after the flag has been hoisted to the staff head, all members of the detail execute order arms on command of the senior member. The halyards are then secured to the cleat of the staff or, if appropriate, the flag is lowered to half-staff and the halyards are secured. The detail is formed again and then marches to the dismissal area.

8.10.3. **Retreat Ceremony:**

8.10.3.1. The retreat ceremony serves a twofold purpose: signals the end of the official duty day and serves as a ceremony for paying respect to the U.S. flag. Because the time for the end of the duty day varies, the commander designates the time for the retreat ceremony. The retreat ceremony may take place at the squadron area, on the base parade ground, or near the base flagstaff. If conducted within the squadron area, the ceremony usually does not involve a parade. If conducted at the base parade ground, retreat may be part of the parade ceremony. For retreat ceremonies conducted at the base flagstaff, the units participating may be formed in line or massed, depending on the size and number of units and the space available.

8.10.3.2. Shortly before the specified time for retreat, the band and Airmen participating in the ceremony are positioned facing the flagstaff and dressed. If marching to and from the flagstaff, the band precedes the Airmen participating in the ceremony.

8.10.3.3. If the band and Airmen march to the flagstaff, a flag security detail also marches to the flagstaff and halts, and the senior member gives the command "Parade, REST" to the security detail.

8.10.3.4. As soon as the Airmen are dressed, the commander commands "Parade, REST." The commander then faces the flagstaff, assumes the position of the Airmen, and waits for the specified time for retreat.

8.10.3.5. At the specified time, the commander orders the bandleader to sound retreat by commanding "SOUND RETREAT."

8.10.3.6. The band plays retreat. If a band is not present, recorded music is played over the base public address system. During the playing of retreat, junior members of the flag security detail assume the position of attention and move to the flagstaff to arrange the halyards for proper lowering of the flag. Once the halyards are arranged, the junior members of the flag security detail execute parade rest in unison.

8.10.3.7. Uniformed military members not assigned to a formation face the flag (if visible) or the music and assume the position of parade rest on the first note of retreat. Upon completion of retreat, they should assume the position of attention and salute on the first note of the national anthem or "To the Colors."

8.10.3.8. After the band plays retreat, the commander faces about and commands "Squadron (Group, etc.), ATTENTION."

8.10.3.9. The commander then commands "Present, ARMS." As soon as the Airmen execute present arms, the commander faces to the front and also assumes present arms. The members of the flag security detail execute present arms on command of the commander.

8.10.3.10. The band plays the national anthem, or the bugler plays "To the Colors." The junior members of the flag security detail lower the flag slowly and with dignity.

8.10.3.11. The commander executes order arms when the last note of the national anthem or "To the Colors" is played and the flag is securely grasped. The commander faces about, gives the Airmen "Order, ARMS," and then faces to the front.

8.10.3.12. The flag security detail folds the flag as illustrated in Figure 8.17. The senior member of the detail remains at attention while the flag is folded unless needed to control the flag.

8.10.3.13. When the flag is folded, the flag security detail, with the senior member on the right and the flag bearer in the center, marches to a position three paces from the commander. (**Note:** In an informal ceremony, the detail marches three paces from the officer of the day.) The senior member salutes and reports "Sir (Ma'am), the flag is secured." The commander returns the salute, and the flag security detail marches away. The Airmen are then marched to their areas and dismissed.

**8.17. Folding the U.S. Flag**

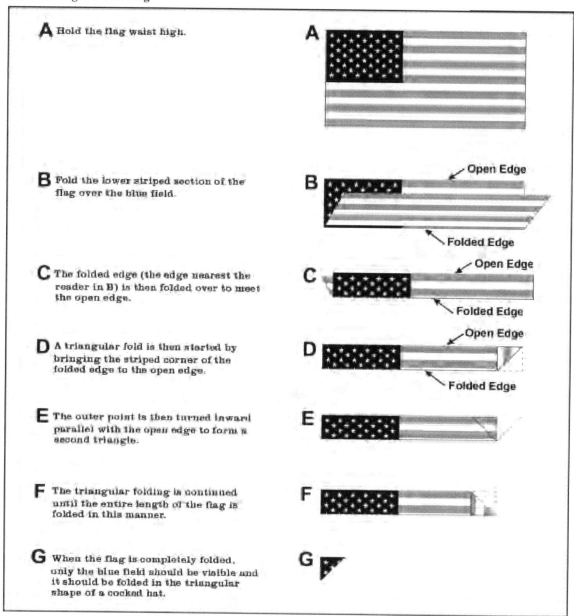

**A** Hold the flag waist high.

**B** Fold the lower striped section of the flag over the blue field.

**C** The folded edge (the edge nearest the reader in B) is then folded over to meet the open edge.

**D** A triangular fold is then started by bringing the striped corner of the folded edge to the open edge.

**E** The outer point is then turned inward parallel with the open edge to form a second triangle.

**F** The triangular folding is continued until the entire length of the flag is folded in this manner.

**G** When the flag is completely folded, only the blue field should be visible and it should be folded in the triangular shape of a cocked hat.

**8.10.4. Lowering the Flag:**

8.10.4.1. When practical, the persons lowering the flag should be one NCO and three Airmen for the all-purpose flag and one NCO and five Airmen for the installation flag.

8.10.4.2. The detail is formed and marched to the flagstaff. The halyards are detached and attended from the leeward side.

8.10.4.3. On the first note of the national anthem or "To the Colors," the members of the detail not lowering the flag execute present arms. The lowering of the flag is coordinated with the playing of the music so the two are completed at the same time.

8.10.4.4. The senior member commands the detail "Order, ARMS" when the flag is low enough to be received. If at half-staff, briskly hoist the flag to the staff head while retreat is sounded and then lower on the first note of the national anthem or "To the Colors."

8.10.4.5. The flag is detached from the halyards and folded. The halyards are secured to the staff.

**8.10.5. Pledge of Allegiance to the Flag.**

The Pledge of Allegiance to the flag, "I pledge allegiance to the flag of the U.S. of America and to the Republic for which it stands, one Nation under God, indivisible, with liberty and justice for all" should be rendered by standing at attention and facing the flag. When not in uniform, persons should remove any non-religious headdress with their right hand and hold it at the left shoulder, with the hand being over the heart. Persons in uniform should remain silent, face the flag, and render the military salute if outdoors and indoors if in formation and wearing appropriate headdress. If indoors and without headdress, military members should stand at attention, remain silent, and face the flag. Military members in uniform do not recite the Pledge of Allegiance to the flag.

**8.10.6. Flag Folding Ceremony.**

Although several flag folding ceremony options are offered by various national interest groups, these are not official Air Force ceremonies. According to Title 4, United States Code, no specific meaning is assigned to the folds of the flag. The Air Force developed a script that provides a historical perspective on the flag. There are no ceremonies in the Air Force requiring a script to be read when the flag is folded. However, when a flag folding ceremony is desired and conducted by Air Force personnel at any location, on or off an installation, this script is the only one that may be used. Refer back to Figure 8.17 for the proper method for folding the U.S. flag and Figure 8.18 for a copy of this script.

**Figure 8.18. Flag Folding Ceremony.**

---

**Flag Folding Ceremony**

**Air Force Script**

For more than 200 years, the American flag has been the symbol of our Nation's unity, as well as a source of pride and inspiration for millions of citizens.

Born on June 14, 1777, the Second Continental Congress determined that the flag of the U.S. be 13 stripes, alternating between 7 red and 6 white; and that the union be 13 stars, white in a blue field representing a new constellation. (1)

Between 1777 and 1960, the shape and design of the flag evolved into the flag presented before you today. The 13 horizontal stripes represent the original 13 colonies, while the stars represent the 50 states of the Union. The colors of the flag are symbolic as well; red symbolizes hardiness and valor; white signifies purity and innocence; and blue represents vigilance, perseverance, and justice. (1)

Traditionally, a symbol of liberty, the American flag has carried the message of freedom, and inspired Americans, both at home and abroad.

In 1814, Francis Scott Key was so moved at seeing the Stars and Stripes waving after the British shelling of Baltimore's Fort McHenry that he wrote the words to The Star Spangled Banner. (2)

In 1892 the flag inspired Francis Bellamy to write the "Pledge of Allegiance," our most famous flag salute and patriotic oath. (2)

In July 1969 the American flag was "flown" in space when Neil Armstrong planted it on the surface of the moon. (2)

Today, our flag flies on constellations of Air Force satellites that circle our globe, and on the fin flash of our aircraft in harm's way in every corner of the world. Indeed, it flies in the heart of every Airman who serves our great Nation. The sun never sets on our U.S. Air Force, nor on the flag we so proudly cherish. (2)

Since 1776, no generation of Americans has been spared the responsibility of defending freedom… Today's Airmen remain committed to preserving the freedom that others won for us for generations to come.

By displaying the flag and giving it a distinctive fold we show respect to the flag and express our gratitude to those individuals who fought, and continue to fight for freedom, at home and abroad. Since the dawn of the 20th century, Airmen have proudly flown the flag in every major conflict on lands and skies around the world. It is their responsibility…our responsibility…to continue to protect and preserve the rights, privileges, and freedoms that we, as Americans, enjoy today.

The U.S. flag represents who we are. It stands for the freedom we all share and the pride and patriotism we feel for our country. We cherish its legacy as a beacon of hope to one and all. Long may it wave.

*Legend:*

(1) *From a report Secretary of Congress Robert Thompson wrote to define the Seal of our Nation (1777).*

(2) *Based upon historical facts.*

---

**8.11. Air Force Ceremonies.**

The Air Force has many different types of ceremonies that are unique customs of our military profession. Some of these ceremonies are very formal and elaborate, while others are quite simple and personal. Award, decoration, promotion, reenlistment, and retirement ceremonies are a few of the most common within the Air Force.

### 8.11.1. Award Ceremony.

An award ceremony affords an opportunity to recognize a member's accomplishments. The commander or other official determines whether to present an award at a formal ceremony or to present it informally. Many units present awards during commander's call. Because there are no specific guidelines for an award presentation, commanders and supervisors must ensure the presentation method reflects the significance of the award.

### 8.11.2. Decoration Ceremony:

**8.11.2.1. Basic Guidelines.** Decoration ceremonies formally recognize service members for meritorious service, outstanding achievement, or heroism. A formal and dignified ceremony is necessary to preserve the integrity and value of decorations. When possible, the commander should personally present the decoration. Regardless of where the presentation is conducted, the ceremony is conducted at the earliest possible date after approval of the decoration. All military participants and attendees should wear the uniform specified by the host. If in doubt, the Service Dress rather than the Airman Battle Uniform is recommended. At the commander's discretion, a photographer may take pictures during the ceremony.

**8.11.2.2. Procedures.** Although decoration ceremonies may differ slightly from one unit to another, they normally begin by announcing "ATTENTION TO ORDERS." All members in attendance stand at attention and face the commander and the recipient. The commander's assistant reads the citation while the commander and recipient stand at attention. After the citation is read, the commander and recipient face each other, and the commander affixes the medal on the individual's uniform. The commander next extends personal congratulations and a handshake while presenting the decoration certificate. The recipient salutes the commander, and the commander returns the salute to conclude the formal part of the ceremony. Attendees are then invited to personally congratulate the recipient and enjoy any refreshments provided.

### 8.11.3. Promotion Ceremony:

**8.11.3.1. Basic Guidelines.** Promotions are significant events in the lives of military people. Commanders and supervisors are responsible for ensuring their personnel receive proper recognition. Many of the guidelines for promotion ceremonies are the same as for decoration ceremonies. Because most promotions are effective the first day of the month, the promotion ceremony is customarily conducted on the last duty day before the promotion. Some bases hold a base-wide promotion for all promotees; many organizations have operating instructions detailing how promotion ceremonies will be conducted.

**8.11.3.2. Procedures.** The national anthem, reaffirmation of the Oath of Enlistment, and the Air Force Song are options that add decorum to the event.

### 8.11.4. Reenlistment Ceremony:

**8.11.4.1. Basic Guidelines.** Unit commanders will honor all reenlistees through a dignified reenlistment ceremony. The Airman may request any commissioned officer to perform the ceremony and may invite guests. The member's immediate family should be invited. This reinforces the fact that when a member makes a commitment to the Air Force, the family is also making a commitment. Any regular, reserve, guard, or retired commissioned officer of the U.S. Armed Forces may perform the ceremony, which may be conducted in any place that lends dignity to the event. The U.S. flag must form a backdrop for the participants. Reenlistees and reenlisting officers must wear an authorized uniform for the ceremony. **Exception:** The uniform requirement is optional for retired officers.

**8.11.4.2. Procedures.** The core of the ceremony is the Oath of Enlistment. The oath is recited by the officer and repeated by the reenlistee. The reenlistee and the officer administering the oath must be physically collocated during the ceremony. Once completed, the officer congratulates the reenlistee and invites the other attendees to do the same. Refreshments may be served.

### 8.11.5. Retirement Ceremony:

**8.11.5.1. Basic Guidelines.** Recognition upon retirement is a longstanding tradition of military service. Each commander makes sure members leave with a tangible expression of appreciation for their contributions to the Air Force mission and with the assurance they will continue to be a part of the Air Force family in retirement. Anyone involved in planning a retirement should consult AFI 36-3203, *Service Retirements,* for complete details. The following paragraphs are extracts from AFI 36-3203:

**8.11.5.1.1.** Commanders are responsible for ensuring members have a retirement ceremony to recognize their contributions. They must offer the retiring member the courtesy of a formal ceremony in keeping with the customs and traditions of the Service. If possible, a general officer conducts the ceremony. Ceremonies held as part of formal military formations, such as retreats and parades, are further encouraged if conditions permit.

8.11.5.1.2. During the retirement ceremony, the member receives a certificate of retirement, a U.S. Flag, the Air Force retired lapel button, Certificate of Appreciation for Service in the Armed Forces of the U.S., and appropriate awards, decorations, honors, and letters of appreciation. If possible, avoid using "dummy" elements that the member cannot keep. Family members and friends should be invited and encouraged to attend the ceremony. Furthermore, the member's spouse is customarily presented with a certificate of appreciation for the support and sacrifices made during the member's career.

8.11.5.1.3. Commanders follow formal ceremony procedures unless the member prefers otherwise. If the member doesn't want a formal ceremony or for any reason (leave or hospitalization) can't be present for duty on the retirement date, the commander personally presents all decorations and any awards or honors to the member at another time. The retirement certificate is not mailed to the member's retirement address unless there is no other choice.

8.11.5.2. **Procedures.** AFPAM 34-1202 outlines an approved sequence of events for indoor retirement ceremonies. Figure 8.19 provides a general guideline that may be used to assist in planning a retirement ceremony as well as many other ceremonies.

**Figure 8.19. General Guideline for Planning a Retirement Ceremony.**

- Appoint someone to set up the ceremony.
- Notify the honoree to ensure the date and times are good. Select and reserve a location for the ceremony.
- Determine whom the honoree would like to assist with the ceremony honors and have the honoree extend the invitation.
- Mail personal invitations to guests (optional) or use AFIT's "E-Invitations" free web application at: https://einvitations.afit.edu/generator/index.cfm.
- Ensure all award elements and certificates are ready. Select an emcee and individuals to act as escorts to any special guests as required.
- Request photographic support from the multimedia center.
- Ensure media equipment, if appropriate, is available. Recommend a "walk through" of the actual ceremony.
- Order refreshments.
- Print programs and make or obtain signs for seating and parking for special guests. Verify the guest list with the honoree and obtain special guest information (relationship, title, and correct spelling of name). Provide guest information, agenda, proposed remarks, applicable biographies or personnel records, and honoree's personal data to the officiating officer and emcee.
- Perform a "dry run" of the ceremony with all key players.
- Set up the location at least 2 hours before the ceremony. Meet with the honoree to go over last-minute details.
- The honoree and special guests often meet with the officiating officer just before the ceremony. The ceremony begins with the emcee announcing their arrival at the ceremony location.
- The emcee welcomes everyone and introduces the special guests.
- The emcee or officiating officer provides career highlights of the honoree.
- The emcee reads the special order of the honoree and the officiating officer performs ceremony procedures.
- Photos are taken throughout the ceremony.
- The honoree provides remarks.
- The emcee thanks everyone for coming and invites participants to congratulate the honoree and enjoy the refreshments.

8.11.5.2.1. Common ceremonies recognizing an individual, such as a retirement ceremony, routinely combine official actions that maintain the dignity and respect of long standing Air Force traditions with a member's desire to personalize the ceremony for family and invited guests.

**8.12. Special Ceremonies and Events.**

The Dining-In, Dining-Out, and Order of the Sword Induction ceremonies are social events that have become valued traditions in the military.

### 8.12.1. The Dining-In and Dining-Out:

8.12.1.1. The only difference between a Dining-In and Dining-Out is that nonmilitary spouses, friends, and civilians may attend a Dining-Out. The Dining-In is a formal dinner for military members only. The present Dining-In format had its beginnings in the Air Corps when General Henry H. "Hap" Arnold held his famous wingdings. The association of Army Air Corps personnel with the British and their Dining-In during World War II also encouraged their popularity in the Air Force. Members now recognize the Dining-In as an occasion where ceremony, tradition, and good fellowship serve an important purpose.

8.12.1.2. Specifically, these ceremonies provide an occasion for Air Force members to meet socially at formal military functions. They also provide an excellent means of saying farewell to departing members and welcoming new ones, as well as providing the opportunity to recognize individual and unit achievements. These are effective in building and maintaining high morale and esprit de corps. Military members who attend these ceremonies must wear the mess dress or the semiformal uniform. Civilians wear the dress specified in the invitations.

### 8.12.2. The Order of the Sword Induction Ceremony.

Induction into the Order of the Sword is an honor reserved for individuals who have provided outstanding leadership and support to enlisted members. The induction ceremony occurs at a formal evening banquet held to honor the inductee as a "Leader among Leaders and an Airman among Airmen." The entire event is conducted with the dignity that reflects its significance as the highest recognition enlisted member can bestow on anyone. Each command has an Order of the Sword and develops their own selection and induction procedures.

## 8.13. Drill:

### 8.13.1. Introduction to Drill.

For the purpose of drill, Air Force organizations are divided into elements, flights, squadrons, groups, and wings. Drill consists of certain movements by which the flight or squadron is moved in an orderly manner from one formation to another or from one place to another. Standards such as the 24-inch step, cadence of 100 to 120 steps per minute, distance, and interval were established to ensure movements are executed with order and precision. The task of each person is to learn these movements and execute each part exactly as described. Individuals must also learn to adapt their own movements to those of the group. Everyone in the formation must move together on command.

### 8.13.2. Drill and Ceremony.

While the term "ceremony" was defined earlier in this chapter, you should be note that certain ceremonies use drill. In these events, ceremonies not only honor distinguished persons and recognize special events, but also demonstrate the proficiency and training state of the Airmen. Ceremonies are an extension of drill activities. The precision marching, promptness in responding to commands, and teamwork developed on the drill field determine the appearance and performance of the group in ceremonies. The following paragraphs cover only the basic aspects of drill. For more information, see AFMAN 36-2203, *Drill and Ceremonies*.

### 8.13.3. Types of Commands:

8.13.3.1. **Drill Command.** A drill command is an oral order that usually has two parts: the preparatory command and the command of execution. The preparatory command explains what the movement will be. When calling a unit to attention or halting a unit's march, the preparatory command includes the unit designation. In the command "Flight, HALT," the word "Flight" is the preparatory command and, at the same time, designates the unit. The command of execution follows the preparatory command. The command of execution explains when the movement will be carried out. In "Forward, MARCH," the command of execution is "MARCH."

8.13.3.2. **Supplementary Command.** A supplementary command is given when one unit of the element must execute a movement different from other units or the same movement at a different time. Examples include: "CONTINUE THE MARCH" and "STAND FAST."

8.13.3.3. **Informational Command.** An informational command has no preparatory command or command of execution and is not supplementary; this command is used to direct others to give commands. Examples are: "PREPARE FOR INSPECTION" and "DISMISS THE SQUADRON."

8.13.3.4. **Mass Commands.** The mass commands help develop confidence, self-reliance, assertiveness, and enthusiasm by making the individual recall, give, and execute proper commands. Mass commands are usually confined to simple movements, with short preparatory commands and commands of execution carried out simultaneously by all elements of a unit. Each person is required to give commands in unison with others as if this person alone were giving the commands to the entire element. The volume of the combined voices encourages every person to perform the movement with snap and precision.

**8.13.4. General Rules for Giving Commands.**

When giving commands, the commander is at the position of attention. Good military bearing is necessary for good leadership. While marching, the commander must be in step with the formation at all times. The commander faces the Airmen when giving commands except when the element is part of a larger drill element or when the commander is relaying commands in a ceremony.

**8.13.5. Drill Positions:**

8.13.5.1. **Attention.** To come to attention, bring the heels together smartly and on line. Place the heels as near each other as the conformation of the body permits and ensure the feet are turned out equally to form a 45-degree angle. Keep the legs straight without stiffening or locking the knees. The body is erect with hips level, chest lifted, back arched, and shoulders square and even. Arms hang straight down alongside the body without stiffness and the wrists are straight with the forearms. Place thumbs, which are resting along the first joint of the forefinger, along the seams of the trousers or sides of the skirt. Hands are cupped (but not clenched as a fist) with palms facing the leg. The head is kept erect and held straight to the front, with the chin drawn slightly so the axis of the head and neck is vertical; eyes are to the front with the line of sight parallel to the ground. The weight of the body rests equally on the heels and balls of both feet. Silence and immobility are required.

8.13.5.2. **Rest Positions.** There are four positions of rest: parade rest, at ease, rest, and fall out. The commander and members of the formation must be at the position of attention before going to any of the rest positions. To resume the position of attention from any of the rests (except fall out, for which the commander uses the command "FALL IN"), the command is "Flight, ATTENTION."

8.13.5.2.1. **Parade Rest.** (The command is "Parade, REST.") On the command "REST," members of the formation raise the left foot from the hip just enough to clear the ground and move smartly to the left so the heels are 12 inches apart, as measured from the inside of the heels. Keep the legs straight but not stiff and the heels on line. As the left foot moves, bring the arms, fully extended, to the back of the body, uncupping the hands in the process; extend and join the fingers, pointing them toward the ground. Face the palms outwards. Place the right hand in the palm of the left, right thumb over the left to form an "X." Keep the head and eyes straight ahead and remain silent and immobile.

8.13.5.2.2. **At Ease.** On the command "AT EASE," members of the formation may relax in a standing position, but they must keep the right foot in place. Their position in the formation will not change; silence is maintained.

8.13.5.2.3. **Rest.** On the command "REST," the same requirements for at ease apply, but moderate speech is permitted.

8.13.5.2.4. **Fall Out.** On the command "FALL OUT," individuals may relax in a standing position or break ranks. They must remain in the immediate area; no specific method of dispersal is required. Moderate speech is permitted.

**8.13.6. The Flight as the Basic Drill Unit.**

The first phase of drill involves teaching basic movements, facings, and positions either as an individual or as a member of an element. The second phase of drill merges the individual with others to form a flight in which base formations and marching are learned. The flight is composed of at least two, but no more than four, elements. This formation is the most practical drill group.

**8.13.7. Formation of the Flight:**

8.13.7.1. A flight forms in a line formation at the command of "FALL IN" (Figure 8.20). **Note:** Usually, the flight sergeant forms and dismisses the flight formation.

8.13.7.2. On this command, each Airman will fall in and establish their dress, cover, interval, and distance. Once established, each Airman executes an automatic ready front on an individual basis and remains at the position of attention.

8.13.7.3. The flight commander will then size the flight. Once all members are properly sized and in column formation (Figure 8.21), the flight commander brings the flight back to line formation.

8.13.7.4. To align the flight in line formation, the commands are "Dress Right, DRESS" and "Ready, FRONT."

8.13.7.5. The flight commander verifies the alignment of each rank then marches to three paces beyond the front rank, faces toward the flight, and commands "Ready, FRONT." With as few movements as possible, the flight commander then takes the normal position in front of the flight by the most direct route.

**Figure 8.20. Flight in Line Formation.**

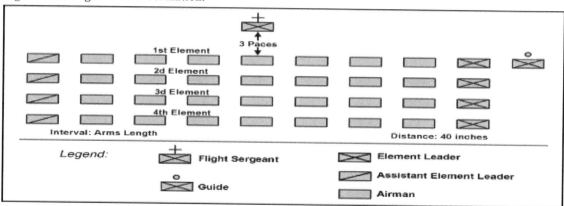

8.13.8. **Open Ranks:**

8.13.8.1. The command "Open Ranks, MARCH" is only given to a formation when in line at normal interval. On the command "MARCH," the fourth rank stands fast and automatically executes dress right dress. The third rank takes one pace, the second rank takes two, and the first rank takes three paces forward. The flight commander aligns the flight, then commands "Ready, FRONT."

8.13.8.2. The inspector and commander proceed to inspect the flight, if required.

8.13.8.3. After inspecting the entire flight, the inspector marches off to the right flank (element leaders) of the flight. The flight commander calls the flight to attention. The flight commander then commands "Close Ranks, MARCH." On the command "MARCH," the first rank stands fast. The second rank takes one pace forward and halts at the position of attention. The third and fourth ranks take two and three paces forward, respectively, and halt at attention.

*Section 8E—Honor Guard, Protocol, Distinguished Visitors, and Military Ceremonies*

**8.14. Base Honor Guard Program:**

8.14.1. The primary mission of the base honor guard program is to employ, equip, and train Air Force members to provide professional military funeral honors for Regular Air Force, retired members, and veterans of the U.S. Air Force. The Base Honor Guard Program is a mandatory Air Force program and is the responsibility of the installation commander. Members are usually volunteers from the installation host and tenant units, with selections generally coming from the installation's Airman Basic to Technical Sergeant pool. The base honor guard emphasizes the importance of military customs and courtesies, dress and appearance, and drill and ceremonies.

**Figure 8.21. Flight in Column Formation.**

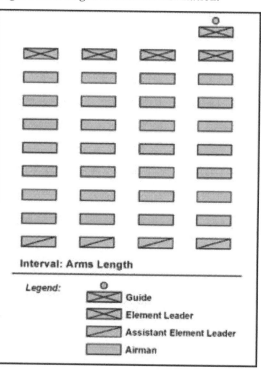

8.14.2. The origins of the base honor guard can be traced to May 1948 when Headquarters Command, U.S. Air Force, directed the creation of an elite ceremonial unit comparable to those of the other Services. The first base honor guard was activated within the 1100th Air Police Squadron, Bolling Field, Washington District of Columbia, and was responsible for maintaining an Air Force ceremonial capability in the National Capitol Region. However, other Air Force installations worldwide approached ceremonial responsibilities and military funeral honors quite differently.

8.14.3. In January of 2000, public law was implemented, providing for all veterans to receive, at a minimum, a funeral ceremony that includes the folding of a U.S. flag, presentation of the flag to the veteran's family, and the playing of "Taps."

## 8.15. Protocol Defined.

Protocol is the set of rules prescribing good manners in official life and in ceremonies involving governments and nations and their representatives. Protocol is an internationally recognized system of courtesy and respect. Protocol for the military and government agencies is a code of traditional precedence, courtesy, and etiquette in matters of military, diplomatic, official, and celebratory ceremonies. Military protocol encompasses the knowledge, accumulation and application of established service customs. In modern practice, protocol combines the traditional codes of conduct with contemporary etiquette and courtesy. The goal is to avoid disputes, insults, embarrassment, and distractions by following a set of objective and generally accepted criteria. As times change, so do the manners of the people; protocol must keep pace with developing official life. Though only a guide, the following sections will help you avoid protocol pitfalls.

## 8.16. Distinguished Visitors (DV):

8.16.1. A DV may be defined as any: (1) general or flag officer; (2) government official with rank equivalent to a brigadier general or higher; (3) foreign military officer or civilian designated a DV by the Under Secretary of the Air Force for International Affairs (SAF/IA); and (4) visitor or group designated by the commander. Also, persons of lower rank, but in certain positions, may be given DV status. At base level, for example, colonels, civilian equivalents, and the Command Chief Master Sergeant may be designated as DV by the commander. Many distinguished dignitaries, military and civilian, domestic and foreign, visit Air Force installations for festive occasions and official business. Reducing the frequency of ceremonial honors rendered official visitors at field installations is of high importance. In the interest of economy and efficiency, such ceremonies as parades, honor cordons, motorcades, and other ceremonies that involve large numbers of Airmen and equipment will be held to an absolute minimum when officials entitled to such honors visit military installations. In general, full honors are reserved for statutory appointees and general or flag officers of the military Services, foreign dignitaries, and occasions when ceremonies promote international good will. The installation commander determines which types of honors are rendered. Enlisted personnel are frequently appointed as project NCOs for ceremonies, officials at social events, or escorts for visiting DVs.

8.16.2. Project NCOs represent their organization or their base and are responsible for assisting DVs. A smooth visit requires planning before the visit. Review AFI 34-1201 and AFPAM 34-1202 for further guidance on responsibilities and proper procedures. Contact guests beforehand to find out if they desire special arrangements. The base protocol office may also need to know guests' transportation needs. Other duties may include preregistering guests, meeting them upon arrival, and escorting them to their next destination.

8.16.3. Place a tentative itinerary and welcome package in the guest quarters. Include such items as a recent base newspaper, unit or base history, telephone numbers of base facilities, maps of the base and local area, and most importantly, the visit point of contact information. Also appropriate are biographies on the installation or host commander and Command Chief Master Sergeant, host Professional Military Education commandants and program managers, and Chief Master Sergeants and first sergeants (in the case of a senior enlisted DV, such as the Chief Master Sergeant of the Air Force). Include instructions on operating difficult-to-use appliances or machines, using the telephone system, and computer connection information in the guest quarters.

8.16.4. Give a thorough prebriefing to the guest speaker at a special function, such as a Dining-In. Guests may have several commitments other than the primary project. If so, make sure they have schedules that allow time for meetings, telephone calls, meals, changes of clothes, coffee breaks, occasional rest periods, and transportation. Common practice is to leave 2 hours between the end-of-the-day activities and the start of evening functions.

8.16.5. Determine transportation time by physically traveling from place to place before the schedule is set. Allow extra time for boarding vehicles and transferring baggage or luggage. For large official parties, be sure to brief all drivers on the schedule and give explicit directions so they can operate independently if they become separated. Ensure they "dry run" the routes to avoid delays due to roadwork, stoplight outages, or road closures. Arrange the lodging checkout time and bill payment method. Arrange flight meals if the guests are leaving by military aircraft and desire this service. Smooth visits can make a lasting positive impression. If you run into difficulty or have questions, do not hesitate to contact the base protocol office.

8.16.6. A DV's visit is an important event in the day-to-day life of an organization. Everyone wants to make a good impression whether the visitor is a representative of Congress, foreign dignitary, or city mayor. Problems with these visits are avoided through strict attention to detail from the preplanning for arrival to luggage handling, dinner arrangements, and departure plans. Remember, you never get a second chance to make a good first impression.

## 8.17. General Information.

The enlisted corps has a variety of programs to recognize individuals for outstanding performance, achievements, contributions, and promotions to the senior noncommissioned officer grades. AFI 36-2805, *Special Trophies and Awards*, provides information on a variety of programs but is not all-inclusive. Senior noncommissioned officers should become familiar with the induction of newly promoted Master Sergeants into the "Top 3." They should also become familiar with the Order of the Sword Ceremony (reference AFI 36-2824, *Order of the Sword Programs*) and retirement ceremonies.

## 8.18. Order of the Sword:

### 8.18.1. Background:

8.18.1.1. The Order of the Sword is patterned after an order of chivalry founded during the Middle Ages—the Swedish Royal Order of the Sword. The rank of NCO was established in the early 12th century. In 1522, Swedish King Gustavus I enjoined the noblemen commissioned by him to appoint officers to serve him. Those appointed were accountants, builders, crafts people, teachers, scribes, and others conducting the daily kingdom affairs. The system worked so well it was incorporated into the Swedish Army as a way to establish and maintain a cohesive, disciplined, and well-trained force. This force ensured the protection of lives and property in the kingdom.

8.18.1.2. Ancient NCOs would honor their leader and pledge their loyalty by ceremoniously presenting him with a sword. The sword—a symbol of truth, justice, and power rightfully used—served as a token for all to see and know that here was a "leader among leaders." The ceremony became known as The Royal Order of the Sword. The first recorded use in the U.S. was in the 1860s when General Robert E. Lee was presented a sword by his command.

### 8.18.2. The Current Ceremony.

The Royal Order of the Sword ceremony was revised, updated, and adopted by Air Force NCOs in 1967. The Order of the Sword was established by the Air Force enlisted force to recognize and honor military senior officers, colonel or above, and civilian equivalents, for conspicuous and significant contributions to the welfare and prestige of the Air Force enlisted force mission effectiveness as well as the overall military establishment. The Order of the Sword is the highest honor and tribute NCOs can bestow upon an individual.

### 8.18.3. Approved Swords.

The only approved swords are at the Air Force level (Air Force Sword) and major command level (Major Command Sword). The Air Force Sword is reserved for those deserving senior leaders who serve outside the major command structure. The Chief Master Sergeant of the Air Force maintains the Air Force Sword. The Major commands maintain the Major Command Swords and ensure they are reserved for those deserving senior leaders who serve or have served within the awarding major command. Each major command establishes additional guidelines not already covered in AFI 36-2824. An Order of the Sword executive committee is responsible for developing guidelines, nomination procedures, approval or disapproval of any nominations submitted, and protocol of the induction ceremony. The committee must also approve the nomination. The Chief Master Sergeant of the Air Force or major command's Command Chief Master Sergeant (depending on level of award), is known as the "keeper of the sword," and usually chairs the committee.

### 8.18.4. Nomination and Selection.

NCOs wishing to nominate a qualified officer or civilian for induction into the Order of the Sword should contact their Command Chief Master Sergeant and refer to AFI 36-2824 for processing procedures. (**Note:** Do not inform the nominee of the possible induction.) The nomination folder should include a cover memorandum, biographical sketch, and brief justification. Ensure the nomination is thorough enough so the committee can carefully weigh the individual's merits. The Chief Master Sergeant of the Air Force or major command Chief Master Sergeant (depending on level of award) informs the nominating organization of the decision and provides appropriate guidance and procedures as necessary.

### 8.18.5. Preparation for the Ceremony.

Once the nomination is approved, a ceremony committee will form and begin planning the ceremony. Preparations required for the Order of the Sword ceremony are similar to those for the Dining-In discussed in this chapter. Host NCOs are responsible for planning, executing, and paying for the ceremony. This includes the dinner, awards and presentations to be made to the honoree, ceremonial equipment (such as individual swords), and printed proclamations.

### 8.18.6. Induction Ceremony.

This evening affair usually consists of a social period, formal dinner, and induction ceremony. The required dress is the mess dress or semiformal uniform. The ceremony should be well rehearsed to reflect formality, dignity, and prestige. Four key participants have speaking parts and other duties: the Chief Master Sergeant of the mess, first sergeant, duty sergeant, and sergeant at arms. Major command directives provide specific guidance for NCOs serving in these positions.

8.18.7. **Permanent Recognition in the Order of the Sword.**

The Chief Master Sergeant of the Air Force maintains the official list of Order of the Sword recipients. Each sponsoring command maintains a master sword designed for their ceremonies. This sword is on display at each command's headquarters. A nameplate commemorating the command's inductions is affixed to its command master sword.

**8.19. Conclusion.**

Military customs and courtesies are proven traditions, acts of respect and courtesy, and signs of the mutual respect and fraternity that exist among military personnel. Military customs and courtesies play an extremely important role in building morale, esprit de corps, discipline, and mission effectiveness. This chapter outlines customs and courtesies, providing an extensive but not all-inclusive outline of what makes the Air Force and the people special. These ceremonies represent many customs and traditions of our Air Force heritage. They are very real aspects of life, and, in the aggregate, form the special culture and lifestyle uniquely characteristic of the military profession. This guidance is offered to empower you with the knowledge that can add comfort to your daily social interactions. Apply using common sense. The guidelines in this chapter can help avoid protocol pitfalls.

**Chapter 9**

**THE NONCOMMISSIONED OFFICER**

*Section 9A—Overview*

**9.1. Introduction:**

9.1.1. Noncommissioned officers (NCO) are the backbone of the Air Force. The organization's success or failure, strengths or weaknesses can be directly related to the effectiveness of its NCOs. This chapter begins by discussing the philosophy, purpose, and structure of the enlisted force. Next, it explores the ranks, roles, responsibilities and developmental levels for Junior Enlisted Airmen, NCOs and senior noncommissioned officers. In addition, it briefly describes those special positions entrusted to senior NCO, such as Air Force Career Field Manager, first sergeant, Command Chief Master Sergeant, and Chief Master Sergeant of the Air Force.

9.1.2. Regardless of rank, every enlisted Airman supports the Profession of Arms to defend the interests of the state, by force and death, when required. This charge is unique to the military profession, and is a calling that requires devotion to service and willingness to sacrifice far beyond that required in other professions. The military as a profession and its core values and supporting ideas are concepts that epitomize the "NCO." Finally, the purpose for including this chapter within AFH 1, *Airman* is to provide enlisted Airmen reference material to support their promotion tests.

*Section 9B—The Enlisted Force Structure*

**9.2. Philosophy:**

9.2.1. The enlisted force is a diverse corps of functionally and operationally specialized Airmen in the Profession of Arms. Despite the differences across functional and operational lines, there is a compelling need for a deliberate and common approach to force development, career progression, and the assumption of increased supervisory and leadership responsibilities. To best leverage our resources we must have a consistent, well-defined set of expectations, standards, and opportunities for growth for *all* Airmen, regardless of rank or specialty. The enlisted force structure provides this consistency and common approach. It defines us as *Airmen first, specialists second.*

9.2.2. All elements of the enlisted force structure reflect the Air Force core values (Integrity First, Service Before Self, and Excellence in All We Do), and are essential to the profession of arms. The core values are the basis for Air Force policies, guidance, and overall focus.

**9.3. Purpose of the Force Structure:**

9.3.1. The enlisted force structure provides the framework for a force structure that best meets mission requirements, while developing institutional and occupational competencies.

9.3.2. The enlisted force structure defines the tiers, ranks, terms of address, roles, expectations, key positions and approved duty titles for the enlisted force.

9.3.3. Additionally, the enlisted force structure provides a framework for supervisors as they set standards during initial feedback sessions, evaluate progress during mid-term feedback sessions, and document performance on annual reports.

**9.4. Air Force Leadership Levels.**

9.4.1. The Air Force operates in a dynamic global context across multiple domains requiring leadership skills at three distinct levels: tactical expertise, operational competence, and strategic vision. These levels emphasize a different mix of qualities and experience. The leadership level at which an Airman operates determines the institutional competencies (see paragraph 9.20) required to lead Airmen in mission accomplishment. As shown in Figure 9.1, as Airmen progress from the tactical expertise to strategic vision leadership levels, emphasis on the use of institutional competencies shifts from personal to organizational, with a generally consistent focus on people/team competencies. The nature and scope of leadership challenges as well as preferred leadership methods differ based on the level of leadership and duties. In addition, these levels apply across the entire spectrum of the enlisted force structure (Figure 9.2).

9.4.2. **Tactical Expertise Level.**

This level is predominantly direct and face-to-face and focused on personal competencies. At the tactical expertise level, Airmen gain a general understanding of team leadership and an appreciation for organization leadership. They master their core duty skills, develop experiences in applying those skills, and begin to acquire the knowledge and experience that will produce the qualities essential to effective leadership. Airmen at the tactical expertise level gain the training, education and experience to become the Air Force's primary technicians and specialists. They learn about themselves as leaders and how their leadership acumen can affect others through the use of ethical leadership.

They assimilate into the Air Force culture and adopt the Air Force Core Values. Airmen at this level focus on honing followership abilities, motivating subordinates and influencing peers to accomplish the mission while developing a warrior ethos. They learn about themselves and their impact on others in roles as both follower and leader in addition to developing their communication skills. The primary focus at the tactical expertise level is accomplishing the missions as effectively and efficiently as possible using available personnel and resources.

**Figure 9.1. Air Force Leadership Levels**

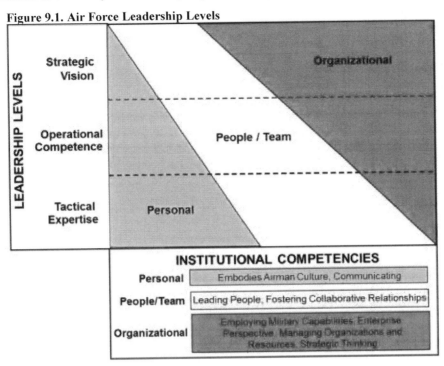

**Figure 9.2. Enlisted Force Development**

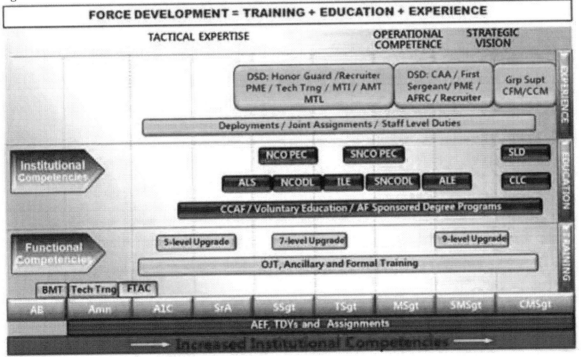

### 9.4.3. Operational Competence Level.

The full-spectrum of institutional competencies is balanced across the operational competence leadership level. At this level, Airmen understand the broader Air Force perspective and the integration of diverse people and capabilities in operational execution. They transition from specialists to leaders with a broader enterprise perspective who understand Air Force operational capabilities. Based on a thorough understanding of themselves as leaders and followers, Airmen apply an understanding of organizational and team dynamics. They lead teams by developing and inspiring others, taking care of people, and taking advantage of diversity. They foster collaborative relationships through building teams and coalitions, especially within large organizations, and negotiate with others, often external to the organization. Airmen operating at this leadership level normally work below the major command or Headquarters Air Force levels. The majority of enlisted Airmen operate at the tactical expertise and operational competence levels.

### 9.4.4. Strategic Vision Level.

At this level, Airmen combine highly developed personal and people/team institutional competencies to apply broad organizational competencies. They develop a deep understanding of Air Force capabilities and how Airmen achieve synergistic results and desired effects with their operational capabilities. They also understand how the Air Force operates within joint, multinational, and interagency relationships. At the strategic vision level, an Airman employs military capabilities, applying the operational and strategic arts with a thorough understanding of unit capabilities, the Air Force at large, and joint and coalition forces. They have an enterprise perspective with a thorough understanding of the structure and relationships needed to accomplish strategic objectives. The strategic vision level focuses on the effects an Airman can have across a major command, a theater, the Air Force, or even other Services or the Department of Defense. The Chief Master Sergeant of the Air Force (CMSAF) and few other senior NCOs assigned to higher headquarters operate at this level.

## 9.5. Enlisted Force Structure Tiers, Ranks and Roles.

The enlisted force structure is comprised of three distinct and separate tiers, each correlating to increased levels of education, training, and experience, which build increasing levels of proficiency. The tiers are Junior Enlisted Airmen, Noncommissioned Officer, and Senior Noncommissioned Officer, with multiple ranks in each tier. Each rank includes an official abbreviation and term of address, as outlined below. Unofficial terms for ranks are not appropriate terms of address (e.g., Tech, Senior, etc.); however, Airmen senior or equivalent to the member may use first names and/or call signs. The three tiers correlate to increased leadership and managerial responsibilities, with each tier building on the responsibilities of the previous one. Therefore, senior NCOs are expected to have mastered NCO responsibilities. Likewise, NCOs are expected to have mastered Junior Enlisted Airmen responsibilities. The primary goal in each tier is mission accomplishment.

### 9.5.1. The Junior Enlisted Airman Tier.

This tier consists of airman basic, airman, airman first class, and senior airman. Initial enlisted accessions enter the Air Force in this tier (airman basic, airman, or airman first class), and focus on adapting to military requirements, being part of the profession of arms, achieving occupational proficiency, and learning how to be highly productive members of the Air Force. In this tier, Airmen prepare for increased responsibilities and ensure they are trained, qualified, and ready to operate, both at home station and in an expeditionary environment. Junior Enlisted Airmen are introduced to the institutional competencies and continue to broaden their technical skills.

#### 9.5.1.1. Airman Basic and newly enlisted Airmen.
Airmen basics, as well as Airmen who initially enlist into the Air Force at the airman or airman first class rank, are primarily adapting to the requirements of the military profession, acquiring knowledge of military customs, courtesies, and Air Force standards, as well as striving to attain occupational proficiency. At their first duty station, they perform basic tasks under close supervision. The written abbreviation for airman basic is "AB" and the official term of address is "Airman Basic" or "Airman."

#### 9.5.1.2. Airman.
Airmen are still learning and adapting to the military profession, and are expected to understand and conform to military standards, customs, and courtesies. Airmen begin to show occupational proficiency at basic tasks and still require significant supervision and support. The written abbreviation is "Amn" and the official term of address is "Airman."

#### 9.5.1.3. Airman First Class.
Airmen first class fully comply with Air Force standards and devote time to increasing their skills in their career fields and the military profession, while becoming effective team members. After a short time at their first duty station, they are often skilled on numerous tasks. Continued supervision is essential to ongoing occupational and professional growth. Typically, the 5-skill level is earned at this grade. The written abbreviation is "A1C" and the official term of address is "Airman First Class" or "Airman."

9.5.1.4. **Senior Airman.** Senior airmen commonly perform as skilled technicians and trainers. They begin developing supervisory and leadership skills through progressive responsibility, Airman Leadership School (ALS), individual study, and mentoring. Senior Airmen strive to establish themselves as effective trainers through the maximum use of guidance and assistance from officer and enlisted leaders. They may serve as first-line supervisors upon completion of ALS. The written abbreviation is "SrA" and the official term of address is "Senior Airman" or "Airman."

9.5.2. **The NCO Tier, Ranks and Roles.**

This tier consists of staff sergeant and technical sergeant. NCOs continue occupational growth and become expert technicians while developing as leaders, supervisors, managers, and mentors in the profession of arms. Additionally, NCOs ensure they keep themselves and subordinates trained, qualified, and ready to deploy and operate at home station and in an expeditionary environment. In this tier, NCOs understand and internalize institutional competencies in preparation for increased responsibilities, while pursuing professional development through a variety of means, including Enlisted PME.

9.5.2.1. **Staff Sergeant.** Staff sergeants are primarily highly skilled technicians with supervisory and training responsibilities. Typically, at this rank they earn the 7-skill level. They must continuously strive to further their development as technicians, supervisors, and leaders through professional development opportunities, including distance learning and/or in-residence Air Force Enlisted PME and Senior Enlisted Joint PME. They are responsible for their subordinates' development and the effective accomplishment of all assigned tasks. They must ensure proper and effective use of all resources under their control to ensure the mission is effectively and efficiently accomplished. They should consider broadening opportunities through the Development Special Duty selection process. The written abbreviation is "SSgt" and the official term of address is "Staff Sergeant" or "Sergeant."

9.5.2.2. **Technical Sergeant.** Technical sergeants are often their organizations' technical experts. They continuously strive to further their development as technicians, supervisors, leaders and mentors through professional development opportunities, including distance learning and/or in-residence Air Force Enlisted PME and Senior Enlisted Joint PME. They should consider broadening opportunities through the Development Special Duty selection process. The written abbreviation is "TSgt" and the official term of address is "Technical Sergeant" or "Sergeant."

9.5.3. **The Senior NCO Tier, Ranks and Roles.**

This tier consists of master sergeant, senior master sergeant, chief master sergeant and Chief Master Sergeant of the Air Force. Senior NCOs serve as leaders in the profession of arms. They advise, supervise and mentor others to further grow and develop junior enlisted Airmen and NCOs under their charge. In this tier, senior NCOs continue professional development through a variety of means, including Enlisted PME. They have a great deal of leadership experience they use to leverage resources and personnel against a variety of mission requirements. Senior NCOs participate in decision-making processes on a variety of technical, operational, and organizational issues.

9.5.3.1. **Master Sergeant.** Master sergeants are technical experts, transitioning from first-line supervisors to leaders of operational competence. This rank carries significantly increased responsibilities and requires a broad perspective and greater leadership and management skills. MSgts are expected to accomplish the mission through the employment of teams by merging subordinates' talents, skills, and resources with other teams' functions. MSgts must complete an Associate's Degree from the Community College of the Air Force in their current Air Force Specialty, if not already earned, to become eligible for promotion to SMSgt. MSgts continue their professional development through distance learning and/or in-residence Air Force Enlisted PME courses. They are also eligible to attend sister-service or International Senior NCO PME, and are encouraged to complete Senior Enlisted Joint PME II. They should consider broadening opportunities through the Development Special Duty selection process. The written abbreviation is "MSgt" and the official term of address is "Master Sergeant" or "Sergeant."

9.5.3.2. **Senior Master Sergeant.** Senior master sergeants are key, experienced, operational leaders skilled at merging teams' talents, skills, and resources with other organizations. Senior Master Sergeants continue to develop their leadership and management skills and earn their 9-skill level. Senior Master Sergeants continue their professional development through distance learning and/or in-residence Air Force enlisted PME courses. They are also eligible to attend sister-service or International senior NCO PME, and are encouraged to complete Senior Enlisted Joint PME II. The written abbreviation is "SMSgt," and the official term of address is "Senior Master Sergeant" or "Sergeant."

9.5.3.3. **Chief Master Sergeant.** Chief master sergeants serve in the highest enlisted rank and hold strategic leadership positions with tremendous influence at all levels of the Air Force. They continue to develop personal leadership and management skills to prepare for ever increasing positions of responsibility. They are charged with mentoring and developing junior enlisted personnel and strongly influence the professional development of junior officers. They bring substantial operational and occupational experience as well as strong institutional skills to their organizations and assigned tasks. All newly selected Regular Air Force (RegAF) Chief Master Sergeants will attend the Chief Master Sergeant Leadership Course. Air Force Reserve and Air National Guard Chief Master Sergeants will apply for attendance through their commands. Chief Master Sergeants serve in key leadership positions such as Combatant Command Senior Enlisted Leader, Command Chief Master Sergeant, Group Superintendent, PME Commandants, Functional and Career Field Managers. The written abbreviation is "CMSgt" and the official term of address is "Chief Master Sergeant" or "Chief."

**9.5.3.4. Chief Master Sergeant of the Air Force.** The CMSAF is the senior enlisted leader of the Air Force and takes precedence over all enlisted members. The CMSAF provides leadership to the enlisted force and advises the Chief of Staff of the Air Force, Secretary of the Air Force, Chairman Joint chief of Staff, and the Secretary of Defense on enlisted matters. The CMSAF communicates with the force, serves on boards and committees for numerous organizations affecting Airmen, testifies before congress, and is the Air Force career field manager for command chief master sergeants and group superintendents. The CMSAF also consults with sister service senior

**Figure 9.3. CMSAF**

enlisted advisors on issues affecting all enlisted members; engages with foreign military leadership regarding theater security cooperation and partner nation development efforts; represents the Air Force to the American public, professional organizations and the media; and manages the Air Force Order of the Sword Program. The written abbreviation is "CMSAF" and the official term of address is "Chief Master Sergeant of the Air Force" or "Chief."

The idea of creating a CMSAF position surfaced as early as 1964 when the Air Force Association's Airman Advisory Council presented the idea. At that time, Air Force leadership rejected the proposal, fearing that such a position would undermine the formal chain of command. Purposeful action did not come until 1966 when Congressman Mendel Rivers introduced a bill that would mandate each of the Services to appoint a senior NCO. Congressman Rivers became convinced that the Air Force needed to follow the example of the Marine Corps (which had created the position of Sergeant Major of the Marine Corps in 1957) and the Army (which had created the position of Sergeant Major of the Army in 1965) and appoint a senior enlisted advisor to the Chief of Staff of the Air Force. Although the Rivers bill never passed, the Air Force recognized the tremendous support behind the proposal. On 24 October 1966, Chief of Staff of the Air Force General John P. McConnell announced the newly created position of CMSAF. In April 1967, Chief Paul W. Airey became the first to wear the unique insignia with the wreath around the star. Over the next decade, support for the office grew among senior leaders and within the enlisted force. Today, the CMSAF wears the chevron depicted in Figure 9.3. To date, 17 individuals have previously served in this office. The present CMSAF, Kaleth O. Wright, took office in February 2017.

**9.5.3.4.1. CMSAF Paul Wesley Airey:**

9.5.3.4.1.1. Paul Wesley Airey enlisted in the Army Air Forces as a radio operator on 16 November 1942. By the height of World War II, he was serving as an aerial gunner aboard B-24 bombers. While in Europe, Airey and his crew were shot down over Vienna, Austria, captured, and held prisoner by the Germans from July 1944 to May 1945. During the Korean conflict, he was awarded the Legion of Merit for creating a means of constructing equipment from salvaged parts, improving corrosion control of sensitive radio and radar components. Following the war, Airey took the job of first sergeant, a position he later said was one of the most important in the Air Force. He subsequently served as first sergeant for six squadrons at four bases over the next 12 years before being appointed to the highest NCO position.

**CMSAF Paul W. Airey**
April 1967 – July 1969
Died: 11 March 2009

9.5.3.4.1.2. Upon assuming his new responsibilities, CMSAF Airey began tackling the problem of personnel retention, an issue he identified as one of the greatest challenges he faced. The first-term reenlistment rate was the lowest it had been in 12 years, but Airey did not attribute the great decline to the unpopularity of the war in Vietnam. He felt it was the consequence of "poor pay, numerous remote assignments, good civilian employment opportunities, and an inequitable promotion system." He became an advisor to a committee to investigate and recommend a more equitable system. His efforts helped produce the Weighted Airman Promotion System which was adopted in 1970, eliminating local enlisted promotion boards and equalizing promotion opportunities across career fields. In retirement, Airey continued to be an enlisted advocate and spoke to Airmen around the force. CMSAF Airey died in 2009.

### 9.5.3.4.2. CMSAF Donald L. Harlow:

9.5.3.4.2.1. Born in Waterville, Maine, Donald L. Harlow was the youngest of nine children. At age 22, after working a variety of jobs to help support his mother and pay his tuition at a private preparatory school, he was drafted into the Army Air Corps. Serving as an armament and gunnery instructor, he taught cadets to fieldstrip and reassemble their weapons and to synchronize firing guns through aircraft propellers. He transferred to the personnel career field in 1945 and advanced to the grade of Staff Sergeant before his February 1946 discharge from active duty. During the Korean War, Harlow was recalled to active duty, holding various positions in the personnel career field. At 16 years of service, he was promoted to Chief Master Sergeant and was the personnel Sergeant Major for Headquarters United States European Command and the Sergeant Major for the Executive Services Division, Office of the Vice Chief of Staff.

**CMSAF Donald L. Harlow**
August 1969 – September 1971
Died: 18 June 1997

9.5.3.4.2.2. As the second to take the reins, CMSAF Harlow continued to cut a path through the misunderstanding, confusion, and mistrust that surrounded the CMSAF Ever vigilant, he campaigned for and refined the newly established Weighted Airman Promotion System, garnered continued flight pay for NCOs attending in-residence PME and worked toward equal per diem for enlisted and officers. During Vietnam, he directed his attention to where he felt it was most needed: young Airmen and their issues, including racial tension, assignment concerns, and promotion problems. Known for his no-nonsense approach and keen ability to listen, Harlow advised the Chief of Staff of the Air Force on matters of true concern to the enlisted force. While many of his recommendations did not result in policy changes during his tenure, he planted the seeds for future change. After retiring, Chief Harlow was a strong lobbyist for enlisted equality. CMSAF Harlow died in 1997.

### 9.5.3.4.3. CMSAF Richard D. Kisling:

9.5.3.4.3.1. Richard D. Kisling and his 10 siblings were raised on a farm in Iowa during the Great Depression and the dust bowl years. The patriotism he developed during his childhood was called on when he was drafted into the Army's combat infantry in 1945 during the effort to reconstitute the number of soldiers driving through France. After training and deployment times, Kisling arrived in France a month before the war in Europe ended. His unit assumed responsibility for negotiating the repatriation of displaced Soviets. From there, Kisling separated from the service for civilian life. After a few months spent missing the camaraderie, he reenlisted for a brief stint in the Army. In 1947, he joined the Army Air Forces, serving first as a clerk and later a personnel specialist. Upon his promotion to Senior Master Sergeant in September 1958, he was among the first group of Air Force enlisted members to wear the super grades of Senior Master Sergeant and Chief Master Sergeant.

**CMSAF Richard D. Kisling**
October 1971 – September 1973
Died: 3 November 1985

9.5.3.4.3.2. Once assigned to the Pentagon, CMSAF Kisling found the enlisted force struggling through the development of a new Air Force. After talking with several base officials, it was determined that the Air Force needed to develop their NCOs like they did their officers. So Kisling placed concerns for NCO professional development in the forefront of discussion at the Pentagon. His persistence paid off when the first senior NCO academy was approved by Congress in 1972. The Academy officially opened its doors in January 1973; however, before the Academy opened its doors, the original plan was to restrict its attendance to first sergeants. In the end, Kisling won the battle of making professional development available to all senior NCOs. His concern for such enlisted issues as housing, pay, promotions, education and training, and assignments earned him the respect of his peers and the nickname, "the GI's man in Washington." CMSAF Kisling died in 1985.

### 9.5.3.4.4. CMSAF Thomas N. Barnes:

**CMSAF Thomas N. Barnes**
October 1973 – July 1977
Died: 17 March 2003

9.5.3.4.4.1. Thomas N. Barnes grew up in the war-related industries town of Chester, Pennsylvania. In 1949, he joined the newly created United States Air Force as an aircraft maintainer specializing in hydraulics. His first duty station found him at the leading edge of United States Air Force integration efforts, as one of the first African-Americans to join the unit. Barnes' unit was flying Korean War support missions. Unbeknownst to others in his squadron, a crew pal taught him the art of flight engineering and let him fly resupply and medical evacuation missions. By his tour's end, Barnes had gained flight engineer certification, accumulated 750 flight hours over enemy territory and earned the Air Medal. He was the first CMSAF with direct Vietnam experience and the first African-American to serve in the highest enlisted post of a military service. The Chief of Staff of the Air Force consecutively extended him in 1975 and in 1976.

9.5.3.4.4.2. CMSAF Barnes' notable contribution came in the area that inspired his greatest passion and ranked among his largest challenges: working to ensure equality among the ranks and races. He took great pride in the part he played in bringing about the Air Force Social Actions Program in 1969. He labored to eliminate barriers for women and convince the Air Force to use them in nontraditional roles. He understood the value of continuing to educate Airmen and believed no one should advance in rank without PME, working to establish the service's firm commitment to enlisted PME. Recognized throughout the force for his ability to communicate with anyone, Barnes made listening to Airmen a priority. At the beginning of his tenure, the question most asked of Barnes was, "What programs will you implement for the blacks?" "The answer was 'None'," Barnes recalls. "I told them I work for all blue suiters." After his retirement, Barnes remained actively engaged in Air Force issues. CMSAF Barnes died in 2003.

### 9.5.3.4.5. CMSAF Robert D. Gaylor:

9.5.3.4.5.1. Growing up in Indiana, Robert D. Gaylor wanted to travel and learn a skill. He enlisted in the Air Force in 1948, a transition time for America and the military. As he arrived at basic training, President Truman issued Executive Order 9981, *Establishing the President's Committee on Equality of Treatment and Opportunity In the Armed Forces*, calling for equality of opportunity in the United States military. Gaylor had had no experience with segregation or integration and he would witness the long journey to full integration. His first duty was as a military policeman and he excelled throughout his career, advancing to the rank of Master Sergeant with only 7 years and 7 months of service. Serving as an instructor at basic training and the NCO Academy convinced him that special duties help prepare NCOs for greater leadership roles. In 1976, as a member of the Air Force Manpower and Personnel Center, Gaylor traveled extensively, giving 275 leadership talks annually.

**CMSAF Robert D. Gaylor**
August 1977 – July 1979

9.5.3.4.5.2. CMSAF Gaylor's goal as the senior enlisted man was to feel the pulse of the enlisted force and serve as a conduit of information. He addressed low morale and the weak military public image head on. He educated the force on the hazards of substance abuse and continued to raise confidence and shift attitudes within the force. He is credited with securing a policy that allowed Senior Airman to transport their families at government expense during permanent change of station moves, a solid step toward improving quality of life. He educated the force in order to eliminate the stereotypes and prejudices working against equal opportunities for minorities and women. Finally, Gaylor promoted leadership. He traveled extensively, talking to Airmen about taking pride in their military careers. He believes one of the most important roles a former CMSAF can play is that of a link between the United States Air Force of the past and today's service. Gaylor continues to meet and serve Airmen, conducting more than 40 Air Force base visits each year.

### 9.5.3.4.6. CMSAF James M. McCoy:

**CMSAF James M. McCoy**
August 1979 – July 1981

9.5.3.4.6.1. James M. McCoy was raised in the midwest, attending high school in Atchison, Kansas, and college at St. Benedicts College in Atchison and St. Ambrose College in Davenport, Iowa. He seriously considered a vocation in the priesthood, but in 1951, during the height of the Korean War, he enlisted in the United States Air Force as a radar operator. When the war ended, the Air Force had too many operators and needed military training instructors. McCoy volunteered and, with only 6 years of active duty experience, found himself in charge of five groups of training instructors. He continued working within the PME system, serving as NCO preparatory school commandant and as an NCO academy instructor before returning to the personnel training field in 1973. A year later he was selected as one of the United States Air Force's 12 Outstanding Airmen of the Year. He then became Strategic Air Command's first senior enlisted advisor. While there, McCoy was a member of the Air Force Management Improvement Group, chaired by CMSAF Barnes, which formed to discuss management issues and propose solutions. As a result, enlisted PME expanded into five phases.

9.5.3.4.6.2. With the public still questioning the military involvement in Vietnam, the Air Force was experiencing the lowest recruiting year ever; retention rates were also dropping when CMSAF McCoy took office. His first challenge was to improve those numbers. In late 1979, along with former CMSAF Kisling, he testified before Congress that people were not reenlisting in the Air Force because they could not make ends meet on enlisted pay. McCoy worked with recruiters to get the right people in the Air Force and sought to improve the PME system from basic training to the NCO and senior NCO level. During his tour as CMSAF, the Stripes for Exceptional Performers Program was instituted to provide incentive and an alternate promotion option for enlisted members. In addition to visiting Airmen, he placed great value on being involved with the Pentagon staff. He expanded the list of boards and conferences where he believed the CMSAF should have a role. In retirement, McCoy remains at the forefront of Air Force issues, having served in leadership positions with Air Force professional organizations and speaking to Airmen throughout the force.

### 9.5.3.4.7. CMSAF Arthur L. "Bud" Andrews:

9.5.3.4.7.1. In January 1953, out of a sense of patriotism and a desire to grow and develop, Arthur "Bud" L. Andrews enlisted in the Air Force. During basic training, his training instructor asked for volunteers to serve as APs. Thinking AP meant "air police," Andrews raised his hand. As it turned out, the training instructor wanted area policemen. He spent the next 3 months picking up cigarette butts outside the barracks. He eventually had an opportunity to enter the military police force, where he served most of the next 14 years. In 1959, while working as an investigator, Andrews was credited with solving a murder committed by an Airman Second Class. By 1970, Andrews had served tours in Morocco, Thailand, and Vietnam; became a first sergeant; and was promoted to the rank of Senior Master Sergeant. During his career he spent a decade as a first sergeant.

**CMSAF Arthur L. Andrews**
August 1981 – July 1983
Died: 26 October 1996

9.5.3.4.7.2. Upon assuming his new position, CMSAF Andrews' top priority could be described as getting back to basics. He believed the most vexing problems (such as terms of pay, benefits, recruitment, and retention) had been addressed and were evolving to meet Airmen's needs. While he continued to advise the Chief of Staff of the Air Force on quality-of-life improvements, he began to focus on cultural change. He felt it was time for Airmen to "think *we* instead of *me, me, me*." He wanted people to focus on "how we're supposed to dress, act, and react toward subordinates and superiors, and how we're supposed to do our jobs." He challenged NCOs to "take care of their people and to accomplish the mission." He further suggested that NCOs look at themselves if they were dissatisfied with their jobs. He dispelled the days of "leadership by stress" and applauded PME for creating a smarter force. Andrews believed the CMSAF needed to know the issues firsthand, which kept him traveling extensively around the Air Force. CMSAF Andrews died in 1996.

### 9.5.3.4.8. CMSAF Sam E. Parish:

**CMSAF Sam E. Parish**
August 1983 – June 1986

9.5.3.4.8.1. Sam E. Parish was raised and educated in north Florida. In 1955, at age 17, he joined the Air Force as a ground weather equipment operator. His first assignment at Wiesbaden Air Base, Germany, brought him into an experimental program to cross train as a weather observer. That experiment led to a career. In 1960, he became the youngest 7-skill level in his career field and continued to excel. While the chief observer for the 7th Weather Squadron in Heidelberg, Germany, he was quickly promoted to Senior Master Sergeant, and at age 31, Parish made Chief Master Sergeant. He was a member of the first senior NCO academy class, and was selected as the Air Weather Service Senior Enlisted Advisor in 1973. He returned to Germany in 1976 as the Consolidated Base Personnel Office Personnel Sergeant Major, and in 1977 became the senior enlisted advisor for the United States Air Forces in Europe, where he established the United States Air Forces in Europe First Sergeant of the Year program. Parish later served as the 40th Air Division and Strategic Air Command senior enlisted advisor.

9.5.3.4.8.2. CMSAF Parish tackled a range of enlisted personnel issues during his tenure. One such issue was the fixed-phase point for promotion to Senior Airman, which would promote qualified Airmen to Senior Airman at a set point in their initial enlistment, allowing them a chance to be selected for Staff Sergeant during their first enlistment. He also obtained Chief of Staff of the Air Force approval to allow flight line personnel to wear a functional badge on their uniform, which led to United States Air Force members in all specialties being able to wear functional badges identifying their career fields. He also obtained Chief of Staff of the Air Force approval to establish the John Levitow Award for each level of PME and to implement the First Sergeant of the Year Program Air Force-wide. He was known as a straight shooter who did not waste time trying to figure out what people wanted to hear. Instead, he told them what they needed to hear. To Parish, the CMSAF is the most important job in the Air Force from an enlisted program perspective. In retirement, he continues to support Airmen by attending service functions and visiting bases throughout the Air Force.

### 9.5.3.4.9. CMSAF James C. Binnicker:

9.5.3.4.9.1. James C. Binnicker, raised in Aiken, South Carolina, joined the Civil Air Patrol in high school with aspirations of becoming a pilot. Cadet of the Year honors earned him a scholarship to attend flight school and the right to represent his state as a foreign exchange cadet in Great Britain. But, in 1957, doctors detected a high frequency hearing loss, disqualifying him from the program. To stay close to his passion, he joined the Air Force in the personal equipment, later called life support, career field. By 1964, Binnicker cross trained into air operations, planning flights for missions to Vietnam. While serving in Vietnam from 1968 to 1969, he served as NCOIC of operations for the 22d Tactical Air Support Squadron, and later as a Vietnamese-speaking linguist at the Republic of Vietnam Armed Forces Language School in Saigon. While in Vietnam, he set his sights on becoming the CMSAF and, as such, being an advocate for enlisted Airmen. He also served as a first sergeant and base Sergeant Major at Seymour Johnson Air Force Base, North Carolina. In 1977, on the recommendation of CMSAF Thomas Barnes, he became the sole enlisted member of the newly established President's Commission on Military Compensation. In addition, he spent over 7 years as the senior enlisted advisor for the 4th Tactical Fighter Wing, 12th Air Force, Pacific Air Forces, and Tactical Air Command.

**CMSAF James C. Binnicker**
July 1986 – July 1990
Died: 21 March 2015

9.5.3.4.9.2. CMSAF Binnicker's first order of business was tackling the Airman performance report, a system of ratings from 1 to 9. In an effort to more accurately differentiate between Airmen, the enlisted performance report was created, along with a system to provide and document performance feedback. Next, Binnicker set his sights on admitting Master Sergeants to the senior NCO academy. He believed giving Airmen all the responsibility they could handle would result in attracting and retaining higher quality people in the Air Force. He also worked to give minorities and women more responsibilities throughout the Air Force. The Chief of Staff, United States Air Force recognized Binnicker as a staunch advocate and spokesman for enlisted issues. His commitment to Airmen did not change following his retirement in 1994. He stayed abreast of issues affecting the enlisted force and visited PME classes to talk with students worldwide. In addition, he served as president and chief executive officer for the Air Force Enlisted Village until his death in March 2015.

**9.5.3.4.10. CMSAF Gary R. Pfingston:**

**CMSAF Gary R. Pfingston**
August 1990 – October 1994
Died: 23 June 2007

9.5.3.4.10.1. Gary R. Pfingston played minor league baseball before enlisting in the Air Force as an aircraft mechanic. During his first assignment as a B-52 crew chief at Castle Air Force Base, California, he went to work one day with a pack of cigarettes and $2, and did not return home for 30 days because the Cuban Missile Crisis sent the base into lockdown. Ten years later, Pfingston worked aircraft maintenance in Thailand, reconfiguring B-52s to carry conventional bombs in what became known as "iron belly" modifications. In 1973, he returned to the states and spent the next 8 1/2 years as a military training instructor, and later, chief of the military training division. During an assignment to Andersen Air Force Base, Guam, Pfingston broke his back, was hospitalized for 147 days, and returned to duty as the first sergeant. Future assignments had Pfingston taking part in the first ability to survive and operate exercise in a chemical environment and serving as a senior enlisted advisor.

9.5.3.4.10.2. CMSAF Pfingston's focus during his tenure was the Air Force drawdown and budget. Holding the highest enlisted position during Desert Storm, he worked to restore basic allowance for subsistence to the troops living in field conditions and increasing the Servicemember's Group Life Insurance, but the toughest challenge he faced was the Air Force downsizing. To avoid involuntary separations, Pfingston worked to implement the Voluntary Separation Incentive and Special Separation Bonus Programs. His idea to provide career paths and milestones in line with the officer career model, led to the career field education and training plan, three-level and seven-level technical schools for all career fields, and mandatory in-residence PME schools. He also found himself involved with issues such as homosexuals serving in the military, Air Force specialty codes opening up to women, assignment policies including the Enlisted Quarterly Assignments Listing (EQUAL) and EQUAL-Plus, and even the introduction of the new senior NCO stripes. Pfingston remained active in what he called the "communication chain" of former CMSAFs advocating for the enlisted force after his retirement. CMSAF Pfingston died in 2007.

**9.5.3.4.11. CMSAF David J. Campanale:**

9.5.3.4.11.1. Worcester, Massachusetts, native David J. Campanale said he had the world by the throat after high school. A promising athlete, when a baseball career fell through, his mother encouraged him to join the Air Force in 1970. Campanale completed aircraft maintenance technical school despite poor study habits and breaking his collarbone playing football. He credits his supervisors at his first base with turning his attitude around. Campanale sought challenges, volunteering for several tours to Andersen Air Force Base, Guam, in support of B-52 Arc Light missions in Southeast Asia. He later volunteered to transfer to aerial repair. As he rose through the ranks, Campanale earned the distinguished graduate award at both the NCO academy and senior NCO academy and was stripes for exceptional performer-promoted to Master Sergeant. He later served as a senior enlisted advisor, a role called "richly rewarding."

**CMSAF David J. Campanale**
October 1994 – November 1996

9.5.3.4.11.2. The year CMSAF Campanale began his tour, the military launched the new TRICARE health program. The change introduced many questions and a great deal of anxiety. He led the charge to alleviate those feelings through education. Also, when Congress threatened to change the retirement system to "High One" effectively reducing retirement pay, Campanale quickly responded. With senior leader support, Campanale stood before Congress in the successful fight against the proposed change. Another important recruitment and retention milestone was adoption of the one-plus-one dormitory standard, which gave each Airman his or her own room. Not a proponent of long speeches, while visiting bases he encouraged questions rather than delivering a speech, which created meaningful dialogue. He believes anyone can become CMSAF and offers those who want to follow in his footsteps this piece of advice: Be honest and keep your promise. Campanale continues to actively mentor Airmen serving today.

### 9.5.3.4.12. CMSAF Eric W. Benken:

**CMSAF Eric W. Benken**
November 1996 – August 1999

9.5.3.4.12.1. Raised in Cincinnati, Ohio, after graduating high school Eric W. Benken moved to Houston, Texas, to join his parents. Struggling to find a good paying job out of the area, he joined the Air Force as an administrative specialist. Although first assigned to Ellington Air Force Base, Texas (less than 25 miles from Houston), he would get his chance to travel 9 months later, on orders to Ching Chuan Kang Air Base, Taiwan. During his tour, he deployed to South Vietnam, where he spent his 20th birthday. As the United States Air Forces Europe senior enlisted advisor, he facilitated the highly successful beddown of forces during the Bosnia Operation Joint Endeavor. He led numerous quality-of-life initiatives, including eliminating/remodeling a third of the United States Air Forces Europe zero-privacy dormitories, making way for the newly developed one-plus-one dormitories. During his assignment, Benken crafted the NCO Professional Development Seminar, an effort to fill the career education void between Airman Leadership School and the NCO academy.

9.5.3.4.12.2. During his tenure as CMSAF, he focused heavily on fundamental discipline, getting back to basics, and changing the culture of the Air Force to meet new expeditionary requirements. He championed Warrior Week at basic training and ensured funding for a simulated deployed location at Lackland Air Force Base, Texas. He instituted changes in the First Sergeant Academy curriculum, focusing on deployment responsibilities. He believed changing the title "senior enlisted advisor" to "Command Chief Master Sergeant" and adding the star to the chevron were critical to the success of these positions, in garrison and on the battlefield. CMSAF Benken engaged Congress and special interest groups on numerous fronts, ultimately defeating attempts to alter basic military training gender-integrated training, and reversing the diminished retirement system of 1986. Other significant challenges included ensuring TRICARE met health care needs, and modernizing the force with a limited budget. He believed Air Force leaders should focus on the future and take steps to prepare the force for the next century. Benken served as the first co-chair of the Air Force Retiree Council, currently serves on the board of directors for the Airmen Memorial Foundation and the Mission Readiness Organization Executive Advisory Council, and continues to speak at a variety of Air Force functions.

### 9.5.3.4.13. CMSAF Jim Finch:

9.5.3.4.13.1. Jim Finch entered the Air Force from East Hampton, New York, expecting to do only a 4-year hitch. He planned to learn a trade and see what the world had to offer and move on. Finch spent the early part of his career in the "bomb dumps" as a missile maintenance crew chief before becoming a PME instructor. After 4 years of teaching, Finch moved to the Leadership and Management Development Center at Maxwell Air Force Base Alabama. While there, he helped develop a correspondence version of the NCO preparatory course, and taught new PME instructors. He was subsequently selected as the Air Force NCO PME functional manager at the Air Force Military Personnel Center. While there, he was involved in restructuring the PME program from four to three levels and implementing procedures to create Airman Leadership School and allow Master Sergeants to attend the senior NCO academy. Finch later served as an NCO Academy commandant, the 11th Air Force senior enlisted advisor, and Air Combat Command, Command Chief Master Sergeant.

**CMSAF Frederick J. Finch**
August 1999 – June 2002

9.5.3.4.13.2. When CMSAF Finch took the reins, the Air Force was moving from a cold war to an expeditionary mindset. He implemented CMSAF Benken's basic training Warrior Week vision to help new recruits understand that the expeditionary Air Force was not a temporary concept. He credits the program's success to the men and women at Lackland candidates and gave commanders more selection flexibility. Known as a man of vision, he spent 3 years focusing on enlisted members' concerns, and implementing programs to improve future preparedness. Finch recognized that the armed forces had to change to meet changing threats to national security. He believed future-focused leaders were paramount to success and made significant contributions to ensure the force developed that kind of leader. Finch maintains his vision for Airmen by serving on boards of Air Force-associated organizations, visiting Air Force members worldwide, and supporting current CMSAF agendas.

#### 9.5.3.4.14. CMSAF Gerald R. Murray:

**CMSAF Gerald R. Murray**
July 2002 – June 2006

9.5.3.4.14.1. Gerald R. Murray, a native of Boiling Springs, North Carolina, grew up on his grandfather's farm. Graduating high school in 1974, he briefly attended college, married his school sweetheart, and worked in textile mills and construction before entering the Air Force as an F-4 aircraft crew chief in 1977. Murray's performance and capabilities were quickly recognized by his promotion to Senior Airman below the zone, and selection as an F-16 aircraft maintenance instructor. He continued to excel as the senior F-16 crew chief on "Victor Alert" at Incirlik Air Base, Turkey, and later as an A-10 squadron production superintendent. Deployed in support of Operations Desert Shield and Desert Storm, he played a key role as the combat turn director at the most forward operation location in theater, garnering the Bronze Star, and later the Air Force General Lew Allen Trophy. After standing up a new A-10 squadron at Moody Air Force Base, Georgia, Murray's performance and leadership were recognized again when he was pulled from the flight line to serve as the 347th Wing Senior Enlisted Advisor and Command Chief Master Sergeant. He later served as the command Chief Master Sergeant at 5th Air Force, United States Forces Japan, and Pacific Air Forces Command.

9.5.3.4.14.2. An evolving expeditionary air force and a changed world after the 11 September 2001 terrorist attacks were catalysts for change during Murray's tenure. Murray refocused basic military training and PME toward expeditionary combat principles and took a leading role in developing a new physical fitness program to improve Air Force-wide capabilities and readiness. Additionally, Murray led efforts to balance the enlisted force structure by increasing high-year tenure for four enlisted grades, bringing back the career job reservation and NCO retraining programs, and redistributing senior NCO promotions in critical and unbalanced Air Force specialty codes. Understanding the need to maintain strong leadership, he initiated a deliberate approach to NCO professional development; led changes to the management of Chief Master Sergeants, including alignment under the Air Force Senior Leaders Management Office, and added a Chief Master Sergeant's leadership course to the enlisted PME continuum. In retirement, Murray remains active in shaping Airmen development, serving with Air Force professional organizations and continuing to speak throughout the force.

#### 9.5.3.4.15. CMSAF Rodney J. McKinley:

9.5.3.4.15.1. Rodney J. McKinley grew up in Mt. Orab, Ohio, and originally entered the Air Force in 1974 as a medical technician. He separated from the Air Force in 1977 to pursue his education. He returned to active duty in 1982 as an aircraft maintenance specialist and served in various aircraft maintenance positions at Myrtle Beach Air Force Base, South Carolina, and Clark Air Base, Philippines. In 1991, he became a first sergeant, a position he held for the next 10 years, with assignments at Myrtle Beach Air Force Base, South Carolina; Ghedi Air Base, Italy; Tinker Air Force Base, Oklahoma; and Ramstein Air Base, Germany. Chief McKinley then served as a command Chief Master Sergeant at Ramstein Air Base, Germany; Langley Air Force Base, Virginia; and 11th Air Force at Elmendorf Air Force Base, Alaska. In February 2003, during the early days of Operation Iraqi Freedom, he deployed as Command Chief Master Sergeant to the 379th Air Expeditionary Wing, Southwest Asia. Before being selected as the 15th CMSAF, he was the Pacific Air Forces Command Chief Master Sergeant at Hickam Air Force Base, Hawaii.

**CMSAF Rodney J. McKinley**
June 2006 – June 2009

9.5.3.4.15.2. During his tenure, CMSAF McKinley was an advocate for winning the Global War on Terrorism, developing and taking care of Airmen, and modernizing aging air, space, and cyberspace assets. CMSAF McKinley focused on properly organizing, training, and equipping Airmen during a time when many were being tasked outside their core competencies. His efforts to improve the enlisted evaluation system resulted in the first major changes to feedback and performance report forms since 1990. CMSAF McKinley also advocated for an educated enlisted corps and strongly encouraged Airmen to pursue their Community College of the Air Force degree earlier in their careers. A strong advocate for the "American Airman" spirit, he opened the door for creation of the Airman's Creed, which codified core Air Force beliefs and articulated the warrior ethos. His vision led to the creation of the Enlisted Heroes Walk on the parade field at Lackland Air Force Base, Texas, and the return of the enlisted collar brass and Good Conduct Medal. CMSAF McKinley also pursued improvements in Airman health and fitness, wounded warrior care, child care, spousal employment opportunities, and accompanied and unaccompanied housing.

### 9.5.3.4.16. CMSAF James A. Roy:

**CMSAF James A. Roy**
June 2009 – January 2013

9.5.3.4.16.1. James A. Roy grew up in Monroe, Michigan, and originally entered the Air Force in 1982 as a heavy equipment operator. He served in various civil engineer positions at MacDill Air Force Base, Florida; Osan Air Base, Republic of Korea; Kunsan Air Base, Korea; Andersen Air Force Base, Guam; and Keesler Air Force Base, Mississippi. He returned to the site of his original technical training—Fort Leonard Wood, Missouri—as an instructor and instructor supervisor. As a Senior Master Sergeant, he transferred into personnel as the military personnel flight superintendent, Keesler Air Force Base, in 1999. From there, Chief Roy served as a Command Chief Master Sergeant at wing, numbered Air Force, and unified combatant command levels. These assignments included Columbus Air Force Base, Mississippi; Charleston Air Force Base South Carolina; Langley Air Force Base, Virginia; and 5th Air Force and United States Forces Japan, at Yokota Air Base, Japan. In October 2004, he deployed as the 386th Air Expeditionary Wing, Southwest Asia Command Chief Master Sergeant. He then served as the United States Pacific Command senior enlisted leader at Camp H.M. Smith, Hawaii.

9.5.3.4.16.2. Chief Roy's key focus areas included ensuring Airmen were ready for joint and coalition operations; deliberately developing Airmen through education, training and experience; and building a culture of resiliency within Airmen and their families. He worked to expand and solidify training and engagement in joint and coalition environments, which helped enhance the employability of Airmen in the increasingly joint and coalition warfighting environment. He also stressed the importance of updating and expanding distance-learning opportunities, and developed and promoted the Enlisted PME-Next construct, designed to close the gap in PME following Airman Leadership School.

### 9.5.3.4.17. CMSAF James A. Cody:

9.5.3.4.17.1. James A. Cody grew up in Lakeville, Massachusetts, and entered the Air Force in 1984 as an air traffic controller. He served in various air traffic control positions at Ramstein Air Base, Germany; Pease Air Force Base, New Hampshire; Vandenberg Air Force Base, California; Osan Air Base, Republic of Korea; Incirlik Air Base, Turkey; Langley Air Force Base, Virginia; and MacDill Air Force Base, Florida. In April 2002, he deployed as the superintendent of the Joint Task Force–Southwest Asia Combat Airspace Management Cell. Chief Cody then served as a Command Chief Master Sergeant at a task force; wing; numbered Air Force; and major command level. These included assignments to Travis Air Force Base, California; MacDill Air Force Base, Florida; 18th Air Force at Scott Air Force Base, Illinois, and Air Education and Training Command at Joint Base San Antonio-Randolph, Texas.

**CMSAF James A. Cody**
January 2013 – February 2017

9.5.3.4.17.2. Immediately upon assuming the position, Chief Cody committed to the continued evolution of the enlisted force. He identified various policies and processes, and with the support of the Air Force Chief of Staff and Enlisted Board of Directors moved each of them forward to ensure the enlisted force was prepared for future challenges. He focused on the deliberate development of Airmen, evolving enlisted PME to a blended learning model, and establishing Developmental Special Duties, which ensured top Airmen were in leadership positions that best leveraged their proven performance across the force. He heightened the conversation surrounding work/life balance and the importance of finding a reasonable and sustainable demand signal for Airmen, and strengthened care and support programs for Wounded Warriors, including Airmen with invisible wounds such as TBI and/or PTSD. Additionally, Chief Cody moved the Enlisted Evaluation System and Weighted Airman Promotion System forward to ensure they served today's Air Force, and Airmen. He led the biggest changes to both systems since their inception in 1970, ensuring job performance was the greatest factor towards promotion.

**CMSAF Kaleth O. Wright**
February 2017 – Present

**9.5.3.4.18. CMSAF Kaleth O. Wright:**

9.5.3.4.18.1. Kaleth O. Wright grew up in Columbus, Georgia and entered the Air Force in 1989 as a dental technician. He served in a variety of dental positions at Pope Air Force Base, North Carolina; Osan Air Base, Republic of Korea; and Kadena Air Base, Japan. In 2001, he became a professional military education instructor, serving in various positions at the Kisling Noncommissioned Officer Academy, Kapaun Air Station, Germany. He returned to his primary Air Force Specialty in 2004, serving as the Dental Flight Chief at Pope Air Force Base, North Carolina, squadron superintendent at Osan Air Base, Republic of Korea, Joint Base Elmendorf-Richardson, Alaska and Kadena Air Base, Japan where he also served as the Superintendent of the 18th Mission Support Group. He was selected as the Command Chief Master Sergeant for the 22d Air Refueling Wing, McConnell Air Force Base, Kansas in 2012 and served as the Command Chief, 9th Air and Space Expeditionary Task Force - Afghanistan, Kabul, Afghanistan in 2014. In 2015, he became the Command Chief Master Sergeant for 3d Air Force and 17th Expeditionary Air Force, Ramstein Air Base before becoming the Command Chief Master Sergeant of U.S. Air Forces in Europe and U.S. Air Forces Africa. He has deployed in support of Operations DESERT SHIELD/STORM and ENDURING FREEDOM.

**9.6. Junior Enlisted Airmen Responsibilities.** Junior enlisted airmen must:

9.6.1. Demonstrate a foundational understanding of what it means to be an Airman in the profession of arms. Understand, accept and embody the Air Force core values, Airman's Creed and exhibit professional behavior, military bearing, respect for authority and high standards of dress and personal appearance, both on- and off-duty, at home and abroad. Correct other Airmen who violate standards.

9.6.2. Accept, execute, and complete all duties, instructions, responsibilities, and lawful orders in a timely and efficient manner. Place the requirements of official duties and responsibilities ahead of personal desires.

9.6.3. Detect and correct conduct and behavior that may place themselves or others at risk, and issue lawful orders when placed in charge of a work activity or task involving other junior enlisted airmen.

9.6.4. Begin to learn and demonstrate the institutional and occupational competencies outlined in Air Force Doctrine Document 1-1, *Leadership and Force Development*; AFMAN 36-2647, Table A2.2; and the appropriate Career Field Education and Training Plan. These competencies are gained through a combination of education (e.g., PME and academic programs), training (e.g., basic military training and career development courses, and experience (e.g., primary and special duty and professional organization participation).

9.6.5. Meet all pre-deployment and mission requirements and maintain the highest level of technical readiness. Attain and maintain a skill level commensurate with rank, as well as a high degree of proficiency in duties outlined in the Career Field Education and Training Plan.

9.6.6. Increase personal resilience by understanding and mastering the social, physical, mental and spiritual domains of comprehensive airmen fitness, and encouraging others to do the same.

9.6.6.1. Be mentally ready to accomplish the mission. Issues that can affect and detract from mental readiness are quality of life, financial problems, sexual harassment or assault, discrimination, stress, marital problems and substance abuse. These issues can prevent Airmen from focusing on the mission, diminish motivation, erode a positive attitude and reduce work quality. Be aware of warning signs and seek appropriate assistance through the chain of command, chaplain, medical community and helping agencies, and help others do the same.

9.6.6.1.1. Be alert for signs of depression or suicide. If depressed or suicidal, seek immediate assistance. Practice and teach the DoD Ask, Care and Escort concept for suicide prevention. Ask - "Are you thinking about harming yourself or others?" Care -calmly take control of the situation, show genuine concern and listen. Escort (not direct) - the person to mental health, the chaplain, or First Sergeant. Call for help but never leave the person alone. junior enlisted airmen are critical to suicide prevention efforts.

9.6.6.1.2. Be alert for behavioral changes and/or signs of traumatic stress in themselves and others, and seek assistance.

9.6.6.2. Be physically ready to accomplish the mission. Actively participate in the Air Force fitness program and always meet Air Force fitness standards by maintaining a year-round physical conditioning program that emphasizes total fitness, to include: aerobic conditioning, muscular fitness training and healthy eating.

9.6.6.3. Be socially ready to accomplish the mission. Build relationships and networks that promote well-being and optimal performance. Teamwork, communication, connectedness and social support are key components of social readiness.

9.6.6.4. Be spiritually ready to accomplish the mission. Spiritual readiness is the proactive practice of establishing a sense of purpose or personal priorities to develop the skills needed in times of stress, hardship and tragedy. Spiritual readiness may or may not include religious activities.

9.6.7. Be a knowledgeable Airman. Stay informed on issues affecting the Air Force using Air Force media sources (e.g., af.mil and my.af.mil). Ensure no discredit to the Air Force or compromise of operational security when using personal and government information systems, including social media.

9.6.8. Contribute to a culture and climate of dignity and respect by supporting and enforcing a zero tolerance policy for sexual harassment, sexual assault, and discrimination. Know and understand the wingman concept. Airmen take care of fellow Airmen. A good wingman shares a bond with other Airmen and intervenes to maintain an environment free of any behaviors that hinder an Airman's ability to maximize their potential and contribution. Positively support one another, both on- and off-duty.

9.6.9. Demonstrate effective followership by enthusiastically supporting, explaining and promoting leaders' decisions. Develop innovative ways to improve processes and provide suggestions up the chain of command that will directly contribute to unit and mission success. Promote a culture of innovation and continuous process improvement to identify and resolve deficiencies.

9.6.10. Continue to pursue personal and professional development through education and involvement. Promote camaraderie, embrace esprit de corps and act as an Air Force ambassador (e.g., join professional organizations and/or participate in organization and community events).

**9.7. NCO Responsibilities**. In addition to all junior enlisted Airmen responsibilities, NCOs must:

9.7.1. Lead and develop subordinates and exercise effective followership in mission accomplishment. NCOs have the authority to issue lawful orders to complete assigned tasks in accordance with Article 92 of the Uniform Code of Military Justice.

9.7.2. Increase knowledge and understanding of, and mentor junior enlisted airmen on the institutional and occupational competencies required to accomplish the mission. These competencies are gained through a combination of education (e.g., academic programs and PME), training (e.g., on-the-job training), and experience (e.g., mentoring and/or participating in professional organizations).

9.7.3. Increase personal and subordinates resilience by championing the social, physical, mental and spiritual domains of comprehensive airman fitness and encouraging others to do the same.

9.7.3.1. Champion social readiness. Develop and lead team-building or networking activities in the unit and encourage subordinates to participate in outside social engagements.

9.7.3.2. Champion physical readiness. Lead the way by promoting, supporting, and participating in unit physical training activities and the Air Force fitness program. Incorporate physical training into the teams' duty schedules as the mission allows.

9.7.3.3. Champion mental readiness. Be actively aware of issues in subordinates that can impact mental readiness and mission effectiveness. Address issues negatively impacting mental readiness, and take positive steps to resolve them in a responsible manner.

9.7.3.4. Champion spiritual readiness to help accomplish the mission. Allow for and encourage subordinates to develop spiritual skills needed in times of stress, hardship and tragedy. This may or may not include religious activities.

9.7.4. Demonstrate and facilitate a climate of effective followership by willingly owning, explaining and promoting leaders' decisions. Develop innovative ways to improve processes, reduce costs and improve efficiency and provide suggestions up the chain of command that will directly contribute to unit and mission success.

9.7.5. If senior in grade, accept responsibility for assuming the role of leader. Responsibility and accountability increase commensurate with grade. Within enlisted grades, NCOs take rank and precedence over all junior enlisted Airmen and other NCOs according to rank. Within the same grade, use: date of rank, total active federal military service date, pay date, and date of birth, in this order, to determine seniority. **NOTE:** In some circumstances NCOs who are lower in rank may be placed in charge of other NCOs of the same grade (i.e., a Technical Sergeant, with a date of rank of 1 Apr 08, is placed in charge of a fellow Technical Sergeant, with a date of rank of 1 Apr 07). When placed in charge by commanders, these NCOs have the authority to issue lawful orders appropriate for mission accomplishment.

9.7.6. Take an active leadership and supervisory role by investing in subordinates. Stay professionally engaged with subordinates on a daily basis both on and off-duty. Understand a subordinate's environment by visiting living spaces and installation support facilities (e.g., dining facilities, chapel centers, recreation centers, dormitories, and enlisted clubs) to be familiar with off-duty opportunities and living conditions. Mentorship is a critical component of leadership; NCOs must use professional and personal experiences to positively mentor others.

9.7.7. Train and develop subordinates to ensure they are technically ready to accomplish the mission, and guide and instruct them to ensure they are prepared to accept increased levels of authority and responsibility.

9.7.8. Remain keenly aware of individual and group dynamics affecting readiness and safety. Identify those exhibiting high-risk behaviors, intervene, and deter further unsafe practices.

9.7.9. Appropriately recognize and reward individuals whose military conduct and duty performance clearly exceed established standards. Ensure subordinates are held accountable when they do not meet established standards.

9.7.10. Provide feedback and counseling to subordinates on performance, career opportunities, promotions, benefits, and entitlements. Feedback and counseling are required utilizing the Airman Comprehensive Assessment. However, continuous informal and formal feedback, mentorship, and counseling opportunities exist to optimize a subordinate's potential and performance. On an annual basis, NCOs must discuss and provide a copy of the Air Force Benefits Fact Sheet to subordinates during feedback.

9.7.11. Promote a culture of Airmen who are flexible and capable of mastering multiple tasks and mission requirements. Pursue opportunities outside primary Air Force Specialty Code, encourage retraining as needed to balance the force and meet mission requirements. Promote a culture of innovation and continuous process improvement to identify and resolve deficiencies.

9.7.12. Complete and promote PME and professional enhancement courses to develop and cultivate leadership skills and military professionalism. Continue personal and subordinate development.

**9.8. Senior NCO Responsibilities.** In addition to meeting all junior enlisted Airmen and NCO responsibilities, senior NCOs must:

9.8.1. Epitomize excellence, professionalism, pride, and competence, serving as a role model for all Airmen to emulate. Reflect the highest qualities of a leader and professional and provide highly effective leadership. A senior NCO's primary purpose is mission accomplishment. Senior NCOs must lead people and manage programs while maintaining the highest level of readiness to ensure mission success.

9.8.2. Translate leaders' direction into specific tasks and responsibilities their teams can understand and execute. Senior NCOs must study leaders' decisions to understand their rationale and goals. They then must fully leverage their personal experience and knowledge to more effectively accomplish the mission.

9.8.3. Help leaders make informed decisions. Senior NCOs must draw upon their knowledge and experience to provide constructive input to best meet the challenges facing their organizations.

9.8.4. Be an active, visible leader. Deliberately develop junior enlisted Airmen, NCOs, fellow senior NCOs and Company Grade Officers into better followers, leaders, and supervisors.

9.8.5. Secure and promote PME and professional enhancement courses for themselves and subordinates to develop and cultivate leadership skills and military professionalism. Provide for subordinates to study Career Development Course and PME material during duty time, when appropriate. Complete an associate's degree through the community College of the Air Force, if not already earned, and continue development for self and subordinates through available education, leadership lectures and seminars, and the Chief of Staff of the Air Force Reading List.

9.8.6. Support civilian and commissioned officers' continued development by sharing knowledge and experience to best meet the organization's mission requirements. Build and maintain professional relationships with both, striving to create effective leadership teams.

9.8.7. Ensure money, facilities and other resources are utilized in an effective and efficient manner and in the best interest of the Air Force. Plan resource utilization, replenishment, and budget allocation to ensure personnel are provided the equipment and resources needed to effectively accomplish the mission. Understand, manage, and explain manning requirements and capabilities. Promote a culture of innovation and continuous process improvement to identify and resolve deficiencies.

9.8.8. Promote responsible behaviors within all Airmen. Readily detect and correct unsafe or irresponsible behaviors that impact unit or individual readiness. Promote peer involvement in detecting and correcting those behaviors, and recognize and reward Airmen who properly employ risk management philosophies.

9.8.9. While every Airman has a duty and obligation to act professionally and meet all Air Force standards at all times, senior NCOs have a special obligation and responsibility to ensure the Air Force retains a climate and culture of dignity and respect, as outlined in AFPD-1, *Air Force Culture*. Senior NCOs who fail to monitor, correct and advise subordinates and leaders when needed have not executed their responsibility.

**9.9. Enlisted Duty Titles.** When properly applied, duty titles facilitate a quick understanding of a person's role and level of responsibility. Enlisted duty titles are assigned based upon the scope of responsibility and the duties being performed. The following duty titles are the official, authorized duty titles for the enlisted force. Exceptions include special positions listed in AFI 36-2618, Chapter 10 and limited instances when a person's position or duties do not meet the criteria listed below. In such circumstances, enlisted personnel will have a duty title that most accurately reflects their day-to-day duties. When published, duty titles specified in functional directives will be utilized.

9.9.1. Supervisor. Used for junior enlisted Airmen and NCOs who are first line supervisors (e.g., Heavy Equipment Supervisor and Shift Supervisor). Junior enlisted airmen will not have the duty title "Supervisor" unless they are at least a SrA, an ALS graduate, and supervise the work of others.

9.9.2. Noncommissioned Officer in Charge. Used only for NCOs and senior NCOs in charge of a work center or element. Noncommissioned Officers in Charge typically have subordinate supervisors (e.g., Noncommissioned Officer in Charge, Installation Security and Noncommissioned Officer in Charge, Outbound Assignments). Noncommissioned Officer in Charge is also used for those whose primary duty is a unit-wide program or function management (e.g., Noncommissioned Officer in Charge, Unit Training Management and Noncommissioned Officer in Charge, Resource Management) even if they do not directly supervise personnel.

9.9.3. Section Chief. Used for NCOs and senior NCOs in charge of a section with at least two subordinate work centers or elements (e.g., Section Chief, Network Control Center). Section chiefs are typically senior NCOs and the rank will vary depending upon the size of the section (number of enlisted personnel, number of work centers, and scope of responsibilities).

9.9.4. Flight Chief. Used for NCOs and senior NCOs who are the enlisted leaders of a flight (e.g., Flight Chief, Information Systems Flight; and Flight Chief, Operations Flight). Flight chiefs are typically senior NCOs and the rank will vary depending upon the size of the flight (number of enlisted personnel, number of work centers, and scope of responsibilities).

9.9.5. Superintendent. Used for senior NCOs in charge of squadron or wing level functions when having oversight of functions within their respective units. Superintendents are typically a Chief Master Sergeant and occasionally a Senior Master Sergeant or Master Sergeant at squadron level and below (e.g., Aircraft Maintenance Squadron Superintendent and Command Post Superintendent). Only senior NCOs will hold the duty title of Superintendent.

9.9.6. Manager. In addition to the special senior NCO positions of Air Force Career Field Manager and Major Command Functional Manager, the title of manager is used for NCOs and senior NCOs who are program, project, and policy managers at Numbered Air Forces, Major Command, Direct Reporting Unit, Field Operating Agency, Joint Staff, or Air Staff levels. They may or may not have personnel working for them and may be the enlisted leader of the branch, division, or directorate (e.g., Manager, Intelligence Systems Integration and Manager, Joint Operations Analysis and Planning).

9.9.7. Chief. Used for Chief Master Sergeants who are program, project, or policy managers at Numbered Air Forces, Major Command, Direct Reporting Unit, Field Operating Agency, Joint Staff, or Air Staff. They may or may not have personnel working for them and may be the enlisted leader of the branch, division, or directorate (e.g., Chief, Air Force Enlisted Force Development; and Chief, Airmen Assignments). **NOTE**: Senior Enlisted Advisor, Senior Enlisted Leader and Chief Enlisted Manager duty titles are only used when holding a designated and approved position. Approved use of the title Senior Enlisted Advisor or Senior Enlisted Leader is not always synonymous with the role of a Command Chief Master Sergeant.

**9.10. Special Enlisted Positions.** Enlisted Airmen may serve in a variety of special leadership or duty positions outside of their functional specialty. These positions include, but are not limited to:

9.10.1. **Chief Master Sergeant of the Air Force.** The Chief Master Sergeant of the Air Force is the senior enlisted leader of the Air Force and takes precedence over all enlisted members. The Chief Master Sergeant of the Air Force provides leadership to the enlisted force and advises the Chief of Staff of the Air Airforce, Secretary of the Air Force, Chairman Joint Chief of Staff, and the Secretary of Defense on enlisted matters. The Chief Master Sergeant of the Air Force communicates with the force, serves on boards and committees for numerous organizations affecting Airmen, testifies before Congress, and is the Air Force career field manager for command chief master sergeants and group superintendents. The Chief Master Sergeant of the Air Force also consults with sister service senior enlisted advisors on issues affecting all enlisted members; engages with foreign military leadership regarding theater security cooperation and partner nation development efforts; represents the AF to the American public, professional organizations and the media; and manages the AF Order of the Sword Program. The written abbreviation is "CMSAF" and the official term of address is "Chief Master Sergeant of the Air Force" or "Chief."

9.10.2. **Command Chief Master Sergeant and Senior Enlisted Leader**. The Command Chief Master Sergeant is the senior enlisted leader in a wing, Numbered Air Force, Major Command, Direct Reporting Unit, Field Operating Agency, state or other similar organization. The equivalent to a Command Chief Master Sergeant in a Combatant Command or Joint Task Force is a Combatant Command or Joint Task Force Senior Enlisted Leader. The Command Chief Master Sergeant and/or Senior Enlisted Leader provides general supervision to the command's enlisted force and is responsible for advising commanders and staff on mission effectiveness, professional development, recognition, key enlisted Airmen nominations and hires, accelerated promotions, performance evaluations, military readiness, training, utilization, health, morale, and welfare of the organization's enlisted, and takes action to address shortfalls or challenges. They also regularly visit Airmen, to include traveling to geographically separated units/elements; interact with sister service counterparts; serve as a liaison to and work closely with the local community; actively lead in the organization's fitness program; and ensure the enlisted force is ready to meet deployment requirements. RegAF Command Chief Master Sergeant and/or Senior Leaders serve on the enlisted force distribution panel by advising the senior rater and panel on enlisted Airmen's potential to serve in the next higher grade. They assist and advise in the selection and nomination of enlisted Airmen for positions of greater responsibility, to include developmental special duties. The Command Chief Master Sergeant is the functional manager for group superintendents and first sergeants in their organization. The Command Chief Master Sergeant performs other duties as required/directed by their commander.

9.10.3. **Group Superintendent**. Group Superintendents provide leadership, management, and general supervision of the organization's enlisted force; and guidance in organizing, equipping, training, and mobilizing the group to meet home station and expeditionary mission requirements. RegAF superintendents may support and advise the squadron commanders and superintendents prior to the enlisted force distribution panel on promotion eligible Airmen's performance and potential to serve in the next higher grade. They also assist and advise in the selection and nomination of enlisted Airmen for positions of greater responsibility, to include developmental special duties. Total Force superintendents manage and direct resource activities; interpret and enforce policies and applicable directives; establish control procedures to meet mission goals and standards; and actively support and maintain robust recognition programs. They work in concert with other enlisted leaders such as squadron superintendents and first sergeants to oversee the readiness, training, health, morale, welfare, and quality of life of assigned personnel. They represent the commander at various meetings, visit Airmen in the group, participate on advisory councils and boards, interact with sister service counterparts as required, and actively lead in the organization's fitness program. They perform other duties as directed by the group commander.

9.10.4. **Commandant**. Commandants are assigned at each ALS, NCOA, collocated PME Center, senior NCOA, and the First Sergeant Academy. They implement and enforce policies, procedures, and directives directly related to the accomplishment of the school's course of instruction. They analyze data; provide direction and vision; and ensure effectiveness via curriculum evaluations, faculty mentoring, student achievement/feedback, and contact with senior leaders. Additionally, they coordinate frequent visits from high-ranking military and civilian leadership.

9.10.5. **Enlisted Engagement Manager/International Affairs**. Enlisted Engagement Managers plan, coordinate, and conduct enlisted engagements with partner nations on behalf of Secretary of the Air Force, International Affairs. They serve at the Major Command and Headquarters Air Force.

9.10.6. **Enlisted Legislative Fellows**. Enlisted Legislative Fellows are senior NCOs who receive instruction and hands-on experience on Capitol Hill through education and development activities consisting of an intensive orientation of Congress; a full time assignment to the staff of a member, committee, or support agency of congress in Washington D.C.; and periodic seminars throughout the assignment. They write and develop research for potential legislative issues of immediate or ongoing concern to the Air Force and nation. The Enlisted Legislative Fellows are assigned to the Legislative Liaison, Office of the Secretary of the Air Force.

9.10.7. **Command Chief Master Sergeant Executive Assistant**. Command chief executive assistants perform assistant duties in support of a Command Chief Master Sergeant or Combatant Command Senior Enlisted Leader at the wing, Numbered Air Force, Direct reporting uniting/Field Operating Agency, Major Command and Combatant Command levels, as well as the Chief Master Sergeant of the Air Force. They serve as personal assistants who oversee tasks requiring attention and pass pertinent data, information, and insight from the staff to the Command Chief Master Sergeant and/or Senior Leader, as well as other duties as required.

9.10.8. **Defense Attaché**. Defense attachés serve in United States embassies in countries around the world. They manage and maintain Defense Attaché Office budget and fiscal data, maintain Defense Attaché Office information files; coordinate United States Naval ship visits and United States military aircraft over-flight and landing clearances with host country officials; coordinate office support requirements with embassy officials; and perform office administrative and support duties according to Defense Intelligence Agency standards.

9.10.9. **Inspections Superintendent**. The inspections superintendent provides feedback, support, and assistance to the Inspector General and Director of Inspections for implementing the Air Force Inspection System at Field Operating Agency/Direct Reporting Units, wings and wing equivalents, major Commands, and Headquarters Air Force. They advise the Inspector General and Director of Inspections on all activities related to the Air Force Inspections Systems.

9.10.10. **Language and Culture Advisor**. Language and culture advisors serve as key advisors and consultants to commanders and supervisors on issues pertaining to foreign language and regional culture. They prepare written reports, briefs and summaries based on specific requirements, and serve as an interpreter/translator as required.

9.10.11. **Enlisted Aide**. Enlisted aides perform tasks and details that, if performed by general or flag officers, would be at the expense of the officer's primary military and official duties. Duties relate to the support of military and official responsibilities of the general or flag officer and include assisting with the care, cleanliness, and order of assigned quarters, uniforms and military personal equipment, as well as planning, preparing, arranging, and conducting official social functions and activities, such as receptions, parties, and dinners.

9.10.12. **Protocol Specialist**. Protocol specialists provide expertise and support for all protocol matters at the installation, wing, Numbered Air Force, Major Commands, and Headquarters levels. They perform, manage and direct all administrative and procedural protocol duties and responsibilities, and provide protocol support for distinguished visitors at all levels. Support includes escort duties, and planning and executing program itinerary visits, official ceremonies and special events.

9.10.13. **Unit Deployment Manager (UDM)**. UDMs are the principal advisor to the organization commander on all issues related to deployment readiness and execution. They implement and execute commander-directed deployment actions for assigned personnel and cargo; monitor and maintain unit deployment readiness statistics; implement commander, Major Commands, and Headquarters Air Force deployment readiness guidance; and exercise general supervision over assigned squadron personnel in all matters related to deployment readiness and execution.

9.10.14. **Missile Facility Manager**. Missile facility managers supervise daily activities at the missile alert facility. They perform routine equipment inspections and emergency operating procedures, and respond to actions directed by the missile combat crew to ensure proper operations of the facility.

9.10.15. **Courier**. Couriers safeguard and deliver armed forces courier service material. They provide adequate protection for material from receipt through delivery or to storage, and caution handlers to exercise care in storing material. Couriers verify each item by identification number when receipting for or delivering material, and maintain constant surveillance over material in custody on the courier route.

9.10.16. **Airman Dorm Leader (ADL).** ADLs perform full time as a manager of Air Force unaccompanied housing facilities. They are responsible for daily operations to include mentoring residents and assisting them in their adjustment to military life; ensuring residents comply with directives and military living standards; and assessing good order and discipline. They also manage facilities and bases areas; perform budget and program execution; and maintain supplies, furnishings, and equipment necessary for providing quality facilities.

**9.11. Developmental Special Duties.** Enlisted Airmen in the rank of SSgt through MSgt may have the opportunity to serve in one of ten developmental special duty positions. Developmental special duties are identified as such due to their unique leadership roles and the Airman's responsibility to mentor and mold future leaders. To ensure the highest quality Airmen are assigned to these positions, the Air Force has implemented a nomination process. The nomination process provides commanders, through their respective major command, an opportunity to nominate their best Airmen to fill these critical positions while providing a developmental career path. The Developmental Special Duties are:

9.11.1. **Academy Military Training NCO.** Academy Military Training NCOs lead, mentor, instruct, develop, and supervise United States Air Force Academy cadets. They serve as the principal advisor to the Cadet Squadron Commander on all issues relating to cadets. Academy Military Training NCOs prepare cadets to support mission requirements, provide military training, and exercise general supervision and leadership to ensure cadet and squadron success.

9.11.2. **Airman and Family Readiness Center NCO.** Airman and Family Readiness Center NCOs are the principal military advisor to the Airman and Family Readiness Center director and staff on matters regarding readiness, resilience, and deployment of Airmen and their families. They support the Airman and Family Readiness Center's overall functional mission to ensure programs and services are responsive, and they develop and provide personal and family readiness services related to pre-deployment, deployment, sustainment, redeployment, reintegration, and post-deployment education and consultation.

9.11.3. **USAF Honor Guard**. Honor guard Airmen represent the Air Force at ceremonies where protocol or custom dictate using an honor guard or military escort. They symbolize the United States Air Force to American and foreign dignitaries at public ceremonies; participate in Air Force and joint service arrival and departure ceremonies for the President, foreign heads of state, and other national or international dignitaries; and perform military funeral honors for USAF Regular Air Force, retired personnel, and veterans according to prescribing publication. Honor guard NCOs lead and supervise Airmen serving on the United States Air Force Honor Guard team performing duties described above. **NOTE:** RegAF USAF Honor Guard NCOs are selected through the Developmental Special Duty nomination process.

9.11.4. **Career Assistance Advisor (CAA)**. CAAs serve at the wing level and are responsible for managing CAA and First Term Airman Center programs, as well as advising commanders and supervisors on force management and professional enhancement. CAAs also advise Airmen on career progression and planning, monitor mandatory pay and benefits briefing programs, and conduct advertising and publicity programs.

9.11.5. **First Sergeant**. First sergeants provide a dedicated focal point for all readiness, health, morale, welfare, and quality of life issues within their organizations. At home station and in expeditionary environments, their primary responsibility is to build and maintain a mission-ready force. First sergeants derive their authority from the unit commander and advise the commander, command chief master sergeant, and other enlisted Airmen on morale, discipline, mentoring, well-being, recognition, and professional development. They ensure the enlisted force understands the commander's policies, goals, and objectives, and conduct quality force reviews on all enlisted performance reports, decoration recommendations, and other personnel actions. Working with their fellow senior NCOs and supervisors, first sergeants ensure equitable and effective discipline, and the highest esprit de corps. First sergeants work closely with CCMs to prepare the organization's enlisted force to best execute all assigned tasks. They actively participate in the First Sergeant Council and other activities that support the needs of the military community.

9.11.6. **Military Training Instructor (MTI)**. MTIs are responsible for shaping newly enlisted trainees into Airmen ready to serve in the United States Air Force. They must exhibit the highest levels of professional behavior, military bearing, respect for authority, and dress and personal appearance. They plan, organize, and direct basic and initial military training, and determine requirements for training, facilities, space, equipment, visual aids, and supplies. They instruct trainees in dormitory setup, drill, and other training subjects using demonstration-performance and lecture methods, and inspect and evaluate military training activities, personnel, and facilities.

9.11.7. **Military Training Leader (MTL)**. MTLs supervise all assigned non-prior service Airmen during technical training. They evaluate standards of conduct, performance, military bearing, and discipline while scheduling and conducting military training functions. They establish incoming, outgoing, and student entry briefings; conduct individual and group interviews; motivate personnel to develop military attitudes, effective human relations, and social skills for improving interpersonal and military relations; and assist students in their personal adjustment to military life.

9.11.8. **Professional Military Education (PME) Instructor**. PME instructors use informal lectures, case studies, teaching interviews, guided discussions, and a variety of other teaching methods to provide the PME instruction and education necessary to facilitate knowledge and understanding of the Air Force institutional competencies. They plan, organize, and direct PME programs at ALS, NCOA and Senior NCOA. PME instructors are responsible for developing and delivering PME courses that develop the institutional competencies for enlisted Airmen along their career continuum. As role models for other Airmen, PME instructors must exhibit the highest levels of professional behavior, military bearing, respect for authority, and dress and personal appearance.

9.11.9. **Recruiter**. The Air Force recruiter is the first Airman most potential enlistees will ever meet. They represent the Air Force in communities across America and must exhibit the highest levels of professional behavior, military bearing, respect for authority and dress and personal appearance. They are responsible for interviewing, screening, testing and evaluating applicants from civilian sources; assisting and participating in special events such as state and municipal ceremonies, exhibits, fairs, parades, centennials and sporting events; and performing other duties as required to achieve recruiting goals.

9.11.10. **Technical Training Instructor**. Technical training instructors provide initial skills training and education for their Air Force specialty. They are technical experts in their career field with an Associate's Degree from the community College of the Air Force. They work closely with Air Force career field managers to develop training and education requirements necessary to award the 3-skill level; and plan, organize, and direct the training of all non-prior service Airmen and career Airmen cross-training into a new Air Force specialty.

**9.12. Airmanship.**

9.12.1. Airmanship Defined. The Army has soldiers. The Navy has sailors. The Marine Corps has marines. The Air Force has Airmen. From the Airman Basic to the Four-Star General, we in the Air Force are all Airmen. As Airmen, we are part of a professional subculture and we demonstrate various disciplines in defense of our Nation through something we call Airmanship. Airmanship is the mindset, evident in our behaviors, that causes us to proudly exhibit the highest levels of professional service to our country.

**Figure 9.4. Airmanship**

9.12.1.2. What exactly is this mindset? The dictionary defines mindset as *"a mental disposition or attitude that predetermines one's responses and interpretations of situations."* In the case of Airmanship, that mental disposition or attitude (mindset) is what we think and how we feel about membership in the profession of arms, and that mindset is reflected in our behavior. A genuine belief in the **oath of enlistment**, an embracement of Air Force **core values** as your own, commitment to the **profession of arms** and an unstoppable determination known as **warrior ethos** are the hallmarks of that mindset. Such a mindset produces pride, selfless service, and care for our country. This mindset is what we aspire to create and sustain in order to perpetuate behaviors necessary for mission accomplishment.

9.12.1.3. Our behavior is a direct result of our mindset (belief, commitment, embracement, and willingness), and demonstrates our personal commitment to membership in the profession of arms. Adherence to and enforcement of standards, the willingness to fulfill all responsibilities, impeccable wear of the uniform, readiness to perform mission objectives, and perpetuation of the Air Force culture provide a clear picture of what we expect Airman behavior to look like. (See Figure 9.4).

**9.12.2. Airmen's Week (Airmanship 100).** Airmen's Week is the first phase in CSAF's larger "Culture of Excellence" initiative; Airmen's week is the first touch-point in career-long continuum of professionalism development. Airmen's Week is a stand-alone course that commences immediately following Basic Military Training (BMT) but before Airmen start technical training. Every Airman (including Guard & Reserve) graduating from BMT has attended Airmen's week, which began on 23 Mar 2015.

**9.12.2.1. Mission and Goals.** Airmen's Week equips Airmen to transition from a solid BMT foundation to the personalization of integrity, service, and excellence. It enables them to apply our core values to real-world situations and demonstrate the dignity, respect, and pride that all Airmen should have in themselves and others. Airmen's Week challenges these Airmen to examine their personal values and decision-making framework to embrace the Airmen's Creed. The goal is a more professional, resilient Airman, inspired by our heritage, committed to the Air Force core values, and motivated to deliver Airpower for America.

**9.12.2.2. Curriculum.** Airmen's Week is a 31-hour course with a curriculum designed to utilize "affective learning" methods which require Airmen to not only respond to/engage with material presented, but also demand they make a value judgment on it. This highly-interactive environment is focused on the application of AF Core Values, ethical decision-making, and "Airmanship".

**9.13. We Are All Recruiters (WEAR) and Recruiters Assistance Programs (RAP):**

9.13.1. The We Are All Recruiters (WEAR) Program may grant individuals permissive temporary duty status if they participate in an event that directly enhances the recruiting mission. All Airmen, regardless of their Air Force specialty, are recruiters. A WEAR event is an event where the interaction of Air Force personnel educates and increases public awareness of the Air Force and could potentially provide numerous leads for recruiters. Approval for WEAR is limited to those events where Airmen are directly speaking to potential applicants or influencers about Air Force opportunities. Applicants are defined as individuals within the 17- to 39-year-old range; and influencers are defined as parents, community leaders, teachers, counselors, coaches, etc. WEAR events are approved on an individual basis. For those events where multiple Airmen are attending, each attendee must submit a package for approval. WEAR requests must be first approved by the individual's commander in accordance with AFI 36-3003, *Military Leave Program.* Requests are then routed through Air Force Recruiting Squadron Public Affairs to the Air Force Recruiting Squadron commander. The Air Force Recruiting Squadron commander is the approval authority for all WEAR packages. Members may receive up to 14 days permissive TDY to attend a WEAR event. For more information, see AFI 36-3003, or visit www.recruiting.af.mil and review the WEAR fact sheet.

9.13.2. The Recruiter Assistance Program (RAP) is an active-duty leave program, run by the Air Force Recruiting Service, where an Airman directly supports an Air Force recruiter. The Air Forces grants up to 12 days of nonchargeable leave, including one weekend, in accordance with AFI 36-3003, *Military Leave Program*. RAP is open to Airmen of all ranks interested in participating and having a positive impact on recruiting. RAP is beneficial to the Air Force and to participants because Airmen can be a major influence in bringing the Air Force story to their hometown or place of previous residence by helping recruiters make contacts and develop leads. RAP duties may include participation in question-and-answer sessions, making presentations, or providing testimonials of their Air Force experiences to high school and college students. For more information about RAP, see AFI 36-3003 or visit www.recruiting.af.mil and review the RAP fact sheet.

## Section 9C—Enlisted Professional Military Education (PME)

## 9.14. United States Air Force Enlisted Professional Military Education.

Air Force enlisted PME compliments training, experience, and other educational programs to provide enlisted leaders a continuum of learning via progressive courses concentrated on developing leadership, Airmanship and military professionalism. Enlisted PME courses provide professional education to enlisted Airmen at specific and critical career points, and thus play a vital role in preparing them for increased supervision, leadership, and management challenges. More specifically, enlisted PME develops Air Force institutional competencies and subcompetencies vital to the knowledge and skills required for critical thinking, sound decision making and strategic thinking to provide the Air Force with agile combat support. More than 67,000 enlisted Airmen complete enlisted PME courses each year. For more information about Air Force enlisted PME programs and policies, see AFI 36-2301, *Developmental Education*.

9.14.1. **Thomas N. Barnes Center, Enlisted PME Academic Affairs.**

The Thomas N. Barnes Center for Enlisted Education, enlisted PME academic affairs is located at Maxwell Air Force Base-Gunter Annex Alabama. Academic affairs provides enlisted PME program development, faculty development, and operational program management for four resident and three distance learning courses. Academic affairs also conducts studies and advises Air Force and other key leaders on numerous issues and policies pertaining to Air Force and joint enlisted PME matters. They can be reached via the Barnes Center for Enlisted Education home page at http://www.au.af.mil/au/barnes.

9.14.1.1. **Mission and Vision.** The academic affairs mission is to educate enlisted Airmen to accomplish the Air Force mission. The academic affairs vision is educational excellence for Airmen…developing enlisted airpower leaders for America.

9.14.1.2. **Curriculum.** Enlisted PME academic affairs provides comprehensive programs (curricula, evaluation, analysis, instructor development) for each level of enlisted PME. These programs consist of thorough and rigorous academic courses that use performance evaluations and objective examinations to determine how well students achieve instructional objectives. For the NCO Intermediate Leadership Experience and senior NCO Advanced Leadership Experience, the principle instructional methods include experiential activities, problem-centered leadership laboratories, personal reflection, guided discussion, case study analysis, and writing assignments.

9.14.1.3. **Academic Credit.** Airmen receive academic credit for completing enlisted PME courses through the Community College of the Air Force, which is accredited through the Southern Association of Colleges and Schools. Enlisted PME schools provide the Community College of the Air Force with class graduate data, and the Community College of the Air Force automatically updates individual records and transcripts with academic credits.

9.14.2. **Enlisted PME Resident Courses:**

9.14.2.1. **Airman Leadership School.** The Airman Leadership School is the first level of enlisted PME that enlisted Airmen complete as they progress through their Air Force careers. On 1 October 1991, Air University established a standardized Airman Leadership School program that replaced the NCO Preparatory Course and the NCO Leadership School. Airman Leadership Schools operate at almost every installation across the Air Force.

9.14.2.1.1. **Mission.** The Airman Leadership School mission is to prepare Senior Airmen to be professional, warfighting Airmen able to supervise and lead Air Force teams to support the employment of air, space, and cyberspace power.

9.14.2.1.2. **Curriculum.** Airman Leadership School is a 192-hour course with a curriculum designed to develop a mindset and associated skills to meet four core graduate attributes: (1) Expeditionary Airman, (2) Supervisor of Airmen, (3) Professional Airman, and (4) Supervisory Communicator. Currently, Airman Leadership School graduates earn 9 semester hours of college credit with Community College of the Air Force.

9.14.2.2. **NCO Academy.** In 1955, Leadership Schools were established across the Air Force to provide non-commissioned officers leadership and management training required to assume day-to-day mission execution responsibilities. The stand-up of these Leadership Schools (which later became NCO Academies) coincided with the release of the first Enlisted Force Structure which established the leadership roles and responsibilities of enlisted Airmen at each grade. In November 1993, operational control of stateside NCO Academies transferred from the various major commands to Air Education and Training Command. Air Education and Training Command assigned all stateside NCO Academies to the College for enlisted PME (now the Barnes Center for Enlisted Education). In addition to the five Barnes Center-operated academies located at Lackland, Sheppard, Tyndall, Keesler and Peterson Air Force Bases; the Air National Guard operates one NCO academy at McGhee-Tyson Air Force Base; Pacific Air Force Command operates three at Hickam, Kadena and Elmendorf Air Force Bases; and United States Air Forces in Europe operates one at Kapaun Air Station.

9.14.2.2.1. **Mission.** The NCO academy mission is to prepare junior enlisted leaders to be adaptable for current and future leadership and management challenges in order to operate [think/act] critically in complex and ambiguous environments. NCOs must successfully complete the NCO academy Distance Learning Course and meet attendance requirements published in AFI 36-2301, *Developmental Education* in order to attend the Intermediate Leadership Experience.

9.14.2.2.2. **Curriculum.** The NCO academy program encompasses the NCO academy Intermediate Leadership Experience (ILE). ILE represents comprehensive junior NCO institutional competency development and further develops the knowledge gained from the distance learning course. The ILE is 198-hour course that includes guided discussion classroom methodology, experiential exercises, case study analysis, and immersive leadership development laboratories designed to improve an NCOs competence, confidence and will to exercise assigned leadership responsibilities.

9.14.2.3. **Air Force Senior NCO Academy.** The Air Force established the Air Force Senior NCO academy in 1972 to enhance development of senior NCOs through PME. In January 1973, the Air Force Senior NCO Academy conducted their first class of 120 senior NCOs at Maxwell Air Force Base-Gunter Annex Alabama. Presently, the Air Force Senior NCO academy trains up to 2,250 Air Force senior NCOs, (Senior Master Sergeants, Senior Master Sergeant selects, and selected Master Sergeants), Navy and Coast Guard chief petty officers, Marine Gunnery Sergeants and above, and international senior NCOs annually. Senior NCOs successfully complete the senior NCO distance learning course and meet attendance requirements published in AFI 36-2301, Developmental Education in order to attend the Air Force Senior NCO Academy Advanced Leadership Experience.

9.14.2.3.1. **Mission.** The Air Force Senior NCO academy mission is to develop joint and coalition senior enlisted leaders to influence mission success in dynamic service environments.

9.14.2.3.2. **Curriculum.** The Air Force Senior NCO Academy program encompasses the Senior NCO academy Advanced Leadership Experience (ALE). ALE represents comprehensive institutional competency development and further develops the knowledge gained from the current Senior NCO distance learning course. The Air Force Senior NCO Academy delivers the 200-hour ALE honing senior enlisted leader skills with education that helps prepare them to be adaptable, critically thinking, and strategically relevant in their operating environment. Successful students are able to apply their understanding of concepts covered in the prerequisite distance learning course as well as additional concepts instructed during the ALE. ALE prepares senior NCOs for increased leadership responsibility in the joint, combined, and interagency operating and strategic environment.

9.14.2.4. **Chief Master Sergeant Leadership Course.** The Chief Master Leadership Course (CLC), located on Maxwell-Gunter Air Force Base, Alabama, is the capstone and pinnacle level of enlisted professional military education. The CLC was first launched in 2004 as an 8-day resident course taught at the Air Force Senior NCO Academy. The course was suspended in 2011 and re-established in 2013 as a 33-week facilitated distance learning course which started on 16 November 2013 and ended 12 September 2014. Currently, the CLC provides new Chief Master Sergeants with foundational, strategic-level leadership competencies invaluable to fly, fight, and win in the employment of air, space, and cyberspace. The CLC conducts seven classes per year, educating 750 total force Chief Master Sergeants annually. The CLC is designed for students selected for promotion to Chief Master Sergeant. The expected learning outcomes for the course are to provide Chief Master Sergeants a broad perspective of the Air Force mission as it relates to national security established by our nation's senior leaders to all levels of Airmen.

9.14.2.4.1. **Mission.** The CLC mission is to provide Chief Master Sergeants the education to bridge operational-to-strategic perspectives of the Air Force. The CLC vision is to develop Chief Master Sergeants into strategic level leaders and to inspire them to effectively lead, manage and mentor today's Airmen.

9.14.2.3.2. **Curriculum.** The course consists of five modules: Educational Theories, National Security, Strategic Leadership, Synchronized Engagement, and Integrated Development. The CLC is a 20-day residence course, preceded by a 15-day, self-paced, non-facilitated, distance learning lesson. The CLC demands extensive self-study, critical creative thinking, communication, and interpersonal skills.

9.14.3. **Enlisted PME Distance Learning Courses.**

Students completing enlisted PME distance learning courses gain additional knowledge about their increasing responsibilities as supervisors, leaders and managers as prescribed in AFI 36-2618, *The Officer and Enlisted Force Structures*. Enlisted PME distance learning course policies are available on the Air University Education Support Web page at http://www.aueducationsupport.com/ics/support/default.asp?deptID=8405 .

9.14.3.1. **Airman Leadership School (Course 3).** The Airman Leadership School distance learning Course 3 provides professional military education to prepare Senior Airmen to supervise and foster a commitment to the military profession. The Airman Leadership School curriculum addresses 165 educational competencies and is designed to develop a mindset and associated skills with respect to four core attributes of a professional NCO: (1) Professional Airmen, (2) Expeditionary Airmen, (3) Supervisor of Airmen, and (4) Supervisory Communicator. The Airman Leadership School distance learning course is open to Air National Guard and Air Force Reserve Senior Airmen and Staff Sergeants. The course is not available for Regular Air Force personnel. Course 3 is administered by the Air Force Career Development Academy and is managed by Barnes Center for Enlisted Education. Students must pass two course exams by attaining the minimum passing score of 70 percent on each exam. Course 3 graduates earn 8 Community College of the Air Force semester hours of college credit.

9.14.3.2. **NCO Distance Learning Course.** The NCO distance learning institutional competency development required to prepare each junior enlisted leader to be professional, warfighting Airmen who can lead and manage Air Force units in the employment of air and space power and is a prerequisite for attendance to the NCO Academy. NCO distance learning course is 168 contact hours of individual study and consists of three modules: (1) Course Introduction, (2) Leadership and Management, and (3) Operational Airman. The course is open to the total force. To successfully complete this course, students are required to pass three module exams, demonstrating curriculum mastery by attaining the minimum passing score of 70 on each exam. NCO distance learning course graduates earn 9 CCAF semester hours of college credit.

9.14.3.3. **Senior NCO Distance Learning Course.** The Senior NCO Distance Learning Course provides institutional competency development required to prepare Senior NCOs to lead the enlisted force at the tactical and operational levels. The curriculum's design heightens students' appreciation and understanding of the three attributes of the Senior NCO: (1) Self Awareness, (2) Leadership and Management, and (3) Joint Warfighter. This course is open to the total force. Completion of the Senior NCO Distance Learning Course is a prerequisite to attend the Air Force Senior NCO Academy. To successfully complete this course, students are required to pass three module exams, demonstrating curriculum mastery by attaining the minimum passing score on each exam Senior NCO Distance Learning Course graduates earn 4 Community College of the Air Force semester hours of college credit.

## 9.15. Senior Enlisted Joint PME.

Chairman Joint Chiefs of Staff Instruction 1805.01B, *Enlisted Professional Military Education Policy*, requires all enlisted personnel operating in joint, interagency, multinational, and coalition warfighting organizations to learn joint concepts. Enlisted personnel learn joint concepts at each enlisted PME level to improve their ability to operate effectively as part of the joint force and to meet joint force needs. Senior enlisted joint PME provides Senior NCOs a more comprehensive joint education to prepare them for assignments to joint billets at the senior enlisted leader or command senior enlisted leader level.

9.15.1. **Mission and Goals.**

Senior enlisted joint PME provides Chairman Joint Chiefs of Staff-sponsored assignment-oriented educational opportunities for enlisted leaders serving in, or designated to serve in, joint and combined organizations. Senior enlisted joint PME is web-based and is designed to expose enlisted personnel to joint education, prepare them to succeed by improving their ability to operate effectively as part of a future joint force, and prepare them to supervise multiple Service members. Senior enlisted joint PME is available to total force personnel in grades E-5 through E-9. Senior enlisted joint PME courses are offered entirely on line and are accessible from anywhere at any time via the Internet. **Note:** Students must complete rank-required service enlisted PME before enrolling in Senior enlisted joint PME.

9.15.2. **Curriculum.**

Senior enlisted joint PME consists of two courses of instruction referred to as senior enlisted joint PME I and II and is hosted by Joint Forces Staff College on Joint Knowledge Online. Senior enlisted joint PME I emphasizes curriculum commensurate with E-5/E-7 Joint Assignment responsibilities. Senior enlisted joint PME II is focused on preparing E-7/E-9 enlisted members for their senior leadership roles in Joint Assignments. Senior enlisted joint PME I and II has learning areas and objectives in (1) National Strategic Overview, (2) Joint Interagency, Intergovernmental, and Multinational Capabilities (3) Foundations of Joint Operations and (4) Joint Force Leadership. For more information or to enroll, go to https://jkodirect.jten.mil/Atlas2/faces/page/login/Login.seam.

### Section 9D—Military Ethics

### 9.16. Introduction.

Military ethics is about each Airman doing what is right and just for our country, Air Force, and unit. Our Air Force, driven towards excellence by competence and character, is built upon thousands of good Americans that have volunteered to defend our country. These Airman realize truth and integrity are more than buzz words; those words are the focal point of our moral compass. As General John D. Ryan, the 16th Air Force Chief of Staff, said "any order to compromise integrity is not a lawful order." Airmen must have the courage to be the type of people we ought to be. Ethical Airmen are not focused on personal successes or virtues.

9.16.1. As an Airman serving proudly in the Profession of Arms, you definitely know the difference between right and wrong. The Air Force provides guiding rules and standards through an ethical code. An ethical code guides us in our daily decision making. Our ethical code is prescribed throughout our Air Force Core Values, Oath of Enlistment, Oath of Office, Air Force Instructions, and the Uniform Code of Military Justice. You'll be faced with decisions. Some decisions you will have to make. Other decisions you will help your wingmen make. These decisions might be related to your mission, your personal life, or the interest of your peers. The choice you make can be successful when you're utilizing sound ethical principles.

9.16.1.1. Sound ethical principles are rooted in our Air Force Core Values. Our core values of Integrity First, Service Before Self, and Excellence In All We Do clearly define our identity. Every Airman learns to cherish our core values when they enter our profession. They begin by reading the core values, then understanding the core values, and finally living the core values. Expanding upon our core values lead us to virtues we must practice and demonstrate in our lives.

9.16.1.2. Integrity First is a character trait and the willingness to do what is right even when no one is looking. Integrity is your moral compass and inner voice of self-control. The virtues of honesty, courage, and accountability stem from Integrity First. Honesty means our words must be unquestionable so we preserve the trust that unites us through common goal and purpose. Courage is about doing the right thing despite fear and empowers us to make ourselves better. Accountability instills our responsibility while maintaining transparency and ownership for our actions.

9.16.1.3. Service Before Self tells us professional duties take precedence over personal desires. The virtues of duty, loyalty, and respect blossom from Service Before Self. Duty is our obligation to perform what is required for the mission; sometimes having to make sacrifices in ways that no other profession has or will. Loyalty is our internal commitment to the success and preservation of something bigger than ourselves, ordered as country, Air Force, and unit. Respect requires us to treat each other with dignity and value them as individuals, knowing all Airmen possess fundamental worth as human beings.

9.16.1.4. Excellence In All We Do directs us to develop a sustained passion for the continuous improvement and innovation that propels the Air Force, as well as ourselves, beyond the capabilities of our adversaries. The virtues of mission, discipline, and teamwork are the cornerstone of Excellence In All We Do. Mission encompasses operations, product, and resource excellence; must accomplish our duties correctly while practicing fiscal responsibility. Discipline is an individual commitment to uphold the highest standards of personal and professional conduct, which we demonstrate with attitude, work ethic, and continuous improvement. Required is teamwork at every level to complete the mission and we must recognize the interdependency of each Airmen's contribution toward the mission and strive for organizational excellence.

9.16.1.5. An ethical dilemma is a situation where one is forced to choose between at least two alternatives. Three general causes of ethical dilemmas are uncertainty, competing values, and potential harm. Uncertainty is the result of not having all the facts pertaining to the situation, having no experience dealing with the situation, or not having a clearly established policy, procedure, or rule for deciding how to choose. Competing values occur when our personal values conflict with those of our institution, subordinates, peers, or supervisors; however, the mark of a true professional is maintaining high professional standards despite conflicting values. Potential harm relates to the intentional and unintentional consequences caused by your actions; you should always think through second and third order consequences of your actions. When facing an ethical dilemma, Dr. James H. Toner provides us the framework of ethical principles for decision making.

9.16.2. According to Dr. James H. Toner, former Professor of International Relations and Military Ethics, Air War College, military ethics is rooted in the three Os: *owing, ordering,* and *oughting.*

9.16.2.1. Military ethics cannot properly exist without the concept of owing. If we, as Airmen, know who and why we owe, we are able to recognize the obligation, responsibility, and duty which give rise to moral thinking and ethical reasoning. Airmen must understand they owe a debt of gratitude to our country, family, service, chain of command, and comrades. Additionally, from the pioneers of aviation to the selfless sacrifice of battlefield Airmen, we owe to those who came before us and those we serve with today to strive for "excellence in all we do". Furthermore, this is a reflection of the core value "service before self" as identified in the Airman's Creed: *I am faithful to a proud heritage, a tradition of honor, and a legacy of valor.*

9.16.2.2. The second O is for ordering, or what Dr. Toner calls moral structuring and ethical priorities. In other words, are you putting your priorities in the right order? Many illegal activities or easily prevented mistakes are the result of a leader's failure to order wisely and well. As defenders of freedom and justice, we take an oath to defend the Constitution of the United States, and to obey the President and the officers appointed over us, in that order. As Airmen, our highest priority is to serve our country. We can never sacrifice the good of our nation for the good of our service, our superiors, or ourselves. According to Dr. Toner, the proper ordering of our priorities should be country, Air Force, and then unit. Dr. Toner explains that to understand this concept, look at the service tape on your uniform and notice the United States always comes before Air Force. We pronounce the same when we recite our Airman's Creed: *I am an American Airman, I am a warrior, I have answered my nation's call.*

9.16.2.3. The final O, oughting, is the understanding of what Airmen ought to do every day. What Airmen do may not be what they ought to do and this may sound simple, but military hierarchies insist upon obedience to orders and total discipline. Ethics, however, objects to this, insisting upon conditional and contextual obedience to orders, which ought to be obeyed, if lawful. The *Manual for Courts-Martial*, Rule 916, states "It is a defense to any offense that the accused was acting pursuant to orders unless the accused knew the orders to be unlawful or a person of ordinary sense and understanding would have known the orders to be unlawful." Our core values help guide us in the direction of what we ought to do.

9.16.3. To support our concept of ordering, we are introduced to the three Ps: *principle, purpose,* and *people.*

9.16.3.1. Our principle, which is truth telling and honorable service, is always first. Truth telling goes hand in hand with our core value of "integrity first", which is the foundation of trust. Trust unites us as Airmen and permits you to grow a strong wingman bond. Honorable service is detailed in the Code of Conduct, which in and of itself is an ethical guide. Just ask Captain Scott F. O'Grady, who was shot down behind enemy lines.

9.16.3.2. Our purpose as Airmen, clearly defined as mission accomplishment and duty, is why our service exists. From hot air balloons to wooden propellers to turbofan engines, Airmen have risen to the challenge at hand. We are the Tuskegee Airmen that never let an escorted bomber get shot down. We are the liberators of the oppressed as evidenced in Operation Desert Storm. We are the future of advanced warfare which we proudly proclaim in the Airman's Creed: *I am an American, My mission is to fly, fight, and win.*

9.16.3.3. Our people make all of this possible. Just look to the walls of the Enlisted Heritage Research Institute to see this is true. Staff Sergeant William H. Pitsenbarger gave his life aiding and defending a unit of soldiers pinned down by an enemy assault. Sergeant John L. Levitow disregarded his own wounds and saved the lives of his entire crew. Senior Airman Jason D. Cunningham gave his life so that others may live. Airman First Class Elizabeth N. Jacobson made the ultimate sacrifice while guarding a convoy of American service men and women. These heroic Airmen personified this passage from the Airman's Creed: *I am an American Airman, guardian of freedom and justice, my nation's sword and shield, its sentry and avenger, I defend my country with my life.*

9.16.4. To assist our decision making, we incorporate the three Rs: *rules, results,* and *realities.*

9.16.4.1. First, obey the rules because the rules are the accepted moral norms. However, we can't create rules for every possible situation. When facing an ethical dilemma and asking yourself "What ought I do?" reflect on the core values to idealize the person we want to be and the example we want to set.

9.16.4.2. Additionally, results are the goals of country, Air Force, and unit and our responsibility as Airmen is to accomplish the mission. However, in the climate of decentralized execution, our responsibility is to figure out how to accomplish the mission. Do not make decisions based on self-interests.

9.16.4.3. Finally, realities are inputs that effect our decision-making. We must use our self-awareness to realize who we are and what we do; because, what we do is who we are and who we are is what we do. If your moral compass needs calibration, your decision will not direct you on the right path. When your moral compass is well maintained, you will guide your country, Air Force, and unit upon a righteous path.

9.16.5. To put the three Os into action, we utilize the three Ds: *discern*, *declare*, and *do*.

9.16.5.1. We must discern, or recognize, the correct path to lead our Airmen on. Attentive wingmen utilize critical thinking to discern. Remember to properly *order* your thinking.

9.16.5.2. We must declare the correct path as we have discerned the correct path. Effective leaders educate and promote the growth of their team. Your inclusion of team members will enhance the change process.

9.16.5.3. Then we must do what we have discerned and declared. Spirited warriors accomplish the mission. We speak these truths when reciting the Airman's Creed: *I am an American Airman, wingman, leader, warrior, I will never leave an Airman behind, I will never falter, and I will not fail.*

9.16.6. As Airmen, we owe those who wore the uniform before us. We are free today because others sacrificed their time, effort, and lives to make our country what our country is, and we must continue the fight to ensure our country stays strong and secure. We must also order our priorities so we are able to overcome any temptation to stray from our military norms and values. Finally, we should always do what we ought to do.

9.16.6.1. When contemplating what to do, considering your possible courses of action is important. By listing your possible decisions that could correct the situation, you can quality check your ideas to take the most moral path. Put each of your courses of action to the test. Dr. Robert M. Hicks, former Deputy Director of the Civil Air Patrol, Chaplain Services, identified three tests we can use to check the morality of our actions.

9.16.6.2. The network test consists of asking yourself, "How would this decision look when aired on the news?" If your actions were broadcast on the evening news, would you be proud of your actions or ashamed of your actions? Would your actions discredit yourself or those we owe? If you find the answer to be the latter, then your decision doesn't pass the network test.

9.16.6.3. The United States of America test focuses on asking yourself, "Is this decision good for America? Is this decision good for the United States Air Force? Is this decision good for my unit? Is this decision good for me?" If you take this course of action, are you properly ordering your priorities? Would your actions promote the virtues of Service Before Self (duty, loyalty, and respect)? If you can't answer this with a resounding yes, this might not be the best decision.

9.16.6.4. The divine test deals with asking yourself, "Would I feel good about the decision when I give account for my life?" When telling the story of your proud and honorable service to our country, would you include conversation about this decision? Would you feel guilt or loss of trust from this action? If you can't answer this with a positive input, the course of action fails the divine test.

9.16.6.5. Utilizing the information provided to you should provide you with a clear path of understanding on how to make ethical decisions. What is important to keep your focus on are two main areas of honorable service: your commitment to the Profession of Arms and your ability to make ethical choices. You can build your own ethical knowledge while fostering that of your peers. Remind yourself and your peers of the reason you do what you do, as found in the Oath of Enlistment or Oath of Office. Declare the importance of adhering to established ethical codes, relying on them when faced with a choice between right and wrong. Use Dr. Toner's model and Dr. Hicks' three tests when making ethical choices.

9.16.7. Military ethics is not about others, but is about *you* knowing what is true and doing what is right; about being the man or woman who leads the kind of life *you* can be proud of.

## Section 9E—*Enlisted Force Development*

## 9.17. Introduction.

Enlisted Force Development is a life-cycle approach to developing innovative Airmen prepared to accomplish the Air Force mission and lead in a rapidly evolving global environment while attempting to meet both personal and professional needs. Deliberate development is essential throughout an Airman's career and satisfied through education on institutional competencies, training on functional competencies, a varied array of experiential opportunities, and force developmental tools. When developing Airmen, what is essential is to ensure they take full advantage of the abundant opportunities and resources that exist both functionally and institutionally. What is imperative from an enterprise perspective, is to look at how Airmen progress through their career fields and then into operational and strategic leadership positions.

9.17.1. Functionally, the Air Force develops technical experts through career field progression and succession planning. From the earliest stages of their careers, Airmen and their supervisors must comprehend the progression path for technical and professional development. In the majority of career fields, the progression roadmap and developmental pyramid provide sufficient direction to produce Airmen qualified for their current duties and for future responsibilities. Incumbent upon Career Field Managers is to routinely review their progression strategy to ensure their career field's technical requirements are being satisfied.

9.17.2. Institutionally, we strive to develop experienced leaders. As Airmen demonstrate expertise and potential, they should be encouraged to take on more responsibility and increased leadership roles. Developmental opportunities such as deployments, joint assignments and headquarters staff assignments offer a unique perspective on how the Air Force functions. Furthermore, special duty assignments provide skills and insight beneficial to an Airman's future capabilities.

9.17.3. Additionally, educational opportunities exist throughout an Airman's career which contribute to individual overall development. Enlisted Professional Military Education, developmental education, civilian education and other self-improvement programs such as the United States Air Force Library Digital Media Program and Air Force Credentialing Opportunities On-Line enhance the knowledge and capabilities of Airmen.

9.17.4. Effective career progression and Airman Development are dependent upon frank conversations between supervisors and subordinates regarding career field and institutional requirements, personal qualifications and goals, and available developmental opportunities. Routine counseling and performance feedback sessions should include these discussions.

## 9.18. Enlisted Force Development Oversight:

### 9.18.1. The Enlisted Force Development Panel.

The Enlisted Force Development Panel is responsible for guiding enlisted force development initiatives. The Enlisted Force Development Panel is charged to review, evaluate, and make recommendations to senior Air Force leaders regarding concerns, programs and initiatives relating to the education, training and experiences impacting enlisted Airman Development. The Enlisted Force Development Panel is hosted by the Chief, Enlisted Force Development and co-chaired by the Chief Master Sergeant of the Air Force and the Director, Force Development (Air Force/A1D). Panel members include Command Chief Master Sergeants from the combatant command and major command level as well as from the Air Force Reserve Command and the Air National Guard. Additionally, there are Career Field Managers and representatives from Air Education Training Command, Air University, Second Air Force, Basic Military Training, Air Force Personnel Center and Headquarters Air Force. A former Chief Master Sergeant of the Air Force attends as a strategic advisor.

## 9.19. Enlisted Force Development Tools.

In 2010, the Enlisted Force Development Panel recommended initiating Enlisted Development Teams to enable the enlisted force to deliberately develop senior enlisted leaders. According to Chief Master Sergeant of the Air Force James A. Roy, "The purpose of deliberate development is to grow our senior noncommissioned officers and grow the next generation of senior enlisted leaders to meet the highly technical and very complex leadership challenges the Department of Defense and the United States Air Force face in the future." In 2011, pilot Enlisted Development Teams were established in eight career fields, focusing on specialties associated with the nuclear enterprise. In 2012, Air Force/A1 and the Vice Chief of Staff approved Enlisted Development Teams for all Air Force specialty codes, with execution across the enlisted force expected to be complete by 2017. Enlisted Development Teams are designed to leverage the development of qualified Airmen with the leadership capacity and acculturation necessary to support current and projected mission requirements. Career Field Managers use Enlisted Development Teams to perform progression and succession planning to place Airmen in key leadership and developmental positions based on defined education, training, experience and performance requirements. Placing "the right people in the right place at the right time" is imperative.

### 9.19.1. MyVECTOR.

Formerly known as the Career Path Tool, MyVECTOR is a Total Force, force development, experience tracking, enterprise solution that supports the Secretary of the Air Force and Chief of Staff of the Air Force development priorities. MyVECTOR is a web-based career planning and force development tool which allows individuals greater transparency into their development and career management. In addition to being the enterprise information technology tool used to support Career Field Managers and development teams, MyVECTOR also offers robust mentoring capabilities. The reconfigured online platform has a modern look and feel, with the new configuration supporting not only the traditional by-name request method of requesting a mentor, but also providing a mentor-matching capability based on weighted characteristics identified by the Airman searching for a mentor. MyVECTOR also has a real-time Mentoring Plan, discussion forums, a bullet tracker to document accomplishments, and the ability to dialogue on-line with your mentor. A resource page is also available to assist both parties with mentoring questions and relationships.

9.19.2. **Enlisted Career Path Pyramid.**

The Enlisted Career Pyramid (Figure 9.5) is a display of training, education, and experience which enlisted Airmen will encounter throughout their career. This career path pyramid provides Airmen with an understanding of current and future opportunities for continuing development.

**Figure 9.5. The Enlisted Career Path**

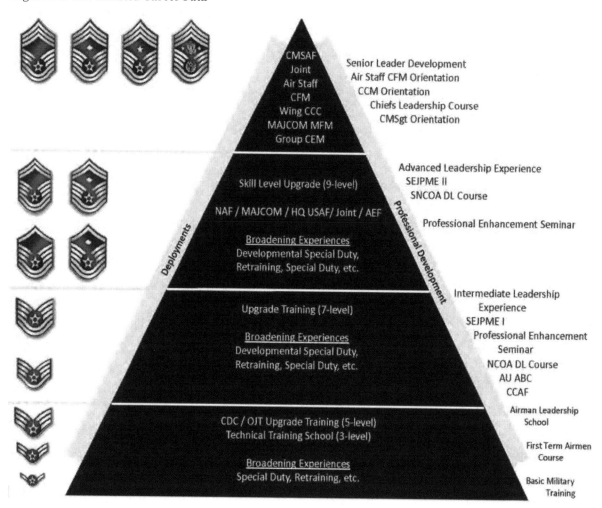

## 9.20. Institutional Competencies.

Institutional competencies prepare Airmen to operate successfully across the widest array of Air Force tasks and requirements. These competencies provide a common language and a set of priorities for consistency across the Air Force. The Air Force's institutional competencies are key to ensuring the ability of Airmen to operate successfully in a constantly changing operational environment. They are broadly applicable and span all occupations, functions, and organizational levels. These competencies place the institutional responsibilities into a context of how the individual should be developed and form the framework for force development in the Air Force. The institutional competency list consists of 8 competencies and 25 sub-competencies. They are grouped into three categories: personal, people/team, and organizational.

9.20.1. **Personal Competencies.**

Personal competencies (Figure 9.6) are those institutional competencies leaders need in face-to-face and interpersonal relationships that directly influence human behavior and values. These are foundational institutional competencies learned at the tactical level that will continue to play a critical role as leaders move to the operational competence and strategic vision levels. Personal competencies are essential for individual contribution, for building cohesive units and for empowering immediate subordinates. Each competency below is followed by the relevant subcompetencies with definitions.

**Figure 9.6. Institutional Competencies – Personal**

| Competency | Subcompetency | Definition |
|---|---|---|
| **Embodies Airman Culture** | **Ethical Leadership** | • Promotes Air Force core values (integrity first, service before self, excellence in all we do) through goals, actions, and referent behaviors |
| | | • Develops trust and commitment through words and actions |
| | | • Accountable for areas of responsibility, operations of unit, and personal actions |
| | | • Maintains checks and balances on self and others |
| | **Followership** | • Comprehends and values the essential role of followership in mission accomplishment |
| | | • Seeks command, guidance and/or leadership while providing unbiased advice |
| | | • Aligns priorities and actions toward chain of command guidance for mission accomplishment |
| | | • Exercises flexibility and adapts quickly to alternating role as leader/follower: follower first, leader at times |
| | **Warrior Ethos** | • Exhibits a hardiness of spirit despite physical and mental hardships–moral and physical courage |
| | | • Continuously hones their skills to support the employment of military capabilities |
| | | • Displays military/executive bearing, self-discipline, and self-control |
| | **Develops Self** | • Assesses self to identify strengths and developmental needs |
| | | • Seeks and incorporates feedback on own performance; aware of personal impact on others |
| | | • Continually increases breadth and depth of knowledge and skills; develops life-long learning habits |
| **Communicating** | **Speaking and Writing** | • Articulates ideas and intent in a clear, concise, and convincing manner through both verbal and written communication |
| | | • Adjusts communication approach to unique operational environment and audience needs |
| | | • Effectively creates communication bridges between units, organizations, and institutions |
| | **Active listening** | • Fosters the free exchange of ideas in an atmosphere of open exchange |
| | | • Actively attempts to understand others' points of view and clarifies information as needed |
| | | • Solicits feedback to ensure that others understand messages as they were intended |

**9.20.2. People/Team Competencies.**

This group of competencies (Figure 9.7) involves more interpersonal and team relationships. They represent competencies that, when combined with the personal competencies, are essential as leaders move on to lead larger groups or organizations. People/team leadership competencies are usually exercised more indirectly than personal leadership competencies. Leaders use these competencies to set the organizational climate. Each competency below is followed by the relevant subcompetencies definitions.

**Figure 9.7. Institutional Competencies – People/Team**

| Competency | Subcompetency | Definition |
|---|---|---|
| Leading People | Develops and Inspires Others | • Helps and motivates others to improve their skills and enhance their performance through feedback, coaching, mentoring, and delegating<br>• Empowers others and guides them in the direction of their goals and mission accomplishment<br>• Inspires others to transcend their own self-interests and embrace personal sacrifice and risk for the good of the organization and mission |
| | Takes Care of People | • People first--attends to the physical, mental, ethical, and spiritual well-being of fellow Airmen and their families<br>• Creates an environment where Airmen take care of Airmen 24/7, 365 days a year, including leaders, peers, and subordinates; integrates wellness into mission accomplishment<br>• Establishes work-life balance through time management and setting clear expectations and priorities |
| | Diversity | • Leverages differences in individual characteristics, experiences, and abilities<br>• Leverages diversity for mission accomplishment and fosters an inclusive environment<br>• Shows respect for others regardless of the situation; treats people in an equitable manner |
| Fostering Collaborative Relationships | Builds Teams and Coalitions | • Builds effective teams for goal and mission accomplishment and improves team performance<br>• Contributes to group identity while fostering cohesiveness, confidence, and cooperation<br>• Sees and attends to the interests, goals, and values of other individuals and institutions<br>• Develops networks and alliances that span organizational, Service, department, agency, and national boundaries |
| | Negotiating | • Understands the underlying principles and concepts applied before, during, and after a negotiation<br>• Attains desired mission outcomes while maintaining positive, long-term relationships with key individuals and groups<br>• Uses appropriate interpersonal styles and methods to reduce tension or conflict between two or more people, anticipates and addresses conflict constructively, and anticipates and prevents counter-productive confrontations<br>• Persuades and influences others; builds consensus; gains cooperation; effectively collaborates |

9.20.3. **Organizational Competencies.**

These competencies (Figure 9.8) represent those applicable at all levels of the Air Force but are most in demand at the strategic level. Strategic leaders apply organizational competencies to establish structure and articulate strategic vision. Effective organizational competency skills include technical competence on force structure and integration; on unified, joint, multinational, and interagency operations; on resource allocation; and on management of complex systems. In addition, they apply to conceptual competence in creating policy and vision and interpersonal skills emphasizing consensus building and influencing peers and other policy makers, both internal and external to the organization. This level is the nexus of warfighting leadership skills for the Air Force. Also, this level is achieved through having learned the lessons from the other types of institutional competencies (i.e., personal and people/team). Each competency below is followed by the relevant subcompetencies that define definitions.

**Figure 9.8. Institutional Competencies – Organizational**

| Competency | Subcompetency | Definition |
|---|---|---|
| Employing Military Capabilities | Operational and Strategic Art | • Understands and applies operational and strategic art in conventional and irregular warfare, peacekeeping, and homeland operations<br>• Demonstrates expertise in integrating and leveraging doctrine, concepts, and capabilities within an effects-based approach to operations<br>• Utilizes innovation and technology in the employment of lethal and nonlethal force |
| | Leverage Technology | • Understands how the Air Force traditionally uses technology (i.e., scientific knowledge, technological expertise, engineering skills, and mathematical and analytical capabilities) to reshape and rethink possibilities and advance military objectives.<br>• Comprehends the skill sets critical for developing and transitioning technology to meet airpower, joint, interagency, and coalition mission requirements.<br>• Recognizes windows of opportunity for the application of technology to provide innovative solutions to enhance efficiency and effectiveness, as well as maintain current and future superiority. |
| | Unit, Air Force, Joint, and Coalition Capabilities | • Considers and applies capabilities of the Air Force across air, space, and cyberspace<br>• Understands how Air Force capabilities relate and complement other Service capabilities<br>• Understands interdependencies and interoperability across Services, agencies, departments, and coalition partners |
| | Non-adversarial Crisis Response | • Recognizes the national security implications of peacekeeping operations, humanitarian relief operations, and support to civil authorities, both foreign and domestic<br>• Understands the need for engagement before and after warfighting or crisis response, the need for integrated involvement with interagency and multinational partners, and the need for multipurpose capabilities that can be applied across the range of military operations |
| Enterprise Perspective | Enterprise Structure and Relationships | • Understands the organizational structure and relationships between the Air Force, the Department of Defense, joint staff, the combatant commands, the defense agencies, and other elements of the defense structure<br>• Understands how one's function or unit fits into its parent organizations<br>• Understands how one's parent organization relates to its external environment—supporting and supported organizations, the public, Congress, etc. |
| | Government Organization and Processes | • Understands essential operating features and functions of the Air Force, DOD, the national security structure, other related executive branch functions, and Congress, to include leadership and organization; roles of members, committees, and staffs; authorization, appropriation, and budget processes; acquisition policy and procedures; and interdependencies and relationships |
| | Global, Regional, and Cultural Awareness | • Conscious of regional and other factors influencing defense, domestic, and foreign policy<br>• Seeks to understand foreign cultural, religious, political, organizational, and societal norms and customs<br>• Develops linguistic skills |
| | Communication Synchronization | • Informs and appropriately influences key audiences by synchronizing and integrating communication efforts to deliver truthful, timely, accurate, and credible information, analysis, and opinion<br>• Formulates the institutional message, telling the Air Force story |
| Managing Organizations and Resources | Resource Stewardship | • Identifies, acquires, administers, and conserves financial, informational, technological, material, warfare, and human resources needed to accomplish the mission<br>• Implements "best practice" management techniques throughout the organization |
| | Change Management | • Embraces, supports, and leads change<br>• Understands the change management process, critical success factors, and common problems and costs<br>• Perceives opportunities and risks before or as they emerge |
| | Continuous Improvement | • Originates action to improve existing conditions and processes, using appropriate methods to identify opportunities, implement solutions, and measure impact<br>• Supports ongoing commitment to improve processes, products, services, and people<br>• Anticipates and meets the needs of both internal and external stakeholders |

| Competency | Subcompetency | Definition |
|---|---|---|
| Strategic Thinking | Vision | • Takes a long-term view and builds a shared vision that clearly defines and expresses a future state |
| | | • Provides innovative and creative insights and solutions for guiding and directing organizations to meet institutional needs |
| | | • Formulates effective plans and strategies for consistently achieving goals and maximizing mission accomplishment |
| | | • Anticipates potential threats, barriers, and opportunities; encourages risk-taking |
| | Decision-making | • Identifies, evaluates, and assimilates data and information from multiple streams and differentiates information according to its utility; uses information to influence actions and decisions |
| | | • Uses analytic methods in solving problems and developing alternatives |
| | | • Makes sound, well-informed, and timely decisions despite conditions of ambiguity, risk and uncertainty |
| | | • Analyzes situations critically to anticipate second and third order effects of proposed policies / actions |
| | | • Establishes metrics to evaluate results and adapts and implements feedback |
| | Adaptability | • Maintains effectiveness when experiencing major changes in work tasks or environment |
| | | • Adjusts to change within new work structures, processes, requirements, and cultures |
| | | • Responds quickly and proactively to ambiguous and emerging conditions, opportunities, and risks |

## Section 9F—The Profession of Arms: An Airman's Perspective

### 9.21. America's Guardians:

9.21.1. Since the Nation's birth, our military has had the constitutional duty to ensure national survival, defend lives and property, and promote vital interest at home and abroad. To provide for the common defense, all of America's military services strive for excellence in how they organize, train, and equip their forces to fight and win the Nation's wars. All are vital, interdependent components of a mighty joint team, united by a tradition of honor, valor, and devotion.

9.21.2. The Air Force exists to fly, fight, and win to achieve strategic, operational, and tactical objectives unhindered by time, distance, or geography. The Air Force's mission is to "deliver sovereign options for the defense of the United States of America and global interests—to fly and fight in Air, Space, and Cyberspace." Thereby, jointly with our brothers and sisters in arms—Soldiers, Sailors, Marines, and Coast Guardsmen—we underwrite the strategy of defending the homeland and assuring allies, while dissuading, deterring, and defeating enemies.

### 9.22. Professionalism or Profession of Arms.

No profession asks more of their members than the Profession of Arms. We are warriors, we have answered our Nation's call; no one puts more on the line to defend freedom than the men and women of the United States Armed Forces.

> As members of the joint team, we Airmen are part of a unique profession that is founded on the premise of service before self. We are not engaged in just another job; we are practitioners of the profession of arms. We are entrusted with the security of our Nation, the protection of our citizens, and the preservation of its way of life. In this capacity, we serve as guardians of America's future. By its very nature, this responsibility requires us to place the needs of our service and our country before personal concerns.

> Our military profession is sharply distinguished from others by what General Sir John Hackett has termed the "unlimited liability clause." Upon entering the Air Force, we accept a sacred trust from the American people.

> We swear to support and defend the Constitution of the United States against all enemies, foreign and domestic. We take this obligation freely without any reservations. We thereby commit our lives in defense of America and her citizens should that become necessary.

> No other profession readily expects its members to lay down their lives for their friends, families, or freedoms. But our profession readily expects its members to willingly risk their lives in performing their professional duties. By voluntarily serving in the military profession, we accept unique responsibilities.

> Inherent in all this is the individual's willingness to subordinate personal interests for the good of one's unit, one's Service, and one's Nation. We can ill afford individuals who become "sunshine soldiers" or

*get focused on careerism. Instead, we need professionals who strive to be the best at their current job and who realize they attain individual advancement through the success of their unit or work center.*

General Ronald R. Fogleman
Former Air Force Chief of Staff

## 9.23. The Airman's Perspective:

9.23.1. Throughout our history, the Air Force has always had a perspective or mindset different than the surface components of national military power, and this is based on a long history of lessons learned in peace and war. Specifically, airpower in application is fundamentally different from other forms of military power. Second, inherent flexibility allows the force to be applied independently or in concert with other forms of military power. Third, can be most effective if applied for the right reasons and in the right concentrations at the right time and place to achieve effects on the battlefield. Therefore, since Air Force forces are employed differently, in different mediums, at different speeds and closure rates and over greater distances. These forces must be applied by those who truly appreciate the breadth and scope in the application of that power. Finally, Airman should have fluent knowledge of these aspects of Air Force capabilities.

9.23.2. Airmen are essential to the Air Force institution and the successful execution of their mission. To understand and actively advocate the Airman's perspective on the use of airpower to achieve objectives as directed by proper authority is important. All Airmen share the same goal—to accomplish their organization's mission. In order to defend the United States and global interests, Airmen should be prepared to fly and fight in air, space, and cyberspace. Using the Airman's perspective gives Airmen a distinctive advantage when performing this mission of the Air Force. Airmen bring not only knowledge, skills, and abilities that allow them to accomplish this mission, but a manner of approaching mission accomplishment unique to those educated, trained, and experienced in bringing airmindedness to all actions they perform. An Airman brings a perspective to performing the Service's mission that compounds his or her effectiveness in a manner best suited to support a commander.

9.23.3. Upon entering the Air Force, members take an oath signifying their personal commitment to support and defend the Constitution of the United States and a commitment and willingness to serve their country for the duration of their Air Force career. The oath is a solemn promise to do one's duty and meet one's responsibilities. The oath espouses the responsibility to lead others in the exercise of one's duty.

9.23.4. Building warrior leaders who have the competencies and skills to understand the complexity of expeditionary operations and the successful execution of airpower capabilities in unilateral, joint, or coalition operations is a responsibility shared by the Air Force and individual Airmen. Also, Airmen must be able to use scarce resources effectively to deliver required air, space, and cyberspace effects. The development of this warrior ethos is an individual and organizational responsibility.

9.23.5. When Air Force forces are employed in various operational environments, they offer basic characteristics that, when exploited, are fundamental to the successful conduct of war and peace. These characteristics, when molded into viable force capabilities and executed by knowledge-enabled Airmen, enhance the overall ability of the joint team to achieve success when called upon. Therefore, each Airman should understand and be able to articulate the full potential and application of Air Force capabilities required to support the Air Force mission and meet United States national security objectives.

## 9.24. The Warrior Ethos:

9.24.1. The central focus of the profession of arms is warfighting. As Airmen, we have a special responsibility to ensure the most lethal Air Force the world has ever seen flies and fights the right way. Airmen have inherited an Air Force forged through the ingenuity, courage, and strength of Airmen who preceded them. An Airman's duty is to continue to provide the Nation and the next generation of Airmen an equally dominant Air Force. Doing so requires Airmen to fully understand the profession of arms they have chosen, the commitment they made by taking an oath of office, and the acceptance to live according to the Air Force's core values. This is the warrior ethos and a mindset designed to build the confidence and commitment necessary to shape professional Airmen able to work as a team to accomplish the mission. This mindset is shaped by an expeditionary service during combat, humanitarian response, disaster relief operations, and by the lessons learned from those operations. The warrior ethos is also developed and sustained over the course of a career through a continuum of learning and associated development experiences, including a wide variety of assignments, focused training and education, exhibiting pride in the Air Force uniform, physical conditioning, and understanding Air Force symbols, history, and culture.

9.24.2. Airmen share a history of service, honor, and sacrifice. From the earliest days of airpower to the heights of space, Airmen have built an extraordinary heritage that forms the foundation for the Service's boundless horizon. Even though we are technology focused, we value quality over quantity. We embrace change and through transformation and innovation ensure a viable Air Force for the future. Airmen firmly grounded in the core values and ingrained with the warrior ethos react to combat stresses, operational deployment pressures, and daily home station demands with valor, courage, and sacrifice. We all have these characteristics, which surface often during times of great difficulty or unforeseen circumstances. While many acts of valor, courage or sacrifice go unseen, others helped shape the finest traditions of the Air Force. They should be recognized not only as part of United States Air Force history, but also to illustrate that any Airman may be called upon to perform above and beyond in the profession of arms.

## 9.25. Valor.

Valor is the ability to face danger or hardship in a determined and resolute manner and is commonly known as bravery, fearlessness, fortitude, gallantry, heart, nerve, and many other terms. Valor is the willingness to step outside of one's comfort zone to deal with an unexpected situation. Such situations can happen almost anywhere. Valor exists in places other than on the battlefield; an Airman can exhibit valor when presented with unusual circumstances in the daily routine of life. When acting with valor, one expresses the qualities of a hero or heroine.

*In the summer of 2005, Senior Airman Shea Dodson wanted to do more than his assigned administrative duties inside of Baghdad's Green Zone. The call was out for volunteers to provide security for ongoing convoys, so Airman Dodson raised his hand. After some intense just-in-time training, he was performing security detail for his first convoy. On this mission, Airman Dodson put that training to good use. When a suspected vehicle-borne suicide bomber raced toward the convoy, he fired .50 caliber rounds into the engine block no fewer than four times, disabling the vehicle. During the same mission, his unit became mired in traffic near a high-rise development. He noticed movement above and saw an Iraqi armed with an AK-47 creeping toward the edge of a balcony overlooking the convoy. Airman Dodson immediately engaged with indirect warning fire from his M-16, hitting the wall next to the suspected insurgent's head. The armed Iraqi dove for cover and never returned. When the convoy arrived at its final destination, a children's school, he continued with a complete security sweep of the perimeter houses to ensure it was clear. Airman Dodson remained on armed watch as his team handed out school supplies to the kids in the open courtyard. By 2 PM that same day, Airman Dodson was back at his desk, keeping track of critical data for the commanding general of the Multinational Security Transition Command–Iraq. It was all in a day's work for this dedicated Airman.*

Quotations from the Air Force Memorial in Washington, DC

*Saving the lives of your fellow Airman is the most extraordinary kind of heroism that I know.*

General Curtis E. LeMay (b. 1906 – d. 1990)
Former Air Force Chief of Staff

*When I think of the enlisted force, I see dedication, determination, loyalty, and valor.*

Paul W. Airey
(b. 1923 –d. 2009)
First Chief Master Sergeant of the Air Force

*As I prepare for this...mission, I am a bit homesick... Mother and Dad, you are very close to me, and I long so to talk to you. America has asked much of our generation, but I'm glad to give her all I have because she has given me so much.*

Sergeant Arnold Rahe, U.S. Army Air Forces, WWII
Killed in France; from a letter to his parents

## 9.26. Courage.

Courage is about the ability to face fear, danger, or adversity. Three types of courage are critical in the profession of arms: personal, physical, and moral. Personal courage is about doing what's right even at risk to one's career. Physical courage is the ability to overcome fears of bodily harm to get the job done, or willingness to risk yourself for someone else's sake in battle or the course of everyday life. Finally, moral courage is the ability to stand by the core values when moral courage may not be the popular thing to do. Integrity breeds courage when and where the behavior is most needed. More often than not, courage is manifested as an act of bravery on the battlefield as Airmen face the challenges present in combat.

*While on a special mission in Southwest Asia in 2005, Technical Sergeant Corey Clewley was loading cargo on his aircraft when he saw a Romanian C-130 experience a hard landing. Unbeknownst to the Romanian crew, the aircraft brakes caused a fire, causing Sergeant Clewley to spring into action. He instructed a fellow loadmaster to inform his aircraft commander of the situation and to ensure that someone contacted the control tower of the fire while he and a crew chief grabbed fire extinguishers and ran toward the burning aircraft. The Romanian C-130 fire intensified as it spread to the aircraft's fuselage and ruptured the hydraulic brake line. Despite the danger to himself, Sergeant Clewley got within a few feet of the flames and attempted to suppress the fire. His sense of urgency tripled when he realized the C-130 crew was still inside the aircraft and was unable to get out of the burning aircraft. He saw a member of the crew mouthing 'please, please' and pointing to the troop exit door. Sergeant Clewley refocused his attention to that area and began suppressing the fire, enabling the crew to safely exit the aircraft. He continued to keep the fire under control until the fire department arrived. Sergeant Clewley credits the team effort that kept the incident from becoming a deadly event and never considered the risk to his own life as he worked to save a crew and aircraft that was not part of his responsibility, his service, or even his Nation. He noted that saving the lives of the people on board was more important than who owned the aircraft.*

> Quotations from the Air Force Memorial in
> Washington, District of Columbia

## 9.27. Sacrifice:

9.27.1. Sacrifice involves a willingness to give your life, time, or comfort to meet others' needs. Personal sacrifice occurs on many levels, but is commonly evident in the heroic actions of Airmen in combat. Day-to-day deployed garrison activities also present opportunities to put others' needs before individual wants.

*Everyday people can confront their fears, pains and uncertainties with courage or cower to the daily decisions facing them. Just being here (at Manas Air Base), you have overcome many challenges with your courage that helped prepare you to contribute to your Nation in tangible ways. You faced basic training, skills training, and deployment to a location worlds away from your normal life. All have taken courage and prepared you for the impact you are making...your decisions, your actions, your sacrifices of the luxuries of home, friends, and family do make a difference. Every day, the Airmen of Manas, from Airman Basic to Colonel, make decisions that have an impact on the Global War on Terrorism! Without the contributions of the individual soldier who pays the price to secure freedom for the many, the mission does not get done. Simply put...because Airmen have courage...because Airmen make sacrifices...because Airmen are not intimidated by challenges...because YOU have the courage to live a life of sacrifice for the ideals of a nation, the mission is accomplished day in and day out.*

> Major James Hall, Commander, Detachment 1,
> 317th Expeditionary Airlift Squadron
> Manas AB, Kyrgyzstan

*They knew not the day or hour nor the manner of their passing when far from home they were called to join that great band of heroic Airmen that went before.*

> Quotations from the Air Force Memorial in
> Washington, District of Columbia

*...Am going on a raid this afternoon...there is a possibility I won't return...do not worry about me as everyone has to leave this earth one way or another, and this is the way I have selected. If after this terrible war is over, the world emerges a saner place...pogroms and persecutions halted, then I'm glad I gave my efforts with thousands of others for such a cause.*

> Inscription from the American Cemetery
> and Memorial, Cambridge, England
> Sergeant Carl Goldman, U.S Army Air Forces,
> WWII, B-17 Gunner, Killed in Western Europe;
> from a letter to his parents

*...Our military families serve right alongside those of us in uniform. A special thank you to all the spouses and children and moms and dads out there praying for your loved ones in harm's way – we add our prayers, too, for their safe return.*

> General Richard B. Myers
> Former Chairman, Joint Chiefs of Staff

9.27.2. Exemplifying the Air Force core values, Senior Airman Jason Cunningham, an Air Force pararescueman performed actions during Operation Enduring Freedom that earned him the thanks of a grateful Nation, at the cost of his life. The Air Force Cross is awarded to United States and Foreign military personnel and civilians who have displayed extraordinary heroism in one of the following situations: while engaged in action against a United States enemy, while engaged in military operations involving conflict with a foreign force, or while serving with a Friendly nation engaged in armed conflict against a force in which the United States is not a belligerent party. The Air Force Cross is awarded when the heroic actions fall just short of warranting the Congressional Medal of Honor. Only 24 Airmen have been awarded the Air Force Cross, the service's highest award, and only two, including Cunningham have received the award since the end of the Vietnam War. Below is the citation for Senior Airman Jason Cunningham's Air Force Cross.

---

CITATION TO ACCOMPANY THE AWARD OF

THE AIR FORCE CROSS

(POSTHUMOUS)

TO

JASON D. CUNNINGHAM

The President of the United States of America, authorized by Title 10, Section 8742, U.S.C., awards the Air Force Cross to Senior Airman Jason D. Cunningham for extraordinary heroism in military operations against an opposing armed force while serving as a pararescueman near the village of Marzak in the Paktia Province of Afghanistan on 4 March 2002. On that proud day, Airman Cunningham was the primary Air Force Combat Search and Rescue medic assigned to a Quick Reaction Force tasked to recover two American servicemen evading capture in austere terrain occupied by massed Al Qaida and Taliban forces. Shortly before landing, his MH-47E helicopter received accurate rocket-propelled grenade and small arms fire, severely disabling the aircraft and causing it to crash land. The assault force formed a hasty defense and immediately suffered three fatalities and five critical casualties. Despite effective enemy fire, and at great risk to his own life, Airman Cunningham remained in the burning fuselage of the aircraft in order to treat the wounded. As he moved his patients to a more secure location, mortar rounds began to impact within fifty feet of his position. Disregarding this extreme danger, he continued the movement and exposed himself to enemy fire on seven separate occasions. When the second casualty collection point was also compromised, in a display of uncommon valor and gallantry, Airman Cunningham braved an intense small arms and rocket-propelled grenade attack while repositioning the critically wounded to a third collection point. Even after he was mortally wounded and quickly deteriorating, he continued to direct patient movement and transferred care to another medic. In the end, his distinct efforts led to the successful delivery of ten gravely wounded Americans to life-saving medical treatment. Through his extraordinary heroism, superb airmanship, aggressiveness in the face of the enemy, and in the dedication of his service to his country, Senior Airman Cunningham reflected the highest credit upon himself and the United States Air Force.

---

## 9.28. Profession of Arms Conclusion:

9.28.1. We must remember that above all else, we are Airmen first. We, more than anyone else, understand the price that is paid for freedom. Airmen, more than anyone else, understand the sacrifices that come from willingly serving our country. Finally, Airmen more than anyone else, understand the meaning of belonging to the Profession of Arms.

9.28.2. We must learn from history. Our shared touchstone of warrior virtues and single, unifying purpose remain unchanged: fly, fight, and win. We must remain true to the legacy of valor and devotion, so boldly written with contrails and smoke across the skies from Ploesti and Schweinfurt, through MiG Alley and downtown Hanoi, to Kandahar and Baghdad. This legacy defines our role in the American way of war—to risk the lives of Airmen to kick down the opponent's door so thousands need not die.

### Section 9G—Personal Professionalism

*The ultimate source of air and space combat capability resides in the men and women of the United States Air Force. We owe it to ourselves to continue our professional development to continue to hone our quality edge.*

General John Jumper
Former Air Force Chief of Staff

## 9.29. Readiness:

9.29.1. One of the telltale signs of a military professional is preparation. When the time comes to use their skills, military professionals are ready because they took advantage of opportunities to gain experience. Every military member will have opportunities to serve. Those opportunities may be mundane, exciting, or inconvenient, but each will provide a chance to gain experience and improve readiness levels.

9.29.2. Often, opportunities to serve do not look particularly exciting or rewarding, but they hold the seeds of greatness. Doing such tasks builds the experience level needed to sharpen judgment and discernment. Military members should be open to a variety of experiences in order to grow in all areas of life (physical, mental, emotional, and spiritual). Military professionals cannot be disconnected from the world and must remember that the cost of choosing one path may be the opportunity to take another.

9.29.3. The military professional who stands ready to make critical decisions and is able to perform under pressure is usually the one who took advantage of unique opportunities that arose. From past experiences, professionals build the confidence, judgment, courage, and integrity they need to act professionally. Will they always feel ready? Probably not, but most will likely say they wish they had more experience upon which to base their decisions or improve their performance. Most experience is gained by accepting opportunities as they come, even when conditions are not perfect.

9.29.4. Certainly, no one can do everything. Members must select wisely to prevent overloading and burnout. They can round out their perspective vicariously by sharing others' experiences through reading. Charles, Archduke of Austria, pointed to this thought when he said, "A great captain can be formed only by long experience and intense study; neither is his own experience enough—for whose life is…sufficiently fruitful of events to render his knowledge universal?"

**9.30. Chief of Staff, United States Air Force Professional Reading Program:**

9.30.1. In 1996, General Fogleman created the Chief of Staff, United States Air Force Professional Reading Program to develop a common frame of reference among Air Force members—officers, enlisted, and civilians—to help each become better, more effective advocates of air and space power. Each Chief of Staff, United States Air Force since then has enhanced and continued the Chief of Staff, United States Air Force's Professional Reading Program. In 2012, General Norton A. Schwartz revised the list by adding books; films; technology, entertainment, design briefings; and online resources.

9.30.2. This program can help launch a career-long reading habit or be used to supplement previous readings. Listed materials cover various topics, although the majority detail air and space power from its genesis to recent times. These sources provide great examples of leadership to illustrate qualities Airmen should emulate. The list includes insight into Air Force history, analyze ongoing conflicts and their relevancy to the future, furnish organizational and leadership success stories, and provide lessons learned from recent conflicts. The more you study, the better you will understand the background behind the Air Force's core competencies and the better equipped you will be to form and express your own opinions.

9.30.3. The Headquarters Air Force Historian (HQ USAF/HO) is responsible for day-to-day management of the reading list. The reading list is particularly relevant as civilian men and women take on more responsibility in these times of global terrorism and international conflict. Most of the books were chosen because of their readability. Their selection does not reflect Chief of Staff, United States Air Force or United States Air Force endorsement of the authors' views or interpretations. Access the updated reading list and a brief summary of new selections at http://www.af.mil/library/csafreading/index.asp. Air University will supply each Air Force library with multiple copies of each new book on the list.

**9.31. Core Values:**

9.31.1. Core values are at the heart and soul of the military profession: *integrity first, service before self, and excellence in all we do.* Such values are closely intertwined since integrity provides the bedrock for our military endeavors, and is fortified by service to country. This in turn fuels the drive for excellence. In light of the demands placed upon our people to support United States security interests around the globe, the concept of "service before self" needs further discussion. As members of the joint team, Airmen are part of a unique profession founded on the premise of service before self. Airmen are not engaged in just another job: they are practitioners of the profession of arms. They are entrusted with the security of the Nation, the protection of their citizens, and the preservation of their way of life. In this capacity, they serve as guardians of America's future, and this responsibility requires Airmen to place the needs of service and country before personal concerns.

9.31.2. The military profession is sharply distinguished from others by what General Sir John Hackett has termed the "unlimited liability clause." Upon entering the Air Force, Airmen accept a sacred trust from the American people. They swear to support and defend the Constitution of the United States against all enemies, foreign and domestic. They take this obligation freely without any reservations and thereby commit their lives in defense of America and their citizens.

9.31.3. No other profession expects their members to lay down their lives for their friends, families, or freedoms. By voluntarily serving in the military profession, Airmen accept unique responsibilities. In today's world, service to country requires not only a high degree of skill, but also a willingness to make personal sacrifices. Airmen work long hours to provide the most combat capability possible for the taxpayer dollar. Military professional's duties require them to go temporary duty or permanent change of station to harsh locations to meet national security needs; are on call 24 hours a day, 7 days a week; and when called, deploy to the far corners of the globe without complaint.

9.31.4. Inherent in all of this is individual willingness to subordinate personal interests for the good of the unit, Service, and Nation. Airmen can ill afford "sunshine soldiers," or those who focus on careerism. Instead, the military needs professionals who strive to be the best at their current job, and who realize they attain individual advancement through the success of their unit or work center. Careerism can be most damaging in the case of leaders. If subordinates perceive leaders are consumed with career concerns, they will be unwilling to forgo personal goals for the good of the unit and the Air Force. This situation is only aggravated by attempts to serve "through a position" or to do a quick "touch and go" in a key job simply to fill out a resume. Ultimately, the mission will suffer with potentially devastating consequences.

9.31.5. So, what is the payoff for placing service before self? The paycheck or the benefits is not what keeps the professionals going. Professionals remain with the Air Force because of the intangibles: the satisfaction gained from doing something significant with their lives, the pride in being part of a unique organization that lives by high standards, and the sense of accomplishment gained from defending the Nation and their democratic way of life.

## 9.32. Conclusion:

9.32.1. This chapter discusses the philosophy, purpose, and structure of the enlisted force and examines the NCO in terms of rank and precedence, legal authority, and general and specific responsibilities. Also briefly described is the special positions of trust senior NCOs may hold, such as Air Force career filed manager, first sergeant, Command Chief Master Sergeant, and Chief Master Sergeant of the Air Force, and concludes with a discussion of the profession of arms.

9.32.2. The word "professional" should inspire all enlisted members to aspire to the ideal of service and expertise. Professional status comes to people at different times in their lives and careers. Furthermore, professionalism is achieved through continuous study, practice, and experience. Overall, the military seems to fit strongly into the professional category, but at what point can an individual claim professional military status? Professional status is expressed by attitudes and commitments, and by internalizing military values. Studying and understanding these factors are vital to the senior NCO and the future of the United States Air Force. Every senior NCO has an obligation to the United States, to the Air Force, and to his or her supervisor and subordinates to be the very best professional possible.

9.32.3. Future military members must educate themselves through study, experience, and by observing others. They must learn to accept responsibility for their actions and those of their subordinates, and to take appropriate action, never hiding behind excuses. Their focus must be on devoted service to the Nation, not on pay, working conditions, or their next assignment. Only then will they move toward achieving the ideal of professionalism.

**Chapter 10**

**LEADERSHIP**

*Section 10A—Overview*

**10.1. Introduction.**

As the old adage "a born leader" implies, those who lead were intended to, or *supposed* to, lead since the day they were born; but how could that be true? Is leadership a characteristic shared only by those gifted enough to lead or is it simply defined by a person's position and authority? After all, given the authority anyone can command, but what sort of influence does one who merely commands and directs have on those who follow? In all actuality, leadership is an ability we all can develop and a leader's effectiveness is often determined by the actions of those who choose to follow. Leadership is a delicate mix of art and science requiring people-oriented attributes, interpersonal communication, and an undeniable character that motivates, or wills, others to follow. This chapter examines the art and science of leadership and includes information to assist Airmen in understanding what leadership is, how it pertains to the Air Force mission, and why it is important to the institution of airpower. This chapter continues with a brief explanation of the differences, and interrelationships between leadership and management, offers an opportunity to assess one's leadership qualities, and advice on how to become a more effective leader. Furthermore, it explains the concept of vision, empowerment, and provides information pertaining to leadership flexibility and followership. Lastly, we will explore ways to effectively manage change and mentor followers.

*Section 10B—Leadership*

**10.2. The Art and Science of Leadership.**

Merriam-Webster's dictionary defines the word *lead* as "to guide on a way especially by going in advance" or "to direct on a course or in a direction." A leader is considered a person "who directs a military force or unit" and/or "who has commanding authority or influence." With this in mind, we can explain the act of leading in the Air Force as "the art and science of accomplishing the Air Force mission by motivating, influencing, and directing Airmen." This highlights two central elements: (1) the mission; objective, or task to be accomplished; and (2) the Airmen who will accomplish it. All aspects of leadership should support the Air Force mission and its Airmen. Successful leaders recognize that people are the most valuable resource and, without them; the organization fails. Therefore, the Air Force relies on its members to develop as leaders for today, and tomorrow. The extent of a person's development is dependent on his or her status within the organization (whether as an officer, enlisted, or civilian), and the level of responsibility he or she has. Most enlisted members function at the tactical level where their technical skills are combined with their direct influence on subordinate members in daily operations and at war.

> *"Good leaders are people who have a passion to succeed....To become successful leaders, we must first learn that no matter how good the technology or how shiny the equipment, people-to-people relations get things done in our organizations. People are the assets that determine our success or failure. If you are to be a good leader, you have to cultivate your skills in the arena of personal relations."*
>
> General Ronald R. Fogleman
> Former Air Force Chief of Staff

10.2.1. **Set the Example.**

Effective leadership takes more than simply "talking the talk." Leadership is modeling, or setting the example for others in word and action. For many, this is considered the toughest part of leading. However, in order to be successful, leaders must evaluate themselves and work on their shortcomings. Effective leaders *lead* rather than drive people. They make fair and firm decisions that are in the best interest of good order, discipline, and successful accomplishment of the mission. A leader's responsibilities go further than just being responsible for accomplishing the mission. Effective leaders are not only expected to accomplish the mission, but to do so with a minimal cost in resources, such as people, materiel, and money. While no one expects the leader to be perfect, a leader cannot demand the best from others if he or she cannot perform as expected.

10.2.2. **Motivate Intrinsically.**

Intrinsic motivation is encouraging others to act, not because they have to; but because they want to. The Air Force continuously adapts in new and innovative ways to conduct daily operations, and requires leaders who can initiate and sustain change. To motivate intrinsically, consider ways to get others to embrace ideas, strategies, and initiatives.

### 10.2.3. Involvement.

A leader's success is reflected in the efficiency, productivity, morale, and enthusiasm demonstrated by the followers and a leader's involvement is essential to maximizing worker performance and the mission. Leaders become a positive influence when they are actively involved in their Airmen's careers. Although service members are obligated to "obey the orders of the President of the U.S. and the orders of the officers appointed over [them]," they respond more positively and with extra effort to those who genuinely care about them. In today's environment of technology and specialization, most leaders tend to find this environment allows them to neglect the need of knowing their subordinate members of the organization, and show sincere concern in their problems, career development, and welfare.

### 10.2.4. Learning from Failure.

Leadership is all about risks and rewards and effective leaders realize that failure is possibly one of the greatest learning tools an organization has for achieving success. With every risk there is the potential for failure; however, these are the moments which shed light on the faults that exist within an organization, its processes, and procedures. Effective leaders realize that learning from failure empowers change and inspires efforts to improve. Therefore, leaders never fear failure, they embrace it.

### 10.2.5. Transparency.

Direction, decisions, and actions are rarely challenged if the leader's intentions are transparent. Transparency is accomplished by integrating regular communication, shared decision-making, mutual consensus, and healthy debate. Airmen should know the reason decisions were made and how that decision will impact them and the organization. Transparent leaders should not micromanage, give credit where credit is due, and take accountability when things fail.

### 10.2.6. Flexibility.

Top-down, authoritative organizations is a classic example of rigid and stubborn leadership and usually results in resentment and animosity, especially during times of change. Leaders who are flexible listen to other points of view, bend when necessary, and are not afraid to change course if things are not going well.

### 10.2.7. Resilience.

Leaders at every level within an organization constantly face challenges, changes, and criticisms. There will always be times of uncertainty, deviation, turmoil, and at times, conflict. Therefore, resilient leaders must possess a combination of compassion and thick skin.

### 10.2.8. Accountability.

Good things come to those who are accountable, and leaders play an important part in ensuring accountability in the workplace. Promoting accountability in the workplace includes establishing clear roles and responsibilities, cultivating a sense of pride and ownership among the members and teams within the organization, providing regular feedback to subordinates, and leading with integrity and by positive example are all responsibilities of a leader. Accountability does not focus on the discipline and punishment associated with being unaccountable; but rather, concentrates on creating, and sustaining, a continuously learning and always improving organization.

*"Give people opportunities to take pride in their work and personal growth. People want to do well at their job; you have to help them do that."*

Robert D. Gaylor
Former Chief Master Sergeant of the Air Force #5

## 10.3. Leadership Self-Evaluation.

To successfully accomplish the responsibilities of a position, one must first understand what is expected of them. The following is a list of questions that offer a perspective as to what is expected of a leader and assist aspiring leaders develop particular skills. Only the most honest responses to these questions will reveal one's definite strengths and potential weaknesses. Positively and proactively responding to the results will provide direction upon which to concentrate efforts to improve.

10.3.1. Do I have the courage to make tough decisions and stand by them?

10.3.2. Am I flexible when dealing with changing situations?

10.3.3. Can I remain enthusiastic and cheerful when I am confronted with seemingly impossible tasks?

10.3.4. Am I willing to do my best with what seems to be inadequate means?

10.3.5. Can I inspire people to achieve outstanding results?

10.3.6. Am I willing to take reasonable risks to allow my Airmen to grow and become more productive?

10.3.7. Am I willing to let my Airmen be creative?

10.3.8. Does my manner invite communication?

10.3.9. Do I really listen? Can I withhold judgment until I have all the facts?

10.3.10. Am I willing to accept my Airmen's failures as my own, yet immediately recognize their successes as theirs?

10.3.11. Am I able to do many things at one time? Can I manage a complex job?

10.3.12. Can I carry out orders as well as give them?

## 10.4. Advice to Leaders.

There are no secrets or "magic formulas" to successful leadership. Rather, leadership is an individual and personal choice and everyone develops their own unique leadership style. Although the best advice is to just be yourself, all ambitious leaders can always benefit from the wise words of others. In 1976, while he was Commander in Chief, Pacific Air Forces, General Louis L. Wilson, Jr., wrote the following timeless advice:

### 10.4.1. Be Tough.

Set your standards high and insist that your people measure up. Have the courage to correct those who fail to do so. In the long run, your people will be happier. Almost certainly morale will be higher, your outfit better, and your people prouder.

### 10.4.2. Get Out from Behind Your Desk.

See for yourself what is going on in your work center. Your Airmen will see that you are interested in their problems, work conditions, and welfare. Many of your people problems will go away if you practice this point.

### 10.4.3. Search Out the Problems.

If you think there are no problems in your organization, you may be ignorant to problems that are not obvious. The trick is to find them. Foster an environment that encourages people to bring problems to you.

### 10.4.4. Find the Critical Path to Success.

Get personally involved in issues on a priority basis. Let your influence be felt on make-or-break issues in your organization. Avoid the "activity trap"—do not spend your valuable time on inconsequential or trivial matters. Weigh in where it counts.

### 10.4.5. Be Sensitive.

Listen to your people. Communicate with them and be perceptive to their needs. Learn to recognize problems and seek out ideas. Be innovative. Recognize that effective communication involves shared perceptions. Do not be afraid to empathize when necessary. Listen, listen, and listen!

### 10.4.6. Do Not Take Things for Granted.

Do not assume things have been fixed—look for yourself. Furthermore, do not assume problems will stay fixed. The probability is high that fixed problems will recur, so regularly monitor your processes.

### 10.4.7. Do Not Alibi.

Remember, you and your people will never be perfect. People will make mistakes, so do not be defensive about things that are wrong. Nothing is more disgusting than the individual who can do no wrong and has an alibi for anything and everything that goes awry.

### 10.4.8. Do Not Procrastinate.

Do not put off those hard decisions because you are not willing to make them today; as they will not be any easier tomorrow. This does not mean you should make precipitous or unreasonable decisions just to be prompt. However, once you have arrived at what you believe is correct, get on with it. Do not block progress.

### 10.4.9. Do Not Tolerate Incompetence.

Once people demonstrate laziness, disinterest, or an inability to get the job done, you must have the courage to terminate their assignments. You cannot afford to do less. On the other hand, when your people are doing good work, recognize the good work and encourage them. Certainly they will do even better.

### 10.4.10. Be Honest.

When talking to your people be candid and insist that they do likewise. They set their behavior patterns based upon your example. Nothing is more disastrous than garbled information, half-truths, and falsifications. Make sure your people know where you stand on this matter. Encourage them to come to you if they have questions about what is going on in the unit. You must create an atmosphere of trust and confidence. Finally, be honest with yourself—do not gimmick reports and figures to make things look good on paper. Advice from a successful leader can be a beneficial tool to the aspiring leader, but where the aspiring leader applies this tool will determine his or her success. The perfect place to start is Air Force standards.

## 10.5. Air Force Standards.

Air Force standards of conduct, discipline, and customs and courtesies reflect the Air Force's broad heritage and traditions. Air Force leaders must not only know these standards, they must enforce them. While current Department of Defense and Air Force policies provide specific guidance on standards, leaders must be familiar with the following:

### 10.5.1. Mission.

The Air Force's mission is to fly, fight, and win…in air, space, and cyberspace. To achieve strategic, operational, and tactical objectives unhindered by time, distance, and geography; the Air Force employs six distinctive capabilities of Air and Space Superiority, Global Attack, Rapid Global Mobility, Precision Engagement, Information Superiority, and Agile Combat Support. The three Air Force Core Values of Integrity First, Service before Self, and Excellence in All We Do, enables Airmen to effectively execute their responsibilities and accomplish the mission.

### 10.5.2. Oath.

Upon entering the Air Force, each member voluntarily takes a sworn oath of enlistment. With every oath, enlisted members reaffirm their belief and public commitment to the following:

*I, (name), do solemnly swear (or affirm) that I will support and defend the Constitution of the U.S. against all enemies, foreign and domestic; that I will bear true faith and allegiance to the same, and that I will obey the orders of the President of the U.S. and the orders of the officers appointed over me according to regulations and the Uniform Code of Military Justice. So help me God.*

### 10.5.3. Way of Life.

Airmen are on duty 24 hours a day, 365 days a year; and if so directed by a competent authority, must report for duty at any time, at any location, for as long as necessary to complete the task at hand. Due to the importance of the Air Force mission, the dangers associated with military service, and the national and international influence and potential implications relevant to global operations; the Air Force enforces more restrictive rules and elevated standards than those found in the civilian community. Individuals unable to maintain these higher standards, or are deemed not compatible with military service will not be retained in the Air Force.

### 10.5.4. Chain of Command.

The chain of command provides the authority, communications, and control necessary to accomplish the mission-related tasks at every echelon of the Air Force. Each level is responsible for all lower levels and accountable to all higher levels. The chain will not work without loyalty at every level. The key to an effective chain of command is trusting the system and resolving issues at the lowest possible level.

### 10.5.5. Conduct.

The Air Force's mission is critical to national security, global stability, and international relations. Therefore, each member has specific responsibilities for accomplishing their part in the mission. Airmen carry out orders, perform specific duty-related tasks, and uphold Air Force standards. Supervisors enforce these standards and ensure their Airmen understand and fulfill them at all times. Standards of conduct apply to both on-duty and off-duty behavior.

### 10.5.6. Professional Relationships.

To maintain a successful and effective military organization, the Air Force depends on professional relationships among all its members (both military and civilian). All interactions and relationships must support the mission and operational effectiveness of the Air Force. Officers and Enlisted alike must ensure their relationships with coworkers, superiors, and subordinates do not portray favoritism or impropriety. Excessive socialization and undue familiarity, whether real or perceived, degrades morale, team cohesion, and leadership effectiveness.

## 10.6. Leadership Versus Management.

*"Leaders are people who do the right thing. Managers are people who do things right."*

> Warren G. Bennis, Ph.D.
> Founding Chair, The Leadership Institute,
> University of Southern California

### 10.6.1. Which Is More Important?

Leadership and management are simply not the same thing. Successful organizations include and depend on elements of control, trust, administration, development, standardization, innovation, compliance, and inspiration. Leadership and management go hand in hand in producing these elements which promote mission success. Throughout military history, there have been accounts of leadership and management in action. For instance, during the D-Day Invasion of Normandy on 6 June 1944, some believe this invasion was an effective use of management which moved the U.S. and coalition forces onto the beaches, and the inspirational leadership is what moved them forward. So which is more important?

### 10.6.2. Roles of Leadership and Management.

To better understand the roles of leadership and management, consider them in terms of behavior, personal characteristics, and organizational situation.

#### 10.6.2.1. Behavior:

10.6.2.1.1. Managerial behaviors focus on building organizational mechanisms that mesh together like the parts of a complex timepiece whereas leadership behaviors concentrate on effectively moving the hands of the timepiece to display the correct time. The behavioral focus of each is clearly important; but, while the manager may be preoccupied with the precision of the process, the leader concentrates on the inertial forces that affect the process.

*"Management is getting people to do what needs to be done. Leadership is getting people to want to do what needs to be done."*

> Warren G. Bennis, Ph.D.
> Founding Chair, The Leadership Institute,
> University of Southern California

The words of Field Marshal Sir William Slim, who led the British Fourteenth Army in the conquest of Burma in World War II, are worthy of note:

*"Leadership is of the spirit, compounded of personality and vision. Management is of the mind, more a matter of accurate calculation, statistics, methods, timetables, and routines."*

> Field Marshal Sir William Slim
> British Fourteenth Army
> Burma, World War II

10.6.2.1.2. Managers use the management process to control people by pushing them in the right direction. Leaders motivate and inspire people to keep moving in the right direction by satisfying human needs. In order to achieve a vision, leaders tailor their behavior toward their followers' needs for achievement, sense of belonging, recognition, self-esteem, and control over their lives. Bennis offers an appropriate summary of this behavioral characteristics comparison in Figure 10.1.

10.6.2.2. **Personal Characteristics.** Figure 10.1 also illustrates a comparison of successful leaders and managers, as researched by Professor Robert White, Indiana University. Neither type of behavior is exclusively positive or negative. Figure 10.1 suggests that leaders must have a grasp of management and leadership skills to be successful. Moreover, the two cannot (and should not) be separated. In other words, leadership is an art that includes management. The best managers tend to become good leaders because they develop leadership abilities and skills through practicing good management techniques. Similarly, seldom is there an effective leader who is not also a good manager. Successful leaders humanize their management skills with inspiration, empowerment, and vision through charisma.

**Figure 10.1. Managers and Leaders: A Comparison.**

| BENNIS'S BEHAVIORAL CHARACTERISTICS COMPARISON | |
| --- | --- |
| **Managers** | **Leaders** |
| Administer | Motivate |
| Maintain | Develop |
| Control | Inspire |
| **WHITE'S PERSONAL CHARACTERISTICS COMPARISON** | |
| **Managers** | **Leaders** |
| Problem solvers | Analyze purposes and causes |
| Statistics driven | Values driven |
| Seek conflict avoidance | Accept and invite conflict |
| Thrive on predictability | Ambiguous |
| Ensure organizational objectives are achieved (even if they disagree with them) | Ensure their objectives and those of the organization become one and the same |

10.6.2.3. **Organizational Situation.**

10.6.2.3.1. What are the organizational implications of management and leadership? Leaders launch and steer the organization toward the pursuit of goals and strategies while managers ensure the resources needed are readily available and efficiently used. Managers are responsible for organizing projects, staffing positions with qualified individuals, communicating plans, delegating responsibilities, and devising systems to monitor implementation. Leadership supports these actions by aligning the personnel's needs, wants, emotions, and aspirations with the task. They understand the vision are committed and encourage others. (**Note:** The concept of vision is discussed in paragraph 10.8.)

10.6.2.3.2. To be successful, an organization needs both leadership and management. For an organization, strong leadership with weak management is no better, and sometimes worse, than the opposite. The challenge is to achieve a balance of strong leadership and capable management. While not the most effective approach, a peacetime military can survive with good administration and management up and down the hierarchy, coupled with good leadership concentrated at the top. On the other hand, a wartime force must have competent leadership at all levels, particularly at the tactical level of war. Good management brings a degree of order and consistency to key issues like readiness, availability, and sustainment. However, no one has yet figured out how to manage people into battle. They must be led.

## 10.7. Leadership Qualities:

10.7.1. **Positive Attitude.**

Leaders must demonstrate the attitude they hope to see emulated by their followers. In doing so, this same attitude will be more easily adopted by their Airmen. Enthusiasm is contagious and can deliver energy to all aspects of organizational operations. Although encouragement is normally considered an action, encouragement is actually attitude related. The inclination to encourage Airmen, as well as oneself, is a powerful motivator and satisfies human needs. Effective leaders constantly embrace positive goals and display a positive attitude.

10.7.2. **Values.**

The degree to which trust, loyalty, and integrity are present in the leadership of an organization directly relates to the organization's effectiveness. Leadership is the capacity to generate and sustain trust, and trust is dependent upon reliability. Indicators of reliability, such as punctual attendance at all meetings, prompt attention to correspondence, and meeting task deadlines translate into the level of trust people have in one another. Trust must also be balanced with a willingness to remove people who cannot be trusted and to make tough decisions when necessary. While the right decision is not always the easiest decision, Airmen respect leaders for doing the right thing and reward leadership with their own trustworthiness and loyalty. Like trust, the doors of loyalty swing both ways. Leaders cannot demand unwavering loyalty of their followers without being willing to return loyalty to them. Integrity is a consistent and honest demonstration of personal commitment to the organization and its vision. Therefore, leaders should be ever mindful of the ramifications of their behavior and strive to epitomize the Air Force core value of *Integrity First*.

**10.7.3. Character.**

The character traits of effective leaders include charisma, compassion, and courage. Effective leadership is a combination of competence and character. Lack of character, however, will most often prevent individuals from becoming great leaders.

*"But what if the leader, government-appointed or self-appointed, shouts, "Follow me!" and no one does? When do men sometimes follow him, and shout enthusiastically too? Something called "character" must be apparent in the leader. The followers must like him and want to be like him, or want him to like them. When it's over, they want him—private, sergeant, lieutenant, or even General Eisenhower—to clap them on the shoulder and say he's proud of them."*

Paul Fussell, Ph.D.,
The Great War and Modern Memory

**10.7.3.1. Charisma.** According to Webster, charisma is a special characteristic of leadership that inspires allegiance and devotion. Charisma can be effective, but is not a cure-all for leadership needs. German sociologist Max Weber's research noted that charisma is often contrary to authority; superiors consequently frown on it. Additionally, once it becomes "old hat" to Airmen, charisma's attraction and powers wane. Further, Airmen can easily spot disingenuous charisma, a characteristic that eventually erodes mission effectiveness.

**10.7.3.2. Compassion.** Compassion is the sympathetic pity and concern for the sufferings or misfortunes of others. Coupled with understanding, compassion is an important leadership trait. Because the human psyche bruises easily, most Airmen withhold their true feelings, often to the point of distress. Additionally, if Airmen do not share their feelings, NCOs will struggle to help Airmen improve their performance. Compassion promotes healthy, open, and honest communication and provides the stimulus to discuss one's inner thoughts and feelings.

**10.7.3.3. Courage.** Courage can take many forms. Leaders must demonstrate both moral and physical courage not only in combat and in high-risk situations, but in day-to-day life. Leadership requires the courage to address sub-standard performance or unacceptable behavior, to welcome new ideas, do what is ethically right when others prefer to do otherwise, and to be honest. Acts of courage inspires others to be courageous as well and helps them to maintain composure in stressful situations and provides the stimulus and encouragement to endure hardships.

**10.7.4. Credibility.**

Credibility is the quality of being trusted and believed in. Credible leaders must exercise and demonstrate humility, commitment to the organization and mission, and optimize operations by tapping into the unique strengths of each team member. Occasionally, leaders must "get their hands dirty" alongside their followers which also bolsters credibility. However, credibility is very fragile and takes years to earn through persistent, consistent, and patient leadership and can easily be lost with one thoughtless action, decision, or behavior. In the present era, leaders are challenged to demonstrate their credibility even more. Successful leaders earn credibility through leading by example and taking responsibility.

**10.7.4.1. Leading by Example.** Leaders lead by example. Leaders can be positive role models when they lead by example and pay attention to what they believe is important. Through positive behavior, leaders show others that they live by their values. They reinforce their credibility when they do not dwell on the effort they have put forth. Plus, Airmen are impressed when leaders do not exhibit undue strain in difficult circumstances.

**10.7.4.2. Taking Responsibility.** A crucial element of a leader's credibility is taking responsibility not only for his or her individual actions, but also for those of the Airmen.

*"All this has been my fault. It is I who have lost this fight, and you must help me out of it the best way you can."*

Attributed to General Robert E. Lee,
Kent Masterson Brown's *Retreat from Gettysburg*

**10.8. Vision.**

Air Force leaders must have a collective vision; a vision that empowers, inspires, challenges, and motivates followers to the highest levels of commitment and a continuous process improvement environment. Therefore, we must embrace and communicate the Air Force Smart Operations for the 21st Century vision. The vision for Air Force Smart Operations for the 21st Century is to establish a continuous process improvement environment in which all Airmen are actively eliminating waste and continuously improving processes. These improvements must be centered on the core missions Airmen are responsible for conducting; specifically to maintain the asymmetric advantages and capabilities the Air Force delivers in air, space, and cyberspace. We need to ensure we are also driving efficiencies and improvements across the board. Therefore, we must use the right tools and techniques to see and attack problems and leverage opportunities for improvement and employ our greatest resource: innovative, dedicated Airmen.

### 10.8.1. What Is Vision?

10.8.1.1. Vision is helping people believe they can accomplish their goals in the anticipation of a better future as a result of their own efforts. Inspiration is one way to convey vision. To better understand this concept, consider the following examples: President Franklin D. Roosevelt's announcement in May 1940 that the U.S. would produce 50,000 planes a year, and President John F. Kennedy's 1961 announcement of the U.S. intention to put a man on the moon within the decade. Both goals were breathtaking, perhaps impossible by most standards, and yet both were achieved. In each case, the dramatic announcement and the infectious inspiration bred helped achieve the goal.

10.8.1.2. The ability to form mental images of a possible outcome and to translate these images into a reality through leadership and action is a unique feature of the human brain. A leader should constantly anticipate the influences, trends, and demands that affect the vision over the next month, year, even decade. Unfortunately, a common leadership error is to become preoccupied with the present at the expense of the future. To be of realistic value, the vision must be logical, deductive, and plausible. Vision must be specific enough to provide real guidance to people, but unbounded enough to encourage initiative and demonstrate relevancy to a variety of conditions. Leaders without vision are doomed to perpetuate complacency. They fail to prosper because they continue doing things as they have always been done.

### 10.8.2. Implementing the Vision.

While senior leadership has the authority and responsibility to change the system as a whole, leaders at lower levels direct supervisors and subordinates to tasks more appropriate to the challenges of the new age. To do this, the leaders must communicate the vision to the unit, shop, or work center. Leaders are responsible for bolstering their Airmen's courage and understanding. However, launching a vision cannot be a single effort. Those who work for and with the leader are excellent sources of ideas. Leaders can prepare the organization for potential changes to come and disarm resistance to change by soliciting suggestions and promoting wide participation.

*"A great leader's courage to fulfill his vision comes from passion, not position."*

John C. Maxwell
*The 21 Irrefutable Laws of Leadership*

### 10.8.3. The Downside.

Even a clearly articulated and achievable vision may flounder if appropriate resource management and leadership practices do not accompany the vision. Sometimes the vision becomes an obsession and, as a result, adversely affects leader and follower judgment. What is crucial about the vision is not the originality, but, how well the vision serves the mission requirements, strategic goals of the unit, and the Air Force as a whole.

### 10.8.4. Maintaining the Vision.

Every leader needs to establish an enduring vision. A vision that meets the organization's needs at the time of implementation, over time, is unlikely to be applicable without changes. There is no regular schedule for vision revision. However, a wise leader does not wait for the alarm to sound before considering alternatives. Rather, the vision-forming process should be continual. Leaders should encourage personnel of all ranks, levels, and occupations to help articulate the vision. The experience will prove invaluable as unit members are promoted into more responsible, higher-level positions and continue to build an effective path to the future. On the other hand, the vision should not be arbitrarily modified. If the vision works and is consistent with environmental and technological developments, the vision should be affirmed and supported. As technology and our environment continue to evolve, our vision and leadership style must keep pace.

## 10.9. Empowerment:

### 10.9.1. Empowerment Defined.

Empowerment is a force that energizes people and provides responsibility, ownership, and control over the work they perform. Some individuals interpret empowerment as merely the delegation of authority. Delegation is not empowerment; however, effective empowerment does require good delegation. Assigning people tasks, along with the freedom and authority needed to creatively accomplish the tasks, is the essence of empowerment. Consequently, empowerment is often confused with participative leadership—emphasizing sensitivity to needs, involving people, and asking people for help. While empowerment includes these concepts, empowerment goes much further and allows workers to become stakeholders in the organization's vision. Once they are committed to this vision, organization members begin to participate in shaping and fashioning the vision into a shared vision. This synergistically developed vision motivates people to focus on the future and what the future holds, not simply because they *must*, but because they *want* to. For this approach to be successful, leaders must always be open and receptive to ideas and suggestions that could improve or refine the organization's vision.

### 10.9.2. Essence of Empowerment.

10.9.2.1. The essence of empowerment requires both leaders and followers to identify with their respective share of the organization's goals. The military is traditionally an authoritarian organization. The need for rapid decision-making and crisis response normally necessitates a traditional hierarchical framework. However, complex hierarchical frameworks do not always result in rapid decisions. Furthermore, the continual transformation of leader-follower roles is heralding an environment that allows both leaders and followers to more effectively realize organizational goals and objectives.

10.9.2.2. Effective empowerment is not new. Truly great leaders of the past never directly told their people how to do their jobs. Rather, they explained what needed to be done and established a playing field that allowed their people to achieve success on their own. Consequently, the follower's success became a success for the leader and the organization as well. While the responsibility for task completion may be on the leader's shoulders, the burden of getting the job done is shared by all. Therefore, the adage, "It's lonely at the top," is applicable to a leader who does not recognize the strengths of his or her people. Airmen can supply the details and express concerns that help overcome barriers to achieving visionary goals and mission accomplishment. When leaders solicit input, they discover the knowledge, interest, and parameters of support.

### 10.9.3. Guidelines to Empowerment.

Empowerment enhances organizational performance by promoting contributions from every member of the organization. Trust is the cornerstone of the mutually dependent relationship shared by leaders and followers. Therefore, the leader must be flexible and patient in introducing empowerment. By delegating decisions to those closest to the issues and by allowing Airmen flexibility in how they implement the vision, the leader successfully allows others to take ownership of the vision and experience pride in achieving the vision. Thus, the leader must maintain a firm grip on operational requirements and strategic planning. The leader must also realize that not everyone is willing or ready to accept the reins of empowerment. To realize their potential in fulfilling the vision, empowered followers need sufficient training on the task at hand. Otherwise, they are doomed to fail. On the other hand, Airmen who have expert knowledge in a particular field should be encouraged to use this knowledge and improve the vision where and when possible. Recognition is a key factor in perpetuating improvements. Hence, an important facet of empowerment is the appropriate recognition of contributions Airmen make to maximize mission success.

### 10.9.4. Potential Pitfalls.

Empowerment is frequently misunderstood and applied inappropriately. Empowerment is often associated with a laissez-faire style of leadership (abdicating responsibility for tasks to Airmen who are left to their own devices). This fire-and-forget approach to empowerment demonstrates a total absence of leadership. Conversely, empowerment is a leader-subordinate relationship that requires even more refined supervisory skills than traditional autocracy. People continually need direction, knowledge, resources, and support. Furthermore, empowerment and vision cannot be imposed. To do so would breed compliance rather than commitment. From an application standpoint, many leaders seek consensus as a means to empower their people. However, while consensus is assumed to be good because consensus represents what the group as a whole wants, consensus is usually safe and free of innovative ideas. Additionally, consensus can divert an organization from their true goal or vision. The adage that "a camel is a horse built by consensus" is not so farfetched. Leaders do not seek consensus—they build it.

## 10.10. Learning:

### 10.10.1. The Leader's Responsibilities.

Life in the military incorporates a perpetual requirement for continued training and education. Effective leaders must accept the responsibility of being both a master student and master teacher and should influence others by example. Training is used to communicate and implement the organization's vision and values at the supervisory and subordinate levels. Training is not only fundamental in focusing the organization's strategic vision, but also helps develop the capabilities of the Airmen who make the vision a reality. Both formal and informal training do more than augment a unit's level of technical expertise. By providing the skills Airmen need to be successful, organizations realize increased energy and motivation.

10.10.2. **Fostering Growth.**

10.10.2.1. Leaders foster professional growth by insisting their Airmen focus attention on the aspects of a situation, mission, or project they control. This is not to say tasks should be limited in scope or challenge. On the contrary, some adventure should be an integral part of every job. In order to motivate Airmen to learn and excel, leaders should provide challenging and enlightening experiences. Consequently, some supervisors want to tell an Airman what to do to improve. While this may impress the follower with the leader's knowledge, telling an Airman what to do to improve creates an unnecessary dependence on the leader and critically limits the follower's value of the experience.

10.10.2.2. The role of the leader in fostering growth is to identify and analyze knowledge and improvement opportunities. This will ensure advancements are permanent and pervasive, not temporary and specific. Leaders encourage the learning process by formally recognizing individual and unit successes, no matter how large or small. A more formal and direct way for the leader to encourage the subordinate to learn is by setting standards. Standards have the multiple effects of providing feedback to the leader on performance, ensuring quality control of unit output, and giving Airmen a goal and inspiration for developing and performing to do their best.

*People want to know what is expected of them. No one goes to work and says, "I am going to do a lousy job today." People work to succeed, and they need to know how you measure that success. Allow for a few mistakes because people must be given the latitude to learn.*

General H. Norman Schwarzkopf, Jr., Retired
Former Commander, U.S. Central Command

10.10.3. **Developing Airmen:**

10.10.3.1. To develop Airmen, a leader must:

10.10.3.1.1. Train replacements (the next generation).

10.10.3.1.2. Develop an understanding of roles and responsibilities.

10.10.3.1.3. Be an advisor and mentor.

10.10.3.1.4. Provide an opportunity for growth and promotion.

10.10.3.1.5. Clarify expectations.

10.10.3.1.6. Strengthen service identity.

10.10.3.1.7. Allow Airmen to make decisions and experience leadership.

10.10.3.1.8. Encourage and facilitate formal education.

10.10.3.2. An important milestone in any Airman's development process is to experience a significant challenge early in his or her career. Developing Airmen for leadership positions requires much work over long periods of time. Identifying people with leadership potential early in their careers and then determining the appropriate developmental challenges for them is the first step. Leaders must recognize and diagnose the capabilities of each Airman in their unit or organization. Those capabilities may include any skills, talents, experiences, personality temperaments, etc., the Airman may have that can contribute to current and future mission accomplishment. Leaders must also diagnose the developmental needs of Airmen, then assist them with personal and professional developmental needs that fulfill current or future job/role and responsibilities. Professional development needs may include off-duty education, Professional Military Education, specific skill training, additional training, professional development seminars/courses, and communication skills, etc. Personal developmental needs may include relationships, interpersonal skills, communication skills, supervisory skills, off-duty education, etc. Today's effective leaders had opportunities early in their careers that required them to lead, take risks, and learn from their triumphs and failures. In business, successful corporations do not wait for leaders to come along. Rather, they actively seek out people with leadership potential and expose them to career experiences designed to develop their skills. However, leaders must caution themselves against becoming preoccupied with finding and developing *young* leadership potential. Leaders must guard against overlooking the "late bloomer" whose leadership potential was not evident early on. A late bloomer's combination of maturity, experience, and untapped potential is a valuable asset to any organization.

10.10.4. **Dealing with Setbacks:**

10.10.4.1. To learn and improve, people need to be encouraged to try new things; sometimes their efforts will fail. A fundamental aspect of empowerment is acknowledging the right to fail. Obviously, some common sense is required. There can be no tolerance for violating regulations, jeopardizing safety, or failing due to a lack of effort. However, if the setback is the result of a failed attempt, applaud the initiative and dissect the setback so the Airman can learn from what went wrong. Unfortunately, the fear of failure prevents many otherwise capable individuals from pursuing their creativity and innovation. An Airman's dedication to improving his or her abilities is quite a valuable asset to an organization. Followers must remain optimistic, even in times of adversity.

10.10.4.2. Some people believe the key to success is to avoid failure. Consequently, they stay with the things they know and do well rather than risk failure by trying something new. The surest way to stifle creativity and innovation is to allow fear to perpetuate complacency. Airmen count on the experience and understanding of strong leaders in dealing with setbacks. There is no substitute for being able to say to an Airman, "I know what you're feeling, I've experienced similar setbacks. Here is how I chose to deal with the situation, and these are what the consequences of my actions were. Reflecting back on the situation, here is what I would do now if I had the chance to do things over."

## 10.11. Dealing with Change:

10.11.1. Leaders must be the chief transformation officers in their organizations and learn everything there is to know about the change before dealing with the change can even take place. Furthermore, they must learn how to deal with the emotions that result from the chaos and fear associated with change. Putting new processes in place is not enough. The people supporting these processes must be motivated to meet the challenge and support the change. To achieve that, leaders must maintain a clear understanding of the present and a clear focus on the future.

10.11.2. The leader must create an organizational climate conducive to change by explaining the limitations or shortfalls of the present process and the possibilities and benefits of the proposed change. Next, the leader must facilitate the change itself: walk Airmen through the change, explain the details, and answer questions. Finally, the leader should reward those who comply with the change and refocus those who do not. Tough-minded optimism is the best quality a leader can demonstrate when coping with change. Leaders coping with change should:

10.11.2.1. Involve people in the change process.

10.11.2.2. Fully explain the reason for change.

10.11.2.3. View change positively.

10.11.2.4. Create enthusiasm for the change.

10.11.2.5. Facilitate change (avoid forcing it).

10.11.2.6. Be open-minded and experiment with alternatives.

10.11.2.7. Seek out and accept feedback.

10.11.2.8. Never get complacent.

## 10.12. The Air Force Core Values.

The Air Force core values are the bedrock of leadership in the Air Force. The core values are a statement of those institutional values and principles of conduct that provide the moral framework within which military activities take place. The professional Air Force ethic consists of three fundamental and enduring values of integrity, service, and excellence. This ethic is the set of values that guides the way Air Force members live and perform. Success hinges on the incorporation of these values into the character of every Airman. In today's time—compressed, dynamic, and dangerous operational environment—an Airman does not have the luxury of examining each issue at leisure. He or she must fully internalize these values to be able to automatically act in all situations to maintain integrity, to serve others before self, and to perform with excellence and encourage others to do the same. The Air Force core values—Integrity First, Service Before Self, and Excellence In All We Do—represent the commitment each Airman makes when joining the Air Force. These values provide a foundation for leadership, decision-making, and success, whatever the level of assignment, difficulty, or dangers presented by the mission.

*All Airmen are men and women of character. Our enduring Air Force Core Values provide a touchstone as we rise to meet current and future challenges, threats, and opportunities. As America's Airmen, it is imperative that we maintain the moral high ground—our Nation depends on it.*

Michael W. Wynne
Former Secretary of the Air Force

*Core Values help those who join us to understand right from the outset what's expected of them. Equally important, they provide all of us, from Airman to four-star general, with a touchstone—a guide in our own conscience—to remind us of what we expect from ourselves. We have wonderful people in the Air Force. But we aren't perfect. Frequent reflection on the core values helps each of us refocus on the person we want to be and the example we want to set.*

> General Michael E. Ryan, Retired
> Former Air Force Chief of Staff

### 10.12.1. Integrity First.

Integrity is the willingness to do what is right even when no one is looking. Integrity is the "moral compass," the inner voice, the voice of self-control, and the basis for the trust imperative in today's Air Force. Integrity is the single most important part of character. Integrity makes Airmen who they are and what they stand for, and is as much a part of their professional reputation as their ability to fly or fix jets, operate the computer network, repair the runway, or defend the airbase. Airmen must be professional, in and out of uniform. Integrity is not a suit that can be taken off at night or on the weekend or worn only when important to look good. Instead, what makes integrity critical is when we least expect to be tested. People are watching us, not to see us fail but to see us live up to their expectations; anything less risks putting the heritage and reputation of the Air Force in peril. Integrity is the ability to hold together and properly regulate all the elements of one's personality. A person of integrity acts on conviction, demonstrating impeccable self-control without acting rashly. Integrity encompasses many characteristics indispensable to Airmen.

*There will be demands upon your ability, upon your endurance, upon your disposition, upon your patience...just as fire tempers iron into fine steel so does adversity temper one's character into firmness, tolerance and determination.*

> Senator Margaret Chase Smith, Lieutenant Colonel
> U.S. Air Force Reserve

### 10.12.2. Service before Self:

10.12.2.1. As an Air Force core value, service before self represents an abiding dedication to the age-old military virtue of selfless dedication to duty, including putting one's life at risk if called to do so. The service-before-self value deals with accepting expeditionary deployments and assignments. Service before self does not mean service before family. Airmen have a duty to their families just as strong as that to the service. The difference is there are times when service to the nation requires subordinating the needs of the family. Their responsibilities to their families include ensuring they are cared for when Airmen are home or deployed.

10.12.2.2. This value also demands that each Airman keep faith in the system. This does not imply that we follow our leaders blindly and not sometimes question what we are doing. Airmen must always place trust in the processes, procedures, and other Airmen to get the job done in the right way. Airmen must understand that an organization can only achieve excellence in an atmosphere free from fear, unlawful discrimination, sexual harassment, intimidation, hazing, or unfair treatment. Airmen must show loyalty to their leadership, fellow Airmen, and the Air Force as a whole, including showing commitment to the Constitution, military chain of command, and to both the President and Secretary of Defense.

*I have been recognized as a hero for my ten minutes of action over Vietnam, but I am no more a hero than anyone else who has served this country.*

> A1C John L. Levitow, lowest-ranking Air Force
> Medal of Honor Recipient

### 10.12.3. Excellence In All We Do:

10.12.3.1. This core value demands Airmen constantly strive to perform at their best. They should always strive to exceed standards objectively based on mission needs. This demands a continuous search for new and innovative ways to accomplish the mission without jeopardizing morale and loyalty.

10.12.3.2. Personally, Airmen seek out and complete developmental education. They constantly work hard to stay in their best physical, mental, emotional, spiritual, and moral shape. Airmen continue to enhance their professional competencies and are diligent to maintain their job skills, knowledge, and personal readiness at the highest possible levels. They understand that when members of an organization work together to successfully reach a common goal, excellence is achieved and no Airman wins the fight alone. Each organization must foster a culture that emphasizes a team mentality while simultaneously maintaining standards and accomplishing the mission. Realizing that people are our most precious resource, Airmen are responsible for ensuring they are trained, fit, focused, and ready to accomplish the mission safely and effectively.

*The power of excellence is overwhelming. It is always in demand and nobody cares about its color.*

General Daniel 'Chappie' James
First African-American USAF Four-Star General

### 10.12.4. Air Force Viewpoint.

The Air Force recognizes these core values as universal and unchanging in the profession of arms. They provide the standards used to evaluate the ethical climate of all Air Force organizations. Finally, when needed in the cauldron of war, they are the beacons that light the path of professional conduct and the highest ideals of integrity, service, and excellence.

## Section 10C—Followership and Mentoring

### 10.13. Introduction.

Preoccupation with leadership often prevents us from considering the nature and importance of followership. At some point, everyone is a follower. Few leaders became successful without first having learned followership skills. Therefore, leaders must recognize the importance and qualities of followership, the needs of followers, and ways to promote followership.

### 10.14. Importance of Followership.

Today's leader has the almost impossible task of keeping up with ever-changing technology while coping with leadership demands. In many cases, the leader is not the most technically skilled person in the unit. He or she likely has personnel with advanced technological skills and capabilities. People are our most valuable resource. Today's junior members have knowledge, skills, and abilities that open unlimited opportunities to maximize work center effectiveness. Therefore, leaders must tap into this resource by nurturing and developing their Airmen's capabilities and fostering their willingness to improve organizational effectiveness.

### 10.15. Qualities of Followership.

The following 10 qualities are essential for good followership. However, this list is neither inflexible nor exhaustive:

#### 10.15.1. Organizational Understanding.

Effective followers must be able to see how their work contributes to the organization's big picture.

#### 10.15.2. Decision-making.

Followers must be able to make sound decisions using a team approach.

#### 10.15.3. Communication Skills.

Followers must have effective communication skills. These skills are crucial when working in a team environment, especially when providing feedback to team members.

#### 10.15.4. Commitment.

Being able to successfully contribute to the organization, while striving to achieve personal goals, requires a strong level of follower commitment.

#### 10.15.5. Problem Solving.

A broader scope of responsibility to help identify and resolve work center problems requires followers to share their knowledge, skills, and experience.

#### 10.15.6. Integrity.

Followers must demonstrate loyalty and a willingness to act according to accepted beliefs. Integrity requires one to identify and be true to values.

#### 10.15.7. Adaptability.

Ever-changing roles, missions, and systems require followers to be adaptable to change without being paralyzed by the stress of not knowing all the answers.

#### 10.15.8. Self-Employment.

Followers must take responsibility for their own careers, actions, and development.

10.15.9. **Courage.**

Followers must have the confidence and guts to do and say the right things at the right times.

10.15.10. **Credibility.**

By demonstrating competency in their words and deeds, followers earn trust and an honorable reputation.

## 10.16. Follower Needs.

Successful leaders must devote attention to what their Airmen want and expect. Otherwise, leaders may lose the opportunity to capitalize on their talents or lose their Airmen's respect. Followers need to know they can count on their leaders when the going gets tough. Furthermore, respect is a two-way street; followers also want to be respected. Followers treated as if they are not important, or who perceive that they are not important, lose their willingness and desire to perform. Leaders demonstrate belief in their Airmen by: (1) maintaining or enhancing their Airmen's self-esteem; (2) listening carefully to their Airmen and responding with empathy; and (3) asking for their Airmen's help and encouraging their involvement. A few moments of sincerity and thoughtfulness go a long way toward satisfying Airmen's basic needs. Followers perform best when they want to be in a unit, not when they are trapped in the unit.

## 10.17. Ways to Promote Followership.

Empowered followership, like motivation, requires a joint effort between leaders and the individuals they lead. This effort must be continuously promoted. Leaders must listen and respond to the ideas and needs of their followers, and followers are similarly required to listen and respond to the ideas and needs of their leaders. Mutual trust is the axis around which this synergistic relationship revolves; the benefits reaped are plentiful. Team requirements are best served when the leader helps followers develop their own initiatives, encourages them to use their own judgment, and allows them to grow and become more effective communicators. As a result of promoting empowered followership, follower skills such as troubleshooting, problem solving, information gathering, conflict resolution, and change management will improve dramatically. Another way to promote empowered followership is by getting out among the Airmen and sharing their interests. Airmen respond to leaders who show sincere interest in them. The success of great leaders depends on their ability to establish a base of loyal, capable, and knowledgeable followers.

## 10.18. Mentor Defined.

A mentor is a trusted counselor or guide. Mentoring, therefore, is a relationship in which a person with greater experience and wisdom guides another person to develop both personally and professionally. The long-term health of the Air Force depends upon the experienced member developing the next in line. Air Force mentoring is governed by AFMAN 36-2643, *Air Force Mentoring Program*.

## 10.19. Mentoring Scope:

10.19.1. Mentoring helps prepare people for the increased responsibilities they will assume as they progress in their careers. Mentoring is not a promotion enhancement program; mentoring is an ongoing process and not confined to the formal feedback required by AFI 36-2406, *Officer and Enlisted Evaluation Systems*, and AFI 36-1001, *Managing the Civilian Performance Program*. Moreover, mentoring is a professional development program designed to help each individual reach his or her maximum potential. Professional development is not a new concept and occurs at every echelon and activity. AFI 36-2909, *Professional and Unprofessional Relationships,* and AFI 36-703, *Civilian Conduct and Responsibility*, explains the standards regarding professional relationships. In particular, mentoring is part of a professional relationship because mentoring fosters communication between subordinates and supervisors concerning careers, performance, duties, and missions. Finally, mentoring enhances morale and discipline and improves the operational environment while maintaining respect for authority.

10.19.2. Air Force mentoring covers a wide range of areas, such as career guidance, technical and professional development, leadership, Air Force history and heritage, air and space power doctrine, strategic vision, and contributions to joint warfighting. Therefore, Air Force mentoring includes knowledge of the military ethics and an understanding of the Air Force's core values: Integrity First, Service Before Self, and Excellence In All We Do.

10.19.3. Commanders and supervisors must encourage Airmen to read and comprehend air and space power literature, such as Air Force doctrine and operational warfighting publications and the books in the Chief of Staff of the Air Force Professional Reading Program.

## 10.20. Assignment of Mentors:

10.20.1. The immediate supervisor or rater is the primary mentor (coach, counselor, guide, role model) for each of his or her Airmen. This designation in no way restricts the subordinate's desire to seek additional counseling and professional development advice from other sources or mentors. Supervisors and commanders must make themselves available to Airmen who seek career guidance and counsel.

10.20.2. Key to the mentoring process is direct involvement by the commander and supervisor. Commanders and supervisors must continually challenge their Airmen to improve. They must provide clear performance feedback and guidance in setting realistic near-, mid-, and long-term professional and personal development goals.

10.20.3. Several programs exist to help the commander and supervisor focus attention on an Airman's professional development. Among these are performance feedback, PME, academic education opportunities, assignment policies, recognition programs, and the individual's own personal development actions. Additionally, many organizations, programs, and associations are dedicated to the advancement and education of military professionals. The first sergeant, base education center, and Airman and Family Readiness Center can provide lists and contact information for organizations that support military development. Leaders should also ensure that Airmen are aware of specific tools available to them such as MyVector which enables web based mentoring, career planning, and knowledge sharing.

## 10.21. Mentoring Responsibilities.

Air Force leaders have an inherent responsibility to mentor future leaders. Supervisors must take an active role in their Airmen's professional development. They must assist their people by providing realistic evaluations of both performance and potential. Supervisors must also be positive role models. At minimum, mentoring consists of a discussion of performance, potential, and professional development plans during the performance feedback session. The feedback should include promotion, PME, advanced degree work, physical fitness, personal goals and expectations, professional qualities, next assignment, and long-range plans, at minimum. Mentors must distinguish between individual goals, career aspirations, and realistic expectations. Each individual defines a successful career differently. There are numerous paths to meet individual career and success goals. Foremost, however, individuals must focus on Air Force institutional needs. The Air Force must develop people skilled in the employment and support of air and space power and how this meets national security needs. While there is nothing wrong with lofty goals, mentors must ensure personnel realize what high but achievable goals are.

## 10.22. Professional Military Education and Academic Education.

PME and academic education enhance performance in each phase of professional development and build on the foundation of leadership abilities shown during the earlier stages of an individual's career. The role of PME in professional development is to prepare individuals to take on increased responsibilities appropriate to their grade and to enhance their contribution to the Air Force. Members should focus on enhancing professional competence and becoming superior leaders, while expanding their operational employment of air, space, and cyberspace power knowledge. Post-secondary degrees (associate, bachelor's, master's, or other advanced academic degrees) are important to professional development to the extent that they enhance the degree holder's job and professional qualifications. A degree directly related to an individual's primary specialty area or occupational series is most appropriate because this type of degree adds to his or her depth of knowledge. This is why senior noncommissioned officers are required to complete the Senior Noncommissioned Officer Academy by correspondence or in residence and obtain a Community College of the Air Force degree (any specialty) to receive a senior rater endorsement on their performance reports. (**Note:** This requirement is the minimum criteria for endorsement consideration and does not guarantee automatic endorsement.) A master's or doctorate degree in management or more general studies enhances job performance for personnel reaching the highest grade levels, where duties may require broader managerial skills. In some career fields, advanced formal education is a prerequisite for certain jobs.

## 10.23. Professional Associations.

Many private organizations develop professional skills and associations for individuals in many career fields and technical specialties. Membership in such associations may provide additional opportunities for mentoring as well as broaden technical expertise. Most Air Force bases have private organizations for each rank tier (for example, Top III (Master Sergeant-Chief Master Sergeant)).

## 10.24. Evaluation and Performance Feedback.

Air Force evaluation systems are designed to accurately appraise performance. Substantive, formal feedback is essential to the effectiveness of the evaluation systems. Performance evaluation systems are an integral part of mentoring and professional development. Performance feedback is designed to provide a realistic assessment of performance, career standing, future potential, and actions required to help the ratee reach the next level of professional development.

## 10.25. Promotion Selection.

The Weighted Airman Promotion System outlines the requirements for promotion selection (Staff Sergeant through Master Sergeant) and provides feedback score sheets to enlisted members considered for promotion. These score sheets help the individual to determine professional development needs. Selection for promotion to Senior Master Sergeant and Chief Master Sergeant is accomplished using an integrated weighted and central selection board system. In addition to the weighted score, the central selection board evaluates each individual using the "whole person concept." Board scores are determined by considering performance, leadership, breadth of experience, job responsibility, professional competence, specific achievements, and education. The board score is added to the weighted score to determine order of merit for promotion.

### 10.26. The Military Assignment System.

The mentor and the individual should both focus on obtaining an assignment that enhances professional development and meets Air Force needs without necessarily keying on a specific position or location. The individual is expected to do well in his or her current assignment. When an individual becomes eligible for reassignment, he or she should address assignment preferences with their supervisor. Assignments should complement the individual's professional development needs and be second only to mission requirements. Supervisors can use the career field education and training plan to help develop career path guidance.

### 10.27. Recognition, Awards, and Decorations.

Military members are eligible for consideration for various decorations throughout their careers. However, supervisors should not submit recommendations just to "do something for their people." Supervisors should restrict recommendations to recognitions of meritorious service, outstanding achievement, etc., that clearly place the individual above his or her peers.

### *Section 10D—Developmental Counseling*

### 10.28. Airman Development.

Airman leadership development is one of the most important responsibilities of every Air Force leader. Developing future leaders should be one of the highest priorities of a leader. The future of the Air Force rests on the shoulders of those prepared for greater responsibility.

### 10.29. Purpose.

Developmental counseling is a shared effort. Leaders assist Airmen in identifying strengths and weaknesses and creating plans of action. Leaders then support them throughout the plan implementation and assessment. However, to achieve success, Airmen must be forthright in their commitment to improve and candid in their own assessment and goal setting.

### 10.30. Leader Responsibilities.

Leaders coach Airmen the same way athletic coaches improve their teams: by identifying weaknesses, setting goals, developing and implementing plans of action, and providing oversight and motivation throughout the process. Effective coaches or leaders must thoroughly understand the strengths, weaknesses, and professional goals of their Airmen. Air Force leaders conduct counseling to help Airmen become better members of the team, maintain or improve performance, and prepare for the future. To conduct effective counseling, leaders should develop a counseling style using the characteristics listed in Figure 10.2. This approach is very similar to the art of leadership coaching. Coaching is a growing field in the Air Force. The Air Force Academy can provide more information about coaching as they have a new Mosaic Coaching Program. An overview of this program is available at http://www.usafa.edu.

**Figure 10.2. Characteristics of Effective Counseling.**

| Purpose: | Clearly define the purpose of the counseling. |
|---|---|
| Flexibility: | Fit the counseling style to the character of each subordinate and to the relationship desired. |
| Respect: | View Airmen as unique, complex individuals, each with a distinct set of values, beliefs, and attitudes. |
| Communication: | Establish open, two-way communication with Airmen using spoken language, nonverbal actions, gestures, and body language. Effective counselors listen more than they speak. |
| Support: | Encourage Airmen through actions while guiding them through their problems. |

**10.31. The Leader as a Counselor.**

Air Force leaders must demonstrate certain qualities to be effective counselors. These qualities include respect for Airmen, self-awareness, cultural awareness, empathy, and credibility.

**10.31.1. Respect for Airmen.**

Allowing Airmen to take responsibility for their own ideas and actions is a show or respect and helps create mutual respect in the leader-subordinate relationship. Mutual respect improves the chances of changing or maintaining behavior and achieving goals.

**10.31.2. Self-Awareness.**

Leaders must be fully aware of their own values, needs, and biases before counseling Airmen. Self-aware leaders are less likely to project their biases onto Airmen. Also, aware leaders are more likely to act consistently with their own values and actions.

**10.31.3. Cultural Awareness.**

Leaders need to be aware of the similarities and differences between individuals of different cultural backgrounds and how these factors may influence values, perspectives, and actions. Unfamiliarity with cultural backgrounds may hinder leaders in addressing cultural issues, especially if they generate concerns within the organization or hinder team-building. Cultural awareness enhances a leader's ability to display empathy.

**10.31.4. Empathy.**

Empathy is to be understanding of and sensitive to another person's feelings, thoughts, and experiences to the point that you can almost feel or experience them yourself. Leaders with empathy can put themselves in their Airman's shoes and see a situation from the other person's perspective. Understanding the Airman's position can help the Airman develop a plan of action that fits his or her personality and needs—one that works for the Airman. Not fully comprehending a situation from the Airman's point of view gives a leader less credibility and influence. As a result, the Airman is less likely to commit to the agreed-upon plan of action.

**10.31.5. Credibility.**

Leaders achieve credibility by being honest and consistent in their statements and actions. Using a straightforward style and behaving in a manner that Airmen respect and trust makes a leader credible. Leaders can earn credibility by repeatedly demonstrating a willingness to assist and being consistent in what they say and do. To influence Airmen without credibility is difficult.

**10.32. Leader Counseling Skills.**

Leaders should seek to develop and improve their own counseling abilities. The techniques needed to provide effective counseling vary from person to person and session to session. However, general skills needed in almost every situation include active listening, responding, and questioning.

**10.32.1. Active Listening.**

During counseling, leaders must actively listen. By actively listening, leaders communicate verbally and nonverbally that they have received the message. To learn more about active listening, refer to Chapter 14, *Communicating in Today's Air Force*.

**10.32.2. Responding.**

A leader responds both verbally and nonverbally to communicate understanding and to clarify and confirm what has been said. Verbal responses consist of summarizing, interpreting, and clarifying the message. Nonverbal responses include eye contact and occasional gestures such as a head nod.

**10.32.3. Questioning.**

Although questioning is a necessary skill, use this skill with caution. Too many questions can aggravate the power differential between a leader and an Airman and place the Airman in a passive mode. The Airman may also react to excessive questioning as an intrusion of privacy and become defensive. During a leadership development review, ask questions to obtain information or to get the Airman to think about a particular situation. Generally, questions should be open-ended to evoke more than a "yes-or-no" answer. Well-posed questions may help to verify understanding, encourage further explanation, or help the Airman move through the stages of the counseling session.

**10.33. Types of Developmental Counseling.**

Developmental counseling can be categorized based on the topic of the session. Event-oriented counseling and performance and professional growth counseling are the two major categories of counseling.

**10.33.1. Event-Oriented Counseling.**

Event-oriented counseling involves a specific event or situation and may precede events such as applying for a special duty assignment or attending a school. This type of counseling may follow events such as a noteworthy duty performance, a problem with performance or mission accomplishment, or a personal problem. Event-oriented counseling includes, but is not limited to:

**10.33.1.1. Counseling for Specific Instances.** Sometimes counseling is connected to specific instances of superior or substandard duty performance or behavior. Leaders must tell Airmen whether or not their performance met the standard and what they did right or wrong (e.g. performance feedback counseling). The key to successful counseling for specific performance is to conduct the counseling as close to the event as possible. Leaders should counsel Airmen for specific examples of superior as well as substandard duty performance.

**10.33.1.2. Crisis Counseling.** Leaders may conduct crisis counseling to get an Airman through the initial shock after receiving negative news, such as notification of the death of a loved one. Listening and, as appropriate, providing assistance may greatly assist the Airman dealing with a crisis.

**10.33.1.3. Referral Counseling.** Referral counseling helps Airmen work through a personal situation and may or may not follow crisis counseling. Referral counseling may also act as preventive counseling before the situation becomes a problem. Usually, the leader assists the Airman in identifying the problem and refers the subordinate to the appropriate resource, such as legal services, a chaplain, or an alcohol and drug counselor.

**10.33.2. Performance and Professional Growth Counseling.**

During performance and professional growth counseling, conduct a review of an Airman's duty performance during a certain period and set standards for the next period. Rather than dwelling on the past, focus the session on the Airman's strengths, areas needing improvement, and potential.

**10.34. Approaches to Counseling.**

An effective leader approaches each Airman as an individual. Different people and different situations require different counseling approaches. Three approaches to counseling include nondirective, directive, and combined. These approaches differ in the techniques used, but they all fit the definition of counseling and contribute to the overall purpose. The major difference between the approaches is the degree to which the Airman participates and interacts during a counseling session. Figure 10.3 summarizes the advantages and disadvantages of each approach.

**10.34.1. Nondirective.**

The nondirective approach is preferred for most counseling sessions. During the counseling session, listen rather than make decisions or give advice. Clarify what is said. Cause the Airman to bring out important points to better understand the situation. When appropriate, summarize the discussion. Avoid providing solutions or rendering opinions; instead, maintain a focus on individual and organizational goals and objectives. Ensure the Airman's plan of action supports those goals and objectives.

**10.34.2. Directive.**

The directive approach works best to correct simple problems, make on-the-spot corrections, and correct aspects of duty performance. The leader using the directive style does most of the talking and tells the Airman what and when of doing something. In contrast to the nondirective approach, the leader directs a course of action for the Airman. Choose this approach when time is short, when you alone know what to do, or if an Airman has limited problem-solving skills. Finally, directive is appropriate when an Airman is immature, insecure, or needs guidance.

**10.34.3. Combined.**

In the combined approach, the leader uses techniques from both the directive and nondirective approaches, adjusting them to articulate what is best for the Airman. The combined approach emphasizes the Airman's planning and decision-making responsibilities. With your assistance, the Airman develops a plan of action. Listen, suggest possible courses, and help analyze each possible solution to determine the good and bad points. Then help the Airman fully understand all aspects of the situation and encourage the Airman to decide which solution is best.

**Figure 10.3. Counseling Approach Summary Chart.**

| Approach | Advantages | Disadvantages |
|---|---|---|
| **Nondirective** | • Encourages maturity<br><br>• Encourages open communication<br><br>• Develops personal responsibility | • Is more time consuming<br><br>• Requires greatest counselor skills |
| **Directive** | • Is the quickest method<br><br>• Is good for people who need clear, concise direction<br><br>• Allows counselors to actively use their experience | • Does not encourage Airmen to be part of the solution<br><br>• May treat symptoms, not problems<br><br>• May discourage Airmen from talking freely<br><br>• The counselor provides the solution, not the Airman |
| **Combined** | • Is moderately quick<br><br>• Encourages maturity<br><br>• Encourages open communication<br><br>• Allows counselors to actively use their experience | • May take too much time for some situations |

## 10.35. The Counseling Process.

The four stages of the counseling process are identify the need for counseling, prepare for counseling, conduct the counseling session, and follow up.

### 10.35.1. Identify the Need for Counseling.

Conduct developmental counseling whenever the need arises for focused, two-way communication aimed at Airman development. Developing Airmen consists of observing their performance, comparing performance to the standard, and then providing them feedback in the form of counseling.

### 10.35.2. Prepare for Counseling.

Successful counseling requires preparation. To prepare for counseling:

10.35.2.1. **Select a Suitable Place.** When scheduling counseling, consider an environment with minimal interruptions and free from distractions.

10.35.2.2. **Schedule the Time.** When possible, counsel an Airman during the duty day. Counseling after duty hours may be rushed or perceived as unfavorable. The length of time required for counseling depends on the complexity of the issue. Generally, a counseling session should last less than 1 hour. If you need more time, schedule a second session.

10.35.2.3. **Notify the Airman well in Advance.** The Airman should know why, where, and when the counseling session will take place. Counseling following a specific event should happen as close to the event as possible.

10.35.2.4. **Organize the Pertinent Information.** Solid preparation is essential to effective counseling. Review all pertinent information including the purpose of the counseling, facts and observations about the Airman, identification of possible problems, main points of discussion, and the development of a plan of action. Focus on specific and objective behaviors the Airman must maintain or improve upon as well as a plan of action with clear, obtainable goals.

10.35.2.5. **Plan the Counseling Approach.** There are as many approaches to counseling as there are leaders. The directive, nondirective, and combined approaches to counseling were addressed earlier. Use a strategy that suits the Airman and the situation.

10.35.2.6. **Establish the Right Atmosphere.** The right atmosphere promotes two-way communication between a leader and Airman. To establish a relaxed atmosphere, offer the Airman a seat or something to drink. Sit in a chair facing the Airman rather than behind a desk because a desk can be perceived as a barrier. Some situations, however, make an informal atmosphere inappropriate. For example, a more formal atmosphere is normally used to give specific guidance and reinforces the leader's rank, position, and authority.

### 10.35.3. Conduct the Counseling Session.

Be flexible when conducting a counseling session. Often, counseling for a specific incident occurs spontaneously as leaders encounter Airmen in their daily activities. Good leaders take advantage of naturally occurring events to provide Airmen with feedback. Even when you have not prepared for formal counseling, you should follow the four basic components of a counseling session:

10.35.3.1. **Open the Counseling Session.** The best way to open a counseling session is to clearly state the purpose. Establish the preferred setting early in the session by inviting the Airman to speak.

10.35.3.2. **Discuss the Issues.** Attempt to develop a mutual understanding of the issues with the Airman. This is best developed by letting the Airman do most of the talking. Use active listening; respond and question without dominating the conversation. Aim to help the Airman better understand the subject of the counseling, such as duty performance, a problem situation and the impact, or potential areas for growth. Both you and the Airman should provide examples or cite specific observations to reduce the perception that is unnecessarily biased or judgmental. However, when the issue is substandard performance, make it clear how the performance did not meet the standard and then develop a plan of action.

10.35.3.3. **Develop a Plan of Action.** A plan of action identifies a method for achieving a desired result and specifies what the Airman must do to reach the goals set during the counseling session. The plan of action must be specific. The plan of action should show the Airman how to modify or maintain his or her behavior.

10.35.3.4. **Record and Close the Session.** Documentation serves as a reference to the agreed-upon plan of action and the Airman's accomplishments, improvements, personal preferences, or problems. To close the session, summarize key points and ask if the Airman understands the plan of action. Invite the Airman to review the plan of action and what you, as the leader, expect from him or her. With the Airman, establish any follow-up measures necessary to support the successful implementation of the plan of action. These may include providing the Airman with resources and time, periodically assessing the plan, and following through on referrals. Schedule any future meetings, at least tentatively, before dismissing the Airman.

### 10.35.4. Follow up.

The counseling process does not end with the counseling session. Follow up continues through implementation of the plan of action and evaluation of results. After counseling, support the Airman as he or she implements the plan of action. Support may include teaching, coaching, or providing time and resources. Observe and assess this process and possibly modify the plan to meet goals. Appropriate measures after counseling include follow-up counseling, making referrals, informing the chain of command, and taking corrective measures.

## 10.36. Leveraging Diversity.

Our work environment today is more diverse than ever. The Air Force team is comprised of military, civilians, and contractors. Leaders can find themselves dealing with a workforce ranging from 18-year-olds to those with 18 or more years of experience. The challenge is to incorporate everyone's specific talents into a cohesive and optimal workforce. We must recognize that people are vital to an organization's success. Consequently, we need to understand the motivations and interests of this diverse workforce.

10.36.1. People are motivated for their reasons, not yours. What sparks interest and passion in one person does not necessarily ignite the next person. Effective leaders take time to recognize what excites others, leverages their talent to the organization, and cultivate a work culture that recognizes and appreciates differing perspectives and approaches to solving problems. Consider this: the Air Force attracts people from every aspect of society, culture, and social status. When, where, and how someone was raised impacts their value system. None of these variables are under a supervisor's direct control. Supervisors cannot change someone's inherent characteristics, but they can change how to lead these people as a cohesive team. Foremost, leaders must create a hospitable climate that promotes respect and inclusion. This will reduce dysfunctional tension and increase team productivity. Specifically, how can this be achieved?

10.36.2. The first step in leading a diverse organization is to form common ground or a shared set of assumptions, which will form the framework within to communicate. The common ground is the organization itself, the vision, goals, rules, regulations, processes, and procedures that govern what the unit does to achieve mission requirements. Clear guidelines improve communication, reduce confusion, provide purpose, and define desired outcomes. A team must have a clear sense of direction or else there will be mass confusion with everyone going in different directions.

10.36.3. Having established common ground, we must increase awareness and expel stereotypes. Examples include younger employees are "wet behind the ears," know nothing, have no respect or loyalty, lack experience, have no credibility, and cannot be trusted with much responsibility. At the other end of the social spectrum, older employees are considered less motivated to work hard, are nothing but deadwood, resistant to change, cannot learn new methods/technology, plateau at 40, should be fired after 50, and are 'fire proof.' Stereotypes ignore differences among the individuals in a group. The workplace has no room for such stereotypes. Instead, leaders must acknowledge the richness and benefits of diversity.

10.36.4. People are different. There is no way to make them fit into a single mold, nor is there any reason to. We do not live in a world of carbon-copied people. To effectively manage a diverse workforce, we must acknowledge differences. However, we should focus more on what we have in common.

10.36.5. Use everyone's experiences and background as a resource. Diversity of experience and background ensures diverse ways of looking at problems. Managing our workforce diversity can result in higher productivity, improved performance, more creativity, more innovations, and reduced stress. Giving emphasis to diversity without threatening our unity is the proper way to strengthen the ties that bind the team together. Sensitivity, mutual respect, and common trust coupled with communication are the prime ingredients to integrating our Airmen.

10.36.6. Former Chief of Staff, U.S. Air Force, General John P. Jumper stated, "Air Force diversity is a critical warfighting and readiness issue. Maximizing the benefits of diversity is a mission imperative. We expect Air Force leaders to challenge any policy, practice, or process that limits the growth and development of potential leaders from all groups." Industry studies have consistently revealed that heterogeneous or diverse groups are more innovative than homogeneous groups because they view improvement opportunities from multiple perspectives. Managing diversity is determining which differences matter in enriching a product or service. Productivity is an outcome of respect and inclusion. Former Chief of Staff, U.S. Air Force, General Ronald Fogleman said, "People are the assets that determine our success or failure. If you are to be a good leader, you have to cultivate your skills in the arena of personal relations." The skilled leader deals effectively with all races, nationalities, cultures, disabilities, ages, and gender.

## Section 10E—Full Range Leadership Development (FRLD)

### 10.37. Full Range Leadership Development.

A full range of leadership behaviors is essential in today's complex world. Therefore, developing full range leadership potential throughout the workforce has become a principal initiative in several of today's most successful organizations, to include the U.S. Air Force. Though the leadership theories of the past were very successful, today's Air Force depends on highly effective Airmen with the flexibility and capability to operate throughout a spectrum of leadership styles. FRLD was adopted because the best parts of past leadership theories are combined.

10.37.1. FRLD is unique and requires us to view leadership as a system made up of three core elements: the leader, the follower, and the situation. The components of the FRLD system are interdependent of one another. Its success relies not only on the leader's actions, but also the follower and the situation. FRLD requires today's leaders to consider the follower and each situation and be willing to:

10.37.1.1. Develop relationships with leadership, peers, and subordinates.

10.37.1.2. Take advantage of opportunities as they come available.

10.37.1.3. Efficiently use available resources.

10.37.1.4. Properly evaluate situations and the performance of followers.

10.37.1.5. Reward appropriately (and discipline accordingly).

10.37.1.6. Identify improvement areas in one's self, their followers, and the work place.

10.37.2. The FRLD Model (Figure 10.4) includes five leadership behaviors ranging from the passive, less effective Laissez-Faire behavior to the more active and effective Transformational Leadership behavior.

10.37.2.1. **Laissez-Faire.** Laissez-faire leaders view the development and needs of their subordinates as someone else's concern. They tend to pass on and abandon their responsibilities and remain indifferent toward important issues. They are hesitant to make decisions and are usually absent from their place of work, which negatively affects relationships with peers and subordinates.

10.37.2.2. **Management by Exception-Passive.** This leadership behavior is the *"if it isn't broke, don't fix it"* leadership style. Here, leaders elect to sit back, observe, and wait for things to go wrong before taking action. They intervene only when policies or rules are broken. Management by Exception-Passive is a little more effective than

Laissez-Faire because subordinates know that leadership will hold them accountable if they fail to meet standards of performance or comply with policies and procedures.

**Figure 10.4. Full Range Leadership Model.**

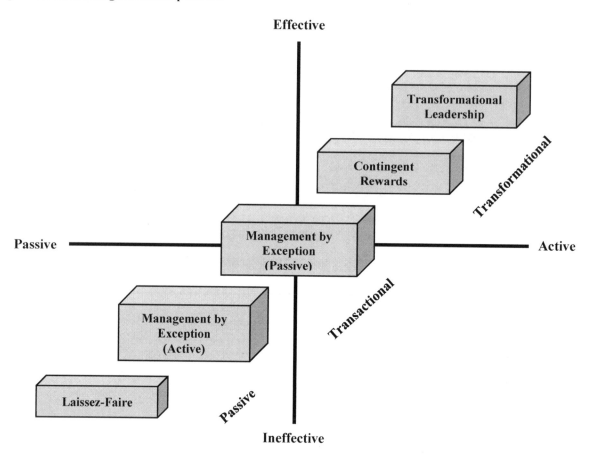

10.37.2.3. **Management by Exception-Active.** This leadership behavior ensures leaders keep personnel and processes in control. They monitor and govern subordinates through forced compliance with rules, regulations, and expectations for meeting performance standards. Management by Exception-Active exists in a structured system with detailed instructions, careful observation, and very *active* supervision. Furthermore, this leadership behavior reduces organizational uncertainties, avoids unnecessary risks, and ensures important goals are being achieved. This transactional leadership behavior reduces the temptation for employees to avoid their duties or act unethically and aids members in meeting defined performance objectives.

10.37.2.4. **Transactional Leadership and Contingent Rewards.** Transactional leadership and contingent rewards involve the constructive *transaction* between a leader and his or her followers. These transactions are "contracts" where the leader sets goals, identifies ways for the subordinate to reach these goals, and supports the follower along the way. The follower is then required to perform their assigned tasks to a specified performance level and, when they achieve their leader's expectations, the leader reinforces the positive behavior by providing a reward. In other words, the reward is contingent upon the follower performing assigned tasks to expectations.

10.37.2.5. **Transformational Leadership.** The transformational leader offers followers a vision and inspires their mission. This type of leadership inspires followers to exceed their goals and promotes positive, meaningful changes. There are four components of transformational leadership, called the *4 I's*: Individualized Consideration, Intellectual Stimulation, Idealized Influence, and Inspirational Motivation.

10.37.2.5.1. **Individualized Consideration (*Nurturing*).** Individualized consideration is where leaders treat their followers as individuals with different needs, abilities, and aspirations and not just as a part of a group of subordinates. They empathize with and support each follower while maintaining healthy communication. Using Individualized Consideration, leaders 'nurture' followers by acting as mentor or coach.

10.37.2.5.2. **Intellectual Stimulation (*Thinking*).** Intellectual Stimulation is the degree to which a leader values their subordinates' rationality and intellect, seeking different perspectives and considering opposing points of view. Using Intellectual Stimulation, leaders stimulate and encourage creativity in their followers, encourage followers to be independent thinkers, and are not afraid to take risks and solicit ideas from their followers.

10.37.2.5.3. **Inspirational Motivation (*Charming*).** This leader behavior involves developing and articulating visions that paint an optimistic and enthusiastic picture of the future that is appealing and inspiring to followers. These visions elevate performance expectations and inspire followers to put forth extra effort to achieve the leader's vision.

10.37.2.5.4. **Idealized Influence (*Influencing*).** Transformational leaders are charismatic and act as positive role models that "walk the walk." They exhibit high levels of moral behavior, virtues, and character strengths, as well as a strong work ethic. They represent the organization's values, beliefs, and purpose in both words and actions. They set aside personal interests for the sake of the group.

10.37.3. Developing these five leadership behaviors begins by understanding each of them and knowing when, or when not, to apply them. In addition, possessing the flexibility and capability to implement each style is critical to successfully leading others, depending on the follower and the situation. Though a more passive approach may be appropriate at times, transformational leaders actively and effectively develop the followers today to become the leaders of tomorrow.

## *Section 10F—Mentorship*

## 10.38. Essential Principles.

Mentoring is a leadership obligation and responsibility. Through mentoring, senior leaders pass on their experience and wisdom to junior members as well as philosophy, traditions, shared values, quality, and lessons learned. Mentoring provides the framework for the professional development of competent, future Air Force leaders. Mentoring is an ongoing process and perhaps the most powerful method leadership can use to shape the future. A mentor is a trusted advisor, teacher, counselor, friend, parent, and/or the more senior person in the relationship. In organizations, mentorship can apply to all leaders and supervisors who are responsible for getting their work done through other people. The assisted individual is usually referred to as the protégé: a student or pupil who learns from the mentor. Understanding mentoring principles is essential to practical implementation.

## 10.39. The Mentoring Process.

The mnemonic at Figure 10.5 demonstrates the concepts of effective mentoring. (Mnemonics are memory aids that help us remember the various aspects of a concept. The elements of effective mentoring, expressed as verbs, correspond to the letters in the word itself.) The following paragraphs describe each element and clarifies the meaning of a mentor.

10.39.1. **Model.**

**Figure 10.5. Mentoring Model.**

| |
|---|
| **M**odel |
| **E**mpathize |
| **N**urture |
| **T**each |
| **O**rganize |
| **R**espond |
| **I**nspire |
| **N**etwork |
| **G**oal-set |

An effective mentor must first lead by example. When serving as a role model, make no mistake that actions speak much louder than words. Mentoring requires the mentor and protégé to spend a significant amount of time together. Here, the protégé is constantly observing and learning from the mentor's words and actions. The opportunity to see how the mentor deals with a variety of situations is an important part of the process. Therefore, the mentor must show the protégé how a mature professional handles various challenges and opportunities. In turn, protégés must be willing to learn, seek assistance, and apply what they have learned.

10.39.2. **Empathize.**

Mentoring involves much more than merely teaching. Mentors must empathize, showing genuine compassion for their protégés. Mentors who remember what it was like when they were new and inexperienced are more effective in assisting others in their professional development. Empathy cultivates strong bonds between mentors and protégés and fosters the mutual commitment that exemplifies mentoring.

10.39.3. **Nurture.**

Nurturing also emphasizes a caring attitude. Like a farmer and his or her crops, the mentor nurtures the protégé. One cannot expect to sow a rich crop without investing ample time, patience, and labor. Certainly these points seem rather obvious, but are often the most neglected elements. Some mentors often find themselves too busy to provide the time and effort to effectively mentor their protégés. Therefore, we must not expect an expert-level performance from someone who has not received appropriate amounts of attention, training, and time from a mentor. Remember, for people to apply, internalize, and value what they have learned takes time.

10.39.4. **Teach.**

Many people, regardless of their knowledge and experience level, find teaching uncomfortable and extremely stressful. Thankfully, some time-tested methods provide a solid benchmark for instruction. Consider these five simple steps when teaching and training protégés: (1) organize the material into logical; systematic, units of manageable size; (2) correct errors immediately; (3) frequently review previously covered material and relate the material to the current lesson; (4) include practical exercises to help the protégé exercise the newfound knowledge; and (5) evaluate the protégés' comprehension often, formally and informally, and provide detailed feedback on their progress.

10.39.5. **Organize.**

Mentors must first be organized before helping others become organized. Hence, a systematic, methodical approach is essential. An organized mentor knows from the very beginning what he or she wants to achieve, focusing every aspect of the process on this goal. The time and effort spent organizing thoughts and materials into a logical, building-block sequential plan of lessons aimed at a precisely defined target pays big dividends in the form of improved learning and developmental experiences for the protégé.

10.39.6. **Respond.**

Mentoring is a two-way communication process that requires mentors to actively listen to the protégés' questions and provide useful and timely responses. There may be times when the protégé is reluctant to ask a particular question. Therefore, effective mentors must remain alert to recognize nonverbal behaviors and subtle communication cues. Rather than sitting back and waiting for the protégé to ask questions, be proactive. Anticipate the needs, problems, and concerns of protégés and take care of them immediately.

10.39.7. **Inspire.**

A mentor should be more than just a good role model, teacher, or helpful acquaintance. Genuine mentoring encompasses an element of inspiration. Inspirational mentors have a profound impact on their protégés that encourages them to transform into a more improved being. Inspiration is one of the characteristics that distinguishes leaders from managers. The best mentors most likely become the best leaders because they are able to inspire others.

10.39.8. **Network.**

A good mentor introduces and "connects" a protégé to other people who can also provide guidance, support, resources, and opportunities. Networking is a vital function that provides protégés a head start on establishing themselves in their professional community. Building a solid network of friends, acquaintances, and associates takes time; the earlier a protégé can cultivate this, the better.

10.39.9. **Goal-Set.**

Many young, inexperienced people do not understand the importance of setting goals. Oftentimes, they lack the expertise to establish specific, achievable, and realistic goals. Therefore, mentors must help their protégés understand why goals are important; establish short- and long-term goals that are specific, achievable, and realistic; and be available to assist them in achieving their goals.

## Section 10G—Strategic Leadership

## 10.40. Definition of Strategic Leadership.

Strategic leadership plays a critical role in propelling today's Air Force through and beyond the 21st century. Strategic leadership is such a broad concept, that we may not be able to define, but we can certainly recognize strategic leadership in action. Noel Tichy, Director of the Global Leadership Program at the Ross School of Business, offers a comprehensible depiction as to what a strategic leader is:

> "Strategic leaders guide the achievement of their organizational vision within a larger enterprise by directing policy and strategy, building consensus, acquiring and allocating resources, influencing organizational culture, and shaping complex and ambiguous external environments. They lead by example to build effective organizations, grow the next generation of leaders, energize subordinates, seek opportunities to advance organizational goals, and balance personal and professional demands."

## 10.41. Components of Strategic Leadership:

10.41.1. Enlisted leaders apply the strategic leadership components of core values, competencies, and actions at the tactical, operational, and strategic levels every day. Leadership at the tactical level is predominantly direct and face-to-face. As leaders ascend the organizational ladder to the operational level, leadership responsibilities become more complex and sophisticated. Strategic leaders have a responsibility to large organizations and systems and are expected to conceptualize and integrate a variety of issues to accomplish the mission.

10.41.2. Core values form the foundation of leadership (paragraph 10.12), coupled with competencies (personal, people/team, and institutional leadership) and actions. Personal leadership focuses on interpersonal relations that directly influence human behavior and values. People/team leadership involves more interpersonal relations and team relationships. Leaders using this competency tailor resources to organizations and programs. Institutional leadership is about establishing structure, allocating resources appropriately, and articulating the organizational vision.

10.41.3. Actions include training and educational activities designed to develop strategic leadership abilities. Early career development focuses on personal competencies at the tactical level. At the operational stage, personal leadership continues, but the Air Force begins to emphasize people/team leadership development and introduces institutional leadership competencies. At the strategic level, the greatest emphasis is on developing institutional leadership competencies, primarily through education designed to help leaders form accurate frames of reference, make sound decisions, uncover underlying connections between general issues, and think creatively, innovatively, and critically about new solutions and options.

## 10.42. Strategic Leadership:

10.42.1. At the strategic level, Airmen must combine highly developed occupational capabilities with competencies gained earlier in their careers to lead and direct exceptionally complex and multi-tiered organizations. Strategic leaders must understand Air Force missions and how operational capabilities and Airmen are integrated to achieve synergistic results and desired effects. Strategic leaders are also expected to demonstrate a highly developed and insightful understanding of personal and team leadership.

10.42.2. The successful strategic leader is the quintessential communicator, using all means of communication. Whereas leaders at lower levels of the organization remain focused on the short term, strategic leaders must have a future focus, spending much of their time looking forward, positioning the organization for long-term success.

10.42.3. Strategic leaders seek education and other opportunities to enhance their understanding and appreciation of strategic leadership, its responsibilities, functions, and impact on the organization. They fully understand their role in shaping climate and culture through vision, policy, communication, education, coaching, mentoring, and personal example.

## 10.43. Conclusion.

To *lead* means *to act as a guide* or to guide; a *leader* is defined as "a person who leads, directs, commands, or guides a group or activity." These are simple definitions, but the implications of poor or ineffective leadership are devastating to mission success. Given the authority, anyone can command. Leading, however, is a delicate art calling for people-oriented attributes that many find difficult to develop and impossible to acquire. With determination and practical experience, you can develop your leadership skill sets. Commanders depend on noncommissioned officers to lead Airmen and accomplish the mission. This chapter discussed the art of leadership, effective leadership, interrelationship of leadership and management, leadership qualities, and the concept of vision, and provided an overview on empowerment and learning. Also provided was information on leadership flexibility and followership, dealing effectively with change, the critical relationship between leadership and core values, mentoring, and counseling. These concepts are fundamental to the mission of the Air Force, as well as the careers and futures of the enlisted force.

# Chapter 11

## OFFICER AND ENLISTED EVALUATION SYSTEMS AND CIVILIAN PERFORMANCE PROGRAM

### Section 11A—Overview

**11.1. Introduction:**

11.1.1. The officer and enlisted evaluations, and civilian appraisals deal directly with the Air Force's most precious resource—people. Supervisors must help their subordinates understand their strengths and weaknesses and how their efforts contribute to the mission. Supervisors must employ the officer and enlisted evaluation systems, and civilian performance program in everyday situations to help develop their subordinates. This chapter addresses the importance of correctly using the officer and enlisted evaluation systems, and civilian performance program, by identifying responsibilities, outlining the performance feedback process, and provides additional information as outlined in governing AFIs 36-2406, *Officer and Enlisted Evaluation Systems* and 36-1001, *Managing the Civilian Performance Program* respectively.

11.1.2. The officer and enlisted evaluation systems, and civilian performance program provides:

11.1.2.1. Meaningful feedback to individuals pertaining to what is expected of them, advice on how well they are meeting expectations, and advice on how to better meet these expectations.

11.1.2.2. A reliable, long-term, cumulative record of performance and potential based on performance.

### Section 11B—General Considerations (Officer and Enlisted Evaluation Systems)

**11.2. Purpose.**

The Officer and Enlisted Evaluation Systems have varied purposes. The first is to establish performance standards and expectations for ratees, meaningful feedback on how well the ratee is meeting those expectations, and direction on how to better meet those established standards and expectations. The second is to provide a reliable, long-term, cumulative record of performance and promotion potential based on that performance. The third is to provide officer Central Selection Boards, senior NCO evaluation boards, the Weighted Airman Promotion System, and other personnel managers' with sound information to assist in identifying the best qualified officers and enlisted personnel for promotion, as well as other personnel management decisions. The fourth is to document in the permanent record any substantiated allegation of a sex-related offense against an Airman, regardless of grade, that results in conviction by courts-martial, non-judicial punishment, or other punitive administrative action.

11.2.1. To accomplish these purposes, the evaluation system focuses on performance. How well the individual does his or her job, and the qualities the individual brings to the job, are of paramount importance to the Air Force. Performance is most important for successful mission accomplishment and important for development of skills and leadership abilities and in determining who will be selected for advancement through assignments, promotions, and other personnel actions. The evaluation system emphasizes the importance of performance in several ways--using periodic performance feedback, as the basis for formal evaluations, and, for officers, through performance-based promotion recommendations.

11.2.2. Effective evaluators must have an adequate understanding of Officer Evaluation System (OES), Enlisted Evaluation System (EES), or both, depending on who they supervise. OES/EES training was implemented in May 96 to help supervisors fulfill their evaluation responsibilities. Unit commanders are responsible for ensuring all first-time supervisors receive mandatory OES/EES training (as appropriate for their position) within 60 days of being appointed as a rater. Additionally, Air Force members should receive annual recurring OES/EES training. How and when this training is conducted is at the discretion of the unit commander. To assist commanders, OES/EES Training Guides are located on the myPers Website.

**11.3. Forms Used:**

11.3.1. **Performance Evaluation Forms Used (see AFI 36-2406 for additional details of each form):**

11.3.1.1. AF Form 77, *Letter of Evaluation*, is a multipurpose evaluation form.

11.3.1.2. AF Form 78, *Air Force General Officer Promotion Recommendation* is used to document performance and promotion recommendations for certain general officers.

11.3.1.3. AF Form 475, *Education/Training Report* is used to document periods when Airmen are in education or formal training.

11.3.1.4. AF Form 707, *Officer Performance Report (Lieutenant thru Colonel)*; AF Form 910, *Enlisted Performance Report (Airman Basic thru Technical Sergeant)* (EPR); AF Form 911, *Enlisted Performance Report (Master*

*Sergeant thru Senior Master Sergeant)* (EPR), or AF Form 912 *Enlisted Performance Report (Chief Master Sergeant)* (EPR), are used to document potential and performance over the course of a ratee's career. For enlisted only, use ratee's grade or projected grade on the static close-out date to determine which form to use.

11.3.1.5. AF Form 709, *Promotion Recommendation Form (PRF)*, used to assess an officer's performance-based potential and to recommend promotion from a senior rater (or in case of Colonel ratees, from the head of the Management Level or designated representative) to central selection boards.

11.3.1.6. AF Form 724, *Airman Comprehensive Assessment Worksheet (Second Lieutenant thru Colonel)*, AF Form 931, *Airman Comprehensive Assessment (ACA) Worksheet (Airman Basic thru Technical Sergeant)*, and AF Form 932, *Airman Comprehensive Assessment Worksheet (Master Sergeant thru Chief Master Sergeant)*.

11.3.1.7. AF Form 3538, *Retention Recommendation Form* is used in conjunction with AFI 36-2406 and HQ Air Force Personnel Center Retirements and Separations Branch guidelines, to document performance-based differentiation and retention recommendations, to assist in involuntary separation and/or retirement boards (Force Shaping, Reduction in Force, or Selective Early Retirement boards). This form is only used at the discretion of the Secretary of the Air Force. See AFI 36-2406 and AFI 36-3203, *Service Retirements*, for details.

11.3.1.8. AF Form 948, *Application for Correction/Removal of Evaluation*, is used by Regular Air Force, and Reserve personnel to substitute, correct or remove an evaluation when the applicant does not have access to the Virtual Military Personnel Flight or Virtual Personnel Center application process.

11.3.2. **Purpose and Their Use:**

11.3.2.1. **Airman Comprehensive Assessment Worksheet.** Airman Comprehensive Assessment Worksheets include the AF Form 724, AF Form 931, and AF Form 932, and are used to document formal communication regarding an assessment of an Airman's responsibilities, accountability, Air Force culture, critical role in support of the mission, individual readiness and performance between raters and ratees (see AFI 36-2406, Chapter 2 for details).

11.3.2.2. **Performance Evaluations.** Performance evaluations include the AF Form 707, AF Form 910, AF Form 911, AF Form 912, AF Form 77, and AF Form 475. These forms are used to document performance and potential as well as provide information for making promotion recommendation, selection, or propriety actions, selective continuation, involuntary separation, selective early retirement, assignment, school nomination and selection, and other management decisions.

11.3.2.3. **Promotion Recommendation Forms.** Use promotion recommendation forms for promotion purposes only, and include the AF Form 78, and AF Form 709. These forms are removed from the Officer Selection Record following the promotion board which they were accomplished for, and are stored electronically. AF Forms 709 will be used for historical, legal, and appeal purposes only.

11.3.2.4. **Retention Recommendation Forms.** Use AF Form 3538, *Retention Recommendation* for involuntary separation/retirement board (Force Shaping, Reduction in Force, or Selective Early Retirement boards) only. These forms are removed from the Officer Selection Record following the board which they were accomplished for, and are stored electronically. These Retention Recommendation Forms will be used for historical, legal, and appeal purposes only.

11.3.2.5. **Enlisted Retention Recommendation Form.** Use AF Form 3538E, *Enlisted Retention Recommendation* for involuntary separation/retirement boards (Force Shaping, Enlisted Retention Board, Quality Force Review Board). These forms are removed from the selection record following the board for which they were accomplished, and are stored electronically. These forms will be used for historical, legal, and appeal purposes only.

11.4. **General Guidelines:**

11.4.1. **Access to Evaluations.** Evaluations are For Official Use Only and are subject to the Privacy Act. They are exempt from public disclosure under DoD Regulation 5400.7/Air Force Supplement (AFSUPDODR 5400-7), DoD Freedom of Information Act Program and AFI 33-332, *Privacy Act Program*. Only persons within the agency who have a proper need to know may read the evaluations. The office with custodial responsibility is responsible for determining if a person's official duties require access. See Chapter two for access to the Airman Comprehensive Assessment (ACA) Worksheets.

11.4.2. **Classified Information and Security Classification.** Do not enter classified information in any section of the evaluation; this includes any type of evaluation forms, attachments to evaluations, referral documents, or endorsements to referral documents. If an entry would result in the release of classified information, use the word "Data Masked" in place of that entry. The Personnel Accounting Symbol code alone is unclassified, however this code will only be entered on the ratee. In the Senior Rater Identification block enter five asterisks, (*****). In those cases where the evaluator is with a classified organization or location, enter "Data Masked" for organization nomenclature and nothing more.

11.4.3. **Bullet Format.** Bullet format is mandatory. Use bullet format as specified in the appropriate table for the evaluation being accomplished. Bullets are limited to a minimum of one line and a maximum two lines per bullet and white space is authorized. Main bullets begin at the left margin and will have one space after the "-". If unfamiliar with the proper bullet format, refer to "The Bullet Background Paper" in AFH 33-337, *The Tongue and Quill*. Although the *Tongue and Quill* allows three lines per bullet, evaluations will not have more than two lines per bullet.

11.4.4. **Special Formatting.** Do not underline, capitalize, or use bold print, unusual fonts or characters, multiple exclamation marks, or headings to emphasize comments, except as required to identify proper names, publication titles, etc.

11.4.5. **Ratee Identification Data.** The name will be in all uppercase. The remaining data (grade, unit, location) will be in upper/lower case.

11.4.6. **Type and Font:**

11.4.6.1. Type all evaluations using the electronic version of the form from the AF Publications website.

11.4.6.2. Forms will be typed using *"Times New Roman."*

11.4.6.3. Forms will be typed using 12-pitch font. You must use computerized versions with proportional spacing, provided a 12-pitch font is used.

11.4.6.4. Handwritten Evaluations.

11.4.6.4.1. Evaluations may be handwritten, only when authorized by HQ Air Force Personnel Center/DP3SP or Air Reserve Personnel Center/DPT, as appropriate (exception: President of the United States/Vice President of the United States may handwrite evaluations).

11.4.6.4.2. When authorized, print or legibly write entries.

11.4.6.4.3. Use only dark blue or black reproducible ink.

11.3.6.4.4. HQ Air Force Personnel Center/DP3SP or Air Reserve Personnel Center/DPT will not approve requests if a computerized form, typewriter, or word processor is available.

11.4.7. **Nicknames and Acronyms:**

11.4.7.1. Nicknames. Do not use call signs, code names or unusual nicknames on evaluations. However, nicknames which are a form of the ratee's name are permitted. **Example:** Bill/Will for William, Jim for James, Chris for Christopher/Christine, Pat for Patrick/Patricia, etc. are authorized.

11.4.7.2. Acronyms. Uncommon acronyms must be spelled out; however, if space is limited, define the acronyms in the proper section of the applicable form. **Note:** The AF evaluation forms allow the evaluators to explain uncommon acronyms in the Remarks section of the forms. When acronyms are used, the acronyms must be listed alphabetically.

11.4.7.2.1. When used, first spell out and follow with the acronym; e.g. Personnel Support for Contingency Operations.

11.4.7.2.2. Acronyms or abbreviations common throughout the Air Force, such as CGO, NCO, CONUS, TDY, etc., are not required to be spelled out first.

11.4.8. Optional Notes and Stamps. *"Wet Signature Evaluation Only."* When used enter optional notes at base level such as "MilPDS/System Processed," administrative review initials, date stamps, etc., only in the top margin. Air Force Personnel Center or Air Reserve Personnel Center level optional notes will be placed only in the bottom margin.

11.4.9. Send requests for deviations or waivers through the wing commander or the comparative level to HQ Air Force Personnel Center/DP3SP (or appropriate ANG/AFR office) who in turn will forward the request to appropriate office of primary responsibility listed in AFI 36-2406.

11.5. **Evaluator Requirements:**

11.5.1. **Number of Evaluators:**

11.5.1.1. Officer Performance Reports (OPR) will have three evaluators, unless the rater or additional rater is also the reviewer/senior rater.

11.5.1.2. Enlisted Performance Reports (EPR) will have at least two evaluators, unless the rater qualifies as a single evaluator.

11.5.1.2.1. For Chief Master Sergeant, no more than two evaluators (the rater and senior rater) will evaluate the ratee's performance.

11.5.1.2.2. For Master Sergeant through Senior Master Sergeant, no more than four evaluators (the rater, additional rater, unit commander/military or civilian director/other authorized reviewer and final evaluator) will evaluate the ratee's performance.

11.5.1.2.3. For Airman Basic through Technical Sergeant, no more than three evaluators (rater, additional rater, and forced distributor) will evaluate the ratee's performance.

11.5.1.3. AF Form 78 and AF Form 3538 forms require two evaluators.

11.5.1.4. Promotion Recommendations Forms and Training Reports only require one evaluator. **Exceptions:** The preceding requirements must be strictly adhered to, unless: commander disagrees with the ratings; the evaluation is referred and the commander is *not* the evaluator named in the referral document, *Referral Reviewer*; or the reviewer is senior to the commander and refers the evaluation.

11.5.2. **Evaluators and Minimum Grade Requirements:**

11.5.2.1. **Rater.** The official in the rating chain designated by management to provide periodic ACA and initiate performance evaluations. Typically the ratee's immediate supervisor.

11.5.2.1.1. **Military Raters:**

11.5.2.1.1.1. **For officers.** The rater must be an officer of the United States or a foreign military service serving in a grade equal to or higher than the ratee.

11.5.2.1.1.2. **For enlisted.** The rater must be an officer or an NCO of the United States or a foreign military service serving in a grade equal to or higher than the ratee.

11.5.2.1.1.2.1. The rater must be at a minimum, in the grade of E-5 or higher, unless para 11.5.2.1.1.2.2. applies.

11.5.2.1.1.2.2. Senior Airman, Regular Air Force and Air Reserve Components may serve as raters only if they have completed Airmen Leadership School.

11.5.2.1.2. **Civilian Raters:**

11.5.2.1.2.1. **For Officers:**

11.5.2.1.2.1.1. Under the General Schedule (GS) system, raters must be a civilian serving in a grade equal to or higher than the ratee.

11.5.2.1.2.2. **For Enlisted:**

11.5.2.1.2.2.1. A civilian rater must be at least a GS-5 or a comparable grade or higher and must be in a position higher than the ratee in the rating chain.

11.5.2.1.2.2.2. For Master Sergeant – Chief Master Sergeant, a civilian rater must be at least a GS-11 or above.

11.5.2.1.3. Management may appoint a rater of the United States or a foreign military service serving in the same grade as the ratee without regard to date of rank.

11.5.2.2. **Additional Rater (*Rater's Rater*):**

11.5.2.2.1. The official designated by management to provide periodic ACA and initiate a performance evaluation on a rater and will be no higher in organization than the reviewer/senior rater.

11.5.2.2.2. The second evaluator in the rating chain, after the rater, to endorse a performance evaluation. The second evaluator in the rating chain must be the rater's rater unless one of the exceptions as stated in AFI 36-2406 applies.

11.5.2.2.3. **Military Additional Raters:**

11.5.2.2.3.1. **For officers.** The additional rater must be an officer of the United States or a foreign military service serving in a grade equal to or higher than the rater, and in a grade higher than the ratee. An O-6 of the United States or a foreign military service may be the additional rater for an O-6.

11.5.2.2.3.2. **For enlisted:**

11.5.2.2.3.2.1. When the rater's rater does not meet this requirement, the additional rater will be the next evaluator in the rating (supervisory) chain that meets the minimum grade requirement.

11.5.2.2.3.2.2. AF Form 910, *Enlisted Performance Report (Airman Basic Thru Technical Sergeant)*. The additional rater must be an officer, Senior NCO (E-7 or above) of the United States or a foreign military service serving in a grade equal to or higher than the rater.

11.5.2.2.3.2.3. AF Form 911, *Enlisted Performance Report (Master Sergeant Thru Senior Master Sergeant)*. The additional rater must be equal or higher in grade than the ratee and a Senior NCO (E-7) or above; or an officer of the United States or a foreign military service serving in a grade equal to or higher than the rater.

11.5.2.2.3.2.4. AF Form 912, *Enlisted Performance Report (Chief Master Sergeant)*. The rater must be an E-9 (Chief Master Sergeant or equivalent) or above; or an officer of the United States, or a foreign military service serving in a grade equal to or higher than the ratee. The final evaluator must be the senior rater; final evaluator may not be delegated to a lower level evaluator.

11.5.2.2.4. **Civilian Additional Raters:**

11.5.2.2.4.1. **For Officers.** The additional rater must be an officer of the United States or a foreign military service serving in a civilian grade equivalent equal to or higher than the rater, and in a grade higher than the ratee.

11.5.2.2.4.1.1. Under the General Schedule (GS) system, additional raters must be at least a GS-9 or equivalent for company grade officers and GS-11 or equivalent for field grade officers.

11.5.2.2.4.2. **For enlisted.** A civilian additional rater must be serving in a civilian grade equivalent, equal to or higher than the rater.

11.5.2.2.4.2.1. For Technical Sergeant and below. A civilian Additional Rater must be at least a GS-7 (or equivalent) or above.

11.5.2.2.4.2.2. For Master Sergeant-Senior Master Sergeant. A civilian Additional Rater must be at least a GS-12 (or equivalent) or above.

11.5.2.3. **Reviewer/Senior Rater/Final Evaluator.** All senior raters must be the person holding the senior rater position designated by the Management Level for the ratee's assigned organizational Personnel Accounting Symbol.

11.5.2.3.1. Senior Raters/Reviewer/Final Evaluator. **Note:** The Head of a Management Level (normally Major Command Commander) must designate all Senior Rater positions. Appointment of command (G-Series orders) does not authorize Senior Rater status.

11.5.2.3.1.1. **For officers.** The reviewer must be the ratee's senior rater and will be the final evaluator on the OPR. **Exceptions:** When the rater or additional rater is also the senior rater, the OPR will close-out at this level (see AFI 36-2406, Table 3.1). Also, when a senior rater refers the evaluation, the officer named in the referral memorandum becomes the final evaluator, unless he/she refers the evaluation again. See definitions of *Reviewer, Senior Rater, Final Evaluator and Rating Chain* in AFI 36-2406, Attachment 1 for additional information.

11.5.2.3.1.1.1. For Lieutenant Colonels and Colonels (except ANG). The reviewer must be the first general officer (includes a Brigadier General select confirmed by the senate), or equivalent, in the rating chain who has been designated as a senior rater by the Management Level.

11.5.2.3.1.1.2. For Lieutenants through Majors (except ANG). The reviewer must be the first Colonel (or equivalent) in a wing commander (or equivalent) position who has been designated as a senior rater, as determined by the Management Level.

11.5.2.3.1.1.3. For ANG Colonels, the first GO in the rating chain will review the OPR.

11.5.2.3.1.1.4. For ANG officers, Lieutenant Colonel and below, the reviewer will be the wing or group commander. For a member assigned to a unit where there is no parent wing or group headquarters in-state, the state Adjutant General will establish an equivalent command-level review authority.

11.5.2.3.1.1.5. HQ AFRC may deviate and assign Senior Rater levels as appropriate for AFR unit assigned Majors and below.

11.5.2.3.1.2. **For enlisted:**

11.5.2.3.1.2.1. Master Sergeant through Senior Master Sergeant. The final evaluator must be, at a minimum, an officer serving in the grade of O-4, civilian equivalent, (GS-12), or higher, but no higher in organization than the senior rater. For Active Guard Reserve and non-Active Guard Reserve, the final evaluator must be at a minimum the full-time unit commander. If there is no full-time unit commander, the final endorser will be the senior full-time officer serving in the grade of O-4, civilian equivalent, (GS-12), or higher, but no higher in organization than the senior rater. Exception: The CMSAF may endorse EPRs as a senior rater and may also serve as the final evaluator.

11.5.2.3.1.2.2. An additional rater who meets the minimum grade requirement *may* close out the evaluation. However, an official higher in the rating chain than the additional rater, may serve as the reviewer/final evaluator, if authorized. In any case, the reviewer/final evaluator may not be higher in the organizational structure than the senior rater.

11.5.2.3.2. **Civilian Raters:**

11.5.2.3.2.1. **For officers.**

11.5.2.3.2.1.1. For Majors and below. A civilian Senior Rater/Reviewer/Final Evaluator must be serving as a wing commander or equivalent in a Senior Rater position designated by the Management Level and at least a GS-15.

11.5.2.3.2.1.2. For Lieutenant Colonels and Colonels. A civilian Senior Rater must be the first Senior Executive Service or equivalent in the rating chain in a Senior Rater position designated by the Management Level.

11.5.2.3.2.2. **For enlisted.**

11.5.2.3.2.2.1. For Master Sergeant – Senior Master Sergeant. A civilian final reviewer must be at least a GS-12.

11.5.2.3.2.2.2. For Master Sergeant – Senior Master Sergeant. A civilian Senior Rater must be serving as a wing commander or equivalent, in a Senior Rater position designated by the Management Level and at least a GS-15.

## 11.6. Responsibilities:

11.6.1. **Commander.** The commander of a unit must review the record of all personnel, regardless of grade, assigned to and/or transferred into his or her command to ensure knowledge of and familiarization with the Airman's history of sex-related offenses resulting in conviction by courts-martial, non-judicial punishment, or other punitive administrative action in order to reduce the likelihood of repeat offenses will escape the notice of current, subsequent, or higher level commanders. This responsibility will be conducted by the immediate commander of the Airman at the lowest unit level. Sex-related offenses include violations of Article 120 of the Uniform Code of Military Justice (rape, sexual assault, aggravated sexual contact and abusive sexual contact), Article 125 (forcible sodomy, which is forced oral or anal sex, and bestiality), Article 120a (stalking), Article 120b (rape and sexual assault of a child), Article 120c (other sexual misconduct, which includes indecent viewing/recording/ broadcasting, forcible pandering, and indecent exposure) or attempts to commit any of those offenses. These responsibilities will not be delegated.

11.6.2. **General Evaluator/Reviewer Responsibilities.** All evaluators and reviewers are responsible for performing an administrative review of all evaluations and if necessary, return them for correction/completion before sending them to the next level. As a minimum, this review must ensure:

11.6.2.1. All applicable blocks are completed (marked, dated, and signed).

11.6.2.2. Evaluations contain accurate information (particularly in the rate identification and job description sections).

11.6.2.3. Spelling accuracy and proper bullet structure.

11.6.2.4. Evaluations do not contain inappropriate comments or recommendations.

11.6.2.5. The information in the evaluation is accurate and not inflated.

11.6.2.6. Evaluations are properly referred, when necessary.

11.6.2.7. Evaluations are accomplished IAW AFI 36-2406.

11.6.3. **Rater:**

11.6.3.1. For officer evaluations, there must be a minimum number of days supervision; see AFI 36-2406, Tables 3.3 and 3.4 for the type of evaluation being prepared. There is no minimum number of days supervision required for enlisted evaluations.

11.6.3.2. Ensures the ratee is aware of who is in his or her rating chain.

11.6.3.3. Must provide an ACA IAW AFI 36-2406. Official documented ACA does not preclude a rater from performing day-to-day verbal assessments. Additionally, raters are required to perform an assessment at the time the evaluation is presented to the ratee. This assessment at the time the evaluation is presented, may be, but is not required to be officially documented on the ACA worksheet. If geographically separated, assessments can be performed electronically or telephonically.

11.6.3.4. Must consider the contents of any Unfavorable Information File and/or Personal Information File, if applicable, before preparing the performance evaluation.

11.6.3.5. Assess and documents the ratee's performance, what the ratee did, how well he or she did it, and the ratee's potential based on that performance, throughout the rating period. The rater differentiates through an evaluation of performance.

11.6.3.6. Receives meaningful information from the ratee and as many sources as possible (i.e. Letter of Evaluations from those who previously supervised the ratee during the reporting period, the first sergeant, etc.), especially when the rater cannot observe the ratee personally. The ratee is encouraged to provide the rater with inputs on specific accomplishments.

11.6.3.7. Considers the significance and frequency of incidents (including isolated instances of poor or outstanding performance) when assessing total performance.

11.6.3.8. Differentiates between ratees with similar performance records; especially when making promotion, stratification, assignment, Developmental Education and retention recommendations.

11.6.3.9. Although some evaluators may not know any other ratee serving in a particular grade and Air Force Specialty Code, they may rate according to their opinions and impressions of the general level of performance of Air Force personnel in the various grades.

11.6.3.10. Records the ratee's performance for the rating period on the applicable form.

11.6.3.11. A rater's failure to perform one or more of the above responsibilities alone will not form the basis for a successful appeal.

11.6.4. **Additional Rater:**

11.6.4.1. There is no minimum number of days supervision required. Exception: See AFI 36-2406.

11.6.4.2. Must be aware of the contents of any Unfavorable Information File and/or Personal Information File, if applicable, and returns evaluation to the rater for reconsideration, if appropriate, to ensure an accurate, unbiased, and an uninflated evaluation.

11.6.4.3. Completes Section V of the OPR, Section VIII of the AF Form 910, Section VII of the AF Form 911 and Section IV of the AF Form 912 by concurring or non-concurring with the rater and making comments.

11.6.4.4. Assumes the responsibilities of the rater when applicable IAW AFI 36-2406. Note: This does not include Permanent Change of Station, Permanent Change of Assignment, Separation or Retirement of the rater.

11.6.4.5. See AFI 36-2406 if the additional rater changes after the close out date of the evaluation.

11.6.5. **Reviewer/Senior Rater/Final Evaluator:**

11.6.5.1. There is no minimum number of days supervision required.

11.6.5.2. Must be aware of the contents of any Unfavorable Information File and/or Personal Information File, if applicable, and returns evaluation to the rater for reconsideration, if appropriate, to ensure an accurate, unbiased, and an uninflated evaluation.

11.6.5.3. Obtains additional information, if necessary, from competent sources such as the ratee's second and third line supervisor, etc.

11.6.5.4. When appropriate, nonconcurs with previous evaluators and makes comments.

11.6.5.5. Approves (Senior Rater) unit mission descriptions for the Promotion Recommendation Form.

11.6.5.6. Directs the additional rater to assume rater's responsibilities IAW AFI 36-2406.

11.6.5.7. Completes performance evaluations as required. See applicable chapters and/or references cited in AFI 36-2406.

11.6.6. **First Sergeant or Designated Senior NCO:**

11.6.6.1. Will not assume rater/additional rater responsibilities. Exception: There is absolutely no one else available.

11.6.6.2. Will be aware of the contents of the Unfavorable Information File and/or Personal Information File if applicable, on all enlisted evaluations and returns the evaluation to the rater for reconsideration, if appropriate, to ensure an accurate, unbiased, and an uninflated evaluation.

11.6.6.3. Will review all enlisted evaluations before the commander's review and advise the commander of any quality force indicators.

11.6.6.4. Senior NCOs may *only* be designated for organizations for which no 8F000/First Sergeant authorization exists. Additional duty first sergeants will not complete evaluation reviews in-lieu of an organization's 8F000/First Sergeant. Exception: Interim first sergeants, additional duty first sergeants, or designated Senior NCOs may complete evaluation reviews when the organization's 8F000/First Sergeant is unavailable due to extended absence (e.g. deployment, lengthy training, or lengthy convalescent leave).

11.6.7. **Ratee:**

11.6.7.1. The ratee is equally responsible for ensuring they know their rating chain and that they received a timely ACA.

11.6.7.2. Ratee Review. Evaluations must be reviewed by the Ratee prior to becoming a matter of record. This is the time to review for typos, spelling, and inaccurate data and bring it to the attention of the Rater. If the data is administratively accurate and it is just a matter of the Ratee disagreeing with the content, the Rater is not required to change their assessment. When the Ratee signs the evaluation, he or she is not concurring with the content, but rather acknowledging receipt of the completed evaluation and is certifying that the Ratee has reviewed the evaluation for administrative errors. If the Ratee disagrees with the content, (comments and/or ratings) the Ratee may file an appeal IAW AFI 36-2406, after the evaluation becomes a matter of record. NOTE: An ACA form is not required upon completion of the OPR/EPR. The OPR/EPR serves as official documentation of the feedback provided to the Ratee.

**11.7. Rater/Ratee Accountability.**

Raters ensure Airmen they supervise receive an ACA to improve performance and contributions to mission accomplishment. To assist raters in preparing evaluations, all commissioned officers and enlisted members who are on active duty or in an active status in a Reserve Component, shall report (in writing) to their rater within 72 hours, any conviction for a violation of a criminal law of the United States or violations of a criminal law of any other country— whether or not the member is on active duty or in an active status at the time of the conduct that provides the basis for the conviction—to the member's rater (first-line military supervisor) or summary courts-martial convening authority. In the case of a member of the individual ready reserve, standby reserve, or ANG, all commissioned officers and enlisted members shall report (in writing) to their wing commanders (or equivalent), in accordance with the requirements below within 30 days. (Note: While the National Defense Authorization Act provision only extended the mandatory reporting to E-7s and above, the Secretary of the Air Force has determined that any member within the United States Air Force must report covered convictions, therefore, extends the mandate to all grades).

11.7.1. **When to Document.** In deciding whether to document adverse information on the performance evaluation, evaluators must consider the vast majority of Airmen serve their entire career with honor and distinction; therefore, failure to document misconduct which reflects departure from the core values of the Air Force is a disservice to all Airmen competing for promotion. Additionally, evaluators must consider items listed below when assessing performance and potential, and specifically mention them in evaluations when appropriate.

11.7.1.1. Impact of the misconduct on the Air Force mission (Did the mission suffer in any way? Was unit morale affected?).

11.7.1.1.1. All commissioned officers, and enlisted members above the pay grade of E-6 (E-7 and above), who are on active duty or in an active status in a Reserve Component, shall report in writing any conviction of such member for a violation of a criminal law of the United States—whether or not the member is on active duty or in an active status at the time of the conduct that provides the basis for the conviction—to the member's first-line military supervisor or summary court-martial convening authority, or in the case of a member of the individual ready reserve, standby reserve, or ANG to the Air Reserve Personnel Center or Air National Guard Bureau, whichever is applicable, in accordance with the requirements below.

11.7.1.1.2. For purposes of this policy, the term "conviction" includes a plea or finding of guilty, a plea of *nolo contendere (no contest),* and all other actions tantamount to a finding of guilty, including adjudication withheld, deferred prosecution, entry into adult or juvenile pretrial intervention programs, and any similar disposition of charges.

11.7.1.1.3. For purposes of this policy, a criminal law of the United States includes any military or other Federal criminal law; any State, district, commonwealth, or territorial or equivalent criminal law or ordinance; and any criminal law or ordinance of any county, parish, municipality, or local subdivision of any such authority, other than motor vehicle violations that do not involve a court appearance.

11.7.1.1.4. Regular Air Force members shall submit reports within 15 days of the date the conviction is announced, even if sentence has not been imposed or the member intends to appeal the conviction. Air Reserve Component members not on active duty but in an active status shall submit reports at the first drill period after the date the conviction is announced, or within 30 days of the date the conviction is announced, whichever is earlier, even if sentence has not been imposed or the member intends to appeal the conviction. All members who must submit evidence of their conviction, must maintain evidence of compliance with this requirement.

11.7.1.1.5. In the event a commander or military law-enforcement official receives information that a covered member of the Armed Forces under the jurisdiction of another military department has become subject to a conviction for which a report is required by this section, the commander or military law-enforcement official receiving such information shall forward it to the member's immediate commander. If the member's immediate commander cannot be readily identified, the commander or military law-enforcement official receiving the information shall forward it to the office designated by the member's military department identified as required below.

11.7.1.1.6. Each Service shall institute procedures to ensure that the members covered by the law comply with its requirements and the policy set forth in this instruction. These procedures shall include points of contact for other military departments to comply with the notification requirements above. Each Service shall also establish points of contact to which Reserve Component members in the individual ready reserve or standby reserve who may not know the identity or address of their first line military supervisor or summary court-martial convening authority may provide information of a conviction covered under this policy.

11.7.1.2. Impact of the misconduct on the Air Force as an institution (Did it bring discredit on the Air Force?).

11.7.1.3. Impact of the misconduct on, and its relationship to the ratee's duties (Did it affect the ratee's ability to fulfill his or her duties?).

11.7.1.3.1. Impact of the misconduct on the Air Force mission (Did the mission suffer in any way? Was unit morale affected?).

11.7.1.3.2. Impact of the misconduct on the Air Force as an institution (Did it bring discredit on the Air Force?).

11.7.1.3.3. Impact of the misconduct on, and its relationship to the ratee's duties (Did it affect the member's ability to fulfill his or her duties?).

11.7.1.3.4. Grade, assignment and experience of the ratee (Is the ratee in a "sensitive" job? Did the ratee "know better"?).

11.7.1.3.5. Number of separate violations and frequency of the misconduct (Is this an isolated or repeated incident?).

11.7.1.3.6. Consequences of the misconduct (Did it result in death, injury, or loss of/damage to military or civilian property?).

11.7.1.3.7. Other dissimilar acts of misconduct during the reporting period (Is the ratee establishing a pattern of misconduct?).

11.7.1.3.8. Existence of unique, unusual or extenuating circumstances (Was the misconduct willful and unprovoked, or were there aggravating factors or events?).

11.7.1.4. Grade, assignment, and experience of the ratee (Is the ratee in a "sensitive" job? Did the ratee "know better"?).

11.7.1.5. Number of separate violations and frequency of the misconduct (Is this an isolated or repeated incident?).

11.7.1.6. Consequences of the misconduct (Did it result in death, injury, or loss of/damage to military or civilian property?).

11.7.1.7. Other dissimilar acts of misconduct during the reporting period (Is the ratee establishing a pattern of misconduct?).

11.7.1.8. Existence of unique, unusual, or extenuating circumstances (Was the misconduct willful and unprovoked, or were there aggravating factors or events?).

11.7.2. **What to Report.** Adverse Actions: For the purpose of this policy, "adverse action" includes:

11.7.2.1. Reportable Civilian Offenses. A conviction of a Federal criminal law; any State, district, commonwealth, or territorial or equivalent criminal law or ordinance; or any criminal law or ordinance of any county, parish, municipality, city, township, or local subdivision of any such authority, and convictions of any foreign criminal law; other than convictions for motor vehicle violations that do not require a court appearance. Specifically, convictions required to be reported include the following: 1) any finding of guilt; 2) any plea of guilty; 3) any plea of no contest or *nolo contendere*; 4) any plea of guilty in exchange for a deferred prosecution or diversion program, and/or; 5) any other similar disposition of civilian criminal charges.

11.7.2.1.1. Any citation or violation of a motor vehicle offense which ultimately results in a conviction of a lesser included offense (resulting from the original citation) is not reportable if the lesser included offense would not have required a court appearance. For example, a member who is charged with reckless driving (an offense requiring a court appearance), but is found guilty of speeding (an offense not requiring a court appearance) has not been convicted of an offense requiring reporting. Commanders and/or supervisors who have questions regarding whether a particular conviction triggers the mandated comment should consult with their staff judge advocate.

11.7.2.1.2. In the event a commander or military law-enforcement official receives information that a member of the Air Force, under the jurisdiction of another military department, has become subject to a conviction for which a report is required by this section, the commander or military law-enforcement official receiving such information shall forward it to the member's immediate commander. If the member's immediate commander cannot be readily identified, the commander or military law-enforcement official receiving the information shall forward it to the office designated by the member's military department identified as required below.

11.7.2.1.3. Procedures shall be instituted to ensure members covered by the law comply with its requirements and the policy as stated in this instruction. These procedures shall include points of contact for other military departments to comply with the notification requirements above. Points of contact shall also be established with the Reserve Component members in the individual ready reserve or standby reserve who may not know the identity or address of their first line military supervisor or summary court-martial convening authority may provide information of a conviction covered under this policy.

11.7.2.2. Complaints of sex-related offenses against a member, regardless of grade, resulting in conviction by court-martial, non-judicial punishment, or punitive administrative action require a mandatory notation on the member's next EPR, OPR, or Training Report, and Promotion Recommendation Form (if not already documented on an evaluation or court-martial in the officer's selection record). Sex-related offenses include violations of Article 120 of the Uniform Code of Military Justice (rape, sexual assault, aggravated sexual contact and abusive sexual contact), Article 125 (forcible sodomy, which is forced oral or anal sex, and bestiality), Article 120a (stalking), Article 120b (rape and sexual assault of a child), Article 120c (other sexual misconduct, which includes indecent viewing/recording/ broadcasting, forcible pandering, and indecent exposure) or attempts to commit any of those offenses. The effective date of the requirement for notation is 26 Dec 13.

11.7.2.3. If a member has been convicted by a court-martial or if the Senior Rater decides to file any adverse information in an Airman's Officer Selection Record or Senior Non-Commissioned Officer Selection Record, comments relating to the ratee's behavior are mandatory on the ratee's next OPR, EPR or Training Report, and Promotion Recommendation Form (if not already documented on an evaluation or court-martial in the Officer Selection Record or Senior Non-Commissioned Officer Selection Record). The evaluation becomes a referral for the OPR, EPR, and Training Report. Comments are also required on Airmen who have been convicted of a "reportable civilian offense" that: 1) is a sexual offense that is the same as, or closely related to, Uniform Code of Military Justice, Articles 120, 120a, 120b, 120c, 125, or attempts to commit any of those offenses; 2) carries a possible sentence of confinement for more than one year, or death; or 3) resulted in a sentence that included unsuspended confinement. For guidance on interpreting this paragraph and sub-paragraphs, supervisors and commanders should consult the servicing staff judge advocate.

11.7.2.3.1. A rater is not required to comment on the conviction in a current report if, during a previous rating period, the rater already commented on the underlying misconduct that ultimately resulted in the conviction. For example: In a case where a member is arrested and charged with Driving Under the Influence by off-base officials who decline to waive jurisdiction, the member's commander issues the member an Letter of Reprimand based on the evidence, and then comments on the Driving Under the Influence Letter of Reprimand in the ratee's next evaluation. Then, the downtown prosecution results in a conviction during a future reporting period. In such a case, the rater is not required to comment on the Driving Under the Influence conviction because the underlying misconduct that led to the conviction was already addressed in a previous evaluation.

11.7.3. **Extraordinary Cases**. Raters may request a waiver of the mandatory requirement to document civilian convictions for good cause. The waiver request will route from the rater, through any required additional rater and the ratee's commander, to the ratee's Senior Rater. The Senior Rater may either deny the waiver request or endorse the request and forward to the Major Command Commander (or in the case of reports within Air Force District of Washington, United States Air Force Academy, or any Direct Reporting Unit or Field Operating Agency reporting to an activity on the Air Staff, to the Vice Chief of Staff of the Air Force, or in the case of the ANG, to the Director, Air National Guard). The Director, Air National Guard may delegate this authority to the respective state's Adjutant General, or equivalent for Territories and the District of Columbia, who will make determinations after consultation with the Director, Air National Guard, or the Deputy Director, Air National Guard. Both the nature and the outcome of the offense for each approved waiver will remain on file with the Director, Air National Guard. No further delegation is authorized.

11.7.3.1. If the Senior Rater denies the waiver request, the decision regarding the waiver request is final and may not be appealed or considered further. This does not prevent an individual from challenging any completed report in any other appropriate forums, e.g., Evaluation Reports Appeal Board, Air Force Board for Correction of Military Records.

11.7.3.1.1. When the Senior Rater endorses the waiver request and forwards it to the final approval authority (Major Command Commander, Vice Chief of Staff, or Director, Air National Guard), the final approval authority can either approve the exception, allowing the exclusion of any comments in the EPR, OPR, Training Report, and Promotion Recommendation Form, or deny the request, resulting in the mandatory inclusion of comments regarding the ratee's criminal behavior.

11.7.3.1.2. The final approval authority is delegable to the Major Command/CV or, in the case of the Air Force/CV, to the Air Force/CVA; no further delegation beyond a The Adjutant General, or equivalent, is authorized for the ANG. The decision of the approval authority is the final decision for such waiver requests and may not be appealed or considered further. This does not prevent an individual from challenging any completed report in any other appropriate forums, e.g., Evaluation Reports Appeal Board, Air Force Board for Correction of Military Records.

11.7.3.1.3. In order to approve any waiver requests, the approval authority must issue a written finding that the mandatory comments for the specific criminal conviction are not in the best interests of the Air Force and that the inclusion of any such comments would unduly harm the ratee. Upon final decision, the final approval authority will forward the waiver documentation to Air Force Personnel Center/DP3SP via email and Air Force Personnel Center/DP2SSM via email. Written waiver approvals will be filed in the member's Master Personnel Records Group for the sole purpose of documenting the final approval.

11.7.4. **Comments.** In all cases, when comments are included in performance evaluations, they must be specific, outlining the event and any corrective action taken. Comments such as "conduct unbecoming…" or "an error in judgment led to an off-duty incident…" are too vague. Examples of valid comments are "Master Sergeant Smith drove while intoxicated, for which he received an Article 15" and "Capt Jones made improper sexually suggestive and harassing comments to a squadron member, for which he received a letter of reprimand."

11.7.5. **Organizational Climate.** Organizational climate is defined as the way in which members in a unit perceive and characterize their unit environment. All Airmen are responsible for creating an organizational climate in which every member is treated with dignity and respect, and one that does not tolerate unlawful discrimination, sexual harassment, or sexual assault in any form. NCOs and officers are not only responsible for creating this environment but are also accountable for it. NCOs and officers can build a healthy organizational climate by: communicating clear direction at all levels of supervision; adhering to and enforcing standards; not tolerating and, when necessary, appropriately responding to any form of sexual harassment, sexual assault, hazing, unlawful discrimination, or any other conduct harmful to the good order and discipline of the unit; being accountable for their actions; and cultivating an environment where teamwork, unity and cohesiveness are the standard practice.

11.7.5.1. All NCO and officer evaluators will assess their ratee(s) on what the member did to ensure a healthy organizational climate.

11.7.5.2. Commanders at every level have an even greater responsibility to create a healthy climate in their command. Additionally, they are responsible for ensuring adherence to Sexual Assault Prevention Program directives. Command climate, just like organizational climate, is the perception of a unit's environment by its members. Commanders are ultimately responsible for the good order and discipline in their unit and have unique responsibility and authority to ensure good order and discipline. Therefore, evaluators must take this special responsibility and authority into consideration when evaluating a commander's effectiveness in ensuring a healthy command climate.

11.7.6. **Equal Opportunity and Treatment.** The expectation is fair and equal treatment of all and enforcement of the same behavior in subordinates. Evaluators must consider a member's commitment to Equal Opportunity and Treatment when evaluating performance and making a promotion recommendation. The goal is to ensure fair, accurate, and unbiased evaluations to help ensure the best qualified members are identified for positions of higher responsibility. Evaluations must reflect serious or repeated occurrences of discrimination, to include sexual harassment, as prescribed in AFI 36-2706, *Military Equal Opportunity Program.*

*Section 11C—Performance Feedback*

**11.8. Purpose.**

ACA is formal communication between a rater and ratee to communicate responsibility, accountability, Air Force culture, an Airman's critical role in support of the mission, individual readiness, and performance feedback on expectations regarding duty performance and how well the ratee is meeting those expectations to include information to assist the ratee in achieving success. It is intended to increase Airmen interaction and support at all levels. If done correctly, mentorship will create and sustain a culture of belonging. The ACA is also intended to provide Airmen an opportunity to discuss their personal and professional goals. Raters document the session on the ACA worksheet and use the Performance Feedback in Section VI to assess or discuss the objectives, standards, behavior, and performance with the ratee. Providing this information helps an individual contribute to positive communication, improve performance, and grow professionally. The following information applies to all military personnel.

**11.9. Responsibilities:**

11.9.1. The ratee will:

11.9.1.1. Know when ACA sessions are due.

11.9.1.2. If a ratee requests a feedback session, the rater will provide one within 30 days of receipt of the request, provided 60 days have passed, since the last feedback session (i.e., Ratee Requested).

11.9.1.3. Notify the rater and, if necessary, the rater's rater, when required or requested ACA did not take place.

11.9.1.4. Complete Section III on their own and review Section IX (*AB thru Technical Sergeant*) or VIII (*Master Sergeant thru Chief Master Sergeant*) for joint communication. Sign the ACA and rater's copy of the ACA notice indicating the date the supervisor conducted the ACA session.

11.9.2. The rater will:

11.9.2.1. Conduct ACA sessions as required by this instruction. In addition, ACA sessions will be conducted at the ratee's request or when deemed necessary (provided 60 days have passed since the last ACA session [i.e., Rater Directed]).

11.9.2.2. Prepare for, schedule, and conduct ACA sessions (avoid conflicts with TDY, leave, etc., when possible), regardless of whether the rater received an ACA notice.

11.9.2.3. Understand Air Force standards and expectations and consider them when providing ACA to personnel.

11.9.2.4. Provide realistic assessments to help the ratee improve performance and grow professionally and personally. Realistic assessments include in-depth discussions with the ratee and written comments on the ACA worksheet, not just marks on the form.

11.9.2.5. Provide the original completed and signed ACA worksheet to the ratee.

11.9.2.6. Retain a copy of the signed and dated ACA notice and worksheet. The Midterm ACA is a required, mandatory supporting document to be routed with the Performance Evaluation (EPR/OPR), however, will not be made a matter of the official record. In addition, the Rater will retain a copy of the initial and midterm ACA as this may be needed for any future appeals.

11.9.2.7. The ACA is a communication tool and is not to be used to discover or document behavior which may result in administrative or judicial action. NOTE: It is important that behavior representing a significant deviation from expected standards is recorded in other administrative forms (i.e. Letter of Reprimand, Letter of Counseling, Letter of Admonishment, Memorandum for Record, etc.).

11.9.2.8. Provide the ratee with the most current Air Force Benefits Fact Sheet.

11.9.3. The rater's rater will:

11.9.3.1. Monitor personnel to ensure raters properly conduct ACA sessions.

11.9.3.2. Conduct ACA sessions when:

11.9.3.2.1. A lower-level rater is not available due to unusual circumstances.

11.9.3.2.2. Officially assuming the subordinate rater's responsibilities.

11.9.4. The unit commander will:

11.9.4.1. Administer the ACA program.

11.9.4.2. Monitor raters and ratees to ensure ACA sessions are conducted properly.

11.9.4.3. Consider disciplining and removing from supervisory positions those raters who fail to conduct documented ACA sessions.

11.9.5. The Military Personnel Section will:

11.9.5.1. Provide ACA notices to raters and ratees. ANG does not currently have standardized automated process to create ACA notices for raters and ratees. ANG Military Personnel Sections may utilize an alternate form of communication to notify all raters and ratees of ACA schedules.

11.9.5.2. Not be required to maintain repository for ACAs for personnel assigned to wing.

11.9.6. Unit will:

11.9.6.1. At the unit commander's request, develop a tracking mechanism to ensure ACAs are conducted. It is the responsibility of individual raters to maintain copies of all completed ACAs and all signed ACA notices (or appropriate statements) on their assigned ratees (Regular Air Force only).

## 11.10. Who Requires an ACA.

ACAs are mandatory for officers, second lieutenant through colonel, and all Regular Air Force and Air Reserve Component personnel. If an individual requests an ACA session, the rater will provide one within 30 days of receipt of the request, provided 60 days have passed since the last ACA session. Do not prepare an ACA when a ratee is a captive, patient, prisoner, absent without leave, etc. For student officers receiving AF Forms 475, ACA is not required, but may be given at the discretion of the commander of the school. For student enlisted personnel, in approved initial skills training or advanced skills training courses an ACA is not required, but may be given at the discretion of the commander of the school. For those performance evaluations completed on non-rated initial skills training or advanced skills training course students, academic progress reports, such as the AETC Form 156 Student Training Report, captured in the Technical Training Management System or an equivalent document utilized by non-AETC institutions of instruction, will serve in-lieu of the mandatory mid-term ACA. ACAs are *not* required for Airmen who have Permanent Change of Station to prisoner status in a long term military confinement facility owned by the Air Force Security Forces Center.

## 11.11. Guidance for Conducting ACA Sessions.

ACA sessions will be conducted face-to-face. EXCEPTION: Raters may conduct sessions by telephone only in unusual circumstances where face-to-face sessions are impractical, such as when the rater and ratee are geographically separated or the rater and/or ratee is on extended TDY. When a telephonic session is conducted, the rater forwards the ACA worksheet to the ratee to complete Section III and review for discussion Section VII. The finalized form is forwarded to the ratee within 10 calendar days after the session.

## 11.12. When to Hold Documented ACA Sessions. See Table 11.1.

## 11.13. The ACA Notice:

11.13.1. The rater should receive a computer-generated ACA notice 30 days after supervision begins (identifying initial or follow-up ACA sessions as required) and again halfway between the time supervision began and the projected performance report close-out date (identifying mid-term ACA session requirement). This notice serves to remind raters that an ACA session is due; however, failure to receive an ACA notice does not justify failing to hold a required session.

11.13.2. Since the ratee shares the responsibility to ensure ACA sessions are conducted, an ACA notice is also sent to the ratee, through his or her unit, 30 days after sending the notice to the rater (for officers) or concurrently with the notice sent to the rater (for enlisted).

**Table 11.1. Airman Comprehensive Assessment Requirements**

| R U L E | A | B |
|---|---|---|
| | **If the ratee is** | **then the ratee requires the following feedback** |
| 1 | a Chief Master Sergeant or a Colonel. | Initial (See Note 1 & Note 4) |
| 2 | a Master Sergeant or Senior Master Sergeant, Major or Lieutenant Colonel. | Initial (See Note 1 & Note 4) Midterm (See Note 4) |
| 3 | an Airman basic, Airman or Airman First Class (who has already received an EPR), a Senior Airman through Technical Sergeant, a Lieutenant through Captain. (see notes 6 and 7 ) | Initial (See Note 1) Midterm (See Note 2) End-of-reporting period (See Note 3) |
| 4 | an Airman Basic, Airman or Airman First Class (with less than 20 months TAFMS) | Initial (See Note 1) Midterm (See Note 5) |
| 5 | an Airman Basic through Colonel | Requested by Ratee (See Note 8) |
| 6 | an Airman Basic through Colonel | When determined necessary by the rater |

**Notes:**

1. The rater must conduct the initial feedback session within the first 60 days he or she *initially* begins supervision. This will be the ratee's only *initial* feedback until they have a change of reporting official. For Chief Master Sergeants and Colonels, this is the only feedback required.

2. The rater must conduct the midterm feedback session midway between the date supervision begins and the projected close-out date of the next EPR/OPR.

3. The rater conducts an End-of Reporting Period feedback session when an evaluation has been accomplished. This session must be conducted within 60 days of the close-out of the evaluation and serves two distinct purposes. The first purpose is to review and discuss with the ratee the previous reporting period and resulting EPR/OPR. The second purpose is to establish expectations for the new reporting period. Note Officers Only: If the evaluation is due to a Change of Reporting Official, the new rater will be required to do an initial feedback in addition to the feedback performed by the previous rater during the presentation of the evaluation. This feedback may be accomplished using the AF Form 931/932/724, but is not required to be documented.

4. Air Reserve Component personnel are not required an ACA if member is pending action IAW AFI 36-3209, *Separation Procedures for Air National Guard and Air Force Reserve Members.*

5. After the initial feedback session is conducted, conduct a (midterm) feedback session every 180 days until the rater writes an EPR or a Change of Reporting Official occurs.

6. If the ratee is due an annual evaluation and the period of supervision is less than 150 days, the rater conducts the feedback session approximately 60 days before the projected evaluation close-out date.

7. Officers Only: If the ratee is getting a Change of Reporting Official evaluation and time permits, the rater will hold a feedback session within 60 days of the close-out date, but not later than 30 days prior.

8. When a ratee requests a feedback session, the rater must conduct a session within 30 days of the ratee's request if at least 60 days have passed (at the rater's discretion) since the last feedback session.

## 11.14. Which ACA Form to Use:

11.14.1. For Lieutenant through Colonel, use AF Form 724.

11.14.2. For a Master Sergeant thru Chief Master Sergeant, use AF Form 932.

11.14.3. For Technical Sergeant and below, use AF Form 931.

**11.15. Preparing the ACA Worksheet.** The ACA worksheet should, as thoroughly as possible, outline the issues discussed during the ACA session; however, it is primarily a guide for conducting the assessment session, not a transcript. Therefore, omission of an issue from the form does not, by itself, constitute proof that the issue was not discussed.

11.15.1. The ACA worksheet may be handwritten or typed by the rater providing the assessment.

11.15.2. Section I, Personal Information, is self-explanatory. Fill in all required data.

11.15.3. Section II, Types of Assessment. In the appropriate box, indicate whether the assessment is initial, mid-term, follow-up, ratee requested, or rater directed.

11.15.4. Section III, Self-Assessment is completed by the ratee. This area provides information to the rater on where the ratee assesses themselves, and assists the rater with information when accomplishing the overall assessment.

11.15.5. Section IV, Airman's Critical Role in Support of the Mission. This section is used to convey to the ratee their critical role in achieving mission success.

    11.15.5.1. Organizational Climate Assessment. It is mandatory for raters to include expectations for contributing to a healthy organizational climate for Airmen up to the grade of Senior Airman. Raters must also ensure that NCOs and Officers are accountable for creating a healthy organizational climate. Raters must ensure that every commander knows he/she is responsible for, and will be held accountable for, ensuring their unit has a healthy command climate.

11.15.6. Section V, Individual Readiness Index. Documents the Airmen's readiness status and Air and Space Expeditionary Force Indicator. Place an "E" in this block if member is an Enabler. Discuss importance of meeting deployment requirements.

11.15.7. Section VI, Performance: Leadership/Primary Duties/Followership/Training, covers those qualities and skills required of all personnel. The Performance: Leadership/Primary Duties/Followership/Training has five sub-sections for Technical Sergeant and below, and eight sub-sections for Master Sergeant thru Chief Master Sergeant, to select from each performance factor. The rater places a mark in the appropriate block which indicates the ratee's level of performance.

    11.15.7.1. Since the primary purpose of the initial ACA session is to establish expectations for the upcoming rating period, a rater is not expected to have already developed a clear-cut opinion of an individual's performance by the time the session is conducted. Therefore, raters will mark the "Initial" block in Section II, Type of Assessment, and will leave blocks in Section VI, Performance: Leadership/Primary Duties/Followership/Training blank, while discussing each area, and the performance expectations for the rate in each area during the feedback session.

    11.15.7.2. For all other ACA types, the rater will indicate how the ratee is meeting the established expectations by marking one block under each main heading. These markings translate to an aggregate rating on the performance evaluation, and provide an indication of how the ratee is meeting the expectations set forth by the rater while providing the basis for the ACA session discussion.

11.15.8. AF Form 931, Section VII, *Followership/Leadership*, documents an Airman's ability to lead and develop subordinates and exercise effective followership in mission accomplishment. The Followership/Leadership section has four sub-sections to select from for each performance factor. The rater places a mark in the appropriate block which indicates the ratee's level of performance.

11.15.9. AF Form 931, Section VIII, and AF Form 932, Section VII, *Whole Airman Concept*, consider the Airman's interpersonal relations that directly influence behavior and values, level of effort to improve themselves personally and professionally, and their devotion and enthusiasm. This section has three sub-sections for both Airman Basic thru Technical Sergeant, and Master Sergeant thru Chief Master Sergeant to select from for each performance factor. The rater places a mark in the appropriate block which indicates the ratee's level of performance.

11.15.10. AF Form 931, Section IX, and AF Form 932, Section VIII, *Knowing Your Airman*, provides questions designed to facilitate open communication between the ratee/rater and may trigger areas and/or specific items which need to be probed in more depth. These questions are not intended to be all encompassing. The purpose is to help start the conversation on the particular item, not make it an interrogation. AF Form 931 items 6 and 7 are designed to receive feedback from the ratee and to set specific expectations for the ratee's growth.

*Section 11D—Civilian Performance Evaluation*

**11.16. Civilian Performance Appraisal Program.** Defense Department civilian employees are getting a new, standardized performance appraisal program as part of the department's New Beginnings initiative. New Beginnings seeks to improve communication between supervisors and employees, provide more transparent processes and improve recruiting, developing and rewarding DoD employees. Once the program is fully implemented additional information will be provided within the 2019 rewrite for AFH 1, *Airman.* Continue to use AFI 36-1001, *Managing the Civilian Performance Program* until your conversion into the new program.

**11.17. Conclusion.**

This chapter covers the officer and enlisted evaluation systems and civilian performance program, and provides supervisors the information needed to employ the officer and enlisted evaluation systems, and civilian performance program in everyday situations to help develop their subordinates. The chapter addressed the importance of correctly using the officer and enlisted evaluation systems, and civilian performance program, by identifying responsibilities, outlining the performance feedback process, and provides additional information as outlined in governing AFIs 36-2406, *Officer and Enlisted Evaluation Systems* and 36-1001, *Managing the Civilian Performance Program* respectively.

## Chapter 12

## TRAINING AND EDUCATION

*Section 12A—Overview*

### 12.1. Introduction.

A "job" does not guarantee success, however, effective On the Job Training; Job Knowledge, Job Proficiency and Job Experience will ultimately lead to a successful career and with continued Education and Training, a solid national defense. On-the-job training (OJT) has been around since the beginning of history and has been used in the United States by both public and private industries for many years. Today, most successful companies have effective OJT programs because OJT works. Well-trained workers mean higher production, positive morale, greater profits, and higher wages. Air Force training costs millions of dollars annually, for good reason. To accomplish the mission, whether that means satellites in orbit, planes in the air, reports to higher headquarters, or vehicles on the road, training is a must. In addition to OJT, training management covers upgrade training, skill levels, retraining, and training responsibilities, forms, and documentation. Finally, each base education office provides Service members with educational opportunities in which they may voluntarily participate during off-duty time or other times, as authorized by military policies. The base education office also provides information on financial assistance and commissioning programs.

*Section 12B—Training Management*

### 12.2. Education and Training Purpose.

Skilled and trained personnel are critical to the Air Force in providing a strong national defense capability. The Air Force OJT program provides training for personnel to attain knowledge and skill qualifications required to perform duties in their specialty.

### 12.3. Strategy.

Develop, manage, and execute realistic and flexible training programs to produce a highly skilled, motivated force capable of carrying out all tasks and functions in support of the Air Force mission. These programs should provide the foundation for Air Force readiness.

### 12.4. Training and Mission Accomplishment.

Training is an integral part of the unit's mission. An effective training program requires commander and supervisory involvement at all levels.

### 12.5. Training and Airman Career Program.

Supervisors must take an active role in the trainee's career progression and explain the relationship between training and career progression. While the supervisor's primary responsibility is to plan a program that outlines specific short-term, mission-related goals for the trainee, overall success depends on the supervisor's ability to advise and assist Airmen in reaching their long-range career objectives.

### 12.6. Training Components.

The Air Force OJT program consists of three components:

12.6.1. **Job Knowledge**—satisfied through career development courses (CDC) designed to provide career knowledge, general task, and deployment/unit type code task knowledge applicable to the Air Force specialty code that is gained through a planned program of study involving CDCs or technical references listed in the applicable career field education and training plan (CFETP) across a wide spectrum of subjects pertaining to a career field. When CDCs are not available, trainees study the applicable technical references identified by the supervisor and/or CFETP.

12.6.2. **Job Proficiency**—hands-on training provided on the job, allowing the trainee to gain proficiency in tasks performed in the work center.

12.6.3. **Job Experience**—gained during and after upgrade training to build confidence and competence.

### 12.7. Upgrade Training.

Upgrade training is the key to the total training program. It leads to award of the higher skill level and is designed to increase skills and abilities. Air Force specialty code upgrade training requirements for award of 3-, 5-, 7-, and 9-skill levels are outlined in Chapter 4 of AFI 36-2201, *Air Force Training Program*, AFI 36-2101, *Classifying Military Personnel (Officer and Enlisted),* and the applicable CFETP.

12.7.1. **Apprentice.**

Airmen must complete an initial skills course for award of the 3-skill level. Retraining into an Air Force specialty code may be accomplished via OJT alone only when specified in the retraining instructions and as approved by the Air Force Career Field Manager or the Air Reserve Component career field functional manager. Personnel retraining via OJT may be awarded a 3-skill level when they complete knowledge training on all tasks taught in the initial skills course and other tasks and mandatory requirements identified by the Air Force Career Field Manager.

12.7.2. **Journeyman.**

Airmen must complete mandatory CDCs if available and applicable mandatory core tasks identified in the CFETP. Award of the 5-skill level also requires completion of a minimum of 12 months in upgrade training and mandatory requirements listed in the Air Force Enlisted Classification Directory. Additionally, the member must be recommended by the supervisor and approved by the commander. Individuals in retraining status, training status code (Training Status Code F), are subject to the same training requirements. **Exception:** The member must complete a minimum of 9 months in upgrade training.

12.7.3. **Craftsman.**

To be a craftsman, the member must be at least a staff sergeant; complete mandatory CDCs, if available; and complete applicable mandatory core tasks identified in the CFETP. Award of the 7-skill level also requires completion of: a 7-skill level craftsman course (if Air Force specialty code requires it); mandatory requirements listed in the Air Force Enlisted Classification Directory; and a minimum of 12 months in training. Additionally, the member must be recommended by the supervisor and approved by the commander. Individuals in retraining status (Training Status Code G) are subject to the same training requirements. **Exception:** The member must complete a minimum of 6 months in upgrade training.

12.7.4. **Superintendent.**

For award of the 9-skill level, the member must be at least a senior master sergeant and meet mandatory requirements listed in the Air Force Enlisted Classification Directory, be recommended by the supervisor, and be approved by the commander.

## 12.8. Retraining Program.

The retraining program is designed to balance the number of personnel in specific grades and year groups of the Air Force specialty. Once retraining is approved and the Airman has been assigned duty in the new specialty, upgrade training begins. With minor exceptions, training requirements are identical for retrainees and standard upgrade trainees.

## 12.9. Training Responsibilities:

12.9.1. **Unit Training Manager (UTM).**

The UTM is the commander's key staff member responsible for overall management of the training program. UTMs serve as training consultants to all unit members and determine if quality training programs are in effect within all sections. UTMs:

12.9.1.1. Develop, manage, and conduct training in support of in-garrison and expeditionary mission requirements; advise and assist commanders and unit personnel in executing their training responsibilities; and conduct a staff assistance visit of the unit's training program every 18 months.

12.9.1.2. Interview newly assigned personnel within 30 days (60 days for Air Reserve Component) to determine training status and CDC enrollment/progression requirements. Initiate Air Force Form 623, *Individual Training Record,* six-part folders (when required by the Air Force Career Field Manager), or approved electronic equivalent, for all trainees entering upgrade training for the first time and provide to the supervisor. Conduct a comprehensive trainee orientation according to AFI 36-2201 for trainees initially entering upgrade training within 60 days of assignment (90 days for Air Reserve Component). UTMs must also manage the unit CDC program and conduct a training progress review with the supervisor and trainee at the 24th month of upgrade training to evaluate status.

12.9.1.3. Ensure all work centers have a master training plan. Assist work centers in developing a master training plan to plan, manage, and execute training activities.

12.9.2. **Supervisor.**

Supervisors have the single greatest impact on mission accomplishment. They must share their experiences and expertise to meet mission requirements and provide a quality training program to the trainee. Supervisors must plan, conduct, and evaluate training. Supervisors will:

12.9.2.1. Use CFETPs (or approved electronic equivalent) to manage work center and individual training and develop master training plans to ensure completion of all work center duty position requirements (for example, 100 percent task coverage). The supervisor must also integrate training with day-to-day work center operations and consider trainer and equipment availability, training opportunities, and schedules.

12.9.2.2. Conduct and document work center training orientation within 60 days of new assignment (120 days for Air Reserve Component). Also, conduct and document an initial evaluation of newly assigned personnel's trainee qualifications within 60 days of initial permanent change of station or permanent change of assignment (120 days for Air Reserve Component).

12.9.2.3. Select trainers (and certifiers as required by the Air Force Career Field Manager) based on skill qualifications with the assistance of the UTM.

12.9.2.4. Administer the CDC program for assigned trainees.

12.9.2.5. Maintain Air Force Form 623, six-part folder, or other approved training record for Airmen in the grades of airman basic through technical sergeant (or personnel in combat ready duty positions, if required by the Air Force Career Field Manager) and senior noncommissioned officers in retraining status, or as directed by the Air Force Career Field Manager. Before submitting members for upgrade, ensure the trainee, as a minimum, meets all mandatory requirements as defined in the Air Force Enlisted Classification Directory, CFETP, and the Air Force job qualification standard (AFJQS).

12.9.3. **Trainer.**

The trainer and supervisor may be the same individual. If necessary, the supervisor may assign someone else to provide the training. Trainers are selected based on their experience and ability to provide instruction to the trainees. Additionally, they must maintain task qualification and complete the Air Force Training Course. Trainer responsibilities include planning, conducting, and documenting training; preparing and using teaching outlines or task breakdowns, as necessary; developing evaluation tools; and briefing the trainee and supervisor on the training evaluation results.

12.9.4. **Task Certifier.**

Task certifiers provide third-party certification and evaluation on tasks identified by the Air Force Career Field Manager, if applicable. The certifier must conduct additional evaluations and certify qualification on those designated tasks. Certifiers must be at least a staff sergeant with a 5-skill level or civilian equivalent, attend the Air Force Training Course, and be capable of evaluating the task being certified. Certifiers will develop evaluation tools or use established training evaluation tools and methods to determine the trainee's ability and training program effectiveness and will brief the trainee, supervisor, and trainer on the training evaluation results.

12.9.5. **Trainee.**

The trainee is the focal point of the Air Force training program. Trainees must make every effort to become qualified to perform in their Air Force specialty. The success and quality of trainee training greatly depends on the relationship between the supervisor, trainer, and trainee. Trainees must:

12.9.5.1. Actively participate in all opportunities for upgrade and qualification training.

12.9.5.2. Comprehend the applicable CFETP requirements and career path.

12.9.5.3. Obtain and maintain knowledge, qualifications, and appropriate skill level within the assigned specialty.

12.9.5.4. Budget on- and off-duty time to complete assigned training tasks, particularly CDC and self-study training requirements, within established time limits.

12.9.5.5. Request assistance from the supervisor, trainer, and UTM when having difficulty with any part of training.

12.9.5.6. Acknowledge and document task qualification upon completion of training.

12.10. **Training Forms and Documents.**

Training documentation is important to personnel at all levels because it validates the status of training and task qualification. Documentation also helps management assess mission capability and readiness, and it defines requirements for individual career progression.

12.10.1. **Air Force Form 623.**

The Air Force Form 623 (or electronic equivalent) is the standard folder used as a training record. The form reflects past and current qualifications and is used to determine training requirements. Supervisors maintain the Air Force

Form 623 for all assigned personnel according to AFI 36-2201. The form is available to all personnel in the chain of command, including the UTM, upon request. Return the form to the member upon separation, retirement, commissioning, or promotion to master sergeant, unless otherwise directed by the Air Force Career Field Manager. **Exception:** Do not give Air Force Forms 623 containing classified information to the individual.

### 12.10.2. Career Field Education and Training Program (CFETP).

The CFETP is a comprehensive core document identifying life-cycle education and training requirements, training support resources, core and home station training, and deployment/Unit Type Code task requirements for a specialty. Supervisors use the CFETP to plan, prioritize, manage, and execute training within the career field. CFETPs are used to identify and certify all past and current qualifications. Keep at least one copy of the entire CFETP (Part I and II), in the work center for general access and master training plan development. Unless otherwise directed by the Air Force Career Field Manager, work center supervisors may file only Part II of the CFETP, with cover page and identification page, in the Air Force Form 623, or equivalent form. If the CFETP is divided into distinct sections (by aircraft, duty position, or mission, etc.) then file only the sections applicable to the individual, such as current/past qualifications, and current upgrade/duty position training requirements.

12.10.2.1. **Part I.** Provides information necessary for overall management of the specialty and is maintained as part of the work center master training plan.

12.10.2.2. **Part II.** Contains the specialty training standard identifying the duties, tasks, and technical references to support training, AETC-conducted training, core and home station training tasks, deployment/Unit Type Code tasks, and correspondence course requirements.

### 12.10.3. Air Force Job Qualification Standard (AFJQS).

The AFJQS is a training document approved by the Air Force Career Field Manager for a particular job type or duty position within an Air Force specialty.

### 12.10.4. Air Force IMT 623A, *On-the-Job Training Record Continuation Sheet.*

Use Air Force IMT 623A, or automated version, to document an individual's training progress. The form reflects status, counseling, and breaks in training. The supervisor and/or trainer and the trainee must sign and date all entries.

### 12.10.5. Air Force IMT 797, *Job Qualification Standard Continuation/Command JQS.*

Air Force IMT 797 is a continuation of the CFETP, Part II, or AFJQS. This form defines locally assigned duty position, home station training, and deployment/Unit Type Code requirements not included in the CFETP, Part II.

### 12.10.6. Air Force IMT 803, *Report of Task Evaluations.*

Evaluators use Air Force IMT 803 to conduct and document completion of task evaluations during training staff assistance visits, when directed by the commander, or when task certification requires validation. File completed evaluations conducted on a single trainee by the supervisor/trainer or task certifier in Air Force Form 623 until upgraded or no longer applicable to the current duty position.

### 12.10.7. Air Force IMT 1098, *Special Task Certification and Recurring Training.*

Supervisors use Air Force IMT 1098 to document selected tasks requiring recurring training or evaluation. Air Force and major command directives may identify tasks contained in the CFETP that require special certification, recurring training, or evaluation.

### 12.10.8. Master Training Plan.

The master training plan employs a strategy for ensuring all work center job requirements are completed by using a master task listing. The master training plan provides milestones for tasks and CDC completion, and prioritizes deployment/Unit Type Code, home station training, upgrade, and qualification tasks.

## 12.11. Career Development Course Program Management:

### 12.11.1. Purpose and Scope:

12.11.1.1. CDCs are published to provide the information necessary to satisfy the career knowledge component of OJT. These courses are developed from references identified in the CFETP that correlate with mandatory knowledge items listed in the Air Force Enlisted Classification Directory. CDCs must contain information on basic principles, techniques, and procedures common to an Air Force specialty code. They do not contain information on specific equipment or tasks unless the specific equipment or task best illustrates a procedure or technique having utility to the entire Air Force specialty code.

12.11.1.2. Headquarters Air University/A4L electronically publishes an "Air Force specialty code listing of CDC requirements, identifying all mandatory CDCs for skill-level upgrade." The list is available on the Headquarters Air University/A4L website at http://www.au.af.mil/au/afiadl/ under the Course and Admin Information tab.

12.11.2. **CDC Administration:**

12.11.2.1. If available, supervisors will use CDCs to satisfy career knowledge requirements for upgrade training.

12.11.2.2. If a CDC becomes available after entering upgrade training, the individual does not have to take the CDC, unless specified by the Air Force Career Field Manager.

12.11.2.3. The UTM will ensure trainees are enrolled in required CDC material within 45 days of in-processing (within 60 days for overseas units).

12.11.2.4. Within 10 duty days of receipt, the UTM issues CDC material to the supervisor and trainee and briefs them on proper use of the CDC and documents the trainee's Air Force IMT 623A or equivalent automated training record.

12.11.2.5. The supervisor determines volume sequence of study, sets the overall course completion schedule, and develops a tracking system to monitor progress. Each volume must be completed within 30 days. (**Exception:** The UTM may grant an extension due to mission requirements. Air Reserve Component and individual mobilization augmentees have 60 days.) If necessary, the supervisor determines the reason for slow progress, counsels the trainee, documents the counseling on Air Force IMT 623A or automated version, and places the trainee in supervised study.

12.11.2.6. The trainee answers the unit review exercise questions. The unit review exercise is an "open book" teaching device. The trainee transfers answers to the field scoring sheet. The supervisor scores the unit review exercise, conducts review training on the areas missed, fills in the bottom of the scoring sheet, places the field scoring sheet in the Air Force Form 623 or automated training records, counsels the trainee, and documents Air Force IMT 623A or automated version. The supervisor will conduct a comprehensive review of the entire CDC with the trainee in preparation for the course examination and documents the review on the Air Force IMT 623A or automated version.

12.11.2.7. The supervisor will notify the UTM to schedule and order the course examination.

12.11.2.8. If the trainee receives a satisfactory result, the supervisor conducts and documents review training, then signs and places the course examination scorecard in the Air Force Form 623 or automated training records until the trainee completes upgrade training or qualification training.

12.11.2.9. If the trainee receives an unsatisfactory result, the unit commander, with help from the UTM or base training manager, interviews the supervisor and trainee to determine reason for failure and corrective action required within 30 days from initial notification (90 days for Air Reserve Component and individual mobilization augmentees). The supervisor documents the counseling on Air Force IMT 623A or automated version, places the trainee in supervised review training, and forwards a copy of the evaluation to the base training office.

12.11.2.10. If the trainee receives a second unsatisfactory course examination result, the unit commander, with assistance from the UTM or base training manager, interviews the supervisor and trainee to determine reason for failure within 30 days from initial notification (90 days for Air Reserve Component and individual mobilization augmentees). After reviewing the facts, the unit commander decides on one of the following options: (1) Evaluate for possible CDC waiver (do not place trainee into Training Status Code T); (2) Withdraw the Airman for failing to progress, place into Training Status Code T, and pursue separation; (3) Withdraw the Airman for failing to progress, place into Training Status Code T, request Air Force specialty code withdrawal, and recommend retraining or return to a previously awarded Air Force specialty code; or (4) Withdraw Airman for failing to progress, place into Training Status Code T, reevaluate at 90 days, and pursue either option 1, 2, or 3 as appropriate.

## Section 12C—*Community College of the Air Force*

## 12.12. Community College of the Air Force:

12.12.1. The Community College of the Air Force is the largest community college in the world and is the only community college in the Department of Defense exclusively for enlisted personnel. The mission of the Community College of the Air Force is to offer and award job-related associate in applied science degrees and other academic credentials that enhance mission readiness, contribute to recruiting, assist in retention and support the career transitions of Air Force enlisted members. Community College of the Air Force awards the associate in applied science degree to enlisted members of the Regular Air Force, Air National Guard, and Air Force Reserve Command. Community College of the Air Force offers over 70 degree programs in 5 general areas: (1) Aircraft and Missile Maintenance; (2) Allied Health; (3) Electronics and

Telecommunications; (4) Logistics and Resources; and (5) Public and Support Services. Enlisted Airmen may only participate in degree programs specifically designed for their Air Force occupational specialty. Community College of the Air Force also offers programs and other academic credentials that support professional development, professional certification, and recognition opportunities.

12.12.2. The Community College of the Air Force was activated in 1972 to gain academic recognition for formal technical training conducted by Air Force schools. From 1980 to 2004, Community College of the Air Force was independently accredited by the Southern Association of Colleges and Schools Commission on Colleges. Today, Community College of the Air Force shares in Air University's regional accreditation through the Southern Association of Colleges and Schools Commission on Colleges.

12.12.3. The Community College of the Air Force administrative center is located at Maxwell Air Force Base, Gunter Annex, Alabama. More than 6,500 instructors assigned to more than 100 affiliated schools deliver more than 2,000 degree-applicable courses for which collegiate credit is earned. Each year more than 1.6 million semester hours are earned in Community College of the Air Force classrooms. To date, Community College of the Air Force has awarded more than 480,000 associate of applied science degrees.

12.12.4. **Associate in Applied Science Degree.** Associate degrees earned in professional, technical or terminal programs are frequently called associate of applied science degrees. The educational standard for the associate in applied science degree is to be designed for those students who plan to seek employment based upon the competencies and skills attained through these programs and to offer the academic, technical and professional knowledge and skills required for job acquisition, retention and advancement. While not designed to meet the needs of students who transfer to a four-year institution, portions of these programs may do so. Community College of the Air Force offers and awards the associate in applied science degree designed to provide graduates with knowledge, skills and theoretical background for enhanced performance as technicians within their respective Air Force occupational specialty. This is accomplished by combining collegiate credit earned through completed formal technical training courses delivered at affiliated military schools and general education courses completed from accredited civilian colleges. Since enlisted Airmen are constantly relocating in performance of their duties, Community College of the Air Force provides a means for them to complete degree requirements regardless of where they are assigned. One way the Community College of the Air Force helps enlisted Airmen to progress toward completing degree requirements while deployed, on temporary duty, or at multiple duty locations is through General Education Mobile. General Education Mobile identifies civilian colleges that provide distance learning courses approved by the Community College of the Air Force in meeting degree program general education requirements. This prevents Airmen from completing unnecessary courses that would not apply toward degree graduation requirements, eliminates waste of military tuition assistance funds, and prevents wasting Airmen's time and efforts.

12.12.5. Enlisted Airmen are automatically registered in the Community College of the Air Force degree program designed for their Air Force occupational specialty during the fourth week of Basic Military Training. Each degree program consists of 64 semester hours and combines Air Force formal technical training and education with a core of general education requirements obtained from accredited civilian colleges or nationally recognized examination programs. To graduate, students must complete the 64 semester-hour academic requirements, hold at least the Journeyman 5-skill level (or equivalent), and have a minimum of 16 semester hours of Community College of the Air Force residency credit applied toward the degree program. Residency is defined as credit earned in a Community College of the Air Force affiliated school or credit awarded for occupational specialty progression. Table 12.1 identifies the requirements for the typical Community College of the Air Force degree and the semester-hour requirements in each subject area.

12.12.6. **Collegiate Credit.** Community College of the Air Force awards collegiate academic credit for degree-applicable courses delivered at affiliated military schools. However, not all Air Force training courses are awarded Community College of the Air Force academic credit. The college accepts credit in transfer from accredited colleges to be applied toward specific degree program requirements. General education courses accepted in transfer from civilian colleges must meet Southern Association of Colleges and Schools Commission on Colleges accreditation and Community College of the Air Force requirements. Refer to the Community College of the Air Force General Catalog for policies concerning acceptance of civilian general education courses in transfer. Community College of the Air Force also researches and awards technical credit for degree-applicable federal and civilian professional credentials (certifications, licensures, and registries). Students may earn Community College of the Air Force collegiate credit for specific national professional credentials that are approved by the college to satisfy applicable degree program technical education and program elective requirements. To determine which professional credentials can be awarded credit and used in a specific degree program, refer to the current Community College of the Air Force General Catalog at http://www.au.af.mil/au/barnes/ccaf/.

Table 12.1. CCAF Degree Program Structure.

| ITEM | A | B |
|------|---|---|
| | Degree Requirements | Semester Hours Needed |
| 1 | Technical Education | 24 |
| 2 | Leadership, Management & Military Studies | 6 |
| 3 | Physical Education | 4 |
| 4 | Program Electives | 15 |
| | **General Education Requirements** | |
| 5 | Oral Communication | 3 |
| 6 | Written Communication | 3 |
| 7 | Mathematics | 3 |
| 8 | Social Science | 3 |
| 9 | Humanities | 3 |
| | | Total:   64 |

## 12.13. Professional Credentials and Credentialing Programs:

### 12.13.1. Professional Development.

Credentialing is a critical element of enlisted professional development. During the certification process, enlisted Airmen gain advanced levels of knowledge and skills beyond their job qualification training. Blending Air Force technical training and education with industry-based skill sets and professional certification processes benefits the Air Force by molding a more diverse and qualified workforce to maintain critical and valuable national defense assets. The Airman benefits by being provided the education and credentials needed in highly technical Air Force career fields. The Airman will also possess highly valued skills needed by industry when he or she transitions out of the Air Force. The end result is industry benefits immensely by receiving a highly trained, qualified, experienced, and disciplined employee, which is a valuable payback of investments. To support documentary evidence of training, skills, and practical experience, Airmen are highly encouraged to maintain records of all previous and current education, training, and qualifications.

### 12.13.2. Credentialing Programs.

Community College of the Air Force offers credentialing programs that assist enlisted Airmen in broadening their professional development. These programs directly support the mission of Community College of the Air Force in that credentialing of enlisted Airmen enhances combat readiness, contributes to recruiting and retention, and supports career transitions. Additional credentialing information is available on Community College of the Air Force website at http://www.au.af.mil/au/barnes/ccaf/certifications.asp.

12.13.2.1. **Air Force Airframe & Powerplant Certification Program.** Community College of the Air Force offers the Air Force Airframe & Powerplant Certification Program for aircraft maintenance technicians in specific occupational specialties. The program is designed to bridge gaps between Air Force education, training, and experience, and Federal Aviation Administration eligibility requirements per Title 14, Code of Federal Regulations, Part 65, *Certification: Airmen Other Than Flight Crewmembers;* Section 65.77, *Experience Requirements.* The program benefits the Air Force by broadening the skill sets and professional development of Air Force technicians, producing a more rounded and diverse aircraft maintenance professional. Furthermore, the Federal Aviation Administration and Joint Service Aviation Maintenance Technician Certification Council entered an agreement approving military appointees to administer all Federal Aviation Administration certification knowledge tests to eligible military personnel. Through the agreement, all Federal Aviation Administration certification knowledge tests are administered free of charge to regular, guard, and reserve component personnel of the United States Armed Services; United States military retirees; United States military dependents; Department of Defense civilians; and Department of Homeland Security civilians.

12.13.2.2. **Community College of the Air Force Instructional Systems Development Certification Program.** Community College of the Air Force offers the Instructional System Development certification program for curriculum developers, writers, and managers formally assigned to affiliated schools to develop and manage Community College of the Air Force degree-applicable courses. This certification is a professional credential that validates the education and training required to develop and manage Community College of the Air Force collegiate courses and the practical experience gained in planning, developing, implementing, and managing instructional systems.

12.13.2.3. **Community College of the Air Force Instructor Certification Program.** Community College of the Air Force offers an instructor certification program for qualified instructors assigned to affiliated schools to teach Community College of the Air Force degree-applicable courses. This certification is a professional credential that validates the instructor's extensive faculty development training, education, qualification, and practical teaching experience required to teach a Community College of the Air Force course. The program consists of three specific levels of achievement and is offered to qualified officer, enlisted, civilian, and other Service instructors.

12.13.2.4. **Professional Manager Certification Program.** Community College of the Air Force offers the Professional Manager Certification Program to qualified Air Force noncommissioned officers. This certification is a professional credential that validates the noncommissioned officer's advanced level of education and experience in leadership and management, as well as professional accomplishments, required to effectively manage enlisted Airmen and critical national defense assets. The program provides a structured professional development track that supplements enlisted professional military education and the Career Field Education and Training Plan.

12.13.3. **Air Force Credentialing Opportunities On-Line (Air Force COOL).**

Community College of the Air Force manages the Air Force Credentialing Opportunities On-Line program, which provides an online research tool designed to increase Airmen's awareness of federal and national professional credentials (certifications, licensures, and registries) available to their Air Force occupational specialty. Air Force Credentialing Opportunities On-Line, accessible at https://afvec.langley.af.mil/afvec/Public/COOL/Default.aspx, also provides information concerning program funding for specialty-related credentials, civilian occupational equivalencies, credentialing agencies, and professional organizations. Air Force Credentialing Opportunities On-Line program does not provide funding for mandatory credentials required to attain an Air Force occupational specialty or duty position. Other information contained on the Air Force Credentialing Opportunities On-Line website can be used to:

12.13.3.1. Gain background information on civilian credentials, including eligibility requirements and resources to prepare for the exams.

12.13.3.2. Identify credentials related to an Air Force occupational specialty.

12.13.3.3. Learn how to fill gaps between Air Force training and experience and civilian credentialing requirements.

12.13.3.4. Get information on funding opportunities to pay for credentialing exams and associated fees.

12.13.3.5. Learn about resources available to help gain employment in a specific civilian occupation.

12.13.4. **Joint Service Aviation Maintenance Technician Certification Council:**

12.13.4.1. Community College of the Air Force is a charter member of the Joint Service Aviation Maintenance Technician Certification Council and serves as the co-chair to the council. The Aircraft Maintenance Air Force Career Field Manager (Air Force/A4LF) also serves as co-chair.

12.13.4.2. The Department of Defense and United States Coast Guard chartered the Joint Service Aviation Maintenance Technician Certification Council to standardize the Federal Aviation Administration Airframe & Powerplant certification process for military personnel and provide direction and resources necessary to ensure military personnel meet Federal Aviation Administration Airframe & Powerplant certification eligibility requirements.

12.13.4.3. The Joint Service Aviation Maintenance Technician Certification Council serves as a functional advisory body to each respective United States military Service's aviation maintenance division and headquarters Federal Aviation Administration which represents military interests in future Federal Aviation Administration decisions or policy changes affecting the Airframe & Powerplant certification process. The council also promotes certification opportunities offered by other nationally recognized credentialing agencies related to military aviation maintenance occupational specialties.

12.13.4.4. Responsibilities of the Joint Service Aviation Maintenance Technician Certification Council are to:

12.13.4.4.1. Ensure Federal Aviation Administration's continued recognition of formal military aviation maintenance technical training and practical experience.

12.13.4.4.2. Review aircraft maintenance technicians' training and experience from a Federal Aviation Administration certification perspective and ensure continued recognition of formal military aviation maintenance technical training and practical experience.

12.13.4.4.3. Serve as the focal point for Federal Aviation Administration Airframe & Powerplant certificate authorization for military members.

12.13.4.4.4. Maintain Department of Defense and United States Coast Guard continuity and relationship with headquarters Federal Aviation Administration in matters related to Title 14, Code of Federal Regulations, Part 65.

12.13.4.4.5. Provide direction and resources necessary to ensure technicians meet Federal Aviation Administration eligibility requirements.

12.13.4.4.6. Develop, maintain and publish a policies and procedures manual to ensure continuity is maintained throughout the life of the program.

12.13.4.4.7. Promote and, if appropriate, develop and administer other certification programs deemed of value to military aviation maintenance occupational specialties.

## 12.14. Air Force Virtual Education Center.

The Air Force Virtual Education Center, accessible at https://afvec.langley.af.mil/afvec/Home.aspx, is the Air Force's premier website for providing information about education benefits and hosts the Air Force Credentialing Opportunities On-Line. It provides students one-stop shopping for all higher education and credentialing needs. Airmen may log on to the Air Force Virtual Education Center to create their own account and gain access to online customer service tools. These services include requesting official Community College of the Air Force transcripts, printing unofficial Community College of the Air Force transcripts, viewing the Community College of the Air Force degree web progress report, and accessing the civilian course conversion table. Airmen can also log on and view their personal education records, which include courses taken, tuition caps, and degree plans. This is the site for Airmen to apply on line for military tuition assistance for college courses and Air Force Credentialing Opportunities On-Line funding for specialty-related and leadership/management credentials.

*Section 12D—Education*

## 12.15. Educational Financial Assistance.

The Voluntary Education Program supports long-range Air Force goals for maintaining a high-quality force and enhancing professional and personal development, recruitment, retention, and readiness. The Air Force offers three programs for enlisted personnel to help defray the cost of obtaining off-duty education:

12.15.1. **Military Tuition Assistance.**

To assist individuals in furthering their education, the Air Force provides a tuition assistance program (with some restrictions) to all eligible Air Force members. As of 1 October 2014, the Air Force pays the cost of tuition only at accredited institutions not to exceed the hourly and annual caps established by DoDI 1322.25, *Voluntary Education Programs,* and AFI 36-2649, *Voluntary Education Program.* These funds are not taxed thus lowering the tax deduction in an Airman's paycheck. Air Force members cannot use tuition assistance to purchase textbooks, ebooks, career development courses/DVDs, references/instructional materials, electronic equipment/supplies, certificate/license examinations and all fees regardless of applicability to course enrollment or institutional reimbursement policy. Students using military tuition assistance whose tuition exceeds the semester hour cap may use the top-up benefit in their Montgomery GI Bill or Post 9/11 GI Bill to cover the remaining portion.

12.15.2. **Montgomery GI Bill.**

Eligible individuals who entered the service for the first time on or after 1 July 1985 are enrolled in the Montgomery GI Bill. Members who participate have their pay reduced by $100 a month for the first 12 months. What looks like a contribution of $1,200 is actually a little more than $900 because no taxes are paid on the $1,200. Participants may also elect to contribute an additional $600, which adds a maximum of $5,400 to the total benefit package. In-service use of the Montgomery GI Bill is permitted after 2 years of continuous Regular Air Force. Benefits expire 10 years after separation or retirement. **Note:** The amount of the total benefit is adjusted each year in relation to the cost of living index.

12.15.3. **Post-9-11 GI Bill.**

Eligible individuals who were on Regular Air Force on or after 11 September 2001 may choose to enroll in this new GI Bill. This program allows some Airmen to transfer GI Bill benefits to dependents if they have sufficient retainability. The details and benefits of this GI Bill are not the same as the Montgomery GI Bill. The decision to move to this program is irrevocable, so Airmen are requested to get full details from the Veteran's Administration at www.va.gov.

## 12.16. College Credit by Examination.

Military members may earn college credits through examination. Individuals may earn up to as much as 60 semester hours of college credit at no financial cost by doing well on the examinations. However, the amount of semester hours accepted by an academic institution is dependent on the policies of the accepting institution. The two major types of examinations available to military personnel are as follows:

12.16.1. **Defense Activity for Nontraditional Education Support (DANTES).**

The DANTES subject standardized tests are a series of tests for obtaining academic credit for college-level knowledge. The DANTES subject standardized tests are essentially course achievement tests. Each DANTES subject standardized tests is based on several textbooks commonly used for a course of the same or similar title. Some of the DANTES subject standardized tests include law enforcement, business, natural science, social science and history, and mathematics.

12.16.2. **The College-Level Examination Program (CLEP).**

The CLEP measures college-level competency. The "general" CLEP tests measure college-level achievement in the five basic areas required for college freshmen and sophomores: English composition, humanities, mathematics, natural science, and social science and history. Additional tests are available in subject areas that include business, English literature, information systems, sociology, psychology, history, management, and foreign language.

## 12.17. Enlisted-to-Air Force Institute of Technology (AFIT) Program:

12.17.1. The Enlisted-to-AFIT Program is a unique element of enlisted force development that enhances the future total force. In conjunction with other professional Education and Training programs, AFIT science, engineering, and management graduate degrees further develop an NCO's technical and managerial skills. The program's purpose is to enhance combat capability through career field core competency augmentation to provide the Air Force with highly proficient NCOs technically experienced in their career field and highly educated through AFIT graduate degree programs. Enlisted-to-AFIT Program degrees range from 18 to 24 months depending upon a student's undergraduate degree and prerequisite course work and are limited to master's degree programs offered at the resident campus, Wright-Patterson Air Force Base Ohio.

12.17.2. To be nominated for this program, the member must be a Regular Air Force Technical Sergeant (or select) or above with a minimum of 8 years of total active federal service. The nominee must have completed a 7- skill level upgrade, a Community College of the Air Force degree, and a bachelor's degree from a regionally accredited institution. Additionally, he or she must be serving in an Air Force specialty code approved for program participation by Headquarters Air Force, Force Development Directorate, with no adverse quality force actions within the previous 36 months, have a minimum of 24 months' time on station, and must be able to obtain 3 years of retainability from the projected AFIT graduation date. For more information on the program, eligibility criteria, and nomination procedures, go to http://www.afit.edu/EN/ADMISSIONS/Default.cfm?l=enl.

## 12.18. Air Force Educational Leave of Absence Program.

An indefinite suspension of the Air Force Educational Leave of Absence Program covered under AFI 36-2306, *Voluntary Education*, Para 7.8, Attachment 8 and AFI 36-3003, *Military Leave Program*, Para 14.13. This suspension applies to any new or current applications in the coordination process. Members currently participating in the program will be reviewed for continuation in the program on a case by case basis. These members should continue in the program until contacted by Air Force Personnel Center/DPSIM.

## 12.19. Commissioning Programs.

Enlisted members can obtain a commission while on Regular Air Force through one of the various commissioning programs. A few of the most common programs include:

12.19.1. **Officer Training School.**

Eligibility for a commission through Officer Training School requires military members to possess a baccalaureate or higher degree from an accredited college or university. AFI 36-2013, *Officer Training School (OTS) and Enlisted*

*Commissioning Programs (ECPS),* contains specific guidance. Additionally, the base education services office has information and can provide assistance.

### 12.19.2. Leaders Encouraging Airmen Development (LEAD).

The LEAD Program delegates authority to unit and wing commanders to nominate highly qualified Airmen to become Air Force officers via United States Air Force Academy attendance. Depending on level of qualifications, nominations may lead to direct entry to United States Air Force Academy, entry to the United States Air Force Academy Preparatory School, or referral to other programs.

### 12.19.3. Scholarships for Outstanding Airmen to Reserve Officer Training Corps (SOAR) Program.

SOAR offers Regular Air Force enlisted personnel the opportunity to earn a commission while completing their bachelor's degree as an Air Force Reserve Officer Training Corps cadet. Those selected separate from the Regular Air Force Air Force and join an Air Force Reserve Officer Training Corps detachment to become full-time college students. The Air Force provides them with a tuition and fees scholarship of up to $15,000 per year, an annual textbook allowance, and a monthly nontaxable stipend. Award of this scholarship is for 2 to 4 years, depending on how many years remain in the student's bachelor's degree program. Airmen with some or no college credit may apply for the program. A limited number of SOAR selects are offered a scholarship with no tuition cap. This program is open to students in any major. Upon graduation and completion of the program, students are commissioned as second lieutenant and returned to Regular Air Force (typically within 60 days of commissioning) for at least 4 years.

### 12.19.4. Air Force Reserve Officer Training Corps Airman Scholarship and Commissioning Program.

This program allows military members to receive an Air Force Reserve Officer Training Corps scholarship to attend a college or university of their choice, provided the college or university offers an Air Force Reserve Officer Training Corps program. If selected for this program, the member is discharged from Regular Air Force and enlisted into the Air Force Inactive Obligated Reserve. Upon completion of the degree and the Air Force Reserve Officer Training Corps requirements, the member receives an Air Force commission.

## 12.20. Air University Associate-to-Baccalaureate Cooperative Program (AU-ABC).

### 12.20.1. Vision.

The vision of Air Force leaders is to provide distance learning and bachelor's degree opportunities for Airmen. The AU-ABC aligns with this Air Force vision and meets the Air University near-term goal of providing enhanced educational opportunities for our enlisted force. The AU-ABC initiative establishes partnerships between the Air Force and accredited civilian higher education institutions to offer baccalaureate degree opportunities via distance learning. AU-ABC links Airmen who have completed associate degrees to "military supportive" baccalaureate programs. AU-ABC applies Community College of the Air Force associate degree credit toward baccalaureate degrees and requires participants to complete no more than 60 semester hours after having earned an Associate of Applied Science degree. AU-ABC degree programs are linked to one or more Air Force-relevant degree programs currently offered by Community College of the Air Force. To participate, registrants must be serving in the Regular Air Force, Air Force Reserves, or Air National Guard. Baccalaureate degree requirements may be completed after a student retires or separates from the Air Force.

### 12.20.2. Program Plans.

AU-ABC programs are classified in the three following categories:

12.20.2.1. **Category I.** The program is designed for Airmen who have completed an associate of applied science degree with the Community College of the Air Force. These students are unconditionally guaranteed that no more than 60 semester hours of credit will be required to complete a baccalaureate degree.

12.20.2.2. **Category II.** This option is designed primarily for Airmen who are currently enrolled in and pursuing a Community College of the Air Force associate of applied science degree. Students should complete the Community College of the Air Force requirements in general education and program elective areas with specifically identified prerequisite course work listed in the partnering institution's baccalaureate degree plan. Upon completion of their Community College of the Air Force degree, students are guaranteed that no more than 60 semester hours of credit will be required to complete a baccalaureate degree if they follow the posted AU-ABC degree plan.

12.20.2.3. **Category III.** This option includes baccalaureate degree programs that require Community College of the Air Force associate of applied science graduates who have met all other AU-ABC specifications to complete more than 60 semester hours of credit beyond the associate of applied science. **Note:** The degrees in this category must still link to one or more Community College of the Air Force associate of applied science programs. Go to https://rso.my.af.mil/afvecprod/afvec/SelfService/MyAFVEC.aspx for more information on AU-ABC.

**12.21. Conclusion.**

Supervisors at every level must ensure Airmen successfully accomplish their training requirements within established timelines. This chapter focuses on that responsibility, highlighting key training responsibilities, forms, and documentation. Supervisors must ensure their Airmen understand their educational benefits and options, including programs identified in this chapter: Community College of the Air Force, Air Force Virtual Education Center, financial assistance, college credit by examination, Air Force Educational Leave of Absence, and various commissioning programs.

. **Chapter 13**

**RESOURCE MANAGEMENT**

*Section 13A—Overview*

**13.1. Introduction.**

With the constant focus on efficiency, the Air Force must get the greatest return from every investment. People are one of the most important resources. This chapter provides valuable information to consider when managing resources and personnel. Also, everyone must safeguard Air Force property and protect it from fraud, waste, and abuse; and resource management requires all members be sensitive to environmental issues. This chapter provides an overview of resource management and identifies many of the Air Force environmental programs.

*Section 13B—Traits of a Healthy Team*

**13.2. Introduction.**

As leaders, we must develop effective teams to accomplish the mission. While building effective teams, we must cultivate a healthy team spirit. The spirit in which a team operates influences every stage of team development and can ultimately determine whether mission goals are met. A healthy team spirit is the engine that runs high performance teams. Five critical attributes are present in all healthy teams: trust, ethical behavior, critical judgment, sharing, and cooperation. While each is essential in building a healthy team spirit, trust is the core of all healthy team interaction.

**13.3. Trust:**

13.3.1. Trust is essential in forming any good relationship; teamwork requires good relationships with a high degree of trust. Team members must share mutual confidence in the integrity and ability of teammates. They also need to feel comfortable enough to take risks, think outside the box, and share their thoughts and ideas without fear of being shut down or discounted. Freedom to communicate openly, honestly, and directly within the group is the hallmark of a trust-based team. Individuals must understand the importance of utilizing effective communication skills to develop the level of trust needed for the teams to grow. These communication skills include positive listening habits such as maintaining good eye contact, recalling essential information, allowing individuals to speak freely with minimal to no interruptions, as well as responding in the appropriate manner. In her book *"Teams at Work,"* author, organizational consultant, and Institute for Planning and Development founder Dr. Suzanne Zoglio wrote "Nothing reduces trust in a group faster than members saying one thing within the group and something else outside the group. When members are assertive enough to say what they need to say directly to the appropriate people and to refrain from talking behind each other's backs, trust is enhanced."

13.3.2. Team members may respond to other team members they do not trust by alienating them, ignoring their inputs, and withholding vital information. Trust is important in creating a healthy team because information needs to be shared and accepted in good faith. Feedback must also be exchanged between members in an open and sincere manner without fear of harsh criticism. Without trust, a team's efforts can be sabotaged and progress brought to a grinding halt. Leaders can promote a trusting atmosphere by being trustworthy and by trusting their workers. Additionally, by valuing individual differences and encouraging open and honest communication, leaders empower their teams to solve problems innovatively through a shared sense of collaboration that is free of self-preservation and one's own personal interest.

13.3.3. While there are many strategies that can be utilized for building trust within a team, leaders should focus their efforts on leading by example and developing a trusting relationship within the team; communicate openly and honestly; know team members and establish a good rapport with team members; discourage cliques or divisions within the team; and finally, discuss trust issues with the team. Remember, trust is earned and can be lost.

**13.4. Ethical Behavior.**

We lose trust in people because of behaviors that reduce our respect for them. Such behaviors are usually unethical and kill the spirit of the team. Ethical behaviors, on the other hand, conform to accepted principles of right and wrong that govern our profession. Team members who exhibit honesty, integrity, and concern for doing what is right behave ethically. In his book *"Essentials of Management,"* author and Professor of Management, College of Business at Rochester Institute of Technology, Andrew J. DuBrin said "To a strong team player, getting the group task accomplished is more important than receiving individual recognition." He also outlined the underlying reasons as to why unethical behavior arises in the team. The primary cause can be closely contributed to one's "values".

13.4.1. Ethics and values operate as a synchronous unit and is often driven by individual personal interests within the team. Teams will often experience turmoil when self-interest or greed enters the team; unconscious biases may lead to stereotypes and affect the judgement of the team; and the likelihood that a team may rationalize or make unethical decisions to complete the task or reach their goal. When teams operate with high standards and moral values, they increase trust and therefore work cohesively.

## 13.5. Sharing Information:

13.5.1. If teams are to succeed, they must openly share information inside and outside the group. This sharing of information involves both active listening and talking. According to Professor DuBrin, "Information sharing help other team members do their job well and also communicates concern for their welfare." Leaders' best demonstrate concern for the welfare of other team members when they actively listen. "The active listener strives to grasp both the facts and feelings behind what is being said," Professor DuBrin added. Active listening and information sharing encourage positive, open, and sincere communication among team members.

13.5.2. Teams must communicate. Team members need to safely assert themselves and share their ideas. Teams that don't allow honest, open sharing quickly lose their effectiveness. As a result, some team members may purposely withhold vital information or disengage from the team. This may cause confusion, frustration, and the inability to complete tasks within teams. While sharing information between team members is essential in producing effective, well-thought-out plans. Also essential is for the leader to share information with team members. When leaders hold on to information, they can create an inaccurate, incomplete, or totally wrong picture of the expected outcome to team members. Information sharing yields better results. Leaders can increase team success by giving members complete access to all necessary data, discouraging the discounting of ideas and feelings, and encouraging the practice of active listening and valuing individual differences.

## 13.6. Critical Judgment.

When we share information, someone is bound to criticize our ideas. For a team to be effective, constructive criticism should be accepted and encouraged. Professor DuBrin said, "A high performance team demands sincere and tactful criticism among members. The willingness to accept constructive criticism increases self-awareness and improves team effectiveness." Critical judgment enables teams to accept intra-group feedback (criticism) and outside evaluations, necessary to examine processes and practices. By using critical feedback, teams can redirect their focus and energy, and correct problems quickly rather than letting them intensify.

13.6.1. Giving constructive criticism occurs when teams focus on the problem or behavior and not necessarily personal opinions; when the negative feedback is given at the appropriate time and is not introduced during a later stage of team development; and lastly when the individual is given an opportunity to observe and self-correct the problem. Critical judgment is essential to ensure teams consistently focus in the right direction.

## 13.7. Cooperation:

13.7.1. Cooperation is critical if teams are to combine diverse backgrounds, skills, and approaches to meet the challenges, customer requirements, and mission changes. Cooperation yields synergistic results and reduces the time it takes to reach a desired outcome. Dr. Zoglio said, "At work there are so few solo opportunities; most challenges require the cooperation of many people. Team members must rely on each other to follow through on assignments, produce quality results, share creative ideas, and contribute to a pleasant work environment." Leaders who encourage cooperation show team members that others have very important contributions to the goals of the unit. Team members may also come to understand how dependent they are on one another in reaching mission objectives.

13.7.2. Dr. Zoglio further states that successful teams manage differences through win/win negotiating and reach decisions by consensus, rather than voting. Successful teams have few turf wars, little competitiveness, and an ability to forgive and forget. Cooperation breeds shared ownership for performance results, and achieving objectives increases team pride and a healthy team spirit. Conversely, competition hinders the cooperative process, as some team members attempt to outshine others to gain extra attention. Such "all-starring" leads to in-fighting, making the team less productive. "All-starring" may also be evidence of a power struggle. To reduce power-play behavior, leaders should reemphasize each team member's specific roles and responsibilities, which eliminates potential barriers to cooperation.

## 13.8. Healthy Team Spirit Summary.

Cultivating a healthy team spirit requires trust, ethical behavior, critical judgment, sharing, and cooperation. Trust is at the heart of any healthy team interaction. Team members must feel comfortable with, and confident in, one another to be able to fully participate and share their ideas and feelings. Positive group member behaviors establish the climate of trust needed to develop a healthy team spirit. Ethical behavior requires members do what is legally, morally, and professionally right for one another and the organization. Such behavior is essential to the communication a team needs to accomplish its goals. Leaders must establish a healthy team spirit to drive performance and develop effective teams to accomplish the mission.

*Section 13C—Managing Resources Other Than Personnel*

**13.9. Resource Management System:**

13.9.1. **Resource Management System Defined.**

Resource management system does not refer to a single system. Instead, the Air Force resource management system involves various systems focusing on outputs and resources used, managers effectively using resources, measuring actual performance compared to planned performance, and using financial plans and accounting to enhance management controls at each organizational level. The resource management system provides a way to establish priorities, choose policies, and act to get the desired results and required resources at an acceptable cost. Resource management system elements include the execution plan, management and accounting systems, participatory and committee management, resource management teams, and resource management training.

13.9.2. **Resource Management System Duties.**

Air Force managers oversee activities that cost money; however, in terms of resources, resource management system duties refer to the stewardship of money, manpower, and equipment. Being an effective steward involves more than legal accountability. Headquarters, United States Air Force and major commands make decisions about using resources. Although base-level resource managers do not control initial allocation of all their resources, they must effectively manage these resources.

13.9.2.1. **Commanders.** Financial management is inherent to command. Commanders review, validate, and balance the execution plan to ensure successful financial management. They must actively review financial programs for each work center (responsibility center) that reports to them and improve resource management by inquiring about program conditions, reviewing causes, weighing alternatives, and directing action. They must also ensure resource management system success by allocating sufficient resources to resource management system training and resource management team efforts.

13.9.2.2. **Comptrollers.** Comptrollers support the organization's mission and the Air Force by providing sound financial management and advice to the commander and staff. They promote responsible and proper financial management to ensure economical and efficient use of resources consistent with statutory and regulatory requirements. They apply policies and procedures that enable the organization to carry out accounting, budget, and cost functions.

13.9.2.3. **Responsibility Center Managers.** Responsibility center managers plan, direct, and coordinate subordinate organizations' activities. They analyze subordinate organizational plans, identify imbalances in resource distribution, analyze alternative actions, and balance programs.

13.9.2.4. **Cost Center Managers.** The cost center is the basic production flight or work center. The cost center manager regulates the consumption of work hours, supplies, equipment, and services to do the tasks within their cost center. Cost center managers shift resources to or from various production tasks within the cost center to ensure the proper mix or to provide the emphasis required.

13.9.2.5. **Resource Advisors.** Resource advisors monitor and help prepare resource estimates. They help develop obligations and expense fund targets, monitor the use of resources in daily operations compared to projected consumption levels, and serve as the primary point of contacts on resource management matters pertaining to their responsibility center. Resource advisors are appointed in writing by the responsibility center manager.

13.9.3. **The Financial Management Board.**

Established by the senior or host commander at each base, the financial management board determines program priorities and ensures effective allocation of resources. The financial management board reviews and approves or disapproves recommendations made by the financial working group to ensure balanced, valid financial programs and to consider all known or anticipated requirements.

13.9.4. **The Financial Working Group.**

Composed of both line and staff resource advisors and responsibility center managers, the financial working group manages commodities and resources integral to the operating activities of the base or unit. The financial working group develops requirements and revisions for the base or unit execution plan, reviews all appropriated fund execution plans, and makes recommendations to the financial management board for final approval. Additionally, the financial working group presents recommendations to the financial management board for unfunded requirement prioritization and fund target adjustments between responsibility centers, and base-level budgetary guidance. The financial working group provides technical guidance to base activities on using their primary responsibility resources.

## 13.10. Effective Use of Government Property:

### 13.10.1. Supply Discipline.

Air Force members must have a supply discipline to conserve, protect, and maintain available government supplies, equipment, and real property for operational requirements. The Air Force's mission makes it imperative that all military and civilian personnel operate and maintain government systems, equipment, supplies, and real property in the best possible condition, in constant readiness, and in the absolute minimum quantity necessary to accomplish assigned tasks. Commanders and supervisors at all levels are responsible for prudent management, control, storage, and cost-effective use of government property under their control.

### 13.10.2. Roles.

Commanders, subordinates, supervisors, and individuals must:

13.10.2.1. Accurately maintain property records to reflect a current inventory and condition of property.

13.10.2.2. Ensure personnel carefully and economically use and safeguard property.

13.10.2.3. Provide adequate security, protection, and storage for property.

13.10.2.4. Make recommendations for preventing fraud, waste, and abuse.

### 13.10.3. Custodial Management of Public Property.

A property custodian is any person designated by the organization commander or chief of staff agency responsible for government property in his or her possession. A custodian must plan and forecast requirements to meet mission goals, prepare and forward materiel requests to the proper agency, sign custody receipts or listings for property charged to his or her organization, report losses or irregularities relating to property to his or her immediate commanders or accountable officers, and take action to reconcile and correct property records. A custodian may be held liable for the loss, destruction, or damage of any property or resources under his or her control.

## 13.11. Financial Management:

### 13.11.1. Use of Resources.

Air Force commanders and supervisors are responsible for the efficient and economical use of all resources in their organizations. Commanders and supervisors directly influence the budgeting, allocation, composition, and distribution of these resources. It should be noted that every Air Force member is directly involved in and responsible for managing resources.

### 13.11.2. Cost-free Resources.

In the following types of instances, everyone has a principal responsibility to ensure resources are used in the most cost-effective manner. Keep in mind, all Air Force resources, at one time or another, had some kind of cost charged to get into the Department of Defense inventory. Some resources may appear to be cost-free assets because Airmen:

13.11.2.1. May not either control the determination or allocation of these resources (real property, weapon systems, and manpower).

13.11.2.2. May not have the authority to change the mix of the total resources allocated.

### 13.11.3. The Operating Budget.

The operating budget covers costs associated with the operation of all Air Force organizations. The approval by higher headquarters gives obligation authority to accomplish the mission. The budget program operates on a fiscal year basis (fiscal year represents the period beginning the first day of October and ending the last day of the following September [1 October through 30 September].)

## 13.12. Fraud, Waste, and Abuse:

### 13.12.1. Fraud, Waste, and Abuse Defined.

The Air Force loses millions of dollars in money and resources every year due to individuals abusing the system, wasting precious resources, and committing acts of fraud. Fraud, waste and abuse is:

13.12.1.1. Fraud. Any intentional deception designed to unlawfully deprive the Air Force of something of value or to secure from the Air Force for an individual a benefit, privilege, allowance, or consideration to which he or she is not entitled. Such practices include, but are not limited to:

13.12.1.1.1. Offering, paying, accepting bribes or gratuities, or evading or corrupting inspectors or other officials.

13.12.1.1.2. Making false statements, submitting false claims, or using false weights or measures.

13.12.1.1.3. Using deceit, either by suppressing the truth or misrepresenting material facts, or deprive the Air Force of something of value.

13.12.1.1.4. Adulterating or substituting materials and falsifying records and books of accounts.

13.12.1.1.5. Conspiring to carry out any of the actions in paragraphs 13.12.1.1.1 through 13.12.1.1.4.

13.12.1.1.6. Engaging in conflict of interest cases, criminal irregularities, and the unauthorized disclosure of official information relating to procurement and disposal matters. **Note:** For purposes of this handbook, the definition can include any theft or diversion of resources for personal or commercial gain.

13.12.1.2. **Waste.** The extravagant, careless, or needless expenditure of Air Force funds or the consumption of Air Force property that results from deficient practices, systems controls, or decisions is waste. Waste also includes improper practices not involving prosecutable fraud. **Note:** Consider wartime and emergency operations when explaining possible waste. For example, legitimate stockpiles and reserves for wartime needs, which may appear redundant and costly, are not considered waste.

13.12.1.3. **Abuse.** The intentionally wrongful or improper use of Air Force resources is abuse. Examples include misuse of rank, position, or authority that causes the loss or misuse of resources such as tools, vehicles, computers, or copy machines.

13.12.2. **Preventing Fraud, Waste and Abuse.**

Preventing fraud, waste and abuse is of primary concern. Detection and prosecution serve to deter fraudulent, wasteful, or abusive practices; however, the key element of the program is to prevent the loss of resources. The Secretary of the Air Force, Inspector General, provides policy guidance, develops procedures, and establishes and evaluates the Air Force complaints and fraud, waste and abuse programs. In turn, inspector generals at every level are responsible for establishing and directing the Air Force complaints and fraud, waste and abuse programs. Air Force personnel have a duty to promptly report fraud, waste and abuse to an appropriate supervisor or commander, to an Inspector General or other appropriate inspector, or through an established grievance channel. Fraud, waste and abuse complaints may be reported to the Air Force Audit Agency, the Air Force Office of Special Investigations, security forces, or other proper authorities. Further, all military and civilian members must promptly advise the Air Force Office of Special Investigations of suspected criminal misconduct or fraud. The Air Force Office of Special Investigations investigates criminal allegations.

13.12.3. **Fraud, Waste and Abuse Complaints:**

13.12.3.1. **Resolution.** As with personal complaints, Air Force members should try resolving fraud, waste and abuse issues at the lowest possible level using command channels before addressing them to a higher level or the Inspector General. Individuals may submit:

13.12.3.1.1. Fraud, waste and abuse disclosures by memorandum, in person, or by fraud, waste and abuse hotlines.

13.12.3.1.2. Complaints anonymously.

**Note:** Making a disclosure or complaint requires factual, unbiased, and specific information. Individuals must understand they are submitting official statements within Air Force channels. Therefore, they remain subject to punitive action (or adverse administrative action) for knowingly making false statements and for submitting other unlawful communications. Information in a disclosure or complaint to an Inspector General is protected.

13.12.3.2. **Complainant Privacy.** The complainant's privacy is safeguarded to the maximum extent practicable to encourage voluntary cooperation and promote a climate of openness in identifying issues requiring leadership intervention. The Inspector General has the responsibility to safeguard the personal identity and complaints of individuals seeking assistance or participating in an Inspector General process such as an investigation. While this does not mean the communications made to an Inspector General are privileged or confidential, it does mean that disclosure of those communications (and the identity of the communicant) is strictly limited to an official need-to-know basis.

13.12.3.3. **Disclosure.** This information is not disclosed unless required by law or regulation, when necessary to take adverse action against a subject, with the approval of the Secretary of the Air Force, Inspector General.

13.12.3.4. **Summary of the Results.** Individuals making a complaint may request a summary of the results from the office to which the complaint was made. However, witnesses (including complainants and subjects) do not have unrestricted access to reports, complainants, and subjects, or any other case file information by virtue of their status as a witness. They have access to Inspector General records as provided for by the Freedom of Information Act and Privacy Act.

13.12.3.5. **Whistleblower Rights.** Whistleblower witnesses have additional rights. The nature of the allegation and findings will determine what information is releasable. All information released is according to Freedom of Information Act and Privacy Act. "Third-party" complainants are not entitled to a response regarding alleged wrongs not directly affecting them unless authorized to receive via a Freedom of Information Act or a Privacy Act release.

13.12.3.6. **Inspector General Channels.** If the Inspector General receives a complaint or disclosure more appropriate for another channel may be referred to that channel by the receiving Inspector General. When Inspectors General refer complaints to command or other more appropriate resolution channels, Inspectors General notify complainants of the referral, except for anonymous complainants.

**13.13. Air Force Environmental Commitment.**

*Leadership at all levels and across all mission operations and support organizations must use the Air Force Environmental Management System's approach to comply with environmental laws, regulations and policy, reduce risks to the mission, and continuously improve environmental management performance. Operationalizing environmental management means ensuring that environmental quality is a consideration by Airmen in all activities the Air Force undertakes.*

General Carrol H. Chandler                           Terry A. Yonkers
Vice Chief of Staff                                  Assistant Secretary, Installations, Environment and Logistics

13.13.1. **Air Force Policy.**

The United States Air Force is a leader and devoted guardian of the environment. As trustee to over 8 million acres of natural habitat, the Air Force takes considerable measures to defend and enhance America's rich natural resources and cultural heritage. Over the last 20 years, the Air Force has followed a compliance-based approach to environmental management resulting in an unparalleled record of responsiveness to regulation, community interests, and ecological needs. Yet, to meet current and future mission requirements, the Air Force environmental program must ensure environmental resources, such as air, land, and water, are available to meet operational needs. This approach allows the Air Force to *sustain, restore, and modernize* their environmental resources, or "natural infrastructure," in full compliance and support of military readiness challenges.

13.13.2. **Department of Defense and Air Force Programs.** Per Executive Order 13693, *Planning for Federal Sustainability in the Next Decade,* the Department of Defense and Air Force established and maintained an environmental management system. In accordance with Executive Order 13693, the Air Force will continue to implement and maintain environmental management system to achieve the performance necessary to sustain compliance, reduce risk, and continuously improve to achieve sustainability goals. AFI 32-7001, *Environmental Management,* implements the environmental management system framework and provides guidance and procedures applicable to all Air Force installations within the United States to include the territories, and in foreign countries. See Figure 13.1 for the environmental management system vision, programs, and guidance. The environmental management system sustains and enhances mission capability by:

13.13.2.1. Maintaining compliance with all applicable environmental laws, regulations, and policy requirements. Typically installations will meet environmental Code of Federal Regulations promulgated by the Environmental Protection Agency and implemented by the States.

13.13.2.2. Reducing compliance burden by implementing pollution prevention solutions that reduce the quantity and impact of pollutants.

13.13.2.3. Sustaining natural, cultural, built, and human resources.

13.13.2.4. Incorporating environmental management system and environmental, safety, and occupational health considerations into installation Air Force Smart Operations 21 lean events to improve mission capacity and prevent waste.

13.13.2.5. Providing community outreach to increase awareness of environmental issues.

13.13.2.6. Incorporating environmental management system elements into specific operations of appropriate organizational levels and installations.

13.13.2.7. Meeting or exceeding current Office of Management and Budget, Department of Defense, and Air Force performance measures.

Figure 13.1. Environmental Management System Vision, Programs, and Guidance.

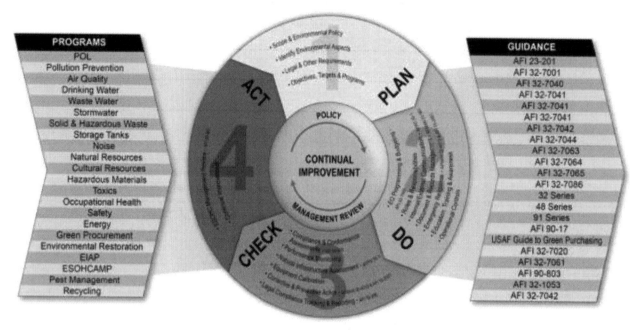

### 13.13.3. Air Force Planning.

The Air Force environmental management system will integrate environmental impact analysis, operational risk management, and prevention of pollution methodologies in order to institute sustainable practices across the Air Force mission and reduce both environmental risk and the Air Force's environmental footprint, and accommodate new mission as required. Key actions for installation/major command organizations include:

13.13.3.1. Documenting aspects and impacts for the installation's activities, products, and services. Aspects are elements of the activities, products, and services that can interact with the environment and produce either a negative or positive environmental impact.

13.13.3.2. For aspects classified as significant, ensure actions to formally manage as part of the environmental management system, including setting objectives and targets and establishing action plans. This helps identify the investment to resource.

13.13.3.3. The environmental programming and budgeting process provides the necessary resources to achieve the goals and objectives of the Air Force strategic plan, the organizational-level, multi-site or installation environmental management system, or other major program objectives. Environmental requirements are entered into Air Force-approved programming tools/software following Civil Engineering operations and maintenance programming guides and supplemental budgeting policy and guidance.

### 13.13.4. Air Force Operational Controls/Performance Monitoring.

Installations shall ensure adequate operational controls are in place to control, mitigate, or prevent negative environmental impacts. Operational controls may be physical (e.g., barrier, secondary containment), engineering (e.g., alarm system), or administrative (e.g., standard operating procedure, management plan, checklist).

13.13.4.1. Develop and implement procedures to prevent non-compliance, adverse environmental impacts, and/or to achieve stated objectives and targets or performance measures.

13.13.4.2. Implement environmental monitoring and performance measures to ensure an environmental self-assessment process to maintain compliance and improve business processes.

13.13.4.3. Ensure self-assessment of all environmental aspects of recurring business processes and readiness for inspections under the commanders' self-inspection and Air Force Inspector General's Unit Effectiveness Inspection Programs, in accordance with AFI 90-201, *The Air Force Inspection System*.

*Section 13D—Planning, Programming, Budgeting, and Execution*

### 13.14. Planning, Programming, Budgeting, and Execution Philosophy.

The ultimate objective of the planning, programming, budgeting, and execution process is to provide the best mix of forces, equipment, manpower, and support attainable within fiscal constraints according to Department of Defense Directive 7045.14, *The Planning, Programming, Budgeting and Execution (PPBE) Process*. The goal of the planning, programming, budgeting, and execution process is to achieve the defense objectives established by the President and the Secretary of Defense in the strategic planning and joint planning guidance. The Air Force uses a unique process for implementing the planning, programming, budgeting, and execution—the Air Force corporate structure. This structure increases management effectiveness by applying judgment and experience to programs, resource limitations, and other program adjustments. This enables senior leadership to assess alternative ways to achieve the planning, programming, budgeting, and execution objective. The Air Force develops their program to achieve defense objectives established by the President and the Secretary of Defense as well as internal Air Force strategic planning objectives. The formulation of the Air Force budget is a complicated and time-consuming endeavor. Planning, programming, budgeting, and execution is a shared process within the Air Force with significant responsibility delegated to the Director of Programs, Deputy Chief of Staff for Plans and Programs (AF/A8P), and the Deputy Assistant Secretary for Budget, Office of the Assistant Secretary of the Air Force for Financial Management and Comptroller (SAF/FMB).

### 13.15. Planning, Programming, Budgeting, and Execution Process.

The planning, programming, budgeting, and execution process is the Department of Defense's resource allocation system. This process has a framework that decides on future capabilities and provides an opportunity to reexamine prior decisions in light of evolving threats, economic conditions, and security concerns. Finally, planning, programming, budgeting, and execution is an iterative process consisting of four interrelated and overlapping phases: planning, programming, budgeting, and execution.

#### 13.15.1. Planning.

The Air Force translates top-down guidance into meaningful plans and requirements for which a program for the future year's defense program can be developed. Planning defines and examines alternative strategies and analyzes external conditions and trends. Planning provides the means to anticipate changes and understand the long-term implications of near-term choices and decisions. Streamlined planning and assessment documents help prioritize objectives, assess strategies, and provide the link between planning and programming. Within the concept of planning, programming, budgeting, and execution, planning also provides a program objective against which the Air Force can measure program execution success.

#### 13.15.2. Programming.

Through the programming processes, the Air Force and other military department's link planned requirements with the resources needed to provide them. Inevitably, this will involve tradeoffs beyond those agreed to in the planning process. By programming, the Air Force matches available resources (fiscal, manpower, and materiel) against validated requirements to achieve the strategic plan and submit program proposals. Planning policies and guidance are addressed and initial program costs are established. The key objective of programming is to develop a balanced, capabilities-based Air Force program in the form of the Air Force program objective memorandum. In addition, through the programming processes, the Air Force defends the program objective memorandum during program review and budget review and adjusts the program as a result of the Office of the Secretary of Defense reviews and changing national and international situations.

#### 13.15.3. Budgeting.

The budgeting phase of planning, programming, budgeting, and execution occurs concurrently with the programming phase. Each Department of Defense component submits a proposed budget estimate simultaneously with a program objective memorandum. The budgeting phase (formulation and justification) provides a platform for a detailed review of a program's pricing, phasing, and overall capability to be executed on time and within budget. The budgeting process principally addresses the years to be justified in the President's budget. Three things happen in the preparation of the budget estimate submission. First, Air Force budget analysts identify situations where the program has put Air Force resources at risk of Office of the Secretary of Defense or Congressional reduction. Second, the comptroller applies the latest inflation figures, flying hour and manpower rates, etc. Third, the program is put into the Office of the Secretary of Defense budget format and budget justification documentation is prepared. Once these steps are complete, the final position is called the program objective memorandum/budget estimate submission or program budget review. The budgeting phase continues with the program budget review submission and fact-of-life changes via notification document in the off-year. Secretary of the Air Force for financial management and comptroller is the Air Force lead for budget and budget execution.

13.15.4. **Budget Execution.**

Budget execution focuses on running the Air Force day to day. Execution is carried out at the Headquarters Air Force, field operating agency, major command, primary support unit, wing, and unit level. The Air Force major commands (including the Headquarters Air Force) are allocated their share of obligation authority to execute their missions in accordance to approved integrated priority lists for those programs that are centrally managed. Because the budget being executed in any given year was actually compiled over a year earlier, you should logically assume some assumptions on which the budget was based will have changed. Because change is anticipated, Congress allows some flexibility within the operating budgets to move resources without requiring their permission but installations are expected to execute to the integrated priority list for centrally managed programs. One key part of budget execution is the major command's operations and maintenance operation plan. Air Force program execution is reviewed during major command budget execution reviews in February, April (concurrent with the internal Air Force midyear review), and July.

## 13.16. Planning, Programming, Budgeting, and Execution Summary.

Every leader contributes to the planning, programming, budgeting, and execution process. Within this system, leaders help establish and forecast a budget to ensure sufficient funds are available to accomplish the mission. Thoughtful and accurate estimates on the local level are extremely important in reflecting the overall Air Force needs. Wise day-to-day resource management is essential to having an effective planning, programming, budgeting, and execution process.

*Section 13E—Manpower Management and Competitive Sourcing*

## 13.17. Manpower Resources.

Manpower is a constrained resource that comprises a large portion of the Air Force Budget. All missions and programs compete for limited authorized military and civilian end-strength, established grade distributions, and must comply with other guidelines as directed by Congress. Manpower must be programmed in accordance with validated manpower requirements, and within fiscal limits and acceptable risk identified in defense planning and programming guidance.

## 13.18. Chain of Responsibilities.

The Directorate of Manpower, Organization and Resources, Program Development Division (Headquarters Air Force/A1MP) allocates programmed manpower resources by command identifier, program element code, resource identification code, and country State code to the commands directing implementation of approved programs. Major commands and equivalents translate these manpower resources into manpower authorizations by updating the unit manpower document. The installation manpower and organization flight is the liaison between installation agencies and the major command A1M staff for all manpower and organization issues.

## 13.19. Manpower Resource Levels:

13.19.1. **Changing Manpower Allocations.**

Command-specific military and civilian manpower requirements must be validated by the major command A1M and approved by Headquarters Air Force A1M before they can be used in the programming and resourcing process. Before manpower allocations can be changed, the requesting organization must give reasons for the requested change. The major command must propose specific tradeoffs if the initiative requires an increase in military or civilian manpower.

13.19.2. **Accommodating Temporary Manpower Requirements.**

End-strength will not be programmed to accommodate cyclical or temporary requirements. Instead major commands and equivalents should use other means to accomplish their short term mission or surge workload to include: (1) use available funds and command civilian employment plans to employ civilians; (2) utilize overtime, temporary full-time, part-time, or over-hire of civilian personnel; (3) seek support from the Air Reserve Component via Military Pay Appropriation funds; (4) utilize temporary duty military and civilian personnel; and (5) seek contract service.

## 13.20. Requirements Determination:

13.20.1. **General Concept.**

Manpower and organization flight personnel assist Air Force commanders and functional managers at all levels in mission accomplishment by objectively quantifying manpower requirements for the distribution of Air Force manpower resources. Key services of this competency include peacetime manpower standards development, wartime manpower requirements, and commercial services management actions (for example, public-private competition, in-sourcing, and business process reengineering). The foundation of any manpower requirements determination effort is the application of Continuous Process Improvement methodologies to a function's processes to make process improvements.

**13.20.2. Determining Manpower Requirements:**

13.20.2.1. The Air Force manpower requirements determination process systematically identifies minimum-essential manpower required for the most effective and economical accomplishment of approved missions and functions within organizational and resource constraints. To accomplish this, Headquarters Air Force functional managers work with Headquarters Air Force A1M to determine the appropriate manpower management tool consistent with resources needed to develop the manpower standard; the required mix of military, civilian, and/or contract services; and the required military category (officer or enlisted) and grade.

13.20.2.2. Determining the correct amount of military manpower required to meet the Air Force's most stringent wartime missions is key to achieving the National Military Strategy and the Defense Planning Guidance. The Defense Planning Guidance defines the planning scenarios used to size and shape the Total Force. These include the amount of military needed for deployment and fight in-place missions for the given scenario. Manpower requirements are sized for the most demanding phase of the scenario construct, including all rotational forces needed for prolonged conflicts. These scenarios drive force structure and manpower military mix budgeting decisions.

**13.20.3. Organization:**

13.20.3.1. The Air Force must be organized to best use available resources. This requires simple, streamlined structures designed for seamless transition from peace to war. The principal characteristics desired in Air Force organizations include mission orientation, unambiguous command, decentralization, agility, flexibility, simplicity, and standardization.

13.20.3.2. Manpower standards are established to ensure work center operations are efficient and standardized to create the most efficient organization. The ultimate goal of organizational performance is mission accomplishment. Resource requirements reflected in a manpower standard should be based on organization and process design, which most effectively and efficiently accomplishes the mission. Improving mission effectiveness while maintaining or improving efficiency should be the goal of any modification to a function's current organizational or process design. Efficiency does not necessarily mean decreasing resources but rather improving the return on the resources used.

**13.20.4. Performance Improvement.**

Improving performance requires both planning and execution. For organizational change effort effectiveness, they generally must include some redesign and/or coordination on five fronts. These fronts are related organizational areas to consider. A change on one front may require actions or changes on another. For example, changing a process may also require some training or retraining (people front); the process improvement may affect how technology is used (technology front); or the process design may require updates to regulations (policy, legislation, regulation front). The five fronts (see figure 13.2) are:

13.20.4.1. **Organization and People.** Human resources are the key to future viability and organizational growth in a continuously learning environment. Although processes and other front factors may change, focus should remain on providing workers with appropriate knowledge, skills, experiences, and tools. This will empower them to learn and act, which will tie their rewards to the organization's values and measures.

13.20.4.2. **Technology.** Technology is a crucial enabling factor that allows compression of cycles, lead time, distance, and broader access to information and knowledge assets. Technology also eliminates barriers between customers and suppliers.

13.20.4.3. **Policies, Legislation, and Regulations.** Changing existing policies, regulations, and legislation may be required for new processes.

13.20.4.4. **Physical Infrastructure.** The physical facilities, equipment, and tools should be designed to support and maximize changes in workflow, information technology, and human resources.

13.20.4.5. **Process.** The flow of work and information into, and throughout the organization must be redesigned using standard Continuous Process Improvement methodologies like Business Process Engineering, Lean, Six Sigma, and Theory of Constraints.

**Figure 13.2. Performance Improvement Fronts**

- Reduce the number of distinct departments or groups
- Organize into teams and develop multi-skilled workers
- Provide appropriate incentives for employees
- Empower individuals and measure performance in relation to the process

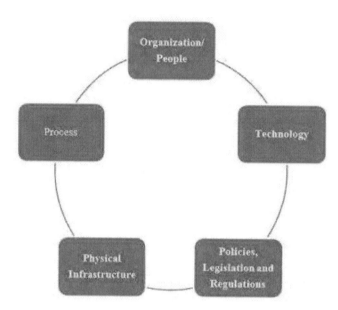

- Eliminate bottlenecks
- Move work in a continuous flow
- Organize work in parallel
- Move activities closer to the customer

- Improve quality and timeliness of information
- Streamline process flow
- Empower knowledgeable workers
- Enable new geographic arrangements of work tasks
- Facilitate communication with customers and suppliers

- Modify physical facilities to facilitate material movements
- Match equipment capabilities to change in workflow
- Improve tools and work areas to fit skills and responsibilities

- Change policies to accommodate new technology and skills
- Use information to influence regulations and legislation
- Alter rules that govern relationships with other entities

## 13.21. Unit Manpower Document.

The unit manning document, used to help manage manpower resources, is a computer product that lists unit funded and unfunded manpower requirements, and contains many data elements that identify the unique position attributes. These attributes include position number, Air Force specialty code, functional account code, office symbol code, grade, personnel accounting symbol, reason code, etc. The unit manning document is the primary document that reflects the manpower required to accomplish the unit mission. The installation manpower and organization office will periodically, or upon request, supply a unit with an updated unit manning document. Supervisors should routinely check the unit manning document for accuracy and use it to track their authorized manpower strength. Headquarters Air Force A1M and the Air Force Manpower Analysis Agency often produce reports based on unit manning document data; continuous review of coding is critical for proper position management. See Figure 13.3.

## 13.22. Manpower Management for Senior Leaders:

### 13.22.1. Keeping Unit Manpower Documents Current.

The unit manpower document displays current and projected requirements and can be configured to display desired fields in various formats. Unit commanders and supervisors may request a unit manpower document from the installation manpower and organization flight on an as-needed basis. Typically, the unit manpower point of contact serves as the liaison between the unit and manpower and organization flight; thus, work center supervisors should coordinate any unit manpower document changes, etc., with their unit manpower point of contact.

**Figure 13.3. Unit Manpower Document.**

| Pos Number | CID | CID Title | MNT Title | PAS | Unit Long Name | Base | RIC | OSC | OSC Title | GRD | AFSC | AFSC Title | OFF | ENL | CIV | Total |
|---|---|---|---|---|---|---|---|---|---|---|---|---|---|---|---|---|
| 0001269909 | 09 | AF PERSONNEL CTR | FUNDED | FFF2 | 1 MANPOWER RQMNTS SQUADRON | JBSA RANDOLPH | 0160 | CC | COMMANDER | GS-06 | 3A171 | ADMINISTRATION, CRAFTSMAN | | | 1 | 1 |
| 0001272909 | 09 | AF PERSONNEL CTR | FUNDED | FFF2 | 1 MANPOWER RQMNTS SQUADRON | JBSA RANDOLPH | 0004 | CC | COMMANDER | LTCOL | 038P73 | COMMANDER, PERSONNEL | 1 | | | 1 |
| 0001295609 | 09 | AF PERSONNEL CTR | FUNDED | FFF2 | 1 MANPOWER RQMNTS SQUADRON | JBSA RANDOLPH | 0160 | CC | COMMANDER | GS-13 | 038P3 | PERSONNEL | | | 1 | 1 |
| 0001269009 | 09 | AF PERSONNEL CTR | FUNDED | FFF2 | 1 MANPOWER RQMNTS SQUADRON | JBSA RANDOLPH | 0104 | MRA | MANPOWER REQUIREMENTS FLIGHT A | MSGT | 3S373 | MANPOWER CRAFTSMAN | | 1 | | 1 |
| 0001269109 | 09 | AF PERSONNEL CTR | FUNDED | FFF2 | 1 MANPOWER RQMNTS SQUADRON | JBSA RANDOLPH | 0104 | MRA | MANPOWER REQUIREMENTS FLIGHT A | SSGT | 3S353 | MANPOWER JOURNEYMAN | | 1 | | 1 |
| 0001269509 | 09 | AF PERSONNEL CTR | FUNDED | FFF2 | 1 MANPOWER RQMNTS SQUADRON | JBSA RANDOLPH | 0160 | MRA | MANPOWER REQUIREMENTS FLIGHT A | GS-11 | 3S393 | MANPOWER SUPERINTENDENT | | | 1 | 1 |
| 0001270509 | 09 | AF PERSONNEL CTR | FUNDED | FFF2 | 1 MANPOWER RQMNTS SQUADRON | JBSA RANDOLPH | 0160 | MRA | MANPOWER REQUIREMENTS FLIGHT A | GS-11 | 3S393 | MANPOWER SUPERINTENDENT | | | 1 | 1 |
| 0001271209 | 09 | AF PERSONNEL CTR | FUNDED | FFF2 | 1 MANPOWER RQMNTS SQUADRON | JBSA RANDOLPH | 0104 | MRA | MANPOWER REQUIREMENTS FLIGHT A | TSGT | 3S373 | MANPOWER CRAFTSMAN | | 1 | | 1 |
| 0001271409 | 09 | AF PERSONNEL CTR | FUNDED | FFF2 | 1 MANPOWER RQMNTS SQUADRON | JBSA RANDOLPH | 0004 | MRA | MANPOWER REQUIREMENTS FLIGHT A | LT | 038P3 | PERSONNEL | 1 | | | 1 |
| 0001271509 | 09 | AF PERSONNEL CTR | FUNDED | FFF2 | 1 MANPOWER RQMNTS SQUADRON | JBSA RANDOLPH | 0104 | MRA | MANPOWER REQUIREMENTS FLIGHT A | MSGT | 3S373 | MANPOWER CRAFTSMAN | | 1 | | 1 |
| 0001272309 | 09 | AF PERSONNEL CTR | FUNDED | FFF2 | 1 MANPOWER RQMNTS SQUADRON | JBSA RANDOLPH | 0160 | MRA | MANPOWER REQUIREMENTS FLIGHT A | GS-11 | 3S393 | MANPOWER SUPERINTENDENT | | | 1 | 1 |
| 0001272409 | 09 | AF PERSONNEL CTR | FUNDED | FFF2 | 1 MANPOWER RQMNTS SQUADRON | JBSA RANDOLPH | 0104 | MRA | MANPOWER REQUIREMENTS FLIGHT A | SSGT | 3S353 | MANPOWER JOURNEYMAN | | 1 | | 1 |
| 0001272509 | 09 | AF PERSONNEL CTR | FUNDED | FFF2 | 1 MANPOWER RQMNTS SQUADRON | JBSA RANDOLPH | 0160 | MRA | MANPOWER REQUIREMENTS FLIGHT A | SMSGT | 3S393 | MANPOWER SUPERINTENDENT | | 1 | | 1 |
| 0001272609 | 09 | AF PERSONNEL CTR | FUNDED | FFF2 | 1 MANPOWER RQMNTS SQUADRON | JBSA RANDOLPH | 0104 | MRA | MANPOWER REQUIREMENTS FLIGHT A | TSGT | 3S373 | MANPOWER CRAFTSMAN | | 1 | | 1 |
| 0001273009 | 09 | AF PERSONNEL CTR | FUNDED | FFF2 | 1 MANPOWER RQMNTS SQUADRON | JBSA RANDOLPH | 0004 | MRA | MANPOWER REQUIREMENTS FLIGHT A | CAPT | 038P3 | PERSONNEL | 1 | | | 1 |
| 0001273709 | 09 | AF PERSONNEL CTR | FUNDED | FFF2 | 1 MANPOWER RQMNTS SQUADRON | JBSA RANDOLPH | 0160 | MRA | MANPOWER REQUIREMENTS FLIGHT A | GS-12 | 038P3 | PERSONNEL | | | 1 | 1 |
| 0001273809 | 09 | AF PERSONNEL CTR | FUNDED | FFF2 | 1 MANPOWER RQMNTS SQUADRON | JBSA RANDOLPH | 0160 | MRA | MANPOWER REQUIREMENTS FLIGHT A | GS-12 | 038P4 | PERSONNEL, STAFF | | | 1 | 1 |
| 0001264709 | 09 | AF PERSONNEL CTR | FUNDED | FFF2 | 1 MANPOWER RQMNTS SQUADRON | JBSA RANDOLPH | 0160 | MRC | MANPOWER REQUIREMENTS FLIGHT C | GS-12 | 038P4 | PERSONNEL, STAFF | | | 1 | 1 |
| 0001269309 | 09 | AF PERSONNEL CTR | FUNDED | FFF2 | 1 MANPOWER RQMNTS SQUADRON | JBSA RANDOLPH | 0104 | MRC | MANPOWER REQUIREMENTS FLIGHT C | MSGT | 3S373 | MANPOWER CRAFTSMAN | | 1 | | 1 |
| 0001269409 | 09 | AF PERSONNEL CTR | FUNDED | FFF2 | 1 MANPOWER RQMNTS SQUADRON | JBSA RANDOLPH | 0104 | MRC | MANPOWER REQUIREMENTS FLIGHT C | TSGT | 3S373 | MANPOWER CRAFTSMAN | | 1 | | 1 |
| 0001270809 | 09 | AF PERSONNEL CTR | FUNDED | FFF2 | 1 MANPOWER RQMNTS SQUADRON | JBSA RANDOLPH | 0104 | MRC | MANPOWER REQUIREMENTS FLIGHT C | SSGT | 3S353 | MANPOWER JOURNEYMAN | | 1 | | 1 |
| 0001270909 | 09 | AF PERSONNEL CTR | FUNDED | FFF2 | 1 MANPOWER RQMNTS SQUADRON | JBSA RANDOLPH | 0104 | MRC | MANPOWER REQUIREMENTS FLIGHT C | SSGT | 3S353 | MANPOWER JOURNEYMAN | | 1 | | 1 |
| 0001271009 | 09 | AF PERSONNEL CTR | FUNDED | FFF2 | 1 MANPOWER RQMNTS SQUADRON | JBSA RANDOLPH | 0104 | MRC | MANPOWER REQUIREMENTS FLIGHT C | TSGT | 3S373 | MANPOWER CRAFTSMAN | | 1 | | 1 |
| 0001271609 | 09 | AF PERSONNEL CTR | FUNDED | FFF2 | 1 MANPOWER RQMNTS SQUADRON | JBSA RANDOLPH | 0160 | MRC | MANPOWER REQUIREMENTS FLIGHT C | GS-11 | 038P3 | PERSONNEL | | | 1 | 1 |
| 0001272009 | 09 | AF PERSONNEL CTR | FUNDED | FFF2 | 1 MANPOWER RQMNTS SQUADRON | JBSA RANDOLPH | 0160 | MRC | MANPOWER REQUIREMENTS FLIGHT C | GS-12 | 038P3 | PERSONNEL | | | 1 | 1 |
| 0001272109 | 09 | AF PERSONNEL CTR | FUNDED | FFF2 | 1 MANPOWER RQMNTS SQUADRON | JBSA RANDOLPH | 0160 | MRC | MANPOWER REQUIREMENTS FLIGHT C | GS-13 | 038P3 | PERSONNEL | | | 1 | 1 |
| 0001272209 | 09 | AF PERSONNEL CTR | FUNDED | FFF2 | 1 MANPOWER RQMNTS SQUADRON | JBSA RANDOLPH | 0160 | MRC | MANPOWER REQUIREMENTS FLIGHT C | GS-12 | 038P3 | PERSONNEL | | | 1 | 1 |
| 0001272709 | 09 | AF PERSONNEL CTR | FUNDED | FFF2 | 1 MANPOWER RQMNTS SQUADRON | JBSA RANDOLPH | 0104 | MRC | MANPOWER REQUIREMENTS FLIGHT C | TSGT | 3S373 | MANPOWER CRAFTSMAN | | 1 | | 1 |
| 0001297809 | 09 | AF PERSONNEL CTR | FUNDED | FFF2 | 1 MANPOWER RQMNTS SQUADRON | JBSA RANDOLPH | 0160 | MRC | MANPOWER REQUIREMENTS FLIGHT C | GS-11 | 3S393 | MANPOWER SUPERINTENDENT | | | 1 | 1 |
| 0001269709 | 09 | AF PERSONNEL CTR | FUNDED | FFF2 | 1 MANPOWER RQMNTS SQUADRON | JBSA RANDOLPH | 0104 | MRD | MPWR REQUIREMENTS FLT D | MSGT | 3S373 | MANPOWER CRAFTSMAN | | 1 | | 1 |
| 0001269809 | 09 | AF PERSONNEL CTR | FUNDED | FFF2 | 1 MANPOWER RQMNTS SQUADRON | JBSA RANDOLPH | 0104 | MRD | MPWR REQUIREMENTS FLT D | TSGT | 3S373 | MANPOWER CRAFTSMAN | | 1 | | 1 |
| 0001270209 | 09 | AF PERSONNEL CTR | FUNDED | FFF2 | 1 MANPOWER RQMNTS SQUADRON | JBSA RANDOLPH | 0160 | MRD | MPWR REQUIREMENTS FLT D | GS-12 | 038P3 | PERSONNEL | | | 1 | 1 |
| 0001270309 | 09 | AF PERSONNEL CTR | FUNDED | FFF2 | 1 MANPOWER RQMNTS SQUADRON | JBSA RANDOLPH | 0160 | MRD | MPWR REQUIREMENTS FLT D | GS-12 | 038P3 | PERSONNEL | | | 1 | 1 |
| 0001270609 | 09 | AF PERSONNEL CTR | FUNDED | FFF2 | 1 MANPOWER RQMNTS SQUADRON | JBSA RANDOLPH | 0004 | MRD | MPWR REQUIREMENTS FLT D | CAPT | 038P3 | PERSONNEL | 1 | | | 1 |
| 0001270709 | 09 | AF PERSONNEL CTR | FUNDED | FFF2 | 1 MANPOWER RQMNTS SQUADRON | JBSA RANDOLPH | 0004 | MRD | MPWR REQUIREMENTS FLT D | LT | 038P3 | PERSONNEL | 1 | | | 1 |
| 0001271109 | 09 | AF PERSONNEL CTR | FUNDED | FFF2 | 1 MANPOWER RQMNTS SQUADRON | JBSA RANDOLPH | 0104 | MRD | MPWR REQUIREMENTS FLT D | MSGT | 3S373 | MANPOWER CRAFTSMAN | | 1 | | 1 |
| 0001272809 | 09 | AF PERSONNEL CTR | FUNDED | FFF2 | 1 MANPOWER RQMNTS SQUADRON | JBSA RANDOLPH | 0160 | MRD | MPWR REQUIREMENTS FLT D | GS-11 | 3S393 | MANPOWER SUPERINTENDENT | | | 1 | 1 |
| 0001294509 | 09 | AF PERSONNEL CTR | FUNDED | FFF2 | 1 MANPOWER RQMNTS SQUADRON | JBSA RANDOLPH | 0104 | MRD | MPWR REQUIREMENTS FLT D | SSGT | 3S353 | MANPOWER JOURNEYMAN | | 1 | | 1 |
| 0001294709 | 09 | AF PERSONNEL CTR | FUNDED | FFF2 | 1 MANPOWER RQMNTS SQUADRON | JBSA RANDOLPH | 0104 | MRD | MPWR REQUIREMENTS FLT D | SSGT | 3S353 | MANPOWER JOURNEYMAN | | 1 | | 1 |
| 0001294909 | 09 | AF PERSONNEL CTR | FUNDED | FFF2 | 1 MANPOWER RQMNTS SQUADRON | JBSA RANDOLPH | 0104 | MRD | MPWR REQUIREMENTS FLT D | TSGT | 3S373 | MANPOWER CRAFTSMAN | | 1 | | 1 |
| Total | | | | | | | | | | | | | 5 | 21 | 16 | 42 |

**13.22.2. Funded and Unfunded Requirements and the Enlisted Grades Allocation Program:**

13.22.2.1. The terms "manpower requirement" and "manpower authorization" are often misunderstood. A manpower requirement is a statement of manpower needed to accomplish a job, workload, mission, or program. The two types of manpower requirements are funded and unfunded. Funded manpower requirements are those that have been validated and allocated. Funded manpower requirements are also known as authorizations. Unfunded requirements are validated manpower needs that are deferred because of budgetary constraints.

13.22.2.2. Some actions not only affect authorization levels but can also impact funded grades. The enlisted grades allocation program is designed to ensure enlisted grades are equitably allocated to Headquarters Air Force, major commands, field operating agencies, and direct reporting units, and at the same time not exceed constraints. A grade imbalance between what is required and what is funded (authorized) can occur as a result of legislative and budgetary constraints on the allocated grades. For example, Chief Master Sergeants are constrained to 1 percent of the total enlisted force.

13.22.2.3. Headquarters Air Force implements congressional and Department of Defense grade constraints by creating grade factors. Two types of factors created and distributed are: (1) overall command grade factors for each enlisted grade; and (2) career progression group factors for each Air Force specialty code to the first three digits. Command grade factors ensure authorized grades do not exceed command-ceiling constraints. The career progression group factors ensure equitable allocation of the grades within each Air Force specialty code in each command. Both types of factors are applied to the budgeted end-strength. Air Force career field managers can recommend adjustments to Head Quarters Air Force A1M, Directorate of Manpower, Organization and Resources. When making adjustments, they must maintain a zero balance of total grades allocated for each command. Commands may engage in grade swaps, via the Air Force career field manager, which in-turn may impact the respective factors. The factors themselves cannot be swapped.

**13.23. Initiating and Tracking Manpower Changes:**

13.23.1. Periodically, a unit may need to change an existing requirement on the unit manning document. An authorization change request (may also be referred to as "manpower change request") is used to request this change. The unit point of contact identifies the requested change and provides detailed justification to the servicing manpower, organization and resources flight. The manpower and organization section evaluates the request, enters it into the manpower programming and execution system, and makes a recommendation for approval or disapproval to the major command.

13.23.2. Many actions necessitate an authorization change request. Some of the most frequent are Air Force specialty code changes, position realignments, redistribution of funding from a funded requirement to an unfunded requirement, and grade conversions. Many factors must be considered when a unit proposes a change. Common considerations include: (1) determining how the change affects the organizational structure; (2) ensuring the manpower realignment does not exceed the requirements allowed by Air Force manpower standards; (3) ensuring the requested change complies with current programming guidelines; and (4) ensuring the requested change does not adversely impact the unit's ability to deploy or perform its wartime mission.

13.23.3. Changes to the unit manning document must be processed within resource constraints (i.e. no net increase in resources) minus no net increase in resources, grades, etc. For example, if a unit wants to fund a position that is currently unfunded, a funded position must be identified for conversion to unfund and detailed rationale for the change provided. The servicing manpower and organization flight will work closely with the unit point of contact when developing an authorization change request. Unit commander approval of authorization change request actions is required prior to submission of the authorization change request to the major command point of contact with the exception of actions resulting from a public-private competition or in-sourcing initiative.

13.23.4. Approved changes to the unit manning document are reflected by an authorization change notice generated by the manpower programming and execution system. The authorization change notice provides details of the approved change and the rationale for the change. The manpower and organization flight will, in turn, provide a copy of the authorization change notice to the affected unit's point of contact. If the request is disapproved, the major command provides rationale to the submitting unit through the servicing manpower and organization flight.

### 13.24. Manpower and Organization Flight.

The installation manpower and organization flight performs a variety of functions to help effectively manage manpower resources. The core competencies of the manpower and organization flight encompass organization structure, requirement determination, program allocation and control, and process improvement. Personnel within the manpower and organization flight provide day-to-day manpower resource management services to include unit manning document management, assisting with authorization change requests, authorization change notices, and organizational structure changes. Manpower and organization flight personnel also provide other management services, such as performance management, commercial activity services, Airmen Powered by Innovation Program, Continuous Process Improvement and management advisory studies.

### 13.25. Commercial Services Management:

#### 13.25.1. Purpose.

Commercial services management is a program designed to improve functions using a variety of management tools including competitive sourcing, in-sourcing, and post-competition accountability. The three principal goals of commercial services management are to sustain readiness, improve performance and quality by doing business more efficiently and cost effectively, and focus available personnel and resources on core Air Force missions. Commercial services management will not affect military-essential skills or those functions that are inherently governmental.

13.25.1.1. Military Essential skills are defined as skills that:

13.25.1.1.1. Directly contribute to the prosecution of war (combat or direct combat support).

13.25.1.1.2. Exercise Uniform Code of Military Justice authority.

13.25.1.1.3. By law must be filled with military personnel.

13.25.1.1.4. Are military by custom or tradition (for example, bands and honor guards).

13.25.1.1.5. Are needed to support overseas rotations and to sustain certain career fields.

13.25.1.1.6. Are not available in the private sector.

13.25.1.2. **Inherently Governmental Function.** The Federal Activities Inventory Reform Act of 1998 defines an inherently governmental function as one that is so intimately related to the public interest as to require performance by federal government employees. Functions may include the determination of budget policy, guidance, and strategy; the determination of the content and application of policies and regulations; the selection of individuals for federal government employment; and obligating money on behalf of the government. For example, warranted contracting officers are inherently governmental because they are responsible for making decisions on behalf of the government. They are the signature authority for committing government funds. The entire contracting staff, however; does not necessarily satisfy the same criteria. Contracting personnel who research and provide information, advice, etc., to the warranted contracting officers do not necessarily have to be government personnel.

## 13.26. Competitive Sourcing Process.

AFI 38-203, *Commercial Activities Program*, defines a structured process for determining whether to perform work in-house or through contract.

### 13.26.1. Competitive Sourcing Study:

13.26.1.1. A competitive sourcing study is a public-private competition that compares the total cost of the in-house government operation of an activity to the total cost of private sector performance of the same activity. The study results determine whether a commercial activity can be done more economically and efficiently by contract or by an in-house workforce.

13.26.1.2. During the competitive sourcing study, the in-house government operation is reengineered into a most efficient organization and submitted in the competition as the agency's tender which is the government's proposal for how it will perform the work. The process of developing a most efficient organization emphasizes innovation in meeting the requirements laid out in the solicitation for the work being completed. The most efficient organization is allowed latitude in its organization and processes outside of the standard Air Force structure to enable greater efficiency and effectiveness.

### 13.26.2. Competitive Sourcing Impact:

13.26.2.1. Air Force policy is to minimize both the adverse effects on personnel and the disruption to the affected organizations. Adversely affected personnel are provided the right of first refusal for contractor jobs, for which they are qualified, in the event the government is unable to place them in other federal positions.

13.26.2.2. Competitive sourcing generates savings by finding more efficient ways to accomplish a particular function. A competitive sourcing study also frees up military personnel to perform other core military essential activities. In a competitive sourcing study, the mission remains essentially unchanged; the composition of the workforce is what changes. Where blue suiters were initially performing the mission, the resulting service provider will be made up of either civil servants or private sector contract employees.

## 13.27. In-sourcing:

### 13.27.1. Origin and Authorization:

13.27.1.1. In-sourcing is the conversion of a contracted function to Department of Defense civilian or military performance, or any combination thereof. Although OMB Circular A-76 provides a structured process for converting contracts to in-house performance through public-private competition, 10 United States Code, Section 2463, *Guidelines and Procedures for Use of Civilian Employees to Perform Department of Defense Functions*, permits Department of Defense components to convert contracts without applying the Circular's requirements. 10 United States Code, Section 2463 provides for special consideration to using Department of Defense civilian employees to perform any function that is currently performed by a contractor and meets any of the following criteria:

13.27.1.1.1. Has been performed by Department of Defense civilian employees at any time during the previous 10 years.

13.27.1.1.2. Is closely associated with the performance of an inherently governmental function.

13.27.1.1.3. Has been performed pursuant to a contract awarded on a noncompetitive basis.

13.27.1.1.4. Has been determined by a contracting officer to have been performed poorly during the 5 years preceding the date of such determination, because of excessive costs or inferior quality.

13.27.1.2. Furthermore, in accordance with the Deputy Secretary of Defense memorandum, In-sourcing contracted services-implementation guidance, contracted functions found to be inherently governmental, exempt from contract performance, unauthorized personal services, or experiencing problems associated with contract administration shall be in-sourced regardless of cost.

### 13.27.2. In-sourcing Business Case Analysis:

13.27.2.1. An insourcing Business Case Analysis compares the cost of a contracted function to the cost of Department of Defense civilian employees to perform the same activity. The Business Case Analysis justifies the decision to in-source when based on cost. Included in the Business Case Analysis are certifications validating contract cost, in-house manning, available labor pool, and activity meets the requirements of a valid and enduring mission requirement. Installations and major commands develop Business Case Analysis, and Air Force manpower analysis agency validates Business Case Analysis as part of the Air Force in-sourcing approval process. Cost models are built using COMPARE, an Air Force manpower analysis agency provided tool that incorporates guidance and factors to estimating and comparing the full costs of civilian and military manpower and contract Support.

13.27.2.2. If new or expanded requirements or functions performed under contract are determined to be inherently governmental or exempt from private sector performance for reasons stated in DoDI 1100.22, *Policy and Procedures for Determining Workforce Mix*, the functions shall be converted to government performance without an economic analysis. In all other cases a cost comparison is required and serves as the key component of the Business Case Analysis.

## 13.28. Responsibilities.

Headquarters Air Force A1M is responsible for implementing the Air Force commercial services management program. Air Force manpower analysis agency develops and maintains tools, templates, and guidebooks to enable the field to execute the program, administers the inherently governmental/commercial activities inventory, monitors post competition accountability, and provides field support on commercial services management initiatives. Major command A1M is the manpower function responsible for providing commercial services management oversight at command levels and providing guidance to manpower and organization flights for implementation of the commercial services management program at the respective wings.

*Section 13F—Government Property and Equipment*

## 13.29. General Responsibilities:

13.29.1. The Air Force mission requires that all military and civilian personnel operate and maintain Government systems, equipment, supplies, and real property in the best possible condition, in constant readiness, and in the absolute minimum quantity necessary to accomplish assigned tasks.

13.29.2. Commanders must manage public property under their control, including proper care and use, provide instructions to subordinates on their specific responsibilities, and maintain records that may be audited. Commanders and supervisors establish controls to eliminate uneconomical equipment management, ensure all personnel are taught proper care and safeguard principles, and enforce these principles. Logistics readiness squadrons offer training on a variety of topics for different management levels. Commanders appoint representatives and ensure the representatives attend the proper training. For example, primary and alternate equipment custodians attend mandatory Block III computer-based training accompanied by a supplemental Block III training provided by the logistics readiness squadron's equipment accountability element.

13.29.3. The Air Force equipment management system provides a standard equipment management system applicable to all Air Force activities. This system is web-enabled and requires a password for access. Air Force equipment management system provides worldwide visibility of all in-use and warehoused equipment assets and is used to report capitalized asset depreciation, determine equipment requirements based on Air Force allowance standards, support the budget and buy program, and report equipment types and quantities required to accomplish the mission. The allowance standards are provided both online in the Air Force equipment management system and offline via compact disk. The allowance standards include specific items and authorized quantities required for the wartime and peacetime needs of each unit.

## 13.30. Property Accounting.

The organization commander or equivalent designates a property custodian for Government property used by the unit and listed on allowance standard documents. Upon assuming responsibility and at least annually, the designated property custodian must perform an inventory of all assets. The custodian signs the custodian authorization/custody receipt listing acknowledging completion of the inventory and signifying all items listed are being used properly and maintained in serviceable condition. After the inventory is completed, the custodian signs the acknowledgement of responsibility block which allows the custodian to become accountable for the property physically in possession, then obtains the commander's signature as validation that the inventory took place and actions are underway to resolve discrepancies. The property custodian is relieved of responsibility only when the account is transferred to another custodian, issues or turns in items and obtains a signed receipt, or provides authorized adjustment documents (turn-in receipts, transfer documents, etc.).

## 13.31. Report of Survey.

A report of survey is used to research and investigate the cause of loss, damage, destruction, or theft of Government property and to determine if the cause of loss was attributable to an individual's negligence or abuse. The final report is used to assess financial liability against the persons responsible or to relieve them from liability if there is no evidence of negligence, willful misconduct, or deliberate unauthorized use of the property. The report of survey also serves as a source document to adjust accountable records and provides a tool for commanders to identify deficiencies requiring corrective action to prevent recurring incidents. AFMAN 23-220, *Reports of Survey for Air Force Property,* identifies procedures for processing a report of survey and implementing the report of survey program.

13.31.1. **When to Complete a Report of Survey:**

13.31.1.1. With some exceptions, a report of survey must be completed for all Government property lost, damaged, destroyed, or stolen. The property can be real or personal. Air Force real property includes buildings and items attached to them, such as air-conditioners and compressors. Anything not real property, such as parkas, tools, desks, equipment, and vehicles is personal property.

13.31.1.2. A report of survey is not necessary when:

13.31.1.2.1. The individual responsible for the loss or damage makes voluntary payment, and loss, damage, destruction, or theft of property is $500 or less. This policy does not prevent the initiation of a report of survey if the loss is less than $500, evidence of negligence, or a systematic loss of property by the same individual over a period of time.

13.31.1.2.2. Investigation of the loss, damage, or destruction of a vehicle indicates no evidence of gross negligence, willful misconduct, or deliberate unauthorized use. The commander may still take action against individuals in these cases using punitive or administrative options.

13.31.1.2.3. Do not use assessment of financial liability as a form of disciplinary action.

13.31.2. **Initiating a Report of Survey:**

13.31.2.1. Generally, the organization possessing the lost or damaged property is responsible for initiating a report of survey even if the property is deployed or issued on a hand-receipt outside the organization.

13.31.2.2. Depending on the organizational structure, the commander normally initiates the proceedings by appointing an investigating official. The investigating official will be an officer, senior NCO, or civilian employee (General Schedule-7, Wage Grade-9, Wage Leader-5, or Wage Supervisor-1 or above). The investigator must be a disinterested, impartial individual who has no interest or involvement in the custodianship, care, accountability, or safekeeping of the property in question.

13.31.3. **Report of Survey Investigation.**

At a minimum, the investigating official will perform the following steps during an investigation:

13.31.3.1. Develop the facts in the case which will lead to the findings and recommendations. The investigator must interview any persons with knowledge of the case if they are in the immediate area. This includes the person who may have lost, damaged, destroyed, or stolen the property.

13.31.3.2. Obtain written statements from persons interviewed and obtain sworn statements in accordance with the *Manual for Courts-Martial,* Appendix 2, Section 936. This section authorizes the investigator to swear witnesses.

13.31.3.3. Ensure the findings and the recommendations are supported by the testimony of persons involved and that the testimony leads logically to the findings and recommendations.

13.31.3.4. Determine if financial liability should be assessed based strictly on the facts and circumstances of the case. If financial liability is recommended based on value on the property involved and not the fact that financial liability generally is limited not to exceed one month's pay or by statements made to the investigating officer by the person involved and the assessment of financial liability will cause personal hardship. **Note:** Reducing the recommended assessment of financial liability is a command prerogative and not within the purview of the investigating officer.

13.31.4. **Liability:**

13.31.4.1. All Air Force members and employees can be held liable for the loss, damage, or destruction of Government property proximately caused by their negligence, willful misconduct, or deliberate unauthorized use.

13.31.4.2. Persons who have lost, damaged, destroyed, or stolen Government property valued at $500 or less may voluntarily pay for the property.

13.31.5. **Processing the Report of Survey:**

13.31.5.1. After the investigation is complete, the investigating official allows the persons involved to review the case and provide verbal or written information to refute the findings and recommendations. In the process of refuting the findings of a report of survey, an Airman may seek advice from the local area defense counsel.

13.31.5.2. The report of survey is then processed to the appointing authority to assign financial responsibility against the individual charged or relieve him or her from responsibility. If financial responsibility is assessed, refer the report of survey to the legal office for review.

13.31.5.3. At the time the report of survey is submitted for acknowledgment by the individual charged, he or she is advised the report of survey action may be appealed to the next level in the chain of command above the person who assigned the financial liability assessment.

*Section 13G—Facility Management*

## 13.32. Installation Commander Responsibilities.

The installation commander has overall responsibility and accountability for the operation of an Air Force installation. The major command and installation commander, assisted by the base civil engineer, are responsible for the following:

13.32.1. Develop, operate, maintain, and control the use of Air Force facilities in compliance with applicable Department of Defense and Air Force policies and procedures.

13.32.2. Develop comprehensive asset management plans, identify facility lifecycle requirements, implement applicable common levels of service, assess the impact of asset condition on mission support through the use of key performance indicators, and develop and execute real property construction, sustainment, restoration, and modernization programs.

## 13.33. Responsibilities of the Using Organization:

13.33.1. Successful facility management relies heavily upon the using organization. The using organization's unit commander will ensure requirements for real property alterations, additions, or new construction are identified to the base civil engineer or wing commander when required.

13.33.2. The unit commander designates in writing an officer, E-5 and above, or civilian equivalent, as primary and alternate facility managers for each facility assigned to the organization. In multipurpose facilities, the major user should be assigned as the primary facility manager. Other organizations using a portion of a multipurpose facility are encouraged to appoint an alternate facility manager for their respective area.

13.33.3. Work that alters real property in any way, to include modifications or repair, requires approval from the base civil engineer. Facility managers submit work requests to the base civil engineer customer service unit utilizing established processes. The base civil engineer determines the execution method for work that is approved.

13.33.4. Emergency work, defined as work that corrects an issue that poses an immediate threat to mission, life, safety, or health will be identified to customer service unit by the quickest means possible, to include verbal or phone communication. All other forms of work will be identified to the customer service unit by the facility manager utilizing the Air Force Form 332, *Base Civil Engineer Work Request*, or designated information technology systems.

## 13.34. Base Civil Engineer Squadron Responsibilities:

13.34.1. The base civil engineer is charged to provide, operate, maintain, restore, and protect the built and natural infrastructure necessary to support the Air Force mission. As such, the base civil engineer serves as the focal point for all construction, sustainment, restoration, and modernization of facilities identified as real property and associated real property installed equipment.

13.34.2. The base civil engineer's customer service unit typically manages the installation's facility manager program. They provide initial and recurring training for facility managers, which covers facility manager roles and responsibilities and identifies the processes and procedures required for submitting work requests.

13.34.3. The base civil engineer's customer service unit receives and reviews all incoming work requests for validity, verifies scope, and ensures the work request is coordinated with the appropriate agencies such as fire, safety, and environmental. If the work request is approved, it will be executed in-house by the operations flight or as a contract managed by the engineering flight.

13.34.4. In-house work will either be direct scheduled or planned. Direct scheduled work does not need detailed planning and can be sent directly to the required shop for execution. An example of a direct scheduled work is fixing a leaky faucet. Planned work is typically more complex and requires detailed planning, scheduling of multiple shops, and lead time for material acquisition. An example of planned work is relocating a doorway and associated exit signs to accommodate the new layout. In-house work is prioritized for execution based on impact to the overall mission and as labor, materials, and funding become available.

13.34.5. When work exceeds the scope or capability of the operations flight, the work request will be classified as a project and sent to the base civil engineer's engineering flight where it will compete against other projects for execution as a contract.

13.34.6. The base civil engineer ensures changes to real property are captured and updated in the real property inventory. The real property inventory must be complete and up-to-date with source documentation for audit purposes to support financial improvement and audit readiness.

**13.35. Planning and Programming Facility Projects:**

13.35.1. Planning refers to the identification of facility work to satisfy current and future mission requirements. The base civil engineer uses several methods to identify facility requirements including annual space utilization surveys, biennial commander's facility assessments, environmental compliance status assessments, asset management plans, and user- or occupant-identified requirements.

13.35.2. During programming, the authority and resources necessary to accomplish the planned work are acquired. After the requirements are identified, the base civil engineer develops facility project proposals and presents them to the installation commander for validation, prioritization, and approval by the proper authority. A key element of programming facility requirements is proper work classification. Work authorization, approval levels, and fund sources vary with work classification. Real property maintenance work is classified as maintenance, repair, or construction. Operations and maintenance appropriation-funded unspecified minor military construction projects may not exceed $1,000,000. The threshold for using operation and maintenance funding for laboratory revitalization unspecified minor military construction projects is $4,000,000.

**13.36. Real Property Records:**

13.36.1. Air Force leadership, Department of Defense, and Congress utilize real property inventory to make planning, programming, and budgeting decisions.

13.36.2. The real property inventory forms an audit trail that begins when a facility is constructed and includes all costs for any alterations and improvements accomplished by military construction and minor construction, to include self-help or government purchase card work. A complete real property inventory consists of all sites, lands, and facilities for which the Air Force has real property accountability, regardless of the organization using or funding the facility or land.

13.36.3. Any activity leading to real property inventory additions, updates, or deletions must have proper approval documentation from the base civil engineer and filed with the real property officer as directed. In most instances these actions are accomplished by the civil engineer squadron. However, when services are procured by government purchase card or other means the facility manager will assist with accomplishing these actions.

*Section 13H—Energy Conservation Program*

**13.37. Air Force Need for Program.**

The Federal government, as the Nation's largest energy consumer, must significantly improve their energy management in order to save taxpayer dollars and reduce emissions that contribute to air pollution and global climate change. In encouraging effective energy management in the Federal government, the Energy Policy Act of 2005, the Security Act of 2007, and Executive Order 13693 *Planning for Federal Sustainability in the Next Decade,* strive to achieve the following goals:

13.37.1. **Energy Efficiency and Greenhouse Gases Reduction Goal.**

Improve energy efficiency through reduction of facility energy intensity (British thermal units per year per square foot) by 2.5 percent annually through the end of fiscal year 2025, or a total of 25 percent by the end of fiscal year 2025, relative to Air Force energy use in fiscal year 2015. Continue to reduce facility energy intensity by 1.5 percent annually from fiscal year 2015 to fiscal year 2020, or a total of 37.5 percent relative to Air Force energy use in fiscal year 2003. Reduce greenhouse gas emissions 40% by fiscal year 2025, relative to a 2008 baseline for most facilities.

13.37.2. **Sustainable Design and Development:**

13.37.2.1. All new construction and major renovation of facilities must comply with Air Force sustainable design and development policy, 2 June 2011, and incorporate sustainable practices. These facilities must become net-zero energy facilities (renewable generation offsets all fossil fuel) by 2030. Fifteen percent of existing facility inventory must incorporate sustainable practices by the end of fiscal year 2025.

13.37.2.2. Agency acquisition of goods and services must incorporate the use of sustainable environmental practices, including acquisition of bio based, environmentally preferable, energy efficient, water efficient, and recycled content products. This includes the use of paper with at least 30 percent recycled content.

13.37.3. **Vehicles.**

Petroleum consumption is to be reduced by 30 percent through the end of fiscal year 2025 as compared to fiscal year 2014. Alternative (nonpetroleum-based) fuel use is to be increased by 10 percent annually. Zero emissions vehicles should account for 20 percent of all new agency passenger vehicle acquisitions by 2025.

13.37.4. **Renewable Energy.**

The Energy Policy Act of 2005 established that in fiscal year 2007 through fiscal year 2009, 3 percent of electrical consumption be generated by renewable sources; in fiscal year 2010 through fiscal year 2012, 5 percent and 7.5 percent thereafter. Executive Order 13693 outlines the goal of 30 percent of facility electric consumption come from renewable sources by 2025 and Title 10, United States Code, Section 2911, *Energy Performance Goals and Master Plan for the Department of Defense,* sets a goal of 25 percent of electrical energy consumption generated by renewable sources by fiscal year 2025.

13.37.5. **Petroleum.**

Through life-cycle cost-effective measures, each agency shall reduce the use of petroleum within its facilities. Agencies may accomplish this reduction by switching to a less greenhouse gas-intensive, nonpetroleum energy source, such as synthetic or renewable energy sources.

13.37.6. **Electronic Products.**

Electronic products procured must be at least 95 percent compliant with electronic product environmental assessment tool standards. Energy Star features of computers must be enabled. Use environmentally sound practices when disposing of electronic equipment.

13.37.7. **Source Energy.**

The Federal government shall strive to reduce total energy use and associated greenhouse gas and other air emissions, as measured at the source.

13.37.8. **Water Conservation.**

Beginning in fiscal year 2008, reduce potable water consumption intensity (gallons per square foot) relative to fiscal year 2007, through life-cycle cost-effective measures by 2 percent annually through the end of fiscal year 2025, or 36 percent by the end of calendar year 2025. Reduce industrial, landscaping, and agricultural water consumption by 2 percent annually or 30 percent by the end of fiscal year 2025 relative to a baseline of consumption in fiscal year 2010.

**13.38. Air Force Compliance with Policy.**

Compliance with energy management policy is assessed by taking measurements in two areas: mobility energy and facility (utility) energy. (**Note**: Water usage is included in the definition of energy management.)

13.38.1. **Mobility Energy.**

The policy to reduce mobility energy will be assessed by measuring actual petroleum consumption. Consumption will be measured in barrels and include aircraft and vehicle operations.

13.38.2. **Facility Energy.**

The policy to reduce facility energy will be assessed by measuring utility consumption to include electricity, coal, natural gas, petroleum, water, etc. Consumption will be measured in million British thermal units per square foot (or gallons per square foot) and will include all installation facilities except privatized housing and facilities meeting Department of Energy exclusion requirements.

**13.39. Conclusion:**

13.39.1. With the constant emphasis on efficiency, the Air Force must get the greatest return from every investment. The Air Force invests in people and other resources, all of which must be managed wisely. This chapter provided an overview of responsibilities and outlined a few of the many Air Force management objectives.

13.39.2. All supervisors, managers, and commanders are responsible for safeguarding Air Force resources and exercising sound resource management practices. Remember, the amount of money spent and the other resources used (manpower, facilities) affect the entire mission. Leaders have a daily role to play in the overall system. They must plan for future requirements and ensure allocated resources are used properly. If correctly accomplished, the result will be a stronger and more efficient Air Force.

**Chapter 14**

**COMMUNICATING IN TODAY'S AIR FORCE**

*Section 14A—Overview*

**14.1. Introduction:**

14.1.1. Your success as a military leader depends on your ability to think critically and creatively; it is also crucial to communicate your intentions and decisions to others. The ability to communicate clearly—to write, speak, and actively listen—greatly impacts your capacity to inform, teach, motivate, mentor, and lead those around you. Communicating your intent and ideas so that others understand your message and act on it is one of the primary qualities of leadership.

14.1.2. Communication is the process of sharing ideas, information, and messages with others. In the Air Force, most communication involves speaking and writing. Any communication can be broken into three parts: the sender, the message, and the audience. For communication to be successful, the audience must not only receive the message, but the audience must interpret the message in the way the sender intended.

14.1.3. This chapter begins by examining the fundamentals of better communication, both written and spoken. Then the chapter focuses on written communications in general terms and outlines certain methods that can be used to improve writing style. Finally, it provides an overview and samples of the types of correspondence the noncommissioned officer (NCO) is likely to deal with in daily activities. This is not an exhaustive text and is meant as an overview, consult AFH 33-337 *The Tongue and Quill.*

*Section 14B—The Principles and Seven Steps for Effective Communication*

**14.2. Principles of Effective Communication.**

Everyone must understand what makes communication succeed and fail. Most mistakes are caused by forgetting one of the five principles of good communication. This section addresses the five core principles, focused, organized, clear, understanding, and supported (FOCUS) (Figure 14.1).

**Figure 14.1. FOCUS Principles**

| **Strong Writing and Speaking:** |
|---|
| **Focused** |
| Address the issue, the whole issue, and nothing but the issue. |
| **Organized** |
| Systematically present your information and ideas. |
| **Clear** |
| Communicate with clarity and make each word count. |
| **Understanding** |
| Understand your audience and its expectations. |
| **Supported** |
| Use logic and support to make your point. |

14.2.1. **Focused.**

The first hallmark of good communication is that the communication is focused. The sender has a clear idea of the purpose and objective, locks on target, and stays on track.

14.2.2. **Organized.**

Good organization means your material is presented in a logical, systematic manner. When writing or speaking is not well organized, audiences become easily confused or impatient and may stop reading or listening. Even if you are providing useful, relevant information, your audience may underestimate the value of the information and your credibility.

14.2.3. **Clear.**

This principle covers two interrelated ideas. First, to communicate clearly, we need to understand the rules of language; how to spell and pronounce words, and how to assemble and punctuate sentences. Second, we should get to the point, not hide our ideas in a maze of words.

14.2.4. **Understanding.**

Understanding their current knowledge, views, and level of interest in the topic helps when sharing ideas with others. Understanding what is expected with the format and length of response, due date, level of formality, and any staffing requirements helps when you have been asked to write a report.

14.2.5. **Supported.**

Use logic and support to make your point. Support and logic are the tools used to build credibility and trust with your audience. Nothing cripples a clearly written, properly punctuated paper quicker than a fractured fact or a distorted argument.

## 14.3. Overview.

Like many things, good communication requires preparation. There are seven steps that will help every Airman become a better communicator, both in written correspondence and in speaking abilities (Figure 14.2). The first four steps lay the groundwork for the drafting process.

## 14.4. Step 1—Analyze Purpose and Audience.

Once the need for communication is determined, step 1 requires you to be clear on your purpose and know or understand your audience. Those who have mastered the art of communication stay focused on their objective and approach audience analysis seriously.

**Figure 14.2. Seven Steps for Effective Communication**

1. Analyze Purpose and Audience
2. Research Your Topic
3. Support Your Ideas
4. Organize and Outline
5. Draft
6. Edit
7. Fight for Feedback and Get Approval

### 14.4.1. Choose the Purpose.

Most Air Force writing or speaking is either to direct, inform, persuade, or inspire. Your task is to think about the message you want to send (the what) and make some sort of determination what your purpose is (the why). Once you decide the purpose, you will know where to place the emphasis and what the tone of your communication should be (Figure 14.3).

**Figure 14.3. Determining Purpose**

**To Direct**—*Directive communication* is generally used to pass on information describing actions you expect to be carried out by your audience. The emphasis in directive communication is clear, concise directions and expectations of your audience.

**To Inform**—The goal of *informative communication* is to pass on information to the audience. The emphasis in informative communication is clear, direct communication with accurate and adequate information tailored to the education and skill levels of the audience. Audience feedback and interaction may be appropriate in some situations to make sure they "got the message."

**To Persuade**—*Persuasive Communication* is typically used when you are trying to "sell" your audience on a new idea, new policy, new product or a change in current operations.

**To Inspire**—One final purpose for writing or speaking that doesn't get much attention, but is frequently used in the military is to *inspire*. The emphasis in inspirational communication is delivery, a thorough knowledge of your topic and likewise your audience.

### 14.4.2. Draft the Purpose Statement.

One way to make sure you are clear on your objective is to write a *purpose statement*, which is one sentence that captures the essence of what you are trying to do—your "bottom line." Developing a clear purpose statement will:

14.9.2.1. Help you FOCUS as you develop your communication.

14.9.2.2. Help your audience *focus* when you deliver your message.

### 14.4.3. Know Yourself.

Realizing your own strengths and weaknesses will help you meet your communication goals.

### 14.4.4. Know Your Organization.

In the military, we rarely act or speak in a vacuum. Often we represent our organization, unit, or functional area and must understand them and accommodate their views, capabilities, or concerns in our communications.

### 14.4.5. Know Your Audience.

The receiving audience falls into one of four sub-categories. Depending on the type of communication and coordination needed, you may or may not deal with each one of these:

14.4.5.1. Primary receiver—the person you directly communicate with, either verbally or in writing.

14.4.5.2. Secondary receiver—people you indirectly communicate with through the primary receivers.

14.4.5.3. Key decision makers—the most powerful members of the audience; the ones that really make the decisions. Knowing who they are will help focus your attention and potentially your delivery in larger briefings and certain written communication.

14.4.5.4. Gatekeepers—people in the chain who typically review the communication before the communication reaches the intended audience. Knowing who they are and what their expectations are can save you embarrassment and help ensure your success in the long run.

14.4.6. **Succeed With Your Audience.**

Some tips are:

14.4.6.1. **Rank.** Differences in military rank can be a real barrier to communication in the Air Force. Many of us become tongue-tied when communicating with those senior in rank, and cursory or impatient with those who are junior in rank. We must constantly remind ourselves we are all communicative equals and should strive to be candid, direct, and respectful with everyone.

14.4.6.2. **Jargon.** Tailor to your audience. Do not overestimate the knowledge and expertise of your readers, but do not talk down to them either. Be careful with excessive use of career-field specific jargon and acronyms.

14.4.6.3. **Be Inclusive.** Remember our diverse force. Sometimes we inadvertently exclude members of our audience by falling into communication traps involving references to race, religion, ethnicity, or sex. Remember this concept when designing your visual support. Knowing your audience and adhering to good taste and sensitivity will keep you in check.

14.4.6.4. **Tone.** This is not just what you say, but how you say it. Closely tied to the purpose of your communication is the tone you take with your audience. Speakers have gestures, voice, and movements to help them communicate. Writers only have words on paper. How many times have you seen colleagues get bent out of shape over a misunderstood e-mail? Why? Because the nonverbal signals available during face-to-face communication are absent. Recognize this disadvantage in written communication and pay close attention to the tone.

14.4.6.5. **Courtesy.** The first rule of writing is to be polite. Forego anger, criticism, and sarcasm—strive to be reasonable and persuasive. Try not to deliberately embarrass someone and avoid with a more tactful choice of words.

14.4.6.6. **Make it Personal.** When appropriate, use pronouns to create instant rapport, show concern, and keep your reader involved. Using pronouns also keeps your writing from being monotonous, dry, and abstract. The pronouns you will probably use the most are you, yours, we, us, and our. Use I, me, and my sparingly. One rule of business writing is to put your audience first; so, when possible, avoid using I as the first word of an opening sentence and avoid starting two sentences in a row with we or I unless you are trying to hammer home a point.

14.4.6.7. **Formal.** ("To be, or not to be") versus Informal ("hey dude"). Different communication situations require different levels of formality. The informal tone is more like a conversation between you and your reader and is characterized by clear, direct, active language. In today's Air Force, most of your writing will be informal, though ceremonies and awards may require more elaborate (formal) language. Whether your tone is formal or informal, you still need to follow the accepted rules of grammar.

14.4.6.8. **Be Positive.** To cultivate a positive tone give praise where praise is due, acknowledge acceptance before focusing on additional improvements, and express criticism in the form of helpful questions, suggestions, requests, recommendations, or clear directives rather than accusations. Your audience always appreciates sincerity and honesty.

14.5. **Step 2—Research Your Topic.**

Whether your goal is to persuade or inform, you will need more than fancy words to win the day—you will need substance as well as style. Once you're clear on your purpose and audience (Step 1), you will need to research your topic to uncover information that will support your communication goals. Before you begin the research, refer to the five approaches to researching below for the best method for accomplishing researching.

14.5.1. **Approach 1.** Review purpose and scope of the overall project. Sometimes your purpose and scope will evolve as you learn more about the topic, and you may need to do some preliminary research just to get smart enough to scope out the effort.

14.5.2. **Approach 2.** Assign a deadline as you can easily get lost in the research process. Don't do an outstanding job of data retrieval, then a marginal job on the presentation because you ran out of time.

14.5.3. **Approach 3.** Ask the boss. Even if you can eventually find the answer on your own, save some time by asking your supervisor for suggestions on where to start.

14.5.4. **Approach 4.** Determine what is known. Before you look for answers outside yourself, look in the mirror. You may already have valuable knowledge about an assigned research project. When relying on personal knowledge, be sure to identify and guard against any biases you may have.

14.5.5. **Approach 5.** Determine where to look for information. Coworkers and base personnel are easy because you can meet with them face-to-face. Office files and references in paper form and on your computer network may be valuable sources of information. Finally, the internet and library offer an unlimited supply of information.

## 14.6. Step 3—Support Your Ideas.

Once you have researched your topic and collected information, you need to figure out how to use what you have found to meet your communication goals. Individual pieces of evidence are used to build your argument. When identifying some common types of evidence, they may include:

14.6.1. **Definition.** A definition is a precise meaning or significance of a word or phrase.

14.6.2. **Testimony.** A testimony uses the comments of recognized authorities to support your claim. These comments are sometimes direct quotations or paraphrases, but direct quotations tend to carry more weight with listeners or readers.

14.6.3. **Statistics.** The use of statistics provides a summary of data that allows your audience to better interpret quantitative information. Statistics can be very persuasive and provide excellent support if handled competently. Keep them simple and easy to read and understand. Also, remember to round off your statistics whenever possible and document the exact source of your statistics.

14.6.4. **Example**. An example is a specific instance chosen to represent a larger fact in order to clarify an abstract idea or support a claim. Good examples must be appropriate, brief and attention arresting. Quite often they are presented in groups of two or three for impact.

14.6.5. **Fact.** A fact is a noncontroversial piece of data that can be confirmed by observation or by talking to communally accepted authorities. Be careful to distinguish facts from inferences, and handle inferences you would like to use in your research as testimony, not fact.

14.6.6. **Explanation:**

14.6.6.1. **Analysis.** The analysis is the separation of a whole into smaller pieces for further studies; clarifying a complex issue by examining one piece at a time.

14.6.6.2. **Comparison and Contrast.** Use comparison to dramatize similarities between two objects or situations, and contrast to emphasize differences.

14.6.6.3. **Description.** A description is to tell about something in detail, to paint a picture with words, typically more personal and subjective than a definition.

## 14.7. Step 4—Organize and Outline.

Select a pattern that enables you and your readers to move systematically and logically through your ideas from beginning to conclusion. Some of the most common organizational patterns are listed below. Your purpose, the needs of your audience, and the nature of your material will influence your choice of pattern.

14.7.1. **Topical.**

Use the topical format to present groups of ideas, objects, or events by categories.

14.7.2. **Compare or Contrast.**

Use the compare and contrast style when you need to discuss similarities and differences between topics, concepts, or ideas.

14.7.3. **Chronological.**

When using the chronological pattern, you discuss events, problems, or processes in the sequence of time in which occurrences take place or should take place (past to present or present to future).

14.7.4. **Sequential.**

A step-by-step approach, sequential is similar to the chronological pattern. Use this approach to describe a sequence of steps necessary to complete a technical procedure or process.

14.7.5. **Spatial or Geographical.**

When using spatial or geographical pattern, you will start at some point in space and proceed in sequence to other points. This pattern is based on a directional strategy—north to south, east to west, clockwise or counterclockwise, bottom to top, above and below.

14.7.6. **Problem and Solution.**

Use the problem and solution pattern to identify and describe a problem and one or more possible solutions, or an issue and possible techniques for resolving the issue. Discuss all facets of the problem, such as origin, characteristics, and impact.

14.7.7. **Reasoning and Logic.**

State an opinion and then make your case by providing support for your position. Use the reasoning and logic pattern when your mission is to present research that will lead your audience down the path to your point of view.

14.7.8. **Cause and Effect.**

Use the cause and effect pattern to show how one or more ideas, actions, or conditions lead to other ideas, actions, or conditions.

**14.8. Step 5—Draft.**

A draft is not the finished product, and each sentence does not have to be polished and perfect. The focus is to get your ideas down on paper. Do not obsess about grammar, punctuation, spelling, and word choice—this all comes later. You do not have to fix every mistake you see. By periodically checking your outline, you are less likely to lose focus and include irrelevant information. Break up your draft into a three-part structure—introduction, body, and conclusion.

14.8.1. **Introduction.**

The introduction captures your audience's attention, establishes rapport, and announces your purpose. Therefore, the introduction sets the stage and tone for your message and the direction you plan to take the audience. A typical introduction has three components: stage-setting remarks, a purpose statement, and an overview.

14.8.1.1. Stage-setting remarks sets the tone, captures the audience's attentions, and encourages the audience to read further. Stage-setting remarks are optional and can be omitted in very short messages.

14.8.1.2. The purpose statement is the one sentence you would keep if you had only one. Moreover, the purpose statement specifically states your purpose, thesis, or main point.

14.8.1.3. The overview clearly presents your main points, previews your paragraph sequence, and ties your main points to your purpose.

14.8.2. **Body.**

This is the heart of your message and includes the main ideas about your subject and supporting details under each main idea. The body, depending on the purpose and subject, will typically consist of several paragraphs. As a general rule a separate paragraph is formed for each main idea.

14.8.3. **Conclusion.**

The conclusion is the last and often neglected part of well-arranged communication. An effective conclusion often summarizes the main points discussed in the body, and leaves the reader with a sense of closure. Conclude your communication with positive statements based on your preceding discussion and avoid bringing up new information. The introduction and conclusion should balance each other without being identical.

14.8.4. **Effective Paragraphs:**

14.8.4.1. Paragraphs are the primary vehicles for developing ideas. They group related ideas into single units of thought, separate one unit of thought from another, and alert readers that the writer is shifting to another phase of the subject.

14.8.4.2. Each paragraph contains a topic sentence, preferably at the beginning, that prepares the reader for the rest of the paragraph and provides a point of focus for support details, facts, figures, and examples. Use supporting ideas to prove, clarify, illustrate, and develop your main point. The objective is to help the readers see the paragraphs as integrated units rather than a mere collection of sentences.

14.8.5. **Plain Language.**

Prepare all Air Force correspondence using plain language. Plain language means using logical organization; common, everyday words (except for necessary technical terms); "you" and other pronouns; the active voice; and short sentences.

### 14.8.6. Transitions.

One way to make sure your paragraphs flow together, both internally and externally, is by using transitions in the form of words, phrases, or sentences. Internal transitions are used within a sentence to improve the flow, while external transitions are used to link separate paragraphs together within the body of the communication.

### 14.8.7. Effective Sentences.

To draft clear and concise sentences, choose clear and concise words and phrases to make up your sentences. There are three considerations to make when drafting sentences: active voice, smothered verbs, and parallelism.

14.8.7.1. **Write Actively.** The active voice shows the subject as the actor, reaches out to the reader and gets to the point quickly with fewer words. Whereas the passive voice shows the subject as receiver of the action.

**EXAMPLES:**

| Instead of: | Your support is appreciated… |
| | The IG team will be appointed… |
| | It is requested that you submit… |
| Use: | I appreciate your support… |
| | Colonel Crawford will appoint the IG team… |
| | Please submit… |

14.8.7.2. **Smothered Verbs.** Make your verbs do the work for you. Weak writing relies on general verbs that take extra words to complete their meaning. Keep verbs active, lively, specific, concise and out in front, not hidden.

**EXAMPLES:**

| Instead of: | The IG team held a meeting to give consideration to the printing issue. |
| | Use that format for the preparation of your command history. |
| | The settlement of travel claims involves the examination of orders. |
| Use: | The IG team met to consider the printing issue. |
| | Use that format to prepare your command history. |
| | Settling travel claims involves examining orders. |

14.8.7.3. **Parallel Construction.** Use a consistent pattern when making a list. If your sentence contains a series of items separated by commas, keep the grammatical construction similar. Violations occur when writers mix things and actions, statements and questions, and active and passive instructions. The key is to be consistent.

**EXAMPLES:**

| Needs Work: | The functions of a military staff are to advise the commander, transmit instructions, and implementation of decisions. |
| Acceptable: | The functions of a military staff are to advise the commander, transmit instructions, and implement decisions. |
| Needs Work: | The security force member told us to observe the speed limit and we should dim our lights. |
| Acceptable: | The security force member told us to observe the speed limit and to dim our lights. |

### 14.8.8. Writer's Block.

If you occasionally suffer from writer's block, you are not alone—many experienced writers have a hard time getting started. The five fears that lead to writer's block are fear of failure, fear of rejection, fear of success, fear of offending, and fear of running out of ideas. Some ways to overcome writer's block are:

14.8.8.1. Brainstorm or "free write" to get your creative ideas flowing.

14.8.8.2. Write just the topic sentences for each paragraph.

14.8.8.3. Avoid procrastination.

14.8.8.4. Don't worry about page length, word count, or some other constraint on the first draft.

14.8.8.5. Bounce ideas off a friend or coworker.

14.8.8.6. Use visuals, like pictures or diagrams, to show meaning.

14.8.8.7. Develop rituals or routines to get in the mood for writing.

## 14.9. Step 6—Edit the Draft.

One way to make sure you edit efficiently is to read your document at least three times to allow yourself to really look hard at the problem areas that could mess up your product. In the first pass, look at the big picture; in the second pass, look at paragraph construction; and in the third pass look at sentences, phrases, and words.

14.9.1. **First Pass: The Big Picture.**

Pay attention to the arrangement and flow of ideas. Here are some ideas to think about:

14.9.1.1. Ensure the purpose statement answers the original tasker.

14.9.1.2. Review the introduction to ensure it contains the purpose statement.

14.9.1.3. Compare the introduction and conclusion to make sure they go together without sounding identical. The introduction should declare the purpose, and the conclusion should show the readers the purpose was accomplished.

14.9.1.4. When checking for relevance and completeness, ensure the paragraphs clearly relate to the purpose statement, contain all main points, and are arranged in a consistent order.

14.9.2. **Second Pass: Paragraph, Structure, and Clarity.**

In the second pass, check whether the main points and supporting ideas are appropriately organized in paragraphs. For each paragraph, focus on the following areas:

14.9.2.1. **Unity of Focus.** Ensure there is only one main point of the paragraph and all the information in the paragraph relates enough to be in the same paragraph.

14.9.2.2. **Topic Sentence.** Ensure the paragraph has one sentence that captures the central idea of the paragraph.

14.9.2.3. **Supporting Ideas.** Ensure sentences expand, clarify, illustrate, and explain points mentioned or suggested in each main idea. The paragraph should have enough details to support the central idea without any extra sentences that are irrelevant to the main point. Also, ensure all transitional words, phrases, and clauses improve the flow and show proper relationships. Finally, the paragraph should contain three to seven sentences.

14.9.3. **Third Pass: Sentences, Phrases, and Words.**

Look at the details and concentrate on the small stuff that can sabotage your communication. These details include the passive voice, unclear language, excessive wordiness, grammatical errors, and spelling mistakes. Read the paper out loud. This requires the communicator to slow down and use two senses—seeing and hearing which increases the chances of catching errors. What one sense misses, the other will pick up.

## 14.10. Step 7—Fight for Feedback and Get Approval.

Fighting for feedback and getting approval are both activities that are part of life in the Air Force. Feedback and coordination are closely linked. If the communicator does a good job at fighting for feedback, the coordination process becomes much smoother. The biggest benefit to fighting for feedback is getting a second pair of eyes to review the communication. Even the best writers and speakers cannot see where the communication can be made stronger as they become too close to the communication. Coworkers are usually a good choice because of their familiarity with the issue and jargon. Also, asking a trusted agent or someone you consider an expert in a specific area of the communication, such as grammar, is another choice to obtain feedback.

14.10.1. **Feedback.**

To give effective feedback, refer to the following:

14.10.1.1. First, effective feedback is consistent, objective, and sensitive to the stated purpose. If asked to review a package, make sure you understand what the person wants from your review and stick to it.

14.10.1.2. Second, distinguish between necessary, desirable, and unnecessary changes. A page full of red marks is hard to interpret. Instead, give the author a sense of what really needs to be changed.

14.10.1.3. Third, avoid using general statements. Instead, pinpoint specific problems such as awkward sentences, grammar, etc.

14.10.1.4. Fourth, concentrate on improving the message's content, not the style or personal preferences of the author (unless the author has asked you specifically to comment on writing style). Before providing feedback, refer to the feedback philosophies in Figure 14.4.

**Figure 14.4. Feedback Philosophies**

---

**Feedback:** Should describe rather than judge.

Is both positive and negative. A balanced description of other people's work considers both strong and weak points.

Strive for being specific rather than general. Highlight or underline specific items you want to bring to the author's attention.

Direct at behavior the author can control. A suggestion to improve the briefing room's temperature, for example, is probably beyond the author's control.

---

14.10.2. **Supervisor-Subordinate Feedback.**

Responsibility as a supervisor requires the need to be tactful and patient, especially when approving and disapproving subordinate's communications. A supervisor is obligated to help subordinates improve their work. This obligation may mean helping them to revise or rewrite their communication, especially if they are inexperienced.

14.10.3. **Get Approval.**

Formal coordination gives affected individuals a chance to comment, and helps ensure the best course of action is presented to the decision maker. To do this you get other offices to approve what you are proposing through the coordination process. Only after the package is fully coordinated can you provide the boss with the best course of action and tell them who is supporting that action.

*Section 14C—Writing*

**14.11. Common Writing Formats.**

The principles of effective communication apply equally well to written and spoken communications. This section will not repeat these principles but will provide the basic formats of written Air Force communication. These formats are the most common and familiar ways of preparing all official and personal correspondence and memorandums.

14.11.1. **Official Memorandum.**

Official memorandums are used to communicate with all Department of Defense agencies. In addition, use official memorandums to conduct official business outside the government with vendors or contractors when the personal letter is inappropriate (Figure 14.5).

14.11.1.1. Use printed letterhead, computer-generated letterhead, or plain bond paper. Only type or print on one side of the paper using black or blue-black ink, and use 10 to 12-point Times New Roman font for text.

14.11.1.2. Neatly and legibly correct minor typographical errors in ink on all correspondence—do not redo correspondence to correct a typographical error that does not change intent. Redo correspondence to correct a minor error only if the correction is sufficiently important to justify the time, purpose, and expense.

14.11.2. **Personal Letter.**

Use the personal letter when your communication needs a personal touch or when warmth or sincerity is essential. You may use the personal letter to write to an individual on a private matter for praise, condolence, sponsorship, etc. Keep the personal letter brief, preferably no longer than one page, include a salutation element (Dear Xxxx), and a complimentary close element (usually Sincerely).

**Figure 14.5. The Official Memorandum.**

# DEPARTMENT OF THE AIR FORCE
## AIR FORCE OCCUPATIONAL MEASUREMENT SQUADRON

24 June 2016

MEMORANDUM FOR ORG/SYMBOL

FROM:  ORG/SYMBOL
        Organization
        Street Address
        City ST 12345-6789

SUBJECT: Sample Memorandum Format (Not exactly scaled/spaced. Consult AFH 33-337 *The Tongue and Quill*)

1. Place the date on the right side of the memorandum 1.75 inches from the top of the page and 1 inch from the right margin.

2. Type the MEMORANDUM FOR caption in all caps on the second line below the date. Leave two spaces and then add the recipient's organization abbreviation and office symbol (ORG/SYMBOL)

3. Type the FROM caption in all caps two line spaces below the last line of the MEMORANDUM FOR caption. After the FROM element, leave two spaces followed by the (ORG/SYMBOL) and then the full mailing address of the originator.

4. Type the SUBJECT caption in all caps, on the second line below the FROM caption.

5. Begin the text on the second line below the SUBJECT caption. Number and letter each paragraph and subparagraph.

6. Type the signature element at least three spaces to the right of page center, five lines below the last line of text. Type the name in UPPERCASE and include grade and service on the first line, the duty title on the second line, and the name of the office or organization level on a third line (if not announced in the heading).

7. Type "Attachments:" at the left margin, three lines below the signature element. Do not number when there is only one attachment; when there are two or more attachments, list each one by number in the order referred to in the memorandum. Describe each attachment briefly. Cite the office of origin, type of communication, date, and number of copies (in parentheses) if more than one.

                                  *John D. Bray*
                                  JOHN D. BRAY, GS-13, DAF
                                  Human Resources Manager

2 Attachments:
1. HQ USAF/DP Memo, 24 Jun 2016
2. AFOMS/CC Msg, 122300Z Mar 16

14.11.3. **Memorandum for Record (MFR or MR).**

The MFR has three forms: the separate-page MFR, the explanatory note, and the compact note.

14.11.3.1. **Separate-Page Memorandum for Record.** The separate-page MFR is based on the official memorandum but omits the "FROM:" since the writer is both the sender and receiver. This MFR is an in-house document to record information that would otherwise not be recorded in writing (for example, a telephone call, results of a meeting, or information passed to other staff members on an informal basis). People who work together every day generally pass most information to their coworkers verbally, but there are times when information should be recorded and kept on file. A memorandum for record is the right tool for this purpose. Figure 14.6 illustrates the format for the separate page MFR.

**Figure 14.6. Separate Page Memorandum for Record.**

MEMO FOR RECORD

1 July 2013

SUBJECT: Preparing a Separate-Page Memorandum for Record

1. Use a separate-page memorandum for record to fulfill the functions discussed on the preceding page.

2. Type or write the memorandum for record on a sheet of paper in this format. Use 1-inch margins all around and number the paragraphs if there is more than one. A full signature block is not necessary, but the memorandum for record should be signed.

*Carolyn R. Brown*

CAROLYN R. BROWN
ASCS/DE

14.11.3.2. **Explanatory Note Memorandum for Record.** The explanatory note memorandum for record is usually on the file copy of most correspondence (Figures 14.7 and 14.8). This memorandum for record gives the reader a quick synopsis of the purpose of the correspondence, tells who got involved, and provides additional information not included in the basic correspondence. By reading both the basic correspondence and the memorandum for record, readers should understand enough about the subject to coordinate on or sign the correspondence without having to call or ask for more information. If the basic correspondence really does say everything, an explanatory memorandum for record may not be required. However, some organizations require you to acknowledge that you have not merely forgotten the memorandum for record by including "memorandum for record: Self-explanatory" on the file copy.

**Figure 14.7. Explanatory Note.**

MEMO FOR RECORD

28 Jun 16

Omit the subject when typing the explanatory note memorandum for record on the record copy. If space permits, type the memorandum for record and date two lines below the signature block. When there is not enough space, type "MFR ATTACHED" or "MFR ON REVERSE" and put the memorandum for record on a separate sheet or on the back of the record copy if it can be read clearly. Number the paragraphs when there are more than one. The signature block is not required; merely sign your last name after the last word of the memorandum for record.

*Brown*

**Figure 14.8. Compact Note.**

Compact Note Memorandum for Record: When you have a very brief memorandum for record and not enough space on the bottom of your correspondence, use this tighter format. Sign your last name followed by the date.

**14.12. Writing Accomplishment—Impact Bullet Statements.**

At some point in your career, you may be required to write bullet statements for an enlisted performance report; Air Force IMT 1206, *Nomination for Award;* bullet background paper; or other Air Force communication. The key to writing an effective bullet statement consists of three steps:

14.12.1. **Step 1: Extract the Facts.**

Getting started can be the hardest part of bullet statement writing. The key is to collect all of the information you can find relevant to the actual accomplishment. First, gather as much information as you can, then sort through the information collected. When sorting the information:

14.12.1.1. Isolate and record the specific action the person performed.

14.12.1.2. Mark the action with a power verb that best describes the action (for example, repaired, installed, designed, etc.).

14.12.1.3. Document related numerical information (number of items fixed, dollars saved, man-hours expended, people served, pages written, etc.).

14.12.1.4. Document how this accomplishment impacted the bigger picture and broader mission of the unit, group, wing, installation, command or Air Force.

14.12.1.5. Once captured, review each item and test to see if the item is truly associated with the single accomplishment identified earlier.

14.12.2. **Step 2: Build the Structure.**

The next step is to take the sorted information and organize the information into an accomplishment-impact bullet. There are two components: the accomplishment element and the impact element.

14.12.2.1. **Accomplishment Element.** The accomplishment element should always begin with an action and only focus on one single accomplishment. Most of the time this action takes the form of a strong action verb such as conducted, established, or led. If you need to give action verbs an added boost, you can use an adverb such as actively, energetically, or swiftly to modify the verb. For a more complete list of verbs and adverbs, refer to Air Force Handbook 33-337, *The Tongue and Quill.*

14.12.2.2. **Impact Element.** The impact element part of the bullet statement explains how the person's actions have had an effect on the organization. The impact element can show varying levels of influence, such as the person's actions connected to significant improvements to a work center's mission, a unit's mission, or as broad as the entire Air Force.

14.12.3. **Step 3: Streamline the Final Product.**

Streamlining the final product is refining the bullet statement to make it accurate, brief, and specific.

14.12.3.1. **Accuracy.** For anything to be accurate, it must be correct. Avoid exaggerating the facts.

14.12.3.2. **Brevity.** When editing for brevity, use the shortest, clearest, yet most descriptive words to the reader and reduce unnecessary words.

14.12.3.3. **Specificity.** Convey the facts in detail; resist the urge to estimate or generalize. Instead, use exact numbers or dollar amounts.

*Section 14D—Face-to-Face: Speaking and Listening*

## 14.13. Air Force Speaking.

This section focuses on spoken communication—both speaking and listening.

### 14.13.1. Verbal Communication.

An effective voice drives home ideas or information. The speaker has control over such things as rate, volume, pitch, and pause. The techniques used to create interest and help increase communication include:

14.13.1.1. **Rate.** There is no correct rate of speed for every speech; however, consider this: the average processing rate is 500 words per minute and the average speaking rate is 180 words a minute. Speak too slowly, and the audience will lose interest; on the other hand, speak too fast and the speech will become unintelligible. The key is to vary the rate of speech to hold the audience's attention and to add emphasis.

14.13.1.2. **Volume.** Another verbal technique that can give emphasis to a speech is volume. If possible, check out the room to know how loudly you must talk, remembering you will need to talk louder with a crowd since the sound is absorbed. Remember your voice will carry further when the room is empty versus full. If the audience must strain to hear you, they will eventually tune you out from utter exhaustion. Speak louder or softer to emphasize a point—a softer level or lower volume is often the more effective way to achieve emphasis.

14.13.1.3. **Pitch.** The use of notes, higher or lower, in the voice is called pitch. Speakers use pitch changes in vowels, words, or entire sentences. Use a downward (high to low) inflection in a sentence for an air of certainty, and an upward (low to high) inflection for an air of uncertainty. Variety in speech pitch helps to avoid monotone and to capture the listener's attention.

14.13.1.4. **Pause.** The pause technique gives the speaker time to catch his or her breath and the audience time to collect the speaker's ideas. The pause technique serves the same function as punctuation in writing. Short pauses usually divide points within a sentence and longer pauses note the ends of sentences. The speaker can also use longer pauses for breaks from one main point to another, from the body to the conclusion of the speech, or to set off an important point worthy of short reflection.

14.13.1.5. **Articulation and Pronunciation.** Articulation is the art of expressing words distinctly. Pronunciation is the ability to say words correctly. People can articulate their thoughts and still mispronounce words while doing so. Unfortunately (and unfairly), many people consider word pronunciation or mispronunciation a direct reflection on the speaker's intelligence. If you are not sure of the pronunciation, consult a current dictionary.

14.13.1.6. **Length.** The length of a presentation is crucial. A key rule in verbal communication is short and sweet. Be prepared, know what you want to say, then say what you want to say with your purpose and audience in mind.

### 14.13.2. Nonverbal Communication.

Actually presenting the talk is the hardest part for many people. How can body movement, voice, and sincerity enhance a presentation? Communications experts tell us that over half of our meaning may be communicated nonverbally. Although nonverbal meaning is communicated through vocal cues, much meaning is carried by the physical behaviors of eye contact, body movement, and gestures.

14.13.2.1. **Eye Contact.** This is one of the most important factors in nonverbal communication. Nothing will enhance the delivery more than effective eye contact with the audience. Eye contact is important for three reasons. First, lets the listeners know the speaker is interested in them. Second, effective eye contact allows you to receive nonverbal feedback from the audience. Third, effective eye contact enhances the credibility of the speaker.

14.13.2.2. **Body Movement.** Good body movement is important because body movement catches the eye of the listener. Effective body movement can be described as free and purposeful. While not essential, the speaker should feel free to move around in front of the audience. When looking at note cards, speakers should drop their eyes, not their head.

14.13.2.3. **Gestures.** Gestures are the purposeful use of the hands, arms, shoulders, and head to reinforce what is being said. Effective gestures are both natural and purposeful. Fidgeting with a paperclip, rearranging or shuffling papers, and constantly clicking a pen are distracting to the audience.

### 14.13.3. Delivery Formats.

Your approach to delivery of the spoken message is usually affected by several factors, including the time you have to prepare and the nature of the message. Three common delivery formats are:

14.13.3.1. **Impromptu.** Speaking when we respond during a meeting or "take the floor" at a conference. Speakers may do this when they have to speak publicly without warning or with only a few moments' notice. To do impromptu speaking well requires a great amount of self-confidence, mastery of the subject, and the ability to "think on your feet." A superb impromptu speaker has achieved the highest level in verbal communications.

14.13.3.2. **Prepared (Formally Extemporaneous).** Prepared speaking or briefing refers to those times when we have ample opportunity to prepare. This does not mean the person writes a script and memorizes the script, but prepared delivery does require a thorough outline with careful planning and practicing. The specific words and phrases used at the time of delivery, however, are spontaneous and sound very natural.

14.13.3.3. **Manuscript.** A manuscript briefing is the delivery format that requires every word spoken to be absolutely perfect. The disadvantage of a manuscript briefing is that people demonstrate a tendency to lack spontaneity, lack eye contact, and they stand behind the lectern with their script.

14.13.4. **Types of Speaking.**

Types of speaking used in the Air Force include briefing, teaching lecture, and formal speech.

14.13.4.1. **Briefing.** The best military briefings are concise and factual. Their major purpose is to inform listeners about a mission, operation, or concept. Some briefings direct or enable listeners to perform a procedure or carry out instructions. Other briefings advocate, persuade, or support a certain solution and lead the audience to accept the briefing. Every good briefing has the qualities of accuracy, brevity, and clarity. Accuracy and clarity characterize all good speaking, but brevity distinguishes the briefing from other types of speaking. A briefer must be brief and to the point and should anticipate some of the questions that may arise. If a briefer cannot answer a question, he or she should not attempt an off-the-top-of-the-head answer. Instead, he or she should admit to not knowing the answer and offer to provide the answer later.

14.13.4.2. **Teaching Lecture.** The teaching lecture is the method of instruction most often used in the Air Force. As the name implies, the primary purpose of a teaching lecture is to teach students about a given subject. Teaching lectures are either formal or informal. Formal lectures are generally one-way with no verbal participation by the students. Informal lectures are usually presented to smaller audiences and allow for verbal interaction between the instructor and students.

14.13.4.3. **Formal Speech.** A formal speech generally has one of three basic purposes: to inform, persuade, or entertain. The informative speech is a narration concerning a specific topic but does not involve a sustained effort to teach. Orientation talks and presentations at commander's call are examples of informative speeches. The persuasive speech is designed to move an audience to believe in or take action on the topic presented. Recruiting speeches to high school graduating classes and court-martial summations are speeches primarily developed to persuade. The entertaining speech gives enjoyment to the audience. The speaker often relies on humor and vivid language to entertain listeners. A speech to entertain is appropriate at a Dining-Out.

14.14. **Effective Listening:**

14.14.1. **Understanding the Listening Process.**

To better understand the listening process, let's begin by distinguishing between hearing and listening. Hearing occurs when your ears pick up sound waves being transmitted by a speaker or some other source. Hearing requires a source of sound and an ear capable of perceiving sound. Hearing does not require the conscious decoding of information.

14.14.2. **Listening To Make Sense.**

Listening, on the other hand, involves making sense out of what is being transmitted. Listening involves not only hearing, it involves attending to and considering what is heard. Effective listening is an active process. Active listening involves exerting energy and responding appropriately in order to hear, comprehend, evaluate, and remember the message.

14.14.3. **The Importance of Listening.**

Listening is especially important in the Air Force, and actually in any military unit. Success is literally a matter of life and death, and we routinely maintain/operate equipment worth millions of dollars. Receiving, comprehending, and remembering spoken information is critical. Any miscommunication is potentially catastrophic. Effective listening helps to build the trust and mutual respect needed to do our jobs. Military personnel must understand their team members and the situation. Leaders with good listening skills often make better decisions and have a stronger bond with their Airmen.

14.14.4. **Pick the Right Tool for the Job: Informative, Critical, or Empathic Listening.**

There are different situations where listening is important and different reasons to listen. Everyone must understand the importance for acknowledging and identifying these differences because appropriate listening behaviors in one situation are sometimes inappropriate in another situation.

14.14.4.1. **Informative Listening.** In informative listening, the listener's primary concern is to understand information exactly as transmitted. A successful listening outcome occurs when the listener understands the message exactly as the sender intended. Suggestions for improving informative listening are to:

14.14.4.1.1. **Keep an Open Mind.** If the primary goal is to understand the message, set aside your preconceptions about the topic and just listen.

14.14.4.1.2. **Listen as if You Had to Teach It.** Typically, we expend more effort to understand a subject when we know that we have to teach a subject to someone else. By taking this approach, we have the mental fortitude to focus longer, ask questions when we do not understand, and think more deeply on a topic.

14.14.4.1.3. **Take Notes.** Focus on main points, and do not attempt to capture everything.

14.14.4.1.4. **Respond and Ask Appropriate Questions.** Good informative listening questions help you clarify and confirm your understanding of the message.

14.14.4.1.5. **Exploit the Time Gap Between Thinking and Speaking Speeds.** The average speaking rate is 180 words per minute; the average processing rate is 500 words per minute. Use this extra time to mentally repeat, forecast, summarize, and paraphrase the speaker's remarks.

14.14.4.2. **Critical Listening.** Critical listening is usually thought of as the sum of informative listening and critical thinking. The listener is actively analyzing and evaluating the message the speaker is sending. Critical listening is appropriate when seeking input to a decision, evaluating the quality of staff work or a subordinate's capabilities, or conducting research. Suggestions for improving critical listening are to:

14.14.4.2.1. **Take Notes.** As with informative listening, focus on main points, and do not attempt to capture everything.

14.14.4.2.2. **Listen as if You Had to Grade It.** One of the few things more difficult than teaching is grading another's work. By taking this approach, we have the mental fortitude to focus longer, ask questions when we do not understand, and think more deeply on a topic.

14.14.4.2.3. **Exploit the Time Gap Between Thinking and Speaking Speeds.** Critical listening is different from informational listening in that you need to try to understand first and evaluate second. Even when you are listening critically, do not mentally argue with the speaker until the message is complete.

14.14.4.2.4. **Ask Appropriate Questions.** Good critical listening questions will be probing in nature to thoroughly evaluate the intellectual content of the speaker's message.

14.14.4.3. **Empathic Listening.** Empathic listening is often useful when communication is emotional or when the relationship between speaker and listener is just as important as the message. Use this type of listening as a first step in the listening process, a prerequisite to informational or critical listening. Empathic listening is often appropriate during mentoring and nonpunitive counseling sessions and is very helpful when communicating with family members.

## Section 14E—Electronic Communications and the Internet

### 14.15. E-mail.

E-mail is defined as the electronic transmission of information over computer-based messaging systems. Recent technological advancements have increased opportunities for more timely, efficient, and effective text-based communications. These advancements facilitated the explosive growth of e-mail use throughout the Air Force at all levels. To uphold a commitment to secure messaging, the Air Force has established guidelines to ensure standardized and responsible use by all Air Force members.

### 14.16. Identity Management.

A vital element for messaging security is the implementation of public key infrastructure and common access cards for identity management. Public key infrastructure allows for the authentication of the sender identity using a digital signature and the encryption and decryption of the message. Users of Department of Defense electronic messaging are directed to follow current Air Force guidance for the use of public key infrastructure to sign and encrypt e-mail.

### 14.17. Defense Message System.

The defense message system is the core messaging system of record for the Department of Defense and the Air Force.

Defense message system is a flexible, commercial-off-the-shelf based application that provides messaging services to all Department of Defense users (including deployed tactical users) and interfaces to other United States government agencies, allied forces, and defense contractors.

## 14.18. Air Force Organizational Messaging.

Organization simple mail transfer protocol mailboxes may be used for all organizational messaging requirements unless usage of defense message system is required in support of combatant command responsibilities.

## 14.19. Individual Responsibilities.

All government communications systems are subject to monitoring, interception, search, and seizure for all authorized purposes. Government-provided messaging systems are for official use and limited authorized personal use only. Individuals must:

14.19.1. Maintain responsibility for the content of their electronic messages and ensure that messages sent adhere to acceptable use of Internet-based capabilities.

14.19.2. Maintain sent and received information according to Air Force records management directives. Emails may be subject to requests under the freedom of information act, litigation, and court orders. If requested, individuals are responsible for reviewing messages in email accounts and all backups to locate responsive material.

14.19.3. Adhere to local policy on sending electronic messages to a large number of recipients. Digital images, as well as mass distribution of smaller messages, may delay other traffic, overload the system, and subsequently cause system failure.

14.19.4. Adhere to local policy when sending an electronic message to mail distribution lists. Use web pages or electronic public folders for unofficial electronic messages (i.e., booster club activities, etc.).

14.19.5. Only reply to electronic messages that absolutely require a response and minimize the use of the Reply to All function.

14.19.6. Bear sole responsibility for material sent.

14.19.7. Properly coordinate and staff electronic messages according to local directives.

14.19.8. Take appropriate action on non-delivery notices or message rejects to ensure messages reach the intended recipient.

14.19.9. Not auto-forward electronic messages from the .mil domain to a commercial internet service provider.

14.19.10. Not indiscriminately release electronic messaging addresses to the public. For further information reference the Air Force Freedom of Information Act; Release of Email Addresses.

## 14.20. Privacy Act Information.

The Privacy Act of 1974 requires agencies to provide safeguards to ensure the security and confidentiality of records and to protect individuals against an invasion of personal privacy. Exercise caution before transmitting personal information over e-mail to ensure the message is adequately safeguarded. When information is so sensitive and personal, e-mail is not the proper way for transmitting this information. When sending personal information over e-mail within Department of Defense, ensure:

14.20.1. There is an official need.

14.20.2. All addressees (including "cc" addressees) are authorized to receive personal information under the Privacy Act.

14.20.3. "For official use only" is added to the beginning of the subject line, followed by the subject, and apply the following statement at the beginning of the e-mail: "This e-mail contains for official use only information which must be protected under *The Privacy Act* and AFI 33-332." Do not indiscriminately apply this statement to e-mails and use only in situations when you are actually transmitting personal information.

## 14.21. E-mail Protocol.

E-mail protocol provides guidelines for proper behavior while on-line. There are many ways to make social blunders and offend people when you are posting. Respect the social culture, and remember that the net is multicultural. Nuances get lost in transmission.

14.21.1. **Rule 1—Be Clear and Concise:**

14.21.1.1. Make sure the subject line communicates your purpose. Be specific and avoid ambiguous titles.

14.21.1.2. Lead with the most important information. If the goal is to answer a question, then paste the question at the top of the page for clearer understanding.

14.21.1.3. Use topic sentences if the e-mail has multiple paragraphs.

14.21.1.4. Be brief and stick to the point. Address the issue, the whole issue, and nothing but the issue.

14.21.1.5. Use bold, italic, or color to emphasize key points.

14.21.1.6. Choose readable fonts. Use 12 point or larger when possible.

14.21.2. **Rule 2—Watch Your Tone:**

14.21.2.1. Be polite. Treat others as you want to be treated. Think of the message as a personal conversation.

14.21.2.2. Be careful with humor, irony, and sarcasm. Electronic postings are perceived much more harshly than they are intended, mainly because the receiver cannot see the sender's body language or hear the tone of voice, or any other nonverbal cues that make up 90 percent of interpersonal communications.

14.21.2.3. DON'T SHOUT. Do not write using all CAPITAL LETTERS—this is the e-mail equivalent of shouting and is considered rude.

14.21.2.4. Keep the email clean and professional. E-mail is easily forwarded. Harassing, intimidating, abusive, or offensive material is unacceptable.

14.21.3. **Rule 3—Be Selective About What Message You Send and Do Not:**

14.21.3.1. Discuss controversial, sensitive, for official use only, classified, personal, Privacy Act, or unclassified information requiring special handling of documents.

14.21.3.2. Forget operations security. Remember operations security, even unclassified information, when brought together with other information, can create problems in the wrong hands.

14.21.3.3. Create junk mail, forward email, or put email on a bulletin board.

14.21.3.4. Create or send chain letters. They waste time and tie up the system.

14.21.3.5. Use e-mail for personal ads.

14.21.4. **Rule 4—Be Selective About Who Gets Your Message:**

14.21.4.1. Reply to specific addressees to give those not interested a break.

14.21.4.2. Use "reply all" sparingly.

14.21.4.3. Get permission before using large mail groups.

14.21.4.4. Double-check the address before mailing, especially when selecting from a global list where many people have similar last names.

14.21.5. **Rule 5—Check Your Attachments and Support Material:**

14.21.5.1. Ensure all information is provided the first time to keep from repeating e-mail just to add another fact.

14.21.5.2. Before sending ensure that you have attached the attachments; this is the most common mistake.

14.21.5.3. Cite all quotes, references, and sources. Respect copyright and license agreements.

14.21.6. **Rule 6—Keep Your E-mail Under Control:**

14.21.6.1. Sign off the computer when you leave your workstation.

14.21.6.2. Create mailing lists to save time.

14.21.6.3. Read and delete files daily. Create an organized directory on your hard drive to keep mailbox files at a minimum. Ensure record copies are properly identified and stored in an approved filing system.

14.21.6.4. Acknowledge important or sensitive messages with a reply to sender; for example, Thanks, done, I will start working the details in the email immediately, etc.

14.21.6.5. When away from your e-mail for an extended period, consider setting up an "Auto Reply" message to let people know how long you will be unavailable via e-mail, as well as providing alternate points of contact for questions that require immediate answers or response.

**14.22. The Internet.**

Use of the Web or web technologies continues to increase as a technique for obtaining and disseminating information worldwide. The Web or Internet provides the capability to quickly and efficiently disseminate information to and access information from a variety of governmental and nongovernmental sources. Web content must be managed in compliance with all information management policies and procedures.

14.22.1. **Use of Internet Resources by Government Employees.**

The Internet provides an indispensable source for information from a variety of governmental and nongovernmental sources. The Air Force goal, within acceptable risk levels, is to provide maximum accessibility to Internet resources for personnel requiring access for official business.

14.22.2. **Appropriate Use.**

Government-provided hardware and software are for official use and limited authorized personal use only. Limited personal use must be of reasonable duration and frequency that have been approved by the supervisors and do not adversely affect performance of official duties, overburden systems or reflect adversely on the Air Force or the Department of Defense.

14.22.3. **Inappropriate Use.**

Using the Internet for other than official or authorized purposes may result in adverse administrative or disciplinary action. The following are specifically prohibited:

14.22.3.1. Use of Federal government communications systems for unauthorized personal use.

14.22.3.2. Uses that would adversely reflect on the Department of Defense or the Air Force such as chain letters, unofficial soliciting, or selling except on authorized Internet-based capabilities established for such use.

14.22.3.3. Unauthorized storing, processing, displaying, sending, or otherwise transmitting prohibited content. Prohibited content includes: pornography, sexually explicit or sexually oriented material, nudity, hate speech or ridicule of others on the basis of protected class (e.g., race, creed, religion, color, age, sex, disability, national origin), gambling, illegal weapons, militancy/extremist activities, terrorist activities, use for personal gain, and any other content or activities that are illegal or inappropriate.

14.22.3.4. Storing or processing classified information on any system not approved for classified processing.

14.22.3.5. Using copyrighted material in violation of the rights of the owner of the copyrights. Consult with the servicing Staff Judge Advocate for fair use advice.

14.22.3.6. Unauthorized use of the account or identity of another person or organization.

14.22.3.7. Viewing, changing, damaging, deleting, or blocking access to another user's files or communications without appropriate authorization or permission.

14.22.3.8. Attempting to circumvent or defeat security or modifying security systems without prior authorization or permission (such as for legitimate system testing or security research).

14.22.3.9. Obtaining, installing, copying, storing, or using software in violation of the appropriate vendor's license agreement.

14.22.3.10. Permitting an unauthorized individual access to a government-owned or government-operated system.

14.22.3.11. Modifying or altering the network operating system or system configuration without first obtaining written permission from the administrator of that system.

14.22.3.12. Copying and posting of for official use only, controlled unclassified information, critical information), and/or personally identifiable information on Department of Defense–owned, operated, or controlled publically accessible sites or on commercial Internet-based capabilities.

14.22.3.13. Downloading and installing freeware/shareware or any other software product without designated accrediting authority approval.

14.22.4. **Malicious Logic Protection.**

Protect information systems from malicious logic (e.g., virus, worm, Trojan horse) attacks by applying a mix of human and technological preventative measures. Scan approved removable media devices for viruses before and after use if scans are not automated. Report any suspected information systems abnormalities (i.e., antivirus errors, virus alerts, unexpected file size increases, unexpected disk access, strange activity by applications, etc.) immediately to the organizational information assurance officer.

14.22.5. **Operations Security and the Internet.**

When accessing internet-based capabilities using Federal Government resources in an authorized personal or unofficial capacity, individuals shall comply with operations security guidance (AFI 10-701, *Operations Security*) and shall not represent the policies or official position of the Air Force or Department of Defense.

*Section 14F—Conducting an Effective Interview*

## 14.23. Introduction.

Many Air Force positions require a job interview. Knowing how to prepare for and conduct yourself during this process can go a long way toward helping you get that special duty or some other much-coveted job in the Air Force. This section is designed to help you prepare for and succeed in conducting an effective Air Force interview:

14.23.1. **Purpose of Interviews.**

So, you've found a new job in the Air Force—one that requires special talents and experience; one that requires you to gather letters of recommendation, submit a resume, and provide copies of your last five enlisted performance reports (EPR); *and* one that requires you to sit through a job interview. If you've ever completed a special duty assignment or worked at certain headquarters assignments, chances are you've already sat through a job interview. However, for many Airmen out there, the Air Force job interview is a new experience—one requiring preparation, practice, and perseverance.

14.23.1.1. Before you set off for that interview, there are a few things you will need to understand about the interview process. First, you need to understand the purpose of the job interview. All job interviews are designed with one goal in mind: to find the right person for a particular job. As military members, many of you will sit through job interviews to get that special job or position you've been looking for. Understanding that employers may have to interview several member for the position, should give you some respect for the process and help you understand that your goal in an interview is to convince the interviewer that *you* are the right person for the job.

14.23.1.2. The second thing you should know about interviews is that they are a two-way process. You are not only interviewing for a job; you are interviewing the prospective employer to see if you actually want the job. Are you willing to spend the next 2-3 years of your career in this organization? Are you willing to work under the conditions laid out in the job description? Are you willing to make a permanent change of station for the position? There are a host of other concerns you should have in mind when preparing for the interview, many of which should center on your desire for the job and working in the new organization.

14.23.1.3. Third, you need to understand that interviews are information-sharing events between you and the interviewer. Your job is to convince the interviewer that your unique knowledge, skills, and abilities are a perfect match for the position you're seeking. Conversely, the interviewer's job is to sift through reams of information gathered from numerous interviews and eventually match the *right* person to the position. The interviewer is basically asking each interviewee the same question: "Why should I hire *you*?" while all interviewees are also highlighting their particular skills for the job.

14.23.2. **Types of Interviews.**

As you've just read, the purpose of the interview is to find the best person for the job. However, interviews can be conducted in several different ways.

14.23.2.1. **Face-to-face Interviews:**

14.23.2.1.1. Face-to-face interviews usually take place in one of two formats: the individual interview or the panel interview. The individual interview may be the person who will supervise you or someone higher in the chain of command. Hiring decisions are often made based on this type of interview. Count on discussing your skills, experience, and training, and how they all relate to the job.

14.23.2.1.2. A selection panel or board interview is frequently used when organizations are filling a managerial position. Usually, three or more people sit on the board, and all candidates are asked the same questions. A selection board interview usually involves more structured questions than an individual interview. This interview can be stressful because you have to answer questions from several people. Be sure to make eye contact with everyone on the panel. When answering a question, you should make eye contact with the person asking the question.

14.23.2.2. **Phone Interviews:**

14.23.2.2.1. The phone interview is another strategy organizations use to select highly qualified Airmen. In this situation, the hiring organization interviews applicants over the phone. These interviews are sometimes used to make first-round cuts to the applicant pool.

14.23.2.2.2. If you apply for a special assignment, chances are the location will be away from your current assignment. In this case, the hiring organization usually conducts the entire interview over the phone. In these situations, there are no second chances to make a good impression, and decisions are based strictly on the phone interview.

14.23.3. **Interviewing:**

14.23.3.1. **Pre-interview Preparations:**

14.23.3.1.1. One of the first things you need to do to prepare for any Air Force job interview is to carefully study the job advertisement or position description. This provides you with information on the particular knowledge, skills, and abilities for which the hiring organization is looking. What experience or skills are required for the job? Do you have the required experience or skills? Note the key responsibilities of the job and try to match your knowledge, skills, and abilities to those requirements and you should make the connections now because you will be asked to do the very same thing during the interview. This first step helps you understand how your talents measure up to the requirements for the position you're seeking.

14.23.3.1.2. The next step is to gather all required information and documentation for the application process. In many cases, you will need to submit past EPRs, a personnel report on individual personnel, a resume, letters of recommendation, and a cover letter. A targeted resume and letters of recommendation should highlight your particular knowledge, skills, and abilities, and relate them to the position for which you're applying. A cover letter should target one or two strengths not mentioned in your EPRs, resume, or letters of recommendation.

14.23.3.1.3. One important aspect to consider before the interview is to conduct research on the mission and history of the hiring organization before the interview. Who are the commander and senior enlisted members of the organization? How large is the organization? What are the mission and vision statements? If you know someone who works in the organization, you should call him or her and ask some particular questions about the organization. Are there any mission changes in the foreseeable future? How many enlisted personnel are assigned there? Has the organization done anything noteworthy in the past 2 or 3 years? The more you know about the organization, the better job you will do of convincing potential employers that you care about the organization, as well as the job you're seeking.

14.23.3.1.4. When preparing for any interview, think about and write down your strengths and weaknesses. Identify two or three strengths that target the knowledge, skills, and abilities in the job advertisement. Next, identify one or two weaknesses that can be turned into strengths (for example, I'm detail oriented but not a micromanager). Putting your strengths and weakness on paper allows you to study and become intimately familiar with them and builds your confidence as you prepare for the interview. As you write down your strengths and weaknesses, develop specific examples that highlight your skills. You will be asked to provide examples of your experience during the interview. Developing examples *before* the interview can only help make the interview flow more smoothly.

14.23.3.1.5. Use job descriptions and bullets from past EPRs to develop possible questions employers might ask during the interview. Remember, employers know exactly what they are looking for, and they are using the interview process to find the right person to fill the position. Put yourself in the interviewer's shoes and develop a set of questions you would ask if you were them. Then, develop answers to the questions you just came up with. If your EPRs were sent as part of the application package, you can bet some of the questions will be targeted toward specific achievements highlighted. Include specific, concrete examples that not only highlight your skills but also tie directly to the specific requirements of the job. Some examples of areas to concentrate on are: (1) problem-solving skills; (2) thoughts on Air Force transformation; (3) team-building skills; (4) how you support the Chief of Staff of the Air Force priorities; (5) leadership philosophy; (6) ability to adapt and work in fast-paced environments; (7) handling criticism; and (8) decision making ability.

14.23.3.1.6. Also, be able to answer the following questions: Why should I hire *you*? How soon can you report? If applicable, how does your family feel about the move? Where do you see yourself in 2 to 3 years? Are there any personal issues that may prevent you from accepting or performing in this position?

14.23.3.1.7. Develop a list of questions to ask potential employers. Interviewers expect candidates to ask intelligent, thoughtful questions concerning the organization and the nature of the work. The nature and quality of your questions reveals your interest in the organization and the position you're seeking. Ensure your questions are employer-centered; avoid self-centered questions that might indicate you are primarily interested in knowing about the benefits of the position. Potential questions should center on (1) duties and responsibilities of the job; (2) possible mission changes in the organization; (3) chain of command or lines of responsibility; (4) unique requirements of the organization; and (5) a typical day in the organization.

14.23.3.1.8. Finally, you need to practice, practice, practice. Practice how you will get out of your car. Practice how you will walk into the room. Practice how you will answer questions. Practice how you will ask questions. Practice your nonverbals. Practice anything you think you will do before, during, or after the interview. This will make you more comfortable and confident and will help you perform better during the interview. If possible, have friends and family conduct mock interviews. Practice in front of a mirror if mock interviews are impossible or impractical. The bottom line here is practice, practice, practice!

14.23.3.2. **Listening Skills.** Listening during the interview is as essential to your success as talking openly and honestly about knowledge, skills, and abilities. Concentrate on what is being said and how it is said, rather than how you are doing. By listening to the interviewer's statements, comments, and questions, you gain a better understanding of the organization and what workplace would be like to work there. If you pay close attention, you can probably hear the "questions behind the questions" your interviewer asks. In other words, pay close attention and read between the lines for what is ***not*** being said in the interview, and you can probably pick up useful nuggets of information that can benefit you during the interview. For instance, if the interviewer continually asks about your ability to develop and motivate teams or seems to refer to getting teams to work better, you may pick up a possible team-development issue within the organization. With this information, you can sell your ability to lead and motivate teams and possibly land yourself the job.

14.23.4. **The Actual Interview.**

As mentioned earlier, most will be interviewed in one of two ways: by phone or in person. If conducted by phone, the interview begins the moment you pick up the phone and ends once you hang up. On the other hand, personal interviews begin the moment you get out of your car and end when you drive out of the parking lot. Either way, the interview is the one best chance you have of "selling yourself" to any potential employer. Whether you interview by phone or in person, there are certain rules you should keep in mind: (1) keep your answers concise; limited to about 2-3 minutes; (2) provide specific examples of your skills and achievements; (3) tie your strengths to the requirements of the job; (4) ask questions; (5) maintain a conversational tone throughout the interview; and (6) keep important documents nearby (such as EPRs, resumes, letters of reference, etc.).

14.23.4.1. **The Phone Interview.**

To some, the phone interview may seem less important than a personal interview because the interview is conducted from different locations and removed from direct observation of the interviewer. However, in many aspects, the phone interview is more difficult than a personal interview. For instance, in a personal interview you can usually gauge how the interview is going by paying attention to the interviewer's nonverbals. On the other hand, with a phone interview there are no visual cues to tell you how you are doing. Therefore, there are some areas you will have to pay close attention to if you want to successfully navigate through a phone interview. Here are a few tips to help you succeed:

14.23.4.1.1. Smile during the interview, just as you would in a personal interview. While hiding behind a phone allows you to disguise your body language, there is no way you can disguise your vocal cues due to nonverbals. Smiling during a phone interview keeps you energetic and helps project enthusiasm.

14.23.4.1.2. Keep a mirror in front of you during the interview. This allows you to see your own expressions and will help to ensure you are smiling and paying attention to your body language. Just because the interviewer can't see you doesn't mean he or she is not listening for details of your nonverbal responses during the interview. A mirror also ensures you conduct yourself in much the same way you would in a personal interview. You would not put your feet on a desk during a personal interview, would you? Of course not! So keep your feet off your desk during a phone interview. Believe it or not, your body posture naturally reflects in your voice. If your posture is slacking while you are on the phone, you can bet your vocal tone will convey that. Keeping a mirror in front of you will help you focus on your body language and nonverbal responses.

14.23.4.1.3. Know when to speak, and then when to stop. In a personal interview, you can usually tell from the interviewer's nonverbals when you need to wrap up an answer or move on. Phone interviews are often filled with long, silent pauses. Do not feel that you need to fill that dead space with conversation. Pay close attention to the tone of the interviewer's voice and know when to stop talking and move on.

14.23.4.1.4. Develop notes for telephone interviews. These notes should include a list of your strengths and weaknesses and how your skills match organizational needs. Develop a list of potential questions employers might ask, along with possible responses. Practice delivering responses so that you will be ready to give polished answers in a clear confident tone. Do not memorize canned answers since they are likely to sound canned over the phone. Instead, use the script to trigger appropriate responses that sound both spontaneous and energetic. Do not forget to ask questions. Questions for potential employers should be part of your script and should be kept readily available during the interview. Keep in mind, the real key to success in any interview is practice.

14.23.4.2. **The Personal Interview:**

14.23.4.2.1. In many cases, personal interviews begin the moment you get out of your car and do not end until you drive away. Many prospective employers will observe you as you walk from your car to the front door of the building or office. Others will purposely let you sit in a waiting area for 10 to 20 minutes. All of this is designed to create tension and provide the employer an opportunity to observe your bearing before the actual interview begins. We cannot overstate that you are on the interviewing clock even though you are not sitting in an interviewing room.

14.23.4.2.2. In job interviews, potential employers judge you on how you look and act, not just on what you say. Your actions, mannerisms, and appearance are reflected in your body language. They give nonverbal information about your work-related skills, attitudes, and values. Research shows that 65 percent of meaning in any interaction is conveyed nonverbally. In many interviews, nonverbal cues are just as important as verbal information in determining who is hired. After all, each person the organization interviews is probably qualified for the job. Therefore, you want to appear *more* qualified than anyone else—do not let your nonverbals cost you a job.

14.23.4.2.3. The first thing required for the interview is to ensure you are wearing the proper uniform. You should get this information before the interview, but check before the interview to make sure. Your dress and appearance is the first nonverbal message you send to any employer, so ensure you are squared away and nothing is out of place.

14.23.4.2.4. Offer a firm (but not *too* firm), warm, whole-hand handshake. Shake hands with both men and women the same way. You would not give men and women different salutes, so do not offer them different handshakes. Practice your handshake before the interview.

14.23.4.2.5. Make eye contact with the interviewers. Your eyes are your most powerful communication tools, and many interviewers use eye contact to determine enthusiasm, sincerity, and possible inconsistencies in your responses. If you use natural eye contact, the interview will become more like a conversation between acquaintances and you will get over some of your nervousness.

14.23.4.2.6. Sit up straight, but not stiff, and lean slightly forward toward the interviewer. As the interview progresses, you may want to mirror the body language of the interviewer. If the interviewer takes a more relaxed posture, then you should relax too—but not too much. If the interviewer is more formal, then you need to mirror that formal behavior.

14.23.4.2.7. Use natural gestures. If you normally use your hands to gesture as you talk, do so during the interview. Gestures help you relax, convey enthusiasm, and release nervous energy. Be careful, though, to avoid nervous gestures such as drumming your fingers, playing with a pencil, jingling the change in your pocket, tapping your feet, etc.

14.23.4.2.8. Speak clearly and evenly—not too fast, but not too slow. Expression is a powerful way to show enthusiasm. Do not speak in a monotone voice. Allow your volume to rise and fall, and pronounce words clearly. Use good grammar and diction, and always think before you speak. The interviewer will assess your communication skills based on how clearly you express yourself.

14.23.4.2.9. Notice the nonverbal cues of the interviewer. His or her facial expressions will let you know how well he or she is listening and may give you clues as to how you are doing. For instance, if the interviewer seems distracted or inattentive, you will need to shorten your answers, use examples, or ask questions.

14.23.4.2.10. As the interview ends, take 2 to 3 minutes to summarize. This gives you a chance to end the interview on a positive note, convey your interest in the position, and sell yourself one more time. During the summary, recap one or two of the key points of the interview and restate how your experience and skills match those required for the position.

14.24. **Post-interview Actions:**

14.24.1. Once the interview is complete, two things will increase your chances of success and help you learn from your experience. First, send a short (two or three paragraphs) thank-you note to the organization with which you interviewed. The letter should be typed or handwritten and should express your gratitude for the interview opportunity. Restate your interest in the position and highlight any particularly noteworthy points made in your conversation or anything you wish to further clarify. This is also an opportunity to add anything you forgot or wish you had said in the interview. Close the letter by mentioning that you will call in a few days to inquire about the employer's decision. Always mail the letter within a day or two of the interview.

14.24.2. The second thing is to make a few notes about the interview. Record some of the questions asked and how you answered them. Write down your strong and weak points from the interview. Make a list of what made the interview successful, what you would change, and what you need to improve. These notes can be invaluable information for you to review and work on for future interviews.

## 14.25. Interview Conclusion.

The job interview is the most important step in any job-search process. Many Airmen will undergo the rigors of an interview for special positions during the course of their careers. Understanding the purpose of the job interview and your role in successfully planning for and conducting a proper interview can greatly increase your chances of landing a coveted job in the Air Force.

*Section 14G—Staff-Level Communication*

## 14.26. Spoken Communication via the Meeting.

Meetings are used to share information, solve problems, plan, brainstorm, or motivate. Whatever their purpose, you need to know some basics about conducting an effective meeting.

### 14.26.1. Planning the Meeting.

Success or failure in a meeting can usually be traced to the planning phase. The key issues associated with planning a meeting are listed below. As you review these items, remember to check on what are standard operating procedures in your organization. Meetings come in all flavors—from totally spontaneous to highly structured and ceremonial. Most are in the middle. If a group has been meeting regularly for a while, try to find out how they have done business in the past.

14.26.1.1. **Decide if the Meeting is Appropriate.** If you can achieve the goal by speaking face-to-face with one or two people, scheduling a formal meeting might not be necessary. If the goal is to just pass on information, consider if sending an e-mail is a viable and appropriate substitute for the meeting.

14.26.1.2. **Define the Purpose.** Every meeting should have a purpose and if there is no purpose, you should not meet. When thinking about the purpose, define in terms of the product wanted at the end of the meeting and what purpose will the product be used for.

14.26.1.3. **Decide Who Should Be Invited.** Invite only those directly involved in the issues being discussed. If you are trying to solve a problem or make a decision on a controversial issue, make sure you have adequate representation from all groups who have a voice in the decision. If you only invite people with one point of view, your meeting will run smoothly, but your decision may not stand up later.

14.26.1.4. **Decide Where and When the Meeting Should Occur.** Ensure the time is convenient for the people who are required to be there, keep the meeting under an hour, or plan for breaks. Finally, reserve the room.

14.26.1.5. **Plan for Capturing Meeting Information.** If this is not a routine meeting with an appointed recorder, take a moment to think about how you will capture the meeting information, both in the meeting itself and afterwards.

14.26.1.5.1. **Capturing Information during the Meeting.** This can be done by using standard note-taking procedures. Ensuring your meeting place has either a dry erase board, butcher paper, or other note-taking capabilities will assist in getting this accomplished.

14.26.1.5.2. **Capturing Information after the Meeting.** Meeting minutes capture the process and outcome of the meeting. Minutes "close the loop" on the meeting and let the attendees know what was decided.

14.26.1.6. **Send Out an Agenda.** Create an agenda and send the agenda to attendees no later than 1 or 2 days before the meeting. The agenda should include the date, time, location, and purpose of the meeting. This advance notice gives everyone an opportunity to prepare their thoughts and know where the meeting is going before they get there.

### 14.26.2. Running the Meeting.

Avoid dragging out a meeting unnecessarily.

14.26.2.1. **Start on Time; Stay on Time.** Meetings should start on time with an upbeat note, so do not wait for tardy attendees. State your desired outcome.

14.26.2.2. **Follow the Agenda.** People generally don't like when a meeting deviates from the agenda. Review the agenda in the opening minutes of the meeting to remind everyone of the goals and plan for the meeting.

14.26.2.3. **Understand Group Dynamics.** If you are in charge of a group that will meet over a period of time, you should learn the basics about group dynamics. In group dynamics which will be experienced in meetings, teams or groups move through predictable stages. To avoid frustration, becoming familiar with these stages is important.

14.26.2.3.1. **Forming Stage.** When a team is forming, members cautiously explore the boundaries of acceptable group behavior. The forming stage is a stage of transition from individual to member status, and of testing the leader's guidance, both formally and informally. Because so much is going on to distract the members' attention in the beginning, the team accomplishes little, if anything, that is concerned with the project goals. Do not be overly concerned; this is perfectly normal!

14.26.2.3.2. **Storming Stage.** Probably the most difficult stage for the team is the storming stage. The team members begin to realize the task is different and more difficult than imagined and they become testy, accusatory, or overzealous. Impatient about the lack of progress, but still too inexperienced to know much about decision making or the scientific approach, members argue about what actions the team should take. They try to rely solely on their personal and professional experience, resisting any need for collaborating with other team members. Their behavior means team members have little energy to spend on progressing toward the team's goal, but they are beginning to understand one another.

14.26.2.3.3. **Norming Stage.** During the norming stage, members reconcile competing loyalties and responsibilities. They accept the team, team ground rules (or "norms"), their roles in the team, and the individuality of fellow members. Emotional conflict is reduced as previously competitive relationships become more cooperative. As team members begin to work out their differences, they now have more time and energy to spend on the project. Thus, they are able to at last start making significant strides.

14.26.2.3.4. **Performing Stage.** By the time of the performing stage, the team has settled their relationships and expectations. At last, team members have discovered and accepted each other's strengths and weaknesses and learned what their roles are. The team is now an effective, cohesive unit. They can begin performing—diagnosing and solving problems, and choosing and implementing changes. You can tell when your team has reached the performing stage because you start getting a lot of work done—finally!

14.26.3. **Follow up: Preparing Meeting Minutes.**

Follow up involves sending out meeting minutes and starting the whole cycle over again. Prepare meeting minutes in the official memorandum format. Minutes are a clear summary of the participants' comments and document planned or completed actions.

14.26.3.1. Date the minutes the day they are distributed. The names of members present may be listed in two columns to save space.

14.26.3.2. Place information regarding a future meeting in the last paragraph.

14.26.3.3. When a person signs a paper as a member of a board or committee, the signature element indicates that person's status on that board or committee, not any other position the person may hold. To approve the minutes, type "Approved as written" two lines below the recorder's signature block, followed by the approving authority's signature block.

14.26.3.4. Minutes are typed either single or double-spaced, with additional space between items of business and paragraphs.

14.26.3.5. The format should be neat and orderly, paying particular attention to uniformity of margins and text.

14.26.3.6. Spell names correctly, use acceptable grammar, and construct and punctuate sentences well. All verbs should be in past tense.

14.26.3.7. The order of the minutes usually coincides with the order of the agenda and generally includes items such as:

14.26.3.7.1. Kind of meeting (regular, special, etc.).

14.26.3.7.2. Day, date, time, and place of meeting.

14.26.3.7.3. The word "Minutes" in the heading.

14.26.3.7.4. Name of the meeting body.

14.26.3.7.5. Opening paragraph; that is, The Executive Committee met for_____ meeting on day, date, and time.

14.26.3.7.6. Members present and absent.

14.26.3.7.7. Action taken on last meeting's minutes.

14.26.3.7.8. Reports.

14.26.3.7.9. Current business, with complete discussions and conclusions.

14.26.3.7.10. Old business, with discussions, and follow up, as recommended.

14.26.3.7.11. New business, with discussions and recommendations.

14.26.3.7.12. Adjournment.

### Section 14H—Instruments of Written Communication

### 14.27. Bullet Background Paper.

The bullet background paper is an excellent tool designed to present concisely written statements centered on a single idea or to present a collection of accomplishments with their respective impacts. Refer to Figure 14.9 for additional information on the bullet background paper.

### 14.28. Air Force IMT 1768, *Staff Summary Sheet.*

Use the staff summary sheet to summarize staff work, request action, or forward information. Staff summary sheets often contain several handwritten notes before reaching the approval authority; therefore, they do not require the same level of perfection (error-free typing, etc.) as the correspondence they may cover. Refer to Air Force Handbook 33-337 for information on filling out the staff summary sheet.

### 14.29. Electronic Staff Summary.

Electronic staff summary requiring your group or wing commander's signature should be sent through your internal channels via e-mail. The office of primary responsibility transmits the package via e-mail to the first reviewer to coordinate and comment. The first reviewer should forward (never reply) the package with comments (if any) to the next reviewer. This procedure is repeated until the last reviewer has coordinated on the package. The last reviewer forwards the entire package back to the office of primary responsibility.

### 14.30. Trip Report.

A trip report describes a temporary duty trip to another location and includes the purpose, travelers, itinerary, discussions, and conclusions or recommendations.

### 14.31. Staff Study Report.

Use the staff study report to analyze a clearly defined problem, identify conclusions, and make recommendations. Not all organizations routinely use a staff study report, but it is an accepted format for a problem-solution report in both Air Force and Joint Staffs. The staff study report should represent completed staff work. This means the staff member has solved a problem and presented a complete solution to the boss. The solution should be complete enough that the decision maker has only to approve or disapprove.

**Figure 14.9. Instructions for Preparing a Bullet Background Paper.**

---

**BULLET BACKGROUND PAPER**

**ON**

**THE BULLET BACKGROUND PAPER**

An increasingly popular version of the background paper is the "bullet" background paper. The bullet format provides a concise, chronological evolution of a problem, a complete summary of an attached staff package, or main thrust of a paper.

Main ideas (Function) follow the introductory paragraph and may be as long as several sentences or as short as one word (such as "Advantages").

- Secondary items follow with a single dash and tertiary items follow with multiple indented dashes. Secondary and tertiary items can be as short as a word or as long as several sentences.

- Format varies.

    - Center title (all capital letters); use 1-inch margins all around; single-space the text; double-space between items—except double-space title and triple-space to text; and use appropriate punctuation in paragraphs and complete thoughts.

    - Headings such as SUBJECT, PROBLEM, BACKGROUND, DISCUSSION, CONCLUSION, or RECOMMENDATION are optional.

Keys to developing a good background:

- Write the paper according to the knowledge level of the user; that is, a person who is very knowledgeable on the subject won't require as much detail as one who knows very little.

- Emphasize main points.

- Attach additional support data; refer to it in the background.

- Require minimum length to achieve brevity with short transitions.

- End with concluding remarks or recommendations.

Include an identification line (author's grade and name, organization, office symbol, telephone number, typist's initials, and date) on the first page 1 inch from the bottom of the page.

SMSgt Williams/MDSS/SGSD/123-9876/mcw/1 Dec 17

---

**14.32. Conclusion.**

Clear, concise, well-thought-out, and well-composed communication is essential for meeting the needs of today's Air Force. We are all involved in speaking and writing to some extent. Therefore, we must become proficient at the methods we use. The meeting is an important forum for providing information, solving problems, and answering questions. Written communication is also another area crucial to meeting the Air Force mission. Fortunately, we have several instruments at our disposal to help us with the process. The staff summary sheet, bullet background paper, trip report, and staff study report all serve a useful purpose and are tools that help facilitate staff-level communication.

# Chapter 15

# PERSONNEL PROGRAMS

*Section 15A—Overview*

## 15.1. Introduction.

15.1.1. The Air Force requires military members to be prepared to serve and support the mission at all times. Force support organizations ensure Airmen and their families are cared for, pay and entitlements are properly addressed, and their individual rights are secure. Airmen need to comprehend the enlisted assignments, family care, reenlistment and retraining opportunities, benefits and services, personnel records and individual rights, the awards and decorations program, and the enlisted promotion systems programs and policies. Each of these areas has an impact, in some form or fashion, on every Airman; therefore, understanding the individual nuances associated with each of these programs is a necessity for all Airmen. The senior NCO promotion program, manpower management and requirements, competitive sourcing, and civilian personnel management programs, are all necessary areas of focus for our aspiring senior NCOs. A basic understanding of these subject areas are required to effectively lead Airmen and manage programs.

15.1.2. The Air Force mission requires military members to be prepared for service at all times. Mission support organizations ensure Airmen's families are cared for; pay and entitlements are properly addressed; and individual rights are secured. This chapter includes information on enlisted assignments, family care, reenlistment and retraining opportunities, benefits and services, personnel records, individual rights, the awards and decorations program, and the enlisted promotion system.

*Section 15B—Enlisted Assignments*

## 15.2. General Information.

Qualified Airmen must be in the right jobs at the right time to accomplish the Air Force mission. The Air Force classifies and assigns Airmen worldwide as equitably as possible to ensure a high state of readiness. The Air Force also recognizes a need for special assignment considerations to take care of Air Force Airmen with exceptional needs. The Air Force uses a coherent and logical classification system to identify valid manpower requirements, to identify and describe each Air Force occupational specialty, to ensure minimum prerequisite standards are set for each specialty, and to ensure qualified Airmen are placed into each specialty. While the primary consideration in selecting Airmen for reassignment is the Airmen's qualifications to accomplish the mission, the Air Force also considers additional factors:

15.2.1. To the maximum extent possible, the Air Force assigns Airmen on a voluntary basis and in the most equitable manner feasible.

15.2.2. The Air Force equitably distributes involuntary assignments among similarly qualified Airmen to minimize family separation and to avoid creating a severe personal hardship on Airmen.

15.2.3. Limitations may be established on involuntary selection for permanent change of station following some temporary duties to allow Airmen to attend essential military and personal pre-permanent change of station requirements, as well as to reduce Airmen and family turbulence.

## 15.3. Assignment Authority.

The Department of Defense allocates funds, delegates authority, and directs policies for the permanent change of station assignment of Airmen to satisfy national security requirements. Permanent change of station assignments may also be directed to ensure equitable treatment of Airmen, such as permanent change of station from overseas to the continental United States upon completion of the prescribed overseas tour. Air Force Instruction 36-2110, *Assignments,* is the governing instruction for operational (including rotational), training (including formal education and professional military education) and force structure assignments.

### 15.3.1. Assignment Requests.

The director of assignments (or equivalent) in coordination with major commands, field operating agencies, and direct reporting units is authorized to initiate assignments for Airmen currently assigned to major commands, field operating agencies, or direct reporting units to fill valid vacant manpower authorizations. Air Force Personnel Center is the final approval authority for Airman assignments. The Airman Assignment Division is the final approval authority for Airman assignments in the grades of Senior Master Sergeant and below. The Chiefs Group is the final approval authority for Chief Master Sergeant and Chief Master Sergeant-select assignments.

15.3.2. **Distribution of Personnel.**

Airmen are distributed to meet the overall needs of the Air Force according to law and Department of Defense and Air Force directives and instructions; as equitably as possible between major commands, within a specialty and grade; according to guidance from the Air Staff functional area office of primary responsibility; and as directed by the designated assignment authority outlined in AFI 36-2110.

## 15.4. Assignment Policy and Procedures:

15.4.1. **Equal Opportunity.**

The Air Force assigns Airmen without regard to color, race, religious preference (except chaplains), national origin, ethnic background, age, marital status (except military couples), spouse's employment, education or volunteer service activities of spouse, or gender (except as provided for by statute or other policies). This applies to both permanent change of station and temporary duty assignments. The primary factor in selecting Airmen for permanent change of station is the Airmen's qualifications to fill a valid manpower requirement and perform productively in the position for which being considered. When Airmen with the required qualifications are identified, then permanent change of station eligibility criteria and other factors are considered.

15.4.2. **Special Experience Identifier.**

The special experience identifier system complements the assignment process and is used in conjunction with grade, Air Force specialty code, Air Force specialty code prefixes and suffixes, etc., to match uniquely qualified Airmen to jobs with special requirements. Special experience identifiers may be used when specific experience or training is critical to the job, and no other means is appropriate or available. The special experience identifier system is also used to rapidly identify Airmen to meet unique circumstances, contingency requirements, or other critical needs. Manpower positions are coded with a special experience identifier to identify positions that require or provide unique experiences or qualifications. The personnel records for the Airmen who earn a special experience identifier are similarly coded.

15.4.3. **Security Access Requirement.**

Manpower positions often require Airmen assigned to have access to a specified level of classified information. However, sometimes the urgency to fill a position does not allow selection of Airmen using permanent change of station eligibility criteria and subsequent processing (and/or investigation) for access at the specified level. Under these circumstances, selection may be necessary from among Airmen who currently have access or can be granted access immediately.

15.4.4. **Grade, Air Force Specialty Code, and Skill-Level Relationship for Assignment.**

Chief Master Sergeants and Chief Master Sergeant-selects may be assigned in any Air Force specialty code or chief enlisted manager code they possess or are qualified to be awarded. Normally, Airmen in the grade of Senior Master Sergeants and below are selected for assignment in their control Air Force specialty code. Airmen with an incompatible grade and control Air Force specialty code skill level because of retraining or reclassification are selected for assignment and allocated against requirements commensurate with their grade, regardless of their control Air Force specialty code skill level. Normally, Airmen are selected based on their grade and skill level. Chief Master Sergeants fill chief enlisted manager code positions; Senior Master Sergeants fill 9-skill level positions; Master Sergeants and Technical Sergeants fill 7-skill level positions; Staff Sergeants and Senior Airman fill 5-skill level positions; and Airman First Class, Airman, and Airman Basic fill 3-skill level positions.

15.4.5. **Volunteer Status and Permanent Change of Station Eligibility.**

Within a group of qualified Airmen who meet the minimum eligibility criteria for permanent change of station selection, volunteers are selected ahead of nonvolunteers. Furthermore, nonvolunteers qualified to fill a requirement who meet the minimum permanent change of station eligibility criteria are selected ahead of qualified volunteers who do not meet permanent change of station eligibility criteria. For example, time on station is a permanent change of station eligibility requirement. A qualified volunteer who meets the minimum time on station requirement is considered first in order of longest on station. Next, the qualified nonvolunteer who meets the time on station requirement in the order of longest on station, and finally the qualified volunteer who does not meet the time on station requirement may be considered; however, qualified volunteer will require a time on station waiver.

15.4.6. **Chief Master Sergeant Development.**

Headquarters Air Force/DPE uses the Chief Master Sergeant assignment policies to support the continued development of Chief Master Sergeants. Because Chief Master Sergeants are Air Force senior leaders, these policies are comparable with other senior leader assignment and development methods. Policies include:

15.4.6.1. **Three-year Limits for Headquarters Staff and Special Duty Tours.** Chief Master Sergeants serving in major command, Headquarters Air Force, and Joint Staff positions, as well as special duty positions will be limited to serving 3-year tours. This increases the opportunities for Chief Master Sergeants to serve in these positions, enhancing their development. Additionally, this improves the flow of field experience into headquarters staff positions and staff experience into base-level units.

15.4.6.2. **Date Eligible for Return from Overseas (DEROS) Management.** DEROS adjustment requests, like DEROS extensions, indefinite DEROSs, and in-place consecutive overseas tours, are closely scrutinized for Chief Master Sergeants and only considered if in the best interest of the Air Force and supportive of Chief Master Sergeant development. Subsequently, DEROS adjustments are not routinely approved for Chief Master Sergeants.

15.4.6.3. **Home-Basing Requests.** In addition to closely scrutinizing DEROS adjustment requests, the Chiefs Group also uses the same criteria to review home-basing requests, which are also not routinely approved. The same rationale used in paragraph 15.4.6.2 applies.

15.4.6.4. **Nominative Selection for Strategic-Level Assignments.** Specific strategic-level assignments such as Air Force career field managers and command Chief Master Sergeants are filled using a nominative selection process. The hiring authority for these positions requests nominations from appropriate organizations, frequently each major command. Each organization then identifies their most qualified Chief Master Sergeants for the advertised position and nominates them to the hiring authority. The hiring authority then selects the best Airman for the job. This highly competitive process ensures a significant level of visibility and senior leader involvement in selecting Chief Master Sergeants to serve in these top positions.

15.4.6.5. **Command Chief Master Sergeant Assignments.** Command Chief Master Sergeant assignments are 2-year minimum and 3-year maximum tours. This ensures an appropriate balance between fresh enlisted leadership and leadership stability within organizations.

15.4.7. **First-Term Airmen.**

First-Term Airmen serving an initial enlistment of 4 or more years may not be given more than two assignments in different locations following initial basic and skill training during their first 4 years of service, regardless of tour length. First-Term Airmen who make two permanent change of station moves are permitted an additional permanent change of station in conjunction with an approved humanitarian reassignment or a join spouse assignment, as a volunteer, or when the permanent change of station is a mandatory move. Low-cost moves are excluded from the two-move count.

15.4.8. **Availability and Deferment.**

Airmen are considered available for reassignment on the first day of the "availability" month. Deferments may be authorized, when possible in most grades and Air Force specialty codes, to maintain an equitable assignment system and also support the need for stability in certain organizations or functions. The reasons for deferments vary. Deferments are normally approved to preclude an Airman's permanent change of station while suitability to remain on Regular Air Force is evaluated or during a period of observation or rehabilitation. Deferments also exist for such things as completion of an educational program or degree, witness for a court-martial, accused in a court-martial, control roster, Article 15 punishment, base of preference program, retraining, humanitarian reasons, etc. AFI 36-2110 contains a complete list of deferments.

15.4.8.1. **Humanitarian Reassignment, Expedited Transfers and Exceptional Family Member Program Reassignment or Deferment.** Policies and procedures concerning humanitarian reassignment, Expedited Transfers and Exceptional Family Member Program reassignment or deferment are outlined in AFI 36-2110. These policies and procedures include but are not limited to:

15.4.8.1.1. The Humanitarian Program provides reassignment or deferment for Airmen to help them resolve severe short-term problems involving a family member. The problem must be resolvable within a reasonable period of time (normally 12 months); the Airman's presence must be considered absolutely essential to resolve the problem; and the Airman must be effectively utilized in his or her control Air Force specialty code at the new assignment. Family members under the humanitarian program are limited to spouse, children, parents, parents-in-law, and those people who have served "in loco parentis." A person "in loco parentis" refers to one who has exercised parental rights and responsibilities in place of a natural parent for at least 5 years before the Airman's or spouse's 21st birthday, or before the Airman's entry to the Regular Air Force, whichever is earlier. While brothers and sisters are not included in the definition of family member for humanitarian consideration, a request involving a brother's or sister's terminal illness will be considered as an exception to policy.

15.4.8.1.2. The Exceptional Family Member Program is a separate and distinct program from humanitarian policy. The Exceptional Family Member Program is based on an Airman's need for special medical or educational care for a spouse or child that is required long term, possibly permanently. Therefore, this program is not a base-of-choice program, as assignment decisions are based on manning needs of the Air Force at locations where the special medical or educational needs for a spouse or child can be met. The Air Force's commitment and responsibilities under the Exceptional Family Member Program requires mandatory enrollment and identification of exceptional family members. Under the Exceptional Family Member Program, an Airman may receive a reassignment if a need arises for specialized care that cannot be met where currently assigned. A deferment from an assignment may be provided for a newly identified condition if the Airman's presence is considered essential. The purpose of such a deferment is to allow the Airman time to establish a special medical treatment program or educational program for the exceptional family member. When granted, the initial period of deferment is usually 12 months, after which an Airman may be reconsidered for permanent change of station, if otherwise eligible.

15.4.8.1.3. Expedited Transfers are a separate and distinct program from the humanitarian policy and applies to only Regular Air Force members who are sexually assaulted and file an unrestricted report. The Airman may request an Expedited Transfer with assistance from the Sexual Assault Prevention and Response Office. If an Airman is the victim of stalking or other sexual misconduct (i.e. indecent viewing, visual recording, or broadcasting; forcible pandering; indecent exposure) and files a report, the Airman may also request an expedited transfer with assistance from the Victim and Witness Assistance Program in the installation's Legal Office. An expedited transfer request initiated on behalf of another will not be accepted. Only exception applies to the vice wing commander applying on behalf of the alleged offender. To enhance protection for the sexual assault victim, potential reassignment of the alleged offender shall be considered by the vice wing commander (or equivalent), balancing interests of the sexual assault victim and the alleged offender. An Airman (victim or alleged offender) will generally only be delayed from departing permanent change of station when they are required to remain for completion of a criminal or disciplinary investigation or action in which they are the subject. All assignment action codes must be removed from the Airman's personnel file in order to facilitate permanent change of station eligibility. Retraining or cross-flow actions will be considered under this program on a case by case basis as the goal for transferring the Airman is a timely reassignment with minimal disruption to an Airman's career and family.

15.4.8.2. **Base of Preference (Enlisted Only).** The first-term Airmen base of preference program is a reenlistment incentive. The Career Airman base of preference program is an incentive for other Airmen to continue an Air Force career. First-term Airmen in conjunction with reenlistment or retraining may request a permanent change of station from continental United States-to-continental United States or permanent change of station from overseas-to-continental United States. First-term Airmen in the continental United States (only) may request a base of preference to remain in place. A permanent change of station base of preference is not authorized from continental United States-to-overseas or overseas-to-overseas. An in-place base of preference is not authorized for Airmen assigned overseas. Career Airmen may request a base of preference to remain in place at a continental United States location or a permanent change of station base of preference for continental United States-to-continental United States assignment.

15.4.8.3. **Assignment of Military Couples (Join Spouse).** Each Airman of a military couple serves in his or her own right. This means military couples must fulfill the obligations inherent to all Airmen. They are considered for assignments to fill valid manning requirements and must perform duties that require the skills in which they are trained. Provided these criteria are met, military couples may be considered for assignments where they can maintain a joint residence. Military couples share the responsibility for reducing family separation. They should not make decisions on future service, career development, or family planning based on the assumption they will always be assigned to the same location or that join spouse assignment is guaranteed.

15.4.8.4. **Voluntary Stabilized Base Assignment Program (Enlisted Only).** The Voluntary Stabilized Base Assignment Program provides Airmen a stabilized tour in exchange for volunteering for an assignment to a historically hard-to-fill location. Application procedures are listed in AFI 36-2110.

15.4.8.5. **Extended Long Overseas Tour Length.** The extended long overseas tour volunteer program applies to Airmen who volunteer for permanent change of station overseas to a long-tour location (one where the accompanied tour length is 24 months or more, and the unaccompanied tour length is more than 15 months). Airmen who volunteer for an extended long overseas tour agree to serve the standard tour length plus an additional 12 months. Tour lengths for various overseas locations are listed in the Joint Travel Regulation, Volume 1, Appendix Q. Extended long overseas tour volunteers are considered ahead of standard overseas tour volunteers according to the priorities shown in AFI 36-2110. The 12-month extended tour period is in addition to the normal (accompanied or unaccompanied) long tour length the Airman must serve. A change in status affects the service retainability that must be obtained and the tour length the Airman will be required to serve. The requirement for additional service retainability may require an Airman to extend or reenlist and could affect selective reenlistment bonus calculation.

**15.4.8.6. Educational Deferment.** Airmen who have not yet been selected for a permanent change of station may request deferment from assignment selection when they have nearly completed a vocational program or college degree requirements.

**15.4.8.7. High School Senior Assignment Deferment Program.** The High School Senior Assignment Deferment Program allows Senior Master Sergeants and below and officers through Lieutenant Colonel to apply for a 1-year assignment deferment. Back-to-back deferments may be possible and military-married-to-military spouses may also apply. As in all situations, however, the needs of the Air Force will come first and will be the determining factor in granting deferments. Requests will be considered on a case-by-case basis, and deferments will be approved where possible.

**15.4.8.8. Temporary Duty.** AFI 36-2110 provides instructions regarding temporary duty procedures. The maximum temporary duty period at any one location in a 12-month period is 180 days unless the Secretary of the Air Force grants a waiver. To the degree possible, Airmen are not selected for involuntary overseas permanent change of station while performing certain kinds of temporary duty. Additionally, if selected for involuntary permanent change of station after one of these temporary duties, the report no later than date will not be within 120 days of the temporary duty completion date.

**15.4.8.9. Dependent Care and Adoption.** All Airmen ensure dependent care arrangements are made when they are separated because of temporary duty or permanent change of station. Military couples with dependents and single Airmen sponsors are expected to fulfill their military obligations on the same basis as other Airmen. They are eligible for worldwide duty and all assignments for which they qualify. To ensure all Airmen remain available for worldwide duty, they must have workable plans to provide parent-like care for their dependents as outlined in AFI 36-2908, *Family Care Plans*. Airmen who cannot or will not meet military commitments due to family needs will be considered for discharge. Airmen adopting children are given a limited time to complete the official adoption process and facilitate bonding. Airmen may be authorized deferment during the 6-month period following the date a child is officially placed in the Airmen's home. Airmen may also be authorized up to 21 days of permissive temporary duty that can be used in conjunction with ordinary leave.

**15.4.9. Time on Station and Service Retainability.**

Minimum time on station requirements exist to provide continuity to an Airman's member's unit and, to the degree possible, reasonable periods of stable family life for Airmen. Further, upon selection for permanent change of station, an Airman must have or be able to obtain certain minimum periods of obligated service depending on the type of permanent change of station move. This committed service retainability ensures an Airman has a period of Regular Air Force remaining long enough to offset the costs associated with a permanent change of station. Minimum time on station provides continuity to the gaining unit and stability to Airmen and their families following permanent change of station. Some types of permanent change of station require time on station periods or obligated service periods more or less than the normal limits. Refer to AFI 36-2110 for the time on station and retainability requirements for specific types of permanent change of station.

**15.4.9.1. Continental United States-to-Continental United States Permanent Change of Station.** For most permanent change of station moves within the Continental United States, first-term Airmen and career Airmen must have at least 48 months of time on station, with the exception of first-term Airmen applying eligible for the first-term Airmen base of preference program. Special circumstances, such as completion of a training course in permanent change of station status, have different time on station minimums. The service retainability requirement for a Continental United States-to-Continental United States permanent change of station is 24 months regardless of career status.

**15.4.9.2. Continental United States-to-Overseas Permanent Change of Station.** First-term Airmen must have at least 12 months of time on station to go from Continental United States to overseas. Career Airmen require 24 months of time on station before an overseas permanent change of station. When notified of permanent change of station selection, Airmen must have or be eligible to obtain sufficient service retainability to complete the full prescribed overseas tour length elected Airmen who do not have retainability may decline to obtain retainability or, if eligible, may retire instead of accepting a permanent change of station. Declining to obtain retainability for permanent change of station will affect a career Airman by making him or her ineligible for promotion and reenlistment. First-term Airmen become ineligible for most voluntary assignments. Airmen who are eligible and desire that their dependents accompany them at government expense during their overseas tours must serve the "accompanied by dependents" overseas tour length. This tour is normally longer than the unaccompanied tour. Electing to serve the longer accompanied tour requires the Airman to obtain the obligated service retainability for the longer tour. Airmen who are either ineligible or decline to obtain the service retainability for the accompanied tour length will not receive approval for dependent travel at the government's expense or command sponsorship.

15.4.9.3. **Overseas-to-Overseas Permanent Change of Station.** If an Airman is serving overseas and is a volunteer for a permanent change of station consecutive overseas tour or in-place consecutive overseas tour, the Airman must complete the full-prescribed tour at the current location and the full-prescribed overseas tour at the new location or another full tour in place.

15.4.9.4. **Overseas-to-Continental United States Reassignment.** Reassignment from overseas to continental United States requires the Airman, in most cases, to have or obtain at least 12 months of obligated service retainability. The exceptions are those Airmen serving at a dependent restricted short tour location of 12 months Airmen who do not have retainability will be retained in the overseas area involuntarily until their date of separation.

15.4.10. **Enlisted Quarterly Assignments Listing (EQUAL) and EQUAL-Plus.**

EQUAL provides Airmen a listing of the assignment requirements available for upcoming assignment cycles and allows them the opportunity to align personal preferences to actual Air Force needs. The listing identifies what assignments, by Air Force specialty code and grade, are available at particular locations. The EQUAL-Plus supplements the EQUAL and is used to advertise requirements for special duty assignments, joint and departmental assignments, short-notice oversea assignments, and all Chief Master Sergeant assignments. EQUAL-Plus shows upcoming requirements, any special qualifications an Airman needs to be eligible for selection, the available locations, reporting instructions, and points of contact for additional information. Both lists can be viewed on the Air Force Personnel Services Web page at https://gum-crm.csd.disa.mil/app/landing.

15.4.11. **Assignment Preferences (Enlisted Only).**

Chief Master Sergeants and Chief Master Sergeant-selects volunteer for assignments on EQUAL-Plus by notifying their assignment noncommissioned officer at Headquarters Air Force Senior Leadership Management Office. Notification can be made via telephone, e-mail, datafax, or electronic message. Senior Master Sergeants and below will use the view/change assignment preference update feature in the virtual military personnel flight to record continental United States or overseas assignment preferences. To enhance the chance for selection to a desired location, Airmen should consult the EQUAL and EQUAL-Plus listings. Upon completion of the update, a notice is produced and available for print. (**Note:** Each Airman is individually responsible for the currency and accuracy of assignment preferences.) When a change in status occurs such as marriage, the Airman should update preferences accordingly. Outdated preferences or no preferences on file will not be the basis for release of an Airman from an assignment for which selected.

15.4.11.1. **Home-Basing and Follow-On Assignment Programs.** The purpose of these programs is to reduce permanent change of station costs, reduce permanent change of station turbulence, and increase stability for Airmen and their families by providing advance assignment consideration. The servicing military personnel section must brief all eligible Airmen selected for or electing to serve an unaccompanied overseas tour of 15 months or less on these programs. Airmen must either apply or decline to apply for these programs in writing. AFI 36-2110, Attachment 5, contains more information on these programs.

15.4.11.2. **Assignment of Family Members.** Assignment of family members to the same duty location or unit is not prohibited, however, family members will not be assigned where one family member will or may hold a command or supervisory position over another family member. Such assignments result in, or may create a perception of, preferential treatment or loss of impartiality, thereby compromising the integrity of command and supervisory functions.

15.4.12. **Permanent Change of Station Cancellation by the Air Force:**

15.4.12.1. Once an Airman is selected for permanent change of station and orders are published, cancellation of the assignment could impose a hardship on the Airman. Normally, a permanent change of station is not cancelled within 60 days of the projected departure date unless the Airman cannot be effectively used at the projected location. The assignment office of primary responsibility may authorize the cancellation.

15.4.12.2. If the Airman indicates a hardship will exist as a result of the cancellation, then the military personnel section will direct the Airman to prepare a written statement containing the details of the hardship. The statement should be coordinated through the unit commander to the military personnel section. Upon receipt, the military personnel section advises the assignment office of primary responsibility, who considers reinstatement of the original assignment, to provide an alternate assignment or confirms cancellation and provides the reasons why the Airman is required to remain at the present base.

15.4.12.3. AFI 36-2110 contains additional information and also contains guidance in the case where an Airman has departed from his or her previous duty station and is en route to the new location.

*Section 15C—Family Care Plans*

## 15.5. Policy.

Department of Defense policy is that the member is responsible for the care of family members during deployments and temporary duty, as at all other times. Failure to produce a family care plan within 60 days of the discussion with the commander, supervisor, or commander's designated representative may result in disciplinary action and/or administrative separation. In addition to a required family care plan, military members are strongly encouraged to have a will.

## 15.6. Members Who Must Have a Family Care Plan.

Single-member parents with custody of children and bear sole or joint responsibility, and military couples with dependents must have a family care plan. Members who are solely responsible for the care of a spouse, elderly family member, or adult family member with disabilities who is dependent on the member for financial, medical, or logistical support (housing, food, clothing, transportation, etc.) must also have a family care plan. This includes family members who have limited command of the English language, are unable to drive, or gain access to basic life-sustaining facilities. Members whose family circumstances or personal status change must notify their commander as soon as possible but no later than 30 days after any change in circumstance or personal status requires them to establish a family care plan.

## 15.7. Family Care Plans.

These plans must include provisions for short-term absences (such as temporary duty for schooling or training) and long-term absences (such as operational deployments) and designate a caregiver for the affected family members. Financial arrangements may include powers of attorney, allotments, and other documents necessary for logistical movement of the family or caregiver should any of these arrangements become necessary. Additional items may be required to fit individual situations.

15.7.1. **Required Counseling:**

15.7.1.1. **New Duty Station.** Commanders or first sergeants counsel all Airmen with family members on AFI 36-2908 during inprocessing. During this counseling, commanders and first sergeants must stress the importance of, and confirm the need for, family care certification by completing Air Force IMT 357, *Family Care Certification.* Commanders or first sergeants may not delegate counseling requirements. **Note:** For members who are geographically separated from the commander's location, commanders may delegate, in writing, the authority to counsel members and certify the Air Force IMT 357 to detachment or operating location chiefs.

15.7.1.2. **Annual Briefing.** The commander or first sergeant is required to annually brief, individually, all military members who require an Air Force IMT 357 about their family care responsibilities. During this briefing, the commander or first sergeant signs the Air Force IMT 357 each time the plan is reviewed and certified, determining the actual workability of the family care plan. The member signs and dates the Air Force IMT 357 to document the briefing was completed.

15.7.2. **Remedial Action.**

Members who fail to make adequate and acceptable family care arrangements will have disciplinary or other actions taken against them.

## 15.8. Who Must Document Their Family Care Plan on the Air Force Form 357.

Air Force members to included Department of Defense Civilian Expeditionary Workforce members who meet the following criteria will develop and maintain a Family Care Plan:

15.8.1. Single parents who have custody of a child and bear sole or joint responsibility for the care of children under the age of 19 or others unable to care for themselves in the absence of the member.

15.8.2. Dual-military couples with dependents.

15.8.3. Married service members with custody or joint custody of a child whose non-custodial biological or adoptive parent is not the current spouse of the Member, or who otherwise bear sole responsibility for the care of children under the age of 19 or for other unable to care for themselves in the absence of the member. *EXAMPLE*: The military member had a child with, or adopted a child with a previous spouse and then they divorced or separated. Then the military member gained full or partial custody of the child.

15.8.4. Members primarily responsible for dependent family members and meet one or more other criteria outlined AFI 36-2908, paragraph 1.2.

15.8.5. Civilian and contractor personnel in emergency essential positions are strongly encouraged to establish family care plans consistent with this instruction. Civilian and contractor personnel should also avail themselves and their caregivers of the information, support, and resources provided by the Airman and Family Readiness Center and social service organizations within legal constraints.

**15.9. When to Implement the Family Care Plan.** Air Force members will implement their family care plan when required to be absent from their family members. This includes single parents or military couples assigned to a family-member-restricted area and activation of noncombatant evacuation operations or other emergency evacuation situations if assigned overseas with family members.

**15.10. Duty Deferments.** To assist Air Force military members in the development of family care plans and establishing a pattern of childcare, service members shall receive the following deferments from duty:

15.10.1. Military mothers of newborns receive a 4-month deferment from duty away from the home station for the period immediately following the birth of a child.

15.10.2. Single service members, or one member of a dual-military couple who adopts, receive a 4 month deferment from duty away from the home station from the date the child is placed in the home as part of the formal adoption process.

15.10.3. Reserve Component members who are mothers of newborns, single Reserve Component members who adopt, and one member of a dual-military couple in the Reserve Component who adopts shall receive a 4-month deferment from involuntary call to Regular Air Force immediately following the child's birth or placement in the home.

15.10.4. Air Force military members, who may be deployed in an area for which imminent danger pay is authorized, may request a deferment of deployment due to unforeseen family circumstances in accordance with DoDI 1342.19.

**Section 15D—Reenlistment and Retraining Opportunities**

**15.11. Selective Reenlistment Program.**

The selective reenlistment program applies to all enlisted personnel and the objective is to ensure the Air Force retains only Airmen who consistently demonstrate the capability and willingness to maintain high professional standards.

15.11.1. **Selective Reenlistment by Category.**

In the Air Force, reenlistment is a privilege, not a right. The selective reenlistment program provides a process by which commanders/civilian directors and supervisors evaluate all first term, second term, and career Airmen. First-term Airmen receive selective reenlistment program consideration when they are within 15 months of their expiration of term of service. Second term and career Airmen with less than 19 years of total active federal military service are considered within 13 months of the original expiration of term of service. Career Airmen also receive selective reenlistment program consideration when within 13 months of completing 20 years of total active federal military service. Once career Airmen have served beyond 20 years of total active federal military service, they receive selective reenlistment program consideration each time they are within 13 months of their original expiration of term of service.

15.11.2. **Responsibilities:**

15.11.2.1. **Unit Commander/Civilian Director.** The unit commander/civilian director has total selective reenlistment program selection and nonselection authority for all Airmen and may non-select any Airman for reenlistment at any time outside of their selective reenlistment program window. Reenlistment intent or retirement eligibility has no bearing on the selective reenlistment program consideration process. Unit commanders/civilian directors approve or deny reenlistment and ensure selection or nonselection decisions are consistent with other qualitative decisions (such as promotion) and are based on substantial evidence. Commanders/directors consider enlisted performance report ratings, unfavorable information from any substantiated source, the Airman's willingness to comply with Air Force standards, and the Airman's ability (or lack thereof) to meet required training and duty performance levels when determining if a member may reenlist. Commanders/directors may reverse their decisions at any time. Commanders/directors do not use the selective reenlistment program when involuntary separation is more appropriate.

15.11.2.2. **Immediate Supervisor.** Supervisors provide unit commanders/directors with recommendations concerning the Airman's career potential. The supervisor's rater may perform the duties required by the immediate supervisor if the immediate supervisor is on leave or temporary duty. To ensure Airmen meet quality standards, immediate supervisors review the report on individual personnel and the Air Force Form 1137, *Unfavorable Information File Summary* (if applicable). They then evaluate duty performance and leadership abilities.

### 15.11.3. Procedures:

15.11.3.1. **Selection.** The military personnel section sends each unit a selective reenlistment program consideration roster that identifies assigned Airmen who require selective reenlistment program consideration. The military personnel section also sends a report on individual personnel for each Airman being considered. The unit forwards the report on individual personnel to supervisors so that each supervisor's reenlistment recommendation can be documented. The supervisor should carefully evaluate the Airman's duty performance and review the Airman's personnel records before making a recommendation to the commander. A supervisor who decides to recommend the Airman for reenlistment places an "X" in the appropriate block, signs the report on individual personnel, and returns the report to the unit commander. The commander reviews the recommendation and evaluates the Airman's duty performance, future potential, and other pertinent information. The commander selects the Airman for reenlistment by annotating and signing the selective reenlistment program roster. The commander's signature on the roster constitutes formal selection. The commander sends the selective reenlistment program roster to the military personnel section for processing.

15.11.3.2. **Nonselection.** If the supervisor decides not to recommend an Airman for reenlistment, he or she initiates an Air Force Form 418, *Selective Reenlistment Program Consideration for Airmen in the Regular Air Force/Air Force Reserve*, and completes Section I and Section II and forwards to the commander. The commander reviews the recommendation and other pertinent data and decides whether to select the Airman. If the commander does not select the Airman for reenlistment, the commander completes Section III of the Air Force Form 418 and informs the Airman of the decision. During the interview, the commander must make sure the Airman understands the right to appeal the decision. The Airman must make known his or her intention within three workdays of the date the Airman acknowledges the nonselection decision. The Airman must submit the appeal to the military personnel section within 10 calendar days of the date he or she renders the appeal intent on the Air Force Form 418, Section V. The commander sends the Air Force Form 418 to the military personnel section after the Airman signs and initials the appropriate blocks.

### 15.11.4. Appeals.

Airmen have the right to appeal selective reenlistment program nonselection decisions. The specific appeal authority is based on an Airman's total active federal military service. First-term Airmen and career Airmen who will complete at least 20 years of total active federal military service on their current expiration of term of service appeal selective reenlistment program nonselection to their respective group commanders. The Airman's respective wing commander is the selective reenlistment program appeal authority for second term and career Airmen who will complete fewer than 16 years of total active federal military service on their current expiration of term of service. The Secretary of the Air Force is the selective reenlistment program appeal authority for second term and career Airmen who will complete at least 16 years of total active federal military service but fewer than 20 years of total active federal military service on their current expiration of term of service. The decision of the appeal authority is final. The appeal authority's decision is documented on the Air Force Form 418, and the Airman is advised of the outcome.

## 15.12. Enlistment Extensions.

Any Airman serving on a Regular Air Force enlistment may request an extension if he or she has a service-directed retainability reason and in the best interest of the Air Force. Extensions are granted in whole-month increments. For example, if the individual needs 15 ½ months of retainability for an assignment, the individual must request a 16-month extension. Voluntary extensions for all Airmen are limited to a maximum of 48 months per enlistment. In the event Air Force specialty codes are constrained, Air Staff may limit first-term Airmen extensions to a specified period. Certain situations (such as citizenship pending) may warrant exceptions to policy. Once approved, an extension has the legal effect of the enlistment agreement by extending the period of obligated service. Extensions can only be canceled if the reason for the extension no longer exists, given the Airman has not entered into the extension. For example, if a member was approved for an extension due to an assignment and that assignment was canceled, the member could then cancel the extension within 30 calendar days provided they have not entered into the extension period.

## 15.13. High Year of Tenure.

High year of tenure provides the Air Force with another method of stabilizing the career structure of the enlisted force. High year of tenure essentially represents the maximum number of years Airmen may serve in their current grade AFI 36-3208, *Administrative Separation of Airmen*, contains waiver provisions for Airmen who believe they have sufficient justification to warrant retention beyond their high year of tenure, but the majority of Airmen are not permitted to reenlist or extend their enlistments if their new date of separation exceeds their high year of tenure. Airmen may be eligible to request an extension of enlistment to establish a date of separation at high year of tenure too separate or retire. Normally, Airmen must be within 2 years of their high year of tenure before they can extend.

## 15.14. Selective Retention Bonus.

The selective retention bonus is a monetary incentive paid to enlisted members to attract reenlistments in, and retraining into, critical military skills with insufficient reenlistments to sustain the career force in those skills. Headquarters United States Air Force adds and deletes skills from the selective retention bonus list as requirements change. The military personnel section is the best source of information on selective retention bonus skills.

### 15.14.1. Zones.

The selective reenlistment bonus is paid in four zones based on total active federal military service:

15.14.1.1. Zone A applies to Airmen reenlisting between 17 months and 6 years.

15.14.1.2. Zone B applies to Airmen reenlisting between 6 and 10 years.

15.14.1.3. Zone C applies to Airmen reenlisting between 10 and 14 years.

15.14.1.4. Zone E applies to Airmen reenlisting between 18 and 20 years.

### 15.14.2. Computing Selective Retention Bonus Awards.

The Air Force calculates the selective retention bonus on the basis of monthly base pay (the rate in effect on the date of discharge [day before reenlistment date] or the day before an extension begins) multiplied by the number of whole years incurred on reenlistment, multiplied by the selective retention bonus multiple for the skill. The selective retention bonus is only payable for obligated service not exceeding 24 years of active service. The maximum selective retention bonus payable to eligible Airmen is $90,000 per zone. Eligible Airmen may receive a selective retention bonus in each zone but only one selective retention bonus per zone (for example, they can receive the last zone A payment and the first zone B payment during the same year). The Air Force, based on current policy directives, may pay up to 100 percent of the bonus amount (less tax) at the time of reenlistment or extension and the remaining percent in equal installments on the anniversary of the reenlistment or extension date.

## 15.15. Career Job Reservation Program.

Because of various career force size and composition restrictions, there are times when the Air Force must place a limit on the number of first-term Airmen who may reenlist. The Career Job Reservation Program exists to assist in the management of first-term Airmen reenlistments, by Air Force specialty code, in order to prevent surpluses and shortages. The Career Job Reservation Program can be active or suspended based on Air Force requirements. When active and in use the program details are as follows:

### 15.15.1. When to Apply for a Career Job Reservation.

Headquarters United States Air Force meets management requirements by establishing and maintaining a career job requirements file for each Air Force specialty code. Air Force specialty codes career job requirements are distributed over a 12-month period. All eligible first-term Airmen must have an approved Career Job Reservation in order to reenlist. Airmen are automatically placed on the Career Job Reservation waiting list on the 1st duty day of the month during which they complete 35 months on their current enlistment (59 months for 6-year enlistees), but no later than the last duty day of the month during which they complete 43 months on their current enlistment (67 months for 6-year enlistees To keep their approved Career Job Reservation, Airmen must reenlist on or before the Career Job Reservation expiration date.

### 15.15.2. Career Job Reservation Waiting List.

When the number of Career Job Reservation applicants exceeds the number of available quotas, Air Force Personnel Center must use a rank-order process to determine which Airmen will receive an approved Career Job Reservation. Airmen compete for a Career Job Reservation in their respective initial term of enlistment group (4-year or 6-year enlistee). Applicants are ranked using the following factors: unfavorable information file (automatic disqualifier), top three enlisted performance reports, current grade, projected grade, date of rank, total active federal military service date. Applicants are placed on the Air Force-wide career job applicant waiting list when there are no Career Job Reservations available. An Airman's position on the waiting list is subject to change as his or her rank order information changes or as new Airmen apply. Airmen may remain on the Career Job Reservation waiting list until their 43rd month on their current enlistment (67 months for 6-year enlistees Supervisors should encourage Airmen to pursue retraining into a shortage skill if a Career Job Reservation is not immediately available.

15.15.3. **Career Job Reservation in an Additionally Awarded Air Force Specialty Code.**

When Airmen are placed on the Career Job Reservation waiting list in their Air Force specialty code, they may request a Career Job Reservation in an additionally awarded Air Force specialty code if quotas are readily available, the Air Force specialty code is different from their control Air Force specialty code, and they possess at least a 3-skill level in the Air Force specialty code.

## 15.16. Air Force Retraining Program.

Retraining is a force management program used primarily to balance the enlisted career force across all Air Force specialty codes and ensure sustainability of career fields. Retraining also provides a means to return disqualified Airmen to a productive status. Additionally, the program allows a limited number of Airmen the opportunity to pursue other career paths within the Air Force. The Air Force encourages Airmen to voluntarily retrain first, however, the needs of the Air Force may require Airmen to be involuntarily retrained to meet sustainment objectives.

15.16.1. **First-Term Airmen Retraining Program.**

The first-term Airmen Retraining Program is designed to retrain first-term Airmen in conjunction with a reenlistment, into skills where shortages exist and additionally, allows a limited number of Airmen the opportunity to pursue other career paths in the Air Force. Airmen maybe selected for involuntary retraining based on Air Force needs to balance the force. Airmen may apply not earlier than the 1st duty day of the month during which they complete 35 months of their current enlistment (59 months for 6-year enlistees), but not later than the last duty day of the 43rd month of their current enlistment (67 months for 6-year enlistees). On the last duty day of each month, Air Force Personnel Center runs a retraining board to select the most eligible Airmen. This is not a physical board, but a computer based one. Applications are prioritized on quality indicators; e.g., most recent enlisted performance report (EPR) rating; current grade; projected grade; next two EPR ratings; Date of Rank; Total Active Federal Military Service Date; Aptitude Qualification Examination score in the applicable area (electrical, mechanical, administrative, general or combination in accordance with Air Force Enlisted Classification Directory, Part II, Attachment 4 (Additional Qualifications)); requested Air Force Specialty Code preferences.

15.16.2. **NCO Retraining Program.**

The NCO retraining program is designed to retrain second term and career Airmen from overage Air Force specialties into shortage specialties to optimize the enlisted force to best meet current and future mission needs. Airmen possessing a secondary, or additional Air Force Specialty Code in a shortage skill, may be returned to the shortage skill if in the best interest of the Air Force. This program consists of two phases: Phase I (voluntary) and Phase II (involuntary). Retraining objectives are determined by Air Staff.

15.16.3. **Online Retraining Advisory.**

The online retraining advisory is a living document found on MyPers that is maintained by the Air Force Personnel Center. The advisory is readily available and a key tool to advise members of retraining opportunities. AFI 36-2626, *Airman Retraining Program*, establishes retraining eligibility and application procedures.

*Section 15E—Benefits and Services*

## 15.17. Veterans Affairs Benefits.

The Veterans Affairs offers a wide range of benefits to the Nation's veterans, service members, and their families. Veterans Affairs benefits and services fall into these major categories: disability benefits, education benefits, vocational rehabilitation and employment, home loans, burial benefits, dependents' and survivors' benefits, life insurance, and health care. Airmen requiring specific information on their Veterans Affairs benefits can retrieve information at www.va.gov. Contact the closest Veterans Affairs department for eligibility requirements.

15.17.1. **Disability Compensation.**

A tax free monetary benefit paid to Veterans with disabilities that are the result of a disease or injury incurred or aggravated during active military service. Compensation may also be paid for post-service disabilities that are considered related or secondary to disabilities occurring in service and for disabilities presumed to be related to circumstances of military service, even though they may arise after service. Generally, the degrees of disability specified are also designed to compensate for considerable loss of working time from exacerbations or illnesses. The benefit amount is graduated according to the degree of the Veteran's disability on a scale from 10 percent to 100 percent (in increments of 10 percent). Compensation may also be paid for disabilities that are considered related or secondary to disabilities occurring in service and for disabilities presumed to be related to circumstances of military service, even though they may arise after service. Generally, the degrees of disability specified are also designed to compensate for considerable loss of working time from exacerbations or illnesses. If you have dependents, an additional allowance may be added if your combined disability is rated 30% or greater. Your compensation may be offset if you receive military retirement pay, disability severance pay, or separation incentive payments. Finally, additional information is available at http://www.benefits.va.gov/compensation/.

### 15.17.2. Educational Benefits.

The Veterans Affairs offers a variety of education benefits to service members and veterans to pursue a higher education during or following their service. Benefit programs include the Post-9/11 GI Bill, Montgomery GI Bill, Reserve Educational Assistance Program, and Survivors' and Dependents' Educational Assistance. The Yellow Ribbon GI Education Enhancement Program (Yellow Ribbon Program) is a provision of the Post-9/11 Veterans Educational Assistance Act of 2008. This program allows institutions of higher learning (degree-granting institutions) in the United States to enter voluntarily into an agreement with Veterans Affairs to fund tuition and fee expenses that exceed Veterans Affair's maximum amount payable. More information is available at http://explore.va.gov/education-training.

### 15.17.3. Vocational Rehabilitation and Employment.

Airmen may receive services to help with job training, employment accommodations, resume development, and job seeking skills coaching. Other services may be provided to assist Veterans in starting their own businesses or independent living services for those who are severely disabled and unable to work in traditional employment. For more information on these services visit their web site at http://www.benefits.va.gov/vocrehab/index.asp.

### 15.17.4. Home Loans.

The Veterans Affairs helps service members, Veterans, and eligible surviving spouses become homeowners. Their mission is to serve Airmen, they provide a home loan guaranty benefit and other housing-related programs to help Airmen buy, build, repair, retain, or adapt a home for their own personal occupancy. Veterans Affairs Home Loans are provided by private lenders, such as banks and mortgage companies. Veterans Affairs guarantees a portion of the loan, enabling the lender to provide you with more favorable terms. For additional information on eligibility and how to apply visit their web site at http://www.benefits.va.gov/homeloans/index.asp.

### 15.17.5. Burial Benefits.

Burial benefits available include a gravesite in any of the 134 Veteran Affairs national cemeteries with available space, opening and closing of the grave, perpetual care, a Government headstone or marker, a burial flag, and a Presidential Memorial Certificate, at no cost to the family. Some Veterans may also be eligible for burial allowances. Cremated remains are buried or inurned in national cemeteries in the same manner and with the same honors as casketed remains. Burial benefits available for spouses and dependents buried in a national cemetery include burial with the Veteran, perpetual care, and the spouse or dependents name and date of birth and death will be inscribed on the Veteran's headstone, at no cost to the family. Eligible spouses and dependents may be buried, even if they predecease the Veteran. The Veterans family should make funeral or cremation arrangements with a funeral provider or cremation office. Any item or service obtained from a funeral home or cremation office will be at the family's expense. Some additional information is available at http://www.cem.va.gov/burial_benefits/.

### 15.17.6. Dependency and Indemnity Compensation.

This is a tax-free monetary benefit generally payable to a surviving spouse, child, or parent of service members who died while on Regular Air Force, Regular Air Force for training, or inactive duty training, or to survivors of Veterans who died from their service-connected disabilities. Parents Dependency and Indemnity Compensation is an income-based benefit for parents who were financially dependent on of a Service member or Veteran who died from a service-related cause. For information on eligibility and how to apply click on this link Dependency and Indemnity Compensation.

### 15.17.7. Life Insurance.

The Veterans Affairs mission is to serve service members, Veterans, and their families, by providing valuable life insurance benefits to give service members, and Veterans, the peace of mind that comes with knowing their family is protected. These life insurance programs were developed to provide financial security for service members families given the extraordinary risks involved in military service. For additional information on the different life insurance benefits available and the eligibility, and how to apply for them click on this link www.benefits.va.gov.

15.17.8. **Health Care:**

15.17.8.1. The transition from receiving care within the Military Healthcare System into the Veterans Health Administration can be challenging and at times confusing. Therefore, for caregivers to understand some of the basic differences between the two is helpful.

15.17.8.2. Military health care, known as TRICARE, is operated through the Department of Defense and provides medical care for Regular Air Force and retired members of the military and their dependents. The Department of Veterans Affairs Veterans Health Administration provides health care for enrolled veterans and their eligible family members through a network of hospitals and clinics across the country.

15.17.8.3. The two departments work together, but have different eligibility criteria, health benefits and costs.

15.17.8.4. Also, important is understanding the Veterans Administration consists of three separate organizations: Veterans Affairs Healthcare, Veterans Affairs Benefits, and Veterans Affairs National Cemeteries.

15.17.8.5. Enrollment in the Veterans Affairs healthcare system meets the requirement for having health care coverage under the new health care law, Affordable Care Act that went into effect on 1 October 2013. Additional information on the Affordable Care Act and Veterans Affairs can be found on the Veterans Affairs website: www.va.gov/aca.

## 15.18. Retirement Benefits.

Enlisted members are eligible to retire if they have 20 years of total active federal military service and there are no restrictions per AFI 36-3203. Enlisted members must apply for retirement. Otherwise, they will separate on their date of separation or expiration of term of service. Officers must have 20 years of total active federal military service and 10 years of total active federal commissioned service to be eligible to retire. A retirement application may be submitted through virtual military personnel flight up to 12 months, but no less than 120 days, before the desired retirement date. Every individual who hopes to retire one day should be familiar with this information. The retirement application is not all-inclusive, and there are exceptions. Every military member should seek personal counseling from the Total Force Contact Center before making firm plans.

15.18.1. **Place of Retirement.**

In general, a member may retire in the continental United States. Members assigned to a duty station in the continental United States retire at the duty station. If the member is overseas, the member and family can proceed to the final continental United States home of selection. If the member elects to retire overseas and live permanently in that country, he or she must comply with command and host government residency rules before the date of retirement.

15.18.2. **Retired Pay.**

The date initially entered military service normally determines which of the existing retirement pay plans applies to a member. Date initially entered military service is the date an individual was initially enlisted, inducted, or appointed in a regular or reserve component of a uniformed service as a commissioned officer, warrant officer, or enlisted member. The date initially entered military service is a fixed date that is not subject to adjustment because of a break in service. Current active military personnel will fall under one of the retirement plans described in Table 15.1.

## 15.19. Survivor Benefit Plan:

15.19.1. Military pay stops when a member dies. Established by Congress on 21 September 1972, the survivor benefit plan provides a monthly income to survivors of retired military personnel upon the member's death. The survivor benefit plan is a government program for retiring members to ensure their eligible survivors receive a portion of their military retired pay in the form of a monthly annuity after their death. The plan was structured so a surviving spouse cannot outlive the annuity, and cost-of-living adjustments are incorporated to offset inflation. Regular Air Force members with a spouse or dependent children are automatically covered by the survivor benefit plan at no cost while they remain on Regular Air Force. The member's death must be classified in line of duty in order for an annuity to be payable if the member is not yet retirement eligible (has not accrued 20 years of Regular Air Force) on the date of death. The annuity payable is 55 percent of the retired pay the member would have been entitled to receive if retired with a total disability rating on the date of death. An annuity may also be payable if the member's death is classified not in line of duty, as long as the member was retirement eligible on the date of death. In this case, annuity payable is 55 percent of the retired pay the member would have been entitled to receive if retired for years of service on the date of death. The surviving spouse of a member who dies in the line of duty while on Regular Air Force may request the survivor benefit plan be paid only to the member's children, avoiding the reduction caused by a spouse's receipt of dependency and indemnity compensation, the survivor benefits paid by the Department of Veteran Affairs when a member's death is determined to have resulted from a service-connected cause.

**Table 15.1. Retirement Pay Plans.**

| LINE | A<br>Plan | B<br>Eligibility (as determined by date initially entered military service) | C<br>Retired Pay Formula | D<br>Cost-of-Living Adjustment (note 1) |
|---|---|---|---|---|
| 1 | Final Basic Pay | Entered service before 8 September 1980 | 2.5 percent multiplied by the years of service plus 1/12 x 2.5 percent for each additional full month, multiplied by final basic pay of the retired grade (Title 10, United States Code, Section 1406) | Full inflation protection; cost-of-living adjustments based on consumer price index |
| 2 | High-3 (note 2) | Entered service on or after 8 September 1980 and before 1 August 1986 | 2.5 percent multiplied by the years of service plus 1/12 x 2.5 percent for each additional full month, multiplied by the average of the highest 36 months of basic pay (note 3) (Title 10, United States Code, Section 1407) | |
| 3 | High-3 with Redux/Career Status Bonus option*<br><br>*Instead of retiring under High-3, these members may choose to receive the career status bonus at 15 years of service in exchange for agreeing to serve to at least 20 years of service and then retiring under the less generous Redux plan. The member may elect a lump sum of $30K, two payments of $15K, three payments of $10K, four payments of $7.5K, or five payments of $6K | Entered service on or after 1 August 1986 | High-3: 2.5 percent multiplied by the years of service plus 1/12 x 2.5 percent for each additional full month, multiplied by the average of the highest 36 months of basic pay<br><br>OR<br><br>*Redux/ career status bonus option: 2.0 percent multiplied by the years of service plus 1/12 x 2.0 percent for each additional full month, (for the first 20 years of active service) plus 3.5 percent for each additional full month (for service beyond 20 years), multiplied by the average of the highest 36 months of basic pay. At age 62, retired pay is recalculated to what would have been under the High-3 Pay Plan. | High-3: Full inflation protection; cost-of-living adjustments based on consumer price index<br><br>OR<br><br>*Redux/ career status bonus option: partial inflation protection; cost-of-living adjustments based on consumer price index minus 1 percent. At age 62, retired pay is adjusted to reflect full cost-of-living adjustments since retirement. Partial cost-of-living adjustments then resumes after age 62. |

Notes:
1. Cost-of-living is applied annually to retired pay.
2. High-3 is a reference to the average of the high 3 years or, more specifically, the high 36 months of basic pay as used in the formula.
3. If a member is demoted or an officer is retired in a lower grade as a result of an Officer Grade Determination, the retired pay plan is Final Basic Pay of the lower, retired grade (Title 10, United States Code, Section 1407(f)).

15.19.2. The survivor benefit plan is the only program that enables a portion of military retired pay to be paid to a member's survivors. Prior to retiring, each member must decide whether to continue survivor benefit plan coverage into retirement. If electing coverage, survivor benefit plan premiums are assessed and automatically deducted from the member's monthly retired pay. Premiums are government-subsidized and deducted from a participating member's retired pay before taxes.

15.19.3. Survivor benefit plan premiums and beneficiary annuity payments depend on what is called the "base amount" elected as the basis of coverage. A service member's base amount can be the full monthly retired pay or a portion of retired pay, down to $300. Full coverage means full-retired pay is elected as the base amount. The base amount is tied to a member's retired pay; therefore, when retired pay receives cost-of-living adjustments, so does the base amount, and as a result, so do premiums and the annuity payments.

15.19.4. Generally the survivor benefit plan is an irrevocable decision. However, under limited circumstances, you may withdraw from the survivor benefit plan (Figure 15.1) or change your coverage. As a survivor benefit plan participant, you have a 1-year window to terminate survivor benefit plan coverage between the second and third anniversary following the date you begin to receive retired pay. The premiums you paid will not be refunded, and an annuity will not be payable upon your death. Your covered spouse or former spouse must consent to the withdrawal. Termination is permanent, and participation may not be resumed under any circumstance barring future enrollment. The survivor benefit plan also has a "paid-up" feature that permits members who have attained age 70 and who have paid survivor benefit plan premiums for 360 months to stop paying premiums but remain active participants in the plan. Additional information can be attained through the local military personnel section office or the Airman and Family Readiness Center.

**Figure 15.1. Stop Coverage.**

Premiums stop when there is no longer an eligible beneficiary in a premium category, such as:

- Children are all too old for benefits and have no incapacity, or

- A spouse is lost through death or divorce, or

- An insurable interest person dies, or coverage is terminated.

## 15.20. Airman and Family Readiness Center:

15.20.1. **Airman and Family Readiness Center Support and Services.** Airman and Family Readiness Center support services are designed to assist commanders in assessing and supporting the welfare of the military community and building a strong sense of community and support within the Air Force. The Airman and Family Readiness Center supports mission readiness by helping Airmen and their families adapt to the challenges and demands of expeditionary operations and the military lifestyle. Airman and Family Readiness Centers work with the unit leadership to assess unit strengths, resources, and concerns. Airman and Family Readiness Centers help to identify issues and trends that affect community readiness and personal preparedness by working with a wide range of civilian and military agencies. Airman and Family Readiness Centers provide services that support work/life issues and facilitate community readiness, resilience and personal preparedness. Core services include:

15.20.1.1. Members are required and spouses are encouraged to attend mandatory family readiness deployment briefings that educate Airmen and their families on all phases of deployment and critical aspects of reunion and reintegration. The briefings include information on: (1) preparing for deployment; (2) sustainment and support and services for family members including extended family; and (3) mandatory reintegration briefings and continuing services that help Airmen prepare for reuniting with their families, friends and communities and for handling combat stressors.

15.20.1.2. Employment Assistance supports Airman and their families in achieving short and long-term employment, referral for education/training, and development of career goals. Airman and Family Readiness Centers provide: employment skills counseling and skills development workshops to prepare customers for portable careers in the private and public sectors; resources for self-employment, information on small business and entrepreneurial opportunities and links to alternatives to paid employment such as volunteerism and education.

15.20.1.3. Airman and Family Readiness Centers offer information, education, and personal financial counseling to help individuals and families maintain financial readiness and build resilience. Each installation has a staff member with a nationally recognized financial counselor certification for more complicated financial issues.

15.20.1.4. Airman and Family Readiness Center staff, in partnership with civilian and military school liaison officers, advocate for the educational needs of military children and assist Airmen and families with information and referrals regarding local school districts and other educational options and assist with educating school personnel on the unique issues impacting military children.

15.20.1.5. Personal and Work services promote community wellness and assist with the readiness and resiliency of the force across the life cycle. Services include intervention, prevention/enrichment consultation and skill building education designed to enhance work-life competencies for individuals, couples, and families. Focus is on promotion, enrichment and improvement of the balance between work and home to increase quality of life and resilience.

15.20.1.6. The Key Spouse Program is an official Air Force unit family readiness program designed to enhance mission readiness and resilience and establish a sense of community. The commander's initiative is what promotes partnerships with unit leadership, families, volunteer Key Spouses, the Airman and Family Readiness Center, and other service agencies.

15.20.1.7. Relocation assistance provides pre-departure and post-arrival services allowing members to make informed decisions and preparations. Referrals will include but are not limited to: temporary housing services, government or private home finding services, child care, medical and medically-related services, spouse employment assistance, cultural and community orientation, schooling, legal, personal property shipment and information on educational and volunteer opportunities.

15.20.1.8. The Transition Assistance Program provides service members with the knowledge, skills, and abilities to empower them to make informed career decisions, be competitive in a global work force, and become positive contributors to their community as they transition from military service and reintegrate into civilian life. Eligible members who have completed their first 180 days or more of continuous Regular Air Force are eligible for the following transition goals, plans, and success components: (1) preparation counseling; (2) Department of Labor Employment Workshop; (3) Veterans Administration benefits briefings I & II; and (4) Capstone.

15.20.1.9. The Airman and Family Readiness Center assists the installation commander and collaborates with other base volunteer agencies to recruit, train, place, and recognize volunteer service. The Air Force Volunteer Excellence Award is a commander's program to recognize volunteer contributions in the local civilian community or military community.

15.20.1.10. Crisis assistance provides immediate, short-term assistance to individuals and families with challenging life situations.

15.20.1.11. Military Family Life Counselors provide confidential non-medical, short-term, solution focused counseling and briefings that augment counseling services provided by other agencies.

15.20.1.12. Air Force Aid Society assistance. The Air Force Aid Society serves as the official charity of the Air Force as a private, nonprofit organization which promotes the Air Force mission by helping to relieve financial distress of Air Force members and their families as a step toward a lasting solution to their financial problems. The Society also assists Airmen and their families with their educational goals, and looks for opportunities to improve Quality of Life through proactive programs.

15.20.1.13. Casualty assistance representatives and survivor benefit plan counselors provide counseling on benefits offered by a wide variety of programs including Department of Veterans Affairs, Social Security Administration, Internal Revenue Service, Department of Health and Human Services, and state and local agencies, and provide all retiring personnel and their spouses' information on survivor benefit plan.

15.20.1.14. Airman and Family Readiness Center staff works with the Air Force Wounded Warrior Program to ensure that participants in the Warrior & Survivor Care program are provided one-on-one assistance.

15.20.1.15. The Exceptional Family Member Program is a three component program with medical, assignments, and family support. Exceptional Family Member Program-Family Support and /or Airman and Family Readiness Centers provide coordination of family support services on and off the installation to exceptional family members who have physical, developmental, and emotional, or intellectual impairments/disabilities.

15.20.1.16. Air Force Families Forever provides immediate and long-term bereavement care, service and support to identified family members of Airmen who die while serving on Regular Air Force.

15.20.2. **Emergency Assistance.** Airman and Family Readiness provides immediate, short- and long-term assistance promoting recovery and the return to a stable environment and mission readiness status for Department of Defense personnel and their families following an all-hazards incident. The Airman and Family Readiness Center, under direction of Wing leadership, activates and supports an Emergency Family Assistance Center which is the central point for delivery of services, coordination of family assistance services and continuous family assistance information

## 15.21. American Red Cross.

American Red Cross services to the Armed Forces program provide support to service members and their families in times of crisis. While serving 1.4 million Regular Air Force personnel and their immediate family members, the American Red Cross also reaches out to the 1.2 million members of the National Guard and Reserve and their immediate family members who reside in nearly every community in the United States and territories of the United States. The core service is emergency communication messages. All American Red Cross services to military members and their families are provided free of charge 365 days a year, 24 hours a day. The American Red Cross assists Regular Air Force personnel, National Guard members, Reservists, Reserve Officer Training Corps, United States Army Corps of Engineers, United States Coast Guard, United States Public Health Service, and veterans. See Figure 15.2 for services available to inactive and active service members.

15.21.1. Use the following guidance to contact the American Red Cross for assistance.

15.21.1.1. Regular Air Force members stationed in the United States and family members residing with them call 877-272-7337 (toll free).

15.21.1.2. Family members who do not reside in the service member's household, members of the National Guard and Reserve, retirees and civilians call their local American Red Cross chapter, which is listed in local telephone books and online at http://www.redcross.org/where/where.html.

15.21.1.3. Regular Air Force members and Department of Defense civilian's stationed overseas and family members residing with them call base or installation operators or the American Red Cross office at the overseas location.

15.21.1.4. The caseworker will need the following information concerning the service member:

15.21.1.4.1. Full name.

15.21.1.4.2. Rank/rating.

15.21.1.4.3. Branch of service (Army, Navy, Air Force, Marines, and Coast Guard).

15.21.1.4.4. Social security number or date of birth.

15.21.1.4.5. Military address.

15.21.1.4.6. Information about the deployed unit and home base unit (for deployed service members only).

**Figure 15.2. Red Cross Services**

---

**Emergency Communication Services**

When a military family experiences a crisis, the American Red Cross is there to assist by providing emergency communications 24 hours a day, 365 days a year. The American Red Cross relays urgent messages containing accurate, factual, complete and verified descriptions of the emergency to service members stationed anywhere in the world, including ships at sea, embassies and remote locations. American Red Cross emergency communications services keep military personnel in touch with their families following the death or serious illness of an immediate family member, the birth of a service member's child or grandchild or when a family experiences other emergencies.

No matter where a military member and their family are stationed, they can rest assured the American Red Cross will deliver their notifications in times of crisis. Even if the service member receives notification of an emergency through an e-mail or a phone call, American Red Cross-verified information assists commanding officers in making a decision regarding emergency leave. Without this verification, the service member may not be able to come home during a family emergency.

**Financial Assistance**

The American Red Cross works under partnership agreements with the Air Force Aid Society, Army Emergency Relief, Coast Guard Mutual Assistance, and Navy-Marine Corps Relief Society to provide quality, reliable financial assistance to eligible applicant's 24-hours/7-days a week/365 days a year. Types of assistance include financial assistance for emergency travel, burial of a loved one, assistance to avoid privation, etc.

**Coping with Deployments**

Psychological First Aid for Military Families was developed out of the American Red Cross's continuing commitment to serve military families. This course was designed specifically for the spouses, parents, siblings, and significant others of service members. This Red Cross service provides useful information on how to strengthen your ability to successfully respond to the challenges that military family members may encounter throughout the deployment cycle. It also explains how to provide psychological first aid to others experiencing stressful feelings or events.

**Reconnection Workshops**

Reintegration support that provides materials focusing on Working Through Anger, Communicating Clearly, Exploring Stress and Trauma, Relating to Children and Identifying Depression. The workshops focus on individuals and small groups and are designed to help family members reconnect and service members reintegrate successfully. Led by licensed, specifically trained Red Cross mental health workers, each session addresses a topic military families have found relevant to the reunion adjustment.

**Veterans Claims for Benefits**

The American Red Cross provides assistance and information in preparing, developing, and obtaining sufficient evidence to support applicants' claims for veterans' benefits and also assists claimants who seek to appeal to the Board of Veterans' Appeals.

(continued on next page)

## Section 15F—Personnel Records and Individual Rights

### 15.22. Personal Information File:

15.22.1. Commanders and supervisors perform many personnel management functions requiring them to keep files on assigned personnel. AFI 36-2608, *Military Personnel Records System,* authorizes the use and maintenance of the commander's or supervisor's personal information files. Unit commanders or equivalents maintain discretion to create personal information files on all assigned personnel, but personal information files are mandatory for officer personnel who receive a letter of admonishment or a letter of counseling. If a personal information file is established, use of Air Force Form 10A, *Personnel Information File, Record of Performance, Officer Command Selection Record Group*, is required. Contents are governed by AFI 36-2608. Custodians must keep the personal information files current and secured in a locked area or container to protect against misuse or unauthorized access.

15.22.2. According to the Privacy Act of 1974, a person who is the subject of the record may request access to this record at any time. Individuals have the right to review their personal information file at any time and challenge or question the need for documents in the file. The contents are available to commanders, raters, first sergeants, senior raters, Air Force Office of Special Investigations, and staff judge advocate personnel as warranted. The release and review of the personal information file contents in these instances are for "official business" or "routine use" according to AFI 33-332, *Air Force Privacy and Civil Liberties*.

15.22.3. Guidance provided according to the Air Force Records Disposition Schedule (https://www.my.af.mil/afrims/afrims/afrims/rims.cfm) for retaining and disposing of the personal information file.

### 15.23. The Privacy Act:

15.23.1. The Privacy Act of 1974 as amended (http://www.justice.gov/opcl/1974privacyact-overview.htm) establishes a code of fair information practices that govern the collection, maintenance, use, and dissemination of personal information about individuals that is maintained in systems of records by federal agencies. Privacy Act System of Records is defined in the Act as "a group of any records under the control of any agency from which information is retrieved by the individual's name, number, or unique identifier". Individual is defined in the Act as "a citizen of the United States or an alien lawfully admitted for permanent residence." Privacy Act rights are personal to the individual who is the subject of the record and cannot be asserted derivatively by others. Note, however, the parent of any minor, or the legal guardian of an incompetent, may act on behalf of that individual. The Privacy Act prohibits the disclosure of information from a system of records absent the written consent of the subject individual.

15.23.2. The Privacy Act limits the collection of information to what the law or Executive Orders authorize. System of Records Notices must be published in the Federal Register allowing the public a 30-day comment period. Such collection must not conflict with the rights guaranteed by the First Amendment to the United States Constitution. A Privacy Act statement must be given when individuals are asked to provide personal information about themselves for collection in a system of records.

15.23.3. In addition to specifying disclosure procedures, the Privacy Act governs the maintenance of systems of records. The Act provides individuals with a means by which to seek access to and amend their records and sets forth agency record-keeping requirements. Individuals have the right to request access or amendment to their records in a system. Personally identifiable information in a system of records must be safeguarded to ensure "an official need to know" access of the records and to avoid actions that could result in harm, embarrassment, or unfairness to the individual. The law limits the uses of records to the purposes that are stated in the System of Records Notices, as published in the Federal Register. System of Records Notices for Air Force records systems can be found at http://dpcld.defense.gov/Privacy/SORNs.aspx. Department of Defense personnel may disclose records to other offices in the Department of Defense when there is "an official need to know" and to other federal government agencies or individuals when a discloser of record is a "routine use" published in the System of Records Notices or as authorized by a Privacy Act exception. In addition, information may be released for a disclosed specified purpose with the subject's consent. The Office of Primary Responsibility of the data should keep an account of all information they've released.

15.23.4. For further information, definitions, exemptions, exceptions, or responsibilities and procedures for safeguarding and reporting of personally identifiable information breaches, consult AFI 33-332, *Air Force Privacy and Civil Liberties Program*. The Office of Management and Budget defines a personally identifiable information breach as, "A loss of control, compromise, unauthorized disclosure, unauthorized acquisition, unauthorized access, or any similar term referring to situations where persons other than authorized users and for an other than authorized purpose have access or potential access to personally identifiable information, whether physical or electronic."

### 15.24. Freedom of Information Act.

The Freedom of Information Act provides access to federal agency records (or parts of these records) except those protected from release by nine specific exemptions. Freedom of Information Act requests are written requests that cite or imply the Freedom of Information Act. The law establishes rigid time limits for replying to requesters and permits assessing fees in certain instances. The Freedom of Information Act imposes mandatory time limits of 20 workdays to either deny the request or release the requested records. The law permits an additional 10-workday extension in unusual circumstances specifically outlined in the Freedom of Information Act. (**Note:** Denials require notification of appeal rights. Requester can file an appeal or litigate.) Refer to Air Force Manual 33-302, *Freedom of Information Act Program*, for specific policy and procedures on the Freedom of Information Act and for guidance on disclosing records to the public.

### 15.25. Air Force Board for Correction of Military Records:

15.25.1. The Air Force Board for Correction of Military Records is the highest level of administrative review and powerful, yet simple system for correcting military records. Unless procured by fraud, their decision is final and binding on all Air Force officials and government agencies. The Air Force Board for Correction of Military Record's authority, jurisdiction, and policy are explained in AFI 36-2603, *Air Force Board for Correction of Military Records*. Air Force Pamphlet 36-2607, *Applicants' Guide to the Air Force Board for Correction of Military Records*, contains additional information.

15.25.2. With few exceptions, most records generated by the Air Force may be corrected by the Air Force Board for Correction of Military Records; however, an applicant must exhaust other reasonably available administrative avenues of relief prior to applying to the Air Force Board for Correction of Military Records. For instance, Enlisted Performance Reports may be voided, upgraded, or rewritten; discharges and reenlistment/reentry eligibility codes may be upgraded; survivor benefit plan elections may be changed; leave may be credited; Article 15 actions may be voided; reinstatement into the Air Force may be achieved, etc. Records may be changed, voided, or created as necessary to correct an error or to remove an injustice, and applicable monetary benefits are recomputed based on the records changed. The Air Force Board for Correction of Military Records cannot, however, change the verdict of a courts-martial imposed after 5 May 1950 but may, on the basis of clemency, change the punishment imposed by the final reviewing authority.

15.25.3. Because the Air Force Board for Correction of Military Records is the highest level of administrative appeal in the Air Force, Applicants must first exhaust other administrative remedies before applying to the Air Force Board for Correction of Military Records. Otherwise their application (DD Form 149, *Application for Correction of Military Record Under the Provisions of Title 10, United States Code, Section 1552*) will be returned without action. For example, Enlisted Performance Report appeals must first be submitted through Evaluation Reports Appeal Board, under the provisions of AFI 36-2401, *Correcting Officer and Enlisted Evaluation Reports*. Applicants should consult AFPAM 36-2607 and or consult with their Force Support Squadron to determine which administrative avenues of relief are available to them depending on the nature of the correction sought.

15.25.4. Application to the Air Force Board for Correction of Military Records is a simple process. However, favorable consideration of the application depends on all the facts and circumstances of the case and how well the request is supported by documentary evidence. The Air Force Board for Correction of Military Records is not an investigative body and except in those rare cases where a personal appearance is granted and testimony is taken, and the decision is based on the evidence contained in the case file. This normally consists of the applicant's submission (e.g. statements, arguments, documentary evidence, etc.), military record, and advisory opinion(s) from the Air Force office of primary responsibility. There is a presumption of regularity on the part of the government and absent evidence to the contrary is assumed that all government officials exercised their duties in accordance with law and policy. Because of this, the applicant bears the burden of providing sufficient evidence to establish the existence of an error or an injustice in record. The type and extent of evidence necessary to support the case depends on the nature of the request.

15.25.5. Cases are reviewed in executive session by a panel of three members, randomly selected from the Air Force Board for Correction of Military Records membership. These members, General Schedule-15s and above, the majority of whom are members of the Senior Executive Service cadre, are appointed from the executive part of the department and serve at the discretion of the Secretary. However, service on the board is a collateral, volunteer duty. Applicants may request a personal appearance before the Air Force Board for Correction of Military Records; however, a personal appearance is not a statutory right and is granted solely at the discretion of the Board, predicated on the finding the applicant's presence, without or without counsel, will materially add to the Board's understanding of the issue(s) involved. Few personal appearances are granted and the decision to conduct such a hearing is made at the time the Board initially adjudicates the application. During deliberations, which are conducted in Executive Session, Board members decide whether the applicant has first exhausted all available avenues of administrative relief; whether the application has been timely filed and if not, whether the failure to do so should be waived in the interest of justice; whether the provisions of Title 10, United States Code, Section 1034 apply to the case, and whether an error or an injustice exists. The Board is a recommending body on all cases and will vote to grant, partially grant, and deny the requested relief. If the board recommends favorable relief, the case is forwarded to the Secretary of the Air Force's designee for final decision. Applicants have the right to request reconsideration of the Board's decision; however, reconsideration is granted only if the applicant can provide newly discovered relevant evidence that was not reasonably available when the original application was submitted.

15.25.6. Applications formally considered by the Air Force Board for Correction of Military Records are processed within 10 to 18 months. Title 10, United States Code, Section 1557, *Timeliness Standards for Disposition of Applications Before Corrections Boards,* provides oversight and clearance deadlines for the correction of military records review and decision. After fiscal year 2010, 90 percent of the cases must be completed within 10 months.

## 15.26. Air Force Discharge Review Board:

15.26.1. The Air Force Discharge Review Board affords former Air Force members the opportunity to request review of their discharge (except for a discharge or dismissal by general court-martial). The objective of a discharge review is to examine an applicant's administrative discharge and to change the characterization of service, the reason for discharge, and the re-enlistment code (when applicable), based on standards of propriety or equity. Bad conduct discharges, given as a result of a special court-martial, may be upgraded on clemency factors.

15.26.2. A personal appearance before the Air Force Discharge Review Board is a statutory right. The applicant or the applicant's counsel may appear before the board in Washington District of Columbia (Joint Base Andrews Naval Air Facility Washington, Maryland) or at a regional location. The Board conducts regional boards via video teleconference. The application can also be considered on a record review basis prior to a request for personal appearance, whereupon the board will review the case based on documentation in the military record and any additional evidence provided by the applicant. The Air Force Discharge Review Board procedures allow the applicant latitude in presenting evidence, witnesses, and testimony in support of the applicant's case.

15.26.3. Airmen separated under circumstances (except retirement) that make them ineligible for reenlistment and officers discharged under adverse conditions are briefed by the Military Personnel Section at the time of their discharge about the Air Force Discharge Review Board process. They are provided with a discharge review fact sheet and an application (DD Form 293, *Application for the Review of Discharge from the Armed Forces of the United States*).

15.26.3.1. No minimum waiting period is required to submit an application.

15.26.3.2. No provisions exist to automatically upgrade a discharge.

15.26.3.3. The military will not pay travel expenses to Air Force Discharge Review Board hearing sites.

15.26.3.4. The military will not bear the cost of private counsel.

15.26.3.4.1. Members may engage counsel at their own expense; however, a number of organizations provide counsel at no cost or a representative to assist applicants. These include national service organizations such as the American Legion, Disabled American Veterans, and Veterans of Foreign Wars.

15.26.3.5. There is a Department of Defense Electronic Reading Room for the Military Departments Boards for the Corrections of Military/Naval Records and the Discharge Review Boards. The Reading Room contains the decisional documents for each of the Boards from October 1998. The personally identifiable information has been removed (redacted) from these documents. The Reading Room site is: http://boards.law.af.mil/.

15.26.3.6. Former Members with Post-traumatic Stress Disorder or Traumatic Brain Injury. In the case of a former member of the armed forces who, while serving on Regular Air Force as a member of the armed forces, was deployed in support of a contingency operation and who, at any time after such deployment, was diagnosed by a physician, clinical psychologist, or psychiatrist as experiencing post-traumatic stress disorder or traumatic brain injury as a consequence of that deployment, a board established under this section to review the former member's discharge or dismissal shall include a member who is a clinical psychologist or psychiatrist, or a physician with training on mental health issues connected with post-traumatic stress disorder or traumatic brain injury (as applicable).

15.26.3.7. **Former Members with Mental Health Diagnoses.** In the case of a former member of the armed forces who was diagnosed while serving in the armed forces as experiencing a mental health disorder, a board established under this section to review the former member's discharge or dismissal shall include a member who is a clinical psychologist or psychiatrist, or a physician with special training on mental health disorders.

### 15.27. The Virtual Military Personnel Flight.

The Virtual Military Personnel Flight is a suite of applications that provides the ability to conduct some of the Airmen's personnel business on line. Examples of applications available now include application for humanitarian reassignment, duty history inquiry, overseas returnee counseling, and reenlistment eligibility inquiry.

*Section 15G—Awards and Decorations*

### 15.28. Introduction.

Air Force members make many personal and professional sacrifices to ensure the Air Force accomplishes its mission. Acts of valor, heroism, exceptional service, and outstanding achievement deserve special recognition. The Air Force Awards and Decorations Program, AFI 36-2803, *The Air Force Awards and Decorations Program*, is limited to recognizing units, organizations, or individuals. This program is designed to foster morale, provide incentive, and esprit de corps. Individuals or units considered for awards and decorations under this program must clearly demonstrate sustained and superior performance. Questions about the Air Force Awards and Decorations Program may be directed to the servicing military personnel section.

### 15.29. Awards:

15.29.1. **Service and Campaign Awards.**

These awards recognize members for honorable active military service for participation in a campaign, period of war, national emergency, expedition, or a specified significant peacetime military operation. They also recognize individuals who participate in specific or significant military operations and who participate in specific types of service while serving on Regular Air Force or as a member of the Reserve forces. Individuals should keep copies of their temporary duty and permanent change of station orders and travel vouchers to help prove entitlement to service and campaign awards. Additional service and campaign awards can be found in AFI 36-2803, *The Air Force Awards and Decorations Program or on the Air Force "myPers" website.*

15.29.1.1. **Global War on Terrorism Expeditionary Medal and the Global War on Terrorism Service Medal.** Two of the most common service awards worn by Air Force members today are the Global War on Terrorism Expeditionary Medal and the Global War on Terrorism Service Medal. They were established on 12 March 2003. The Global War on Terrorism Expeditionary Medal is awarded to members who deployed on or after 11 September 2001 for service in Operations ENDURING FREEDOM, IRAQI FREEDOM, or NEW DAWN. The Global War on Terrorism Service Medal is awarded to members who participated in the Global War on Terrorism operations outside of the designated area of eligibility for the Global War on Terrorism Expeditionary Medal, Afghanistan Campaign Medal and Iraq Campaign Medal, on or after 11 September 2001 and a date to be determined.

15.29.1.2. **Afghanistan Campaign Medal and the Iraq Campaign Medal.** Two other service medals being issued are the Afghanistan Campaign Medal and Iraq Campaign Medal. The Afghanistan Campaign Medal and Iraq Campaign Medal were established on 29 November 2004 and recognize service members who serve or have served in the respective countries in support of Operations ENDURING FREEDOM, IRAQI FREEDOM, or NEW DAWN. Effective 1 May 2005, members deployed to Afghanistan or Iraq receive the respective campaign medal in lieu of the Global War on Terrorism Expeditionary Medal. Campaign stars are worn on the ribbons to designate official campaign periods as established by the Department of Defense. An Arrowhead Device is authorized to denote participation in a combat parachute jump, helicopter assault landing, combat glider landing, or amphibious assault landing, while assigned or attached as a member of an organized force carrying out an assigned tactical mission.

15.29.1.3. **Korea Defense Service Medal.** In February 2004, Department of Defense approved the Korea Defense Service Medal for Regular Air Force, Air Force Reserve, and Air National Guard personnel as recognition for military service in the Republic of Korea and the surrounding waters after 28 July 1954 and a future date to be determined.

15.29.1.4. **Humanitarian Service Medal.** The Humanitarian Service Medal is awarded to members of the United States Armed Forces and their Reserve components who, after 1 April 1975, distinguished themselves as individuals or members of United States military units or ships by meritorious direct participation in a significant military act or operation of humanitarian nature. "Direct participation" is any member assigned directly to the humanitarian operation providing hands-on participation. A bronze service star denotes subsequent awards. A listing of approved operations for the Humanitarian Service Medal are identified in DoDM 1348.33, *Manual of Military Decorations and Awards*.

**15.29.2. Unit Awards.**

These awards are presented to United States military units that distinguish themselves during peacetime or in action against hostile forces or an armed enemy of the United States. To preserve the integrity of unit awards, they are approved only to recognize acts or services that are clearly and distinctly outstanding by nature and magnitude. The acts or services recognized must place the unit's performance above that of other units similar in composition and mission and be of such importance that they cannot be appropriately recognized in any other way. Only one unit award is awarded for the same achievement or service. The unit's entire service must have been honorable during the distinguished act. An organization may display the award elements of a unit award. Designated subordinate units of the organization may also share in the award; however, higher organizations may not. All assigned or attached people who served with a unit during a period for which a unit award was awarded are authorized the appropriate ribbon if they directly contributed to the mission and accomplishments of the unit. Questions concerning eligibility to wear a specific unit award may be directed to the local military personnel section. The five most common unit awards worn by Air Force members today are Gallant Unit Citation, the Meritorious Unit Award, the Air Force Outstanding Unit Award, the Air Force Organizational Excellence Award, and the Joint Meritorious Unit Award.

**15.29.2.1. Gallant Unit Citation.** The Gallant Unit Citation was approved by the Secretary of the Air Force in March 2004 and is awarded to Air Force units for extraordinary heroism in action against an armed enemy of the United States while engaged in military operations involving conflict with an opposing foreign force on or after 11 September 2001. The unit must have performed with marked distinction under difficult and hazardous conditions in accomplishing its mission so as to set it apart from and above other units participating in the same conflict. The Gallant Unit Citation will normally be earned by units that have participated in single or successive actions covering relatively brief time spans.

**15.29.2.2. Meritorious Unit Award.** The Meritorious Unit Award was also approved by the Secretary of the Air Force in March 2004 and is awarded to Air Force units for exceptionally meritorious conduct in performance of outstanding achievement or service in direct support of combat operations for at least 90 continuous days during the period of military operations against an armed enemy of the United States on or after 11 September 2001. Superior performance of normal mission alone will not justify award of the Meritorious Unit Award. Service in a combat zone is not required, but service must be directly related to the combat effort. The Meritorious Unit Award is not awarded to any unit or unit component previously awarded the Air Force Outstanding Unit Award, Air Force Organizational Excellence Award, or unit awards from other Service components for the same act, achievement, or service.

**15.29.2.3. Air Force Outstanding Unit Award.** The Air Force Outstanding Unit Award was established and awarded in the name of the Secretary of the Air Force 6 Jan 1954. The Air Force Outstanding Unit Award is awarded only to numbered units or numbered Air Forces, air divisions, wings, groups, and squadrons. To be awarded the Air Force Outstanding Unit Award, an organization must have performed meritorious service or outstanding achievements that clearly set the unit above and apart from similar units. Commanders must annually review the accomplishments of their eligible subordinate units and recommend only those units that are truly exceptional. Only 10 percent of similar units assigned to a command are recommended annually. Commanders send Air Force Outstanding Unit Award recommendations to their major commands for consideration. Certain recommendations for the Air Force Outstanding Unit Award are exempt from annual submission. These are recommendations for specific achievements, combat operations, or conflict with hostile forces.

**15.29.2.4. Air Force Organizational Excellence Award.** The Air Force Organizational Excellence Award was established and awarded in the name of the Secretary of the Air Force 6 Jan 1954. The Air Force Organizational Excellence Award has the same guidelines and approval authority as the Air Force Outstanding Unit Award. The Air Force Organizational Excellence Award is awarded to unnumbered organizations such as a major command headquarters, a field operating agency, a direct reporting unit, the Office of the Chief of Staff, and other Air Staff and deputy assistant chief of staff agencies. Only 10 percent of similar units assigned to a command are recommended annually.

**15.29.2.5. Joint Meritorious Unit Award.** The Joint Meritorious Unit Award was established 4 June 1981 and is awarded in the name of the Secretary of Defense to recognize joint units and activities such as a joint task force for meritorious achievement or service superior to that normally expected. Air Force members assigned or attached to the joint unit or joint task force awarded a Joint Meritorious Unit Award may be eligible to wear the Joint Meritorious Unit Award ribbon.

### 15.29.3. **Achievement Awards.**

These awards recognize members for achieving or meeting specific types of pre-established criteria or requirements of qualification, service, performance, or conduct. Air Force members must meet specific eligibility requirements and criteria. The Military Personnel Section determines and verifies eligibility for the various types of achievement awards and makes the appropriate entry into personnel records. The military personnel section also procures and provides the initial issue of all achievement medals and ribbons. Additional achievement awards can be found in AFI 36-2803.

15.29.3.1. **Air Force Longevity Service Award.** The Air Force presents the Air Force Longevity Service Award every 4 years to members who complete honorable active Federal military service.

15.29.3.2. **Air Force Overseas Ribbon.** The Air Force awards these ribbons to individuals who have completed an overseas (long or short) tour.

15.29.3.3. **Air Force Training Ribbon.** The Air Force awards this ribbon to members who have completed an Air Force accession training program (since 14 August 1974), such as basic military training, officer training school, Reserve Officer Training Corps, United States Air Force Academy, or Medical Services, Judge Advocate, or Chaplain orientation.

### 15.29.4. **Special Trophies and Awards.**

The Air Force also sponsors various special trophies and awards programs. Special trophies and awards are unique in that the commanders of major commands, field operating agencies, and direct reporting units must nominate individuals to compete for these awards. In most cases, commanders submit nominations annually. The competition among the nominees is keen. The commander's nomination alone serves as a meaningful recognition because nomination places the individual in competition with the best in the Air Force or the Nation. Some examples of special trophies and awards are the 12 Outstanding Airmen of the Year Award and the Lance P. Sijan Award. AFI 36-2805, *Special Trophies and Awards*, lists various special trophies and awards programs.

### 15.29.5. **Foreign Decorations.**

The policy of the Department of Defense is that awards from foreign governments may be accepted only in recognition of active combat service or for outstanding or unusually meritorious performance only upon receiving the approval of Department of the Air Force.

## 15.30. Decorations:

### 15.30.1. **What Is a Decoration?**

Formal recognition for personal excellence that requires individual nomination and Air Force or Department of Defense approval. Decorations are awarded in recognition for acts of valor, heroism, courage, exceptional service, meritorious service, or outstanding achievement that clearly place members above their peers and be of such importance that the person cannot receive proper recognition in any other way. When an individual is being considered for a decoration, the determining factors are level of responsibility, achievements, accomplishments, manner of performance, and the impact of the accomplishment. Each decoration has specific performance requirements for award, and an individual may receive only one decoration for any act, achievement, or period of service. Specific criteria for each decoration are in AFI 36-2803.

### 15.30.2. **Recommending an Individual for a Decoration.**

Any person, other than the individual being recommended, having firsthand knowledge of the act, achievement, or service may recommend or contribute to a decoration recommendation by providing evidence or statements through the supervisor and chain of command of the member being recommended. However, this obligation primarily falls on the immediate supervisor. The three most common decorations are the Air Force Achievement Medal, the Air Force Commendation Medal, and the Meritorious Service Medal. Every unit, wing, and major command has specific submission criteria and procedures for these three decorations. For specific guidance, contact your commander support staff or the force management section at the local force support squadron or military personnel section.

## *Section 15H—Airman Promotion System*

## 15.31. Objective.

The enlisted promotion system supports Department of Defense directive 1304.20, *Enlisted Personnel Management System (EPMS),* by helping to provide a visible, relatively stable career progression opportunity over the long term; attracting, retaining, and motivating to career service, the kinds and numbers of people the military services need; and ensuring a reasonably uniform application of the principle of equal pay for equal work among the military services. This section addresses the program elements of the Regular Air Force Airman.

## 15.32. Promotion Quotas.

Promotion quotas for the top five grades (Staff Sergeant through Chief Master Sergeant) are tied to fiscal-end strength and are affected by funding limits, regulatory limits, and the number of projected vacancies in specific grades. The Department of Defense limits the number of Airmen the Air Force may have in the top five grades. Public law (Title 10, United States Code, Section 517) limits the number of Airmen who may serve in the Regular Air Force in the top two enlisted grades. The authorized daily average of enlisted members on Regular Air Force (other than for training) in pay grades E-8 and E-9 in a fiscal year may not be more than 2.5 percent and 1.25, respectively.

## 15.33. Promotion Cycles and General Eligibility Requirements.

The Air Force establishes promotion cycles to ensure timely periodic promotions and to permit more accurate forecasting of vacancies. Promotion cycles also balance the promotion administrative workload and provide cutoff dates for eligibility. The basis for promotion eligibility is proper skill level, sufficient time in grade, sufficient time in service, and a recommendation by the immediate commander. Table 15.2 lists time in service, time in grade, and significant dates of promotion. Table 15.3 lists minimum eligibility requirements for each grade.

**Table 15.2. Time in Service and Time in Grade Requirements, Promotion Eligibility Cutoff Dates, and Test Cycles for Promotion to Airman through Chief Master Sergeant.**

| RULE | A<br>For Promotion To | B<br>Time in Service | C<br>Time in Grade | D<br>Promotion Eligibility Cutoff Dates | E<br>Test Cycle |
|---|---|---|---|---|---|
| 1 | Airman | --- | 6 months | NA | NA |
| 2 | Airman First Class | --- | 10 months | NA | NA |
| 3 | Senior Airman | 36 months | 20 months or 28 months | NA | NA |
| 4 | Staff Sergeant | 3 years | 6 months | 31 March | May - June |
| 5 | Technical Sergeant | 5 years | 23 months | 31 January | February - March |
| 6 | Master Sergeant | 8 years | 24 months | 30 November | February - March |
| 7 | Senior Master Sergeant | 11 years | 20 months | 30 September | December |
| 8 | Chief Master Sergeant | 14 years | 21 months | 31 July | September |

## 15.34. Promotion Ineligibility.

There are many reasons why an Airman may be considered ineligible for promotion, such as approved retirement, declination for extension or reenlistment, court-martial conviction, control roster action, not recommended by the commander, failure to appear for scheduled testing without a valid reason, absent without leave, etc. When individuals are ineligible for promotion, they cannot test; cannot be considered if already tested; and the projected promotion, if already selected, will be canceled.

## 15.35. Promotion Sequence Numbers.

The Air Force Personnel Center assigns promotion sequence numbers to Airmen selected for promotion to Staff Sergeants through Chief Master Sergeant based on date of rank, total active federal military service date, and date of birth. Supplemental selectees are assigned promotion sequence numbers of .9 (increment previously announced) or .5 (unannounced future increment).

## 15.36. Accepting Promotion.

Airmen who accept a promotion are eligible for reassignment and selective retraining in the projected grade. Selectees to the grade of Master Sergeant and Senior Master Sergeant will incur a 2-year Regular Air Force service commitment from the effective date of promotion. In addition, members with 18 or more years of total active federal military service will be required to obtain 2-years retainability to serve the 2-year Regular Air Force service commitment. Selectees to the grade of Chief Master Sergeant will incur a 3-year Regular Air Force service commitment from the effective date of promotion and will be required to obtain 3-years retainability (regardless of total active federal military service) to serve the 3-year Regular Air Force service commitment. Within 10 workdays after selection for promotion you are required to accept or decline the promotion.

Table 15.3. Minimum Eligibility Requirements for Promotion. (Note 1)

| RULE | A<br>If promotion is to the rank of ( note 2) | B<br>and the Primary Air Force Specialty Code as of Promotion Eligibility Cutoff Dates is at the | C<br>and time in current grade is computed on the first day of the month before the month promotions are made | D<br>and the Total Active Federal Military Service Date is on the first day of the last month of the promotion cycle (see note 3) | E<br>and the Airman has | F<br>and following mandatory education is complete (see note 7) | G<br>then |
|---|---|---|---|---|---|---|---|
| 1 | Senior Airman | 3 level (note 4) | not applicable | 1 year | | | The Airman is eligible for promotion if recommended in writing, by the promotion authority He or she must serve on Regular Air Force in enlisted status as of the promotion eligibility cutoff date, serving continuous Regular Air Force until the effective date of promotion, and is not in a condition listed under AFI 36-2502, Table 1.1 on or after the promotion eligibility cutoff date; must be in promotion eligibility status code X on effective date of promotion (see note 8). |
| 2 | Staff Sergeant | 5 level (note 5) | 6 months | 3 years | | | |
| 3 | Technical Sergeant | 7 level (note 5) | 23 months | 5 years | | | |
| 4 | Master Sergeant | 7 level | 24 months | 8 years | | | |
| 5 | Senior Master Sergeant | 7 level (note 5) | 20 months | 11 years | 8 years cumulative enlisted service (total enlisted military service date) creditable for basic pay (see note 5) | Senior NCO Academy and Associates Degree from Community College of the Air Force (note 8 and 9) | |
| 6 | Chief Master Sergeant | 9 level (note 5) | 21 months | 14 years | 10 years cumulative enlisted service (total enlisted military service date) creditable for basic pay (see note 5) | Associates Degree from Community College of the Air Force (note 8 and 9) | |

See notes on next page

*NOTES:*

1. Use this Table to determine standard minimum eligibility requirements for promotion consideration Headquarters United States Air Force may announce additional eligibility requirements The individual must serve on enlisted Regular Air Force and have continuous Regular Air Force as of promotion eligibility cutoff date.

2. The high year of tenure policy applicable as of promotion eligibility cutoff date may affect promotion eligibility in grades Senior Airman and above.

3. Use years of satisfactory service for retirement in place of total active federal military service date to determine promotion eligibility for Air National Guard and Air Force Reserve Airmen ordered to Regular Air Force under 12301(a).

4. Airman First Class must meet skill level requirements by the effective date of promotion for Senior Airman Senior Airman must meet skill level requirements by the promotion eligibility cutoff date for Staff Sergeant Staff Sergeants test and compete for promotion to Technical Sergeant if they have a 5-skill level as of promotion eligibility cutoff date; however, they must have a 7-skill level before promotion Master Sergeants and Senior Master Sergeants must meet minimum skill-level requirements listed above. In some case, commanders may waiver this to allow them to compete for promotion Airmen demoted to Senior Airman, Staff Sergeant, or Technical Sergeant will not have their high year of tenure adjusted to make them eligible to compete for promotion. Airmen who are demoted past their high year of tenure for that grade will not be afforded an opportunity to promotion test If demoted an Airman's high year of tenure will be established in accordance with AFI 36-3208.

5. Service in a commissioned, warrant, or flight officer status is creditable for pay. Such service does not count for this requirement (38 Comptroller General 598). Airmen may be considered for promotion who meet this requirement on the first day of the last month promotions are normally made in the cycle. Actual promotion does not occur earlier than the first day of the month following the month the Airman completes the required enlisted service. This applies if the select had a sequence number in an earlier promotion increment; however, if the Airman meets the required enlisted service on the first day of the month, the date of rank and effective date is that date.

6. If a temporary duty student meets the requirements of this table but does not maintain satisfactory proficiency, the military personnel section that services the Airman's temporary duty unit informs the military personnel section servicing the Airman's unit of assignment.

7. To satisfy promotion eligibility requirements, enlisted professional military education will be completed by in-residence for promotion to Staff Sergeant and by correspondence for promotion to Senior Master Sergeant. All professional military education may be completed in-residence or by correspondence. If selected, the projected promotion will be placed into withhold, if the 12-month Enlisted Professional Military Education Policy enrollment expires before the promotion sequence number consummates. The promotion sequence number will be removed if Enlisted Professional Military Education Policy is not completed by the end of the promotion cycle.

8. Completion of the United States Army Sergeants Major Academy, the United States Navy Senior Enlisted Academy, the United States Coast Guard Chief Petty Officers Academy, United States Marine Corps Staff NCO Academy, or approved comparable international courses are equivalent to Senior NCO Academy.

9. The Community College of the Air Force degree can be in any discipline Degree must be conferred (awarded) by Community College of the Air Force on or before the promotion eligibility cut-off date.

## 15.37. Declining Promotion.

Airmen may decline a promotion in writing any time prior to the effective date. The declination letter must include name, social security number, promotion cycle, promotion sequence number (if already selected), and a statement of understanding that reinstatement will not be authorized.

## 15.38. Enlisted Professional Military Education Completion.

Airmen who fail to complete Phase 2 and/or Phase 3 enlisted PME distance learning prior to the established suspense are considered ineligible for promotion. Airmen selected for promotion to Staff Sergeant must complete in-resident enlisted professional military education (Airman Leadership School) before assuming the rank of Staff Sergeant unless the member is granted an enlisted professional military education waiver. There is no PME requirement to sew on Technical Sergeant or Master Sergeant; however, the Airman must not have a Promotion Eligibility States code 2 for failure to complete Phase 2 or 3 distance learning by the suspense date. If they have a Promotion Eligibility code 2 on or after promotion eligibility cut-off date they are ineligible for the cycle. Airmen pending promotion consideration to the rank of Senior Master Sergeant must complete Phase 3 Senior NCO Academy or equivalent/sister service/international enlisted professional military education (correspondence or in-residence) on or before the promotion eligibility cut-off date to remain eligible for promotion. In the case that an Airman has a promotion sequence number and has not completed their required distance learning by the suspense date, he or she will be placed into a promotion withhold status. The withhold status will be removed upon course completion or it will expire at the end of the promotion cycle where the line number will be cancelled.

**15.39. Promotion by Grade:**

15.39.1. **Airman and Airman First Class.**

The Air Force normally promotes eligible Airmen recommended by their commander on a noncompetitive basis. An Airman Basic must have 6 months of time in grade to be eligible for promotion to Airman. The time in grade requirement for an Airman to be eligible for promotion to Airman First Class is 10 months. There are different phase points for individuals graduating from basic military training as Airman or Airman First Class that correspond with their earlier promotions. Individuals initially enlisting for a period of 6 years are promoted from Airman Basic or Airman to Airman First Class upon completion of either technical training, or 20 weeks of technical training (start date of the 20-week period is the date of basic military training completion), whichever occurs first.

15.39.2. **Senior Airman.**

The Air Force promotes Airman First Class to Senior Airman with either 36 months of time in service and 20 months of time in grade or 28 months of time in grade, whichever occurs first. They must possess a 3-skill level and be recommended by their unit commander. Airman First Class may compete for early advancement to Senior Airman if they meet the minimum eligibility criteria outlined in the aforementioned Table 15.3. If promoted to Senior Airman below the zone, their promotion effective date would be 6 months before their fully qualified date. Individuals are considered in the month (December, March, June, or September) before the quarter (January through March, April through June, July through September, or October through December) they are eligible for below the zone promotion.

15.39.3. **Staff Sergeant and Technical Sergeant.**

Promotion to the grades of Staff Sergeant through Technical Sergeant occurs under one of two programs: the Weighted Airman Promotion System or Stripes for Exceptional Performers.

15.39.3.1. **Weighted Airman Promotion System.** Airmen compete and test under Weighted Airman Promotion System in their control Air Force specialty code held on the promotion eligibility cutoff date. The Weighted Airman Promotion System consists of up to four weighted factors: specialty knowledge test, promotion fitness examination, decorations, and enlisted performance reports. Each of these factors is "weighted" or assigned points based on its importance relative to promotion. The promotion fitness examination and specialty knowledge test account for 200 points. The promotion fitness examination contains a wide range of Air Force knowledge, while the specialty knowledge test covers Air Force specialty code broad technical knowledge. Table 15.4 shows how to calculate points. The Air Force makes promotions under Weighted Airman Promotion System within each Air Force specialty code, not across them. This means those eligible compete for promotion only with those individuals currently working in their Air Force specialty code. Selectees are individuals with the highest scores in each Air Force specialty code, within the quota limitations. If more than one individual has the same total score at the cutoff point, the Air Force promotes everyone with that score.

15.39.3.2. **Stripes for Exceptional Performers Program.** The Stripes for Exceptional Performers Program, established in 1980, is designed to meet those unique circumstances that, in the commander's judgment, clearly warrant promotion. Under Stripes for Exceptional Performers, commanders of major commands and field operating agencies and senior officers in organizations with large enlisted populations may promote a limited number of Airmen with exceptional potential to the grades of Staff Sergeant through Technical Sergeant (each major command determines their own procedures and Stripes for Exceptional Performers selection levels). The commander must ensure personnel who are promoted meet eligibility requirements including completion of the appropriate enlisted professional military education. An individual may not receive more than one promotion under any combination of promotion programs within a 12-month period. (**Exception:** A Senior Airman must serve 6 months of time in grade before being promoted to Staff Sergeant.) Isolated acts or specific achievements should not be the sole basis for promotion under this program. Stripes for Exceptional Performers promotion opportunities are limited, therefore Commanders are encouraged to recognize and promote their exemplary performers who meet the minimum promotion eligibility criteria. Date of rank and effective date is the date the selection authority announces the promotion.

**Table 15.4. Calculating Weighted Points and Promotion Factors for Promotion to Staff Sergeant through Technical Sergeant.**

| RULE | A<br><br>If the factor is | B<br><br>then the maximum score is |
|---|---|---|
| 1 | Specialty Knowledge Test | 100 points. Base individual score on percentage correct (two decimal places). (note 1) A minimum specialty knowledge test score of 40 points is required (a combine score of 90 specialty knowledge test/Promotion Fitness Exam points is required). (note 2) |
| 2 | Promotion Fitness Exam | 100 points. Base individual score on percentage correct (two decimal places). (note 1) A minimum Promotion Fitness Exam score of 40 points is required (a combine 90 points specialty knowledge test/Promotion Fitness Exam is required) Airmen testing Promotion Fitness Exam only are required to score a minimum of 45 points (note 2). |
| 3 | Decorations | 25 points. Assign each decoration a point value based on order of precedence. (note 3)<br>Medal of Honor: 15<br>Air Force, Navy, or Distinguished Service Cross: 11<br>Defense Distinguished Service Medal, Distinguished Service Medal, Silver Star: 9<br>Legion of Merit, Defense Superior Service Medal, Distinguished Flying Cross: 7<br>Airman, Soldier, Navy-Marine Corps, Coast Guard Bronze Star, Defense/Meritorious Service Medals, Purple Heart: 5<br>Air, Aerial Achievement, Air Force Commendation, Army Commendation, Navy-Marine Corps Commendation, Joint Services, or Coast Guard Commendation Medal: 3<br>Navy - Marine Corps, Coast Guard, Air Force, Army, or Joint Service Achievement Medal: 1 |
| 4 | Enlisted Performance Reports | 250 points. Multiply each enlisted performance report's point value (note 4), preceding the promotion eligibility cutoff date, not to exceed 3 reports, by the time-weighted factor for that specific report When the maximum three enlisted performance reports are calculated the time weighted factors begins with 50 percent (.50) for the most recent report, 30 percent (.30) for the middle or second most recent report, and 20 percent (.20) for the bottom report (50% - 30% -20%). After calculating each report, add the total weighted point value of each report for a sum. When an Airman is in their second year of eligibility, and/or when only two reports are calculated, the time weighted factor begins with 60 percent (.60) for the top or most recent report and 40 percent (.40) for the bottom report (60% - 40%). When an Airman is in their first year of promotion eligibility and/or when only one enlisted performance report is calculated, the time weighted factor is 100 percent. (notes 1 and 4)<br>**Example:** Enlisted performance report string (most recent to oldest): Promote Now + Must Promote + Promote<br>Promote Now [250] x .50 = 125 weighted points<br>Must Promote [220] x .30 = 66 weighted points<br>Promote          [200] x .20 = <u>40 weighted points</u><br>                                         231 points |

**Notes:**

1. Cutoff scores after the second decimal place. Do not use the third decimal place to round up or down.

2. Airmen that score the minimum 40 points on either the specialty knowledge test or Promotion Fitness Exam (when taking both examinations) must score a minimum of 50 on the other one, in order to meet the minimum combine score of 90 For those testing Promotion Fitness Exam only a minimum score of 45 is required (combine score of 90 when doubled). Airmen that fail to obtain the minimum score are considered promotion ineligible.

3. The decoration closeout date must be on or before the promotion eligibility cutoff date. The "prepared" date of the DECOR 6 recommendation for decoration printout must be before the date Headquarters Air Force Personnel Center made the selections for promotion. Fully document resubmitted decorations (downgraded, lost, etc.) and verify they were placed into official channels before the selection date.

4. Promote Now = 250, Must Promote = 220, Promote = 200, Not Ready Now = 150, Do Note Promote = 50.

5. Only count evaluations received during each grade's period of promotion eligibility. Do not count non-evaluated periods of performance, such as break in service, report removed through appeal process, etc., in the computation. For example, compute an enlisted performance report string of 4B, XB, 5B the same as 4B, 5B, 4B enlisted performance report string.

15.39.4. **Master Sergeant, Senior Master Sergeant and Chief Master Sergeant.**

Consideration for promotion to the grades of Master Sergeant, Senior Master Sergeant and Chief Master Sergeant is done through a two-phased process. Phase I is similar to the Weighted Airman Promotion System evaluation for Staff Sergeant and Technical Sergeant, although some promotion factors differ. Phase II consists of a central evaluation board held at Air Force Personnel Center using the whole-person concept. All promotion eligibles for each cycle are reviewed by the central evaluation board. The Air Force selects senior NCOs with the highest scores in each Air Force specialty code for promotion, within the quota limitations. If more than one senior NCO has the same total score at the cutoff point, the Air Force promotes everyone with that score. Table 15.5 (Master Sergeant cycle) and Table 15.6 (Senior Master Sergeant/Chief Master Sergeant cycles) detail how points are calculated.

## 15.40. Weighted Airman Promotion System Testing:

### 15.40.1. **General Responsibilities and Score Notices.**

Preparing for promotion testing is solely an individual responsibility. Weighted Airman Promotion System score notices are a means to give Airmen a report of their relative standing in the promotion consideration process and should never be provided to or used by anyone other than the individual and his or her commander. An Airman's scores cannot be disclosed without the Airman's written consent. Commanders support staff, first sergeants, supervisors, etc., are not authorized access to an Airman's Weighted Airman Promotion System scores. The commander has the specific duty to notify Airmen of promotion selection or nonselection results and may need to review their score notices to determine status. Commanders must restrict their use of the scores to notification and advisory counseling on behalf of the Airman and must not allow further dissemination of scores. Individuals may retrieve a copy of their score notice on the virtual military personnel flight after the initial promotion selection for the current cycle.

### 15.40.2. **Individual Responsibilities.**

Personal involvement is critical. As a minimum, all Airmen testing must:

15.40.2.1. Know their promotion eligibility status.

15.40.2.2. Maintain their specialty and military qualifications to retain their eligibility.

15.40.2.3. Use a self-initiated program of individual study and effort to advance their career under Weighted Airman Promotion System.

15.40.2.4. Obtain all current study references for a particular promotion cycle.

15.40.2.5. Review the annual Enlisted Promotions References and Requirements Catalog to check availability and receipt of correct study references.

15.40.2.6. Be prepared to test the first day of the testing window and throughout the testing cycle. Members who will be unavailable during the entire testing cycle due to a scheduled temporary duty must be prepared to test prior to temporary duty departure even if the temporary duty departure is before the first day of the testing cycle. Airman may opt to test early provided the correct test booklets are available.

15.40.2.7. Ensure they receive at least 60 days of access to study materials prior to testing.

15.40.2.8. (For Master Sergeant, Senior Master Sergeant and Chief Master Sergeant eligibles) Ensure their selection folder at Air Force Personnel Center is accurate and complete.

**Table 15.5. Calculating Weighted Points and Promotion Factors for Master Sergeant.**

| R U L E | A | B |
|---|---|---|
| | If the factor is | then the maximum score is |
| 1 | Specialty Knowledge Test | 100 points. Base individual score on number correct (two decimal places). (note 1) A minimum specialty knowledge test score of 40 points is required (a combine score of 90 specialty knowledge test/Promotion Fitness Exam points is required). (note 2) |
| 2 | Promotion Fitness Exam | 100 points. Base individual score on number correct (two decimal places). (note 1) A minimum Promotion Fitness Exam score of 40 points is required (a combine score of 90 points specialty knowledge test/Promotion Fitness Exam is required). Airmen testing Promotion Fitness Exam only are required to score a minimum of 45 points (note 2). |
| 3 | Decorations | 25 points. Assign each decoration a point value based on order of precedence. (note 3) <br> Medal of Honor: 15 <br> Air Force, Navy, or Distinguished Service Cross: 11 <br> Defense Distinguished Service Medal, Distinguished Service Medal, Silver Star: 9 <br> Legion of Merit, Defense Superior Service Medal, Distinguished Flying Cross: 7 <br> Airman, Soldier, Navy-Marine Corps, Coast Guard Bronze Star, Defense/Meritorious Service Medals, Purple Heart: 5 <br> Air, Aerial Achievement, Air Force Commendation, Army Commendation, Navy-Marine Corps Commendation, Joint Services, or Coast Guard Commendation Medal: 3 <br> Navy - Marine Corps, Coast Guard, Air Force, Army, or Joint Service Achievement Medal: 1 |
| 4 | Board Score | 450 points. Each panel member scores each record, using a 6- to 10-point scale and half-point increments. An individual's record may receive a panel composite score (3 members) from a minimum of 18 (6 - 6 - 6) to a maximum of 30 (10 - 10 - 10) points. The composite score (18 to 30 points) is later multiplied by a factor of 15, resulting in a total board score (270 to 450). <br><br> **Example:** <br> Panel composite score 8 + 8.5 + 8 = 24.5 <br> 24.5 x 15 = <br> 367.5 Board Score |

**Notes:**

1. Cutoff scores after the second decimal place. Do not use the third decimal place to round up or down.

2. Airmen that score the minimum 40 points on either the specialty knowledge test or Promotion Fitness Exam (when taking both examinations) must score a minimum of 50 on the other one, in order to meet the minimum combine score of 90. For those testing Promotion Fitness Exam only a minimum score of 45 is required (combine score of 90 when doubled). Airmen that fail to obtain the minimum score will be rendered a promotion non-select.

3. The decoration closeout date must be on or before the promotion eligibility cutoff date. The "prepared" date of the DECOR 6 recommendation for decoration printout must be before the date Headquarters Air Force Personnel Center made the selections for promotion. Fully document resubmitted decorations (downgraded, lost, etc.) and verify they were placed into official channels before the selection date.

**Table 15.6. Calculating Weighted Points and Promotion Factors for Senior Master Sergeant and Chief Master Sergeant.**

| R U L E | A | B |
|---|---|---|
| | **If the factor is** | **then the maximum score is** |
| 1 | United States Air Force Supervisory Exam | 100 points. Base individual score on correct (note 1). A minimum score of 45 points is required (note 2). |
| 2 | Decorations/ Awards | 25 points. Assign each decoration a point value based on order of precedence as follows (note 3): Medal of Honor: 15 Air Force, Navy, or Distinguished Service Cross: 11 Defense Distinguished Service Medal, Distinguished Service Medal, Silver Star: 9 Legion of Merit, Defense Superior Service Medal, Distinguished Flying Cross: 7 Airman, Soldier, Navy-Marine Corps, or Coast Guard Bronze Star, Defense/Meritorious Service Medals, Purple Heart: 5 Air, Aerial Achievement, Air Force Commendation, Army Commendation, Navy-Marine Corps Commendation, Joint Services Commendation, or Coast Guard Commendation Medal: 3 Navy - Marine Corps Achievement, Coast Guard Achievement, Air Force Achievement, Army Achievement, or Joint Service Achievement Medal: 1 |
| 3 | Board Score | 450 points. Each panel member scores each record, using a 6- to 10-point scale and half-point increments. An individual's record may receive a panel composite score (3 members) from a minimum of 18 (6 - 6 - 6) to a maximum of 30 (10 - 10 - 10) points. The composite score (18 to 30 points) is later multiplied by a factor of 15, resulting in a total board score (270 to 450).  **Example:** Panel composite score 8 + 8.5 + 8 = 24.5  24.5 x 15 =  367.5 Board Score |

**Notes:**
1. Cut off scores after the second decimal place. Do not use the third decimal place to round up or down.
2. A minimum United States Supervisory Exam score of 45 is required to maintain promotion eligibility. Airmen that fail to obtain the minimum score will be rendered a promotion non-select.
3. The decoration closeout date must be on or before the promotion eligibility cutoff date. The signed date by the higher official endorsing the recommendation on the DECOR 6 must be before the date Headquarters Air Force Personnel Center announced the selections for promotion. Fully document resubmitted decorations (downgraded, lost, etc.) and verify they were placed into official channels before the selection date.

### 15.40.3. Data Verification Record.

The military personnel section will instruct eligible Airmen to obtain and review his or her data verification record on virtual military personnel flight to verify the data used in the promotion selection process. Each eligible Airman must review the data verification record and the master personnel records in the Automated Records Management System (automated records management system)/Personnel Records Display Application and report any errors to the military personnel section. If an error is noted, the Airman must immediately contact his or her military personnel section for assistance. The military personnel section will update Military Personnel Data System with the correct data. Except for updating enlisted performance report data, each change will produce an updated promotion brief at Air Force Personnel Center and update the data verification record on virtual military personnel flight. The Airman's receipt of the updated data verification record ensures changes were made. Airmen should verify the updated information. Supplemental promotion consideration may not be granted if an error or omission appeared on the data verification record and the individual took no corrective or follow-up action before the promotion selection date for Staff Sergeant through Technical Sergeant, and before the original evaluation board for Master Sergeant, Senior Master Sergeant and Chief Master Sergeant. Individuals may retrieve a copy of their data verification record on virtual military personnel flight before the initial promotion selection for the current cycle.

## 15.41. Study Materials:

### 15.41.1. Enlisted Promotions References and Requirements Catalog.

Published annually on 1 October, the *Enlisted Promotions References and Requirements Catalog* lists all enlisted promotion tests authorized for administration and the study references associated with these tests. Only publications used to support questions on a given promotion test are listed. There are three types of tests discussed in the catalog;

Promotion Fitness Examinations, United States Air Force Supervisory Examinations, and specialty knowledge tests. The study references for the Promotion Fitness Examinations and United States Air Force Supervisory Examinations are the grade-specific study guides derived from AFH 1, *Airman* and the study references for specialty knowledge tests are a combination of career development courses and/or technical references. Career development courses used as study references may be different from those issued for upgrade training. The catalog also contains administrative and special instructions for test control officers. The *Enlisted Promotions References and Requirements Catalog* is available at https://www.omsq.af.mil/.

15.41.2. **Distribution of Weighted Airman Promotion System Career Development Courses and Non-Career Development Courses Study References.**

The Air Force Career Development Academy is tasked with providing each promotion eligible member access to Weighted Airman Promotion System career development courses. Weighted Airman Promotion System career development courses are available on-line at http://cdc.aetc.af.mil/. The site is updated to coincide with release of the *Enlisted Promotions References and Requirements Catalog*. Non-career development course study reference materials, such as Air Force instructions or technical orders, should be available on-line at http://www.e-publishing.af.mil or other approved repositories. Commercial publications, such as medical references, should be available at unit or base level. Individuals may ask their unit Weighted Airman Promotion System monitor to order any study reference listed in the catalog that is not locally available. According to AFI 36-2605, *Air Force Military Personnel Testing System*, promotion eligible Airmen should have access to their reference materials at least 60 days before the scheduled test date. If not, the Airman may request a delay in testing.

15.42. **Promotion Test Development:**

15.42.1. **Test Developers.**

The Airman Advancement Division, Joint Base San Antonio-Randolph, Texas, produces all Air Force enlisted promotion tests, which are written by Airmen for Airmen. Although the tests are developed at Airman Advancement Division, senior NCOs from across the Air Force travel to Joint Base San Antonio-Randolph to develop and validate the test questions. For specialty knowledge tests, senior NCO subject-matter experts are selected based on their specialties and job experience. For Promotion Fitness and United States Air Force Supervisory Examinations, Chief Master Sergeants are selected based on Air Force demographics, extensive experience, and major command representation. Test development specialists provide psychometric and developmental expertise required to ensure the tests are credible, valid, and fair to all examinees. All enlisted promotion tests are revised annually.

15.42.2. **Test Development Process.**

Airman Advancement Division test development specialist's work closely with Air Force career field managers to stay abreast of changes affecting career fields which may impact promotion test development. At the beginning of a test development project, the most current tests are administered to the subject-matter experts. This gives subject-matter experts the point of view of the test takers and helps them evaluate how the test content relates to performance in their specialties. They carefully check the references of each question. Only after this is accomplished do they begin developing new test questions. Every question on a test comes from one of the publications listed in the *Enlisted Promotions References and Requirements Catalog*.

15.42.3. **Specialty Knowledge Tests.**

Specialty knowledge tests measure important job knowledge required of Staff Sergeants, Technical Sergeants, and Master Sergeants in a particular specialty. Senior NCOs from each career field, guided by test development specialists, develop tests for their Air Force specialty using the specific career field education and training plan, occupational analysis data, and their experiences to tie test content to important tasks performed in the specialty.

15.42.4. **Promotion Fitness Examination and United States Air Force Supervisory Examination.**

The Promotion Fitness Examination measures military and supervisory knowledge required of Staff Sergeants, Technical Sergeants, and Master Sergeants. The United States Air Force Supervisory Examination evaluates practical military, supervisory, and managerial knowledge required for the top two non-commissioned grades. Chief Master Sergeants from across the Air Force, guided by test development specialists, develop these tests using the Military Knowledge and Testing System chart and their experience.

15.43. **Promotion Test Administration and Scoring.**

Promotion tests are administered to all Airmen competing for promotion to the grades of Staff Sergeant through Chief Master Sergeant. To the greatest extent possible, test administration procedures are standardized to ensure fairness for all members competing for promotion. Strict procedures are used for handling, storing, and transmitting test booklets and answer sheets to preclude the possibility of loss or compromise. All promotion tests are electronically scored at Air Force Personnel Center following thorough quality control steps to ensure accurate test results for each member. The test scanning and scoring process contains many safeguards to verify accuracy, including hand-scoring a percentage of answer sheets (pulled randomly), and physically reviewing answer sheets. Because of the difficulty of the tests, some individuals may receive scores they believe do not reflect their study efforts. Likewise, some members may receive the same score as the previous year. Information concerning verification of test scores is contained in AFI 36-2605.

### 15.44. Air Force Enlisted Promotion Test Compromise.

Group study (two or more people) is strictly prohibited. This prohibition protects the integrity of the promotion testing program by ensuring promotion test scores are a reflection of each member's individual knowledge. Enlisted personnel who violate these prohibitions are subject to prosecution under Article 92 of the Uniform Code of Military Justice for violating a lawful general regulation. Conviction can result in a dishonorable discharge, forfeiture of all pay and allowances, and confinement for up to 2 years. Information concerning enlisted promotion test compromise is contained in AFI 36-2605. In addition to group study, specific test compromise situations include, but are not limited to:

15.44.1. Discussing the contents of a specialty knowledge test, promotion fitness examination, or United States Air Force supervisory examination with anyone other than the test control officer or test examiner. Written inquiries or complaints about a test are processed through the test control officer.

15.44.2. Sharing pretests or lists of test questions recalled from a current or previous specialty knowledge test, promotion fitness examination, or United States Air Force supervisory examination; personal study materials; underlined or highlighted study reference material; and commercial study guides with other individuals.

15.44.3. Although the Air Force does not recommend or support commercial study guides, they may be used to prepare for promotion testing. Placing commercial study guide software on government computers is prohibited because doing so implies Air Force sanctioning of the guides. Additionally, there are prohibitions against developing commercial study guides.

15.44.4. Creating, storing, or transferring personal study notes on government computers. Government computers may be used to view electronic versions of official study references such as this pamphlet, Air Force instructions, Air Force policy directives, technical orders, etc.

**Note:** Training designed to improve general military knowledge, such as NCO of the quarter or Senior Airman below the zone boards, does not constitute group study as long as the intent of the training is not to study for promotion tests. Likewise, training to improve general study habits or test-taking skills is permissible if the training does not focus on preparing for promotion tests. However, individuals may not collaborate in any way or at any time to prepare for promotion testing.

### 15.45. Supplemental Promotion Actions.

Air Force Personnel Center conducts in-system promotion consideration on a monthly basis. Supplemental evaluation boards for promotion to the grades of Master Sergeant, Senior Master Sergeant, and Chief Master Sergeant are conducted on a semiannual basis. Remember, supplemental promotion consideration may not be granted if the error or omission appeared on the data verification record, or in the senior NCO selection record, located in the personnel records display application, and the individual did not take the necessary steps to correct the error prior to promotion selection or prior to the evaluation board. Fully documented supplemental consideration requests, to include proof of corrective or follow-up actions taken by the individual to correct the error, are submitted to the military personnel section, in writing, with the recommendation of the individual's unit commander. The military personnel section forwards the request to Air Force Personnel Center for final approval.

### 15.46. Occupational Analysis Program.

15.46.1. The Air Education and Training Command, Occupational Analysis Division houses the Air Force Occupational Analysis Program, governed by AFI 36-2623, *Occupational Analysis*. The purpose of the Occupational Analysis Program is to equip senior leaders and managers of Air Force personnel and training programs with objective, fact-based information about Air Force occupations and civilian occupational series. The role of occupational analysis is to conduct occupational studies; develop survey instruments, analyze the data collected, and provide actionable Air Force specialty information. Decision makers associated with training program responsibilities for an Air Force specialty use occupational survey data to establish, validate, and adjust training. Decision makers associated with personnel programs for an Air Force specialty use occupational survey data to justify or change personnel policies and to refine, or maintain occupational structures. Occupational survey data is provided to the Air Education and Training Command, Airman Advancement Division to ensure enlisted promotion tests are relevant, fair, and reliable.

15.46.2. As noted in AFPD 36-26, *Total Force Development*, paragraph 1.1.6., the Department of the Air Force adopted the Instructional System Development process to develop Air Force training programs. The Occupational Analysis Program is the **singularly unique Air Force entity** which collects, analyzes, and reports the job/occupational performance factors which are defined, measured, and applied within Instructional System Development. The Occupational Analysis Program is integral to providing an objective and factual orientation for three force development tenets inherent to AFPD 36-26, *Total Force Development*: (1) capabilities-based training (used to identify knowledge needed and specific tasks necessitating training to meet job performance requirements); (2) personnel classification and utilization (used to identify tasks performed at each career stage and to validate occupational structures); and (3) promotion testing (used to identify operationally relevant duties and tasks for test development to promote and retain the best Airmen). (Figure 15.3.)

**Figure 15.3. Occupational Analysis Data: Hierarchy of Impact**

15.46.3. The Occupational Analysis Division conducts occupational studies on enlisted Air Force specialties on a periodic basis, typically a 3- to 4-year cycle, and upon request (if out of cycle). Special studies, to include officer Air Force specialties and civilian occupational series, are conducted upon request. Career field leaders and subject matter experts are key to the process in developing the content of the survey instruments. Occupational surveys are administered to all eligible personnel in the targeted Air Force specialty or civilian occupational series through direct email (AFNet).

15.46.3.1. Data Presentation and Applications.

15.46.3.1.1. Occupational survey results are reported in occupational analysis reports. Occupational analysis reports data includes information on the duties and responsibilities performed by career field members in the form of task statements and duty areas. Collectively, this data describe the work performed by career field members in their jobs (Air Force Specialty Code) and throughout each stage of their career. Additionally, occupational survey data provides supporting information on when and how members should be trained to perform their jobs. Enlisted career field training personnel use occupational survey data (e.g., skill-level member data) as the primary source of empirical data to support decisions on *what* type of training is needed, *who* needs the training, and to what *depth* the training should be taught...*Right Skills * Right Time * Right Place.*

15.46.3.1.2. Career field leaders at specialty training requirements team sessions and/or utilization and training workshops are primary users of occupational survey data. These conferences of career field leaders, and training and personnel specialists evaluate existing training requirements for relevancy and efficacy. Based on occupational survey data, conference attendees make changes to career field education and training plans, career development course content, and the Air Force Specialty/Air Force Specialty Code description of duties, responsibilities, and qualifications as depicted in their respective Air Force Classification Directory (Enlisted. officer, or civilian Office of Personnel Management Handbook).

15.46.3.1.3. Occupational survey data is also crucial in the development and validation of specialty knowledge test content—integral to the Weighted Airman Promotion System. Occupational survey data are the objective source of job information available to specialty knowledge test development teams to construct promotion examinations that meet the requirements for relevance, fairness, and reliability. The Occupational Analysis Program produces a collective measure of occupational survey data which identifies mission essential tasks (areas of work) that suggests this data should serve as the basis for relevant promotion test content.

15.46.3.1.4. The Occupational Analysis process and data application are conducted IAW AFI 36-2623, *Occupational Analysis* and supported by AFPD 36-26, *Total Force Development*, AFMAN 36-2234, *Instructional System Development (ISD)*, and AFH 36-2235, Vol 9, *ISD Application to Technical Training*. Additionally, the Occupational Analysis process supports the requirements referenced in AFI 36-2201, *Air Force Formal Training*, AFI 36-2101, *Classifying Military Personnel (Officer and Enlisted)*, AFI 36-2605, *Air Force Military Personnel Testing System*, and AETCI 36-2641, *Technical and Basic Military Training Development*.

15.46.4. All career field members have pivotal roles with the constructive outcomes of occupational studies. Airmen of a career field being surveyed must devote the necessary time and commitment in completing their assigned occupational surveys. As stated previously, the data collected from each Airman, each survey participant, translates into operationally relevant training programs for their Air Force Specialty Code, and fair and reliable promotion tests for their career field under Weighted Airman Promotion System.

15.46.5. View your career field information by visiting the Air Force Occupational Analysis Program website: oa.aetc.af.mil/, select enlisted products, and find your Air Force Specialty's occupational analysis reports to gain valuable insights into the duties and responsibilities of your career field, and other career fields across the Air Force. In addition to the duties and tasks performed, and equipment and systems operated within a career field, you can also view job satisfaction information, work-life balance data, and the rationale behind *why* Airmen are reenlisting or separating from the Air Force. This information brings great value should you be considering career broadening through retraining.

*Section 15I—Senior NCO Promotion Program*

**15.47. Individual Responsibility:**

15.47.1. The importance of individual responsibility cannot be overemphasized. Each individual is responsible for ensuring he or she is properly identified as eligible for promotion consideration. (See AFI 36-2502, for minimum eligibility requirements for promotion.) Those eligible should have the current study reference materials, know when the testing cycle starts, ensure the information in their selection folder at Air Force Personnel Center is accurate and complete, study as needed, and test when scheduled.

15.47.2. Those eligible for promotion to Master Sergeant, Senior Master Sergeant and Chief Master Sergeant should obtain their data verification record (Figure 15.4) through virtual military personnel flight. The data verification record displays current career information as of the promotion eligibility cutoff date, some of which is included in the senior NCO evaluation brief (Figure 15.5) reviewed by the evaluation board.

15.47.3. Along with reviewing the data verification record, eligibles should review their senior NCO selection folder documents filed in automated records management system and personnel records display application to ensure data is accurate and appropriate documents are filed. Promotion eligibles should notify their military personnel section of any errors.

**15.48. Promotion Criteria:**

15.48.1. As noted in the aforementioned Tables 15.5 (MSgt), 15.6 (SMSgt/CMSgt) show how to calculate weighted factors for promotions and Table 15.3 shows the minimum eligibility requirements for promotion to Senior Master Sergeant and Chief Master Sergeant.

15.48.2. Senior Master Sergeants being considered for promotion to Chief Master Sergeant will compete for promotion in the chief enlisted manager code of the control Air Force specialty code they held as of the promotion eligibility cutoff date. Master Sergeants being considered for promotion to Senior Master Sergeant will compete for promotion in the superintendent level of the control Air Force specialty code they held as of the promotion eligibility cutoff date. Individuals with a reporting identifier or special duty identifier, designated as their control Air Force specialty code on the promotion eligibility cutoff date, will compete within that reporting identifier or special duty identifier.

**Figure 15.4. Sample Senior NCO Promotion Data Verification Record.**

Enlisted Data Verification Record

The following data is reflected in your Weighted Airman Promotion System Record. The data reflected is as of the Promotion Eligibility Cutoff Date and may not be the same as what is in the Military Personnel Data System.

The information reflected on this data verification record will be used in the promotion process for the cycle indicated. Review this data in detail, especially your control Air Force specialty code, decorations, Professional Military education and education data and retain for your personal records. Information reflected is as of Promotion Eligibility Cutoff Date, except a projected retirement date will continue to be updated until the actual promotion brief is produced (about 30-45 days prior to the board). The evaluation board reviews all reports closing out up to 5 years prior to Promotion Eligibility Cutoff Date. Any additional reports are listed for your information only. If you have recently retrained or entered a Special Duty Identifier, your control Air Force specialty code effective date is the date you departed for training. If you detect any errors or have any questions, contact your customer service center or personnel representative immediately. Your personal involvement is a must—it's your promotion

This is considered an official document and it is your responsibility to verify your promotion information.

### GENERAL INFORMATION          AS OF: 03 AUG 2013

**NAME:** SMITH, JOHN A.                    **RANK:** SMSG                 **SSAN:** XXX-XX-4321
**UNIT:** DET DPSO AF PERSONNEL CTR FO,     **DATE OF RANK:** 01 NOV 2011  **PROMOTION CYCLE:** 13E9
   RANDOLPH AFB, TX 78150-0000

**PROMOTION ELIGIBILITY CUTOFF DATE (PECD):** 31 JUL 2013
**PROMOTION ELIGIBILITY STATUS:** ELIGIBLE - PENDING TEST(S)

### DUTY INFORMATION

**PECD UNIT:** 0007 FORCE SPT SQ            **DUTY TITLE:** SUPT, MILTARY PERSONNEL FLT
DYESS AFB, TX 78150-0000                    **DUTY LEVEL:** W/B

### AIR FORCE SPECIALTY CODE (AFSC) INFORMATION:

**PRIMARY AFSC:** 3S091   **CONTROL AFSC:** 3S0X0   **DUTY AFSC:** 3S091   **PROMOTION AFSC:** 3S0X0

### CAREER INFORMATION

**TOTAL ACTIVE FEDERAL MILITARY SERVICE DATE:** 01 MAY 1990   **PROJECTED RETIREMENT SEPARATION DATE:**
**HIGH YEAR TENURE DATE:** MAY 2016                                 **RETIREMENT REASON:**

### PROFESSIONAL MILITARY EDUCATION

| COURSE | DATE COMPLETED |
|---|---|
| USAF SENIOR NCO ACADEMY | DEC 2003 |
| NCO ACADEMY | JUL 2001 |
| AIRMAN LEADERSHIP SCHOOL | MAY 1995 |

### ACADEMIC EDUCATION

| LEVEL | SPECIALTY | DATE |
|---|---|---|
| AA ASSOCIATE DEGREE | HUM RES MGT/PERS ADM | MAY 2005 |

### DECORATIONS                                              EPR

| DECORATIONS | TOTAL AWARDED | CLOSING DATE | REASON | RATING | CLOSEOUT DATE |
|---|---|---|---|---|---|
| MERIT SVC MED | 1 | 10 AUG 2006 | PCS | 5B | 21 DEC 2006 |
| AF COMM MED | 4 | 01 OCT 2000 | PCS | 5B | 21 DEC 2005 |
| AF ACHIEV MED | 1 | 01 AUG 1989 | ACH | 5B | 21 DEC 2004 |
| NAVY ACH MED | 2 | 19 JUN 1997 | ACH | 5B | 15 NOV 2003 |
| | | | | 5B | 15 NOV 2002 |

### ASSIGNMENT HISTORY

| EFF DATE | DAFSC | DUTY TITLE | COM LV | ORGANIZATION |
|---|---|---|---|---|
| 05 May 2005 | 3S091 | SUPERINTENDENT, MPS | WB | 0008 MISSION SUPPORT SQ |
| 19 Nov 2004 | 3S071 | NCOIC, ACFT MXS/NUM CEM MATTER | H2 | AF WIDE SPT |
| 20 Nov 2002 | 3S071 | NCOIC, GENERAL INTEL ASGNS | H2 | AF PERSONNEL CTR |
| 31 Dec 2000 | 3S071 | NCOIC COMMANDER'S SUPPORT STAFF | 2E | AF LEGAL SER AG |
| 31 Dec 1999 | 3S051 | NCOIC, AFLSA ORDERLY ROOM | 2E | AF LEGAL SER AG |

**Figure 15.5. Senior NCO Evaluation Brief.**

PRIVACY ACT OF 1974 (AS AMENDED) APPLIES

AIR FORCE SENIOR NCO EVALUATION BRIEF

**PREPARED:** 01-OCT-13    **BOARD NUMBER:** 5616.00    **CYCLE:** 13E9

**PERSONAL DATA**

NAME: SNCO BRIEF

SSAN: 123456789

**AFSC DATA**

CONTROL AFSC: 3S091

PROMOTION AFSC: 3S0X0

**GRADE DATA**

GRADE: SMS

DOR: 01 NOV 2011

**SERVICE DATA**

TAFMSD: 01 MAY 1990
HIGH YEAR TENURE: 01 MAY 2016
PROJ RET DATE
RET REASON:

**DUTY DATA**

DAFSC: 3S091    DUTY TITLE: SUPERINTENDENT, MPF
DUTY LEVEL: W/B    UNIT: 0007 FORCE SUPPORT SQ
EFF DATE: 2 JUN 2011    DYESS AFB TX

**ACADEMIC EDUCATION**

*(will not be utilized for MSgt Evaluation Board)*

| LEVEL | SPECIALTY | DATE |
|---|---|---|
| BACH DEGREE | HUM RES MGT/PERS ADM | 200607 |
| ASSOCIATE DEGREE | HUM RES MGT/PERS ADM | 200501 |
| ASSOCIATE DEGREE | INFORMATION SYSTEMS MGT | 199606 |

**DECORATIONS**

| TYPE | NBR | CLOSE DATE | REASON |
|---|---|---|---|
| MERIT SVC MED | 1 | 10 AUG 2006 | PCS |
| AF COMM MED | 3 | 01 OCT 2000 | PCS |
| AF ACHIEV MED | 4 | 30 SEP 2006 | ACH |
| ARMY ACHV MED | 1 | 23 AUG 1996 | ACH |

**SENIOR NCO ACADEMY**

COMPLETED: YES

*(will not be utilized for MSgt Evaluation Board)*

**CCAF DEGREE**

AWARDED: YES

*(will not be utilized for MSgt Evaluation Board)*

**ASSIGNMENT HISTORY**

| EFF DATE | DAFSC | DUTY TITLE | LVL | ORGANIZATION | |
|---|---|---|---|---|---|
| 05 MAY 2010 | -3S091 | SUPERINTENDENT, MPS | WB | 0008 | MISSION SUPPORT SQ KUNSAN ABS SKORE |
| 17 NOV 2009 | -3S071 | MISSING PERSONS PGM MANAGEMENT | H2 | 0000 | AF PERSONNEL CTR FO RANDOLPH AFB TX |
| 01 JUL 2009 | -3S071 | MISSING PERSONS PGM MANAGEMENT | H2 | 0000 | AF PERSONNEL CTR FO RANDOLPH AFB TX |
| 21 FEB 2009 | -3S071 | MISSING PERSONS PGM MANAGEMENT | H2 | 0000 | AF PERSONNEL CTR FO RANDOLPH AFB TX |
| 22 JAN 2006 | -3S071 | SECT CHIEF, BCMR/SSB/REGAF APPTS | H2 | 0000 | AF PERSONNEL CTR FO RANDOLPH AFB TX |
| 28 FEB 2004 | -3S071 | NCOIC, AFBCMR APPEALS & SSB SEC | H2 | 0000 | AF PERSONNEL CTR FO RANDOLPH AFB TX |
| 31 JUL 2003 | -3S071 | NCOIC, AFBCMR APPEALS SECTION | WB | 0000 | AF PERSONNEL CTR FO RANDOLPH AFB TX |
| 03 AUG 1999 | -3S071 | NCOIC, COMMANDER SUPPORT STAFF | WB | 0065 | MISSION SUPPORT SQ LAJES FLD PORTU |

15.48.3. The board considers academic education completed on or before the promotion eligibility cutoff date. Up to three academic education levels can be reflected on the senior NCO evaluation brief. When the academic education level is updated in the personnel data system, the promotion file is updated and a new data verification record and evaluation brief is produced to reflect the change. If the Community College of the Air Force degree was awarded by Community College of the Air Force or any other accredited college requirements were completed before the promotion eligibility cutoff date but the evaluation brief was completed within 10 days of the board convening date, the education services office will update the personnel data system. The individual must notify the Air Force Personnel Center by message of this update. This information is then used to post the senior NCO evaluation brief filed in the senior NCO selection folder. Promotion eligible Airmen are responsible for ensuring this data is posted on their data verification record and evaluation brief.

15.48.4. The promotion eligibility cutoff date is used to determine content of the selection folder and information on promotion evaluation briefs. The number of enlisted performance reports included is limited to those reports closed out 5 years before the promotion eligibility cutoff date (maximum of 10 enlisted performance reports). Approved decorations, resubmissions, or decorations being upgraded must be submitted and placed into official channels before the selection date. The data shown on the senior NCO evaluation brief includes the member's name, social security number, grade, date of rank, Air Force specialty information, service dates (to include projected retirement date), academic education level, decorations, duty information, duty history, and professional military education/Community College of the Air Force completion.

## 15.49. Evaluation Board.

The evaluation board is very important because the evaluation board accounts for over half the total score. Understanding how board members are selected, the evaluation board process, and those areas considered by board members can provide valuable insight into what is required to get promoted.

15.49.1. **Selection of Board Members.**

The number of promotion eligible personnel identified by major command and Air Force specialty codes determines the number and career field backgrounds of the board members. Board members are divided into panels, each consisting of one colonel and two Chief Master Sergeants. The board president is always a general officer. Before evaluating records, board members are briefed on the task objective, eligible population profile, and selection folder content. Board members are then sworn to complete the board's task without prejudice or partiality. They also participate in an extensive trial-run process to ensure scoring consistency before evaluating any "live" records.

15.49.2. **Areas the Board Considers.**

The board looks at performance, education, breadth of experience, job responsibility, professional competence, specific achievements, and leadership. In each area, the individual has control over the information the board reviews. Individuals therefore—not board members—are responsible for their own promotions by ensuring the board receives the most current updates.

15.49.2.1. **Performance.** The evaluation board reviews all enlisted performance reports for the 5 years preceding the promotion eligibility cutoff date. The board members consider all aspects of the enlisted performance report— job description (key duties, tasks, and responsibilities), individual rating factors, periods of supervision, overall evaluations, levels of endorsements, and each narrative word picture. If the person is an exceptional performer, the enlisted performance reports should convey to the board that he or she has demonstrated the highest qualities required of a leader and manager.

15.49.2.2. **Education.** When considering educational opportunities, enlisted members should focus on a degree program that complements their career field and enhances their ability to do their job. When the board evaluates academic education as part of the whole-person assessment, the most important consideration should be the degree to which the education enhances the member's potential to serve in the next higher grade.

15.49.2.3. **Breadth of Experience.** This factor refers to the individual's overall professional background, experience, and knowledge gained during his or her career to the present. Board members consider knowledge and practical experience in areas other than the current Air Force specialty code. If the eligible individual remained in one career field, board members consider whether he or she had wide exposure across the career field. Board members also consider potential to fill other types of jobs, as well as supervisory and managerial experience.

15.49.2.4. **Job Responsibility.** This factor does not refer entirely to the career field's command-level positions, although experience at this level is a consideration. Many base-level jobs demand just as much of an individual as jobs at higher command levels. Consideration is primarily given to what was asked of the individual and how well the individual accomplished the task. Did the job require significant decisions, or was it a job in which the individual routinely carried out the decisions of others? Is the individual a proven, effective leader, responsible for directing the work of others, or is the person responsible only for his or her own performance?

15.49.2.5. **Professional Competence.** What do rating and endorsing officials say about the individual's expertise? Is it truly outstanding? How much does the individual know about the job, and how well does he or she accomplish it? The Air Force Chief of Staff has emphasized the need for careful selection of individuals for promotion to the senior NCO grades. Therefore, those selected must be the best qualified. They must have sufficient leadership and managerial experience to prepare them for the challenges they, and the Air Force, face.

15.49.2.6. **Specific Achievements.** These are often recognized in the form of awards and decorations. However, many other significant accomplishments are often addressed in the enlisted performance report's narrative comments. Such recognition, either in the form of decorations or narrative comments, can help board members identify truly outstanding performers.

15.49.2.7. **Leadership.** Board members use their judgment, expertise, and maturity when reviewing records to assess a member's potential to serve in a higher grade. In particular, board members evaluate leadership potential. How well does he or she manage, lead, and interact with peers and subordinates? What have rating officials said about the person's leadership qualities and potential? What haven't they said?

## 15.50. Evaluation Process:

### 15.50.1. Trial Run.

As previously mentioned, board members are given two selected sets of records to score as a practice exercise before the actual scoring process. Using the whole-person concept, they score the records using secret ballots. This process helps establish a scoring standard they can apply consistently throughout the board process.

### 15.50.2. Scoring:

15.50.2.1. After the trial run is completed and discussed, panels begin the actual scoring of live records. The same panel evaluates all eligibles competing in a chief enlisted manager code or Air Force specialty code. Each panel member scores each record, using a 6- to 10-point scale and half-point increments. An individual's record may receive a panel composite score (3 members) from a minimum of 18 (6-6-6) to a maximum of 30 (10-10-10) points. The composite score (18 to 30 points) is later multiplied by a factor of 15, resulting in a total board score (270 to 450). Using a secret ballot, panel members score the record individually with no discussion. Records are given to each panel member, and after they are scored, the ballots are given directly to a recorder. This ensures each panel member has scored each record independently.

15.50.2.2. A record scored with a difference of more than 1 point between any of the panel members (for example, 8.5, 8.0, and 7.0) is termed a split vote and is returned to the panel for resolution. At this point, all panel members may discuss the record openly among themselves. This allows them to state why they scored the record as they did. Only those panel members directly involved in the split may change their scores. If panel members cannot come to an agreement on the split vote, they give the record to the board president for resolution. This ensures consistency of scoring and eliminates the possibility that one panel member will have a major impact (positive or negative) on an individual's board score.

15.50.2.3. Actual scores will vary between panels; the specific reason why certain panels scored the way they did cannot be determined because this is a subjective decision. However, because a single panel reviews each chief enlisted manager code or Air Force specialty code, all records within a chief enlisted manager code or Air Force specialty code are evaluated under the same standard. Some panels may award high scores, while others may award low ones. Therefore, whether a panel scores "easy" or "hard" is not significant. The important part of the final board score is how one eligible compares to his or her peers in the final order of merit. This allows each eligible to see how competitive he or she was.

15.50.2.4. Because each board is completely independent, board members do not know how an individual scored or ranked during the previous cycle. Each board arrives at their own scoring standard. However, as long as everyone competing in a chief enlisted manager code or Air Force specialty code is looked at under the same standard, fair and equitable consideration is ensured. A number of factors affect board scores from year to year—new panel members with different thought processes, previous promotion eligible with changed or improved records, and a large pool of new eligibles. As a result, board scores do vary (often significantly) from one board to the next.

15.50.2.5. Board members do not have access to the weighted scores of individuals competing for promotion. Their primary concern is to align all eligible in a relative order of merit, based on their panel score, within their chief enlisted manager code or Air Force specialty code. When board members leave, they do not know who was selected. They only know they have reviewed and scored each record within the standard that evolved from the trial run.

15.50.3. **Not Fully Qualified Process:**

15.50.3.1. A process associated with enlisted promotion boards often misunderstood is the not fully qualified process. As previously stated, senior NCO evaluation board members use the whole-person concept to align promotion eligible in a relative order of merit within their chief enlisted manager code or Air Force specialty code based on the quality of each promotion eligible's senior NCO evaluation record. Also, board members are formally charged to ensure individuals are not only best qualified, but also fully qualified to assume the responsibilities of the next higher grade.

15.50.3.2. If the board determines an individual is not fully qualified based on an evaluation of the record, the individual is rendered not fully qualified for promotion. In this case, Air Force Personnel Center removes the individual from promotion consideration and deactivates his or her promotion record, rendering the individual ineligible for promotion. The parent major command and military personnel section are then notified of the board's decision in writing. The parent major command must immediately notify the individual through the unit commander. The board is not allowed to disclose the exact rationale for their findings. However, factors contributing to the decision can be as general as an overall noncompetitive record when compared to peers or as specific as a demonstrated substandard performance and disciplinary problems. Additionally, the chief enlisted manager may have a very small number of eligibles and the board has exercised the authority to prevent promotion by default. In any event, the member is ineligible for that cycle.

15.50.4. **Post-Board Processing.**

After the board is finished, the weighted factor scores are combined with the board scores. This completely electronic operation builds an order of merit listing by total score within each chief enlisted manager code or Air Force specialty code, and the overall promotion quota is then applied to each list. After the selection results are approved, the data is transmitted to the military personnel section. Questions regarding the Master Sergeant, Senior Master Sergeant, and Chief Master Sergeant promotion selection process should be directed to the military personnel section career development element.

15.50.5. **Score Notice.**

All eligible personnel receive a score notice that reports how they compare to their peers in their chief enlisted manager code or Air Force specialty code in the specific promotion cycle. To determine weak areas, individuals can also compare their scores with the promotion statistics available in the military personnel section and/or posted on the Internet via the virtual military personnel flight. Personnel can access the virtual military personnel flight through the Air Force Personnel Center Web site at https://gum-crm.csd.disa.mil.

**15.51. Supplemental Promotion Actions:**

15.51.1. Reviewing the data verification record and senior NCO selection folder and taking prompt action to correct any errors provides the evaluation board the most accurate career assessment. However, if data errors or omissions occur, supplemental promotion consideration may be granted. Supplemental consideration is not granted if the error or omission appeared on the data verification record or in the automated records management system/personnel records display application and appropriate corrective and follow-up action was not taken prior to the board convening.

15.51.2. Table 15.7 provides specific information concerning supplemental consideration. Requests for supplemental consideration are submitted in writing containing the unit commander's recommendation and processed through the military personnel section. In addition, the military personnel section can answer questions about the data verification record, which may eliminate the need for supplemental consideration.

**Table 15.7. Reasons for Supplemental Consideration by the Senior NCO Evaluation Board.** (Note 1)

| RULE | A<br>If the item is | B<br>and correction is to | C<br>then consideration by the supplemental evaluation board is |
|---|---|---|---|
| 1 | Professional Military Education (note 2) | add the Senior NCO or NCO Academy course | authorized. |
| 2 | Enlisted Performance Report | add, remove, or make a significant change | |
| 3 | Academic education | show increased academic level (note 3) | |
| | | correct academic specialty (note 3) | |
| | | change year of completion | not authorized. |
| 4 | Decoration | add a decoration citation (This is not authorized if the citation or order was filed or if the decoration was listed on the brief used by the board.) (note 3) | authorized. |
| 5 | Projected retirement data (individuals who were eligible and considered by original board) | delete a projected retirement that is not valid at the time the board met | |
| | | delete a projected retirement that was valid when the board convened, but was later withdrawn | not authorized. |
| | | change the projected retirement date | |
| 6 | Any eligibility factor | render an Airman eligible (as of the promotion eligibility cutoff date) who was erroneously ineligible when the board convened | authorized. |
| 7 | Projected high year of tenure date (for individuals who were ineligible because of an high year of tenure date and not considered by the original board) | show approved extension of high year of tenure date (and reason is best interest of the Air Force) | |

**Notes:**

1. Do not allow supplemental consideration for Airmen needing more than the maximum board score (450 points) for selection.

2. Give credit if the Airman takes the end-of-course examination on or before the promotion eligibility cutoff date and successfully completes the course, even if this end-of-course examination is not scored until after the promotion eligibility cutoff date. The MilPDS will not change; only the individual's promotion record.

3. Prior to rescoring the record, panel members consider the type of error, degree of impact on the promotion score, and the points needed for selection. Records the panel considers, but chooses not to rescore, are non-selectees.

## 15.52. Weighted Airman Promotion System Testing:

### 15.52.1. General Responsibilities and Score Notices.

Preparing for promotion testing is solely an individual responsibility. Weighted Airman Promotion System score notices are a means to give Airmen a report of their relative standing in the promotion consideration process and should never be provided to or used by anyone other than the individual and his or her commander. An Airman's scores cannot be disclosed without the Airman's written consent. Commanders support staff, first sergeants, supervisors, etc., are not authorized access to an Airman's Weighted Airman Promotion System scores. The commander has the specific duty to notify Airmen of promotion selection or non-selection results and may need to review their score notices to determine status. Commanders must restrict their use of the scores to notification and advisory counseling on behalf of the Airman and must not allow further dissemination of scores. Individuals may retrieve a copy of their score notice on the virtual military personnel flight after the initial promotion selection for the current cycle.

### 15.52.2. Individual Responsibilities.

Personal involvement is critical. As a minimum, all Airmen testing must:

15.52.2.1. Know their promotion eligibility status.

15.52.2.2. Maintain their specialty and military qualifications to retain their eligibility.

15.52.2.3. Use a self-initiated program of individual study and effort to advance their career under Weighted Airman Promotion System.

15.52.2.4. Obtain all current study references for a particular promotion cycle.

15.52.2.5. Review the annual Enlisted Promotions References and Requirements Catalog to check availability and receipt of correct study references.

15.52.2.6. Be prepared to test the first day of the testing window and throughout the testing cycle. Members who will be unavailable during the entire testing cycle due to a scheduled temporary duty must be prepared to test prior to temporary duty departure even if the temporary duty departure is before the first day of the testing cycle. Airman may opt to test early provided the correct test booklets are available.

15.52.2.7. Ensure they receive at least 60 days of access to study materials prior to testing.

15.52.2.8. (For Master Sergeant, Senior Master Sergeant and Chief Master Sergeant promotion eligibles) Ensure their selection folder at Air Force Personnel Center is accurate and complete.

15.52.3. **Data Verification Record.**

The military personnel section will instruct eligible Airmen to obtain and review his or her data verification record on virtual military personnel flight to verify the data used in the promotion selection process. Each eligible Airman must review the data verification record and the master personnel records in the Automated Records Management System/Personnel Records Display Application and report any errors to the military personnel section. If an error is noted, the Airman must immediately contact his or her military personnel section for assistance. The military personnel section will update Military Personnel Data System with the correct data. Except for updating enlisted performance report data, each change will produce an updated promotion brief at Air Force Personnel Center and update the data verification record on virtual military personnel flight. The Airman's receipt of the updated data verification record ensures changes were made. Airmen should verify the updated information. Supplemental promotion consideration may not be granted if an error or omission appeared on the data verification record and the individual took no corrective or follow-up action before the promotion selection date for Staff Sergeant through Master Sergeant, and before the original evaluation board for Senior Master Sergeant through Chief Master Sergeant. Individuals may retrieve a copy of their data verification record on virtual military personnel flight before the initial promotion selection for the current cycle.

**Section 15J—Civilian Personnel Management and Programs**

**15.53. Civilian Personnel Services.**

The Air Force provides most civilian personnel services from two sources: installation civilian personnel flights, usually located in the force support squadron, and Air Force Personnel Center. Air Force activities collocated on an Air Force installation with a civilian personnel flights, or within the same locality, are to be served by that civilian personnel flights. When an activity is not collocated or located near a civilian personnel flights, services are to be provided by the nearest civilian personnel flights. Civilian Personnel Sections must service all civilian employees to ensure they are all included in the Air Force Civilian Personnel Program. Exceptions to the civilian personnel servicing arrangements are to be submitted to Air Force/A1C for approval due to impact on Reduction in Force retention and bargaining unit representation. This includes arrangements to centralize or decentralize civilian personnel servicing arrangements.

**15.54. Civilian Resource Management:**

15.54.1. While military pay is centrally managed by Headquarters United States Air Force, civilian pay is a budget line item at major command, field operating agency, and installation level, as well as at Headquarters United States Air Force. The availability of performance payout and numbers of authorized civilian positions comprise the base line for civilian employment levels. Civilian Pay funds are needed for civilian overtime; performance awards; special act awards; notable achievement awards, retention, recruitment, and relocation bonuses; student loan repayment program, seasonal and longer-term overhires; and voluntary separation incentive payments to minimize involuntary reduction-in-force separations and severance pay for affected employees as the result of reduction in force. Accurate requirement projections and development of employment plans are critical to support the workload demand within budget, while executing work years, end strength and civilian pay resource.

15.54.2. Civilian resource management is a team effort. Commanders and senior leaders depend on human resource officers, financial managers, and manpower officers to recommend effective use of employees, funds, and manpower authorizations to meet mission requirements. Major commands and installations use a corporate board structure, meeting at least quarterly, to manage annual appropriations, revolving funds, or reimbursements used for civilian employment costs.

15.54.3. When funds are available, civilian overhire positions can be established to handle peak workloads, recurring annual programs, military manning shortfalls, or other short-notice requirements that cannot be met through normal manpower requirements or personnel assignment processes. Most overhire positions are filled using temporary appointments (not to exceed 1 year). If the workload continues beyond a year, term appointments of up to 5 years may be used. Permanent appointments to overhire positions are unusual, although a permanent employee may be placed in an overhire position in a reduction-in-force.

## 15.55. Job Descriptions:

15.55.1. Civilian employees, except those above grade General Schedule-15 do not have a rank. Instead, they take the grade of the position they occupy. Since the position is graded, not the employee, detailed written job descriptions are the basis for determining pay, qualification requirements, performance expectations, and appraisal ratings.

15.55.2. Position descriptions historically have covered duties, responsibilities, and supervisory controls. The Air Force has expanded the scope of core personnel documents to include performance standards, qualifications required for recruitment, and training requirements for a new employee in the position.

15.55.3. Supervisors are responsible for core personnel documents accuracy, and for implementing standard core personnel documents from a growing library of these documents. Air Force Personnel Center/DPIC (formally AFMA/MAH) coordinates standard core personnel document content with appropriate Headquarters United States Air Force functional representatives before issuing new standard core personnel documents. Supervisors who select standard core personnel documents save the time required to write a new document and the time a position classification specialist would need to determine the correct pay plan or schedule, occupation series or code, and grade. Standard core personnel documents can also be used as templates for a unique core personnel documents that requires a new classification analysis.

15.55.4. Air Force civilian personnel sections with relatively large numbers of serviced civilian personnel retain position classification authority and responsibilities until they transition to Air Force Personnel Center/DPIC. Air Force Personnel Center/DPIC performs classification support for installations with smaller civilian employee populations. From either source, supervisors can seek assistance in developing core personnel documents or selecting or modifying standard core personnel documents.

## 15.56. Filling Jobs:

15.56.1. Vacant civilian positions are filled based on an organization's needs using a variety of recruitment sources and appointing authorities consistent with applicable laws, regulations, directives and policies as established by the Office of Personnel Management, Department of Defense, and Department of the Air Force. Referral and selection priorities must be observed when filling competitive service positions. Employees with mandatory selection or priority referral rights normally include those adversely affected by reduction-in-force through involuntary separation or demotion. These priorities may also include transfer of function declinations or transfer of work outside the commuting area, overseas returnees, reduction-in-force reclassification, civilian spouses, or spouses of Regular Air Force military following a change in duty location. Supervisors work in concert with their servicing Human Resource specialist in the civilian personnel sections or Air Force Personnel Center to determine appropriate recruitment sources. A vacancy for competitive fill actions is announced, candidates are screened by Air Force Personnel Center, and one or more lists of candidates are referred to the supervisor.

15.56.2. Based on their qualifying experience and/or education, civilians can enter civil service at different pay grade levels. The competitive staffing process used by the Air Force and other Federal agencies determines the relative qualifications of the candidates and refers only the best qualified for selection. Office of Personnel Management provides agencies with qualification standards written broadly for government-wide application. The standards are covered by either a Group Standard (multiple occupations) or by Individual Occupation. The Group Standards cover occupations under Professional and Scientific, Administrative and Management, Technical and Medical Support, Clerical and Administrative Support and Student Trainee positions. Some occupations have education requirements identified in the qualification standards. The level of education is dependent upon the duties and the grade of the position. Many jobs in professional and related occupations require a 4-year college degree. Some of these occupations including engineers, physicians and surgeons, and biological and physical scientists require a bachelor's or higher degree in a specific field of study. 5 United States Code, Section 3308 prohibits requiring education for positions that are competed, unless Office of Personnel Management has determined the duties of a scientific, technical, or professional position cannot be performed by an individual who does not have the prescribed minimum education. The minimum qualification requirements are listed on job announcements which may include specific job-related work experience, education level, medical or physical standards, training, security, certifications and/or licensure requirements.

15.56.3. Competitive placements require collaboration between supervisors and human resource specialists at the civilian personnel sections or the Air Force Personnel Center. Human resource specialists advise supervisors regarding recruitment sources. The minimum area of consideration includes Department of Defense-wide, Transfer and Reinstatement eligibles for all locally and centrally managed permanent positions. Exceptions to the standard area of consideration will be limited to positions subject to the Developmental Team process, career broadener/intern outplacements and placements to minimize adverse action.

15.56.4. Once established priority requirements are cleared, the vacancy is announced for competitive actions. The supervisor is issued a candidate referral list of qualified candidate names. Once the supervisor receives the candidate referral list, he or she may confer with the human resource specialist for interview procedures. If an interview is used as part of the selection process, the supervisor arranges the interview. Interviews are required for all General Schedule-14 and General Schedule-15 positions. Should the selecting official choose to interview, questions must be approved by the civilian personnel sections prior to use. All candidates should be asked the same questions, and the interview periods should be of relatively equal length. Some interview requirements may be defined by a locally negotiated agreement with the representative union.

15.56.5. Centrally managed career programs cover most vacancies in grades General Schedule-12 through General Schedule-15. Senior functional managers set career development and placement policies for employees in career program covered positions. These positions are subject to the same recruitment processes as non-centrally managed positions.

## 15.57. Training and Development.

Air Force policy provides for necessary training to improve skills needed in employee performance. Supervisors are responsible for determining training requirements and working with the civilian personnel sections or education and training function to identify appropriate training sources. Organizational funds must often be used to support training needs; however, civilian training funds are often available.

15.57.1. **Identifying Training Requirements:**

15.57.1.1. Conducted annually is a training-needs survey which provides the supervisor an opportunity to project training requirements for the upcoming fiscal year. Due to unforecasted mission requirements, however; supervisors may request an out-of-cycle training need at any time during the year.

15.57.1.2. Although first-line supervisors are the key individuals in determining development needs, they may need additional guidance from higher-level management, other supervisors, or the employees themselves. The servicing employee development specialist is available to assist in training needs analysis and identification of methods and training sources.

15.57.1.3. Not all training and developmental needs can or should be met through Air Force sponsorship. Employees are responsible for independently pursuing training and education that will prepare them for promotion or develop them for career transitions. Such self-development activity is employee initiated and accomplished during off-duty hours. Supervisors should encourage civilian employees to participate in self-development activities, when appropriate. Civilian tuition assistance is available in some major commands and field operating agencies.

15.57.2. **Training Sources:**

15.57.2.1. **Primary Training Sources.** Once training needs are identified, the next step is to determine training sources. The three primary sources of training are agency (Air Force), interagency, and nongovernment. Training away from the work site is requested, approved, and documented using Standard Form 182, *Authorization, Agreement and Certification of Training.*

15.57.2.2. **Agency Training.** Agency training is conducted by the employer (Air Force) and may include on-the-job training, in-house training, and Air Force formal schools. On-the-job training and in-house training are often the most effective because the supervisor tailors the training to meet the specific job requirements. On-the-job training usually is as casual as giving a few pointers to a new worker or as formal as a fully structured training program with timetables and specified subjects. Therefore, on-the-job training can include directing employees to appropriate publications for self-study. Some functional activities also use in-house training. This type of training is very effective when a large number of employees need instruction on common aspects of occupational skill requirements.

15.57.2.2.1. **Air Force Formal Schools.** More formalized agency classroom training is available through Air Force formal schools listed in the Web-based *Education and Training Course Announcements (ETCA)* located at https://etca.randolph.af.mil/. Career field management programs plan for and sponsor developmental assignments, tuition assistance, formal training, and education to develop current and future managers. Leadership and management developmental opportunities, including intermediate service school and senior service school, are available to eligible high-potential civilian employees. Information is available at www.afciviliancareers.com.

15.57.2.3. **Interagency Training.** This training may be needed if agency sources are not adequate to meet identified training needs. Interagency training includes all training sponsored by other United States government agencies. Office of Personnel Management, the United States Departments of Army and Navy, and the United States Departments of Labor and Agriculture are just a few sources from which to obtain training.

15.57.2.4. **Nongovernmental Training.** Federal regulations require agencies to consider and select government training sources before turning to nongovernment alternatives. However, nongovernment sources may be considered when agency or interagency courses cannot satisfy the training need or when nongovernment training is more advantageous. Nongovernment sources incorporate a wide range of seminars, conferences, courses, and workshops, as well as curricula offered by private educational institutions.

## 15.58. Performance, Conduct, and Discipline:

### 15.58.1. Performance Planning, Appraisals, and Awards for Employees.

The employee is advised of the duties and responsibilities of the job and the supervisor's performance expectations in their core personnel document. Employees receive annual appraisals on how well they perform their duties. Supervisors may reward employees for performing their duties well. A performance award is a management option to recognize high performance.

15.58.1.1. Supervisors set the performance elements (duties and tasks) for the civilian employees they supervise. In developing an employee's performance elements, supervisors determine the major and important requirements of the employee's job based on the employee's direct contribution to organization or work unit objectives.

15.58.1.2. Performance standards prescribe how a particular element or duty must be accomplished. Set by supervisors, the standards must reflect levels necessary for acceptable performance. When possible, supervisors should identify observable behaviors that lead to success on the job. **Note:** Elements and standards are documented in writing on Air Force Form 860, *Civilian Performance Plan*, if a core personnel document is not used.

15.58.1.3. The performance appraisal is the basis for personnel actions to identify and correct work performance problems, recognize and reward quality performance, improve productivity, and grant periodic pay increases. Supervisors review the employee's performance of each element and rate the performance against each element's standards and then render an overall summary rating. AFI 36-1001, *Managing the Civilian Performance Program*, provides guidance for evaluating civilian employee performance for General Schedule and Federal Wage System employees.

15.58.1.4. Performance awards (performance cash award, time-off award, and quality step increase) can be used as tools to motivate General Schedule and Federal Wage System employees to perform above an acceptable level as well as compensate them for performing beyond expectations. Effective management of the performance awards program can help improve productivity and morale in the organization.

15.58.1.5. Poor performance must be corrected. Employees who fail one or more performance elements are administered an unacceptable appraisal and will have an opportunity to improve. Causes for poor performance are identified (medical conditions, training deficiencies, etc.). However, if performance does not improve to a satisfactory level, the employee may be removed from the position. Placement in another position at the same or lower grade is possible. Separation from civilian employment is also possible.

### 15.58.2. Personal Conduct:

15.58.2.1. **Standards of Conduct.** AFI 36-703, *Civilian Conduct and Responsibility*, and the Department of Defense 5500.7-R, *Joint Ethics Regulation*, cover activities that are mandatory for civilian employees and activities that are prohibited. Employees are required to comply with standards of conduct in all official matters. Employees are expected to maintain high standards of honesty, responsibility, and accountability and to adhere to the Air Force core values of *Integrity First, Service Before Self, and Excellence In All We Do*.

15.58.2.2. **Required Activities.** Among required activities are: furnishing testimony in official investigations and hearings consistent with protections against self-incrimination; paying lawful debts and taxes; being present for work unless authorized to be absent; complying with health, safety, and all other proper instructions regarding work; presenting a positive public image and complying with reasonable dress and grooming standards; and maintaining professional relationships with fellow workers, subordinates, and supervisors.

15.58.2.3. **Prohibited Actions.** Prohibited actions follow the guidance in federal laws and government-wide regulations, as well as Department of Defense and Air Force instructions. Discrimination and sexual harassment, drug and alcohol abuse, misuse of government purchase cards, misuse of government computers, vehicles and other equipment, taking bribes, conducting personal business at work, and criminal behavior off-duty that reflect adversely on Air Force employment are among the prohibited activities. The Air Force does not attempt to list all possible forms of improper conduct but warns employees that misconduct will not be tolerated.

15.58.3. **Discipline:**

15.58.3.1. Disciplinary action is taken to correct employee misconduct or performance when the employee can control the essentials of the performance problems and has the skills, knowledge, and capacity to perform well but is unwilling to do so. Guidance is in AFI 36-704, *Discipline and Adverse Actions*.

15.58.3.2. The Air Force goal in the area of civilian discipline is to maintain a constructive work environment. If a disciplinary or adverse action must be taken against a civilian employee, this action must be done without regard to race, color, religion, sex, national origin, age, disability, or other factors (such as marital status or politics). Actions based on an employee's inability to perform because of a physical or mental disability should only be taken when the employee's disability cannot be reasonably accommodated.

15.58.3.3. The employee must receive advance notice of impending actions. Disciplinary or adverse actions must be prompt and equitable and comply with the intent and letter of all governing requirements, and respect must be given to the private nature of the actions.

15.58.3.4. Proper administration of discipline is a chief concern of labor organizations representing Air Force employees. Procedures governing disciplinary and adverse actions are common features of most Air Force labor-management agreements. Moreover, a basic tenet of federal labor relations law states that an employee who is a member of a bargaining unit has a right to union representation, upon the employee's request, during an investigatory interview where the employee reasonably believes disciplinary action may result from the interview.

15.58.3.5. Oral admonishment, the least severe disciplinary action, is often adequate to improve work habits or correct behavior. For significant misconduct or repeated infractions, a written reprimand may be an appropriate penalty. Written reprimands are recorded in the employee personnel record for a specified period, as directed by AFI 36-704, or an applicable negotiated labor-management contract.

15.58.3.6. Suspension is a disciplinary action that may be imposed for more serious infractions when the situation indicates that a lesser penalty is not adequate. A suspension is a particularly severe disciplinary action that places the employee in a nonpay and nonduty status, usually for a specific length of time. Employees accused of serious crime may be suspended indefinitely until criminal justice is complete.

15.58.3.7. For employees who have received oral admonishments, written reprimands, or suspensions and whose behavior continues to be inappropriate, or for such a onetime egregious event of misconduct, removal may occur. Like all other disciplinary actions, the supervisor must ensure the disciplinary action is warranted and well documented. Reprimands, suspensions, and removals must be coordinated with the civilian personnel sections and the staff judge advocate so a procedural violation or an administrative oversight does not jeopardize a valid disciplinary action.

15.59. **Working Conditions:**

15.59.1. **Pay:**

15.59.1.1. Civilian employees are paid every 2 weeks. General Schedule employee pay is expressed as an annual salary and high cost areas have higher pay rates. All General Schedule pay rates in the United States include locality pay and pay rates overseas do not include locality pay and are approximately 10 percent lower than United States rates. General Schedule pay scales normally increase in January through the legislative process.

15.59.1.2. The Federal Wage System consists of wage grade, wage leader, and wage supervisor. The Federal Wage System pay is expressed as hourly wage rates. Federal Wage System rates vary more between local areas than General Schedule. Federal Wage System rates may also be increased annually but on an area-by-area basis throughout the year.

15.59.1.3. Both General Schedule and Federal Wage System have steps in each grade. Employees progress through the steps via longevity. The General Schedule grades have 10 steps. Within grade or step increases start at 1-year intervals, but slow to 3-year intervals in the higher steps. Federal Wage System grades have five steps. Federal Wage System within grade increases start at 6-month intervals and slow to 2-year intervals.

15.59.1.4. Pay for overtime is at time-and-a-half or 1.5 times base pay. Overtime pay for General Schedule employees is capped at 1.5 times the GS-10, step 1, pay rate; for employees with rates of basic pay greater than the basic pay for General Schedule-10, step 1, the overtime hourly rate is the greater of either the hourly rate of basic pay for General Schedule-10, step 1, multiplied by 1.5, or the employee's hourly rate of basic pay. Instead of overtime pay, an employee may receive compensatory time off for each hour of overtime worked. Work at night, on Sunday, and on a federal holiday earns extra pay.

15.59.2. **Work-Hours:**

15.59.2.1. Civilian work hours are more precisely defined and less flexible than those of Regular Air Force military personnel. Civilian work schedules are defined in such terms as administrative workweek, basic workweek, regular tour of duty, uncommon tour of duty, and part-time tour of duty. Most civilians work a regular tour of duty. Normally, this is five 8-hour days, Monday through Friday. Uncommon tours of duty (a 40-hour basic workweek that includes Saturday and/or Sunday or fewer than 5 days, but not more than 6 days of a 7-day administrative workweek) are authorized when necessary for mission accomplishment.

15.59.2.2. Special circumstances permit part-time, intermittent, or special tours of duty. Installation and tenant commanders establish, by written order, daily work hours to include designated rest and lunch periods. Two types of alternate work schedules can be implemented by organization commanders. Flexible work schedules allow employees to start and end work at different times. Compressed work schedules cover 80 hours in a pay period in fewer than 10 workdays. The most common schedule has four 9-hour days each week, an 8-hour day in 1 week, and a regular day off in the other week. AFI 36-807, *Weekly and Daily Scheduling of Work and Holiday Observances,* covers work scheduling.

15.59.3. **Absence and Leave:**

15.59.3.1. Civilian employees earn 13 days of sick leave each year and 13, 20, or 26 days of annual leave, depending on their length of service. Annual leave accumulation is capped at 30 days for most General Schedule and Federal Wage System employees. Employees working overseas can accumulate 45 days. There is no cap on sick leave accumulation.

15.59.3.2. Annual leave is used for vacations and/or personal reasons and should be approved in advance of being taken, unless emergency conditions exist. Leave is charged and taken in 15-minute increments. Sick leave for medical appointments or care for a family member should be scheduled and approved in advance except in cases of emergency. Illness or injury that keeps an employee away from work should be reported to a supervisor during the first two hours of the duty day.

15.59.3.3. Absence for jury duty, dismissals for extreme weather conditions, or absences excused by the installation commander are not charged to annual leave. Employees who have earned compensatory time for overtime or time-off awards should schedule absences to use that time like they schedule annual leave. Absence and leave are covered in AFI 36-815, *Absence and Leave.*

**15.60. Unions in the Air Force:**

15.60.1. Approximately 70 percent of Air Force civilian employees are covered by labor agreements between unions and installations or major commands. As such, they are members of the bargaining unit, even if they are not dues-paying union members. Unions have legal status under federal law. Guidance is included in AFI 36-701, *Labor Management Relations.*

15.60.2. A labor relations officer or specialist in the civilian personnel sections is the usual liaison between supervisors and other management officials and union officials. The job can be full-time or part of a larger assignment. The labor relations officer speaks for management in routine communications with the union and with parties outside the Air Force who have roles in labor contract negotiations and dispute resolution.

15.60.3. A variety of union officials may act for, and make commitments for, unions. These include elected officers such as the president, vice president, and treasurer; and appointed officials such as stewards and union delegates to special meetings or projects. As part of a democratic organization, the union official may be required to present issues to a committee, such as a bargaining committee for approval. At other times, the official may have been delegated authority to make commitments. One of the duties of union officials is to raise employee concerns in the early stages of policy formulation and to resolve employee complaints. Managers should strive to work with union officials, particularly where grievances have been filed, in a professional, nondefensive manner.

15.60.4. Management and union representatives negotiate collective bargaining agreements (contracts) covering grievance procedures, use of official time for union matters, use of Air Force resources by unions such as office space, telephone, and computers, and other local or major command-wide items of interest impacting the working conditions of bargaining unit employees. These contracts bind both sides with agreements subject to interpretation by third parties outside

Department of Defense and Air Force; for example, the Federal Labor Relations Authority and/or arbitrators. Contracts do not cover pay, benefits, or other matters governed by Federal laws and government-wide regulations. However, revised Air Force instructions that differ from provisions in a contract may need to be negotiated. In recent years, civilian performance appraisal changes were not implemented at some installations until conclusion of lengthy negotiations between management and unions.

## 15.61. Dispute Resolution:

15.61.1. Civilian employees have a variety of avenues to resolve disputes. Labor-management contracts must include a negotiated grievance procedure that must be used by members of the bargaining unit. Most start with an option to seek resolution using outside neutral facilitators or mediators (alternative dispute resolution). Formal grievances follow two or more steps before one side decides to refer the dispute to a paid, outside arbitrator. Costs are usually shared equally by the union and management, so union decisions to pursue arbitration are not routine. Subject to challenge on points of law or contract terms, arbitrators' decisions are final.

15.61.2. Supervisors, managers, and employees who are not covered by a collective bargaining agreement, or who are not members of the bargaining unit follow different grievance procedures. AFI 36-1203, *Administrative Grievance System,* covers the administrative grievance process. Administrative grievances are decided by Air Force officials, usually the installation commander or designee, although outside fact finders may be used at management's option.

15.61.3. A number of personnel decisions, for example, nonselection for promotion and performance recognition, are excluded from administrative grievances and most negotiated grievance procedures. Appeals of adverse actions covered by legal appeal rights are also excluded from the administrative grievance system. The Merit System Protection Board hears appeals of suspensions without pay of more than 14 days, demotions (change to lower grade), and removals. Disputes pursued as grievances cannot be duplicated as equal employment opportunity complaints and vice versa. Appeals of adverse actions that include allegations of discrimination may be reviewed by both Merit System Protection Board and the Equal Employment Opportunity Commission.

15.61.4. A different route is taken to resolve union/management disputes concerning the statutory rights of either party. The Federal Labor Relations Authority investigates charges of unfair labor practice brought by either union or management. The union files most unfair labor practice charges when managers or supervisors are accused of changing working conditions or calling formal meetings without proper notice to the union. If found guilty, management may be required to revert back to the previous working condition, and the organization commander, including a wing commander, can be required to post an admission of managements wrong doing on official base bulletin boards.

## 15.62. Conclusion:

15.62.1. The Air Force mission requires military members to be prepared for service at all times. Force support organizations ensure Airmen's families are cared for, pay and entitlements are properly addressed, and their individual rights are secure. This chapter included information on enlisted assignments, family care, reenlistment and retraining opportunities, benefits and services, personnel records and individual rights, the awards and decorations program, and the Airman Promotion system.

15.62.2. This chapter continued with the Senior NCOs Promotion Program, identifying how manpower requirements are quantified and how supervisors initiate changes, and using competitive sourcing to maximize cost-effectiveness, efficiency and enhance mission capability by taking advantage of services available through the private commercial sector. This chapter also introduced civilian personnel management, covering such areas as job descriptions, filling positions, training, performance, conduct, and discipline; and working conditions, equal employment opportunity working conditions, and unions. Senior NCOs require a basic understanding of the subject areas to effectively lead.

# Chapter 16

# WING SUPPORT

## Section 16A—Overview

### 16.1. Introduction.

Wing Support is filled with information every Airman can use on a daily basis to assist them along in their career. Air Force Portal, entitlements, legal services, ground safety along with risk management, and the procedures for prevention of and response to sexual assault are some of the topics covered. The chapter serves as a great guide to assist you if you shall ever need information on any of these topics. More importantly though, as you become supervisor, mentor or friend having a working knowledge of topics covered in this chapter is vital to helping you be a great Wingman.

## Section 16B—Air Force Portal

### 16.2. Air Force Portal Simplifies Access:

16.2.1. In 2000, the United States Air Force launched the Air Force Portal to simplify access to information. The mission of the Air Force Portal is to provide ready access to the latest Air Force information, services, and combat support applications. Since first introduced, the Air Force Portal has changed the way we do business. Every day this technology helps us connect, collaborate, and perform our duties in service to our nation. Access is available anytime, anywhere, from any Internet-connected computer whether at home, at the office, or deployed with a valid Department of Defense public key infrastructure certificate, such as a common access card.

16.2.2. The Air Force Portal provides a single point of entry to Web-based information, self-service applications, collaboration and networking tools, and combat support systems, many without requiring a separate user identification and password. Users have access to key applications like total force awareness training, myPay, Air Force virtual education center, Air Force fitness management system, virtual military personnel flight, LeaveWeb, Training Business Area, Enterprise-Solution-Supply and many more. On the library page, you can access online periodicals, do research, and find valuable education and training materials. The Portal is the entry point to the Global Combat Support System Air Force. The goal of Global Combat Support System Air Force is to provide timely, accurate, and trusted combat support information to joint and Air Force commanders at all echelons.

16.2.3. Tremendous growth continues, with the number of active registered Air Force and Department of Defense users now over 725,000, with over 400,000 average logins per week, and serving millions of web pages per day. Provides one location for all areas—information, collaboration, and applications—so you can do your job, manage your career, and live your life in the Air Force.

## Section 16C—Military Pay, Allowances, and Entitlements

### 16.3. Military Pay and Allowances.

Department of Defense 7000.14-R, Volume 7A, *Military Pay Policy—Active Duty and Reserve Pay,* The Joint Travel Regulation and Air Force Manual 65-116, Volume 1, *Defense Joint Military Pay System Active Component FSO Procedures*, contain guidance on pay and allowances and related entitlements.

16.3.1. **Military (Basic) Pay:**

16.3.1.1. Basic pay is the fundamental component of military pay and typically, the largest component of a member's pay. Every member is entitled to basic pay while on Regular Air Force, with some exceptions such as: during periods of unauthorized absence, excess leave, or after an enlistment expires. Annual military pay raises are set by Congress and the President in the National Defense Authorization Act. In accordance with Federal Law (37 United States Code 1009) the January 1 annual pay raise will automatically match the private sector wage increases, as measured by the Employment Cost Index for the previous year. If, because of national emergency or serious economic conditions affecting the general welfare, the President may submit a plan to Congress requesting a lower annual pay raise.

16.3.1.2. Grade and length of military service determine the actual rate of basic pay. Military pay date is important because this date determines the length of service for pay purposes. In general, the pay date should be the same date the individual entered on Regular Air Force if he or she had no prior service before entering the Air Force. However, if the individual previously served in certain governmental agencies the Air Force adjusts the pay date to reflect credit for these periods. Periods of absence without leave, desertion, and sickness or injury due to personal misconduct will result in negative pay date adjustments.

16.3.2. **Leave and Earnings Statement.**

Defense Finance and Accounting Service Form 702, *Defense Finance and Accounting Service Military Leave and Earnings Statement*, is a comprehensive statement of a member's entitlements, deductions, allotments, leave information, tax-withholding information, and Traditional Thrift Savings Plan and the Roth Thrift Savings Plan information. Verify and keep your leave and earnings statement each month with increased attention when returning from deployment or when making changes such as marriage, divorce, or birth of a child. If your pay varies significantly and you don't understand why or if you have any questions, consult your servicing finance office. The myPay system allows members to view their leave and earnings statement as well as initiate changes to selected items affecting their pay.

## 16.4. Military Allowances and Entitlements.

Allowances are monies provided for specific needs such as food or housing. Monetary allowances are provided when the government does not provide for that specific need. For example, the quantity of government housing is not sufficient to house all military members and their families. Those who live in government housing do not receive full housing allowances. Those who do not live in government housing receive allowances to assist with the cost of obtaining commercial housing. The most common allowances are basic allowance for subsistence and basic allowance for housing. Most members receive both of these allowances, and in many cases, these allowances comprise a significant portion of the member's total pay. Other than continental United States cost-of-living allowance, allowances are not taxable, which is an additional embedded benefit of military pay.

16.4.1. **Basic Allowance for Subsistence.**

Basic allowance for subsistence is a nontaxable allowance used to offset the cost of the service member's meals. Most junior grade enlisted members assigned to single-type government quarters at their permanent duty station are required to eat in the government dining facilities, receive basic allowance for subsistence, and are charged the discounted meal rate which is deducted from their pay. When certified by the commanding officer or designee, members are allowed to claim reimbursement for missed meals.

16.4.2. **Housing Allowances.**

Housing allowances are based on member's grade, dependency status, and duty location. The location determines whether the allowance is basic allowance for housing or overseas housing allowance. In some cases, members who are not able to take their families to the permanent duty station are eligible for payment of family separation housing allowance in addition to basic allowance for housing or overseas housing allowance.

16.4.2.1. **Basic Allowance for Housing.** The intent of basic allowance for housing is to provide uniformed service members accurate and equitable housing compensation based on housing costs in local civilian housing markets. This allowance is payable when government quarters are not provided. Many Air Force installations have privatized their quarters, meaning that private contractors have taken over much of the previously Air Force-owned-and-operated family housing. Members in these privatized quarters are entitled to basic allowance for housing, and the rental agreement requires a rent amount not to exceed the basic allowance for housing entitlement paid via allotment. Members without dependents residing in government single-type quarters are entitled to partial basic allowance for housing unless the quarters (including government-leased quarters) exceed the minimum standards of single quarters for their grade. Members living in single-type government quarters who pay court-ordered child support may qualify for differential (basic allowance for housing-Differential). The leave and earning statement displays the basic allowance for housing rate below the heading ENTITLEMENTS, listed as basic allowance for housing. The PAY DATA portion of the leave and earning statement shows the basic allowance for housing type and basic allowance for housing dependents, as well as other housing-related data.

16.4.2.2. **Overseas Housing Allowance.** Overseas housing allowance is a cost reimbursement-based allowance to help defray housing costs incident to assignments to a permanent duty station outside the United States. Members are reimbursed actual rental costs not to exceed the maximum overseas housing allowance rate for each locality, grade, and dependency status. There are two types of allowances paid under overseas housing allowance: move-in housing allowance and monthly overseas housing allowance including a utility/recurring maintenance allowance. The location move-in housing allowance (for those who qualify) is based on the average "move-in" costs for members. The monthly overseas housing allowance is the rent, up to the rental allowance at a permanent duty station, plus the utility/recurring maintenance allowance.

16.4.2.3. **Family Separation Housing.** The purpose of family separation housing is to pay a member for added housing expenses resulting from enforced separation from dependents. There are two types of family separation housing: family separation housing –basic allowance for housing and family separation housing-overseas housing allowance. Family separation housing –basic allowance for housing is payable in a monthly amount equal to the without-dependent basic allowance for housing rate applicable to the member's grade and permanent duty station. Family separation housing-overseas housing allowance is payable in a monthly amount up to the without-dependent overseas housing allowance rate applicable to the member's grade and permanent duty station. For additional guidance, consult the Joint Travel Regulation at http://www.defensetravel.dod.mil/site/travelreg.cfm.

### 16.4.3. Clothing Replacement Allowance.

Enlisted military members receive an annual allowance to help maintain, repair, and replace initial issue uniform items as necessary. There are two types of clothing replacement allowance: clothing replacement allowance Basic, a preliminary replacement allowance paid annually between the 6th and 36th month of Regular Air Force; and clothing replacement allowance Standard, an allowance that automatically replaces clothing replacement allowance Basic after 36 months of Regular Air Force. Entitlement to either allowance depends on the individual's "entered on Regular Air Force date" in his or her master military pay account. This allowance is paid at the end of the member's anniversary month and appears on the leave and earning statement opposite CLOTHING under the ENTITLEMENTS heading.

### 16.4.4. Family Separation Allowance.

Family separation allowance is a type of allowance payable to members with dependents in addition to any other allowance or per diem to which a member may be entitled. Family separation allowance has three different categories: family separation allowance-restricted, family separation allowance-serving on ships, and family separation allowance-temporary. A member may not receive more than one payment of family separation allowance for the same period, even though qualified for family separation allowance-restricted and family separation allowance-serving on ships or family separation allowance-temporary. The purpose of family separation allowance is to compensate qualified members for added expenses incurred because of an enforced family separation. Members are eligible for family separation allowance-restricted if transportation of dependents, including dependents acquired after effective date of orders, is not authorized at government expense, and the dependents do not live in the vicinity of the member's permanent duty station. Family separation allowance-serving on ships applies to members serving on ships away from the homeport continuously for more than 30 days. A member is eligible for family separation allowance-temporary if the member is on temporary duty away from the permanent station continuously for more than 30 days, and the member's dependents are not residing at or near the temporary duty station. This includes members required to perform a period of the temporary duty before reporting to their initial station of assignment.

### 16.4.5. Station Allowances outside the Continental United States.

The aim of overseas station allowances is to help defray the higher than normal cost of living or cost in procuring housing in overseas areas. Allowances the Department of Defense authorizes only at certain overseas locations include temporary lodging allowance and cost-of-living allowance. Members receive information regarding their specific entitlements during in-processing at the new location. Members may also receive information from their local finance office upon notification of a pending overseas assignment.

### 16.4.6. Continental United States Cost-of-Living Allowance.

Continental Unites States cost-of-living allowance is payable to members assigned to designated "high cost" areas within the continental Unites States. For additional information, see Joint Travel Regulation, chapter 8.

## 16.5. Special and Incentive Pay.

A number of special and incentive pays recognize certain aspects of duty, including, but not limited to hazardous duty incentive pay, imminent danger pay, special duty assignment pay, enlisted flying duty incentive pay, and hardship duty pay-location. Also included are enlistment and reenlistment bonuses.

## 16.6. Deductions.

The two general categories of payroll deductions are involuntary and voluntary deductions.

### 16.6.1. Involuntary Deductions:

#### 16.6.1.1. Withholding Income Tax:

16.6.1.1.1. Department of Defense 7000.14-R, Volume 7A, Chapter 44, outlines specific taxable and nontaxable items. All "pay" is considered income for federal and state income tax purposes (for example, basic pay, incentive pay, special pay, lump-sum payment of accrued leave, and separation pay). Allowances considered nontaxable on 9 September 1986 remain nontaxable. For example, basic allowance for subsistence remains nontaxable and continental United States cost-of-living allowance is taxable.

16.6.1.1.2. The leave and earning statement reflects the current month and year-to-date income for social security, federal income tax, and state income tax purposes under the headings "FICA TAXES," "FED TAXES," and "STATE TAXES" in the middle of the form. Defense Finance and Accounting Service is responsible for ensuring the leave and earning statement provides the necessary pay and entitlement information.

16.6.1.2. **Federal Insurance Contributions Act (FICA) Taxes.** The FICA requires federal agencies to withhold FICA (Social Security and Medicare) taxes from the basic pay of military members covered by the Social Security Act and to pay matching FICA taxes to the Social Security Administration.

16.6.1.3. **Federal Income Tax Withholding (FITW).** FITW is used to provide for national programs such as defense, community development, and law enforcement. The FITW complies with the Treasury Department Circular E as implemented in military service directives. A member may authorize an additional monthly amount of FITW.

16.6.1.4. **State Income Tax Withholding (SITW).** The tax laws of the state where the member is a legal resident determine whether the member must pay state taxes. The amount withheld depends upon the state tax rate. One-time payments may also be subject to state tax. The state for tax purposes is reflected in the first column on the leave and earning statement under STATE TAXES.

16.6.1.5. **Armed Forces Retirement Home (AFRH).** Monthly deductions from the pay of regular enlisted members, up to a maximum of $1, are set by the Secretary of Defense after consulting with the AFRH Board. The money helps support the United States Soldiers', Airmen's and Naval Homes.

16.6.2. **Voluntary Deductions:**

16.6.2.1. Military members may establish voluntary deductions such as allotments to help administer their personal finances. Effective January 1, 2015, members are not authorized to start allotments for the purchase, lease, or rental of personal property. Personal property includes vehicles (e.g., automobiles, motorcycles, or boats), appliances or household goods (e.g., a washer, dryer, furniture), electronics (e.g., laptop, tablet, cellphone, or television), and other consumer items that are tangible and movable. Members may also have an allotment for a personal savings program, support of family members, and payment of insurance premiums. Members may control certain discretionary allotments through myPay however, there can be no more than one discretionary allotment to the same allottee. Nondiscretionary allotments have limited uses, such as charitable contributions, loan repayment to the Air Force Aid Society, garnishment for commercial debts, and delinquent travel charge card debt.

16.6.2.2. To allow for sufficient processing time, allotments should be requested about 30 days before the desired month. Occasionally, an allotment transaction may occur after the cutoff date for the mid-month payday. This will result in the entire amount of the allotment being deducted from the end-of-month pay. Normally, if the member is paid twice a month, the allotment is deducted in equal amounts from the mid-month and end-of-month pay. If the individual receives pay once a month, the entire amount is deducted from the monthly paycheck. There are certain cutoff dates that affect when allotments can be processed. Contact your local finance office for assistance.

16.6.2.3. The maximum amount of service members' Group Life Insurance coverage is $400,000 and members are covered, by law, at the maximum rate unless they decline or reduce coverage. Service members' Group Life Insurance automatically insures an eligible member against death when the member is performing Regular Air Force or Regular Air Force for training for an ordered period of more than 30 days. However, an individual may choose less coverage in amounts divisible by $50,000 or elect no coverage, but he or she must do so in writing. Additionally, family service members' Group Life Insurance covers spouses and dependent children when the eligible member also participates in Service members' Group Life Insurance coverage, including military spouses. There is a monthly deduction for spousal coverage: the amount of the deduction depends on the amount of coverage. Each child is covered in the amount of $10,000 at no cost to the member. The member may not elect to insure any child for less than $10,000. Service members' Group Life Insurance and Family service members' Group Life Insurance premiums are deducted from members' military pay each month. The military personnel section is the office of primary responsibility for administering the program.

16.7. **Military Pay Schedules:**

16.7.1. **Regular Payments.**

Military members are paid on a monthly basis with the option to receive payments once or twice per month. Members receive a statement (net pay advice) of the net amount pay and the financial organization to which statement was sent at mid-month (if receiving a payment) and a comprehensive statement of pay, the leave and earning statement, at the end of the month via myPay. These statements are created centrally by Defense Finance and Accounting Service. Military members must understand the pay system has processing cutoff dates that affect updates to their pay. The cutoff date is the day when Defense Finance and Accounting Service stops processing transactions against pay accounts for the current period so the regular payroll process can begin. The cutoff is necessary to compute, prepare, and transfer funds. While the cutoff dates fluctuate from month to month, they are generally around the 6th for the mid-month payday and the 20th for the end-of-month payday.

### 16.7.2. Local, Partial, and Emergency Partial Payments.

Local cash payments are normally only authorized for overseas areas where on base military banking facilities are not readily available. Exceptions may be granted for members assigned to classified or contingency operations where the exigencies of their assignments may require local cash or partial payments. Under extenuating circumstances, a stateside member may receive an emergency partial payment if the payment is deemed time sensitive and required within 24 hours due to an unforeseen set of circumstances. The member's commander may authorize immediate cash payments up to the amount of accrued entitlement to date when deemed appropriate to the mission. Non-cash partial payments may be made, via electronic funds transfer and deposited into the member's financial institution, normally in 2 to 3 business days. Partial payments are limited to the amount of pay and allowances the member has accrued to the date of the payment. Partial payments are recouped in full on the next available payday.

### 16.7.3. Permanent Change of Station Advance Payments.

Advance payments of pay and allowances provide members with funds to meet extraordinary expenses incident to a government-ordered relocation that are directly related to the permanent change of station and not covered by other entitlements. A permanent change of station advance payment is an advance of up to 3 months of basic pay, less the mandatory deductions of FICA, FITW, SITW, Air Force Retirement Home, and all known debts currently being deducted. Airman First Class and below must have the approval of their immediate commander for advance pay. If the desired repayment period is greater than 12 months or the amount requested is greater than 1 month's basic pay, then all members must have the approval of their immediate commander. Repayment periods greater than 12 months are only approved in cases of financial hardship. **Note:** Individual billed account government travel charge card usage is authorized and highly encouraged for all permanent change of station related expenses.

## 16.8. Permanent Change of Station Allowances:

### 16.8.1. Transportation Allowance.

When military members are ordered to perform a permanent change of station, they may receive a variety of travel allowances. Some of these allowances include:

16.8.1.1. **Government-Procured Transportation.** Available United States-certificated air carriers must be used for all commercial air transportation of persons/property when the government funds the air travel. When the authorizing/order-issuing official determines United States-certificated air carriers are unavailable, commercial air transportation on a non-United States-certificated air carrier may be authorized/approved. Documentation explaining why United States-certificated air carrier service is not available must be provided to the traveler. Endorsements on the travel orders or government travel procurement document made in accordance with service guidance are acceptable. Travel time for travel by government conveyance (except government automobile) or common carriers obtained by government-procured transportation is allowed for the actual time needed to travel over the direct route including necessary delays for the transportation mode used.

16.8.1.2. **Use of Privately Owned Conveyance.** Uniformed service policy is to authorize/approve (as distinguished from permit) privately owned conveyance travel if acceptable to the member and advantageous to the government based on the facts in each case. Other allowable travel and transportation options include government conveyance or commercial carrier. Reimbursement of parking fees, ferry fares, road, bridge and tunnel tolls is authorized for privately owned conveyance over the most direct route between the stations involved. The member is also authorized a flat per diem at the standard continental United States rate for each permanent change of station travel day between authorized points, up to the allowable travel time.

16.8.1.3. **Personally Procured Transportation.** Department of Defense policy mandates the use of the commercial travel office for all official transportation requirements. A member who, despite the Department of Defense policy, procures common carrier transportation at personal expense for official travel is authorized reimbursement (except transoceanic travel in which no reimbursement is authorized) up to the amount authorized. However, reimbursement must not exceed the cost for the authorized transportation and accommodations over a usually traveled direct route according to a schedule necessary to meet the requirements of the order. Commands/units are expected to take appropriate disciplinary action when a member and (or) an authorizing/order-issuing official fail to follow the regulations concerning commercial travel office use. Consult the Joint Travel Regulation for additional information.

16.8.1.4. **Mixed Modes.** When both government-procured and personally procured modes of transportation are used, the Air Force uses a combination of rules governed by the Joint Travel Regulation. The local Financial Service Office can provide specific guidance.

16.8.2. **Dependent Travel.**

A military member receives monetary allowance in lieu of transportation and flat rate per diem for the official distance dependents travel with him or her by privately owned vehicle. If dependents purchase commercial common carrier transportation, the member may be reimbursed for the actual cost of the transportation, not to exceed the cost the government would have incurred for ordered travel, and the member receives a per diem allowance for dependents. When the Air Force restricts travel of dependents to a location overseas, dependents may move at government expense to any place (called the Designated Location, which must be approved and listed on the permanent change of station authorization) within the continental United States the member designates. With special approval, dependents may move outside the continental United States.

16.8.3. **Dislocation Allowance.**

This allowance is paid at a rate determined by the Secretary of Defense and payable to all members with dependents when dependents relocate their household goods in conjunction with a permanent change of station. It is also payable to members without dependents if they are not assigned permanent government quarters upon arrival at the new permanent duty station.

16.8.4. **Temporary Lodging Expense and Temporary Lodging Allowance.**

A member arriving or departing permanent change of station at a location within the continental United States may receive temporary lodging expense to help defray the added living expenses incurred while occupying temporary lodging. A member arriving or departing permanent change of station at a location outside the continental United States may receive temporary lodging allowance to help defray the added living expenses incurred while occupying temporary lodging. Temporary lodging expense is paid on a travel voucher. Temporary lodging allowance is paid in military pay and is reflected on the leave and earning statement.

16.8.5. **Shipment of Household Goods.**

A member ordered on a permanent change of station move may ship household goods within certain weight limitations at government expense. Authorized weight allowances normally depend on the grade of the member and whether he or she has dependents. A member may be reimbursed for personally arranging for the shipment of household goods. Claims should be prepared and submitted according to service instructions. The government's cost limit is based on the member's maximum household goods weight allowance (that is, if the member transports household goods in excess of the authorized weight allowance, all payments are based on the authorized weight allowance).

16.8.6. **Shipment of Unaccompanied Baggage.**

This provision refers to the portion of the permanent change of station weight allowance ordinarily transported separately from the major or bulk of household goods and usually is transported by an expedited mode. When the expedited transportation mode is commercial air, a maximum of 1,000 pounds (net), may be transported.

16.8.7. **Shipment of Privately Owned Vehicle.**

When authorized, members may ship one privately owned vehicle at government expense when ordered to go on a permanent change of station to, from, or between locations overseas. Privately owned vehicle storage may be provided or authorized for personally arranging when shipment is prohibited or restricted.

16.8.8. **Mobile Home Shipment.**

Members who own a mobile home should contact the traffic management office to arrange transportation. In certain circumstances, members may arrange or contract personally for the movement of the mobile home. Shipment of a mobile home is in lieu of household goods transportation.

16.9. **Temporary Duty Entitlements:**

16.9.1. **Per Diem.**

This allowance helps defray the cost of quarters, meals, and certain incidentals, Per diem rates depend on the temporary duty location. Travelers are paid a prescribed amount for meals and incidental expenses plus the actual amount for lodging, not to exceed the maximum lodging rate for the specific location. The rates depend on the availability of government facilities, such as quarters and dining facilities.

16.9.2. **Transportation.**

Policy mandates that uniformed service members use available commercial travel offices to arrange official travel. The mode of transportation used between the points designated in the travel order will determine the transportation entitlement. On the other hand, if the member receives authorization to travel at personal expense, he or she will receive a reimbursement limited to what cost the government would have incurred for the authorized mode of travel. Consult the transportation office or commercial travel office for assistance.

16.9.3. **Miscellaneous Reimbursable Expenses.**

Reimbursable travel related expenses include travel from home or place of lodging to the servicing transportation terminal by taxi, limousine, bus, or privately owned vehicle; passports, and visas; and rental vehicles when authorized on travel orders.

16.9.4. **Temporary Duty Expenses:**

16.9.4.1. When the temporary duty is completed, the traveler is responsible for electronically filing a voucher (Defense Travel System) or preparing his or her DD Form 1351-2, *Travel Voucher or Subvoucher*, to claim reimbursement for official travel within 5 business days upon return to permanent duty station. The traveler is responsible for the truth and accuracy of the information. When the traveler signs the form (and this signature authority must never be delegated), he or she attests that the statements are true and complete and that he or she is aware of the liability for filing a false claim. All claims and attached statements shall be completed using ink, typewriter, or computer-generated forms. The member is expected to pay the amount billed from the government travel charge card company upon receipt of the monthly statement.

16.9.4.2. Electronic funds transfer is the mandatory means by which a travel claim is settled. The split disbursement option in Defense Travel System, which permits direct payment via electronic funds transfer to the government travel charge card contractor for charges incurred on the individual billed account government travel charge card and to the cardholder for any residual amount will be utilized. Spilt disbursement enables travelers to elect the amount of money to be forwarded to the government travel charge card contractor. In cases where the traveler is temporary duty for 45 days or more, he or she shall file an interim voucher (or have scheduled partial payments setup in Defense Travel System) every 30 days and use split disbursement to pay the bill. An extended temporary duty trip is no excuse for late payment of the government travel charge card bill.

**16.10. The Government Travel Charge Card Program:**

16.10.1. **Purpose.**

The travel card program is intended to facilitate and standardize the use by Department of Defense travelers of a safe, effective, convenient, commercially available method to pay for expenses incident to official travel, including local travel. The travel card is used to improve Department of Defense cash management, reduce Department of Defense and traveler administrative workloads, and facilitate better service to Department of Defense travelers. In addition, because of the refund feature of the travel card program, the program results in cost savings for the Department.

16.10.2. **Agency Program Coordinators.**

An agency program coordinator is an individual (uniformed member, employee, contractor, or foreign national) designated in writing by a commander or director as responsible for the management of the travel card program. Agency program coordinators are responsible to manage the travel card program within their hierarchy in accordance with Department of Defense Financial Management Regulation, Volume 9, Chapter 3 and understand policies and procedures set forth in the Air Force government travel charge card guide, and the Department of Defense Financial Management Regulation.

16.10.3. **Card Use.**

Unless otherwise exempted, all Department of Defense personnel are required to use the government-sponsored, contractor-issued government travel charge card for all expenses arising from official government travel. These expenses include lodging, transportation expenses, local ground transportation, and rental car expenses authorized on travel orders. The cardholder, while in a travel status, may use the card for nonreimbursable incidental travel expenses such as rental movies, personal telephone calls, exercise fees, and beverages when these charges are not part of a separate room billing or meal and are reasonable.

16.10.3.1. Government travel charge cardholders obtain cash, as authorized, through automated teller machines, rather than obtaining cash advances from a Department of Defense disbursing officer.

16.10.3.2. Travelers may use the government travel charge card at a specified network of automated teller machine to obtain cash needed to pay for "out-of-pocket" travel-related expenses. The travel card vendor assigns a personal identification number to each cardholder, together with card issuance to permit automated teller machine access. Automated teller machine advances will not be obtained earlier than 3 working days before scheduled travel and are limited to authorized expenses exempt from mandatory card usage (meals, incidentals, miscellaneous expenses, etc.). The travel card vendor will charge the cardholder a transaction fee for automated teller machine use. This includes international transaction fees made as a result of any foreign currency conversion. These charges, which appear on the cardholder's billing statement, are typically part of the incidental expense portion of per diem and are therefore no longer separate reimbursable expenses. In addition, some banks charge a service fee for automated teller machine access. This fee is also part of the incidental expense portion of per diem and are no longer reimbursable.

16.10.4. **Card Abuse.**

Commanders or supervisors will not tolerate the misuse of the Department of Defense government travel charge card. Cardholders who misuse their Department of Defense government travel charge card are subject to appropriate administrative or disciplinary action. The cardholder will only use the government travel charge card while in official travel status.

16.10.5. **How to Pay the Card Company.**

The travel card vendor provides detailed monthly bills. Cardholders are responsible for payment in full of outstanding balances due in the monthly billing statement from the travel card vendor. Payments should be made promptly (within the current billing cycle). Military service members who travel temporary duty and use government credit cards must use the split disbursement feature within Defense Travel System, which automatically pays the credit card vendor for credit card charges while on official travel. Cardholders must designate the total outstanding balance incurred while traveling as split-disbursement when filing their vouchers. A late fee per billing cycle may be assessed for individually billed accounts that are 75 days past the closing date of the account statement on which the charges first appeared.

16.10.6. **Travel Card Considerations during a Permanent Change of Station.**

Individuals are required to use the government travel charge card during a permanent change of station. Credit limit increases and deferred payment options are available to accommodate the extended travel times of a permanent change of station move. The individual is still responsible for keeping the bill current while in a permanent change of station status. The cardholder must notify the losing agency program coordinator before departing the old duty station and gaining agency program coordinator upon reporting to the new duty station. The losing agency program coordinator will update the travel card account to "mission critical" status and set a future date in the travel card company's Electronic Access System to deactivate the cardholder's account based on permanent change of station travel order report no later than date. The agency program coordinator will also submit a transfer request to the travel card vendor so the individual is removed from that unit's reporting hierarchy level. The gaining agency program coordinator will ensure the transfer request is processed by the travel card vendor when the member arrives so the account information can be updated. The gaining agency program coordinator will also clear the deactivation date within the travel card vendor's Electronic Access System.

16.10.7. **Delinquencies:**

16.10.7.1. Cardholders are responsible for payment in full of the amount stated on the monthly billing statement. The travel card vendor will submit to Defense Finance and Accounting Service accounts that are 126 days past due for Salary-offset processing. The travel card vendor may also initiate pay garnishment proceedings through the judicial system against cardholder accounts over 126 days delinquent. Upon written request of the travel card vendor, Department of Defense may act on their behalf and collect by payroll deduction from the amount of pay owed to the cardholder any funds the cardholder owes to the travel charge card vendor as a result of delinquencies not disputed by the cardholder on the government travel charge card.

16.10.7.2. If the travel card vendor cannot initiate pay garnishment proceedings and the cardholder account is over 210 days delinquent, the travel card vendor will charge off the account and report the delinquency to the credit bureau. The debt will then be collected through a third party collection agency assigned by the travel card vendor.

16.10.8. **Collection of Debts:**

16.10.8.1. **Debts to the Federal Government.** An Air Force member who owes debts to the federal government or instrumentalities of the government does not have to give his or her consent for the Air Force to collect. Generally, for debts that exceed $100, the individual must be given due process (that is, the individual must receive notification of the pending collection of a debt and be given a chance to repay the debt before any withholding action occurs). However, due process need not be completed before the start of a collection action if an individual's estimated date of separation is not sufficient to complete collection and the Air Force would be unlikely to collect the debt. Due process may not apply when the collection action can be completed within two monthly pay periods. The Air Force may also collect debts involving any federal agency, portions of a reenlistment bonus not served, delinquent hospital bills for family members, excess shipment of household goods, loss or damage to government property, and erroneous payments made to or on behalf of the member by the Air Force.

16.10.8.2. **Waiver and Remission Provisions.** Military members may request relief from valid debts by applying for waiver or remission of the debt. The local financial services office has specific guidance and can provide assistance regarding these programs.

16.10.8.3. **Waiver of Claims for Erroneous Payments of Pay and Allowances.** When a member receives erroneous pay or allowances, he or she may apply for a waiver of claims by the United States. A waiver may be granted when there is no indication of fraud, misrepresentation, fault, or lack of good faith on the part of the member or any other person having an interest in obtaining a waiver of the claim. Defense Finance and Accounting Service will rule on all waivers. When filing for a waiver, the collection of the indebtedness must be started.

16.10.8.4. **Remission.** A Regular Air Force or separated member, or his or her commander, may apply for remission of a member's indebtedness to the United States. The Air Force may not remit or cancel any debt due to non-collection of court-martial forfeiture. In addition to the circumstances creating the debt and the issue of good faith on the part of the member, financial hardship may be a factor for consideration.

## 16.11. The United States Air Force Uniformed Thrift Savings Plan:

### 16.11.1. Purpose.

The Thrift Savings Plan is a retirement savings and investment plan established for federal employees as part of the Federal Employees' Retirement Act of 1986. Participation in the plan for uniformed service members is authorized by law. The plan offers Traditional Thrift Saving Plan, tax-deferred advantages similar to those in an individual retirement account or 401(k) plan. Traditional Thrift Saving Plan contributions can be taken out of pay before taxes are computed; as a result, individual tax obligations are reduced. Roth contributions are taken out of your paycheck after your income is taxed. When you withdraw your funds at a future date, your contributions will be tax-free since you already paid taxes on the contributions.

### 16.11.2. Participating in the Traditional and Roth Thrift Saving Plan.

A member is authorized to contribute from 1 to 92 percent of their basic pay. Members are not permitted to contribute more than 92 percent of their basic pay so that required deductions of Social Security and Medicare can be made. If a member is contributing to the Thrift Saving Plan from basic pay, the member is also authorized to contribute bonuses, incentive, or special pay. As of January 2017, the maximum Thrift Savings Plan contribution amount for 2017 is $18,000 for deferred and Roth contributions and up to $54,000 total combined deferred/exempt Traditional and Roth contributions. The amounts contributed to the traditional and Roth Thrift Savings Plan must be stated as a whole percent. Members have the ability to manage their Thrift Savings Plan via myPay; those requiring customer assistance for Thrift Savings Plan pay-related questions, leave and earning statement interpretations, and financial issues may contact their financial service office.

### 16.11.3. Education and Awareness.

The Personal Financial Readiness is a core service of the Airman and Family Readiness Center and they offer information, education, and personal financial counseling to help individuals and families maintain financial stability and reach their financial goals.

## Section 16D—Leave Management

## 16.12. Policy.

As stated in AFI 36-3003, *Military Leave Program*, lengthy respites from the work environment tend to have a beneficial effect on an individual's psychological and physical status. Therefore, an effective leave program is an essential military requirement. According to Department of Defense Instruction 1327.6, *Leave and Liberty Policy and Procedures*, all officers in command, major headquarters, and the military departments shall ensure that secondary and nonessential efforts, though desirable in themselves, do no prevent an effective leave program.

## 16.13. Accruing Leave.

The Air Force can pay members for unused leave at certain points in their careers, such as reenlistment, retirement, separation under honorable conditions, or death. By law, members may receive accrued leave payment up to a maximum of 60 days during their military careers. However, the department of Defense policy expresses Congressional concern that members use leave to relax from the pressures of duties and not as a method of compensation. **Note:** Members do not earn leave when they are absent without official leave, in an unauthorized leave status, in confinement as a result of a court-martial sentence, in an excess leave status, or on appellate leave under Title 10, United States Code, Section 876a, *Leave Required to Be Taken Pending Review of Certain Court-Martial Convictions.*

## 16.14. Special Leave Accrual.

Special leave accrual earned in combat zones may be kept for 4 fiscal years; special leave accrual earned in support of operations may now be kept for 2 fiscal years. An additional one-time special leave accrual sell-back is authorized for enlisted service members. Under this provision, an enlisted service member may sell back up to 30 days of special leave accrual. Such a sell back counts toward the service member's cap of 60 days over a career. This provision has no termination date. Members lose any leave in excess of 60 days at the end of the fiscal year unless they are eligible for special leave accrual. Eligible members who lose leave on 1 October may have only that portion of leave restored that could not possibly have been used before the end of the fiscal year not to exceed 120 days. The wing or vice commander has final approval authority and may be delegated no lower than the first O-6 in the chain of command. Major command or field operating agency directors of personnel or equivalents (Colonel or above) will approve special leave accrual for their organizations. Any commander in the chain of command may deny a member's request for special leave accrual without referring the member to a higher-level authority when the request does not meet the criteria for special leave accrual consideration. Members are eligible for special leave accrual if any of the following circumstances exist:

16.14.1. A member who serves on Regular Air Force while entitled to hostile fire/imminent danger pay for a continuous period of at least 120 days are authorized to retain such leave (not to exceed 120 days) until the end of the third fiscal year following the fiscal year in which the duty assignment in terminated.

16.14.2. Members assigned to a non-hostile fire and/or non-imminent danger pay area for a continuous period of at least 120 days are authorized to retain such leave up to 120 days but not to exceed the total number of continuous days assigned to the unit or qualifying duty until the end of the second fiscal year in which the duty assignment is terminated.

## 16.15. Beginning and Ending Leave.

Leave must begin and end in the local area. The term "local area" means the place of residence from which the member commutes to the duty station on a daily basis. This also applies to leave en route to a permanent change of station or temporary duty assignment. In this case, the local area, as defined at the old and new permanent duty station, applies. The old permanent duty station is for beginning leave; the new permanent duty station is for ending leave. Making a false statement of leave taken may result in punitive action under the Uniform Code of Military Justice. Regardless of the amount of leave authorized, Finance calculates leave based on the actual date of departure and date of return. General rules on charging leave are as follows:

16.15.1. Use Air Force Form 988, *Leave Request/Authorization*, for all types of leave and permissive temporary duty when LeaveWeb cannot be used. (See AFMAN 65-116, Volume 2, *Defense Joint Military Pay System (DJMS) Unit Procedures Excluding FSO*, Chapter 7, for information concerning LeaveWeb.) (**Exception:** When members take leave en route with permanent change of station or temporary duty travel, the financial service office uses the travel voucher to determine authorized travel and chargeable leave.) Nonduty days and holidays are chargeable leave days if they occur during an authorized period of leave. If leave includes a weekend, a member cannot end leave on a Friday and begin the leave again on Monday. Further, unit commanders will not approve successive Monday through Friday leaves (or periods of leave surrounding other nonduty days) except under emergency or unusual circumstances as determined by the unit commander.

16.15.2. A member who is unable to report to duty upon expiration of leave because of illness or injury must advise the leave approving authority. The next of kin, attending physician, representative at the nearest medical treatment facility, or American Red Cross representative may act on the member's behalf when the member is incapacitated and unable to provide notification. Upon returning from leave, the member must present a statement from the nearest medical treatment facility or attending physician regarding the member's medical condition. (**Note:** The unit commander evaluates the statement before authenticating the leave document.) If a member on leave requires hospitalization or quarters status, leave is not charged while hospitalized or on quarters. Chargeable leave ends the day before and starts again the day following hospitalization or quarter's status, regardless of the hour of admission or discharge or release from quarters. The unit commander issues an amended leave authorization, if required.

16.15.3. The military personnel section and Air Force Personnel Center/DPFCM (Missing Persons Branch) change the member's leave status to absent without official leave when the member fails to return to duty at the end of his or her leave period.

**16.16. Extension of Leave.**

The member must ask, orally or in writing, for an extension of leave. The extension must be requested sufficiently in advance of expiration of leave authorized to permit the member to return to duty at the proper time if the approval authority disapproves the extension.

**16.17. Recall from Leave.**

Unit commanders may recall members from leave for military necessity or in the best interest of the Air Force. Refer to the joint travel regulation to determine if travel and transportation allowances apply. If the unit commander authorizes the member to resume leave after the member completes the duty that resulted in recall, a new Air Force Form 988 or orders must be prepared.

**16.18. Types of Leave.**

AFI 36-3003 outlines many types of leave, such as:

16.18.1. **Annual Leave.**

Another name for "ordinary" leave is annual leave. Normally, members request leave, as accruing (earning), within mission requirements. Members use annual leave to take vacations, attend to parental family needs such as illnesses, celebrate traditional national holiday periods, attend spiritual events or other religious observances, or as terminal leave with retirement or separation from Regular Air Force.

16.18.2. **Advance Leave.**

Advance leave is leave granted based on a reasonable expectation that a member will accrue at least that much leave during the remaining period of active military service. The purpose of advance leave is to enable members to resolve emergencies or urgent personal situations when they have limited or no accrued leave. When a member has taken all the advance leave that represents what he or she will be accruing during the remaining period of active service, unit commanders change member's leave status from advance to excess leave. The financial service office stops or collects, if applicable, all pay and allowances paid after the member's leave status changes from advance to excess leave.

16.18.3. **Convalescent Leave.**

Convalescent leave is an authorized absence normally for the minimal time needed to meet the medical needs for recuperation. Convalescent leave is not chargeable leave. Unit commanders normally approve convalescent leave based on recommendations by either the medical treatment facility authority or physician most familiar with the member's medical condition. When a member elects civilian medical care at personal expense and an Air Force physician determines the medical procedure as elective by military medical treatment facility authorities, such as cosmetic surgery, the member must use ordinary leave for all absences from duty, including convalescence. When medical authorities determine a medical procedure is necessary, such as childbirth, and the member elects civilian medical care, the commander, upon the recommendation by either the medical treatment facility authority or the attending physician most familiar with the member's medical condition may grant convalescent leave.

16.18.4. **Emergency Leave.**

Emergency leave is chargeable leave granted for personal or family emergencies involving the immediate family. Unit commanders approve emergency leave; however, commanders can delegate leave approval to no lower than the first sergeant for enlisted personnel. Normally, verification by the America Red Cross is not necessary. However, when the official granting leave has reason to doubt the validity of an emergency situation, he or she may request assistance from the military service activity nearest the location of the emergency or, when necessary, from the American Red Cross. The initial period of emergency leave is usually for no more than 30 days with possible extensions of an additional 30 days. If the individual needs an extension while on emergency leave, he or she must contact the unit commander or first sergeant for approval. Unit commanders should advise members to apply for a humanitarian or exceptional family member reassignment or hardship discharge if the leave period is more than 60 days. Air Force Personnel Center approves emergency leave if leave requested results in a member having a cumulative negative leave balance of over 30 days. The member may not request emergency leave for reasons such as attending court hearings or the resolution of marital or financial problems; the member may, however, request ordinary leave for these situations. Situations when emergency leave is normally authorized include but are not limited to:

16.18.4.1. To visit a terminally ill person in the immediate family of either the member or the member's spouse.

16.18.4.2. When there has been a verified death in the member's immediate family or the spouse's immediate family.

16.18.4.3. Because the member or someone in the member's or spouse's immediate family has a life-threatening condition due to an accident, illness, or major surgery or is admitted to an Intensive Care Unit due to a major illness or accident.

16.18.4.4. Because the member is affected by a natural disaster, such as a hurricane, tornado, flood, or earthquake, and a severe or unusual hardship would result if the member failed to return home.

16.18.5. **En Route Leave.**

En route leave is ordinary leave members use in connection with permanent change of station, including their first change of station upon completion of technical training. Members may request advance leave when they do not have enough accrued leave to use as en route leave. Normally, the losing unit commander approves up to 30 days en route leave with any change of station move if the leave does not interfere with the reporting date to either a port or new assignment. Members who complete basic or technical training may request at least 10 days of leave en route if their first duty station is in the continental United States. They may request at least 14 days if going to an overseas assignment.

16.18.6. **Terminal Leave.**

Terminal leave is chargeable leave taken in conjunction with retirement or separation from Regular Air Force. The member's last day of leave coincides with the last day of Regular Air Force. Normally, a member does not return to duty after terminal leave begins. The amount of leave taken cannot exceed the leave balance at the date of separation. See AFI 36-3003 for guidance.

16.18.7. **Excess Leave.**

Excess leave is leave members normally use for personal or family emergency situations when members cannot request advance leave. Excess leave is a no-pay status; therefore, entitlement to pay and allowances and leave accrual stops on the member's first day of excess leave. A member will not receive disability pay, if injured, for time spent on excess leave. The period of excess leave will not count toward the fulfillment of any Regular Air Force service commitment.

16.18.8. **Environmental and Morale Leave.**

Environmental and morale leave is leave authorized at overseas installations where adverse environmental conditions require special arrangements for leave in desirable places at periodic intervals. The environmental and morale leave taken is ordinary leave. Funded environmental and morale leave is charged as ordinary leave, but members are authorized to use Department of Defense-owned or -controlled aircraft; plus, travel time to and from the environmental and morale leave destination is not charged as leave. Unfunded environmental and morale leave is also charged as ordinary leave, but members are authorized space-available air transportation from the duty locations, and travel time to and from the leave destination is charged as leave.

16.19. **Regular and Special Passes.**

A pass period is an authorized absence from duty for a relatively short time and starts from the end of normal work hours on a duty day and ends at the beginning of normal work hours the next duty day. There are no mileage restrictions. However, approval authorities may require members to be able to return to duty within a reasonable time in the event of an operational mission requirement such as a recall, unit alert, or unit emergency.

16.19.1. **Regular Pass.**

A regular pass starts after normal work hours on a given day and stops at the beginning of normal work hours the next duty day. This includes nonduty days Saturday, Sunday, and a holiday for up to 3 days total if a member normally works Monday through Friday or up to 4 days for a member who works a nontraditional work schedule, such as a compressed workweek. The combination of nonduty days and a public holiday may not exceed 4 days. Department of Defense or higher management levels may determine that a Monday or Friday is compensatory (comp) time off when a holiday is observed on a Tuesday or Thursday, in which case a regular pass may consist of a weekend, a comp day off, and a public holiday.

16.19.2. **Special Pass.**

Unit commanders may award 3- or 4-day special passes for special occasions or circumstances, such as reenlistment or for some type of special recognition or compensatory time off. They may delegate approval to a level no lower than squadron section commander, deputies, or equivalents. Special passes start after normal work hours on a given day. They stop at the beginning of normal work hours on either the 4th day for a 3-day special pass or the 5th day for a 4-day special pass. A 3-day special pass can be Friday through Sunday, Saturday through Monday, or Tuesday through Thursday. A 4-day special pass can be Thursday through Sunday or Saturday through Tuesday or Friday through Monday. This applies to a normal Monday through Friday workweek. Passes may be taken in conjunction with leave without a duty day between the pass and leave period. The member must be physically present in the local area when departing and returning from leave. The pass can be taken before or after leave, but not both.

**16.20. Permissive Temporary Duty.**

Permissive temporary duty is an administrative absence for which funded temporary duty is not appropriate. Commanders may not authorize permissive temporary duty in place of leave or a special pass or in conjunction with special passes. Normally, Air Force Form 988 is used for all types of permissive temporary duties. See AFI 36-3003 for complete information.

16.20.1. **Authorized PTDYs.**

Types of authorized permissive temporary duties include, but are not limited to:

16.20.1.1. Traveling to or in the vicinity of a new permanent duty station to secure off-base housing before the member out-processes the old permanent duty station. (Generally, members request permissive temporary duty after signing in at the new permanent duty station.)

16.20.1.2. Accompanying a dependent patient or military member patient to a designated medical treatment facility not in the local area when the medical authority deems permissive temporary duty essential.

16.20.1.3. To attend a Department of Defense sponsored employment assistance seminar under the Transition Assistance Program when the member cannot schedule one locally and when the member will separate or retire within 180 days.

16.20.1.4. Attending national conventions or meetings hosted by service-connected organizations such as the Military Officer Association, Air Force Sergeants Association, or the Noncommissioned Officers Association.

16.20.2. **Permissive Temporary Duty Not Authorized.**

Members are not authorized permissive temporary duties:

16.20.2.1. To search for a house in a close proximity permanent change of station move.

16.20.2.2. In conjunction with a permissive reassignment.

16.20.2.3. To attend a professional military education graduation when the graduate is a coworker, friend, or military spouse.

16.20.2.4. To attend a change of command or retirement ceremony. **Note:** The presiding official for a military retirement ceremony may be authorized permissive temporary duty.

**16.21. Post-Deployment/Mobilization Respite Absence:**

16.21.1. Post-Deployment/Mobilization Respite Absence is in support of the Secretary of Defense utilization of the total force policy. The program applies to creditable deployments and mobilizations underway on, or commencing after, 19 January 2007.

16.21.2. The Secretary of Defense has directed establishment of programs to recognize members who are required to mobilize or deploy with a frequency beyond established rotation goals and Post-Deployment/Mobilization Respite Absence as a new category of administrative absence.

16.21.3. The concept of operations is to establish a yearly rotation goal of a deployment-to-dwell ratio of 1:2. That is, for every 1 year a service member of the active component is deployed, he or she must have 2 years at his or her home station. The yearly mobilization-to-dwell ratio goal for the Reserve Component is 1:5 years. Post-Deployment/Mobilization Respite Absence earned under these conditions is considered administrative absence.

16.21.4. For the purpose of accruing Post-Deployment/Mobilization Respite Absence under this program, the Department of the Air Force defines criteria as creditable deployments/temporary to the land areas of Afghanistan or Iraq on or after 19 January 2007, but before 1 October 2011. Aircrew participating in missions into, out of, within or over the area of eligibility in support of military operations, count each day of operation as 1 day of eligibility. Deployment is defined as a member temporary duty under contingency, exercise, and deployment orders to these locations.

16.21.5. Creditable time continues to accrue during periods of rest and relaxation, leave, and for temporary duties outside of Afghanistan or Iraq of 30 consecutive days or less.

16.21.6. For qualifying deployments and mobilizations beginning on or after 1 October 2011, Active Component Airmen who, on the first day of their current deployment, had deployed in excess of 12 months out of the previous 36 months, and who meet the other eligibility criteria contained in AFI 36-3003, qualify for Post-Deployment/Mobilization Respite Absence.

## 16.22. Program Administration:

16.22.1. Commanders can only delegate ordinary leave approval to the lowest supervisory level to meet the needs of the unit. Supervisors should train personnel on the requirements of the leave program and ensure they know how to use, LeaveWeb and the Air Force Form 988 to request leave and permissive temporary duty.

16.22.2. Before approving leave, supervisors should ensure members requesting leave have a sufficient leave balance. Also, they must ensure members provide a valid address and emergency telephone number where they can be reached. Before signing the Air Force Form 988, follow the unit's procedures to obtain a leave authorization number. Leave numbers normally will not be given earlier than 14 days prior to the leave effective date. Members on leave should use risk management principles to assess all hazards and control risks before excessive or hazardous travel, especially when traveling by automobiles. Also, supervisors should make sure the member has sufficient funds to return to duty on time. If the documentation is not processed digitally, the unit leave monitor sends Part I with authorization number to the servicing finance office and gives Part II to the member after obtaining a leave authorization number. The supervisor retains Part III for completion after the member returns from leave.

16.22.3. When the member returns from leave, the supervisor determines how the member's actual leave dates compared to the first and last days of chargeable leave reported on Air Force Form 988, Part I. The member signs Part III, and the supervisor certifies the dates of leave and sends Part III to the commander support staff for processing. If there is a change in the actual number of days the member took, supervisors will follow the instructions listed in Part III. **Note:** The Air Force adopted the current method of recording leave to prevent fraud in the leave reporting system.

16.22.4. LeaveWeb is an Air Force system that automates the method of requesting and processing leave (in lieu of using the hard copy Air Force Form 988). Under LeaveWeb, the member requests ordinary leave which generates an e-mail to his or her supervisor. The supervisor approves or disapproves the leave and, if approved, sends the leave information to the unit leave monitor to validate. Once validated, the leave is sent electronically to finance. The member prints a copy of the approved leave form to hand-carry during leave. Upon returning from leave, the member completes the necessary updates in LeaveWeb and forwards the e-mail to his or her supervisor for endorsement. This electronic process reduces waste in materials as well as man-hours.

## Section 16E—Equal Opportunity

## 16.23. Equal Opportunity Policy:

16.23.1. The Air Force is a richly diverse community consisting of Airmen, military and civilian, with widely varied backgrounds, beliefs, multicultural influences, and many unique life experiences. Airmen are most effective when they are working in an environment that promotes teamwork, inclusion, and mutual respect. Therefore, we must train and prepare our Airmen to view human relation issues and circumstances more broadly. This will allow them to effectively understand, engage, and defeat any potential adversary or personal situation with intelligence and integrity.

16.23.2. The Equal Opportunity Program proactively engages all Airmen in the pursuit of equal opportunity. The Air Force Equal Opportunity Program has been developed to foster and support equal opportunity, the Air Force Core Values and Airman's Creed, and must be carried out in the day-to-day actions of all personnel. The Air Force will not tolerate unlawful discrimination and unlawful harassment or reprisal against individuals who engage in protected activity. Airmen must actively make workplace professionalism a top priority and take proactive steps to prevent, correct and eliminate unlawful discriminatory behavior. Air Force Equal Opportunity policy compliance is a function of leadership.

## 16.24. Equal Opportunity Program Objectives:

16.24.1. The primary objective of the program is to eradicate unlawful discrimination. The Equal Opportunity office will assist commanders at all levels in conducting a continuing campaign to eradicate every form of unlawful discrimination or harassment from the workplace. In order to promote a workplace free of unlawful discrimination, to include sexual harassment, the Equal Opportunity office will take proactive steps to ensure all available efforts are in place (for example, human relations education, commander's calls, climate assessments).

16.24.2. The program also seeks to foster a positive human relations environment. The Equal Opportunity office will use the Human Relations Climate Assessment Subcommittee Installation Equal Opportunity Assessment Summary and Defense Equal Opportunity Management Institute Organization Climate Survey tool to evaluate positive and negative factors in the local environment. Human relations education is also provided through proactive measures to ensure all employees and management personnel understand the need for a positive human relations environment.

### 16.25. Unlawful Discrimination:

16.25.1. Unlawful discrimination against military members includes any unlawful action that denies Equal Opportunity to persons or groups based on their race, color, religion, national origin, sexual orientation or sex (including sexual harassment). This type of discrimination can occur in a variety of forms to include: in writing, verbal, or in a combination. Unlawful discrimination can occur on or off base.

16.25.2. Unlawful discrimination against Department of Defense civilian employees includes any unlawful employment practice that occurs when an employer fails or refuses to hire or promote, discharges, or otherwise discriminates against any individual with respect to compensation, terms, conditions, or privileges of employment; or limits, segregates, or classifies employees or applicants for employment in any way that deprives or tends to deprive any individual of employment opportunities or otherwise adversely affects his/her status as an employee because of race, color, religion, national origin, sex, (including sexual harassment, pregnancy, gender identity, and sexual orientation age (40 or older), genetic information, physical or mental disability, or reprisal.

16.25.3. Unlawful discrimination can also include the use of disparaging terms regarding an individual's birthplace, ancestry, culture, or the linguistic characteristics common to a specific ethnic group. The use of terms that degrade or connote negative statements pertaining to race, color, religion, national origin, sex, age, genetic information, and mental or physical disability can constitute unlawful discrimination. These terms include insults, printed material, visual material, signs, symbols, posters, or insignia.

16.25.4. The operational language of the Air Force is English. Air Force personnel must maintain sufficient proficiency in English to perform their official/military duties. All official communications must be understood by everyone who has a need to know their content. Commanders may require Air Force personnel to use English only when such use is clearly necessary and proper for the performance of military duties. Accordingly, commanders, supervisors, and managers at all levels must not require the use of English for personal communications unrelated to official duties.

### 16.26. Sexual Harassment:

16.26.1. Sexual harassment is a form of sex discrimination that involves unwelcome sexual advances, requests for sexual favors, and other verbal or physical conduct of a sexual nature when:

16.26.1.1. Submission to such conduct is made either explicitly or implicitly a term or condition of a person's job, pay, or career.

16.26.1.2. Submission to or rejection of such conduct by a person is used as a basis for career or employment decisions affecting this person.

16.26.1.3. Such conduct has the purpose or effect of unreasonably interfering with an individual's work performance or creates an intimidating, hostile, or offensive working environment.

16.26.2. This definition emphasizes that workplace conduct, to be actionable as an "abusive work environment," harassment need not result in concrete psychological harm to the victim, but rather need only be so severe or pervasive that a reasonable person would perceive, and the victim does perceive, the work environment as hostile or offensive. Workplace is an expansive term for military members and may include conduct on or off duty, 24 hours a day.

16.26.3. Any person in a supervisory or command position who uses or condones any form of sexual behavior to control, influence, or affect the career, pay, or job of a military member or civilian employee is engaging in sexual harassment. Similarly, any military member or civilian employee who makes deliberate or repeated unwelcome verbal comments, gestures, or physical contact of a sexual nature in the workplace is also engaging in sexual harassment.

### 16.27. Military Equal Opportunity Complaint Process:

16.27.1. **Authorization.**

Only military personnel, their family members, and retirees may file military Equal Opportunity complaints. To file a complaint, the individual must be the subject of the alleged unlawful discrimination or sexual harassment. Third parties, to include commanders, supervisors or co-workers, may not file a complaint on behalf of another individual. The Equal Opportunity office will refer all third party individuals who are aware of specific allegations of military Equal Opportunity policy violations to their respective chain of command. The Equal Opportunity office will not accept military complaints from military members, family members or retirees if their concern is related to their off-base or Department of Defense civilian employment.

16.27.2. **Military Informal Complaint Procedures**.

The purpose of the military informal complaint process is to attempt resolution at the lowest possible level.

16.27.2.1. To informally resolve unlawful discrimination and sexual harassment complaints, individuals may orally address or prepare written correspondence to the alleged offender, request intervention by a coworker, opt to use the alternate dispute resolution process, or use the chain of command (for example, request assistance from the supervisor, first sergeant, or commander).

16.27.2.2. There is no time limit for filing informal complaints and no requirement for commander approval before accepting informal complaints.

16.27.2.3. Informal sexual harassment complaints must be processed in accordance with Title 10, United States Code, Section 1561, *Complaints of Sexual Harassment: Investigation by Commanding Officers* and complaint allegations must be forwarded to the applicable General Court-Martial Convening Authority. The commander must initiate a Commander Directed Investigation. The Equal Opportunity office will serve as Subject Matter Experts for commanders and organizations conducting sexual harassment investigations. The Commander Directed Investigation process for sexual harassment complaints must be complete within 14 calendar days.

16.27.3. **Military Formal Complaint Procedures:**

16.27.3.1. The purpose of the military formal complaint process is to enable military members, retirees and their family members to formally present allegations of unlawful discrimination and sexual harassment to the Equal Opportunity office with the goal of attempting resolution through a complaint clarification process.

16.27.3.1.1. Complaint clarification is the process of gathering information regarding a formal military complaint or hotline complaint to determine whether a "preponderance of evidence" exists to demonstrate that unlawful discrimination or sexual harassment occurred. The complaint clarification includes interviewing or taking statements from complainants, potential witnesses, alleged offenders and anyone else who may have information relevant to the case. The Equal Opportunity office may use information gathered from other investigations in conjunction with (but not in lieu of) their own clarification process to establish a preponderance of credible evidence.

16.27.3.1.2. The clarification results are forwarded to the Staff Judge Advocate for a legal sufficiency review. Once the review is complete, the alleged offender's commander receives the complaint for final action, if appropriate.

16.27.3.1.3. The entire complaint clarification process for unlawful discrimination complaints must be completed within 20 duty days. This includes 9 duty days for the Equal Opportunity office to conduct a clarification, 6 duty days for legal review, and 5 duty days for commander action, if required.

16.27.3.1.4. Formal sexual harassment complaints must be processed in accordance with Title 10, United States Code, Section 1561, *Complaints of Sexual Harassment: Investigation by Commanding Officers*. The complaint clarification process for sexual harassment complaints must be complete within 14 duty days. This includes 6 duty days for the Equal Opportunity office to conduct a clarification, 4 duty days for legal review, and 4 duty days for commander action, if required.

16.27.3.2. Military formal complaints must be filed within 60 calendar days of the alleged offense. The installation commander may waive the time limits for good cause based on a memorandum with sufficient justification provided by the complainant and submitted through the Equal Opportunity office.

**16.28. Civilian Complaint Process.**

Only Air Force employees, former employees, and applicants for employment may file civilian Equal Opportunity complaints. An aggrieved person can file a complaint if discriminated against on the basis of race, color, religion, sex, (including pregnancy, gender identity, and sexual orientation) national origin, age (40 and older), or disability, or if subjected to sexual harassment or retaliated against for opposing discrimination or for participating in the complaint process. Additionally, an employee can file a complaint under Title II of the Genetic Information Nondiscrimination Act of 2008, which prohibits genetic information discrimination for any aspect of employment, including hiring, firing, pay, job assignments, promotion, layoff, training, fringe benefits, or any other term or condition of employment. To harass or retaliate against a person because of his or her genetic information is illegal under the Genetic Information Nondiscrimination Act.

16.28.1. **Civilian Informal Complaint Procedures:**

16.28.1.1. The purpose of the civilian informal complaint process is to provide for the prompt, fair and impartial processing and resolution of complaints, consistent with legal obligations under Title 29, Code of Federal Regulations, Part 1614, *Federal Sector Equal Employment Opportunity*. The objective is to seek opportunities to resolve issues at the lowest organizational level at the earliest possible time.

16.28.1.2. The Equal Opportunity office will work with management and the staff judge advocate in an attempt to resolve the complainant's concerns. The Equal Opportunity office must complete the informal complaint process within 30 calendar days of the complaint being filed unless the complainant grants an extension not to exceed 60 additional calendar days.

16.28.1.3. If the matter is not resolved to the complainant's satisfaction before the end of the authorized period, including extensions, the complainant is issued a notice of right to file a formal complaint.

16.28.2. **Civilian Formal Complaint Procedures:**

16.28.2.1. A formal complaint must be filed at the installation where the alleged discrimination occurred. In order for the complaint to be processed at the formal stage, the initial contact must be within 45 calendar days of the date of the matter alleged to be discriminatory or, in the case of a personnel action, within 45 calendar days of the effective date or when he or she becomes aware of the personnel action. The complaint must describe the actions or practices that form the basis of the complaint that was discussed with the Equal Opportunity office during the informal complaint process.

16.28.2.2. The complaint must be filed with the Equal Opportunity director or designee within 15 calendar days of the complainant receiving the notice of right to file a formal complaint.

16.28.2.3. The Air Force is required to process civilian formal Equal Opportunity complaints in accordance with Title 29, Code of Federal Regulations, Part 1614 and Equal Employment Opportunity Management Directive 110. The Equal Employment Opportunity Commission requires federal agencies to discharge certain responsibilities once a civilian formal Equal Opportunity complaint has been filed.

16.28.2.4. The Equal Opportunity office must process all formal complaints expeditiously and make a determination whether to accept, dismiss, or partially dismiss a complaint or portion of a complaint to allow an investigation to be completed within 180 calendar days from the date of filing.

16.29. **Equal Opportunity and Treatment Incident:**

16.29.1. An Equal Opportunity and Treatment Incident is an overt, adverse act, occurring on or off base, directed toward an individual, group, or institution which is motivated by or has overtones based on race, color, national origin, religion, sexual orientation or sex which has the potential to have a negative impact on the installation human relations climate. An Equal Opportunity and Treatment Incident may include subjects other than military members such as retirees and family members.

16.29.2. The Air Force classifies these incidents as minor, serious, or major based on: the number of participants, property damage, physical injury, assault, arson, and/or an act resulting in death. Vandalism (degrading graffiti), hate group activity, discriminatory epithets, signs, symbols, or the use of slurs based on race, color, national origin, religion, sexual orientation or sex may be classified as an Equal Opportunity and Treatment Incident.

*Section 16F—Legal Services*

16.30. **Legal Office.**

Legal offices provide legal assistance in connection with personal civil legal matters to support and sustain command effectiveness and readiness. Under Title 10, United States Code, Section 1044, the ability to offer legal assistance and legal services to the eligible categories of personnel is contingent upon the availability of legal staff resources and regulations as may be prescribed by the Secretary of the Air Force.

16.31. **Personal Legal Readiness.**

Legal readiness is the state of legal preparation in which Air Force members are ready to deploy, both in their personal and mission capacities. Legal readiness involves the member's awareness of the personal legal issues that may arise in preparation for or during a deployment and the remedies available to avoid or lessen any adverse effects of those issues. This is usually provided through legal assistance available to Regular Air Force members, reservists, and guardsmen on federal Regular Air Force, their dependents, and civilian employees stationed overseas and their families. Personnel tasked for deployment at their bases are briefed on preparing their personal and family legal affairs for deployment. Subject areas include, but are not necessarily limited to, wills; service members Group Life Insurance designations; general and special powers of attorney; medical planning, including advance medical directives (living wills and medical or health care powers of attorney), and designation of anatomical gifts; guardians or in loco parentis powers of attorney to ensure care of minor children; landlord-tenant matters; income exclusions and/or tax return filing extensions applicable to potential deployment locations; property and financial affairs management; protections under the Servicemembers Civil Relief Act; protections under the Uniformed Services Employment and Reemployment Rights Act for reserve personnel deploying; and ensuring important documents are maintained in safe, secure, and reasonably accessible locations.

**16.32. Complaints of Wrongs under Article 138, Uniform Code of Military Justice.**

The Uniform Code of Military Justice, Article 138, is another provision for protecting individuals' rights. Members of the Armed Forces who believe they have been wronged by their commanding officers may request redress under the provisions of Article 138. AFI 51-904, *Complaints of Wrongs under Article 38, Uniform Code of Military Justice* implements Article 138. Any member of the armed forces who believes himself wronged by his commanding officer, and who, upon due application to that commanding officer, is refused redress, may complain to any superior commissioned officer, who shall forward the complaint to the officer exercising general court-martial jurisdiction over the officer against whom the complaint is made. The officer exercising general court-martial jurisdiction shall examine into the complaint and take proper measures for redressing the wrong complained of; and he shall as soon as possible, send to the Secretary concerned a true statement of that complaint, with the proceedings had thereon.

16.32.1. A member may use Article 138 when a discretionary act or omission by his or her commander adversely affects the member personally. Examples include acts that violate law or regulation; those that exceed the legitimate authority of the commander; ones that are arbitrary, capricious, or an abuse of discretion; or those that clearly apply administrative standards unfairly. However, the Article 138 complaint system will not provide redress for:

16.32.1.1. Submissions related to acts or omissions that were not initiated, carried out, or approved by the member's commander;

16.32.1.2. Submissions seeking reversal or modification of non-discretionary command actions. For example, mandatory filings of adverse information in an unfavorable information file are not reviewed under Article 138, Uniform Code of Military Justice.

16.32.1.3. Submissions challenging the actions of the commander complained against which addressed an Article 138 application for redress, or actions by the General Court-Martial Convening Authority on an Article 138 complaint;

16.32.1.3.1. However, a submission alleging that the commander or General Court-Martial Convening Authority failed to act on or forward a formal complaint, will be considered under Article 138, Uniform Code of Military, as a new application for redress against the commander or General Court-Martial Convening Authority, as appropriate.

16.32.1.4. Submissions filed on behalf of another person; and.

16.32.1.5. Submissions requesting disciplinary action against another person.

16.32.2. A member who believes himself or herself wronged by the action of his or her commander, before submitting a complaint under Article 138, must apply in writing through channels to that commander for redress of the grievance. A complaint (in writing) to that commander, or his or her designated representative, is sufficient. Absent unusual circumstances, the member must apply for redress within 90 days of the member's discovery of the wrong complained of and the complaint should contain all available supporting evidence.

16.32.2.1. If the commander who allegedly wronged the member is no longer in command of the member, the member must still submit the initial application for redress to the commander who allegedly wronged the member, regardless of that commander's current position or duty location, or the member's current position or duty location.

16.32.3. The commander complained of may consider other reliable evidence, in addition to matters submitted by the member. Such additional evidence will be attached to the file so the member and the commander's general court-martial authority can review the complaint.

16.32.4. Not later than 30 days after receipt of the initial application for redress, the commander must notify the member in writing that:

16.32.4.1. A decision regarding the requested relief has been deferred to allow for the completion of further fact gathering. Such notice of a deferral shall be sent every 30 days until such fact gathering proceeding is completed. Such notice prohibits the member from requesting General Court-Martial Convening Authority review, as provided in AFI 51-904, paragraph 6.3, until 90 days have elapsed from the initial application for redress; or

16.32.4.2. The redress requested is granted, or

16.32.4.3. The requested relief is wholly or partially denied because:

16.32.4.3.1. The requested relief is not warranted;

16.32.4.3.2. The submission is outside the scope of Article 138, Uniform Code of Military Justice;

16.32.4.3.3. The submission is untimely; or

16.32.4.3.4. There is a more appropriate channel for reviewing the complaint.

16.32.5. If the commander denies the requested relief because there is a more appropriate channel for reviewing the complaint or the commander lacks authority to grant the requested relief, the commander must:

16.32.5.1. Forward the submission (including any supporting evidence) to the appropriate processing office or officer, if any, with authority to grant the requested relief.

16.32.5.2. Return the submission (including any supporting evidence) to the member and direct the member to the appropriate office or officer, if any, with authority to grant the requested relief.

16.32.5.3. If appropriate, inform the member of his or her right to file an application with the Air Force Board for Correction of Military Records, in accordance with AFI 36-2603, *Air Force Board for Correction of Military Records*, and AFPAM 36-2607, *Applicants' Guide to the Air Force Board for Correction of Military Records (AFBCMR)*.

16.32.6. In all cases, keep a copy of the request, the supporting evidence, and the action taken.

16.32.7. If the member's commander wholly or partially denies an initial application for redress under Article 138, Uniform Code of Military Justice, the member must request General Court-Martial Convening Authority review within 30 days after receiving the commander's written response denying, in whole or in part, the initial application for redress.

16.32.8. If after 30 days from the submission of the initial application for redress, the member has received no response from the commander who allegedly wronged the member, the member must request General Court-Martial Convening Authority review within 60 days from the date the initial application for redress was submitted.

16.32.9. If the member's commander has notified the member that a decision regarding the requested relief has been deferred, the member may only request General Court-Martial Convening Authority review after 90 days from the initial application for redress.

16.32.10. The member may submit the formal Article 138 complaint directly to the General Court-Martial Convening Authority exercising jurisdiction over the commander against whom the initial application for redress was made, or through any superior commissioned officer.

16.32.11. Untimely formal complaints under Article 138, Uniform Code of Military Justice, will be denied without a determination on the merits of the submission and returned to the member, unless the General Court-Martial Convening Authority waives the time requirement for good cause.

16.32.12. Not later than 60 days after receipt of the formal complaint, the General Court-Martial Convening Authority must notify the member that:

16.32.12.1. A decision regarding the requested relief has been deferred to allow for the completion of a proceeding or inquiry, or completion of a review by another authority. Such notice shall be sent every 60 days until such proceeding, inquiry, or review is completed. Once the proceeding, inquiry, or review is completed, the General Court-Martial Convening Authority must notify the member of his or her decision within 60 days.

16.32.12.2. The requested relief is granted; or

16.32.12.3. The requested relief is denied, in whole or in part, because:

16.32.12.3.1. The requested relief is not warranted;

16.32.12.3.2. The submission is outside the scope of Article 138, Uniform Code of Military Justice;

16.32.12.3.3. The submission is untimely; or

16.32.12.3.4. There is a more appropriate channel for reviewing the complaint.

*Section 16G—Ground Safety*

**16.33. Mishap Prevention Program:**

16.33.1. **Purpose.**

The purpose of the Air Force Mishap Prevention Program is to minimize the loss of Air Force resources and protect Air Force people from death, injuries, or occupational illnesses by managing risks on- and off- duty. This program applies to all operations except where otherwise prescribed or specified in Status-of-Forces Agreements. Continuing to meet this goal is critical to our mission effectiveness. The challenge of deployments, technologically advanced combat systems, and changing duty requirements demands strong on-duty mishap prevention programs. Off-duty mishap prevention must also adapt to meet the challenges posed by motor vehicles, sports and recreation, and other off-duty activities. All Air Force personnel have responsibilities in the mishap prevention program as aligned within the Air Force Safety Management System and will utilize sound risk management principles, processes, tools, and techniques to assess and mitigate risk associated with both on- and off-duty activities. The Air Force Safety Management System is a mishap prevention framework mandated by AFI 91-202, *The US Air Force Mishap Prevention Program.* The Air Force Safety Management System conceptualizes the mishap prevention effort in four pillars. These pillars are: Policy and Leadership, Risk Management, Assurance, and Promotion and Education.

**Figure 16.1 Air Force Safety Management System**

16.33.1.1. The purpose of the Air Force Safety Management System is to utilize the four pillars, as depicted in Figure 16.1, as a framework for structuring the Air Force mishap prevention programs and activities used to minimize risk and reduce the occurrence and cost of injuries, illnesses, fatalities and property damage. Leadership implements the Air Force Safety Management System by providing guidance and goals, establishing safety responsibility and accountability, applying risk management to all activities, and promoting the Air Force Safety Management System throughout the organization. This implementation of the Air Force Safety Management System prevents mishaps and preserves combat capability. Managing mishap prevention activities requires goal setting, planning, executing, and measuring performance in a Plan Do Check Act continuous improvement process.

16.33.1.2. Plan Do Check Act is an iterative four-step management method used for the control and continuous improvement of processes and products. Leaders from the squadron to the headquarters will use the Plan Do Check Act methodology to ensure that continuous improvement is being accomplished.

16.34.1.3. The desired end result of the Air Force Safety Management System framework is mishap prevention. Mishaps cost money, cost lives, and degrade mission and morale. All mishaps are preventable whether they occur off duty or on duty. Commanders, supervisors, and individuals must ensure a robust safety culture permeates through all activities.

16.33.2. **Mishap Defined.**

An Air Force mishap is an unplanned occurrence, or series of occurrences, that results in occupational illnesses or death or injury to Air Force personnel, or damage to Department of Defense property.

16.33.2.1. **Class A Mishap.** Direct mishap cost totaling $2,000,000, destruction of a Department of Defense aircraft, or a fatality or permanent total disability.

16.33.2.2. **Class B Mishap.** Direct mishap costs totaling $500,000 or more but less than $2,000,000, a permanent partial disability, or inpatient hospitalization of three or more personnel

16.33.2.3. **Class C Mishap.** Direct mishap cost totaling $50,000 or more but less than $500,000, or a nonfatal injury or illness that results in one or more days away from work.

16.33.2.4. **Class D Mishap.** Direct mishap cost totaling $20,000 or more but less than $50,000, or a recordable injury or illness not otherwise classified as a Class A, B, or C mishap.

16.33.3. **Mishap Prevention Responsibilities.**

Commanders, functional managers, supervisors, and individuals will enforce established safety rules and carry out required Air Force Safety Management System responsibilities identified within AFI 91-202. They will enforce rules, criteria, procedures, and safety standards to help eliminate unsafe acts or conditions. An effective mishap prevention program depends on individuals integrating mishap prevention principles at every functional level, and taking personal and collective responsibility for complying with and enforcing applicable safety standards.

16.33.3.1. **Safety Office.** At the installation level, safety staffs, host and tenant unit, implement mishap prevention programs for all Air Force units as prescribed by AFI 91-202 and applicable host tenant support agreements. The occupational safety staff consists of career safety professionals who are first-term and career Airmen trained in the enlisted safety career field (Air Force Specialty Code 1S0X1), as well as Department of Air Force civilians. With the assistance of the commanders, supervisors, and individuals, the host safety office staff provides oversight of the safety program and provides support and guidance to help eliminate unsafe acts or conditions. When mishaps occur, the safety staff ensures all mishaps are investigated and reported. **Note**: Air Force safety investigations are for mishap prevention purposes only--not for punitive actions or pecuniary liability.

16.33.3.2. **Commanders.** Commanders at all levels are responsible for implementing the United States Air Force mishap prevention program in accordance with the framework of the Air Force Safety Management System.

16.33.3.2.1. **Installation Commanders.** Installation commanders provide safe and healthful workplaces for all installation employees; ensure leadership at all levels is held accountable for enforcing safety and occupational health standards, and chair the installation safety council and/or environment, safety, and occupational health council.

16.33.3.2.2. **Commanders below installation level.** Commanders below installation level implement a safety and health program in their unit, or area of responsibility. Where commanders are not authorized fulltime safety personnel, they will appoint a primary and alternate unit safety representative to assist them in implementing their safety program. They also ensure a proactive mishap prevention program is implemented to include procurement and proper use of personal protective equipment, and worker/facility compliance with applicable standards.

16.33.3.3. **Supervisors.** Supervisors understand and enforce the safety and health standards that apply to their areas, operations, and operations involving their subordinates. They use risk management techniques to analyze work environments and job tasks for hazards; the job safety analysis will be used as part of this process. They review work processes annually, when new tasks or equipment are added, or when existing tasks change. They develop a work-center-specific Job Safety Training Outline on safety, fire prevention/protection, and health requirements. Supervisors will document and maintain completed training in the work area, and will conduct and document monthly spot inspections of the work areas. They report all mishaps that occur in work areas, off-duty mishaps involving assigned personnel, and related subsequent employee absences to the supporting safety office, and ensure the proper forms are completed if a mishap involves a civilian employee.

16.33.3.4. **Individuals.** Individuals hold a vital role in preventing mishaps. A failure to intervene when a potential unsafe act is identified is a failure to protect. Every Air Force member is accountable for considering their personal safety and the safety of others when participating in on and off-duty activities. Individuals are responsible for complying with all safety instructions, technical orders, job guides, and operating procedures. They identify and report hazardous conditions that place Air Force personnel or property at risk to supervision and/or using the Air Force Form 457, *USAF Hazard Report,* when necessary. Individuals will report personal injury, property damage, and any suspected exposure to biological, chemical, or nuclear hazardous materials to their supervisors as soon as practical, but not to exceed 24 hours. Individuals should immediately report to their supervisor a physical or mental condition that they feel could impact safe job performance. Individuals will use personal protection equipment for job tasks as identified by supervision. Apply risk management principles in both on- and off-duty activities to enhance the safety and wellbeing of themselves and other personnel.

## 16.34. Human Factors:

16.34.1. **Overview.**

Human factors is about people in their living and working environments, and how features of individual's tools, tasks, and working environment influence human performance. The Air Force leverages standardized Department of Defense Human Factors Analysis and Classification System codes to determine errors contributory or causal in Air Force mishaps. Through a systematic root cause(s) analysis, human factors deficiencies can be identified,

406       **1 OCTOBER 2017   AFH1**

mitigation strategies can be applied, organizational cultures can be improved, and processes can be established to interrupt chains of events and avoid mishaps. To improve human performance and use Human Factors Analysis and Classification System effectively, we must understand the different hazards that exist and how to properly mitigate risks along potential mishap pathways.

16.34.2. **Root Cause(s) Analysis.**

The Air Force uses four levels to determine the root cause(s) of a mishap when dealing with Human Factors Analysis and Classification System: Organizational Influences, Supervision, Preconditions, and Acts:

16.34.2.1. **Organizational Influences** are factors in a mishap if the communications, actions, omissions, or policies of upper-level management directly or indirectly affect supervisory practices, conditions or actions of the operator(s) and result in a system failure, human error, or an unsafe situation.

16.34.2.2. **Supervision.** Unsafe supervision can stem from failure to correct known problems, inappropriately planned operations, inadequate supervision, and supervisory violations.

16.34.2.3. **Preconditions** are factors in a mishap if conditions of the operators/individuals, environmental factors, or personnel factors affect practices, conditions, or actions of individuals and result in human error or an unsafe situation.

16.34.2.4. **Acts** are the active failures or actions committed by the operator which complete the mishap event sequence and fall into two categories: violations and errors. Violations factor into mishaps when personnel disregard rules and instructions leading to unsafe acts.

16.34.2.5. Through the four levels of Human Factors Analysis and Classification System, we can not only determine mishap root cause(s) for mishaps that have taken place, but more importantly, we can leverage Human Factors Analysis and Classification System to identify hazards early, mitigate risks on our on- and off-duty activities, and proactively avoid mishaps altogether.

16.34.2.6. Figure 16.2 is a diagram describing the complex factors by which the holes in the "cheese" can align resulting in a mishap. Many mishaps have strong correlations to previous mishaps. If we know what the failures or "holes" are, we can develop controls to minimize the risk of similar mishaps happening in the future.

## 16.35. Accountability.

We cannot tolerate reckless behavior or unwise decisions. All Airmen must take personal responsibility and be held accountable for their actions. Supervisors will ensure military and civilian personnel understand the implications of poor decisions and the importance of compliance. Commanders will ensure personnel are aware of Air Force instruction requirements and enforce compliance. Violations by military personnel are punishable under the Uniform Code of Military Justice and may also be considered misconduct during line-of-duty determinations. **Note:** Safety investigations are for mishap prevention purposes only. Commanders may direct an additional investigation and use factual information (time, speed, position, weather, etc.) and information obtained elsewhere (non-privileged witness statements, police reports, etc.) for disciplinary purposes (Letter of Reprimand, Article 15, etc.).

**Figure 16.2. Complex Factors that can Lead to a Mishap.** (Adapted from Reason, J (1990). Human Error. Cambridge University Press)

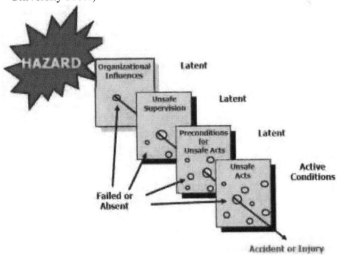

16.35.1. **Potential Impact of Not in Line of Duty Determination.**

A member who is injured due to his or her own misconduct stands to lose substantial benefits. If a member dies due to his or her own misconduct, the family stands to lose benefits. Regular pay, disability retirement pay, disability severance pay, veterans' benefits, and survivor benefit plan payments may be reduced or lost. The Servicemember who is permanently disabled due to injury or illness while not in the line-of-duty faces discharge without benefits or further medical care.

16.35.2. **How to Protect Yourself and Your Family.**

Think before you act. Driving while under the influence is obvious misconduct. You do not have to be intoxicated to be found not in the line-of-duty. Speeding, recklessness, and failure to use personal protective equipment resulting in injury may lead to disciplinary action. Your career, your family's well-being, and most importantly your life depend on you making wise decisions.

**16.36. Occupational Safety Program:**

16.36.1. Supervisors are responsible for training, establishing work methods and job instructions, assigning jobs, and supervising personnel. They are in the best position to identify hazards, assess risks associated with those hazards, and correct unsafe work practices or safety deficiencies that would impede mission success.

16.36.2. One of the greatest influences on successful mission accomplishment is a highly trained workforce that recognizes the importance of safety precautions and procedures and adheres to standards incorporating the basic elements of risk management.

16.36.3. Safety training may be integrated into task performance training or conducted separately. Before any operation begins and any safety training can take place, the supervisor must determine where people may be injured or equipment damaged. A job safety analysis is used to evaluate each work task not governed by a technical order or other definitive guidance and when a new work task or process is introduced into the workplace. If unsafe and unhealthful working conditions exist, eliminate or control them through engineering, administrative controls, or personal protective equipment. Commanders and supervisors must provide personal protective equipment for Air Force military members and civilian employees. The use of personal protective equipment is appropriate only if other controls are not possible or practical.

16.36.4. Supervisors must document safety training. The method of documentation may include, but is not limited to, the Air Force Form 55, *Employee Safety and Health Record*, electronic mediums such as Air Force forms/MAF LOG C2/CAS-B/G081 or locally developed products. If the Air Force Form 55 is mandated for use as the training documentation device, the entity that mandated the form usage will prescribe the requirement in writing to include entries that require signatures, e.g., hazard communication, respirator, low powered industrial, lockout/tagout, fall protection, confined spaces, radiation safety, laser safety, etc. **Note**: Signature of the supervisor or the person who conducted the training; other documents may require the initials of the individual and trainer/supervisor.

**16.37. Hazard Identification and Reporting:**

16.37.1. Mishap prevention begins with hazard identification. As a supervisor, a good way to know where to begin identifying hazards is to study historical workplace injury and fatality trends. The installation safety office can offer personalized workplace mishap trending. Injury and illness trends are also released annually by The Occupational Safety & Health Administration in conjunction with the Bureau of Labor Statistics. In 2014, the six most common ways workers died on the job are:

16.37.1.1. Transportation mishaps (traffic mishaps), 1,976 fatalities.

16.37.1.2. Falls (one level to another; slips and trips), 819 fatalities.

16.37.1.3. Workplace violence (homicides), 771 fatalities.

16.37.1.4. Contact with objects (struck by, struck against), 723 fatalities.

16.37.1.5. Exposure to harmful substances (chemicals), 385 fatalities.

16.37.1.6. Fire (fires, smoke, explosions), 147 fatalities.

16.37.2. On and off duty Airmen are not immune to injury, illness, and death. Off duty, the most common way Airmen are injured or die is from vehicle related mishaps. On duty, Airmen experience injuries and death similar to national workplace statistics: falls, vehicle mishaps, and struck by objects. Injuries, illnesses, and fatalities can be eliminated through hazard identification. Hazard identification not only includes understanding how injuries occur, but also understanding and enforcing safety standards. Although not all inclusive, to ensure the safety of all, commanders, supervisors, and Airmen at all levels will:

16.37.2.1. Keep areas around exit doors and passageways free of obstructions. Ensure the exit route leads to a public way.

16.37.2.2. Remove from service ladders with broken or missing steps, rungs or cleats, broken side rails, or other defects.

16.37.2.3. Frequently check the third and/or grounding prong is secure, especially on items unplugged frequently. Do not cut off the prong, or use an adapter to allow a three-prong plug to fit a two-prong receptacle, since this negates third-wire grounding protection.

16.37.2.4. Only use multi-receptacle surge protectors to power computers and related equipment such as lights and or fans. Do not use surge protectors or extension cords with high current items such as coffee makers, refrigerators, microwave ovens, heaters, food preparation equipment, etc.

16.37.2.5. Ensure Personal Protective Equipment is worn appropriately and where needed (fall protection gear, eye protection, etc.)

16.37.2.6. Ensure Technical Orders, Air Force Instructions, and other regulations are followed.

16.37.2.7. Seek to identify and correct hazards such as missing guards, areas where falls are likely, missing and damaged safety equipment, confined space areas, and falling or loose objects/debris.

16.37.3. Report hazards to the responsible supervisor or local agency. If the hazard is eliminated on the spot, no further action is required; sharing information with other units or agencies may prevent duplicating hazards and deficiencies elsewhere and is recommended. If the hazard presents imminent danger, the supervisor or individual responsible for that area must take immediate action to correct the situation or apply interim control measures. Report hazards to the safety office that cannot be eliminated immediately using Air Force Form 457, *USAF Hazard Report*, by telephone, or in person. Reports can be submitted anonymously. The Chief of Safety will determine the appropriate safety, fire, or health discipline to investigate the hazard report. The investigator discusses the hazard report with the member who submitted the report (if known), the responsible supervisor or manager, and other parties involved to validate the hazard and determine the best interim controls and corrective action.

16.37.4. Air Force Form 457, *USAF Hazard Report*, must be readily available to all unit personnel in the work center. The investigator must respond within 10 duty days in writing about the corrective action or plans, and conduct follow-up reviews until the corrective action is completed.

## 16.38. Traffic Safety:

16.38.1. The Air Force Traffic Safety program is aimed at preventing and reducing traffic mishaps using a wide-range of mishap prevention program specifically focusing on driving behaviors and risk management. Off-duty traffic mishaps are the leading cause of Air Force fatalities, with motorcycle mishaps accounting for approximately half of all AF traffic fatalities. This is an alarming fact, considering Air Force motorcycle riders, account for only 9 percent of the Air Force population.

16.38.2. Reckless driving behaviors (i.e. driving under the influence, speeding, distracted driving, lack of training) are the leading cause in over 75 percent of all private motor vehicle mishaps. Distracted driving (primarily cell phone usage/text messaging) has increased in recent years and according to the National Safety Council was involved in 26 percent of all 2014 motor vehicle mishaps. Several tools are available to help supervisors in educating Airmen in safe driving practice, including Motorcycle training classes, Motorcycle Unit Safety Tracking Tool, Travel Risk Planning System and several online/classroom traffic safety courses.

## Section 16H—Risk Management

## 16.39. Definition.

Risk management is a decision-making process to systematically evaluate possible courses of action, identify risks and benefits, and determine the best course of action for any given situation. Risk management enables commanders, functional managers, supervisors, and individuals to maximize capabilities while limiting risks through application of a simple, systematic process appropriate for all personnel and functions in both on- and off-duty situations. Appropriate use of risk management increases an organization's and individual's ability to safely and effectively accomplish their mission/activity while preserving lives and precious resources.

16.39.1. **Risk Management Principles.**

Four principles govern all actions associated with risk management. These principles are the cornerstone of effective risk management and are applicable 24-hours a day, 7-days a week, 365-days a year (24-7-365) by all personnel, for all on- and off-duty operations, tasks and activities.

16.39.1.1. **Accept No Unnecessary Risk.** Unnecessary risk comes without a commensurate return in terms of real benefits or available opportunities and will not contribute meaningfully to mission or activity accomplishment, and needlessly jeopardizes personnel or other assets. All Air Force missions and daily routines involve risk. The most logical choices for accomplishing a mission are those that meet all mission requirements while exposing personnel and resources to the lowest acceptable risk; take only those risks that are necessary to accomplish the mission or task. However, we cannot and should not be completely risk averse; even high risk endeavors may be undertaken when there is a well-founded basis to believe that the sum of the benefits exceeds the sum of the costs. Balancing benefits and costs is a subjective process and tied intimately with the factors affecting the mission or activity; therefore, personnel with prior knowledge and experience of the mission or activity must be engaged whenever possible in making risk decisions to ensure a proper balance is achieved.

16.39.1.2. **Make Risk Decisions at the Appropriate Level.** Although anyone can make a risk decision that impacts their personal well-being, some risk acceptance decisions must be made by an appropriate decision-making authority that can effectively allocate resources and implement controls to mitigate or eliminate risks associated with an operation/activity. Making risk decisions at the appropriate level also establishes clear accountability. Leaders and individuals must be aware of how much risk they can accept and when to elevate risk management decisions to a higher level. Those accountable for the success or failure of the mission or activity must be fully engaged in the risk decision process.

16.39.1.3. **Integrate Risk Management into Operations and Planning at All Levels.** Integrate risk management into planning at all levels and as early as possible. This provides the greatest opportunity to make well informed risk decisions and implement effective risk controls. To effectively apply risk management, commanders, supervisors, and personnel must dedicate time and resources to integrate risk management principles into planning, operational processes and day-to-day activities. Risk assessments of operations and activities are most successful when they are accomplished in the normal sequence of events (the pre-planning of a mission or activity) by individuals directly involved in the event, and not as a last minute or add-on process. Any amount of pre-planning that can be accomplished, even in a time constrained environment is better than no planning at all.

16.39.1.4. **Apply the process cyclically and continuously.** Risk management is a continuous process applied across the full spectrum of military training and operations, base operations functions, and day-to-day activities and events both on and off duty. This cyclic process is used to continuously identify and assess hazards, develop and implement controls, evaluate outcomes, and provide feedback to our Airmen to save lives and preserve combat resources.

16.39.2. **Risk Management Levels.**

The principles, goals and fundamental concepts of risk management highlight the universal application of risk management concepts both on- and off-duty. There are two primary levels of risk management (*Deliberate* and *Real-Time*) that dictate the level of effort and scope that should normally be undertaken when evaluating risk(s). Figure 16.3 depicts the basic relationship of these levels and how they relate across the strategic (long-term) to tactical (short-term) spectrums. The controls/resources and issues shown below the risk management levels are examples of resources and impacts that might apply across the planning and execution timelines. As the diagram shows, Deliberate and Real-Time risk management are interrelated when making risk management decisions; they are separated only at the point where the planning phase transitions to the execution phase of the mission/activity. A strong, effective risk management process involves careful and deliberative planning coupled with effective, real-time risk management. This full spectrum approach ensures comprehensive risk mitigation and the likelihood of mission/activity success.

16.39.2.1. **Deliberate Risk Management.** Deliberate risk management refers to pre-mission/activity planning and involves the full formal application of the complete 5-Step risk management process outlined in paragraph 16.39.3. This process can range from an in-depth planning process involving thorough hazard identification, detailed data research, diagram and analysis tools, formal testing, and long-term tracking of the risks associated with an operation, activity or system, down to normal day-to-day operations/activity planning that utilize the same 5-Step risk management process, but require less time and resources to complete. Generally associated with strategic-level planning, in-depth risk management planning is reserved for complex operations/systems, high priority/high visibility situations or circumstances in which hazards are not well understood. In-depth risk management is normally implemented well in advance of the planned system, mission, event, or activity and is normally reserved for more complex and risky efforts (such as large troop/unit movements, airshow planning, system development, tactics and training curricula development, scheduled vacations, organized camping/hiking activities, scheduled home repairs, etc.). As the situation, operation, or activity becomes less complex, familiar and/or closer to execution, deliberate risk management planning becomes simplified and the focus shifts to ensuring near-term hazards and mitigation strategies are considered. Across the spectrum of deliberate risk management, we must always include the experience, expertise, and knowledge of experienced personnel to identify known hazards/risks and strategies to effectively mitigate risks for the specific mission, activity, or task in both on- and off-duty situations. Although pre-planning is always desired for any situation, we must also consider how we deal with risk management once we begin the execution phase of an activity.

**Figure 16.3. Relationship of Risk Management Levels**

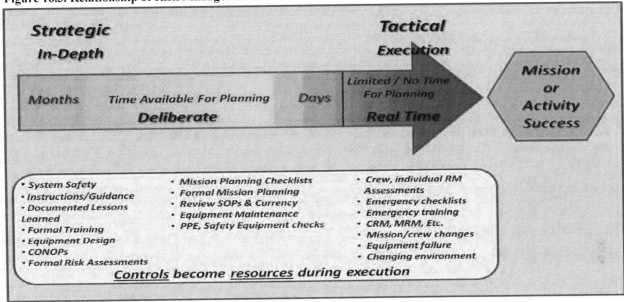

16.39.2.2. **Real-Time.** This level of risk management is always associated with risk management decisions made in "Real-Time" during the "execution" or tactical phase of training, operations, emergency/crisis response situations, or off-duty activities where there is normally little or no time to conduct formal/deliberate risk management planning. Real-time is usually an informal, mental risk assessment that is done "on the fly" (i.e. short-notice taskings, weather/natural phenomena driven activities, emergency responses, spontaneous off-duty activities, etc.) using basic risk management process steps to identify and mitigate hazards in the new or changing situation. As time is normally constrained or limited in these situations, deliberate risk management planning is impractical. Imperative to the Real-Time situations, is that individuals are able to efficiently and effectively apply risk management concepts to mitigate risks. To enhance recall of critical risk management steps, the Air Force has adopted an easy to remember mnemonic (ABCD discussed in paragraph 16.39.4.) to assist personnel in making sound risk management decisions during "Real-Time" and to provide a description of the Air Force real-time risk management process that is appropriate during the "execution" of a mission or activity and/or time-constrained situations.

16.39.3. **5-Step Risk Management Process.**

Risk Management is a continuous, systematic decision informing process consisting of five primary steps (Figure 16.4) that define the formal risk management process primarily associated with deliberative risk management planning and forms the basis for real-time risk management process considerations. The following is a brief description of the 5-Step risk management process:

16.39.3.1. **(Step 1) Identify the Hazards.** Step one of the risk management process involves application of appropriate hazard identification techniques in order to identify hazards associated with the operation or activity. Hazards can be defined as any real or potential condition that can cause mission degradation, injury, illness, death to personnel or damage to or loss of equipment/property. Key aspects of this step include:

16.39.3.1.1. Mission/Task Analysis: Review current and planned operations and/or tasks associated with the mission or activity.

16.39.3.1.2. List Hazards: Identify and list hazards and/or factors that may lead to dangers and risks associated with the operation or activity.

**Figure 16.4. 5-Step Risk Management**

16.39.3.1.3. List Causes: List the causes associated with each identified hazard, and try to identify the root cause(s) against which to apply risk management strategies.

16.39.3.2. **(Step 2) Assess the Hazards.** The assessment step involves the application of quantitative and/or qualitative measures to determine the probability and severity of negative effects that may result from exposure to risks/hazards and directly affect mission or activity success. Assessing hazards can be a formalized or intuitive process. Key aspects of this step include:

16.39.3.2.1. Assess Hazard Exposure: Evaluate the time, proximity, volume or repetition involved to determine the level of exposure to hazards.

16.39.3.2.2. Assess Hazard Severity: Determine severity of the hazard in terms of potential impact on personnel, equipment, or mission/activity.

16.39.3.2.3. Assess Probability: Determine the probability that the hazard will cause a negative event of the severity assessed above. Probability may be determined through estimates or actual numbers (if available).

16.39.3.2.4. Assess Risk Levels: Determine the level of risk associated with the hazard as related to Severity and Probability. The level of risk will vary from "extremely high" as associated with frequent exposure and catastrophic effects to "low" as associated with unlikely exposure and negligible effects.

16.39.3.2.5. Complete Risk Assessment: Combine severity and probability estimates to form a risk assessment for each hazard. By combining the probability of occurrence with severity, a matrix is created where intersecting rows and columns define a Risk Assessment Matrix. Figure 16.5 provides one example of a Risk Assessment Matrix; color coding, coupled with numeric values is one way to ensure the matrix is readable in both color and grayscale formats. Risk Assessment Matrices can take different forms and must be designed to fit the organization or situation as warranted. Note: A complete and in-depth description of the Risk Assessment Matrix can be found in AFPAM 90-803, *Risk Management (RM) Guidelines and Tools*.

**Figure 16.5. Sample Risk Assessment Matrix**

| Risk Assessment Matrix | | | | PROBABILITY<br>Frequency of Occurrence Over Time | | | | |
|---|---|---|---|---|---|---|---|---|
| | | | | A<br>Frequent<br>(Continuously experienced) | B<br>Likely<br>(Will occur frequently) | C<br>Occasional<br>(Will occur several times) | D<br>Seldom<br>(Unlikely; can be expected to occur) | E<br>Unlikely<br>(Improbable; but possible to occur) |
| SEVERITY | Effect of Hazard | Catastrophic<br>(Death, Loss of Asset, Mission Capability or Unit Readiness) | I | EH | EH | H | H | M |
| | | Critical<br>(Severe Injury or Damage, Significantly Degraded Mission Capability or Unit Readiness) | II | EH | H | H | M | L |
| | | Moderate<br>(Minor Injury or Damage, Degraded Mission Capability or Unit Readiness) | III | H | M | M | L | L |
| | | Negligible<br>(Minimal Injury or Damage, Little or No Impact to Mission Readiness or Unit Readiness) | IV | M | L | L | L | L |
| | | | | Risk Assessment Levels<br>EH=Extremely High H=High M=Medium L=Low | | | | |

16.39.3.3. **(Step 3) Develop Controls and Make Decisions:** Step three involves the development and selection of specific strategies and controls that reduce or eliminate risk. Effective mitigation measures reduce one of the three components (Probability, Severity or Exposure) of risk. Risk mitigation decisions must be made at the appropriate level for the identified risk. The higher the risk, the higher the decision-level needs to be to ensure that an appropriate analysis of overall costs to benefits has been carefully weighed. Keep in mind there is no "cookie-cutter" approach or specific standard for establishing levels of risk management decision authority across the Air Force. Critical is that leadership/decision makers ensure the levels of decision authority are aligned appropriately for mission requirements and experience levels of the personnel conducting operations/activities under their responsibility. Decision levels may vary within a command for differing operations/activities if training requirements, mission sets or activities are divergent enough to warrant separate standards (for example, Air Education and Training Command, Air Force Special Operations Command, etc.). Decision makers must ultimately choose the most mission supportive risk controls, consistent with risk management principles that provide the best solution for the given hazards. Risk decisions must never be delegated to a lower level for convenience or when the situation dictates senior-level involvement; exceptions may be considered in time critical situations where delays might endanger lives, resources or equipment. Key aspects of this step include:

16.39.3.3.1. Identify Control Options: Starting with the highest-risk hazards as assessed in Step 2, identify as many risk control options as possible for all hazards. Each hazard should have one or more controls that can effectively eliminate, avoid, or reduce the risk to an acceptable level.

16.39.3.3.2. Determine Control Effects: Determine the effect of each control on the risk(s) associated with the hazard. With controls identified, the hazard should be re-assessed taking into consideration the effect the control will have on the severity and or probability. This refined risk assessment determines the residual risk for the hazard (assuming the implementation of selected controls). At this point, consider the cost (personnel, equipment, money, time, etc.) of the control and the possible interaction between controls; do they work together?

16.39.3.3.3. Prioritize Risk Controls: For each hazard, prioritize those risk controls that will reduce the risk to an acceptable level. The best controls will be consistent with mission objectives and optimize use of available resources (manpower, material, equipment, funding, time).

16.39.3.3.4. Select Risk Controls: For each identified hazard, select those risk controls that will reduce the risk to an acceptable level. As in prioritizing controls, the best controls will be consistent with mission/activity objectives and optimum use of available resources (outlined above).

16.39.3.3.5. Make Risk Control Decision: Analyze the level of risk for the operation/activity with the proposed controls in place. Determine if the benefits of the operation/activity now exceed the level of risk the operation/activity presents. Be sure to consider the cumulative risk of all the identified hazards and the long term consequences of the decision. If the cost of the risk(s) outweighs the benefits, re-examine the control options to see if any new or modified controls are available. If no additional controls are identified, inform the next level in the chain of command that, based on the evaluation, the risk of the mission exceeds the benefits and should be modified. When notified of a situation in which risk outweighs the benefit, the next level in the chain of command must assist and implement required controls, modify/cancel the mission, or accept the identified risks based on a higher level of the risk-benefit equation. Keep in mind that as circumstances change for a given mission/activity, the benefit-to-risk comparison must also be made to ensure that previous "Go/No-Go" decisions are valid.

16.39.3.4. **(Step 4) Implement Controls.** Once control measures have been selected, an implementation strategy must be developed and carried out. The strategy must identify the: who, what, when, where and costs associated with the control measure. For mission-related controls, accountability must be emphasized across all levels of leadership and personnel associated with the action so that there is clear understanding of the risks and responsibilities of commanders and subordinates alike. There must always be accountability for acceptance of risk regardless of circumstances. Key aspects of this step include:

16.39.3.4.1. Make Implementation Clear: Provide a roadmap for implementation, a vision of the end state, and describe successful implementation. Deployed the control measure in a method the intended audience can understand.

16.39.3.4.2. Establish Accountability: Accountability is a critically important area of risk management. The accountable person is the one who makes the decision (approves the control measures), and hence, the right person (appropriate level) must make the decision. Also, be clear on who is responsible at the unit or execution level for implementation of the risk control. Individuals involved in a specific risk management process must be aware of who is responsible and accountable at each stage of an operation/activity and when (if possible) decisions will be elevated to the next level.

16.39.3.4.3. Provide Support: To be successful, command/leadership must be behind the control measure(s) put in place. Provide the personnel and resources necessary to implement the control measures. Incorporate sustainability from the beginning and be sure to deploy the control measure along with a feedback mechanism that will provide information on whether the control measure is achieving the intended purpose.

16.39.3.5. **(Step 5) Supervise and Evaluate.** Risk management is a process that continues throughout the life cycle of a system, mission, or activity. Leaders and supervisors at every level must fulfill their respective roles to ensure controls are sustained over time. Key aspects of this step include:

16.39.3.5.1. Supervise: Monitor the operation/activity to ensure:

16.39.3.5.1.1. The controls are effective and remain in place.

16.39.3.5.1.2. Changes which require further risk management are identified.

16.39.3.5.1.3. Action is taken when necessary to correct ineffective risk controls and reinitiate the risk management steps in response to new hazards.

16.39.3.5.1.4. Risk and controls are re-evaluated anytime the personnel, equipment, or mission/activity change or new actions are anticipated in an environment not covered in the initial risk management analysis.

16.39.3.5.1.5. There is continuity of selected risk management controls during leadership changes. Ensuring outgoing leaders share knowledge, experiences, and lessons with incoming leaders provides positive transition of risk acceptance and less volatility to the operation or activity when these changes occur.

16.39.3.5.2. Evaluate: The risk management process review/evaluation must be systematic. After assets are expended to control risks, a cost benefit review must be accomplished to see if risk and cost are in balance. Significant changes in the system are recognized and appropriate risk management controls are reapplied as necessary to control the risks. Effective review/evaluation will also identify whether actual costs are in line with expectations and how the controls have affected mission performance (good or bad). Other considerations:

16.39.3.5.2.1. Every risk analysis will unlikely be perfect the first time. When risk analyses contain errors of omission or commission, it is important that those errors be identified and corrected.

16.39.3.5.2.2. Measurements are necessary to ensure accurate evaluations of how effectively controls eliminate hazards or reduce risks. When available, After-Action reports, surveys, and in-progress reviews are excellent tools for measurements. To be meaningful, measurements must quantitatively or qualitatively identify reductions of risk, improvements in mission success, or enhancement of capabilities.

16.39.3.5.3. Feedback: A review by itself is not enough; a feedback system must be established to ensure that the corrective or preventative action taken was effective and that any newly discovered hazards identified during the mission/activity are analyzed and corrective action taken. Feedback informs all involved as to how the implementation process is working and whether or not the controls were effective. Feedback can be in the form of briefings, lessons learned, cross-tell reports, benchmarking, database reports, etc. Without this feedback loop, we lack the benefit of knowing if the previous forecasts were accurate, contained errors, or were completely incorrect. Commanders, supervisors and individuals must work with appropriate risk management process managers, Instructors/Advisors to ensure effective risk management feedback and cross tell is collected and distributed to enhance future operations, and activities.

### 16.39.4. Real-Time Risk Management Process or ABCD Model.

The 5-Step risk management Process is the cornerstone of all risk management decisions and lays the framework for conducting formalized risk assessments normally associated with the deliberative level of risk management. Although real-time risk management is also founded on the 5-Step risk management process, streamlining the steps is essential in situations where risk decisions need to be made quickly and in Real-Time. The real-time risk management process or ABCD model provides individuals with an easy to remember mnemonic that walks them through the essential steps of the RM wheel to: "**A**ssess the situation, **B**alance controls, **C**ommunicate, and **D**ecide and **D**ebrief the risk management decision: **ABCD**." This simple and easy to remember memory jogger provides individuals with a means to evaluate risks and formulate mitigation strategies in a short time and can be easily applied in both on- and off-duty situations. Figure 16.6 provides a graphic example of the relationship between the 5-Step risk management Process and real-time risk management process using the ABCD model.

16.39.4.1. **Assess the Situation.** Assessing risk in a time-critical environment typically occurs when a planned activity is already underway or when the complexity or perception of overall risk is low. Effective assessment requires the key elements of hazard/risk identification and understanding the negative effects associated with those hazards/risks. Individuals must seriously consider the activity or action in which they are about to engage and choose appropriate mitigation strategies to meet the hazards they identify. In real-time risk management process, a complete assessment of the situation requires three stages of situational awareness in a relatively short time: (a) Perception of what is happening; (b) Integration of information and goals; and (c) Projection into the future. Unlike Deliberate risk management, where there is ample time to assess potential situations, an individual's ability to discern the situation and apply available resources quickly and effectively that can mean the difference between success or failure. This first step of the real-time risk management process/ABCD model effectively combines the first two steps of the 5-Step risk management Process.

**Figure 16.6. The 5-Step Risk Management Process as related to the Real-Time Risk Management Process/ ABCD Model.**

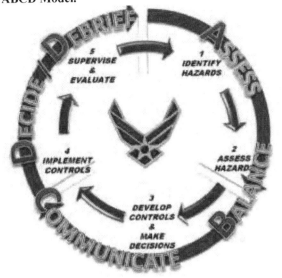

16.39.4.2. **Balance Controls.** The second step of the real-time risk management process/ABCD model is specifically tied to making risk control decisions (Step 3 of the 5-Step risk management process) to mitigate or eliminate the risks identified in assessing the hazards of the activity. After assessing the situation, personnel must consider all available controls (resources) to facilitate mission or activity success and how to manage them. Controls/resources can vary in scope and availability from situation to situation. The better-prepared individuals are prior to an activity, the more likely they will have more controls/resources available to create multiple redundancies or "blocks" to effectively eliminate or mitigate potential risks in real-time. As an example, this equates to having a good understanding of the situation, being properly trained, wearing correct personal protective equipment, knowing personal limitations, and having a "Wingman" to support their effort. Each of these controls/resources serves as a layer of protection and enhances a decision maker's ability to balance risk versus reward through proper preparation and understanding of the situation and options. When making these considerations, Airmen must communicate with their team and leadership to ensure all options and resources are effectively utilized in making a sound, yet timely risk decision.

16.39.4.3. **Communicate.** The third step of the real-time risk management process/ABCD model is to communicate. This communication can take various forms such as Real-Time communication with leadership to discuss problems and/or intentions, internal team/crew communication to discuss Real-Time hazards and mitigation options, or an individual internalizing their current situation and taking time to evaluate if they are heading down the right path. This step assumes individuals and/or teams carefully consider options and controls available to them in Real-Time situations, and that they are aware of how perception and communication skills change in unanticipated and changing environments. Perception and communication skills are adversely affected as individuals become increasingly stressed and lose situational awareness. Feeling undo pressure to succeed or to continue with a plan when anticipated conditions require "mid-stream" changes can have similar effects on individuals and/or team members as they try to compensate. In these high stress situations, communication skills diminish as individuals channelize attention and lose awareness of the overall situation; they can experience tunnel vision and be unable to multitask effectively to deal with the changing circumstances. Understanding this, individuals and teams who are thrust into these situations can better prepare, anticipate, and identify if they or others are losing situational awareness and make corrections. This awareness enables individuals to communicate with teammates and leadership in Real-Time situations, and allows them to take a step back and reevaluate options. Asking questions such as: "Who needs to know about the situation?" "Who can help or assist?" "Who can provide back-up?" or "Can this be done differently?" are just a few examples of the considerations that must be made prior to implementing a mitigation strategy in real-time.

16.39.4.4. **Decide and Debrief:**

16.39.4.4.1. The final step of the real-time risk management process/ABCD model is to make the decision to continue, modify or abandon the mission/activity based upon Real-Time circumstances and conditions. Unlike step 4 of the 5-Step risk management process where an implementation strategy is carefully developed and carried out through identification of the who, what, when, where and cost associated with the control prior to an activity, real-time risk management process relies on the individual or small group taking immediate or near immediate action to mitigate risk(s) in real-time. This aspect alone can make real-time risk management process decisions riskier than deliberate risk management decisions. Individuals must realize this and make every effort to deliberately weigh risk decisions before taking action to ensure they are selecting the best course of action.

16.39.4.4.2. Sometimes the original plan must be modified or changed to account for unforeseen issues in order to assure success. Although minor changes or modifications to a plan or strategy may be easily implemented, others may require higher authority (if available) to properly weigh the risk and determine the best course of action. Accountability under these circumstances rests solely with the individual(s) involved in the activity and their responsibility is to fully understand the scope and limits of their Go/No-Go decision and act accordingly. As such, the acceptance of risk and associated consequences needs to be taken seriously with the understanding that any adverse outcome from a selected course of action may not only affect the individual, but greatly impact loved ones, co-workers, and ultimately their valuable contribution to the Air Force mission. Although the goal for any mission or activity is to operate safely and achieve success, all Airmen must consider the possibility of abandoning the mission or activity if the situation appears too risky or too costly to continue and there are no reasonable options or strategies to change/alter the circumstances in the time remaining to conduct the mission/activity.

16.39.4.4.3. As with the formal 5-Step risk management process, both leadership and personnel involved in a mission/activity must ensure that the feedback loop or "debrief" aspect of the "D" is performed. This vital process step ensures individuals follow through and complete the ABCD mnemonic loop by identifying what worked, what did not work, and ensures documented lessons learned are disseminated. Debriefs will improve performance, mitigate risks in future activities, and are essential in completing the ABCD loop. Asking questions such as: "Was our assessment accurate?" "Were we lucky?" "How well did we use the controls/resources?" "Was the communication effective?" and "What can we do to improve the events in the future?" are a few examples of questions that leaders, crews/teams, and individuals can ask in debriefs to ensure future activities are improved and risks are reduced.

### Section 16I—Sexual Assault

**16.40. Air Force Policies and Procedures for Prevention of and Response to Sexual Assault:**

16.40.1. Sexual Assault Is a Crime.

The United States Air Force does not tolerate sexual assault. Sexual assault is criminal conduct that falls well short of the standards America expects of the men and women in uniform and violates Air Force Core Values. Inherent in the Air Force Core Values of Integrity First, Service Before Self and Excellence in All We Do, is respect: self-respect, mutual respect, and respect for the Air Force as an institution.

16.40.2. Sexual Assault.

The following definition of sexual assault has been directed by the Department of Defense and is for education and training purposes only. This definition does not affect in any way the definition of any offense under the Uniform Code of Military Justice. Commanders are encouraged to consult with their staff judge advocate for complete understanding of this definition in relation to the Uniform Code of Military Justice.

*Sexual assault is defined as intentional sexual contact, characterized by the use of force, threats, intimidation, or abuse of authority or when the victim does not or cannot consent. As used in this Instruction, the term includes a broad category of sexual offenses consisting of the following specific Uniform Code of Military Justice offenses: rape, sexual assault, aggravated sexual contact, abusive sexual contact, forcible sodomy (forced oral or anal sex), or attempts to commit these offenses.*

*Consent is defined as words or overt acts indicating a freely given agreement to the sexual conduct at issue by a competent person. An expression of lack of consent through words or conduct means there is no consent. Lack of verbal or physical resistance or submission resulting from the accused's use of force, threat of force, or placing another person in fear does not constitute consent. A current or previous dating relationship or the manner of dress of the person involved with the accused in the sexual conduct at issue shall not constitute consent. There is no consent where the person is sleeping or incapacitated, such as due to age, alcohol or drugs, or mental incapacity.*

**16.41. Installation Sexual Assault Response Coordinator.**

The Installation sexual assault response coordinator is an Air Force civilian employee or Air Force officer reporting to the installation Commander, who serves as the commander's central point of contact at installation level or within a geographic area to ensure appropriate care is coordinated and provided to adult victims of sexual assault, perpetrated by someone other than the victim's spouse, same sex domestic partner, and/or unmarried intimate partner, and tracks the services provided to a victim from the initial report through final disposition and resolution. The installation sexual assault response coordinator ensures the implementation of the sexual assault prevention and response program, to include sexual assault awareness, prevention and response training. Installation sexual assault response coordinators are trained and credentialed.

**16.42. Victim Advocate:**

16.42.1. A victim advocate provides non-clinical crisis intervention, referral, and ongoing non-clinical support to adult sexual assault victims, perpetrated by someone other than the victim's spouse, same sex domestic partner, and/or unmarried intimate partner. Support will include providing information on available options and resources to victims. The victim advocate, on behalf of the sexual assault victim, provides liaison assistance with other organizations and agencies on victim care matters and reports directly to the sexual assault response coordinator when performing victim advocacy duties. The Air Force has two types of victim advocates: sexual assault prevention and response victim advocates and Volunteer victim advocates. Both will be trained and credentialed.

16.42.1.1. The sexual assault prevention and response victim advocate is a fulltime general service civilian employee selected and trained by the sexual assault response coordinator, who provides essential support, liaison services and care to victims.

16.42.1.2. Volunteer victim advocates are military and Department of Defense civilian employee volunteers selected and trained by the sexual assault response coordinator, who provide essential support, liaison services and care to victims. The victim advocate reports directly to the sexual assault response coordinator while carrying out sexual assault advocacy responsibilities.

## 16.43 Reporting Options.

The Air Force is committed to ensuring adult victims are protected, treated with dignity and respect, and provided support, advocacy, and care. To achieve these objectives, the Air Force has two reporting options: Unrestricted and Restricted Reporting. Unrestricted Reporting of sexual assault allegations activate victim services and accountability responses, and are essential to eliminating the crime. However, in some cases Unrestricted Reporting may represent a barrier for victims to access services, when the victim desires no command or Air Force law enforcement involvement. Consequently, the Air Force recognizes a fundamental need to provide a confidential disclosure vehicle via the Restricted Reporting option. Airmen who make a Restricted Report have access to all victim care services, but no investigation will be opened and the chain-of-command will not be notified. Regardless of whether the victim elects restricted or unrestricted reporting, confidentiality of medical information will be maintained.

## 16.44. Special Victims' Counsel.

In 2013, the Air Force created the first program to provide adult and child victims of sexual assault with legal representation to assist them. Special Victims' Counsel provide legal assistance services through experienced, licensed, and independent legal counsel from the reporting process, in the investigation, during the prosecution, and through the appellate process. Sexual Assault Response Coordinators, military criminal investigators, trial counsel and victim witness liaison personnel must inform a sexual assault victim that they have the opportunity to be represented free of charge. A sexual assault victim may request Special Victims' Legal Counsel representation at any time. Special Victims' Counsel deliver victim-centered advice and advocacy through comprehensive, independent representation to sexual assault victims worldwide, assist them in obtaining support and recovery resources, and promote greater confidence in the military justice process and the United States Air Force.

## 16.45. Response to an Allegation of Sexual Assault:

16.45.1. Any military member or civilian employee, other than those authorized to receive confidential communications or otherwise exempted by operation of law, regulation, or policy, who receives a report of a sexual assault incident about a subordinate in the individual's supervisory chain will report the matter to the sexual assault response coordinator, Commander, and Air Force Office of Special Investigations. Failure to comply may result in administrative action or action under the Uniform Code of Military Justice. Military members or civilian employees who become aware of a sexual assault incident, not involving a subordinate in the supervisory chain, are strongly encouraged, but not required to report the incident to the installation sexual assault response coordinator or encourage the victim to do so.

16.45.2. Upon notification, the sexual assault response coordinator will immediately respond or direct a trained and credentialed victim advocate to respond to the victim. When contacted by the sexual assault response coordinator and/or victim advocate, a sexual assault victim may decline any or all sexual assault prevention and response services or request a different advocate, to include gender specific, if one is available. Unless assistance is declined, the sexual assault response coordinator and/or victim advocate will provide the victim accurate information on the sexual assault response process, including the option of unrestricted or restricted reporting, as applicable. The sexual assault response coordinator and/or victim advocate will inform the victim of the availability of healthcare treatment, including the option of a sexual assault forensic examination, and a Special Victims Counsel.

## 16.46. Reporting Option Eligibility:

16.46.1. The following individuals are eligible for both the Unrestricted and Restricted Reporting option within the SAPR Program.

16.46.1.1. Regular Air Force members who were victims of sexual assault perpetrated by an acquaintance or stranger (non-intimate partner), victim's spouse, same sex domestic partner, and/or unmarried intimate partner.

16.46.1.1.1. Military members, who are on Regular Air Force, but who were victims of sexual assault prior to enlistment or commissioning, are eligible to receive sexual assault prevention and response services under either reporting option. Support to an Regular Air Force service member is available regardless of when or where the sexual assault took place.

16.46.1.2. Regular Air Force members' dependents, 18 and older, who are eligible for treatment in the medical healthcare system, at installations in the continental United States and outside of the continental United States, by an acquaintance or stranger (non-intimate partner), victim's spouse, same sex domestic partner, and/or unmarried intimate partner.

16.46.1.3. Air Force Reserve component members in Title 10 status who are sexually assaulted when performing active service and inactive duty training will be eligible to receive full sexual assault prevention and response support services from a sexual assault response coordinator and/or volunteer victim advocate.

16.46.1.3.1. If reporting a sexual assault that occurred prior to or while not performing active service or inactive training when not in Title 10 status, Air Force Reserve component members will be eligible to receive limited sexual assault prevention and response support services from a sexual assault response coordinator and/or victim advocate. Local laws and regulations apply when the member is in Title 32 status.

16.46.1.4. Air Force civilian employees who are victims of sexual assault regardless of their duty station location.

16.46.1.4.1. Air Force civilian employees who are victims of sexual assault are not eligible for non-emergency medical services or legal services unless the reporting individual is otherwise a beneficiary.

## 16.47. Restricted Reports:

16.47.1. The Department of Defense has directed the implementation of confidentiality in the form of a Restricted Reporting option. This enables eligible victims to report allegations of sexual assault to specified personnel, without triggering an investigation. This reporting option is intended to remove barriers to medical care and support while giving the victim additional time and increased control over the release and management of personal information.

16.47.2. The Air Force makes every effort to treat victims of sexual assault with dignity and respect, to protect their privacy to the maximum extent of the law, and provide support, advocacy, and care.

## 16.48. Receiving a Restricted Report:

16.48.1. Only sexual assault response coordinators, sexual assault prevention and response victim advocates, volunteer victim advocates and Healthcare Personnel may receive restricted reports of sexual assault. While communications with chaplains or other individuals may be entitled to privileged status under the Military Rules of Evidence or other statues and regulations, such communications are not restricted reports. Chaplains and other individuals entitled to privileged communications are not authorized to accept a report of sexual assault; however communication related to the incident is protected. Before such communications can be considered a restricted report, the restricted report must be reported or forwarded to a sexual assault response coordinator for determination of eligibility.

16.48.2. If a victim tells Healthcare Personnel that a sexual assault has occurred, the Healthcare Personnel will notify the sexual assault response coordinator in cases of acquaintance or stranger (non-intimate partner) sexual assault. The requirement of AFI 44-102, *Community Health Management*, to report incidents of sexual assault to the Air Force Office of Special Investigations or other authorities as appropriate is expressly waived for restricted reports.

16.48.3. A victim advocate who is contacted by a victim wishing to make a restricted report but who has not been assigned by the sexual assault response coordinator to serve as the victim advocate for that individual will not enter into a discussion of the circumstances but will immediately refer the victim to the sexual assault response coordinator. The victim advocate is not required to report the initial contact to command or law enforcement.

## 16.49. Notification to Command of a Restricted Report.

Within 24 hours of receipt of a restricted report of an alleged acquaintance or stranger (non-intimate partner) sexual assault, the sexual assault response coordinator will notify the installation or host wing commander that a restricted report of an alleged sexual assault has been made and provide only non-identifiable information. Non-identifying information under the restricted reporting option is intended to provide commanders with general environmental information about the number and types of sexual assaults on the installation and is to be used to provide a better understanding of incidents of sexual assault. Neither commanders nor law enforcement may initiate investigations based on information about restricted reports provided by sexual assault response coordinators.

## 16.50. Unrestricted Reports.

Any report of a sexual assault made through normal reporting channels, including the victim's chain of command, law enforcement, and the Air Force Office of Special Investigations or other criminal investigative service is considered an Unrestricted Report. Any report of sexual assault made through the sexual assault response coordinator, victim advocate, or Healthcare Personnel by an individual who elects an Unrestricted Report and designates so in writing on the Victim Reporting Preference Statement will be forwarded to the Air Force Office of Special Investigations. The individual to whom the Unrestricted Report was made will notify the sexual assault response coordinator in cases of acquaintance or stranger (non-intimate partner) sexual assault.

**16.51. Use of Information:**

16.51.1. In cases of an unrestricted report of a sexual assault or information concerning a sexual assault is otherwise known, information concerning the victim and the offense will only be provided to governmental entities or persons with an established official need to know. Those who are deemed to have an official need to know in the Air Force routinely include: law enforcement; the commanders and first sergeants of the victim and the alleged assailant; legal personnel; the sexual assault response coordinator and victim advocate; and healthcare providers as required to perform their respective duties. The intent of this restriction is to protect the privacy of the victim.

16.51.2. Commanders notified of a sexual assault through an Unrestricted Report must take immediate steps to ensure the victim's physical safety, emotional security, and medical treatment needs are met and that the Air Force Office of Special Investigations or appropriate criminal investigative agency and sexual assault response coordinator are notified (in cases of spouse, same sex domestic partner, and/or unmarried intimate partner sexual assaults are referred to Air Force Family Advocacy Program). The appropriate commanders should determine whether temporary reassignment or relocation of the victim or alleged assailant is appropriate.

16.51.3. In cases where the victim consults the sexual assault response coordinator, prior to disclosure to the chain of command, law enforcement, Air Force Office of Special Investigations, or other criminal investigative service, and the victim does not elect a reporting option, the sexual assault response coordinator is not under any obligation or duty to inform investigators or commanders about the report and will not produce the report or disclose the communications surrounding the report.

**16.52. Addressing Victim Collateral Misconduct in Sexual Assault Cases:**

16.52.1. An investigation into the facts and circumstances surrounding an alleged sexual assault may produce evidence that the victim engaged in misconduct like underage drinking or other related alcohol offenses, adultery, drug abuse, fraternization, or other violations of instructions, regulations, or orders. According to the Uniformed Code of Military Justice, the *Manual for Courts-Martial*, and Air Force instructions, commanders are responsible for addressing misconduct in a manner that is consistent and appropriate to the circumstances.

16.52.2. Commanders have the authority to determine the appropriate disposition of alleged victim misconduct, to include deferring disciplinary action until after disposition of the sexual assault case. When considering what corrective actions may be appropriate, commanders must balance the objectives of holding members accountable for their own misconduct with the intent to avoid unnecessary additional trauma to sexual assault victims and the goal of encouraging reporting of sexual assaults. The gravity of any collateral misconduct by the victim, and the impact on good order and discipline, should be carefully considered in deciding what, if any, corrective action is appropriate. Commanders should consult with the servicing staff judge advocate prior to taking any action regarding collateral misconduct.

**16.53. Prevention and Response for the Deployed Environment:**

16.53.1. The Air Force will identify trained military sexual assault response coordinators (and/or trained civilian sexual assault response coordinators who volunteer) for Air Expeditionary Force rotational support for global contingency operations consistent with requirements established by the commander of Air Force forces. Normally, each Air Expeditionary Wing will warrant at least one sexual assault response coordinator requirement. For deployments smaller than an Air Expeditionary Force, deployed commanders must provide a sexual assault response capability consistent with Air Force requirements.

16.53.2. Home station unit commanders must ensure Air Force members are trained on both annual sexual assault and response training requirements and pre-deployment prior to any deployment.

**16.54. Conclusion.**

This chapter discussed some of the aspects of wing support including the Air Force Portal, military pay and allowances, leave management, LeaveWeb, military equal opportunity, legal services, ground safety, risk management, and policies and procedures for prevention of and response to sexual assault. Supervisors need to ensure their Airmen understand the value of applying the knowledge outlined in this chapter.

**Chapter 17**

**DRESS AND APPEARANCE**

*Section 17A—Overview*

**17.1. Introduction:**

17.1.1. Dress and personal appearance standards immediately identify us as United States Air Force Airmen. These standards are intended to ensure all Airmen maintain a distinctive, plain, standardized appearance. Deeply rooted in our Air Force heritage our dress and personal appearance standards provide visible examples of self-discipline, commitment and a willingness to set aside individuality for the betterment of the whole. Wearing the Air Force uniform means carrying on a tradition that identifies the person as a member of a historical profession, a close-knit society, quietly assured of his or her competence and professionalism.

17.1.2. The Air Force uniform developed slowly into what is worn today. During this evolution, the uniform design changed from one with many devices and accouterments to one with very few embellishments. The present Air Force uniform with authorized badges, insignia, and devices is plain yet distinctive, presenting the appearance of a military professional. Wearing the Air Force uniform means carrying on a tradition—one that identifies the person as a member of a historical profession, a close-knit society, quietly assured of his or her competence and professionalism. This chapter identifies the most common uniform items and combinations for enlisted members. **Note:** Consult AFI 36-2903, *Dress and Personal Appearance of Air Force Personnel*, for official guidance.

*Section 17B—Individual Responsibilities*

All Air Force members in uniform will adhere to standards of neatness, cleanliness, safety, uniformity, military image, and present the appearance of a disciplined service member. Air Force members will procure and maintain all mandatory clothing items, follow local supplements and procedures, and keep uniforms neat, clean, pressed, buttoned, and properly maintained. Members will not stand or walk with hands in pockets of any uniform combination (other than to insert or remove items). While walking in uniform use of personal electronic media devices, including ear pieces, speaker phones or text messaging is limited to emergencies or when official notifications are necessary. Military customs and courtesies take precedence. (**Exception:** Earphones are authorized during individual physical training when wearing the physical training uniform.) Air Force members will not smoke or use smokeless tobacco products, drink, or eat while walking in uniform. This also applies when Airmen are required to wear civilian clothes to perform assigned duties.

**17.2. When to Wear the Uniform:**

17.2.1. **Military Duties.**

As a rule, Air Force members must wear a uniform while performing military duties. Installation commanders will provide (at no cost) to enlisted members required organizational and functional items directed for wear. When members perform duty on other services' installations, they must comply with order of dress for that service, provided their standards are not less restrictive than the Air Force.

17.2.2. **Traveling.**

Wearing a uniform is optional when a member is departing from a military airfield on Department of Defense aircraft or United States government commercial contracted flights. Those who choose to wear civilian clothing will ensure items are neat, clean, and appropriate for inflight operations, the mode of travel, and the destination. Examples of inappropriate clothing include: ripped, torn, frayed, or patched clothing; tank tops, shorts, short skirts, undergarments worn as outer garment, bathing suits, and any garments which are revealing or display obscene, profane, or lewd words or drawings. The Airman Battle Uniform (ABU) is acceptable when traveling between military installations.

**17.3. Uniform Wear Restrictions.**

Airmen will not wear uniform items that do not meet Air Force specifications. Additionally, Air Force members may not wear uniform items to further political activities; for private employment or commercial interests; while participating in public speeches, interviews, picket lines, marches or rallies; or at any public demonstration when the perception may exist that the Air Force sanctions the cause.

**17.4. Personal Grooming Standards:**

17.4.1. **Hair.**

Hair will be clean, well-groomed, neat and present a professional appearance. If dyed, hair will look natural. Hair will not contain an excessive amount of grooming aids, touch the eyebrows, or protrude below the front band of properly worn headgear. **Exception:** Hair may be visible in front of the women's flight cap.

17.4.1.1. **Men.** Men's hair must have a tapered appearance on the sides and back, both with and without headgear. Hair will not exceed 1¼ inches in bulk, regardless of length, and will not exceed ¼ inch at the natural termination point. Hairstyles that are extreme, faddish, or violate safety requirements are not permitted. Men's hair will not touch the ears; only closely cut or shaved hair on the back of the neck may touch the collar. The block cut is permitted with tapered appearance. Men are also authorized cleanly shaven heads, military high-and-tight, or flat-top haircuts. Men will not have any visible items in, or attached to, their hair.

17.4.1.2. **Women.** Women must style their hair to present a professional appearance. Hair will not be worn in an extreme or faddish style, or violate safety requirements. Hair cannot extend below an invisible line drawn parallel to the ground at the bottom edge of the shirt collar, regardless of length. Hairstyles may include wear of conservative hairpins, combs, headbands, elastic bands, scrunchies, and barrettes. However, the items must match the individual's hair color. Women may not have shaved heads, military high-and-tight, or flat-top haircuts. Minimum length is ¼ inch, and hair will not exceed 3 inches in bulk. Long hair worn in a bun will be secured with no loose ends. When hair is in a ponytail, the hair must be pulled all the way through the elastic band, hang naturally downward, and not extend below the collar. Bangs and side-swept hair will not touch the eyebrows.

17.4.1.3. **Wigs/Hairpieces/Extensions.** Wigs, hairpieces, and extensions must meet the same standards required for natural hair. They must be of good quality, fit properly, and not exceed limits stated for natural hair. Synthetic hair is not authorized when prohibited by safety and mission. Wigs will not be used to cover unauthorized hairstyles.

17.4.2. **Beards, Mustaches, and Sideburns (Men):**

17.4.2.1. Beards are not worn except when authorized by a commander, on the advice of a medical official, for health reasons. If authorized by the commander, members must keep facial hair trimmed not to exceed ¼ inch in length. If granted a shaving waiver, members will not shave any facial hair in a manner as to give a sculptured appearance. Commanders and supervisors will monitor treatment progress to control shaving waivers.

17.4.2.2. Mustaches, if worn, will not extend downward beyond the lip line of the upper lip or extend sideways beyond a vertical line drawn upward from both corners of the mouth.

17.4.2.3. Sideburns, if worn, will be neatly trimmed and tapered in the same manner as the haircut. They will be straight and of even width (not flared) and end in a clean-shaven horizontal line. They will not extend below the bottom of the orifice of the ear opening.

17.4.3. **Cosmetics (Women).**

Cosmetics must be conservative and in good taste and will not be worn in field conditions.

17.4.4. **Fingernails.**

Fingernails must be clean, well-groomed, not exceed ¼ inch in length past tip of finger, and not interfere with duty performance or hinder proper fit of prescribed safety equipment or uniform items.

17.4.5. **Nail Polish (Women).**

When worn, nail polish will be a single color that complements skin tone. Bright red, orange, purple, black, and other extreme colors are not authorized. Decorations are prohibited, but French manicures are authorized.

**17.5. Tattoos and Brands:**

17.5.1. **Unauthorized Types.**

Tattoos and brands, anywhere on the body, that are obscene or advocate sexual, racial, ethnic, or religious discrimination or commonly associated with gangs, extremist, and/or supremacist organizations, are prohibited in and out of uniform. Tattoos and brands that are prejudicial to good order and discipline or of a nature that tends to bring discredit upon the Air Force are prohibited in and out of uniform.

### 17.5.2. Inappropriate Types.

Excessive tattoos and brands must not be exposed or visible (includes being visible through the uniform) while in uniform. Excessive is defined as any tattoo or brand that exceeds ¼ coverage of the exposed body part and those above the collarbone and readily visible when wearing an open-collar uniform.

### 17.5.3. Violations.

Failure to observe the mandatory provisions listed below are a violation of Article 92, Uniform Code of Military Justice. Violations for the following types of tattoos and brands are as follows:

17.5.3.1. **Unauthorized.** Any member who obtains unauthorized tattoos will be required to remove them at his or her own expense. Depending on the circumstances, commanders may seek Air Force medical support for voluntary tattoo removal. Members who fail to remove unauthorized tattoos in a timely manner will be subject to involuntary separation.

17.5.3.2. **Inappropriate.** Members are not allowed to display excessive tattoos that would detract from an appropriate professional image while in uniform. Commanders will use AFI 36-2903 to assist in determining appropriate military image and acceptability of tattoos displayed by members in uniform. Air Force members with existing tattoos that do not meet standards must keep them completely covered using current uniform items (for example, long-sleeved shirt or blouse, pants or slacks, dark hosiery, etc.) or volunteer to remove tattoos. Members who do not comply with these requirements are subject to disciplinary action.

## 17.6. Body Piercing.

Body piercing standards are provided below:

**Note:** In uniform, women are authorized to wear one set of earrings as described in paragraph 17.15.1.

### 17.6.1. In Uniform.

Members are prohibited from attaching, affixing, or displaying objects, articles, jewelry, or ornamentation to or through the ear, nose, tongue, eyebrows, lips, or any exposed body part (includes visible through the uniform). Women may wear one set of earrings.

### 17.6.2. In Civilian Attire:

17.6.2.1. **Official Duty.** Members are prohibited from attaching, affixing, or displaying objects, articles, jewelry, or ornamentation to or through the ear, nose, tongue, eyebrows, lips, or any exposed body part (includes being visible through clothing). Women may wear one set of earrings.

17.6.2.2. **Off Duty on a Military Installation.** Members are prohibited from attaching, affixing, or displaying objects, articles, jewelry, or ornamentation to or through the ear (males), nose, tongue, eyebrows, lips, or any exposed body part (includes being visible through clothing).

### 17.6.3. Imposing More Restrictive Standards.

Major command commander's may impose more restrictive standards for tattoos/brands/body markings and body ornaments, on or off duty, in those locations where Air Force-wide standards may not be adequate to address cultural sensitivities (e.g., overseas). Additionally, major command commanders may impose more restrictive standards on those performing highly visible special mission requirements or special duty positions (for example, more restrictive standards for permanently assigned recruiters, reserve officer training corps cadre, Officer Training School cadre, United States Air Force Academy cadre, military training instructors, military training leaders, instructors in any training environment, etc.).

**Note:** According to AFI 36-2903, individuals are prohibited from intentionally pursuing body alterations or modifications that result in a visible, physical effect that disfigures, deforms, or otherwise detracts from a professional military image.

## Section 17C—Uniform and Accessory Standards

## 17.7. Mess Dress Uniform.

The mess dress is an optional uniform for enlisted personnel. This uniform is worn for social or official functions (for example, "black tie" events); a tuxedo or evening gown is the civilian equivalent. Nametag and headgear are not worn. Enlisted may wear the semiformal service dress if they do not have a mess dress. Refer to AFI 36-2903 for semiformal wear instructions. When in mess dress, saluting is not required. Mess dress items include:

17.7.1. **Jacket.**

The jacket for men and women is semi-fitted, single-breasted, having a straight back with three wing and star buttons positioned diagonally on each side of the coat. Women's jackets have a satin shawl collar and lapels. Men's jackets have a front link chain closure with button on each end while women's jackets have no front link chain closure. For both men and women, sleeves end ¼ to ½ inch below the wrist. Men wear 4-inch chevrons. Women wear 3½ or 4-inch chevrons. The jacket and trousers or skirt must match in shade and material. Accouterments include occupational, duty, miscellaneous badges, and command insignia. Aeronautical, space, cyber, missile operations, and chaplain badges are mandatory. Miniature medals will be worn.

17.7.2. **Trousers (Men).**

The trousers are high rise with side pockets, ⅞ inch blue striping, and no cuffs or pleats.

17.7.3. **Skirt (Women).**

The skirt is ankle length (no higher than the ankle, no longer than the bottom of the heel). Furthermore, the skirt has a one-panel front and a one- or two-panel back, is straight hanging, and has a seam on the left side split to the top of the knee. Women may also wear an A-line style without the split.

17.7.4. **Shirt/Blouse.**

The shirt or blouse is a conventional white long-sleeved dress type with a turndown collar and French cuffs with pleats. Women may wear the long-sleeved blouse with barrel cuffs. Wearing a shirt or blouse with a military crease is prohibited.

17.7.5. **Tie.**

Men will wear the blue satin bow tie. The blue satin inverted-V tie tab with self-fastening tails is mandatory for women.

17.7.6. **Cuff Links.**

Cuff links are mandatory for men; optional for women, with the mess dress uniform. They will either be silver, satin finish or highly polished with the "wing and star" design; silver, highly polished with the Air Force symbol; or plain silver, highly polished, commercial design with dimensions and shape similar to the "wing and star" cuff links.

17.7.7. **Studs.**

Studs are mandatory for men; optional for women. They can be either pearl centered, silver rimmed, highly polished, satin finished or plain silver, highly polished, commercial design with dimensions and shape similar to the pearl centered studs. The finish must match cuff links.

17.7.8. **Cummerbund.**

Men and women will wear the blue satin cummerbund, pleated and without design, with the open edge of the pleats facing upward.

17.7.8.1. **Suspenders.** Men must wear suspenders. They will be solid white, blue, or black and will not be visible when wearing the jacket.

17.7.8.2. **Shoes.** Men will wear low quarters, and women will wear pumps. See AFI 36-2903 for additional shoe requirements. Boots are not authorized.

17.7.8.3. **Outer garments and Accessories.** Men and women may wear the top coat or all-weather coat, black scarf, black gloves, blue winter cap, and black earmuffs. Women may carry handbags. Men will wear socks, and women will wear hose.

**17.8. Service Dress Uniform.**

This uniform consists of the blue service coat and trousers/slacks or skirt (women), light blue long- or short-sleeved shirt, and polyester herringbone twill tie for men or tie tab for women. With arms hanging naturally, the sleeves of the service coat will end ¼ to ½ inch below the wrist. Ensure the bottom edge of the coat extends 3 to 3½ inches below the top of the thigh.

17.8.1. **Mandatory Accouterments.**

Mandatory accouterments to be worn with the service dress coat are:

17.8.1.1. **"U.S." Lapel Insignia.** The "U.S." lapel insignia is placed halfway up the seam, resting on but not over the seam. The "U.S." letters are parallel with the ground. Enlisted "U.S." insignia have circles around the "U.S." and officer "U.S." insignias do not.

17.8.1.2. **Nametag.** The nametag is metal engraved, brushed satin finish with blue letters; center metallic nametag on right side between the sleeve seam and the fold of the lapel. Bottom of nametag is parallel with bottom of ribbons.

17.8.1.3. **Ribbons.** Center ribbons resting on but not over the edge of the welt pocket. Wear a maximum of four devices on each ribbon. Wear all authorized ribbons and devices.

17.8.1.4. **Chevrons.** Center the sleeve chevron (4 inch for men; 3 ½ or 4-inch for women) halfway between the shoulder seam and elbow when the arm is bent at a 90-degree angle.

17.8.1.5. **Chaplain, Aeronautical, Space, Cyberspace, and Missile Operations Badges.** Chaplain, aeronautical, space, cyberspace, and missile operations badges are mandatory.

17.8.2. **Accouterments:**

17.8.2.1. **Badges.** Air Force members are highly encouraged to wear their current occupational badge. Chaplain, aeronautical, space, cyberspace, and missile operations badges are mandatory; others are optional. Wear highly polished badges only, midsized or regular; do not mix sizes. (**Note:** The oxidized heritage wings are authorized for wear. Midsized or regular badges may be worn with the medical badge.) Center the aeronautical, occupational, or miscellaneous badge ½ inch above the top row of ribbons. Center an additional badge ½ inch above the first one. Men center the duty or miscellaneous badge 1½ inches below the top of the welt pocket, and/or on the right side centered 1½ inches below the nametag. Center a third badge ½ inch above the nametag. Women wear duty or miscellaneous badges centered ½ inch above the nametag and centered ½ inch apart. No more than four badges will be worn at one time.

17.8.2.2. **Tie (Men).** The necktie is mandatory. A tie tack or clasp is optional. Authorized tacks/clasps include the Air Force symbol, grade insignia, or wing and star. If worn, center between the bottom edge of the knot and bottom tip of the tie.

17.8.2.3. **Tie Tab (Women).** Wear of the blue satin inverted-V tie tab is mandatory.

## 17.9. Service Uniform.

The service uniform consists of the light blue, long- or short-sleeved shirt/blouse, and trousers/slacks or skirt (women).

### 17.9.1. Short-Sleeved Shirt/Blouse.

Sleeves must barely touch, or come within 1 inch of touching the forearm when the arm is bent at a 90-degree angle. The tie (men) and tie tab (women) are optional unless the short-sleeved shirt is worn with the service dress uniform. Mandatory accouterments include:

### 17.9.2. Nametag.

Men will center the blue nametag on, but not over, the edge of the right pocket. Women will center the blue nametag on the right side, even with to 1½ inches higher or lower than the first exposed button.

### 17.9.3. Chevrons.

Center the 3½-inch sleeve chevron halfway between the shoulder seam and bottom edge of sleeve.

### 17.9.4. Chaplain, Aeronautical, Space, Cyberspace, and Missile Operations Badges.

Chaplain, Aeronautical, space, cyberspace, and missile operations badges are mandatory.

### 17.9.5. Optional Accouterments.

Optional accouterments include:

17.9.5.1. **Ribbons.** Men center ribbons resting on, but not over, the edge of the left pocket between the left and right edges. Women center ribbons on the left side parallel with the ground, aligning the bottom of the ribbons with the bottom of the nametag. Air Force members may wear only authorized awards and devices when wearing ribbons. Ribbons are optional; however, if any are worn, all ribbons and devices must be worn. Ribbons must be clean, unfrayed, and not have a visible protective coating. Wear the ribbon with the highest precedence nearest the lapel on the top row. Ribbons are not worn on outer garments such as raincoats, all-weather coats, or lightweight blue jackets. For additional information on placement and arrangement of ribbons, see AFI 36-2903.

17.9.5.2. **Badges.** A maximum of four earned badges may be worn on any blue service uniform. A maximum of two badges may be worn on the left side of the uniform above ribbons, or the pocket if ribbons are not worn. Wear only aeronautical, occupational, and miscellaneous badges in this location. Aeronautical and space badges are worn above occupational and miscellaneous badges. When more than one aeronautical badge is worn, the second badge becomes optional. A maximum of two occupational badges may be worn; the badge representing the current career field (regardless of level earned) is worn in the top position. **Exception:** Chaplain and aeronautical badges are always worn in the top position when wearing two occupational badges. With the exception of the heritage wings, wear highly polished badges only, midsized or regular size, and do not mix sizes. **Note:** The medical badge may be worn with midsized or regular badges.

17.9.5.3. **Men.** Chaplain, aeronautical, space, cyberspace and missile operations badges are mandatory. Others are optional. Center aeronautical, occupational, miscellaneous, etc., badge ½ inch above ribbons or pocket if not wearing ribbons. Center an additional badge ½ inch above the first one. Center the duty or miscellaneous badge on the lower portion of the left pocket, between the left and right edges and bottom of the flap and bottom of the pocket, and on the right pocket between the left and right edges and bottom of the flap and bottom of the pocket. **Exception:** The missile badge is worn centered on the left pocket only.

17.9.5.4. **Women.** Chaplain, Aeronautical, Space and Cyberspace badges are mandatory. Others are optional. Center the aeronautical, occupational, miscellaneous, etc., badge ½ inch above ribbons, or center badge parallel to the nametag if not wearing ribbons. Center an additional badge ½ inch above the first one. Center the duty and miscellaneous badge ½ inch above the nametag. **Exception:** The missile badge can be centered 1½ inches below bottom of ribbons or on the right side ½ inch above the nametag.

17.9.5.5. **Long-Sleeved Shirt/Blouse.** The collar of the shirt/blouse shows ¼ or ½ inch above the coat collar, with arms hanging naturally and sleeves extended to ¼ to ½ inch below the wrist. The man's shirt has two pleated pockets and convertible cuffs. The woman's blouse will have a tapered fit. A tapered fit is optional for men. Military creases are prohibited. **Note:** The mandatory and optional accouterments are the same as the short-sleeved shirt/blouse. **Exception:** The tie or tab is mandatory when wearing the long-sleeved shirt/blouse.

17.9.5.6. **Tie (Men):**

17.9.5.6.1. The polyester or silk herringbone twill tie is mandatory when wearing the service dress uniform, the semiformal uniform, and the long-sleeved shirt.

17.9.5.6.2. The tie must not have a design or sheen and can be 2 or 3 inches wide and may be tapered at the center with a pointed end. The fabric can be polyester, silk, wool, synthetic, or a blend. Woven and pre-tied ties are optional.

17.9.5.7. **Tie Tab (Women).** The tie tab is a blue inverted-V, constructed of a polyester herringbone, with self-fastening tails. This tie tab is mandatory when wearing the service dress uniform, the semiformal uniform, and the long-sleeved blouse.

17.9.5.8. **Trousers (Men) and Slacks (Women).** The trousers are trim-fitted. The slacks fit naturally over the hips for women with no bunching at the waist or bagging at the seat. The bottom front of the trousers/slacks rests on the front of the shoe or boot with a slight break in the crease. The bottom back of the trousers/slacks is approximately ⅞ inch longer than the front. The silver tip of the belt extends beyond the buckle facing the wearer's left for men and right for women, with no blue fabric showing between the buckle and belt tip.

17.9.5.9. **Skirt (Women).** The skirt hangs naturally over the hips with a slight flare. Skirt length is no shorter than the top of the kneecap or longer than the bottom of the kneecap. The silver tip of the belt extends beyond the buckle facing the wearer's right, with no blue fabric showing between the buckle and belt tip.

## 17.10. Flight Cap.

The flight cap is worn slightly to the wearer's right with the vertical crease of the cap in line with the center of the forehead, in a straight line with the nose. The cap is approximately 1 inch from the eyebrows. When not worn, tuck the cap under the belt (on the wearer's left side for men, and either side for women) between the first and second belt loops. Do not fold the cap over the belt.

## 17.11. Hosiery (Women).

Hosiery must be worn with the skirt. Hosiery must be a commercial sheer nylon in neutral, dark brown, black, off-black, or dark blue shades that complement the uniform and the individual's skin tone. Do not wear patterned hose.

## 17.12. Footwear:

### 17.12.1. Low Quarters.

Shoes are black oxford, lace-up style with a plain rounded toe or plain rounded, capped toe. Low quarters have no design and are smooth or scotch-grained leather or manmade material with an optional high gloss or patent finish. The sole will not exceed ½ inch in thickness, and the heel will not be higher than 1 inch (measured from the inside front of the heel). The shoe may have a low wedge heel. Plain black socks without design are worn with low quarters. **Note:** Women may wear hose.

### 17.12.2. Pumps (Women).

Pumps are authorized for wear with the blue service uniform. The pumps will be a plain black commercial design without ornamentation, made of smooth or scotch-grained leather or man-made material, high gloss or patent finish. The height of heels should be no higher than 2½ inches (measured from inside sole of the shoe to the end of the heel lift). Faddish styles will not be worn (extreme toes, pointed, squared, or extreme heel shapes).

### 17.12.3. Black Combat Boots.

The black combat boot can be worn with the service dress and services uniforms when not wearing a skirt, maternity service dress and/or maternity jumper. Laces will either be tied and tucked in the boot or tied and wrapped around the boot. No "bowtie" boot laces. Logos will be the same color as the boot. Boots must be black, with or without safety toe, plain rounded toe, or rounded capped toe with or without perforated seam. They may have a high gloss or patent finish.

## 17.13. ABUs.

The ABU replaces the temperate and hot weather battle dress uniform and the desert camouflage uniform. ABUs may be worn off base for short convenience stops and when eating at restaurants where people wear comparable civilian attire. Do not wear ABUs off base to eat in restaurants where most diners wear business attire or when going to establishments that operate primarily to serve alcohol. The basic ABU configuration is ABU shirt, trousers, patrol cap, T-shirt, rigger belt, boots, and socks. The ABU is a wash-and-wear uniform. Starching and hot pressing of the ABU is prohibited. Light ironing and center creasing of enlisted chevrons is authorized.

### 17.13.1. ABU Coat (Shirt).

The long-sleeved ABU shirt sleeves may be rolled up. If rolled up, the cuffs will remain visible and the sleeve will rest at, or come within 1 inch of the forearm when the arm is bent at a 90-degree angle. The ABU shirt may be removed in the immediate work area as determined appropriate by local leadership.

#### 17.13.1.1. Accouterments:

17.13.1.2. **Tapes.** Center the "U.S. AIR FORCE" tape immediately above the left breast pocket. Center the nametape (last name only) immediately above the right breast pocket. Cut off or fold tapes to match pocket width.

17.13.1.3. **Chevrons.** Center the chevron (4 inch for men; 3½ or 4 inch for women) halfway between the shoulder seam and elbow when the arm is bent at a 90-degree angle. When sleeves are rolled up, chevrons do not need to be fully visible, but rank must be distinguishable.

17.13.1.4. **Badges.** Chaplain, aeronautical, space, cyberspace and missile operations badges are mandatory; all other occupational and qualification badges and patches are optional. No more than a combined total of three chaplain, aeronautical, space, cyberspace, missile operations or occupational, or qualification badges and/or graduate patches will be worn on the wearer's left. If authorized, the Security Forces, Fire Protection and Office of Special Investigations duty shields, missile and/or excellence-in competition badge will be worn on the wearer's left pocket of the ABU. No other items are authorized in this location. The duty shield or badge will be centered between the bottom of the pocket flap, bottom of the pocket and left and right edges. Third and/or fourth qualification badges may be worn on the right pocket or above the nametape (as appropriate).

17.13.1.5. **Trousers.** Trousers must be evenly bloused (gathered in and draped loosely) over or tucked into the top of the combat boots to present a bloused appearance. The belt may extend past the buckle.

17.13.1.6. **Patrol Cap.** ABU patrol caps are authorized headgear for wear with the ABU. Organizational caps are not authorized. **Exception:** REDHORSE and Combat Arms Training and Maintenance (on the range only). Mixing and matching of the ABU and REDHORSE ABU cap is authorized.

17.13.1.7. **T-shirt.** ABU T-shirts are tan desert sand-colored, crew neck. *Exception:* Squadron commanders may authorize wear of standardized color morale t-shirts on Friday or during special events.

17.13.1.8. **Boots.** ABU sage green boots are authorized for wear with all utility uniforms. Desert tan boots will not be worn with the ABU unless authorized by the Theater commander for wear only in theater.

17.13.1.9. **Socks.** ABU sock color is sage green when worn with the sage green or tan boots. Plain white socks may be worn under the sage green socks as long as the white socks are not visible.

## 17.14. Physical Training Uniform and Improved Physical Training Uniform.

Physical Training Uniform/Improved Physical Training Uniform (short- or long-sleeve) T-shirt will be tucked in when worn with the shorts or running pants. Physical Training Uniform/Improved Physical Training Uniform shorts lining may be removed, but do not modify other physical training items. Short, mid and full length solid black or dark blue form fitting sportswear (i.e. spandex, lycra or elastic) may be worn and visible under physical training running shorts. Jacket, when worn, must be zipped at least halfway. Socks will be white or black, any length, and may have small conservative trademark logos. Hats and winter caps (knit) are authorized during personal physical training. Commanders determine authorized headgear during organized physical training. The uniform items are authorized for wear with conservative civilian attire during individual/personal physical training or while off duty. No offensive wording, graphics or photos are authorized on any item worn with the physical training gear. Bandanas and other similar headscarves and headgear are not authorized unless due to medical waiver condition. Athletic style shoes are mandatory. For additional guidance, refer to AFI 36-2903.

## 17.15. Accessory Standards:

### 17.15.1. Jewelry.

Bracelets (no wider than ½ inch) and watches must be conservative, not present a safety hazard, and be worn around the wrist. No more than three rings may be worn. Rings are worn only at the base of the finger. Thumb rings are not authorized. Necklaces may be worn if concealed under a collar or undershirt. Women are authorized to wear small spherical, conservative, round diamond, gold, white pearl or silver earrings with any uniform combination. Earrings must be worn as a matching set and should fit tightly without extending below the earlobe, except for the connecting band on clip earrings.

### 17.15.2. Eyeglasses and Sunglasses.

Eyeglasses, sunglasses, and wraparound sunglasses with conservative ornamentation are authorized. Frames may be black or brown material or gold or silver wire. Brand name glasses may be worn with a small logo on the frames or lens, which must be of the same color. Sunglasses must have conservative lenses and frames; faddish styles and mirrored lenses are prohibited. Sunglasses are not permitted in formation, except when authorized by a commander or commandant on the advice of a medical official for medical reasons (for example, Photorefractive Keratectomy or Lasik surgery). Eyeglasses and sunglasses must not be worn around the neck, or on the top or back of the head or exposed hanging on the uniform. Eyeglasses and sunglasses will be worn in the manner for which they were made.

### 17.15.3. Additional Items:

17.15.3.1. Pencils and pens must be concealed except when carried in the appropriate compartments of the ABU. Electronic devices worn on the uniform must be solid black, silver, dark blue, or gray, or covered in black, silver, dark blue, or gray, and must be conservative. Only one electronic device at a time may be worn on the uniform belt. While walking in uniform use of personal electronic media devices, including ear pieces, speaker phones, and/or text messaging is limited to emergencies or when official notifications are necessary. Military customs and courtesies take precedence. **Exception:** Headphones and earphones (iPods, Mp3, etc.) are authorized while wearing the physical training uniform during individual or personal physical training in the fitness center or on designated running areas unless prohibited by the installation commander.

17.15.3.2. Lanyards for access passes, badges, and common access cards must be plain, dark blue or black with silver or plastic small conservative link chains and clear plastic. Green may also be worn with the ABU. These attachments must not present a safety issue. Umbrellas must be plain, black, and carried in the left hand. Attaché cases, gym bags, and backpacks are carried in the left hand, on the left shoulder, or both shoulders (must not interfere with rendering the proper salute). Olive drab, sage green and ABU pattern are authorized colors for gym bags. Olive drab, sage green and ABU pattern are an authorized color for back packs and any authorized color back pack may be worn/carried with any uniform. A conservative manufacturer's logo is allowed.

## 17.16. Conclusion.

This chapter covered many common areas of interest in our Air Force uniforms. The information contained in this chapter is not the governing directive with regard to uniform wear. Refer to the most current edition of AFI 36-2903 for specific guidance and authority.

# Chapter 18

# FIT FORCE

## Section 18A—Overview

### 18.1. Introduction.

This chapter covers the fitness program, proper nutrition, substance abuse, tobacco use, suicide prevention, posttraumatic stress disorder, reintegration from deployment, medical care, and the Wingman concept. Air Force members must be physically fit to support the Air Force mission. Commanders and supervisors must incorporate fitness into the Air Force culture to establish an environment for members to maintain physical fitness and health to meet expeditionary mission requirements and deliver a fit-and-ready force. The annual fitness assessment provides commanders with a tool to assist in the determination of overall fitness of their military personnel.

## Section 18B—Physical Fitness and Fitness Components

### 18.2. Physical Fitness, Optimal Performance and Mission Readiness.

Adequate physical fitness levels ensure every Airman can properly support the Air Force mission while performing at optimal capacity. The goal of the fitness program is to motivate all members to participate in a year-round physical conditioning program emphasizing total fitness to include proper aerobic conditioning, muscular fitness training, and healthy eating. An active lifestyle will increase productivity, optimize health, and decrease absenteeism while maintaining a higher level of readiness.

### 18.3. Physical Fitness.

The five major components of fitness are cardiorespiratory endurance, body composition, muscular strength, muscular endurance, and flexibility. Warm-up and cool down are also essential components of a complete physical fitness program.

18.3.1. Cardiorespiratory endurance is the ability to perform large muscle, dynamic, moderate-to-high intensity exercise for prolonged periods.

18.3.2. Body composition is the relative portion of the body comprised of fat and fat-free tissue.

18.3.3. Muscular strength is the maximum force generated by a specific muscle or muscle group.

18.3.4. Muscular endurance is the ability of a muscle group to execute repeated contractions over a period of sufficient time duration to cause muscular fatigue.

18.3.5. Flexibility is the maximum ability to move a joint freely, without pain, through a range of motion.

### 18.4. Aerobic Fitness.

A successful cardiorespiratory endurance exercise program should address modality (type of exercise), volume (frequency multiplied by duration) and intensity.

18.4.1. **Mode.**

Select activities that involve a large proportion of total muscle mass, maximize use of large muscles, (*e.g.,* muscles around the thigh and hip), involve dynamic, rhythmic muscle contractions, and minimize static (no movement) contraction and use of small muscles. Examples are running, cycling, swimming, rowing, jogging, vigorous walking, indoor aerobic exercise machines, and some sports *if* they are continuous in nature.

18.4.2. **Volume (frequency multiplied by duration).**

Accomplish moderately intense aerobic activity 30 minutes a day, five days a week *or* vigorously intense aerobic activity 20 minutes to 25 minutes a day, 3 days a week *and* muscle fitness exercise (see below), or an equivalent combination of moderately and vigorously intense aerobic activity. For additional and more extensive health and fitness benefits, accomplish moderately intense aerobic activity 300 minutes (5 hours) a week, or accomplish vigorously intense aerobic activity 150 minutes a week, or an equivalent combination. Generally, the minimal levels of exercise volume and intensity above are necessary to maintain health and fitness, while the higher levels are necessary to improve health and fitness.

18.4.3. **Intensity.**

Intensity refers to how hard one exercises. Moderately intense aerobic activity equates to continuous exercise that raises heart and respiratory rates, initiates sweating (varies with climate), and permits conversation; vigorously intense aerobic activity elicits higher physiological responses and permits light or broken conversation. Intensity, considered the most important variable in training, may be prescribed as a percentage of maximum velocity, or percentages of physiological variables, i.e., a percent of maximal volume of oxygen consumed (%VO$_2$ max) or percent of maximal heart rate (%heart rate max). One formula for determining exercise intensity by heart rate is presented in Figure 18.1.

**Figure 18.1. Heart Rate Formula.**

220 - age = maximum heart rate for Airmen under 40 years of age.

Max heart rate = 208 – 0.7(age) for Airmen age 40 years and above.

Measure resting heart rate for three to four days shortly after waking for a 60 second period, while in the same body position each day. Take an average of the measures.

- Calculate heart rate range. Heart Rate Range = Maximal heart rate – Resting heart rate.

- Calculate minimum, optimal (target), and do-not-exceed (safety) exercise heart rates:

- Minimum exercise heart rate = (50% Heart Rate Range) + Resting heart rate.

- Optimal exercise heart rate = (75% Heart Rate Range) + Resting heart rate.

- Do-not-exceed exercise heart rate = (85% Heart Rate Range) + Resting heart rate.

For example, a 30 year old Air Force member with a Resting heart rate of 70 beats a minute calculates Maximal heart rate as 220 – 30 = 190 beats a minute and heart rate Range as 190 – 70 = 120. Applying the equations:

- Minimum exercise heart rate = 50% (120) + 70 = 60 + 70 = 130 beats a minute.

- Optimal exercise heart rate = 75% (120) + 70 = 90 + 70 = 160 beats a minute.

- Do-not-exceed exercise heart rate = 85% (120) + 70 = 102 + 70 = 172 beats/min.

Therefore, this individual should keep exercise heart rate above 130 beats a minute, but below 172 beats a minute, targeting 160 beats a minute for at least 20 minutes to 25 minutes 3 days a week. Unfit individuals should start at the lower end of the heart rate Range. As fitness level increases, the resting heart rate will decrease, therefore increase the intensity percentage from low (50%) towards optimal (75%). Also, base fitness personnel can help fine tune these calculations taking into account medications, risk of injury, and individual preferences and objectives.

## 18.5. Muscular Strength and Endurance Training.

A successful strength and endurance training program should include the principles of specificity, regularity, recovery, balance, and variety.

### 18.5.1. Principle of Specificity.

A strength training program should provide resistance to specific muscle groups that need to be strengthened. These groups can be identified by doing a simple assessment of functional movement. The Airman slowly does work-related or functional movements he or she wants to improve upon. An example would be the Airman whose job requires them to bend over, pick up an object, and place it in an overhead position. This work-related task has the functional movement of a squat and an overhead press with a weight. By incorporating these moves into a strength training program, the Airman can improve strength and, therefore, improve work-related tasks while reducing injuries by being conditioned in those muscles needed to perform the work. If the Airman's performance of a task is not adequate, or if he/she wishes to improve, strength training for the identified muscles will be beneficial. In this way, he/she ensures maximum carryover value to his/her warrior tasks.

### 18.5.2. Principle of Regularity.

Exercise must be done regularly to produce a training effect. Sporadic exercise may do more harm than good. Airmen can maintain a moderate level of strength by doing proper strength workouts only once a week for a short period of time if they have already established a strong baseline level of muscular fitness. However, three workouts per week are best for optimal gains. The principle of regularity also applies to the exercises for individual muscle groups. An Airman can work out three times a week, but when different muscle groups are exercised at each workout, the principle of regularity is violated and gains in strength are minimal. Airmen should strive for exercising the same muscle group a minimum of twice each week.

### 18.5.3. **Principle of Recovery.**

Consecutive days of hard resistance training for the same muscle group can be detrimental. The muscles must be allowed sufficient recovery time to adapt. Strength training may be done every day only if the exercised muscle groups are rotated, so the same muscle or muscle group is not trained (exercised) on consecutive days. There should be at least a 48-hour recovery period between workouts for the same muscle groups. For example, the legs can be trained with weights on Monday, Wednesday, and Friday and the upper body muscles on Tuesday, Thursday, and Saturday. Recovery is also important within a workout. The recovery time between different exercises and sets depends, in part, on the intensity of the workout. Normally, the recovery time between sets should be 30-180 seconds.

### 18.5.4. **Principle of Balance.**

When developing a strength training program, remember the importance of including exercises to work all the major muscle groups – in both the upper and lower body. You should not work just the muscle groups in the upper body, with the idea running will strengthen the legs. Most muscles are organized into opposing pairs; activating one muscle results in a pulling motion, while activating the opposing muscle results in the opposite or pushing movement. When planning a training session, one training technique is to follow a pushing exercise with a pulling exercise resulting in movement at the same joints. For example, follow an overhead press with a lateral pull-down exercise. This technique helps ensure good strength balance between opposing muscle groups which may, in turn, reduce the risk of injury. Sequence the program to exercise the larger muscle groups first, then the smaller muscles.

### 18.5.5. **Principle of Variety.**

Using different equipment, changing the exercises, and altering the volume/intensity are good ways to add variety – and they may also produce better results. The Airmen should periodically substitute different exercises for given muscle groups. For example, Airmen can do squats with a barbell instead of leg presses on a weight machine. Also, for variety or due to necessity (for example, when in the field), they can switch to partner-resisted exercises or another form of resistance training. However, avoid frequent fundamental changes as Airmen may become frustrated if they do not have enough time to adapt or to see improvements in strength.

## 18.6. **Flexibility Training:**

18.6.1. Flexibility is an important component of any fitness program. Many activity-related injuries have their root in lack of flexibility. Think of muscles as rubber bands. When they are cold, they are rigid and brittle. When warm, they stretch and retract more easily. Conducting a good warm-up before exercising and a good cool down upon completion will help prevent injury and reduce muscle soreness.

18.6.2. Regardless of your current fitness level, you should always begin your exercise sessions with a warm-up and end it with a cool down. Recommendations are listed in paragraphs 18.8.1 and 18.8.2. below.

## 18.7. **Body Composition.**

The two largest contributing factors to maintaining a positive body composition are exercise and diet.

18.7.1. A combination of exercise and diet is the best way to lose excessive body fat. Losing 1-2 pounds a week is a realistic goal best accomplished by reducing caloric intake and increasing energy expenditure. In other words, eat less and exercise more. Dieting alone can cause the body to believe the body is being starved. In response, the body tries to conserve its fat reserves by slowing down its metabolic rate and, as a result, loses at a slower rate.

18.7.2. Airmen must consume a minimum number of calories from all the major food groups, with the calories distributed over all the daily meals – including snacks and drinks. This ensures an adequate consumption of necessary vitamins and minerals. A male, not under medical supervision, requires a caloric intake of at least 1,500; women require at least 1,200 calories and Airmen should avoid diets failing to meet these criteria.

18.7.3. There is no "quick and easy" way to improve body composition. Losing fat safely takes time and patience.

18.7.4. Exercise not only burn calories, but helps the body maintain its useful muscle mass and may help keep the body's metabolic rate high during dieting. Fat is best utilized during aerobic exercise. Aerobic exercise, which uses lots of oxygen, is the best type of activity for burning fat. Aerobic exercise includes jogging, walking, swimming, bicycling, cross-country skiing, rowing, stair climbing, and jumping rope. Anaerobic activities, such as sprinting or lifting heavy weights, burn little, if any, fat.

**18.8. Warm-up and Cool Down:**

18.8.1. **The Warm-up.**

Before beginning any vigorous physical activity, you should prepare your body for exercise. The dynamic warm-up increases the flow of blood to the muscles and tendons, thus helping reduce the risk of injury and increasing the joint's range of motion and positively affects the speed of muscular contraction. The following is the recommended sequence of dynamic warm-up activities for 5-7 minutes before vigorous exercise:

18.8.1.1. Slowly jog in place or walk for 1-2 minutes. This causes a gradual increase in the heart rate, blood pressure, circulation, and increases the temperature of the active muscles.

18.8.1.2. Slowly rotate joints (for example, arm circles, knee and ankle rotations) to gradually increase their range of motion; work each major joint for 5-10 seconds.

18.8.1.3. Slowly mimic the activities to be performed. For example, lift a lighter weight to warm up before lifting the heavier one; this helps prepare the neuromuscular pathways. The dynamic warm-up increases the flow of blood to the muscles and tendons, helping reduce the risk of injury, increasing the joint's range of motion, and positively affects the speed of muscular contraction.

18.8.2. **Cool Down.**

18.8.2.1. Do not stop suddenly after vigorous exercise, but gradually bring your body back to a resting state by slowly decreasing the intensity of the activity. After running, for example, you should walk for 1-2 minutes. Stopping exercise suddenly can cause blood to pool in the muscles, thereby reducing blood flow to the heart and brain. This may cause fainting or abnormal heart rhythm and this could lead to serious complications.

18.8.2.2. Repeat the stretches done in your warm-up to help ease muscle tension and any immediate feeling of muscle soreness; be careful not to 'over-stretch'. The muscles are warm from activity and could be over-stretched to the point of injury.

18.8.2.3. Hold stretches 15-30 seconds or more during your cool down to improve flexibility.

18.8.2.4. Do not limit flexibility training to the cool down periods. Stretching is one form of exercise that takes very little time relative to the benefits gained and may be done easily at home or work. Repetitive movements at work or having a more sedentary job can increase tension in specific muscle groups, which would benefit from mild stretching during the course of the day.

**18.9. Unit Physical Fitness Training Program:**

18.9.1. Commander-driven physical fitness training is the backbone of the Air Force physical fitness program. The program promotes aerobic and muscular fitness, flexibility, and optimal body composition of each Airman in the unit. Safety must be an overarching concern throughout physical training and assessment.

18.9.2. The program will meet the current ability level of the members while encouraging and challenging members to progress to a higher fitness level. The 1.5-mile timed run, 2-kilometer walk, abdominal circumference, push-up, and sit-up assessments are designed to measure the effectiveness of the physical training program. However, training should not be limited to the assessment activities.

18.9.3. The unit fitness program will incorporate the guidelines established in AFI 36-2905, *Fitness Program*, to develop general fitness, prevent boredom, and decrease repetitive strain injuries. Finally, the program must ensure a safe environment for training by assessing traffic patterns, use of headphones or other personal equipment, temperature, availability of water and first aid, and awareness of emergency procedures. In addition, you should consider individual safety issues, such as medical limitations and level of ability.

**18.10. Physical Fitness Standard:**

18.10.1. The Air Force uses a composite fitness score based on aerobic fitness, muscular strength/endurance, and body composition (using abdominal circumference measurements) to determine overall fitness. Overall fitness is directly related to health risk, including risk of disease (morbidity) and death (mortality). A composite score of 75 or greater, in addition to meeting the minimum component scores, represents the minimum accepted for health, fitness, and readiness levels. Health and readiness benefits continue to increase as body composition improves and physical activity and fitness levels increase. Members are encouraged to optimize their readiness status and posture by improving their overall fitness. Age and gender-specific fitness score charts are provided in AFI 36-2905, Attachment 10. **Note:** Meeting the minimum component scores does not constitute the minimum points required to earn a composite passing score. Scoring the minimum component values in all components will not generate enough points to earn a composite score of 75 or greater.

The minimum components are established to ensure members test adequately in all components and avoid "asymmetrical fitness" (i.e. excelling in some and disregarding others).

18.10.2. Airmen will receive a composite score on a 0-100 scale based on the following maximum component scores: 60 points for aerobic fitness assessment, 20 points for body composition, 10 points each for the muscular fitness assessment components, push-ups and sit-ups. Use the following formula to determine the score: composite score = total component points achieved multiplied by 100 and divided by total possible points.

18.10.3. Airmen with a medical profile prohibiting them from performing one or more components of the fitness assessment will have a composite score calculated on the tested components.

18.10.3.1. **Exemptions.** Biannually, members must complete a composite fitness assessment. Exemptions are designed to categorize members as unable or unavailable to train or test, for reasons beyond the control of the member or commander, for a limited time period as outlined in AFI 36-2905.

18.10.3.2. **Component Exemptions.** The commander, in consultation with the fitness program manager, may grant members exemption from aerobic and muscle fitness components based on medical recommendation according to AFI 36-2905 for a time-limited period. Other fitness assessment components will still be assessed.

18.10.4. Composite scores represent a health-based fitness level. As the fitness level increases, Airmen are able to tolerate extremes in temperature, fatigue, and stress while optimizing performance in the deployed environment. Refer to Table 18.1 for fitness levels.

18.10.5. Members must have a current fitness score on file prior to deployment. Member will not be considered "exempt" in the deployed location until their current fitness assessment expires. If a member fails their fitness assessment before deploying and their officer performance report/enlisted performance report closes out after the deployment starts, the commander has the discretion to annotate a non-current/failing fitness assessment within the reporting period on the evaluation. Additionally, the commander has the discretion to document the evaluation as a referral for a non-current/failing fitness assessment at the evaluation close-out date or enlisted performance report static close out date in accordance with AFI 36-2406, *Officer and Enlisted Evaluation Systems*.

18.10.6. Any failures will be annotated in Air Force fitness management system and will be considered against the individual. However, if an Airman reaches the 91-day mark after the unsatisfactory fitness assessment, but before the evaluation closes out, the unsatisfactory score is no longer current and the commander has the discretion to annotate a non-current/failing fitness assessment within the reporting period on the evaluation. Additionally, the commander has the discretion to document the evaluation as a referral for a non-current/failing fitness assessment at the evaluation close-out date or enlisted performance report static close out date. For Satisfactory and Excellent scores, deployed Airmen become "exempt" only when they reach the first day of the month, seven/thirteen calendar months following the previous official fitness assessment rating.

**Table 18.1. Scoring Chart**

| ITEM | A Fitness Levels | B Scores | C Currency of Fitness Testing |
|------|------------------|----------|-------------------------------|
| 1 | Excellent (all 4 components or on a chronic profile) | Composite score ≥ 90, all component minimums met | Within 12 months |
| 2 | Excellent (3 or less components and not a chronic profile) | Composite score ≥ 90, all component minimums met | Within 6 months |
| 3 | Satisfactory | Composite score ≥ 75-89.99, all component minimums met | Within 6 months |
| 4 | Unsatisfactory | Composite score < 75, and/or one or more component minimums not met | Within 90 days |

**18.11. Physical Fitness Assessment:**

18.11.1. Installations will develop a local plan, signed by the installation commander, for unit commanders to appoint physical training leaders to augment the fitness assessment cell for the purpose of administering fitness assessments. Fitness assessment cell augmentees will conduct fitness assessments and designated fitness assessment cell personnel will provide oversight. Fitness assessment cell augmentees *will not* test members from their own unit. The fitness assessment cell will conduct the fitness assessments for all Airmen. Where no fitness assessment cell exists, fitness assessments should be conducted by a certified physical training leader from another unit; arrangements of this nature will be determined by local leadership.

18.11.2. The fitness screening questionnaire will be completed no earlier than 30 calendar days (90 days for Air Reserve Component, but no later than 7 days prior to the fitness assessment, to provide time for medical evaluation, when indicated. Failure to complete the fitness screening questionnaire does not invalidate the fitness assessment.

18.11.3. Medical providers may recommend temporary medical exemptions for medical conditions preventing an Airman from safely participating in specific physical conditioning programs or in a component of the fitness assessment. Assessment for participation in fitness activities should be made at each visit to prevent the member from having to return for clearance or exemption at a later date.

18.11.4. Pregnant Airmen will engage in physical activity to maintain cardiovascular and muscular fitness throughout the pregnancy and postpartum period according to medical provider recommendations. Exercise regimens will consist of routines inclusive of physical training and nutrition counseling. Airmen are exempt from the fitness assessment during pregnancy and for 180 days after the delivery date.

## 18.12. Assessment Procedures.

All components of the fitness assessment must be completed within a 3-hour window on the same day. If extenuating circumstances occur (for example, rapidly changing or severe weather conditions, natural disasters, emergencies, safety issues, etc.), then all components must be completed within 5 duty days. Reserve members must be in a duty status for fitness assessments. The body composition component is the first component of the fitness assessment includes measuring height, weight, and abdominal circumference which must be the first component assessed in the fitness assessment. The muscular fitness components (push-ups and sit-ups) may be accomplished before or after the 1.5-mile run or 2-kilometer walk. There is a minimum 3-minute rest period between components. The assessment components should be scheduled to allow adequate rest for members on irregular or shift work hours.

18.12.1. **Body Composition Assessment:**

18.12.1.1. **Height and Weight.** Height and weight are obtained by fitness assessment cell members.

18.12.1.2. **Abdominal Circumference.** The abdominal circumference measurement is used to obtain the body composition component score. Fitness assessment cell members, or trained augmentees, will take the abdominal circumference measurement in a private room or a partitioned area. See AFI 36-2905 for the abdominal measurement procedures.

18.12.2. **Aerobic Assessment:**

The run and walk will be performed on an approved distance course. Aerobic fitness is measured with a 1.5-mile run, according to procedures outlined in AFI 36-2905. All members will complete the 1.5-mile timed run unless medically exempted. Members medically exempted from the run and cleared for an alternate assessment will, upon recommendation by the exercise physiologist/fitness program manager, complete the 2-kilometer walk, according to procedures in AFI 36-2905. Airmen who perform the 2-kilometer walk will not be allowed to run (that is, at least one foot must be in contact with the ground at all times) or the fitness assessment will be terminated. The 2-kilometer walk is the only authorized alternative. **Note:** The member does not select the assessment method. The fitness program manager determines which assessment to use based on the member's profile.

18.12.3. **Muscular Fitness Assessment:**

Upper body muscular strength and endurance are measured with a 1-minute timed push-up assessment; abdominal muscular strength and endurance is measured with a 1-minute timed sit-up assessment.

## 18.13. Ongoing Education and a Supportive Environment:

Physical fitness education will be incorporated into training programs and unit physical training. Ongoing commander emphasis and a supportive environment are essential to maintain force health and fitness.

18.13.1. **Information and Support.**

Information can be found at http://www.afpc.af.mil/affitnessprogram/index.asp.

18.13.2. **Environment.**

The installation environment will be conducive for all members to maintain a healthy lifestyle, and a community-based education and awareness program that addresses optimal nutrition, body composition, and fitness evident to all members. Programs will be available to Air Reserve Component personnel.

## 18.14. Unit Key Players.

The unit physical training program success depends on many people, including the unit commander, unit fitness program manager, physical training leader, immediate supervisor, and the individual.

### 18.14.1. Unit Commander.

The unit commander promotes, supports, and ensures unit fitness program integrity and provides an environment that is conducive to healthy lifestyle choices; provides an overall work environment for a community supportive of optimal nutrition and fitness by providing access to facilities providing healthy foods and encourages Airmen to participate in physical fitness during the duty day; and implements and maintains a unit physical training program according to guidelines in AFI 36-2905.

### 18.14.2. Unit Fitness Program Manager.

The unit fitness program manager oversees the administration of the fitness program for the unit, notifies the unit commander if members fail to attend scheduled fitness appointments, and provides fitness metrics and unit status reports to the unit commander monthly.

### 18.14.3. Physical Training Leaders:

18.14.3.1. The physical training leader completes the initial physical training leader course before overseeing and conducting the unit fitness program and maintains currency by receiving annual refresher course or upon change of duty station, whichever comes first. Air Reserve Component physical training leaders at co-located bases will receive initial and refresher training from Regular Air Force fitness program managers. If not feasible for Air Reserve Component physical training leaders to receive in person training, they will complete distance learning training as coordinated through the Air Force Medical Operations Agency and the supporting base fitness program manager.

18.13.3.2. Physical training leaders must complete basic life support and automated external defibrillator training before attending the physical training leader certification course. They must maintain currency while serving as physical training leaders.

### 18.14.4. Individual.

Individuals must maintain individual year-round physical fitness through self-directed and unit-based fitness programs and proper nutrition standards according to AFI 36-2905. Individuals must also meet Air Force fitness minimum standards and attend all required fitness program appointments.

## Section 18C—Nutrition

## 18.15. Nutrition.

Overweight and obesity in the United States has been declared a threat to National Security. Nearly 27% of 17 to 24 year olds are too overweight to serve in the military. The Department of Defense is not immune as 48% of Airmen are assessed as overweight and 14% obese. Imbalance of calorie intake and physical activity are the primary causes for unintended weight gain and an increase potential health risk. Airmen are responsible to be mission ready at all times and must recognize that food is the fuel that supports our performance and ability to complete the mission. To understand how nutrition affects the body, Airmen must understand the following basic concepts: calories, the functions of nutrients, and how to customize nutrient intake to support performance.

### 18.15.1. Nutrition Basics: MyPlate.

**Figure 18.2. MyPlate Food Guidance System.**

The United States Department of Agriculture's MyPlate food guidance system (Figure 18.2) provides practical information to help individuals build healthier diets. MyPlate emphasizes fruits, vegetables, grains, protein foods, and dairy groups in appropriate portions. The United States Department of Agriculture's website, www.choosemyplate.gov has user-friendly tools and resources on topics such as weight management and calories, physical activity, tracking your diet and healthy eating tips.

### 18.15.2. Calorie Intake.

18.15.2.1. The Dietary Guidelines for Americans summarizes and synthesizes knowledge about individual nutrients and food into a set of recommendations for healthy eating. The 2015 version provides recommendations under 5 main messages; (1) Follow a healthy eating pattern across the lifespan; (2) Focus on variety, nutrient density, and amount; (3) Limit calories from added sugars and saturated fats and reduce sodium intake; (4) Shift to healthier food and beverage choices; (5) Support healthy eating patterns for all.

18.15.2.2. Maintaining a healthy weight is key to Airmen's' health and readiness. The Air Force recognizes abdominal circumference as one of the most specific indicators of disease risk in adults because abdominal fat is a predictor of obesity-related diseases. In addition to meeting military appearance standards, overweight and obese Airmen have increased risk of high blood pressure, high blood cholesterol, heart disease, stroke, Type 2 diabetes, arthritis, breathing problems and certain types of cancer. Gradual improvements in diet, physical activity and lifestyle are easier to incorporate and more likely to be maintained. This can be achieved by following the key dietary guideline recommendations to consume a healthy eating pattern that accounts for all foods and beverages within an appropriate calorie level. A healthy eating pattern includes: a variety of vegetables from all the subgroups-dark green, red and orange, legumes (beans and peas), starchy, and other; fruits, especially whole fruits; grains, at least half of which are whole grains; fat-free or low-fat dairy, including milk, yogurt, cheese, and/or fortified soy beverages; a variety of protein foods, including seafood, lean meats and poultry, eggs, legumes (beans and peas), and nuts, seeds and soy products; oils.

18.15.2.3. Maintaining a healthy energy balance is important. Calories from foods and beverages need to be balanced with calories burned through metabolism and physical activity to meet weight goals—less calories to lose weight, balanced calories to maintain weight and more calories to gain weight. If weight loss is desired, creating a calorie deficit of 500-1000 calories a day through diet and/or exercise should lead to a healthy weight loss of 1 to 2 pounds per week. The Supertracker in www.choosemyplate.gov can provide individuals with healthy calorie recommendations and assist in tracking food intake and physical activity.

### 18.15.2.4. Macronutrients.

Macronutrients make up the bulk of the diet and supply energy as well as many essential nutrients. Carbohydrates and protein provide 4 calories per gram and fats provide 9 calories per gram.

### 18.15.2.4.1. Carbohydrates.

18.15.2.4.1.1. Carbohydrates are the primary fuel source your body uses during exercise. An appropriate amount of carbohydrates is important to maintain glycogen stores for energy reserve. Carbohydrates increase blood glucose levels and supply energy. Simple carbohydrates increase blood glucose levels rapidly while complex carbohydrates increase blood glucose levels slowly over a longer time. Simple carbohydrates are often found in packaged or processed foods, examples are; table sugar, brown sugar, corn syrup, honey, fruit drinks, soft drinks and candy. Added sugars are simple sugars added to foods or beverages when they are processed or prepared and should account for less than 10% of calories per day. Complex carbohydrates can be found in fruits, breads, cereals, grains, milk and starchy vegetables (potatoes, corn, peas, and squash). Healthy carbohydrates contain fiber and whole grains and limited added sugars. The recommended serving size is about the size of the palm of your hand and contains approximately 15 grams of carbohydrate; sizes differ with sweets and vegetables. The general recommendation for carbohydrate intake is 45-65% of total calories.

18.15.2.4.1.2. Fiber is classified as soluble or insoluble. Soluble fiber attracts water and turns to gel during digestion. Therefore, soluble fiber lowers low-density lipoprotein/bad cholesterol and prolongs stomach emptying time so sugar is released and absorbed more slowly. Additionally, fiber can be found in oatmeal, oat bran, nuts and seeds, dry beans and peas, and most fruits. Insoluble fiber adds bulk to the stool and helps food pass more quickly through the stomach and intestines. Finally, fiber can be found in whole wheat bread, barley, brown rice, seeds, and in most vegetables and fruits. The average American consumes 12-15 grams per day, whereas the recommended total fiber intake is 20-35 grams per day.

### 18.15.2.4.2. Protein.

Proteins are used by our bodies for tissue maintenance, replacement, function and growth of our muscles. If our body is not getting enough calories from dietary sources or tissue stores, protein may be used for energy. The general recommendation for protein intake is 10-35% of total calories or 0.8 to 1.2 grams/kilograms body weight to meet daily needs. Protein can be found in meats, poultry, fish, legumes, tofu, eggs, nuts and seeds, milk and milk products, and grains. Individuals should focus on lean meats and low fat milk products to reduce saturated fats. The recommended serving size of meat is the size of a deck of cards and contains about 21 grams of protein. One 8 ounce glass of milk contains 8 grams of protein.

18.15.2.4. **Fats.**

18.15.2.4.1. Fats are a major energy source and help our bodies maintain temperature and protect organs from trauma. Balanced fat intake is essential to maintain energy reserve. Fats can be found in oils, high fat cuts of meat, baked sweets, whole-fat milk and cream, butter, cheeses, nuts and seeds, avocados, and fish. The general recommendation for fats is 20-35% of total calories. The differences between the four categories of fats are important to understand; saturated fats, trans fats, polyunsaturated fats, and monounsaturated fats.

18.15.2.4.2. Diets higher in saturated fats have been linked to coronary heart disease. Saturated fats should make up less than 10% of your daily calories, foods that contain more saturated fats are usually solid at room temperate and can be found in high-fat cheeses, high-fat cuts of meat, whole-fat milk and cream, butter, ice cream, and palm and coconut oils.

18.15.2.4.3. Trans fats have also been linked to coronary heart disease and intake of these fats should be kept as low as possible. They can be found in small amounts in the fatty parts of meat and milk products and in foods that contain partially hydrogenated oils. Trans fats can be made from vegetable oils through a process called hydrogenation and are found in foods such as frozen pizzas, frozen pies, cookies, and margarine, spreads and other processed foods.

18.15.2.4.4. Eating more unsaturated fan can reduce your risk for heart disease and improve high-density lipoprotein/good cholesterol levels. Unsaturated fats are typically liquid at room temperature and include monounsaturated and polyunsaturated fats. Unsaturated fats typically come from plant sources such as canola oil, olive oil, nuts, seeds, flaxseed, and avocado but is also present in fish such as trout, herring, and salmon.

18.15.2.5. **Sodium.**

Americans consume about 3,400 milligrams of sodium every day, mostly in the form of salt found in processed foods- canned foods, soups, cheese, bread, prepared mixes and deli meats. The Dietary Guidelines for Americans recommends that adults limit their sodium intake to 2,300 mg per day-about the amount in one teaspoon of table salt. Certain "at-risk" groups including adults over the age of 51, African Americans, and people who have high blood pressure, diabetes, or kidney disease should limit their sodium intake to about 1,500 milligrams per day. High sodium intake raises blood pressure which is a major risk factor for the nation's leading cause of death – heart disease. The best way to ensure a low sodium diet is to eat whole foods such as fresh or frozen fruits and vegetables; lean, unprocessed poultry and fish; unsalted nuts; whole grains; and low-fat dairy products such as skim milk or yogurt.

18.15.2.6. **Fluid.**

Water is essential for life, in fact the body is made up of over 60% water. Water has no calories and is needed to transport nutrients throughout your body via blood plasma, while also assisting many of your body's other functions, including waste elimination. Depending on age, sex, race, and body composition water needs differ. The exact percentage is different for males and females and from one person to another with a range of 45-75%. Taking these factors into account, daily water balance for each individual also depends on the total difference between water gain and water loss. Water gains occur from consumption of liquids, foods, and the body's natural production of water. Water losses occur from the following sources: sweat, respiration, gastrointestinal, and renal. The body is in constant demand for water and this demand increases when you exercise, when you are ill, and in environmental conditions, such as humidity and altitude. For a generally healthy individual, the Dietary Reference Intakes, recommend a total daily water consumption (combination of drinking water, beverages, and food) for women, 19-70 years of age, as 2.7 liters per day and for men, 19-70 years of age, as 3.7 liters per day.

18.15.2.7. **Caffeine.**

Caffeine is a stimulant present in a variety of products including coffee, tea, colas, energy drinks, dietary supplements, over-the-counter medications, and some foods. According to the Human Performance Resource Center, daily caffeine intake up to 400 mg has been found safe for healthy adults and non-pregnant/non-lactating women. Caffeine used in moderation with a dose of up to 200 mg has been shown to improve cognitive performance in individuals. A cup of coffee typically has 100 mg of caffeine. Be aware that taking large doses of caffeine, roughly 400–500 mg, at one time can result in a serious condition known as "caffeine intoxication." Symptoms of caffeine intoxication can include nausea, vomiting, agitation, nervousness, or headache. Excessive caffeine intake can be life-threatening and could potentially cause electrolyte imbalance or high levels of acid in the blood which could cause seizures.

18.15.2.8. **Energy Drinks versus Sport Drinks.**

Energy drinks and sports drinks are both marketed by manufacturers to improve performance. Evidence as to the effect of energy drinks on athletic performance is inconsistent. Be aware, case studies have reported seizures after heavy consumption of energy drinks. Energy drinks usually carry a "warning" due to the use of stimulants such as caffeine, green tea extract, guarana seed extract, yerba mate, acacia rigidula, taurine, ginseng or other proprietary "energy boost blends." Proprietary blends can contain novel, untested ingredients, along with botanicals, amino acids, proteins, peptides, or extracts. Additionally, vitamins and minerals (e.g. B-vitamins and magnesium) may be added, leading to excessive intakes. Energy drinks are not meant to hydrate. Sports drinks, or carbohydrate-electrolyte beverages, are designed to hydrate and do not contain caffeine unless otherwise stated. Sports drinks generally contain a mixture of carbohydrates (14 to 19 grams per 8-ounce serving), sodium (115-175 mg per 8-ounce serving), and potassium (20-98 milligrams per 8-ounce serving) which has been shown to improve exercise performance. If eight liters of sweat are lost per day or higher intensity exercise lasts greater than 60 minutes, a carbohydrate-electrolyte beverage may be needed. In conclusion, the safest solution is to avoid energy supplements and learn more about electrolytes and carbohydrate fueling strategies to decide which sport drink (not energy drink) is the best choice for you.

18.15.2.9. **Alcohol.**

Excessive drinking can be harmful to your health and may increase the risk for high blood pressure, liver cirrhosis and several forms of cancer. The Dietary Guidelines for Americans advise limiting alcohol to one drink per day for women and two drinks per day for men. The serving size for beer is 12 ounces, wine is 5 ounces and 80 proof distilled spirits is 1.5 ounces. The average serving of alcohol generally has about 150 calories. Additionally, alcohol has 7 calories per gram and can be a significant contributor caloric consumption in the diet. Alcohol may lead to excess weight gain, increased risk for chronic diseases, osteoporosis, stress injuries, and impaired short and long term cognitive function.

18.15.3. **Performance Nutrition Basics.**

Nutrition plays an important role in maintaining health and performance, particularly exercise. This next section builds upon the basic nutrition principles and focuses on fueling strategies that will help enhance and optimize physical performance. The basics of performance nutrition focus on fluid hydration and timing of fueling strategies (before, during, and after exercise).

18.15.3.1. **Fluid Requirements with Exercise.**

Exercise substantially increases fluid loss, placing greater demands on fluid replacement; so that proper hydration before, during, and after intense workouts is critical. Decrements in performance starts to occur with fluid losses of 2% of body weight degrades both cognitive and mental performance. One liter of water is equivalent to 1 kilogram (2.2 pounds) of body weight. An example would be a 150 pound individual losing 3 pounds of body weight through sweat losses which would equate to 1.36 liters of fluid. During exercise, sweat rate losses can vary from 0.3-2.4 liters. Fluid losses are dependent on exercise intensity, genetic predisposition, fitness status, acclimation of heat, altitude, clothing, and other environmental conditions. Dehydration occurs with fluid losses of greater than 2% of body weight and increases risk for heat illness, exhaustion and stroke. In general, for activities less than 60 minutes, water is the best beverage for hydration. If you are doing more than 60 minutes of continuous exercise, then you may benefit from a sports drink to replace electrolytes and carbohydrates. Also know that a while dehydration can affect performance and be life threatening, the same can occur on the opposite end of the spectrum with excess fluid consumption. Excess fluid can lead to over-hydration resulting in symptoms such as chills, vomiting, dizziness, disorientation, altered mental status, fatigue, headache, and even death. According to the United States Army Research Institute of Environmental Medicine, regardless of how hot it is or how hard you are working, you should limit fluids to no more than 6 cups an hour and 48 cups a day. The key with fluid intake is to aim to replace losses and monitor signs and symptoms of under/over hydration. Determine how much water is lost by taking a weight measurement (without clothes/gear) before and after a hard training workout. Drink 16 ounces of fluid for every pound of weight lost.

18.15.3.2. **Pre-, During, and Post-event Eating Strategies.**

Following appropriate eating strategies based on event timing and exercise intensity can help improve performance. Avoid drastic changes in diet before a fitness test or mission; try out new foods and strategies during training times.

18.15.3.2.1. **Pre-exercise:** The purpose of a pre-exercise beverage, snack or meal is to provide enough fluid to maintain hydration and enough carbohydrates to maintain proper blood sugar levels during activity. A pre-exercise meal (includes some carbs, protein and low or moderate fat) should be consumed 3 to 4 hours before starting the activity. This allows time for the body to digest the food. A small amount of protein before exercise may reduce muscle soreness later. Pre-exercise snacks/beverages should be consumed 30 to 60 minutes before an activity. The snacks and beverages consumed one hour before should contain mainly carbohydrates since they are digested quickly and turned to energy-giving glucose. Snack examples are bananas or other fruits (grapes, applesauce, and peaches), graham crackers, pretzels, or low fiber dry cereal. Avoid foods with fat and fiber in a pre-exercise snack to minimize possibility of an upset stomach.

18.15.3.2.2. **During Exercise:** During exercise duration of less than 45 minutes, carbohydrate consumption is not warranted. In sustained high intensity exercise with a duration of 45-75 minutes, small amounts of carbohydrates during activity (sports drinks and products) may enhance performance, but does not provide a source of fuel. During endurance exercise of 1-2.5 hours in length, carbohydrate intake provides a source of fuel. The recommended intake of carbohydrates for events 1-2.5 hours in length is 30-60 grams per hour. In ultra-endurance events, greater than 2.5-3 hours in length, carbohydrate intakes of up to 90 grams per hour can improve performance.

18.15.3.2.3. **Post-exercise/Recovery:** If exercising at a low or moderate intensity for less than a half hour a post workout beverage or snack is not necessary. However, if the exercise routine is rigorous and lasts for more than 45 minutes, a snack or light meal will help in recovery. This "recovery" meal helps replenish the carbohydrates burned during exercise and converts them into a storage form (glycogen) for later use. Adding protein to the meal or snack helps rebuild muscle tears that occur during exercise. Following exhaustive exercise a minimum of 24 hours is required to replace the glycogen stores lost in training. Timing and the ratio of carbohydrate to protein are also important factors to consider. The critical window of refueling is within 45 minutes of finishing your exercise. High glycemic foods are the most effective for restoring glycogen. An optimal composition of a post recovery beverage or snack is a 4:1 carbohydrate to protein ratio. This means that for every 4 grams of carbohydrates there should be 1 gram of protein. A great example is the recovery beverage chocolate milk. A regular 8 ounce glass of chocolate milk contains about 29 grams of carbohydrates and 8 grams of protein, a 3.6:1 carbohydrate/protein ratio. In contrast, a regular 8 ounce glass of milk contains 12 grams of carbohydrates and 8 grams of protein, a 1.5:1 carbohydrate/protein ratio. Other examples of simple post-workout snacks include low fat yogurt, trail mix (cereal, nuts and dried fruit) and water, or string cheese and a fruit bar with water. Hydration repletion should also be a priority. Recovery fluids should include sodium and potassium. Examples of these types of fluids are: water, juices, sports beverages, coffee, tea, soups, and water containing foods such as fruits and vegetables.

18.15.3.3. **Supplements.**

18.15.3.3.1. The use of dietary supplements continues to be popular among members of the military. The term dietary supplement includes many products, such as vitamins, minerals, herbs, botanicals, amino acids, or other substances, and are sold as pills, powders, bars, packs, gels, drinks, or shakes. The Food and Drug Administration does not test products before they are sold in stores or via the internet; this lack of oversight means there is no guarantee that what you purchase is what you get. Knowing the "red flags" when choosing a dietary supplement is important. First, be aware that the most popular types of supplements- bodybuilding, performance enhancement, sexual enhancement, and weight loss products, are the ones most likely to be "tainted" with prescription drugs, heavy metals, or other undeclared ingredients. Second, avoid products that have ingredients listed as "blends," "proprietary blends," or "delivery systems" on the label. These blends do not specify the amount of each ingredient in the blend and increase the risk of overdosing on ingredients such as creatine or caffeine. Third, be wary of products that promise a "quick fix" or amazing results that seem too good to be true. Fortunately, there are third party verification/certification companies that will test the purity and/or quality of the product, so look for those types of labels on your products (Figure 18.3). Remember, climate and stress may alter the effects of dietary supplements, especially in a deployed environment which can increase the risk of having a bad reaction to a product.

**Figure 18.3. Purity/Quality Labels for Products**

18.15.3.3.2. The Department of Defense has created a resource called the Operation Supplement Safety campaign, which is designed to educate the military community about dietary supplements and how to choose supplements wisely. Convenient, reliable, and science-based information can be found at http://hprc-online.org/opss. Airmen on flying status must consult with their flight surgeon; however, all Airmen are encouraged to discuss dietary supplement use with their healthcare provider or base nutrition professional in order to avoid any drug-supplement interactions for safety reasons.

*Section 18D—Substance Use/Misuse*

**18.16. Alcohol and Drug Abuse Prevention and Treatment and Drug Demand Reduction Programs:**

18.16.1. Alcohol and Drug Abuse Prevention and Treatment and Drug Demand Reduction programs include substance use/misuse prevention, education, treatment, and urinalysis testing. Substance use/misuse prevention and treatment policies and programs are thoroughly integrated into every facet of Air Force core values, quality of life, and force management. These policies have been in place for over two decades and have evolved to meet changing conditions within the Air Force. Our members are held to the highest standards of discipline and behavior, both on and off duty. Individuals who experience problems related to substance use/misuse will receive counseling and treatment as needed; however, all Air Force members are held accountable for unacceptable behavior.

18.16.2. The Alcohol and Drug Abuse Prevention and Treatment Program objectives are to promote readiness, health, and wellness through the prevention and treatment of substance misuse and abuse; minimize the negative consequences of substance misuse and abuse to the individual, family, and organization; provide comprehensive education and treatment to individuals who experience problems attributed to substance misuse or abuse, to restore function and return identified substance abusers to unrestricted duty status or assist them in their transition to civilian life.

## 18.17. Policy on Drug Abuse:

18.17.1. Department of Defense policy is to prevent and eliminate drug and alcohol abuse and dependence from the Department of Defense. Such abuse and dependence are incompatible with readiness, the maintenance of high standards of performance, and military discipline. Drug abuse is defined as the illegal, wrongful, or improper use, possession, sale, transfer, or introduction onto a military installation of any drug defined in AFI 90-507, *Military Drug Demand Reduction Program.* "Wrongful" means without legal justification or excuse.

18.17.2. Studies have shown that products made with hemp seed and hemp seed oil may contain varying levels of tetrahydrocannabinol, an active ingredient of marijuana which is detectable under the Air Force Drug Testing Program. To ensure military readiness, the ingestion of products containing or products derived from hemp seed or hemp seed oil is prohibited. Failure by military personnel to comply with the prohibition on the ingestion of products containing or products derived from hemp seed or hemp seed oil is a violation of Article 92, Uniform Code of Military Justice.

18.17.3. To ensure military readiness, safeguard the health and wellness of the force, and to maintain good order and discipline in the Service, the knowing use of any intoxicating substance, other than the lawful use of alcohol or nicotine products, that is inhaled, injected, consumed, or introduced into the body in any manner to alter mood or function, is prohibited. These substances include, but are not limited to, controlled substance analogues (for example, designer drugs such as "spice" that are not otherwise controlled substances); inhalants, propellants, solvents, household chemicals, and other substances used for "huffing;" prescription or over-the-counter medications when used in a manner contrary to their intended medical purpose or in excess of the prescribed dosage; and naturally occurring intoxicating substances (for example, Salvia divinorum). The possession of any intoxicating substance described in this paragraph, if done with the intent to use in a manner that would alter mood or function, is prohibited. Failure by military personnel to comply with the prohibitions contained in this paragraph is a violation of Article 92, Uniform Code of Military Justice.

18.17.4. All patients diagnosed with a substance use disorder and entered into the Alcohol and Drug Abuse Prevention and Treatment Program will be recommended for limited duty, indicating the patient is not worldwide qualified.

## 18.18. Policy on Alcohol Abuse.

Air Force policy recognizes that alcohol abuse negatively affects public behavior, duty performance, and/or physical and mental health. The Air Force provides comprehensive clinical assistance to eligible beneficiaries seeking help for an alcohol problem.

### 18.18.1. Alcohol and Drug Abuse Prevention and Treatment Program.

AFI 44-121, *Alcohol and Drug Abuse Prevention and Treatment (ADAPT) Program* provides guidance for the identification, treatment, and management of personnel with substance use problems and describes Air Force policy regarding alcohol and drug abuse.

### 18.18.2. Drunk Driving.

AFMAN 31-116, *Air Force Motor Vehicle Traffic Supervision*, applies to everyone with military installation driving privileges. AFMAN 31-116 establishes guidance on court hearing procedures, convictions, non-judicial punishment, civilian administrative action, or appropriate punishment for violation of impaired and intoxicated driving policies. If a member has a blood alcohol percentage of 0.05 but less than 0.10, the person is presumed to be impaired. Intoxicated driving is operating a motor vehicle under intoxication caused by alcohol or drugs. There is a 1-year driving privilege suspension for driving or being in physical control of a motor vehicle while under the influence of intoxicating liquor 0.10 percent or greater. **Note:** In the United States, if a state uses a more stringent standard (for example, 0.08 instead of 0.10), Air Force units will use the lower standard. Overseas, the limit is 0.10 unless the Secretary of Defense sets a lower limit.

**18.19. Identification and Referral:**

18.19.1. **Recognizing and Referring Personnel for Substance Use and Abuse:**

18.19.1.1. Each person is responsible for exercising good judgment in the use of alcohol when not otherwise restricted by public law or military directive. The Air Force reviews members' drinking habits that affect public behavior, duty performance, or physical and mental health. The Air Force provides non-punitive assistance to members seeking help for an alcohol problem. In assessing potential drug- and alcohol-related problems, the supervisory role is to identify subordinates with problems early and to motivate them to seek and accept help.

18.19.1.2. As depicted in Figure 18.4, many signs and symptoms of substance use/misuse exist. However, the presence of these signs, though common indicators of substance use/misuse, does not always substantiate a substance use problem. To note all the behavioral symptoms that may suggest substance use/abuse or precisely define their sequence and severity is impossible. They are exactly as stated—signs and symptoms. Do not use these signs to make a conclusive substance use diagnosis. This responsibility lies with the Alcohol and Drug Abuse Prevention and Treatment Program personnel. If any of these signs are present, it may suggest a potential problem exists for the member. Talk with the member and explain why you are concerned. Fear of discussing concerns is normal, but discussing the concern is important to address the concern early before the problem gets out of control. Document and discuss specific instances of unusual behavior with the supervisor, first sergeant, or unit commander. This will help expedite the care a subordinate may need. When additional professional assistance is needed, do not hesitate to document and then refer troubled subordinates to the Alcohol and Drug Abuse Prevention and Treatment Program. **Note:** Help must be offered to every individual. Any time a person acknowledges a substance use problem, notify the supervisor, first sergeant, or unit commander.

**Figure 18.4. Signs and Symptoms of Substance Use/Misuse.**

| | | |
|---|---|---|
| Arrests or legal problems | Failed attempts to stop or cut down | Memory loss |
| Concerns expressed by family, friends | Financial irresponsibility | Morning drinking and hangovers |
| Denial or dishonesty about use | Frequent errors in judgment | Suicidal thoughts or behaviors |
| Deteriorating duty performance | Health problems related to drinking | Unexplained or frequent absences |
| Dramatic mood swings | Increased use of alcohol | Violent behavior |

18.19.2. **Identifying Individuals with Substance use Disorders or Misuse.**

For the Air Force to have an effective substance use prevention and treatment program, there must be a means of identifying service members experiencing problems with substance use. Although commanders play a major role in identifying substance abusers, members should be aware of how commanders must proceed in various circumstances. Due to the nature of the position noncommissioned officers hold within the unit, they also play an important part in the identification process. There are basically five identification methods:

18.19.2.1. **Medical Care Referrals.** Medical personnel must notify the unit commander and the Alcohol and Drug Abuse Prevention and Treatment program manager when a member:

18.19.2.1.1. Is observed, identified, or suspected to be under the influence of drugs or alcohol while seeking medical care.

18.19.2.1.2. Receives treatment for an injury or illness that may be the result of substance use/misuse.

18.19.2.1.3. Is suspected of abusing substances.

18.19.2.1.4. Is admitted as a patient for alcohol or drug detoxification.

18.19.2.2. **Commander's Identification.** Unit commanders will refer all service members for assessment when substance use or misuse is suspected to be a contributing factor in any misconduct; for example, driving under the influence, public intoxication, drunk and disorderly, spouse or child abuse and maltreatment, underage drinking, positive drug test, or when notified by medical personnel. When commanders or supervisors fail to refer a member with suspected or identified substance use problems, this places the member at increased risk for developing more severe substance use problems and may jeopardize the safety of others and ultimately mission accomplishment.

18.19.2.3. **Drug Testing.** The Air Force conducts drug testing of personnel according to AFI 90-507, *Military Drug Demand Reduction Program*. Drug testing is most effective as a deterrent. Therefore, Air Force military members are subject to testing regardless of grade, status, or position. Inspection testing is the best deterrent presently available against drug abuse. Military members may receive an order or voluntarily consent to provide urine samples at any time. Military members who fail to comply with an order to provide a urine sample are subject to punitive action under the Uniform Code of Military Justice. Commander-directed testing should only be used as a last resort because the results cannot be used in actions under the Uniform Code of Military Justice, or administrative actions, including adverse characterization of administrative discharges such as (General) or under other than honorable conditions.

18.19.2.3.1. **Inspection under Military Rule of Evidence 313.** Inspection testing is the most common method of testing in the Air Force. Drug testing is random and unpredictable. In general, an inspection is an examination conducted as an incident of command, the primary purpose of which is to determine and ensure the security, military fitness, or good order and discipline of the unit, organization, or installation. Individuals are selected at random using a nonbiased selection process. Commanders may also select work sections, units, or segments of the military population to provide urine samples. Commanders may use the positive result of a urine sample to refer a member for a substance use evaluation, as evidence to support disciplinary action under the Uniform Code of Military Justice or administrative discharge action, and as a consideration on the issue of characterization of discharge in administrative discharges.

18.19.2.3.2. **Probable Cause.** Probable cause requires a search and seizure authorization from the appropriate commander to seize a urine specimen. Probable cause exists when there is a reasonable belief that drugs will be found in the system of the member to be tested. Consult with the staff judge advocate regarding procedures for determining whether probable cause exists. Results may be used for Uniform Code of Military Justice or to characterize administrative discharges.

18.19.2.4. **Medical Purposes.** Results of any examination conducted for a valid medical purpose including emergency medical treatment, periodic physical examination, and other such examinations necessary for diagnostic or treatment purposes may be used to identify drug abusers. Results may be used as evidence to support disciplinary action under the Uniform Code of Military Justice, or administrative discharge action according to AFI 90-507, Table 7.1. These results may also be considered on the issue of characterization of discharge in separation proceedings.

18.19.2.5. **Self-identification.** Air Force members with substance use problems are encouraged to seek assistance from the unit commander, first sergeant, substance use counselor, or a military medical professional. Self-identification is reserved for members who are not currently under investigation or pending action because of an alcohol-related incident. Following the assessment, the Alcohol and Drug Abuse Prevention and Treatment program manager will consult with the treatment team and determine an appropriate clinical course of action.

18.19.2.5.1. **Drugs.** An Air Force member may voluntarily disclose evidence of personal drug use or possession to the unit commander, first sergeant, substance use counselor, or a military medical professional. Commanders will grant limited protection for Air Force members who reveal this information with the intention of entering treatment. Commanders may not use voluntary disclosure against a member in an action under the Uniform Code of Military Justice or when weighing characterization of service in a separation. Disclosure is not voluntary if the Air Force member has previously been:

18.19.2.5.1.1. Apprehended for drug involvement.

18.19.2.5.1.2. Placed under investigation for drug abuse. The day and time when a member is considered placed under investigation is determined by the circumstances of each individual case. A member is under investigation, for example, when an entry is made in the security forces blotter, when the security forces investigator's log shows an initial case entry, or when the Air Force Office of Special Investigations opens a case file. Furthermore, a member is considered under investigation when he or she has been questioned about drug use by investigative authorities or the member's commander, or when an allegation of drug use has been made against the member.

18.19.2.5.1.3. Ordered to give a urine sample as part of the drug-testing program in which the results are still pending or have been returned as positive.

18.19.2.5.1.4. Advised of a recommendation for administrative separation for drug abuse.

18.19.2.5.1.5. Entered into treatment for drug abuse.

18.19.2.5.2. **Alcohol.** Commanders must provide sufficient incentive to encourage members to seek help for problems with alcohol without fear of negative consequences. Self-identified members will enter the Alcohol and Drug Abuse Prevention and Treatment assessment process and will be held to the same standards as others entering substance use education, counseling, and treatment programs.

**18.20. Leadership Responsibilities.**

The supervisor's role in the treatment process does not end with identifying and referring members. Though the supervisor is not charged with providing treatment, daily interaction with his or her personnel and the treatment team can have a significant impact on the success of the treatment efforts. Identifying individuals who need treatment is a critical first step in helping them break free of the tremendously potent cycle of denial, negativity, and increased substance use. However, entering treatment is only a first step. A member's substance use problem did not develop overnight and took time, as will treatment and recovery. The supervisor must remain focused on the member's duty performance, attendance in the program, and maintenance of standards. One of the most critical components to a member's treatment is the treatment team meeting. Commander and/or first sergeant and supervisor involvement in the treatment team meeting at key points in the patient's treatment and recovery are important. The commander or first sergeant and the supervisor must be involved at program entry, termination, and anytime there are significant treatment difficulties with the patient. The primary objective of the treatment team is to guide the clinical course of the patient's treatment after examining all the facts. The treatment team consists of the commander, supervisor, member's counselor, medical consultants, other appropriate helping agencies, and the member.

**18.21. Substance Use Assessment.**

The central purpose of the substance use assessment is to determine the patient's need for treatment and level of care required. Alcohol and Drug Abuse Prevention and Treatment staff members conduct the substance use assessment within seven calendar days of notification. Alcohol and Drug Abuse Prevention and Treatment program managers conduct required reviews of the patient's medical records and all documentation provided by the Alcohol and Drug Abuse Prevention and Treatment staff on a priority basis. Information gathered during the assessment will form the basis for patient diagnosis, treatment planning, and delivery of substance use services.

**18.22. Substance Use Treatment.**

Substance use treatment is divided into two services: nonclinical and clinical.

**18.22.1. Nonclinical Services.**

All active duty members involved in alcohol-related misconduct will be referred for a substance use assessment. Members who do not meet diagnostic criteria for a substance use disorder will receive alcohol counseling targeted (secondary) prevention and education. All decisions about length and number of visits of targeted prevention and education will be based on thorough assessment and determination of risk and is tailored for the individual. There will be at least two follow-up appointments of a minimum of 30 minutes duration to reassess risk, assess progress, and as appropriate, conduct a follow-up review of the educational components. If the client is assessed to need more services, there should be follow-ups with progress updates depending on the client's needs. The focus of these appointments is not treatment. They are designed to be targeted (individual) prevention, education, and reassessment. In addition to the initial assessment, a required alcohol education module will be completed within 2 weeks following the assessment. The alcohol education module includes information on Air Force policy, understanding the relationship between consumption, metabolism and intoxication, and physiological effects of alcohol on brain and body.

18.22.1.1. Additional counseling addressing bio-psychosocial issues identified in the assessment may be prescribed. Length of involvement will be determined based on the patient's presenting problems and agreed-upon treatment or behavioral contract.

18.22.1.2. Individuals being processed for separation are provided appropriate medical care (e.g., detoxification) before separation. Separation action is not postponed because of a member's participation in the Alcohol and Drug Abuse Prevention and Treatment Program.

**18.22.2. Clinical Services:**

18.22.2.1. Patients meeting the Diagnostic Statistical Manual 5 diagnostic criteria for a substance use disorder will be entered into substance use treatment with the level and intensity of care determined by the Alcohol and Drug Abuse Prevention and Treatment program manager using current American Society of Addiction Medicine criteria. The philosophy is to place personnel with substance use problems in the least intensive or restrictive treatment environment possible appropriate to their therapeutic needs.

18.22.2.2. Depending on the member's needs, variable lengths of stay or duration of treatment are provided within an array of treatment settings. The treatment program will reflect a multidisciplinary approach to assist the patient to achieve full recovery, free of the negative effect of the substance use. Treatment plans are individually tailored to meet patient's needs. Family involvement is strongly encouraged.

18.22.2.3. Individuals diagnosed with a substance use disorder will refrain from the use of alcohol during the initial phase of treatment and are strongly encouraged to continue to abstain during aftercare. Total abstinence is a critical treatment goal; however, because of the nature of alcoholism, relapses into drinking behavior are not uncommon and should be anticipated. A relapse by itself is not sufficient reason for program failure; however, relapses must be considered a significant threat to the patient's treatment and dealt with appropriately.

18.22.2.4. Involvement in self-help recovery groups (such as 12-step, rational recovery) is encouraged as an adjunct to treatment. The frequency of attendance is determined by the treatment team with the patient.

## 18.23. Detoxification Prior to Treatment.

Patients being referred for inpatient treatment will be assessed to determine the level of detoxification services required. To the greatest extent possible, patient detoxification will be managed on an outpatient basis prior to inpatient treatment. Patients assessed as requiring medically managed detoxification (inpatient) will be entered into an appropriate medical facility.

## 18.24. Completing the Program:

### 18.24.1. Successful Completion.

Patients will not be considered to have successfully completed treatment until they meet the Diagnostic Statistical Manual criteria for early full remission. Based on Diagnostic Statistical Manual criteria, the treatment team determines patient progress toward agreed-upon goals and issues as stated in the treatment plan and determines when the patient is effectively in recovery and no longer requires program resources.

### 18.24.2. Failing the Program:

18.24.2.1. The treatment team determines a patient to have failed the program based on a demonstrated pattern of unacceptable behavior, inability, or unwillingness to comply with their treatment plan, or involvement in alcohol or drug-related incidents after receiving initial treatment. The determination a patient has failed treatment is based on the patient's repeated failure to meet and maintain Air Force standards (behavior), rather than solely on the use of alcohol. An individual who has failed the Alcohol and Drug Abuse Prevention and Treatment Program will be considered for administrative separation by his or her commander.

18.24.2.2. Decisions regarding aftercare services will be based on a current assessment of status and will include establishment of an aftercare treatment plan identifying specific goals, interventions, and means to assess interventions.

## 18.25. Management of Personnel with Substance use Disorders.

The commander is responsible for all personnel and administrative actions pertaining to patients involved in the Alcohol and Drug Abuse Prevention and Treatment Program, to include assignment availability, promotion eligibility, reenlistment eligibility, Personnel Reliability Program, security clearance, etc. Application of administrative restrictions should be based on the establishment of an unfavorable information file or control roster resulting from the member's unacceptable behavior and not solely based on their involvement in the Alcohol and Drug Abuse Prevention and Treatment Program.

## 18.26. The Line of Duty Determination.

A member's substance use misconduct can lead to a line of duty determination. A line of duty determination is a finding made after an investigation into the circumstances of a member's illness, injury, disease, or death. The finding concludes: (1) whether or not the illness; injury, or disease existed prior to service and if an existed prior to service condition was aggravated by military service; (2) whether or not the illness, injury, disease, or death occurred while the member was absent from duty; and (3) whether or not the illness, injury, disease, or death was due to the member's own misconduct. The line of duty determination protects the interests of both the member and the United States Government. A line of duty determination may impact disability retirement and severance pay, forfeiture of pay, period of enlistment, as well as veteran benefits. Additional guidance may be found in AFI 36-2910, *Line of Duty (Misconduct) Determination.*

## Section 18E—Tobacco Use

## 18.27. Air Force Goal for Tobacco Use.

The Air Force's goal is a tobacco-free force. Tobacco use is the single most preventable cause of disease and death in the United States. Every year, in the United States, tobacco use is responsible for about 1 in 5 deaths (at least 480,000 deaths per year, of which an estimated 41,000 of these deaths are from secondhand smoke exposure).

## 18.28. Effects of Tobacco Use:

18.28.1. Optimal health and total fitness are force multipliers and critical to the military mission. Tobacco use, including but not limited to cigarettes, cigars, spit tobacco (also known as smokeless tobacco or "chew"), and electronic cigarettes (e-cigarettes), is inconsistent with the Air Force's goal of a mission-ready, healthy and fit force. Tobacco use affects all bodily systems, not just the mouth and lungs. Some types of cancer, cardiovascular diseases and many types of other diseases, have been linked to tobacco use. For the military member, tobacco use decreases endurance, night vision and fine motor coordination (for example, the coordination needed to hold a weapon steady), increases the risk of injuries (such as fractures) and post-operative respiratory complications, and impairs (or slows) wound healing. Additionally, the Environmental Protection Agency classifies tobacco smoke as a class "A" carcinogen. This means smoking causes cancer. Smoking is an obvious cancer threat to the smoker; but, more importantly, it poses a cancer threat to the individual who chooses not to smoke. Tobacco not only harms the user but can also cause cancer or contribute to cardiovascular disease in those who breathe the exhaled smoke called environmental tobacco smoke.

18.28.2. While studies by the Centers for Disease Control and Prevention and the National Institutes of Health have shown a decline in cigarette smoking, the use of other forms of tobacco has significantly increased. The increased use of smokeless tobacco is based on the faulty assumption of less hazardous. Smokeless tobacco actually contains 28 different cancer-causing agents (carcinogens). Oral cancers affect 30,000 people annually, and one person dies every hour as a result of this disease. The 5-year survival rate is very low. Only 50 percent of persons are alive at 5 years after diagnosis.

18.28.3. Nicotine found in tobacco products is addictive. Nearly one-half of all smokers in the United States have tried to quit in the past year. Because of the powerful physical and psychological addiction, quitting can be a challenge. The longer one uses tobacco, the more difficult cessation can be. Therefore, never using products containing nicotine is the best prevention. The United States Surgeon General has found that nearly 100 percent of adults who smoke every day started smoking when they were 26 years of age or younger, reinforcing prevention in our younger Airmen is critical to reducing tobacco prevalence in the Air Force.

## 18.29. Cost of Tobacco use to the Air Force.

The significant costs associated with tobacco use are both physical and financial. TRICARE has estimated that tobacco use costs the Department of Defense $1.7 billion annually because of increased healthcare utilization and decreased work productivity (due to smoking breaks and illness). No less significant is the fact that the cost of smoking a pack a day for a year is 1-month's base pay for an Airman Basic.

## 18.30. Air Force Standards.

AFI 40-102, *Tobacco Use in the Air Force*, expands tobacco-free environments. Tobacco use on a military installation is restricted to designated tobacco areas. Tobacco use is prohibited on military treatment facility campuses; within 50 feet of a building entry, sidewalk, or parking lot; within 100 feet of a playground; on all recreational facilities, including athletic complexes, golf courses, and beaches; in all lodging rooms, lodging and unaccompanied housing common areas, and temporary lodging facility units; and family housing if serviced by a common air-handling unit. Installation commanders are authorized to designate all unaccompanied housing as nonsmoking. The Air Force prohibits all students in technical training, accession, and graduate medical education programs from using tobacco products while in duty uniform, and prohibits tobacco use at all times during basic military training. Not using tobacco should be the Air Force norm to promote mission readiness, health, and productivity. Commanders are expected to support Airmen trying to quit tobacco products. Installation health promotion programs provide strategies for education, motivation, and intervention to discourage tobacco use. Formal, structured tobacco cessation programs designed to assist members in breaking the addiction to tobacco products are available.

### Section 18F—Medical Care

## 18.31. The Military Health System:

18.31.1. The military health system is a national leader in health care, health education, training, research, and technology. The military health system mission, vision, and overall strategy focus Department of Defense resources on providing a highly ready system of health that supports our nation's military mission—anytime, anywhere.

18.31.2. The military health system supports the operational mission by fostering, protecting, sustaining, and restoring health. The military health system provides the direction, resources, health care providers, and other means necessary for promoting the health of the beneficiary population. These include developing and promoting health awareness issues to educate customers, discovering and resolving environmentally based health threats, providing health services (including preventive care, problem intervention services, and pastoral care and religious support), and improving the means and methods for maintaining the health of the beneficiary population by constantly evaluating the performance of the health support. The military health system supports all uniformed service personnel, retirees, and their families.

**18.32. The Defense Health Agency:**

The Defense Health Agency is a joint Combat Support Agency that supports the military medical services and manages the execution of health policy issued by the Assistant Secretary of Defense for Health Affairs. The Defense Health Agency supports the delivery of integrated, affordable, and high-quality health services to military health system beneficiaries. In addition, the Defense Health Agency executes responsibility for shared services, functions, and activities of the military health system and other common clinical and business processes in support of the military services. The Defense Health Agency additionally serves as the program manager for the TRICARE health plan.

**18.33. The Air Force Medical Services:**

18.33.1. The Air Force medical services mission is to enable medically fit forces, provide expeditionary medics, and improve the health of all we serve to meet our Nation's needs.

18.33.2. The Air Force medical services vision is to ensure that our patients are the "Healthiest and Highest Performing Segment of the United States by 2025."

18.33.3. The Air Force medical services objectives are to:

18.33.3.1. Promote and sustain a Healthy and Fit Force.

18.33.3.2. Prevent Illness and Injury.

18.33.3.3. Restore Health.

18.33.3.4. Optimize Human Performance.

18.33.4. The Air Force medical service is increasingly called upon to deliver medical capabilities throughout the range of military operations. Diverse medical missions consist of civil-military operations, global health engagement, or humanitarian assistance/disaster relief as part of joint or multinational operations. The Air Force medical service provides the joint forces with several distinct capabilities around the globe, including: health services support, en route casualty support, and health care to eligible beneficiaries.

**18.34. TRICARE Program:**

TRICARE is the worldwide health care program serving uniformed service members and retirees, their family members, survivors, plus certain former spouses entitled to TRICARE benefits. TRICARE programs are also available to Air Reserve Component members and their families. TRICARE is a force multiplier for the military health system that fills gaps in military health care using networks of civilian health care professionals, facilities, pharmacies, and suppliers. These civilian networks help enable the Department of Defense to provide beneficiaries with access to high-quality health care services even while uniformed medics are serving abroad in contingency operations. Comprehensive, current information on the TRICARE program can be found at www.tricare.mil.

**18.35. TRICARE Regions.**

TRICARE is available in the United States and overseas locations. Each TRICARE region has a managed care support contractor that administers and coordinates health care services with network and non-network civilian hospitals and providers.

**18.36. TRICARE Plans.**

Several TRICARE health plan options are available to eligible beneficiaries. Availability for each depends on the sponsor's military status and residence. The three primary health care options offered to eligible beneficiaries are TRICARE Prime, TRICARE Standard, and TRICARE Extra.

18.36.1. **TRICARE Prime.**

TRICARE Prime is the managed care option and offers the most affordable and comprehensive health coverage to beneficiaries. Active duty members and their families do not pay enrollment fees, annual deductibles, or copays for care, unless they seek care in the network without a primary care manager referral. Each Prime enrollee is assigned a primary care manager who is responsible for providing routine, non-emergency, and urgent health care. The primary care manager is responsible for submitting referrals for specialty care and establishing medical necessity when needed. The primary care manager also coordinates with the regional TRICARE contractor, when necessary, to find specialists in the network. TRICARE Prime also has time and distance standards for urgent, routine, and specialty care to ensure beneficiaries can conveniently access care when the care is needed. Other Prime benefits include travel reimbursement for some specialty care, and a point-of-service option that permits enrollees to seek care from any provider without a referral; however, the point-of-service option carries significantly higher deductibles and cost shares then those under TRICARE Standard. TRICARE Prime is the only health plan option available to active duty service members.

18.36.1.1. **TRICARE Prime Remote.** TRICARE Prime Remote is a stateside health plan option for active duty service members and active duty family members who live and work 50 miles or one-hour drive time from a medical treatment facility in a TRICARE Prime Remote designated zip code.

18.36.1.1.1. **Active Duty Service Members.** Uniformed service members on extended active duty orders who meet TRICARE Prime Remote qualifications are required to enroll in TRICARE Prime Remote. In some cases where geographic boundaries create undue hardship for travel, active duty service members living closer than 50 miles may be eligible for TRICARE Prime Remote.

18.36.1.1.2. **Active Duty Family Members.** Active duty family members residing with their TRICARE Prime Remote-enrolled sponsors are eligible for TRICARE Prime Remote for active duty family members and must enroll to enjoy the benefit. Family members enrolled in TRICARE Prime Remote for active duty family members may remain enrolled even if the sponsor receives unaccompanied permanent change of station orders as long as they continue to reside in the same TRICARE Prime Remote location.

18.36.1.2. **TRICARE Overseas Program Prime Remote.** TRICARE overseas program offers Prime coverage to active duty service members permanently assigned to designated remote locations and their eligible command-sponsored family members. Only active duty family members who meet the Joint Travel Regulation definition of command sponsored are eligible for TRICARE overseas program Prime Remote enrollment.

18.36.2. **TRICARE Standard and Extra and TRICARE Overseas Program Standard.**

TRICARE Standard and Extra are fee-for-service plans available to eligible non-active duty beneficiaries throughout the United States. TRICARE Standard is the stateside program and TRICARE Overseas Program Standard is the overseas program. Enrollment is not required and coverage is automatic as long as the beneficiary is eligible and registered in the Defense Eligibility and Enrollment System. When using TRICARE Standard and Extra, the beneficiary may visit any TRICARE-authorized provider within the network or outside the network. Care within military medical treatment facilities is on a space-available basis only. Referrals for health care are not needed under these two health plans, but some services may require prior authorization. The network status of the provider being seen determines whether the beneficiary will be charged copays under TRICARE Standard or TRICARE Extra. When visiting a non-network provider, the Standard option is being used and Standard copays apply. When visiting a network provider, the Extra option is being used and the beneficiary will pay less out of pocket as compared to non-network providers. Additionally, when using network providers, the provider will file all medical claims on behalf of the beneficiary and the beneficiary will not be liable for any charges outside of the TRICARE copay and deductible.

18.36.3. **TRICARE Reserve Select.**

TRICARE Reserve Select plan is a premium-based health plan available for purchase worldwide and offers a TRICARE Standard-like benefit. TRICARE Reserve Select is available for purchase by qualified members of the selected Reserve for themselves and their eligible family members. Members must not be enrolled or eligible to enroll in the Federal Employee Health Benefits Program.

18.36.4. **TRICARE Young Adult.**

The TRICARE Young Adult program is a premium-based health care plan available for purchase by qualified dependents when dependents "age out" of TRICARE eligibility. TRICARE Young Adult offers TRICARE Prime and TRICARE Standard coverage worldwide. TRICARE Young Adult includes medical and pharmacy benefits, but excludes dental coverage.

18.36.4.1. Young adult dependents may generally purchase TRICARE young adult coverage when the following criteria are met:

18.36.4.1.1. The young adult is a dependent of a TRICARE-eligible uniformed service sponsor.

18.36.4.1.2. Unmarried.

18.36.4.1.3. At least 21 (or age 23 if previously enrolled in a full-time course of study at an approved institution of higher learning and if the sponsor provides at least 50 percent of the financial support), or has not yet reached age 26.

18.36.4.2. Young adult dependents may not purchase TRICARE young adult coverage when they are:

18.36.4.2.1. Eligible to enroll in an employer-sponsored health plan as defined in TRICARE Young Adult regulations.

18.36.4.2.2. Eligible for a different TRICARE program.

18.36.3.2.3. Married.

## 18.37. TRICARE Dental Program.

The TRICARE Dental Program is a voluntary, premium-based dental insurance plan and offers dental coverage for a wide range of services to active duty family members, Guard/Reserve members, and their eligible family members. Active duty service members (and Reservists called to active duty for more than 30 days) are not eligible for TRICARE Dental Program. Beneficiaries will pay monthly premiums and cost-shares. Monthly premiums vary based on sponsor and member status. All dental care is provided by civilian dentists, and either the dentist or the patient is required to file claims for reimbursement.

### Section 18G—Suicide Prevention

## 18.38. Suicide Defined.

The Centers for Disease Control and Prevention defines suicide as death caused by self-directed injurious behavior with an intent to die as a result of the behavior.

## 18.39. Suicide Demographics.

In any given year, roughly 40,000 Americans die by suicide, almost twice as many as are killed by homicide. The military is not exempt from the problem of suicide. Suicide remains a leading cause of concern and preventable form of death among Air Force personnel. During the last five years (2011 - 2015) the Air Force lost between 43- 63 Airmen per year to death by suicide. This equates to 12.9 to 20.3 suicides for every 100,000 Airmen. The Air National Guard and Air Force Reserve components have lost an average of 25 Airmen per year. Additionally, the Air Force has lost an average of 18 civilian employees to death by suicide over the last five years. Within the Air Force, the most common stressors experienced by those who die by suicide are relationship problems, legal problems, mental health problems, financial hardship and work problems. Air Force data shows that while all age, rank, gender and ethnic groups are represented suicide is most common amongst young, junior enlisted Caucasian males.

## 18.40. Effect on the Military.

When suicides occur in the Air Force, they may result in a number of serious consequences, which include:

18.40.1. First and foremost, a preventable loss of human life.

18.40.2. Second, the grief and loss to the deceased's family, friends, co-workers, and military community.

18.40.3. Third, a direct impact on mission capability through loss of the deceased's skills, experience, and productivity.

## 18.41. Dynamics of Suicide.

18.41.1. The reasons for considering suicide will vary from person to person. All people experience stressors (i.e., challenges or problems) and distress (i.e., the negative feelings associated with stressors). Research tends to identify that risk for suicide is associated with feeling isolated/not belonging, the belief that the individual is or will become a burden and an acquired capability both in access to a means to die and overcoming the fear of dying. Other factors associated with suicide are new or worsening stressors/distress combined with an inability to problem solve/cope. The Air Force promotes and supports Airmen who resolve their problems and challenges in healthy, safe, and constructive ways. To that end, the Air Force has developed many resources to help Airmen and their families resolve these problems.

18.48.2. Airmen must know the importance of recognizing that anyone can become suicidal, regardless of how well they have managed military or personal stress previously. If an Airman experiences stressors or problems that overwhelm their ability to cope, it may result in feeling distressed, alone, and a burden to others. This may increase vulnerability and susceptibility to suicide.

## 18.42. Protective Factors.

18.42.1. Protective factors are strengths or resources which the individual possesses or practices which enhance resilience and reduce distress. Common protective factors include:

18.42.1.1. Sense of belonging.

18.42.1.2. Good, healthy support from family, friends, and fellow Airmen.

18.42.1.3. Effective problem solving skills and coping strategies.

18.42.1.4. Individual's belief that he/she has control over his/her own life and actions.

18.42.1.5. Willingness to seek help early.

18.42.1.6. Focus on the future.

18.42.1.7. Believe things will get better.

18.42.1.8. Lack of access to means to hurt yourself.

18.42.1.9. Cultural/religious/spiritual beliefs that discourage suicide and support self-preservation.

18.42.2. Demographic factors are personal and unchangeable by the individual. They include aspects such as gender or age. Common stressors are experiences which may increase risk. They include experiences such as problems in a relationship or legal problems. Risk factors are personal characteristics which reduce resilience or increase susceptibility to illness and suicide. Risk factors include a history of mental illness or use of substances. Warning signs are sudden and signify a person is in distress and requires support. Warning signs include sudden changes such as sleep difficulties or sudden discipline problems (See Figure 18.5.).

**Figure 18.5. Demographic Factors, Common Stressors, Risk Factors and Warning Signs.**

| Demographic Factors | Common Stressors | Risk Factors | Warning Signs |
| --- | --- | --- | --- |
| Male | Relationship Problems | Mental Illness | Social Isolation |
| Young | Legal Problems | Substance Use | Changes in Sleep |
| Single | Financial Problems | Increased Alcohol Use | Poor Work Performance |
| Rank E1-E4 | Workplace Problems | Trauma History | Sudden Discipline Problems |
| | | Family History of Suicide | Anger |

## 18.43. Common Problems.

18.43.1. **Legal Problems.** Being under investigation for a suspected criminal offense is extremely stressful. Legal problems almost always entail some type of career impact and can be cause for administrative action by the Air Force. Military members who face serious legal problems often worry about public disgrace, a very real threat to their careers, their freedom, or their ability to find work if separated from the Air Force. While criminal charges carry realistic consequences, some individuals may begin thinking of the worst possible outcome whether realistic or not. This increased stress (real or perceived) is why they need more support from their command, unit, and Air Force community regardless of the crime for which they have been investigated/charged/convicted.

18.43.2. **Financial Problems.** Financial problems can be a stressor and a cause of distress. Alert commanders often recognize this as symptomatic of a possible broader pattern of problems or poor decision-making. Financial problems can also be a symptom of other problems such as gambling or substance misuse/addiction.

18.43.3. **Relationship Problems.** Relationship problems are the most common stressor type among Air Force members who have died by suicide. An abrupt loss, like a break up in a romantic relationship is a frequently seen stressor. A healthy, happy and supportive relationship can be an important protective factor against many other kinds of stress. When relationships are troubled they may add to personal stress/distress and/or make other stressors more challenging to manage.

18.43.4. **Work and Administrative Problems.** Work and administrative problems (e.g., failure to complete tasks, poor performance or showing up to work late) have been noted in many Air Force suicides. These work related stressors may be a sign of other problems (e.g., alcohol or relationship problems) and/or they may influence or increase feelings of hopelessness and isolation. Feelings of hopelessness and isolation increase vulnerability and susceptibility to suicide. An Airman facing administrative problems like fitness testing failures may feel his career and future are at risk. Airmen must be able to identify and understand the seriousness of workplace or administrative problems. Front line leaders and fellow Airmen should understand the challenges that an Airman may be experiencing and act to provide support.

18.43.5. **Mental Health Problems.** Studies in non-military populations have tended to show that up to 90% of individuals dying from suicide have evidence of past mental health problems. This has led to the assumption that mental health problems lead to suicide. While many individuals who die by suicide have a mental health history the majority of individuals with a mental health history will not attempt or die by suicide. Mental health problems are common among Airmen who die by suicide. Despite the difficulty to fully quantify mental health problems among Airmen who die by suicide, since Airmen may avoid seeking mental health care and/or may under-report their symptoms. Most mental health problems treated in the Air Force are not severe and many mental health visits are related to difficulties with life stresses rather than a serious mental illness. However, individuals with significant mental illness are at increased risk of suicide. Therefore, Airmen with symptoms of a mental illness must understand the importance of seeking help early and complying with their treatment plans. Effective treatments for mental illness are available and can reduce risk of suicide.

### 18.44. Facts about Air Force Suicides.

18.44.1. **Planned versus Unplanned.** Suicides may be unplanned (impulsive) or planned. In unplanned suicides, there may be little or no warning. These may be very difficult to predict or prevent and can be associated with excessive use of alcohol or other substances. In planned suicides, an individual may take the time to plan out the aspects of their death, like updating a will or checking on life insurance. While these are normal activities for most adults to undertake, a pattern of behavior in an Airman that indicates he is "putting his affairs in order" may indicate consideration of suicide. There are often some indicators in either planned or unplanned suicides that can be detected. See the list of risk factors to identify potential changes.

18.44.2. **Communication of Intent.** Not every Airman who dies by suicide will communicate their intention to end their life. Some may make suicidal statements (e.g., stating that others would be better off without them), or send texts, use voicemails, social media posts or leave a note. Sometimes suicidal individuals talk about themes of death and suicide, without referring to themselves. In other cases, the deceased may not communicate their intent at all. The increase in the use of electronic communications presents another medium for people to communicate suicidal thoughts or intentions as well as new opportunities for alert Airmen to intervene. Any suicidal remark should be taken very seriously and followed up on. Some people are reluctant to ask a person whether they are having thoughts of suicide because of the fear that they will give someone the idea. Substantial research indicates that this is not the case. The opposite is true: asking a person if they are having thoughts of suicide may prevent a suicide by getting the person the care they need.

18.44.3. **Time of Year versus Unpredictable Variability.** Statistically, suicide is a rare occurrence. Because of the infrequent, suicide rates in small populations (e.g. a major command) vary quite randomly. This often leads people to try to find factors like time of year to explain rises and dips in rate. One such myth is that suicide is more common during the holidays when people may feel more alone and isolated. This is not true. Personal factors like the ones described above are much more important. Vigilance must be maintained year round.

18.44.4. **Changes in Behavior versus no Change in Behavior.** A common myth is that once an Airman has made the decision to die by suicide, they may appear calm, as if all their problems have been resolved. This may be true for some, but not all. Airmen need to be observant for any sudden changes in behavior or attitude in their fellow Airman. These changes should be attended to in a supportive manner to ensure the individual is not considering suicide.

### 18.45. Self-injurious Behavior and Suicide Attempts.

Self-injurious behavior (i.e., cutting, burning) is any behavior that intentionally causes harm to the individual regardless of the severity of the injury. A suicide attempt is any behavior whose intent is to end the individual's life, regardless of the outcome. Any self-injury or suicide attempt should be treated as serious as the severity of injury is not an accurate indicator of the person's potential risk or intent. These injuries warrant immediate medical and command attention and should be addressed and reported without delay.

### 18.46. Every Airman's Responsibilities.

In the Air Force, each Airman has the responsibility to identify and support other Airmen (Regular Air Force, Air National Guard, Air Force Reserve, Civilians and Family Members) in times of need. Each Airman must be aware of the following: (1) Command is available and trained to provide support to Airmen in need, or those attempting to support their Airmen; (2) The Air Force established numerous resources aimed at resolving problems and stressors. Airmen can access these resources through chaplains, medical services or command leadership; (3) Airman can access counseling through Military One Source (1-800-342-9647) as well as Military Family Life Counselors; and (4) National resources like the Military Crisis line (1-800-273-8233, Press 1). Early identification combined with proactive problem solving enhances careers. Early intervention increases the probability of success, and is most likely to save a life; similarly, this helps maintain the balance promoted through the four domains of Comprehensive Airmen Fitness (Social, Mental, Physical and Spiritual). There are a number of identifiable risk factors and warning signs. These may include: (1) multiple stressors or an intense stressor, sudden mood or behavior changes; (2) giving away personal effects; and (3) making statements about suicide/suggesting it would be better if the individual were not alive. Safety is increased when an at-risk Airman has limited access to means of self-harm (e.g., firearms or potentially dangerous medications). Command and Legal should be part of this process. Any sudden purchase of lethal means can be a very significant warning sign that should be questioned and reported.

18.46.1. The people most likely to spot a person at risk for suicide are the ones who interact with that person on a daily basis (e.g., friends, coworkers or immediate supervisors). These individuals are best positioned to notice changes in an at-risk Airman's behavior, mood, and performance. Engage with that person, find out what caused the observed changes, assist in choosing resources to resolve stressors, and communicate concerns with the chain of command as appropriate.

18.46.2. Know your resources and encourage appropriate help-seeking from installation and other support agencies to resolve the challenges. Challenges and stressors are a normal part of each person's life. You are encouraged to engage with fellow Airman and know how they generally look and behave. When you notice there is a problem, assist your fellow Airman in finding help to resolve the challenge early.

## 18.47. Military Leadership Role in Preventing Suicide:

18.47.1. While suicide prevention is the ultimate responsibility of every Airman, the Air Force has identified that leadership support and action across the levels of command are critical to the goal of reducing suicide in the Air Force.

18.47.2. The Air Force Suicide Prevention program is based on leadership action. Leaders at all levels are responsible for implementing this program. Successful risk identification rests with the Airman's most immediate associates and his or her first-line supervisors who see and interact with them on a daily basis and are in a position to see any changes in behavior or performance that may signal a problem. Open communication between Airmen and their supervisors, especially in an environment where there is genuine concern for everyone's well-being, is vitally important.

18.47.3. Frontline supervisors have tremendous and complex responsibilities in our high ops tempo Air Force, executing the mission and taking care of their subordinates. Effective training and strong leadership can enhance the support that an Airman will receive. Some factors that can challenge effective supervision are: (1) tunnel vision on the mission to the exclusion of subordinate needs; (2) not being engaged with their Airmen; (3) difficulty recognizing risk factors and warning signs; (4) lack of knowledge of Air Force supported resources and the true impact of seeking help on an Air Force career; and (5) inappropriately "protecting" the Airman from the consequences of their actions or failing to take proper action. Some examples of inappropriate supervisor actions are supervisors telling subordinates to avoid seeking mental health assistance as this will hurt their career, helping subordinates hide alcohol and drug misuse problems, promoting the avoidance of installation helping services and possible safe and constructive resolution of problems. The majority of the time, seeking help appropriately does not have long-term negative career impact. In fact, seeking help can improve performance and enable people to better solve problems. Supervisors should engage in problems early to ensure subordinates get the help they need to maintain peak performance.

18.47.4. When risk is identified, appropriate professional resources can be obtained and applied to the problem. The Air Force has invested in the development of outstanding helping resources whose purpose is to support individuals in distress, leaders in enhancing safety, promoting balance in the four domains of Comprehensive Airmen Fitness and preventing suicide. Appropriate intervention will vary depending on the nature of the problem and degree of risk. Sometimes situations require services from multiple support agencies (e.g., Mental Health, Airman & Family Readiness and Chaplains, etc.). The Airman's Guide for Assisting Personnel in Distress provides resources to help supervisors and Airmen guide personnel to appropriate helping agencies and is available at: airforcemedicine.af.mil/airmansguide.

## 18.48. Actions to Mitigate Suicide Risk.

While not every suicide can be prevented, definite steps can be taken by Air Force personnel to reduce risk in Air Force populations. The following actions can be taken to support Airmen in resolving life's challenges and reducing the number of suicides: (1) Knowing your co-workers; their usual mood and behaviors, and how they are functioning; (2) Being able to recognize early signs of risk, stress and distress; (3) Engaging with Airmen to determine what may be stressful or problematic; (4) Assisting Airmen with choosing the most appropriate resource to help resolve the problem; and (5) Following up with Airmen to ensure the stressors are resolving and new ones are not taking their place.

## 18.49. Psychological Services.

Mental Health Services are designed to be a force multiplier in the Air Force. Seeking care for a mental health problem is a sign of strength and increases the likelihood of recovery while reducing risk for suicide. More than 12% of Air Force personnel voluntarily seek mental health services each year.

18.49.1. At the installation level, mental health clinic staff members typically perform a risk assessment on all individuals who come in for services as well as screen for suicide at follow up appointments. The services and treatment provided at mental health clinics play an important role in suicide prevention, but the healthcare system does not own the problem and can only act if aware of the problem. This means individuals at risk must either seek help themselves or be brought into the healthcare system by others. Suicide prevention is the responsibility of the entire Air Force community.

18.49.2. A common fear is that seeking care at the mental health clinic will have negative impact on the person's career. A 2006 study (Rowan, A.B. & Campise R. L., 2006) reviewing more than 1,000 self-referred mental health cases found that in 89 percent of cases there was no contact at all between the mental health clinic and the patient's unit. In 97% of cases there was no negative impact on career. Confidentiality is governed by AFI 44-172 *Mental Health.*

18.49.3. Mental health providers are required by DoDI 6490.08, *Command Notification Requirements to Dispel Stigma in Providing Mental Health Care to Service Members*, to disclose safety (for example, suicidal or violent thoughts) and fitness for duty issues to commanders, but all other information is private. For more information on the limitations of confidentiality see DoDI 6490.08. Willingness to seek help when needed is a sign of good judgment and strength.

18.49.4. In an effort to promote help-seeking by Airmen who are experiencing legal or administrative problems, the Air Force instituted the Limited Privilege Suicide Prevention Program in accordance with AFI 44-172. This program allows Airmen who are under investigation to receive mental health care without risk of further incriminating themselves.

## 18.50. Air Force Suicide Prevention Program:

The Air Force Suicide Prevention Program is an evidence based approach which requires that all personnel take an active role in reducing suicide.

18.50.1. **Suicide Prevention Program's History.** In May 1996, General Thomas S. Moorman, Air Force Vice-Commander, commissioned an integrated product team composed of all functional areas of the Air Force. He requested General Charles H. Roadman (Air Force Surgeon General) chair the 75-member committee and develop suicide prevention strategies. The suicide prevention integrated product team quickly realized suicide was not a medical problem, but instead was a community problem. To establish an effective program, they designed a line program owned by the Chief of Staff of the Air Force with the Air Force Surgeon General as the office of primary responsibility. The program was founded upon the concept that decreasing suicides required a community/Public Health approach in which prevention and assistance were offered long before someone became suicidal.

18.50.2. **Air Force Suicide Prevention Summit**. In 2015, in response to a concern about rising suicide rates, the Air Force convened a Suicide Prevention Summit, bringing together subject matter experts from DoD, the Military Services, federal agencies including the National Institute for Mental Health and Centers for Disease Control and academic researchers and theorists, to address the issue of suicide in the Air Force and move the program forward. Based on the recommendations of the Summit, six interconnected Suicide Prevention Lines of Effort were identified and six corresponding working groups were formed under oversight of the Air Force Integrated Delivery System and Community Action information Board. These Lines of Effort's included: (1) Integrate Prevention; (2) Strengthen Airman Culture; (3) Leverage Strength-Based Communication; (4) Enhance Civilian Support Services; (5) Targeted Resilience Outreach; and (6) Improve Medical Care of At-risk Airmen. The 11 elements were retained as the core of the program while a wide range of initiatives were established and executed under the Lines of Effort framework to enhance the effectiveness of suicide prevention.

18.50.3. **Air Force Suicide Prevention Program Elements.** In order to combat suicide, the suicide prevention integrated product team developed and implemented 11 overlapping initiatives or elements, as published in AFI 90-505, *Suicide Prevention Program.* These 11 initiatives are designed to foster an Airman culture under commander-led action groups which can be grouped into three broad categories:

18.50.3.1. **Leadership and Community.** Leadership Involvement, Unit-based Preventive Services, Airman Culture, Suicide Event Tracking and Analysis, Post Suicide Response (Postvention), Integrated Delivery System, Community Action Information Board and Commanders Consultation Assessment Tool.

18.50.3.2. **Education.** Addressing Suicide Prevention through Professional Military Education, Guidelines for Commanders: Use of Mental Health Services.

18.50.3.3. **Protections for those under Investigation.** The Investigative Interview Policy and Limited Privilege Suicide Prevention Program. The Investigate Interview policy directs that following any investigative interview, the Air Force investigators (e.g., Air Force Office of Special Investigations, Inspector General, Security Forces, and Equal Employment Opportunity) must hand-off the accused directly to the member's commander, or first sergeant through person-to-person documented contact. Limited Privilege Suicide Prevention Program is available to those who are under investigation or have been formally charged with a crime. This protection allows individuals at risk of suicide to access mental health services with confidentiality of what is discussed during that time that the individual is deemed to be at risk.

## 18.51. Intervention Model.

Suicide prevention is everyone's responsibility. For effective suicide prevention, we need to create a culture that encourages early help-seeking behavior and develop a community that provides assistance long before someone becomes suicidal. The model listed below was developed to assist Airmen in intervening when an Airman is experiencing stress, distress and challenges.

### 18.51.1. The Ask, Care, and Escort (ACE) Model.

To facilitate personal engagement in suicide prevention, the Air Force has developed the acronym, ACE, to help people remember the key steps.

18.51.1.1. **Ask.** When you see or hear any of the warning signs discussed in this section, or are aware of risk factors in someone's life, ask questions to learn more about the person's problems or concerns. If you have any concerns about someone's safety, calmly but directly ask the question, "Are you thinking of killing/hurting yourself?" Asking about suicide gives people permission to talk about a subject that may otherwise be difficult to bring up and lets the Airman know you are ready to discuss what they are experiencing. Do not promise to keep thoughts of suicide a secret. Airmen need to remember the importance of sharing these concerns with command and professionals who can help the person.

18.51.1.2. **Care.** Showing care and concern for those at risk is important. Simply taking the time to ask about problems, and asking specifically about suicide shows caring and concern. If someone acknowledges thoughts of suicide, listen to them and allow them to share what is troubling them. Avoid making judgmental statements, such as "you wouldn't do something so stupid" or immediately trying to solve their problem or talk them out of suicide. If they have shared thoughts of suicide with you, accept that they are in distress, listen to their concerns, and begin the process of getting them help. You should also identify if they have a plan for suicide, what the plan is, and attempt to remove anything that might be used for self-harm, such as weapons or medications. First, understand there are many potential means for self-harm and recommend you take reasonable steps to secure the potential means of suicide while not putting yourself in harm's way. If you are not able to secure the potential means of self-harm, or you have significant concern about the individual's safety, then command and emergency services need to be contacted.

18.51.1.3. **Escort.** After asking about suicide and showing concern, the final step is to escort the person to command, or a professional support agency that can provide appropriate assistance. Do not leave him or her alone, or send the person alone to a chaplain or mental health clinic as he or she may change his or her mind on the way. At most bases, chaplains and mental health professionals are on call through the command post, and evaluations can be conducted in local emergency rooms if on-base services are not accessible. If an Airman reveals that he or she is thinking about suicide, this is a life or death emergency and command must be contacted. If a distressed Airman will not agree to go with you, you should contact your chain of command or emergency services for help to ensure the person's safety.

18.51.2. Understanding the appropriate steps to suicide risk prevention and the available Air Force approved resources can aid in saving the career and life of a fellow Airman. Engage the Airman to understand the problem. Utilize leadership to support safety and good decision-making. In non-crisis situations utilize resources such as chaplain services, Military Family Life Counselors or Military One Source. If an Airman is in crisis utilize emergency services including Air Force, local civilian or national resources, 911, emergency room, mental health clinic or Military Crisis Line (1-800-273-8255) to provide professional support to an Airman in distress.

## Section 18H—Posttraumatic Stress Disorder (PTSD)

### 18.52. Posttraumatic Stress Disorder Components.

Understanding the difference between operational stress and Post Traumatic Stress Disorder (PTSD) is important. Most individuals who experience a traumatic event in an operational environment will have some reaction and some signs of "stress" like problems with sleep or troublesome memories; however, the majority of individuals exposed to a traumatic event will not develop PTSD. PTSD is a complex mental health diagnosis made by trained professionals for individuals meeting specific diagnostic criteria. Prolonged or repeated exposures to stressful or traumatic events increase the chance of stress reactions, and if over looked or untreated can lead to mental health symptoms to include recurrent and unwanted thoughts, images and dreams, exaggerated startle response, and avoidance of situations or activities that remind the individual of aspects of the traumatic event. PTSD also causes persistent mood symptoms, including feelings of depression, foreshortened sense of the future, and an inability to express the full range of emotions. This latter symptom is often noticed by friends and family members who are more likely to notice a mood or behavioral change in the individual with PTSD. Since the dawn of time, people have experienced traumatic events and many have the skills and resources to deal with them. For this reason most stress reactions resolve on their own or with minimal assistance, especially when identified early. Therefore, the benefit to the individual, unit and mission is to recognize and respond to stressors and stress-related symptoms proactively when they are present in the unit or individual. However, do not assume that simply because someone has been exposed to trauma, they will inevitably develop PTSD. If symptoms from a traumatic event emerge, they usually emerge within the first 30 days of the trauma and for someone to develop delayed onset PTSD in the absence of any initial symptoms is unusual. Some of the symptoms of PTSD you might notice in yourself or your wingmen are listed below. Depending on many factors, like the severity and number of exposures, for a small subset of individuals, stress reactions do not resolve on their own, and symptoms of PTSD may develop. The Diagnostic and Statistical Manual-5 defines PTSD by eight criteria: (1) stressor (there must be a traumatic incident the person was exposed to); (2) intrusive symptoms (the person persistently re-experiences the event); (3) avoidance (the person attempts to avoid reminders of the event); (4) negative alterations in cognitions (thoughts) and mood; (5) alterations in arousal and reactivity (like irritability, easy startle and sleep difficulties); (6) duration (persistence of symptoms greater than one month); (7) functional significance (impact to functional areas (e.g., social, occupational)); and (8) exclusion (disturbance not due to medication, substance use or other illness). As with most mental health diagnoses, other conditions must first be ruled-out before a diagnosis of PTSD can be made. This includes the effects of medication, alcohol or a co-existing medical condition that shares some of the symptoms of PTSD.

## 18.53. PTSD Incidence.

New rates of diagnosed PTSD continue to remain relatively low (under 1%) among total force Airmen, but differ by gender and career group. Women are twice as likely to be diagnosed with PTSD as men, and specific career fields show elevated rates of PTSD, including special investigators, medical, and support personnel. Deployment is a risk factor for PTSD because deployment increases the likelihood of exposure to trauma. However, an important note is that most people who develop PTSD experience a non-combat trauma such as interpersonal violence which can occur in a number of different environments.

## 18.54. Prevention.

The prevention of PTSD occurs by fostering resilient coping responses to stress. The more psychologically capable the individual is to withstand a stressful situation, the less likely that individual is to develop PTSD. An internal locus of control, the belief that and commitment to life values, and a supportive peer network are all factors that bolster the stress response and enable Airmen to go through trauma without negative consequences. Further, the ability to recognize stress reactions and intervene when they are present is important in the prevention of PTSD and other mental health issues. This is based on the theory that preparation for trauma helps to "insulate" the individual and gain a sense of control or mastery over the environment. Deploying Airman receive just in time training on stress reactions, psychological first aid, and referral resources through online Pre-Deployment mental health training (in Advanced Distributed Learning Service). Additionally, post deployment training (currently provided by installation mental health staff) focuses on the reintegration back into home life and work after a deployment and how to recognize stress reactions and symptoms that can remain or emerge following a deployment where there have been potentially traumatic experiences. Critical to the prevention of PTSD is for leaders to clearly communicate mission details and expectations to the extent possible so that deploying Airmen can anticipate their deployment experiences and practice adaptive coping responses prior to exposure to trauma. Preparation also helps Airman evaluate the possible difficulties they may experience during deployment and develop a plan for managing those difficulties before they occur.

### 18.54.1. Risk and Protective Factors.

18.54.1.1. There are many factors that can make an individual more vulnerable to negative effects of traumatic experiences and to eventually develop PTSD. Some of these include ongoing life stresses, lack of social support, history of a psychiatric disorder/or family history of one, and past stresses like prior combat exposure, and even childhood history of abuse. Each individual has different personal strengths and resilience skills that help him or her deal with traumatic experiences. Therefore, each unit is a sum of these strengths and each deployed unit should capitalize on these strengths. Understanding your personal strengths and vulnerabilities and those of the others in your unit allows you to intervene early after a traumatic event and seek out the support needed for resolving stress reactions. Remember, risk factors or even exposure to horrific events do not equal a diagnosis of PTSD.

18.54.1.2. Effective unit leadership is a critical factor in preventing PTSD. A cohesive unit with solid leadership, clear operational goals, and frequent communication can reduce risk. Leadership which stresses and Airmen who practice good self-care (getting regular and adequate sleep, eating a balanced diet, and having adequate time for rest and relaxation) along with the use of positive stress management skills can help reduce operational stress and decrease the risk of PTSD. Informed leaders can actively impact their units to reduce the risk of PTSD and other related problems to their Airmen by ensuring they are engaged and working as a team.

### 18.54.2. Operational Stress Reactions.

Operational stress reactions can be experienced by both individuals exposed to a traumatic event or those individuals/units with a high operational tempo where the requirements of battle have kept them from having adequate downtime. Stress reactions may be evident in different forms and may range from mild to severe. Below are some of the reactions to be aware of to ensure early intervention.

18.54.2.1. Physical signs like rapid breathing or shortness of breath, feeling dizzy, headaches, feeling nauseated, profuse sweating or sweaty palms, and rapid heart rate.

18.54.2.2. Mental signs like sleep disturbance, poor attention and concentration, poor problem solving, confusion, hyper-vigilance, and nightmares.

18.54.2.3. Emotional signs like irritability and blaming others, fear or anxiety, feeling overwhelmed, feeling guilt, denial, agitation, and feelings of sadness (depressed mood).

18.54.2.4. Behavioral signs like withdrawal, change in communication, increased alcohol consumption, change in appetite, emotional outbursts, jumpiness or being easily startled, and suspiciousness.

18.54.3. **Psychological First Aid.**

Psychological first aid is designed to reduce the initial distress caused by a traumatic event and can be used for ongoing operational stress where individuals may exhibit stress reactions. Psychological first aid supports individuals with stress reactions by teaching adaptive coping and recovery skills that can easily be implemented. For individuals whose stress reactions aren't resolving in a short period of time, additional support from Mental Health or the Combat & Operational Stress Control unit should be encouraged. Tenets of psychological first aid include the following:

18.54.3.1. **Safety.** Provide a physically and emotionally safe place (as the operational environment allows) for individuals to recuperate emotionally following a traumatic event. This may be as simple as designating a tent/shelter away from the incident with food, water and a place to relax.

18.54.3.2. **Needs.** Learn what the Airmen's needs and concerns are by listening to them with compassion and responding with a calm voice. Are they worried about someone? Do they want to make a phone call?

18.54.3.3. **Availability.** Make yourself available. For example, offer to go to the gym, dining facility, play games, morale tent, or just be there to talk/listen.

18.54.3.4. **Support.** Encourage Airmen to stay connected with peers and social support, this maybe in the deployed setting or at home.

18.54.3.5. **Coping.** Provide basic coping skills that empower others to make decisions for one's self and restoration back to 'normal' state. Lead by example using self-care mentioned earlier.

18.54.3.6. **Services.** Finally, link individual with supportive services, if needed. These include Chaplains, first sergeants, or Mental Health.

18.54.4. **Pre-Exposure Preparation.**

18.54.4.1. The goal of Pre-Exposure preparation is to enhance resilience through anticipating and understanding normal responses to unusual stressors which might include exposure to battle or a mass accident scene with human casualties. Individuals are better prepared, are calmer and feel more in control when they have some advance knowledge of what to expect on scene and what stress reactions are normal and to be expected. Pre-Exposure preparation focuses on preparing Airmen for a particular mission or incident by providing relevant (and sometimes graphic) details applicable to the probable upcoming mission or situation. In preparing Airmen for a mission, Pre-Exposure preparation training will educate the Airman on three key steps to support successful performance under stress by: (1) Being aware of the individual's functioning and changes in functioning (such as changes in their behavior, sleep, or mood); (2) Identifying and practicing positive stress management behaviors (such as getting proper sleep, nutrition, and exercise); and (3) Avoiding unhelpful coping behaviors (such as excessive alcohol usage, poor sleep or eating practices, etc). Pre-Exposure preparation should be tailored to the unit and specific mission in order to be relevant and effective.

18.54.4.2. Units that have a moderate or higher chance of exposure to traumatic events as part of their duties can enhance their psychological resilience and risk of operational stress with the following preparation principles:

18.54.4.2.1. **Engage in Realistic Training.** Get Airmen ready for the tasks they will perform in the operational environment. Train using simulated or actual exposure to realistic events, such as body handling, survival training, and mock captivity training, as appropriate for the unit's mission.

18.54.4.2.2. **Strengthen Perceived Ability to Cope.** Feeling competent to do one's job in an operational environment is critical. Discuss reasons for realistic training. Enhance the individual's sense of competency by training to the point until the Airmen feels competent and has gained a sense of mastery. If possible, include the teaching of coping skills during operational training in order to increase the likelihood that the Airmen will use those skills when needed.

## 18.55. Treatment.

Today, there are treatments available for PTSD that have been demonstrated through rigorous scientific research to be high effective. These are referred to as Evidence-Based Treatments. The Air Force has supported training in two Evidence-Based Treatments by requiring training in one or more Evidence-Based Treatments during mental health residency programs in psychiatry, psychology, and social work. Direct accession providers receive training in Evidence-Based Treatments during their first assignment through a collaborative arrangement with the Center for Deployment Psychology. The two Evidence-Based Treatments that are taught to all mental health providers in the United States Air Force are: (a) Cognitive Processing Therapy; and (b) Prolonged Exposure. These are among the Evidence-Based Treatments that have been recommended as first-line treatment of PTSD by the Veterans Affairs/Department of Defense Clinical Practice Guidelines based on a detailed review of the scientific literature. Typical treatment protocols include 10-12, weekly sessions with a trained provider in a supportive, therapeutic environment. Most research indicates that Evidence-Based Treatments reduces PTSD symptoms by approximately 50% and that this improvement is sustained over several months to years. In many cases, Airmen diagnosed with PTSD and treated with Evidence-Based Treatments will "lose" the PTSD diagnosis and will notice that symptoms either disappear entirely, or are sub-threshold and do not interfere with quality of life. If properly treated, the majority of Airmen diagnosed with PTSD never require a medical board.

## Section 18I—Stress Management

## 18.56. Stress Defined.

18.56.1. At some point in your life, you have probably experienced stress. Long work days, increased deployments, and financial issues are just a few of the things that can make you feel stressed. The frequency of stress and the significant negative effect stress can have on people and organizations make this a major concern of enlisted leaders at all levels. The importance at the organizational level is because stress can negatively affect performance, organizational effectiveness, and mission accomplishment. On a personal level, experiencing stress over an extended period of time can lead to health problems and affect your overall quality of life. Therefore, the importance is to personally and professionally recognize stress and to learn how to manage stress effectively.

18.56.2. Stress is a dynamic concept that dates back to earlier this century. According to Jerrold S. Greenberg in his book *Comprehensive Stress Management*, the concept of stress is based on the research of two individuals named Walter Cannon and Hans Selye. Cannon, a physiologist at Harvard Medical School, was the first person to describe the body's reaction to stress. He identified this reaction as a response to a perceived threat that prepared the body for flight or fight. Later research conducted by Selye, an endocrinologist widely regarded as the father of stress research, concluded that the body's reaction to stress was the same regardless of whether the source was good or bad, positive or negative. He also provided us with a useful definition of stress. According to Selye, stress can be defined as "the nonspecific response of the body to any demand for change." The demand in Selye's definition is commonly called a stressor.

18.56.3. A stressor can be more accurately defined as any factor (demand) that has the potential to cause stress. This factor can be positive, such as getting promoted, or negative, such as getting fired. The causes of stress is from either positive or negative factors. Selye labeled the stress experienced from positive factors eustress. Eustress results from exhilarating experiences and is the stress of winning and achieving. He labeled the stress experienced from negative factors distress. Distress includes the stress of losing, failing, overworking, and not coping effectively. When you start to feel "stressed out," distress is usually the type of stress you are feeling.

18.56.4. We are in daily contact with many types of stressors. For the most part, we can categorize them into two major areas: organizational stressors and extra-organizational stressors.

18.56.4.1. Organizational stressors are the type of factors experienced in the work environment. For Airmen today, that could range from short-notice deployments to hazardous working conditions. Imagine how you would feel if your commander informed you that you would deploy in a week, or how you might feel if your work environment was bombarded with loud noises all day. If these types of situations regularly happen to you and you have not developed effective ways to cope with them, you could experience stress.

18.56.4.2. Extra-organizational stressors are the type of factors experienced outside the work environment. Three major extra-organizational stressors are family, marital, and financial issues. Family and marital issues can run the gamut from minor illness to conflicting roles in the family to a death in the family. Similarly, financial problems can run from the minor to the catastrophic. These types of stressors are important because while they usually occur outside of the duty section, if not properly managed, they can affect performance at work.

18.56.5. How do you know if you are stressed? Stress reactions appear in four different categories: cognitive, emotional, behavioral, and physical. The key to recognizing stress is to know understand what is normal for you so that you can recognize when something has changed. The combined presence of symptoms determines the degree of the problem.

Indicators (Figure 18.6) may be isolated reactions or combinations among the four categories. Finally, the duration, frequency, and intensity of the symptoms could make dealing with stress difficult.

18.56.6. Being able to recognize the symptoms of stress is important, not only for yourself, but for your Airmen, as well. The earlier you identify what stress does to your body and state of mind, the earlier you can employ stress reduction techniques.

**Figure 18.6. Common Symptoms of Stress.**

| Cognitive | Emotional | Behavioral | Physical |
|---|---|---|---|
| Memory Problems | Apathy | Appetite changes | Frequent illness |
| Inability to concentrate | Anxiety | Increased arguments | Headaches |
| Poor judgment | Depression | Increased smoking | High blood pressure |
| Seeing only the negative | Irritability | Neglecting self-care | Increased heart rate |
| Anxious or racing thoughts | Job dissatisfaction | Social withdrawal | Physical exhaustion |
| Constant worrying | Memory problems | Substance abuse | Sleep disturbances |
| | Mental fatigue | Violence | Weight gain/loss |

18.56.7. Stress management programs and methods vary, but they all tend to have common goals. Individual stress management methods aim at strengthening your ability to manage stressors and the stress response. Organizational stress management methods aim more at altering potential stressors themselves. Because organizational and extra-organizational stressors are interrelated and influence each other, attention to both stress management methods is vitally important.

**18.57. Individual Stress Management Methods:**

18.57.1. **Planning.**

You can reduce stress by identifying potential stressors before they cause problems. Once you identify stressors, you can develop strategies to avoid their effects while achieving your goals. For example, if you are stressed by crowds and long lines, don't plan to visit the commissary on or just after payday. If you get extremely upset when you are recalled in the middle of the night, having the latest recall roster and procedures readily available at all times may help reduce the amount of stress you feel. While planning can't prevent stress that occurs as an event is happening, planning is extremely valuable in preventing stress before a stressor occurs.

18.57.2. **Time Management.**

Not having enough time to complete a task can be a significant stressor for some people. If time management is an issue for you, you can reduce stress by using effective time management skills and tools, like developing a task list and prioritizing tasks.

18.57.3. **Overload Avoidance.**

For most people to eliminate, or at least reduce, the effects of overload-related stressors is relatively simple. For a start, identify and avoid busy work, delegate or empower others when possible, learn to say no, and attempt to negotiate unreasonable deadlines.

18.57.4. **Relaxation.**

Relaxation can help you manage stress and stay alert, energetic, and productive. When you relax, you reduce mind and body tension. By incorporating relaxation skills into your daily routines, you can train your body to respond differently to stress. Relaxation techniques, such as meditation, reading, and listening to music, can improve your heart rate, regulate your blood pressure, and decrease your respiratory rate. If you are experiencing stress in your life, taking the time to relax can reduce the negative effects of stress on your health.

18.57.5. **Exercise and Good Nutrition.**

Regular exercise combined with a healthy diet is an effective stress management technique. Exercise can provide an outlet for excess energy and tension caused by stress. Eating nutritious foods ensures your body has the nutrients needed to manage stress, and helps prevent overeating. Exercising and eating a balanced diet help your body become more resistant to the negative results of stress, such as high blood pressure, heart attacks, and frequent illness.

18.57.6. **Strong Social Support Networks.**

Having a strong social support network such as family, friends, social clubs, peers etc. can help you manage stress. Being able to discuss your problems with people who care about you and your wellbeing can help reduce your stress by giving you a more positive outlook, suggest solutions to your problems, or just listen. Just talking about your problems and letting them out can help release any built-up tension and may make you see the situation or problem more clearly.

## 18.58. Organizational Stress Management Methods.

As an Airman or a supervisor, your approach to dealing with stress can help reduce your and your subordinates' stress levels. You can begin by identifying potential stressors in the work environment and developing strategies to remove or reduce them. Here are a few examples of organizational stress management methods you can use:

### 18.58.1. Job Design.

If you identify potential sources of stress associated with tasks, ask yourself if there is a need for each task and if the task is feasible. Eliminate the task if not needed. If the task is feasible, ask yourself how important job design is and prioritize. If your job requires you and/or your subordinates to work long hours, consider using elements of job enrichment, like giving adequate time off or periodic breaks to help reduce potential stress. If within your power restructure the job to better accommodate individual needs and the abilities of your Airmen to help reduce stress and enhance productivity.

### 18.58.2. Improving the Work Environment.

Numerous physical factors within a work environment can be potential stressors. Some of these stressors cannot be eliminated, but you may be able to reduce them. Examine such environmental factors as temperature, noise, light levels, and make necessary improvements.

### 18.58.3. Improving Organizational Communication.

A lack of information can be a significant stressor. As a supervisor, you should do your best to keep your subordinates informed about anything that could impact their lives. In addition, you should practice good communication skills, like active listening, being open minded and avoiding prejudging, and humility. These skills not only will help reduce stress, but also promote trust, cooperation, and teamwork within the work center.

### 18.58.4. Personnel Selection and Job Placement.

Having the wrong person in a job position can create a great deal of stress for the individual and others. When possible, you should carefully match individuals to a position they are qualified for based on their skills, level of experience, and rank. In the military, this might not be the easiest thing to do, but you should keep in mind the potential stress-related benefits of having the right person in the right position.

### 18.58.5. Workplace Conflict.

Having conflict with co-workers can cause serious stress within the work center. Look for ways to help resolve any issues you or subordinates may have with others. Sit down and talk with the person with whom you are having conflict with, listen to their point of view and understand what the other person is saying, communicate your point of view in a calm and professional way, and try to come to an agreement or compromise. If the conflict can't be resolved amongst yourselves you may need to have a mediator to help resolve the issue.

### 18.58.6. Substance Abuse Programs.

Sometimes stress can cause people to resort to excessive amounts of alcohol and/or drugs which can have a dramatically negative effect on mission, morale, and readiness. All supervisors are responsible and accountable for managing substance abusers in accordance with applicable directives and getting them the help they need.

## Section 18J—Redeployment Support Process

## 18.59. Purpose.

The positive and sustained care, control, and discipline of each Airman is the purpose of the redeployment support process. The goal is to ensure personnel readiness throughout the air and space expeditionary force cycle by providing timely support for our military members and their families. Redeployment support is an ongoing process, not a homecoming event. The intent is to provide continuous, integrated support from the area of responsibility to home station and to assist in the transition from the deployed environment to family life and work site.

## 18.60. Recovery.

After periods of arduous duty and protracted periods of deployment, a lengthy respite from the deployment environment has a beneficial effect on an individual's psychological and physical status. An immediate recovery period also provides time for the returning Airman to tend to personal needs neglected during lengthy periods away from home. Each major command is responsible for establishing and publishing personnel recovery (leave, passes, attribution, and retention) policies for returning combat forces. See AFI 36-3003, *Military Leave Program*, for guidance.

## 18.61. Reconstitution.

Although recovery is important to support returning forces as they transition back to their normal environment, they also must be reconstituted for further deployment possibilities, including surge requirements. This process entails planning that will return units back to full combat capability in a short time. While there is no one correct rule set for reconstitution planning, consideration must be given to prioritizing and restoring levels of consumables expended during the crisis, and recovering lost training. Every base/unit must assess their own situation based on such variables as the magnitude, duration, and intensity of a crisis, consumption rates, and the type of deployment location (fixed versus austere base). See AFI 10-401, *Air Force Operations Planning and Execution*, for further guidance on reconstitution.

## 18.62. Scope.

The Air Force redeployment support process applies to deployed area of responsibility and home stations. All personnel deployed to an area of responsibility, to continental United States locations in support of contingencies, and to remote assignments are included. Key determinants for participation are lengthy family separation and significant family related stressors prior to reintegration. Community Action Information Board and Integrated Delivery System helping agencies complete specified activities to support redeployed Regular Air Force, Air National Guard, Air Force Reserve, military and civilian personnel, their family members, and units during the air and space expeditionary force cycle. Readjustment from duty in the area of responsibility requires structured recovery time and activities for members and families prior to leave or temporary duty.

## 18.63. Redeployment Support Process Timeline.

Figure 18.7 provides a template for commander responses and actions, and Community Action Information Board and Integrated Delivery System members' activities at the critical redeployment, recovery, reintegration, and reconstitution junctures. Subsequent sections provide detailed information on roles and responsibilities.

**Figure 18.7. Redeployment Support Timeline.**

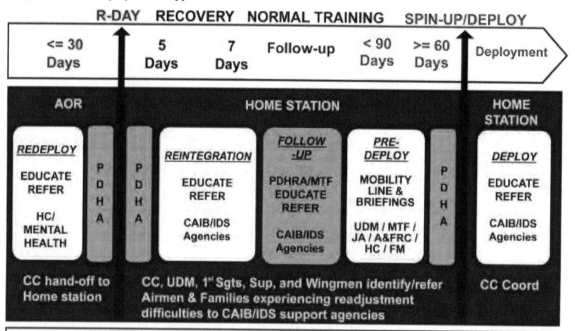

**18.64.  Home Station Community Action Information Board and Integrated Delivery System Agency Responsibilities.**

Figure 18.7 outlines the air and space expeditionary force cycle, and specifies commander and Community Action Information Board or Integrated Delivery System agency critical juncture activities. The Air and Space Expeditionary Force Online (https://aef.afpc.randolph.af.mil/default.aspx) is a critical source of deployment information, education, and training.

18.64.1. **Personnel Readiness.**

Personnel readiness begins reintegration, and develops the reception station. Personnel readiness will ensure procedures are established to account for members returning from deployments. These procedures will be incorporated into installation reconstitution planning and the installation deployment plan. Returning units and individuals will in-process with the installation personnel readiness element within 2 duty days of redeployment day. The installation personnel readiness element will update the date of return to home station for all individuals in Deliberate and Crisis Action Planning and Execution Segments on the date of notification of return according to AFI 36-3802, *Personnel Readiness Operations*.

18.64.2. **Chaplain Service.**

Chaplain Corps members support personnel, families, and base populations during contingencies according to AFI 52-104, *Chaplain Service Readiness*. At home station following deployment, chaplain service members provide follow-up support, reintegration and reunion ministries, and other programs to strengthen families and enhance individual spiritual health. Post-deployment services at Air Force Reserve Command wings will be coordinated with the reserve wing deployment support program point of contact.

18.64.3. **Airman and Family Readiness Center.**

18.64.3.1. The Airman and Family Readiness Center provides mobility and deployment assistance to help single and married Department of Defense personnel and families meet predeployment, deployment, and post deployment challenges, according to AFI 36-3009, *Airman and Family Readiness Centers*. Services help reduce stress and deal with separation and reintegration, increase individual and family morale and unit cohesion, and support operational readiness.

18.64.3.2. Airman and Family Readiness Centers use electronic media and hard copies to help develop reintegration educational material and provide materials support to the chaplain and mental health services in the area of responsibility.

18.64.3.3. During deployments, Airman and Family Readiness Center staffs tailor support to commanders, units, and families; work with local school authorities and teachers to help them understand stressors unique to children of deployed military; provide a myriad deployment support programs; and distribute commercial, printed materials addressing deployment. Upon request, one-on-one counseling is available. The Airman and Family Readiness Center staff provides support to the parents and siblings of single Airmen.

18.64.3.4. Post deployment assistance is linked to pre-deployment activities, particularly early intervention to educate families, single members, and units on concerns related to reunion and reintegration. The Airman and Family Readiness Center staff monitors family coping skills, assists potential at-risk families, and collaborates with Community Action Information Board and Integrated Delivery System agencies to ensure smooth family reunions.

18.64.4. **Force Support Squadron and Family Member Program Protocols.**

These protocols help bases respond to increased childcare needs during contingencies and during the Air and Space Expeditionary Force cycle, in accordance with AFI 34-144, *Child and Youth Programs*. Childcare providers receive training on caring for children who are experiencing family separation and reintegration, or whose parents are working extended hours.

**18.65. Conclusion.**

This chapter began with the Air Force Fitness Program. Next, the chapter included information on exercising and proper nutrition to create a healthy lifestyle. This chapter included information on substance abuse, tobacco use, medical care, suicide prevention, PTSD, stress management, redeployment and Airman and Family Readiness Center programs. Air Force policy is to ensure Air Force members and their families are physically fit and of sound mind and body to enhance mission accomplishment.

## Chapter 19

## SECURITY

*Section 19A—Overview*

### 19.1. Introduction.

The purpose of security is to never permit the enemy to acquire unexpected advantage…The lethal consequences of enemy attack make the security of friendly forces a paramount concern. Security applies to all members of the Air Force at all times. In certain positions, Airmen are required to handle classified information; at other times, Airmen may be required to serve in a foreign country. Such is the diversity of security. This chapter covers information assurance, installation security, and antiterrorism. These topics are essential to the Air Force mission and the security of all resources. Along with information presented in Chapters 5, Emergency Management Program, and 6, Standards of Conduct, this information helps ensure Air Force forces are prepared to face any adversary.

*Section 19B—Information Assurance*

### 19.2. Information Assurance:

19.2.1. Information assurance refers to the measures that protect and defend information and information systems by ensuring their availability, integrity, confidentiality, authentication, and non-repudiation. These measures include providing for restoration of information and information systems by incorporating protection, detection, and reaction capabilities.

19.2.2. The Air Force implements and maintains the information assurance program to secure information and information technology assets. The Air Force achieves these objectives through the effective employment of its core information assurance disciplines of computer security, communications security, and TEMPEST (formerly known as emissions security).

### 19.3. Computer Security:

19.3.1. **Definition.**

Computer security consists of measures and controls that ensure confidentiality, integrity, and availability of information systems assets including hardware, software, firmware, and information being processed, stored, and communicated.

19.3.1.1. Limited Authorized Personal Use. Government-provided hardware and software are for official use and limited authorized personal use only. Limited personal use must be of reasonable duration and frequency that have been approved by the supervisors and do not adversely affect performance of official duties, overburden systems or reflect adversely on the Air Force or the Department of Defense.

19.3.1.2. All personal use must be consistent with the requirements of Department of Defense 5500.7-R, Joint Ethics Regulation.

19.3.1.3. Internet-based capabilities are all publicly accessible information capabilities and applications available across the Internet in locations not owned, operated, or controlled by the Department of Defense or the Federal Government. Internet-based capabilities include collaborative tools such as simple notification service, social media, user-generated content, social software, e-mail, instant messaging, and discussion forums (e.g., YouTube, Facebook, MySpace, Twitter, Google Apps, etc.).

19.3.1.4. When accessing Internet-based capabilities using Federal Government resources in an authorized personal or unofficial capacity, individuals shall comply with operations security guidance (AFI 10-701, *Operations Security*) and shall not represent the policies or official position of the Air Force or Department of Defense.

19.3.2. **Information Systems.**

An information system is a discrete set of information resources organized for the collection, processing, maintenance, use, sharing, dissemination or disposition of information. Note: Information Systems also include specialized systems such as industrial/process controls systems, telephone switching and private branch systems, and environmental control systems.

19.3.3. **Countermeasures.**

Every Air Force information system has vulnerabilities (system security weaknesses) and is susceptible to exploitation (to gain access to information or disrupt critical processing). A countermeasure is any action, device, procedure, or technique that meets or opposes (i.e. counters) a threat, vulnerability or attack by eliminating, preventing, or minimizing damage, or by discovering and reporting the event, so corrective action(s) can be taken.

19.3.4. **Threats.**

Not all threats to our national security are conventional in nature. Threats include, but are not limited to any circumstance or event with the potential to adversely impact organizational operations (including mission, functions, image, or reputation), organizational assets, individuals, other organizations, or the Nation through an information system via unauthorized access, destruction, disclosure, modification of information and/or denial of service.

19.3.5. **Malicious Logic Protection.**

The Air Force must protect information systems from viruses and other forms of malicious logic by using a combination of human and technological countermeasures to ensure the protection is maintained throughout the lifecycle of the information system.

19.3.5.1. **Infection.** The invasion of information systems applications, processes, or services by a virus or malware code causing the information system to malfunction.

19.3.5.2. **Detection.** A signature or behavior-based antivirus system that signals when an anomaly caused by a virus or malware occurs.

19.3.5.3. **Reaction.** If you are notified of a virus or malware detection, immediately notify your information system security officer and follow local procedures.

19.3.6. **General Protection of Information Systems.**

All authorized users must protect information systems against tampering, theft, and loss. Protection from insider and outsider threats occurs by controlling physical access to the facility and data.

19.3.6.1. Ensure user access to information system resources and information is based upon their security clearance and need to know. Ensure protection of applicable unclassified, sensitive, and/or classified information using encryption according to the applicable Federal Information Processing Standard (FIPS) 140-2, *Security Requirements for Cryptographic Modules*.

19.3.6.2. Protect against casual viewing of information. Place devices that display (or output) classified and sensitive information in a location that deters unauthorized individuals from reading the information. Ensure buildings and rooms that contain information systems are locked during non-duty hours. Classified information systems should be stored in a General Services Administration approved safe or in buildings or areas cleared for open storage of classified.

19.3.7. **Removable Media Control.**

Storage media includes, but is not limited to, compact discs, external storage drives, and universal serial bus drives (memory sticks, jump drives, pen drives, etc.). These devices have memory storage capability and are categorized as removable media. Because of the capacity of their memory storage and their portable nature, these devices pose an increased risk of data tampering, theft, or loss. At a minimum, personnel must use these preventive measures:

19.3.7.1. Safeguard, mark, and label removable media according to the requirements for the highest level of information ever contained on the media using applicable information security guidance.

19.3.7.2. Report loss or suspected loss of removable media containing sensitive information according to applicable information security guidance from your local security manager or information systems security officer.

19.3.7.3. Clear, sanitize, or destroy removable media used to store sensitive information before releasing to unauthorized personnel or outside Department of Defense or Air Force control. Contact your local information systems security officer for guidance and procedures.

19.3.7.4. Use your local security guidance before attaching any removable media or storage device to an information system.

19.3.7.5. Do not use disguised removable media or storage devices. Air Force policy defines disguised as a device designed to look like anything other than removable media or a storage device (for example, watch, pen, flashlight, etc.).

19.3.8. **Mobile Computing Devices.**

Mobile computing devices are information systems such as portable electronic devices, laptops, smartphones, and other handheld devices that can store data locally and access Air Force managed networks through mobile access capabilities. While many mobile computing devices may have specific security policy and procedures governing their use, all of these devices should follow the same basic requirements.

19.3.8.1. All wireless systems (including associated peripheral devices, operation systems, applications, network connection methods, and services) must be approved prior to processing Department of Defense information. The information systems security officer will maintain documented approval authority and inventory information on all approved devices.

19.3.8.2. All mobile computing devices (not assigned or in use) must be secured to prevent tampering or theft.

19.3.8.3. Users of mobile devices will sign a detailed user agreement outlining the responsibilities and restrictions for use.

### 19.3.9. Public Computing Facilities or Services.

Do not use public computing facilities or services (Internet cafés and kiosks, hotel business centers, etc.) to process government-owned unclassified, sensitive, or classified information. Public computing facilities or services include any information technology resources not under your private or United States governmental control. Use of these resources to access Web-based government services (Outlook® messaging software, Web applications, etc.) constitutes a compromise of login credentials and must be reported as a security incident according to the current Air Force guidance on computer security.

## 19.4. Communications Security.

Communications security refers to measures and controls taken to deny unauthorized persons information derived from information systems of the United States government related to national security and to ensure the authenticity of such information systems. Communications security protection results from applying security measures (i.e., crypto security, transmission security, and emission security) to communications and information systems generating, handling, storing, processing, or using classified or sensitive information, the loss of which could adversely affect the national security interest. Communications security also entails applying physical security measures to communications security information or materials.

### 19.4.1. Cryptosecurity.

Cryptosecurity is a component of communications security resulting from the provision and proper use of technically sound cryptosystems.

### 19.4.2. Transmission Security.

Transmission security is a component of communications security resulting from the application of measures designed to protect transmissions from interception and exploitation by means other than cryptoanalysis. Examples of transmission security measures include using secured communications systems, registered mail, secure telephone and facsimile equipment, manual cryptosystems, call signs, or authentication to transmit classified information.

### 19.4.3. Physical Security.

Physical security is the part of communications security resulting from the use of all physical measures necessary to safeguard communications security material from access by unauthorized persons. Physical security measures include the application of control procedures and physical barriers. Physical security also ensures continued integrity, prevents access by unauthorized persons, and controls the spread of communications security techniques and technology when not in the best interest of the United States and allies of the United States. Common physical security measures include verifying the need to know and clearance of personnel granted access, following proper storage and handling procedures, accurately accounting for all materials, transporting materials using authorized means, and immediately reporting the loss or possible compromise of materials.

## 19.5. TEMPEST (formerly known as Emissions Security).

**TEMPEST** is protection resulting from all measures taken to deny unauthorized persons information of value that may be derived from the interception and analysis of compromising emanations from crypto equipment, information systems, and telecommunications systems. The objective of emissions security is to deny access to classified and, in some instances, unclassified information that contain compromising emanations within an inspectable space. The inspectable space is considered the area in which it would be difficult for an adversary with specialized equipment to attempt to intercept compromising emanations without being detected. TEMPEST countermeasures (classified/unclassified equipment separation, shielding, grounding, etc.) are implemented to reduce the risk of compromising emanations escaping the inspectable space. The TEMPEST countermeasures must be validated by the Certified TEMPEST Technical Authority prior to any classified processing in the facility.

*Section 19C—Installation Security*

**19.6. Operations Security:**

### 19.6.1. Operations Security Defined:

19.6.1.1. Operation security is a process of identifying, analyzing, and controlling critical information indicating friendly actions associated with military operations and other activities to:

19.6.1.1.1. Identify those actions that can be observed by adversary intelligence systems.

19.6.1.2.2. Determine what specific indications could be collected, analyzed, and interpreted to derive critical information in time to be useful to adversaries.

19.6.1.3.3. Select and execute measures that eliminate or reduce to an acceptable level the vulnerabilities of friendly actions to adversary exploitation.

19.6.1.2. Operation security is closely integrated and synchronized with other influence operations capabilities to protect operations and is not a collection of specific rules and instructions that can be applied to every operation.

### 19.6.2. Purpose.

The purpose of Operation security is to reduce the vulnerability of Air Force missions by eliminating or reducing successful adversary collection and exploitation of critical information. Operation security applies to all activities that prepare, sustain, or employ forces during all phases of operations.

### 19.6.3. Operational Context.

Operational effectiveness is enhanced when commanders and other decision makers apply Operation security from the earliest stages of planning. Operation security involves a series of analyses to examine the planning, preparation, execution, and post execution phases of any operation or activity across the entire spectrum of military action and in any operational environment. Operation security analysis provides decision makers with a means of weighing the risk to their operations. Decision makers must determine the amount of risk they are willing to accept in particular operational circumstances in the same way as operations risk management allows commanders to assess risk in mission planning.

### 19.6.4. Signature Management Methodology Defined:

19.6.4.1. Signature management is the active defense or exploitation of operational profiles resident at a given military installation. Defense of operational profiles is accomplished by implementing protective signature management measures to deny adversary collection of critical information.

19.6.4.2. Base profiling is a process within signature management that identifies the local operating environment and captures process points that present key signatures and profiles with critical information value. This process is the deliberate effort to identify functional areas and the observables they produce to contribute to the overall signature of day-to-day activities and operational trends.

### 19.6.5. Implementing Operation Security.

Air Force forces can be under observation at their peacetime bases and locations, in training or exercises, while moving, or when deployed to the field conducting actual operations. Operation security methodology provides systematic and comprehensive analysis designed to identify observable friendly actions that could reveal intentions or capabilities. Air Force units utilize the base profiling process to identify vulnerabilities and indicators of their day-to-day activities. With this understanding, Air Force operation security program managers use the signature management methodology to apply measures and/or countermeasures to hide, control, or simulate indicators. Therefore, operation security principles must be integrated into operational, support, exercise, and acquisition planning. Operation security is incorporated into day-to-day activities to ensure a seamless transition to contingency operations. The operation security process consists of five distinct steps:

19.6.5.1. Identify critical information.

19.6.5.2. Analyze threats.

19.6.5.3. Analyze vulnerabilities.

19.6.5.4. Assess risk.

19.6.5.5. Apply appropriate operation security countermeasures.

19.6.6. **Operation Security Indicators.**

Operation security indicators are friendly, detectable actions, and open-source information that can be interpreted or pieced together by an adversary to derive critical information. The five basic characteristics of operation security indicators that make them potentially valuable to an adversary include:

19.6.6.1. **Signatures.** This characteristic of an indicator is identifiable or to stand out.

19.6.6.2. **Associations.** The relationship of an indicator to other information or activities.

19.6.6.3. **Profiles.** Each functional activity generates their own set of more-or-less unique signatures and associations. The sum of these signatures and associations is the activity's profile.

19.6.6.4. **Contrasts.** Any differences observed between an activity's standard profile and most recent or current actions.

19.6.6.5. **Exposure.** Refers to when and for how long an indicator is observed. The longer an indicator is observed, the better chance an adversary can observe the indicator and form associations and/or update the profile of operational activities.

**19.7. Information Security.**

All personnel in the Air Force are responsible for protecting classified information and controlled unclassified information under their custody and control.

19.7.1. **Classified Information.** Information shall be classified only to protect national security. There are three levels of classification: Top Secret, Secret, and Confidential. Information may only be classified by either original classification or derivative classification. Each individual is responsible for providing the proper safeguards for classified information, reporting security incidents, and understand the sanctions for noncompliance.

19.7.1.1. **Top Secret.** Top Secret shall be applied to information the unauthorized disclosure of which reasonably could be expected to cause exceptionally grave damage to the national security that the original classification authority is able to identify or describe.

19.7.1.2. **Secret.** Secret shall be applied to information the unauthorized disclosure of which reasonably could be expected to cause serious damage to the national security that the original classification authority is able to identify or describe.

19.7.1.3. **Confidential.** Confidential shall be applied to information the unauthorized disclosure of which reasonably could be expected to cause damage to the national security that the original classification authority is able to identify or describe.

19.7.1.4. **Original Classification.** Original classification is the initial decision by an original classification authority that an item of information could reasonably be expected to cause identifiable or describable damage to the national security subjected to unauthorized disclosure and requires protection in the interest of national security. Only officials designated in writing may make original classification decisions.

19.7.1.5. **Derivative Classification.** Air Force policy is to identify, classify, downgrade, declassify, mark, protect, and destroy classified information consistent with national policy. Controlled unclassified information will also be protected per national policy, DoDM 5200.01, Volumes 1 and 4, *Department of Defense Information Security Program: Overview, Classification, and Declassification*, February 24, 2012 and DoDM 5200.01, Volume 2 and 3, *Department of Defense Information Security Program*, February 24, 2012, Incorporating Change 2, March 19, 2013, *Department of Defense Information Security Program*, and AFI 16-1404, Air Force *Information Security Program*, provide the guidance for managing classified information and controlled unclassified information. Within the Department of Defense all cleared personnel are authorized to derivatively classify information provided they have received initial training before making derivative classification decisions and refresher at least once every 2 years. Derivative classification is the incorporating, paraphrasing, restating, or generating classified information in a new form or document and is not photocopying or otherwise mechanically or electronically reproducing classified material. Derivative classifiers must use authorized types of sources for making decisions. One of the most important responsibilities of derivative classifier is to observe and respect the classification determinations made by an original classification authority.

19.7.1.6. **Marking Classified Information.** All classified information shall be clearly identified by marking, designation, or electronic labelling in accordance with DoDM 5200.01, Vol 2, *Department of Defense Information Security Program: Marking of Classified Information*. Markings are used to:

19.7.1.6.1. Alert holders to the presence of classified information.

19.7.1.6.2. Identify, as specifically as possible, the exact information needing protection.

19.7.1.6.3. Indicate the level of classification assigned to the information.

19.7.1.6.4. Provide guidance on downgrading (if any) and declassification.

19.7.1.6.5. Give information on the sources of and reasons for classification.

19.7.1.6.6. Notify holders of special access, control, or safeguarding requirements.

19.7.1.6.7. Promote information sharing, facilitate judicious use of resources, and simplify management through implementation of uniform and standardized processes.

19.7.1.7. **Specific Markings on Documents.** Every classified document must be marked to show the highest classification of information contained within the document. The marking must be conspicuous enough to alert anyone handling the document that the document is classified. Every document will contain the overall classification of the document, portion markings indicating the classification level of specific classified information within the document, the originating office, date of origin, and downgrading instructions, if any, and declassification instructions. The three most common markings on a classified document are the banner lines, portion markings, and the classification authority block.

19.7.1.7.1. **Banner Lines.** Are conspicuously placed at the top and bottom of the outside of the front cover (if any), title page (if any), first page, and on the outside of the back cover (if any or last page of each classified document. These markings are usually centered on the page. Examples of Banner Markings in DoDM 5200.01, Volume 2, *DoD Information Security Program*: *Marking of Classified Information* for an illustration.

19.7.1.7.2. **Portion Marks.** Every subject, title, paragraph, section, tab, attachment, classified signature block, bullets, tables and pictures in every classified document shall be marked to show the highest level of classification contained within the document. Use these symbols in uppercase letters to indicate the highest classification level in the portion: (TS) for Top Secret, (S) for Secret, and (C) for Confidential. Examples of Portion Markings in DoDM 5200.01, Volume 2, *Department of Defense Information Security Program*: *Marking of Classified Information*, for illustration.

19.7.1.7.3. **Classification Authority Block.** This block appears on the face of each classified United States document unless otherwise stated in DoDM 5200.01, Volumes 1-4. There are two types of classification authority blocks. One is used by an original classifier and the other by a derivative classifier. Original classification authority block will contain a: Classified By (name of classifier), Reason, Downgrade To (if any), and Declassify On line. Refer to DoDM 5200.01, Volume 2, *Department of Defense Information Security Program*: *Marking of Classified Information*, for an illustration of an Originally Classified Document. Derivative classification authority block will contain a: Classified by (name of classifier), Derived From (identify sources), Downgrade To (if any) and Declassify On lines. Refer to DoDM 5200.01, Volume 2, *Department of Defense Information Security Program*: *Marking of Classified Information*, for an illustration of an Derivatively Classified Document.

19.7.1.8. **Challenges.** Personnel should submit challenges of classification to their security manager or the classifier of the information if substantial reason exists to indicate the document has been classified improperly or unnecessarily

19.7.1.9. **Safeguarding.** Everyone who works with classified information is personally responsible for taking proper precautions to ensure that unauthorized persons do not gain access to classified information. There are two primary types of protection that must be employed at all times: (1) store the information using approved means; or (2) having it under the personal observation and control of an authorized individual.

19.7.1.9.1. **Access to Classified Information.** Before granting access to classified information the person must have: (1) security clearance eligibility; (2) a signed Standard Form 312, *Classified Information Non-Disclosure Agreement*; and (3) a need-to-know. The individual's responsibility with authorized possession, knowledge, or control of the information is to determine whether the person receiving the information has been granted the appropriate security clearance access by proper authority.

19.7.1.9.2. **Protection When Under Personal Observation or Control.** An authorized person shall keep classified material removed from storage under constant surveillance. The authorized person must place coversheets on classified documents not in secure storage to prevent unauthorized persons from viewing the information. The following forms will be used to cover classified information outside of storage: Standard Form 703, *Top Secret*, Standard Form 704, *Secret*, and Standard Form 705, *Confidential*.

19.7.1.9.3. **End-of-Day Security Checks.** Use Standard Form 701, *Activity Security Checklist*, to record the end of the day security check if you are appointed to conduct the check. This form is required for any area where classified information is used or stored. Ensure all vaults, secure rooms, and containers used for storing classified material are checked.

19.7.1.9.4. **Security Incidents Involving Classified Information.** Anyone finding classified material out of proper control must take custody of and safeguard the material and immediately notify his or her commander, supervisor or security manager. The terms associated with security incidents are formally defined DoDM 5200.01 Volume 3. The following general characterizations are provided:

19.7.1.9.4.1. **Infraction.** An infraction is a security incident involving failure to comply with requirements which cannot reasonably be expected to, and does not, result in the loss, suspected compromise, or compromise of classified information. An infraction may be unintentional or inadvertent and does not constitute a security violation, if left uncorrected, can lead to security violations or compromises. Infraction requires an inquiry to facilitate immediate corrective action but does not require an in-depth investigation.

19.7.1.9.4.2. **Violation.** Violations are security incidents that indicate knowing, willful, and negligent for security regulations, and result in, or could be expected to result in, the loss or compromise of classified information. Security violations require an inquiry and/or investigation.

19.7.1.9.4.3. **Compromise.** A compromise is a security incident (more specifically, a violation) in which there is an unauthorized disclosure of classified information (i.e., disclosure to a person(s) who does not have a valid clearance, authorized access, or a need to know).

19.7.1.9.4.4. **Loss.** A loss occurs when classified information cannot be physically located or accounted for (e.g., classified information/equipment is discovered missing during an audit and cannot be immediately located).

19.7.1.9.5. **Data Spills**. Classified data spills occur when classified data is introduced either onto an unclassified information system or to an information system with a lower level of classification, or to a system not accredited to process data of that restrictive category.

19.7.1.9.6. **Information Appearing in the Public Media.** If classified information appears in the public media, including on public Internet sites, or if approached by a representative of the media, personnel shall be careful not to make any statement or comment that confirms the accuracy of or verifies the information requiring protection. Immediately report the matter to your supervisor, security manager, or commander, but do not discuss with anyone who does not, in the case of classified information, have an appropriate security clearance and need to know.

19.7.2. **Controlled Unclassified Information.**

In addition to classified information, certain types of unclassified information also require application of access and distribution controls and protective measures for a variety of reasons. Such information is referred to collectively as controlled unclassified information. Requirements, controls, and protective measures developed for Department of Defense controlled unclassified information (i.e., For Official Use Only), (Law Enforcement Sensitive, Department of Defense Unclassified Controlled Nuclear Information, and LIMITED DISTRIBUTION) as well as some of those developed by other Executive Branch agencies are found in DoDM 5200.01 Volume 4. The originator of a document is responsible for determining at origination whether the information may qualify for controlled unclassified information status. Before provided to the public all Department of Defense unclassified information must be reviewed and approved for release.

19.7.2.1. **For Official Use Only Information.** For official use only information is the most commonly used controlled unclassified information category in the Air Force and Department of Defense. For official use only information is a dissemination control applied by the Department of Defense to unclassified information when disclosure to the public of that particular record, or portion thereof, would reasonably be expected to cause a foreseeable harm to an interest protected by one or more of the Freedom of Information Act Exemptions 2 through 9. Refer to DoDM 5200.01, Volume 4, *Department of Defense Information Security Program: Controlled Unclassified Information* for additional information on Freedom of Information Act exemptions.

19.7.2.2. **Marking For Official Use Only information.** Information that has been determined to qualify for official use only status shall be indicated by markings.

19.7.2.2.1. Each document will identify the originating office to allow someone receiving the document to contact the office if questions or problems about the designation or marking arise.

19.7.2.2.2. FOR OFFICIAL USE ONLY or UNCLASSIFIED//FOR OFFICIAL USE ONLY will be marked at the bottom of the outside of the front cover (if there is one), the title page, the first page, and the outside of the back cover (if there is one).

19.7.2.2.3. Internal pages shall be marked FOR OFFICIAL USE ONLY. If internal pages contain UNCLASSIFIED//FOR OFFICIAL USE ONLY or UNCLASSIFIED// For Official Use Only information the marking must appear at both the top and bottom.

19.7.2.2.4. Subjects, titles, and each section, part, paragraph, or similar port shall be marked using the parenthetical notation (For Official Use Only) or (U// For Official Use Only if it contains For Official Use Only information).

19.7.2.3. **Access to For Official Use Only.** No person may have access to information designated as For Official Use Only information unless they have a valid need for access in connection with the accomplishment of a lawful and authorized Government purpose. The final responsibility for determining whether an individual has a valid need for access to information designated for official use only status rests with the individual who has authorized possession, knowledge, or control of the information.

19.7.2.4. **Protection of For Official Use Only.** During work hours, reasonable steps shall be taken to minimize the risk of access by unauthorized personnel, i.e. not leaving for official use only status information unattended where unauthorized personnel are present. After working hours, store the information in unlocked containers, desks, or cabinets if the building is provided security by Government or Government-contract personnel. If building security is not provided or deemed inadequate, store the information in locked desks, file cabinets, bookcases, or locked rooms.

## 19.8. Personnel Security:

19.8.1. The Personnel Security Program entails policies and procedures that ensure military, civilian, and contractor personnel who access classified information or occupy a sensitive position are consistent with interests of national security. It involves the investigation process, adjudication for eligibility, and the continuous evaluation for maintaining eligibility. Commanders and supervisors must continually observe and evaluate their subordinates with respect to these criteria and immediately report any unfavorable conduct or conditions that come to their attention that might bear on the subordinates' trustworthiness and eligibility to occupy a sensitive position or have eligibility to classified information.

19.8.2. The Department of Defense Central Adjudication Facility is the designated adjudicative authority to grant, deny, and revoke security clearance eligibility. Eligibility is adjudicated using the Department of Defense 13 Adjudicative Guidelines while applying the whole person concept and mitigating factors. Individuals are granted due process and may appeal if the security clearance eligibility is denied or revoked. Refer to the AFI 31-501, Personnel Security Program Management for details.

19.8.2.1. The Department of Defense 13 Adjudicative Guidelines include the following topic areas:

19.8.2.1.1. Allegiance to the United States.

19.8.2.1.2. Foreign Influence.

19.8.2.1.3. Foreign Preference.

19.8.2.1.4. Sexual Behavior.

19.8.2.1.5. Personal Conduct.

19.8.2.1.6. Financial Considerations.

19.8.2.1.7. Alcohol Consumption.

19.8.2.1.8. Drug Involvement.

19.8.2.1.9. Psychological Conditions.

19.8.2.1.10. Criminal Conduct.

19.8.2.1.11. Handling Protected Information.

19.8.2.1.12. Outside Activities.

19.8.2.1.13. Use of Information Technology.

19.8.3. All personnel with clearance eligibility are subject to continuous evaluation. This requires reporting post investigation information that falls within the Department of Defense 13 Adjudicative Guidelines to the security manager.

19.8.3.1. The Commander will report all continuous evaluation information related to the 13 Adjudicative Guidelines to the Department of Defense Central Adjudication Facility via the security manager.

## 19.9. Industrial Security:

### 19.9.1. Policy.

Air Force policy is to identify in classified contracts specific government information and sensitive resources that must be protected against compromise or loss while entrusted to industry. AFI 31-601, *Industrial Security Program Management,* assigns functional responsibilities and establishes a system of review that identifies outdated, inappropriate, and unnecessary contractual security requirements. Policy also outlines and provides guidance for establishing on-base integrated contractor visitor groups.

### 19.9.2. Scope.

The security policies, requirements, and procedures identified in AFI 31-601 are applicable to Air Force personnel and on-base Department of Defense contractors performing services under the terms of a properly executed contract and associated security agreement or similar document, as determined appropriate by the installation commander.

## 19.10. Integrated Defense Program:

19.10.1. The Air Force Integrated Defense Program is the integration of multidisciplinary active and passive, offensive and defensive capabilities, employed to mitigate potential risks and defeat adversary threats to Air Force operations within the base boundary and the base security zone. These threats include, but are not limited to, terrorist, insiders, criminals, and foreign intelligence and security services. To integrate Integrated Defense efforts with other Air Force capabilities to achieve synergistic effects using an all-hazards approach is critical. Potential hazards to an installation include, but are not limited to, chemical biological radiological nuclear-high yield explosive attacks, natural and man-made disasters, major accidents, and accidental or deliberate release of hazardous materials, toxic industrial materials or chemicals (see AFPD 31-1, *Integrated Defense*). Integrated Defense is a fundamental battle competency for all Airmen, whether garrison or deployed. The teaming of Integrated Defense forces creates a united, seamless defense stronger than the defensive efforts of individuals/or individual units. This effort ensures all Airmen are trained to defend themselves and integrate into defense operations while in garrison or deployed. Installation commanders determine the effects required of Integrated Defense operations at Air Force installations based on a four-step process that involves:

19.10.1.1. Determining and prioritizing the criticality of installation assets.

19.10.1.2. Analyzing the threats and operating environment.

19.10.1.3. Assessing the installation's vulnerabilities to the threats.

19.10.1.4. Making prudent integrated defense decisions based on the risk estimate. The integrated defense risk management process is critical in order for the installation commander to make the best use of limited resources and personnel available to execute the Integrated Defense mission.

19.10.2. Integrated defense is an "all-Airmen" program. However, Air Force Security Forces have enterprise lead in Integrated Defense operations. The defense force commander synchronizes integrated defense operations with emergency and consequence management activities articulated in applicable Air Force and Department of Defense publications.

19.10.3. The goal of Integrated Defense is to neutralize security threats within the base boundary and the base security zone in order to ensure unhindered Air Force operations. Through Integrated Defense, commanders must: (1) minimize mission degradation from threat activity within the base boundary and coordinate necessary security operations support within the base security zone when the base security zone is not congruent with the base boundary; (2) minimize loss of life and injury from threat activity; and (3) protect government property and personnel from hostile and criminal acts.

19.10.4. Integrated Defense does not stand alone to protect personnel and resources; planners create an effective security program by coordinating with other Department of Defense and Air Force programs. Furthermore, the protection and defense of air bases requires the coordinated effort of emergency management, antiterrorism, and other mission support function forces under the mission assurance umbrella. This coordinated planning provides a seamless progression of mission assurance programs and completes the installation's defense in depth picture.

19.10.5. Joint Publications define the base boundary as a line that delineates the surface area of a base for the purpose of facilitating coordination and deconfliction of operations between adjacent units, formations, or areas. See Figure 19.1 for an example of a base boundary configuration. Therefore, the base boundary is not necessarily the base perimeter. Rather, the base boundary should be established based upon the factors of mission, enemy, terrain and weather, troops and support available, time available, civil considerations, specifically balancing the need of the base defense forces to control key terrain with their ability to accomplish the mission. These measures decrease the likelihood of fratricide, prevent noncombatant casualties, and minimize damage to the property of friendly civilians. Boundaries may not necessarily coincide with the fenced perimeter, property lines or legal boundaries. Nevertheless, while tactical considerations will ideally determine Integrated Defense boundaries, the defense force commander will strictly adhere to legal, jurisdictional, host nation constraints, commander's intent, and higher echelon orders and directives when conducting operations within the base boundary.

19.10.6. The base security zone is an Air Force unique concept and term to be used intraservice only. The Air Force uses the planning term base security zone to describe the area of concern around an air base and to support the establishment and adjustment of the base boundary. The base security zone is the area outside the base perimeter from which the base may be vulnerable from standoff threats (for example, mortars, rockets, man portable aerial defense systems). The installation commander should identify the base security zone and coordinate via the operational chain of command with local, state, federal agencies (within the continental United States) or host nation or area commander (outside the continental United States) for the base security zone to be identified as the base boundary. If the base boundary does not include all of the base security zone terrain, the installation commander is still responsible for either mitigating (through coordination with local, state, federal agencies (continental United States) or the area commander or host nation (outside the continental United States) or accepting the risks of enemy attack from the terrain outside the base boundary. The base security zone, in the simplest terms, is the area from which a threat can launch an attack against base personnel and resources or aircraft approaching/departing the base. Air-minded forces must consider the base security zone for planning constructs continental United States, outside the continental United States, and at contingency locations. Threats vary in the Integrated Defense continuum from peacetime to wartime, regardless of the location of our installations.

**Figure 19.1. Base Boundary Configuration**

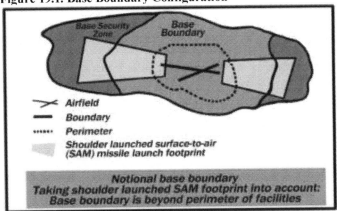

19.10.6.1. Optimally, the base security zone and the base boundary are the same, but that is not always the case. The base security zone may, for planning purposes, incorporate more geographical area than the base boundary. For example, there may be key terrain outside the base boundary from which adversaries can impact air operations.

19.10.6.2. For terrain outside the base boundary, but within the base security zone, the defense force commander should coordinate with local, state, federal agencies (continental United States) or host nation or area commander (outside the continental United States) to conduct base defense tasks within the area. If these forces/agencies are not available due to competing requirements, then the defense force commander should coordinate via their operational chain of command with the appropriate area commander to conduct the base defense task. When defense forces operate outside the base boundary, the appropriate area of operations commander should exercise tactical control over those forces for base defense purposes only. Joint and coalition forces entering the base boundary should inform the base defense operations center before they enter, and monitor the base defense operations center's communication net while operating in the area.

19.10.6.3. The base defense operations center is the command and control center for Integrated Defense operations during routine and emergency operations. The defense force commander will establish a base defense operations center to coordinate and direct, via their operational chain of command, the tactical control of Integrated Defense forces and supporting capabilities. All functions performed by central security control, the law enforcement desk, or other security forces control centers will be performed by the base defense operations center at all locations, home station and deployed.

## 19.11. Integrated Defense Effects:

19.11.1. Commanders execute Integrated Defense with the objective of achieving nine desired effects based on the risk management process described in paragraph 19.12. Those effects are:

19.11.1.1. **Anticipate.** Anticipate threat intentions and actions (Intelligence Preparation of the Operational Environment or crime trend analysis).

19.11.1.2. **Deter.** Deter threat activity through active community policing (e.g., Eagle Eyes Program), boundary and internal circulation control, controlled area marking, prudent physical security measures.

19.11.1.3. **Detect.** Detect threats through the use of lighting, Intrusion Detection Systems/Early Warning Systems, closed-circuit television, etc.

19.11.1.4. **Assess.** Assess to identify friend or foe using cameras, posted sentries, response forces, integrated delivery system, etc.

19.11.1.5. **Warn.** Warn friendly forces of adversary activity through systems such as mass notification, radio, public address, commander's access channels, voice, hand and arm signals, cellular telephones, instant messenger/short message system texting, etc.

19.11.1.6. **Defeat.** Defeat threats through appropriate, progressive force application; coordinated security force response; and integration of total force.

19.11.1.7. **Delay.** Delay adversaries using a layered application of barriers, obstacles, technology, physical security measures, and forces (defense-in-depth).

19.11.1.8. **Defend.** Defend assets through threat- and effects-based planning that integrates all friendly forces into a single, comprehensive plan by ensuring friendly forces are trained and qualified on Arming and Use of Force. Also, ensure the fighting positions are positioned where prudent based on risk analyses.

19.11.1.9. **Recover.** Recover from adversarial events by applying effective command and control, and developing and exercising comprehensive emergency management plan 10-2.

19.11.2. These effects are not randomly applied to an installation instead they are deliberately achieved through innovative and reliable tactics, techniques, and procedures based on the Integrated Defense risk management process and analysis.

19.11.3. Ideally, defense forces receive such good intelligence they are able to anticipate any and all threats. As this is unlikely, attaining subsequent Integrated Defense desired effects is necessary. For instance, it would be preferred to deter a threat; but if that does not succeed, the next ideal effect would be to detect the threat. Once the threat is detected, assessment by forces occurs. Friendly forces are then warned of the threat and attempts are made to defeat, or eliminate, the threat. If the threat cannot be defeated, it must be delayed. If not possible, defensive measures must be taken to mitigate the effects of the threat. Recovery actions are then implemented to consolidate and reorganize friendly forces and restore operations.

19.11.4. The intelligence fusion cell is an action group whereby the security forces staff S-2 (intelligence) function coordinates with subject matter experts from the Intelligence and Air Force Office of Special investigations communities to collaborate and conduct intelligence preparation of the operational environment. The goal is to leverage information and intelligence to support the timely identification of indicators and warnings of emerging localized threats. The intelligence fusion cell and the products of the fusion cells are the primary information sources that directly support the defense force commander in making immediate, proactive decisions for Integrated Defense planning.

19.11.5. Intelligence preparation of the battlefield/battlespace is an analytical methodology that provides predictive intelligence to warfighters for use in planning and executing operations. A systematic, four-step process, intelligence preparation of the battlefield/battlespace's bottom line intent is to support operational decisions by providing analyzed information regarding the threat and environment in a given set of circumstances. Intelligence preparation of the battlefield/battlespace is the primary mechanism used to achieve the Integrated Defense desired effect of "anticipate." Furthermore, this analytical methodology is a continuous process, enabling the commander to visualize: (1) the spectrum of friendly and adversarial capabilities and weakness; (2) how they are affected by a variety of environmental factors (for example; (3) weather, light, terrain, political and social conditions), and (4) the logical predictions of the most likely and most dangerous enemy course of action.

19.11.6. Intelligence preparation of the battlefield/battlespace is a continuous, four-part process: (1) defines the operating environment; (2) describes the operating environment's effects; (3) evaluates the enemy; and (4) determines enemy course of action. The examples below should be collected, analyzed, and applied to the tactical situation, as a minimum.

19.11.6.1. **Part 1.** This part is comprised of comprehensive lists, dispositions, and capabilities (offensive and defensive) of tasked friendly forces and other forces (for example, host nation military and police forces, local, state, national agencies [continental United States] and host nation [outside the continental United States]) that contribute to the security of the installation and are available to contribute during enemy surges (for example, increased force protection conditions; terrain and weather (including light data); and background data on the operating environment to include history, demographics, socioeconomic data, religious groups, etc. Incident and emergency response plans should also be identified in Part 1 for later consideration during war-gaming conducted during Intelligence Preparation of the Battlespace Part 4.

19.11.6.2. **Part 2.** Analyze the data collected in Part 1 and describe how the factors affect operations, equipment, and personnel. Whenever possible, use color-coded stoplight charts that use green, yellow, and red coding to describe aspects of operations or effects on personnel and equipment. For example, use mission capable (green), partially mission capable (yellow), or non-mission capable (red).

19.11.6.3. **Part 3.** Collect historical data and existing intelligence analyses (for example, Defense Intelligence Agency country reports or Air Force Office of Special Investigations defense threat assessments of the operating environment, or other reports about adversaries capable of operating in the geographic area of concern. Consider the capabilities and weaknesses of each specific group without assuming that all enemy forces collaborate. Consider and analyze the effects of the operating environment (gathered in Part 1 and analyzed in Part 2) on each individual adversary.

19.11.6.4. **Part 4.** Consider all data collected in the previous three parts and make logical predictions of enemy course of actions. For each adversary assessed to be present and capable, establish a prediction of the most likely and most dangerous enemy course of actions. Then, through a process of war-gaming, establish friendly courses of action that would effectively meet the commander's intent in defeating the predicted enemy course of actions.

## 19.12. Integrated Defense Risk Management Process.

The integrated defense risk management process provides installation commanders, integrated defense working groups, defense force commanders and defense planners the ability to produce effects-based, integrated defense plans by using a standardized model to identify risks and develop risk management strategies. These strategies leverage finite resources against adaptive threats to protect Air Force resources and personnel. The integrated defense risk management process identifies at risk assets and aids the integrated defense working groups in generating the criticality assessment and the risk assessment products. A risk reduction decision based on a clear understanding of what is important, the estimated threat, and how the asset might be damaged/destroyed, is then developed through a logical process involving asset criticality assessment, threat assessment, and vulnerability assessment. The integrated defense risk management process analyzes an installation's defense capabilities and provides options to mitigate security risks, such as additional tactics, techniques, and procedures, facility hardening, technology insertion, etc.

19.12.1. The integrated defense risk management process has four main components: (1) the risk assessment (as described above); (2) the risk tolerance decision; (3) courses of action determination; and (4) decision and implementation. All four components are directly influenced by the evolving situation monitored through the Intelligence Preparation of the Battlespace cycle. As such, new information, assessments, or decisions can be assimilated into the integrated defense risk management process at any point, which may alter the execution of Integrated Defense. These four components are performed in the following seven steps:

19.12.1.1. **Step 1: Develop the Criticality Assessment.** The criticality assessment identifies assets worthy of protection whose loss or damage would have a negative impact on the mission. Fundamental to this evaluation is the criteria used to measure asset value or consequence of loss. Typical criteria include mission criticality, impact on national defense, replace-ability, monetary value, and relative (or intrinsic) value.

19.12.1.2. **Step 2 and Step 3: Develop the Threat Assessment and Vulnerability Assessment.** Threat multiplied by vulnerability determines the probability of loss (or damage) of the asset. Threats are generally considered in terms of adversaries and their tactics (for example, hackers, terrorists, criminals, protestors). To know if adversaries pose a threat requires information about their operational capability, intentions, activity, operating environment, and history. Vulnerabilities are weaknesses that can be exploited by an adversary because of inadequate security, lax or complacent personnel trends, vulnerable software or hardware, and insufficient security policies or procedures. **Note:** Identification and evaluation of existing threats and vulnerabilities are identified during Parts 1 through 3 of the intelligence preparation of the operational environment process and may be supplemented with other documents, such as antiterrorism vulnerability assessments.

19.12.1.3. **Step 4: Develop the Risk Assessment.** Once all previous assessments (criticality, threat, and vulnerability) are completed and studied together to provide a complete picture of the risks to an asset, the risk assessment can be developed. A quantitative measurement of risk can be determined using the following equation: risk = asset criticality multiplied by (threat multiplied by vulnerability).

19.12.1.4. **Step 5: Risk Tolerance Decision.** At this point in the integrated defense risk management process, the commander may have enough data to enable an informed risk tolerance decision. But if information required to assess risks is deficient, a command critical intelligence requirement should be developed or modified to guide the intelligence community's collection efforts. In today's resource-constrained environment, some risks must be accepted. However, some risks cannot be tolerated due to their frequency or severity of consequence. The installation commander's intent for Integrated Defense will define the level of tolerance. For risks exceeding the commander's tolerance level, countermeasures will be developed in the next step to render these risks more acceptable.

19.12.1.5. **Step 6: Present Countermeasure Courses of Action.** This step presents and evaluates options for reducing risks. While risks can be alleviated by reducing the asset's criticality or mitigating the threat, eliminating vulnerabilities is the area that can have the most impact on the installation commander's risk tolerance decision. At this time, the integrated defense working group can develop various countermeasure courses of action to remove or mitigate vulnerabilities and reduce unacceptable risks. An estimate of risk reduction (i.e., benefit of risk reduction) can be prepared, along with showing the costs associated with courses of action implementation.

19.12.1.6. **Step 7: Decision and Implementation.** This is the most important step in the integrated defense risk management process. During this step, the installation commander selects the course of actions that will bring the risks within his/her tolerance level, and directs resources to implement the decision. Closely tied with step 7 is continuous assessment. This feedback loop posits that risk management is not an event or tangible product, but rather a continuous cycle. The implementation of countermeasure courses of action will sometimes change the installation's risk posture in unexpected or unintended ways. By immediately identifying changes to the installation's critical assets, threats and vulnerabilities, decision makers can continually refine the installation's risk posture.

19.12.2. Integrated Defense provides flexible planning and execution opportunities that allow owners/users of protection level 1 (PL1) non-nuclear, protection level 2 (PL2), protection level 3 (PL3), and protection level 4 (PL4) assets to become actively involved in the defense of their areas.

19.12.3. The integrated defense risk management process provides a more precise understanding of how the three risk factors of threat, vulnerability and asset criticality relate to each other at each installation. Understanding the relationships between these factors, as well as continually analyzing the operating environment, assists commanders in mitigating, accepting, and reducing risks to appropriate levels.

19.12.4. Operationalize force protection intelligence in order to maintain optimal situational awareness throughout the base boundary and base security zone. This can be accomplished for the defense force commanders through the development of a robust intelligence/information collaboration, analysis, and fusion capability.

**19.13. Security Protection Levels:**

19.13.1. **Protection Level 1 (PL1).**

PL1 is assigned to those resources for which the loss, theft, destruction, misuse, or compromise would result in unacceptable mission degradation to the strategic capability of the United States or catastrophic consequences for the nation. Examples of PL1 resources are nuclear weapons in storage, mated to a delivery system, or in transit; designated command, control, and communications facilities; and aircraft designated to transport the President of the United States. PL1 security must result in the greatest possible deterrence against hostile acts. This level of security will provide maximum means to detect and defeat a hostile force before it is able to seize, damage, or destroy resources.

19.13.2. **Protection Level 2 (PL2).**

PL2 is assigned to resources for which the loss, theft, destruction, misuse, or compromise would result in significant mission degradation to the war fighting capability of the United States. Examples of PL2 resources are nonnuclear alert forces; designated space and launch systems; expensive, few in number, or one-of-a-kind systems or facilities; and intelligence-gathering systems. PL2 security must result in significant deterrence against hostile acts. This level of security will ensure a significant probability of detecting and defeating a hostile force before PL2 is able to seize, damage, or destroy resources.

19.13.3. **Protection Level 3 (PL3).**

PL3 is assigned to resources for which the loss, theft, destruction, misuse, or compromise would result in mission degradation to the United States warfighting capability. Examples of PL3 resources are non-alert resources that can be generated to alert status, such as F-16 fighters; selected command, control, and communications facilities, systems, and equipment; and non-launch-critical or non-unique space launch systems. PL3 security must result in a reasonable degree of deterrence against hostile acts. This level of security ensures the capability to impede a hostile force and limit damage to resources.

19.13.4. **Protection Level 4 (PL4).**

PL4 is assigned to operational or mission support resources that directly or indirectly support power projection assess and the war fighting mission for which the loss, theft, destruction, misuse, or compromise would adversely affect mission capability. Examples of PL4 resources are facilities storing Category I, II, or III sensitive conventional arms, ammunition, and explosives; fuels and liquid oxygen storage areas; and Air Force accounting and finance vault areas. PL4 resources are secured by containing them in controlled areas with owners/users being responsible for security. Security forces provide response to threats. This level of security must reduce the opportunity for theft of or damage to resources.

## Section 19D—Antiterrorism Program

### 19.14. Air Force Antiterrorism Program Defined.

The program seeks to deter or limit the effects of terrorist acts against the Air Force by giving guidance on collecting and disseminating timely threat information, providing training to all Air Force members, developing comprehensive plans to deter and counter terrorist incidents, allocating funds and personnel, and implementing antiterrorism measures.

### 19.15. Antiterrorism Training and Exercises.

At least annually, commanders conduct comprehensive field and staff training to exercise antiterrorism plans, to include antiterrorism physical security measures, Continuity of Operations Program, Critical Asset Risk Management and emergency management plans. Antiterrorism training and exercises shall be afforded the same emphasis as combat task training and executed with the intent to identify shortfalls affecting the protection of personnel, assets and information against terrorist attack and subsequent antiterrorism consequence management efforts. Antiterrorism, an area of responsibility specific training, particularly pre-deployment training, should include terrorism scenarios specific to the deployed location and based on current enemy Tactics, Techniques, and Procedures, and lessons learned. Additionally, the current baseline through force protection condition Charlie measures shall be exercised annually at installations and self-supported separate facilities.

### 19.16. Threat Information Collection and Analysis:

19.16.1. Commanders shall task the appropriate organizations under their command to gather, analyze, and disseminate terrorism threat information, as appropriate. To support the commander, the Services should continuously ensure forces are trained to maximize the use of information derived from law enforcement liaison, intelligence, and counterintelligence processes and procedures. This includes intelligence procedures for handling priority intelligence requests for in-transit units as well as implementation of procedures to conduct intelligence preparation of the space and mission analysis.

19.16.2. Identifying the potential terrorism threat to Department of Defense personnel and assets and how the hazards affect the mission is the first step in developing an effective antiterrorism program. Commanders at all levels who understand the threat can assess their ability to prevent, survive, and prepare to respond to an attack. A terrorism threat assessment requires the identification of a full range of known or estimated terrorist threat capabilities (including the use or threat of use of chemical, biological, radiological, nuclear, or high-yield explosives and weapons of mass destruction). In addition to tasking appropriate agencies to collect information, commanders at all levels can and should encourage personnel under their command to report information on individuals, events, or situations that could pose a threat to the security of Department of Defense personnel, families, facilities, and resources.

19.16.3. At the strategic level, the Deputy Chief of Staff for Intelligence, Surveillance and Reconnaissance (Air Force/A2) and the Director for Intelligence, Surveillance, and Reconnaissance Strategy, Doctrine and Force Development (Air Force/A2D) is responsible for ensuring the timely collection processing, analysis, production, and dissemination of foreign intelligence, current intelligence, and national-level intelligence information concerning terrorist activities, terrorist organizations, and force protection issues. These efforts will focus on, but not be limited to, transnational and state-sponsored entities and organizations. The Air Force Office of Special Investigations is the lead Air Force agency for collection, investigation, analysis, and response for threats arising from terrorists, criminal activity and foreign intelligence and security services. Air Force Office of Special Investigations is primarily focused on countering adversary intelligence collection activities against United States forces and will act as the Air Force single point of contact with federal, state, local and foreign nation law enforcement, counterintelligence, and security agencies.

### 19.17. Department of Defense Random Antiterrorism Measures Program.

Installation commanders shall develop and implement a random antiterrorism measures program that will include all units on the installation. The intent of the random antiterrorism measures program is to provide random, multiple security measures that consistently change the look of an installation's antiterrorism program. Random antiterrorism measures introduce uncertainty to an installation's overall force protection program to defeat surveillance attempts and make random antiterrorism measures difficult for a terrorist to accurately predict our actions. The random antiterrorism measures program shall be included in antiterrorism plans and tie directly with all force protection condition (including force protection condition normal) to ensure continuity and standardization should threats require Air Force-wide implementation. Random antiterrorism measures times for implementation, location, and duration shall be regularly changed to avoid predictability. Random antiterrorism measures execution shall be broad based and involve all units and personnel. Antiterrorism officers are required to monitor, track, and analyze random antiterrorism measures implementation efforts. Installation commanders will develop procedures to ensure random antiterrorism measures are being conducted and reported to the Antiterrorism officers.

### 19.18. General Antiterrorism Personal Protection.

Always keep a low profile and avoid publicity. Avoid going out in large groups; be unpredictable. Vary daily routines to and from home and work. Be alert for anything suspicious or out of place. Avoid giving unnecessary personal details to anyone unless their identity can be verified. Be alert to strangers who are on government property for no apparent reason. Refuse to meet with strangers outside your workplace. Always advise associates or family members of your destination and anticipated time of arrival when leaving the office or home. Report unsolicited contacts to authorities and do not open doors to strangers. Memorize key telephone numbers. Be cautious about giving out information regarding family travel places or security measures. When overseas, learn and practice a few key phrases in the local language.

### 19.19. Home and Family Security.

Your spouses and children should always practice basic precautions for their personal security. Familiarize your family with the local terrorist threat, and regularly review protective measures and techniques. Ensure everyone in the family knows what to do in any type of emergency. Restrict the possession of house keys. Lock all entrances at night, including the garage. Keep the house locked, even if you are at home. Destroy all envelopes or other items that show your name, rank, or other personal information. Remove names and rank from mailboxes. Watch for unfamiliar vehicles cruising or parked frequently in the area, particularly if one or more occupants remain in the vehicle for extended periods.

### 19.20. Telephone Security.

Post emergency telephone numbers on the telephone and preprogram telephone numbers for security forces, local police, fire department, hospitals, and ambulances. Do not answer your telephone with your name and grade. Report all threatening phone calls to security officials and the telephone company. Attempt to ascertain any pertinent information about the caller. For example, background noise, accent, nationality, or location.

### 19.21. Travel Overseas.

When traveling overseas, travel in small groups and try to be inconspicuous when using public transportation and facilities. Dress, conduct, and mannerisms should not attract attention and be generally similar to that worn by the people in the area. Avoid spontaneous gatherings or demonstrations; stay away from known trouble. Know emergency telephone numbers, local dialing instructions, and ensure family members carry a list of telephone numbers with them at all times.

### 19.22. Suspicious Packages or Mail.

Look for an unusual or unknown place of origin; no return address; excessive amount of postage; abnormal size or shape; protruding strings; aluminum foil; wires; misspelled words; differing return address and postmark; handwritten labels; unusual odor; unusual or unbalanced weight; springiness in the top or bottom; inflexibility; crease marks; discoloration or oily stains; incorrect titles or title with no name; excessive security material; ticking, beeping, or other sounds; or special instruction markings, such as "personal, rush, do not delay, or confidential" on any packages or mail received. Additionally, be vigilant for evidence of powder or other contaminants. Never cut tape, strings, or other wrappings on a suspect package. If the package has been moved, place the package in a plastic bag to prevent any leakage of contents. If handling mail suspected of containing chemical or biological contaminants, wash hands thoroughly with soap and water. Report suspicious mail immediately and make a list of personnel who were in the room when the suspicious envelope or package was identified.

### 19.23. Ground Transportation Security.

Criminal and terrorist acts against individuals usually occur outside the home and after the victim's habits have been established. Your most predictable habit is the route you travel from home to your place of duty or to commonly frequented local facilities. Always check for tampering of the interior and exterior of your vehicle before entering the vehicle. Also check the tires and trunk for fingerprints or smudges. If you detect something out of the ordinary, do not touch anything. Immediately contact the local authorities. When overseas, select a plain car. Avoid using government vehicles when possible. Do not display decals with military affiliations and do not openly display military equipment. Keep your doors locked at all times. Do not let someone you do not know direct you to a specific taxi. Ensure taxi is licensed and has safety equipment (seat belts at a minimum). Ensure face of driver and picture on license are the same. Travel with a companion.

### 19.24. Commercial Air Transportation Security Overseas.

Before traveling overseas, consult the Department of Defense Foreign Clearance Guide Department of Defense 4500.54-M, available at fcg.pentagon.mil to ensure you know and can meet all requirements for travel to a particular country. Get an area of responsibility specific threat briefing from your security officer, antiterrorism officers, or the appropriate counterintelligence or security organization prior to traveling overseas. This briefing is required prior to travel overseas and must occur within 3 months of travel. Use office symbols on orders or leave authorization if the word description denotes a sensitive position. Use military contractor United States flag carriers. Avoid traveling through high-risk areas. Do not use rank or military address on tickets. Do not discuss military affiliation. Have proper identification to show airline and immigration officials. Do not carry classified documents unless absolutely mission essential. Dress conservatively; do not wear distinct military items (wear long-sleeved shirts if you have United States-affiliated tattoos). Carry plain civilian luggage; avoid military-looking bags, or bags with logos or decals.

## 19.25. Human Intelligence and Counterintelligence.

Human Intelligence is a category of intelligence derived from information collected and provided by human sources. Human resources intelligence is also called Human Intelligence and is the intelligence derived from the intelligence collection discipline that uses human beings as both source and collectors, and where the human being is the primary collection instrument. Counterintelligence is information gathered and activities conducted to protect against espionage, other intelligence activities, sabotage, or assassinations conducted by or on behalf of foreign governments or elements thereof, foreign organizations or foreign persons, or international terrorist activities.

### 19.25.1. Threat Areas:

19.25.1.1. **Espionage.** The act of obtaining, delivering, transmitting, communicating, or receiving information about national defense with intent or reason to believe the information may be used to the injury of the United States or to the advantage of any foreign nation.

19.25.1.2. **Subversion.** An act or acts inciting military or civilian personnel of the Department of Defense to violate laws, disobey lawful orders or regulations, or disrupt military activities with the willful intent thereby to interfere with, or impair the loyalty, morale, of discipline, of the Military Forces of the United States.

19.25.1.3. **Sabotage.** An act or acts with intent to injure, interfere with, or obstruct the national defense of a country by willfully injuring or destroying, or attempting to injure or destroy, any national defense or war material, premises, or utilities, to include human and natural resources.

19.25.1.4. **Terrorism.** The calculated use of unlawful violence or threat of unlawful violence to inculcate fear; intended to coerce or intimidate governments or societies in the pursuit of goals that are generally political, religious, or ideological.

### 19.25.2. The Human Intelligence Effort:

19.25.2.1. **Interrogation.** Interrogation is the systematic effort to procure information to answer specific collection requirements by direct and indirect questioning techniques of a person who is in the custody of the forces conducting the questioning. Proper questioning of enemy combatants, enemy prisoners of war, or other detainees by trained and certified Department of Defense interrogators may result in information provided either willingly or unwittingly.

19.25.2.2. **Source Operations.** Designated and fully trained military Human Intelligence collection personnel may develop information through the elicitation of sources, to include: "walk-in" sources, who without solicitation make the first contact with Human Intelligence personnel; developed sources that are met over a period of time and provide information, based on operational requirements; unwitting persons, with access to sensitive information.

19.25.2.3. **Debriefing.** Debriefing is the process of questioning cooperating human sources to satisfy intelligence requirements, consistent with applicable law. The source usually is not in custody and usually is willing to cooperate. Debriefing may be conducted at all echelons and in all operational environments. Through debriefing, face-to-face meetings, conversations, and elicitation, information may be obtained from a variety of human sources.

19.25.2.4. **Document and Media Exploitation.** Captured documents and media, when properly processed and exploited, may provide valuable information such as adversary plans and intentions, force locations, equipment capabilities, and logistical status. The category of "captured documents and media" includes all media capable of storing fixed information to include computer storage material. This operation is not a primary Human Intelligence function but may be conducted by any intelligence personnel with appropriate language support.

### 19.25.3. Incident Reporting.

AFI 71-101, Volume 4, *Counterintelligence,* requires individuals who have reportable contacts or acquire reportable information to immediately (within 30 days of the contact) report the contact or information, either verbally or in writing, to Air Force Office of Special Investigations. "Contact" means any exchange of information directed to an individual, including solicited or unsolicited telephone calls, email, radio contact, and face-to-face meetings. Examples include:

19.25.3.1. Contact for any reason other than for official duties with a foreign diplomatic establishment, whether in the United States or abroad.

19.25.3.2. A request by anyone (regardless of nationality) for illegal or unauthorized access to classified or unclassified controlled information.

19.25.3.3. Personal contact with an individual (regardless of nationality) who suggests that a foreign intelligence or any terrorist organization may have targeted him or her or others for possible intelligence exploitation.

19.25.3.4. Information indicating military members, civilian employees, or Department of Defense contractors have contemplated, attempted, or effected the deliberate compromise or unauthorized release of classified or unclassified controlled information.

19.25.4. **Air Force Office of Special Investigations Responsibility.**

The Air Force Office of Special Investigations initiates and conducts all counterintelligence investigations, operations, collections, and other related activities for the Air Force. In the United States, the Air Force Office of Special Investigations coordinates these activities when appropriate with the Federal Bureau of Investigation. Outside the United States, Air Force Office of Special Investigations coordinates these activities with the Central Intelligence Agency and the Federal Bureau of Investigation, as appropriate. The Air Force Office of Special Investigations is also the installation-level training agency for counterintelligence awareness briefings and is the sole Air Force repository for the collection and retention of reportable information.

## 19.26. Protection of the President and Others:

19.26.1. As a result of a formal agreement between the Department of Defense and United States Secret Service, individuals affiliated with the Armed Services have a special obligation to report information to the Secret Service pertaining to the protection of the President of the United States. This obligation is specified in AFI 71-101, Volume 2, *Protective Service Matters.*

19.26.2. Air Force members and civilian employees must notify their commanders, supervisors, or the Air Force Office of Special Investigations of information concerning the safety of anyone under the protection of the United States Secret Service. This includes the President and Vice President, the President- and Vice President-elect, and visiting heads of foreign states or foreign governments. Additionally former United States Presidents and their spouses for their lifetimes, except that protection of a spouse shall terminate in the event of remarriage unless the former President did not serve as President prior to January 1, 1997, in which case, former Presidents and their spouses for a period of not more than ten years from the date a former President leaves office. The type of information to report includes:

19.26.2.1. Threats, incidents, or demonstrations against foreign diplomatic missions (embassies, chanceries, consulates) in the United States or territories of the United States and the use or attempted use of bodily harm, assassination, or kidnapping as a political weapon.

19.26.2.2. Civil disturbances which may require the use of Federalized National Guard or United States military personnel to maintain or restore public order.

19.26.2.3. United States citizens or residents who have renounced or indicated a desire to renounce the United States government and who are characterized by emotional instability, violent anti-United States sentiment, or a propensity toward violence. Others who should be reported are military members or civilian employees of the Armed Forces being separated or discharged or retired who are deemed a threat by a competent authority (installation or hospital commander).

19.26.3. The Air Force Office of Special Investigations is the point of contact between the Air Force and the United States Secret Service. Any information of interest to the United States Secret Service that comes to the attention of Air Force commanders and supervisors must be reported to the nearest Air Force Office of Special Investigations unit as soon as possible.

## 19.27. Conclusion.

Security responsibility applies to all members of the Air Force at all times. This chapter covered information assurance, installation security, and force protection. These topics are essential to the Air Force mission and to the security of all its resources. All Air Force members must be versed in security principles, apply them to all aspects of their work, and be conscious of how it affects their personal lives. Proper security measures directly contribute to Air Force readiness.

# Chapter 20

# AIR FORCE KNOWLEDGE

## Section 20A—Overview

### 20.1. Introduction.

Air Force knowledge is important because it provides the framework of information required to understand the basic infrastructure of the Air Force such as weapon systems, vocabulary, and some Air Force heritage. In these few pages, you will find a small sampling of the knowledge you will need to be a successful Airman. I encourage you to study the priceless information contained in these pages as well as other sources such as the Air University (http://www.au.af.mil/au/awc/awcgate/awc-ldr.htm). Understanding this Air Force knowledge will give you the power to unleash the Airman inside you, live a career of success, and leave a lasting legacy for future generations to follow.

## Section 20B—Mission Design Series

### 20.2. Tail Flashes.

The majority of major commands require assigned aircraft to hold identifiers as depicted in Technical Order 1-1-8, *Application and Removal of Organic Coatings, Aerospace and Non-Aerospace Equipment*. The composite listing of unit identifiers are identified in Table 20.1., and show past and current Air Force aircraft tail unit identifiers.

**Table 20.1. Tail Flashes Unit Identifiers.**

| CODE | AIRCRAFT | UNIT/ LOCATION/ COMMAND |
|---|---|---|
| AC | F-16C/D | 177 FW Atlantic City, NJ (ANG) |
| AF | T-41D, TG-10C, TG-15A/B, UV-18B, T-51A, T-53A, TG-16A | 306 FTG USAF Academy, CO (AETC) |
| AK | F-16C/D | 354 FW Eielson AFB, AK (PACAF) |
| AK | KC-135R | 168 ARW Eielson AFB, AK (ANG) |
| AK | E-3, F-22, C-12F, C-17 | 3 WG Elmendorf AFB, AK (PACAF) |
| AK | F-22 | 477 FG Elmendorf AFB, AK (AFRC) |
| AK | C-17, C-130, HH-60 | 176 AW Elmendorf, AK (ANG) |
| AL | F-16C/D | 187 FW Dannelly Field, AL (ANG) |
| AP | T-1A, T-6 | 479 FTG Pensacola NAS, FL (AETC) |
| AV | F-16C/D | 31 FW Aviano AB, Italy (USAFE) |
| AZ | F-16C/D | 162 WG Tucson IAP, AZ (ANG) |
| AZ | MQ-1 | 162 WG, 214 RG, Davis Monthan AFB, AZ (ANG) |
| BB | U-2S, TU-2S, T-38A, RQ-4, MC-12 | 9 RW Beale AFB, CA (ACC) |
| BB | RQ-4 | 9 RW, Det 1, Anderson AB, Guam (ACC) |
| BB | RQ-4 | 9 RW, Det 4, Sigonella NAS, Italy (ACC) |
| BD | B-52H | 307 BW, Barksdale AFB, LA (AFRC) |
| CA | MQ-9 | 163 ATKW, March ARB, CA (ANG) |
| CA | F-15 | 144 FW, Fresno Airport, CA (ANG) |
| CB | T-1A, T-6, T-38C | 14 FTW Columbus AFB, MS (AETC) |
| CH | MQ-1, MQ-9 | 432 WG Creech AFB, NV (ACC) |
| CO | F-16C/D | 140 WG Buckley ANGB, CO (ANG) |
| DC | F-16C/D | 113 WG Andrews AFB, MD (ANG) |

| CODE | AIRCRAFT | UNIT/ LOCATION/ COMMAND |
|---|---|---|
| DM | A-10C | 355 FW Davis-Monthan AFB, AZ (ACC) |
| | EC-130H | 55 WG, 55 ECG Davis-Monthan AFB, AZ (ACC) |
| DY | B-1B | 7 BW, Dyess AFB, TX (AFGSC) |
| ED | F-16C/D, B-1, B-2, B-52H, C-12, F-22, T-38 | 412 TW, Edwards AFB, CA (AFMC) |
| EG | F-35 | 33 FW Eglin AFB, FL (AETC) |
| EL | B-1B | 28 BW Ellsworth AFB, SD (AFGSC) |
| EN | T-6, T-38C | 80 FTW Sheppard AFB, TX (AETC) |
| ET | F-15C/E, F- 16C/D, A-10C, UH-1N | 96 TW Eglin AFB, FL (AFMC) |
| FC | UH-1N | 58 SOW, 336 TRG, Fairchild AFB, WA (AETC) |
| FE | UH-1N | 90 MW F.E. Warren AFB, WY (AFGSC) |
| FF | F-22 | 1 FW Langley AFB, VA (ACC) |
| | F-22 | 192 FW Langley AFB, VA (ANG) |
| FL | HC-130P, HH-60G | 920 RQW Patrick AFB, FL (AFRC) |
| FM | F-16C/D | 482 FW Homestead ARB, FL (AFRC) |
| FR | TH-1H | 58 SOW, 23 FTS Fork Rucker, AL (AETC) |
| FT | HH-60G, HC-130J | 23 WG, 563 RQG, Davis-Monthan AFB, AZ (ACC) |
| | A-10C, HC-130J, HH- 60G | 23 WG Moody AFB, GA (ACC) |
| | HH-60G | 23 WG, 563 RQG, Nellis AFB, NV (ACC) |
| GA | E-8C | 116 ACW Robins AFB, GA (ANG) |
| | E-8C | 461 ACW Robins AFB, GA (ACC) |
| GF | RQ-4 | 9 RW, 69 RG Grand Forks, ND (ACC) |
| HH | KC-135R, F-22, C-17 | 154 WG Hickam AFB, HI (ANG) |
| | C-17, F-22A | 15 AW Hickam AFB, HI (PACAF) |
| HL | F-16C/D, F-35A | 388 FW Hill AFB, UT (ACC) |
| | F-16C/D, F-35A | 419 FW Hill AFB, UT (AFRC) |
| HO | MQ-1, MQ-9 | 49 WG Holloman AFB, NM (ACC) |
| ID | A-10C | 124 FW Gowen Field, Boise ID (ANG) |
| IN | A-10C | 122 FW Fort Wayne, IN (ANG) |
| JZ | F-15C/D | 159 FW NAS JRB New Orleans, LA (ANG) |
| KC | A-10C | 442 FW Whiteman AFB, MO (AFRC) |
| LA | B-52H | 2 BW Barksdale AFB, LA (AFGSC) |
| LF | F-16C/D, F-35A | 56 FW Luke AFB, AZ (AETC) |
| MA | F-15C/D | 104 FW Barnes ANGB, MA (ANG) |
| MD | A-10C | 175 WG Warfield ANGB, MD (ANG) |
| MI | A-10C | 127 WG Selfridge ANGB, MI (ANG) |
| MM | UH-1N | 341 MW Malmstrom AFB, MT (AFGSC) |
| MO | F-15E | 366 FW Mountain Home AFB, ID (ACC) |
| MT | B-52H | 5 BW Minot AFB, ND (AFGSC) |
| | UH-1N | 91 MW Minot AFB, ND (AFGSC) |
| NY | MQ-9 | 174 ATKW Hancock Field, NY (ANG) |
| OF | OC/RC/TC/WC-135, E-4B | 55 WG Offutt AFB, NE (ACC) |
| OH | F-16C/D | 180 FW Toledo Express Airport, OH (ANG) |

| CODE | AIRCRAFT | UNIT/ LOCATION/ COMMAND |
|---|---|---|
| OK | E-3B/C | 552 ACW Tinker AFB, OK (ACC) |
|  | F-16C/D | 138 FW Tulsa Airport, OK (ANG) |
|  | E-3B/C | 513 ACG Tinker AFB, OK (AFRC) |
| OS | A-10C, F-16C/D | 51 FW Osan AB, South Korea (PACAF) |
| OT | F-15C, F-16C/D | 53 WG – 85 TES Eglin AFB, FL (ACC) |
|  | A-10C, F-15C/D/E, F-16C/D, F-22, F-35 | 53 WG – 422 TES Nellis AFB, NV (ACC) |
|  | F-35 | 53 WG - 31 TES Edwards AFB, CA (ACC) |
|  | B-1B | 53 WG – 337 TES Dyess AFB, TX (ACC) |
|  | B-52 H | 53 WG – 49 TES Barksdale AFB, LA (ACC) |
| RA | T-1A, T-6, T-38C | 12 FTW Joint Base San Antonio, TX (AETC) |
| SA | F-16C/D | 149 FW Joint Base San Antonio, TX (ANG) |
| SD | F-16C/D | 114 FW Joe Foss Field, SD (ANG) |
| SJ | F-15E | 4 FW Seymour Johnson AFB, NC (ACC) |
| SP | F-16C/D | 52 FW Spangdahlem AB, Germany (USAFE) |
| ST | F-16C/D, F-15C/D, A-10C (Ground Trainers) | 82 TW Sheppard AFB, TX (AETC) |
| SW | F-16C/D | 20 FW Shaw AFB, SC (ACC) |
| TX | MQ-1 | 147 RW Ellington Field, TX (ANG) |
|  | F-16C/D | 301 FW NAS Fort Worth JRB Carswell Field, TX (AFRC) |
| TY | F-22, T-38A | 325 FW Tyndall AFB, FL (AETC) |
| VN | T-1A, T-6, T-38C | 71 FTW Vance AFB, OK (AETC) |
| WA | A-10C, F-15C/D/E, F-16C/D, F-35 | 57 WG Nellis AFB, NV (ACC) |
| WI | F-16C/D | 115 FW Truax Field, WI (ANG) |
| WM | B-2, T-38A | 509 BW Whiteman AFB, MO (AFGSC) |
| WP | F-16C/D | 8 FW Kunsan AB, South Korea (PACAF) |
| WW | F-16C/D | 35 FW Misawa AB, Japan (PACAF) |
| XL | T-1A, T-6, T-38C | 47 FTW Laughlin AFB, TX (AETC) |
| YJ | C-12J, C-130H, UH-1N | 374 AW Yokota AB, Japan (PACAF) |
| ZZ | F-15C/D, E-3B/C, KC-135R, HH-60G | 18 WG Kadena AB, Japan (PACAF) |

### 20.3 - Mission Design Series (MDS).

The MDS designator is an official Department of Defense recognized alpha-numeric symbol designation of a military defense aerospace vehicle. A standardized set of symbols, established by the Secretary of Defense, are used for solely designating military defense aerospace vehicles categorized as: aircraft (standard or non-standard), guided missiles, rockets, probes, boosters, and satellites. The designator describes the aerospace vehicle in two components where the components are separated by a dash. The first component, comprised only of alpha characters, describes the mission of the vehicle. The second component, comprised of both alpha-numeric characters, describes the design number and design series of the vehicle.

**Aerospace Vehicle Mission Design Series Designators for Aircraft**

Example: **YF-22**

| Y =Status Prefix | F = Basic Mission | 2 = Design Number | 2 = Design Number |
| --- | --- | --- | --- |

| STATUS PREFIX | MODIFIED MISSION | BASIC MISSION | VEHICLE TYPE |
| --- | --- | --- | --- |
| G - Permanently Grounded<br>J - Special test (temporary)<br>N - Special test (permanent)<br>X - Experimental<br>Y - Prototype<br>Z - Planning | A - Attack<br>C - Cargo/Transport<br>D - Director<br>E - Special Electronic installation<br>F - Fighter<br>H - Search/Rescue<br>K - Aerial Refueling<br>L - Cold Weather<br>M - Multi-mission<br>O - Observation<br>P - Patrol<br>Q - Drone<br>R - Reconnaissance<br>S - Antisubmarine<br>T - Trainer<br>U - Utility<br>V - Staff<br>W - Weather | A - Attack<br>B - Bomber<br>C - Cargo/Transport<br>E- Special Electronic installation<br>F - Fighter<br>O - Observation<br>P - Patrol<br>R - Reconnaissance<br>S - Antisubmarine<br>T - Trainer<br>U - Utility<br>X - Research | G - Glider<br>H - Helicopter<br>S - Space plane<br>V - VTOL/STOL<br>Z - Lighter-than-air |

## Heritage of the Roundel

| | | |
|---|---|---|
| **1906-1916** | **1918 – 1920** | **1917, 1921-1941** |
| Used with and without white background circle. In use at the time of the Mexican Border Campaign. | The official American insignia during World War I and began to be phased out in 1919. | Introduced prior to the American entry into World War I and officially readopted after the war. |
| **1942-1943** | **1942-1943** | **1943** |
| The red center of the 1921-1941 insignia was removed unofficially in December 1941 and officially in May 1942 to avoid confusion with Japanese insignia. | Some aircraft in the European and Mediterranean theaters unofficially incorporated a yellow surround in the British style. | Between 29 June and 14 August, the official national insignia incorporated white sidebars and an overall red surround. |

| | |
|---|---|
| **1943-1947** | **1947-Present** |
| The red surround of the official insignia was quickly changed to a blue surround. During its 4 years of use, this insignia appeared on more aircraft than all its predecessors combined. | With the reorganization of the Defense Department and the creation of the United States Air Force, red bars were added to the official national insignia. |

**Low Visibility**

Beginning in the late seventies low visibility markings have been introduced officially and unofficially on the aircraft of the United States Air Force and other services. These grey insignia appear in their various forms on the majority of aircraft in the United States Air Force inventory.

### 20.4. Current Weapon Systems, Space Systems, and Missile and Munition Systems.

**Airpower is "the ability to project military power or influence through the control and exploitation of air, space, and cyberspace to achieve strategic, operational, or tactical objectives."** The proper application of airpower requires a comprehensive doctrine of employment and an Airman's perspective. As the nation's most comprehensive provider of military airpower, the Air Force conducts continuous and concurrent air, space, and cyberspace operations. The air, space, and cyberspace capabilities of the other Services serve primarily to support their organic maneuver paradigms; the Air Force employs air, space, and cyberspace capabilities with a broader focus on theater-wide and national-level objectives. Through airpower, the Air Force provides the versatile, wide-ranging means towards achieving national objectives with the ability to deter and respond immediately to crises anywhere in the world.

| Current Weapon Systems |
| --- |

**A-10**
**Thunderbolt II**

A-10C is a close air support platform used to support troops in contact with enemy forces. The A-10 performs secondary roles of Air Interdiction, Airborne Forward Air Control, and Combat Search and Rescue. This aircraft has excellent maneuverability at low air speeds and altitude, and is a highly accurate and survivable weapons-delivery platform.

**AC-130**
**Gunship**

The AC-130U/W/J gunships' primary missions are close air support, air interdiction, and armed reconnaissance. Other missions include perimeter and point defense, escort, landing, drop and extraction zone support, forward air control, Combat Search and Rescue. The AC-130 gunship has a combat history dating back to Vietnam.

**B-1B**
**Lancer**

The B-1B is a multi-mission bomber carrying the largest payload of both guided and unguided weapons in the Air Force inventory. The B-1B's blended wing/body configuration, variable-geometry wings and turbofan afterburning engines, combine to provide long range, maneuverability and high speed while enhancing survivability.

**B-2**
**Spirit**

The B-2 Spirit is a multi-role bomber capable of delivering both conventional and nuclear munitions. The penetrating flexibility and effectiveness inherent in manned bombers is what the B-2 provides. The low-observable, or "stealth," characteristics give it the unique ability to penetrate an enemy's most sophisticated defenses and threaten its most valued, and heavily defended, targets.

## B-52
### Stratofortress

The B-52H is a long-range, heavy bomber that can perform a variety of conventional or nuclear missions including strategic attack, close-air support, air interdiction and offensive counter-air. For more than 40 years, B-52 Stratofortresses have been the backbone of the manned strategic bomber force for the United States. The B-52 is capable of dropping or launching the widest array of weapons in the United States inventory.

## C-5
### Galaxy

The C-5A/B/C Galaxy and C-5M Super Galaxy is one of the largest aircraft in the world and the largest airlifter in the Air Force inventory. The C-5 is used for strategic intertheater delivery of outsized and oversized cargo and passengers. Ground crews are able to load and off-load the C-5 simultaneously at the front and rear cargo openings, reducing cargo transfer times.

## C-17
### Globemaster III

The C-17 is capable of rapid strategic delivery of troops and all types of cargo to main operating bases or directly to forward bases in the deployment area. The aircraft can perform tactical airlift and airdrop missions and can transport litters and ambulatory patients during aeromedical evacuations when required.

## B-2 Spirit

Stealth, multi-role bomber. The B-2 is able to deliver both nuclear and conventional munitions, and is capable of attacking an enemy's war-making potential, in the first critical hours of a conflict. This aircraft is the Air Force's only all-weather hard/deeply buried conventional strike capability.

## C-21
### Learjet

A cargo and passenger airlift aircraft employed for short ranges and into short fields. This aircraft can be configured to transport litters during medical evacuations.

### C-130J
### Hercules

The C-130H/J Hercules primarily performs the tactical portion of the airlift mission. The aircraft is capable of operating from rough, dirt strips. Basic and specialized versions of the aircraft perform diverse roles including airlift support, Antarctic resupply, aeromedical missions, weather reconnaissance, aerial spray missions, firefighting duties for the United States Forest Service and natural disaster relief missions.

### C-146A
### Wolfhound

The C-146A Wolfhound's primary mission is to provide United States Special Operations Command flexible, responsive and operational movement of small teams needed in support of Theater Special Operations Commands (TSOC). Airlift missions are conducted by Air Force Special Operations Command aircrews to prepared and semi-prepared airfields around the world. The aircraft can carry a maximum of 27 passengers or 6,000 pounds of cargo, or up to four litter patients.

### E-3
### Sentry AWACS

The E-3 is a deployable airborne command and control battle management platform employed at the tactical level of war. Airborne Warning and Control System provides all altitude surveillance, warning, and battle management for worldwide air combat operations. The E-3 directs, coordinates, and controls joint and combined forces and operations.

### E-4B
### NAOC

The National Airborne Operations Center is designed as a highly survivable node of the National Military Command System. The E-4 provides critical Command and Control mission support in case of national emergency and provides support to coordinate actions by civil authorities during crisis response.

**Current Weapon Systems (continued)**

### E-8C Joint STARS

Joint Surveillance and Target Attack Radar System (Joint STARS) is a joint Army/Air Force program designed to enhance battle management by providing air/land component commanders with near real-time wide-area surveillance and targeting information on moving and stationary ground targets.

### EC-130H Compass Call

The EC-130H Compass Call is an airborne tactical weapon system using a heavily modified version of the C-130 Hercules airframe. The system disrupts enemy command and control communications and limits adversary coordination essential for enemy force management. The Compass Call system employs offensive counter-information and electronic attack capabilities in support of United States and coalition tactical air, surface, and special operations forces.

### EC-130J Commando Solo

EC-130J Commando Solo aircraft conduct Military Information Support Operations (MISO) and civil affairs broadcasts in FM radio, television and military communications bands. These missions are typically flown at night to reduce probability of detection in politically sensitive or hostile territories.

### F-15 Eagle

F-15C/D is a dual engine, all weather, extremely maneuverable fighter designed to gain and maintain air superiority. The F-15C/D has electronic systems and weaponry to detect, acquire, track and attack enemy aircraft while operating in friendly or enemy-controlled airspace.

### F-15E
### Strike Eagle

F-15E is a dual engine, air-to-ground, air-to-air, all weather, fighter designed for close air support, strategic attack, and interdiction roles. The F-15E has the capability to fight its way to a target over long ranges, destroy enemy ground positions and fight its way out. The aircraft uses two crew members, a pilot and a weapon systems officer.

### F-16
### Fighting Falcon

F-16C/D is a single engine multi-role tactical fighter with full air-to-air and air-to-ground combat capabilities. This aircraft provides a relatively low-cost, high-performance weapon system for the United States and allied nations.

### F-22
### Raptor

F-22 is a low observable, highly maneuverable airframe, with advanced integrated avionics, and aerodynamic performance allowing supersonic cruise without using afterburner.

### F-35A
### Lightning II

The conventional takeoff and landing F-35A gives the U.S. Air Force the power to dominate the skies – anytime, anywhere. The F-35A is an agile, versatile, high-performance, multirole fighter that combines stealth, sensor fusion, and unprecedented situational awareness.

### HC-130N/J
### Combat King

The HC-130N King and HC-130J Combat King II are Combat Search and Rescue configured extended-range versions of the C-130 Hercules. They provide in-flight refueling to rescue and Special Operations helicopters and performs tactical delivery of personnel recovery specialists in permissive or hostile environments.

### HH-60G
### Pave Hawk

The primary mission of the HH-60G Pave Hawk helicopter is to conduct personnel recovery operations into hostile environments to recover isolated personnel. The HH-60G is rapidly deployable and has day/night, marginal weather combat capability employed for Combat Search and Rescue, counter-drug, disaster relief, civil search and rescue, and National Aeronautics and Space Administration support operations.

### KC-10
### Extender

The KC-10 provides global in-flight refueling and airlift support for deployment, employment, redeployment, and joint/combined special operations. The KC-10 can transport up to 75 people and nearly 170,000 pounds of cargo a distance of about 4,400 miles unrefueled.

### KC-135R
### Stratotanker

The KC-135 provides the core aerial refueling capability for the United States Air Force and has excelled in this role for more than 50 years. A cargo deck above the refueling system can hold a mixed load of passengers and cargo. Depending on fuel storage configuration, the KC-135 can carry up to 83,000 pounds of cargo and 37 passengers.

## MC-130H
### Combat Talon II

The MC-130H Combat Talon II provides infiltration, exfiltration, and resupply of special operations forces and equipment in hostile or denied territory. Secondary missions include psychological operations and helicopter and vertical lift air refueling. The aircraft features terrain-following and terrain-avoidance radars capable of operations as low as 250 feet in adverse weather conditions.

## MC-130J
### Commando II

The Commando II flies clandestine, low-level air refueling missions for special operations helicopters and tiltrotor aircraft, and infiltration, exfiltration, and resupply of special operations forces by airdrop or airland in politically sensitive or hostile territories. The MC-130J primarily flies missions at night to reduce probability of visual acquisition and intercept by airborne threats. Its secondary mission includes the airdrop of leaflets.

## MQ-1B
### Predator

The Predator is an armed, multi-mission, medium-altitude, long-endurance remotely piloted aircraft. The MQ-1B is employed primarily as an intelligence-collection asset and secondarily against dynamic execution targets. Given its significant loiter time, wide-range sensors, and precision weapons, it provides a unique capability against high-value, fleeting, and time-sensitive targets.

## MQ-9
### Reaper

Like the MQ-1, the MQ-9 is an armed, multi-mission, medium-altitude, long-endurance remotely piloted aircraft, but it is larger and more heavily-armed than the Predator. The MQ-9 can employ both AGM-114 Hellfire missiles and GBU-12 laser-guided bombs. The remotely piloted aircraft can be disassembled and loaded into a single container for deployment worldwide.

**Current Weapon Systems (continued)**

### RC-135
### U/V/W

RC-135V/W Rivet Joint, RC-135U Combat Sent, and RC-135S Cobra Ball are electronic reconnaissance and surveillance platforms employed all over the world to increase battlespace awareness by detecting, identifying and geo-locating signals throughout the electromagnetic spectrum.

### RQ-4
### Global Hawk

The RQ-4 Global Hawk is a high-altitude, long-endurance, remotely piloted aircraft with an integrated sensor suite that provides global all-weather, day or night intelligence, surveillance and reconnaissance capability. Global Hawk's mission is to provide a broad spectrum of intelligence, surveillance and reconnaissance collection capability to support joint forces in worldwide peacetime and contingency operations.

### T-1
### Jayhawk

The T-1A Jayhawk is a medium-range, twin-engine jet trainer used in the advanced phase of specialized undergraduate pilot training for students selected to fly airlift or tanker aircraft. It is also used to support navigator training for the United States Air Force, Navy, Marine Corps and international services.

### T-6A
### Texan II

The T-6A is a single-engine primary flight training aircraft for future United States Air Force and United States Navy pilots. Students learn basic flying skills common in the T-6 before moving on to advanced flight training.

### T-38A/C
### Talon

The T-38 is a twin-engine, high-altitude, supersonic jet trainer used in the advanced phase of specialized undergraduate pilot training for students selected to fly fighter aircraft Air Combat Command, Air Force Material Command, and the National Aeronautics and Space Administration also use the T-38 in various roles other than training.

### U-2S
### Dragon Lady

The U-2 provides high-altitude, all-weather surveillance and reconnaissance. The Dragon Lady delivers critical imagery and signals intelligence throughout all phases of conflict, including peacetime indications and warnings, low-intensity conflict, and large-scale hostilities. Routinely flown at altitudes over 70,000 feet, the U-2 pilot must wear a full pressure suit similar to those worn by astronauts.

### UH-1N
### Iroquois

The UH-1N is a light-lift utility helicopter used to support various missions. The primary missions include: airlift of emergency security forces, security and surveillance of off-base nuclear weapons convoys, and distinguished visitor airlift. Other uses include: disaster response, search and rescue, medical evacuation, airborne cable inspections, support to aircrew survival school, routine missile site support and transport.

### UV-18
### Twin Otter

The UV-18B Twin Otter is the military version of the DeHavilland DHC-6. Carrying a pilot, co-pilot and up to 17 jumpers. The Twin Otter is used to support parachute and airmanship training at the United States Air Force Academy.

### VC-25
### Air Force One

The presidential air transport fleet consists of two specially configured Boeing 747-200B's with the Air Force designation VC-25. When the president is aboard either aircraft, or any Air Force aircraft, the radio call sign is "Air Force One."

**Space Systems**

### Air Force Satellite Control Network (AFSCN)

The Air Force Satellite Control Network is a worldwide network of satellite control stations which uses satellite and terrestrial communication links providing connectivity to over 150 Department of Defense, National, Allied and Civil space vehicles.

### Ballistic Missile Early Warning System (BMEWS)

The Ballistic Missile Early Warning System detects, tracks and warns of ballistic missile launches, launches of new space systems, and provides data on foreign ballistic missile events.

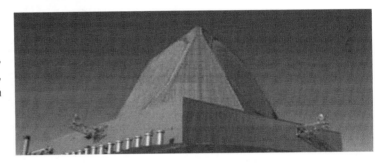

### Defense Meteorological Satellites Program (DMSP)

DMSP provides an enduring and survivable capability, through all levels of conflict, to collect and disseminate global visible and infrared cloud data and other specialized meteorological, oceanographic, and space environment data required to support worldwide DoD operations and high-priority national programs.

### Defense Satellite Communications System and Wideband Global SATCOM (DSCS and WGS)

These constellations of satellites provide worldwide, responsive wideband and anti-jam satellite communications supporting strategic and tactical command, control, communications, and intelligence requirements. Each WGS satellite provides service in both the X and Ka frequency bands, with the unprecedented ability to cross-band between the two frequencies onboard the satellite. Wideband Global SATCOM augments the one-way Global Broadcast Service through two-way Ka-band service.

## Space Systems (continued)

### Defense Support Program and Space Based Infrared System (DSP) and (SBIRS)

DSP and SBIRS supports the defense and intelligence communities through missile early warning, missile defense, battlespace awareness, and technical intelligence mission areas. DSP satellites use an infrared sensor to detect heat from missile and booster plumes against the Earth's background. The SBIRS sensors are designed to provide greater flexibility and sensitivity than the DSP infrared sensor and detect short-wave and mid-wave infrared signals, allowing SBIRS to perform a broader set of missions.

### Evolved Expendable Launch Vehicle (EELV)

The Delta IV, Atlas V and Falcon 9 Evolved Expendable Launch Vehicle provide the Air Force and the nation rapid and reliable access to space with a standardized launch capability.

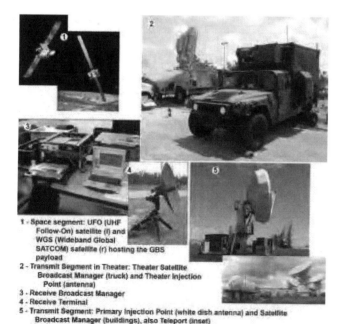

1 - Space segment: UFO (UHF Follow-On) satellite (l) and WGS (Wideband Global SATCOM) satellite (r) hosting the GBS payload
2 - Transmit Segment in Theater: Theater Satellite Broadcast Manager (truck) and Theater Injection Point (antenna)
3 - Receive Broadcast Manager
4 - Receive Terminal
5 - Transmit Segment: Primary Injection Point (white dish antenna) and Satellite Broadcast Manager (buildings), also Teleport (inset)

### Global Positioning System (GPS)

The Global Positioning System is a constellation of orbiting satellites that provides navigation and timing data to military and civilian users all over the world. The constellation is designed and operated as a 24-satellite system, consisting of six orbital planes, with a minimum of four satellites per plane. The system is controlled by the 50th Space Wing, located at Schriever AFB.

**Milstar and Advanced Extremely High Frequency Satellite Communications Systems**

Milstar and AEHF provide the President, Secretary of Defense and the U.S. armed forces with assured, survivable satellite communications (SATCOM) with low probability of interception and detection. Designed to overcome enemy jamming and nuclear effects, Milstar and AEHF are the most robust and reliable SATCOM systems currently employed by the Department of Defense thus ensuring worldwide command and control.

**Perimeter Acquisition Radar Characterization System (PARCS)**

PARCS provides tactical warning and attack characterization of sea-launched and intercontinental ballistic missile attacks against the continental United States. The system supports the space surveillance network by providing space surveillance data, tracking, reporting and space object identification.

**Phased Array Warning System (PAVE PAWS)**

The PAVE PAWS Early Warning Radars are capable of detecting ballistic missile attacks and conducting general space surveillance and satellite tracking. They are able to detect and track both intercontinental and sea-launched missile threats. Early warning and attack characterization data is sent to the United States' Missile Warning and Space Control Centers.

## Missile and Munition Systems

### ADM-160
### Miniature Air-Launched Decoy (MALD)

MALD is a low-cost flight vehicle that is modular, air-launched and programmable. It weighs less than 300 pounds and has a range of approximately 500 nautical miles. MALD protects aircraft and their crews by duplicating the combat flight profiles and signatures of United States and allied aircraft.

### AGM-65
### Maverick Missile

The AGM-65 is an air-to-surface launch and leave tactical missile. Electro-optical, infrared or laser-guided these missiles are used in close air support, interdiction, and enemy defense suppression missions. It provides stand-off capability and high probability of strike against a wide range of tactical targets, including armor, air defenses, ships, transportation equipment and fuel storage facilities.

### AGM-86
### Launched Cruise Missile (ALCM)

The AGM-86 is a subsonic, highly accurate, long range, air-to-surface strategic nuclear missile designed to evade air and ground-based defenses in order to strike targets at any location within any enemy's territory.

### AGM-86C
### Conventional Air-Launched Cruise Missile
### (CALCM)

CALCM provides the warfighter with an adverse weather, day or night, air-to-surface, accurate, long-range conventional (non-nuclear) standoff strike capability against deep and hardened targets.

## AGM-88
### High Speed Anti-Radiation Missile (HARM)

The AGM-88 is an air-to-surface tactical anti-radiation missile used to destroy or suppress enemy radar threats at standoff range homing in on source radar emissions.

## EELV

The Boeing Delta IV and Lockheed Martin Atlas V Evolved Expendable Launch Vehicle provide the Air Force and the nation rapid and reliable access to space with a standardized launch capability.

## AGM-114
### Hellfire Missile

Originally developed for anti-armor use, the laser-guided AGM-114 Hellfire is a family of 100-pound class guided air-to-surface missiles for use against fixed and moving targets. It has multi-mission, multi-target precision-strike ability, and can be launched from multiple both rotary and fixed-wing aircraft including Remotely Piloted Aircraft.

## AGM-129A
### Advanced Cruise Missile (ACM)

The AGM-129A is a subsonic, low-observable air-to-surface strategic nuclear missile with significant range and accuracy. The ACM's external shape is optimized for low observables characteristics and includes forward swept wings and control surfaces, a flush air intake and a flat exhaust.

### AGM-158
#### Joint Air-to-Surface Stand-Off Missile (JASSM)

The AGM-158 is a long range, conventional, air-to-ground, precision standoff missile to destroy high-value, well-defended, fixed and relocatable targets.

### AIM-9M/X
#### Sidewinder

The AIM-9M/X is a fighter-borne supersonic, short range, passive infrared heat-seeking air-to-air missile with a high explosive warhead. The initial production version, designated AIM-9B, entered the Air Force inventory in 1956.

### AIM-120
#### Advanced Medium-Range Air-toAir Missile (AMRAAM)

The AIM-120 is a supersonic, medium range, active radar guided air-to-air missile with a high explosive warhead. It has an all-weather, beyond-visual-range capability that improves the aerial combat capabilities of U.S. and allied aircraft to meet current and future threat of enemy air-to-air weapons.

### GBU-15

The GBU-15 is unpowered glide munition that employs elecro-optical or infrared terminal seeker for a standoff attack of high value ground targets. The rear control section consists of four wings that are in an "X"-like arrangement with trailing edge flap control surfaces for flight maneuvering.

## Missile and Munition Systems (continued)

### GBU-31/32/38/54
### Joint Direct Attack Munition (JDAM)

Joint Direct Attack Munition is a joint Air Force and Navy system used to upgrade the existing inventory of general purpose bombs by integrating them with GPS, laser and inertial guidance system tail kits to provide accurate adverse weather delivery from very low to very high altitudes. JDAM enables multiple weapons to be directed against single or multiple targets on a single pass.

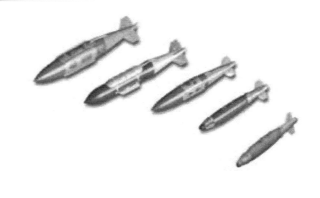

### GBU-39
### Small Diameter Bomb (SDB)

The SDB is an extended range all-weather, 250-pound class, guided munition. The SDB relies on GPS to provide navigation to the target. It is capable of destroying fixed and stationary targets. SDB increases aircraft loadout, decreases the logistical footprint, decreases collateral damage, and improves aircraft sortie generation times.

### GBU-43
### Massive Ordinance Air Blast (MOAB)

The MOAB is a 21,000-pound, guided, high-explosive munition designed for anti-personnel and obstacle clearance purposes. It rests on a cradle inside an airdrop aircraft platform and is extracted by a drogue parachute. After extraction from the aircraft, the MOAB is guided to the target by fixed wings and grid fins.

### GBU-57
### Massive Ordinance Penetrator

The Massive Ordnance Penetrator (MOP) is a 30,000-pound guided, earth-penetrating weapon system designed to accomplish the difficult, complicated mission of reaching and destroying targets in hardened and deeply-buried facilities. The 20.5-foot long bomb carries more than 5,300 pounds of explosives and can reach targets as far as 200 feet underground before exploding.

### LGM-30G
### Minuteman III

The LGM-30G Minuteman intercontinental ballistic missile (ICBM) is an element of the nation's strategic deterrent forces under the control of the Air Force Global Strike Command. The Minuteman III is an inertially guided, intercontinental ballistic missile. Minuteman III is capable of delivering up to 3 multiple independently targetable reentry vehicles. It provides a highly survivable, quick-reaction component to the nuclear Triad.

### PAVEWAY

### Family of Guided Bombs

PAVEWAY series laser-guided bomb kits transform traditional 500, 2,000, and 5,000-pound bomb bodies into precision-guided, air-to-ground munitions for targeting of soft and hardened targets. The PAVEWAY series consists of GBU-10/24/27/28.

### Section 20C—Air Force Information

### 20.5. Air Force Vocabulary

Many industries, such as the medical industry and the computer industry, have their own technical jargon. However, there may be perhaps no other industry in the world that matches up with the amount of industry-specific speech as that possessed by the military. To eliminate confusion terms and acronyms are published as attachments within official Air Force publications.

20.5.1. The Joint Publication (JP) 1-02, *Department of Defense Dictionary of Military and Associated Terms,* sets forth standard United States military and associated terminology to encompass the joint activity of the Armed Forces of the United States. These military and associated terms, together with their definitions, constitute approved Department of Defense terminology for general use by all Department of Defense components.

20.5.1.1 **Purpose.** This publication supplements standard English-language dictionaries and standardizes military and associated terminology to improve communication and mutual understanding within Department of Defense, with other federal agencies, and among the United States and its allies.

20.5.1.2. **Application.** This publication applies to the Office of the Secretary of Defense, the Services, the Joint Staff, combatant commands, Department of Defense agencies, and all other Department of Defense components.

It is the primary terminology source when preparing correspondence, to include policy, strategy, doctrine, and planning documents.

20.5.1.3. **Publication Format.** JP 1-02 is published outlining two basic parts:

20.5.1.3.1. **Terms and definitions.** These are annotated with the source publication.

20.5.1.3.2. **Abbreviations and acronyms.** The source publication establishes the authoritative context for proper understanding and management of the associated term.

20.5.1.4. **JP 1-02 Online Availability and Update Schedule.** JP 1-02 is accessible online as a searchable database and in PDF format at the following Internet address: http://www.dtic.mil/doctrine/dod_dictionary and at the following NIPRNET address: https://jdeis.js.mil/jdeis/. The contents of JP 1-02 are updated on a monthly basis to include any terminology additions, modifications, or deletions made within the previous calendar month in accordance with CJCSI 5705.01.

20.5.2. Military Phonetic Alphabet.

The United States Air Force, as well as all other branches of the United States armed services, currently use the International Civil Aviation Organization alphabet for radio communication. This alphabet was adopted by the United States armed services in 1956, and is currently used by North Atlantic Treaty Organization countries as well as civil aviation around the world. Table 20.1 shows both the code words for each letter and their recommended pronunciation.

**Table 20.1 Phonetic Alphabet**

| Letter | Code Word | Pronunciation |
|--------|-----------|---------------|
| A | Alfa | AL fah |
| B | Bravo | BRAH voh |
| C | Charlie | CHAR lee |
| D | Delta | DEL tah |
| E | Echo | EKK oh |
| F | Foxtrot | FOKS trot |
| G | Golf | Golf |
| H | Hotel | HO tell |
| I | India | IN dee ah |
| J | Juliet | JEW lee ett |
| K | Kilo | KEY loh |
| L | Lima | LEE mah |
| M | Mike | Mike |
| N | November | NOH vem ber |
| O | Oscar | OSS car |
| P | Papa | PAH pah |
| Q | Quebec | keh BECK |
| R | Romeo | ROW me oh |
| S | Sierra | see AIR ah |
| T | Tango | TANG go |
| U | Uniform | YOU nee form |
| V | Victor | VIK ter |
| W | Whiskey | WISS key |
| X | X-ray | EKS ray |
| Y | Yankee | YANG kee |
| Z | Zulu | ZOO loo |

## 20.6. Pledge of Allegiance

**I Pledge Allegiance to the flag
of the United States of America
and to the Republic for which it stands
one Nation under God, indivisible,
with liberty and justice for all**

## 20.7. National Anthem.

**National Anthem
Francis Scott Key**

Oh say can you see,
by the dawn's early light,
What so proudly we hailed
at the twilight's last gleaming?

Whose broad stripes and bright stars,
through the perilous fight
o'er the ramparts we watched
were so gallantly streaming

And the rockets red glare,
the bombs bursting in air,
gave proof through the night
That our flag was still there!

O say does that Star-Spangled banner yet wave?
O'er the land of the free
and the home of the brave!

## 20.8. United States Air Force Hymn.

**United States Air Force Hymn**
Music by Henry Baker
Lyrics by Mary Hamilton

Lord, guard and guide the men who fly
Through the great spaces of the sky;
Be with them traversing the air
In darkening storms or sunshine fair

Thou who dost keep with tender might
The balanced birds in all their flight
Thou of the tempered winds be near
That, having thee, they know no fear

Control their minds with instinct fit
What time adventuring, they quit
The firm security of land;
Grant steadfast eye and skillful hand

Aloft in solitudes of space
Uphold them with Thy saving grace.
O God, protect the men who fly
Thru lonely ways beneath the sky.

## 20.9. High Flight.

**HIGH FLIGHT
by Royal Canadian Pilot Officer John Gillespie Magee, Jr.**

Oh, I have slipped the surly bonds of earth
And danced the skies on laughter-silvered wings;
Sunward I've climbed, and joined
the tumbling mirth of sun-split clouds
and done a hundred things
You have not dreamed of —
wheeled and soared and swung
High in the sunlit silence.

Hov'ring there,
I've chased the shouting wind along, and flung
My eager craft through footless halls of air.
Up, up the long, delirious, burning blue
I've topped the windswept heights with easy grace
Where never lark, or even eagle flew.
And, while with silent, lifting mind I've trod
The high untrespassed sanctity of space,
Put out my hand, and touched the face of God.

## 20.10. The Air Force Song.

**Air Force Song History**

The only official history of the Air Force Song can be found in a copy of a script which was used on radio station WRC broadcast on 23 Feb 1944. Captain Alf Heiburg, leader of the Army Air Corps Band, interviewed Captain Robert Crawford, composer of the "Army Air Corps Song," during this broadcast. Captain Crawford related the story, retold here:

In 1939, when he was a civilian pilot, Robert Crawford was asked by a friend to enter a song contest. While flying his plane to Philadelphia, he composed a simple tune. The next day he wrote lyrics that, when combined with the tune, became what was known as the "Army Air Corps Song." The United States Army Band made the first recordings of the song in 1939. It was later renamed the Army Air Forces Song, and eventually the Air Force Song.

**Air Force Song**

Off we go into the wild blue yonder,
Climbing high into the sun
Here they come zooming to meet our thunder
At'm boys, giv'r the gun!
Down we dive spouting our flame from under
Off with one helluva roar!
We live in fame or go down in flame
Hey! Nothing'll stop the U.S. Air Force!

Minds of men fashioned a crate of thunder
Sent it high into the blue;
Hands of men blasted the world asunder,
How they lived God only knew!
Souls of men dreaming of skies to conquer
Gave us wings, ever to soar.
With Scouts before and bombers galore,
Nothing can stop the U.S. Air Force!

Here's a toast to the host of those who
Love the vastness of the sky,
To a friend we send the message of his
Brother men who fly.
We drink to those who gave their all of old
Then down we roar to score the rainbow's
Pot of gold.

A toast to the host of the men we boast
The U.S. Air Force!
Off we go into the wild sky yonder
Keep the wings level and true
If you live to be a gray-haired wonder
Keep the nose out of the blue
Flying men, guarding our nations's borders
We'll be there, followed by more
In echelon, we'll carry on
Nothing can stop the U.S. Air Force!

## 20.11. Total Force.

20.11.1. American Airmen from each component — Regular Air Force, Air National Guard, and Air Force Reserve — provide seamless airpower on a global scale every day. Over the past two decades, to meet combatant commander requirements and the demands of recurring deployments, the Air Force has increasingly called upon its Total Force. This elevated use of the Air National Guard and Air Force Reserve has transformed a traditionally strategic reserve force into a force that provides operational capability, strategic depth, and surge capacity.

20.11.2. In Total Force Integration associations, the Active and Reserve Components share equipment, facilities and resources, including aircraft, crews and maintenance, to carry out a common mission. In a classic association, the Active Component is the host unit, retaining weapon system responsibility, while sharing the mission with a Reserve or Guard tenant unit. For active associations the Reserve or Guard unit is host, with an Active Component tenant. Integrating with the Active Component in this way yields numerous synergistic benefits to the Air Force's strength, including an improved ability to respond with surge capacity at a moment's notice.

20.11.3. **Air National Guard.**

20.11.3.1. The heritage predates the establishment of the United States Air Force as a separate armed service in 1947: it shares a community-based militia tradition with the Army National Guard that dates from colonial times. State National Guards began forming aviation units as early as 1908, and New York's 1st Aero Company was the first such organization mustered into federal service in 1916. Mobilization for World War I dissolved these state units, although many Guard personnel served in the Army Air Service. With the reorganization of the Army in 1920, the National Guard gained organic aviation units with federal standing. Twenty-nine observation squadrons had activated by the time the United States entered World War II, all absorbed into the Army Air Forces upon mobilization.

20.11.3.2. After federal service in the war, these 29 units became the core of the new Air National Guard, together with 43 more flying squadrons added to the Air National Guard after 1947. In keeping with the National Guard's previous legal status, and in contrast to the Air Force Reserve, the Air National Guard retained a dual role: each state's Air National Guard units remained at the governors' disposal when not called into federal service. In either status, the federal government provided the bulk of the Air Guard's funding. Initially, the Air National Guard's nominal mission was as a short-range, daytime air defense force. In this role, the bulk of the Air National Guard's aircraft were F-47 Thunderbolt and F-51 Mustangs left over from World War II, plus a few light bombers, B-26 Invaders. A small number of early jet fighters soon supplemented the initial propeller-driven force.

20.11.3.3. The Air Guard received its baptism by fire during the Korean War. Sixty-seven flying squadrons and approximately 45,000 Air National Guard members, some 80 percent of the force, were mobilized. Mobilization was complicated: some units took three to six months to become combat ready, and some never did. The Air National Guard still formed a substantial part of the wartime Air Force, with some units serving in combat, while others relieved deploying regular squadrons at home.

20.11.3.4. Based on Korean War experience, senior Air National Guard and Air Force leaders committed to build the Air National Guard into a more effective force, and the Air National Guard received modern equipment and better funding to that end. These efforts came to fruition when President John F. Kennedy mobilized over 21,000 Air National Guard members from 28 squadrons in 1961 as part of the United States response to the Berlin Crisis. The Air National Guard deployed 216 Air National Guard fighter aircraft with support personnel to Europe to reinforce North Atlantic Treaty organization. This movement, Operation Stair Step, was the largest aircraft deployment in Air National Guard history. The entire deployment across the Atlantic Ocean occurred without the loss of a single plane.

20.11.3.5. The war in Vietnam saw a few Air National Guard fighter squadrons deployed, and the Air Guard supplied some of the airlift into the theater. The Air Guard's main role, however, was support for the Air Force's commitments in Europe as the demands of operations in Southeast Asia taxed the regular force. The Air National Guard assumed aerial refueling responsibilities for Air Force fighters in Europe from 1967 to 1977. This effort, Operation Creek Party, demonstrated that the Air Guard could provide sustained support to the Air Force without resorting to mobilization by rotating forces of volunteer personnel operating aircraft drawn from Air National Guard squadrons. This approach remains virtually unchanged today.

20.11.3.6. After the Vietnam War, some significant missions moved to the Air National Guard. Air Guard KC-135 air refueling tankers began participating in the Strategic Air Command's nuclear alert force in 1976. In 1977, the Air National Guard became the primary airlifters for United States Southern Command's Operation Coronet Oak, which continues today. From 1978 to 1990, rotating Air National Guard fighter squadrons assumed responsibility for the air defense of the Panama Canal Zone under Operation Coronet Cove. The Air National Guard participated in Operation Just Cause, the 1989 invasion of Panama to expel its dictator, Manuel Noriega, and to install a democratically elected president. In the 1990s, Air Guardsmen manned radar stations and flew fighter aircraft in Latin America to monitor and report suspected drug-running aircraft. This operational experience served the Air Guard well in the Persian Gulf crisis of 1990-1991. Air National Guard fighters, tankers, airlifters, special operations, aeromedical evacuation, and security forces participated in the air campaign of the Persian Gulf War. During that time, 12,404 Air National Guard members were mobilized and deployed to Southwest Asia, Europe and other overseas locations as well as serving in the continental United States.

20.11.3.7. Following the Persian Gulf War and the end of the Cold War, the Air National Guard continued to operate world-wide, integrated with the Regular Air Force and the Air Force Reserve, jointly with the other services, and combined with North Atlantic Treaty Organization forces. The Air National Guard participated in several major operations involving humanitarian assistance, peacekeeping, and direct combat action. Some operations were extensions of those that involved the Air National Guard earlier in South America, but through the 1990s the Air National Guard gained more commitments, Bolstered by new capabilities, Air Guard flying and support units helped maintain the no-fly zones over Iraq, provided humanitarian assistance in Somalia and Rwanda, and supported peacekeeping forces in the Balkans and Haiti. The Air Force's global mobility operations involved Air National Guard tanker and airlift forces on a daily basis. In 1997, the Air National Guard assumed responsibility for manning First Air Force, which maintained the air defenses of the continental United States. President Bill Clinton also mobilized 4,870 Air Guardsmen during the Kosovo War in 1999.

20.11.3.8. The Air National Guard played a critical role in the immediate United States response to the terrorist attacks of 11 September 2001 and the subsequent global military actions. In the immediate aftermath of 9/11, the Air National Guard improvised a greatly strengthened continental air defense system and bore the main burden of sustaining it. The combination of fighter patrols and 24-hour alerts at 26 Air National Guard bases across the United States put heavy stress on the Air National Guard fighter force in both training and readiness, but the wide geographic dispersal of its fighter units and its long standing role in continental air defense made the Air National Guard the right organization to execute the mission.

20.11.3.9. The Air National Guard's aviation and support units also played critical roles in the wars in Afghanistan (Operation Enduring Freedom) and Iraq (Operation Iraqi Freedom). Flying and non-flying Air National Guard units deployed repeatedly to every operating base supporting those wars. When Operation Enduring Freedom began 7 October 2001, the Air National Guard participated in the initial combat operations in Afghanistan and have continued to participate in the mission ever since. Air National Guard airlift, tankers, A-10 and F-16 units, special operations, rescue, civil engineer, security forces, combat communication and many other units have repeatedly deployed to the region over the course of that war. When the United States invaded Iraq on 20 March 2003, the Air National Guard had 18,552 members on Regualr Air Force participating in the invasion and serving in Afghanistan and other overseas operations. The six Air National Guard A-10 units participated in combat operations in Iraq and Afghanistan simultaneously. During the invasion of Iraq, the only A-10 presence in Afghanistan was an Air National Guard unit. Air Guard F-16C Block 30 fighters and a few A-10s equipped with Litening 2 targeting pods – a capability developed independently by the Air National Guard - provided air support for special operations units operating in the western desert of Iraq looking for SCUD missiles. In addition, Air National Guard F-16C Block 30 aircraft provided a unique capability as the last United States aircraft equipped with Theater Airborne Reconnaissance System pods. Intelligence Surveillance and Reconnaissance in general was a growing capability for deployed Air National Guard forces with the proliferation of Remotely Piloted Aircraft systems like the Predator.

20.11.4. **Air Force Reserve.**

20.11.4.1. Since formal establishment of the Air Force Reserve in April 1948, the Air Force Reserve has amassed a rich heritage with heroic accounts of responding to natural disasters, humanitarian crisis, and combat operations. Our history is also a study of changing, adapting, and evolving from a strategic force held in "reserve" into an operational Reserve force with the most advanced weapons systems.

20.11.4.2. Today, Citizen Airmen perform leading roles in military operations, humanitarian crisis and disaster relief around the globe. The Air Force Reserve consists of officers, enlisted and civil servants who are tasked by law to fill the needs of the armed forces whenever more units and people are required than are available within the Regular Air Force. More than 860,000 people make up the Ready, Standby, Retired and Regualr Air Force Retired Reserve. This includes nearly 70,000 Selected Reservists who are "ready-now" participating in every job specialty and on the front lines of daily military operations around the globe. The Air Force Reserve is a combat-ready force of Citizen Airmen, stationed locally at over 60 locations throughout the United States and serving globally for every Combatant Command in air, space and cyberspace.

20.11.4.3. The Chief of Air Force Reserve, Headquarters Air Force, Pentagon, serves as the principal advisor on reserve matters to the Secretary of the Air Force and Air Force Chief of Staff. The Chief of Air Force Reserve is also dual-hatted as the Commander of Air Force Reserve Command, located at Robins Air Force Base, Georgia. The Commander of Air Force Reserve Command is responsible for organizing, training, and equipping all Air Force Reserve units. Air Force Reserve Command is composed of three Numbered Air Forces, a Force Generation Center, the Air Reserve Personnel center, 35 flying wings, 1 space wing, 1 Special Operations Wing, 11 flying groups, and 4 independent groups.

20.11.4.4. Circa 1917: The National Defense Act of 1916 directed the creation of an Officers Reserve Corps, an Enlisted Reserve Corps and the nation's Air Service Reserve Program. For the first time, Reserve Corps were clearly a federal reserve force and not militia. The Reserve Corps were established on March 22, 1917, just weeks before the United States formally entered World War I. By the end of the war, more than 11,000 of Army Air Service pilots who fought were reserve officers. Notably, the First Reserve Aero Squadron deployed in the summer of 1917 for action in France. Later, the squadron went on to fight in the Pacific Theater in World War II, served at the forefront of the nuclear deterrence mission in the Cold War, and, still serving today as the 26th Space Aggressor Squadron, is the oldest squadron in the Air Force Reserve.

20.11.4.5. 1941: Reservists played a critical role in World War II. In the war's early days 1,500 reserve pilots along with 1,300 non-rated officers and 400 enlisted Airmen were activated into the Army Air Corps. These included the legendary Jimmy Doolittle who was ordered to Regualr Air Force to work in Detroit to convert automobile manufacturing plants into aircraft factories and later went on to lead "Doolittle's Raiders," the first American bombing attack on the Japanese mainland.

20.11.4.6. 1948: In a joint directive signed by General Omar Bradley, the Army Chief of Staff, and General Carl Spaatz, the Air Force Chief of Staff, dated April 14, 1948 the Army Air Corps Reserve was transferred to the Air Force officially becoming the Air Force Reserve.

20.11.4.7. 1950: The young Air Force Reserve was barely two years old when it mobilized nearly 147,000 reservists, many who were World War II veterans, for the Korean War from 1950 to 1953. The Armed Forces Reserve Act of 1952 refined the use of the Reserve Components in time of war or national emergency and established three levels of Air Force reservists – ready, standby, and retired.

20.11.4.8. 1960's: In 1961, President John F. Kennedy called up the Air Force Reserve in response to the Berlin crisis. The mobilization included five Air Force Reserve C-124 aircraft units and 5,613 reservists. By 1962, an additional mobilization of 14,220 reservists and 422 aircraft were supporting operations during the Cuban Missile Crisis. Most experts believe that the mobilization had the effect of deterring war. Beginning in the early 1960s, the Air Force Reserve provided strategic airlift as well as counterinsurgency, close air support, tactical mobility, interdiction, rescue and recovery, intelligence, medical, maintenance, aerial port and air superiority until the United States ended its involvement in the Vietnam War.

20.11.4.9. 1970's: In August 1970, the Department of Defense implemented the Total Force Policy and the Air Force Reserve became a multi-mission force flying the same modern aircraft as the active Air Force. In March 1973, Air Force Reserve C-141 and C-9 associate aircrews, medical, aeromedical, casualty assistance, legal, chaplain, and intelligence personnel supported Operation Homecoming—the return of the American prisoners of war from North Vietnam. That same year, the Air Force Reserve proved the concept of Global Mobility by flying hundreds of strategic airlift missions during the Arab-Israeli War.

20.11.4.10. 1980's: For the most part, the nation was at peace for the next few years with the Air Force Reserve periodically engaged in emergency-response and humanitarian missions. This included the rescue and return of more than 700 American students from Grenada and evacuation of wounded Marines from Lebanon in 1983, the aerial-refueling of F-111 aircraft during the El Dorado Canyon raid on Libyan-sponsored terrorists in 1986, and Operation Just Cause that ousted Panama's General Noriega in 1989-1990.

20.11.4.11. 1990's: Nearly 23,500 Air Force Reservists were mobilized, and 15,000 volunteered for service in support of Operations Desert Shield and Desert Storm, in response to Saddam Hussein's invasion of Kuwait in 1990. This began more than twenty years of continuous combat operations in Southwest Asia, while simultaneously conducting numerous emergency-response and humanitarian missions. These included combat operations over Bosnia, Serbia, and Kosovo, and Haiti as well as the evacuation of Clark Air Force Base during the eruption of Mount Pinatubo, and significant contributions to disaster relief operations in former Soviet republics, southern Turkey and northern Iraq, Somalia, and Haiti.

20.11.4.12. 2001: When terrorists attacked the United States on Sept. 11, 2001, Air Force reservists responded in full measure. Air Force Reserve F-16 fighter aircraft flew combat air patrols to protect American cities while KC-135 tankers and Airborne Warning and Control System aircraft supported security efforts. In October 2001, Operation Enduring Freedom began as United States military forces entered Afghanistan to combat the Taliban and eliminate terrorist sanctuaries. In March 2003, Operation Iraqi Freedom began in order to end Saddam Hussein's regime. Air Force Reserve units and reservists played key roles in all combat operations as Air Force Reserve MC-130 Combat Talon aircraft became the first fixed-wing aircraft to penetrate Afghan airspace while Air Force Reserve F-16 crews performed the first combat missions. In 2004, more than 140 Air Force Reserve Combat Convoy Airmen served in the 1059th Air Expeditionary Force Truck Company. Air Force Reserve Security Forces served throughout Iraq and Afghanistan, and comprised the entire Security Force presence at Kirkuk Air Base with as many as 275 personnel. Air Force Reserve Explosive Ordnance Disposal provided extensive mission support in Iraq and Afghanistan by executing a broad scope of missions within and beyond the base security zone. Air Force Reserve Expeditionary Combat Support capabilities provided airfield operations, cargo and passenger handling, medical, security, intelligence, and personnel services.

20.11.4.13. Today and in recent years, Citizen Airmen have supported every Air Force core function and every Combatant Commander around the world. Air Force reservists were engaged in surge operations in Iraq and Afghanistan. They supported combat and humanitarian missions in Haiti, Libya, Japan, Mali and the Horn of Africa. Also, they've provided national disaster relief at home in the United States after Hurricanes Katrina and Sandy, the gulf oil spill and the wildfires in the western states. Throughout our history, Citizen Airmen have continually volunteered, allaying concerns that reservists would not be available when really needed. Since its inception, the Air Force Reserve evolved from an individual-mobilization-only force into an operational reserve that participates daily in missions around the globe. Today, Air Force reservists safeguard nuclear weapons and guide Global Positioning Satellites. From bases in the United States, reservists fly remotely piloted aircraft in combat half a world away. They track hurricanes out at sea and bring medical supplies and food into disaster areas to save lives around the world. Spanning six and a half decades – with the last two decades of continuous combat – the Air Force Reserve has fulfilled the legacy of early air pioneers and exceeded the potential seen by the visionaries who created it. For more information on the history of the Air Force Reserve, go to: www.afrc.af.mil/library/history/.

*Section 20D—Career Fields*

### 20.12. Career Fields Occupational Badges.

Air Force members are highly encouraged to wear their current occupational badge on all uniform combinations. A maximum of two occupational badges may be worn. When wearing two occupational badges, wear the one representing the current career field (regardless of level earned) in the top position. **Exception:** Chaplains and aeronautical badges are always worn in the top position when wearing two occupational badges. If authorized, place the second occupational badge in top position and centered ½ inch above the first one. Refer to Figure 1.1 for a listing of officer and enlisted occupational badges. Occupational badges are reflective of your Air Force specialty. See AFI 36-2903, *Dress and Personal Appearance of Air Force Personnel* for specific instructions on wear of occupational badges.

**Figure 1.1. Occupational Badges**

| | | |
|---|---|---|
| Acquisition & Financial Management | Air Traffic Control | Band |
| Chaplain Service Support | Civil Engineer | Commander |
| Command & Control | Cyberspace | Cyberspace Support |
| Explosive Ordnance Disposal | Firefighter | Force Protection |
| Force Support | High Altitude Low Opening (HALO) | Historian |

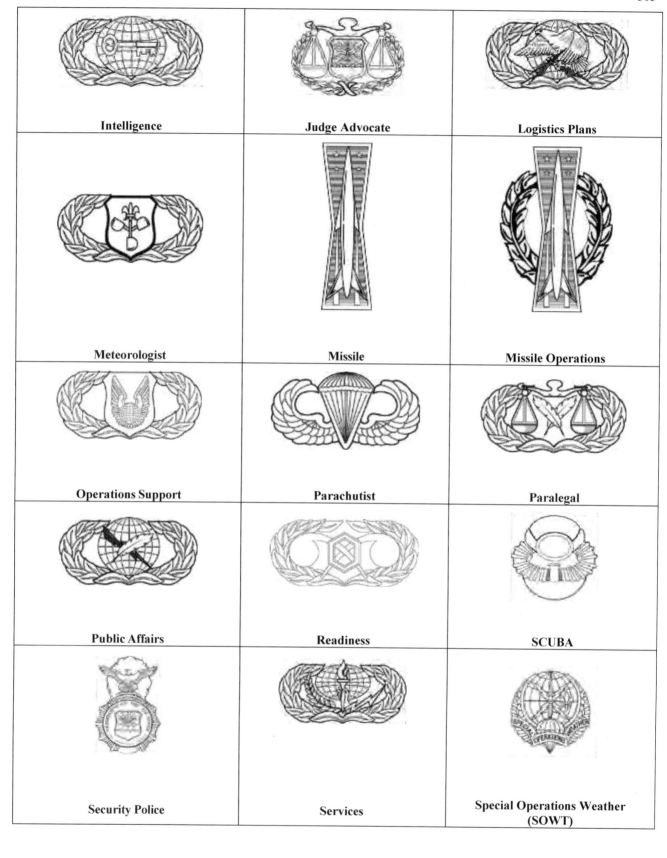

| | | |
|---|---|---|
| Intelligence | Judge Advocate | Logistics Plans |
| Meteorologist | Missile | Missile Operations |
| Operations Support | Parachutist | Paralegal |
| Public Affairs | Readiness | SCUBA |
| Security Police | Services | Special Operations Weather (SOWT) |

| | | |
|---|---|---|
| Space | Space/Missile | Supply Fuels |
| Transportation | Weapons Director | Chaplain Buddhist |
| Chaplain Christian | Chaplain Jewish | Chaplain Muslim |
| Biomedical Science Corps | Dental Corps | Enlisted Medical |
| Medical Service Corps | Nurse Corps | Air Battle Manager |
| Astronaut | Enlisted Aircrew | Flight Nurse |

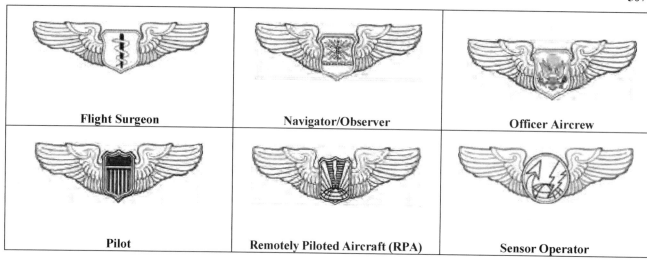

| | | |
|---|---|---|
| **Flight Surgeon** | **Navigator/Observer** | **Officer Aircrew** |
| **Pilot** | **Remotely Piloted Aircraft (RPA)** | **Sensor Operator** |

## 20.13. Specialized Headgear.

20.13.1. The Department of the Air Force approved and authorized its first distinctive uniform for members of the Pararescue career field in 1966. The Air Force approved and authorizing for the combat control distinctive beret uniform in 1973 and began making other concessions of approving other distinctive beret uniforms for other career fields during the 1980s and subsequent decades.

20.13.2. Regardless of specialty or unit the approval of distinctive beret uniform for wear with service uniforms is not intended as self-recognition but as recognition directed towards a group fulfilling the accomplishment of unique duties associated with specific mission roles at an above average level of dependability and reliability. Generally speaking the beret provides recognition of all members of the group being volunteers to perform hazardous duties, completed specific standardized qualification training to provide a unique or extraordinary tactical capability, and willingly sustain strong level of personal and team/unit mission readiness to respond and accomplish quickly.

**Combat Control and Special Tactics Officer (Scarlet)**

**Pararescue and Combat Rescue Officer (Maroon)**

**Security Forces (Blue)**

**Survival, Evasion, Resistance and Escape (SERE) Team (Pewter Green)**

**Tactical Air Control Party (Black)**

**Tactical Liaison Officer (Black)**

**Weather Parachutist (Pewter Gray)**

**20.14. Conclusion.**

Air Force knowledge is important because it provides the framework of information required to understand the basic infrastructure of the Air Force such as weapon systems, vocabulary, and some Air Force heritage. In these few pages, you will find a small sampling of the knowledge you will need to be a successful Airman. I encourage you to study the priceless information contained in these pages as well as other sources such as the Air University (http://www.au.af.mil/au/awc/awcgate/awc-ldr.htm). Understanding this Air Force knowledge will give you the power to unleash the Airman inside you, live a career of success, and leave a lasting legacy for future generations to follow.

**Chapter 21**

**ORGANIZATIONAL MANAGEMENT**

*Section 21A—Overview*

### 21.1. Introduction.

Organizational management is the process of organizing, planning, leading, and controlling resources within an entity with the overall aim of achieving its objectives. Organizational management provides leaders the ability to make decisions and resolve issues in order to be both effective and beneficial. This chapter will provide valuable information leaders need to effectively manage their organizations. This chapter will cover Organizational Design, Managing Organizational change, conflict, problem solving, and project management.

*Section 21B—Organizational Design*

### 21.2. Introduction.

What do you think of when you hear the term Organizational Design? Do you think of your organizational chart? Most people do, but that is only a portion of your organization's design. Organizational design is the process of selecting a formal system of communication, coordination, controls, authority, and assigned responsibilities necessary to achieve the organization's goals. As leaders, we need to understand how to select appropriate organizational designs that facilitate mission accomplishment. To this end, this reading will address how effective organizational design not only facilitates mission accomplishment but also enhances productivity of an organization. First, we will discuss factors leaders should consider when designing their organizations. Then, we will look at four organizational systems or designs, and discuss the organizational factors which determine which design is most appropriate for a given organization. Before we can talk about the different designs, we need to look at what influences or factors affect our design choice.

### 21.3. Design Factors:

21.3.1. There are many factors that influence how we set up our organizations. The first is **organizational strategy (goals).** Professor of Organizational Behavior Dr. Stephen Robbins states, "An organization's strategy is a means to help management achieve its objectives. Since objectives are derived from the organization's overall strategy, it is only logical that strategy and structure should be linked. More specifically, structure should follow strategy." (Robbins: 569) What Dr. Robbins suggests is we need to identify why we are doing what we are doing, how we expect to get there (strategy), and then design our organizations to accomplish that strategy. Why does your organization exist? What are your goals? Does your mission require creativity or control? Do you need to be effective or efficient? Answers to these questions give us a starting point in determining which design the organization should use. Nevertheless, we must consider a few other factors.

21.3.2. Another design factor is the **environment.** When we speak of the environment, we are not talking about the climate or the physical environment. We are talking about what outside forces affect the organization's processes. Are we dependent on other organizations or sections to do our jobs? Is the environment constantly in a state of flux? Are we continually changing or do we do the same processes repeatedly? Professor Richard Daft, author of *Organizational Theory and Design,* calls this the stable-unstable dimension. "An environment's domain is stable if it remains the same over a period of months or years. Under unstable conditions, environmental elements shift abruptly." (Daft: 148) If our routine is unstable, this means the environment is constantly changing, which requires flexibility. If you can set your watch by it, as the cliché goes, then it is stable and allows stricter control. Don't be fooled into thinking that once you identify your environment as stable, it remains that way; it does not. We need to continually scan our environment to identify outside changes that affect our design. Certainly, you can see that the environment helps us determine which design is most appropriate for our organization. Just like goals, the environment works with other factors as well.

21.3.3. The third factor to consider is the **size** of your organization. Early in your career, you learned the term *span of control.* There are only so many people one person can effectively manage. Once you reach a point where you lose effectiveness, new levels of management must be developed and more structure introduced. Let's assume your whole organization is a five-person shop. How many levels of supervision would you need? Probably one. Now add two more workers. Do supervision levels increase? No! How about adding 10, 20, or 100 people? Maybe as the organization grows, so should the level of supervision. There comes a point where your structure becomes so rigid that more workers would require few, if any, additional levels of supervision.

21.3.4. The last factor we will discuss is **technology.** According to Professor Daft, technology refers to the work processes, techniques, machines, and actions used to transform organizational inputs (materials, information, ideas) into outputs (products and services). (Daft: 266) We need to look at what resources we use to accomplish our mission to also help determine the best design for our organizations. If we primarily use new equipment with unknown procedures or outcomes, we would need fewer controls and more flexibility than if we use equipment that is old with known procedures and outcomes. In other words, if the equipment you use is old and well known, more structure could be utilized. If the equipment you use is newer, the outcomes or problems you may encounter require flexibility.

21.3.5. These four factors, strategy, environment, size, and technology, all influence how we should design our organization. Let's shift our attention to four organizational systems or designs we can use to improve unit effectiveness.

## 21.4. Designs.

21.4.1. The first design we will discuss is the **mechanistic design**. Sometimes referred to as the bureaucratic structure, it is vertically structured; communication is basically up and down rather than lateral. As Dr. Robbins puts it, "The mechanistic model ... is synonymous with the bureaucracy in that it has extensive departmentalization, high formalization, a limited information network (mostly downward communication) and little participation by low-level members in decision-making." (Robbins: 569) Departmentalization means grouping our work tasks by specialty. The more specialized the tasks, the more structure is used. By high formalization, we mean a heavy reliance on rules. Let's look at the mechanistic system in the context of the factors discussed earlier. The mechanistic system lends itself well to an organization where strategy or goals are geared toward efficiency; tasks need to be accomplished quickly and accurately. An environment which is quite stable requires little flexibility; therefore, a rigid structure or mechanistic design should be used. If the size of the organization is intermediate to large, more structure is necessary. As discussed earlier, as organizations grow, new levels of supervision must be added to maintain control. Finally, technology is known. What we use to do our jobs is not new. We can predict day to day what will happen and we have procedures to follow to accomplish our tasks. The mechanistic organization is very efficient, and responds to decisions rapidly. Because of the vertical communication, procedures flow from top to bottom rather quickly. This is very effective for emergency services that rely on speed. The mechanistic design has disadvantages as well. Because of the reliance on rules, job satisfaction suffers because subordinates basically do as they are told with little to no discussion. Limited discussion also leads to a poor social or human relations environment as well.

21.4.2. The **organic design** is just the opposite of the mechanistic. This design has horizontal specialization rather than vertical. According to Dr. Robbins, the organic system is "... flat, uses cross-hierarchical and cross-functional teams, has low formalization, possesses a comprehensive information network (utilizing lateral and upward communication as well as downward), and it involves high participation in decision-making." (Robbins: 569) Looking at an organizational chart, you would not see much difference between the mechanistic and the organic design. On the other hand, the interaction within the organization is quite different. The organic organization has extensive cross-communication. There is no clear line drawn for the communication path to follow. As workers need to communicate with others, they do so, free of bureaucratic lines. The organic system allows joint decision-making and encourages subordinates to voice their opinions. Looking back at the factors, the organic organization's strategy is geared toward innovativeness and creativity. The computer software industry is a good example of one that requires a creative rather than a restrictive system. The environment is unstable; with change being the norm rather than the exception. Therefore, an organic system is needed. The size should be small to moderate because this type of organization requires loose rules. Technology is fairly new with outcomes that are unknown, requiring adaptation rather than compliance. The organic system lends itself well to research and development organizations that are creative rather than restrictive. The strengths of an organic organization lie within communication. The sharing of information and participative environment increase worker satisfaction and often produce well-rounded decisions. Unfortunately, the organic design's communication slows down the implementation process. This slow response leads to low efficiency. In addition, the organic organization's flexibility reduces standards. In other words, if the same task is performed every three months, they may be handled differently each time.

21.4.3. There are very few organizations that are purely mechanistic or organic. For this reason, we have another design that incorporates the strengths of both, the **diverse** design. This design is used when the organization needs the rigid structure of the mechanistic organization for one section and the flexibility of the organic for another. For example, the administrative section has specific rules to follow when processing performance reports, decorations, and orders. For this purpose, they would require a mechanistic system. In the same organization, you may have a section that conducts training. The mechanistic system would hinder the creativity required for such a section; therefore, an organic system would be more effective. Because the organization uses both mechanistic and organic systems to accomplish the mission, the organizational design is considered diverse. The diverse organization incorporates the best of both designs to accomplish the mission.

21.4.4. The last design we will look at is the **matrix design**. Basically, developing a matrix is teaming workers from different sections or organizations together to solve problems or serve a function. We do this quite often. The disaster preparedness section, mobility section, and process action teams are good examples of a matrix. The distinguishing factor in a matrix is the chain of command. In the matrix design, subordinates have two bosses. They have their functional boss, who writes their performance report and schedules normal duty hours, and the project boss or team leader. The strength of the matrix design lies in the pooling of expertise and resources, and the weaknesses lie in the confusion of who is in charge; the functional or project boss. One note of caution; the matrix is not a design in itself. Basically the matrix is a design within a design. In other words, an organization designed mechanistically that develops a Process Action Team to work a project does not become a matrix. Actually, they are a mechanistic organization with a matrix. A matrix is usually short-lived, so the overall organizational structure remains intact.

21.4.5. As managers in today's Air Force, your job is to ensure organizations are operating at peak performance. One way of accomplishing that responsibility is to set up organizations effectively. We need to look at our units from the standpoint of our organizational strategy; the environment or an outside influence on our organization, the size of our organization, and the technology or advances in the equipment we use day to day. Once we understand how these factors relate to our organization, we can decide what structure would best accomplish our mission. Is the organization geared toward the rigid mechanistic structure, the flexible organic structure, a combination (the diverse structure), or do we need to use specialized teams to solve a problem as in the matrix structure? These are decisions made by the effective leader. By designing our organizations properly, we are designing the organization that will capitalize on strengths and minimize weaknesses. As you can see, organizational design goes much further than the organizational chart.

### Section 21C—Managing Organizational Change

### 21.5. Introduction.

The British created a civil service job in 1803 requiring a man stand on the White Cliffs of Dover with a spyglass. He was supposed to ring a bell if he saw Napoleon coming. Despite Napoleon's defeat in 1813, the job existed until 1945.

21.5.1. What's wrong with this picture? The scenario illustrates an improvement, not to mention a significant cost-saving opportunity that was ignored for over 130 years! We know change is inevitable. We know changes are taking place every day, all around us. We know change is easy, right? Wrong! As the scenario above shows, change is not automatic and doesn't just happen.

21.5.2. Change can be a complicated and often painful process. Senior enlisted leaders are in key positions to manage change. They have the authority and responsibility to lead and manage organizations, many years of experience, and technical proficiency. However, as leaders, they must also become proficient organizational change managers.

21.5.3. This section explores the change process using the model proposed by renowned social psychologist Kurt Lewin, who recommended leaders view change as a three-stage process: unfreezing, changing, and refreezing.

### 21.6. Stage 1: Unfreezing.

Leaders begin organizational change by unfreezing, which means going where the hurt is—where people feel the pain of poor policies or systems. Organizational change is defined as the adoption of a new idea or behavior by an organization (Daft, 452); the establishment of new norms. These norms can be grouped in various categories, including technology, tasks, structure, and people norms: (1) technology: computers, test equipment, weapons systems, etc.; (2) tasks: general procedures, job steps, checklists, etc.; (3) structure: administrative procedures, evaluation systems, etc.; and (4) people: technical or leadership training, new jobs, etc.

21.6.1. Regardless of what specifically needs to change, the first step is to recognize the need for change and this step is far from easy. Change is appropriate when there is a perceived gap between what the norms are and what they should be. This perception starts the momentum to begin unfreezing.

21.6.2. Unfreezing is a deliberate management activity to prepare people for change. Leaders create an environment where people feel the need for change. This is often the most neglected, yet essential part of unfreezing. A key factor in unfreezing involves making people knowledgeable about the importance of a change and how it will affect their jobs. Leaders must first generate a need in the people who will feel the greatest effect of the change. They do this by pointing out the problems or challenges with current operations. In many cases, people will want to stick to the old norms.

21.6.3. The first reaction to change is usually resistance. Just as change is inevitable, so is resistance to change. An essential element for successful change is having a good plan. Planning enables the change agent to anticipate problems, develop courses of action, and deal with resistance. Resistance can take many forms. Four of the most common are:

21.6.3.1. **Uncertainty.** When faced with impending change, people often experience fear of the unknown, or see the change as a threat to their security: Can I do the new job? Can I operate the new equipment? Will I still have a job?

21.6.3.2. **Self-interest.** People often consider the power they currently have or their role in the existing environment and question the possible loss of power after the change is implemented.

21.6.3.3. **Different Perception/No Felt Need to Change.** Even if you think people recognize the need for change, they may see the situation differently. Outwardly, they may support the change, but inwardly, they resist it.

21.6.3.4. **Over-Determination.** Ironically, organization structure may be a barrier to change. For example, a mechanistic structure that relies on strict procedure and lines of authority may be so rigid that it inhibits change.

21.6.4. When making change, success depends on managing and reducing resistance, and a change agent becomes vitally important. Leaders must accept the role of change agent in order to manage change. Senior enlisted leaders have vast influence on their subordinates, peers, and superiors. Commanders and directors often call upon senior noncommissioned officers to change an organization, to "make it happen." Here are five proven methods leaders employ to reduce and manage resistance to change:

   21.6.4.1. **Education and Communication.** Educating people about the need for, and expected results of, a change should reduce their resistance. Open communication is necessary throughout the change process and helps reduce uncertainty.

   21.6.4.2. **Participation and Involvement.** Leaders reduce resistance by actively involving those affected in designing and implementing change. Involving people in the process may be time-consuming, but should help commit them to the new program.

   21.6.4.3. **Facilitation and Support.** Introduce the change gradually, if possible. Provide additional training if needed. Reinforce and encourage people as much as possible. Remember the power of high expectations.

   21.6.4.4. **Negotiation and Agreement.** Offer incentives to those who continue to resist the change. Negotiated agreements can help remind everyone of the changes they agreed upon should resistance return.

   21.6.4.5. **Coercion.** This technique involves using force to get people to accept change. This is a last resort because compulsion negatively affects attitudes, and has long-term negative consequences. Coerced compliance requires constant leadership oversight to ensure the change remains in effect.

21.6.5. There are usually many factors to consider, whether maintaining current norms (the status quo) or changing current norms. The change agent must analyze restraining (opposing) forces and devise ways to reduce them to overcome resistance. At the same time, leaders must recognize and strengthen driving (supporting) forces—those forces pushing toward change. After analyzing the forces for and against change and developing a strategy to deal with them, leaders can attend to the change itself. Leaders improve the chance of success when they break the change into sequential steps. This approach provides visible success early, which may encourage people to support the rest of the change program.

21.6.6. The unfreezing stage should be addressed whenever change is imminent. Careful planning is an essential element of unfreezing, improving chances of success and decreasing the likelihood of having to repeat the unfreezing stage. Your plan should include a set of evaluation standards to measure the degree of success or failure of the change. An evaluation with clear goals and objectives can help assess the success of change and help determine appropriate rewards when the change has been completed.

## 21.7. Stage 2: Changing.

This stage involves modifying technology, tasks, structure, or distribution of people. This is the movement from the old state, or the previous norms, to the new state. During the changing stage, the organization installs new equipment, restructures work centers, or implements a new performance appraisal system. In short, changing is anything that alters the status quo.

21.7.1. Your role as change agent in this stage is to monitor the change as it occurs and pay close attention to the people most affected by it. If you've implemented the change too early, you'll know it by watching the people's reactions. If some link in the system isn't ready to handle the change, production may bog down. A few irate callers from other branches or units will let you know in a hurry!

21.7.2. In this stage, ensure the plan unfolds as intended. Even the best plans go awry for one reason or another. Remember, the importance of you being involved as the change is implemented and be ready to deal with problems that may arise.

21.7.3. Provide support at this stage. Some people may be traumatized by the actual implementation, so you should provide encouragement and advice as needed. The same techniques used to overcome resistance to change (paragraph 21.6.4) apply here, too.

21.7.4. Go back to the unfreezing stage if the change isn't going well. Going back or regrouping is better than pressing on with a change that causes more problems than it fixes. The change agent must decide whether (and when) to move forward. You must keep tabs on things or you won't be in a position to make this decision. Don't just plan to change, flip the switch, and let the chips fall where they may.

## 21.8. Stage 3: Refreezing.

The final stage in the change process is refreezing. Just because you implemented a change and it appears to be going smoothly doesn't mean the job is done. You must lock in (or refreeze) the desired outcomes and the new norms so they become permanent.

21.8.1. Without refreezing, people often return to the old ways. Consider an Airman who completes 7-skill level upgrade training and learns the proper way to perform key tasks in his or her work center. The proper way may differ from the way the work center completes the tasks. The Airman may be inclined to conform to the old way rather than make waves: old behaviors take over and nothing changes. Actively encouraging the use of new techniques and reinforcing them encourages others to use them, essentially freezing the new behavior. A critical step in refreezing is evaluating results. Did the change have the desired effect? If so, press on. If not, the new process may need more support, instruction, training, time, etc.

21.8.2. Having developed strategies to evaluate results in Stage 1 of the change process, now is time to implement them. Positively reinforcing desired outcomes is crucial. Reward people when they do something right; this strengthens the correct behaviors and helps freeze them into place. In many cases, the change agent can call attention to the success of the change and show where it works. Highlighting successful change helps remove lingering resistance and prevents people from returning to the old way of doing things.

21.8.3. In some cases, even what appears to be successful change management fails in the end. Years ago, a company bought new computer equipment for the typing pool, replacing the old electric typewriters with word processing stations. The new technology included color monitors, advanced software, and high-speed printers. Everyone was carefully trained. The new equipment was installed for half the typists at first, then the other half got their new equipment, and the supervisors (change agents) provided support and encouragement all the way. Soon the section was turning out professional correspondence in half the time it previously took. Successful change, you say. Unfortunately, it wasn't. To cut down on the noise from the printers, portable dividers were installed between workstations. This isolated the typists from coworkers, who used to be able to converse back and forth unimpeded. As a result, the previous social system, which was one of harmony, turned into one of unhappy isolation. Both the people and the work suffered, and the change plan had to be modified.

21.8.4. Do you think the change agents anticipated this outcome and planned for it? Probably not, but they really weren't at fault. After all, no one can anticipate everything. The example serves to remind us of the importance of refreezing. The change agent must evaluate results, reinforce the desired outcomes, and make constructive modifications as needed.

21.8.5. A change agent has a tough job. Carefully planning change; however, can make it as painless as possible. Managing change is one of the most important responsibilities you have. Using this three-stage process can help you manage the inevitable changes, rather than letting the changes manage you.

## *Section 21D—Conflict Management*

## 21.9. Introduction.

Conflict is inevitable in every organization, and is often necessary to reach high levels of performance. Dr. Kenneth Thomas, author of *Conflict and Conflict Management, the Handbook of Industrial and Organization Psychology* (1976), defines conflict as the "process that results when one person (or a group) perceives that another person or group is frustrating, or about to frustrate, an important concern." Conflict involves incompatible differences between parties that result in interference or opposition. Such differences can motivate for positive change or decrease productivity.

### 21.9.1. Destructive Versus Constructive Conflict.

Conflict can be constructive or destructive and becomes destructive when it results in "barriers" to cooperation and communication. This destroys morale and diverts energy away from important tasks and initiatives. On the other hand, conflict can be constructive when managed effectively. Positive conflict results in problem solutions, greater understanding, and enhanced communication between individuals or groups. In the past, managers were trained to avoid conflict because of its negative repercussions. This continues to challenge managers today as they work feverishly to avoid it altogether. However, managing conflict effectively offers benefits to the organization like reducing organizational chaos and stimulating work activity and productivity. Therefore, to manage conflict successfully, we must first understand some of the sources of conflict.

### 21.9.2. Sources of Conflict.

Many factors may result in or increase the probability of conflict within an organization. These factors manifest themselves in combination with other factors, making it potentially difficult to identify the specific source of the conflict. Many researchers, however, agree that conflict originates with one or more of the following stimulants:

**21.9.2.1. Communication Factors.** We often hear that many problems occur due to a failure in, or a lack of, communication. However, on closer examination, this usually accounts for a very small portion of the conflicts reported. The real crux of the problem is miscommunication; for example, when communication is misinterpreted, inaccurate, or incomplete. For personnel to perform at their very best, they need constructive, comprehensible, and accurate information; anything less results in frustration, stress, and failure. Remember, conflict is defined as frustration of an important concern, whether real or perceived. Consider your organization and the conflicts that erupted because of poor communication. Now consider what happens when the communication process fails altogether. Did the outcomes result in conflict?

**21.9.2.2. Structural Factors:**

**21.9.2.2.1. Size.** Research shows that organizational size affects the people who work there. Like an elevator that reaches its maximum capacity, the larger the organization, the more people there is to cause and participate in conflict. With more personnel comes more opinions, perspectives, perceptions, etc. As a result, larger organizations may have unclear goals, more rigid structures, increased specialization, more levels of supervision, and increased opportunities for information to become distorted as it passes through each organizational echelon.

**21.9.2.2.2. Participation:**

21.9.2.2.2.1. The more people interact and participate, the more noticeable their differences become. This can also lead to disputes and conflict, partly because although people may attempt to participate does not necessarily mean their ideas are heard or accepted. This rejection can spark frustration and conflict among members. However, this situation also has the potential to increase productivity if workers become more creative or competitive and search for better ways to enhance overall unit performance. This is productive conflict versus destructive conflict.

21.9.2.2.2.2. We want people to challenge the status quo, to seek better ways to do business, and to continually improve processes. This supports our core value, *excellence in all we do*. Such efforts also support our *service before self* core value, in that we must be willing to set aside old ways and personal differences in order to listen to the ideas of others, to include our newest Airman. We must be willing to change, put self-interests aside, and do what is right for the Air Force.

**21.9.2.3. Line-Staff Distinctions.** Diverse backgrounds and roles can create conflict. According to Dr. Thomas, this is very noticeable in the line and staff functions because the roles are so different. Overall, line personnel are concerned with production and are usually more loyal to the company. Staff functions usually involve creativity; therefore, staff personnel are usually more critical of the organization. Moreover, since there are usually different requirements for staff and line functions, there are different types of backgrounds for each. These differences in values, training, background, etc., can lead to conflict. Consider how line and staff personnel view organizational goals. Line personnel normally are more concerned with the immediate or short-range goals, whereas staff personnel are more concerned with long-range or strategic goals. These differences in background and viewpoints can trigger conflict.

**21.9.2.4. Rewards.** Earning rewards involves a level of competition, which can lead to conflict. Healthy competition is not the problem. However, the individuals and groups who perceive that the rewards were given unfairly or in favor of someone else can often lead to conflict. For example, one person or department receives recognition that others feel they deserved but did not receive.

**21.9.2.5. Resource Interdependence.** Most likely, we have all had to compete for resources at one time or another. When people compete for scarce resources and each party feels they have a greater need, conflict may arise. Oftentimes, negotiations fail as each party assumes a directive, or authoritarian position as they compete for the resource.

**21.9.3. Personal Behavior Factors.**

Conflict can arise because of individual differences, such as goals and objectives, perceptions, values, and personalities. Three such differences, in particular, may facilitate behaviors that cause conflict: values, perception, and personality.

**21.9.3.1. Values.** Values are very important to people and will determine their behavior. When people's values are questioned, criticized, or opposed, conflict can result. Some values, such as religion and politics, seem to incite the biggest arguments and can lead to fights, but even less emotion-based values can cause conflict. For example, a worker who values high quality work may see him or herself due a reward for the quality of the work. Conflict may occur if the unit emphasizes quantity over quality and rewards someone else instead.

**21.9.3.2. Perception.** Values also affect how people perceive situations and other people. If a person perceives others as lazy and incompetent, how he or she responds to that perception may cause problems. A person's perception of what constitutes fairness, quality of work, or constructive techniques can lead to conflict if these perceptions differ significantly from others or what the organization has defined for those factors.

21.9.3.3. **Personality.** We have all heard about people who couldn't get along because of a personality conflict and this isn't uncommon. Put certain personalities together and you are asking for conflict. Two personality types especially conflict-prone are the highly authoritarian individual and the low self-esteem individual. The highly authoritarian personality may antagonize coworkers by escalating otherwise trivial differences. The low self-esteem personality may feel threatened by others and therefore overreact. Either type of behavior can create interpersonal conflict in an organization.

## 21.10. Five Styles of Conflict Management:

21.10.1. Now that we have an idea of what conflict is and what causes it, we can examine some ways to manage it. In the book, "*Conflict and Negotiation Processes in Organizations,*" *Handbook of Industrial and Organizational Psychology* (1992), Dr. Thomas suggests five major conflict management styles: competing (or forcing), collaborating, accommodating, avoiding, and compromising. Dr. Thomas uses a two-dimensional framework to compare these styles. The first dimension refers to the degree of cooperation a manager exhibits, measuring from uncooperative to cooperative. The second dimension measures assertiveness on a scale from nonassertive (passive) to assertive (active). Being cooperative refers to how willing a person or group is to satisfy the other's needs. For example, if Person A gives into the needs of Person B, Person A is considered cooperative. If Person A assumes a "my way or the highway" approach, he or she is considered uncooperative.

21.10.2. From these two dimensions, we can devise a way to manage conflict based on the situation. Just as situational leadership is based on task and relationship behavior, conflict management is situational and is based on assertive and cooperative behavior. With this in mind, let's look at the five styles used to manage conflict.

21.10.2.1. **Competing (or Forcing).** This style attempts to overwhelm an opponent with formal authority, threats, or the use of power. Its underlying features are being highly assertive and uncooperative.

21.10.2.2. **Collaborating.** The collaborating style involves an attempt to satisfy the concerns of both sides through honest discussion. Creative approaches to conflict reduction, such as sharing resources, may actually lead to both parties being materially better off. For this style to be successful, trust and openness are required of all participants. This style is high in assertive behavior and high in cooperation and seeks a win position for both groups.

21.10.2.3. **Accommodating.** The accommodating style combines low assertiveness and high cooperation. At the simplest level, this style may merely involve giving in to another person's wishes.

21.10.2.4. **Avoiding:**

21.10.2.4.1. The combination of low assertiveness and low cooperation leads to an avoiding style. The person implies that he or she will appear to be neutral and it may not always be possible to adopt a truly neutral position, but a manager may nonetheless prefer to avoid the situation. Although a manager who avoids difficult issues is likely to be resented by his or her Airmen, this strategy may be effective under certain circumstances. For example, a manager may initially stay out of a disagreement to avoid escalating the conflict during a particular phase of development. Later, when he or she judges the time is right, the manager may take a more active role in finding a productive solution.

21.10.2.4.2. Experienced managers recognize that action is not always necessary because some problems dissipate over time or are resolved by other organizational processes. For example, an intense conflict between two Airmen may seem to require intervention by their manager. If the manager knows that one of the individuals will soon be transferred to another department or promoted to another position, ignoring the situation and letting the impending changes resolve the difficulty may be the best solution.

21.10.2.5. **Compromising.** This style involves intermediate degrees of assertiveness and cooperation to partially satisfy both parties' desires and achieve a middle ground. To successfully compromise, both parties must be willing to give up something. Compromising is common during labor and management disputes.

## 21.11. Applying Conflict Management Style:

21.11.1. When deciding which style of conflict management to use, consider a few additional factors. First, consider who you are dealing with. When dealing with a supervisor or a peer, the competing style of conflict management may not be applicable. Also, doubtful any of us could force our commander in a conflict situation. On the other hand, competing may work for a subordinate. You have the legitimate power to enforce a policy. So knowing *who* is important in deciding the style you can use.

21.11.2. Another factor is determining how critical the issue is, also known as the *stakes*. If the issue is critical, you may wish to use the avoiding style at first to carefully consider the options or gather more data. However, because the issue is critical, you cannot avoid it for long. Sooner or later, you will have to confront the issue. Also, if the situation is critical and you know you are right, you may need to use the competing style to force your position. Conversely, if the issue is trivial, you could avoid it or even accommodate the other party. Remember to always consider the *stakes* in the issue.

21.11.3. The final factor is the *situation* itself. In an emergency, the competing style might be necessary because there simply is not enough time to collaborate or compromise. You also cannot avoid an emergency. However, if time is not an issue and the parties are willing to discuss the matter, collaboration may be the best way to deal with the conflict situation because it works best for everyone.

21.11.4. Although people may consider some styles of conflict management more effective (for example, collaborating versus avoiding), all of the conflict management styles are useful, depending on who, the stakes, and the situation. Using these five styles allows us to successfully manage conflict, reduce disorder and chaos, and facilitate creativity and innovative problem solving. Being a conflict management specialist is just another one of the many responsibilities of managers!

### *Section 21E—Problem Solving*

### 21.12. Overview.

The use of Continuous Process Improvement (CPI) increases operational capabilities while reducing associated costs by applying proven methodologies to all processes associated with fulfilling the Air Force mission. Continuous Process Improvement is a comprehensive philosophy of operations built around the concepts that there are always ways a process can be improved to better meet mission/customer requirements; organizations must constantly strive to make those improvements based on performance metrics that align to strategic objectives; and efficiencies should be replicated to the extent practical. Continuous Process Improvement is a hallmark of highly successful organizations and a major graded area in Air Force Inspection System (AFI 90-201, *Air Force Inspection System*) and a commander responsibility in AFI 1-2, *Commander's Responsibilities*.

### 21.13. Continuous Process Improvement uses Structured Problem Solving.

The core of Air Force process improvement is the Practical Problem Solving Method. The Practical Problem Solving Method is a standardized and structured approach to problem solving utilized in commercial industry and adopted by the Air Force. The Practical Problem Solving Method is an 8-step process used to clarify problems, identify root causes, and develop appropriate countermeasures to achieve change. Typically, the Practical Problem Solving Method is illustrated using the A3 format.

### 21.14. Identifying Improvement Opportunities.

Oftentimes the success of an organization relies on its ability to identify opportunities for process improvement. Much like industry partners, the Air Force must strive for continuous process improvement. Customer demand, processing, budgeting, and work force needs are all factors organizations have to effectively manage to survive. The Air Force contends with the same issues as global operations continue: readiness, training, and modernization have to be managed with less monetary freedom. The application of Practical Problem Solving Method provides a methodical approach to identifying opportunities for improvements through all process within the Air Force. Consistently applied, the Practical Problem Solving Method provides an excellent tool to make data-driven decisions with regards to management, process change, and the sharing of best practices.

21.14.1. **Strategic Alignment.** Strategic alignment provides the framework to ensure resources and actions of subordinate levels align to and achieve the strategy, mission, vision, priorities, and objectives of the enterprise. The Strategic Plan identifies the current mission, vision for the future, and prioritizes objectives to get from the current state to the future vision. The Strategic Plan also communicates Commander's intent and assigns responsibility. Imperative is that all improvement efforts align with the organization's efforts to accomplish the overall Strategic Plan's objectives. AFI 1-2, *Commander's Responsibilities,* requires commanders to strive for strategic alignment within their organization.

### 21.15. Practical Problem Solving Method.

The Practical Problem Solving Method (Table 21.1.) is intended to be printed on an 11x17 piece of paper (A3 size) and completed in pencil. An A3 provides a concise single page document for problem identification and validation designed to help organizations build consensus. Its simple design helps the user apply a structured scientific approach, while allowing it to be modified and changed quickly for ease of use. Descriptions of the Practical Problem Solving Method steps follow:

**Table 21.1. Air Force Practical Problem Solving Method.**

| Step | Description |
|------|-------------|
| 1 | Clarify and validate the problem |
| 2 | Break down the problem and identify performance gaps |
| 3 | Set improvement target |
| 4 | Determine root cause |
| 5 | Develop countermeasures |
| 6 | See countermeasures through |
| 7 | Confirm results and process |
| 8 | Standardize successful processes |

**21.15.1. Step 1—Clarify and Validate the Problem:**

21.15.1.1. The critical first step to effective problem-solving is to clearly understand the problem. A problem solving effort that begins with "We all know what the problem is, so just get it fixed now?" sets us up for failure before we begin. This "fly by the seat of your pants approach" leads to several errors. First, because the "obvious solution" is often based purely on the experience level of the problem solver, which misdiagnose the underlying problem. Secondly, this mindset is closed to the possibility of innovative solutions which are better suited to solving the real problem. A well-defined problem statement uses data to identify where the problem is occurring and impact of the problem, and compares performance against a standard with scope and direction. The statement does not make assumptions of a root cause, solution and/or countermeasure and includes visual tools to depict the current state.

21.15.1.2. The Who, What, When, Where, and significance of the problem statement should be validated by data. This is done by collecting and analyzing data to both validate the existence and magnitude of the problem. If data does not exist, the effort should be paused to collect and analyze the needed data *before* moving forward. Tools to consider for Step 1 are Strategic Alignment; Voice of the Customer; Supplier, Input, Process, Output, Customer Diagram; and Value Stream map.

**21.15.2. Step 2—Break Down Problem and Identify Performance Gaps:**

21.15.2.1. Once the problem has been clearly identified and answers the Who, What, When, and Where of the problem statement, efforts are made to further analyze the data in comparison to the voice of the customer. The voice of the customer gives the standard to measure from. The delta between the current state (otherwise known as the voice of the process) and voice of the customer will highlight opportunities for improvements (also called the performance gap). Often, the more thorough the evaluation of a problem in this step, the more effective and concise the Practical Problem Solving Method will be.

21.15.2.2. A critical step in assessing a problem is gathering and reviewing data on the process. Understanding what appropriate data is required and the ability to interpret that data is paramount to performance gap analysis. Step 2 effectively frames and supports the problem in Step 1 using data. Tools to consider for Step 2 are "Go & See" and metrics that help better define the gap between the voice of the customer and voice of the process.

**21.15.3. Step 3—Set Improvement Targets:**

21.15.3.1. Air Force leaders establish a vision of what an organization will strive to become (the Ideal State). In Step 3, process owners and/or project sponsors set improvement targets based on voice of the customer and strategic goals and objectives. Targets help define the required performance levels to achieve the vision. Targets should be challenging but achievable and have certain characteristics: Specific, Measurable, Attainable, Results-focused, and Time-bound (SMART). The project should obtain a vector check upon completion to ensure strategic alignment with the project champion. Tools to consider for Step 3 are Ideal State Map, SMART objectives, setting goals.

**21.15.3.2. SMART Objectives are:**

21.15.3.2.1. **Specific:** Have desirable outputs based on subject matter expert knowledge and experience applicable to the process improvement activity. Specific targets should answer who is involved, what is to accomplish, where it is to be done, when it is to be done (time frame), which (Identify requirements and constraints) and why (Specific reasons, purpose or benefits of accomplishing the goal).

21.15.3.2.2. **Measurable:** Include time frames and data obtainable from specific sources. Establish criteria for measuring progress toward the attainment of each goal. To determine if your goal is measurable, ask questions such as......How much? How many? How will I know when it is accomplished?

21.15.3.2.3. **Attainable:** Resources are available; may have some risk, but success is possible.

21.15.3.2.4. **Results-Focused:** The mission, vision, and goals are linked and meaningful to the user.

21.15.3.2.5. **Time-bound:** Provide date for completion. Targeted dates provide measurable accountability.

**21.15.4. Step 4—Determine Root Cause.**

Air Force leaders often find themselves addressing problems which have been "solved" many times because previous problem-solving efforts were directed at *symptoms* of a problem rather than the *root cause* of the problem. If an aircraft is constantly breaking down and cannot perform its mission, should the goal be to reduce aircraft usage, improve repair cycle time, improve the quality of replacement parts, improve the aircraft design, or improve the aircraft design process? Each step becomes increasingly difficult to evaluate, but each step also has a greater impact in the elimination of the problem. Root cause analysis is a tradeoff between digging as deeply as possible and finding the deepest point still within the team's sphere of influence. The correct root cause should be validated by using the same data used to define the problem in Step 1. Tools to consider for Step 4 are 5 Whys, brainstorming, Pareto Chart, Affinity diagram, fishbone diagram, and control charts.

**21.15.5. Step 5—Develop Countermeasures:**

21.15.5.1. Step 5 is where process changes that directly corrects, influences, affects each of your root causes are developed. Air Force leaders should follow important guidelines to ensure the greatest likelihood of success. A key principle to remember is that the impact of a solution is a combination of the quality of the solution and the acceptance of the solution by the people who must implement it. The relationship is similar to the following formula: (Quality of the solution) x (Acceptance) = Impact. Also, when developing countermeasures strive for process improvement change that is sustainable and repeatable.

21.15.5.2. Address potential root causes with countermeasures which conform to lean principles and are the most practical and effective, "keep it simple." Validate countermeasures will close performance gaps when implemented. Countermeasures should move the organization closer to the ideal state and support strategic plans. Also recommended is to build consensus, when possible and appropriate, with all stakeholders involved. Judiciously involving stakeholders in the development of countermeasures sponsors ownership of the solution and its success. At the end of this step, obtain a vector check from the champion to ensure strategic alignment. The champion approves the countermeasures prior to implementation. Tools to consider for Step 5 are Sort, Straighten, Shine, Standardize, Sustain; brainstorming; multi-voting; Possible, Implement, Challenge, Kill Chart; error-proofing; standard work; cell/flow design; and Future State Map.

**21.15.6. Step 6—See Countermeasures Through.**

Step 6 is seeing countermeasures through execution and tracking of detailed implementation plans for each countermeasure approved in Block 5 of the Practical Problem Solving Method. The champion should be updated regularly on all tasks status until countermeasures have been implemented or deemed unnecessary as target state has been met. Devoting time and resources towards developing an action plan without action should be considered waste. Tools to consider for Step 6 are Sort, Straighten, Shine, Standardize, Sustain; visual management, standard work, cell/flow design, variation reduction, error-proofing, quick changeover, and the rapid improvement event.

**21.15.7. Step 7—Confirm Results and Process:**

21.15.7.1. Step 7 compares the results of implemented countermeasures to the identified performance gaps and improvement targets. Verify the improved process is sustainable and repeatable. Results are measured by data and analyzed to confirm the project's intent. Illustrate confirmed results with appropriate data tool(s) which link back to performance gap(s) in Step 2 and improvement target(s) in Step 3. Tools to consider during step 7 are key performance indicators/metrics and strategic alignment.

21.15.7.2. Processes should be monitored for:

21.15.7.2.1. Performance relative to the baseline developed in Steps 1 and 2.

21.15.7.2.2. Performance relative to SMART targets established in Step 3.

21.15.7.2.3. Performance relative to the solution implementation.

21.15.7.2.4. If you are not meeting targets, you may need to return to Step 4. Incorrect root-cause determination is the most common mistake made during continuous process improvement efforts.

**21.15.8. Step 8—Standardize Successful Processes:**

21.15.8.1. Step 8 is the most commonly skipped and under-completed step of the entire Practical Problem Solving Method. Some people are tempted to take newfound knowledge and skills and immediately move on to the next improvement initiative, skipping the effort to ensure the results are codified.

21.15.8.2. This step is defined by answers to three questions:

21.15.8.2.1. **What is needed to standardize the improvements?** This could be Airmen Powered by Innovation (API) program input, changes to technical orders, Air Force instructions, operating instructions, equipment materiel, or using a different vendor or supplier.

21.15.8.2.2. **How should improvements and lessons learned be communicated?** This could be accomplished through input into Air Force CPI Portal, key meetings, Air Force publications, Public Affairs, chain of command, or SharePoint sites. Leaders should ensure the Wing Process Manager is aware of the success.

21.15.8.2.3. **Were other opportunities or problems identified by the problem-solving model?** This project may have identified additional problem-solving opportunities.

21.15.8.3. Effective problem solving should follow the Practical Problem Solving Method. Attempting to skip, reorder, or shortcut steps invariably leads to suboptimal solutions or failure. Following the Practical Problem Solving Method ensures actions lead to the desired results with minimal waste. It also ensures the results are aligned with the needs of the organization. Properly applied, the Practical Problem Solving Method is aligned to the organization's purpose and activities and increases Air Force combat effectiveness.

21.15.9. **Methodologies.** Air Force CPI incorporates aspects of four major CPI methodologies. A Practical Problem Solving Method solution may simultaneously draw from more than one of the CPI methods.

21.15.9.1. **Lean.** A methodology focused on work flow, customer value, and eliminating process waste; unique from traditional process improvement strategies in that its primary focus is on eliminating non-value added activities.

21.15.9.2. **Six Sigma.** A rigorous, data-driven methodology for process improvement focused on minimizing waste through identifying, controlling, and reducing process variation.

21.15.9.3. **Business Process Reengineering.** A comprehensive process requiring a change in the fundamental way business processes are performed. Business process reengineering identifies unnecessary activities and eliminates them wherever possible.

21.15.9.4. **Theory of Constraints.** A systematic approach to optimize resource utilization by identifying, exploiting, subordinating, elevating, and reassessing constraints (bottlenecks) in the process.

21.15.10. **Practical Problem Solving Method Level of Effort.** Different levels of effort are required to accomplish this method initiative.

21.15.10.1. **Just Do It:** Also called point improvement, this involves one person (or a small team) and can be accomplished in less than a day. Examples could be using torque wrenches instead of adjustable wrenches, or routing paperwork via email instead of the post office or paper distribution channels.

21.15.10.2. **Rapid Improvement Event:** A rapid improvement event consists of a small team of individuals, usually subject matter experts, and can be accomplished in less than a week and is designed to develop and implement countermeasures after appropriate project preparations have been made. Examples could be improving aircraft servicing cycle times, or improving first-time pass yields on task management tool taskers.

21.15.10.3. **Improvement Project:** This setting requires a large team and is conducted over a longer period of time. Examples might be shortening aircraft annual overhaul cycle time or writing software to track annual overhauls.

21.15.11. **Summary.**

Practical Problem Solving Method is a structured method to CPI. It is flexible enough to be effective at any level, from Headquarters Air Force, to the individual Airman. This single-piece of paper approach provides a standardized template for Airmen to solve problems and perform process improvement initiatives. If you have questions on the usage of Practical Problem Solving Method or want to get more training related to CPI philosophies, please contact your local Manpower office for training at your location.

*Section 21F—Project Management*

**21.16. Introduction.**

"Project management? I'm not in the plans and programs business; so why should I worry about managing a project?" These are questions which may be on your mind right now. If so, you may be right, for now. However, you have the likelihood of taking positions in the future which will or do involve the sound management of a multitude of resources. Even if you are not involved in the management of a long-term project involving millions of dollars' worth of resources, the benefits of obtaining knowledge of project management principles and their application will make you a better planner and manager.

In addition, these same skills will easily blend with your other management skills to improve your effectiveness as a manager and a leader. Scores of books have been written on the topic of project management, and this short reading cannot make you fully knowledgeable of all aspects of project management. However, this reading will familiarize you with some of project management's essential terminology and illustrate practical uses of project management principles. Project management cannot be understood unless you know a little bit about the project management language.

## 21.17. Project Management.

Project management uses a unique array of terminology to communicate its principles and use. The first term we should probably clear up right away is the term "project management." According to Hersey and Blanchard in their book *Management of Organizational Behavior,* management is defined as the process of working with and through individuals and groups and other resources to accomplish organizational goals (Hersey and Blanchard: 5). In their book, *Successful Project Managers,* Jeffrey K. Pinto and O.P. Kharbanda define project as a combination of human and non-human resources pulled together in a temporary organization to achieve a specified purpose (Pinto and Kharbanda: 13). Although there are many definitions to choose from, for the purpose of this reading we'll use Pinto and Kharbanda's definition of project management: the process of leading, coordinating, planning, and controlling a diverse and complex set of processes and people in the pursuit of achieving project objectives (Pinto and Kharbanda: 17). With this definition in mind, it may be worthy to examine what project management is not. A project is not a program; programs are ongoing. A project, by definition, is something temporary. Although temporary could be in terms of years, a project is unlike a program. You are involved with many programs in your work centers, and programs are ongoing. A project has a single objective, which has some time frame attached to it. Armed with project management's basic definition, we can now expand on project management's other terms.

21.17.1. Some of the terminology used in project management is contained in the basic steps of project management. These steps are depicted in Figure 21.1 and appear in the book *Fundamentals of Project Management,* by James P. Lewis (Lewis: 7).

**Figure 21.1. Project Management Steps.**

> **Define the Project Objective**
>
> **Develop Solution Options**
>
> **Plan the Project**
> What must be done?
> Who will do it?
> How will it be done?
> When must it be done?
> How much will it cost?
> What do we need to do it?
>
> **Execute the Plan**
>
> **Monitor & Control Progress**
> Are we on target?
> If not, what must be done?
> Should the plan change?
> What else did we learn?
>
> **Close the Project**
> What was done well?
> What should be improved?
> What else did we learn?

21.17.1.1. **Define the Project Objective.** Identify the problem or objective to be solved, or the improvement to be achieved by the project. What client need is being satisfied by the project?

21.17.1.2. **Develop Solution Options.** How many ways might you go about solving the problem? Of the available alternatives, which do you think will best solve the problem? Some decision analysis techniques will come into play here.

21.17.1.3. **Plan the Project.** Planning is nothing more than answering questions—what must be done, by whom, for how much, how, when, and so on.

21.17.1.4. **Execute the Plan.** People sometimes go to great length and effort to put together a plan, but then fail to follow it. Follow your plan.

21.17.1.5. **Monitor and Control Progress.** The project manager must monitor and control by being present and making appropriate decisions. This is where you'll determine whether or not the plan was sound and can make adjustments as necessary.

21.17.1.6. **Close the Project.** Once the objective has been achieved, the project is finished, but there is still a final step that should be taken. It's time for lessons learned—what went well, what didn't, and what should be improved? (Lewis: 7)

21.17.1.7. Ultimately, the goal is to achieve the objective of the project in the most logical, sensible manner. By following these steps, you will succeed. Sound simple? We all know there is more to it than just knowing the steps. Once a realization of the steps of project management is attained, accomplishing these steps requires understanding of some more terminology.

21.17.2. Before you can complete Step 1 of project management, you have to ensure the problem or improvement opportunity is clearly defined by the project objective. You might say that an objective is simply a goal, but in reality, when it comes to project management, an objective has to be more specific than a typical broad goal. According to Marion E. Haynes in her book, *Project Management: From Idea to Implementation,* good objectives are SMART. SMART is an acronym, which stands for Specific, Measurable, Action-oriented, Realistic, and Time-limited.

21.17.2.1. Specific because a good objective says exactly what you want it to say.

21.17.2.2. Measurable because you want to be able to determine whether you have met the objective.

21.17.2.3. Action-oriented by using statements that have action-tense verbs and are complete sentences. In other words, make the objective active voice, not passive voice.

21.17.2.4. Realistic because good objectives must be attainable yet should present a challenge.

21.17.2.5. Time-limited because a specific time should be set by which to achieve the objective (Haynes: 16).

21.17.3. For example, "Accomplish the renovation of the office area" would be an example of a goal you wish to achieve. A SMART objective for such a goal might be: "Renovate the office area by June 30, 200X at a cost not to exceed $12,000." By specifying the objective of the project, you can now determine the constraints you have to operate under.

21.17.4. Constraints are numerous for all activities we endeavor, but constraint consideration is crucial for project management. According to Geoff Reiss in his book, *Project Management Demystified,* quality, time, and cost are the main constraints realized in project management. Quality refers to being in accordance with the requirement - the specifications. Time refers to the amount of time you have to complete the project. Cost, of course, refers to your resource constraints, to include the four M's necessary to complete the project: money, manpower, machinery, and materials. One of these constraints (Quality, Time, and Cost) will be your driver for the project (Reiss: 39). To understand the meaning of driver, let's examine some of National Aeronautics and Space Administration's projects. In the 1960s, a manned vehicle called Sputnik broke through the earth's atmosphere, and the space race began. In an effort to catch-up, time became a driver for National Aeronautics and Space Administration's project to launch a man into space. The amount of money spent or the quality of the materials, although important, did not drive the project. However, during the 1980s, the explosion of the Challenger caused National Aeronautics and Space Administration to change drivers. Now quality became the driver for future projects. The driver for your project will have an impact on the other two constraints affecting your project. Ensure you take this into consideration when making decisions about your project's objective. If time is the driver, the T of your SMART objective needs to be reflective of that driving influence. If quality is your driver, the S of your SMART objective needs to be predominant. How will quality being your driver affect the other constraints? Quality increases the amount of time taken and increases the expense of materials. You must always remain cognizant of the impact one constraint has on another and adjust the management of your project accordingly. Ultimately, your driver and affected constraints will have an impact on the solutions you develop. As the project manager, it is incumbent upon you to provide the leadership and use good team-building techniques to establish a sound project objective and generate the solution options necessary to achieve those objectives. Once these steps have been completed, it will then be time to embark upon the most important and time-consuming aspect of project management—planning.

21.17.5. As indicated earlier, planning the project involves answering several questions. The first of those questions is: what must be done? The answer is contained in the objective of the project, but more specifics are needed. Haynes states that the starting place for answering the question of what must be done is by using a work breakdown structure. A work breakdown structure is a technique based on dividing a project into sub-units, or work packages. Since all the elements required to complete the project are identified in the work breakdown structure, the chances of neglecting or overlooking an essential step are minimized. A work breakdown structure is typically constructed with two or three levels of detail, although more levels are quite common depending on the complexity of the project (Haynes: 25). To illustrate using an elementary example, Figure 21.2 depicts a work breakdown structure for a typical yard project. Granted, a work breakdown structure would not usually be constructed for such a project, but to illustrate the concept, it is best to use something very simple to start with.

21.17.6. Graphically, you can quickly ascertain the necessary tasks to complete the project. Such a structure for your project will permit you, and others who see the work breakdown structure, to readily identify what needs to be done, spot omissions which might later affect the outcome of the project, and make suggestions for improving and expanding the work breakdown structure. How much is too much detail? According to Lewis, the general guideline is that you stop breaking down the work when you reach a point at which you can estimate to the desired degree of accuracy, or at which the work will take an amount of time equal to the smallest units you want to schedule (Lewis: 41 ). Taking Figure 21.2's work breakdown structure as an example, although the 'trim hedge' element of the project is an element that needs to be included as part of the work breakdown structure, it is not necessary to further indicate whether the hedge should be squared or rounded, done from left to right or top to bottom, etc. The amount of breakdown is an element the project manager and the project team must decide upon. Once the work breakdown structure has been tweaked and finalized, the next step is task analysis.

**Figure 21.2. Work Breakdown Structure.**

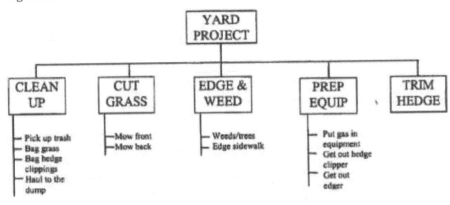

21.17.7. Like the work breakdown structure, the amount of detail needed for the task analysis depends on the task involved and the desires of the project manager and project team. The more complex the project, the greater the importance of detailed task analysis. Figure 21.3 depicts a typical task analysis and details considered using our elementary example task pertaining to the yard project. As you can see from the example, a wealth of information is contained about the task which is not depicted in the work breakdown structure, to include task milestones, more specific information of how the milestones can be measured, and identification of dependent tasks, budgetary concerns, task assignments, and reporting requirements. As the project manager, you can delegate the task analysis for each task to the appropriate person. Once they are compiled, you can make final decisions on task assignments and budgetary concerns. The task analysis is what provides the crucial information for determining how the tasks of the project interrelate. For example, in the case of the yard project, the tasks associated with preparing the equipment must be completed prior to any of the other tasks being accomplished. There is no sense in accomplishing cleanup if you haven't done any of the work yet. Although this example may seem to be common sense, when larger projects are in the planning stage, it is imperative the proper sequencing of tasks occurs prior to beginning a project to ensure the efficiency of the project. You wouldn't want carpet installed in your home prior to painting the ceiling and the walls, right? Once a task analysis has been performed on all tasks associated with the project, the next phase of project management, scheduling, must be conducted.

**Figure 21.3. Task Analysis Worksheet.**

| Task Objective: Clean up | | |
|---|---|---|
| **Task Milestones** | **Measurement** | **Time** |
| 1. Pick up trash | Front & back yards (determine # bags needed) | 15 minutes |
| 2. Bag grass | Front & back yards (determine # bags needed) | 30 minutes |
| 3. Bag hedge clippings | Around hedges bordering property and house (determine # of bags needed, wear gloves) | 15 minutes |
| 4. Haul to dump | Use pickup (ensure driver has directions and vehicle is fueled) | 35 minutes |
| **Task(s) on which this task is dependent:** Cut grass, trim hedge, and edge & weed | | |
| **Task(s) which is (are) dependent on this task:** None | | |
| **Itemized Task Budget:** Cost of gloves – none (already own pair), bags – approximately 15 cents each, and fuel and insurance on pickup – To be Determined | | |
| **Task assigned to:** My teenage son | | |
| *Report to:* Me or adult in attendance | | |

21.17.8. The advent of computer software has made scheduling tasks for projects much easier than it used to be. According to Lewis, until around 1958, the only tool for scheduling projects was the bar chart (Lewis: 50). Figure 21.4 below depicts a simple bar chart constructed from a word-processing software package using a table. As you can see, the time taken to complete a task is depicted graphically as one of the dark colored bars in 5-minute increments.

### Figure 21.4. Gantt Chart.

| Task Name | 5 | 10 | 15 | 20 | 25 | 30 | 35 | 40 | 45 | 50 | 55 | 60 | 65 | 70 | 75 | 80 | 85 | 90 | 95 | 100 | 105 | 110 | 115 | 120 | 125 | 130 | 135 | 140 | 145 | 150 |
|---|---|---|---|---|---|---|---|---|---|---|---|---|---|---|---|---|---|---|---|---|---|---|---|---|---|---|---|---|---|---|
| Gas in equipment | █ | | | | | | | | | | | | | | | | | | | | | | | | | | | | | |
| Get out edger | | █ | | | | | | | | | | | | | | | | | | | | | | | | | | | | |
| Get out hedge clip | █ | | | | | | | | | | | | | | | | | | | | | | | | | | | | | |
| Mow front yard | | | █ | █ | █ | █ | █ | █ | █ | | | | | | | | | | | | | | | | | | | | | |
| Mow back yard | | | | | | | | | | | █ | █ | █ | █ | █ | █ | | | | | | | | | | | | | | |
| Edge weeds/trees | | | █ | █ | █ | █ | █ | █ | | | | | | | | | | | | | | | | | | | | | | |
| Edge sidewalk | | | | | | | | | █ | █ | | | | | | | | | | | | | | | | | | | | |
| Trim hedges | | | █ | █ | █ | █ | █ | █ | | | | | | | | | | | | | | | | | | | | | | |
| Pick up trash | | | | | | | | | | | | | | | | | █ | █ | | | | | | | | | | | | |
| Bag the grass | | | | | | | | | | | | | | | | | █ | █ | █ | █ | █ | | | | | | | | | |
| Hedge clippings | | | | | | | | | | | | | █ | █ | | | | | | | | | | | | | | | | |
| Haul to dump | | | | | | | | | | | | | | | | | | | | | | | | | | █ | █ | █ | █ | █ |

21.17.9. Lewis indicates that prior to the advent of project management software, similar charts were used. Chart such as the one depicted in Figure 21.4., above were called Gantt charts, named after Henry Gantt, the developer of this notational system. Until the advent of computer software packages, Gantt charts had one serious drawback determining the impact of a slip of one task, on the rest of the project was very difficult. To overcome this problem, two methods of scheduling were developed in the late 1950s and early 1960s that used arrow diagrams to capture the sequential and parallel relationships among project activities. One method was called critical path method, developed by DuPont; the other, performance evaluation and review technique, was developed by the Navy and the Booze, Allen and Hamilton Consulting Group. The major difference between the two methods is the ability performance evaluation and review technique has to calculate the probability that an activity will be completed by a certain time, whereas critical path method does not (Lewis: 51). It is important to point out that critical path method is a method of scheduling used when the time for completing each task of the project is well known, whereas performance evaluation and review technique is used when task durations within a project (usually a large project) are unknown or difficult to predict. For example, in the case of the yard project, if you had performed the various tasks before, you would be able to accurately estimate the amount of time it would take to complete the tasks based upon your own personal experience. Therefore, critical path method would be a simpler method for scheduling. However, in the case of a large project where estimates are not based upon personal experience, performance evaluation and review technique might be a more appropriate method for scheduling. According to Haynes, a way to deal with the lack of precision in estimating time is to use a commonly accepted formula for the task. The estimate is derived in the following way (Figure 21.5.):

### Figure 21.5. Formula for the Task.

Let $Tm$ = the most probable time, $To$ = the most optimistic (shortest) time, $Tp$ = the pessimistic (longest) time, and $Te$ = the calculated time estimate. Then The following formula would apply:

$$Te = \frac{T0 + 4Tm + Tp}{6}$$

21.17.10. Once a time duration is determined for each sub-unit of the project, the next step is to determine the earliest and latest starting times for each sub-unit (Haynes: 31). Both critical path method and performance evaluation and review technique methods are used for what is termed network analysis. According to Reiss, network analysis is simply breaking down any project into activities or tasks and then deciding how long each task will take and how each of these activities relate to one another. From this data, you calculate the timing of each element and predict which activities or tasks are vital to the success of the project (Reiss: 46). The analysis (a simple graphical expansion of the task analysis) is depicted using bar charts, critical path method, performance evaluation and review technique, or a combination of the three. For critical path method and performance evaluation and review technique, a common convention used is called activity on arrow or precedence. For the purpose of this reading, we will refer to the technique as strictly *precedence*. To better understand this technique, the following series of diagrams and accompanying explanation is provided. In Figure 21.6 below, the precedence, or task to be accomplished, is indicated on the line between the two circles. According to Reiss, the words written above the line describe the task and are known as the task description. This task or activity (precedence) takes a certain period of time. We call the circles *events* or *nodes*, and they illustrate the completion or the beginning of events. Reiss goes on to say that the circles can also be squares, diamonds, or a variety of other symbols, depending on what technique is being employed (Reiss: 49).

**Figure 21.6. The Precedence or Task**

21.17.11. To expand this concept a little, let's take a look at a slightly more involved example. In Figure 21.7 below, we see an example of how the precedence of 'open garage door' must occur before the next two separate events can begin or reach completion. In other words, for event 4 to take place (the beginning of the precedence's get the car out and get the bike out); the prior precedence 'open garage door' must take place. When a task must be completed before other tasks can begin, that task is said to be a *dependency* task, or *predecessor* task. According to Reiss, the completion of events like 5 & 6, 'get the bike out' and 'get the car out', are dependent upon the task 'open garage door', and therefore follow 'open garage door'. These succeeding tasks are independent of each other in the diagram. In other words, they can be accomplished independently of each other (provided the same person is not accomplishing both tasks) (Reiss: 50). Tasks that are independent of each other can be performed simultaneously if adequate resources are available.

**Figure 21.7. The Precedence or Task Expanded**

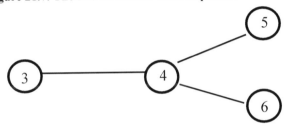

21.17.12. According to Reiss, we can also estimate the amount of time which we think each task will take, and this amount of time we call the duration of the task. When a network diagram is drawn containing nodes connected by tasks labeled with durations, the time each task should happen can be calculated by adding up the durations of the various routes contained within a network. Normally one of these routes will take longer than the other routes. The longest route is referred to as the *critical path*. The completions of the tasks along the critical path are vital to the success of the project, for if any one of those tasks becomes delayed for some reason, the entire project will also be delayed. For example, Figure 21.8 illustrates a network diagram with multiple routes and activity arrows labeled with task completion times.

21.17.12.1. The critical path is indicated in bold (A, C, E, G, I) along the route with the longest total completion times. If the tasks between A and C, C and E, E and G, or G and I should take longer than the time indicated, the total length of time for the entire project will be delayed. Hence, this *critical path* is vital to task completion, so the tasks along this path should receive the most attention during the length of the project.

21.17.13. As indicated earlier by Reiss, squares can be used to represent these events, or nodes. Performance evaluation and review technique makes use of squares to illustrate network analysis (Reiss: 49). In Figure 21.9 below in the network diagram of Figure 21.8 is formatted in performance evaluation and review technique.

**Figure 21.8. Critical Path.**

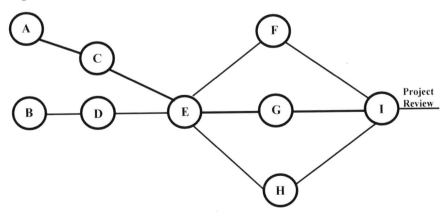

**Figure 21.9. Performance Evaluation and Review Technique.**

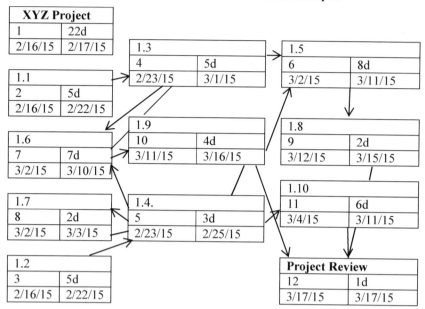

21.17.14. The critical path is identified by the bold-faced box borders and the arrows that lead into and out of them. As you can see from the upper left box labeled XYZ PROJECT, the project is to take 22 days, assuming the critical path durations do not change (Task 1.1 of 5 days + Task 1.3 of 5 days + Task 1.6 of 7 days + Task 1.9 of 4 days + Project Review of 1 day = 22 days). Whether you choose, network diagramming like that depicted in Figures 21.7 and 21.8 or a Gantt chart is insignificant. The important thing to remember is that the tool used should be simple to read and user friendly for your project. For the purpose of the remainder of this reading, we will use a Gantt chart to graphically depict further project discussions. Most project management software packages make use of Gantt charts, but even if you do not have access to project management software, Gantt charts can be easily constructed manually in most word processing and spreadsheet programs. Figure 21.10 below is a Gantt chart from a popular software package that depicts the information displayed previously in Figures 21.8 & 21.9.

21.17.15. The critical path in Figure 21.10 is identified by those tasks whose task names are larger, bold-faced and underlined in the column labeled Task Name. As indicated earlier, the critical path is vital to task completion, so the tasks along this path should receive the most attention during the length of the project. Reiss indicates that activities off the critical path have some freedom of movement without affecting the overall project. These tasks are said to have float or slack. The amount of float is the amount of time the activity can be delayed without affecting the project overall. Critical tasks have no float, and may become critical when their float is entirely consumed by the passage of time. There are two types of float—*free float* and *total float*. Total float is what we have been talking about thus far—the amount of time a task can be delayed without affecting the project's end date (Reiss: 52). (NOTE: In the following examples, the Gantt chart depicted is for a work schedule of Monday through Friday, with weekends being non-duty days.) For example, in Figure 21.10 below, task 1.2 has 2 days of total float. Since it is not along the critical path, if it was to be delayed by 2 days, it would still not cause task 1.6 to be delayed from occurring; thus, its delay would not affect the critical path or the project. Free float is the amount of time a task can be delayed without affecting any tasks at all. Task 1.2 causes the delay of task 1.4; therefore, it has no free float because a delay of this task affects another task. However, task 1.4 has free float for if it was delayed by as much as 2 days, its delay would not have any effect on the accomplishment of another task. Why? Because task 1.3 must be accomplished before tasks 1.5, 1.6, and 1.7 can occur. Since task 1.3 is 5 days and 1.4 is 3 days, if 1.4 was to start 2 days late and still finish in 3 days, it would not hold up the tasks, which are also waiting on the completion of task 1.3. That extra 2 days is called task 1.4's free float. Float (or slack) is a concept which is very beneficial to a project manager. For example, suppose task 1.3 (a critical task) was accomplished by a team of folks. If a couple of team members were unable to perform for some reason (emergency leave, hospitalization, etc.), task 1.4 could be delayed and personnel from the team accomplishing that task could be used for task 1.3. Another possibility might be that computers used for accomplishment of task 1.3 have failed and task 1.4 could be delayed to permit the computer resources to be used for task 1.3. Knowledge of task duration, resources to accomplish the task, and float available for tasks can enable a project manager to make sound decisions to keep the project on schedule or to even shorten the time required to complete the project.

**Figure 21.10. Task Name Gantt Chart.**

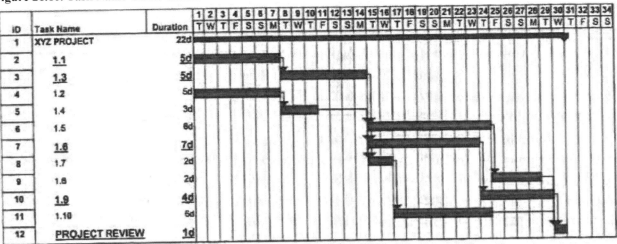

21.17.16. There is a multitude of information available on project management. We have attempted to introduce you to some of the terminology, expound on some project management principles, and illustrate practical uses of project management principles. Remember, project management and program management are not the same thing. Unlike a program, a project is temporary, not ongoing. Project management is the process of leading and managing processes and people in the pursuit of achieving project objectives. The steps of project management include defining the problem, developing solution options, planning the project, executing the plan, monitoring and controlling progress, and closing the project. Project objectives should be SMART — specific, measurable, action-oriented, realistic, and time-limited. For project management, the primary constraints are quality, time, and cost. Of these three constraints, one of them will likely be the driver for a project. The driver of a project will have an impact on the other constraints affecting the project. As a project manager, you must remain constantly aware of the driver and how it impacts the other constraints of the project. With the constraints in mind, it is imperative for the project manager to provide sound leadership and management to develop the solution options necessary to achieve the project objective. Once options are developed, the most important and time-consuming aspect of project management must occur—planning the project. Planning a project involves activities that answer the questions who, what, when, where, and how. Techniques of special importance to use during planning are a work breakdown schedule, task analysis, and scheduling. Scheduling is accomplished in a number of ways, to include Gantt charts, critical path method, and performance evaluation and review technique. Gantt, critical path method, and performance evaluation and review technique are methods used for network analysis. Critical path method and performance evaluation and review technique use a common convention called activity on arrow, or precedence. Regardless of the method used, the route contained in the diagram depicting the longest duration is referred to as the critical path. The completion of the tasks along the critical path is vital to the success of the project, and failure of any one of those tasks to be completed on time results in a delay to project completion. The activities of some tasks off the critical path have some freedom of movement without affecting the overall project. These tasks are said to have float or slack; the two types of float are total float and free float. Total float is the amount of time a task can be delayed without affecting the project's end.

**21.18. Conclusion .**

Organizational management is the process of organizing, planning, leading, and controlling resources within an entity with the overall aim of achieving its objectives. Organizational management provides leaders the ability to make decisions and resolve issues in order to be both effective and beneficial. This chapter provided valuable information leaders need to effectively manage their organizations. This chapter covered Organizational Design, Managing Organizational change, conflict, problem solving, and project management.

**Chapter 22**

**HUMAN RESOURCE DEVELOPMENT**

*Section 22A—Power*

**22.1. Introduction**:

22.1.1. The concept of power in the workforce has a negative connotation and brings to mind such associations as coercion, manipulation, and even corruption. This does not have to be the case. Power has many positive aspects, and everyone can learn to explore and harness different sources of the individual power they have in the workplace. By developing their own sources of power, employees will be less dependent on others for the leadership they need, and thus be better able to take initiative and make greater contributions in their jobs.

22.1.2. Develop your own program called *Situational Self Leadership*, and take a different perspective on power. Develop an understanding that "the sole advantage of power is the ability to do more good." Thus, if you want to do more good for yourself and more good for the people around you, it is important to learn how to tap into your own points of power.

**22.2. Aspects of Power:**

22.2.1. **Position power** is inherent in the authority of the position you have. You have position power when your business card has a title printed on it that indicates you have the power to manage people or command resources. My dad, an officer in the Navy, used to say, "The best leaders are those who have position power and never have to use it."

22.2.2. **Task power** is power that stems from being good at a particular task at work and being able to help others with a process or procedure they may need to do.

22.2.3. **Personal power** comes from your personal character attributes such as strength of character, passion, inspiration, or a personal vision of the future. Personal power is further enhanced by the strength of your interpersonal skills, such as your ability to communicate well and to be persuasive with others.

22.2.4. **Relationship power** comes from association with others through friendship, personal understanding of a colleague, and cultivation of a relationship, nepotism, or reciprocity (trading favors).

22.2.5. **Knowledge power** is about having expertise in an area. This is often through knowing a special skill or group of skills in your job, but is also evidenced by having certain degrees or certifications indicating special training. Knowledge power can often be transferred from job to job or from organization to organization, and is a general type of power.

**22.3. Charting Your Points of Power:**

22.3.1. An enlightening activity is to list a number of workplace situations or conditions where you feel you have the power to influence outcomes or people. Next to each item, categorize the type of power you have in that circumstance.

22.3.2. Now draw a five-pointed star with ten hash marks from the center to the tip of each point. From the center of the star, mark off the corresponding number of responses you listed in your assessment of each type of power. The farthest hash mark you indicate on each arm of the star becomes the new tip of that arm. Connect these new points. The resulting graphic should be some semblance of a star, with certain points having more emphasis and others having less. This will show you your primary points of power at a glance.

22.3.3. If you want to be a real star in the workplace, try to develop a strategy to balance the points of power where you work. Some examples:

22.3.3.1. You have high knowledge power due to expertise in analysis, and are often asked to analyze situations and report your findings in meetings. However, you are weak in personal power and your ability to communicate is poor. Your strategy might be to take a presentation skills course or to ask someone to critique a presentation before you give it to the group.

22.3.3.2. You have high task power and need to present an idea to the head of your department, but are somewhat weak in relationship power. Your strategy could be to ask a coworker who has the ear of the department head to give you feedback on how he or she thinks the department head will react to your idea.

22.3.3.3. You have task power and are working on a very visible project, but you lack position power, which might make it difficult to get support. Your strategy could be to use your task power to solicit a sponsor or champion who will help promote your project and your credibility.

22.3.3.4. You have personal power, but are weak in relationship power. Your strategy might be to use your social skills to network. Ask others for instructions, attend meetings of professional organizations, or schedule lunches to help build relationships.

22.3.4. Take advantage of the points of power where you are strong. Use your power in a positive way to do more good for yourself and those around you. If people throughout your organization are enabled to develop their sources of power, it could create a more even playing field for everyone. Power doesn't have to be concentrated in the hands of a few.

### Section 22B—Unit Morale

### 22.4. Contemporary Motivation:

22.4.1. Contemporary motivation is a simple, three-phased approach to motivation. This approach states that people can be in one of three levels of commitment to the organization—the membership level (at the lowest end), the performance level, or the involvement level (highest level). A person's level of commitment determines how motivated he or she is to accomplish the mission. The more committed a person is to the organization, the more involved he or she is in the organization. Supervisors can help to ensure the proper rewards are provided so individuals can move to, or remain in, a higher commitment level.

22.4.2. Are methods available to measure unit morale or motivation levels? Yes. For instance, the Inspector General uses a climate assessment instrument to assess a unit's morale. Mark Alexander, author of the article, *Organizational Norms, The 1977 Annual Handbook for Group Facilitators* (1977), defines a set of organizational norms and maintains that identifying and evaluating organizational norms will result in a morale score. He identified 10 norms categories, but we will only examine seven. Paragraph 22.5 is an excerpt from the article and norms survey.

### 22.5. Organizational Norms.

Within any organizational situation, behavioral forces influence individual effectiveness and job satisfaction. To a certain extent, these forces are a result of organization requirements that people behave and act in certain ways, that they hold certain values and sentiments, and that they interact with others in a particular manner.

#### 22.5.1. Required and Emergent Behavior.

An organization's required behavior, sentiments, and interactions are not necessarily in effect. Existent or emergent behaviors, sentiments, and interactions, in many cases, have a much greater influence on organization life than required behavior. Emergent behavior correspondingly affects productivity, individual satisfaction, and personal development. Behavioral scientists generally recognize that emergent organizational behavior is determined largely by formation of working group behavioral norms.

22.5.1.1. Norms are desirable behaviors. They are considered acceptable behavior as prescribed by work groups and, in the larger context, by society and its institutions. There are numerous examples throughout work and everyday life of emergent behavior and the underlying norms that cause this behavior.

22.5.1.2. In the work environment, a tendency to establish start and quit times that vary from company policy, or a work group's inclination to establish a quicker or slower pace than required are two often-cited examples. Outside the work situation, normative (or emergent) behavior also occurs, and can be observed in schools, institutions, or anywhere that people come together and interact for a period of time.

#### 22.5.2. Positive or Negative Norms.

From the organization's view, norms can be positive or negative. Recent studies on organizational norms indicate that they can be broken into categories, and that certain types or clusters of positive or negative norms can exist in a given work situation.

22.5.2.1. Positive norms are those that support the organization's goals and objectives and foster behavior directed toward achieving those goals. Norms that support hard work, loyalty, quality, and concern for customer satisfaction are examples of positive norms.

22.5.2.2. Negative norms have just the opposite effect. They promote behavior that works to prevent the organization from achieving its objectives. Negative norms are those that sanction criticism of the company, theft, absenteeism, and low levels of productivity.

**22.6. Norm Categories:**

22.6.1. **Organizational and Personal Pride.**

Norms in this category are associated with an individual's feelings of identification and sense of pride regarding the organization. Positive norms lead the person to see the organization as "his" or "hers." Negative norms are reflected in a "we" and "they" attitude toward the organization and its goals. Examples of positive and negative organizational and personal pride norms are evident in the competition between military organizations. If competition helps the units become better at their missions and exhibit greater morale and motivation, then competition is positive. On the other hand, if competition hampers the mission and leads to reduced morale and motivation, competition is negative.

22.6.2. **Teamwork and Communication.**

These norms are reflected in the visible behaviors where individuals work together (cooperate). Negative norms foster individuality, secrecy, and the belief that success is achieved by an attitude of "every man for himself." Positive norms promote sharing of information and working together to achieve common goals. Thomas Jefferson noted that a candle loses nothing when it lights another candle; that is the real nature of partnership and teamwork: give freely of yourself and you will be rewarded with abundance. Promoting a positive norm is even more critical as all military branches and government agencies work together to counter global threats and to combat terrorism at home and abroad.

22.6.3. **Leadership and Supervision.**

Leadership norms can enhance or hinder effective supervision. Negative norms cause supervisors to assume more active roles, like constantly policing and monitoring Airmen. Positive norms result in supervisors assuming the role of subordinate helpers, trainers, and developers.

22.6.4. **Profitability and Cost Effectiveness.**

This group of norms determines people's behavior with respect to profit and cost consciousness. Positive norms encourage people to save money and reduce costs; negative norms foster a lack of concern for bottom line performance. You may have heard someone say "it's good enough for government work." That is a negative norm that has been perpetuated over the years, but is one our Air Force cannot afford if we are to effectively accomplish our mission of defending the United States and protecting its interests through superior air and space power.

22.6.5. **Customer Relations.**

Norms in this group result in individual behavior that affects the manner in which a customer is served. Positive norms are directed toward maximizing customer satisfaction. Negative norms lead to viewing the customer as an obstacle to be avoided. Air Force basic doctrine tells us the Air Force's air and space core competencies are recognized by our joint "customers." In other words, the total force, joint force, North Atlantic Treaty Organization, and others rely on us to do our job to the best of our ability. If we do not, we cannot fight and win our Nation's wars as we are expected to. Therefore, each organization must cultivate a culture that helps our Airmen, Soldiers, Marines, and Sailors develop a positive customer relations norm to ensure our Nation can meet any challenge in the most effective manner.

22.6.6. **Innovativeness and Creativity.**

This group of norms determines, to a large degree, whether original and creative behaviors are supported and encouraged. Positive norms lead to the stimulation of new ideas and to positive change. Negative norms support the status quo and discourage experimentation. In today's total and joint forces environment, we must encourage everyone to bring innovativeness and creativity to the table in order to meet the dynamic threats that terrorism has brought to our shores.

22.6.7. **Training and Development.**

Positive norms in this group encourage training and view development as essential to the ongoing operation. Negative norms treat development as a nonessential, nice-to-do, but not critical aspect of the operation. We saw firsthand during Hurricane Katrina that training is vitally important to the Department of Homeland Security, the Federal Emergency Management Agency, the United States Army Corps of Engineers, and other natural disaster responders. In addition, Airmen are constantly training with soldiers, sailors, and marines to ensure each branch is better equipped and prepared to fight the global war on terrorism.

## 22.7. Why We Measure Norms:

22.7.1. Understanding that norms exist, that they can be either positive (supportive of organizational goals) or negative (incongruent with organizational goals), and that they can be categorized drives the need to measure those norms and develop a normative profile.

22.7.2. In effect, a normative profile is a statement of organizational strengths and weaknesses on a behavioral level. Understanding their impact on an organization's ability to achieve its goals, you should direct improvement programs toward changing work group norms rather than individual behavior (as is so often the case with organizations' development programs). Once norms change, behavioral change should follow. If a military member's behavior does not support positive organizational norms, the supervisor needs to determine the underlying reasons. The individual's behavior could be a result of unmet needs, a result of discipline problems, or both. In order to be effective operational managers and expeditionary leaders, supervisors must learn to instill positive norms to properly motivate and discipline Airmen.

## Section 22C—Transactional Analysis (TA)

### 22.8. Introduction:

22.8.1. "I'm OK-----You're OK" is a euphemism for Transactional Analysis, also called TA. To some, TA is a nonverbal reaction to communication between husband and wife or parents and children. However, TA is much more than that and can be applied to a business, industrial, or military organization.

22.8.2. TA is a theory of personality as well as a systematic psychotherapy for personal growth and personal change. As TA evolves, this reaction to communication is finding a wide application in organizations and education. TA principles and techniques is used by managers to more fully understand themselves and their relationships with others, which can lead to them becoming happier, healthier, and more productive. TA can be defined by several principles, such as, Ego States, Transactions, Life Positions, Strokes, and Time Structuring. These principles can be utilized to form techniques to improve individual productivity that, in turn, can lead to increased organizational effectiveness.

### 22.9. Ego States:

22.9.1. One area of TA is the study of individual *ego states*. We all know, without being told, that we are different. The underlying theory of TA is the highlighting of those differences. According to Dr. Eric Berne in his book, *Games People Play,* TA analysis states that a human personality is composed of ego states commonly referred to as *Parent, Adult,* and *Child* (PAC). Each ego state is relatively separate from the others and each has its own set of feelings, beliefs, and behavior patterns. Generally, people act in one ego state at a time. In some cases, people may act in two ego states at the same time. The states are produced by the playback of recorded data of past events involving real people, real times, real places, and real feelings. (Beme: 23-28)

22.9.2. Another expert on this subject, Dr. Thomas Harris, does an excellent job of writing about these ego states in his book, *I'm OK—You're OK.* He says the Parent ego state is a way of thinking, acting, feeling, and believing much the same as our parents and is based upon the brain's recordings of our perceptions of our parents' responses. As such, the Parent ego state responds immediately and automatically to childlike behavior. The Parent can be a *critical* Parent or an overly *nurturing* Parent. (Harris: 40-46) Dr. Arnold Kambly in his booklet, *The ABC's of PAC: An Introduction to Transactional Analysis,* refers to the Parent as the taught concepts of life. "We were taught this behavior from watching authority figures in our early childhood." (Harris: I)

22.9.3. Dr. Harris says the Child ego contains our basic desires and needs, and the recordings of the feelings and reactions of our childhood. Oddly enough, this state develops about the same time as the Parent state. The spontaneous dimensions of the Child provide for the joy, motivation, and natural creativity of one's own personality. "Adopted elements of the Child are expressed in feelings and patterns of response to parental stimuli` responses such as rebellion, procrastination, or compliance." (Harris: 47-50) Dr. Kambly refers to this ego state as "the felt concept of life. These are the feelings we have recorded from childhood." (Kambly: I-2) These feelings bring forth our emotions and desires for emotion in others.

22.9.4. According to Dr. Harris, the third state, the Adult ego state, is a way of acting, feeling, and believing that is rather objective. The Adult part of our personality develops later than either that of the Parent or the Child, and continues to develop throughout the lifetime of a healthy person and is the analytical part of our personality that processes current and objective information about our environment. The Adult also edits our archaic recordings in the Parent and Child parts of personality. (Harris: 50-59) Dr. Kambly says the Adult deals with the realities of the world, plus input from the Parent and Child. The Adult deals with the "here and now," in contrast to the other two ego states which come from the past. (Kambly: 3) "The Adult is the learned concept of life. In this case, learned in the Adult is different than the taught of the Parent." (Kambly: 3) Learned refers to a continuous process. The Adult is always learning. The taught Parent ego state was taught once, in the past.

22.9.5. The three ego states appear in our behavior at different times. According to Dr. Harris, a healthy individual maintains a balance among the three. However, some people may be dominated by one of the ego states. This is *contamination*. (Harris: 123-140). According to Dr. Kambly, "contamination takes place when the Parent or Child contaminates the Adult." The Adult makes the decisions, but these decisions are then distorted due to the past tapes of the Parent or Child. Dr. Harris and Dr. Kambly agree that such people have been known to create problems for managers who have to work with them. People with Child-dominated personalities generally do not engage in much rational problem solving. They can be hard to reason with in emotionally charged situations because these people have learned through earlier experiences that they can succeed by being loud, boisterous, or emotional. Parent-dominated people also do not engage in much rational problem solving because they already know what is right and what is wrong. They are overly critical or overly nurturing. Another problem is *exclusion*. This happens when one ego state excludes the others. In this situation, the excluding ego state pushes out the excluded ego states. Dr. Kambly points out that "a healthy person has the ego states separate and discrete. When things go wrong, contamination or exclusion results." (Kambly: 45)

## 22.10. Life Position:

22.10.1. Along with ego states, the term *life position* is associated with TA. Simply stated, life position is how a person feels about oneself and about other people. In the process of growing up, people make some rather basic assumptions about themselves and about others in their environment. The combination of assumptions about oneself and about others is referred to as a life position. Important to state is that the life position has two parts: the feelings of self and feelings toward others. This is different than self-concept or self-esteem, which only deal with self. Life positions tend to be more permanent than ego states. This permanency can create potential problems in an organizational setting where people work together even if their life positions are not complementary. Life positions result from reinforcement received throughout life from expressions of need and responses to expressed needs.

22.10.2. The focus of the book by Dr. Harris (*I'm OK—you're OK*) is on these life positions. "The assumptions are described in terms of "okayness." Thus, individuals are labeled either OK or not OK, whether they refer to themselves or to someone else. OK and not OK equate to value and individual worth. Thus, there are four possible life positions:" (Harris: 66)

    22.10.2.1. I'm not OK—You are not OK = neither of us has value (- -).

    22.10.2.2. I'm not OK—You are OK = I don't have value; you have value (- +).

    22.10.2.3. I'm OK—You are not OK = I have value; you don't have value (+ -).

    22.10.2.4. I'm OK—You are OK = We both have value (+ +).

22.10.3. The fourth life position is ideal because most people with these feelings tend to have a positive outlook on life and are generally successful.

## 22.11. Transactions and Strokes:

22.11.1. According to Dr. Eric Heme, "a situation which results in social intercourse is dubbed a transaction." (Beme: 29) If two or more people encounter each other in a social interaction, sooner or later one of them will speak, or give some indication of acknowledging the presence of the others. Dr. Heme calls this the *transactional stimulus*. Another person says or does something related to this stimulus, and that action is called the transactional response. Therefore, simple TA is concerned with diagnosing which ego states are used in the transaction (stimulus and response). Transactions may involve combinations of ego states and match or replay forms of interactions that develop early in life. Simple transactions are those in which both stimulus and response arise from the Adult states of the parties concerned. These are *parallel* or *complementary*. Also, Child to Parent transactions (and vice versa) is complementary. Complementary means the responses are both appropriate and expected. Some transactions are not complementary. The responses are not expected or appropriate. For example, an Adult-to-Adult stimulus followed by a Child to Parent response is not complementary and is called a *crossed* transaction. These occur when a respondent reacts from an ego state other than the one desired by the initiator. Crossed transactions can cause problems, but they also have a use as you'll see later. Analyzing the transactions to determine the ego states can help determine the life position. As long as transactions remain complementary, communication continues regardless of the content of the transaction. On the other hand, communication ceases as a result of crossed transactions. Dr. Berne's research and experience tell us that crossed transactions are barriers to effective communication and negatively impact the motivation of people, which ultimately results in decreased output.

22.11.2. Consider the following example: The supervisor states, "Staff Sergeant Jones, could you come to a meeting in my office around 1300 today?" Staff Sergeant Jones replies, "Sure." This is an Adult transaction. Communication could continue and the supervisor could say, "Good. I'd like you to brief that idea you submitted to the rest of the staff I really think it will work." On the other hand, Staff Sergeant Jones could have said, "Oh come on, I've already got enough work to do around here. I don't want to sit through another boring meeting." In this case, Staff Sergeant Jones is responding emotionally and not from the Adult ego state. Therefore, effective communication is blocked.

22.11.3. Another type of transaction is called a *stroke.* A stroke is a special form of recognition that one person gives to another. Strokes can *positive* or *negative,* and are common in any organization.

22.11.4. According to Dr. Kambly, positive strokes can be verbal, nonverbal, or physical. They are designed to make the person feel good. They are a type of reward. They can be conditional, which means they are based on a certain condition being met. Telling a worker, "Hey Staff Sergeant Jones, you did a great job putting together the training report." is an example of a positive conditional stroke. Positive conditional strokes modify behavior in that they try to get the person to continue the behavior. Positive strokes can also be unconditional. An unconditional stroke is not based on any condition and is given just for *being,* not for *doing.* Smiling at someone and telling them you're glad to have them as part of the team is a positive unconditional stroke. Positive unconditional strokes are designed to make the person feel good about themselves. Positive unconditional strokes improve self-esteem, which can help lead to a better life position.

22.11.5. Dr. Kambly also reviews the negative strokes people use. Negative strokes are designed to make the person feel bad. They are a type of punishment or rebuke. Just like positive strokes, negative stokes can be conditional or unconditional. A negative conditional stroke is used to modify behavior in that it is used to get the person to stop the behavior. Issuing a reprimand or Article 15 is an example. The act (condition) resulted in the negative conditional stroke. A negative unconditional stroke is aimed at the person, just like the positive unconditional stroke and is an attack against the person and not any specific behavior. Slamming a person, putting them down, or calling them names are all examples of negative unconditional strokes. In professional relationships, there is never a need to use negative unconditional strokes.

22.11.6. Dr. Harris identifies different stroking with the different life positions. He has found that "people of unhealthy life positions tend to overuse certain types of strokes." (Harris: 67- 77) For example, an "I'm OK—You're not OK" person may overuse negative strokes. The reason is obvious. This person thinks they are so much better than everyone else, and they may operate from the critical Parent ego state. On the other hand, an "I'm not OK—You're OK" person may overuse positive strokes. This person sees others as so much better than they are. A problem with overusing positive strokes is that the strokes become plastic or meaningless. If the supervisor is always using them, his or her praise becomes meaningless.

## 22.12. Time Structuring.

Another aspect of TA deals with *time structuring.* According to Dr. Kambly, "if a person lives to be 75 years old, assuming he or she sleeps 8 hours out of every 24, he or she has approximately 50 waking years to spend in some type of time structuring." (Kambly: 9) Dr. Heme states there are several options for a person. These are: Withdrawal, Rituals, Activities, Pastimes, Games, and Intimacy. (Beme: 18-19) A summary of each of these, as taken from Dr. Kambly's booklet, is below.

22.12.1. **Withdrawal.** This involves no risk and has minimal social rewards because there is minimal contact. A person does not have to be alone to be in withdrawal. They can be "lost in the crowd." Withdrawal is not always bad. We all need to get away and relax or be alone at times. However, if this is the primary way a person structures their time, it becomes a problem. This can be dangerous if a person uses it all the time. Some people can be withdrawn prior to suicide.

22.12.2. **Rituals.** Rituals are highly structured and predictable ways to structure time. This can be as simple as walking down the hall and saying, "Hi Jim. How are you today?" Jim then replies, "Hi. I'm fine." This is done out of habit and is predictable. You may not really care how Jim is, and Jim may not actually be "fine." Rituals are okay at times, but if this is all a person does, this is not productive in the work center. Rituals are just small talk about things of little value. So, a person who spends most of their time in rituals does not contribute as much to the work center. Rituals are slightly riskier than withdrawal because there is some interaction. However, the risk is minimal because of the structured and predictable nature of rituals.

22.12.3. **Activities.** These are goal oriented. Activities are things people do to meet mission requirements or goals. They are production orientated. This is where the majority of time should be spent in the work center. People with a healthy life position can spend a lot of time in activities and they expect others to be goal-oriented (activity-centered) also.

22.12.4. **Pastimes.** Pastimes are ways to structure time, such as hobbies, for relaxation. Things we do without a specific goal in mind are all pastimes. Pastimes and activities can be confused. You need to look at the intent of the time structuring. For example, someone playing golf for fun is structuring their time doing a pastime. However, if they are a professional golfer and make money at it, they are engaged in activities. The risk is a bit higher for activities and pastimes than it is for rituals or withdrawal because there are more chances of interaction and more chances for values and differences of opinion to come into play. There are more meaningful transactions during activities and pastimes.

22.12.5. **Games.** Games are a way to structure time in devious or crooked ways to get strokes (which are normally negative). Games are not productive and they result in anger, frustration, jealousy, etc. The risks in games are high because of the anger and hurt feelings that result. Those with unhealthy life positions normally play games. Games, like poor communication, often tend to create organizational problems. A basic understanding of the term *games* is essential to the application of TA in management. In his book *Games People Play,* Dr. Berne refers to a game as "a recurring set of transactions, often repetitious, superficially plausible, with a concealed motivation." (Berne: 48) These types of transactions can be of a type called *ulterior,* meaning there is a hidden or ulterior meaning to the transaction. Basically, games are transactions that are designed to cause an emotional response such as anger or hurt. A game might be as simple as an "I'm not OK—You're OK" person speaking from the Child ego state trying to get others to be the nurturing Parent. Some games get more complex and can even result in death. Given this definition, games become barriers preventing people and organizations from achieving their objectives. Games tend to inhibit full productivity. Using crossed transactions (responding always from your Adult when the game-player is using the Child or Parent) will reduce game-playing. For example, assume someone says, "That's the dumbest idea I've ever heard of. What moron came up with that?" This person is being a critical Parent and not presenting any facts to support the point of view. Using your Adult, you could reply, "What parts of the idea do you find flawed?" or "Can you provide specific data to support your opinion?" These replies use the Adult to seek facts and to focus the person on the *here and now.*

22.12.6. **Intimacy.** This is the most risky, but also the most rewarding type of time structuring and is defined as a close relationship with others free of games and exploitation. Intimacy is being open, honest, and sincere and requires a person at the "I'm OK—You're OK" life position. Intimacy is not just sexual relationships. A person can have sexual relationships and be in a state of withdrawal or ritual. Intimacy is a close personal relationship, and that's why the risk and reward are high.

**22.13. The Work Environment:**

22.13.1. We can now relate the concepts of TA to the environmental process. How do basic concepts of TA apply in business, industrial, or military environments? The most basic application of TA principles is to managerial styles. TA is a powerful tool that can help managers understand the interactive nature of human problems in a work environment so that they can deal with these problems more effectively. Does the supervisory relationship indicate the need for a participative or an authoritarian management style, or does the need indicate another point along the continuum? For an authoritarian style, or *Theory X* management, to work effectively, the manager has to operate as a Parent while workers operate in the Child state. Supervisors have absolute authority while workers are very dependent on direction from above. Thus, the boss is OK but workers are not OK. In this situation, the manager accepts final responsibility for failure. Being dependent, much like a Child, the worker in this situation is protected from making a wrong decision because the boss takes full responsibility for all actions.

22.13.2. There is another view. According to Maslow, Herzberg, and other motivation theorists, the authoritarian style of management frustrates achievement of the higher-level needs of human personality. Therefore, a worker in this situation may find it satisfactory, but may never experience a state of self-fulfillment and growth. A common belief among casual observers is that the condition just described is common in many organizations. The participative or *Theory Y* management style involves Adult-Adult transactions. A two-way flow of communication exists and the worker feels more comfortable in providing his or her input. Subordinates feel a sense of responsibility rather than a feeling of dependency. Because workers influence decisions and share responsibility, they experience a feeling of fulfillment. The corresponding life position is likely I'm OK—You're OK.

22.13.3. A potential exists for crossed transactions in any management setting. In the authoritarian approach, the supervisor may be comfortable in the Parent ego state, but the worker may not enjoy the Child state. The worker may want to operate in the Adult state, and rightfully so. In this situation, Parent-to-Adult communication is disturbed and an unsettled situation occurs. The worker becomes frustrated, leading to unproductive behavior and performance—not a healthy situation for any organization. Thus, a manager with an understanding of TA, and with knowledge of worker ego states based on observation, could possibly head off this type of situation.

22.13.4. Crossed transactions are also possible while using a participative management style. By its very nature, this style encourages employee ego involvement in on-the-job activities. Individuals identify closely with work units and jobs because they are involved in establishing policies and operating procedures. However, even in this style, instances often occur when policies are established and decisions are rendered with rule or no employee involvement—a simple exercise of management prerogative. Such cases provide a fertile ground for crossed transactions when disgruntled employees confront individual managers. Here, the potential is high for responses from the Parent ego state, and the opportunity for conflict exists. Therefore, a skilled manager with an understanding of TA, and with knowledge of worker ego states based on observation, can avoid the conflict by dealing with those situations from a complementary state.

22.13.5. TA has taken hold as a supervisory tool. Initially, it was used mainly to teach employees who deal with the public how to relate better to their customers. Later, managers experimented with TA as a means of improving communications within the company itself. This experimentation has encouraged and reinforced a team concept. This is a participative management style whereby management and workers share the responsibility for decision-making. Some management practitioners view this as cooptation. In other words, it gives workers an equitable "share of the pie." The prevailing philosophy is that workers take ownership for their behavior in supporting policies and following procedures, which results in allowing more focus on productivity while maintaining a high interpersonal working relationship. In TA terms, both management and workers function in the Adult ego state. The resulting impact of this condition on organizations is that the organization is OK. Overall, it can be stated, "Together we are OK. The organization is OK = We all have value."

Summarizing life positions and their relationship to management styles, one might view it in terms of a management matrix similar to that depicted in Table 1.1.

**Table 1.1. Management Matrix**

| STYLE | POSITION | IMPACT ON ORGANIZATION |
|---|---|---|
| Theory X | Management = OK<br><br>Subordinates = not OK | Organization = not OK |
| Theory Y | Management = OK<br><br>Subordinates = OK | Organization = OK |
| Full Participation | (Management + Subordinates) = OK<br><br>Organization = OK | Organization = OK + (Growth and high productivity) |

## 22.14. Conclusions:

22.14.1. Generally, what has been the response to TA? Many executives, after having been exposed to TA training, swear by it; others have not responded as well, and consider it just another buzz word. TA is very difficult to evaluate objectively. Most supervisors are more than willing to prescribe TA training for line employees, but do not show much enthusiasm for applying TA concepts to themselves. Even though there is skepticism, some supervisors have learned that TA is profitable in terms of increasing organizational effectiveness. It's presented here as a tool to add to your management tool box.

22.14.2. The application of TA tracks well with the management theories of Likert, McGregor, and Argyris because use of TA provides opportunities for individuals to grow and mature. Even though some workers prefer to function in the Child state and appear to avoid responsibility, most desire to be treated as adults and to be given more responsibility. Using TA not only provides an opportunity for managers to know their people, but it also helps them to get in touch with themselves. When all parties involved are aware of each other's needs, communication improves. This condition is essential to organizational effectiveness. The effective supervisor focuses on workers' behavior and the modification of that behavior as a means for improving the organizational climate, thereby ultimately increasing overall productivity.

## *Section 22D—Performance Counseling*

## 22.15. Performance Counseling.

Performance Counseling is a systematic, two-way discussion between supervisor and subordinate concerning duty performance as compared to established standards, with the intention of informing the subordinate of his/her past duty performance and cooperatively developing a plan to sustain or improve performance.

## 22.16. The Lost Art of Feedback:

22.16.1. The ability and willingness to communicate effectively is the key to supervisory success. Although communication effectiveness is based on the ability to make and maintain effective contact, regardless of the situation, specific areas of communication require some additional thought and planning.

22.16.2. One of the most important tools for maintaining control and developing people is the proper use feedback. Although feedback has been categorized as positive and negative. Another way to view this is to classify it into supportive feedback (which reinforces an ongoing behavior) and corrective feedback (which indicates that a change in behavior is appropriate). In this sense, all feedback is positive. The purpose of all feedback should be to assist an individual in maintaining or enhancing his or her present level of effectiveness or appropriateness.

22.16.3. Some feedback, by definition, is better than no feedback. There are, however, ways to do it well and ways to do it superbly. Here are some guidelines that can help to sharpen the process. The most important function of feedback is to help the individual who is receiving the feedback to keep in touch with what is going on in the environment.

### 22.16.4. Supportive Feedback:

22.16.4.1. Supportive feedback is used to reinforce behavior that is effective and desirable. An axiom of effective supervision is "Catch them doing something right and let them know it." (Blanchard & Johnson, 1982)

22.16.4.2. One of the most damaging and erroneous assumptions that many supervisors make is that good performance and appropriate behavior are to be expected from the employee, and that the only time feedback is needed is when the employee does something wrong. Therefore, these supervisors never give supportive feedback. If a supervisor was determined to give only one kind of feedback, he or she would be ahead to choose supportive feedback and let corrective feedback go. In other words, if a supervisor stresses errors only, the end result would be, at most, an attempt by employees to do standard, error free work. This accomplishment would not be bad, but there is a better way.

22.16.4.3. If a supervisor concentrated on what the employees were doing well, then superior work is what the employees would become aware of. They would begin to view their work in terms of performing as well and as creatively as possible. What is reinforced has a tendency to become stronger. What is not reinforced has a tendency to fade away. If excellence is actively reinforced and errors are simply mentioned, employees will focus on excellence and tend to reduce errors. The following example of the two types of feedback illustrates the difference.

22.16.4.3.1. **Focus on errors.** "The last three pieces in that batch contained wrong figures. We cannot have that kind of sloppy work in this department."

22.16.4.3.2. **Focus on good work.** This batch looks good, except for the last three pieces, which contain wrong figures. You probably used the wrong formula. Take them back and check them out, just the way you did the first group."

22.16.4.4. Fortunately, however, no one has to make a choice between using only supportive or only corrective feedback.

22.16.4.5. Both are essential and valuable, and it is important to understand how each works so that the maximum gain can be received from the process.

22.16.5. **Corrective Feedback.** Corrective feedback is used to alter a behavior that is ineffective or inappropriate and is essential to the growth process as supportive feedback. A corrective feedback session, although never hurtful if done properly, is not a particularly pleasant experience. Under the best of circumstances, the subordinate will probably feel a little defensive or embarrassed.

22.16.5.1. In giving corrective feedback, the manager should have an option ready to present. When the employee is made aware of the inappropriate behavior, having an immediate alternative can be effective and powerful in shaping behavior. By presenting the alternative immediately after the corrective feedback, the manager is helping the subordinate to come out of a personally uncomfortable situation in the shortest possible time. This protects the dignity of the subordinate. The manager would also be establishing himself or herself as a supporter of good work and good workers, which would go a long way in developing strong, productive, supportive working relationships. Also very important, the manager would be presenting an alternative that the employee might never have considered or that was considered and rejected. This provides for immediate learning. Most important, however, is the fact that the manager would make the employee aware that an alternative was available at the time the employee chose to act otherwise. This awareness can facilitate the employee in taking responsibility for his or her own choices. That is, the employee would realize, "That's right, I could have done it that way." The following example shows how an alternative can be effectively added to the feedback.

22.16.5.2. "When you snapped at Ann in front of the group, she appeared to be very embarrassed and angry. When you must remind an employee to be on time, it's less embarrassing for everyone to discuss it with the employee privately after the meeting."

22.16.6. **Guidelines for Effective Feedback.** The following guidelines are helpful for managers who are trying to improve their feedback skills, and may also be used as a review prior to giving feedback.

22.16.6.1. **Deal in Specifics:**

22.16.6.1.1. Being specific is the most important rule in giving feedback, whether supportive or corrective. Unless the feedback is specific, very little learning or reinforcement is possible. The following examples illustrate the difference in general and specific statements.

*General:* "I'm glad to see that your work is improving."

*Specific:* "I'm pleased that you met every deadline in the last three weeks."

*General:* "You're a very supportive person."

*Specific:* "I appreciate you taking time to explain the contract to our new employee."

*General:* "You're falling down on the job again."

*Specific:* "Last month most of the cost reports were completely accurate, but last week your profit cost figures were wrong."

22.16.6.1.2. The last set is, of course, an example of corrective feedback. General statements in corrective feedback frequently result in hostile or defensive confrontations, whereas specific statements set the stage for problem-solving interaction. Carrying the last illustration one step farther, the manager could add an alternative: "Start checking the typed report against the computer printouts. Some of the errors may be typos, not miscalculations."

22.16.6.1.3. If the employee is to learn from feedback and respond to it, then he or she must see it in terms of *observable* effects. That is, the employee must be able to see clearly how his or her behavior had a direct impact on the group's performance, morale, etc. When the employee sees the point of the feedback objectively, the issue will be depersonalized, and the employee will be more willing to continue with appropriate behaviors or to modify inappropriate behaviors. Although the manager's personal approval ("I'm glad to see...") or disapproval ("I'm disappointed that...") can give emphasis to feedback, it must be supported by specific data in order to effect a change in behavior.

22.16.6.2. **Focus on Actions, Not Attitudes:**

22.16.6.2.1. Just as feedback must be specific and observable to be effective, it must be non-threatening to be acceptable. Although subordinates, like supervisors, are always accountable for their behavior, they are never accountable for their attitudes or feelings. Attitudes and feelings cannot be measured, nor can a manager determine if or when an employee's feelings have changed. For feedback to be acceptable, it must respect the dignity of the person receiving the feedback.

22.16.6.2.2. No one can attack attitudes without dealing in generalities, and frequently attacks on attitudes result in defensive reactions. The following example illustrates the difference in giving feedback on behavior and giving feedback on attitudes.

22.16.6.2.2.1. **Feedback on attitude:** "You have been acting hostile toward Jim."

22.16.6.2.2.2. **Feedback on behavior:** "You threw the papers down on Jim's desk and used profanity."

22.16.6.2.3. An attitude that managers often try to measure is loyalty. Certain actions that seem to indicate loyalty or disloyalty can be observed, but loyalty is a result, not an action and cannot be demanded; it must be earned. Whereas people have total control over their own behavior, they often exercise little control over their feelings and attitudes. They feel what they feel. If a manager keeps this in mind and focuses more energy on things that can be influenced (i.e. employee behavior), changes are more likely to occur.

22.16.6.2.4. The more that corrective feedback is cast in specific behavioral terms, the more it supports problem-solving and the easier it is to control. The more that corrective feedback is cast in attitudinal terms, the more it will be perceived as a personal attack and the more difficult it will be to deal with. The more that supportive feedback is cast in terms of specific behaviors, the higher the probability that those behaviors will be repeated and eventually become part of the person's natural way of doing things.

22.16.6.3. **Determine the Appropriate Time and Place:**

22.16.6.3.1. Feedback of either type works best if it is given as soon as feasible after the behavior occurs. Waiting decreases the impact that the feedback will have on the behavior. The passage of time may make the behavior seem less important to the manager, other important events begin to drain the energy of the manager, and some of the details of the behavior might be forgotten. On the other hand, dwelling on it for a long period could blow it out of proportion. From the subordinates' viewpoint, the longer the wait for the feedback, the less important it must be. The following example illustrates this point.

22.16.6.3.1.1. **Tardy feedback:** "You fell below your quota several times last month."

22.16.6.3.1.2. **Immediate feedback:** "There are only ten products here; your quota for today was fourteen."

22.16.6.3.2. Enough time should be allotted to deal with the issues in their entirety. A manager can undercut feedback effectiveness by looking at the clock and speeding up the input so that an appointment can be met. Answering the telephone or allowing visitors to interrupt the conversation can have the same effect. The manager can also cause unnecessary stress by telling an employee at ten o'clock in the morning "I want to see you at three this afternoon." A more appropriate procedure would be to say, "Would you please come to my office now," or "When you reach a stopping point, drop by my office. I have something good to tell you." In addition to an appropriate time, the setting is also important. The old proverb, "Praise in public, censure in private," is partially correct. Almost without exception, corrective feedback is more appropriately given in private. In the case of supportive feedback, however, discretion is needed. In many instances, praise in public is appropriate and will be appreciated by the subordinate. In other instances, privacy is needed to keep the positive effect from being short-circuited. For example, some people make a virtue out of humility; any feedback that reinforces their sense of worth is embarrassing. Rather than appreciating an audience, this type of employee would find it painful and perhaps resent it.

22.16.6.3.3. Sometimes a norm arises in a work group that prevents anyone from making a big deal out of good work. This does not mean that the group does not value good work, but supportive feedback in private might prevent the employee from feeling he or she was responsible for breaking the norm. In other instances, public praise can cause jealousy, hostility, or tense working relationships. Therefore, a conscious decision should be made about whether or not to give the supportive feedback publicly.

22.16.6.3.4. Another important consideration is the actual location selected for giving the feedback. The delivery of the feedback should match its importance. If the feedback concerns an important action, the manager's office would be better than an accidental encounter in the hall. On the other hand, the manager might convey a quick observation by telling someone at the water fountain, "Say that was beautiful artwork on the Madison report." Choosing the time and place is a matter of mixing a little common sense with an awareness of what is going on.

22.16.6.4. **Refrain from Inappropriately Including Other Issues:**

22.16.6.4.1. Frequently when feedback is given, other issues interfere. When supportive feedback is given, any topic that does not relate to the specific feedback point should not be discussed if it would undercut the supportive feedback. For example, the manager could destroy the good just accomplished by adding, "And by the way, as long as you are here, I want to ask you to try to keep your files a little neater. While you were away, I couldn't find a thing."

22.16.6.4.2. When corrective feedback is given, however, the situation is different. The manager will want the feedback to be absorbed as quickly and easily as possible, with the employee's negative feelings lasting no longer than necessary. Therefore, as soon as the feedback has been understood and acknowledged, the manager is free to change the subject. The manager may want to add, "I'm glad that you see where the error occurred."

22.16.6.4.3. "Now, as long as you are here, I'd like to ask your opinion about ..." This type of statement, when used appropriately, lets the subordinate know that he or she is still valued. Obviously, the manager should not contrive a situation just to add this type of statement, but when the situation is naturally there, the manager is free to take advantage of it.

22.16.6.4.4. In certain situations, it is appropriate to give supportive and corrective feedback simultaneously. Training periods of new employees, performance-appraisal sessions, and times when experienced employees are tackling new and challenging tasks are all good examples of times when both types of feedback are appropriate. Nevertheless, some cautions are necessary.

22.16.6.4.5. Never follow the feedback with the word "but." It will negate everything that was said before it. If appropriate to give supportive and corrective feedback within the same sentence, the clauses should be connected with "and." This method allows both parts of the sentence to be heard clearly and sets the stage for a positive suggestion. The following examples illustrate the difference.

22.16.6.4.5.1. Connected with but: "Your first report was accurate, but your others should have measured up to it."

22.16.6.4.5.2. Connected with and: "Your first report was accurate, and your others should have measured up to it."

22.16.6.4.5.3. Connected with but: "You were late this morning, but Anderson called to tell you what a great job you did on the Miller account."

22.16.6.4.5.4. Connected with and: "You were late this morning, and Anderson called to tell you what a great job you did on the Miller account."

22.16.6.4.6. Alternate the supportive and corrective feedback. Better to mix the supportive feedback with the corrective feedback than to give all of one type and then all of the other when a great deal of feedback must be given. Regardless of which type comes first, the latter will be remembered the most clearly. If a chronic self-doubter is first given supportive feedback and then only corrective feedback, he or she is likely to believe the supportive feedback was given just to soften the blow of the other type. Alternating between the two types will make all the feedback seem more genuine.

22.16.6.4.7. Where feasible, use the supportive feedback to cushion the corrective feedback. When both types of feedback are appropriate, there is usually no reason to start with corrective feedback. However, this does not mean that corrective feedback should be quickly sandwiched in between supportive feedback statements. Each type is important, but frequently supportive feedback can be used as an excellent teaching device for areas that need correcting. This is especially true if the employee has done a good job previously and then failed later under similar circumstances. For example, the manager might say, "The way you helped Fred to learn the codes when he was transferred to this department would be appropriate in training the new employees."

**22.16.7. Principles of Feedback:**

22.16.7.1. Two major principles govern the use of feedback. The first principle, which relates to how feedback is conducted, can be paraphrased, "I can't tell you how you are, and you can't tell me what I see." In other words, the person giving the feedback is responsible to relate the situation as he or she observes it, and the person receiving the feedback is responsible for relating what he or she meant, felt, or thought. The second principle is that feedback supports growth. Let's define what is meant by "I can't tell you how you are, and you can't tell me what I see."

22.16.7.1.1. **Receiving Feedback**: "You Can't Tell Me How I Am."

22.16.7.1.1.1. From the recipient's viewpoint, the first principle is "You can't tell me how I am, and I can't tell you what you see." Although most people realize that giving feedback correctly requires skill and awareness, they are less aware of the importance of knowing how to receive feedback. When receiving feedback, many people tend to argue about, disown, or attempt to justify the information. Statements like "I didn't say that," "That's not what I meant," and "You don't understand what I was trying to do," are attempts to convince the person giving the feedback that he or she didn't see or observe what he or she claims. However, the recipient needs to understand that the observer, whether manager, peer, or subordinate, is relating what he or she experienced as a result of the recipient's behavior. There is nothing wrong with the giver and receiver having different viewpoints. The purpose of feedback is to give a new view or to increase awareness. If an argument ensues and the observer backs down, the recipient is the loser.

22.16.7.1.2. **Giving Feedback:** "You Can't Tell Me What I See."

22.16.7.1.2.1. The object of giving feedback is not to judge the other person, but to report what was seen and heard and what the effects of the behavior were. Personal approval or disapproval, even if important, is secondary.

22.16.7.1.2.2. Feedback should be given directly to the person for whom it is intended. When others are present, the manager sometimes addresses them almost to the exclusive of the intended recipient, who sits quietly and gathers information by eavesdropping. Good contact with the recipient is an essential element in giving feedback.

22.16.7.1.2.3. Never apologize for giving corrective feedback. Corrective or otherwise, feedback is a gift; apologies will discount the importance and lessen the impact. Nevertheless, corrective feedback must be given in a way that does not jeopardize the recipient's dignity and sense of self-worth.

22.16.7.1.2.4. To offer an interpretation of the behavior or a hunch about what the behavior might indicate is sometimes more helpful. Crucially important is to offer the interpretation as a suggestion and never as a judgment or clinical evaluation of the person. Only the recipient is capable of putting it into a meaningful context. For example, the manager might say, "When Pete showed you the error you made; you told him it was none of his concern. I wonder if you were mad at Pete for some other reason." This statement shows the recipient the behavior and allows him or her to consider a possible cause for that behavior.

22.16.7.1.2.5. The appropriate response, as a rule of thumb, is to say "thank you" when either type of feedback is received. Also appropriate of course is to ask for clarity or more detail on an issue.

22.16.7.1.2.6. The purpose of feedback is to help the recipient. Feedback can be thought of as food which is very nourishing. When people are hungry, food is what they need. But when they are full, food is the last thing they want or need. The same applies to ingesting feedback. When people have had enough, they should call a halt. Attempting to absorb all the feedback that might be available, or that various people would like to give, is like forcing food into a full stomach just because someone says, "Please have some more."

22.16.7.1.2.7. The recipient is responsible for demanding specificity in feedback. No feedback should be accepted as legitimate if it cannot be clearly demonstrated by an observable behavior. For example, if someone says, "You're very arrogant," an appropriate response would be "What specifically have I said or done to cause you to think that?" If that response is countered with "I don't know; I just experience you that way," then the accusation should be immediately forgotten. People cannot afford to change just to meet everyone's personal likes or expectations.

22.16.7.1.2.8. In fact, what is impossible is to change to meet everyone's expectations, and the situation becomes compounded as more and more people give their feedback. A single act can generate disparate feedback from different people who observe the behavior. For example, a loud exclamation could be viewed as appropriately angry by one person, overly harsh by another, and merely uncouth by a third. Each person will see it from his or her unique perspective. Therefore, feedback requires action from both the giver and the receiver. Only the giver can tell what he or she observed or experienced, and only the recipient can use the information in deciding whether or not to change the behavior.

22.16.7.1.2.9. For feedback to be effective, the receiver must hear what the giver is saying, weigh it, and then determine whether or not the information is relevant. The following example illustrates how this can be done.

**Department manager:** "Waste in your unit is up by four percent. Are you having any problems with your employees?"

**Supervisor:** "I was not aware of the waste increase. No, I am not having trouble with my employees. I suppose I have been focusing on the quality so much that I lost sight of the waste figures. Thanks for bringing this to my attention."

22.16.7.2. **Feedback Supports Growth.** The second major principle, "feedback supports growth," is important because we cannot always see ourselves as others see us. Although an individual may be the world's foremost authority on himself or herself, there are still parts of the individual that are more obvious to other people. Although people may be more aware of their own needs and capabilities and more concerned about their own welfare than other people are, they are able to stretch themselves and grow if they pay attention to feedback from others. Although feedback may be extremely uncomfortable at the time, the individual can look back later and realize the feedback was the spark that inspired the change that turned his or her career or personal life in a different direction. If the feedback is not rejected or avoided, recipients can discover and develop ways to work that they did not think were available.

22.16.8. **Feedback Strategies:**

22.16.8.1. The strategies suggested here are not step-by-step procedures to be blindly followed. Their purpose is to help in planning and organizing an approach to deal with an issue. They offer a logical and effective sequence of events for the feedback session. The person planning the session must decide on the desired future objective. (The future, however, could be five minutes after the session or two years later.) During the feedback session, attention must be focused on what is happening in terms of the outcome. That is, the focus must be on obtaining the goal, not on sticking to the strategy. This focus allows the giver to change tactics or even modify the original strategy if conditions change or unforeseen events occur. After the strategy is selected, the following three rules should be kept in mind:

22.16.8.1.1. Be clear about what you want in terms of specific, identifiable outcomes for yourself, your subordinate, and the organization.

22.16.8.1 2. Plan what you intend to say and how you intend to conduct the meeting, according to the particular strategy you will use.

22.16.8.1.3. Have the strategy in mind as you engage the individual, but keep it in the background.

22.16.8.2. **Supportive Feedback Strategy.** The following steps are suggested as a strategy for supportive feedback:

22.16.8.2.1. **Acknowledge the specific action to be reinforced.** Immediately let the subordinate know that you are pleased about something he or she did. Be specific and describe the event in behavioral terms. "You finished the project (action) on time (result)."

22.16.8.2.2. **Explain the effects of the accomplishment and state your appreciation.** For the behavior to be reinforced, the person must be able to see the effects of that behavior in specific, observable ways. Your appreciation is important, but as an additional reinforcing element. The main reinforcement is the effect. "It was a major factor in securing the contract (effect), and I am pleased with your outstanding work (appreciation)."

22.16.8.2.3. **Help the subordinate to take full responsibility for the success.** If the employee acknowledges the feedback, this step is accomplished. If the employee seems overly modest, more work is needed. Unless he or she can, to some degree, internalize the success and receive satisfaction from it, very little growth will occur. One approach would be to ask how the success was accomplished or if any problems were encountered and how they were overcome. In talking about what happened, the employee is likely to realize how much he or she was really responsible for. What is important is for both you and the employee to hear how the success was accomplished.

22.16.8.2.4. **Ask if the subordinate wants to talk about anything else.** While the employee is feeling positive and knows that you are appreciative and receptive, he or she may be willing to open up about other issues. The positive energy created by this meeting can be directed toward other work related issues, so take advantage of the opportunity.

22.16.8.2.5. **Thank the subordinate for the good performance.** The final step, again thanking the subordinate for the accomplishment, assures that your appreciation will be uppermost in his or her mind as he or she leaves and returns to the work setting.

22.16.9. **Corrective Feedback Strategy.** The following steps are suggested as a strategy for corrective feedback.

22.16.9.1. **Immediately describe the event in behavioral terms and explain the effect.** Clearly relate in specific, observable, and behavioral terms the nature of the failure or behavior and the effect of the failure or behavior on the work group or organization. If you can appropriately say something to reduce the employee's embarrassment, the employee is more likely to accept the feedback non-defensively.

22.16.9.2. **Ask what happened.** Before assuming that the subordinate is at fault, ask what happened. In many instances, the subordinate is not at fault or is only partially responsible. At worst, the employee is given an opportunity to explain before you proceed; at best, you may receive information that would prevent you from censuring the employee.

22.16.9.3. **Help the subordinate to take full responsibility for the actions.** The more time spent in step 2 (finding out what happened), the easier step 3 will be. The subordinate needs to learn from the experience in order to reduce the probability of a reoccurrence. Unless this step is handled effectively, the subordinate will see himself or herself as a victim, rather than as someone who made a mistake and is willing to correct it.

22.16.9.4. **Develop a plan to deal with the issues.** Once the subordinate has accepted responsibility, the next step is to help rectify the situation. Now that the employee is willing to be accountable for errors, you can collaboratively devise a plan that will help eliminate them. That is, both of you must agree to take action. If you each want the same thing, such as better performance from the subordinate, then both of you are obligated to do something about it. This is also an excellent opportunity to build on the subordinate's strengths (e.g., "I'd like for you to show the same fine attention to safety regulations that you show to job specifications.")

22.16.9.5. **State your confidence in the subordinate's ability**. Once the issue is resolved, end the session by stating your confidence in the ability of the employee to handle the situation. The object is to allow the subordinate to reenter the work setting feeling as optimistic about his or her self as the situation permits. The subordinate must also understand that you will follow up and give additional feedback when the situation warrants.

## 22.17. Conclusion.

Remember, the concept of power in the workforce usually has a negative connotation. It brings to mind such associations as coercion, manipulation, and even corruption. This does not have to be the case. Power has many positive aspects, and everyone can learn to explore and harness different sources of the individual power they have in the workplace. Develop your own sources of power, and employees will be less dependent on others for the leadership they need. Thus, if you want to do more good for yourself and more good for the people around you, it is important to learn how to tap into your own points of power.

**Chapter 23**

**CRITICAL THINKING AND DECISION-MAKING**

*Section 23A—Overview*

**23.1. Introduction:**

23.1.1. Effective Airmanship requires good decision-making. From Airman Basic to General the decisions each of us make every day impact the delivery of airpower. The following chapter is designed to spur development of critical thinking habits in our Airmen and deepen their awareness of the decision-making processes. The habits of mind necessary to become a critical thinker are developed over time; there is no magical process or checklist to follow. Each of us must work every day to make good decisions by consciously applying the intellectual analysis necessary to account for complexities not normally considered and often overlooked.

> *The process of decision-making is as important as the information analyzed. The trap many of us fall into is focusing on the decision, not how the decision should be made.*

23.1.2. Decisions are made by individuals acting alone, in groups, or on behalf of organizations, each of these levels of decision-making present a variety of challenges. The following discussion is intended to highlight these challenges and make you aware of the conscious and unconscious challenges to applying good habits of mind (critical thought) as Airmen every day.

*Section 23B—Critical Thinking and Human Nature*

**23.2. Cognitive Bias:**

23.2.1. In thinking about problems we are seldom the perfectly rational actor we hope to be. Instead we are influenced by a number of factors that shape how we interpret information, weigh its relevance, and ultimately decide upon a course of action or inaction as the situation dictates. Psychologists use the term *bounded rationality* to describe the actual operating state of the human mind. What this means is that we are unable to be comprehensive in our gathering and analysis of information as decision-making models assume. Instead of being truly rational, and making the best possible decision, we end up '*satisficing.*'

23.2.2. Cognitive bias in our decision processes result in several 'traps' decision-makers need to guard against. Some of the more common are:

23.2.2.1. **Overconfidence bias.** Humans are overconfident in their own judgments, often unreasonably so.

23.2.2.2. **Sunk-cost effect.** The tendency to escalate commitment to a course of action you have already made a substantial investment or resources in (time, money, personnel, etc.) despite poor performance.

23.2.2.3. **Availability bias.** Tendency to place too much emphasis on information we have available instead of the information we need during decision-making.

23.2.2.4. **Confirmation bias.** The most prevalent bias, this propensity refers to our tendency to gather and use information that confirms our existing views while downplaying or avoiding information that challenges our working hypothesis.

23.2.2.5. **Anchoring bias.** The unconscious tendency to allow an initial reference point to distort our estimates, even when that initial reference point is completely arbitrary. Starting at an extreme position may act as an anchor for all parties in a decision process or negotiation. In a negotiation, this bias can work in favor of the side that stakes out the initial reference point—both sides tend to use the initial position as a reference point for the solution (i.e. car salesman techniques).

23.2.2.6. **Illusory bias.** Tendency to jump to conclusions about the relationship between two variables when in fact no relationship (correlation) exists.

23.2.2.7. **Hindsight bias.** The tendency to judge past events as easily predictable when in fact they were not easily foreseen. This bias limits our ability to learn from past mistakes and may affect how leaders evaluate subordinate decision-making.

23.2.2.8. **Egocentrism.** When we attribute more credit to ourselves for group or collaborative outcome than an outside party making an unbiased assessment would.

23.2.3. As decision makers Airmen need to be aware of cognitive biases and consciously take steps to guard against their affects. The habitual application of critical thinking methods to the gathering and analysis of information helps reduce our unconscious and natural tendency to satisfice in decision-making. Some techniques to counter cognitive biases include:

23.2.3.1. **After-action reviews** provide powerful learning moments for participants and serve as a forum for feedback to the decision maker about his/her decision style – helping to prevent repetition of mistakes.

23.2.3.2. **Seeking unbiased outside expert input** can help provide a check and balance on reasoning and the interpretation of available information.

23.2.3.3. **Creating a decision environment encouraging candid dialogue** and vigorous debate is perhaps the most effective way to minimize the influence of cognitive bias.

## 23.3. Mental Frames:

23.3.1. Each of us uses mental frameworks and shortcuts to simplify our understanding of a complex world. The use of these frameworks helps us process information quickly and efficiently. Understanding that these frameworks contribute to the bias presented earlier, the following discussion is intended to make you aware of how the frameworks you have built, based on your own unique personal experiences; these experiences shape your own decision-making process and the solutions you derive.

23.3.2. Frames consist of our assumptions about how things are related and how they work. How we frame a problem influences the decisions we make. This effect is particularly noticeable when framing a challenge as either a risk or an opportunity. Research shows that the human mind estimates the expected return when confronted with a risky situation and that we tend to be risk adverse. Our risk aversion and the importance of framing are explained in Prospect Theory.

## 23.4. Prospect Theory.

According to the *Prospect Theory,* framing a situation as a potential gain causes decision makers to act differently than framing same situation as a potential loss. Faced with potential losses most people are willing to take greater risks than when facing with potential gains. The Prospect Theory helps explain our tendency to escalate commitment based on sunk costs instead of making rational evaluations based on how things exist today. Based on sunk cost arguments, leaders often take-on more and more risk, committing additional resources in order to avoid losses even when the chances of success are low.

## 23.5. Risk or Opportunity.

Another implication of framing is how organizations react when faced with changes in the operating environment or mission tasking. At the organizational level, threats to our comfortable framework of assumptions are often met with rigid resistance while changes we see as opportunities are met with flexible and adaptable approaches. Often inaccurate expectations are established as a result of mental frames applied by decision makers. As human beings Airmen are subject to the initial frameworks we establish when confronting change. For good or bad these frameworks act to limit the information we take in, our willingness to fairly and unbiasedly assess information, and ultimately restrict the solution sets we create.

## 23.6. Intuition:

23.6.1. When decision makers use intuition to choose courses of action they are not evaluating a whole series of alternatives and are not selecting solutions based on objective analysis. Intuition is based on previous experience, and matching patterns from these experiences, to cues picked up in the current environment. As patterns are recognized, humans automatically reason by analogy, projecting past situations into our current environment. Based on recognition of patterns, decision makers often select a course of action as if reading a script, instead of exploring a wide range of options. Having decided on an initial preferred course of action, senior leaders often mentally play out the solution; and if it seems feasible, they go with it. For decision makers, intuition is both a powerful guide and a potential decision trap.

23.6.2. When operating in challenging or ambiguous situations, highly experienced professionals often have intuitive reactions to events. Although unable to articulate their unconscious pattern recognition, experts are often correct in their analysis and selection of a course of action despite what a novice may perceive as a lack of information or signals pointing to a contrary course of action. In highly complex and ambiguous situations, however, the complexity obscures pattern recognition and experienced Airmen can mistakenly apply incorrect or outdated models, resulting in poor decision-making. This is especially true when decision makers are operating outside of their experience base, for instance, when leading higher-level organizations or moving from one career field to another.

### 23.7. Key Points to Remember:

23.7.1. Airmen, especially leaders within any organization, must be careful about imposing mental frames on themselves and their team in order to create an environment where critical thinking is exercised. When leaders hold back personal opinions they avoid framing the situation in preconceived ways (that constricts the range of advice and alternatives offered). By consciously avoiding the natural tendency to view change as threatening, intentionally framing change as an opportunity, Airmen are free to exercise the habits of mind necessary to make well informed decisions.

23.7.2. A challenge for Airmen in a position of responsibility is to avoid the human tendency to continue a course of action due to sunk costs; proper use of combined intuitive judgment and formal analysis is one means for avoiding this decision trap. The use of analysis to check intuition is an effective decision-making technique. Formal analysis can check intuition and assures you challenge your intuitive judgment, not confirm it. Conversely, intuition is useful in validating and testing the assumptions that underlie analysis. As Airmen, recognizing the value of intuition is just as critical as guarding against a lack of analysis in the decision-making process. Do not try to replace intuition with rules and procedures; intuition is often compressed experience indicating as of yet unrecognized patterns in the environment. Airmen must routinely and consciously create decision processes with information flowing freely in both directions.

23.7.3. A simple five-step process for communicating intuitive decisions, seeking feedback, and conveying intent is to use the following statements when addressing decision teams:

23.7.3.1. Here's what I think we face.

23.7.3.2. Here's what I think we should do.

23.7.3.3. Here's why.

23.7.3.4. Here's what we should keep our eye on.

23.7.3.5. Now, talk to me.

### 23.8. Analogies:

23.8.1. Analogies are very powerful decision-making tools and often the greatest innovative breakthroughs occur when analogies from one field or domain are applied to others. Reasoning by analogy occurs when we assess a situation and match it to similar experiences we have encountered, assuming that they are alike. At the conscious level, Airmen can deliberately use analogies to frame a decision-making process; they save time and provide clues about possible courses of action and implications, at the unconscious level analogies play a large role in intuition as discussed in the previous section.

23.8.2. The critical thinking trap inherent in the use of analogies is that they can lead us to focus on similarities between events and downplay important differences. Very powerful experiences from our past leave us overly reliant on very salient analogies, even when they no longer fit current situation; thus, blinding Airmen to the requirement to explore and question underlying assumptions.

23.8.3. In order to avoid the temptation to focus on similarities and downplay differences decision makers and their teams should consciously make two lists: one describing similarities and the other describing differences. A second technique is to write down and clearly define what you know, what is unknown, and what you presume about the situation you are analyzing. The objective of both these techniques is to clearly separate fact from assumption and then probe your presumptions carefully. The act of questioning our assumptions in any decision process is, at its heart, how we apply the habits of mind necessary for good critical thought.

### Section 23C—Critical Thinking in Groups

### 23.9. Wisdom of Groups:

23.9.1. Conventional wisdom holds that groups make better decisions than individuals because they draw from a diverse base of talent and experience. Unfortunately, many groups fail to make good decisions because they fail to merge the diverse ideas and recognize potential synergies; the result is a failure to capitalize on the team's diverse talents. When this happens teams can actually make worse decisions than a talented individual. Airmen must be conscious of how group decisions are made and create teams capable of applying critical thought to problems in a group setting.

23.9.2. Airmen engaged in the group decision-making must consciously structure the process to encourage critical thinking. Leaders must begin by deciding:

23.9.2.1. Who should be involved in the decision process?

23.9.2.2. In what sort of environment does the decision take place?

23.9.2.3. How will the participants communicate?

29.9.2.4. How will the leader control the decision process?

23.9.3. Unfortunately, due to bias, a lack of time, framing, personnel shortages, outside pressure, or any number of other reasons leaders often fail to decide 'how to decide?' Instead, they rely on existing decision processes and groups, even though they may be unreliable given the context of the issue.

23.9.4. Some argue that groups are more intelligent than individual experts because the aggregation of their judgment leads to a better answer, even though they are not a group of experts. In some cases this is true, but it is not a given. Several critical preconditions are necessary. To be effective groups of non-experts must:

23.9.4.1. Be diverse.

23.9.4.2. Represent many different disciplines, perspectives, and areas of expertise.

23.9.4.3. Be decentralized.

23.9.4.4. Be able to effectively aggregate all the individual judgments.

23.9.4.5. Contain members who are independent (most important).

23.9.5. Within groups, information-processing problems can prevent the pooling of collective knowledge. Group members tend to discuss areas of common information while failing to surface privately held information for personal reasons or a failure to recognize its importance. Airmen, because of our shared heritage and commitment to teamwork must constantly guard against the trap of ignoring information in an effort to find common ground. Even when data is widely discussed and analyzed, the filtering of data as it moves up the decision chain can prevent decision makers from having access to the nuances of these discussions during the decision process. If as an Airmen you are in positions to make decisions based on the recommendations of groups you should be aware of how the group was set-up and operated and make an effort to understand the decision-making process they used.

23.9.6. **Wisdom of Groups Conclusion.**

Things to be aware of when forming a decision-making team:

23.9.6.1. Individuals must be able to sway others in the crowd, a condition that is often lacking in the organizational decision-making environment.

23.9.6.2. Interdependence and hierarchy of group members can neutralize the benefits group decisions.

23.9.6.3. Pressure to conform and fractionalization of groups into sub groups can prevent honest analysis.

23.9.6.4. The tendency of some individuals to dominate the discussions can inhibit less aggressive members from presenting their ideas, especially if these ideas are call into question the prevailing wisdom of the dominant personalities.

23.9.6.5. Conversely, members that do not feel personally accountable for the group's outcomes may 'free ride' by not presenting their ideas, content to allow others to 'carry the load'.

**23.10.** *Groupthink (Thinking or Conforming):*

23.10.1. *Groupthink* is a well-known decision trap most of us are familiar with—and a major reason groups make flawed decisions. *Groupthink* occurs when tremendous pressures within the team for conformity and a desire for unanimity drive decision-making at the expense of true critical thinking. Without candid dialogue between team members, and real assessment of options, groups tend to spend most of their time tweaking proposed solutions rather than examining evidence and assumptions to create new options. Many factors contribute to groupthink, including the homogeneity of the group, reporting and supervisory chains, and permanent versus long-term nature of the groups involved.

23.10.2. Within groups, especially long standing groups, individuals often self-sensor based on a desire to avoid becoming ostracized and marginalized. As a result, a fallacy develops within the team; each member erroneously believes the other team members unanimously support a decision or course of action, making it harder to present dissenting opinions. If alternative options were previously examined and dismissed, they are rarely reconsidered based on new information or changes in the decision environment.

23.10.3. To avoid group think Airmen must be aware of the below symptoms of *Groupthink*:

23.10.3.1. The group has a feeling of being invulnerable (it cannot fail).

23.10.3.2. Inherent belief that the group is better than rivals (cultural egocentric thought, stereotyping).

23.10.3.3. Rationalization away of disconfirming data and warning signs.

23.10.3.4. The group has a feeling of being unanimous in support for particular views.

23.10.3.5. Majority pressuring those with dissenting views.

23.10.3.6. Group member's self-sensor rather than challenge majority perspective to avoid becoming ostracized or marginalized.

## 23.11. Groupthink Conclusion:

23.11.1. For some decision events, outside consultation may be the only way to avoid groupthink. In other cases, Airmen can work to minimize structural barriers to candid dialogue and reduce groupthink tendencies within their organization.

23.11.1.1. Reduce structural complexity and the information filtering that occurs because of internal organizational barrier and interest groups.

23.11.1.2. Defining roles within decision-making teams, giving responsibility to members for aspects of the analysis process and holding them accountable for representing these perspectives within the group.

23.11.1.3. Reducing homogeneity of team composition to bring in alternative perspectives.

23.11.1.4. Reduce status difference and rating chain conflicts between team members that might squelch candid dialogue.

23.11.1.5. Invite disagreement during the analysis process; a failure to do so will squelch candid dialogue.

## 23.12. Debate and Conflict:

23.12.1. Disagreement between participants in any decision process is necessary to stimulate inquiry and analysis. The challenge for leaders in any decision process is to create constructive conflict while retaining the teamwork and relationships necessary for future decision events. In the decision-making process, debate focused on the issues and ideas at hand (*cognitive conflict*) is constructive; on the other hand, emotional and personal outbursts (*affective conflict*) are not.

23.12.2. A key aspect of managing the decision process is to stimulate *cognitive conflict* to advocate positions and analysis—debating concepts, but not attacking the person representing them. Airmen in leadership positions should clearly establish ground rules for interaction during deliberations and require participants to respect each other's cognitive and analytical styles.

## 23.13. Critical Thinking in Groups Conclusion:

23.13.1. Decision makers must ensure they are not structuring their decision process to minimize conflict at the expense of critical thinking. Leaders set the example by: identifying and articulating the mental models they apply, encouraging others to challenge these models, avoiding prematurely selecting courses of action before debate is finished, and encouraging others to make mistakes. In other words, professional debate is constructive, unprofessional personalization of debate is not. Without adhering to the levels of professionalism expected of Airmen we squelch the critical thinking necessary to innovate and ensure good decision-making.

23.13.2. Some techniques include assigning members to act as adversaries; and/or to advocate multiple scenarios address the problem. These techniques give participants the responsibility to provide contrary perspectives and use varying lenses for information analysis. Dissenters must be encouraged to try to persuade other team members, not senior leadership; this practice stimulates debate and forces critical thinking. However, if employed, senior leaders must guard against the temptation to domesticate dissenters, using them as token "devils advocates."

## Section 23D—Critical Thinking and Organizational Culture

## 23.14. The Inability to Decide.

Many leaders and organizations are plagued by chronic and persistent indecision. Indecision resulting from dysfunctional patterns of behavior manifests itself as one of three harmful organizational cultures: (1) culture of 'no'; (2) culture of 'yes'; and 3) culture of 'maybe.'

23.14.1. **Culture of no.** Organizations with a culture of no have established a decision process where lone dissenters are able to issue non-concurs within the planning process, effectively blocking overall organizational goals because they conflict with internal sub-organizational interests. This culture can arise in organizations where decision meetings focus on dissections of proposals instead of true debate and analysis. Leaders who reward subordinates based on their ability to dissect others ideas without providing alternative courses of action enable and promote a culture of no. Do not forget the importance of being able to differentiate between the use of a "devil's advocate" and the culture of no. In a culture of no, dissenters are trying to tear down or block proposals and ideas, not critique a proposal with the intent of strengthening it.

23.14.2. **Culture of yes.** Within a culture of yes, dissenters tend to stay silent. This silence becomes a tacit endorsement of the proposal without the benefit of analysis and debate. In this form of organizational culture, once a decision is made subordinates later express disagreement to distance themselves from a decision or work to overturn or undermine the implementation of the plan. Airmen operating in this type of culture must understand that silence does not mean assent and watch for those not contributing to the discussion. This type of culture can develop when leadership devalues critical analysis. Overcoming this cultural tendency requires leadership to create constructive conflict within the decision process to surface and analyze concerns and alternative interpretations of evidence.

23.14.3. **Culture of maybe.** Under the culture of maybe, decision makers work to gather as much information as possible, so much so they become trapped in "*analysis paralysis*." Under *analysis paralysis*, decision makers constantly delay action because they think more information and analysis will clarify their choice. This culture tends to develop in organizations facing highly ambiguous situations; or in organizations where competing sections/leaders practice conflict avoidances as opposed to open analysis and debate. In these organizations, decision makers must balance the benefit of gaining more information against the diminishing returns they provide (as opposed to initiating action). While leaders are seldom able to accurately calculate the cost versus benefit of waiting for additional clarity, intuitive judgment serves as a cut-off for unnecessary delay.

23.14.4. **Procedural Justice:**

23.14.4.1. The process by which a decision is made significantly influences implementation and follow-through of the solution. The key aspect to outcome of a critical decision is consensus among the team responsible for enactment. Consensus does not mean unanimity—rather, consensus is a commitment to, and shared understanding of, the desired outcome.

23.14.4.2. Sections above discussed the need for debate and conflict in applying true critical thinking to decisions—and the challenge of keeping the debate constructive. Airmen must also work to make sure the process is fair and legitimate. Even when participants agree with the chosen course of action, if they do not see the process as legitimate they are often disenchanted with the outcome. Procedural fairness provides support to decision makers, especially when they are making unpopular decisions.

23.14.4.3. Fair processes helps build consensus. More importantly, they aid implementation because participants feel that all perspectives have been considered and analyzed. If decision-makers are subjective in their analysis, participants lose faith in the decision process, making it difficult to support the outcome. Providing participants with time and venues to air positions, and a transparent system of weighing different perspectives, is important. In essence, fair process means that the decision maker demonstrates genuine consideration of alternatives. This does not mean debate continues endlessly. When final decisions are made the fairness of the process is what allows Airmen arguing for various positions to rally around the designated way ahead with confidence that the decision maker considered all aspects before making the decision on which course of action to pursue.

23.14.4.4. Procedural legitimacy in decision-making occurs when the decision process is perceived to be in line with an organization's socially accepted norms and desired behavior. Airmen in leadership positions must avoid artificially limiting debate and analysis of information. In order to create an organizational culture of decision legitimacy leaders can do the following:

23.14.4.1. Provide a process road map at the beginning of the decision process.

23.14.4.2. Reinforce and demonstrate an open mind-set.

23.14.4.3. Engage in active listening and make sure others do too.

23.14.4.4. Separate advocacy from analysis.

23.14.4.5. Explain the decision rationale once made.

23.14.4.6. Express appreciation for everyone's participation and how alternative inputs contributed to the process.

23.14.5. **Normal Accidents and Normalizing Deviance.**

Within the United States Air Force, like any other organization decisions made in highly complex tightly integrated environments often have unanticipated consequence. If Airmen are unaware of, or have failed to think through decisions catastrophic failure can be the result. With the understanding of the role all Airmen play in using the habits of mind for critical thinking provided above, the following sections examine two perspectives on decision-making failure—one structural; the other behavioral (Normal Accident Theory, Normalized Deviance).

### 23.14.6. Normal Accident Theory:

23.14.6.1. This theory rests upon the assumption that in any highly complex high-risk organizational structure decision failures are unavoidable. High-risk systems are systems classified by their complexity and the coupling of multiple processes occurring in conjunction with one another. Systems that are interactively complex and tightly coupled are particularly vulnerable to catastrophic failure stemming from mistakes made by decision makers, often small mistakes, which go unrecognized or uncorrected and increasingly skew outcomes as they work their way through the system.

23.14.6.2. In coupled systems tight interactions based on poor decisions can magnify normal accidents into system-wide failure. In simple linear processes, such as an assembly line, failure has a visible impact on the next process but is identifiable and limited. When interactions are nonlinear and affect a variety of other systems, the failure of one component has unanticipated effects on many subsystems. If the subsystems are tightly coupled (highly interdependent) a failure quickly causes changes in multiple systems nearly simultaneously making it hard for leaders to diagnose the symptoms and see the extent of the developing failure. Because Airmen project power globally, anticipation of the impact even minor deviations from procedure or instruction can have is extremely challenging. This is the reason we stress adherence to standard operating procedures and Airmen must apply the habits of critical thinking before deviation from our normal operations – others are counting on our predictability to do their job safely as we work together to advance United States security interests.

### 23.14.7. Normalizing Deviance:

23.14.7.1. This is the gradual acceptance of unexpected events and risk as a normal part of the operating environment. Eventually the deviations are accepted as a normal occurrence and no longer assessed using the habits of mind necessary to identify causes and find solutions. As organizational members become accustomed to the reoccurrence of seemingly minor but unpredicted anomalies in a system they become less concerned with the potential catastrophic effect of more severe failures of the same systems. The classic case is the *Challenger* space shuttle disaster. In this case, the erosion of O-rings was not within acceptable tolerances. However, after its occurrence several times with no catastrophic result, the members of the organization accepted their erosion as a normal and acceptable event, despite deviation from their engineering standards. In this case National Aeronautics and Space Administration, as an organization, was working hard to make space flight feel routine. The organization's culture, combined with cognitive bias and external pressures to make space flight routine led do the normalization of a potentially catastrophic failure.

23.14.7.2. Normalization of deviance is the gradual acceptance of lower standards of performance. This practice produces shortcuts in the way organizations act. These variations then become normal procedures—normalized to the point where the deviance is no longer even noticed. As Airmen we should not accept this practice, we guard against this by continuously questioning the way we do business and digging into any failure to meet the standards we set for performance.

23.14.7.3. Airmen must be aware of the type of organization they operate within and understand its complex interactions. They must consciously identify the "close-calls" and deviances from normal operations. All Airmen must ensure deviations from standards are analyzed as part of the decision-making process to gain an understanding of how to improve programs and implement new decisions.

### 23.14.8. Practical Drift and Ambiguity:

23.14.8.1. **Practical Drift.** Within large organizations, sub-unit leaders at all levels make decisions to maximize efficiency. They establish localized rules and procedures that comply with the overall intent of the organization. Over time these procedures become accepted practice. Similar to *Normalizing Deviance* (discussed above), this practice causes organizational norms to drift. Often, this drift is unproblematic—however, under ambiguous conditions in complex interactive environments, divergence may lead to altered expectations and poor information flow (resulting in catastrophic cross-system failure; e.g. Blackhawk shoot down).

23.14.8.2. Airmen must be aware of how their decisions at the local level tie in with overall organizational goals, standards, and expectations. Leaders must use their awareness of organizational goals and standards to monitor *practical drift* in their areas of responsibility, recognizing disciplined initiative, while maintaining standards consistent with outside expectations. This task becomes difficult when many sub-units work together. Communications breakdowns across large organizations often cause a loss of perspective on how *practical drift* may be creating problems with follow-on unforeseen consequences.

23.14.8.3. The challenge for Airmen of all ranks is that ambiguous threats do not trigger organizational responses. The failure to apply critical thinking to ambiguous threats means that the recovery window between the emergence of the threat and its occurrence as a catastrophic failure may narrow. National Aeronautics and Space

Administration's organizational culture caused leaders to downplay O-ring failure, moving it from a critical to an ambiguous threat. Airmen at all levels must be aware that ambiguous threats may go unaddressed due to information filters caused by structural complexity and inter-organization power dynamics.

23.14.8.4. Airmen in positions of responsibility must work to temper *practical drift* and create a culture where critical thinking is applied to ambiguous threats. This goal can be accomplished by developing processes for identifying and analyzing small problems and failures, treating them as potential indicators of larger problems. Effective techniques include: empowerment of front line troops/workers; and flattening hierarchies to reduce information filtering.

23.14.8.4.1. To further minimize the problems associated with *practical drift*, leaders can also:

23.14.8.4.2. Create and encourage transparency in organizational structures and systems to identify local *practical drift* and understand the "why" behind local standards.

23.14.8.4.3. Avoid '*band-aid*' approaches to small problems – fix the root cause across the system.

23.14.8.4.4. Create a climate of candid dialogue where you review and revisit standards and seek problems.

23.14.8.4.5. Monitor seams where information is handed off between units and organizations.

23.14.8.4.6. Conduct careful after-action reviews focused on process improvement.

## 23.15. Conclusion:

23.15.1. Airmen at all levels participate in decision-making daily. The habits of mind necessary to assure we apply critical thought are something we must consciously foster. Our diverse and highly educated force brings to the table a wide variety of views, experiences, and abilities; providing the United States Air Force a deep pool of talent to draw ideas from. By using the techniques of good decision-making and fostering the development of habits of mind in our Airmen we tap into that rich pool of talent. When time allows we must consciously create processes to think though decisions using critical analysis of all factors, ensuring we focus on doing what is best for the nation and the Air Force. This effort to create habits of mind pays off when we must make decisions quickly and under great pressure. During these times we naturally fall back on the decision-making processes we use every day.

23.15.2. In order to create these good habits of mind Airmen in leadership positions at all levels, from the back shop to the Air Staff, must create an environment where Airmen are free to exercise critical thought. We must guard against organizational cultures and leadership styles designed to simply arrive at a decision and quickly move on. Organizations and leaders focused on the decision, not the decision-making process tend to stifle critical analysis of issues and prevent development of good habits of mind; ultimately causing poor decision-making and negatively affecting the United States Air Force, the Department of Defense, and our nation.

**Chapter 24**

**STUDYING EFFECTIVELY**

*Section 24A—Overview*

**24.1. Introduction.**

Getting the most out of promotion studies is an individual affair. No method will produce the best results for every Airman. Lack of success may have more to do with poorly developed study skills than intellectual ability. This chapter suggests methods for effective studying, but each Airman must determine which methods and strategies work best for him or her. This chapter covers effective study habits, study strategies, the military knowledge and testing system, and a learning style self-assessment instrument to help Airmen prepare for promotion exams. This information is not testable for promotion.

*Section 24B—Effective Study Habits in Eight Easy Steps*

**24.2. General Information.**

Airmen grapple with many issues that may make it difficult to concentrate on studying. To get promoted, you must study for your Promotion Fitness Exam or United States Air Force Supervisory Exam. The key to effective studying is to study smartly. You can begin with these effective study habits.

24.2.1. **Approach Studying with the Right Mindset:**

24.2.1.1. Many people consider studying a necessary task, rather than an enjoyable opportunity to learn, but research indicates that how you approach a task is almost as important as the task itself. Having the right mindset may help you study more effectively.

24.2.1.2. Sometimes you can't force yourself to have the right mindset. During such times, you should take a study break. If you are distracted by other issues, studying will be an exercise in futility. Come back to it when you're not focused on something else.

24.2.1.3. How to improve your study mindset:

24.2.1.3.1. Decide to think positively while you study; remind yourself of your skills and abilities.

24.2.1.3.2. Avoid catastrophic thinking. Instead of thinking, "I'll never have enough time to study for this exam," think "It may be a little late to start studying, but if I do it now, I can still get most of it done."

24.2.1.3.3. Avoid absolute thinking. Instead of thinking "I always mess up," the more objective view is, "I didn't do very well last time. What can I do to improve?"

24.2.1.3.4. Avoid comparing yourself negatively with others.

24.2.2. **Bring Everything You Need; Nothing You Don't:**

24.2.2.1. When you find an ideal place to study, you may bring things you don't need. For example, it may seem ideal to type notes into a computer to refer to later, but computers are a powerful distraction for many people. So ask yourself if you really need a computer to take notes, or can you make do with the old-fashioned paper and pencil.

24.2.2.2. Don't forget the things you need to study for promotion (see the Enlisted Promotion Reference and Requirements catalog, https://www.omsq.af.mil/TE/EPRRC.pdf) to ensure you are studying the correct information. Don't waste time running back and forth to get an important book, paper, or other resource.

24.2.3. **Outline and Rewrite Your Notes.**

Many people find a standard outline format helps them boil information down to its most basic components, and connecting similar concepts makes information easier to remember during an exam. An outline is most effective as a learning tool when you use your own words and structure because everyone connects similar information differently. Failing to outline in your own style and words may result in failure to remember important items.

24.2.4. **Use Memory Games (Mnemonic Devices):**

20.2.4.1. Memory games, such as mnemonic devices, use simple word association to help remember pieces of information. Some people string together words to form an easy-to-remember nonsense sentence. The first letter of each word stands for a piece of the information you're trying to remember. A common military mnemonic device example is "Be My Little General of the Air Force." The first letters of the words help you remember the general officer ranks: Brigadier, Major, Lieutenant, and General.

24.2.4.2. The key to such memory devices is the new phrase or sentence you come up with has to be more memorable and easier to remember than the terms or information you're trying to learn. These don't work for everyone, so if mnemonics don't work for you, don't use them.

24.2.5. **Practice, Practice, Practice.**

The age-old adage "practice makes perfect" is true. You can practice by yourself using practice exams or flash cards (depending on what's available). If a practice exam isn't available, you can make one yourself. However, interactive exercises available at http://pdg.af.mil/ may help you retain information from Air Force Handbook 1, *Airman.* Whatever tools you use, practice can enhance your retention of general military knowledge in the Air Force Handbook 1, *Airman.*

24.2.6. **Make and Stick to a Schedule:**

20.2.6.1. Many people plan to study when they get around to it or have some spare time. If you schedule study time the same way your duty hours are scheduled, you'll find studying is less hassle in the long run. Instead of last-minute cramming sessions, scheduling the same amount of study time every day for 3 to 6 months before your promotion test will be easier and enable you to learn more of the material.

20.2.6.2. Some people study every day, others once or twice a week. Frequency isn't as important as actually studying routinely. Even if you study one day a week for 6 to 8 months, that is better than a massive cram session a few days before the exam.

24.2.7. **Build in Breaks and Rewards:**

20.2.7.1. If you view studying as a chore, it will be natural to avoid it. If, however, you use rewards to help reinforce what you're doing, you may be pleasantly surprised by an attitude change.

20.2.7.2. Start by breaking study time into manageable components. Studying for 4 hours at a time without a break is unrealistic for most people. Studying for an hour followed by a 5-minute break and a snack may be more sustainable and enjoyable for you. Divide study time into segments that make sense and work for you.

20.2.7.3. When establishing your goals, establish rewards as well. Tell yourself specifically what your reward will be if you reach your goal: Maybe "I will have a special dessert tonight if...," or "I will buy a new song online if...," or "I will spend an extra 30 minutes gaming if..." for reaching the established goal. The point is, find a reward that is small but real, and to stick to it. Setting limits on your behavior is a method to teach yourself discipline.

24.2.8. **Stay Healthy and Balanced:**

20.2.8.1. It may seem hard to live a balanced life, but the more balanced your life, the easier every component becomes. If you spend all of your time focused on one thing, your life may become unbalanced. When that happens, everything becomes more difficult.

20.2.8.2. Maintaining a balanced life comes more easily over time, but you can work to improve health and balance by doing what you already know: exercise regularly, eat nutritious food, and get enough sleep. There are no shortcuts to good health.

*Section 24C—Study Strategies*

**24.3. General Information.**

Whether you are studying for a promotion test, specialty knowledge test, or any other test, the following study strategies may help you attain your goals:

24.3.1. **Stay Motivated.**

Studying and learning can take you far in life, yet it can seem so hard to get around to it, and life's constant distractions don't help.

24.3.1.1. **Attention.** Distractions can affect your motivation to study. If you were totally isolated on a desert island, where there was absolutely nothing to do but study, you'd study every word of your subject until you were completely versed in it because there would be nothing to distract you. Having so many choices means—now more than ever—we need to exert willpower.

24.3.1.2. **What Do You Want Out of Life?** To stay motivated, you should think about why you are studying. Presumably, studying is connected to what you want out of life, so ask yourself what you will ultimately get out of those things you do to avoid studying. Your life will be what you make of it.

24.3.1.3. **Feed and Develop Your Mind.** We live in a world surrounded by entertainment options. However, your mind needs the nutrition of study as well as the relaxation of entertainment. When you study well, you find it has its own subtle pleasures and satisfactions apart from the positive results it can bring into your life.

24.3.2. **Use Time Wisely.**

You might have all the time in the world, but if you don't use it wisely, it won't help you to meet your goals. Procrastination is a problem for many students. The following tips may help you deal with this issue:

24.3.2.1. **Clear Your Schedule.** Recognize that your obligations are as important as other people's needs. Set limits to prevent or minimize interruptions. Give full concentration to your studies without feeling guilty for whatever you're not doing.

24.3.2.2. **Get Motivated.** Create a distraction-free work area, and commit to staying there for until you meet the day's study goal. If you get sidetracked, remind yourself how studying will help you achieve your goals.

24.3.2.3. **Prioritize.** Answers to these questions may help you establish a priority list: What must be done first? When is it due? What is worth more in terms of the score? What is worth more in terms of personal, educational or career goals?

24.3.2.4. **Use a Daily "To Do" List.** A "to do" list can help you reach your goals by helping you prioritize your daily tasks. As you complete tasks, check them off your list.

24.3.2.5. **Break Your Study into Chunks.** Estimate how much time you'll need to complete a task, and don't try to do it all at one time. Break it down so that it's achievable without being overwhelming.

24.3.2.6. **It Doesn't Have to Be Perfect.** Some people are so afraid they won't perform perfectly that they don't do anything at all. Make sure you understand your goals. Then evaluate how important your study is and what level of performance is acceptable to you. Then, just do it.

24.3.2.7. **When You Really Hate It, Do It First.** Work on a task you really hate first, while you have more energy. Reward yourself when you complete those items on your daily list.

24.3.3. **Study Environment.**

Once you know when and for how long you will study, commit to a time and place that meets your needs. Make that decision based on whether the environment matches your learning style. See Section 20E of this chapter for information to help you understand your dominant learning style. When establishing a study environment, consider:

24.3.3.1. **Time of Day.** If possible, schedule your most challenging courses and most intense study sessions when you are most alert. Determine if you feel more alert and productive during the morning, midday, or evening, and schedule accordingly.

24.3.3.2. **Posture and Mobility.** Some people prefer to sit at a table or desk (formal posture); others learn more easily sitting comfortably on a sofa or lying on the floor (informal); others need to move around when they study. Some people can sit and study for long periods of time (high persistence), while others need frequent breaks (low persistence). Recognize your posture and mobility needs when you to plan.

24.3.3.3. **Sound.** Not everyone needs to study in a perfectly quiet environment; if you like sound when you study, try to make it an environment where the kinds of sounds won't actually be distracters.

24.3.3.4. **Lighting.** Reading ability can be affected by the amount and type of lighting in your study area, and contrast between text and paper color. Be aware that light does make a difference, and choose a study environment that best matches your learning preferences.

24.3.3.5. **Temperature.** You may not be able to control the room temperature, but you should be aware of your temperature preferences and dress accordingly.

### 24.3.4. Set Goals:

24.3.4.1. **Be a Lifelong Learner.** Technological advances have occurred in exponential leaps over the past century, and the only certainty in life is change. Education is the key to preparing you for change. Your most valuable asset and skill is your ability to learn and apply knowledge gained through education.

24.3.4.2. **Setting Goals.** Setting goals is a good way to accomplish a particularly difficult task, such as developing study skills. Setting SMART goals will have you studying like a pro in no time. SMART goals are:

24.3.4.2.1. **Specific.** Once you identify what you want to work on, narrow that down to a single, specific thing. Working out one problem at a time may make it easier to reach your goal without spreading yourself too thin. "I want to be a better reader" is broad, so a more specific goal would be "I want to improve my reading speed." Write your specific goal on a piece of paper.

24.3.4.2.2. **Measurable.** You won't know if you met your goal if you cannot measure it in some way. For instance, instead of "I want to improve my reading speed," a measurable goal would be "I want to improve my reading speed by 10 words per minute."

24.3.4.2.3. **Action.** This is where you decide how to achieve your goal. Write this part as an explanatory activity. For example, your goal might now be "I want to improve my reading speed by 10 words a minute. I will do this by skimming over words like 'the' and 'an'."

24.3.4.2.4. **Realistic.** Make sure your goals are achievable. "I will improve my reading speed by memorizing every word in the dictionary" is unrealistic for most people. Everyone has limits (time, resources, ability, etc.). Do not ignore limits or you may set unrealistic goals.

24.3.4.2.5. **Timeline.** Set a suspense date, and make sure it is both specific and realistic for you. "I will meet this goal sometime over the summer" is vague. "I will meet this goal by the first day of school next fall," is specific and realistic. Your timeline may be days, months or years, but must be realistic for you and your lifestyle.

### Section 24D—Military Knowledge and Testing System (MKTS)

### 24.4. General Information.

The MKTS chart is critical to the Air Force promotion system. The chart is used to help guide the development of enlisted study guides to support the enlisted promotion system. Enlisted members should use the chart as a study strategy for the preparation of their promotion fitness exam or United States Air Force supervisory exam.

24.4.1. Every 2 years, members from the enlisted board of director's (CMSAF and major command chiefs) review the information contain within the study guides and rate the importance of the information and level of understanding for each promotion grade from Staff Sergeant to Chief Master Sergeant. The MKTS chart is provided to the subject-matter experts tasked to write the promotion fitness exam and United States Air Force supervisory exam.

24.4.2. The MKTS chart is located at attachment 1 of study guides. The MKTS chart also provides the opportunity to provide each enlisted grade a promotion study guide based on the information contained in the chart. These promotion study guides are available at www.studyguides.af.mil for download to prepare for promotion testing.

### Section 24E—Know Your Learning Style

### 24.5. Adult Learning Style Profile.

Adapted from Learning Style Form, developed by Dr. Ray Barsch; University of Northwestern Ohio Virtual College, Learning Styles Evaluation.

24.5.1. The statements in Figure 24.1 are designed to help an individual determine their learning style (visual, auditory, or tactile/kinesthetic). No learning style is better than any other. However, knowing your preferred learning style and tailoring your study sessions to that style will help you retain more of the material. Follow the directions in Figure 24.1 to begin discovering your preferred learning style.

**Figure 24.1. Learning Style Profile.**

**Directions:** Read each statement, and place a check mark in the appropriate box that best matches your feeling about that statement. Work quickly. Do not sit and ponder. There are no right or wrong answers. When finished follow the directions in Figure 24.2 for scoring instructions.

| COMMENTS | OFTEN | SOME-TIMES | SELDOM |
|---|---|---|---|
| 1. I remember things better when people tell them to me than when I read them. | | | |
| 2. I follow written directions better than oral directions. | | | |
| 3. I like to write things down or take notes for visual review. | | | |
| 4. I bear down extremely hard with pen or pencil when writing. | | | |
| 5. I require oral explanations of diagrams, graphs, or visual directions. | | | |
| 6. I enjoy working with tools (cooking, woodworking, mechanical). | | | |
| 7. I am skillful and enjoy developing and making graphs and charts. | | | |
| 8. I like to learn something new by talking rather than reading about it. | | | |
| 9. I remember best by writing things down several times. | | | |
| 10. I can understand and follow directions using maps. | | | |
| 11. I do better at academic subjects by listening to lectures and tapes. | | | |
| 12. I handle objects (coins, keys, pencils) while studying, reading, and conversing. | | | |
| 13. I learn to spell better by repeating the letters aloud, not by writing them. | | | |
| 14. I understand a news article better by reading it than by listening to the radio. | | | |
| 15. I chew gum, smoke, eat, or drink while studying/working. | | | |
| 16. I remember something best by picturing it in my head. | | | |
| 17. I like to make, build, or create things as I learn. | | | |
| 18. I would rather listen to a good lecture or speech than read about the subject. | | | |
| 19. I am good at working and solving jigsaw puzzles and mazes. | | | |
| 20. I prefer listening to news on the radio or TV rather than reading about it. | | | |
| 21. I like to learn mostly by building, making, or doing things. | | | |
| 22. I enjoy researching an interesting subject by reading relevant material. | | | |
| 23. I feel comfortable touching others, hugging, handshaking, etc. | | | |
| 24. I follow oral directions better than written directions. | | | |
| 25. I enjoy learning by going places and seeing things. | | | |
| 26. I like to draw, color, sketch, and paint things. | | | |
| 27. I doodle during meetings, lectures, or while listening on the phone. | | | |
| 28. I enjoy listening to music. | | | |
| 29. I like to shape or make things with my hands (clay, ceramics, dough, etc.). | | | |
| 30. I read aloud (or whisper) to myself when trying to understand new written material. | | | |

**Figure 24.2. Learning Style Score.**

Directions: Place the point value on the line next to its corresponding item number: OFTEN = 5 points; SOMETIMES = 3 points; SELDOM = 1 point. Total each column to arrive at your profile score under each heading. Arrange the column totals, from highest to lowest, on the lines below the column totals.

| AUDITORY | | VISUAL | | TACTILE | |
|---|---|---|---|---|---|
| Question # | Points | Question # | Points | Question # | Points |
| 1 | | 2 | | 4 | |
| 5 | | 3 | | 6 | |
| 8 | | 7 | | 12 | |
| 11 | | 9 | | 15 | |
| 13 | | 10 | | 17 | |
| 18 | | 14 | | 21 | |
| 20 | | 16 | | 23 | |
| 24 | | 19 | | 25 | |
| 28 | | 22 | | 27 | |
| 30 | | 26 | | 29 | |
| TOTAL: | | TOTAL: | | TOTAL: | |
| **Highest Modality:** _____ **Score:** _____ | | **Second Modality:** _____ **Score:** _____ | | **Lowest Modality:** _____ **Score:** _____ | |

24.5.2. A score that reads Visual = 33, Auditory = 24, Tactile = 19, indicates that you are a visual learner, with an auditory learning backup, and some tactile learning. Such people learn best by seeing something. If vision is obscured, visual learners can still learn through listening and tactile modes, but the major and best mode of learning unavailable.

24.5.3. A score that reads Auditory = 30, Visual = 27, Tactile = 20 indicates that you are an auditory learner, with a visual backup, and some tactile learning. Such people learn best by hearing or saying what needs to be learned. Auditory learners can learn by seeing the information, but their best retention occurs when they see the information and repeat it to themselves, or when they hear the material being read aloud. They may also learn very well using audio cassettes, compact disks, or digital media with retention and depth of learning enhanced by visual and tactile input.

24.5.4. A score that reads Tactile = 34, Visual = 27, Auditory = 27 indicates that you are a tactile learner, with auditory and visual backup learning modes. Such people learn best by doing. They may write material they see or hear, take notes during lectures but rarely need to look at them afterwards, or find it easier to recall information if they move around or have something in their hands.

**24.6. Auditory Learners.**

Auditory learners use hearing to process information. When given a choice, strong auditory learners will sit where they can easily hear the speaker and where outside sounds will not interfere. Some auditory learners will sit to one side, on the side of their strongest ear. Many auditory learners find it easy to understand the words from songs on the radio and announcements on public address systems.

24.6.1. **Characteristics:**

24.6.1.1. Prefer to hear information.

24.6.1.2. Have difficulty following written directions.

24.6.1.3. Have difficulty with reading and writing.

24.6.1.4. May not look a speaker in the eye; may turn their eyes away so they can focus on listening.

24.6.2. **Learning Tips:**

24.6.2.1. Use audio cassettes or compact discs for reading and lectures (when available).

24.6.2.2. Participate in discussions, ask questions, and repeat given information.

24.6.2.3. Summarize or paraphrase written material, and record the information.

24.6.2.4. Discuss the material with someone else.

**24.7. Visual Learners.**

Visual learners need to see the big picture. They may choose a seat where they can see the whole stage or the whole screen. They may choose the back seat in a room so everything is out in front, and they can see it all.

24.7.1. **Characteristics:**

24.7.1.1. Need to see it to learn it; must have a mental picture.

24.7.1.2. Have artistic ability.

24.7.1.3. Have difficulty with spoken directions.

24.7.1.4. Overreact to sounds.

24.7.1.5. Have trouble following lectures.

24.7.1.6. May misinterpret words.

24.7.2. **Learning Tips:**

24.7.2.1. Use visuals (graphics, films, slides, illustrations, doodles, charts, notes, flashcards) to reinforce learning.

24.7.2.2. Use multicolored highlighters to organize notes.

24.7.2.3. Write directions down.

24.7.2.4. Visualize words, phrases, sentences to be memorized.

24.7.2.5. Write everything down; review often.

**24.8. Tactile Learners.**

Tactile/kinesthetic learners need to touch and feel things. They want to feel or experience the lesson themselves. Given a choice, strong kinesthetic learners will be right in the middle of the action. They may take things apart to see how they work and put them back together, without directions.

24.8.1. **Characteristics:**

24.8.1.1. Prefer hands-on learning/training.

24.8.1.2. Can put things together without directions.

24.8.1.3. Have difficulty sitting still.

24.8.1.4. Learn better when they can get involved.

24.8.1.5. May be coordinated and have athletic ability.

24.8.2. **Learning Tips:**

24.8.2.1. Make a model, do lab work, role-play.

24.8.2.2. Take frequent breaks.

24.8.2.3. Copy letters and words to learn how to spell and remember facts.

24.8.2.4. Use a computer.

24.8.2.5. Write facts and figures repeatedly.

24.8.2.6. Read and walk, talk and walk, repeat and walk.

**24.9. Conclusion.**

Effective studying does not happen overnight. It requires time and patience. Effective studying habits are learned through trial and error, and people must develop strategies that work for them. Developing effective study habits and strategies, and knowing your learning style should improve your ability to achieve your goals.

## Chapter 25

## PROFESSIONALISM

### Section 25A—Overview

### 25.1 Introduction:

25.1.1. The Profession of Arms requires unique expertise to fulfill our collective responsibility to the American people. It is distinguished from others in society because of our expertise in the justified application of lethal military force and the willingness of those who serve to die for our Nation. Our profession is defined by our values, ethics, standards, skills and attributes.

25.1.2. The U.S. Air Force and its Airmen wield our Nation's most powerful and responsive weapons. Every member of the U.S. Air Force team--Regular Air Force, Guard, Reserve and civilian--is entrusted with the responsibility of preserving U.S. national security. We provide vital skills to help ensure the Air Force is ready to answer our Nation's call. The trust placed by the Nation in our Airmen rests upon confidence in the character and competency of the men and women who serve. To continue this trust we must maintain and project power within the boundaries of a very sacred and honored Air Force ideal…one based on our Air Force Core Values of *Integrity First, Service Before Self* and *Excellence In All We Do*. Guided by these Core Values, the Air Force will continue to develop and inspire our Airmen within the Profession of Arms.

25.1.3. We are worthy of the Nation's trust through actions consistent with our Air Force Core Values summarized in one word: professionalism. As a service we maintain the trust of our Nation by integrating our Air Force Core Values into mission accomplishment daily, infusing professionalism into everything we do. Professionalism describes who we are as a service; how we conduct ourselves and live our lives; and it sets the standards to which all Airmen will be expected to adhere and exceed. Professionalism is about learning to lead oneself…it is not just about what we do but also how we do it. Professionalism within the Air Force is framed by the requirement for trust, loyalty, dignity and personal commitment. Professionalism is the heart and soul of who we are and who we aspire to be every day. Our sense of professionalism underlies the pride we feel when we say *I am an American Airman*.

25.1.4. This Roadmap is universal and reaches across every element and operation within the Air Force. Whether in war or peace, at home or abroad, on or off duty, our Airmen must hold true to the sacred trust our institution requires. A trust that respects all our fellow Airmen strives to bring out the best version of our people, commits to a higher calling of service and holds those who fail to maintain the honor our standards demand fully accountable. As Airmen we continually seek to deepen and foster our commitment to high personal standards of conduct. Ultimately, we instill and value who we are as Airmen within the Profession of Arms as our hallmark to shape and sustain Air Force culture today and well into the future.

25.1.5. In direct support of the objectives outlined in this Roadmap, we established the Profession of Arms Center of Excellence (PACE) as an Air Force-level Center on March 2, 2015. PACE will champion our focused commitment to collaborating, coordinating and developing areas of growth and leadership for all of our Airmen. PACE, working closely with organizations across the Air Force, will help to provide deliberate, institution-wide strategies focused on supporting professionalism efforts with a common goal of enriching and enhancing the Air Force Profession of Arms. As a dedicated champion to the Air Force Profession of Arms, PACE will provide leadership, education and connectivity with current and emerging cylinders of excellence currently focused on enhancing human capital within the unique Profession of Arms. Through PACE, the Air Force senior leadership has a dedicated institution for direct focus and ability to modify specific Air Force requirements within the Profession of Arms. This Roadmap outlines an expectation, mindset and standard for which all future PACE operations will focus. An electronic copy of the Strategic Roadmap is available by clicking on this link.

### Section 25B—Professionalism

### 25.2. Definitions:

25.2.1. Air Force Profession of Arms: (the *Context*)

A vocation comprised of experts in the design, generation, support and application of global vigilance, global reach and global power serving under civilian authority, entrusted to defend the Constitution and accountable to the American people.

25.2.2. Air Force Professional: (the *Identity*)

An Airman (Regular Air Force, Reserve, Guard or civilian) is a trusted servant to our Nation who demonstrates unquestionable competence, adheres to the highest ethical standards and is a steward of the future of the Air Force profession. Air Force professionals are distinguished  by a willing commitment and loyalty to the Air Force Core Values.

25.2.3. Air Force Professionalism: (the *Spirit*)

A personal commitment and loyalty to Air Force standards and expectations framed within  an environment of shared trust, guided by Air Force Core Values.

## 25.3. Professionalism Vision: *Airmen who do the RIGHT thing - the RIGHT way - for the RIGHT reason.*

The future of the U.S. Air Force rests on the degree to which we can continue to attract, recruit, develop and retain individuals committed to the Profession of Arms and Air Force Core Values. Airmen must be trusted professionals with exemplary character, judgment and competence, who hold themselves and their fellow Airmen accountable. As a profession, these characteristics are expected and directed for both individuals who serve in the Air Force as well as for the  institution itself.

## 25.4. Professionalism Mission: *Leaders forging professional Airmen who embody Integrity, Service and Excellence.*

Every Airman, including those who are leaders and those who aspire to lead, will be vital to the  process of developing our personnel. The Air Force will proactively develop each of our Airmen  within a professional culture requiring the highest degree of commitment toward institutional  standards. Our standards require Airmen to make the right choices guided by the Air Force Core Values at all times.

## 25.5. Air Force Profession of Arms Roles and Responsibilities.

Successful implementation of this strategic roadmap will depend on the commitment and engagement of every Airman. This strategic roadmap represents Air Force guidance that applies to operations across all service responsibilities and is designed to be both consistent and enduring for today and the future. In support of the *Goals, Objectives* and *Desired Effects* that follow, this strategic guidance will be applied at all levels of operations throughout education, training and experience through the development of *targeted* programs and practices. The formal roles and responsibilities for this Roadmap are:

25.5.1. **Chief of Staff of the Air Force (CSAF):**  Foster and communicate the continuous vision for  an Air Force steeped in the Air Force Core Values and support an Air Force culture committed to  the highest standards of the Profession of Arms.

25.5.2. **Profession of Arms Center of Excellence (PACE):**  With Direct Liaison Authorized  (DIRLAUTH) to the CSAF, PACE is responsible for collaborating and coordinating an Air Force institutional-wide professionalism strategy; standardizing/synchronizing Air Force-wide professionalism courses; building and providing world-class professionalism tools for local use; and enhancing unit climate assessments with professionalism solutions. PACE will be a collaborative institute that helps to bring together, communicate and assist in supporting the best  practices of multiple agencies across the Air Force who share the effort of enhancing our human capital.

25.5.3. **AF/A1:**  Advocate for required resources and assist PACE in establishing policies guiding the design, development and delivery of this Strategic Roadmap in support of the United States Air Force  Profession of Arms.

25.5.4. **Major Commands/Field Operation Agencies/Direct Reporting Units:** Implement programs and practices that explicitly support this Strategic Roadmap. Develop strategies and  expectations that enable and encourage subordinate agencies (Wing, Group, Squadron, etc.) to successfully operationalize and sustain these Goals, Objectives and Desired Effects.

## 25.6. Air Force Professionalism Goals:

### 25.6.1. Goal 1:  Inspire a strong COMMITMENT to the Profession of Arms.

*Professionalism is based on a shared commitment to standards and Air Force Core Values. Professionals fully understand and embrace the sacred trust the decision to join the Profession of Arms requires. On and off duty, in peace and in war, Airmen embrace and live by the  standards our institution requires.*

25.6.1.1. Deepen the understanding of and loyalty to their oath as a personal commitment to national service (Roadmap Objective 1.1).

25.6.1.1.1. Airmen internalize the commitment to their oath of service (Roadmap Desired Effect 1.1.1.).

25.6.1.2. Preserve the Air Force standards in times of peace and war (Roadmap Objective 1.2).

25.6.1.2.1. Airmen adhere to the Laws of Armed Conflict and Code of Conduct (Roadmap Desired Effect 1.2.1.).

25.6.1.2.2. The institution and Airmen are held accountable for adherence to ethical and legal conduct (Roadmap Desired Effect 1.2.2.).

25.6.1.2.3. Airmen practice moral courage to hold one another accountable (Roadmap Desired Effect 1.2.3.).

25.6.1.3. Inspire our Airmen through Air Force heritage to build pride, perspective and ownership to meet challenges (Roadmap Objective 1.3).

25.6.1.3.1. Air Force heritage is linked to current, relevant topics and operations (Roadmap Desired Effect 1.3.1.).

25.6.1.3.2. Today's victories are strategically communicated and establish tomorrow's heritage (Roadmap Desired Effect 1.3.2.).

25.6.2. **Goal 2: Promote the RIGHT MINDSET to enhance effectiveness and trust.**

*Professionalism is based on one's commitment to the organization and its shared objectives. Serving as an Airman, whether on Regular Air Force, the Reserve, Guard, or as a civilian, is not just a job—it's a profession. We have been given the sacred trust of the American people, and that trust is maintained only when our Airmen conduct themselves with integrity and character. To meet this expectation, all Airmen must build their lives and shape our service on the foundation of our Air Force Core Values: Integrity First, Service Before Self and Excellence in All We Do. All Airmen must develop and sustain a positive attitude, enhance their understanding of airpower and develop professional perspectives that will create and maintain the future force.*

25.6.2.1. Strengthen an Airman's ability to connect Air Force Core Values with mission accomplishment (Roadmap Objective 2.1).

25.6.2.1.1. Commanders and unit leadership establish a climate consistent with Air Force Core Values (Roadmap Desired Effect 2.1.1.).

25.6.2.1.2. Airmen integrate Air Force Core Values with individual performance (Roadmap Desired Effect 2.1.2.).

25.6.2.2. Foster habits that lead to moral courage and ethical judgment (Roadmap Objective 2.2).

25.6.2.2.1. Airmen exercise the character necessary to make sound decisions (Roadmap Desired Effect 2.2.1.).

25.6.2.2.2. The institution and Airmen act consistently and in accordance with the Air Force Core Values to build trust (Roadmap Desired Effect 2.2.2.).

25.6.2.3. Foster mental agility, adaptive behavior and diversity of thought (Roadmap Objective 2.3).

25.6.2.3.1. Airmen use flexible and creative thinking to develop better solutions (Roadmap Desired Effect 2.3.1.).

25.6.2.3.2. Airmen understand and apply critical thinking skills (Roadmap Desired Effect 2.3.2.).

25.6.2.3.3. Organizations harness ingenuity at all levels through various forums (Roadmap Desired Effect 2.3.3.).

26.6.3. **Goal 3: Foster RELATIONSHIPS that strengthen an environment of trust.**

*Trust is the foundation of the Profession of Arms. How we treat one another and how we strive to bring out the best version of our people will determine our ability to meet our shared objective of U.S. national security. As a service, providing opportunities to build healthy relationships throughout the force requires leadership to appropriately prioritize resources and provide clear expectations and guidance at all levels.*

25.6.3.1. Prioritize resources at all levels to equip leaders to enhance the professional environment for their Airmen (Roadmap Objective 3.1).

25.6.3.1.1. Leaders create opportunities for professional interaction and development (Roadmap Desired Effect 3.1.1.).

25.6.3.1.2. Airmen operate in a safe and healthy professional environment (Roadmap Desired Effect 3.1.2.).

25.6.3.2. Prepare Airmen to develop and respect professional peer relationships (Roadmap Objective 3.2).

25.6.3.2.1. Peer-to-peer behavior remains professional on and off duty (Roadmap Desired Effect 3.2.1.).

25.6.3.2.2. Airmen are prepared to appropriately deal with negative peer pressure (Roadmap Desired Effect 3.2.2.).

### 25.6.4. Goal 4: Enhance a CULTURE of shared identity, dignity and respect.

*The Air Force must strengthen its identity as Airmen first, occupational specialty second. Airmen must understand their role in the enduring connection between Airpower and national security. Within this shared identity we must embrace a culture that preserves human dignity as a mission imperative.*

25.6.4.1. Review, train and enforce our Air Force Core Values and professional standards, institutionally and individually (Roadmap Objective 4.1).

25.6.4.1.1. Leaders ensure institutional policy, programs and procedures remain consistent with Air Force Core Values and standards (Roadmap Desired Effect 4.1.1.).

25.6.4.1.2. All Airmen have a common understanding of Air Force Core Values and standards (Roadmap Desired Effect 4.1.2.).

25.6.4.1.3. All Airmen hold each other accountable for adherence to our Air Force Core Values and standards (Roadmap Desired Effect 4.1.3.).

25.6.4.2. Build pride and identity as Airmen protecting U.S. national security (Roadmap Objective 4.2).

25.6.4.2.1. Individuals identify themselves as Airmen first, specialists second (Roadmap Desired Effect 4.2.1.).

25.6.4.2.2. Airmen understand and can articulate their contribution to the Air Force mission and U.S. national security (Roadmap Desired Effect 4.2.2.).

25.6.4.2.3. Airmen interact across specialties and the Total Force in order to identify and attain common goals (Roadmap Desired Effect 4.2.3.).

25.6.4.3. Continually operate in a way that is organizationally and personally inclusive (Roadmap Objective 4.3).

25.6.4.3.1. Airmen value human dignity and treat everyone with respect (Roadmap Desired Effect 4.3.1.).

25.6.4.3.2. Airmen seek and value the contribution of every Airman (Roadmap Desired Effect 4.3.2.).

### 25.6.5. Glossary of Terms:

25.6.5.1. **Air Force Core Values**: Integrity first, Service before self and Excellence in all we do. The Air Force Core Values are more than minimum standards. They inspire us; remind us what it takes to get the mission done. They are the common bond among all professional Airmen, past and present.

25.6.5.2. **Air Force Profession of Arms**: A vocation comprised of experts in the design, generation, support and application of global vigilance, global reach and global power serving under civilian authority, entrusted to defend the Constitution and accountable to the American people.

25.6.5.3. **Air Force Professional**: An Airman (Regular Air Force, Reserve, Guard or civilian) is a trusted servant to our Nation who demonstrates unquestionable competence, adheres to the highest ethical standards and is a steward of the future of the Air Force profession. Air Force professionals are distinguished by a willing commitment and loyalty to Air Force Core Values.

25.6.5.4. **Air Force Professionalism:** A personal commitment and loyalty to Air Force standards and expectations framed within an environment of shared trust, guided by Air Force Core Values.

25.6.5.5. **Airmen**: All members of the Air Force family - officer, enlisted and civilian representing the Regular Air Force, Reserve and Guard. Everyone in our Air Force is critical to what we do.

25.6.5.6. **Desired Effect:** The desired strategic outcome supporting a goal or objective once it has been fulfilled. These are the foundation to developing lines of effort and implementation strategies.

25.6.5.7. **Goal**: An expression of the desired future state of the Air Force in a particular area or theme. Goals define and prioritize broad direction and are inherently long-term in nature.

25.6.5.8. **Mission**: Fundamental reason for being; purpose of the organization/effort, and why it exists beyond present day operations.

25.6.5.9. **Objective**: A major milestone or action required to achieve a goal. Objectives are specific action statements establishing what, not how.

25.6.5.10. **Vision**: Mental image of the future -- the preferred end state -- including how to approach the customer and satisfy the mission, how services are delivered, how to organize and manage people and other resources.

*Section 25C—America's Air Force: A Profession of Arms.*

**25.7 The Little Blue Book.**

First, we must understand that our chosen profession is that of a higher calling, in which we hold ourselves to higher standards. To serve proudly and capably, our commitment to our cause must be unbreakable; it must be bonded in our mutual respect for each other. Throughout our service we are guided and reminded of this awesome responsibility to our nation. The oaths we take remind us that we serve freely in support and defense of our Constitution. Our Air Force Core Values serve as our compass and provide the fortified foundation of our service. We abide by a Code of Conduct that captures our resolve, while our Airman's Creed highlights the strength of our diverse Airmen who fly, fight and win as one Air Force. We are the world's greatest Air Force...powered by Airmen, fueled by innovation; this book serves as a guide to the principles that make us so strong. Wherever you are in your Air Force career, it is a reminder to the meaning of service in our profession...The Profession of Arms.

25.7.1. **A Profession of Arms:**

25.7.1.1. No profession asks more of its members than the Profession of Arms. As we state in our Airman's Creed, we have answered our nation's call. It is a higher calling, and it comes with a higher standard.

25.7.1.2. General Ronald Fogleman, our 15th Chief of Staff once said, "We are not engaged in just another job; we are practitioners of the Profession of Arms. We are entrusted with the security of our nation, the protection of our citizens and the preservation of its way of life. In this capacity, we serve as guardians of America's future. By its very nature, this responsibility requires us to place the needs of our service and our country before personal concerns."

25.7.1.3. That responsibility was given to each and every one of us when we raised our right hand and swore to support and defend the Constitution of the United States. When we joined our Air Force with a sacred oath, we accepted a sacred trust from the American people, one that goes beyond anything else in society. As members of a joint team, our profession is distinguished from others because of our expertise in the justified application of lethal military force and the willingness of those who serve to pay the ultimate sacrifice for our nation. No other profession expects its members to lay down their lives for their friends, families or freedoms...but it's what our profession readily expects.

25.7.1.4. And make no mistake, this is a profession. We are professionals. As volunteers, our sworn obligation is to the Constitution. Fighting America's wars is an ugly business - there is nothing pretty about it, cool about it or glorious about it - but it must be done, and somebody must be good at it. We're good at it. Our status as the world's greatest Air Force was earned by the men and women who have gone before us, and is carried on by every Airman who wears the uniform today.

25.7.1.5. All service men and women belong to the Profession of Arms, from the most junior enlisted to our most senior leaders. We are all accountable for meeting ethical and performance standards in our actions and similarly accountable for our failure to take action, when appropriate. The distinction between ranks lies solely in our level of responsibility and the degree of accountability...not in our level of commitment to the Profession of Arms. We share the common attributes of character, courage and competence. We qualify as professionals through intensive training, education and practical experience. As professionals, we are defined by our strength of character, a life- long commitment to core values and a dedication to maintain our professional abilities through continuous improvement, individually and institutionally.

25.7.1.6. We must remember above all else, we are patriots first. As service men and women we, more than anyone else, understand the price paid for freedom. We, more than anyone else, understand the sacrifices that come from willingly serving our country. We, more than anyone else, understand what it means to serve in the Profession of Arms.

25.7.2. **Respect:**

25.7.2.1. Respect is at the root of the Profession of Arms and bonds every Airman who voluntarily serves. Respect is the feeling of esteem or deference for a person or other entity, but in the Air Force it takes on a greater meaning and importance. Respect is the lifeblood of our profession. Without it, we simply cannot stand strong in the defense of our nation. Mutual respect strengthens our team and eliminates seams that reveal a weakness in the force.

25.7.2.2. Respect in the Profession of Arms goes beyond professional courtesy. It means accepting others for who they are, embracing a heightened personal sense of humility and fostering an environment of inclusiveness in which every Airman is able and eager to offer their skills, abilities and ideas. It means treating the equipment and resources in our possession with care, understanding and embracing the power of diversity and holding those who mistreat others accountable. More than anything, we must respect the humbling mission placed in our hands by the American people, and the impact our weapons and our actions can have around the globe.

25.7.2.3. Our Air Force is a critical part of the greatest fighting force the world has ever known; it's powered by the greatest Airmen the world has ever seen. Through respect for each other, our resources and our mission, we will continue to provide Global Vigilance, Global Reach and Global Power for America.

### 25.7.3. **Air Force Core Values.**

Values represent enduring, guiding principles for which we as individuals or organizations stand. "Core" values are so fundamental that they define our very identity. The United States Air Force has clearly defined its identity by these three simple values: Integrity First, Service Before Self, and Excellence In All We Do.

For those of us who join this proud community of Airmen - whether officer, enlisted, civilian, Active, Guard, or Reserve - being a part of the Air Force family requires we commit to living these values, on and off duty. This is the expectation of our profession, and is the standard against which our fellow service members and the American public hold us. The Air Force Professional is a trusted servant of our Nation who adheres to the highest standards of character, courage and competence. How we act represents to countless others the collective identity of the United States Air Force.

25.7.3.1. **The Challenge. Living the Core Values:**

25.7.3.1.1. Understanding the Core Values is relatively easy. The true challenge is to live them. It's a commitment that never ends, and one that always matters.

25.7.3.1.2. We all have the ability to display integrity, both professionally and personally. We have all placed ourselves in a position to serve a greater purpose. And we all have the innate desire to achieve excellence. Yet there will be moments where living and acting by the Core Values will be challenging.

25.7.3.1.3. These moments are also opportunities to prove, through our actions, that we truly embody these Core Values. In doing so, we honor the heritage and continue the legacy of those who served before us and sacrificed so much. It is through this alignment of our actions with these values that we, as an Air Force, earn the public's trust, strengthen our Service, and accomplish our mission. These are the Core Values of our Air Force.

25.7.3.1.4. Each of these Core Values is further defined by virtues (desired behaviors and characteristics) we must practice and demonstrate in our daily lives, showing we truly do value Integrity, Service and Excellence. Consistently practicing these virtues results in habits of honorable thought and action, producing an Air Force Professional. Air Force Professionalism is a shared belief in, and a commitment to, honorable service based on our Air Force Core Values.

25.7.3.2. **Integrity First:**

25.7.3.2.1. Integrity is simply doing the right thing, all the time, whether everyone is watching or no one is watching. It is the compass that keeps us on the right path when we are confronted with ethical challenges and personal temptations, and it is the foundation upon which trust is built. An individual realizes integrity when thoughts and actions align with what he or she knows to be right. The virtues that demonstrate one truly values integrity include:

25.7.3.2.2. **Honesty is the hallmark of integrity.** As public servants, we are trusted agents. Honesty requires us to evaluate our performance against standards, and to conscientiously and accurately report findings. It drives us to advance our skills and credentials through our own effort. The service member's word must be unquestionable. This is the only way to preserve the trust we hold so dear with each other and with the population we serve.

25.7.3.2.3. **Courage is not the absence of fear, but doing the right thing despite the fear.** Courage empowers us to take necessary personal or professional risks, make decisions that may be unpopular, and admit to our mistakes; having the courage to take these actions is crucial for the mission, the Air Force, and the Nation.

25.7.3.2.4. **Accountability is responsibility with an audience.** That audience may be the American people, our units, our supervisors, our fellow Airmen, our families, our loved ones, and even ourselves. Accountable individuals maintain transparency, seek honest and constructive feedback, and take ownership of the outcomes of their actions and decisions. They are responsible to themselves and others and refrain from actions which discredit themselves or our service.

25.7.3.3. **Service Before Self:**

25.7.3.3.1. Service before self tells us that professional duties take precedence over personal desires. The call to serve is a call to live according to a higher standard. It is not just a job; it is a commitment that takes energy, dedication, and sacrifice. We do not "work" in the Air Force; we serve in the Air Force. A heart and mindset for service allows us to embrace expectations and requirements not levied on the American public or other professions. The virtues that demonstrate one truly values service include:

25.7.3.3.2. Duty is the obligation to perform what is required for the mission. While our responsibilities are determined by the law, the Department of Defense, and Air Force instructions, directives, and guidance, our sense of duty is a personal one and bound by the oath of service we took as individuals. Duty sometimes calls for sacrifice in ways no other profession has or will. Airmen who truly embody Service Before Self consistently choose to make necessary sacrifices to accomplish the mission, and in doing so, we honor those who made the ultimate sacrifice.

25.7.3.3.3. Loyalty is an internal commitment to the success and preservation of something bigger than ourselves. Our loyalty is to the Nation first, the values and commitments of our Air Force second, and finally to the men and women with whom we serve. Loyalty to our leaders requires us to trust, follow, and execute their decisions, even when we disagree. We offer alternative solutions and innovative ideas most effectively through the chain of command. Ultimately, loyalty is demonstrated by helping each other act with honor.

25.7.3.3.4. Respect is treating others with dignity and valuing them as individuals. We must always act knowing that all Airmen possess fundamental worth as human beings. We must treat others with the utmost dignity and respect, understanding that our diversity is a great source of strength.

25.7.3.4. **Excellence In All We Do:**

25.7.3.4.1. Excellence in all we do does not mean that we demand perfection in everything from everyone. Instead, this value directs us to continuously advance our craft and increase our knowledge as Airmen. We must have a passion for continuous improvement and innovation that propels America's Air Force in quantum leaps towards accomplishment and performance.

25.7.3.4.2. **Mission focus encompasses operations, product and resources excellence.** The complex undertaking of the Air Force mission requires us to harness the ingenuity, expertise, and elbow grease of all Airmen. We approach it with the mindset of stewardship, initiative, improvement, pride, and a continued commitment to anticipate and embrace change. Our work areas, our processes, and our interpersonal interactions must be undeniably professional and positive. Our people are the platform for delivering innovative ideas, strategies, and technologies to the fight.

25.7.3.4.3. **Discipline is an individual commitment to uphold the highest of personal and professional standards.** Airmen commit to a life of discipline and self-control. We demonstrate it in attitude, work ethic, and effort directed at continuous improvement, whether it be pursuing professional military education or nurturing ourselves physically, intellectually, emotionally, or spiritually. Each Airman represents the entire Air Force. Our appearance, actions, and words shape the culture of the Air Force and the reputation of the entire military profession.

25.7.3.4.4. **Teamwork is essential to triumph at every level.** Airmen recognize the interdependency of every member's contributions towards the mission and strive for organizational excellence. We not only give our personal best, but also challenge and motivate each other. We carry our own weight, and whenever necessary, help our wingmen carry theirs. We serve in the greatest Air Force in the world, and we embrace the idea that our part of the Air Force meets that world-class standard.

## 25.8. Conclusion.

Continuing to do things the same way we always have is sure to lead to the same results we have already seen. Our Air Force of the 21st Century can't afford to do what we have always done—we must continue to transform ourselves! We must work today to transform the Air Force of tomorrow to meet our next challenges. The foundation of our Air Force professionalism resides in our commitment and the oath we took to serve our country. Let's work together today to strengthen an environment that allows all Airmen to build trust and credibility with the nation they serve and start to forge our place in the future evolution and superiority of our Air Force.

**GINA M. GROSSO, Lt General, USAF**
**DCS, Manpower, Personnel and Services**

**Attachment 1**

**GLOSSARY OF REFERENCES AND SUPPORTING INFORMATION**

**Note:** Below are the references annotated within this publication; however, the complete listing of references by chapter and section are available at www.studyguides.af.mil.

*References*

**Chapter 1, Air Force Heritage**

Air Force Historical Support Division

**Chapter 2, Enlisted History**

USAF Enlisted Heritage Hall

**Chapter 3, Organization**

Title 10 United States Code (U.S.C.) Section 131, 7 January 2011
Title 10 United States Code (U.S.C.) Section 151, 10 Feb 2010
Title 10 United States Code (U.S.C.) Section 152, 7 Jan 2011
Title 10 United States Code (U.S.C.) Section 155, 18 Dec 2014
Title 10 United States Code (U.S.C.) Section 8013, 22 December 2016
Title 10 United States Code (U.S.C.) Section 8031, 26 January 2017
Title 10 United States Code (U.S.C.) Section 8033, 22 December 2016
United States Constitution Section 2, Article 2
DoDD 5100.01, *Functions of the Department of Defense and Its Major Components*, 21 December 2010
AFI 38-101, Air Force Organization, 16 March 2011

**Chapter 4, Air Force Doctrine, Air and Space Expeditionary Force (AEF), and Joint Force**

JP 1, *Doctrine for the Armed Forces of the United States*, 25 March 2013
JP 3-0, *Joint Operations*, 11 August 2011
JP 3-08, *Interorganizational Coordination During Joint Operations*, 12 October 2016
JP 5-0, *Joint Operation Planning*, 11 August 2011
AFDD, Volume 1, *Basic Doctrine*, 27 February 2015
AFPD 10-4, *Operation Planning*, 30 April 2009
AFI 10-401, *Operations Planning and Execution*, 13 March 2012

**Chapter 5, Emergency Management Program**

AFI 10-2501, *Air Force Emergency Management (EM) Program Planning and Operations*, 19 April 2016
AFMAN10-2502, *Air Force Incident Management System (AFIMS) Standards and Procedures*, 26 September 2011
AFMAN 10-2503, *Operations in a Chemical, Biological, Radiological, Nuclear, and High-Yield Explosive (CBRNE) Environment*, 31 May 2012

**Chapter 6, Standards of Conduct**

DoDD 1344.10, *Political Activities by Members of the Armed Forces*, 19 February 2008
DoD 5500.07, *Standards of Conduct*, 29 November 2007
DoD 5500.7-R, *Joint Ethics Regulation (JER)*, 17 November 2011
AFI 1-1, *Air Force Standards*, 12 November 2014
AFI 36-2909, *Professional and Unprofessional Relationships*, 15 June 1206
AFI 51-401, *Training and Reporting to Ensure Compliance with the Law of Armed Conflict*, 5 September 2014
AFI 51-901, *Gifts from Foreign Governments*, 19 December 2016
AFI 51-903, *Dissident and Protest Activities*, 30 July 2015

**Chapter 7, Enforcing Standards and Legal Issues**

Title 10 United States Code (U.S.C.) Chapter 47, Sections 801-946, 5 October 1994
*Uniform Code of Military Justice*
*Manual for Courts-Martial, United States* (2012 Edition)
AFPD 90-2, *Inspector General—The Inspection System*, 11 September 2015
AFI 36-2502, *Airman Promotion/Demotion Programs*, 14 October 2016

AFI 36-2907, *Unfavorable Information File (UIF) Program*, 26 November 2014
AFI 36-3208, *Administrative Separation of Airmen*, 24 June 2016
AFI 51-202, *Nonjudicial Punishment*, 31 March 2015
AFI 90-301, *Inspector General Complaints Resolution*, 8 July 2016

## Chapter 8, Military Customs, Courtesies, and Protocol for Special Events

Title 4 United States Code (U.S.C.), *Flag and Seal, Seat of Government, and the States*, 30 July 1947
Title 10 United States Code (U.S.C.) Section 506, *Seals of Departments or Agencies*, 3 January 2012
Title 18 United States Code (U.S.C.) Part 1 Chapter 25, Section 506, 15 October 1970
Title 36 United States Code (U.S.C.) Sections 101 to 2502, *Patriotic and National Observances and Ceremonies*, 12 August 1998
AFI 34-242, *Mortuary Affairs Program*, 2 April 2008
AFI 34-1201, *Protocol*, 25 January 2013
AFPAM 34-1202, *Guide to Protocol*, 10 January 2013
AFMAN 36-2203, *Drill and Ceremonies*, 19 February 2016
AFI 36-2805, *Special Trophies and Awards*, 29 June 2001
AFI 36-2824, *Order of the Sword Programs*, 14 April 2009

## Chapter 9, Enlisted Force Development

AFDD 1-1, *Leadership and Force Development*, 8 November 2011
AFI 36-2109, *Chief Master Sergeant of the Air Force and Command Chief Master Sergeant Programs*, 14 July 2016
AFI 36-2301, *Developmental Education*, 9 July 2013
AFI 36-2618, *The Officer and Enlisted Force Structures*, 23 March 2012
AU-24, *Concepts for Air Force Leadership*, 23 June 2005
AFDD 1-1, *Leadership and Force Development*, 14 October 2011

## Chapter 10, Leadership

AFDD 1-1, *Leadership and Force Development*, 8 November 2011
AFDD, Volume 2, *Leadership*, 8 August 2015
AFMAN 36-2643, *Air Force Mentoring*, 19 February 2016
AU-2, *Guidelines for Command*, February 2008
AU-24, *Concepts for Air Force Leadership*, 2001
AFM 6-22, *Army Leadership*, 1 October 2006
John C. Kunich and Richard I. Lester, *Leadership and the Art of Mentoring: Tool Kit for the Time Machine*. Journal of Leadership (1999)
John J. Sosik and Don I. Jung. *Full Range Leadership Development: Pathways for People, Profit, and Planet*. Taylor and Francis Group. New York, 2010
Paul Hersey, Kenneth H. Blanchard, and Dewey E. Johnson, *Management of Organizational Behavior: Leading Human Resources*, 8th ed. NJ: Prentice Hall, 2001
Strategic Leadership Primer, Department of Command, *Leadership and Management*, United States Army War College (2010)

## Chapter 11, The Enlisted Evaluation System (EES)

AFI 36-2406, *Officer and Enlisted Evaluation Systems*, 8 November 2016
AFI 36-1001, *Managing The Civilian Performance Program*, 1 July 1999

## Chapter 12, Training and Education

AFI 36-2013, *Officer Training School (OTS) and Enlisted Commissioning Programs (ECPS)*, 22 December 2008
AFI 36-2201, *Air Force Training Program*, 7 August 2013
AFI 36-2305, *Educational Classification and Coding Procedures*, 6 February 2013
AFI 36-2649, *Voluntary Education Program*, 16 August 2016
AFI 36-3003, *Military Leave Program*, 11 May 2016
*Community College of the Air Force 2014-2016 General Catalog Number 20*

## Chapter 13, Resource Management

EO 13423, *Strengthening Federal Environmental, Energy, and Transportation Management*, 17 February 2009
EO 13514, *Federal Leadership on Environmental, Energy, and Economics Performance*, 5 October 2009
DoDD 7045.14, *The Planning, Programming, Budgeting, and Execution (PPBE) Process*, 25 January 2013

AFPD 32-70, *Environmental Quality*, 20 July 1994
AFPD 38-2, *Manpower*, 5 February 2013
AFPD 36-21, *Utilization & Classification of Air Force Military Personnel*, 8 December 2014
AFI 23-111, *Management of Government Property in Possession of the Air Force*, 26 September 2016
AFMAN 23-220, *Reports of Survey for Air Force Property*, 1 July 1996
AFI 32-1001, *Operations Management*, 22 April 2016
AFI 32-1021, *Planning and Programming Military Construction (MILCON) Projects*, 31 October 2014
AFI 32-1032, *Planning and Programming Appropriated Fund Maintenance, Repair, and Construction Projects*, 19 May 2016
AFI 32-10142, *Facilities Board*, 6 October 2016
AFI 32-9005, *Real Property Accountability and Reporting*, 22 March 2016
AFI 36-1401, *Position Classification*, 1 August 1997
AFI 36-3202, *Separation Documents*, 30 September 2009
AFI 38-101, *Air Force Organization*, 16 March 2011
AFI 38-201, *Management of Manpower Requirements and Authorizations*, 30 January 2014
AFI 38-203, *Commercial Activities Program*, 23 June 2016
AFI 38-204, *Programming United States Air Force Manpower*, 21 April 2015
AFI 38-208, Volume 1, *Air Force Management Engineering Program Process*, 10 December 2007
AFI 38-402, *Manpower and Organization Airmen Powered by Innovation*, 5 February 2015
AFI 65-601, Volume 1, *Budget Guidance and Procedures*, 16 May 16
AFI 65-601, Volume 2, *Budget Management for Operations*, 18 May 2012
AFI 90-301, *Inspector General Complaints Resolution*, 8 July 2016
AFPAM 32-1004, Volume 3, *Working in the Operations Flight Facility Maintenance*, 1 September 1998
Bruce D. Sanders, PhD, & Peter R. Scholtes, et al. "*Fine-Tuning Team Spirit*," Supervisory Management. June 1980
Suzanne Willis Zoglio. "*Teams at Work*," Pa, Tower Hill Press, 1993

### Chapter 14, Communicating in Today's Air Force

AFMAN 17-1201, *User Responsibilities and Guidance for Information Systems*, 19 May 2016
AFMAN 17-1301, *Computer Security (COMPUSEC)*, 1 November 2016
AFH 33-337, *Tongue and Quill*, 27 May 2015
Carl S. Savino, and Ronald L. Krannich. *Air Force Blue to Corporate Gray: A Career Guide for Air Force Personnel*. Competitive Edge Services. Fairfax Station, VA. 2006
John A. Kline. *Speaking Effectively: A Guide for Air Force Speakers*. Air University Press. Maxwell Air Force Base, AL. 1989
*Transition Assistance Program (TAP) Workshop Participation Manual*

### Chapter 15, Personnel Programs

Title 5, United States Code, Section 7114, *Government Organization & Employees*, 7 January 2011
Title 10, United States Code, Section 1553, Review of Discharge or Dismissal, 3 January 2012
DoDD 1304.20, *Enlisted Personnel Management System (EPMS)*, 28 July 2005
DoDD 1332.35, *Transition Assistance for Military Personnel*, 29 February 2016
DoDI 1332.28, *Enlisted administrative Separations*, 27 January 2014
DoDI 1342.22. *Military Family Readiness*, 3 July 2012
DoDI 1342.19, *Family Care Plans*, 7 May 2010
DoDI 1342.22, *Military Family Readiness*, 3 July 2012
DoD 1348.33-M, *Manual of Military Decorations and Awards,* 23 November 2010
DoD 5400.7-R/AFMAN 33-302, *Freedom of Information Act Program*, 16 May 2016
AFI 10-216, *Evacuating and Repatriating Air Force Family Members and Other U.S. Noncombatants*, 27 July 2016
AFI 10-403, *Deployment Planning and Execution*, 18 January 2017
AFI 10-2501, *Air Force Emergency Management (EM) Program*, 19 April 2016
AFI 33-332, *Air Force Privacy and Civil Liberties Program*, 17 November 2016
AFPD 36-21, *Utilization & Classification of Air Force Military Personnel*, 8 December 2014
AFPD 36-26, *Total Force Development*, 22 December 2015
AFI 36-1001, *Managing the Civilian Performance Program*, 1 July 1999
AFI 36-1004, *The Air Force Civilian Recognition Program*, 29 August 2016
AFI 36-2101, *Classifying Military Personnel (Officer and Enlisted)*, 18 November 2013
AFI 36-2102, *Base-Level Relocation Procedures*, 24 June 2016
AFI 36-2103, *Individualized Newcomer Treatment and Orientation (INTRO) Program*, 30 April 2012
AFI 36-2110, *Assignments*, 23 Jun 16

AFI 36-2201, *Air Force Training Program*, 7 August 2013
AFPAM 36-2234, *Instructional System Development*, 1 November 1993
AFH 36-2235, Volumes 1-13, *Information for Designers of Instructional Systems*, 1 Nov 2002
AFI 36-2502, *Airman Promotion/Demotion Programs*, 14 October 2016
AFI 36-2603, *Air Force Board for Correction of Military Records*, 5 March 2012
AFI 36-2605, *Air Force Military Personnel Testing System*, 26 January 2015
AFI 36-2606, *Reenlistment in the United States Air Force*, 29 August 2012
AFPAM 36-2607, *Applicants' Guide to the Air Force Board for Correction of Military Records (AFBCMR)*, 3 November 1994
AFI 36-2623, *Occupational Analysis*, 10 September 2012
AFI 36-2626, *Airman Retraining Program*, 13 January 2015
AFI 36-2803, *The Air Force Military Awards and Decorations Program*, 27 January 2017
AFI 36-2805, *Special Trophies and Awards*, 14 March 2013
AFI 36-2908, *Family Care Plans*, 1 October 2014
AFI 36-3006, *Survivor Benefit Plan and Supplemental Survivor Benefit Plan (SSBP)*, 7 October 2009
AFI 36-3009, *Airman Family Readiness Centers*, 18 February 2016
AFI 36-3111, *Air Force Aid Society*, 15 October 2015
AFI 36-3203, *Service Retirements*, 18 September 2015
AFI 36-3202, *Separation Documents*, 30 September 2009
AFI 36-3208, *Administrative Separation of Airmen*, 24 June 2016
AFI 36-401, *Employee Training & Development*, 28 June 2002
AFI 36-701, *Labor Management Relations*, 27 July 1994
AFI 36-703, *Civilian Conduct and Responsibility*, 18 February 2014
AFI 36-704, *Discipline and Adverse Actions*, 22 July 1994
AFI 36-706, *Administrative Grievance System*, 22 May 2014
AFI 36-802, *Pay Setting*, 25 April 2016
AFI 36-807, *Scheduling of Work, Holiday Observances, and Overtime*, 25 August 2015
AFI 36-815, *Absence and Leave*, 8 July 2015
AFI 36-816, *Civilian Telework Program*, 13 November 2013
AETCI 36-2640, *Technical and Basic Military Training Evaluation*, 23 August 2016
AETCI 36-2641, *Technical and Basic Military Training Development*, 23 January 2017
AFI 38-203, *Commercial Activities Program*, 23 June 2016
AFPD 51-12, *Alternative Dispute Resolution*, 5 March 2010
AFI 51-1201, *Alternative Dispute Resolution Processes in Workplace Disputes*, 17 March 2014

## Chapter 16, Wing Support

Title 5, Code of Federal Regulations, Part 1600, *Employee Contributions Elections, Contribution Allocations, and Automatic Enrollment Program*
DoDI 1327.06, *Leave and Liberty Policy and Procedures*, 19 may 2016
DoD 7000.14-R, Volume 7A, *Military Pay Policy and Procedures—Active Duty and Reserve Pay*, April 2016
Dod 7000.14-R, Volume 9, *Travel Policy*, June 2015
The Joint Federal Travel Regulation
AFI 36-2706, *Equal Opportunity Program Military and Civilian*, 5 October 2011
AFI 36-3003, *Military Leave Program*, 11 May 2016
AFI 36-6001, *Sexual Assault Prevention and Response (SAPR) Program*, 18 March 2016
AFI 51-504, *Legal Assistance, Notary and Preventive Law Programs*, 15 December 2016
AFMAN 65-116, Volume 1, *Defense Joint Military Pay System Active Component (DJMS-AC) FSO Procedures*, 22 May 2012
AFI 90-802, *Risk Management*, 8 March 2016
AFPD 91-2, *Safety Programs*, 24 July 2012
AFI 91-202, *The US Air Force Mishap Prevention Program*, 16 February 2016
AFI 91-207, *The US Air Force Traffic Safety Program*, 12 September 2013

## Chapter 17, Dress and Appearance

AFI 36-2903, *Dress and Personal Appearance of Air Force Personnel*, 30 March 2016

## Chapter 18, Fit Force

Title 32, Code of Federal Regulation, Part 199.17, *TRICARE Program*, July 2004
DoDD 1010.04, *Problematic Substance Use by DoD Personnel*, 20 February 2014

AFI 10-403, *Deployment Planning and Execution*, 20 September 2012

AFI 36-2905, *Fitness Program,* 21 October 2013

AFI 36-2910, *Line of Duty (Misconduct) Determination*, 8 October 2015

AFI 36-3802, *Personnel Readiness Operations,* 23 February 2009

AFI 40-102, *Tobacco Free Living*, 4 March 2015

AFI 44-121, *Alcohol and Drug Abuse Prevention and Treatment (ADAPT) Program*, 8 July 2014

AFI 44-172, *Mental Health*, 13 November 2015

AFI 48-123, *Medical Examinations and Standards*, 5 November 2013

AFI 90-505, *Suicide Prevention Program*, 6 October 2014

Accelerating Progress in Obesity Prevention: Solving the Weight of the Nation. Front Matter. Washington, DC: The National Academies Press, 2012.

Actual causes of death in the United States McGinnis JM, Foege WH; JAMA. 1993

Committee on Dietary Supplement Use by Military Personnel. Use of dietary supplements by military personnel. Washington, DC: Food and Nutrition Board, Institute of Medicine; 2008

Committee on Military Nutrition Research. *Fluid Replacement and Heat Stress*. Washington, DC: National Academy of Sciences, Institute of Medicine; 1994.

Deuster P, Maier S, Moore V, Paton J, et al. *Dietary Supplements and Military Divers A Synopsis for Undersea Medical Officers*. 2004.

JS Coombes, & KL Hamilton. *The effectiveness of commercially available sports drinks*. Sports Med. 2000

Kochanek KD, Xu J, Murphy SL, Miniño AM, Kung H-C. Deaths: final data for 2009. *Nat Vital Stat Rep.* 2011

Nawrot P, Jordan S, Eastwood J, Rotstein J, et al. *Effects of caffeine on human health*. Food Additives and Contaminants Part

NIH, NHLBI Obesity Education Initiative. *Clinical Guidelines on the Identification, Evaluation, and Treatment of Overweight and Obesity in Adults.* 1998

Singh A, Bennett T, Deuster P. *Peak Performance Through Nutrition & Exercise*. USUHS, 1999

**Chapter 19, Security**

DoDI 2000.16, *DoD Antiterrorism (AT) Standards*, 17 Nov 2016

DoDM 5200.1-R, Volume 1, *DoD Information Security Program: Overview, Classification, and Declassification*, 24 February 2012

DoDD 8500.1E, *Information Assurance (IA)*, 23 April 2007

DoDI 8500.2, *Information Assurance Implementation*, 6 February 2003

JP 1-02, *DoD Dictionary of Military and Associated Terms*, 15 February 2016

JP 2-0, *Joint Intelligence*, 22 October 2013

JP 3-13, *Operations Security*, 20 November 2014

CJCSG 5260, *A Self-Help Guide to Antiterrorism*, 10 June 2013

AFPD 17-1, *Information Dominance Governance and Management*, 12 April 2016

AFI 16-1404, *Air Force Information Security Program*, 20 May 2015

AFI 16-1406, *Air Force Industrial Security Program*, 30 January 2017

AFMAN 17-1201, *User Responsibilities and Guidance for Information Systems*, 19 May 2016

AFI 10-245, *Antiterrorism (AT)*, 25 June 2015

AFI 10-701, *Operations Security (OPSEC)*, 8 June 2011

AFPD 31-1, *Integrated Defense*, 28 October 2011

AFI 31-101, *Integrated Defense (FOUO)*, 8 October 2009

ACCPAM 31-101, *Physical Security Awareness Training*, 15 February 2011

AFI 31-501, *Personnel Security Program Management*, 17 November 2016

AFI 33-200, *Information Assurance (IA) Management*, 18 October 2016

AFI 71-101, Volume 2, *Protective Service Matters*, 17 December 2015

AFI 71-101, Volume 4, *Counter Intelligence*, 17 December 2015

**Chapter 20, Air Force Knowledge**

JP 1-02, *DoD Dictionary of Military and Associated Terms*, 15 January 2015

AFI 36-2903, *Dress and Personal Appearance of Air Force Personnel*, 18 July 2011

CAFI 21-105, *Fabrication Program*, 5 September 2012

*National Museum of the United States Air Force*

*The Smithsonian Institution*

*The United States Air Force Band*

**Chapter 21, Organizational Management**

AETCI 90-107, *Continuous Process Improvement*, 17 May 2010

CMSgt Ed Welker, Essay "*Managing Organizational Change*" by 2ed. Houghton Mifflin Co., Boston, 1987
Geoff Reiss. *Project Management Demystified*. Taylor & Francis. 2007
J.B., Miner. *Organizational Behavior, Performance and Productivity*. Random House, New York, 1988
J.B., Moorhead, G. and R. W. Griffin, Robbins. *Organizational Behavior*, 2ed. Houghton Mifflin Co., Boston, 1989
James P. Lewis. *Fundamentals of Project Management*. New York: American management Association. 2006
Jeffrey Pinto, & O.P. Kharbanda. *Successful Project Managers*. New York: Van Nostrand Reinhold Company. 1995
J., J. Hunt, and R. Osborn. *Managing Organizational Behavior*. 2ed. John Wiley & Sons, New York, 1985
Marion E. Haynes. *Project Management: From Idea to Implementation*. Kogan Page. 1990
Paul Hersey and Kenneth H. Blanchard. *Management of Organizational Behavior: Utilizing Human Resources*. 6ed. Prentice Hall, Englewood Cliffs, NJ, 1993
Richard L. Daft. *Organization Theory and Design*. West Publishing Co., St. Paul, 1983
Richard L. Daft. *Organizational Theory and Design*, 3rd Ed. New York, West Publishing, 1989
Scholtes, Peter R. *The Team Handbook*. Joiner Associates Inc., Madison, WI, 1988
Stephen P. Robbins. *Organizational Behavior, Concepts, Controversies and Applications*. New Jersey, Prentice Hall, 1996
S.P., Schemerhorn. *Organizational Behavior, Concepts, Controversies, and Applications*. 4ed. Prentice Hall, Englewood Cliffs, NJ, 1989

## Chapter 22, Human Resource Development

Arnold H. Kambly. M.D. *The ABC's of PAC: An Introduction to Transactional Analysis*. MI: The University Center, 1971
Eric Berne. *Games People Play*. NY: Grove Press, Inc. 1967
Gary Johns and Alan M. Saks. *Management of Organization Behavior*, 9th ed.  New Jersey: Prentice Hall. 2007
Hank Karp. The 1987 Annual: Developing Human Resources "*The Lost Art of Feedback*", pp 237-245
John C. Maxwell. *Conflict and Conflict Management Handbook of Industrial and Organizational Psychology*. 1st ed
Paul Hersey and Kenneth H. Blanchard. *Management of Organizational Behavior: Utilizing Human Resources*, 6th ed. NJ: Prentice Hall, 1993
Thomas A. Harris. *I'm OK-You're OK*. NY: Harper and Row Publishers, Inc. 1973
Thomas Gordon. Leader Effectiveness Training, 1977, pp 1-36 & 92-113
William Pfeiffer and John E., Jones. *Essentials of Management*. 9th ed. Ohio: South-Western College 2011

## Chapter 23, Critical Thinking and Decision-Making

Anthony Weston's. *A Rulebook for Arguments*. Fourth Edition. Hackett Publishing Company Inc. Indianapolis IN. 2009
Charles Perrow. *Normal Accidents: Living with High-Risk Technologies*. New York: Basic Books. 1984
James Surowiecki. *The Wisdom of Crowds*. New York: Random House. 2005
Karl Weick. *The Power of Intuition: How to use your Gut Feelings to Make Better Decisions at Work*.  New York: Doubleday. 2003
Michael A. Roberto. *The Art of Critical Decision Making*, Chantilly: The Great Courses. 2009
Scott A. Snook. *Friendly Fire: The Accidental Shootdown of U.S. Blackhawks over Northern Iraq*. Princeton, NJ: Princeton University Press. 2000

## Chapter 24, Studying Effectively

University of Northwestern Ohio Virtual College. *Learning Styles Evaluation*. 14 December 2000

## Chapter 25, Your Legacy as an Air Force Professional Starts Today

Strategic Roadmap: United States Air Force Profession of Arms, May 2015

### *Abbreviations and Acronyms*

**A1**—Manpower and Personnel
**A1C**—Airman First Class
**AB**—Airman Basic
**ABCD**—Assess, Balance, Communicate, and Decide
**ABU**—Airman battle uniform
**ACA**—Airman Comprehensive Assessment
**ACC**—Air Combat Command
**ACE**—Ask, Care, and Escort
**ADL**—Airman Dorm Leader
**AEF**—American Expeditionary Force
**AETC**—Air Education and Training Command
**AFAUX**—Air Force Auxiliary
**AFGSC**—Air Force Global Strike Command

**AFH**—Air Force Handbook
**AFI**—Air Force Instruction
**AFIT**—Air Force Institute of Technology
**AFJI**—Air Force Joint Instruction
**AFJROTC**—Air Force Junior Reserve Officer Training Corps
**AFJQS**—Air Force Job Qualification Standard
**AFMAN**—Air Force Manual
**AFMC**—Air Force Materiel Command
**AFPAM**—Air Force Pamphlet
**AFPD**—Air Force Policy Directive
**AFRH**—Armed Forces Retirement Home
**API**—Airmen powered by innovation
**AFR**—Air Force Reserve
**AFRC**—Air Force Reserve Command
**AFSOC**—Air Force Special Operations Command
**AFSPC**—Air Force Space Command
**ALS**—Airman Leadership School
**AMC**—Air Mobility Command
**Amn**—Airman
**AMT**—Academy Military Training
**ANG**—Air National Guard
**APEX**—Adaptive Planning and Execution
**AU-ABC**—Air University Associate-to-Baccalaureate Cooperative Program
**B-SMART**—balanced, specific, measurable, attainable, results-focused, and time-bound
**CAA**—Career Assistance Advisor
CAP—Civil Air Patrol
**CCM**—Command Chief Master Sergeant
**CDC**—Career Development Course
**CFETP**—Career Field Education and Training Plan
**CGO**—Company Grade Officer
**CJCSM**—Chairman, Joint Chiefs of Staff manual
**CLEP**—College-Level Examination Program
**CMSAF**—Chief Master Sergeant of the Air Force
**CMSgt**—Chief Master Sergeant
**CONUS**—Continental United States
**CPI**—Continuous Process Improvement
**CSAF**—Chief of Staff, United States Air Force
**DANTES** —Defense Activity for Nontraditional Education Support
**DEROS**—Date Eligible for Return from Overseas
**DoD**—Department of Defense
**DODD**—Department of Defense Directive
**DODI**—Department of Defense Instruction
**DODM**—Department of Defense Manual
**DSD**—Developmental Special Duty
**DV**—Distinguished Visitor
**EES**—Enlisted Evaluation System
**EPR**—enlisted performance report
**EQUAL**—Enlisted Quarterly Assignments Listing
**FICA**—Federal Insurance Contributions Act
**FITW**—Federal Income Tax Withholding
**FRLD**—Full Range Leadership Development
**GI**—General Issue
**GS**—General Service
**IG**—Inspector General
**ILE**—Intermediate Leadership Experience
**IMT**—Information Management Tool
**JP**—Joint Publication
**MFR**—Memo for Record
**MKTS**—Military Knowledge and Testing System

**MOPP**—Mission-Oriented Protective Posture
**MSgt**—Master Sergeant
**MTI**—Military Training Instructor
**MTL**—Military Training Leader
**NATO**—North Atlantic Treaty Organization
**NCO**—Noncommissioned Officer
**NCOIC**—Noncommissioned Officer in Charge
**OES**—Officer Evaluation System
**OJT**—On-The-Job Training
**OPR**—Officer Performance Report
**PACAF**—Pacific Air Forces
**PACE**—Profession of Arms Center of Excellence
**PL**—Protection Level
**PME**—Professional Military Education
**PTSD**—Posttraumatic Stress Disorder
**RAP**—Recruiter Assistance Program
**SITW**—State Income Taw Withholding
**SMART**—Specific, Measurable, Attainable, Results-focused, and Time-bound
**SMSgt**—Senior Master Sergeant
**SOAR**—Scholarships for Outstanding Airmen to ROTC
**SrA**—Senior Airman
**SSgt**—Staff Sergeant
**TA**—Transactional Analysis
**TDY**—Temporary Duty
**TSgt**—Technical Sergeant
**UCMJ**—Uniform Code of Military Justice
**UDM**—Unit Deployed Manager
**UIF**—Unfavorable Information File
**U.S.**—United States
**U.S.C.**—United States Code
**USAF**—United States Air Force
**USAFE**—United States Air Forces in Europe
**USS**—United States Ship
**UTM**—Unit Training Manager
**WEAR**—We Are All Recruiters

## Terms

**Abuse**—The intentional, wrongful, or improper use of government resources. Abuse typically involves misuse of rank, position, or authority.

**Aerospace Power**—The synergistic application of air, space, and information systems to project global strategic military power.

**Air Force Members**—All active duty officers and enlisted personnel serving in the United States Air Force.

**Air Force Personnel**—All civilian employees, including government employees, in the Department of the Air Force (including nonappropriated fund activities), and all active duty officers and enlisted members of the Air Force.

**Alignment**—Dress and cover.

**Attrition**—The reduction of the effectiveness of a force by loss of personnel and materiel.

**Capital Case**—An offense for which death is an authorized punishment under the Uniform Code of Military Justice.

**Chain of Command**—The succession of commanding officers from a superior to a subordinate through which command is exercised.

**Coalition**—An ad hoc arrangement between two or more nations for common action.

**Coalition Force**—A force composed of military elements of nations that have formed a temporary alliance for some specific purpose.

**Coherent**—Sticking together; a logical relationship of parts. Paramilitary and military measures, short of overt armed conflict, involving regular forces are employed to achieve national objectives.

**Cohesion**—The act, process, or condition of cohering: *exhibited strong cohesion in the family unit.*

**Command and Control (C2)**—The exercise of authority and direction by a properly designated commander over assigned and attached forces in the accomplishment of the mission.

**Compromise**—The known or suspected exposure of clandestine personnel, installations, or other assets or of classified information or material to an unauthorized person.

**Conflict**—A fight; a battle; struggle.

**Contingency**—An emergency involving military forces caused by natural disasters, terrorists, subversives, or by required military operations. Due to the uncertainty of the situation, contingencies require plans, rapid response, and special procedures to ensure the safety and readiness of personnel, facilities, and equipment.

**Continuum**—A continuous extent, succession, or whole, no part of which can be distinguished from neighboring parts except by arbitrary division.

**Convening Authority**—Commanders, usually above the squadron level, who have the authority to order a court-martial be conducted. The convening authorities consult with the staff judge advocate, determine if trial by court-martial is appropriate, and refer the case to a court-martial which they have created and for which they appoint the judge, court members, as well as the trial and defense counsels.

**Correctional Custody**—The physical restraint of a person during duty or nonduty hours, or both, imposed as a punishment under Article 15, Uniform Code of Military Justice, which may include extra duties, fatigue duties, or hard labor.

**Counterair**—A US Air Force term for air operations conducted to attain and maintain a desired degree of air superiority by the destruction or neutralization of enemy forces. Both air offensive and air defensive actions are involved. The former range throughout enemy territory and are generally conducted at the initiative of the friendly forces. The latter are conducted near or over friendly territory and are generally reactive to the initiative of the enemy air forces.

**Cover**—Individuals align themselves directly behind the person to their immediate front.

**Dereliction of Duty**—The willful neglect of your job or assigned duties.

**Deterrence**—The prevention from action by fear of the consequences. Deterrence is a state of mind brought about by the existence of a credible threat of unacceptable counteraction.

**Distance**—The prescribed space from front to rear between units. The distance between individuals in formation is 40 inches as measured from their chests to the backs of the persons in front of them.

**Doctrine**—Fundamental principles by which the military forces or elements thereof guide their actions in support of national objectives. It is authoritative but requires judgment in application.

**Dress**—Alignment of elements side by side or in line maintaining proper interval.

**Echelon**—A subdivision of a headquarters.

**Element**—The basic formation; the smallest drill unit, comprised of at least 3 individuals, but usually 8 to 12 persons, one of whom is designated as the element leader.

**Endorser**—The evaluator in the rating chain designated to close out the EPR. The minimum grade requirements vary depending upon the ratee's grade.

**Espionage**—The act of obtaining, delivering, transmitting, communicating, or receiving information about the national defense with an intent, or reason to believe, that the information may be used to the injury of the United States or to the advantage of any foreign nation.

**Esprit de Corps**—Devotion and enthusiasm among members of a group for one another.

**Evaluator**—A general reference to any individual who signs an evaluation report in a rating capacity. Each evaluator must be serving in a grade or position equal to or higher than the previous evaluators and the ratee. **Note:** A commander who is junior in grade to the rater will still review the enlisted performance report (see AFI 36-2403).

**Exploitation**—Taking full advantage of success in battle and following up initial gains, or taking full advantage of any information that has come to hand for tactical, operational, or strategic purposes.

**File**—A single column of individuals placed one behind the other.

**Fiscal Year**—A 12-month period for which an organization plans to use its funds. The fiscal year starts on 1 October and ends on 30 September.

**Forensic**—Relating to, used in, or appropriate for courts of law or for public discussion or argumentation. Of, relating to, or used in debate or argument; rhetorical. Relating to the use of science or technology in the investigation and establishment of facts or evidence in a court of law: *a forensic laboratory.*

**Forfeiture of Pay**—A type of punishment where people lose their entitlements to pay for a specified period of time.

**Fraud**—The intentional misleading or deceitful conduct that deprives the government of its resources or rights.

**Functional Area**—Duties or activities related to and dependent upon one another.

**Grievance**—A personal complaint, by a civilian employee, related to the job or working environment and subject to the control of management. This term also includes any complaint or protest based on either actual or supposed circumstances.

**Guide**—The Airman designated to regulate the direction and rate of march.

**Half staff**—The position of the flag when it is one-half the distance between the top and bottom of the staff.

**Hardware**—The generic term dealing with physical items as distinguished from its capability or function, such as equipment, tools, implements, instruments, devices, sets, fittings, trimmings, assemblies, subassemblies, components, and parts.

**Hyper-vigilance**—The condition of maintaining an abnormal awareness of environmental stimuli, post-traumatic stress syndrome, marked by symptoms like frequent nightmares and repetitive anxiety dreams, insomnia, intrusive disturbing thoughts, *hypervigilance*, and being easily startled.

**Information Superiority**—The capability to collect, process, analyze, and disseminate information while denying an adversary's ability to do the same.

**Information Warfare (IW)**—Any action taken to deny, exploit, corrupt, or destroy an adversary's information and information functions while protecting friendly forces against similar actions and exploiting our own military information functions.

**Infrastructure**—A term generally applicable to all fixed and permanent installations, fabrications, or facilities for the support and control of military forces.

**Installation Commander**—The individual responsible for all operations performed by an installation.

**Intelligence**—The product resulting from the collection, processing, integration, analysis, evaluation, and interpretation of available information concerning foreign countries or areas.

**Interdiction**—An action to divert, disrupt, delay, or destroy the enemy's surface military potential before it can be used effectively against friendly forces.

**Internet**—An informal collection of government, military, commercial, and educational computer networks using the transmission control protocol/internet protocol (TCP/IP) to transmit information. The global collection of interconnected local, mid-level, and wide area networks that use IP as the network layer protocol.

**Interrogation**—Systematic effort to procure information by direct questioning of a person under the control of the questioner.

**Interval**—Space between individuals standing side by side. Normal interval is one arm's length. Close interval is 4 inches.

**Joint Force**—A general term applied to a force composed of significant elements, assigned or attached, of two or more military departments, operating under a single joint force commander. See also joint force commander.

**Joint Force Air Component Commander (JFACC)**—The joint force air component commander derives authority from the joint force commander who has the authority to exercise operational control, assign missions, direct coordination among subordinate commanders, redirect and organize forces to ensure unity of effort in the accomplishment of the overall mission. The joint force commander will normally designate a joint force air component commander. The joint force air component commander's responsibilities will be assigned by the joint force commander (normally these would include, but not be limited to, planning, coordination, allocation, and tasking based on the joint force commander's apportionment decision). Using the joint force commander's guidance and authority, and in coordination with other service component commanders and other assigned or supporting commanders, the joint force air component commander will recommend to the joint force commander apportionment of air sorties to various missions or geographic areas.

**Joint Force Commander (JFC)**—A general term applied to a combatant commander, subunified commander, or joint task force commander authorized to exercise combatant command (command authority) or operational control over a joint force. See also joint force.

**Joint Operations**—A general term to describe military actions conducted by joint forces, or by service forces in relationships (such as support, coordinating authority), which, of themselves, do not create joint forces.

**Joint Task Force (JTF)**—A joint force that is constituted and so designated by the Secretary of Defense, a combatant commander, a subunified commander, or an existing joint force commander.

**Logistics**—The science of planning and carrying out the movement and maintenance of forces. In its most comprehensive sense, those aspects of military operations that deal with design and development, acquisition, storage, movement, distribution, maintenance, evacuation, and disposition of materiel; movement, evacuation, and hospitalization of personnel; acquisition or construction, maintenance, operation, and disposition of facilities; and acquisition or furnishing of services.

**Military Operations Other Than War**—Operations that encompass the use of military capabilities across the range of military operations short of war. These military actions can be applied to complement any combination of the other instruments of national power and occur before, during, and after war.

**Military Strategy**—The art and science of employing the armed forces of a nation to secure the objectives of national policy by the application of force or the threat of force.

**Mitigation (of offense)**—To lessen or attempt to lessen the magnitude of an offense.

**Multinational Operations**—A collective term to describe military actions conducted by forces of two or more nations, typically organized within the structure of a coalition or alliance. See also alliance, coalition, and coalition force.

**National Strategy**—The art and science of developing and using the political, economic, and psychological powers of a nation, together with its armed forces, during peace and war, to secure national objectives.

**Nonappropriated Activity**—An activity associated with the government, but whose operation is not directly funded by the government; that is, the NCO open mess, officers open mess, and child care center.

**Nonappropriated Funds**—Funds generated by Department of Defense military and civilian personnel and their dependents and used to augment funds appropriated by the Congress to provide a comprehensive, morale-building welfare, religious, educational, and recreational program, designed to improve the well-being of military and civilian personnel and their dependents.

**Operational Chain of Command**—The chain of command established for a particular operation or series of continuing operations.

**Operational Control (OPCON)**—The transferable command authority that may be exercised by commanders at any echelon at or below the level of combatant command. Operational control is inherent in combatant command (command authority). Operational control may be delegated and is the authority to perform those functions of command over subordinate forces involving organizing and employing commands and forces, assigning tasks, designating objectives, and giving authoritative direction necessary to accomplish the mission. Operational control includes authoritative direction over all aspects of military operations and joint training necessary to accomplish missions assigned to the command. Operational control should be exercised through the commanders of subordinate organizations. Normally this authority is exercised through subordinate joint force commanders and service and/or functional component commanders. Operational control normally provides full authority to organize commands and forces and to employ those forces as the commander in operational control considers necessary to accomplish assigned missions. Operational control does not, in and of itself, include authoritative direction for logistics or matters of administration, discipline, internal organization, or unit training.

**Period of Supervision**—The number of calendar days during the reporting period that the ratee was supervised by the rater.

**Permissive Reassignment**—A permanent change of station at no expense to the government where an individual is given consideration because of personal reasons. Individuals bear all costs and travel in leave status.

**Personnel Reliability (PR)**—A commander's determination of an individual's trustworthiness to perform duties related to nuclear weapons.

**Physiological**—Having to do with the physical or biological state of being.

**Precedence**—Priority, order, or rank; relative order of mission or operational importance.

**Qualification Training**—Actual "hands-on" task performance training designed to qualify an individual in a specific duty position. This portion of the dual channel OJT program occurs both during and after the upgrade training process. It is designed to provide the performance skills required to do the job.

**Rank**—A single line of Airmen standing side by side.

**Rater**—The person designated to provide performance feedback and prepare an enlisted performance report (EPR) when required. The rater is usually the ratee's immediate supervisor.

**Rations in Kind**—The actual food or meal.

**Reconnaissance**—A mission undertaken to obtain, by visual observation or other detection methods, information about the activities and resources of an enemy or potential enemy; or to secure data concerning the meteorological, hydrographic, or geographic characteristics of a particular area.

**Repatriation**—The procedure whereby American citizens and their families are officially processed back into the United States subsequent to an evacuation.

**Sensitive Information**—Data requiring special protection from disclosure that could cause embarrassment, compromise, or threat to the security of the sponsoring power. It may be applied to an agency, installation, person, position, document, materiel, or activity.

**Software**—A set of computer programs, procedures, and associated documentation concerned with the operation of data processing system, such as compilers, library routines, manuals, and circuit diagrams.

**Special Operations (SO)**—Operations conducted by specially organized, trained, and equipped military and paramilitary forces to achieve military, political, economic, or psychological objectives by unconventional military means in hostile, denied, or politically sensitive areas. These operations are conducted during peacetime competition, conflict, and war independently or in coordination with operations of conventional, nonspecial operations forces. Political-military considerations frequently shape special operations, requiring clandestine, covert, or low-visibility techniques, and oversight at the national level. Special operations differ from conventional operations in degree of physical and political risk, operational techniques, mode of employment, independence from friendly support, and dependence on detailed operational intelligence and indigenous assets.

**Staff Judge Advocate (SJA)**—The senior legal advisor on the commander's staff.

**Strategy**—The art and science of developing and using political, economic, psychological, and military forces as necessary during peace and war, to afford the maximum support to policies, in order to increase the probabilities and favorable consequences of victory and to lessen the chances of defeat.

**Subversive**—Anyone lending aid, comfort, and moral support to individuals, groups, or organizations that advocate the overthrow of incumbent governments by force and violence is subversive and is engaged in subversive activity. All willful acts that are intended to be detrimental to the best interests of the government and that do not fall into the categories of treason, sedition, sabotage, or espionage will be placed in the category of subversive activity.

**Tactical Control (TACON)**—Command authority over assigned or attached forces or commands, or military capability or forces made available for tasking, that is limited to the detailed and, usually, local direction and control of movements or maneuvers necessary to accomplish missions or tasks assigned. Tactical control is inherent in operational control. Tactical control may be delegated to, and exercised at any level at or below, the level of combatant command.

**Tactics**—The employment of units in combat; the ordered arrangement and maneuver of units in relation to each other and or to the enemy in order to use their full potentials.

**Terrorist**—An individual who uses violence, terror, and intimidation to achieve a result.

**Theater**—The geographical area outside the continental United States for which a commander of a combatant command has been assigned responsibility.

**Under Arms**—Bearing arms.

**Unmanned Aerial Vehicle**—A powered, aerial vehicle that does not carry a human operator, uses aerodynamic forces to provide vehicle lift, can fly autonomously or be piloted remotely, can be expendable or recoverable, and can carry a lethal or nonlethal payload. Ballistic or semi-ballistic vehicles, cruise missiles, or artillery projectiles are not considered unmanned aerial vehicles.

**War**—Open and often prolonged conflict between nations (or organized groups within nations) to achieve national objectives.

**World Wide Web (WWW)**—Uses the Internet as its transport media and is a collection of protocols and standards that allow the user to find information available on the internet by using hypertext and/or hypermedia documents.

# Rank Insignia of the United States Armed Forces

## ENLISTED

| | E-1 | E-2 | E-3 | E-4 | E-5 | E-6 | E-7 | | E-8 | | E-9 | | | SEA |
|---|---|---|---|---|---|---|---|---|---|---|---|---|---|---|

### AIR FORCE

| E-1 | E-2 | E-3 | E-4 | E-5 | E-6 | E-7 | | E-8 | | E-9 | | | SEA |
|---|---|---|---|---|---|---|---|---|---|---|---|---|---|
| No Insignia — Airman Basic (AB) | Airman (Amn) | Airman First Class (A1C) | Senior Airman (SrA) | Staff Sergeant (SSgt) | Technical Sergeant (TSgt) | Master Sergeant (MSgt) | First Sergeant (FS) | Senior Master Sergeant (SMSgt) | First Sergeant (FS) | Chief Master Sergeant (CMSgt) | First Sergeant (FS) | Command Chief Master Sergeant (CCM) | Chief Master Sergeant the Air Force |

### ARMY

| E-1 | E-2 | E-3 | E-4 | E-5 | E-6 | E-7 | | E-8 | | E-9 | | | SEA |
|---|---|---|---|---|---|---|---|---|---|---|---|---|---|
| No Insignia — Private E-1 (PV1) | Private E-2 (PV2) | Private First Class (PFC) | Corporal (CPL) / Specialist (SPC) | Sergeant (SGT) | Staff Sergeant (SSG) | Sergeant First Class (SFC) | | Master Sergeant (MSG) | First Sergeant (1SG) | Sergeant Major (SGM) | | Command Sergeant Major (CSM) | Sergeant Major of the Army (SMA) |

### MARINES

| E-1 | E-2 | E-3 | E-4 | E-5 | E-6 | E-7 | | E-8 | | E-9 | | | SEA |
|---|---|---|---|---|---|---|---|---|---|---|---|---|---|
| No Insignia — Private (PvT) | Private First Class (PFC) | Lance Corporal (LCpl) | Corporal (Cpl) | Sergeant (Sgt) | Staff Sergeant (SSgt) | Gunnery Sergeant (GySgt) | | Master Sergeant (MSgt) | First Sergeant (1stSgt) | Master Gunnery Sergeant (MGySgt) | | Sergeant Major (SgtMaj) | Sergeant Major of the Marine Corps (SgtMajMC) |

### NAVY

| E-1 | E-2 | E-3 | E-4 | E-5 | E-6 | E-7 | | E-8 | | E-9 | | | SEA |
|---|---|---|---|---|---|---|---|---|---|---|---|---|---|
| No Insignia — Seaman Recruit (SR) | Seaman Apprentice (SA) | Seaman (SN) | Petty Officer 3rd Class (PO3) | Petty Officer 2nd Class (PO2) | Petty Officer 1st Class (PO1) | Chief Petty Officer (CPO) | | Senior Chief Petty Officer (SCPO) | | Master Chief Petty Officer (MCPO) | Force Command Master Chief Petty Officer (FORMC) | Fleet Command Chief Petty Officer (FLTMC) | Master Chief Petty Officer of the Navy (MCPON) |

### COAST GUARD

| E-1 | E-2 | E-3 | E-4 | E-5 | E-6 | E-7 | | E-8 | | E-9 | | | SEA |
|---|---|---|---|---|---|---|---|---|---|---|---|---|---|
| Seaman Recruit (SR) | Seaman Apprentice (SA) | Seaman (SA) | Petty Officer 3rd Class (PO3) | Petty Officer 2nd Class (PO2) | Petty Officer 1st Class (PO1) | Chief Petty Officer (CPO) | | Senior Chief Petty Officer (SCPO) | | Master chief Petty Officer (MCPO) | | Command Master chief (CMC) | Master Chief Petty Officer of the Coast Guard (MCPO-CG) |

# Rank Insignia of the United States Armed Forces
## OFFICERS

| O-1 | O-2 | O-3 | O-4 | O-5 | O-6 | O-7 | O-8 | O-9 | O-10 | Special |
|---|---|---|---|---|---|---|---|---|---|---|

### AIR FORCE

| O-1 | O-2 | O-3 | O-4 | O-5 | O-6 | O-7 | O-8 | O-9 | O-10 | Special |
|---|---|---|---|---|---|---|---|---|---|---|
| Second Lieutenant (2d Lt) | First Lieutenant (1st Lt) | Captain (Capt) | Major (Maj) | Lieutenant Colonel (Lt Col) | Colonel (Col) | Brigadier General (Brig Gen) | Major General (Maj Gen) | Lieutenant General (LtGen) | General (Gen) | General of the Air Force (GAF) |

### ARMY

| O-1 | O-2 | O-3 | O-4 | O-5 | O-6 | O-7 | O-8 | O-9 | O-10 | Special |
|---|---|---|---|---|---|---|---|---|---|---|
| Second Lieutenant (2d Lt) | First Lieutenant (1st Lt) | Captain (Capt) | Major (Maj) | Lieutenant Colonel (Lt Col) | Colonel (Col) | Brigadier General (Brig Gen) | Major General (Maj Gen) | Lieutenant General (LtGen) | General (Gen) | General of the Army (GA) |

### MARINES

| O-1 | O-2 | O-3 | O-4 | O-5 | O-6 | O-7 | O-8 | O-9 | O-10 | Special |
|---|---|---|---|---|---|---|---|---|---|---|
| Second Lieutenant (2d Lt) | First Lieutenant (1st Lt) | Captain (Capt) | Major (Maj) | Lieutenant Colonel (Lt Col) | Colonel (Col) | Brigadier General (Brig Gen) | Major General (Maj Gen) | Lieutenant General (LtGen) | General (Gen) | |

### NAVY

| O-1 | O-2 | O-3 | O-4 | O-5 | O-6 | O-7 | O-8 | O-9 | O-10 | Special |
|---|---|---|---|---|---|---|---|---|---|---|
| Ensign (ENS) | Lieutenant Junior Grade (LTJG) | Lieutenant (LT) | Lieutenant Commander (LCDR) | Commander (CDR) | Captain (CAPT) | Rear Admiral Lower Half (RDML) | Rear Admiral Upper Half (RADM) | Vice Admiral (VADM) | Admiral (ADM) | Fleet Admiral (FADM) |

### COAST GUARD

| O-1 | O-2 | O-3 | O-4 | O-5 | O-6 | O-7 | O-8 | O-9 | O-10 | Special |
|---|---|---|---|---|---|---|---|---|---|---|
| Ensign (ENS) | Lieutenant Junior Grade (LTJG) | Lieutenant (LT) | Lieutenant Commander (LCDR) | Commander (CDR) | Captain (CAPT) | Rear Admiral Lower Half (RDML) | Rear Admiral Upper Half (RADM) | Vice Admiral (VADM) | Admiral (ADM) | Fleet Admiral (FADM) |

## WARRANT OFFICERS

### ARMY

| | | | | |
|---|---|---|---|---|
| Warrant Officer (WO1) | Chief Warrant Officer (CW2) | Chief Warrant Officer (CW3) | Chief Warrant Officer (CW4) | Chief Warrant Officer (CW5) |

### MARINES

| | | | | |
|---|---|---|---|---|
| Warrant Officer (WO) | Chief Warrant Officer (CWO2) | Chief Warrant Officer (CWO3) | Chief Warrant Officer (CWO4) | Chief Warrant Officer (CWO5) |

### NAVY

| | | | | |
|---|---|---|---|---|
| The grade of Warrant Officer (WO) is no longer in use. | Chief Warrant Officer (CWO2) | Chief Warrant Officer (CWO3) | Chief Warrant Officer (CWO4) | Chief Warrant Officer (CWO5) |

### COAST GUARD

| | | | | |
|---|---|---|---|---|
| The grade of Warrant Officer (WO) is no longer in use. | Chief Warrant Officer (CWO2) | Chief Warrant Officer (CWO3) | Chief Warrant Officer (CWO4) | The grade of chief Warrant Officer (CWO-5) is no longer in use. |

# Air Force Awards and Decorations

## Devices

**Bronze Star**

Denotes participation in designated campaign or campaign phases and/or period.

**Silver Star**

Worn in the same manner as the bronze star, but each silver star is worn in lieu of five bronze service star.

**Silver/Bronze Star**

When worn together on a single ribbon, the silver star(s) will be worn to the (observer left) wearer's right of any bronze star(s).

**Bronze Oak Leaf Cluster**

Denotes second or subsequent entitlements of awards.

**Silver Oak Leaf Cluster**

Represents 6th, 11th, etc., entitlements or in lieu of five bronze oak leaf clusters.

**Silver/Bronze Oak Leaf Cluster**

The silver oak leaf Cluster is worn to the (observer left) wearer's right of the bronze oak leaf cluster on the same ribbon.

**"V" Device**

Denotes personal valor (combat heroism) in combat with an enemy of the U.S.

**"V" Device with Other Devices**

The "V" device, when worn on the same ribbon with cluster, is worn to the (observer left) wearer's right of such clusters.

**Arrowhead Device**

Denotes participation in a combat parachute jump, helicopter assault landing, combat glider landing, or amphibious assault landing. Wear device on both service and suspension ribbons when authorized. Point the arrowhead up in a vertical Position.

**Hourglass Device**

A bronze, silver or Gold hourglass with the Roman numeral "X" is worn on the service and suspension ribbon of the Armed Forces Service Medal.

**"M" Device**

Worn on the Armed Forces Reserve Medal to indicate mobilization in support of U.S. military operations or contingencies designated by the Secretary of Defense.

**"Winter Over" Clasp and Disc**

Worn on the suspension ribbon of the Antarctica Service Medal. Wear bronze for first winter, gold for second winter, and silver for third and subsequent winters. The discs are worn on the service ribbon in the same manner as the clasps.

**"N" Device**

Worn on the Nuclear Deterrence Operations Service Medal to indicate direct support to nuclear deterrence operations.

**"N" Device with Other Devices**

The "N" device is worn to the (observer left) wearer's right of such clusters.

Made in the USA
Columbia, SC
24 June 2021